CORPORATE STRATEGY

Visit the *Corporate Strategy, fourth edition* Companion Website at **www.pearsoned.co.uk/lynch** to find valuable **student** learning material including:

- **Chapter overview** including key concepts and definitions
- **Multiple choice questions** to help you test your understanding
- **Case Study Guide** offering help with reading, analysing and presenting cases
- A searchable **online glossary** to explain key terms

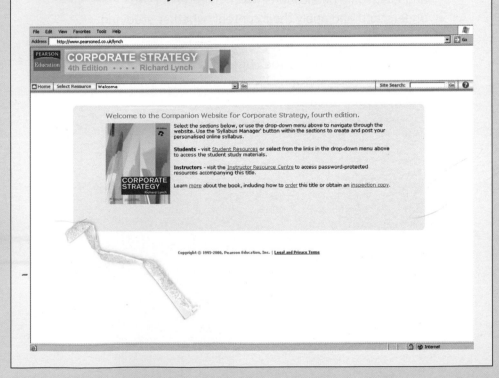

Fourth Edition

CORPORATE STRATEGY

Richard Lynch

FINANCIAL TIMES

An imprint of **Pearson Education**
Harlow, England • London • New York • Boston • San Francisco • Toronto • Sydney • Singapore • Hong Kong
Tokyo • Seoul • Taipei • New Delhi • Cape Town • Madrid • Mexico City • Amsterdam • Munich • Paris • Milan

Pearson Education Limited

Edinburgh Gate
Harlow
Essex CM20 2JE
England

and Associated Companies throughout the world

Visit us on the World Wide Web at:
www.pearsoned.co.uk

First published 1997
Second edition 2000
Third edition 2003
Fourth edition published 2006

ISBN-13: 978-0-273-70178-1
ISBN-10: 0-273-70178-9

British Library Cataloguing-in-Publication Data
A catalogue record for this book is available from the British Library

Library of Congress Cataloging-in-Publication Data
Lynch, Richard L.
      Corporate strategy / Richard Lynch.— 4th ed.
          p. cm.
      Includes bibliographical references and indexes.
      ISBN 0-273-70178-9
      1. Business planning.   2. Strategic planning.   I. Title.

      HD30.28.L92 2006
      658.4′012 — dc22

                                              2005042438

10   9   8   7   6   5   4   3   2
09   08   07   06

Typeset in 9/12 pt Stone Serif by 35
Printed and bound by Graficas Estella, Spain

The publisher's policy is to use paper manufactured from sustainable forests.

Ex umbris et imaginibus in veritatem.
From shadows and imagination to the truth.

JOHN HENRY NEWMAN

Brief contents

Contents

Part 1
INTRODUCTION

Chapter 1
Corporate strategy

Chapter 2
A review of theory and practice

Part 2
ANALYSIS OF THE ENVIRONMENT

Chapter 3
Analysing the environment - basics

Contents

Part 4
THE PURPOSE OF THE ORGANISATION

Part 6
THE IMPLEMENTATION PROCESS

Contents

About this book

This book explores the fundamental decisions that will guide the future of organisations, and how such matters can be identified, evaluated and implemented. It presents a comprehensive, structured and critical approach to strategic management.

Its underlying theme is the need to consider not only the *rational approach* to strategic decision making, but also the *creative aspects* of such decisions – an approach that remains unique to this strategy text. The book argues that both of these are essential to enable students and practising managers to develop successful strategies.

This fourth edition has been substantially revised: a new chapter on public sector strategy – for the first time ever in a strategy text; there are major updates on organisational structure, learning, co-operation and networks, the resource-based view, corporate governance and social responsibility, knowledge, technology, corporate versus business strategy, entrepreneurial strategy and global strategy. There is a new full-colour design. All the cases have been updated, with one-third being completely new. The learning structure has also been revised. An outline of the main changes appears later in this section.

Finally, and for the first time ever in a strategy text, there is an accompanying compact disc. It uses a case study to explore the main areas in greater depth than is possible in a written text, demonstrating how they link together. *Corporate Strategy* continues to break new ground, as it did with the first edition over ten years ago.

OBJECTIVES

The purpose of the book is to provide a comprehensive, well-structured and interesting treatment of strategic management, covering organisations in both the private and public sectors. The text has been specially designed in a modular format to provide both a summary of the main areas and a more detailed treatment for those wishing to explore issues in more depth.

More specifically, the objectives are:

- *To provide a comprehensive coverage of the main study areas in corporate strategy*. For example, the different functional areas of the organisation and important subject areas such as innovation, knowledge and technology strategy are all explored. The exploration of the strategy contributions from the business functions of marketing, human resources, finance and operations (production) remains unique to this text.

- *To present the practical issues and problems of corporate strategy, so that the compromises and constraints of real organisations are considered*. Each chapter contains case studies which both illustrate the principles and raise subjects for group and class discussion. Leadership, corporate governance and ethical issues are amongst the topics explored.

- *To assist organisations to add value to their assets through the development of successful corporate strategy*. The search for best practice in the context of the organisation's resources and constraints is a constant theme.

- *To explore both the rational and the creative approaches to the development of corporate strategy*. This text takes the view that the classical approaches to rational corporate strategy development need to be complemented by the more recent ideas based on crafting strategy development. Knowledge, technology, innovation and entrepreneurship are explored.

- *To stimulate critical appraisal of the major theories, particularly with regard to their practical application in organisations*. Many of the leading conceptual approaches are first described and then subjected to critical comment. The aim is to encourage the reader to think carefully about such matters.

● *To outline the international implications of the corporate strategic process.* Most of the cases have an international dimension and most chapters have a separate section exploring international issues. A special chapter on globalisation explores the specific issues raised by this strategic area.

WHO SHOULD USE THIS BOOK?

The book is intended to provide an introduction to corporate strategy for the many students in this area.

● *Undergraduate students* on Business Studies, modular and other courses will find the subject matter sufficiently structured to provide a route through the subject. No prior knowledge is assumed.

● *MBA students* will find the practical discussions and theoretical background useful. They will also be able to relate these to their own experience.

● *Postgraduate students* on other specialist taught masters' programmes will find that the extensive coverage of theories and, at times, critical comments, together with the background reading, provide a useful input to their thinking.

In addition, the book will appeal to practising middle and senior managers involved in the development of corporate strategy. The case studies and checklists, the structured approach and the comprehensive nature of the text will provide a useful compendium for practical application.

DISTINCTIVE FEATURES

Two-model structure

For some years, there has been disagreement on the approach to be adopted in studying corporate strategy. The *rational* model – strategy options, selection and implementation – has been criticised by those favouring an approach based on the more *creative* aspects of strategy development. Given the lack of agreement between the approaches, *both* models are used throughout this book. They are *both* treated as contributing to the development of optimal corporate strategy: two sides of the same strategic coin.

Modular structure

The subject can be treated in depth by taking each chapter in sequence. Alternatively, the book has been designed to be used as a complete course through the study of *selected chapters only*. The aim has been to make the subject more accessible at first reading to those requiring such an approach. The precise structure is explained in the section on 'How to use this book'.

Clear chapter structure

Each chapter follows the same format: learning outcomes; short introduction; opening case study; later case studies linked to the theory points in the text; a specific project linked with one of the case studies; regular summaries of key strategic principles; chapter summary; review and discussion questions; critical reflection on a key issue in the chapter; recommended further reading; detailed notes and references. There is also a glossary of terms at the end of the book as an aid to comprehension.

Accompanying compact disc

For the first time ever in a strategy text, a compact disc accompanies the text. The CD uses an in-depth case study to explore the main areas of strategy and show how they link together. Strategy is a complex topic with many different approaches – the aim of the CD is to show one way that the strategic decision-making process can be developed from the available data. The CD icon (left) appears in the margin to highlight where the book and CD content link.

Focused case material

There are 80 case studies in this book. Each case has been written or adapted to explore strategy issues relevant to its location in the text. Most cases also have a wider context and there are some longer cases – as outlined on later pages. The shorter cases have been especially designed for the larger class sizes and shorter discussion sessions now prevalent in many institutions. All the cases have been updated for the fourth edition and one-third are completely new.

Key strategic principles and chapter summaries

To aid learning and comprehension, there are frequent summaries of the main learning points under the heading of *key strategic principles*. In addition, at the end of each chapter there is an integrated summary of the areas explored.

International coverage

There is extensive coverage of international strategic issues throughout the book. For ease of teaching and learning, the international theory has generally been placed towards the end of each chapter, but cases and examples are threaded through the text. In addition, there is a separate chapter on the special issues involved in globalisation strategy.

Public sector and not-for-profit strategy

For the first time in a strategy text, there is a separate chapter on this important topic. *Strategic management* principles have been historically developed almost exclusively from a business perspective – for example, competitive advantage, customer-driven strategy and corporate governance. *Public sector* theory has historically had a completely different intellectual foundation – for example, the concepts of the public interest, the legal framework of the state and the role of public administrators. This chapter explores how they can come together. It will be particularly interesting for managers from the public sector studying for a business degree at both undergraduate and postgraduate level.

Critical reflection and recommended further reading

Every chapter ends with a short critical reflection on a key topic in the chapter. In addition, each chapter has a list of recommended further readings. The purpose is to allow the student to debate a topic from the chapter and to explore the subject matter further as the basis for further projects, assignments and dissertations.

Strategic project

Each chapter includes a suggestion for a strategic project. It is linked to a case study in the chapter and shows how the case topic might be extended. The projects are supported by further information available on the internet.

A useful feature of the text remains the selection of some case material from the *Financial Times*. These extracts are the copyright of the *Financial Times*, which has kindly given permission to reproduce them in this book.

Lecturer's guide

This is available to those lecturers adopting this textbook. It includes short commentaries on each chapter and comments on the cases, together with OHP masters.

NEW FOR THE FOURTH EDITION

As a result of the helpful feedback on the three earlier editions, this new edition has been thoroughly updated while maintaining the main structure of the previous edition. The main changes are in three areas – new subject material, pedagogy and case material.

New subject material

- New chapter on public sector strategy (Chapter 18 – Government, public sector and not-for-profit strategies)
- Concise and updated coverage of organisation structure: Chapters 16 and 18 of the previous edition have been combined into one topic (Chapter 16 – Organisational structure and style and people issues).
- Extended and focused coverage of learning-based strategy theories: all the old material in Chapters 11, 15 and 16 has been combined into one chapter and updated – Chapter 15.
- New and extended coverage of the latest strategy topics:
  - Chapter 3: new section on market basics – market size, share and growth
  - Chapter 4: new section on co-operation and network strategy
  - Chapter 6: new and updated material on resource-based view
  - Chapter 8: many detailed textual changes reflecting increased company and financial disclosure and their implications for strategy development
  - Chapter 10: separate, extended sections on corporate governance and ethics/corporate social responsibility
  - Chapter 11: knowledge extended and updated
  - Chapter 11: technology extended and updated
  - Chapter 12: new and extended treatment of the distinction between corporate and business strategy
  - Chapter 15: game theory treated as separate section
  - Chapter 15: network theory extended and treated as separate section
  - Chapter 17: extended discussion on the balanced scorecard
  - Chapter 19: global strategy at company level extended
  - Chapter 20: new section on entrepreneurial strategy

Pedagogy

- New definitions added throughout text to increase learning clarity
- Critical reflection section added to end of each chapter for class discussion and debate
- Free compact disc of extended case study 'Battle for the Breakfast Cereal Market' revised for new edition

Case material

All the cases have been brought up to date and one-third are completely new. All cases have lecturer notes in the *Lecturer's Guide* and any that have been dropped from the previous edition appear on the *Corporate Strategy* website.

ABOUT THE AUTHOR

Richard Lynch is Emeritus Professor of Strategic Management at Middlesex University, London, England. He originally studied at UMIST, Leeds University and the London Business School. He then spent over 20 years in business with well-known companies such as J Walter Thompson, Kraft Jacobs Suchard and Dalgety Spillers in positions in marketing and corporate strategy. During the early 1980s, he was a director of two public companies before setting up his own consultancy company specialising in European and international strategy. In the 1990s he became increasingly involved in Higher Education, eventually taking a full-time position in 1999. He retired from his full-time post in December 2004 but remains active in research and writing. He has written four previous books on international marketing and strategy and a number of publications in research journals.

How to use this book

Corporate strategy is all-embracing and covers every aspect of the organisation, so its study can be both lengthy and time-consuming. This book has been written to guide the reader through from its early stages of development. It can therefore be read from cover to cover; alternatively, it may be more useful to begin by concentrating on certain key *chapters*, which will provide an overview of the process and show the linkages that exist between the different areas. The areas can then be covered in more depth, if required, by reading the *related chapters*.

Key chapters	Related chapters
Part 1	
Chapter 1	Chapter 2
Part 2	
Chapter 3	Chapters 4 and 5
Part 3	
Chapter 6	Chapters 7, 8 and 9
Part 4	
Chapters 10, 11 and 12	None: all important
Part 5	
Chapters 13, 14 and 15	Chapter 16
Part 6	
Chapters 17 and 21	Chapters 18, 19, 20 and 22

The key chapters might form the basis of a 12-week modular course. The longer text including the related chapters might form the basis of a two-seminar programme.

Corporate strategy is complicated because there is no final agreement on what exactly should be included in the topic. There are two main strategic approaches worth mastering before venturing too far into the text. They are summarised in Chapter 1 – the *prescriptive* and the *emergent* strategic approaches. Since these approaches are discussed extensively later in the book, they should be studied in Chapter 1 before moving on to other chapters. If you have trouble understanding these two elements, then you might also like to consult the early part of Chapter 2, which investigates them in more detail.

Each chapter then follows the same basic format:

- *Learning outcomes and introduction*. This summarises the main areas to be covered in the chapter and is useful as a summary of what to expect from the chapter.

- *Opening case*. This is designed to highlight a key strategy issue in the chapter and to provide an example that will then be explored in the text. It is therefore worth reading and using the case questions to ensure that you have understood the basics of the case. You can return to it once you have read the chapter.

- *Key strategic principles*. Each chapter then explores aspects of the subject and summarises them. These can be used to test your understanding of the text and also for revision purposes later.

● *Comment.* After the outline of a major strategic theory, there may be a section with this heading to explain some of the theoretical or practical difficulties associated with that topic. The opinions contained in such a section are deliberately designed to be controversial. The section is meant to make you think about the topic. If you agree with everything I have written, then I have failed!

● *Later case studies.* These are designed to provide further examples and raise additional strategic issues. It is worth exploring the questions.

● *Strategic project.* One of the case studies has been used to suggest a broader strategic project. There is data on the internet to assist the process and your lecturer or tutor will be provided with details on how to access this.

● *Critical reflection.* Each chapter ends with a short section highlighting a key theme of the chapter as the basis for further discussion and exploration. For example, it might form the basis of an essay on a strategy topic or the focus of a seminar after a class lecture.

● *End of chapter questions.* Some are designed to test your understanding of the material in the chapter. Others are present as possible essay topics and require you to undertake some research using the references and reading from the chapter. Some questions have been developed to encourage you to relate the chapter to your own experience: student societies and outside organisations to which you belong can all be considered using the chapter concepts. You may also be able to relate the chapter to your own work experience or to those of other members of your family or friends. All these will provide valuable insights and help you explore the concepts and reality of corporate strategy.

● *Further reading.* This is designed to help when it comes to essay topics and dissertations. This section tries to keep to references in the major journals and books in order to make the process as accessible as possible.

Guided tour of the book

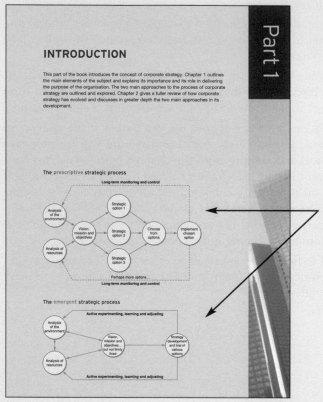

Two-model structure – two models of strategic thought are used throughout the book – *prescriptive* and *emergent*. Both are treated as contributing to the development of optimal corporate strategy.

Key strategic principles – at regular intervals, frequent summaries are given of the main learning points.

Case studies – are woven into each chapter and referred to frequently in order to illustrate how strategic principles do and don't work in practice. There are more than 80 case studies throughout the book and many are new and updated. For ease of reference, see the Guide to the main focus of case studies on page xxvi.

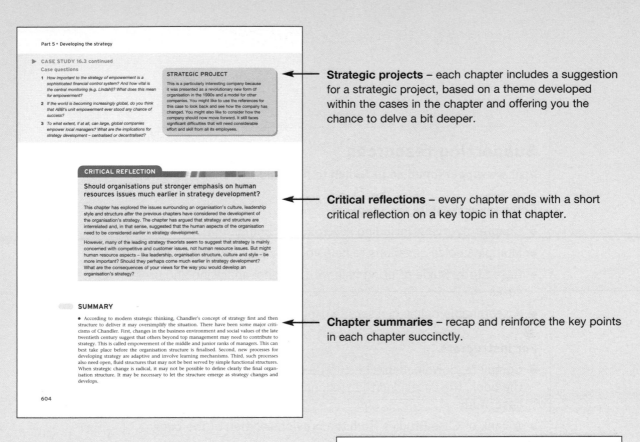

Strategic projects – each chapter includes a suggestion for a strategic project, based on a theme developed within the cases in the chapter and offering you the chance to delve a bit deeper.

Critical reflections – every chapter ends with a short critical reflection on a key topic in that chapter.

Chapter summaries – recap and reinforce the key points in each chapter succinctly.

End-of-chapter **Questions** – test your understanding of the key issues raised in each chapter.

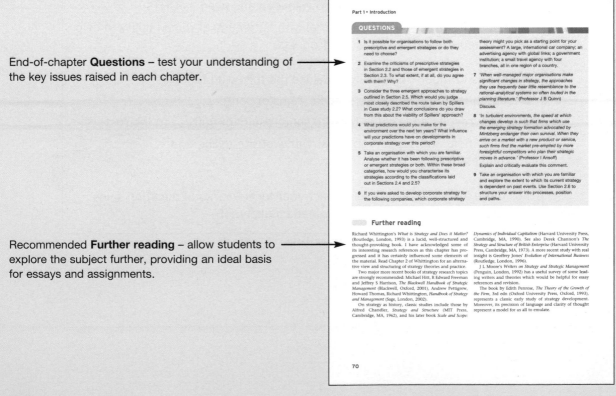

Recommended **Further reading** – allow students to explore the subject further, providing an ideal basis for essays and assignments.

 Student CD-Rom – an extended case study serves as an introduction to Corporate Strategy and provides an overview, showing how the book's themes come together in real life. This icon in the book's margin highlights where the book and CD content link.

Supporting resources

Visit **www.pearsoned.co.uk/lynch** to find valuable online resources

Companion Website for students

- Chapter overview including key concepts and definitions
- Multiple choice questions to help you test your understanding
- Case Study Guide offering help with reading, analysing and presenting cases
- A searchable online glossary to explain key terms

For instructors

- Complete, downloadable Lecturer's Guide, including teaching notes on the book, the cases and the student CD-Rom and suggestions for longer case study
- A bank of Case Studies from the previous edition of the book
- PowerPoint slides that can be downloaded and used as OHTs
- New Testbank of question material with automatic grading facility to help you keep track of your class's progress

Also: The Companion Website provides the following features:

- Search tool to help locate specific items of content
- E-mail results and profile tools to send results of quizzes to instructors
- Online help and support to assist with website usage and troubleshooting

For more information please contact your local Pearson Education sales representative or visit **www.pearsoned.co.uk/lynch**

Guided tour of companion website

Chapter overview including key concepts and definitions

Multiple choice questions to help you test your understanding

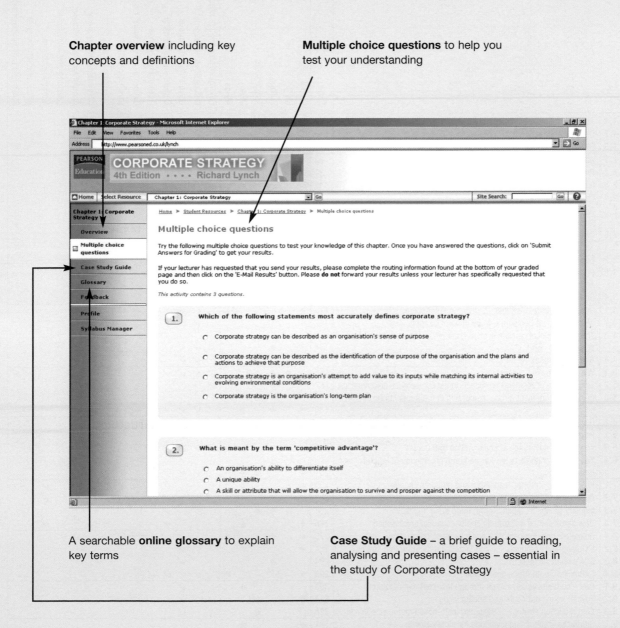

A searchable **online glossary** to explain key terms

Case Study Guide – a brief guide to reading, analysing and presenting cases – essential in the study of Corporate Strategy

Guide to the main focus of case studies

CASE STUDY		Page	Main area covered						Topic or theme													
			Global	UK	Europe	Asia/Pacific	USA	Africa	Emergent/prescriptive process	Competitive environment	Competitive resources	Culture and leadership	Developing purpose	Governance and social responsibility	Strategic options	International and global strategy	Corporate level strategy	Acquisitions and alliances	Learning and knowledge	Managing change	Public and not-for-profit	SMEs and entrepreneurship
1.1	Apple's profitable but risky strategy	3	◆							✔												
1.2	Disaster and recovery: 1 Corporate profit disaster at IBM	10	◆				◆			✔	✔						✔					
1.3	Sky-high strategies of Europe's budget airlines	23		◆	◆					✔	✔											✔
2.1	Attacking a dominant competitor – Nestle and General Mills	33	◆		◆				✔	✔	✔			✔	✔							
2.2	Prescriptive strategic planning at Spillers in the late 1970s	37	◆						✔													
2.3	Prescriptive strategy to build a world airline – Singapore Airlines	42	◆			◆			✔													
2.4	Emergent strategy at Virgin Group	47	◆	◆					✔													
2.5	Building the Subway world franchise using emergent and prescripive processes	55	◆				◆		✔													✔
2.6	Disaster and recovery: 2 The new strategic challenge at IBM	63	◆				◆			✔	✔	✔	✔									
3.1	Strategic bargaining to film *Lord of the Rings*	77	◆							✔												
3.2	Lifecycle impact on strategy in the European ice cream market	86			◆					✔												
3.3	Pan-European steel companies merge to cope with the new competitive environment	90	◆		◆					✔								✔				
3.4	Shaking up Sony: restoring the profits and the innovative fire	107	◆			◆	◆		✔	✔	✔	✔										
4.1	Unilever ice cream defends its global market share	115	◆							✔	✔											
4.2	Web strategy at Boo.com – to be booed? Or applauded?	122	◆							✔	✔											
4.3	The Galileo global satellite system – the result of European co-operation	134	◆		◆				✔	✔												
4.4	Global ice cream: Nestlé goes on the attack	144	◆						✔	✔	✔								✔			
5.1	Will Dyson remain successful?	155		◆	◆				✔	✔	✔	✔										✔
5.2	Two methods of segmenting products in the European ice cream market	167			◆					✔												
5.3	Customer strategy at Airbus: competing in the SuperJumbo aircraft segment	180	◆		◆		◆			✔	✔							✔				
6.1	Resource strategy at GSK: negotiating a merger and making it work	191	◆	◆			◆				✔											
6.2	How three European companies attempt to utilise their resources	199			◆						✔											
6.3	Competitive advantage at Louis Vuitton and Gucci	212	◆						✔	✔	✔											
6.4	Xbox – the strategic battle for the home entertainment market has just begun	231	◆			◆	◆			✔	✔											
7.1	Ford Motors: strategy, leadership and strategic change	239	◆			◆						✔								✔		
7.2	Royal Dutch/Shell – what does it take to bring change?	252	◆		◆							✔		✔						✔		
7.3	Industry groups in Japan, Korea, Hong Kong and Italy	264			◆	◆						✔										
7.4	How Xerox shifted its strategy and changed its organisation	265	◆									✔								✔		
8.1	Heineken: how the company finances its global strategy	273	◆		◆			◆					✔						✔			
8.2	L'Oréal beauty products – using financial data to explore strategy	284	◆									✔	✔									
8.3	SCA's financial objectives	294			◆								✔									
8.4	SABMiller: South Africa goes global	298	◆					◆					✔	✔	✔	✔						
9.1	Dell – competitive advantage through low-cost manufacturing	308				◆									✔							
9.2	Toyota: taking out costs and adding value	315	◆			◆			✔						✔				✔			
9.3	Cost reduction strategy at Bajaj, the India-based motorcycle maker	328				◆									✔							
10.1	Starbucks – sacrificing dividends for global growth	341	◆			◆										✔						
10.2	DaimlerChrysler: what price a global strategy?	348	◆		◆											✔						
10.3	Leadership in action: Jürgen Schrempp of Daimler-Benz	354	◆		◆							✔										
10.4	Citigroup – rebuilding its corporate governance	360	◆			◆								✔	✔							
11.1	Maglev – Shanghai's innovative new transport system	376				◆			✔						✔							
11.2	Developing new knowledge at Nike	382	◆			◆			✔					✔	✔				✔			
11.3	Will traditional retail banks survive the threat of new technologies?	389	◆						✔													
11.4	Revitalising innovation at 3M	394	◆				◆		✔													
11.5	How Philips exploits its technology edge	399			◆	◆																
12.1	Purpose at two conglomerates – General Electric, USA and Siemens, Germany	411	◆		◆		◆								✔		✔					
12.2	Coca-Cola: lowering the fizz in its objectives	423	◆			◆									✔		✔					
12.3	McDonald's restaurants: how to maintain momentum?	431	◆														✔					

CASE STUDY		Page	Main area covered						Topic or theme													
			Global	UK	Europe	Asia/Pacific	USA	Africa	Emergent/prescriptive process	Competitive environment	Competitive resources	Culture and leadership	Developing purpose	Governance and social responsibility	Strategic options	International and global strategy	Corporate level strategy	Acquisitions and alliances	Learning and knowledge	Managing change	Public and not-for-profit	SMEs and entrepreneurship
13.1	Walt Disney: building options for Mickey Mouse	448	◆			◆									✔							
13.2	Generic strategy options analysis: global ice cream	456	◆												✔							
13.3	Market-based strategies in global TV	458	◆						✔													
13.4	Building a global media company at News Corporation	469			◆	◆	◆		✔				✔		✔				✔			
14.1	Nokia – dialling global opportunities in mobile phones	489	◆		◆								✔		✔							
14.2	Eurofreeze evaluates its strategy options: 1	498			◆										✔							
14.3	Where now for Unilever's 'Path to Growth' strategy?	511	◆		◆								✔	✔								
14.4	Eurofreeze evaluates its strategy options: 2	519			◆										✔							
15.1	How Honda came to dominate two major motorcycle markets	530				◆			✔								✔					
15.2	Europe's leading telecom companies: overstretched and under threat	534			◆								✔									
15.3	How GEC Marconi used game theory to make an extra US$3 billion	543			◆										✔				✔			
15.4	Buying travel on-line: choosing a strategy for the internet age	563	◆						✔										✔			✔
16.1	PepsiCo: organising to integrate its acquisitions	574	◆				◆												✔			
16.2	Cisco Systems: benefits of a highly structured organisation?	595	◆				◆												✔			
16.3	How ABB empowered its managers and then reversed the process	602	◆		◆								✔						✔			
17.1	European football: viable strategy badly implemented? Or does the whole strategy need a rethink?	611			◆												✔					
17.2	Strategic planning at Canon with a co-operative corporate style	622			◆													✔	✔			
17.3	Informal strategic controls at Nestlé	630	◆														✔					
18.1	The World Bank: juggling the strategic environment	645	◆																		✔	
18.2	Olympic Games 2012: five cities bid to host the games	658																			✔	
18.3	'Should we close the Kings Theatre?' A tough strategic decision for Portsmouth City Council	668		◆																	✔	
19.1	MTV: more local than global?	680	◆				◆								✔							
19.2	Tate & Lyle plc: globalisation to sweeten the profit line	687	◆	◆											✔							
19.3	Global automotive vehicles – strategy in a mature market	697	◆												✔							
19.4	Global automotive vehicles – the battle between Ford and Toyota	715	◆			◆	◆								✔	✔						
20.1	eBay – the auction market that spans the world	724	◆																✔			
20.2	Recorded music on the internet: only the beginning of the broadband revolution?	736	◆												✔							
20.3	Chocolate maker savours its sweet desserts	741			◆										✔							✔
21.1	Shock tactics at BOC	750	◆																	✔		
21.2	Counting on Carly: part 1	758	◆				◆					✔								✔		
21.3	StanChart chief swept out by culture clash	766		◆		◆						✔								✔		
21.4	Counting on Carly: part 2	777	◆				◆					✔								✔		
22.1	Next steps for Novartis	788	◆		◆	◆								✔			✔					
22.2	Side-effects of age leave Roche reeling	800	◆		◆									✔			✔					✔
2.3	Prescriptive strategy to rescue Britain's ailing NHS	*CASES ON THE COMPANION WEBSITE*		◆																	✔	
2.4	Emergent strategy at Spillers baking			◆					✔			✔										
2.5	The rise and fall of Dalgety			◆													✔					
4.4	The call of Africa grows louder							◆	✔													
7.2	Culture, crisis and power at British Petroleum			◆								✔										
8.4	Improving shareholder wealth at LucasVarity, Burton and Diageo		◆	◆									✔									
10.3	Negotiation ethics at Portsmouth's new millennium tower			◆																	✔	
12.2	Objectives derailed on the Jubilee Line Extension			◆																	✔	
15.4	Mobile Revolution: Vodafone's struggle to maintain its success		◆																✔			
19.1	Globalisation at Giant Bicycles		◆			◆										✔						
19.2	International strategy in the world pulp and paper industry		◆													✔						
20.3	Making an impact in only 100 days			◆																✔	✔	
21.2	Owens-Corning reveals its strategies for change			◆																✔		
21.3	United Biscuits – a shadow of its former self		◆	◆																✔		

Acknowledgements

First edition

During the writing of the first edition of this book, the text has benefited enormously from a panel of reviewers set up by Pitman Publishing. They are: Drs Robert Bood, Vakgroep Bedrijfseconomie, Faculty of Economics, Gronigen University; Stuart Bowie, Bristol Business School, University of the West of England; Ms Maria Brouwer, Department of Economics, Amsterdam University; Bruce Lloyd, Head of Strategy, Business School, South Bank University; Professor Bente R Lowendahl, Department of Strategy and Business History, Norwegian School of Management, Sandvika; Richard Morland, Senior Lecturer in Management, Department of Business Management, Brighton University; Dr Martyn Pitt, School of Management, Bath University; Professor Louis Printz, Department of Organisation and Management, Aarhus School of Business, Denmark; Professor Dr Jacob de Smit, Faculteit der Bedrijtskunde, Erasmus University, Rotterdam; and Bill Ramsay, Associate Fellow, Templeton College, Oxford.

In addition, others have also made a significant contribution: Dr Richard Gregson and Richard Cawley, European Business School, London; Professor Colin Haslam, Royal Holloway College, University of London; Dr Carol Vielba and Dr David Edelshain, City University Business School, London; Adrian Haberberg, University of Westminster, London; Professor Kazem Chaharbaghi, University of East London; Laurie Mullins, University of Portsmouth; and Val Lencioni and Dr Dennis Barker, Middlesex University Business School. I am also grateful to Middlesex University for a part-time sabbatical to write sections of the text.

Since becoming involved in higher education, I have lectured at universities in South East England, Singapore and elsewhere. The concepts and cases have benefited from the comments, challenges and contributions of many students over this time period and I am grateful to them all.

To provide real-life examples, I have been able to draw upon material provided by a number of organisations. In particular, I would like to thank Skandia, Ford Motor Company and Portsmouth City Council. I am also grateful to the *Financial Times* for permission to adapt a number of articles as case studies for use in the book. Numerous other authors and organisations have also given permission for extracts from their work to be used: these are acknowledged appropriately in the text.

Note that Chapter 14 presents a case study of two companies, Eurofreeze and Refrigor. These are wholly fictional names developed for the purposes of the case study. No link is intended with any real company that might be trading under these or similar names in frozen food or other products. As explained in the case, the data is derived from several real cases and has been disguised to protect confidentiality.

The first edition of this book would never have happened without the major support and encouragement of the editorial team at Pearson Education. Their professionalism, experience and knowledge have been invaluable. My thanks go to Catriona King in the very early days and, later, to the invaluable Stuart Hay, together with Simon Lake and Mark Allin. Elizabeth Tarrant worked magnificently on the editorial process, Colin Reed produced an excellent design and Helen Beltran notably improved the text. Finally, Penelope Woolf provided the bedrock of guidance and support on which all else has rested. My thanks to them all.

This book has a history stretching back over a number of years, including the author's experience in nearly 30 years as a line manager and consultant in industry. To all my many colleagues over the years, I offer my grateful thanks for all the lessons learnt.

Second edition

The second edition owes much to those who contributed to the first edition: they are acknowledged above. In addition, a new panel of reviewers set up by the publishers has commented on the second edition and the text has again benefited considerably from their guidance. They are: Greet Asselburgh, Management Department, RUCA Antwerpen; Peter Berends, Faculty of Economics and Business Administration, University of Maastricht; Andy Crane, Cardiff Business School; Steven Henderson, Southampton Institute; Tom Lawton, Royal Holloway, University of London; Judy Slinn, Oxford Brookes University.

In addition to all those named above across the two editions, others have also made a significant contribution to this edition: the many students who have commented on parts of the text; Professor Harold Rose and the Dean, Professor John Quelch, London Business School; Roger Lazenby, Middlesex University Business School; Gerry Scullion, Ulster University; the participants in the two *Financial Times* Corporate Strategy Workshops in early 1999; the anonymous respondents to the academic questionnaire from the publishers on the first edition; John Meehan and one of his student groups in Liverpool John Moores University. In addition to his comments, John has also taken over responsibility for the website that operates in conjunction with this text, for which my thanks.

Various companies and organisations have given permission for their material to be used in the text. They are thanked individually in the text.

Importantly, it is right to acknowledge the immense contribution of the publishers, Pearson Education, to the development of this second edition. Their policy of seeking the highest standards in educational publishing has been crucial to this work. Their significant resource commitment to promote and communicate strategic management writing and research has been a vital element in the development of the second edition. In addition to those named above at the time of the first edition, I am particularly grateful to Jane Powell and Beth Barber for their earlier guidance and advice. More recently, Sadie McClelland and Jacqueline Senior have taken over these roles and moved the process forward with considerable skill. I would also like to record my thanks to David Harrison for the desk editing job at Harlow.

Finally, I want to thank two of my nephews: Christian Lynch, who sorted out my computer software, and Stephen Lynch, who sorted out the hardware. Without them and all the others who have contributed to the text, this second edition would never have happened.

Third edition

Once again, Pearson Education set up a panel to comment on the second edition and provide invaluable comments for the third edition. The guidance of the following is much appreciated: John Ball, Swansea Business School; Jack Colford, Oxford Brookes University; Sandy Cripps, East London Business School; Bo Eriksen, University of Southern Denmark; Joyce Falkenberg, Norwegian School of Economics and Business Administration; Moira Fischbacher, University of Glasgow; Simon Harris, University of Stirling, UK; Paul Jackson, Coventry Business School; Tomi Laamanen, Helsinki University of Technology; Juha Laurila, Helsinki School of Economics; Tim Moran, University of Salford; Robert Morgan, University of Wales, Aberystwyth; Colin M Souster, University of Luton; Barry Witcher, University of East Anglia.

Fourth edition

As with previous editions, Pearson Education set up a panel to comment on the third edition and provide invaluable comments for this new edition. The comments of the following have been much appreciated: Dr. Paul Baines, Middlesex University Business School; Dr David Lal, Aberdeen Business School, The Robert Gordon University; Dr Celine Abecassis-Moedas, Centre for Business Management, Queen Mary-University of London; Bruce Cronin, University of Greenwich Business School; Marcin Wojtysiak-Kotlarski, Collegium of Business

Administration, Warsaw School of Economics; Philippa Collins, School of Management and Languages, Heriot-Watt University; James Rowe, Sunderland University Business School; Dr Denis Harrington, Business Postgraduate Centre, School of Business, Waterford Institute of Technology, Ireland; Dr James Cunningham, Department of Management, National University of Ireland, Galway; Dr Edward Shinnick, National University of Ireland – Cork; Colin Turner, University of Hull; Dr Paul Hughes, The Business School, Loughborough University; Dr Jonathan Moizer, Plymouth Business School, University of Plymouth; Professor Robert E. Morgan, Cardiff Business School, Cardiff University.

Again, it is right to acknowledge the major contribution of the publishers, Pearson Education, to the development of the third and fourth editions. Over the years, many Pearson people have contributed with professionalism, enthusiasm and real interest. For the first two editions, I listed all the major Pearson contributors individually. However, there have now been so many over the years that the list has become somewhat unmanageable. May I therefore simply record my thanks collectively to everyone involved.

Publisher's acknowledgements

We are grateful to the following for permission to reproduce copyright material:

Figures 1.6, 21.7 and 21.8 from *Managing Change for Competitive Success*, Blackwell Publishing Ltd (Pettigrew, A and Whipp, R 1991); Case 2.3, Case 6.3, Case 10.2, Case 13.4, Case 19.4 and Case 21.2 photos Corbis; Table 3.2 from *Implanting Strategic Management*, FT Prentice-Hall, reprinted by permission of the Ansoff Family Trust (Ansoff, I and McDonnell, E 1990); Figure 4.5 adapted from 'On the description and comparison of economic systems', in *Comparison of Economic Systems: Theoretical and Methodological Approaches*, edited by A Eckstein, University of California Press. Copyright © The Regents of the University of California (Koopman, K and Montias, J M 1971); Figure 5.9 courtesy of British Aerospace plc; Case 6.1 GlaxoSmithKline logo reprinted by permission of GlaxoSmithKline; Exhibit 6.2 from *The Economics of Strategy*, Copyright © 1996 John Wiley & Sons, Inc. This material is used by permission of John Wiley & Sons, Inc. (Besanko, D, Dranove, D and Shenley, M 1996); Table 6.2 from 'How much does industry matter?', *Strategic Management Journal*, March 1991, pp64–75, Copyright © 1991 John Wiley & Sons, Inc. Reprinted by permission of John Wiley & Sons, Inc. (Rumelt, R 1991); Table 6.4 after *Gaining and Sustaining Competitive Advantage, 2nd Edition*, reprinted by permission of Pearson Education, Inc. (Barney, J B 2002); Figures 6.10 and 20.2 from 'Sustaining competitive advantage: towards a dynamic resource-based strategy', *Management Decision*, 37(1), pp45–50, with permission from MCB University Press (Chaharbaghi, K and Lynch, R 1999); Case 7.1 photo The Henry Ford; Table 7.2 republished with permission of the Academy of Management, from 'Organizational Strategy, Structure and Process', *Academy of Management Review*, 3, copyright 1978; permission conveyed through Copyright Clearance Center, Inc. (Miles, R E *et al.* 1978); Figure 7.7 from 'Evolution and Revolution as Organisations Grow', *Harvard Business Review*, July–August 1972. Copyright © 1972 by the President and Fellows of Harvard College; all rights reserved. Reprinted by permission of Harvard Business School Publishing (Greiner, L E 1972); Case 8.3 SCA logo and screenshot reprinted by permission of Svenska Cellulosa Aktiebolaget SCA (publ); Table 8.9 from *Strategic Management*, 9th edn © Richard D Irwin, a Times Mirror Higher Education Group, Inc. Company, Burr Ridge, USA, p.31. Adapted with permission of the publisher (Thompson, A and Strickland, A 1996); Case 9.2 photo Toyota (GB) PLC; Exhibit 11.2 reproduced courtesy of Skandia Insurance Company Ltd (publ); Figure 11.4 redrawn from *The Knowledge-Creating Company: How Japanese Companies Create the Dynamics of Innovation*, reprinted by permission of Oxford University Press, Inc. (Nonaka, I and Takeuchi, H 1995); Figure 11.5 adapted from *Wellsprings of Knowledge*, Copyright © 1995 by the President and Fellows of Harvard College; all rights reserved. Reprinted by permission of Harvard Business School Publishing (Leonard, D 1995); Table 12.2 adapted from *Corporate Responsibility*, reprinted by permission of Pearson Education Ltd. (Cannon, T 1994); Exhibit 12.4 reprinted by permission of the Ford Motor Company; Figure 12.9 reproduced by permission of Dr Evert Gummerson; Figure 13.13 redrawn from *The Mind of the Strategist*, reprinted by permission of the McGraw-Hill Publishing Company (Ohmae, K 1983); Case 14.1 photo Nokia; Figure 14.4 reproduced by permission of Arthur D Little Limited; Exhibit 16.6 adapted from 'The Structuring of Organisations' in *The Strategy Process: Concepts and Contexts*, 4th edition, edited by H Mintzberg *et al.*, reprinted by permission of Pearson Education, Inc. (Mintzberg,

H 2003); Exhibit 16.7 republished with permission of Academy of Management, from *An Integrative Framework for Strategy-Making Processes*, *Academy of Management Review*, 17, copyright 1992; permission conveyed through Copyright Clearance Center, Inc. (Hart, S 1992); Figure 17.3 from *The Strategy-focused Organisation*, Copyright © 2001 by the President and Fellows of Harvard College; all rights reserved. Reprinted by permission of Harvard Business School Publishing (Kaplan, R S and Norton D P 2001); Case 17.2 photo Canon (UK) Limited; Figure 17.9 after *Strategic Control*, reprinted by permission of Pearson Education Ltd. (Goold, M and Quinn, J J 1991); Figure 18.3 from *Public Management Reform*, Oxford University Press. By permission of Oxford University Press (Pollitt, C and Bouckaert, G 2000); Figure 19.3 from *The Competitive Advantage of Nations*, Macmillan (Porter, M E 1990); Figure 19.7 after *Managing the Multinational Enterprise: Organization of the Firm and Ownership of Subsidiaries*, reprinted by permission of Basic Books, a member of Perseus Books, L.L.C. and Pearson Education Ltd. (Stopford, J M and Wells, Jr, L T 1972); Case 20.1 screenshot reprinted by permission of eBay Inc.; Case 20.3 screenshot reprinted by permission of Lily O'Briens; Figure 22.4 reprinted by special permission from *The McKinsey Quarterly*, Summer 1980.

We are grateful to the Financial Times Limited for permission to reprint the following material:

Case Study 3.1 'Pete and Ken's excellent adventure. Lord of the Rings looks set to be one of the most profitable movies ever. So why was making it such a big deal?', adapted from Survey – Creative Business, © *Financial Times*, 19 March 2002; headline: 'Boo faces its critics but jury is still out on Net prospects', © *Financial Times*, 3 February 2000; headline: 'Boo's next?', © *Financial Times*, 19 May 2000; Case Study 9.3 Adapted from 'India's scooter giant seeks US style kickstart', © *Financial Times*, 6 July 1998; Case Study 10.3 Adapted from 'Steering straight with his foot to the floor', © *Financial Times*, 26 February 2001; Case Study 11.5 Adapted from 'How Philips exploits its technology edge', © *Financial Times*, 22 March 2001; Case Study 16.2 Adapted from 'Cisco Systems: Benefits of a highly structured organisation?', © *Financial Times*, 12 April 1999; Case Study 20.1 Adapted from 'Ebay, the flea market that spanned the globe', © *Financial Times*, 11 January 2002 and 'Inside Track: Farewell to online utopia: No more "neighbourhood watch" for users of the ebay auction site', © *Financial Times*; Case Study 20.3 Adapted from 'Chocolate maker savours its sweet desserts', © *Financial Times*, 20 April 2004; Case Study 21.1 Adapted from 'Shock tactics at BOC', © *Financial Times*, 29 April 1999; Case Study 21.3 Adapted from 'StanChart chief swept out by culture clash', © *Financial Times*, 1 December 2001; Case Study 22.2 Adapted from 'A dose of bad medicine: side-effects of age leave Roche reeling', © *Financial Times*, 1 June 2001; Figure 3.8 Sony manufacturing operations, © *Financial Times*, 15 November 1995; Figure 9.5 Axle-stand production line at a car accessory factory, © *Financial Times*, 4 January 1994.

BP plc for an extract from the *BP Annual Report and Accounts 2004*; Ford Motor Company Limited for an extract from the *Ford Motor Company 1996 Company Mission, Values and Guiding Principles*; Pearson Education Limited for an extract from *Multinational Enterprises and the Global Economy* by J H Dunning (1993); Penguin Books Limited and Richard Pascale for an extract adapted from his book *Managing on the Edge*; Svenska Cellulosa Aktiebolaget SCA for an extract from the SCA Annual Report and Accounts 1992.

In some instances we have been unable to trace the owners of copyright material, and we would appreciate any information that would enable us to do so.

Chapter 1
Corporate strategy

- What is corporate strategy and why is it important?
- What are the core areas of corporate strategy and how do they link together?
- What makes 'good' corporate strategy?
- To what extent is corporate strategy different in public and non-profit organisations?
- What are the international dimensions of corporate strategy?

Chapter 2
A review of theory and practice

- How have current ideas on corporate strategy evolved?
- What are the main approaches to corporate strategy?
- What are the main prescriptive and emergent theories of strategy?
- How does the theory of corporate strategy relate to corporate practice?

INTRODUCTION

This part of the book introduces the concept of corporate strategy. Chapter 1 outlines the main elements of the subject and explains its importance and its role in delivering the purpose of the organisation. The two main approaches to the process of corporate strategy are outlined and explored. Chapter 2 gives a fuller review of how corporate strategy has evolved and discusses in greater depth the two main approaches in its development.

The prescriptive strategic process

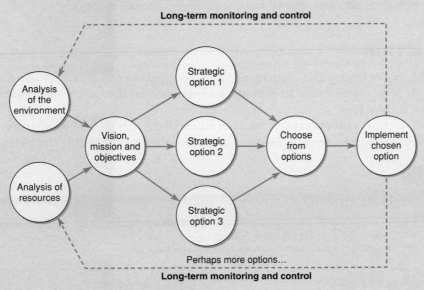

The emergent strategic process

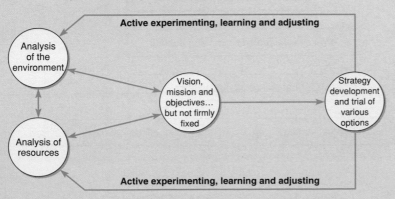

Chapter 1

CORPORATE STRATEGY

Learning outcomes

When you have worked through this chapter, you will be able to:

● define corporate strategy and explain its five special elements;

● explain the core areas of corporate strategy and how they link together;

● distinguish between process, content and context of a corporate strategy;

● identify what makes 'good' corporate strategy;

● outline the extent to which corporate strategy differs in public and non-profit organisations;

● explain the difference between national and international corporate strategy.

INTRODUCTION

Corporate strategy is exciting and challenging. It makes fundamental decisions about the future direction of an organisation: its purpose, its resources and how it interacts with the world in which it operates.

Every aspect of the organisation plays a role in this strategy – its people, its finances, its production methods and its environment (including its customers). In this introductory

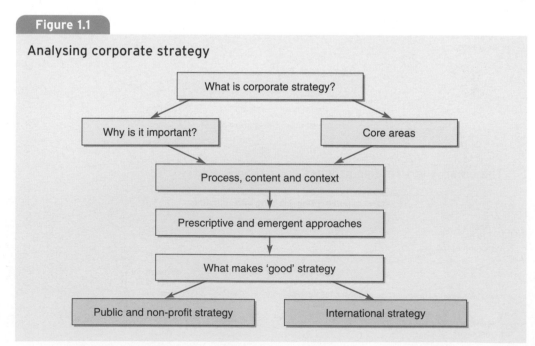

Figure 1.1

Analysing corporate strategy

chapter we examine how these broad areas need to be structured and developed if the organisation is to continue to operate effectively.

Corporate strategy is complicated by the fact that there is considerable disagreement between researchers on the subject and how its elements are linked together. There are two main routes and these are examined in this chapter: the prescriptive process and the emergent process. As a result, two models have been developed to explain the subject. These are shown in the opening diagram to this part of the book (*see* p1).

Part 1

In exploring corporate strategy, it is useful to begin by examining why it is important and what it contains. A useful distinction can also be drawn between its process, content and context. The two main routes are then examined and the key question explored – what makes 'good' strategy? Finally in this chapter, we examine the special characteristics of public and international strategies – *see* Figure 1.1.

CASE STUDY 1.1

Apple's profitable but risky strategy

When Apple's Chief Executive – Steven Jobs – launched the Apple iPod in 2001, he made a significant shift in the company's strategy from the relatively safe market of innovative, premium-priced computers into the highly competitive market of consumer electronics. This case explores this profitable but risky strategy.

Early beginnings

To understand any company's strategy, it is helpful to begin by looking back at its roots. Founded in 1976, Apple built its early reputation on innovative personal computers that were particularly easy for customers to use and as a result were priced higher than those of competitors. The inspiration for this strategy came from a visit by the founders of the company – Steven Jobs and Steven Wozniack – to the Palo Alto research laboratories of the Xerox company in 1979. They observed that Xerox had developed an early version of a computer interface screen with the drop-down menus that are

widely used today on all personal computers. Most computers in the late 1970s still used complicated technical interfaces for even simple tasks like typing – still called 'word-processing' at the time.

Jobs and Wozniack took the concept back to Apple and developed their own computer – the Apple Macintosh (Mac) – that used this consumer-friendly interface. The Macintosh was launched in 1984. However, Apple did not sell or share the software to rival companies. Over the next few years, this non-co-operation strategy turned out to be a major weakness for Apple.

Apple's specialist computers dominate the desktop publishing market segment – here in a design studio in Italy.

In 2001, Apple moved from selling specialist niche computers used in design and desktop publishing into mainstream consumer electronics. This shop façade in Fukuoka, western Japan illustrates the depth of the new competition taken on by this major strategic decision on the part of Apple.

Battle with Microsoft

Although the Mac had some initial success, its software was threatened by the introduction of Windows 1.0 from the rival company Microsoft, whose chief executive was the well-known Bill Gates. Microsoft's strategy was to make this software widely available to other computer manufacturers for a licence fee – quite unlike Apple. A legal dispute arose between Apple and Microsoft because Windows had many on-screen similarities to the Apple product. Eventually, Microsoft signed an agreement with Apple saying that it would not use Mac technology in Windows 1.0. Microsoft retained the right to develop its own interface software similar to the original Xerox concept.

Coupled with Microsoft's willingness to distribute Windows freely to computer manufacturers, the legal agreement allowed Microsoft to develop alternative technology that had the same on-screen result. The result is history. By 1990, Microsoft had developed and distributed a version of Windows that would run on virtually all IBM-compatible personal computers – see Case 1.2. Apple's strategy of keeping its software exclusive was a major strategic mistake that it was determined to avoid when it came to the launch of the iPod.

Apple's innovative products

Unlike Microsoft with its focus on a software strategy, Apple remained a full-line computer manufacturer from that time, supplying both the hardware and the software. Apple continued to develop various innovative computers and related products. Early successes included the Mac2 and PowerBooks along with the world's first desktop publishing programme – PageMaker. This latter remains today the leading programme of its kind. It is widely used around the world in publishing and fashion houses. It remains exclusive to Apple and means that the company has a specialist market where it has real competitive advantage and can charge higher prices.

Not all Apple's new products were successful – the Newton personal digital assistant did not sell well. Apple's high price policy for its products and difficulties in manufacturing also meant that innovative products like the iBook had trouble competing in the personal computer market place.

Apple's move into consumer electronics

Around the year 2000, Apple identified a new corporate strategy to exploit the growing worldwide market in personal electronic devices – CD players, MP3 music players, digital cameras, etc. It would launch its own Apple versions of these products to add high-value, user-friendly software. Resulting products included iMovie for digital cameras and iDVD for DVD-players. But the product that really took off was the iPod – the personal music player that stored hundreds of CDs. And this time, Apple sought industry co-operation rather than keep the product to itself. The iPod was launched in late 2001 and, importantly, was followed by the iTunes Music Store in 2003 in the USA and 2004 in Europe. ITunes was essentially an agreement with the world's five leading record companies to

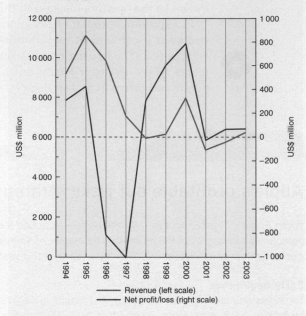

Figure 1.2

Apple Computers – sales and net income 1993-2002

Revenue (left scale)
Net profit/loss (right scale)

allow legal downloading of music tracks using the internet for 99 cents each. This was a major coup for Apple – it had persuaded the record companies to adopt a different approach to the problem of music piracy. At the time, this revolutionary agreement was unique to Apple and was due to the negotiating skills of Steve Jobs, the Apple chief executive, and his network of contacts in the industry. Figure 1.2 shows that Apple's new strategy was beginning to pay off.

So, where is the risky strategy?

By 2005, Apple's music player – the iPod – was the premium-priced, stylish market leader with around 60 per cent of world sales. Its iTunes download software had been redeveloped to allow it to work with all Windows-compatible computers (about 90 per cent of all PCs) and it had around 70 per cent of the world music download market, the market being worth around US$330 million per annum. The company had launched the iPod Mini and the iPod Shuffle to meet demand for lower-priced versions of the same product.

Here lies the strategic risk for Apple. Apart from the classy, iconic style of the iPod, there is nothing that rival consumer electronic companies cannot match. By 2005, all the major companies like Sony, Philips and Panasonic were catching up fast with new launches that were just as stylish, cheaper and with more capacity. Apple's competitors were even reaching agreements with the record companies to provide legal downloads of music from websites. Another example of the likely competition came from the mobile telephone market leader,

Nokia, and the dominant software company, Microsoft. In February 2005, they jointly announced that all new Nokia mobile phones would come with Microsoft's Windows Media 10, allowing downloading of music from PCs onto mobile phones – yet another threat to Apple. However, Apple was the market leader and was able to demonstrate major increases in sales and profits from the development of the iPod and iTunes by early 2005. Apple had sold over 10 million iPods worldwide since the launch in 2001.

Apple's other response was to capitalise on its new popularity by launching a stripped-down version of its basic computer – the MacMini – which would integrate with the iPod and allow customers to migrate to this new, Apple computer. But the *MacMini* came without screen, keyboard and mouse. By the time these costs were included, the product was more expensive than the market leader, Dell. Moreover, mass-market personal computers were operating on wafer-thin profit margins – *see* Case 9.1.

Case questions

1 *What do you think of Apple's strategy? What would you do next if you were responsible for Apple?*

2 *What lessons can other companies learn from Apple's strategies over the years?*

STRATEGIC PROJECT

Apple and the internet music industry

You can combine the Apple case with the case on the internet music industry – Case 20.2 – into a strategic project. You will find more information from the references at the end of the chapter, particularly on web pages. It is particularly important to examine actual and potential competitors – like Dell Computers and Sony launching similar products to the iPod. At the time of preparing this case, neither company had done this, but there were plenty of rumours. Explore questions like: Will Apple continue to dominate this industry? What strategies does it need to adopt? If you were Dell, what would be your launch strategy? Look back at the patchy profit record of Apple over the last ten years – *see* Figure 1.2 – for an indication that the company may not find easy success.

1.1 WHAT IS CORPORATE STRATEGY?

1.1.1 The essence of corporate strategy

Definition ➤ Corporate strategy can be described as the identification of the *purpose* of the organisation and the plans and actions to achieve that purpose.[2] Importantly, this is not the only definition. We will consider an alternative view in the next section. During its early years, Apple's sense of purpose was to provide work for the owners, friends and immediate employees. In later years, the purpose changed as the company grew larger and it was able to seek new customers and broaden its product range. The purpose became a broader concept that included dividends to independent shareholders beyond its original founders and offering its services to a far wider range of customers. In recent years, some companies have taken the view they should have a role in society that goes beyond shareholders, employees and other immediate members of the company.

Corporate strategy consists of two main elements: corporate-level strategy and business-level strategy. Figure 1.3 captures these two important aspects of the topic of corporate strategy. Early commentators such as Ansoff[3] and Drucker[4] clearly refer to both these aspects of strategy: mapping out the future directions that need to be adopted against the resources possessed by the organisation.

- *At the general corporate or headquarters level,* basic decisions need to be taken over what business the company is in or should be in. The culture and leadership of the organisation are also important at this broad general level.[5] For example, Apple at the time of writing was developing a major new strategic initiative in consumer electronics: the basic

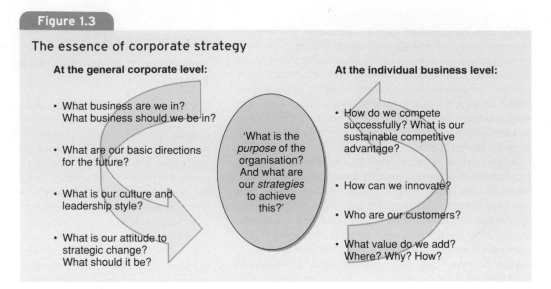

Figure 1.3

The essence of corporate strategy

At the general corporate level:

- What business are we in? What business should we be in?

- What are our basic directions for the future?

- What is our culture and leadership style?

- What is our attitude to strategic change? What should it be?

'What is the *purpose* of the organisation? And what are our *strategies* to achieve this?'

At the individual business level:

- How do we compete successfully? What is our sustainable competitive advantage?

- How can we innovate?

- Who are our customers?

- What value do we add? Where? Why? How?

strategic decision to move further into delivering recorded music, rather than expand in such areas as specialist computing, was taken by the corporate headquarters of Apple at that time. However, Apple Computers had gone through a series of re-organisations to deliver this strategy, so the new strategy was also related to the leadership and culture of the organisation. Corporate-level strategy can also be seen in the following definition of corporate strategy:

> *Corporate strategy is the pattern of major objectives, purposes or goals and essential policies or plans for achieving those goals, stated in such a way as to define what business the company is in or is to be in and the kind of company it is or is to be.*[6]

- *At the business level*, corporate strategy is concerned with competing for customers, generating value from the resources and the underlying principle of the sustainable competitive advantages of those resources over rival companies. For example, Apple in the early twenty-first century was investing heavily in new designs for computers as well as the iPod and iTunes strategy described in Case 1.1. Business-level strategy can be seen in the following definition of corporate strategy:

> *The strategy of the firm is the match between its internal capabilities and its external relationships. It describes how it responds to its suppliers, its customers, its competitors and the social and economic environment within which it operates.*[7]

However, it has to be said that there is no universally agreed definition of strategy.[8] For example, while some strategy writers, such as Campbell and others,[9] have concentrated on corporate-level activity, most strategy writing and research, such as that by Porter,[10] has concentrated on the business level. This book explores *both* levels.

It should be noted that there are writers who use terms other than 'corporate strategy' to define strategy development: 'strategic management', 'business policy', 'competitive strategy', and so on. *Corporate strategy* is used here because it embraces every *type* of organisation – large and small; public, non-profit and privately owned – and it is the most general expression of the *various levels* of strategy, including all the many lower levels within an organisation. This distinction is explored further in Chapter 12.

1.1.2 An alternative view of strategy

Some strategists dispute the approach to strategy described above.[11] Some writers, like Quinn, emphasise the uncertainty of the future and suggest that setting out to identify a single strategy and develop a complete strategic plan may be a fruitless task.[12]

Definition ➤ They see corporate strategy as being essentially entrepreneurial and dynamic, with an element of risk. Corporate strategy can be described as finding market opportunities, experimenting and developing competitive advantage over time. The intended purpose of the strategy may not necessarily be realised in practice. This definition is clearly different from that mentioned earlier. This book tackles these two conflicting definitions and their implications for strategy development, but it focuses more on the first than the second because the first has received more attention in the literature. We explore these two approaches later in this chapter.

1.1.3 The three main areas of strategy

Examining the actions further at the *business level* of corporate strategy and focusing on the first definition, every organisation has to manage its strategies in three main areas:

1 the organisation's internal *resources*;
2 the external *environment* within which the organisation operates;
3 the organisation's ability to *add value* to what it does.

Corporate strategy can be seen as the linking process between the management of the organisation's internal resources and its external relationships with its customers, suppliers, competitors and the economic and social environment in which it exists.[13]

The organisation develops these relationships from its abilities and resources. Hence, the organisation uses its history, skills, resources, knowledge and various concepts to explore its future actions. Figure 1.4 shows some examples of this process.

Resources strategy

The *resources* of an organisation include its human resource skills, the investment and the capital in every part of the organisation. Organisations need to develop corporate strategies to optimise the use of these resources. In particular, it is essential to investigate the *sustainable competitive advantage* that will allow the organisation to survive and prosper against competition. For example, Apple had advantages in the production and marketing of its new iPod music player and associated software that set the standard for the industry. It had also invested heavily in branding its products and the Apple retail stores that sold its products. All these were part of its resources.

Figure 1.4

Some examples of how corporate strategy links the organisation's resources with its environment

Environmental strategy

In this context *environment* encompasses every aspect external to the organisation itself: not only the economic and political circumstances, which may vary widely around the world, but also competitors, customers and suppliers, who may vary in being aggressive to a greater or lesser degree – customers and competitors are particularly important here. In strategy, the word 'environment' does not just mean 'green, preserve the planet' issues, though these are important and are included in the definition.

Organisations therefore need to develop corporate strategies that are best suited to their strengths and weaknesses in relation to the environment in which they operate. For example, Apple faced a highly competitive environment for its computers in relation to the American companies such as Dell and Hewlett Packard. In addition, the company had to cope with changing levels of economic growth in many markets around the world, which influenced the decisions of its customers to purchase new computers.

Some commentators, such as Ohmae,[14] suggest that a corporate strategy is really only needed when an organisation faces competitors: no competitive threat means there is no need for strategy. This is a rather narrow view of strategy and its environment: even a monopoly without competitors could need a strategy to defend its position. With a general move to privatise the nationalised monopolies around the world, corporate strategy may be required for this reason alone. Equally, charitable foundations compete for funds from donors and sometimes for the volunteers that make the wheels turn. A corporate strategy is no less relevant in this context.

Other commentators, such as Mintzberg,[15] have suggested that the environment is so uncertain, particularly at a global level, that it may be impossible to *plan* a long-term corporate strategy. This may need to be *crafted*, i.e. built up gradually through a learning process involving experimentation. The organisation may be seeking to add value by operating effectively, but the ever-changing environment offers little or no possibility for the management to plan in advance. Such commentators argue that unpredictable environments make the task of devising a realistic corporate strategy more than mere planning. Strategies have to be devised to cope with such difficulties.

Adding value

There is a need to explore further the purpose of corporate strategy beyond the requirements of environmental change and management of resources. In essence, the need is to *add value* to the supplies brought into the organisation. To ensure its long-term survival, an organisation must take the supplies it brings in, add value to these through its operations and then deliver its output to the customer.

For example, Apple takes the supplies it buys in – such as components, energy, skills and capital equipment – and then uses its own resources and expertise to create a product from these supplies – such as a computer or an iPod – that has a value which is higher than the combined value of all the supplies which have been used to make the product. Apple adds value and then passes the product on to its customers.

The purpose of corporate strategy is to bring about the conditions under which the organisation is able to create this vital additional value. Corporate strategy must also ensure that the organisation adapts to changing circumstances so that it can continue to add value in the future. The ways in which value can be added and enhanced are crucial to corporate strategy.

Corporate strategy is both an art and a science. No single strategy will apply in all cases. While most organisations would like to build on their skills, they will be influenced by their past experiences and culture, and constrained by their background, resources and environment (just as we are in our own individual lives). Nevertheless, corporate strategy is not without logic, or the application of scientific method and the use of evidence. At the end of the process, however, there is a place for the application of *business judgement*, as in our example, where Apple took a business judgement to go ahead in producing its early design of the iPod music player because the market looked attractive. Later, it took the business judgement that its best strategy was to launch a supply of music – the iTunes web download – in spite of the initial reluctance of the music companies to agree a deal.

1.1.4 Key elements of strategic decisions

There are five key elements of strategic decisions that are related primarily to the organisation's ability to add value and compete in the market place. To illustrate these elements, examples are given from the highly competitive market for video computer games which was worth around US$25 billion globally in 2004:

1 *Sustainable decisions* that can be maintained over time. For the long-term survival of the organisation, it is important that the strategy is sustainable. There would be little point in Microsoft launching its new Xbox games console if the market disappeared after six months. Up to year 2004, the company had spent millions of dollars developing the product and this would take some years to recover.[16]

2 *Develop processes to deliver the strategy.* Strategy is at least partly about *how* to develop organisations or allow them to evolve towards their chosen purpose. For example, Microsoft began by launching Xbox into the US market in Autumn 2001, followed by Japan in early Spring 2002 and Europe about one month later. But the whole strategic decision of Microsoft to compete in this market had been taken years earlier and then major investments were undertaken to achieve this purpose.

3 *Offer competitive advantage.* A sustainable strategy is more likely if the strategy delivers sustainable competitive advantages over actual or potential competitors. Corporate strategy usually takes place in a competitive environment. Even monopolistic government organisations need to compete for funds with rival government bodies. Microsoft was much later in entering the global computer games market than its main rivals, Sony and Nintendo. Microsoft therefore needed some special competitive advantages in its new machine to persuade customers of rival products to change. Initially, it was offering what it claimed to be the best video graphics and the ability to play its games on-line. Subsequently, it has claimed to offer superior games and more computing power than its competitors. Its main rival – Sony PlayStation – then announced a totally new computer chip in 2005 that would beat this advantage. One way of developing competitive advantage is through *innovation* – a constant theme of this book.

4 *Exploit linkages between the organisation and its environment* – links that cannot easily be duplicated and will contribute to superior performance. The strategy has to exploit the many linkages that exist between the organisation and its environment: suppliers, customers, competitors and often the government itself. Such linkages may be contractual and formal, or they may be vague and informal (just because they are not legally binding does not mean they have little importance). In the case of video games machines, Microsoft was able to offer compatibility and connections with its other dominant computer software products: Explorer and Windows XP.

5 *Vision* – the ability to move the organisation forward in a significant way beyond the current environment. This is likely to involve innovative strategies. In the highly competitive video games market, it is vital to have a vision of the future. This may involve the environment but is mainly for the organisation itself: a picture of how video games might look in five to ten years' time will challenge and direct strategic decisions over the intervening period. For Microsoft, its vision of the Xbox would move it from its current involvement primarily with *office* activities like report writing and presentations to new, *home entertainment* applications like video games – thus providing a completely new source of revenue. It is highly likely to involve *innovative* solutions to the strategic issues facing the industry.

In the final analysis, corporate strategy is concerned with delivering long-term *added value* to the organisation.

The key reading at the end of this chapter, taken from the work of Professor John Kay, further explores some essential aspects of corporate strategy.

Key strategic principles

● Corporate strategy can be considered at two levels in the organisation: the corporate level and the business level.

● At the corporate level, corporate strategy is the pattern of major objectives, purposes or goals and the essential policies or plans for achieving those goals. It involves a consideration of what business the company is in or should be in.

● At the business level, corporate strategy is concerned with the match between the internal capabilities of the organisation and its external relationships with customers, competitors and others outside the organisation.

● Strategy is developed by a consideration of the resources of the organisation in relation to its environment, the prime purpose being to add value. The added value is then distributed among the stakeholders.

● There are five key elements of strategy, principally related to the need to add value and offer advantages over competitors: sustainability; process; competitive advantage; the exploitation of linkages between the organisation and its environment; vision. Several of these elements may well involve innovative solutions to strategic issues.

CASE STUDY 1.2

Disaster and recovery: 1

Corporate profit disaster at IBM

In the early 1990s, the world's largest computer company, International Business Machines (IBM), suffered one of the largest profit disasters in corporate history. Essentially, its problems were rooted in poor corporate strategy. This case study examines how IBM got into such a mess. The case study at the end of Chapter 2 shows how IBM managed to turn itself round.

Over the period 1991–93, IBM (US) suffered a net loss of almost US$16 billion (half the total GDP of the Republic of Ireland at that time) – see Figure 1.5. During this period, the company had many of the characteristics of a supposedly good strategy: a dominant market share, excellent employee policies, reliable products (if not the most innovative), close relationships with national governments, responsible local and national community policies, sound finances and extensive modern plant investment around the world. Yet none of these was crucial to its profit problems, which essentially arose from a failure in corporate strategy. This case study examines how this came about: *see* Figure 1.5. The reasons for the major losses are explored in the sections that follow – clearly the company was continuing to sell its products, but its costs were too high and it was unable to raise its prices because of increased competition.

IBM market domination 1970–85

During the 1970s and early 1980s, IBM became the first-choice computer company for many of the world's leading companies: it had a remarkable global market share – approaching 60 per cent. It constructed its computers to its own proprietary standards so that they were incompatible with other computers but helped to maintain the company's domination of the market.

In essence, IBM offered large, fast and reliable machines that undertook tasks never before operated by machinery: accounting, invoicing and payroll. Above all, choosing IBM meant that risk was low for customers: 'No one ever got fired for buying IBM.' Hence, IBM was the market leader in large *mainframe* computers and earned around 60 per cent of its profits from such machines.

Reflecting its dominance of global computer markets, the IBM culture was relaxed and supremely confident of its

Figure 1.5

IBM Computers – sales and net income 1989–93

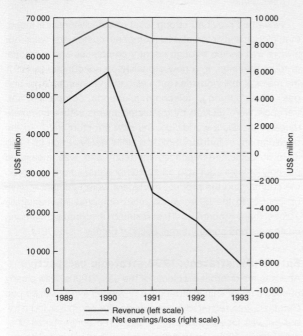

- —— Revenue (left scale)
- —— Net earnings/loss (right scale)

abilities and resources. Because of its sheer size and global reach, the company was split into a series of national companies, each operating with a great degree of independence. This meant that central management control was limited, with many key strategic decisions being taken at national company level. Often, central management did not even know what was happening in key product groups until the end of the year, when all the figures for the group were added up. For major new market developments, the initiative was often taken by IBM's North American subsidiary. Throughout this period, IBM central HQ was content to rely on the success and profitability of its mainframe computer range and observe the rapid growth of another small but related market in which it had no involvement: the personal computer (PC) market.

Development of the PC market

During the late 1970s and early 1980s, small PCs with names like Osborne, Commodore and Sinclair were developed. Some of these were particularly user-friendly – for example, Apple computers. In these early years, IBM preferred to maintain a lofty technical distance. It took the view that the PC market was small and PCs would never handle the mainframe tasks. Some of these small

machines were built around common computer chips and software. Although they did not have the capacity to handle any of the large computational problems of computer mainframes, the PC market was growing fast – over 100 per cent per annum in some years. In the late 1970s, IBM was exploring new growth areas and decided to launch its own small machine onto the market.

The launch of the IBM PC in 1983

Because IBM's existing company structure was large and nationally based and its culture was so slow and blinkered, it chose to set up a totally new subsidiary to manufacture and market its first PC. Moreover, it did not use its own proprietary semiconductor chips and operating software. It acquired them respectively from the medium-sized chip manufacturer Intel (US) and from what was then a small software company called Microsoft (US).

IBM took the view that it was doing Intel and Microsoft and all PC customers a favour by making the IBM designs into the world standard. Indeed, IBM was rather proud of establishing the global benchmark in what was a small specialist market sector, as well as holding the lead in the much larger mainframe market. IBM finally launched its first PC in 1981 without tying either Intel or Microsoft exclusively to itself. The new PC cost US$3,000 and, by today's standards, was very small. Although the claim 'IBM-compatible' quickly became a common standard for most PCs, except Apple, these developments had two consequences for IBM:

1 its worldwide PC standard allowed competitors to produce to a standard design for the first time;
2 no restriction was placed by IBM on Intel and Microsoft supplying similar products to other companies.

In spite of its price (over $1,000) and performance, the new Atari ST was presented as good value for money in 1985. It was compatible with the new IBM-PC standard but did not use Microsoft Windows Software – it used an alternative called GEM, which has now disappeared. The Atari Company itself ceased to trade around 1990.

▶ **CASE STUDY 1.2 continued**

IBM reasoned that these issues did not matter because it would dominate the small PC market just as it did mainframes. In addition, IBM judged that the small PC would never replace the large mainframe, so it posed no significant threat to its main business. As it turned out, the company was at least partially wrong on both counts.

Technological advance and branding in the later 1980s

Although computer markets were driven by new technology, the key development was IBM's establishment of the common technical design mentioned above. This meant that its rivals at last had a common technical platform to drive down costs. IBM was unable or unwilling to find some way of patenting its design. IBM's strategic mistake was to think that its reputation alone would persuade customers to stay with its PC products. However, its competitors were able to exploit the new common IBM-compatible PC design to produce faster, reliable and cheaper machines than IBM, using the rapid advances in technology that occurred during the 1980s.

IBM and other computer companies continued to spend funds branding their products. However, their suppliers, such as Intel and Microsoft, also began to spend significant sums on advertising. Microsoft's 'Windows' was launched in the late 1980s and Intel's 'Pentium' microchip was launched in 1993. Both were destined to dominate their respective markets.

IBM slips into disaster 1986-93

In the late 1980s, IBM recognised the competitive threat from Microsoft and Intel. It launched its own proprietary software, OS/2 Warp, in 1994 to counteract this. It also negotiated with Apple to set up a new computer chip standard, the Power PC Chip, with the aim of attacking Intel. Although both initiatives had some innovations, they were too little and too late. IBM struggled on with the concepts, but the software made little headway against the established Microsoft and the chip was abandoned in the mid-1990s.

By 1993, IBM's advertising was forced into claiming that its PCs used the Microsoft 'Windows' operating system and its computer chips had 'Intel inside'. The IBM PC was just one of many computers in the small-computer market.

New organisation structure: 1991

Recognising the need for change, the company began to develop a new organisational structure in 1991. Up to this time, the organisation had been centred on two central aspects of the company:

1 *Products*. The company provided the most complete range of products from mainframes to telecommunications networks, from PCs to computer software. Each main product group sold its products independently of other groups.
2 *Country*. The company was the leading provider in most countries, with the ability to provide computer solutions tailored at national level for the particular requirements of each country. Each major country had its own dedicated management responsibilities.

While this provided strong local responsiveness, it meant that global and international company customers were not always well served through country companies and individual product offerings. In a new organisation announced in 1991, the major global industries such as banking, insurance, oil and gas, manufacturing, telecommunications companies and transport were tackled by dedicated teams with a *complete range of products* worldwide: the new structure involved the development of Industry Solution Units (ISUs). Each ISU had its own dedicated management team and was measured not only on sales but also on customer satisfaction. However, the country and the product managers were reluctant to give up control to the ISUs, which often operated internationally across many countries. This resulted in confusion among customers and some internal political battles inside IBM.

Future IBM strategy: 1993 strategic perspective

After the major profit problems of the early 1990s, IBM clearly needed a major shift in strategy. A new chief executive, Mr Lou Gerstner, was recruited from outside the computer industry, but he was faced with a major task. The conventional strategic view in 1993 was that the company was too large. Its true strengths were the series of national IBM companies that had real autonomy and could respond to specific national market conditions, and the wide range of good IBM products. But the local autonomy coupled with the large IBM product range meant that it was difficult to provide industry solutions. Moreover, IBM's central HQ and research facility had difficulty in responding quickly to the rapid market and technological changes that applied across its global markets. The ISUs had been set up to tackle this but did not seem to be working. The most common strategy solution suggested for IBM was therefore to break up the company into a series of smaller and more responsive subsidiaries in different product areas – a PC company, a mainframe company, a printer company and so on.

Case questions

1 *Use the five key elements of strategic decisions (see Section 1.1.4) to evaluate IBM's corporate strategy. What conclusions do you draw for these and added value?*

2 *What are the strengths and weaknesses of IBM? And what are the opportunities and threats that it faces from the competitive environment surrounding the company?*

3 *What strategies would you have adopted in 1993 to turn round the situation at IBM? When you have made your choice, you might like to turn to the end of Chapter 2 and see what the company actually did.*

1.2 CORE AREAS OF CORPORATE STRATEGY

Definition ➤ The three core areas of corporate strategy are strategic analysis, strategy development and strategy implementation.

1 *Strategic analysis.* The organisation, its mission and objectives have to be examined and analysed. Corporate strategy provides value for the people involved in the organisation – its *stakeholders* – but it is often the senior managers who develop the view of the organisation's overall objectives in the broadest possible terms. They conduct an examination of the *objectives* and the organisation's *relationship with its environment.* They will also analyse the *resources* of the organisation. This is explored in Chapters 3 to 12.

2 *Strategy development.* The strategy options have to be developed and then selected. To be successful, the strategy is likely to be built on the particular skills of the organisation and the special relationships that it has or can develop with those outside – suppliers, customers, distributors and government. For many organisations, this will mean developing advantages over competitors that are sustainable over time. There are usually many options available and one or more will have to be selected. This is covered in Chapters 13 to 15.

3 *Strategy implementation.* The selected options now have to be implemented. There may be major difficulties in terms of motivation, power relationships, government negotiations, company acquisitions and many other matters. A strategy that cannot be implemented is not worth the paper it is written on. This is explored in Chapters 16 to 22.

If a viable corporate strategy is to be developed, each of these three areas should be explored carefully. For the purpose of clarity, it is useful to separate the corporate strategy process into three sequential core areas, as we have done above. It would be wrong, however, to think of the three core areas as being only sequential. While it is not possible to implement something that does not exist, many organisations will have some existing relationships with customers and suppliers that are well developed, and others that have not yet started. Even small, new companies will want to experiment and negotiate. This means that activities in all three areas might well be simultaneous – implementing some ideas while analysing and developing others.

Table 1.1 lists some of the working definitions used in the three core areas of corporate strategy, some of which will already be familiar to you. To clarify the distinction between the terms, the table also includes the example of an ambitious young manager, showing his/her strategy for career progression. However, the example in Table 1.1 highlights two important qualifications to the three core areas:

1 the influence of judgement and values;

2 the high level of speculation involved in major predictions.

The importance of *judgement and values* in arriving at the mission and objectives shows that corporate strategy is not a precise science. For example, in the hypothetical career example in Table 1.1, the person has a clear view on what is important in life if their ambitions are to be achieved; some people would not share these ambitious values. We examine the role of value judgements further in Chapter 12.

Moreover, corporate strategy may be *highly speculative* and *involve major assumptions* as it attempts to predict the future of the organisation. For example, many of the later stages of the career progression in Table 1.1 involve some very difficult projections – on marriage, family and health, for example – that may well not be achieved. Indeed, given such uncertainties, it is difficult to see the example as anything more than an idealised series of wish-statements. In the same way, in the case of corporate strategy, there may be a largely false and perhaps unrealistic sense of direction.

Some books and research papers on corporate strategy do not recognise this problem and may be guilty of implying that corporate strategy has certainties about the future that it

Table 1.1

Definition of terms used in the three core areas of strategy[18]

	Definition	Personal career example
Mission statement	Defines the business that the organisation is in against the values and expectations of the stakeholders	To become a leading European industrialist
Objectives (or goals)	State more precisely what is to be achieved and when the results are to be accomplished. Often quantified. (Note that there is no statement of how the results are to be attained)	To achieve a directorship on the main board of a significant company by the age of 42
Strategies	The pattern or plan that integrates an organisation's major goals or policies and action sequences into a cohesive whole. Usually deals with the *general principles* for achieving the objectives: why the organisation has chosen this particular route	1 To obtain an MBA from a leading European business school 2 To move into a leading consultancy company as a stepping stone to corporate HQ 3 To obtain a key functional directorship by the age of 35 in the chosen company
Plans (or programmes)	The *specific* actions that then follow from the strategies. They specify the step-by-step sequence of actions to achieve the major objectives	1 To obtain a first-class honours degree this year 2 To take the next two years working in a merchant bank for commercial experience 3 To identify three top business schools by December two years from now 4 To make application to these schools by January of the following year
Controls	The process of monitoring the proposed plans as they proceed and adjusting where necessary. There may well be some modification of the strategies as they proceed	Marriage and children mean some compromise on the first two years above Adjust plans back by three years
Reward	The result of the successful strategy, adding value to the organisation and to the individual	High salary and career satisfaction

does not possess in reality.[19] Some companies also take this approach and work on the basis that strategy is set rigidly for a fixed time period.[20] This does not mean we should not explore the future directions of corporate strategy, just that we should be cautious about their meaning.

Key strategic principles

- The three core areas of corporate strategy are: strategic analysis, strategic development and strategy implementation.
- There are two important qualifications to the three core areas. Judgement and values play an important role in determining the objectives and choice. Moreover, some elements are highly speculative and may involve major assumptions.
- There is considerable overlap between the three core areas, which are separated out for the sake of clarity but, in practice, may operate concurrently.

1.3 PROCESS, CONTENT AND CONTEXT

Research[21] has shown that in most situations corporate strategy is not simply a matter of taking a strategic decision and then implementing it. It often takes a considerable time to make the decision itself and then another delay before it comes into effect. There are two reasons for this. First, *people* are involved – managers, employees, suppliers and customers, for example. Any of these people may choose to apply their own business judgement to the chosen corporate strategy. They may influence both the initial decision and the subsequent actions that will implement it. Second, the *environment* may change radically as the strategy is being implemented. This will invalidate the chosen strategy and mean that the process of strategy development needs to start again.

For these reasons, an important distinction needs to be drawn in strategy development between *process*, *content* and *context*. Every strategic decision involves these three elements, which must be considered separately, as well as together.

Every strategic decision involves:

1 *Context* – the environment within which the strategy operates and is developed. In the IBM case during the 1980s the context was the fast-changing technological development in personal computers.

2 *Content* – the main actions of the proposed strategy. The content of the IBM strategy was the decision to launch the new PC and its subsequent performance in the market place.

3 *Process* – how the actions link together or interact with each other as the strategy unfolds against what may be a changing environment. The process in the IBM case was the delay in tackling the PC market, the slow reaction to competitive actions and the interaction between the various parts of the company as it attempted to respond to competitor actions. Process is thus the means by which the strategy will be developed and achieved.

These three elements are the axes of the same three-dimensional cube of corporate strategy decision making (*see* Figure 1.6).

In most corporate strategy situations, the *context* and *content* are reasonably clear. It is the way in which strategy is developed and enacted – the *process* – that usually causes the most problems. Processes need investigation and are vague and quixotic because they involve people and rapidly changing environments.

The difficulty is compounded by the problem that, during the implementation period, the process can influence the initial strategic decision. For example, as the process unfolded at IBM, competitive actions forced the organisation to make cutbacks that were not originally identified as part of the strategic content.

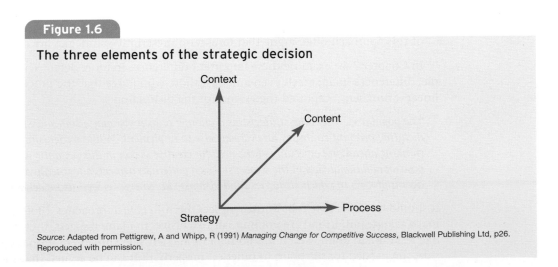

Figure 1.6

The three elements of the strategic decision

Source: Adapted from Pettigrew, A and Whipp, R (1991) *Managing Change for Competitive Success*, Blackwell Publishing Ltd, p26. Reproduced with permission.

At various points throughout this book, the distinction between process, content and context will be useful in clarifying relationships. Much emphasis will be laid on process, which is one of the more difficult parts of strategy.

Key strategic principles

- In corporate strategy development, it is necessary to distinguish between three elements: context, content and process.

- In most corporate strategy situations, the context and content are reasonably clear; it is the process that causes the problem because process may influence the way that people in the organisation develop and implement strategy.

- Process is the way actions link together or interact with each other as the strategy unfolds in the environment, which may itself be changing. It is often one of the more difficult parts of strategy development.

1.4 PROCESS: LINKING THE THREE CORE AREAS

1.4.1 Two different approaches to the process

Part 1

Until now corporate strategy has been presented as a unified, cohesive subject. It is important at this point to explain and explore a fundamental disagreement which exists among commentators over the way that corporate strategy may be developed. Differing views on the content, process and nature of corporate strategy have arisen because of the breadth and complexity of the subject. For the present, the overall distinctions can be summarised as representing two main approaches to corporate strategy development:

1 *The prescriptive approach.* Some commentators have judged corporate strategy to be essentially a linear and rational process, starting with where-we-are-now and then developing new strategies for the future (*see* Jauch and Glueck[22] and Argenti[23]). A prescriptive corporate strategy is one whose *objective* has been defined in advance and whose *main elements* have been developed before the strategy commences.

Definition ➤

2 *The emergent approach.* Other commentators take the view that corporate strategy emerges, adapting to human needs and continuing to develop over time. It is evolving, incremental and continuous, and therefore cannot be easily or usefully summarised in a plan which then requires to be implemented (*see* Mintzberg[24] and Cyert and March[25]). Emergent corporate strategy is a strategy whose *final objective* is unclear and whose *elements* are developed during the course of its life, as the strategy proceeds. The theorists of this approach often argue that long-term prescriptive strategies are of limited value.

Definition ➤

In Chapter 2 we examine these important differences in more detail. There are, for example, differences in approach even amongst those who judge that the process is rational and linear. Mintzberg[26] captured the essence of the distinction:

The popular view sees the strategist as a planner or as a visionary; someone sitting on a pedestal dictating brilliant strategies for everyone else to implement. While recognising the importance of thinking ahead and especially of the need for creative vision in this pedantic world, I wish to propose an additional view of the strategist – as a pattern recognizer, a learner if you will – who manages a process in which strategies (and visions) can emerge as well as be deliberately conceived.

It should be noted here that Mintzberg sees merit in *both* approaches. (Both approaches can make a contribution and are not mutually exclusive. In many respects, they can be said to be like the human brain, which has both a rational left side and an emotional right side. Both sides are needed for the brain to function properly.)[27] It can be argued that the same is true

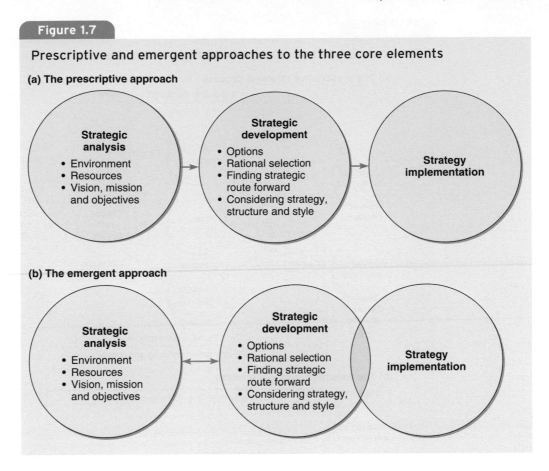

Figure 1.7

Prescriptive and emergent approaches to the three core elements

(a) The prescriptive approach

Strategic analysis
- Environment
- Resources
- Vision, mission and objectives

Strategic development
- Options
- Rational selection
- Finding strategic route forward
- Considering strategy, structure and style

Strategy implementation

(b) The emergent approach

Strategic analysis
- Environment
- Resources
- Vision, mission and objectives

Strategic development
- Options
- Rational selection
- Finding strategic route forward
- Considering strategy, structure and style

Strategy implementation

in corporate strategy. Reference is therefore made to both the prescriptive and emergent approaches throughout this book. However, it should be understood that these are main headings for a *whole series of concepts* of corporate strategy – explored in more detail in Chapter 2.

1.4.2 Impact on the three core areas

1 *The prescriptive approach* takes the view that the three core areas – strategic analysis, strategic development and strategy implementation – are linked together sequentially. Thus it is possible to use the analysis area to develop a strategy which is then implemented. The corporate strategy is *prescribed* in advance (*see* Figure 1.7(a)).

2 The *emergent approach* takes the view that the three core areas are essentially interrelated. However, it is usual to regard the analysis area as being distinctive and in advance of the other two elements. Because corporate strategy is then developed by an experimental process that involves trial and error, it is not appropriate to make a clear distinction between the strategy development and implementation phases: they are closely linked, one responding to the results obtained by the other. These relationships are shown in Figure 1.7(b).

1.4.3 Developing models of corporate strategy

Based on the two approaches, it is possible to develop models to aid in understanding the way that corporate strategy operates. These models are explained here and will then be used throughout this book to structure our examination of corporate strategy.

The two contrasting models are shown in Figure 1.8. Each element of the process is explored in more depth in the chapters of the book that follow.

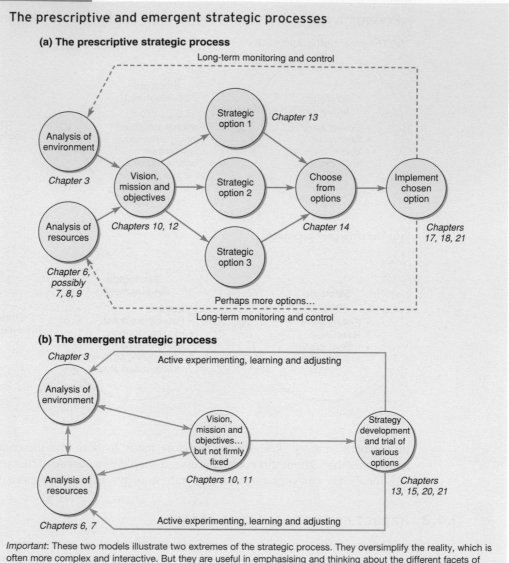

Figure 1.8

The prescriptive and emergent strategic processes

(a) The prescriptive strategic process

Long-term monitoring and control

Analysis of environment

Chapter 3

Strategic option 1 — *Chapter 13*

Vision, mission and objectives

Chapters 10, 12

Strategic option 2

Analysis of resources

Chapter 6, possibly 7, 8, 9

Strategic option 3

Choose from options

Chapter 14

Implement chosen option

Chapters 17, 18, 21

Perhaps more options…

Long-term monitoring and control

(b) The emergent strategic process

Chapter 3

Active experimenting, learning and adjusting

Analysis of environment

Vision, mission and objectives… but not firmly fixed

Chapters 10, 11

Strategy development and trial of various options

Chapters 13, 15, 20, 21

Analysis of resources

Chapters 6, 7

Active experimenting, learning and adjusting

Important: These two models illustrate two extremes of the strategic process. They oversimplify the reality, which is often more complex and interactive. But they are useful in emphasising and thinking about the different facets of the strategic process.

Strategic analysis

The analytical phase of both the *prescriptive* and the *emergent* approach can be divided into two parts:

1 *Analysis of the environment* – examining what is happening or likely to happen outside the organisation, e.g. economic and political developments, competition.

2 *Analysis of resources* – exploring the skills and resources available inside the organisation, e.g. human resources, plant, finance.

These are followed by a third element:

3 *Identification of vision, mission and objectives* – developing and reviewing the strategic direction and the more specific objectives, e.g. the maximisation of profit or return on capital, or in some cases a social service.

Some strategists put this third element *before* the other two.[28] They argue that any organisation first sets out its objectives and then analyses how to achieve them. However, this book takes the view that it is necessary to set objectives in the *context* of the environment and competitive resources of the organisation. For example, a manufacturer of straw hats needs to take account of the very limited demand for that product and the limited likelihood of having superior competitive resources *before* setting its objectives.

So vision, mission and objectives are accepted by both prescriptive and emergent approaches but, at this point, the two processes clearly diverge.

Strategy development and implementation

According to the prescriptive approach, the next step is the formal consideration of the options available to achieve the agreed objectives. This is followed by a rational selection from the options according to identified criteria, in order to arrive at the prescriptive strategy. In most cases, this choice is implemented after considering the necessary organisation, controls and other matters that will be important in practice. The decisions then feed back into the resources and the environment of the organisation – for example, the 'resources' of the strategy might include new factories and new products and the 'environment' might include new customers attracted to the organisation as a result of its new strategy. Both these will have an impact on subsequent strategic decisions and are represented in the model by the outside feedback arrows.

In Figure 1.8(a) the steps in this process can be followed. It should be emphasised, however, that this diagram represents only one description of the approach; there are many different approaches, with strategists unable to agree on the definitive prescriptive route – Chapter 2 explores this in more depth.

Strategy development and implementation – the emergent approach

Essentially, this takes a much more experimental view of the strategy choice and its implementation. It seeks to learn by trial, experimentation and discussion as strategies are developed. There is no final, agreed strategy but rather a series of experimental approaches that are considered by those involved and then developed further. Strategies emerge during a process of crafting and testing.

There is therefore no clear distinction in the emergent approach between the two stages of developing the strategy and its implementation.

Moreover, there is no need to identify a separate stage of discussion involving the leadership, culture and organisation, since all these will occur inevitably during the strategy development and implementation phase. Importantly, there is then a strong link back to the earlier analytical phase, enabling changes in the environment and resources to be reflected quickly in the adaptive, learning strategy. This is shown in Figure 1.8(b).

By definition, there can be no single view of a process that emerges within an organisation – each one will be different. Figure 1.8(b) serves to indicate the circulatory nature of the decision-making process according to this approach. There is no definitive emergent route.

Key strategic principles

- There are two main approaches to corporate strategy development: the *prescriptive* approach and the *emergent* approach. Each complements the other, and both are relevant to the strategy process.

- The *prescriptive* approach takes the view that the three core elements are linked together sequentially. The *emergent* approach regards the three core areas as being essentially interrelated.

- The two approaches can be used to develop models for the corporate strategy process. However, it should be recognised that every model is a compromise and may not reflect all the circumstances that exist in reality.

1.5 WHAT MAKES 'GOOD' STRATEGY?

Given the lack of agreement on a definition of corporate strategy and the difficulty of developing it successfully, it is relevant to explore what makes 'good' corporate strategy. To some, it might appear that there is one obvious answer: 'good' strategy delivers the purpose set out for the strategy in the beginning. However, this begs several important questions:

1 Was the purpose itself reasonable? For example, perhaps the purpose was so easy that any old strategy would be successful.

2 What do we do when it is difficult to define the purpose clearly, beyond some general objective of survival or growth? Such vagueness may make it difficult to test whether a 'good' strategy has been developed.

3 Since the whole purpose of strategy is to explore what we do in the *future*, can we afford to wait until it has been achieved before we test whether it is good?

Essentially, we need some more robust tests of good strategy. These lie in two areas. First, those related to the real world of the organisation and its activities: *application-related*. Second, those that rely on the disciplines associated with the basic principles of *academic rigour*: originality, logical thought and scientific method. It might be argued that academic rigour has no relevance to the real world, but this would be wrong. All organisations should be able to apply these basic principles to the process of strategy development.

1.5.1 Tests of good strategy: application-related

At least three tests are available that provide some means of assessing whether a strategy is good:

1 *The value-added test*. A good strategy will deliver increased value added in the market place. This might show itself in increased profitability, but might also be visible in gains in longer-term measures of business performance such as market share, innovative ability and satisfaction for employees.

2 *The consistency test*. A good strategy will be consistent with the circumstances that surround a business at any point in time. It will take into account its ability to use its resources efficiently, its environment, which may be changing fast or slowly, and its organisational ability to cope with the circumstances of that time.

3 *The competitive advantage test*. For most organisations, a good strategy will increase the sustainable competitive advantage of the organisation. Even those organisations that traditionally may not be seen as competing in the market place – such as charities or government institutions – can be considered as competing for resources. Charities compete with others for new funds, government departments compete with each other for a share of the available government funds.

In practice, such tests can be applied to strategy proposals at any time.

1.5.2 Tests of good strategy: academic rigour

Another five tests might also be employed that relate to the above but are more fundamental to the basic principles of originality, logical thought and scientific method:

1 *The originality test*. The best strategy often derives from doing something totally different. One test that has academic validity is therefore that of originality. However, this needs to be used with considerable caution or it becomes just another excuse for wild and illogical ideas that have no grounding in the topic.

2 *The purpose test*. Even if there are difficulties in defining purpose, it is logical and appropriate to examine whether the strategies that are being proposed make some attempt to

address whatever purpose has been identified for the organisation. Such a definition of purpose might be taken to include the aspirations and ambitions of the leaders of the organisation, along with its stakeholders.

3 *The logical consistency test.* Do the recommendations flow in a clear and logical way from the evidence used? And what confidence do we have in the evidence used? Do we trust such evidence? Might it be unreliable because it has come from a competitor?

4 *The risk and resources test.* Are the risks and resources associated with the strategies sensible in relation to the organisation? They might be consistent with the overall purpose, but involve such large levels of risk that they are unacceptable. Moreover, they may require resources that are substantially beyond those available to the organisation – not just finance, but perhaps people and skills.

5 *The flexibility test.* Do the proposed strategies lock the organisation into the future regardless of the way the environment and the resources might change? Or do they allow some flexibility, depending on the way that competition, the economy, the management and employees and other material factors develop?

While none of these tests is complete in itself, together they provide a way to explore proposals and the many case studies that appear in this book.

Key strategic principles

● The lack of agreement on the precise meaning of corporate strategy makes it difficult to identify what is meant by 'good' corporate strategy. If strategy development is to be beneficial, then a careful exploration and definition of the purpose of the task is essential early in the process. Two areas of test are suggested in this search: application-related and academic rigour.

● *Application-related* might be considered as having three major components: value added, consistency with the environment and the delivery of competitive advantage.

● *Academic rigour* can usefully be considered as having five components: originality, relevance to the defined purpose, logical consistency, risks and resources, flexibility.

1.6 STRATEGY DEVELOPMENT IN PUBLIC AND NON-PROFIT ORGANISATIONS

1.6.1 Public organisations

In many countries around the world, the public sector forms the major part of industrial and commercial activity, e.g. telecommunications services in South Africa and the French government controlling shareholdings in its national electricity and gas companies, although some of these have now been privatised.[29] Since such companies often compete internationally with the private sector, many of the same strategy considerations apply to public and to private organisations. The major difference has been the lack in government-owned institutions of the objective to deliver a profit. The European Commission has now taken the view that state subsidies may not be compatible with the Treaty of Rome, and public organisations have come under increasing pressure to apply commercial criteria.[30] In Europe, there are many organisations in the public sector, ranging from electricity supply in some countries to public health bodies in others. Their individual requirements for strategy development will depend on their precise nature. Certainly those that are being privatised will need to consider this area.

Outside Western Europe, many key industries remain in public ownership. However, the trend in most parts of the world is now towards privatising large public companies in the utilities and telecommunications sectors. The arguments in favour of the change of owner-ship are set out in the *World Bank Report 1994*.[31] The principal impact of privatisation on strategy will depend on the form that privatisation takes. Some companies may still remain monopolies even though they are in the private sector.

The main considerations regarding corporate strategy in public organisations include:

- *Policy and politics*. Some European countries and Asian countries such as India and China are committed to the view that public companies are there to provide a public service. Strategy is therefore directed towards achieving this aim. The political policy of the gov-ernment will guide strategic development.

- *Monopoly suppliers*. Public authorities are often monopoly suppliers of a service. While they may be under pressure to operate efficiently (however that is defined), they may be unable to spend any surplus profits they generate. Moreover, they will be subject to changes in government policy direction and will lack the consistency of private organ-isations as a result. The lack of choice for customers will mean the suppliers are not really subject to the market pressures that affect business strategy in the private sector.

- *Bureaucracy and slower rate of change*. Being part of the public sector may affect the man-agement style and values of managers and the workforce, leading specifically to greater bureaucracy and a slower rate of response to outside pressures.

- *Battle for resources from government*. Much of the real strategy in the public sector across Europe is fought over the allocation of resources from central government. Increases in annual budget allocations or cutbacks in funds affect fundamentally the service and level of investment in physical assets available to the public. There is no reason why such con-siderations should not be subject to strategic scrutiny, but the nature of the evidence and logic may be different.

1.6.2 Non-profit organisations

Both public and private organisations operate in this area: charities, churches, even some educational institutions, for example. Non-profit organisations are usually founded for rea-sons other than commercial considerations: for instance, bird and animal welfare, disease research, international rescue, poverty alleviation. For these reasons, corporate strategy must first recognise and reflect the values held by such organisations.[32] It also needs to understand the voluntary nature of much of this activity and the varied sources of funds often available.

All of these considerations will have a profound effect on corporate strategy. Decision making may be slower and more uncertain. There may be more lobbying of funding bodies over individual decisions. There may be several conflicting objectives that make strategy difficult to develop. The style and expectations of the organisation need to be built into the strategy process. These matters are explored in depth in Chapter 18 of this text.

Key strategic principles

- Public organisations are unlikely to have a profit objective. Strategy is therefore governed by broader public policy issues such as politics, monopoly supply, bureaucracy and the battle for resources from the government to fund the activities of the organisation.

- Strategy in non-profit organisations needs to reflect the values held by the institutions concerned. Decision making may be slower and more complex.

- Within the constraints outlined above, the basic strategic principles can then be applied.

1.7 INTERNATIONAL DIMENSIONS IN CORPORATE STRATEGY

While the principles of corporate strategy can be applied across the world, the international dimensions of strategy do introduce some specific and important considerations.[33]

- *International economies and their impact on trading between nations.* The completion of the Uruguay Round of the General Agreement on Tariffs and Trade in 1994, the enlargement of the EU in the period 2004–2008 and the formation of the North American Free Trade Association in 1994 are all examples of such developments. All may provide opportunities and pose threats for company corporate strategy.

- *International finance, currency and tax.* For example, adverse currency movements alone could severely curtail gains to be made from other aspects of corporate strategy.

- *Economies of scale and production.* Coupled with the lower wage costs available in some countries, these have had a powerful impact on aspects of corporate strategy.

- *Differing cultures, beliefs and management styles around the world.* These are major factors that must form an important part of corporate strategy for international companies. Major strategic problems have arisen where international companies have considered these vital topics too late in the strategy process.

This is not a comprehensive list of major topics, but it does illustrate the specific impact on corporate strategy. Corporate strategy is more complex in international environments, but the same basic principles apply. International issues are explored at the end of most chapters in this text, with a major review being undertaken in Chapter 19.

Key strategic principles

- The international dimensions of corporate strategy make its development more complicated.
- Among the topics that need careful consideration are: international economies and their impact on world trade; international finance; economies of scale derived from global production; differing cultures and beliefs.

CASE STUDY 1.3

Sky-high strategies of Europe's budget airlines

Between 1993 and 1997, European airline markets were steadily freed from government regulations on competition, pricing and services. Following this deregulation process, the new European budget airlines – like Ryanair (Ireland), easyJet (UK), Air Berlin (Germany) and Buzz (Netherlands) – presented some serious competition to Europe's leading airlines. This case explores the attack strategies that threaten the very survival of companies like Lufthansa, British Airways and SAS.

'We make money with falling air fares. And we make stinking piles of money with rising air fares . . . It's scary' – Michael O'Leary, chief executive of Ryanair in year 2000. Although profits at Europe's largest airlines had recovered from the losses of 2001, most of them were still struggling. Two of Europe's leading airlines – Swiss Air and Sabena – went bankrupt in 2001 and the reborn Swiss International Airlines was still in recovery in 2004. The leading Italian airline, Alitalia, was in severe financial difficulties at that time. British Airways had shed over 20 per cent of its workforce by the year 2004 and Lufthansa was under major pressure from budget airlines in its domestic German market. By contrast, the leading budget airlines – Ryanair and easyJet – were making significant profits and ordering new aircraft to expand their European operations. Europe's major air carriers were in major strategic trouble. However, this was not just because of the new budget airlines.

▶ CASE STUDY 1.3 continued

Reasons for the strategic difficulties – high staff costs and poor load factors

Although the budget airlines represented a significant competitive threat to Europe's leading airlines, the problems facing such airlines were more complex than a simple high- versus low-cost strategy. The leading airlines traditionally earned their major profits from their *long-haul* routes – like Amsterdam to New York or London to Singapore. Their *short-haul* routes, i.e. those inside their home countries or within the EU, were rather less profitable. On the long-haul routes, they were able to charge high prices because of special 'open skies' deals that existed between individual EU countries and other nations like the USA. Essentially, country governments in the 1990s signed these deals. They carved up the long-haul markets between countries – like Germany to the USA – between a limited number of airlines and excluded other European and foreign airlines that might offer more competition. The long-haul market was particularly important for some airlines – see Table 1.2.

In addition, each European country controlled flight access to its major airports and gave preferential treatment to its own national carriers – Air France in France, KLM in the Netherlands and so on – thus reducing competition and raising prices. In 2002, the European Commission on behalf of the European Union (EU) challenged these agreements, arguing that they were against the open competition rules of the Treaty of Rome. At the time of writing, the 'open skies' policies still persisted but was likely to come to an end in the next few years. The outcome was still not entirely clear and was associated with political negotiations between the member nations of the EU.

As a result, those airlines with a high proportion of such profitable long-haul routes and destinations – like Lufthansa, British Airways and Air France – were able to earn significant profits and perhaps justify higher numbers of employees. Table 1.3 shows the resulting picture in terms of staff costs in comparison with turnover. Companies like Iberia, SAS and Alitalia had proportionately less long-haul turnover – for example, fewer people wanted to fly from Stockholm to New York than from Frankfurt to New York. Hence, the smaller airlines were unable to benefit to the same extent from such profitable routes. Even so, most European airline companies persisted for many years in maintaining relatively high numbers of staff, though all airlines were now cutting staff. However, Table 1.3 shows that such airlines still had much higher staff numbers than the budget airlines.

In addition to high staff costs, the more recent problem has been 'load factor' – the percentage of seats filled by paying passengers on each aircraft. With a scheduled flight, the aircraft has to keep to a timetable and fly, even if it is half-empty. And three factors reduced passenger numbers dramatically in the last few years:

● *Downturn in the world economy* – leading to fewer business-class travellers. These were the real profit earners as they were willing to pay much higher prices than economy-class passengers for marginal improvements in flight comfort.
● *Tragic events of September 11 2001* – making people and companies reluctant to undertake unnecessary air travel.
● *Increased fuel costs* – for a variety of reasons, airline fuel costs rose significantly over the period and these were reflected in some increase in air fares. However, the main impact of higher fuel costs was on lower profits as the airlines felt unable to pass on all the cost increases to their passengers.

Thus in the period 2001–2004, long-haul flights were not as profitable as in previous years. In addition, the 'open skies' policy still allowed some competition and all airlines were suffering. The problem here was that no airline had any real competitive advantage over its rivals apart from the 'open skies' deals and the rights to land at some national airports.

Market size, growth and share of the leading European airlines – a controlled strategic environment

At one level, the world airline market is large, with total turnover of over US$650 billion. However, this is misleading strategically because most airlines are concentrated in one geographic continent and because there is little growth, for the reasons outlined above. In the past, the 'open skies' deals compensated for this, which meant that many international markets were controlled by small oligopolies of aircraft companies. By co-operating on these leading routes, such airlines were able to hold up their prices and keep out new entrants by government treaty. American airlines inside the USA were even better protected: the US government ruled that only

Table 1.2

The importance of long-haul business for some leading airlines

Airline	Country of origin	Long-haul share of total turnover for airline (%)	Short-haul turnover of total turnover for airline (%)
British Airways	UK	63	37
Air France	France	57	43
Lufthansa	Germany	48	52
Alitalia	Italy	35	65
Iberia	Spain	32	68
SAS	Sweden, Denmark and Norway	15	85

Source: Derived from Annual Report and Accounts – note that figures are only approximate.

Table 1.3

Comparing European airlines – the budget airlines manage with far fewer employees

Airline	Country	Revenue US$ million, year 2003	Employees ('000)	Passengers (millions)	Strategic comment
Lufthansa	Germany	19 100	67	45	Picking up strategies from budget airlines – flexible pay, moving to internet ticket sales, etc.
British Airways	UK	13 800	53	38	Withdrew some operations in 2002 and still cutting back in 2004
Air France	France	16 497	72	43	Under threat from easyJet at Paris/Orly – announced merger with KLM to cut costs but not fully operational for several years
KLM Royal Dutch	Netherlands	7 500	28	20	Merging with Air France in complicated share deal over several years
SAS	Sweden, Denmark and Norway	6 000	20	24	Real competition from Ryanair and easyJet to new destinations in Denmark and Sweden – some high domestic prices: see text
Swiss International	Switzerland	5 100	7	15	Bankrupt 2001 – see text – but reconstituted in 2003/4 with funding from Swiss national and regional government. EasyJet established a new Swiss base in 2005
Iberia	Spain	5 000	25	25	easyJet and Ryanair offer cheap flights to Spanish destinations
Alitalia	Italy	5 000	23	27	Major financial crisis 2004 – not fully resolved at time of writing
Sabena	Belgium	2 500	8	11	Bankrupt 2001 – as a result of cost pressures rather than budget airlines
Virgin Europe	UK	2 000	6	5	Losses at Virgin Europe are not included in these data – low-cost competition Important to distinguish this airline from *Virgin Atlantic*, which was highly profitable and not part of the above
Austrian Airlines	Austria	1 900	4	5	Almost bankrupt in 2003. New strategy in 2004 to focus on serving Eastern European destinations – Hungary, etc.
Finnair	Finland	1 800	9	7	Some competition planned
Two selected budget airlines					
Ryanair	Ireland	840	2*	15	Just look at the passengers carried for the number of employees – turnover and passengers more than doubled since year 2000
EasyJet	UK	1 400	3*	20	Acquired Go Airline in 2003 – included in data here. Turnover more than tripled since year 2000, passengers quadrupled.

* *Note*: the employee numbers for the budget airlines are misleading as they only cover *permanent* employees. Ryanair, in particular, employs some workers on special contracts that do not appear to be fully listed in its annual accounts.

Source: Company Annual Reports and Accounts plus press reports.

▶ **CASE STUDY 1.3 continued**

domestic US airlines could fly between destinations inside the USA, thus excluding all other airlines – not only the European airlines mentioned above but also major world airlines like Japan Airlines and Singapore Airlines.

Beyond such treaty advantages, no airline company had any significant competitive advantage over its rivals. They were all transporting aircraft seats around the world and competing on offering better in-flight meals, higher quality in-flight entertainment, longer seat-room and so on. The problem with all these supposed 'advantages' was that any company could match another over time and none was really sustainable. Moreover, such advantages were often not possible on routes within Europe because the flights were too short. In addition, the European budget airlines decided that what really mattered to customers was ticket prices.

European airline markets: customers and market segmentation

The European airline market can be broadly divided into two main market segments – business customers and leisure/domestic customers. Roughly 80 per cent of all customers fall into the latter category – they are travelling for holiday or domestic reasons such as study or visiting relations. They are important to fill the aircraft but do not represent the most profitable segment of the airline market. According to Tony O'Leary of Ryanair, 'In this business, it's low cost that wins. Ninety nine per cent of people want the cheapest price. They don't want awards for the inflight magazine or the best coffee. The brand? Who cares? It has to be safe, on time and cheap. It's a bus service, it's transport.'

The other 20 per cent are business customers. They are paid for by their companies and are engaged on business-related activities. It is this latter group that is usually prepared to pay for full-fare tickets and travel in greater comfort. For the airlines, the business customers are therefore the most profitable. There is some recent evidence that business customers are increasingly under pressure from their companies to travel on budget airlines. The main difficulty may be that some budget airports are located far from business destinations: for example, the Frankfurt-Hahn German destination of Ryanair from London Stansted is 96 kilometres from the main business centre of Frankfurt.

Perhaps the most important strategic feature of the European airline market is the lack of strong market segments beyond the two above. This makes it difficult to operate dedicated niche strategies that target these segments with special prices, services and related activities. The lack of such segments has made it easier for the budget airlines to attack the leading European companies.

Strategic threat from the budget European airlines

Low-price flights have been available for many years throughout Europe: the holiday charter air companies offered them by taking groups of tourists on holiday using special flights and dedicated aircraft. However, such flights were not available to the general public at scheduled times. This all changed with the *deregulation* of the European airline market in the 1990s. For example, in October 2001 a typical business ticket on a scheduled flight from London Gatwick to Amsterdam cost US$550 on British Airways and US$170 on easyJet – but see the comment on the availability of tickets later in this section. The difficulty of British Airways and all the other leading European airlines is that they were unable to match the budget airline prices and still make a profit just by cutting out newspapers and coffee. Table 1.3 provides a clue – just compare the number of employees at BA and easyJet and then look at the number of passengers carried.

Even amongst the budget airlines, low *price* itself is not a sustainable competitive advantage. However, lower *costs* than competitors are an advantage – as long as they can be maintained. The difficulty is that such a route to competitive advantage is well known. For example, Ryanair copied this

*In May 2005, **British Airways** charged £123 for a return morning/evening flight from London Heathrow to Milan Malpensa Airport. The price for the journey from London Stansted to Milan Bergamo on **Ryanair** around the same time was £89.*

Table 1.4

Some examples of how to keep costs down at Europe's budget airlines

Cost reduction strategy	Reason
Simple fare structure based on single journey – often cheaper if booked early	Makes it easy and cheaper to operate booking and pricing – fill up part of the aircraft and then charge marginal pricing to maximise revenue
Rapid turnaround at the airport – maximum of 25 minutes versus one hour for other airlines	The aircraft only earns profits when it is flying
Operate on routes that only operate point-to-point, so that there are no connecting flights	Connecting flights can mean delays, extra baggage handling costs, more complicated route structures, etc.
Choose airports with low handling charges	Significant savings can be made by avoiding London/Heathrow, Paris/CDG, etc.
No food or newspapers sold or free on the aircraft	Clearing up food and waste paper delays the turnaround time
Few job restrictions – even the pilots may help with baggage	Saves the cost of extra staff
Avoid travel agents and use the internet for booking	Travel agents charge fees and the internet can be used to fill seats quickly at the last minute
Operate high-density seating	More passengers increases revenue
Operate one type of very modern aircraft – often the latest model Boeing or Airbus	Reduces maintenance costs

Source: Press reports – see references for this case at end of chapter.

approach from South West Airlines in the US in the late 1980s: 'We went to look at South West. It was like the road to Damascus. This was the way to make Ryanair work' – Michael O'Leary, chief executive of Ryanair.

Table 1.4 lists some of their cost-reduction practices. Nevertheless, it should be acknowledged that the level of service on the European budget airlines may be barely tolerable for some passengers. In addition, some European airports are far from tourist destinations. However, easyJet and Go both had a deliberate policy of flying to main airports, even if the landing fees are higher. The aim was to attract business travellers. Moreover, the budget airlines often only offer the very low prices on the seats that they have difficulty in filling – just try to book a low-price seat during a main holiday weekend! Perhaps there is not so much competitive advantage on costs over the leading European carriers after all.

Strategic response from Europe's leading airlines up to year 2004: initially some uncertainty but then employ budget airline strategies

In the face of the significant threat to their European routes, the response of the leading European airlines has been somewhat inconsistent. For example, British Airways (BA) decided in 1999 to launch its own low-cost airline, called Go. This was duly set up in 2000. Then in 2001, BA decided that its new strategy was to withdraw from the low-cost end of the market and concentrate on business passengers. The company sold Go to a management buyout in mid-2001. By the end of that year, BA announced a new strategy. It was restructuring its European airlines on low-cost strategic lines, but would not be

setting up a separate airline. 'We will not become a no-frills airline, nor will we launch one' – Rodd Eddington, BA's chief executive. Nevertheless, BA would be reducing its fleet costs, reducing levels of service to economy class passengers and assuming that business class passengers would continue to pay full fare.

Lufthansa's response was different but equally defensive. Its immediate strategy was to offer low prices on its own domestic routes and to match Germania, one of its low-cost rivals. Ryanair then increased its presence in the German market and engaged in a very public battle with Lufthansa. This prompted a warning to Lufthansa from the German competition office about selling seats below costs. In late 2001, Lufthansa withdrew its services from some UK/German routes where it faced heavy competition. In addition, the airline mounted a legal challenge to Ryanair's German advertising that called on Germans not to let 'Lufthansa strip you down to your underpants'. Ryanair obtained 1.5 million German passengers in 2002 and was forecasting 10 million by 2008.

The Dutch airline KLM responded to the budget airline challenge by setting up its own low-cost airline, Buzz. Subsequently, it merged its operations with Air France in order to save overhead costs. However, this merger was complicated and would take some years to have a full impact. Air France itself was concerned when its French competitor, Air Lib, collapsed in France, thus releasing some air landing slots at Paris/Orly airport. easyJet attempted to take all these slots, but was only awarded a portion of them. SAS, Scandinavian Airlines, set up a series of deals with low-cost rivals Maersk in Denmark and Skyways in Sweden. But these arrangements

▶ CASE STUDY 1.3 continued

broke EU competition rules and needed to be renegotiated. Many of Europe's leading airlines have thus far been unable to withstand the strategic challenge of the budget carriers in any substantive way.

In March 2002, a consortium of the leading European airlines launched their own website to sell airline tickets cheaply at the last minute and fill remaining aircraft capacity: it is called opodo and can be viewed at: www.opodo.co.uk. It has proved a significant success in terms of offering a way for the major airlines to reduce booking costs and offer special deals to fill their aircraft. In addition, all airlines have now developed their individual extensive on-line internet booking facilities. The winners have been the ordinary customers; the losers have been the ticket agents who used to handle the bookings. The airlines themselves have gained no competitive advantage from such a move since they all offer the same facility.

Conclusion

In 2001, Ryanair and easyJet carried 7.4 million passengers and 7.1 million passengers respectively. At that time, Ryanair was talking of carrying 40 million passengers annually by 2009–10. easyJet forecast passenger numbers of 30 million by late 2007–8. Other low-cost airlines were also setting ambitious targets. There will be some market growth over this period, but the majority of such passengers can only come from the existing European airline carriers.

© Copyright Richard Lynch 2006. All rights reserved. This case was written by Richard Lynch from published sources only.[34]

Case questions

1 Why is the development of corporate strategy important for the major European airlines?

2 Using the concept of the three major stages of corporate strategy, identify the possible main elements that might appear in a strategic plan for a low-cost airline.

3 What sustainable competitive advantages do the main European airlines possess?

4 What strategies are needed for the main European airlines to survive?

STRATEGIC PROJECT

Some of the world's airlines face severe financial pressures – for example, United Airlines and Alitalia at the time of writing. However, other airlines have managed to cope with such problems – for example, Singapore Airlines and Emirates. Why are some airlines more successful than others? What strategies have they followed? What external circumstances have helped them? You can obtain information to explore this by searching the websites of the major airlines. Then use the issues explored in this case to make a more general search of trends in airline passengers, attitudes of governments to competition, fuel price pressures.

CRITICAL REFLECTION

The nature of corporate strategy

One of the main disputes in Corporate Strategy over the last twenty years concerns the differences between prescriptive and emergent forms of strategy process. Companies argue that they need to have a 'Strategic Plan' in order to plan ahead in terms of both the competitive environment – sales, customers, new products and services – and also of resources – finance and cash, people, factories. Some of these elements take years to develop and put into practice. A clear strategic plan is therefore essential. Essentially this involves a *prescriptive* process to strategy development.

Other companies have a more entrepreneurial and experimental approach to strategy. It is important to sense what is happening in fast-changing markets and to be able to respond to this. In addition, long-term strategic planning often turns out to be mistaken, with unintended outcomes. It is better therefore to be more creative in strategy development and to take an *emergent* approach to the process of strategy development.

What is your view? Which approach is better?

Or do both approaches have merit? If the latter is true, then how do you handle the differences of approach inside the company?

SUMMARY

● In this chapter, we have explored the nature of corporate strategy – linking process between the organisation and its environment – which focuses particularly on value added and the sustainable competitive advantages of the organisation and the need to be innovative. Adding value is of particular importance to most organisations, though for non-profit and government organisations this is not necessarily the case.

● There are three core areas of corporate strategy: strategic analysis; strategic development; and strategy implementation. Although the three core areas are often presented as being strictly sequential, they will be simultaneous in some circumstances. There are two important qualifications to the three core areas: the use of judgement and values to derive the strategy and the need to make highly speculative assessments about the future. Unless handled carefully, these may give a false sense of direction about the future.

● In developing corporate strategy, there is a need to distinguish between process, content and context. Process is the method by which the strategies are derived; content is the strategic decisions then made; context is the environment within which the organisation operates and develops its strategies. Process is usually the area that causes the most problems because it is difficult to measure precisely and because it is crucial to strategy development.

● There is a fundamental disagreement between strategists regarding how corporate strategy can be developed. There are two basic routes: the *prescriptive approach* and the *emergent approach*. The prescriptive approach takes the view that the three core areas are linked together sequentially; the emergent approach regards the three core areas as being inter-related. The two approaches have some common elements in the early stages: analysis and the development of a mission for the organisation. Beyond this, they go their separate ways and lead to two different models for the corporate strategy process.

● Because of the difficulties in defining and developing strategy, it is important to explore what is meant by 'good' strategy in a particular context. There are two main areas that can be used to test whether a strategy is good or not. One area relates to its *application* to delivering the purpose of the organisation. The other area relates to the *academic rigour* with which the strategy has been developed.

● In public sector, government-owned organisations, the strategy is usually governed by broader public policy concerns, rather than profits. In non-profit institutions, strategy needs to reflect the values of the particular organisation; the basic strategic principles can then be applied.

● In international terms, the development of corporate strategy is more complex for a number of reasons, including the impact on trade between nations, financial issues, economies of scale in global production and differing cultures and beliefs. All these make international corporate strategy more complex to develop.

QUESTIONS

1 Summarise the main IBM strategies. Take each element of your summary and compare it against the criterion for a successful strategy in Section 1.5. How does each measure up? Did IBM have a 'good' strategy?

2 As a work assignment, analyse the activities of Apple Computers. Investigate in particular how it has had difficulty staying ahead of its competitors. Compare your answer with the five key elements of strategic decisions in Section 1.1.4.

3 In commenting on strategy, Professor John Kay makes the comment that motivation of employees is not really part of corporate strategy. Do you agree with this? Give reasons for your views.

▶ **Questions continued**

4 Take the three core areas of corporate strategy and apply them to a decision with which you have recently been involved. For example, it might be the organisation of a student activity or the purchase of a major item of equipment. Did you analyse the facts, consider the options and make a selection? Does this description oversimplify the process because, for example, it was necessary to persuade others to spend some money?

5 To what extent do you agree with Professor Mintzberg's description of strategies emerging rather than being prescribed in advance? If you agree with his description, what evidence do you have to support your view? If you disagree, then explain the basis of your rejection.

6 With the three core areas of corporate strategy in mind, identify how the strategy development process might vary for the following types of business: a global company such as IBM; a public service company such as a water provider (which might also be a monopoly); a non-profit organisation such as a student union or society.

7 If corporate strategy is so uncertain and has such a strong element of judgement, is there any point in its formal analysis? What arguments does the chapter use to justify such a process? Using your own value judgement, do you find them convincing?

Further reading

Professor Kay's book *Foundations of Corporate Success* (Oxford University Press, 1993) remains an excellent introduction to the nature of corporate strategy; read the early chapters. In addition, the well-known book of readings and cases by Professors Mintzberg and Quinn, *The Strategy Process* (Prentice Hall, 1991), has a useful selection of material on the nature of corporate strategy; read Chapter 1 in particular. The article by Professor Mintzberg on 'Crafting strategy' in the *Harvard Business Review* (July–Aug 1987) is also strongly recommended.

For the counter-argument to Mintzberg, a useful paper is: Miller, C C and Ireland, R D (2005) 'Intuition in strategic decision making: friend or foe in the fast-paced 21st century', *Academy of Management Executive*, Vol 19, pp19–30, which argues that intuition is troublesome in strategy.

See also Henry Mintzberg and Frances Westley (2001) 'Decision-making: It's not what you think', *Sloan Management Review*, MIT. Another interesting paper: R Duane Ireland, Michael A Hitt, S M Camp, and D L Sexton (2001) 'Integrating entrepreneurship and strategic management actions to create firm wealth', *Academy of Management Executive*, Vol 15, No 1, pp49–63.

Notes and references

1 References for Apple case: Apple Annual Report and Accounts for 2003. Website: www.apple-history.com/history. This website provides much more detail than the case and would be good for student research. *Financial Times* reports: 29 April 2003, p31; 6 April 2004, Creative Business Section, p3; 30 April 2003, p22; 14 October 2004, p29; 19 November 2004, p13; 7 December 2004, p31; 11 January 2005, p26; 12 January 2005, p27; 21 January 2005, p12; 15 February 2005, p1.

2 Adapted from Andrews, K (1987) *The Concept of Corporate Strategy*, Irwin, Homewood, IL, Ch2.

3 Ansoff, I (1969) *Corporate Strategy*, Penguin, Harmondsworth, Ch1.

4 Drucker, P (1961) *The Practice of Management*, Mercury, London, Ch6.

5 Leadership is sometimes ignored as part of the topic of strategy, but is actually extremely important. For example, where would Microsoft be without Bill Gates? It might be argued that 'strategy' should stand separately from 'leadership' but this is like trying to separate an orange from its juice.

6 Andrews, K (1971) *The Concept of Corporate Strategy*, Irwin, Homewood, IL, p28.

7 Kay, J (1993) *Foundations of Corporate Success*, Oxford University Press, Oxford, p4.

8 Further definitions are discussed in Quinn, J B (1980) *Strategies for Change: Logical Incrementalism*, Irwin, Homewood, IL, Ch1.

9 Campbell, A, Goold, M and Alexander, M (1995) 'Corporate strategy: the quest for parenting advantage', *Harvard Business Review*, Mar–Apr.

10 Porter, M E (1985) *Competitive Advantage*, The Free Press, Harvard, MA.

11 See, for example, Quinn, J B (1980) Op. cit.

12 He argues that strategic decisions are those that determine the overall direction of an enterprise and its ultimate viability in the light of the predictable, the unpredictable and the unknowable changes that may occur in its most important environments. Quinn, J B (1980) Op. cit.

13 Kay, J (1993) Op. cit., Ch1.

14 Ohmae, K (1982) *The Mind of the Strategist*, Penguin, Harmondsworth, p36.

15 Mintzberg, H (1987) 'Crafting strategy', *Harvard Business Review*, July–Aug.

16 Harney, A (2002) 'Microsoft fired up for console wars', *Financial Times*, 7 February 2002, p28.

17 Case compiled by the author from the following published sources: Heller, R (1994) *The Fate of IBM*, Warner Books, London (easy to read and accurate); Carroll, P (1993) *The Unmaking of IBM*, Crown, London (rather one-sided); *Financial Times*: 7 Aug 1990, p14; 5 June 1991, article by Alan Cane; 8 Nov 1991, article by Alan Cane and Louise Kehoe; 5 May 1993, p17; 29 July 1993, p17; 14 Mar 1994, p17; 26 Mar 1994, p8; 28 Mar 1994, p15; *Economist*, 16 Jan 1993, p23; *Business Age*, Apr 1994, p76. Note that this case simplifies the IBM story by emphasising the PC aspects. There are further parts to the story that can be read in the references above.

18 Partly adapted from Quinn, J B (1991) *Strategies for Change*, Ch1, and Mintzberg, H and Quinn, J B (1991) *The Strategy Process*, Prentice Hall, Upper Saddle River, NJ.

19 For example, Gilmore, F F and Brandenburg, R G (1962) 'Anatomy of corporate planning', *Harvard Business Review*, 40, Nov–Dec, p61.

20 For example, the IBM Annual Report and Accounts for 1993 took a firm and inflexible view on what was required to recover from its major losses. It was only the arrival of a new chief executive – see Case 2.6 – that revised this picture in a more experimental way.

21 See, for example, Pettigrew, A and Whipp, R (1991) *Managing Change for Competitive Success*, Blackwell, Oxford. See also Mintzberg, H (1987) Op. cit.

22 Jauch, L R and Glueck, W (1988) *Business Policy and Strategic Management*, McGraw-Hill, New York.

23 Argenti, J (1965) *Corporate Planning*, Allen and Unwin, London.

24 Mintzberg, H (1987) 'Crafting strategy', *Harvard Business Review*, July–Aug, p65.

25 Cyert, R M and March, J (1963) *A Behavioural Theory of the Firm*, Prentice Hall, Upper Saddle River, NJ.

26 Mintzberg, H (1987) Op. cit.

27 This analogy was inspired by Professor Mintzberg's brief comment in his article: Mintzberg, H (1994) 'The fall and rise of strategic planning', *Harvard Business Review*, Jan–Feb, p114.

28 See, for example, Thompson, A A and Strickland, A J (1993) *Strategic Management: Concepts and Cases*, 7th edn, Irwin, Homewood, IL.

29 At the time of writing, the South African government was exploring the possibility of privatising its national telecommunications services carrier, Telekom.

30 For example, the EU Barcelona Summit in 2002 was unable to agree on the complete liberalisation of energy markets across the European Union – in spite of discussing the matter for over 20 years and signing the Treaty of Rome in 1957!

31 International Bank for Reconstruction and Development (1994) *World Development Report 1994*, Oxford University Press, New York. The report surveys this area in thoughtful detail.

32 Whelan, T L and Hunger, J D (1991) *Strategic Management*, 2nd edn, Addison-Wesley, Reading, MA, Ch11.

33 Daniels, J D and Radebaugh, L H (1995) *International Business*, 7th edn, Addison-Wesley, Reading, MA.

34 Case written by author from numerous sources including: *The Economist*, Special Survey, 12 June 1993; Annual Report and Accounts of Ryanair, Easyjet, British Airways, Lufthansa, etc; also from some selected *Financial Times* articles: 8 December 1998; 11 November 2000, pp14, 20; 6 August 2001, p24; 11 August 2001, p11; 23 October 2001, p20; 31 October 2001, p14; 23 November 2001, p25; 23 January 2002, p29; 30 January 2002, p23; 1 February 2001, pp8, 24; 7 February 2002, p24; 8 February 2002, p26; 14 February 2002, p22, 15 February 2002, p26; 20 February 2002, p30; 17 May 2002, p32; 17 June 2002, p18 (Letter); 19 June 2002, p4; 1 October 2003, p28; 8 October 2003, p14; 29 January 2004, p27; 4 May 2004, p28; 8 May 2004, pM3; 2 June 2004, p26; 15 June 20004, p21; 28 June 2004, p26; 3 November 2004, p24; 5 January 2005, p11; 21 January 2005, p20; 1 February 2005, p22.

Chapter 2

A REVIEW OF THEORY AND PRACTICE

Learning outcomes

When you have worked through this chapter, you will be able to:

- outline the historical context of corporate strategy;
- describe and evaluate prescriptive strategic practice;
- describe and evaluate emergent strategic practice;
- identify the main theories associated with prescriptive corporate strategy;
- identify the main theories associated with emergent corporate strategy;
- explain the importance of an organisation's history as a part of its strategy.

INTRODUCTION

This chapter provides an overview of corporate strategy theories and practice. Each of the main theories is explored in further detail in later chapters, so it is possible to skip this chapter now and read it later, but you will miss the opportunity to gain an overview of the general theoretical structure of corporate strategy.

To provide a more substantial foundation for corporate strategy development, the prescriptive and emergent approaches of Chapter 1 deserve further exploration. They will benefit from being set against the background of the historical developments that prompted and shaped them.

Even within each route, prescriptive or emergent, there is substantial disagreement among strategists about how corporate strategy can and should be developed. Both routes contain many different interpretations and theories. If the dynamics are to be fully understood, it is important that some of these differences are explored.

Finally, it is argued that corporate strategy can only usefully be understood from a historical perspective. Every organisation's strategy must be seen in the context of its past events, its resources and its experience.

Attacking a dominant competitor: a joint venture strategy by Nestlé and General Mills

Kellogg (US) dominates the world's ready-to-eat breakfast cereal market. In 1989, Nestlé (Switzerland) and General Mills (US) agreed a joint venture to attack the market. The objectives of the new company were to achieve by the year 2000 global sales of US$1 billion and, within this figure, to take a 20 per cent share of the European market. This case examines how this was achieved by the new joint company, Cereal Partners (CP).

Parts 2 and 3

Background

In 1997, Kellogg was the breakfast cereal market leader in the US with around 32 per cent share in a market worth US$9 billion at retail selling prices. By 2002, the company was no longer market leader. Its great rival, General Mills (GM), had finally taken over with a share of 33 per cent while Kellogg's share dropped to 30 per cent. GM had achieved this important strategic breakthrough by a series of product launches over a 15-year period in a market that was growing around 2 per cent p.a. However, by 2004, Kellogg had regained market leadership again by one percentage share point. This reversal was the outcome of some clever marketing by Kellogg coupled with GM being distracted by the consequences of its acquisition of another American food company, Pillsbury, in 2003.

Outside the US, the global market was worth around US$8–10 billion and growing in some countries by up to 10 per cent p.a. However, this was from a base of much smaller consumption per head than in the US. Nevertheless, Kellogg still had over 40 per cent market share of the non-US market. It had gained this through a vigorous strategy of international market launches for over 40 years in many markets. Up to 1990, no other company had a significant share internationally, but then along came the new partnership.

The CD accompanying this text explores the battle for the breakfast cereal market.

Development of Cereal Partners

After several abortive attempts to develop internationally by itself, General Mills (GM) approached Nestlé about a joint venture in 1989. (A joint venture is a separate company, with each parent holding an equal share and contributing according to its resources and skills; the joint venture then has its own management and can develop its own strategy within limits set by the parents.) Nestlé had also been attempting to launch its own breakfast cereal range without much success. Both companies were attracted by the high value added in this branded, heavily advertised consumer market.

GM's proposal to Nestlé was to develop a new 50/50 joint company. GM would contribute its products, technology and manufacturing expertise – for example, it made 'Golden Grahams' and 'Cheerios' in the US. Nestlé would give its brand name, several underutilised factories and its major strengths in global marketing and distribution – for example, it made 'Nestlé' cream products. Both parties found the deal so attractive that they agreed it in only three weeks. The joint venture was called Cereal Partners (CP) and operated outside North America, where GM remained independent.

Over the next twelve years, CP was launched in 70 countries around the world. Products such as 'Golden Grahams', 'Cheerios' and 'Fibre 1' appeared on grocery supermarket shelves. CP used a mixture of launch strategies, depending on the market circumstances: acquisitions were used in the UK and Poland, new product launches in the rest of Europe,

South and Central America and South Africa, and existing Nestlé cereal products were taken over in South-East Asia. To keep Kellogg guessing about its next market moves and to satisfy local taste variations, CP also varied the product range launched in each country. By contrast with Kellogg, CP also agreed to make cereals for supermarket chains, which they would sell as their own brands.

By 2004, CP had reached its targets of US$1 billion profitable sales and 20 per cent of European markets. Kellogg was responding aggressively, especially in the US, where it had regained market leadership. CP was beginning to think that its innovative strategies would repeat US experience: it was beginning to attack a dominant competitor, Kellogg, worldwide.

Case question

Using the description of prescriptive and emergent strategies from Chapter 1 (and Chapter 2 if you need it), decide the following: was CP pursuing a prescriptive strategy, an emergent strategy, or both?

Note: the CD accompanying this text has a detailed analysis of the competitive battle between Kellogg and Cereal Partners. You will find it helpful to look at the CD to answer this question and explore its implications.

HISTORICAL CONTEXT OF STRATEGY

In Chapter 1, we saw that corporate strategy relates the activities of the organisation to the environment in which it operates. As a result of increasing wealth, changes in industrialisation, shifts in the power balance between nations and many other factors, this environment is constantly changing. Corporate strategy and the prevailing logic supporting it will change as the environment surrounding the organisation changes. Before we examine the theories surrounding corporate strategy, it is therefore appropriate to explore those theories in a historical context.

Until the late nineteenth century, organisations that were not owned by the nation state were too small to be considered as corporations. Small artisan factories driven by crafts may have needed strategies to survive and prosper against competitors, but formal corporate strategy did not exist. Table 2.1 shows how matters have developed since that time.

Table 2.1

The development of corporate strategy in the twentieth century, showing important environmental influences

Period	Environment	Strategy and management developments
1900–1910	• Colonial wars • Global trading of commodities	• Beginnings of examination of the management task, e.g. F W Taylor and Henri Fayol
1910–30	• World war and its legacy	• Rise of larger organisations and the consequent need for increased management control
1930s	• Crash: trade barriers erected to protect some countries	• Formal management control mechanisms developed, e.g. budgeting and management accounting, particularly in the US • Early human resource experiments in the US
1940s	• World war and its legacy	• Strong US industry and the birth of formal strategy • Beginnings of organisational theory
1950s	• Sustained economic growth coupled with first European trade and political block: European Economic Community	• First real strategy writings in formal series of papers • Organisational theory is applied to management tasks
1960s	• Continued growth until first oil price rise late in the decade	• Corporate strategy techniques are researched • Separate parallel development in organisational research
1970s	• Growth becomes more cyclical with another oil price shock	• Formal corporate strategy techniques adopted • First research writings objecting to same techniques
1980s	• Far East and global developments • Computer data handling develops fast • Beginnings of moves to privatise government institutions	• Major strategic emphasis on competitive aspects of formal corporate strategy • Search continues for new strategy concepts emphasising the human rather than the competitive aspects of the process
1990s	• Telecommunications, global corporations, high growth in the Pacific Rim but currency problems in Japan • Late 1990s – rise of internet trading and business opportunities	• Global concepts of strategy • Greater emphasis on the organisation's own resources rather than competition as the basis for strategy development • Business opportunities from internet support new strategy concepts of fast-moving markets, hypercompetition and learning mechanisms
2000s	• Global recession followed by recovery • Asian economies, including China and India, begin to grow fast • Collapse of Enron and other companies for ethical reasons	• New emphasis on innovation • Strategists realise that low-wage economies coupled with mature technologies in some industries, like cars, require new strategic approaches • Corporate social responsibility takes greater prominence in strategy

North America, Europe and Japan were more or less the only areas that had begun to industrialise by the end of the nineteenth century. Countries such as China, India, Korea, Malaysia, Singapore, the Philippines, Saudi Arabia, Iran and Iraq, Nigeria and South Africa were still largely without industry; they supplied commodities and raw materials to world markets but had not yet begun to industrialise.[1] Corporate strategy, which is principally associated with increased industrialisation, was therefore more likely to develop in Europe, North America and Japan than other areas around the world.

2.1.1 Corporate strategy in the early twentieth century

During the early twentieth century, particularly in the US and Europe, managers rather than academics began to explore and define the management task. F W Taylor in the US and Henri Fayol in France are examples of senior industry figures who started to research and write on such issues.[2] Taylor and Fayol were industrialists rather than academics, holding senior positions in industry for some years. Around the same time, Henry Ford began experimenting to produce goods more cheaply and fulfil growing market demand. In the period 1908–15[3] he developed strategies that we still recognise today, and included those outlined in Exhibit 2.1. Henry Ford did not believe in major model variations and market segmentation, however, unlike his great rival from the 1920s: General Motors, headed by Alfred P Sloan.[4] Nor did Ford believe in the importance of middle and senior management. He actually sacked many of his senior managers and ultimately left his company in real difficulties when he died.[5] Hence, his rival in the 1920s and beyond, General Motors, was ultimately more successful with other strategies that still exist today (*see* Exhibit 2.1).

Exhibit 2.1

Early strategies still recognised today

From the period 1908–15: Henry Ford

- Innovative technology
- Replacement of men by machines
- Search for new quality standards
- Constant cost-cutting through factory redesign
- Passing on the cost reductions in the form of reduced prices for the model T car

From the period 1920–35: Alfred Sloan and colleagues

- Car models tailored for specific market niches
- Rapid model changes
- Structured management teams and reporting structures
- Separation of day-to-day management from the task of devising longer-term strategy

---

After the First World War came the great economic depression of the 1930s. This brought the need for a new order in international currency and, just as importantly, the desire for larger companies to gain economies of scale. However, much of this was confined to North America and competitive strategy itself was still in its infancy.

2.1.2 Corporate strategy in the mid-twentieth century

The Second World War brought its specialist demands for military equipment, coupled with more destruction across much of Europe and Japan; North and South America went largely unscathed. At this time, the Middle East and Far East still remained largely outside the scope of industrial development. This period was hardly the time for corporate strategists to influence events. Yet strategic game theory had its origins in developing more effective British naval tactics when hunting for German U-boats.

The late 1940s probably witnessed the period of the greatest power of North American industry and companies. It was also the real beginning of corporate strategy development and this then continued into the 1950s. It was accompanied by the reconstruction of industry across Europe and the beginnings of the Asian development period, particularly in Japan. Economists like Penrose[6] were beginning to explore how firms grew, and human behaviourists like Cyert and March[7] suggested that rational economic behaviour was an oversimplified way of considering company development.

By the late 1950s, writers such as Ansoff were beginning to develop corporate strategy concepts that would continue into the 1970s. During the 1960s the early concepts of what would later become one of the main approaches to corporate strategy – *prescriptive corporate strategy* – began to take shape. Ansoff[8] argued that there were environmental factors which accelerated the development of corporate strategy. Two trends can be identified:

1 *The accelerated rate of change.* Corporate strategy provided a way of taking advantage of new opportunities.

2 *The greater spread of wealth.* Corporate strategy needed to find ways of identifying the opportunities provided by the spread of increasing wealth, especially in Europe.

It was during this same period that the early research was conducted which subsequently led to the development of the second main approach to corporate strategy, *emergent corporate strategy*, although this really only came to prominence in the 1970s and 1980s.

2.1.3 Corporate strategy into the twenty-first century

The 1970s saw the major oil price rises. They came as a result of the world's increased need for energy and Middle Eastern success in organising an oil price cartel. The business environment was subject to a sudden and largely unpredicted change that caused some corporate strategists to reconsider the value of prediction in corporate strategy.

The last 20 years have witnessed further environmental developments that are identified briefly in Table 2.1. These trends have had the following effects on corporate strategy:

● *Free market competition.* According to various United Nations and World Bank studies, free market competition has been one element in supporting and encouraging growth in many newly developing countries.[9]

● *Asia–Pacific competition and increased wealth.* Corporate strategy has moved out of being the preserve of North American and European countries. The lower labour costs and greater wealth in countries such as China and India have put pressure on Western and Japanese companies to cut costs or move to such countries. For example, in breakfast cereals, CP has opened factories in Asia to take advantage of low labour costs.

● *Global and local interests.* In addition to economic growth, the world market place has become more complex in cultural and social terms. Markets have become more international, thus making it necessary to balance global interests and local demand variations. For example, in breakfast cereals, CP has adapted its breakfast cereal products to local tastes within its basic worldwide branding.

● *Need to empower and involve employees in strategic decisions.* The higher levels of training and deeper levels of skills of employees mean that they are no longer poorly trained and no longer have difficulty making a contribution to corporate strategy, especially in some Western countries.

● *Greater speed of technical change and rise of new forms of communications.* Technology is changing more quickly and the development of new forms of communication, such as the internet, have revolutionised strategy. For example, both Kellogg and Cereal Partners have developed websites.

● *Collapse of some companies for ethical reasons.* Ethical lapses in some companies, such as Enron in the US, have led to a renewed emphasis on ethical issues in the development and conduct of corporate strategy.

Key strategic principles

● Corporate strategy responds to the environment existing or developing at that time.

● The early twentieth century was characterised by the increased use of science and technology. This was reflected in greater structuring of management and strategy. Mass production of quality products became possible.

● In the mid-twentieth century, the accelerated rate of technological change and the greater spread of wealth led to new demands for formal strategy development.

● In the late twentieth century, there were six distinct pressures on corporate strategy: free market competition; the importance of the Asia–Pacific economies; global competition; greater knowledge and training of managers and employees; greater speed of technical change and rise of new forms of communication; greater recognition of ethical issues in corporate strategy. All six elements in the environment have directed the development of corporate strategy.

CASE STUDY 2.2

Prescriptive strategic planning at Spillers in the late 1970s

Under the guidance of a leading North American consulting company, a strategic corporate planning system was introduced into Spillers plc in 1978–79.[10] *The company had a turnover of around £700 million (US$1,200 million) and had been largely without any form of central direction up to that time.*[11]

Spillers plc consisted of a number of operating companies:

● flour milling and bread baking (Spillers Homepride Flour)
● food coatings (Lucas Food Ingredients)
● meat slaughtering and processing (Meade Lonsdale Group)
● branded petfoods (Winalot)
● restaurant chain (Mario and Franco Italian Restaurants)
● branded canned meats and sauces (Tyne Brand).

The new strategic planning system consisted of an annual plan prepared to a common format by each of the above operating groups. Each plan had to address how it conformed with the Spillers' mission statement and objectives, e.g. with regard to return on capital, market share, capital investment, etc. The plans were gathered together and presented by the operating groups to the Spillers Group Board.

This prescriptive strategy process certainly gave the centre of Spillers a degree of central knowledge and direction that it had never possessed before. It allowed the centre to debate with the senior managers and directors representing the various parts of the group what they judged to be the major strategic issues facing the company. Moreover, for the first time, it gave the company an ability to allocate scarce resources among the competing requests of the operating companies within the group:

● £2 million investment in a new ingredient production line at Lucas Ingredients near Bristol, UK
● £1.5 million investment in a major expansion of the Mario and Franco restaurant chain
● Expansion of Spillers petfood branded products and production facility in Cambridgeshire, UK – estimated cost £3 million capital and a net loss for two years of £2 million in this product group
● £20 million capital requirement spread over three years for a new abattoir at Reading, UK. (The existing facility cannot meet the new higher EU standards in the long term, yet it provides over half the profits of the Spillers Meat Group.)

The company did not have the financial resources to meet all the requests. It had to make a selection; techniques such as portfolio matrices (see Chapter 4) were used to analyse and present the results. Even under the new system, however, few strategic options were ever presented by the operating companies to group headquarters: for example, the proposal was for a new abattoir or nothing. Nevertheless, rational choice was considered by the main board. Moreover, beyond the centre, shareholders could now be told about the future plans and direction of the company. Employees were equally interested in the success of their own areas of the group.

▶ CASE STUDY 2.2 continued

Figure 2.1

Spillers plc: sales and net income levels 1973–79

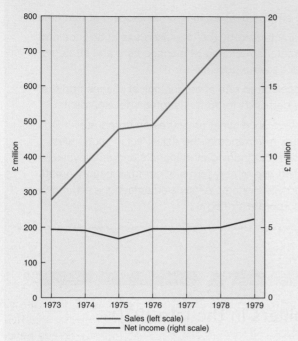

— Sales (left scale)
— Net income (right scale)

Source: Company Annual Report and Accounts.

Group strategic planning at Spillers had not previously existed. The success of Spillers' operating subsidiaries in obtaining funds up to that point had depended upon which operating company had asked first and who happened to make the most attractive financial case at the time when funds were available. Once prescriptive strategic analysis and rational debate were introduced into this process during 1979, the main board at last had a clear picture of the strategies of each major operating company and their requests for funds to implement these proposals. There had been a few complaints by the operating companies that the estimated system had been too rigid. Overall, however, the new Spillers system was fairer and less open to individual favouritism.

In practice, for Spillers in 1979 the prescriptive solutions offered by its corporate strategic planning process were too little and too late; the strategic problems that would ultimately lead to its downfall were already evident.

All of this came to an end when Spillers was at the receiving end of a takeover bid by the UK company Dalgety in 1979. Spillers was swallowed up by an audacious acquisition and its strategic plans were used to provide a useful, if static, picture of what had been acquired. Prescriptive strategic planning had its uses for Dalgety, even if this was not quite the purpose originally intended by Spillers.

Case questions

1 *Using Mintzberg's critique of prescriptive processes, what are the main weaknesses of Spillers' proposals?*

2 *Bearing these in mind, was it a worthwhile exercise for Spillers in your judgement?*

2.2 PRESCRIPTIVE CORPORATE STRATEGY IN PRACTICE

2.2.1 The basic concept

Definition ➤ A prescriptive corporate strategy is one where the *objective* has been defined in advance and the *main elements* have been developed before the strategy commences. However, it should be noted that there are many variations on this basic approach.

● As seen in Chapter 1, prescriptive strategy starts with an analysis of the competitive environment and resources of the organisation. For example, the Spillers company – *see* Case 2.2 – began with data on each market in which the company was engaged.

● This is then followed by a search for an agreed purpose, such as the maximisation of the return on the capital involved in a business (Ansoff, Porter).[12] It should be noted that the objective is not necessarily profit maximisation: for example, in a publicly owned enterprise or social co-operative, the objective could have social service standards as its major aim. One test for prescriptive strategy is to see whether a clearly defined objective has been identified in advance of the commencement of the strategy. In the case of Spillers, the purpose was related primarily to the delivery of profits to shareholders.

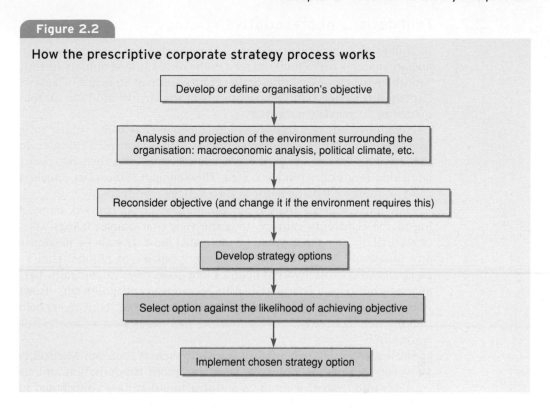

Figure 2.2

How the prescriptive corporate strategy process works

- Against the background of the competitive environment and an agreed purpose, various options are identified to enable the business to achieve the purpose. One option is then selected which is best able to meet the objective. In Case 2.2, the Spillers company never had a complete range of options presented to the group: in this sense, the prescriptive planning was weak.

- The chosen option is implemented by the organisation's managers. At Spillers, the strategic decisions to invest in food ingredients and petfoods were then implemented by building the production plant, launching the agreed products, etc.

This prescriptive process is shown in Figure 2.2. In summary, the advantages of the prescriptive process are that it assists in providing a complete overview of the organisation, thus allowing a comparison with the objectives of the organisation. In turn, this allows an assessment of the resources of the organisation, especially those that deliver competitive advantage, and the allocation of resources that are scarce. Finally, the prescriptive process lends itself to monitoring the implementation and monitoring of an agreed plan.

Key strategic principles

- Prescriptive strategy begins with an analysis of the competitive environment and the competitive resources of the organisation. In this context, the purpose or objective of the strategy is then identified.
- The objective may be adjusted if the environment or other circumstances change.
- To test for prescriptive strategy, it is useful to examine whether a clearly defined, main objective has been identified.
- The advantages of the prescriptive process include the overview it provides; the comparison with objectives; the summary of the demands made on resources; the picture of the choices to be made; and the ability to monitor what has been agreed.

2.2.2 Foundations of prescriptive strategy

In studies of prescriptive strategy, close parallels have been drawn with what happens in *military strategy* – for example, as seen in the early Chinese military historical writings of Sun Tzu; the writings of the nineteenth-century German strategist, Clausewitz,[13] and those of Captain B H Liddell Hart[14] who wrote about the First World War. All these have been have quoted by corporate strategists.[15]

Prescriptive business strategy is sometimes seen as being similar to sending the troops (*employees*) into battle (*against competitors*) with a clear plan (*the prescriptive strategic plan*) that has been drawn up by the generals (*directors*) and then has been implemented (by launching innovatory products, etc.). The Kellogg/CP breakfast cereals strategic battle is a good example – CP doing battle against Kellogg worldwide.

Prescriptive strategic analysis has also borrowed from *economic theory*. Adam Smith, writing in the eighteenth century, took the view that human beings were basically capable of rational decisions that would be motivated most strongly by maximising their profits in any situation.[16] Moreover, individuals were capable of rational choice between options, especially where this involved taking a long-term view. Adam Smith has been quoted with approval by some modern strategists, economists and politicians. However, it should be noted that he lived in the eighteenth century and wrote about an era before modern organisations were conceived: for example, he had never seen a factory; only the craftsman's workshop.[17]

Subsequently, modern strategy theorists, such as Professor Michael Porter[18] of Harvard University Business School, have translated profit maximisation and competitive warfare concepts into strategy techniques and structure that have contributed to prescriptive strategic practice. Porter suggested that what really matters is *sustainable competitive advantage* vis à vis competitors in the market place: only by this means can a company have a successful strategy.

Others have taken this further: for example, the Boston Consulting Group used market data to develop a simple, strategic matrix that presented strategic options for analysis (we will explore this in Chapter 3). One of the early writers on corporate strategy was Professor Igor Ansoff, at that time at Vanderbilt University, Tennessee, who wrote a number of books and papers over the period from 1960 to 1990[19] that explored the practice of prescriptive strategy. Strategists such as Andrews,[20] Chakravarthy and Lorange[21] follow in the long line of those writing about strategic planning systems who employ many of these basic concepts. They are still widely used in many organisations around the world.

2.2.3 Critical comment on prescriptive strategy

Despite the advantages claimed for a prescriptive strategy system operating at the centre of organisations, there have been numerous critics of the whole approach. One of the most insightful is Professor Henry Mintzberg of McGill University, Canada. Along with other commentators,[22] Mintzberg has researched decision making at corporate strategy level and suggested that a prescriptive strategy approach is based on a number of dangerous assumptions as to how organisations operate in practice (summarised in Exhibit 2.2).[23] There is significant research to show that these assumptions are not always correct. For example, the market place can change, or employees may not like an agreed strategy – perhaps because it will mean that they lose their jobs – and will find ways to frustrate it. Given this evidence, theories of *emergent strategy* have developed, as an alternative view of the strategy process.

Although highly critical of the formal prescriptive planning process, Mintzberg has modified his views in recent years and accepted that some strategic planning may be beneficial to the organisation.[24]

Exhibit 2.2

Some major difficulties with the prescriptive strategic process

Mintzberg has identified six major assumptions of the prescriptive process that may be wholly or partially false:

1 *The future can be predicted accurately enough to make rational discussion and choice realistic.* As soon as a competitor or a government does something unexpected, however, the whole process may be invalidated.

2 *It is possible and better to forgo the short-term benefit in order to obtain long-term good.* This may be incorrect: it may not be possible to determine the long-term good and, even if it is, those involved may not be willing to make the sacrifice, such as jobs or investment.

3 *The strategies proposed are, in practice, logical and capable of being managed in the way proposed.* Given the political realities of many companies, there may be many difficulties in practice.

4 *The chief executive has the knowledge and power to choose between options. He/she does not need to persuade anyone, nor compromise on his/her decisions.* This may be extraordinarily naïve in many organisations where the culture and leadership seek discussion as a matter of normal practice.

5 *After careful analysis, strategy decisions can be clearly specified, summarised and presented; they do not require further development, nor do they need to be altered because circumstances outside the company have changed.* This point may have some validity but is not always valid.

6 *Implementation is a separate and distinctive phase that only comes after a strategy has been agreed: for example, a strategy to close a factory merely requires a management decision and then it just happens.* This is extraordinarily simplistic in many complex strategic decisions.

In conclusion, the period of the 1970s was the era when prescriptive corporate strategic planning was particularly strong. Further strategic competitive concepts, such as generic strategies, would be proposed in the 1980s (*see* Chapter 13), but the basic process of analysis, strategic choice, selection and implementation formed the best practice of many companies. The major UK food company, Spillers, was just one example of prescriptive strategy in action (*see* Case study 2.2). Another example of prescriptive strategy is that associated with the development of Singapore Airlines, as a leading world airline, though here the outcomes have not always been those that were intended (*see* Case study 2.3).

Key strategic principles

- A prescriptive strategy is a strategy whose objective has been defined in advance and whose main elements have been developed before the strategy commences.

- The objective may be adjusted if circumstances change significantly.

- After defining the objective, the process then includes analysis of the environment, the development of strategic options and the choice between them. The chosen strategy is then implemented.

- Mintzberg identified six assumptions made by the prescriptive process that may prove suspect in practice and invalidate the process.

CASE STUDY 2.3

Prescriptive strategy to build a world airline – Singapore Airlines

Widely regarded as one of the world's leading airlines, Singapore Airlines started as a small regional airline in 1972. With the backing of the Singaporean government, the company chose to use prescriptive strategies to build its market position. But the outcomes for the company have not always been as predictable as assumed by prescriptive strategy.

When the Prime Minister of Singapore, Mr Lee Kuan Yew (now the distinguished Senior Minister of that country), led his country to break away from the Malaysian Federation in 1965, he realised that a relatively small country of 6 million people needed a strong and distinctive strategy if it was to survive and grow.[25] His government allowed the existing airline – Malaysian–Singapore Airlines – to continue until 1972. At that time, both his government and the government of Malaysia judged that it would be better if the airlines of the two countries followed the distinctive paths set by their separate countries. Two airlines, Malaysian Airlines System (now called Malaysian Airlines) and Singapore Airlines were therefore founded. This case focuses on Singapore Airlines but acknowledges that Malaysian Airlines has also built a major international airline in the period up to 2004.

From its foundation to the present, the Singapore government has held a controlling share (57 per cent through a company called Temasek Holdings) in Singapore Airlines.

© Munshi Ahmed/Corbis

Just like its competitors, Singapore Airlines will typically need years to negotiate, acquire and implement new aircraft and new routes. Prescriptive strategies are essential.

The government has therefore been at the centre of the development strategy of the airline. In 1972, the airline had a fleet of 10 aircraft, a staff of 6,000 and a route network of 22 cities in 18 countries. By 2004, the airline was recognised as one of the world's leading airlines with a fleet of 89 aircraft serving 90 destinations in 40 countries. The company also had 16 more aircraft on order and options on another 45 spread over the years 2005–09. Importantly, its operations base in Singapore – Changhi Airport – was widely regarded as one of the most modern and smooth-running aircraft hub operations in the world. In addition, Singapore Airlines had a strong service reputation with customers based on its use of modern aircraft, attractive in-flight food and extensive provision of in-flight entertainment. What were the strategies that led to this level of success?

The following prescriptive strategies were undertaken for the development of Singapore Airlines on the important assumption that significant growth in world travel would continue:

- From the beginning, the airline decided that it would build a reputation of *superior service* to its rivals. Thus, it introduced free drinks, hot towels and headsets from the outset

in 1972 – such amenities are relatively cheap and quick to introduce. In more recent years, it was one of the first airlines to offer in-flight entertainment screens at each individual seat – even in economy class.

- Substantial investment in *staff training, employee welfare and related activities.* Singapore Airlines took the view that staff were crucial both to in-flight service delivery and also to aircraft safety through expertise in ground and related operations. Equally, as aircraft design changed and in-flight service operations became more complex, the airline recognised a need to update continuously its knowledge and expertise in these areas.

- The investment in a *modern fleet of aircraft* with a policy of always seeking out the latest in terms of technology and aircraft design. For example, the airline introduced the new ultra long-range Airbus A340-500 aircraft in 2004. These planes permit for the first time non-stop flights from Singapore to Los Angeles. Equally, Singapore Airlines will be one of the first airlines to operate the new Jumbo Passenger Jet – the A380-800, *see* Case 5.3 – which will revolutionise long-distance air transport, beginning in the year 2008. Such a strategy carries a number of risks – for example, will the aircraft design actually work? Will it prove acceptable to customers? Will it deliver the cost savings planned?

● Development of *a modern airport* at its main base in Singapore – Changhi Airport – coupled with the related strategy of ensuring that the airport became an efficient handling facility for rival airlines. This would encourage other airlines to base their services at Changhi when seeking stop-over locations on long-haul flights between continents of the world.

● *Co-operation with other airlines* through code-sharing and ticket marketing arrangements to make it easier for customers to travel around the world and to lock them into certain airlines rather than rivals. For example, Singapore Airlines operated code-sharing with Scandinavian Airline Systems (SAS) in 1999. In the following year, Singapore joined the Star Alliance, which included not only SAS but also the dominant German company, Lufthansa, and the major American airline, United Airlines. Co-operation was taken further, with attempts to buy into rival airlines – Singapore unsuccessfully tried to acquire stakes in South African Airways and the Australian airline Ansett in 2000. It then acquired a 49 per cent shareholding in Sir Richard Branson's Virgin Airlines – *see* Case 2.4 – in year 2000 for US$960 million.

The prescriptive strategy assumption that growth in world travel would continue was cast into doubt by two major events. The company's profits suffered twice in consequence – *see* Figure 2.3 for the evidence of the first of these. In 2001, the disastrous attack of September 11 in America caused a major downturn in world air travel. Singapore Airlines was forced to make cuts – 180 pilots and 415 ground crew lost their jobs. In 2003, the fears associated with the highly infectious SARS virus had a severe impact on air travel, especially to Asian destinations, including Singapore. The company was forced to cut back nearly 360 flights per week at one stage during 2003. In this sense, the assumptions of the prescriptive strategies outlined above were not fulfilled due to events outside the control of the company. This does raise the question of whether it is appropriate to rely on prescriptive strategies when events can clearly undermine the strategic outcome in terms of company profitability.

Figure 2.3

Operating outcomes of Singapore Airlines' strategies over the last ten years

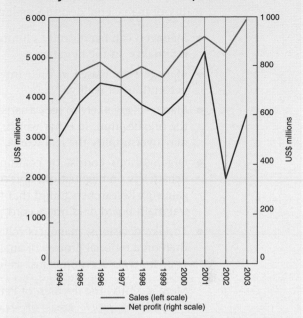

Note: the profit impact of the SARS virus in 2003 is not shown above. It appears in the 2004 accounts, which were not available at the time of writing.

Source: Annual Report and Accounts.

Case questions

1 *What makes the Singapore Airlines strategies prescriptive rather than emergent? Does it matter that the outcomes were not as predictable as assumed by prescriptive strategy?*

2 *Are there any weaknesses in using prescriptive strategy processes to develop strategy at the airline? You might like to use Exhibit 2.2 to answer this question.*

2.3 EMERGENT CORPORATE STRATEGY IN PRACTICE

2.3.1 The basic concept

Definition ➤ Emergent corporate strategy is a strategy whose *final objective* is unclear and whose *elements* are developed during the course of its life, as the strategy proceeds. However, it should be noted that there are many variations on this basic approach.

In the light of the observation that human beings are not always the rational and logical creatures assumed by prescriptive strategy,[27] various commentators have rejected the dispassionate, long-term prescriptive approach. They argue that strategy *emerges*, adapting to human needs and continuing to develop over time. Given this, they argue that there can be only limited meaningful prescriptive strategies and limited value from long-term planning.

Although this approach probably has its roots in the Hawthorn experiments of Elton Mayo in the 1930s,[28] it was not really until the research of Cyert and March in the 1960s[29] and Herbert Simon[30] around the same period that real progress was made. Research into how companies and managers develop corporate strategy in practice has shown that the assumption that strategies are always logical and rational does not take into account the reality of managerial decision making.

● Managers can handle only a limited number of options at any one time – called 'bounded rationality' in the literature.

● Managers are biased in their interpretation of data. All data is interpreted through our perceptions of reality.

● Managers are likely to seek a satisfactory solution rather than maximise the objectives of the organisation. In other words, the profit-maximising assumption of economic theory may oversimplify the real world.

● Organisations consist of coalitions of people who form power blocs. Decisions and debate rely on negotiations and compromise between these groups, termed 'political bargaining'. Researchers found that the notion of strategy being decided by a separate, central main board does not accord with reality.

● To take decisions, managers rely on a company's culture, politics and routines, rather than on a rational process of analysis and choice. (Who you know and how you present your strategic decision is just as important as the content of the strategy.)

More recently, the research of Pettigrew,[31] Mintzberg,[32] Johnson[33] and others has further developed the *people* areas of strategy. Their empirical research has shown that the development of corporate strategy is more complex than the prescriptive strategists would imply: the people, politics and culture of organisations all need to be taken into account. Strategists such as Argyris[34] and Senge[35] have emphasised the *learning* approach to strategy: encouraging managers to undertake a process of trial and error to devise the optimal strategy.

As a result, according to these researchers, corporate strategy can best be considered as a process whereby the organisation's strategy is derived as a result of trial, repeated experimentation and small steps forward: in this sense, corporate strategy is *emergent* rather than *planned*. Figure 2.4 presents a simplified and diagrammatic view of the emergent process. The process then proceeds as market conditions change, the economy develops, teams of people in the company change, etc. Clearly, such a process is hard to define in advance and therefore difficult to analyse and predict in a clear and structured way. For example, when entering new breakfast cereal markets, Cereal Partners in Case 2.1 adopted different strategies in accordance with the particular market circumstances. Equally, Virgin Group tried different product offerings – airlines, trains, bridal gowns, etc – with some being more successful than others.

If the emergent view of the strategy process is correct, then the implications for corporate strategy are profound:[36,37]

1 Strategies emerge from a confused background and often in a muddled and disorganised way: the resulting strategies themselves may therefore be unclear and not fully resolved.

2 The prescriptive strategic process is unlikely to reflect reality: options identified will not be comprehensive and the selection process will be flawed.

3 Considering 'implementation' *after* the rest of the strategy process does not reflect what usually happens.

4 Managers are unlikely to seek the optimal solution: it may not be capable of identification and, in addition, may not be in their personal interests.

5 Working within an organisation's routines and culture will allow the optimal culture to emerge rather than be forced by an artificial planning process.

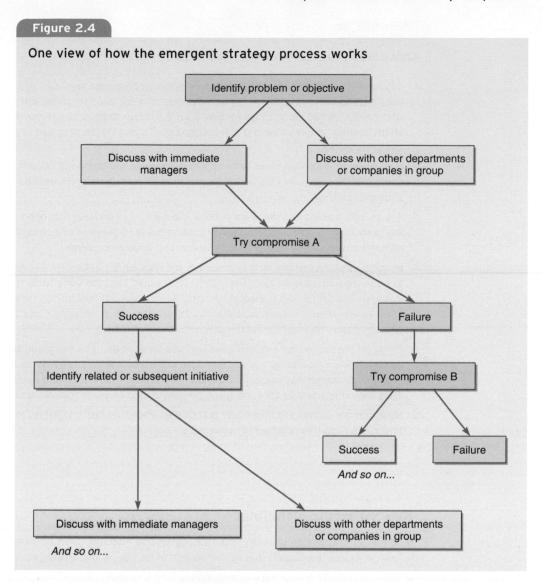

Figure 2.4

One view of how the emergent strategy process works

In summary, the advantages of the emergent strategy process are that it accords with actual practice in many organisations, especially with regard to people issues like motivation. It takes account of the leadership, culture and politics of an organisation. In addition, it also allows strategies to experiment and develop as strategic circumstances change, delivering flexibility during the process.

2.3.2 Critical comment on emergent strategy

Those who favour prescriptive strategic approaches have a number of basic concerns about emergent strategy. These are summarised in Exhibit 2.3.[38]

In practice, many organisations treat the above comments as *limitations* on the prescriptive approach, rather than issues that cannot be overcome. To see how strategy can emerge, you can read Case study 2.4. The strategy of Virgin Group is examined from a long-term perspective over the period 1968–2004. An *extended time perspective* is useful in order to see how strategic decisions take shape according to the emergent approach. Section 2.6 takes this further at the end of this chapter.

Exhibit 2.3

Concerns about the emergent strategic process

1 It is entirely unrealistic to expect board members at corporate level simply to sit back and let operating companies potter along as they wish. The HQ consists of experienced managers who have a *unified* vision of where they wish the group to progress. It may take several steps to arrive at this vision, but the group should make visible progress rather than just muddling along.

2 Resources of the group need to be *allocated* between the demands of competing operating companies; this can only be undertaken at the centre. It therefore demands some central strategic overview.

3 It is entirely correct that there are political groups and individuals that need to be persuaded that a strategy is optimal, but to elevate this process to the level of corporate strategy is to *abdicate responsibility* for the final decisions that need to be taken.

4 In some industries where long time frames are involved for decision making, decisions have to be taken and adhered to or the organisation would become completely muddled: for example, building a new transport infrastructure or telecommunications network may take years to implement. Experimentation may be appropriate in the early years but, beyond this, strategy has to be *fixed* for *lengthy projects*.

5 Although the process of strategy selection and choice has to be tempered by what managers are prepared to accept, this does not make it wrong; rational decision making based on evidence has a greater likelihood of success than hunch and personal whim. Thus the debate should take place but be *conditioned by evidence and logic*.

6 Management control will be *simpler and clearer* where the basis of the actions to be undertaken has been planned in advance.

Key strategic principles

- Emergent corporate strategy is a strategy whose final *objective* is unclear and whose *elements* are developed during the course of its life, as the strategy proceeds.

- The process is one of experimentation to find the most productive route forward.

- Emergent strategy does not have a single, final objective; strategy develops over time.

- In fast-developing markets, the time period may be short; in slow-developing markets, it is likely to be longer.

- To test for emergent strategy, it is essential to examine how the strategy has developed in practice over a defined time period.

- The advantages of the process include its consistency with actual practice in organisations; it takes account of people issues such as motivation; it allows experimentation about the strategy to take place; it provides an opportunity to include the culture and politics of the organisation; it delivers flexibility to respond to market changes.

- Six problems have been identified with the emergent strategic process that make it difficult to operate in practice.

CASE STUDY 2.4

Emergent strategy at Virgin Group

Under the strong and populist leadership of its chief executive, Sir Richard Branson, Virgin Group has pursued an opportunistic strategy to build a company with estimated annual sales of over US$7 billion by 2003. Starting from nothing in 1968, Virgin Group tried a series of strategies over the next 30 years. Their aim was to find opportunities to grow the business on the basis of what became the Virgin brand name and on the strong reputation of its founder and chief executive. The strategic trial-and-error process was essentially emergent, rather than prescriptive. This case outlines some of the main strategies with their successes, failures and continuing business developments.

Background to the early years

After an experimental launch of a student magazine, the young Richard Branson developed a small record mail-order business in 1969 to take advantage of the end of resale price maintenance in the UK. He opened his first record shop two years later and subsequently developed it into the Virgin Megastore chain.[39] At the same time, he was attempting to develop a record label by signing up various pop artists of the time. None of these businesses possessed any clear competitive advantage, though arguably contractual rights to popular musicians and the Virgin brand itself had some real value. He continued to seek business opportunities using the Virgin brand and, by chance, met up with an entrepreneur wishing to develop an airline business. This eventually led to the Virgin airline business with its first route to New York in 1984.[40] In later years, the company moved into a variety of business ventures – from Virgin Bride and Virgin Coke – to Virgin Trains and Virgin mobile telephones – *see* Table 2.2. In terms of its strategy, Virgin Group claims to examine business opportunities carefully, seeking an opportunity for 'restructuring the market and creating competitive advantage'.

Virgin Group has business activities ranging from record retailing to airlines and to mobile telephone services.

Virgin Group's underlying business strategy

The company has developed its strategy over a number of years. Essentially, Virgin takes the view that there are always opportunities available for the hungry business executive. The underlying business logic has been summarised by Branson thus:

> *Business opportunities are like buses . . . There's always another coming along.*[41]

In practice, what this means is that Virgin examines new opportunities to see if the group can offer something 'better, fresher and more valuable' than existing companies. It looks particularly at markets where the existing customers are not always receiving value for money and where the existing companies have in some cases become complacent – trains, insurance and banking for example – and where the new internet might deliver a business opportunity. This means that the main thrust of the strategy has been to find new market opportunities where the company believes its brand name can create competitive advantage. 'Contrary to what people may think, our constantly expanding and eclectic empire is neither random nor reckless. Each new business demonstrates our skill at picking the right market and the right opportunity,' says the Virgin website.

Outcome of emergent strategies: Virgin focuses on geographical expansion

In the last few years, Virgin has focused its strategy on geographical expansion of its existing product portfolio rather than adding products. For example, it has taken its highly successful concept of Virgin Mobile telephones to other countries beyond its UK base. The strategy continues to emerge but in a geographical rather than a product sense.

Case questions

1 *The Virgin emergent approach to strategy development has not always proved successful – Virgin Bride and Virgin Cola, for example, remain relatively small businesses. Does this matter? Do all emergent strategies have to be successful?*

2 *Critically evaluate Virgin Group's strategies over the period of the case study. Was the company wise to spend so much time investing in so many new product areas? What would you have done?*

▶ CASE STUDY 2.4 continued

Table 2.2

Selected business opportunities developed by the Virgin Group

Year	Business opportunity
1968	First issue of *Student* magazine – Branson's first business venture, which was subsequently closed
1970	Start of Virgin Mail Order operation – records sent by mail at cheaper prices than those of record stores
1971	First Virgin Record Store opens in Oxford Street, London, UK
1972	First Virgin Recording Studio
1973	Launch of Virgin Records label plus Virgin Music Publishing – the Sex Pistols were signed in 1977
1984	Virgin Atlantic Airways launched with limited flights between the UK and US
1985	Virgin Holidays founded (travel agency chain in the UK) – Virgin Hotels then followed in 1988
1988	Virgin Megastores opened in UK – Japan followed in 1990
1991	Virgin Publishing (book publishing) begins
1992	Virgin Records sold to the major record company, EMI
1994	Virgin Vodka and Virgin Cola launched with great publicity
1995	Virgin Direct Personal Services founded – sells financial services within the UK
1996	Virgin Trains launched to provide long-distance train services in parts of the UK
1999	Virgin Mobile begins – sells mobile telephone services in the UK by renting space on the network of a competitor; Virgin Bride – a bridal emporium – begins with Sir Richard seeking publicity by being photographed in a white bridal gown
2000	Virgin Cars – a car purchasing website; Virgin Wines – a wine purchasing website; Virgin Cosmetics – 500 products for men and women in the UK Virgin Blue – low cost airline launched in Australia – becomes major success with Initial Public Offering (IPO) in 2003.
2001	Virgin Mobile extends into Singapore
2002	Virgin Mobile extends into the US
2000 onwards	Virgin Group decides to grow its businesses by a *geographic expansion strategy* of existing products and services, rather than launching into further new markets

2.4 SOME PRESCRIPTIVE THEORIES OF CORPORATE STRATEGY

The distinction between prescriptive and emergent strategies explored in the last two sections oversimplifies the reality of strategy development – there are many theories. The next two sections explore some of the theories that underlie this basic distinction. This section examines prescriptive strategy theories, while emergent strategy theories are explored in Section 2.5. It should be noted, however, that there is some overlap between the two areas. This will be explored further later in this chapter. In broad terms, it is useful to identify four main areas of prescriptive strategy theory:

1 industry- and environment-based theories of strategy;

2 resource-based theories of strategy;

3 game-based theories of strategy;

4 co-operation- and network-based theories of strategy.

Figure 2.5

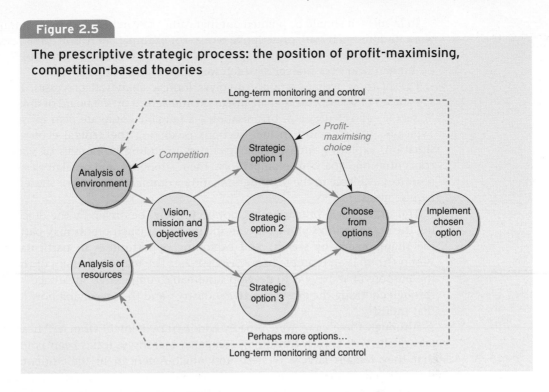

The prescriptive strategic process: the position of profit-maximising, competition-based theories

2.4.1 Industry and environment-based theories of strategy

For some companies, *profitability* is the clear goal, and the content of the corporate strategy therefore addresses this objective; over the long term, this is likely to override all other objectives. This profit is delivered by *selecting and then competing in an industry*. Such theories are commonly called environment-based theories of strategy. Importantly, the word 'environment' here is *not* used in the sense of 'green, sustainability' but means *the external factors acting on the organisation*, markets, competitors, governments, etc. Figure 2.5 shows where the emphasis lies within the context of prescriptive strategy.

Definition ➤

Such concepts derive from the assertion that organisations are rational, logical and driven by the need for profitability. They can be related back to three areas:

1 the eighteenth-century Scottish economist, Adam Smith, and his view that man was rational, logical and motivated by profit;

2 the concepts of military warfare quoted earlier in this chapter that show how the competitive war can be won;

3 the industrial organisational (I/O) model of above average returns to a company deriving from the concept that the most important determinant of company profits was the external environment.

In terms of the development of strategy theory, much of this material only really came together in the 1960s. Igor Ansoff,[43] Alfred Chandler[44] and Alfred Sloan[45] all had an early influence in this area. More recently, writers such as Wheelen and Hunger[46] have laid out the model for rational, analytical and structured development of strategy. During the 1980s, the work of Porter[47] added significantly to this material; he was a dominant influence during this period. Much of his work was based on the study of large companies and the application of industrial economic concepts to strategy, as has been pointed out by Rumelt, Schendel and Teece.[48] Porter's approach relied essentially on the view that the industry in which a firm chooses to compete is the prime determinant of its long-run profitability.[49] This contribution will be examined in greater depth later in the book.

In fairness, it should be pointed out that earlier researchers such as Ansoff never saw their work in quite such stark prescriptive terms. For example, an Ansoff 1968 research paper on corporate strategy[50] refers with approval to the emergent strategy work of Cyert and March on human resources strategies, which we explore later in this chapter.

For all these writers, strategy involves formal, analytical processes. It will result in a specific set of documents that are discussed and agreed by the board of directors (or the public sector equivalent) of an organisation – a tangible corporate plan for some years ahead. Typically, the plan will include sections predicting the general economic and political situation; exploring industry characteristics including economies of scale and degree of concentration; analysing competitors, their strengths and weaknesses; considering the resources available to the organisation; and recommending a set of strategies to meet these requirements.

The strategy will primarily (but not exclusively) be driven by the objective of maximising the organisation's profitability in the long term (such profits may particularly accrue to the shareholders) by seeking and exploiting opportunities in particular industries. The Virgin Group is an example here – *see* Case 2.4. The major argument of the theorists is that the purpose of strategy is to develop sustainable competitive advantage[51] over competitors through choosing the most attractive industry[52] and then resolving how to compete within that industry.

Although these views were broadly endorsed by Kenichi Ohmae,[53] head of the Japanese part of the well-known consulting company, McKinsey, it has been pointed out by Wilks that they remain largely Western and Anglo-American in their orientation.[54] They are primarily concerned with profit and leave only limited room for social, cultural, governmental and other considerations. This view of strategy is therefore unlikely to appeal to countries which demand a higher social content from company plans – for example, within Europe: France, Poland, the Netherlands and Scandinavian countries.

Outside Europe, India has insisted on a strong social content to plans for many years and has only in the last few years come to accept that strong social policies need to be tempered by market forces.[55] Japanese companies also have other criteria, as we have already seen. Malaysian and Singaporean companies with their strong relationships with the governments of their respective countries might well also sacrifice profitability to other objectives, such as building market presence or providing extra training for workers – *see* Case 2.3 on Singapore Airlines.[56] Content for companies in these countries will inevitably be broader.

These nation-state arguments are, however, a matter of degree and do not deny the need to make long-term profits in order to ensure the survival and growth of the enterprise. A more fundamental criticism of profit-maximising theories has been made by Hamel and Prahalad[57] and Kay.[58] They argue that, although competitors are important, the emphasis on competitive industry comparisons essential to such theories is misleading: it simply shows where organisations are weak. Such theories do not indicate how the company should develop its own resources and skills – the key strategic task in their view.

Hannan and Freeman[59] took an opposing view: they argued that markets are so powerful that seeking sustainable competitive advantage for the majority of companies is not realistic; only the largest companies with significant market share can achieve and sustain such advantage. For all the others, complex and detailed strategies are a distraction. Moreover, as soon as all companies have access to Porter's writings on industry analysis, Hamel and Prahalad[60] and Kay[61] have argued that the advantage ceases since all companies have the same knowledge.

From a different perspective, Mintzberg[62] and others have criticised the approach by arguing that this is simply not the way that strategy is or should be developed in practice. Thus human-resource-based theories of strategy would suggest that seeking to maximise performance through a single, static strategic plan is a fallacy. There are no clear long-term mission statements and goals, just a series of short-term horizons to be met and then renewed. Techniques that purport to provide long-term insights may be too simplistic. Using such arguments, Mintzberg in particular has been highly articulate in his criticisms

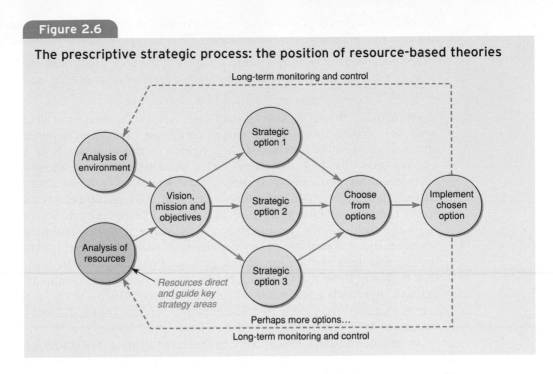

Figure 2.6

The prescriptive strategic process: the position of resource-based theories

of the formal strategic planning process. However, he has subsequently modified his criticisms and accepted that some strategic planning may be beneficial to the organisation.[63] Chapter 3 explores environment-based strategies in more depth.

2.4.2 Resource-based theories of strategy

Definition ➤ Resource-based theories concentrate on the chief resources of the organisation as the principal source of successful corporate strategy. The source of competitive advantage lies in the organisation's resources (*see* Figure 2.6). This does not mean that *all* the resources of an organisation will deliver competitive advantage – perhaps not the canteen or legal facilities at Virgin Group, for example. But *some* of the resources must be able to provide a distinctive competitive advantage in the market place if the company is to deliver above-average profits in that industry – for instance, the Virgin brand name is a unique and powerful resource that allows the company to attract and keep customers.

Writing in the 1960s, Drucker[64] points out that it is important to '. . . build on strength . . . to look for opportunities rather than for problems'. Many basic economic texts have also stressed the importance of resources as the basis for profit development.

One particular aspect of resource-based strategy, emphasised by US and Japanese strategists beginning in the 1960s and 1970s, was operations (manufacturing) strategy and the emphasis on total quality management. Although Henry Ford had developed these areas early in the twentieth century, little emphasis was subsequently given to them. They were probably considered to be too ordinary and insufficiently concerned with overall corporate strategy. (Many strategic texts made no mention of them even in the late 1990s.) Deming, Ishikawa and Taguchi[65] worked on quality issues and Ohno[66] and many others worked on manufacturing strategy issues. Chapter 9 will attempt to redress the balance in this area; some of the major practical advances in corporate strategy during the last 20 years have occurred in this area.

From a different theoretical perspective, resource-based strategy development has emerged as one of the key prescriptive routes in recent years. Possibly as a reaction against the strong emphasis on markets and profit maximising of the 1980s (*see* Section 2.4.1

above), researchers began to argue that the organisation's resources were far more import-ant in delivering competitive advantage:

> The traditional competitive strategy paradigm [e.g. Porter 1980] with its focus on product-market positioning, focuses only on the last few hundred yards of what may be a skill-building marathon.[67]

Wernerfelt,[68] Peteraf,[69] Dierickx and Cool,[70] Kay[71] and others have all explored aspects of what has become known as the *resource-based view* of strategy development. Essentially, although competition is explored, the emphasis in this approach is on the organisation's own resources – its physical resources, such as plant and machinery; its people resources, such as its leadership and skills, and, above all, the ways that such resources interact in organ-isations. It is this combination of resources that delivers competitive advantage, because such a combination takes years to develop and may therefore be difficult for others to copy.

In this context, the resource-based view draws a distinction between the general resources that are available to any organisation, such as accounting skills and basic tech-nology, and those that are special and, perhaps, even unique to the organisation. It argues that it is only those special resources that deliver sustainable competitive advantage. For example, the Nestlé brand name is a unique resource available to Cereal Partners' breakfast cereals and the Virgin name to that company – *see* Case studies 2.1 and 2.4. The resource-based view is explored in Chapter 6.

An important recent development has been the treatment of the *knowledge* of the organ-isation as a key resource.[72] It has been argued that the knowledge possessed by an organisa-tion – its procedures, its technical secrets, its contacts with others outside the organisation – will deliver significant competitive advantages to many organisations. Some strategists have gone so far as to suggest that such knowledge is the only resource that will deliver sus-tainable competitive advantage. While this may be overstated, knowledge is important in strategy development and will be explored in Chapter 11.

2.4.3 Game-based theories of strategy

Definition ➤ Game-based theories of strategy focus on an important part of the prescriptive process – the decision making that surrounds the selection of the best strategic option. Instead of treating this as a simple options-and-choice model, game theory attempts to explore the interaction between an organisation and others as the decision is made – the *game* (*see* Figure 2.7). The theoretical background to such an approach is based on mathematical models of options and choice coupled with the theory of chance.[73]

Game theory begins by recognising that a simple choice of the 'best' strategy will have implications for other companies, such as suppliers and competitors. The consequences for others will be unknown at the time the initial choice is made by the organisation itself. The theory then attempts to model the consequences of such a choice and thereby allow for the choice itself to be modified as the game progresses. Game theory will include not only *com-petitors*, but also other organisations that might be willing to *co-operate* with the organisa-tion. Such a theory considers that the options-and-choice prescriptive model oversimplifies the options and choices available. It will also involve negotiation with others, anticipation of competitive responses and the search for optimal solutions. Such a process may allow all competitors in the market place to win.

Although game theory has been around since the 1940s, it is only relatively recently that it has been applied to strategy. The reason is that the complex world of strategy decisions is difficult to model adequately using the mathematical theory that lies at the foundation of game theory. In the last few years, strategists have begun to explore some key concepts without necessarily modelling every detail using strict mathematical analysis. The results have been some new insights into the prescriptive strategic process that are explored in Chapters 3 and 14. However, game theory still remains only a partial view of a limited part of the strategic process.

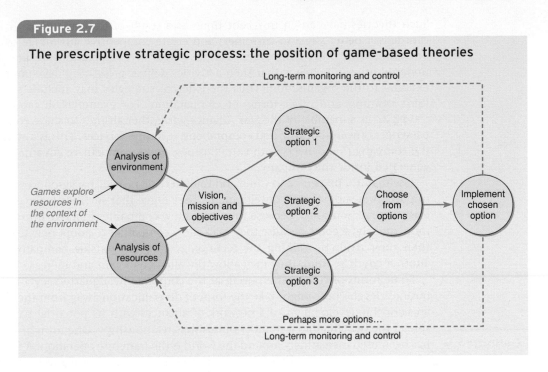

Figure 2.7

The prescriptive strategic process: the position of game-based theories

2.4.4 Co-operation and network theories of strategy

Definition ➤ In a co-operative strategy at least two companies work together to achieve an agreed objective. Co-operation and network theories of strategy seek clearly defined, prescriptive strategies, but they stress the importance of the formal relationship opportunities that are available to organisations. Figure 2.8 shows where they fit into the overall model.

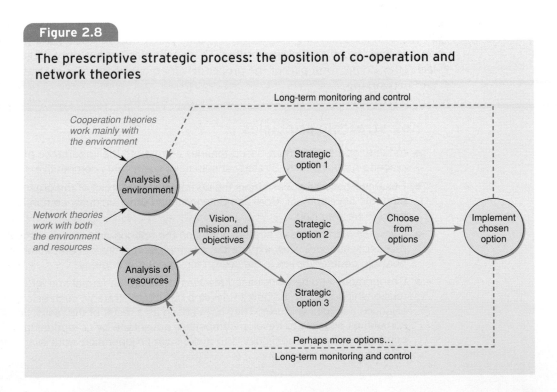

Figure 2.8

The prescriptive strategic process: the position of co-operation and network theories

Such theories have arisen in recent times as a result of the realisation that organisations can deliver better value to customers and create competitive advantage over rivals by co-operating with other companies. Various forms of co-operation are possible. The main underpinning principle is that such activities deliver growth by developing links that are external to the organisation. Thus the external strategies may include strategic alliances, joint ventures and other forms of co-operation. For example, Singapore Airlines – *see* Case 2.3 – is a member of the Star Alliance with other airlines to share computer ticketing, passenger onward-booking and comprehensive airline services. This is a strategy external to the company that delivers both extra business and a competitive advantage that cannot be generated inside the company.

Eisenhardt,[74] Inkpen[75] and Child and Faulkner[76] all provide background on this increasingly important area of strategy development. They argue that such strategies are valuable for at least three reasons: first, because they may allow companies to move into restricted markets more quickly; second, because they may allow companies to adopt new technologies earlier than their rivals by gaining the technology from an outside company – perhaps from another country; third, they may allow the alliance to gain and increase its market power.

Some forms of co-operation occur at the corporate headquarters level rather than at the business level. These might take the form of diversification away from the existing business areas or the development of a network of alliances with its potential partners in order to spread the benefits into a number of business relationships. One form of co-operation that

Definition ➤ has been used increasingly around the world is the franchise operation. A franchise is a form of co-operative strategy in which a firm (the franchisor) develops a business concept and then offers this to others (the franchisees) in the form of a contractual relationship to use the business concept. Typically, the franchisee obtains a tried-and-tested business formula in return for paying a percentage of its sales and agreeing to tight controls from the franchisor over the product range, pricing, etc.[77] Case 2.5 describes the Subway franchise operation.

The main problems with co-operative and network strategies are that they are fragile and risk collapse if the contractual terms have not been carefully developed or one of the partners misrepresents the benefits that it brings to the agreement.[78] Co-operative agreements are explored further in Chapter 4. In addition, it is important to note that some forms of co-operation are *illegal* in most countries around the world. Such illegal activities involve collusion to reduce competition in the market place, thus increasing the prices of the goods on sale and thereby increasing profits. These activities are not only illegal but also unethical. They do *not* form part of the proper development of theories of strategic co-operation and networking.

Key strategic principles

- Industry and environment-based theories emphasise the importance of the market place to deliver profits. Strategy should seek sustainable competitive advantage.

- Resource-based theories stress the competitive resources of the organisation in strategic development. Core competencies and other uniquely competitive resources need to be identified.

- Game-based theories of strategy focus on the options-and-choice stage of the prescriptive model. They explore the commercial realities of competitor reactions and possible counter-moves in the search for an optimal strategy.

- Co-operation and network-based theories focus on the formal and informal relationships that can be built to develop corporate strategy, such as strategic alliances and joint ventures. They have arisen as a result of the realisation that it is sometimes possible to develop competitive advantage by co-operating with rival companies. The main difficulty is to make such co-operation work over time: it often fails for a variety of reasons.

CASE STUDY 2.5

Building the Subway world franchise using emergent and prescriptive processes

Back in 1965, 17-year old Fred DeLuca opened up a sandwich shop called Pete's Super Submarines in Delaware, US. (Non-American readers might like to know that long bread rolls are known as 'submarines' in North America because of their shape.) By 2004, the business had grown into a chain – renamed Subway – with over 22,000 outlets worldwide. It was all done through a mix of emergent and prescriptive strategies.

Subway: the early years

When Fred DeLuca wanted to earn some money in 1965 to pay his college fees, he asked a family friend, Dr Peter Buck, for some advice on what he should do. Dr Buck suggested that he tried to open a sandwich store, having seen a successful operation in the local town. Buck loaned him US$1,000 and the first store was opened in Bridgeport, Connecticut, US in August 1965. It was called Pete's Super Submarines and sold a range of freshly-cut long sandwiches for which the customer could choose the fillings from a range on the counter. Fred himself ran the store and drove regularly to market to buy fresh vegetables and meat – obtaining the right quality at the right prices proved to be important to a successful shop. A second shop followed after one year and then a third in 1967. Importantly, the third shop – now really a 'restaurant' – was in a more visible location. This was found to be vital to success, even if the rents and related costs were higher.

Subway: developing the franchise concept

For the next few years, the store/restaurant experimented with different approaches to its product range, its marketing, its purchase of fresh produce and its in-store production. The company name was changed to 'Subway' and the familiar yellow logo was developed. Essentially, the founders developed a business formula for their sandwich restaurant with the following characteristics:

- Relatively low capital costs around US$80–120,000 compared to around US$1 million for a McDonalds, Jolly Bee or Burger King Restaurant (because the latter need to fit fryers and grills, etc.)
- Around 6–8 employees per store compared to around 15–20 in a typical McDonalds
- Clean and simple design with strong logo – name changed to 'Subway'
- Clear and simple in-store pricing and product presentation – hygiene factors and training are important to ensure that all food is fresh and clean.

This was the basis of the Subway franchise first offered in 1974. Over the next 30 years, Subway grew its operations mainly through franchising. Importantly, it began to experiment with different locations. Typically, a fast-food franchise like McDonalds needs to be located in a high customer traffic area like a shopping mall in order to be profitable because of the high start-up and wage costs. Subway found that its franchise could be operated in smaller and more specialist outlets – such as schools and factories – because of its smaller-scale business formula.

Subway in North America

By the mid-1990s, Subway had more outlets than McDonalds, though each individual outlet had a lower turnover than a McDonalds. The strategic problem for Subway in North

Subs can be bought everywhere from Valdez, Alaska, US to Shanghai, China.

▶

America was that sales growth was beginning to slow around this time. Previous growth had come from opening more outlets but – as McDonalds also discovered: *see* Case 12.3 – eventually a franchise chain like Subway largely runs out of new locations. To tackle this, Fred DeLuca went back to his customers. He learned that an increasing number came to Subway because it offered a low-fat alternative to burgers and French fries. In 1998, Fred used this to develop a marketing campaign that focused on a line of seven low-fat sandwiches. The company claims that the sales were boosted significantly as a result – the precise figures are unclear because the company was private (and remains so to this day). In 2000, the company decided that it still wished to attract customers who wanted a full calorie meal. It therefore developed a range of big-eater sandwiches – for example, steak and cheese. Again, this had a positive impact on sales. By 2004, Subway had around 20,000 outlets in the US and Canada.

Subway: worldwide expansion

In 1984, Subway opened its first franchise operation outside North America – in Bahrain in the Middle East. The company then continued to expand internationally and had opened 2,000 outlets by 2004 in 75 countries: locations included China, India, Australia, New Zealand, Africa, South America, Mexico, Germany and the UK. The opening of the 2000th outlet in 2004 was regarded as being particularly important. 'This milestone shows that we are right on track towards achieving our goals of our worldwide strategic plan and reaching the 7,500 restaurant count by the year 2010,' said Patricia Demarais, Subway's Director of International Business.

Case questions

1 *What precisely makes the development of Subway's strategy both prescriptive and emergent?*

2 *More generally, is it possible for a company to start with an emergent strategy and then develop a prescriptive strategy? Can a company continue with emergent strategies beyond its early years? Should a company continue with such emergent strategies as it continues to grow?*

2.5 SOME EMERGENT THEORIES OF CORPORATE STRATEGY

When strategies emerge from a situation rather than being prescribed in advance, it is less likely that they will involve a long-term strategic plan. This does not mean that there is no planning but rather that such plans are more flexible, feeling their way forward as issues clarify and the environment surrounding the company changes. Planning is short-term, more reactive to events, possibly even more entrepreneurial.

To understand the background to emergent strategy theory, it is useful to look back to the 1970s. At that time, prescriptive strategies with detailed corporate plans were widely used. Suddenly, oil prices rose sharply as a result of a new, strong Middle East oil price consortium. Many industrial companies around the world were hit badly in an entirely unpredictable way; the prescriptive plans were thrown into confusion. Emergent strategies that relied less on precise predictions about the future were sought. More recently, the economic bubble associated with new internet companies has also highlighted the uncertainty of the environment. For this reason, some strategists argue that the whole basis of prescriptive strategy is false. They would claim that, even during periods of relative certainty, organisations may be better served by considering strategy as an emergent process.

For our purposes, we can usefully distinguish four sets of emergent strategy theories:

1 survival-based theories of strategy;

2 uncertainty-based theories of strategy;

3 human-resource-based theories of strategy;

4 innovation and knowledge-based theories of strategy.

2.5.1 Survival-based theories of strategy

Definition ➤ Survival-based strategies regard the survival of the fittest company in the market place as being the prime determinant of corporate strategy. It is about how to survive in an environment which is shifting and changing. There is little point in sophisticated prescriptive

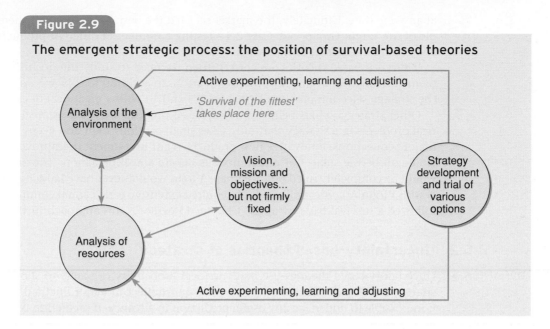

Figure 2.9

The emergent strategic process: the position of survival-based theories

Active experimenting, learning and adjusting

Analysis of the environment

'Survival of the fittest' takes place here

Vision, mission and objectives... but not firmly fixed

Strategy development and trial of various options

Analysis of resources

Active experimenting, learning and adjusting

solutions: much better to dodge and weave as the market changes, letting the strategy emerge in the process. Figure 2.9 shows where the emphasis is placed by survival-based strategies.

As Section 2.4 explained, industry and environment-based approaches are concerned with selecting the optimal strategy to maximise the organisation's profitability and then implementing that strategy. Critics have long known that this simple economic model is far from reality. For example, in the late 1930s, Hall and Hitch[80] surveyed companies and showed that they did not set output at the theoretical maximum level, i.e. where marginal cost equals marginal revenue. This was partly because decisions were not necessarily rational and partly because it was unclear what the revenue and cost relationships were anyway.

However, this does not mean that companies just muddle through. The competitive jungle of the market place will ruthlessly weed out the least efficient companies; survival-based strategies are needed in order to prosper in such circumstances. Essentially, according to the survival-based strategy theorists, it is the market place that matters more than a specific strategy; hence, the optimal strategy for survival is to be really efficient. Beyond this, companies can only rely on chance.

To overcome these difficulties, Henderson[81] suggested that what most companies needed in order to survive in these highly competitive circumstances was differentiation. Products or services that were able to offer some aspect not easily available to competitors would give some protection. However, other strategists doubt that true differentiation is possible because it takes too long to achieve and the environment changes too quickly. In these circumstances, theorists suggest that survival-based strategies should rely on running really efficient operations that can respond to changes in the environment. As Williamson commented:

Economy is the best strategy.[82]

If the environment matters more than a specific strategy, then survival-based strategists argue that the optimal strategy will be to pursue a number of strategic initiatives at any one time and let the market place select the best.[83] Selection of strategy is therefore incorrect according to this theory. It is better to experiment with many different approaches and see which emerges as the best through natural selection. For example, Whittington[84] points to the example of Sony's Walkman strategy in the 1980s. The company launched 160 different versions in the North American market, never retaining more than about 20 versions at any one time. Ultimately, the market selected the best. More recently, there is the example of the Virgin Group – *see* Case 2.4 – testing a number of different products and services and letting the market decide which will survive.

If survival-based theories are correct, then we need to study the organisation's environment carefully (we begin this process in Part 2). In addition to this, we would need to treat the strategy selection process of Chapters 13 and 14 with a great deal of circumspection.

Other strategy writers believe survival-based theories are too pessimistic; there are practical problems in a strategy that only takes small cautious steps and keeps all options open. Major acquisitions, innovative new products, plant investment to improve quality radically would all be the subject of much anxious debate and little action. The bold strategic step would be completely ruled out.[85] Perhaps Virgin would never have launched the highly successful Virgin Atlantic airline, which required extensive early capital commitments, if it had followed a survival-based strategy. Chapter 15 explores this approach further.

2.5.2 Uncertainty-based theories of strategy

Definition ➤ Uncertainty-based theories use mathematical probability concepts to show that corporate strategy development is complex, unstable and subject to major fluctuations, thus making it impossible to undertake any useful prediction in advance. If prediction is impossible, then setting clear objectives for corporate strategy is a useless exercise. Strategy should be allowed to emerge and change with the fluctuations in the environment. Figure 2.10 illustrates where the emphasis lies in such theories.

As a result of the major difficulties in predicting the future environment surrounding the organisation in the 1970s, the development of long-term strategic planning was regarded by some theorists as having little value. Strategic planning could still be used but it had to have much greater flexibility and did not have the absolute certainties of the 1970s. This approach to strategy led not only to survival-based strategies that seek to keep all options open to the last possible opportunity but also to uncertainty-based strategies.

Since the 1960s, chaos theory and mathematical modelling of changing states have been used to map out the consequences of scientific experiments; such procedures were not developed for the business community but for other scientifically oriented topics, as in the mathematical modelling of weather forecasting. Essentially, such techniques were able to demonstrate that, in particular types of uncertain environment, small perturbations in the

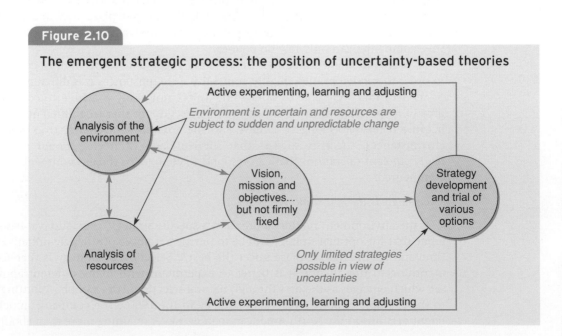

Figure 2.10

The emergent strategic process: the position of uncertainty-based theories

early stages of a process can lead to major variances in the later stages – not unlike the multiplier effect in macroeconomics. A major implication of such environments – often called *chaotic systems* – is that it is simply not possible to predict sufficiently accurately many years ahead (*see* Gleick).[86]

One variant of this approach to strategy is provided by the empirical research study conducted by Miller and Friesen.[87] They found that significant corporate strategy occurs in revolutionary ways: there are sudden major shifts in the whole strategy and organisational structure of the company before they reach a new steady state. From a mathematical perspective, it is possible to model such systems and show that they oscillate between steady and turbulent states. Strebel[88] has used a similar argument, pointing particularly to changes in technology that are likely to lead to 'breakpoints' in the development of the organisation.

Business has been identified as such a chaotic system. Stacey[89] has suggested that the environment of many businesses, particularly those in rapidly growing industries such as computers, is inherently unstable. It will never be possible to forecast accurately profits five or ten years into a new project; hence, for example, the apparent accuracy of discounted cash flows and cash projections is largely spurious. It follows that business strategy has to emerge rather than try to aim for the false certainties of the prescriptive approach.

Several writers, such as Miller and Friesen,[90] have also applied the same arguments to the resources of the organisation. They argue that innovation is vital to successful strategy: this can only be achieved in a significant way if the organisation's resources are subjected to revolutionary change, rather than gradual change. Such an approach is likely to have a chaotic, free-wheeling element whose outcome cannot be planned or predicted by strategy in advance. Chapters 11 and 20 explore revolutionary innovation further.

Some companies would regard this whole approach as being partially true but probably too pessimistic. Although the weather is a chaotic system and cannot be predicted accurately, we do know that the Sahara Desert is hot and dry, Singapore is warmer and more humid than London, and so on. Similarly, it can be argued that there are some certainties about business, even though we are unable to predict accurately. Moreover, organisations (especially large ones) need a basic non-chaotic structure if they are to avoid dissolving into anarchy. Singapore Airlines could not afford to rely on uncertainty-based theory when placing an order for ten new SuperJumbo airliners – *see* Case 2.3 – back in 2003.

There are patterns of behaviour and trends that may be subject to change but can still be predicted with some accuracy. Business strategy may need to emerge and be adaptable, but it is not necessarily totally random and uncertain. However, strategy does need to identify and estimate risk. (We will return to the problem of risk and risk management in Chapter 14.)

2.5.3 Human-resource-based theories of strategy

Definition ➤ These theories of strategy emphasise the *people* element in strategy development and highlight the motivation, the politics and cultures of organisations and the desires of individuals. They have particularly focused on the difficulties that can arise as new strategies are introduced and confront people with the need for change and uncertainty. Figure 2.11 shows where these theories fit into the emergent process. They involve people and occur wherever human resources are prominent; it is therefore difficult to identify a precise position.

We have already examined the important findings of researchers such as Cyert and March[91] and the work of Herbert Simon[92] – corporate strategy needs to have a human-resource-based dimension. Organisations consist of individuals and groups of people, all of whom may influence or be influenced by strategy; they may make a contribution, acquiesce or even resist the corporate strategy process, but they are certainly affected by it. Nelson and Winter[93] developed this theme further, arguing that the options-and-choice model of the prescriptive process was completely misleading:

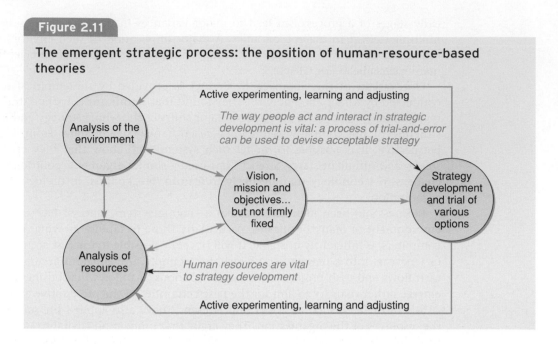

Figure 2.11

The emergent strategic process: the position of human-resource-based theories

It is quite inappropriate to conceive of firm behavior in terms of deliberate choice from a broad menu of alternatives that some external observer considers to be 'available' opportunities for the organization.

The human resource aspects of strategy development will be explored in much greater detail in Chapters 7 and 15. However, according to some writers, these matters are not just about peripheral issues of implementation; they are fundamental to the strategy process itself. Nelson and Winter[94] argued that organisations have in reality limited strategic choice. The strategy available is:

not broad, but narrow and idiosyncratic; it is built on a firm's routines, and most of the 'choosing' is also accomplished automatically by those routines.

Strategic logic is restricted by the processes and people already existing in the organisation.

Mintzberg[95] has also developed this theme and argued that strategy emerges from an organisation as it adapts continuously to its environment. Implementation is not, therefore, some separate phase tacked on to the end of the strategy process, but intermingled with corporate strategy as it develops. Quinn[96] has described this gradualist, emergent approach that accepts that it is looking at only a limited number of feasible options as *logical incrementalism*. In the words of Mintzberg's famous phrase:

Smart strategies appreciate that they cannot always be smart enough to think through everything in advance.

We will explore these areas in greater depth in Chapter 15.

More recently, there has been considerable emphasis on the learning aspect of strategy development. Mintzberg emphasised the importance of learning. After him, Senge[97] and others have developed the learning concept, encouraging managers involved in strategy to undertake a process of trial and error to adopt the optimal strategy (*see* Chapter 21).

The main criticisms of the emergent approach to strategy development listed in Section 2.3 apply especially to human-resource-based strategy. Similar comments may have prompted Mintzberg to move more recently towards the modification of his argument outlined above.[98]

2.5.4 Innovation and knowledge-based theories of strategy

Definition ➤ Innovation and knowledge-based theories of strategy privilege the generation of new ideas and the sharing of these ideas through knowledge as being the most important aspects of strategy development. These theories came to prominence during the 1990s. Innovation here does not just mean inventing new products or production processes: it means the development and exploitation of any resource of the organisation in a new and radical way.[99] In particular, the way that the knowledge of the organisation is used to generate new and radical solutions has come to be recognised as an important contributor to strategy development[100] – 'knowledge' here does not mean data so much as the collective wisdom and understanding of many people in the organisation developed over many years. Figure 2.12 shows where such an approach fits into the emergent strategic process.

According to those favouring innovation and knowledge theories, their advantage is that they begin to tackle a problem that has arisen with other, existing theories. The argument goes that the widespread study of existing theories – like resource-based competitive advantage, for example – means that every company knows about such thinking and therefore there is less chance for such theories to deliver new competitive advantage. By emphasising the new and evolving nature of knowledge and innovation, such theories help to overcome this difficulty. Innovation by its very nature moves forward the traditional thinking of the organisation and thereby delivers the possibility of new competitive advantage. Case study 2.4 shows the way that the Virgin Group was willing to explore new ideas, share knowledge and build new business activities through an innovative approach to business strategy.

In the process of innovating, one important aspect is that of sharing knowledge and ideas. This has been made much easier in the last ten years as a result of the internet and telecommunications technology. This has now developed into an important topic in strategy with real potential to revolutionise strategic thinking. The rise and fall of some internet businesses around the year 2000 has made no difference to the potential of this important strategic route. Chapters 11 and 15 explore these concepts in more depth.

Figure 2.12

The emergent strategic process: the position of innovation and knowledge-based theories

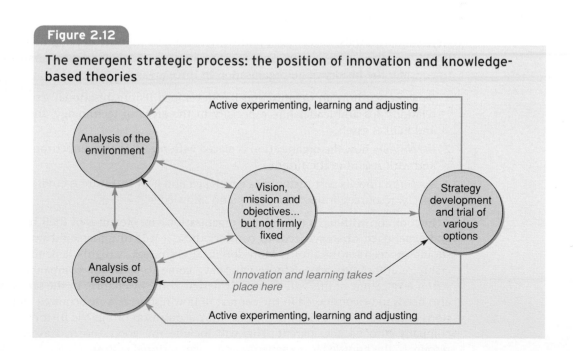

Key strategic principles

- Survival-based theories of strategy are based on the survival of the fittest in the market place. It is difficult to plan strategy actively and possible to survive by differentiation as events unfold.

- Uncertainty-based theories of strategy regard prediction as impossible because of the inherently unstable nature of business and its environment. Strategies must be allowed to react to the changing environment and emerge from the chaos of events. Some would regard this as being a pessimistic view of strategy.

- Human-resource-based theories emphasise the importance of the people element in strategy development. They highlight the motivation, the politics and culture of organisations and the desires of individuals. They also suggest that strategy would benefit from an element of learning and experimentation that empowers individuals.

- Innovation and knowledge-based theories stress the value of radical new strategic thinking in order to move ahead of rivals. The sharing of knowledge through the internet may be an important part of such a process.

2.6 STRATEGY AS HISTORY - THE CONTRIBUTIONS OF PENROSE AND CHANDLER

Definition ➤ According to this view, strategy must, at least in part, be seen as an outcome of the organisation's present resources, its past history and its evolution over time. Back in 1959, before strategy was considered to be a distinct academic subject, the young academic economist Edith Penrose turned traditional economic thinking on its head. She argued that what happened *inside* the firm was just as important as the market place *outside* the firm.[101] Up to this time, it was this latter area that had been the main focus of economics with its consideration of market demand and supply issues. Moreover, in exploring how firms grow, Penrose argued that this was related to a firm's resources, its past history and its evolution over time. Thus the firm's previous history was a key influence on its future development.

In 1962, the US strategist Alfred Chandler published a substantial study of the growth of four great US companies during the early twentieth century:[102] its arguments and language were similar to those of Penrose. Both writers showed that the development of a firm over time is an essential element of understanding strategy. To make sense of strategy, it is useful to consider the history of an organisation in three areas:[103]

1 *the processes*: how an organisation has developed its organisational structure, company relationships and leadership, especially in the areas of technology, institutional assets and market assets;

2 *the position*: how the organisation is placed with regard to its competitors, both at present and with regard to the future;

3 *the paths*: how its past history has developed and how its future is envisaged, covering its special resources, innovative ability and knowledge.

In common with us as individuals, organisations are creatures of their history, resources and experience. Strategy needs to consider these if it is to understand how developments should proceed for the future. More specifically, strategy is highly dependent on the leadership, culture and style of those who have come to form the company, especially at a senior level. Some of this will happen by design, some by chance. In the same way, strategy also needs to be considered in the context of how resources were acquired and market positions obtained.[104] For example, expansion by acquisition brings the history of the acquired company into its new parent. This will include the good and bad aspects of the new resources, the knowledge, experience and organisational culture.

> ## Key strategic principles
>
> - An organisation's previous history is a key determinant of its future development. Future strategy will be grounded in its past resources developed over time.
>
> - In strategy development, it is useful to consider the history of an organisation in three areas: how its *processes* have developed; how the organisation is *positioned* with regard to competitors; and how its *paths* have developed in the past and are envisaged to continue in the future.

CASE STUDY 2.6

Disaster and recovery: 2

The new strategic challenge at IBM

After a disastrous period from 1991 to 1993, the world's largest computer company, IBM, managed to revive its fortunes. But it still faces major strategic challenges over the next few years.

After reporting a net loss of US$16 billion in the three years 1991–93 – *see* Case Study 1.2 – the company made a major profit recovery over the next few years. There were two phases to this process – the period 1995–99 and the period 2000–04. During much of this period, the company had a new leader, Mr Lou Gerstner. He handed over to another leader, Mr Sam Palmisamo, in 2002. The early phase was marked by the strategies of cost-cutting and reshaping the IBM product portfolio towards computer services. The later phase continued along the same route but included more acquisitions and a new strategic vision for the company that remains to be proven. The sections that follow examine how the company has developed and explore how it is now tackling the challenges and opportunities in the global market for computers and services.

Background – the 1990s

During the 1990s, the computer market continued to grow rapidly, with strong demand for small personal computers (PCs), networked computers and large, mainframe machines. In spite of problems elsewhere, IBM had never lost its dominance of the global mainframe computer market. It also continued to manufacture a wide range of products and services from the semiconductors used in computers to the final advice on how a customer's computer network services should be designed and operated, Perhaps it was a stroke of luck for the company that the major development of the internet happened around this time. It provided a means of boosting IBM's most profitable product areas – mainframe computers and computer services – at a time when it was under pressure with its range of small PCs. The IBM case in Chapter 1 explored these issues, so this case picks up the story after that period of major difficulty for the company.

Background – the 2000s

In the late 1990s, the internet 'dot.com' boom turned to bust – *see* Case 4.2 – and a number of computer service companies went out of business. However, even in the new millennium, computer consultancy companies were still enjoying a period of continuing profitable growth and the internet itself was also continuing to grow. Computers and their software were becoming technically more complex. There was also a strategic trend towards *outsourcing*, i.e. companies buying in products from outside, rather than making or servicing them inside the company. From the perspective of the average company, areas like computer services were particularly attractive to outsource because they often required specialist expertise, involved rapidly changing technologies and were crucial to the company's ongoing operations. From the perspective of a major computer supplier like IBM, the costs of computer production continued to reduce rapidly and were subject to increased competition. At the same time, customers were increasingly willing to pay for outsourcing of computer services. Essentially, there was a shift in value added from computer manufacturing to computer services.

New leadership at IBM: Louis Gerstner 1993–2002

After the former chief executive, John Akers, stepped down in 1993, Louis Gerstner was appointed as his successor. The new man came from the food industry and had a strong reputation for knowing how to cut costs. He knew little about the computer industry but said, at the time, that this was no problem. However, he subsequently admitted that his lack of knowledge had been a disadvantage. Importantly for IBM, this was the first time a leader had been appointed from outside the company, with a clear lesson for those remaining inside.

Mr Gerstner began by spending several months reviewing the situation and talking with IBM customers. He wanted to develop a customer-driven strategy (*see* Chapter 5) and devoted the majority of his time to understanding their views. He concluded that the company had great strengths in terms of its people and expertise but had become too stuck in its ways. For example, he arrived at his first IBM meeting wearing

▶ **CASE STUDY 2.6 continued**

a blue shirt to find all his new colleagues wearing white shirts. Why? His colleagues thought that white shirts were the IBM custom. They had forgotten the original IBM instruction, which was to wear the same colour shirts as your customers who some years earlier had been wearing white shirts. The customers had moved on but IBM had not. Mr Gerstner rapidly gained a reputation as a straight-speaking, even gruff, leader.

Gerstner famously concluded in 1993: 'The last thing IBM needs right now is a vision.' The strategy needed to be much more basic if the recovery was to be successful. Over the next year, he and his immediate colleagues then made three major strategic decisions:

1 *IBM would remain one company.* Large customers wanted integrated-technology solutions to their problems and IBM had sustainable competitive advantage in this area. As technology moved faster, with more suppliers and more complex products, customers would increasingly welcome a company like IBM that would combine all this into one customised solution for an individual company. IBM would not therefore be broken up and the main parts would be retained.

2 *IBM would refocus its strategy around its customers.* Complicated corporate strategy was not needed, rather a simple focus on the needs of customers, their technology requirements and, where appropriate, new R&D and new acquisitions. IBM expected to become closer to its leading customers, perhaps even taking over some functions such as data processing and telecommunications network links that were previously run by its customers.

3 *IBM needed all senior managers to work actively for the new focus and structure.* Mr Gerstner said that some managers had appeared to be blocking strategies that were essential for survival: he called it 'pushback'. He actually removed several senior executives during 1993–94.

IBM had already recognised the need to offer one-stop computer service solutions to its major customers back in 1991; Case study 1.2 described the Industry Solution Units (ISUs) that were set up to tackle this. To build on IBM's strength of being able to offer a one-stop technical solution to many major companies, Mr Gerstner confirmed that ISUs were to be the main organisational structure, even though their integrated solutions were more suited to IBM's larger customers. Pushback against the ISUs would no longer be tolerated.

The new organisation culture and structure that began to emerge from this new strategic focus was an essential element of IBM's recovery during the subsequent years. New leadership does bring new strategies. As Figure 2.13 shows, IBM had begun to turn around its fortunes during the latter part of the 1990s. However, by this time, some of the value added in the computer industry had passed irretrievably to Microsoft and Intel – as explained in Case 1.2 in Chapter 1. Although IBM needed further strategies to grow again, the starting point was to implement the strategies for profit recovery in the period 1993–97.

Figure 2.13

The decline of IBM and the growth of Intel and Microsoft

(a) Revenue

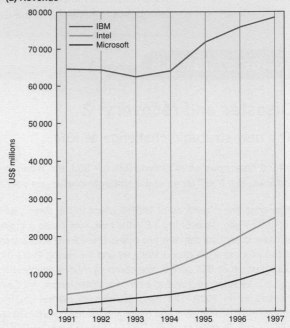

(b) Net profit (less)

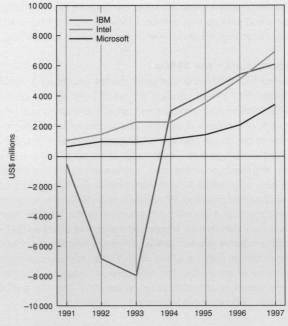

Source: Company accounts.

Summary of the recovery strategies at IBM: 1993–97

In addition to the firm development of ISUs, IBM's recovery from near-disaster came from six main strategies:

1 *New corporate culture* – leaner, more responsive and willing to learn;

2 *Cost cutting.* IBM reduced its workforce by 86,000 to 215,000 in the period 1993–95. The R&D budget was also slashed, especially on the more esoteric products and on some mainframe development. Some of these job losses were accounted for by the sale of companies, rather than outright sackings;

3 *Sale or management buy-out of some peripheral companies* – for example, in hard-disk drives and computer printing peripherals;

4 *Reorganisation of the company away from countries into global product groups.* Economies of scale were delivered by new worldwide product groups working across country boundaries;

5 *Acquisition of companies in fast-growing segments of the computer industry* – for example, IBM acquired the only remaining independent software company of any standing, Lotus Development, for US$3.25 billion cash in 1995;

6 *Investment in the fast-growing segment of computer service outsourcing.* IBM continued to invest in its own activities to act as a major supplier of computer services to non-computer companies – for example, taking over and running the computing services of a major bank for a contractual fee. This service is called outsourcing.

Summary of strategies at IBM: 1998–2004

By the late 1990s, IBM had activities in all computer and related markets. It had software – operating systems, databases, collaboration tools and middleware. It also had hardware, ranging from mainframe computers to small PCs and laptops. Finally, it had the design and manufacture of the microprocessors that went into computers and it had information technology (IT) consultancy. The outcome of this new range of products and services can be seen in the financial results of IBM in the period 1999–2003. The consolidated

IBM Group profitability 1999–2003

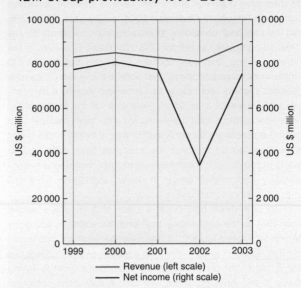

— Revenue (left scale)
— Net income (right scale)

Note: There is a discrepancy between Figure 2.14 and Table 2.3 for the year 2003 in terms of revenue and net income. This arises from the difference between internal and third party sales. Figure 2.14 shows the *overall* picture of the group. Table 2.3 shows the *balance of activities* within the group but overstates the outcome with regard to the overall picture. Table 2.3 can be used to understand where profits are being generated in IBM but the final outcome is more accurately captured in Figure 2.14.

Source: Company accounts.

results are shown in Figure 2.14. They indicate that the company still had weak areas.

The business stabilised over the time period 1998–2004. However, there were a number of factors making it difficult to grow the business – the personal computer part of the business was not making adequate profits; the computer chip-making manufacturing facility was facing heavy competition and losing money. The main IBM business activities are shown in Table 2.3. IBM had to deal with its underperforming

Table 2.3

Breakdown of trading activities of IBM in 2003

All figures in US$ millions

Business activity	Global services – consultancy			Computer hardware	Computer software	Global financing	Enterprise investments	Total for group
	Systems group	Personal systems group	Technology group					
Revenue	45 472	14 839	11 558	3 676	15 924	4 127	1 070	96 666
Pre-tax income	4 499	2 046	(118)	(252)	3 808	1 182	(252)	10 913

Source: Company accounts – see note below Figure 2.14 for comment on total turnover and profitability.

manufacturing areas. In 2002, it therefore negotiated to separate its disc drive business into a joint venture with the Japanese company, Hitachi. In December 2004, it agreed in principle to sell its personal computer manufacturing operations to the Chinese company Lenovo for US$1.75 billion. However, at the time of writing, this deal had not been completed. The US Government was concerned that such a move would transfer national security technology to China and therefore compromise US interests. In addition, there was still the matter of the under-performing IBM interests in chip manufacture. But finding a purchaser for such assets was not easy – this might have changed by the time you read this case. IBM had no plans to move out of mainframe computer manufacture, consultancy and related areas: it judged that these were still important to its future vision.

Although there had been a clear shift in value added from IBM to the chip maker Intel and the software company Microsoft – *see* Figure 2.13, Mr Gerstner (and his successor Mr Palmisano in 2002 – *see* later section) and his colleagues recognised that there was a more profound change taking place in the industry. There was also a shift from computer manufacturing value added into two computer-related areas – software and information technology consultancy. Computer hardware was becoming less profitable with the value added shifting to computer services – this is shown in the 2003 profit figures for the different parts of IBM in Table 2.3. IBM was already involved in both software and information technology consultancy. IBM decided, in view of the attractive profits, to deepen that interest further by examining each of these areas in more depth.

World market for computer software
The total market was estimated to be worth around US$200 billion in 2004. There were three main segments to the market:

- *Operating systems for business computers*: market worth US$30 billion. Market leader Microsoft with 42 per cent market share [Note: this is the *business* computing market, not the *personal* computing market where Microsoft has 90 per cent share]. IBM had an 8 per cent share in 2003 but with plans to increase this. In 2004, it announced a major strategic challenge to Microsoft. It would invest over US$1 billion to attract software developers to co-operate with IBM in software development of various kinds – co-market deals, free software, low-cost development tools and access to large customer accounts. IBM is based on Java and the freely available Linux operating system – a direct attack on Microsoft's proprietary software system.
- *Operating systems for middleware markets*: market worth US$72 billion in 2003. IBM was already market leader here with 17 per cent share; Oracle had 8 per cent and Microsoft 6 per cent. Middleware helps companies tie together various business applications inside companies – financial systems, communications systems, etc. If IBM can gain further advantage here then it can use this to sell other parts of its vertically integrated products and services.

- *Operating systems for applications*: market worth over US$100 billion in 2003. Microsoft was leader here with around 11 per cent of the market; SAP (Germany) was second with 5 per cent. IBM withdrew from this market in the late 1990s as being too complex and specialist. It had no plans to move back into this market in 2004. Beyond the market leaders, the market was fragmented.

IBM's strategy for the years from 2002 onwards was therefore to attack segments of this market. It ignored the segment for applications, but targeted the segments for business computers and middleware. At the time of writing, its strategy was still waiting to show results but the early figures were encouraging.

World market for IT consultancy
The total market was estimated to be worth at least US$1 billion in 2004. IBM was the market leader here with a large activity base in this area during the 1990s. In 2002, IBM paid US$3.5 billion for the consulting services arm of the management accounting company PwC. This brought around 30,000 consultants into IBM and opened up the possibility of moving into outsourcing of computer services beyond mere IT consulting: outsourcing is the new 'vision' of IBM and is explained further below. With regard to the IT consultancy market itself, the market was highly fragmented but had four main forms of competitors:

- *Mainstream management consultancies*: well-known consultants like Bain which had moved into IT consulting
- *Outsourcing companies with consultancy development capabilities*: Accenture, Cap Gemini Ernst and Young, Bearingpoint (formerly within the accountants KPMG), EDS, Wipro (from India)
- *Software vendors who had begun to sell consultancy*: Oracle, SAP and Peoplesoft (subsequently acquired by Oracle)
- *Computer companies*: Hewlett-Packard/Compaq and Dell were also selling consultancy services. HP had even attempted to buy PwC before it was sold to IBM. Case 21.4 describes this in more detail

Because IBM was larger than any other consulting company, all the four types of consultancy outlined above were its potential competitors. IBM's strategy in computer consultancy was to offer a comprehensive service to business clients. It would compete with all four above. At the time of writing, IBM's consultancy operations were the biggest single source of profits in the company – *see* Table 2.3. IBM considered this to be an area with major scope for further development. However, it had first to cope with the retirement of Mr Gerstner and the arrival of a new chief executive.

New leadership at IBM: Sam Palmisano 2002-onwards
In March 2002, Mr Gerstner retired and was replaced by a new chief executive, Mr Sam Palmisano. It was a surprising appointment, given the previous inward-looking IBM culture, because the new leader had himself been with the company

for nearly 30 years. In reality, it is always difficult to recruit a new chief from outside an organisation that is large and complex. Mr Palmisano quickly began to make his own decisions. He disbanded the 12-person management committee that had guided IBM up to that time and voluntarily gave up his own profit-related bonus in order to give higher rewards to his senior managers. His management style was more avuncular, less aggressive than Mr Gerstner. He then developed a vision for the future of IBM that would take the company ten years to fulfil. But he did not abandon the strategies of his predecessor. His strategic vision is explained below. It was based on the IBM understanding of the main forces and trends now developing in computer markets.

IBM's new vision 2003

In 2003, Sam Palmisano announced a new vision for IBM. It was based on the competitive advantages of the company – its vertical integration into most areas of computer activity and its strengths in computing consultancy. The vision was to combine the existing consulting skills and technology leadership of IBM into a totally new computer offering. The company would attempt to develop computer systems that were linked like giant grids and available on demand in the way that water and electricity services were delivered to individual homes and businesses in many parts of the world. The vision was to provide computer service for all companies around the globe 24/7.

Essentially, IBM would be the outsource provider of computer services. For example, IBM signed a contract in 2003 for US$400 million with Procter and Gamble (P&G), the US consumer goods company, to track all its pallets and cartons worldwide and assist that company in improving its service

and reducing its costs to customers like the major grocery supermarkets. P&G would outsource all this activity to IBM and pay a fee for this service. The new IBM vision was potentially very profound: it sought to build on IBM's strengths as a major consultancy and technology provider to become the main supplier of outsourced computer services in all forms as these grew in the twenty-first century.

At the time of writing, customer demand for such a broad-range all-embracing computer service was unclear. An additional problem with the vision was that it was not clear in 2003 whether the customers themselves were able to cope with the concept. 'The on-demand concept is going to be very important eventually. The trouble is that I don't think most companies have the IT architectures mature enough to take advantage of it,' said Jeanne Ross, principal research scientist at the Massachusetts Institute of Technology's Centre for Information Systems Research. In addition and according to some commentators, the technologies required to implement the on-demand computer service vision identified by IBM were still not fully available at IBM itself. Finally, IBM's competitors were not standing still: rivals were also offering extensions to their consultancy services.

IBM strategy conclusions

To the present, the results of IBM's new strategies have been successful, with a major recovery in profitability from the difficulties of the early 1990s. It was also well placed with new growth strategies to develop further into the twenty-first century. But whether its new vision would be achieved was not entirely clear.

Table 2.4 summarises IBM's situation over the years from the early 1980s to the mid 2000s. It shows how IBM's

---

Table 2.4

How IBM's objectives and strategies shifted over time

Period	Summary objective for company	Examples of strategies to achieve objective
Early to mid-1980s	Grow and maintain market dominance	• Invest in branding • Enhance service • Regular new product initiatives
Late 1980s to early 1990s	Survive competitive threat	• Major cutbacks in costbase • Divest peripheral parts
Mid-1990s onwards	Restart growth	• Acquire new companies • Invest further in segments of the software and computer services markets
Late 1990s into 2000s	Develop new vision of 'computer grid' available on demand	• Develop new technologies to realise vision • One-stop computer services shop • Develop alliances and joint ventures • Acquire service companies • Divest under-performing manufacturing parts of the business

Sources for IBM case: See reference[105].

▶ CASE STUDY 2.6 continued

objectives changed and the new strategies that were developed to address the new objectives of the company. Both were changed significantly during this lengthy time frame. Although the strategies are presented as static statements at single points in time, they were more fluid and experimental over this time frame.

Case questions

1 *Where would you place the new strategies of IBM – prescriptive or emergent? And within this, which strategic theory represents the most appropriate explanation of the company's development?*

2 *What are the risks and benefits of the company's new vision? What are the dangers of having a competitive advantage that relies on vertical integration? Will the company succeed?*

3 *Are there any more general lessons to be drawn for companies from the IBM approach of providing industry solutions? Or is this strategy specific to one very large company in an industry that is still evolving?*

STRATEGIC PROJECT

IBM is under increasing strategic pressure from both hardware and software companies. You might like to identify some of the leading, smaller companies from this book such as Microsoft, Dell or Hewlett-Packard. You might then consider how you would attack IBM, if you were one of these companies. You would probably choose to focus on a segment of the market but which segment and why?

CRITICAL REFLECTION

Is the distinction between prescriptive and emergent strategy processes too simplistic to be useful?

This chapter has argued that there is a basic distinction to be made between prescriptive and emergent theories of strategy. However, it explained – *see* the beginning of Section 2.4 – that this basic distinction was simplistic. Many strategy theories rely on much more detailed insights than this simple difference – for example, 'game theory' or 'resource-based theory'. Examples of the specific theories are outlined in Sections 2.4 and 2.5. This might suggest that the basic split between prescriptive and emergent strategies is too simple and serves no useful purpose.

To explore this question, you might like to consider what precisely makes 'good' strategy. The topic – 'What makes good strategy?' in Chapter 1, Section 1.5 – might give you some ideas. You could then apply them to the basic distinction between prescriptive and emergent strategy. You could also apply them to some of the more detailed prescriptive and emergent theories outlined in this chapter.

SUMMARY

● Prescriptive and emergent strategies can be contrasted by adapting Mintzberg's analogy:[106]

Prescriptive strategy is Biblical in its approach: it appears at a point in time and is governed by a set of rules, fully formulated and ready to implement.

Emergent strategy is Darwinian in its approach: an emerging and changing strategy that survives by adapting as the environment itself changes.

Given the need for an organisation to have a corporate strategy, much of this chapter has really been about the *process* of achieving this strategy. As has been demonstrated, there is no common agreement on the way this can be done.

● On the one hand, there is the *prescriptive* process, which involves a structured strategic planning system. It is necessary to identify objectives, analyse the environment and the resources of the organisation, develop strategy options and select among them. The selected process is then implemented. However, there are writers who caution against having a system that is too rigid and incapable of taking into account the people element in strategy.

● On the other hand, there is the *emergent* process, which does not identify a final objective with specific strategies to achieve this. It relies on developing strategies whose final outcome may not be known. Managers will rely more on trial and error and experimentation to achieve the optimal process.

● In the early part of the twentieth century when industrialisation was proceeding fast, the prescriptive process was the main recommended route. As organisations came to recognise the people element and their importance to strategic development, emergent strategies were given greater prominence during the middle part of the century. In recent years, emphasis has switched between market-based routes and resource-based routes in the development of strategy. Social and cultural issues have also become more important as markets and production have become increasingly global in scale. New communications technologies like the internet have led to new opportunities and the need for new strategic concepts. In addition, the collapse of some companies through their lack of regard for the ethics of running a business has led to a new emphasis on ethical issues in the development of corporate strategy.

● Within the *prescriptive* route, four main groups of strategic theory have been identified:

1 *the industry and environment-based route* – the market place is vital to profit delivery;

2 *the resource-based route* – the resources of the organisation are important in developing corporate strategy;

3 *the game theory route* – concentrating on the way that strategic choice is decided and negotiated with others in the market place;

4 *the cooperation and network route* – this stresses the importance of the formal relationship opportunities that are available to organisations.

Each of these has different perspectives on the development of strategy.

● Within the *emergent* route, four main groups were also distinguished:

1 *the survival-based route* – emphasising the 'survival of the fittest' in the jungle of the market place;

2 *the uncertainty-based route* – regards prediction as impossible because of the inherently unstable nature of the environment and the need to have innovative processes;

3 *the human-resource-based route* – places the emphasis on people in strategic development. Motivation, politics, culture and the desires of the individual are all important. Strategy may involve an element of experimentation and learning in order to take into account all these factors.

4 *the innovation and knowledge-based route* – stresses the contribution of new ideas and radical ways of thinking and sharing knowledge if an organisation is to outsmart its competitors.

● Strategy development should also be seen in the historical context of the development of the organisation. A firm's previous history is a key influence on its future development. This can usefully be considered under three broad headings: process, competitive position and paths of past and future resource development.

QUESTIONS

1 Is it possible for organisations to follow both prescriptive and emergent strategies or do they need to choose?

2 Examine the criticisms of prescriptive strategies in Section 2.2 and those of emergent strategies in Section 2.3. To what extent, if at all, do you agree with them? Why?

3 Consider the three emergent approaches to strategy outlined in Section 2.5. Which would you judge most closely described the route taken by Spillers in Case study 2.2? What conclusions do you draw from this about the viability of Spillers' approach?

4 What predictions would you make for the environment over the next ten years? What influence will your predictions have on developments in corporate strategy over this period?

5 Take an organisation with which you are familiar. Analyse whether it has been following prescriptive or emergent strategies or both. Within these broad categories, how would you characterise its strategies according to the classifications laid out in Sections 2.4 and 2.5?

6 If you were asked to develop corporate strategy for the following companies, which corporate strategy theory might you pick as a starting point for your assessment? A large, international car company; an advertising agency with global links; a government institution; a small travel agency with four branches, all in one region of a country.

7 *'When well-managed major organisations make significant changes in strategy, the approaches they use frequently bear little resemblance to the rational–analytical systems so often touted in the planning literature.'* (Professor J B Quinn)

Discuss.

8 *'In turbulent environments, the speed at which changes develop is such that firms which use the emerging strategy formation advocated by Mintzberg endanger their own survival. When they arrive on a market with a new product or service, such firms find the market pre-empted by more foresightful competitors who plan their strategic moves in advance.'* (Professor I Ansoff)

Explain and critically evaluate this comment.

9 Take an organisation with which you are familiar and explore the extent to which its current strategy is dependent on past events. Use Section 2.6 to structure your answer into processes, position and paths.

Further reading

Richard Whittington's *What is Strategy and Does it Matter?* (Routledge, London, 1993) is a lucid, well-structured and thought-provoking book. I have acknowledged some of its interesting research references as this chapter has progressed and it has certainly influenced some elements of the material. Read Chapter 2 of Whittington for an alternative view and structuring of strategy theories and practice.

Two major more recent books of strategy research topics are strongly recommended: Michael Hitt, R Edward Freeman and Jeffrey S Harrison, *The Blackwell Handbook of Strategic Management* (Blackwell, Oxford, 2001), Andrew Pettigrew, Howard Thomas, Richard Whittington, *Handbook of Strategy and Management* (Sage, London, 2002).

On strategy as history, classic studies include those by Alfred Chandler, *Strategy and Structure* (MIT Press, Cambridge, MA, 1962), and his later book *Scale and Scope: Dynamics of Individual Capitalism* (Harvard University Press, Cambridge, MA, 1990). See also Derek Channon's *The Strategy and Structure of British Enterprise* (Harvard University Press, Cambridge, MA, 1973). A more recent study with real insight is Geoffrey Jones' *Evolution of International Business* (Routledge, London, 1996).

J L Moore's *Writers on Strategy and Strategic Management* (Penguin, London, 1992) has a useful survey of some leading writers and theories which would be helpful for essay references and revision.

The book by Edith Penrose, *The Theory of the Growth of the Firm*, 3rd edn (Oxford University Press, Oxford, 1993), represents a classic early study of strategy development. Moreover, its precision of language and clarity of thought represent a model for us all to emulate.

Notes and references

1 Kennedy, P (1990) *The Rise and Fall of the Great Powers*, Fontana Press, London, Ch5. The historical description of this chapter draws on this well-researched and documented book.

2 Urwick, L (ed) (1956) *The Golden Book of Management*, Newman Neame, London. The book contains brief records of the lives and work of 70 of the early management pioneers, including their publications and a comment on their contribution. The historical material in this chapter draws on this work, which is no longer in print.

3 Williams, K, Haslam, C, Johal, S and Williams, J (1994) *Cars: Analysis, History and Cases*, Berghahn Books, New York, Ch7.

4 Abernathy, W J and Wayne, K (1974) 'Limits of the learning curve', *Harvard Business Review*, Sept–Oct, pp109–19.

5 Drucker, P (1961) *The Practice of Management*, Mercury Books, London, Ch10.

6 Penrose, E (1959) *The Theory of the Growth of the Firm*, Basil Blackwell, Oxford.

7 Cyert, R M and March, J G (1963) *A Behavioural Theory of the Firm*, Prentice-Hall, Englewood Cliffs, NJ.

8 Ansoff, H I (1969) *Business Strategy*, Penguin, Harmondsworth.

9 World Bank (1994) *World Development Report 1994*, Oxford University Press, New York, Ch3.

10 The evidence in this case comes from personal experience: the author was senior manager at Spillers plc corporate strategy headquarters and acted as liaison manager with the consultancy company.

11 Lester, T (1979) 'Slow grind at Spillers', *Management Today*, Jan, pp59–114.

12 Ansoff, I (1969) Op. cit. Porter, M E (1980) *Competitive Strategy*, The Free Press, Harvard, MA, Introduction.

13 Clausewitz, C von, *On War*, Routledge and Kegan Paul, London, quoted in Kotler, P and Singh, R (1981) 'Marketing warfare', *Journal of Business Strategy*, pp30–41.

14 Liddell Hart, B H (1967) *Strategy*, Praeger, NY, also quoted in reference 4 above.

15 *See*, for example, James, B G (1985) *Business Warfare*, Penguin, Harmondsworth, also Ries, J and Trout, A (1986) *Marketing Warfare*, McGraw-Hill, Maidenhead.

16 Whittington, R (1993) *What is Strategy – and Does it Matter?*, Routledge, London, p16.

17 Wiles, P J D (1961) *Price, Cost and Output*, Blackwell, Oxford, p78.

18 Porter, M E (1985) *Competitive Advantage*, The Free Press, Harvard, MA.

19 Ansoff, H I (1965) *Corporate Strategy: An Analytical Approach to Business Policy for Growth and Expansion*, McGraw-Hill, New York.

20 Andrews, K (1971) *The Concept of Corporate Strategy*, Irwin, Homewood, IL.

21 Chakravarthy, B and Lorange, P (1991) *Managing the Strategy Process*, Prentice Hall, Upper Saddle River, NJ. The first chapter is usefully summarised in: De Wit, B and Meyer, R (1994) *Strategy: Process, Context and Content*, West Publishing, St Paul, MN.

22 For example, see the following for an extended critique of prescriptive strategy: Stacey, R (1998) *Strategic Management and Organisational Dynamics*, 2nd edn, Pearson Education, London.

23 Mintzberg, H (1990) 'The Design School: reconsidering the basic premises of strategic management', *Strategic Management Journal*, 11, pp176–95.

24 Mintzberg, H (1994) 'The fall and rise of strategic planning', *Harvard Business Review*, Jan–Feb, pp107–14.

25 Lee Kuan Yew (1998) *The Singapore Story*, Simon and Schuster (Asia) Pte.

26 References of Singapore Airlines case: airline website – www.singaporeair.com; Singapore Airlines Annual Report and Accounts 2004.

27 Writing in the 1950s, Herbert Simon was amongst the first to argue that the unreliability and limitations of human decision making made Adam Smith's simple economic assumption that humans would usually take rational decisions somewhat dubious – see reference 30 below.

28 Mayo, E, *Human Problems in Industrial Civilisation*, along with other research on the *Bank Wiring Observation Room*, described in Homans, G (1951) *The Human Group*, Routledge and Kegan Paul, London, ChIII.

29 Cyert, R M and March, J (1963) *A Behavioral Theory of the Firm*, Prentice Hall, Upper Saddle River, NJ.

30 March, J G and Simon, H (1958) *Organisations*, Wiley, New York.

31 Pettigrew, A (1985) *The Awakening Giant: Continuity and Change at ICI*, Blackwell, Oxford.

32 Mintzberg, H (1990) Op. cit.

33 Johnson, G (1986) 'Managing strategic change – the role of strategic formulae', published in: McGee, J and Thomas, H (ed) (1986) *Strategic Management Research*, Wiley, Chichester, Section 1.4.

34 Argyris, C (1991) 'Teaching smart people how to learn', *Harvard Business Review*, May–June, p99 summarises his many earlier papers.

35 Senge, P M (1990) 'The leader's new work: building learning organisations', *Sloan Management Review*, Fall, pp7–22.

36 Lindblom, C E (1959) 'The Science of Muddling Through', *Public Administrative Review*, 19, pp79–88.

37 Whittington, R (1993) Op. cit. He repeats Weick's true story of the Hungarian troops who were lost in the Alps during the First World War but found a map which they used to reach safety. They then discovered that they were using a map of a totally different mountain range, The Pyrenees. Whittington makes the point that taking *some* action, any action, will constitute strategy in these circumstances, even if the particular choice of strategy is wrong. The issue is not whether the *right* strategic choice has been made and then implemented, but rather whether any choice has been made that will give direction to the people concerned.

38 These comments are taken from a variety of sources: the following is probably the best starting point: Ansoff, I (1991) Critique of Henry Mintzberg's 'The Design School', *Strategic Management Journal*, 12, pp449–461.

39 Jackson, T. (1995) *Virgin King: Inside Richard Branson's Business Empire*, HarperCollins, London, p66.

40 Jackson, T. (1995) Op. cit.

41 Jackson, T. (1995) Op. cit.

42 References for Virgin case: Virgin website (www.virgin.com); Jackson, T. (1995) Op. cit.

43 Ansoff, I (1965) *Corporate Strategy*, Penguin, Harmondsworth.

44 Chandler, A (1962) *Strategy and Structure*, MIT Press, Cambridge, MA.

45 Sloan, A P (1963) *My Years with General Motors*, Sedgewick & Jackson, London.

46 Wheelen, T and Hunger, D (1992) *Strategic Management and Business Policy*, Addison-Wesley, Reading, MA.

47 Porter, M E (1980) Op. cit. and (1985) Op. cit.

48 Rumelt, R, Schendel, D and Teece, D (1991) 'Strategic management and economics', *Strategic Management Journal*, 12, pp5–29. This contains an extensive and valuable review of this area.

49 Bowman, E H and Helfat, C E (2001) 'Does corporate strategy matter?' *Strategic Management Journal*, Vol 22, pp1–23.

50 Ansoff, I (1968) 'Toward a strategy theory of the firm', in Ansoff, I (ed) (1969) *Business Strategy*, Penguin, Harmondsworth, p39.

51 Porter, M E (1980) Op. cit.

52 Seth, A and Thomas, H (1994) 'Theories of the firm: implications for strategy research' *Journal of Management Studies*, Vol 31, pp165–191.

53 Ohmae, K (1983) *The Mind of the Strategist*, Penguin, Harmondsworth.

54 Wilks, S (1990) *The Embodiment of Industrial Culture in Bureaucracy and Management*, quoted in Whittington, R (1993) Op. cit., p160.

55 But problems remain: see Luce, E (2002) 'Investment in India "riddled with obstacles"', *Financial Times*, 19 March, p14.

56 *See*, for example, the leading article in the *Financial Times Survey on Singapore*, 24 Feb 1995.

57 Hamel, G and Prahalad, C K (1990) 'The core competence of the corporation', *Harvard Business School Review*, May–June. Their 1994 book *Competing for the Future* (Harvard Business School, Baston, MA) picks up many of the same themes.

58 Kay, J (1993) *Foundations of Corporate Success*, Oxford University Press, Oxford.

59 Hannan, M T and Freeman, J (1988) *Organisational Ecology*, Harvard University Press, Cambridge, MA.

60 Hamel, G and Prahalad, C K (1990) Op. cit.

61 Kay, J (1993) Op. cit.

62 Mintzberg, H (1987) Op. cit.

63 Mintzberg, H (1994) 'The fall and rise of strategic planning', *Harvard Business Review*, Jan–Feb, pp107–14.

64 Drucker, P (1967) Op. cit., Ch9.

65 Slack, N, Chambers, S, Harland, C, Harrison, A and Johnston, R (1995) *Operations Management*, Pitman Publishing, London, p812.

66 Williams, K, Haslam, C, Johal, S and Williams, J (1994) Op. cit., Ch7.

67 Hamel, G and Prahalad, C K (1994) *Competing for the Future*, Harvard Business School Press, Boston, MA.

68 Wernerfelt, B (1984) 'A resource-based view of the firm,' *Strategic Management Journal*, 5(2), pp171–80.

69 Peteraf, M A (1993) 'The cornerstones of competitive advantage', *Strategic Management Journal*, 14, pp179–81.

70 Dierickx, I and Cool, K (1989) 'Asset stock accumulation and sustainability of competitive advantage', *Management Science*, 35, pp1540–51.

71 Kay, J (1994) *Foundations of Corporate Success*, Oxford University Press, Oxford.

72 Nonaka, I (1991) 'The knowledge-creating company', *Harvard Business Review*, Nov–Dec.

73 For a useful and accessible review, *see* Dixit, A K and Nalebuff, B J (1991) *Thinking Strategically*, W W Norton, New York. In addition to the references in Chapter 15, it is important to note that writers like Professor Michael Porter also employed game theory in their work without specifically discussing its theoretical background. *See* Chapter 3 for references to Porter.

74 Eisenhardt, K M (2002) 'Has the strategy changed?' *MIT Sloan Management Review*, Vol 43, No 2, pp88–91.

75 Inkpen, A C (2001) 'Strategic alliances' in: Hitt, M A, Freeman, R E and Harrison, J S (eds) *Handbook of Strategic Management*, Oxford University Press, Oxford.

76 Child, J and Faulkner, D (1998) *Strategies of Co-operation: Managing Alliances, Networks and Joint Ventures*, Oxford University Press, Oxford.

77 Lafontaine, F (1999) 'Myths and strengths of franchising', *Financial Times Mastering Strategy*, Part Nine, 22 November, pp8–10.

78 Dyer, J H, Kale, P and Singh, H (2001) 'How to make strategic alliances work', *MIT Sloan Management Review*, Vol 42, No 4, pp37–43.

79 References for Subway case: Subway web pages 2005 – www.subway.com – (Incidentally, give a clearer idea of the business formula than is possible in a short case); Biddle, R (2001) *Forbes Magazine*, 9 March; web franchise site – www.entrepreneur.com.

80 Hall, R C and Hitch, C J (1939) 'Price theory and business behaviour', *Oxford Economic Papers*, 2, pp12–45, quoted in Whittington, R (1993) Op. cit.

81 Henderson, B (1989) 'The origin of strategy', *Harvard Business Review*, Nov–Dec, pp139–43.

82 Williamson, O (1991) 'Strategising, economising and economic organisation', *Strategic Management Journal*, 12, pp75–94.

83 Hannan, M T and Freeman, J (1988) Op. cit.

84 Whittington, R (1993) Op. cit., p22.

85 Pascale, R (1990) *Managing on the Edge*, Viking Penguin, London, p114.

86 Gleick, J (1988) *Chaos*, Penguin, London.

87 Miller, D and Friesen, P (1982) 'Structural change and performance: quantum versus piecemeal–incremental approaches', *Academy of Management Journal*, 25, pp867–92.

88 Strebel, P (1992) *Breakpoints*, Harvard Business School Press, Boston, MA. A summary of this argument appears in De Wit, B and Meyer, R (1994) Op. cit., pp390–2.

89 Stacey, R (1993) *Strategic Management and Organisational Dynamics*, Pitman Publishing, London.

90 Miller, D and Friesen, P (1984) *Organisations: A Quantum View*, Prentice Hall, Englewood Cliffs, NJ.

91 Cyert, R and March, J (1963) Op. cit.

92 March, J and Simon, H (1958) Op. cit.

93 Nelson, R and Winter, S (1982) *An Evolutionary Theory of Economic Change*, Harvard University Press, Cambridge, MA, p34.

94 Nelson, R and Winter, S (1982) Ibid.

95 Mintzberg, H (1987) 'Crafting strategy', *Harvard Business Review*, July–Aug, pp65–75.

96 Quinn, J B (1980) *Strategies for Change: Logical Incrementalism*, Irwin, Burr Ridge, MN.

97 Senge, P M (1990) Op. cit.

98 Mintzberg, H (1994) Op. cit.

99 Major writers in this area include: Kay, J (1993) *Foundations of Corporate Success*, Oxford University Press, Oxford, Chapter 5. Professor Kay also reviews the earlier work of Professor David Teece – see references at the end of Chapter 5. For a more recent view, Markides C A (2000) *All the Right Moves*, Harvard Business School Press, Boston, MA.

100 Nonaka, I and Takeuchi, H (1995) *The Knowledge-Creating Company*, Oxford University Press, Oxford. See also Davenport, T H and Prusack, L (1998) *Working Knowledge*, Harvard Business School Press, Harvard, MA.

101 Penrose, E (1959) *The Theory of the Growth of the Firm*, Basil Blackwell, Oxford. Note that a third edition of the text was published in 1993 with a new preface by Professor Penrose: it has a historical perspective that is relevant to strategy development.

102 Chandler, A (1962) *Strategy and Structure*, MIT Press, Cambridge, MA. Chandler later developed this perspective further in his 1990 text: *Scale and Scope: Dynamics of Industrial Capitalism*, Harvard University Press, Cambridge, MA.

103 Developed by the author from the concepts outlined in: Teece, D J, Pisano, G and Shuen, A (1997) 'Dynamic capabilities and strategic management', *Strategic Management Journal*, 18(7), pp509–33.

104 The arguments here are not dissimilar to those used by the human-resource-based strategists outlined in Section 2.5.3. See in particular the views of Nelson and Winter.

105 References for IBM Case: Heller, R (1994) *The Fate of IBM*, Warner Books, London (easy to read and accurate); Carroll, P (1993) *The Unmaking of IBM*, Crown, London (rather one-sided); *Financial Times*, 7 Dec 1990, p14; 5 June 1991, article by Alan Cane; 8 Nov 1991, article by Alan Cane and Louise Kehoe; 5 May 1993, p17; 29 July 1993, p17; 14 Mar 1994, p17; 26 Mar 1994, p8; 28 Mar 1994, p15; 31 May 94, p21; 4 Oct 1994, p16; 10 Oct 1994, p23; 25 Oct 1994, p18; 12 Jan 1995, p22; 5 June 1995, p15; 6 June 1995, p21; 13 June 1995, p21; 26 June 1995, p15; 29 Sept 1995, p21; 14 Dec 1996, p9; 18 Feb 1997, p4; 22 Nov 1997, p17; 5 Mar 1998, p17; *The Economist*, 16 Jan 1993, p23; 14 Dec 1996, pp102–3; *Business Age*, Apr 1994, p76; 30 January 2002, pp21, 31; 1 February 2002, p30; 14 February 2002, p31; 12 April 2002, p31; 11 April 2003, p26; 9 July 2003, p13; 25 September 2003, p32; 10 October 2003, p17; 1 December 2003, p21; 2 March 2004, p29; 17 March 2004, p13; 4 May 2004, p28; 6 December 2004, p28; 9 December 2004, p26; 25 February 2005, p26.

106 Mintzberg, H (1990) 'The Design School: Reconsidering the basic premises of strategic management', *Strategic Management Journal*, as adapted by De Wit, R and Meyer, B (1994) Op. cit., p72.

**Chapter 3
Analysing the
environment –
basics**

- What is the environment and why is it important?
- What are the main background areas to be analysed?
- What is the strategic significance of market growth?
- How are the more immediate influences on the organisation analysed?
- How do we analyse competitors?
- What is the role of co-operation in environmental analysis?
- How important is the customer?

**Chapter 4
Analysing
markets,
competition and
co-operation**

- Why is sustainable competitive advantage important in strategy?
- How are competitors analysed and how do we beat them?
- How do competitors compete with each other and what is the nature of the competition?
- What is the role of the product portfolio analysis?
- How important are distributors?
- What are the benefits of co-operative strategies and how do we manage them?
- What influence can the government have on the market and corporate strategy?

**Chapter 5
Developing
customer-driven
strategy**

- Why is customer-driven strategy so important?
- How are customers analysed?
- What contribution do reputation and branding make to strategy?
- What is the role of customer communication in strategy development? What is the strategic role of price and value for money?

Part 2

ANALYSIS OF THE ENVIRONMENT

Both the prescriptive and the emergent approaches to corporate strategy consider an organisation's ability to understand its environment – its customers, its suppliers, its competitors, the organisations with which it co-operates and the social and economic influences in its operations – to be an important element of the strategy process.

This part of the book begins by examining the basic analytical tools and frameworks used in a study of an organisation's environment and then goes on to tackle particular aspects of this task in more detail, namely the basic market and the organisation's competitors and its customers, co-operators and marketing resources.

The prescriptive strategic process

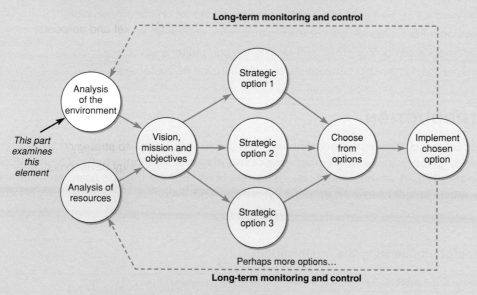

The emergent strategic process

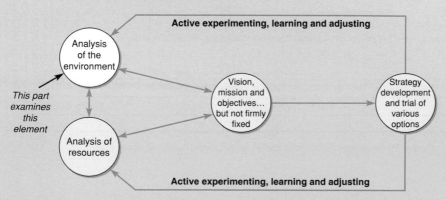

Chapter 3

ANALYSING THE ENVIRONMENT - BASICS

Learning outcomes

When you have worked through this chapter, you will be able to:

- explain why it is important to study the environment of the organisation;
- outline the main environmental influences on the organisation and relate the degree of change to prescriptive and emergent strategic approaches;
- undertake a PESTEL analysis of the general influences on the organisation;
- understand the implications of market growth and market cyclicality for corporate strategy;
- understand the importance of key factors for success in the environment;
- carry out a Five Forces analysis of the specific influences on the organisation;
- develop a Four Links analysis of the organisation's co-operators;
- undertake a competitor profile and identify the competitor's advantages;
- explore the relationship between the organisation and its customers.

INTRODUCTION

In recent years, the term 'environment' has taken on a rather specialised meaning: it involves 'green' issues and the poisoning of our planet by human activity. These concerns are certainly part of our considerations in this book, but we use the term 'environment' in a much broader sense to describe everything and everyone outside the organisation.

Figure 3.1

The seven basic factors influencing the organisation

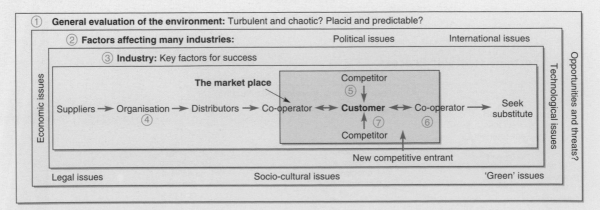

Note: Within an industry, the balance of forces and the interrelationship between the forces can be complex. It is not fully shown above.

This includes customers, competitors, suppliers, distributors, government and social institutions.

Before examining aspects of the environment in depth in Chapters 4 and 5, it is useful to begin by exploring the seven basic factors in the environment that influence corporate strategy (*see* Figure 3.1). As elements of the environment change, the organisation needs to adjust its corporate strategy accordingly. Prescriptive strategies will want to anticipate how the environment will change in the future in order to meet future needs ahead of competing organisations. Emergent strategies will be content with an understanding of the environment.

Part 4

Strategic bargaining to film *Lord of the Rings*

In the highly competitive and risky environment of Hollywood film-making, it is essential to analyse those who have the power to make things happen. This case explores the strategic environment surrounding one of the most profitable films ever made – and how the deal and the movie almost failed.

Background

It was one of the biggest gambles in movie history – handing US$300 million to shoot an epic trilogy in one take to a virtually unknown director with no record of big-budget Hollywood pictures. And letting him do it 7,000 miles away, so that studio executives had little control over what actually happened on the set.

There were plenty of recent examples of how a huge investment in what seemed a sure-fire blockbuster had backfired, leaving massive dents in the studio's finances – *Waterworld*, *Heaven's Gate* and so on. Somehow, though, *Lord of the Rings* did get made and took over US$500 million in its first year as well as winning four Oscars. It is easy to forget the scale of the risk involved and the convoluted strategic bargaining that was necessary before a single scene was shot.

For Peter Jackson, the film's New Zealand-born director, and his agent, Ken Kamins from ICM, the story behind *Lord of the Rings* is one of a project that very nearly failed to see the light of day.

Competitive environment

When Jackson and Kamins set out to make the film in 1995, they first had to secure the rights to JRR Tolkien's novels, *The Fellowship of the Ring*, *The Two Towers* and *The Return of the King*. Producer Saul Zaentz had bought the rights from Professor Tolkien for a rumoured US$15,000 30 years earlier and he had no intention of selling them. Up to that point, Jackson was known only for low-budget horror movies such as *Braindead*. However, an Oscar nomination in 1995 for the screenplay of his US$3.5 million arthouse drama *Heavenly Creatures* had earned him a first-look deal with Harvey Goldstein, head of Miramax, the independent studio allied to Disney. So Jackson and Kamins approached Weinstein that year with the idea for a *Lord of the Rings* adaptation.

'When we told Harvey that Saul held the rights, he was immediately enthusiastic,' says Kamins, 'as he had just helped Saul on *The English Patient* [Miramax had stepped in to pick up the film after Fox, part of News Corporation, dropped it on the eve of production]. That created the moral window by which Harvey could ask. But this wasn't charity either. Saul had Harvey pay a pretty penny – I've been told somewhere in the US$3 million range.'

Outdoor advertising in Hollywood, USA. Even after the strategy was negotiated and implemented, it was important to promote the film

▶ **CASE STUDY 3.1 continued**

New bargaining problems

Having secured the film rights, the Miramax boss sent Jackson and his partner, Fran Walsh, off to write the scripts for a two-part adaptation, with both parts being filmed one after the other. Production research was also to begin in New Zealand. Just when things seemed to be going smoothly, the next wave of problems emerged. 'It soon became clear to Miramax that it was going to be a very expensive proposition,' says Kamins, 'maybe more expensive than their brief as defined by Disney allowed them to get involved in. Harvey then went to Disney and asked whether they would want a partner in the project. When Disney said no, Miramax got concerned about the cost. And of course [started] asking obvious questions: what happens if the first movie doesn't work?'

Faced with such a risky and expensive project, Weinstein asked Jackson to make the trilogy as one film of no more than three hours. Jackson declined, and, instead, he and Kamins asked to take the project to another studio. Weinstein agreed, although he imposed very tough conditions. Says Kamins: 'We had three weeks to set it up somewhere else. Harvey also demanded that the US$12 million that Miramax had already spent in development had to be repaid within 72 hours of the agreement being signed. Now this is highly unusual in the movie business. Normally, a studio would simply pay the former studio a 10 per cent option or they would work out a deal in the budget of the film once the movie got made. Most importantly, he and a partner insisted on 5 per cent of the gross, whether there was one movie, two movies or eight.'

The deal hangs on a knife-edge

With three weeks to find another studio, Jackson and Kamins decided to do two things. While Kamins started submitting the screenplays for the two-part adaptation to every studio in Hollywood, Jackson flew to New Zealand to produce a 35-minute documentary with US$50,000 of his own money. The idea was that, if any of the studios was interested, the documentary would show them where Miramax's US$12 million had gone, and, most importantly, why Jackson was the right director. But Kamins had little success – every studio said no, except two, Polygram and New Line, which was owned by Warner Brothers. Then Polygram pulled out at the last minute: 'So we went to New Line realising that they were the last Popsicle stand in the desert, and them not knowing that,' said Kamins.

But at New Line, they had some luck. Jackson's old friend, Mark Ordesky, turned out to be one of those making the decision. New Line then asked: 'Why are you making two movies? It's three books, so it's three movies.' Negotiations started the next day. Many in the business doubted the sanity of the decision, especially making three rather than two films. 'But Peter's presentation made it clear that he had an absolutely commanding vision for the film . . . You would be surprised how, in the movie business, some of these commitments are made on far less sturdy ground.'

By 2002, AOL Time Warner was estimated to have one of the biggest money-spinners in entertainment history on its hands. New Line and its distribution partners had turned *Lord of the Rings* into a worldwide franchise in the *Star Wars* mould, and were exploiting the brand name across a huge range of platforms – DVD, video games, the internet, merchandise of every sort. The gamble was starting to pay.

Heavily adapted by Richard Lynch from an article by Katja Hofmann in *FT Creative Business*, 19 March 2002, page 10. © *Financial Times* 2002. All rights reserved. Reproduced with permission.

Case questions

1 *Who has the bargaining power in this strategic environment? And who has the co-operating power? Identify and analyse the players – use the concepts from Sections 3.7 and 3.8 to help you.*

2 *What useful strategic concepts, if any, from this chapter can be used in analysing the strategic environment? And what cannot be used? Why?*

3 *If risk and judgement are important in business decisions, can prescriptive strategic analysis be usefully employed?*

3.1 EXPLORING THE COMPETITIVE ENVIRONMENT

3.1.1 Why studying the competitive environment is important

Definition ➤ In strategy, the environment means everything and everyone outside the organisation: competitors, customers, government, etc. Strategists are agreed that an understanding of the competitive environment is an essential element of the development of corporate strategy. It is important to study the environment surrounding the organisation for three main reasons. First, most organisations compete against others – for example, films like *Lord of the Rings* compete against other films for finance from the film studios – *see* Case 3.1. Hence a study of the environment will provide information on the nature of competition as a step

Definition ➤ to developing *sustainable competitive advantage*.[1] Sustainable competitive advantage is an advantage over competitors that cannot easily be imitated. Second, most organisations will perceive *opportunities* that might be explored and *threats* that need to be contained.[2] For example, the *Lord of the Rings* trilogy was seen by some film backers to have more threats than opportunities. Such opportunities and threats may come not just from competitors but also from government decisions, changes in technology and social developments and many other factors. Third, there are opportunities for networks and other linkages, which lead to sustainable co-operation. For example, Peter Jackson met his old friend Mark Ordesky when needing some help in the final negotiations to finance *Lord of the Rings*. Such linkages with others may strengthen an organisation in its environment by providing mutual support.

However, there are three difficulties in determining the connection between the organisation's corporate strategy and its environment.

1 *The prescriptive versus emergent debate.* The first problem arises from the fundamental disagreement about the corporate strategy processes that was explored in Part 1 of this book. Some prescriptive strategists take the view that, in spite of the various uncertainties, the environment can usefully be predicted for many markets. Some (but not all) emergent strategists believe that the environment is so turbulent and chaotic that prediction is likely to be inaccurate and serve no useful purpose. Each of these interpretations implies a quite different status for the same basic topic. This difficulty is explored further in Section 3.2.

2 *The uncertainty.* Whatever view is taken about prediction, all corporate strategists regard the environment as uncertain. New strategies have to be undertaken against a backdrop that cannot be guaranteed and this difficulty must be addressed as corporate strategies are developed. For example, Case 3.1 showed that the risks were so high in financing the film *Lord of the Rings* that nearly every studio declined to finance the film.

3 *The range of influences.* It is conceivable, at least in theory, that every element of an organisation's environment may influence corporate strategy. One solution to the problem posed by such a wide range of factors might be to produce a list of every element. This would be a strategic mistake, however, because organisations and individuals would find it difficult to develop and manage every item. In corporate strategy, the production of comprehensive lists that include every major eventuality and have no priorities has no value. A better solution is to identify the *key factors for success* in the industry and then to direct the environmental analysis towards these factors. This is considered briefly in this chapter and in more depth in Chapter 6.

3.1.2 The main elements of environmental analysis

To analyse an organisation's environment, while at the same time addressing the three difficulties outlined in Section 3.1.1, certain basic analytical procedures can be undertaken (*see* Table 3.1).

3.1.3 The distinction between proactive and reactive outcomes

When analysing the environment, it is useful to draw a distinction between two types of results from the analysis:

1 *Proactive outcomes.* The environmental analysis will identify positive opportunities or negative threats. The organisation will then develop proactive strategies to exploit or cope with the situation. For example, film producers might develop cross financing co-operation as a result of identifying new market opportunities.

2 *Reactive outcomes.* The environmental analysis will highlight important strategic changes over which the organisation has no control but to which, if they happen, it will need to be able to react. For example, new EU legislation on cultural content and investment might influence strategic activity in the European film industry.

In both cases, the environment will need to be analysed but the strategic implications are very different.

Table 3.1

Nine basic stages in environmental analysis

Stage	Techniques	Outcome of stage
1 Environment basics – an opening evaluation to define and explore basic characteristics of the environment (*See* Section 3.2)	Estimates of some basic factors surrounding the environment: • Market definition and size • Market growth • Market share	Basic strategic analysis of: • Scope the strategic opportunity • Establish future growth prospects • Begin to structure market competition
2 Consideration of the degree of turbulence in the environment (*See* Section 3.3)	General considerations: • Change: fast or slow? • Repetitive or surprising future? • Forecastable or unpredictable? • Complex or simple influences on the organisation?	General strategic conclusions • Is the environment too turbulent to undertake useful predictions? • What are the opportunities and threats for the organisation?
3 Background factors that influence the competitive environment (*See* Section 3.4)	PESTEL analysis and scenarios	• Identify key influences • Predict, if possible • Understand interconnections between events
4 Analysis of stages of market growth (*See* Section 3.5)	Industry life cycle	• Identify growth stage • Consider implications for strategy • Identify maturity, overproduction and cyclicality issues
5 Factors specific to the industry: what delivers success? (*See* Section 3.6)	Key factors for success analysis	• Identify factors relevant to strategy • Focus strategic analysis and development
6 Factors specific to the competitive balance of power in the industry (*See* Section 3.7)	Five Forces analysis	• Static and descriptive analysis of competitive forces
7 Factors specific to co-operation in the industry (*See* Section 3.8)	Four Links analysis	• Analysis of current and future organisations with whom co-operation is possible • Network analysis
8 Factors specific to immediate competitors (*See* Section 3.9)	Competitor analysis and product portfolio analysis	• Competitor profile • Analysis of relative market strengths
9 Customer analysis (*See* Section 3.10)	Market and segmentation studies	• Strategy targeted at existing and potential customers

 Part 4a
 Part 4a
 Part 4a
 Part 4a
 Part 4a
 Part 4b
 Part 4b
 Part 4c
 Part 4c

Key strategic principles

● Environmental analysis is important because it helps in developing sustainable competitive advantage, identifies opportunities and threats and may provide opportunities for productive co-operation with other organisations.

● There are three difficulties in studying the environment: the use to which the analysis will be put; uncertainty in the topic; coping with the wide range of environmental influences.

● Environmental analysis can be used to provide a *proactive* strategy outcome or highlight a *reactive* strategic situation that will need to be monitored.

3.2 STRATEGIC ENVIRONMENT – THE BASICS

In order to begin the environmental analysis, it is useful to start with some basic factors that are sometimes forgotten in the academic concepts but contribute to the strategic analysis of the environment.[3] We can divide the basics into three areas:

Part 4a

● Market definition and size
● Market growth
● Market share.

3.2.1 Market definition and size[4]

In analysing the strategic environment, most organisations will want an answer to the basic question – 'What is the size of the market?' This is important because it will assist in defining the strategic task. Markets are usually described in terms of annual sales. From a strategy perspective, a 'large' market may be more attractive than a 'small' market. The words 'large' and 'small' need to be considered carefully – for example, a 'large' opportunity to Peter Jackson who directed *Lord of the Rings* might be US$200 million – *see* Case 3.1; a 'large' opportunity to Warner Brothers who ultimately funded the film and have much broader film interests might be US$1 billion. Despite such problems, it is a useful starting point to attempt to assess the strategic opportunity (or the lack of it).

Measuring market size raises a related problem – how to define the 'market'. For example, is the annual market for *Lord of the Rings* (LOTR) defined as *fantasy films* only – worth, say, US$500 million? Or is the annual LOTR market *all adventure films*, including *Lord of the Rings* but also covering others from James Bond films to those starring Clint Eastwood – worth, say, US$10 billion? The answer will depend on the customers and the extent to which other products are a real substitute. Although some market definitions may seem obvious – for example, 'the ice cream market' would seem to be clearly defined, they need to be treated with care: perhaps another snack will substitute for ice cream and should be included within the definition? This topic is explored further in Section 5.1.

3.2.2 Market growth

In establishing the size of the market, it is also common practice to estimate how much the market has grown over the previous period – usually the previous year. From a strategy perspective, the importance of growth relates to the organisation's objectives. An organisation wishing to grow rapidly might be more attracted to a market growing rapidly. Clearly any such estimate also needs to take into account the argument about market definition made above.

3.2.3 Market share

Although some strategists disagree, a large share of a market is usually regarded as being strategically beneficial.[5] The reason is that a large share may make it possible to influence prices and may also reduce costs through scope for economies of scale, thereby increasing profitability.[6] Clearly, there are definitional problems here – *see* Section 3.2.1 above – but some estimate of market share is desirable from a strategy perspective. In practice, it may difficult to establish a precise market share – for example, the share of the film market taken by *Lord of the Rings* in 2002 will depend on the fact that it was high during the few weeks after its general release and greatest popularity – but this may not matter. From a strategy perspective, the important point is that *Lord of the Rings* took a significant share of the *fragmented* film market. Equally, there will be other strategic circumstances where a *dominant* share may be identified – for example, the market share held by companies supplying domestic water to households – without necessarily being able to measure the precise share. This is explored further in Chapters 4 and 14.

Key strategic principles

- Environmental analysis can usefully begin with a basic assessment of the market definition and size, the market growth and the market share.
- Market definition is important because it will determine the size and scope of the strategic opportunity. Market definition will be defined by a consideration of customers and the availability of substitute products.
- Market growth is commonly estimated early in any strategic analysis because of its importance with regard to the growth objectives of an organisation.
- A basic estimate of market share can be used to estimate whether an organisation has a significant share of a market as a starting point in exploring the strategic implications.

3.3 DEGREE OF TURBULENCE IN THE ENVIRONMENT[7]

Part 4a

At the general level of environmental analysis, it is important to consider the basic conditions surrounding the organisation. Special attention needs to be directed to the nature and strength of the forces driving strategic change – the *dynamics* of the environment. One reason for this consideration is that, if the forces are exceptionally turbulent, they may make it difficult to use some of the analytical techniques – like Porter's 'Five Forces', discussed later in this chapter. Another reason is that the nature of the environment may influence the way that the organisation is structured to cope with such changes.

The environmental forces surrounding the organisation can be assessed according to two main measures:

1 *Changeability* – the degree to which the environment is likely to change. For example, there is low changeability in the liquid milk market and high changeability in the various internet markets.

2 *Predictability* – the degree with which such changes can be predicted. For example, changes can be predicted with some certainty in the mobile telephone market but remain largely unknown in biogenetics.

These measures can each be subdivided further. Changeability comprises:

- *Complexity* – the degree to which the organisation's environment is affected by factors such as internationalisation and technological, social and political complications
- *Novelty* – the degree to which the environment presents the organisation with new situations.

Predictability can be further subdivided into:

- *Rate of change* of the environment (from slow to fast)
- *Visibility of the future* in terms of the availability and usefulness of the information used to predict the future.

Using these factors as a basis, it is then possible to build a spectrum that categorises the environment and provides a rating for its *degree of turbulence* (*see* Table 3.2).

When turbulence is low, it may be possible to predict the future with confidence. For example, film companies like Warner Brothers might be able to use data on their film customers around the world, along with international economic data, to predict future demand for different types of films.

When turbulence is higher, such predictions may have little meaning. The changeability elements influencing the organisation may contain *many* and *complex* items and the *novelty*

Table 3.2

Assessing the dynamics of the environment

	Environmental turbulence	Repetitive	Expanding	Changing	Discontinuous	Surprising
Changeability	*Complexity*	National	National	Regional Technological	Regional Socio-political	Global Economic
	Familiarity of events	Familiar	Extrapolable		Discontinuous Familiar	Discontinuous Novel
Predictability	*Rapidity of change*	Slower than response		Comparable to response		Faster than response
	Visibility of future	Recurring	Forecastable	Predictable	Partially predictable	Unpredictable surprises

Turbulence level	Low 1	2	3	4	5 High

Source: Ansoff, I and McDonnell, E (1990) *Implanting Strategic Management*, FT Prentice-Hall.

being introduced into the market place may be high. For example, new services, new suppliers, new ideas, new software and new payment systems were all being launched for the internet at the same time. Turbulence was high. Predicting the specific outcome of such developments was virtually impossible.

If the level of turbulence is high – called *hypercompetition*[8] by some strategists – and as a result the environment is difficult to study, the analysis recommended in some of the sections that follow may need to be treated with some caution. However, for most fast-growing situations, including the internet, there is merit in at least attempting to understand the main areas of the environment influencing the organisation. It may not be possible to undertake formal predictions but it will certainly be possible to identify the most important elements.

Key strategic principles

- It is important to begin an analysis of the environment with a general consideration of the degree of turbulence in that environment. If it is high, then this will make prediction difficult and impact on prescriptive approaches to strategy development.

- There are two measures of turbulence: changeability, i.e. the degree to which the environment is likely to change; and predictability, i.e. the degree to which such change can be predicted.

- Each of the two measures can then be further subdivided: changeability can be split into complexity and novelty; predictability can be divided into rate of change and visibility of the future. All these elements can then be used to explore turbulence.

3.4 ANALYSING THE GENERAL ENVIRONMENT

Part 4a

In any consideration of the factors surrounding the organisation, two techniques can be used to explore the general environment: these are the PESTEL analysis and scenarios.

3.4.1 PESTEL[9] analysis

It is already clear that there are no simple rules governing an analysis of the organisation. Each analysis needs to be guided by what is relevant for that particular organisation. However, it may be useful to begin the process with a *checklist* – often called a PESTEL analysis – of the **P**olitical, **E**conomic, **S**ocio-cultural, **T**echnological, **E**nvironment and **L**egal aspects of the environment. Exhibit 3.1 presents some of the main items that might be considered when undertaking a PESTEL analysis.

Exhibit 3.1

Checklist for a PESTEL analysis

Political future

- Political parties and alignments at local, national and European or regional trading-block level
- Legislation, e.g. on taxation and employment law
- Relations between government and the organisation (possibly influencing the preceding items in a major way and forming a part of future corporate strategy)
- Government ownership of industry and attitude to monopolies and competition

Socio-cultural future

- Shifts in values and culture
- Change in lifestyle
- Attitudes to work and leisure
- 'Green' environmental issues
- Education and health
- Demographic changes
- Distribution of income

Economic future

- Total GDP and GDP per head
- Inflation
- Consumer expenditure and disposable income
- Interest rates
- Currency fluctuations and exchange rates

- Investment – by the state, private enterprise and foreign companies
- Cyclicality
- Unemployment
- Energy costs, transport costs, communications costs, raw materials costs

Technological future

- Government and EU investment policy
- Identified new research initiatives
- New patents and products
- Speed of change and adoption of new technology
- Level of expenditure on R&D by organisation's rivals
- Developments in nominally unrelated industries that might be applicable

Environmental future

- 'Green' issues that affect the environment
- Level and type of energy consumed – renewable energy?
- Rubbish, waste and its disposal

Legal future

- Competition law and government policy
- Employment and safety law
- Product safety issues

Like all checklists, a PESTEL analysis is really only as good as the individual or group preparing it. Listing every conceivable item has little value and betrays a lack of serious consideration and logic in the corporate strategy process. Better to have three or four well-thought-out items that are explored and justified with evidence than a lengthy 'laundry list' of items. This is why this book does not recommend simple + and – signs and accompanying short bullet points, although these might provide a useful summary.

To the prescriptive strategists, although the items in a PESTEL analysis rely on *past* events and experience, the analysis can be used as a *forecast of the future*. The past is history and corporate strategy is concerned with future action, but the best evidence about the future *may* derive from what happened in the past. Prescriptive strategists would suggest that it is worth attempting the task because major new investments make this hidden assumption anyway. For example, when Warner Brothers invested several hundred million dollars in the first *Harry Potter* film, it was making an assumption that the fantasy film market would remain attractive; it might as well *formalise* this through a structured PESTEL analysis, even if the outcome is difficult to predict.

The emergent corporate strategists may well comment that the future is so uncertain that prediction is useless. If this view is held, a PESTEL analysis will fulfil a different role in *interpreting* past events and their interrelationships. In practice, some emergent strategists may give words of caution but still be tempted to predict the future. For example, one prominent strategist, Herbert Simon, wrote a rather rash article in 1960 predicting that, 'We will have the technical ability, by 1985, to run corporations by machine.'[10] The emergent strategists are correct in suggesting that prediction in some fast-moving markets may have little value. Overall, when used wisely, the PESTEL analysis has a role in corporate strategy.

3.4.2 Scenario-based analysis

In the context of a scenario-based analysis, a scenario is a model of a possible future environment for the organisation, whose strategic implications can then be investigated. For example, a scenario might be developed to explore the question: 'What would happen if broadband allowed every film to be delivered in-home by the year 2020 and demand for multi-screen cinema showings collapsed as a result? What impact would this have on film producers and cinema chains?'

Scenarios are concerned with peering into the future, not predicting the future. Prediction takes the *current* situation and extrapolates it forward. Scenarios take *different* situations with *alternative* starting points. The aim is not to predict but to explore a set of possibilities; a combination of events is usually gathered together into a scenario and then this combination is explored for its strategic significance. The organisation then explores its ability to handle this scenario – not because it necessarily expects it to happen but because it is a useful exercise in understanding the dynamics of the strategic environment. Exhibit 3.2 provides some guidance on the development of scenarios.

Exhibit 3.2

Some guidance on building scenarios

- Start from an *unusual viewpoint*. Examples might include the stance of a major competitor, a substantial change in technology, a radical change of government or the outbreak of war.

- Develop a *qualitative description* of a group of possible events or a *narrative* that shows how events will unfold. It is unlikely that this will involve a quantitative projection.

- Explore the *outcomes* of this description or narrative of events by building two or three scenarios of what might happen. It is usually difficult to handle more than three scenarios. Two scenarios often lend themselves to a 'most optimistic outcome' and a 'worst possible outcome'.

- Include the inevitable *uncertainty* in each scenario and explore the *consequences* of this uncertainty for the organisation concerned – for example, 'What would happen if the most optimistic outcome was achieved?' The PESTEL factors may provide some clues here.

- Test the usefulness of the scenario by the extent to which it leads to *new strategic thinking* rather than merely the continuance of existing strategy.

- Recall that the objective of scenario building is to develop strategies to cope with uncertainty, *not* to predict the future.

Key strategic principles

● The PESTEL analysis – the study of Political, Economic, Socio-cultural, Technological, Environmental and Legal factors – provides a useful starting point to any analysis of the general environment surrounding an organisation. It is vital to select among the items from such a generalised list and explore the chosen areas in depth; long lists of items are usually of no use.

● Prescriptive and emergent strategists take different views on the merits of projecting forward the main elements of the PESTEL analysis. The prescriptive approach favours the development of projections because they are often implied in major strategic decisions in any event. Emergent strategists believe the turbulence of the environment makes projections of limited value.

● A scenario is a picture of a possible future environment for the organisation, whose strategic implications can then be investigated. It is less concerned with prediction and more involved with developing different perspectives on the future. The aim is to stimulate new strategic thought about the possible consequences of events, rather than make an accurate prediction of the future.

CASE STUDY 3.2

Lifecycle impact on strategy in the European ice cream market

During the period up to year 2000, the European ice cream market underwent significant change: some segments were relatively mature while some were experiencing strong growth. The North American market was more mature and fragmented with stronger regional brands. This case study shows how the positions of the main European segments can be plotted in terms of the industry evolution (see Figure 3.2) and how strategies vary from one segment to another.

Figure 3.2

Industry evolution in the European ice cream market

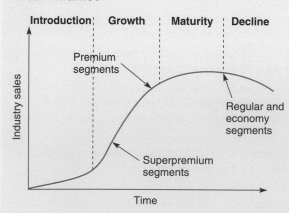

Some ice cream products – like traditional tubs – need little strategic investment. Some ice cream products – like premium ice creams from Häagen-Dazs and Ben & Jerry's – are new to the market and need major support.

The market can be divided into four distinct segments:

- The *superpremium segment*, typified by Häagen-Dazs, was still in the early stages of its growth at this time. New companies were still entering the segment, e.g. Ben and Jerry's from the US had been acquired by Unilever, but it had yet to be launched in some parts of continental Europe. New products were being tried using new methods of carton presentation and new high prices.
- The *premium segment* had developed significantly in 1989 with the introduction of premium-priced *Mars* ice cream. By the year 2000, there were few new companies entering the market. The basic product ranges had become established among the leading players; the strategic battle was for distribution and branding.
- The *regular and economy segments* were typified by Unilever's bulk packs, sold under the name Carte d'Or across much of Europe. These had existed for many years

but were still growing at around 5–6 per cent per annum (still regarded as a growth market according to some definitions). The segment also had a large number of other suppliers, not all of whom were national, let alone European. There was keen competition on price and with own-label products from grocery retailers. There was relatively little product innovation.

Case questions

1 *What strategies are suggested for each segment of the market from the conventional view of the industry life cycle? (Refer to Table 3.3.)*

2 *Thinking of strategy as doing the unconventional, how might you modify the strategies identified in Question 1?*

3.5 ANALYSING THE STAGES OF MARKET GROWTH

Part 4a

The well-known strategic writer, Professor Michael Porter from Harvard University Business School, has described the *industry life cycle* as 'the grandfather of concepts for predicting industry evolution'. The basic hypothesis is that an industry – or a market segment within an industry – goes through four basic phases of development, each of which has implications for strategy – *see* Case 3.2 for an example. These phases can be loosely described as introduction, growth, maturity and decline and are shown in Figure 3.3.

3.5.1 Industry life cycle

The nature of corporate strategy will change as industries move along the life cycle. In the *introductory* phase, organisations attempt to develop interest in the product. As the industry moves towards *growth*, competitors are attracted by its potential and enter the market: from a strategic perspective, competition increases. As all the available customers are satisfied by the product, growth slows down and the market becomes *mature*. Although growth has

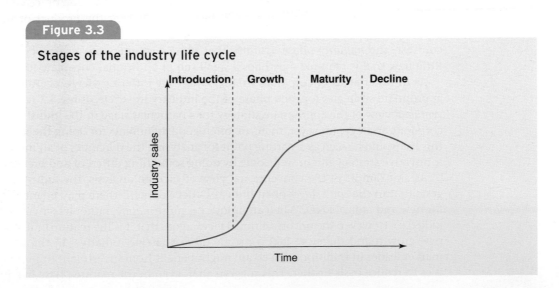

Figure 3.3

Stages of the industry life cycle

Table 3.3

The industry life cycle and its strategy implications – a conventional view

	Introduction phase	Growth phase	Maturity phase	Decline phase
Customer strategy	• Early customers may experiment with product and will accept some unreliability • Need to explain nature of innovation	• Growing group of customers • Quality and reliability important for growth	• Mass market • Little new trial of product or service • Brand switching	• Know the product well • Select on basis of price rather than innovation
R&D strategy	• High	• Seek extensions before competition	• Low	
Company strategy	• Seek to dominate market • R&D and production particularly important to ensure product quality	• React to competition with marketing expenditure and initiatives	• Expensive to increase market share if not already market leader • Seek cost reductions	• Cost control particularly important
Impact on profitability	• High price, but probably making a loss due to investment in new category	• Profits should emerge here but prices may well decline as competitors enter market	• Profits under pressure from need for continuing investment coupled with continued distributor and competitive pressure	• Price competition and low growth may lead to losses or need to cut costs drastically to maintain profitability
Competitor strategy	• Keen interest in new category • Attempt to replicate new product	• Market entry (if not before) • Attempt to innovate and invest in category	• Competition largely on advertising and quality • Lower product differentiation • Lower product change	• Competition based primarily on price • Some companies may seek to exit the industry

slowed, new competitors may still be attracted into the market: each company then has to compete harder for its market share, which becomes more fragmented – that is, the market share is broken down into smaller parts. Sales enter a period of *decline*.

To explore the strategic implications, it is useful to start by identifying what stage an industry has reached in terms of its development. For each stage in the cycle there are a number of commonly accepted strategies (*see* Table 3.3). In the case of ice cream customers in Case 3.2, the *introduction* phase will be used to present the product or service to new customers – perhaps a premium ice cream flavour to those who have never tasted it. By contrast, the *maturity* phase assumes that most customers are aware of the product and little new trial is required – perhaps a small tub of traditional chocolate ice cream.

As in other areas of corporate strategy, there are differing views regarding the choice of appropriate strategies for each phase of the industry life cycle. Table 3.3 represents the *conventional* view of the appropriate strategy for a particular stage in the industry's evolution. In corporate strategy, however, there are often good arguments for doing the *unconventional*, so this list would be seen as a starting point for analysing the dynamics of an industry. The most innovative strategy might well come by doing something different and breaking the mould.

As an example of the conventional view of such an analysis, the industry life cycle suggests that in the *early stages* of an industry's development there may be more opportunities for new and radical R&D. When an industry is more *mature*, rather less investment is needed in R&D.[11] However, the unconventional view argues that it is the mature industry that requires new growth and therefore R&D or some other strategic initiative. In the ice cream case, a market leader in traditional ice cream might benefit from investment in more modern facilities to reduce costs further. This suggests that, even in the mature phase of a market, heavy investment is often necessary to remain competitive in the market. It is for this reason that the life cycle concept can best be seen as a starting point for growth analysis.

It is important to note in the development of strategy the two consequences of the industry life cycle that can have a significant impact on industries:

1 *Advantages of early entry.* There is substantial empirical evidence that the first company into a new market has the most substantial strategic advantage. For example, Aaker[12] quotes a study of 500 mature industrial businesses showing that pioneer firms average a market share of 29 per cent, early followers 21 per cent and the late entrants 15 per cent. Although there are clearly risks in early market entry, there may also be long-term advantages that deserve careful consideration in strategic development.

2 *Industry market share fragmentation.* In the early years, markets that are growing fast attract new entrants. This is both natural and inevitable. The consequence as markets reach maturity is that each new company is fighting for market share and the market becomes more fragmented. Again, this has important implications for strategy because it suggests that mature markets need revised strategies – perhaps associated with a segment of the market (*see* Chapter 5).

For strategic purposes, it may be better to examine different *segments* of an industry, rather than the market *as a whole*, as different segments may be at different stages of the industry life cycle and may require different strategies (*see* the European ice cream industry example in Case study 3.2). For example, it is possible to take a totally different industry such as the global travel industry and apply the same thinking: in recent years, some special-interest holidays, such as wildlife and photography, were still growing strongly whereas standard beach-and-sun holidays were in the mature stage of the life cycle.

3.5.2 Critical comment on the industry life cycle

The concept of the industry life cycle has both supporters and critics. Smallwood[13] and Baker[14] defend its usefulness and offer empirical support for the basic concept. Dhalla and Yuspeh[15] have led the criticisms, some of which certainly have a degree of validity (*see* Exhibit 3.3).

Exhibit 3.3

Criticisms of the industry life cycle

1 It is *difficult to determine the duration* of some life cycles and to identify the precise stage an industry has reached. For example, the Mars Bar was launched in the 1930s and is certainly not in decline – but is it in the growth or mature phase?

2 Some industries miss stages or *cannot be clearly identified* in their stages, particularly as a result of technological change. For example, has the bicycle reached the mature phase or has it reached a new lease of life as the petrol-driven car pollutes city atmospheres?

3 Companies themselves can instigate change in their products and can, as a result, *alter the shape of the curve.* For example, new life has been brought into the camera industry by the introduction of miniaturisation and, more recently, by the use of electronic storage in place of film.

4 At each stage of evolution, the *nature of competition may be different*: some industries have few competitors and some have many, regardless of where they are in the cycle. This may be a far more important factor in determining the strategy to be pursued. For example, in Chapter 5 we will examine the relatively fragmented vacuum cleaner market and the highly concentrated civil aircraft market: both are relatively mature, with corporate strategy being determined not by evolution but by other factors.

There are certainly some difficulties with the industry life cycle approach, but the reason for such an analysis at the corporate strategy level is to identify the *dynamic factors that are shaping the industry's evolution*. The industry life cycle helps us to do this; it will then be possible to compare the organisation's own strategy with this analysis.

Key strategic principles

● The industry life cycle – charting the development of a market from introduction, through growth and maturity to decline – is useful to identify the dynamic factors shaping the industry's evolution, although there are criticisms of its use.

● It also helps to specify the conventional view of the strategies that are appropriate to each stage of the cycle, even if these are then changed for logical reasons.

● Aspects of life cycle analysis that are worthy of special consideration include: the advantages of early entry, the fragmentation of market share as markets mature, the incidence of cyclicality and its effect on demand in mature markets.

CASE STUDY 3.3

Pan-European steel companies merge to cope with the new competitive environment

Until recently, national companies dominated the European steel industry. But the strategic environment has become increasingly competitive, resulting in a series of mergers across the EU. This case explores the pressures to merge.

Government ownership in the 1980s – little competition and loss-making companies

For many years in the latter part of the twentieth century, steel companies were considered to be national assets by national governments: they made the steel that went into a country's defence armaments. In fact, most steel companies were either owned or controlled by their respective national governments across Europe. Then the strategic environment changed in three ways:

1 The threat of war lessened as the old Soviet Union collapsed, so national ownership was no longer so important.

2 It was, at last, recognised that national ownership meant that there was no competitive pressure on steel companies to make a profit – governments and their tax payers simply rescued any steel company making a loss.

3 The advent of the single European market was also a factor: each EU country had signed the *Treaty of Rome* and therefore agreed free and fair cross-border competition. This meant no state subsidies. There was considerable pressure to make this happen in the steel industry from the European Commission and some European member states.

Between 1988 and 1998, most national European steel companies were sold to the private sector. Big job cuts followed as the companies then began to compete without government subsidy and needed to cut their labour costs. This reduced employment in the European steel industry from 900,000 in the early 1970s to around 300,000 in 1998 and around 200,000 in 2003. At least productivity – measured by tonnes of steel produced per worker – went up as a result. But the newly privatised companies still rarely made any profits.

Small national companies – still subsidised and inefficient

Up to the early 1990s, some governments were still giving significant subsidies to prop up their ailing national steel companies. Not only did this keep inefficient companies alive, but it also made it more difficult for the more efficient private companies to make profits. However, governments across the EU finally agreed in 1994 that such state support would largely end.

Although the major European steel companies were officially encouraged to expand further across European borders, some restrictions were kept in place by governments to protect their national companies. Nevertheless, some of the major steel companies moved out of their national markets through merger, acquisition and the purchase of minority shareholdings. Hoogevens in the Netherlands linked up with several German companies. Arbed in Luxembourg exchanged shares with the major Spanish steel producer, CSI. Usinor, the leading French company, purchased small companies in Germany, Spain, Italy and the UK. Some of these were steel

The special steel used in the construction of Portsmouth's new Millennium Tower achieved a much higher profit margin than the standard steel sheet used in making cars.

manufacturing companies and some were steel distributors – aimed at ensuring that Usinor products were widely available in individual national markets. But none of these moves made in the 1990s can explain why substantial losses were still being made by virtually all steel companies in some years. The strategic problems of the 1990s were related to the European strategic environment in the supply and demand for steel.

Steel strategic environment: excess production capacity, low-priced imports, aggressive customers and a downturn in the European economy

For many years, there has been excess steel production capacity in Europe – around 20 million tonnes out of a total demand of around 160–170 million tonnes. Steel production requires substantial capital investment. Plant typically needs to run at high capacity if such investment is to be profitable. Hence, spare production capacity is always a problem. In years like 1995 and 1999, when there was strong demand to take up such capacity, raise prices and protect volumes, the major European steel companies were able to report significantly increased profits. But this attracted companies from Eastern Europe and Asia to export production to Europe, especially when demand was slack in their home countries. The EU was then forced to place restrictions on the amount of steel that could be imported from such areas but only after the European steel companies had started to make losses again.

There was an additional problem: some of the customers of the steel companies had high bargaining power: companies making cars, like Ford and Volkswagen, and domestic appliances, like Merloni and Electrolux, were heavy users of steel across Europe. They could afford to shop around among the steel companies for the best price and there was little differentiation between the steel companies. A basic bar of carbon steel is much the same from any supplier. The sustainable competitive advantage of the major steel producers was usually associated with the efficiency of their production plant and occasionally with the technology that they possessed to produce specialist steels. For the latter, the steel companies were able to charge higher prices and gain higher margins. However, most steel companies make standard products, where the cost of production is the main point of differentiation.

To add to the pressure, the European economy turned down around the year 2000, resulting in lower demand for steel products across the EU. Because prices were previously high, some companies even added to their production capacity. Steel is produced in blast furnaces that rely on economies of scale and production cannot be easily reduced as demand declines. Taking all these factors, it was not surprising that the steel companies were all showing major losses into the new millennium.

Steel company strategic response: merger strategy

In a further attempt to cut costs, the leading European steel companies engaged in series of mergers in recent years – Table 3.4 lists the main activities. Substantial cost reductions were being sought by this means. For example, the merger in early 2002 between France's Usinor, Aceralia of Spain and Arbed of Luxembourg to form a new company called Arcelor was expected to produce annual savings and sales of US$260m in 2003. By 2006, this was expected to rise to US$610m. However, this would only happen if the three companies shed workers and undertook a major reorganisation of plant capacity. At the time of the announcement of the merger, details of these changes were 'deliberately glossed over'. Entirely understandably, this only made the trade unions increasingly nervous and made the cost savings more unlikely. Equally, investors in the three companies had heard previous claims about cost savings without necessarily seeing any profits. In fact, Arcelor then began to rationalise and become profitable. However, the same was not true at another merger – Corus. This company was formed from the Dutch company Hoogevens and the UK company British Steel. Major losses were sustained by Corus in the early 2000s and then the company had some luck.

Change in the strategic environment 2004

Around the year 2004, privatisation of steel mills in Poland and Russia led to reductions in production capacity in those countries, reducing world supply by around 100 million tonnes out of a total of around 800 million tonnes. In addition, China increased its demand for steel by around 25 per cent because

▶ CASE STUDY 3.3 continued

Table 3.4

Western European steel industry: merger strategy

Companies in 1996	Country	Output tonnes million	Companies in 2003	Country	Output tonnes million
British Steel	UK	16	Arcelor	France, Lux and Spain	43
Usinor Sacilor	France	15	Corus	UK and Netherlands	19
Riva	Italy	13	Riva	Italy	16
Arbed	Luxembourg	11	Thyssen Krupp	Germany	16
Thyssen	Germany	9	Salzgitter	Germany	6
Cockerill Sambre	Belgium	6	Voestalpine	Austria	6
Hoogevens	Netherlands	6	Huta Katovice	Poland	5
Krupp Hoesch	Germany	5			
Huta Katovice	Poland	4			
CSI	Spain	4			

See text for details of the main company mergers up to 2003.

of its own fast-growing economy and because it had become a major world manufacturer of articles containing steel. The result was 100 per cent increase in steel prices in many markets around the world. Suddenly, all the European steel companies were able to increase their prices to their customers and significant profits were being made, even at Corus.

Sources: See reference[16].

Case questions

1 *What were the main changes in the strategic environment of the main steel companies? What was their impact on company strategy?*

2 *What were the sustainable competitive advantages of the main steel companies? What implications does this have for the long-term profitability of companies in the industry?*

3 *What does this therefore mean for individual steel company strategy? Is merger strategy the answer?*

3.6 KEY FACTORS FOR SUCCESS IN AN INDUSTRY

Part 4a

In a strategic analysis of the environment, there is an immense range of issues that can potentially be explored, creating a problem for most organisations, which have neither the time nor the resources to cope with such an open-ended task. The analysis can be narrowed down by identifying the *key factors for success* in the industry and then using these to *focus the analysis* on particularly important environmental matters.

The key factors for success (KFS) are those resources, skills and attributes of the organisations in the industry that are *essential* to deliver success in the market place. Success often means profitability, but may take on a broader meaning in some public service or non-profit-making organisations.

KFS are common to all the major organisations in the industry and do not differentiate one company from another. For example, in Case study 3.3, the factors mentioned – low labour costs, a range of specialised steel products, etc. – are common to many steel companies. Such factors will vary from one industry to another. For example, by contrast, in the perfume and cosmetics industry the factors will include branding, product distribution and product performance, but they are unlikely to include low labour costs.

When undertaking a strategic analysis of the environment, the identification of the KFS for an industry may provide a useful starting point. For example, the steel KFS item of 'low labour costs' would suggest an environmental analysis of the following areas:

- general wage levels in the country;
- government regulations and attitudes to worker redundancy, because high wage costs could be reduced by sacking employees;
- trade union strength to fight labour force redundancies.

In the steel industry, these elements of the environment would benefit from careful study, whereas, in the cosmetics and perfume industry, they might have some relevance but would be far less important than other areas.

It is therefore important to identify the KFS for a particular industry. Many elements relate not only to the environment but also to the *resources* of organisations in the industry. For example, 'labour costs' will relate to the numbers employed and the level of their wages in individual companies. To identify the KFS in an industry, it is therefore usual to examine *the type of resources* and *the way that they are employed* in the industry and then to use this information to analyse the environment outside the organisation. Hence, KFS require an exploration of the resources and skills of an industry before they can be applied to the environment. Part 3 of this book will explore resources, while the way in which KFS are developed is covered in greater detail in Chapter 6.

> ## Key strategic principles
>
> - Key factors for success (KFS) are the resources, skills and attributes of an organisation that are essential to deliver success in the market place. They are related to the industry and are unlikely to provide differentiation between organisations in the industry.
> - KFS can be used to identify elements of the environment that are particularly worth exploring.
> - KFS are developed from an examination of the type of resources used and the way in which resources are employed in an industry. They need therefore to be developed from an analysis of the organisation's resources.

3.7 ANALYSING THE COMPETITIVE INDUSTRY ENVIRONMENT – THE CONTRIBUTION OF PORTER

Part 4b

An industry analysis usually begins with a general examination of the forces influencing the organisation. The objective of such a study is to use this to develop the *competitive advantage* of the organisation to enable it to defeat its rival companies. Much of this analysis was structured and presented by Professor Michael Porter of Harvard University Business School.[17] His contribution to our understanding of the competitive environment of the firm has wide implications for many organisations in both the private and public sectors.

This type of analysis is often undertaken using the structure proposed by Porter; his basic model is illustrated in Figure 3.4. This is often called *Porter's Five Forces Model* because he identifies five basic forces that can act on the organisation:

1 the bargaining power of suppliers;
2 the bargaining power of buyers;
3 the threat of potential new entrants;
4 the threat of substitutes;
5 the extent of competitive rivalry.

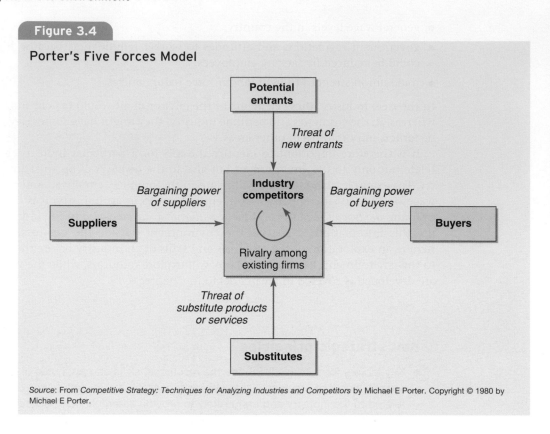

Figure 3.4

Porter's Five Forces Model

Source: From *Competitive Strategy: Techniques for Analyzing Industries and Competitors* by Michael E Porter. Copyright © 1980 by Michael E Porter.

The objective of such an analysis is to investigate how the organisation needs to form its strategy in order to develop opportunities in its environment and protect itself against competition and other threats. Porter himself cautiously described[18] his analysis as being concerned with the 'forces driving industry competition'. However, the general principles can perhaps be applied to public service and not-for-profit organisations where they compete for resources, such as government funding or charitable donations – *see* Chapter 18 for a further discussion of this.

3.7.1 The bargaining power of suppliers

Virtually every organisation has suppliers of raw materials or services which are used to produce the final goods or services. Porter suggested that suppliers are more powerful under the following conditions:

- *If there are only a few suppliers.* This means that it is difficult to switch from one to another if a supplier starts to exert its power.

- *If there are no substitutes for the supplies they offer.* This is especially the case if the supplies are important for technical reasons – perhaps they form a crucial ingredient in a production process or the service they offer is vital to smooth production.

- *If suppliers' prices form a large part of the total costs of the organisation.* Any increase in price would hit value added unless the organisation was able to raise its own prices in compensation.

- *If a supplier can potentially undertake the value-added process of the organisation.* Occasionally a supplier will have power if it is able to integrate forward and undertake the value-added process undertaken by the organisation; this could pose a real threat to the survival of the organisation.

In the case of European steel, suppliers' bargaining powers are in some respects low. There are many sources of supply for raw materials such as coal. However, in terms of energy and iron ore supply, suppliers may have higher bargaining power. For example, Arcelor will rely heavily on energy to smelt the steel and this will come partially from the French national electricity provider, Electricité de France (EdF). If EdF were to raise its electricity prices, the steel company would have no choice but to accept such changes because EdF is a monopoly supplier. By contrast, in the UK, Corus could bargain with several potential suppliers for the supply of electricity because there is a more open market.

Equally, there are only three major suppliers of iron ore in the world. Iron ore is a key ingredient of steel manufacture. In late 2004, the three companies began to raise their prices dramatically by around 70 per cent to their Japanese customers. European and American steel manufacturers expected similar rises in early 2005 because they had low bargaining power.

3.7.2 The bargaining power of buyers

In his model, Porter used the term *buyers* to describe what might also be called the *customers* of the organisation. Buyers have more bargaining power under the following conditions:

- *If buyers are concentrated and there are few of them.* When the organisation has little option but to negotiate with a buyer because there are few alternative buyers around, the organisation is clearly in a weak position: national government contracts in defence, health and education are obvious examples where the government can, in theory at least, drive a hard bargain with organisations.

- *If the product from the organisation is undifferentiated.* If an organisation's product is much the same as that from other organisations, the buyer can easily switch from one to another without problems. The buyer is even more likely to make such a shift if the quality of the buyer's product is unaffected by such a change.

- *If backward integration is possible.* As with suppliers above, the buyer's bargaining power is increased if the buyer is able to backward-integrate and take over the role of the organisation.

- *If the selling price from the organisation is unimportant to the total costs of the buyer.*

In the case of European steel, small companies or private buyers are unlikely to have much bargaining power with companies of the size of Arcelor or Corus; a letter from an individual to Arcelor, threatening to switch from its products to those of Corus or Krupp Thyssen unless its prices are lowered, is unlikely to have much impact – the threat is low. However, if a major steel distributor or steel user, such as an engineering company, were to make such a threat, then it would clearly have to be taken more seriously because of the potential impact on sales. In this latter case, the threat is high. Steel companies have reduced this threat by acquiring most of the leading European steel distributors.

3.7.3 The threat of potential new entrants

New entrants come into a market place when the profit margins are attractive and the barriers to entry are low. The allure of high profitability is clear and so the major strategic issue is that of barriers to entry into a market.

Porter argued that there were seven[19] major sources of barriers to entry:

1 *Economies of scale.* Unit costs of production may be reduced as the absolute volume per period is increased. Such cost reductions occur in many industries and present barriers because they mean that any new entrant has to come in on a large scale in order to achieve the low cost levels of those already present: such a scale is risky. We have already examined the computer and steel industries where such cost reductions are vital.

2 *Product differentiation*. Branding, customer knowledge, special levels of service and many other aspects may create barriers by forcing new entrants to spend extra funds or simply take longer to become established in the market. Real barriers to entry can be created in strategic terms by long-established companies in a market (*see* Chapter 6). Retailers such as IKEA with strong branding and specialist product lines and expertise are examples of companies with differentiated products.

3 *Capital requirements*. Entry into some markets may involve major investment in technology, plant, distribution, service outlets and other areas. The ability to raise such finance and the risks associated with such outlays of capital will deter some companies – for example, the high capital cost of investing in new steal-making machinery in Case 3.3 earlier in this chapter.

4 *Switching costs*. When a buyer is satisfied with the existing product or service, it is naturally difficult to switch that buyer to a new entrant. The cost of making the switch would naturally fall to the new entrant and will represent a barrier to entry. Persuading buyers to switch their purchases of computer software from Microsoft Windows to Apple has an obvious cost and inconvenience to many companies that would need to be overcome. In addition to the costs of persuading customers to switch, organisations should expect that existing companies will retaliate with further actions designed to drive out new entrants. For example, Microsoft has not hesitated to upgrade its products and reduce its prices to retain customers that might otherwise switch.

5 *Access to distribution channels*. It is not enough to produce a quality product; it must be distributed to the customer through channels that may be controlled by companies already in the market. For many years, the leading petrol companies have owned their own retail petrol sites to ensure that they have access to retail customers.

6 *Cost disadvantages independent of scale*. Where an established company knows the market well, has the confidence of major buyers, has invested heavily in infrastructure to service the market and has specialist expertise, it becomes a daunting task for new entrants to gain a foothold in the market. Korean and Malaysian companies are attempting to enter the European car market and face these barriers created by well-entrenched companies such as Ford, Volkswagen and Renault.

7 *Government policy*. For many years, governments have enacted legislation to protect companies and industries: monopolies in telecommunications, health authorities, utilities such as gas and electricity are examples where entry has been difficult if not impossible. The European Commission has been working alongside European governments to remove some but not all such barriers over the last few years.

In the case of the European steel market, it is not easy for small companies to enter the market because there are major economies of scale. For these companies, entry barriers are high. However, technology is now beginning to develop that will allow smaller companies to make steel economically so entry barriers may be reduced.

3.7.4 The threat of substitutes

Occasionally, substitutes render a product in an industry redundant. For example, SmithKline Beecham lost sales from its product Tagamet for the treatment of ulcers, due to the introduction of more effective products – first the introduction of Zantac from Glaxo in the 1980s and then, in the 1990s, Losec from the Swedish company Astra. Tagamet is still on sale as an over-the-counter remedy but its major public health sales have largely ceased. More recently, Losec sales have also suffered as the drug patents protecting prices have come to an end and cheaper low-price substitutes have been launched by rival companies – the so-called 'generic' drugs, sourced from countries like India.

More often, substitutes do not entirely replace existing products but introduce new technology or reduce the costs of producing the same product. Effectively, substitutes may limit the profits in an industry by keeping prices down.

From a strategy viewpoint, the key issues to be analysed are:

- the possible threat of obsolescence;
- the ability of customers to switch to the substitute;
- the costs of providing some extra aspect of the service that will prevent switching;
- the likely reduction in profit margin if prices come down or are held.

In the steel market, there is the possibility of substituting lighter metals such as aluminium for steel, depending on the usage. The threat of substitution may therefore be high but this depends on the technology and end-use.

3.7.5 The extent of competitive rivalry

Some markets are more competitive than others. Higher competitive rivalry may occur in the following circumstances.

- *When competitors are roughly of equal size and one competitor decides to gain share over the others*, then rivalry increases significantly and profits fall. In a market with a dominant company, there may be less rivalry because the larger company is often able to stop quickly any move by its smaller competitors. In the European steel industry, companies are roughly of equal size with no company dominating the market – one of the reasons why rivalry is so intense.

- *If a market is growing slowly and a company wishes to gain dominance*, then by definition it must take its sales from its competitors – increasing rivalry.

- *Where fixed costs or the costs of storing finished products in an industry are high*, then companies may attempt to gain market share in order to achieve break-even or higher levels of profitability. Paper making, steel manufacture and car production are all examples of industries where there is a real case for cutting prices to achieve basic sales volumes – thus increasing rivalry.

- *If extra production capacity in an industry comes in large increments*, then companies may be tempted to fill that capacity by reducing prices, at least temporarily. For example, the bulk chemicals industry usually has to build major new plants and cannot simply add small increments of capacity. In the steel industry, it is not possible to half-build a new steel plant: either it is built or not.

- *If it is difficult to differentiate products or services*, then competition is essentially price-based and it is difficult to ensure customer loyalty. Markets in basic pharmaceutical products such as aspirin have become increasingly subject to such pressures. In the steel market, flat-rolled steel from one manufacturer is much the same as that of another, so competition is price-based. However, where specialist steels are made with unique performance characteristics, the products are differentiated on performance and price rivalry is lower.

- *When it is difficult or expensive to exit from an industry* (perhaps due to legislation on redundancy costs or the cost of closing dirty plant), there is likely to be excess production capacity in the industry and increased rivalry. The European steel industry has suffered from problems in this area during the last few years.

- *If entrants have expressed a determination to achieve a strategic stake in that market*, the costs of such an entry would be relatively unimportant when related to the total costs of the company concerned and the long-term advantages of a presence in the market. Japanese car manufacturing in the EU has advantages for Toyota and Nissan beyond the short-term costs of building plant, as EU car markets were opened to full Japanese competition around the year 2000.

In the European steel market, some sectors of the market clearly have intense rivalry – for example, basic steel products competing on price and possibly service. Overall, an analysis would probably conclude that competitive rivalry was high in the market place, but would certainly seek to explain the differing reasons in the different segments and draw out the implications for strategy.

3.7.6 Strategy implications from the general industry and competitive analysis

In corporate strategy, it is not enough just to produce an analysis; it is important to consider the implications for the organisation's future strategy. Some issues that might arise from the above include:

● *Is there a case for changing the strategic relationships with suppliers?* Could more be gained by moving into close partnership with selected suppliers rather than regarding them as rivals? The Japanese car industry has sought to obtain much closer co-operation with suppliers and mutual cost reduction as a result.[20] (*See* Chapter 9.)

● *Is there a case for forming a new relationship with large buyers?* Manufacture of own-label products for large customers in the retail industry may be undertaken at lower margins than branded business but has proved a highly successful strategy for some leading European companies.[21] Even Cereal Partners (from Chapter 2) is now engaged in this strategy in order to build volume through its plants.

● *What are the key factors for success that drive an industry and influence its strategic development?* What are the lessons for the future that need to be built into the organisation's corporate strategy? We will return to these questions in Chapter 6.

● *Are there any major technical developments that rivals are working on that could fundamentally alter the nature of the environment?* What is the time span and level of investment for such activity? What action should we take, if any?

3.7.7 Critical Comment of the Five Forces Model

Porter's Five Forces Model is a useful early step in analysing the environment, but it has been the subject of some critical comment:

● The analytical framework is essentially *static*, whereas the competitive environment in practice is constantly changing. Forces may move from high to low, or vice versa, rather more rapidly than the model can show.

● It assumes that the organisation's own interests come first; for some charitable institutions and government bodies, this assumption may be incorrect.

● It assumes that buyers (called customers elsewhere in this book) have no greater importance than any other aspect of the micro-environment. Other commentators such as Aaker,[22] Baker[23] and Harvey-Jones[24] would fundamentally disagree on this point: they argue that the customer is more important than other aspects of strategy development and is not to be treated as an equal aspect of such an analysis.

● In general, its starting point is that the environment poses a threat to the organisation – leading to the consideration of suppliers and buyers as threats that need to be tackled. As pointed out above, some companies have found it useful to engage in closer *co-operation* with suppliers; such a strategy may be excluded if they are regarded purely as threats. This is explained more fully in Section 3.8.

● Porter's strategic analysis largely ignores the human resource aspects of strategy: it makes little attempt to recognise, let alone resolve, aspects of the micro-environment that might connect people to their own and other organisations. For example, it considers neither the country cultures, nor the management skills aspects of corporate strategy (*see* Chapter 7).

● Porter's analysis proceeds on the basis that, once such an analysis has been undertaken, then the organisation can formulate a corporate strategy to handle the results: *prescriptive* rather than *emergent*. As we saw in Chapter 2, some commentators would challenge this basic assessment.

In spite of these critical comments, the approach taken in this book is that Porter's model provides a very useful starting point in the analysis of the environment. It has real merit because of the issues it raises in a logical and structured framework. It is therefore recommended as a useful first step in corporate strategy development.

Professor Porter presented his Five Forces Model as an early stage in strategic analysis and development. He followed it with two further analyses: an analysis of *industry evolution* – the extent to which the micro-environment is still growing or has reached maturity[25] – and the study of *strategic groups* within a market. (*See* Chapters 4 and 5.)

> ## Key strategic principles
>
> ● The purpose of industry and competitive strategic analysis is to enable the organisation to develop competitive advantage.
>
> ● Porter's Five Forces Model provides a useful starting point for such an analysis.
>
> ● Suppliers are particularly strong when they can command a price premium for their products and when their delivery schedules or quality can affect the final product.
>
> ● Buyers (or customers) are strong when they have substantial negotiating power or other leverage points associated with price, quality and service.
>
> ● New entrants pose a substantial threat when they are easily able to enter a market and when they are able to compete strongly through lower costs or other means.
>
> ● Substitutes usually pose a threat as a result of a technological or low-cost breakthrough.
>
> ● Competitive rivalry is the essence of such an analysis. It is necessary to build defences against competitive threat.
>
> ● The model has been the subject of some critical comment but it remains a useful starting point for competitive strategic analysis.

3.8 ANALYSING THE CO-OPERATIVE ENVIRONMENT

3.8.1 The four links model

Part 4b

As well as competing with rivals, most organisations also co-operate with others, e.g. through informal supply relationships or through formal and legally binding joint ventures. Until recently, such links were rarely analysed in strategy development – the analysis stopped at Porter's Five Forces and some in-depth studies of one or two competitors (*see* Section 3.9). However, it is now becoming increasingly clear that *co-operation* between the organisation and others in its environment is also important as:

● it may help in the achievement of sustainable competitive advantage;

● it may open up new markets and increase business opportunities;

● it may produce lower costs;

● it may deliver more sustainable relationships with those outside the organisation.

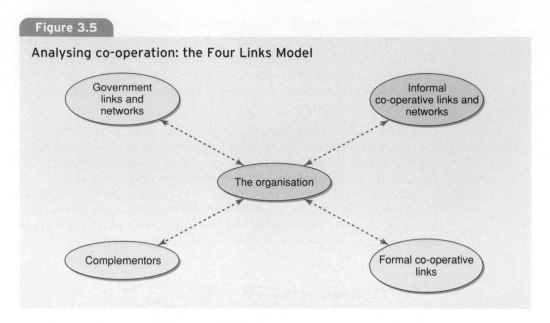

Figure 3.5

Analysing co-operation: the Four Links Model

It should be noted that an extreme form of co-operation – collusion between competitors to rig markets – is illegal in most countries and is not explored further here. But there are many other forms of co-operation that are highly beneficial and should form part of any analysis of the environment. For example, European steel companies have formed joint ventures with Brazilian steel companies for the benefit of both parties, and Krupp Thyssen Stahl is co-operating with its energy suppliers to reduce costs. Moreover, all the main European steel companies are co-operating with the government of the EU on policy matters affecting the industry. Joint ventures, alliances and other formal methods of co-operation are explored in Chapter 4 – *see* Section 4.6.

The basic co-operative linkages between the organisation and its environment can usefully be explored under four headings:

1 informal co-operative links and networks

2 formal co-operative links

3 complementors

4 government links and networks.

The objective of such an analysis is to establish the strength and nature of the co-operation that exists between the organisation and its environment. It can be conducted through the *Four Links Model* – *see* Figure 3.5.

3.8.2 Opportunities and threats from informal co-operative links and networks

Informal co-operative links and networks are the occasions when organisations link together for a mutual or common purpose *without* a legally binding contractual relationship. They have long been recognised as providing an important means of understanding the strategy of the firm.[26] By their nature, they may well occur by accident as well as by design. They will include many forms of contact, ranging from formal industry bodies that represent industry matters with other interested parties – for example, the European Confederation of Iron and Steel Industries – to informal contacts that take place when like-minded individuals from a variety of industries meet at a social function – for example, a local Chamber of Commerce meeting.

The analysis will need to assess the opportunities that such links and networks present. Occasionally, there may also be threats from arrangements. In analysing them, it is the *strength or weakness* of the relationship that matters. For example, in some parts of the world such as Japan and Korea, the networks are called *Keiretsu* and *Chaebol* respectively and have provided strong mutual support to those companies that belong to them. In some services, such as international banking, it is the strength of the network that provides the competitive advantage for those involved in it and excludes those that are not.[27]

3.8.3 Opportunities and threats from formal co-operative linkages

Formal co-operative linkages can take many business forms but are usually bound together by some form of legal contract. They differ from the networks described above in the higher degree of formality and permanence of the link with the organisation. They are shown in alliances, joint ventures, joint shareholdings and many other deals that exist to provide competitive advantage and mutual support over many years. The benefits and problems of such linkages are explored in section 4.6 in the next chapter. Some companies like the UK retailer Marks & Spencer, the Japanese car manufacturer Toyota and the Italian clothing company Benetton have developed such linkages into vital contributors to the uniqueness of their strategies. Suppliers, distributors and other formal co-operators with such companies provide essential products and services at lower prices and higher service levels than those offered to others in the industry. Essentially, formal co-operative linkages develop out of many years of discussion and understanding. They are very difficult for other companies to copy.[28] The *strengths and weaknesses* of such linkages should therefore be measured in terms of their depth, longevity and degree of mutual trust. Although the main interest may come from opportunities offered by such formal linkages, threats may arise from those developed by competitors.

3.8.4 The opportunities and threats presented by complementors

Complementors are those companies whose products add more value to the products of the base organisation than they would derive from their own products by themselves.[29] For example, computer hardware companies are worth little without the software that goes with them – one product *complements* the other. In strategic terms, there may be real benefits from developing new complementor opportunities that enhance both parties and contribute further to the links that exist between them. Typically, complementors come from different industries with different resources and skills that work together to present new and sustainable *joint offerings* to customers. Again, it is the *strengths and weaknesses* of the relationship that need to be analysed. Although the main interest may come from opportunities offered by complementors, threats may arise from the complementor linkages developed by competitors.

3.8.5 Opportunities and threats from government links and networks

Government links and networks concern the relationships that many organisations have with a country's national parliament, regional assemblies and the associated government administrations. In the case of the EU and other international treaties, these clearly extend beyond national boundaries. Such contact may be formal, through business negotiations on investment, legal issues and tax matters. It may also be informal, through representation on government/industry organisations in connection with investment and trade.

Government links and networks can be vital in tax and legal matters, such as the interpretation of competition law. Equally, governments can be important customers of organisations, e.g. in defence equipment and pharmaceuticals. Many organisations have come to devote significant time and effort to developing and cultivating such relationships through lobbying and other related activities. Because of the nature and role of government, it may need to remain relatively remote in its legislative and regulatory dealings with outside organisations. However, it is appropriate to evaluate the degree of co-operation or hostility between government and outside bodies. Thus outside organisations will wish to consider the *opportunities and threats* posed by government activities. These may form a significant part of their corporate strategic development, especially at very senior levels within an organisation.

3.8.6 Critical comment on Four Links Model

At least in part, such a model may not have the precision and clarity of the Five Forces Model and other competitor analyses: networks come and go, complementors may come to disagree, alliances may fall apart and democratic governments fail to be re-elected. All linkage relationships lack the simplicity of the bargaining power and competitive threat analyses of the Five Forces Model. However, the Four Links Model is essentially concerned with co-operation between organisations (*see* Figure 3.5). This will have many facets that go beyond simple bargaining relationships.

Developing such links is likely to involve, at least in part, an emergent approach to strategy development. Linkages may provide opportunities to experiment and develop new and original strategies. They may allow an unusual move in strategy development that will deliver sustainable competitive advantage. Hence, even though they may be imprecise and lacking in the simplicities of economic logic, such linkages deserve careful analysis.

Beyond the analysis of co-operation, companies have now come to recognise that co-operation provides new strategic opportunities. Strategic alliances, joint ventures and other forms of cooperation have been identified as possibilities for strategy development. These are explored in Section 4.6 in the next chapter.

Key strategic principles

- In addition to competing against rivals, most organisations also co-operate with other organisations. Such co-operation can deliver sustainable competitive advantage.

- The main elements that need to be analysed for co-operation are captured in the *Four Links Model*: informal co-operative links and networks, formal co-operative links, complementors and government links and networks.

- *Informal co-operative links and networks* are the range of contacts that arise from organisations joining together informally for a common purpose. *Formal co-operative linkages* are usually bound by some form of legal contract – examples include alliances and joint ventures. *Complementors* are those companies whose products add more value to the products of the base organisation than they would derive from their own products by themselves. *Government links and networks* concern the relationships that exist between national and international governments and organisations, including those concerning tax, legislation and formal government purchasing.

- Such relationships can be measured by the strength of the linkage in the case of the first three. In the case of government, they may be better measured by considering the opportunities and threats posed by the relationship. All such links are often less structured and formalised than those involving competitor analysis but may represent significant areas of long-term competitive advantage.

3.9 ANALYSING ONE OR MORE IMMEDIATE COMPETITORS IN DEPTH

Part 4c

In any analysis of competitors and their relationship to the organisation, it is useful to analyse some immediate and close competitors: this is often called competitor profiling.

3.9.1 Sustainable competitive advantage and strategic resources

Broad surveys of competitive forces are useful in strategy analysis. But it is normal to select a few companies for more detailed examination. The reason is that the sustainable competitive advantage becomes more precise and meaningful when given a specific comparison. Moreover, some rival companies will have *strategic resources* – those resources that set them apart and make them formidable opponents that need to be identified; for example, well-respected brand names like Coca-Cola and Volkswagen, specialist technologies such as laser printer production at the Japanese company Canon, and unique locations of hotels and restaurants, such as those owned by McDonald's. We return to the topic of strategic resources in Chapter 6.

3.9.2 Competitor profiling

As a starting point, it is useful to undertake competitor profiling – that is, the basic analysis of a leading competitor, covering its objectives, resources, market strength and current strategies.

In many markets, there will be more than one competitor and it will not be possible to analyse them all. It will be necessary to make a choice – usually the one or two that represent the most direct threat. In public service organisations where the competition may be for *resources* rather than for *customers*, the same principle can be adopted, with the choice being made among the agencies competing for funds. In small businesses, the need to understand competitors is just as great although here it may be more difficult to identify which company will pose the most direct threat; a *typical* competitor may be selected in these circumstances. Once the choice has been made, the following aspects of the competitor's organisation need to be explored:

- *Objectives*. If the competitor is seeking sales growth or market share growth, this may involve an aggressive stance in the market place. If the company is seeking profit growth, it may choose to achieve this by investing in new plant or by some other means that might take time to implement. If this is the case, there will be less of an immediate impact on others in the market place, but new plant may mean lower costs and a longer-term impact on prices. Company annual reports and press statements may be helpful here in defining what the competitor says it wants to do. These need to be treated with some caution, however, since the company may be bluffing or using some other competitive technique.

- *Resources*. The scale and size of the company's resources are an important indicator of its competitive threat – perhaps it has superior or inferior technology, perhaps overmanning at its plants, perhaps financial problems. Chapter 4 will provide a more detailed checklist in terms of competitive advantage, and Chapter 6 examines resources in more detail.

- *Past record of performance*. Although this may be a poor guide to the future, it is direct evidence that is publicly available through financial statements and stockbrokers' reports.

- *Current products and services*. Many companies buy competing products or services for the sole purpose of tearing them apart. They analyse customers, quality, performance, after-sales service, promotional material and some will even interview former employees – unethical perhaps, but it does happen.

- *Links with other organisations*. Joint members, alliances and other forms of co-operation may deliver significant competitive advantage.
- *Present strategies*. Attitudes to subjects such as innovation, leading customers, finance and investment, human resource management, market share, cost reduction, product range, pricing and branding all deserve investigation. The marketing areas are explored further in Chapters 4 and 5 and resources are examined in Chapters 6 to 9.

Competitor profiling is time-consuming but vital to the development of corporate strategy. Some larger companies employ whole departments whose sole task is to monitor leading competitors. Small businesses also often have an acute awareness of their competitors, although this may be derived more informally at trade meetings, social occasions, exhibitions and so on. In corporate strategy, it is vital to gain a 'feel' for competitors.

3.9.3 Emergent perspectives on competition

One of the main dangers of competitive profiling is that it will be seen as essentially static. In practice, all organisations are changing all the time. Moreover, the competitive profiling process should be regarded as one of discovery and one that never finishes. Emergent perspectives on competitor analysis, which emphasise this changing nature, will deliver useful insights, especially where the environment is changing rapidly. For example, emergent perspectives are *essential* when analysing internet competitors – *see* Case study 20.2.

3.9.4 Outcome of competitor profiling

However imprecisely, it is important to draw up a clear statement of the competitive advantages held by a rival organisation. A useful means of summarising this is the SWOT analysis – *see* Section 13.1.

Key strategic principles

- Competitor profiling is an essential first step in analysing immediate competitors. It will seek to identify the strategic resources of rivals.
- More generally, it will explore the objectives, resources, past performance, current products and services, and present strategies of at least one competitor.
- Competitor profiling should be regarded as an ongoing task. Its emergent nature is particularly important in fast-moving markets.

3.10 ANALYSING THE CUSTOMER AND MARKET SEGMENTATION

Part 4c

Since customers generate the revenues that keep the organisation in existence and deliver its profits, customers are crucial in corporate strategy. In this context it is perhaps surprising that much greater emphasis has been given in some aspects of strategic development to *competition* rather than to the customer.[30] The reason is that the focus of the purchase decision for the customer is a competitive selection between the different products or services on offer. While this is undoubtedly true, it is easy to lose sight of the direct strategic importance of the customer.

There are three useful dimensions to an analysis of the customer:

1 identification of the customer and the market;
2 market segmentation and its strategic implications;
3 the role of customer service and quality.

3.10.1 Identification of the customer and the market

Back in the 1960s, Levitt[31] wrote a famous article that argued that the main reason some organisations were in decline was because they had become too heavily product-oriented, and were not sufficiently customer-oriented. As a result, they defined their customer base too narrowly. To help this process, a useful distinction can be made between:[32]

- *immediate customer base* – for example, those travelling on railways; and
- *wider customer franchise* – for example, those travelling by public transport, including railways, aircraft and buses.

In order to define accurately this aspect of the environment it is important to develop strategies that identify customers and competitors. Ultimately, if the market environment is incorrectly defined, then competitors may creep up and steal customers without the company realising it until it is too late. Furthermore, it is vital to analyse *future* customers as well as the *current* customer profile. Moreover, there are some problems associated with Levitt's concept and these are explained in Chapter 5.

3.10.2 Market segmentation and its strategic implications

Most markets have now moved beyond *mass marketing* – where one product is sold to all types of customer – to *targeted marketing* – where the seller identifies market segments, selects one or more of these and then develops products or services targeted specially at the segment. Market segmentation is the identification of specific parts of a market and the development of different market offerings that will be attractive to those segments[33] – an important element of any market analysis.

Market segmentation is important for strategy for several reasons:

- *Some segments may be more profitable and attractive than others.* For example, large segments may have low profit margins but their size may make them attractive, even at these levels of profitability.
- *Some segments may have more competition than others.* For example, a specialist segment may have only a limited number of competitors.
- *Some segments may be growing faster and offer more development opportunities than others.*

Porter[34] uses market segmentation to draw a basic distinction between two major generic strategies:

1 *broad target segments* that involve large numbers of customers, e.g. basic flat-rolled steel bars that have wide customer demand; and

2 *narrow target segments* that involve small niches in the market place, e.g. small specialist steel products that are sold for their particular performance characteristics at high prices to a small number of buyers.

In conclusion, careful analysis of segments and their characteristics is therefore important (*see* Chapter 5).

Key strategic principles

- In identifying markets, it is important to identify the customer base sufficiently broadly. A useful distinction can be drawn between the immediate customer base and a wider franchise based on product substitution. It is also important to explore future customers as well as the current customer base.
- Market segmentation is fundamental to the development of corporate strategy: some parts of markets may be more attractive than others. Careful analysis of segments and their characteristics is therefore important.

3.11 CONCLUSIONS

Given the amount of analysis that can potentially be undertaken, the question is raised as to whether each aspect of analysis has equal priority. Although there are no absolute rules, it is usually the case that the customer comes first, the immediate competition second and the broader environment surrounding the organisation then follows. In other words, the analytical process might be arranged in the *reverse order* of this chapter. However, it is probably best considered as a circular process – *see* Figure 3.6 – and perhaps in this sense emergent.

In many respects, the real danger in analysing the environment is to limit the process to examining past events and ways of thinking. It is absolutely essential to break out of the current mould and examine alternative routes and ideas. This is particularly likely to be the case if some types of emergent approaches are adopted, because they rely essentially on taking small steps from the current position. As Egan[35] has pointed out:

> While expedient for conditions of relative environmental stability, [the emergent approach] is likely to be unacceptable in periods of discontinuous change. The rapid demise of Nixdorf Computer and Wang Computer should have sent rapid signals to IBM that more of the same was wholly inappropriate in the rapidly changing computer industry.

In this context, the troubles of the world-class Japanese company Sony – *see* Case 3.4 – against a backdrop of rapidly dropping profits in consumer electronics have all the hallmarks of a difficult future.

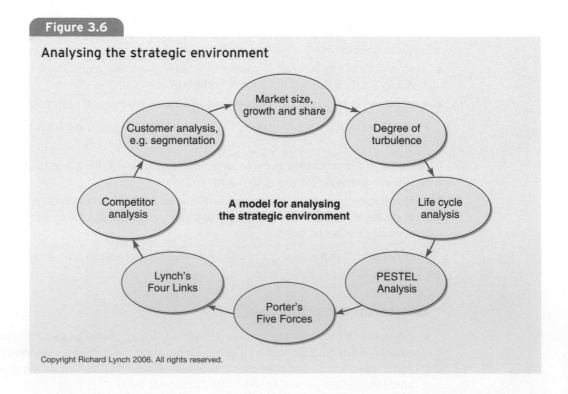

Figure 3.6

Analysing the strategic environment

Shaking up Sony: restoring the profits and the innovative fire

In early 2005, Sony Corporation of Japan did something almost unheard of in Japanese business. It appointed a Welsh-born American citizen as head of the Japanese company along with a new Japanese president. This case explores the reasons for this extraordinary shake up, which aimed to re-establish Sony as one of the world's best-performing and innovative consumer electronics companies.

New American and Japanese leadership

From 1997 to 2005, the Welsh-born American citizen Sir Howard Springer led Sony's American subsidiary. He had brought it back from serious weakness with a programme of reorganisation, cost-cutting and reinvention. He was the person appointed as chairman and chief executive of Sony in 2005.

From 1975 to 2005, the Japanese Sony executive Ryoju Chubachi worked in various positions in the company, most recently as head of Sony's Japanese production plants in the home country and with a brief to improve the group's production technology. Mr Chubachi was well-placed to examine how to help the different parts of Sony work together more efficiently.

In early 2005, Springer was appointed chairman and chief executive and Chubachi was appointed president – just below the chief executive but with a crucial role in the Sony shake-up. At the same time, the previous chairman, Mr Nobuyuki Idei, and seven fellow board members agreed to step down. Only the chief financial officer, Mr Katsumi Ihara, who had previously turned round the Sony Ericsson joint venture, remained from the old board. What were the reasons for this radical change?

Sony's profit problems

To understand why such a major shake-up was required, it is useful to look back at the Sony profit record over the last ten years. In 1995, profits after tax were around US$2.3 billion. In 2004, profits were only around US$1 billion while over the same time period sales had increased from US$45 billion to US$72 billion. Figure 3.7 shows the main problem area: the

Up to recent times, Sony has been one of Japan's most respected and innovative companies

consumer electronics division had sales of over US$47 billion in 2004 but made a net loss of US$339 million. Such a position was simply not sustainable for any length of time. The next section explains the reasons for this very poor situation.

The most profitable part of the Sony company was the Games Division, i.e. PlayStation with sales of US$7.5 billion and a trading profit of US$650 million. In the late 1980s, Sony had added banking and insurance services to its electronics businesses – typical of many Japanese companies at that time. Sony Financial Services, including Sony banking and insurance, was the next largest profit earner in 2004. Around the same time as Sony moved into financial services, the company also acquired CBS Music and Columbia Pictures in the US. The strategic logic here was that of developing a vertically integrated company – from the service that develops the pictures and music to the machines that deliver them in individual homes. These two divisions were re-named Sony Pictures and Sony Music: they were also profitable in 2004. Sony Pictures was responsible for such films as *Men in Black* and *Spiderman* and Sony Music had artists such as Bruce Springsteen, Bob Dylan and Mariah Carey under contract.

Figure 3.7

Breakdown of Sony sales 2004

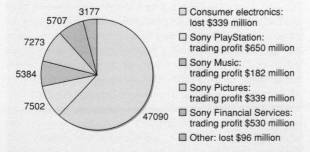

3177
5707
7273
5384
7502
47090

□ Consumer electronics: lost $339 million
□ Sony PlayStation: trading profit $650 million
□ Sony Music: trading profit $182 million
□ Sony Pictures: trading profit $339 million
□ Sony Financial Services: trading profit $530 million
□ Other: lost $96 million

▶ **CASE STUDY 3.4 continued**

> **Table 3.5**

Breakdown of Sony sales 2004 within its consumer electronics division

Type of product	Example of products	Sales 2004 US$ million
Audio products	Sony Walkman, MP3 player	5 996
Video products	Sony video recorders and cameras	9 116
Television and related products	Sony televisions	8 819
Information and communications	Sony personal computers, laptops	8 027
Semiconductors	Used in variety of manufacturing applications	2 435
Components	Microelectronic circuit boards	5 998
Other		6 699
Total		47 090

Source: Sony Annual Report and Accounts 2004. Note that the figures have been marginally adjusted by the author for some inconsistencies between various parts of the accounts. The changes do not alter the fundamental strategic perspective.

For many observers, Sony Consumer Electronics Division was the real problem area. It had worldwide sales of US$47 billion but still managed to deliver a net loss of US$339 million in 2004. Such a performance was simply not sustainable over time and radical strategies were required. Table 3.5 shows the breakdown of the sales within this division: it includes many famous consumer products like the Sony Walkman, Sony digital cameras and Sony televisions. The company did not publish any further detail within the division on precisely which product ranges contributed to the division's profits and losses. However, it was known that the audio products, such as the Walkman, and the television products, like the WEGA model, were under major competitive threat from two sources – first, mature technology coupled with low-wage labour manufacturing: second, totally new digital technology such as that associated with liquid crystal display (LCD) screens for televisions and computers.

Sony had made considerable attempts to reduce its manufacturing costs by relocating its manufacturing to low-wage labour countries – see next section – but had failed to recognise the importance of some of the new technologies. For example, its rival Japanese company, Sharp Electronics, was much further advanced in the development of the LCD technology. Another example was personal computers: Sony had developed a new range of laptops – called the VAIO – with excellent on-screen display. But the company was competing

against companies with lower production costs like Dell Computers and HP/Compaq. Some commentators regarded Sony's strategy as being too little, too late and with too little innovation.

Company background

To understand how Sony came to be in such a position, it is necessary to go back to its early years and the influence of its first chairman, Akio Morita. Sony was founded in Tokyo in 1946 by Mr Morita and his friend, Masaru Ibuka. Sony's technology was primarily the focus of Mr Ibuka and Sony's business development, especially its global expansion, came primarily from Mr Morita. Sony rapidly established itself as one of the most innovative Japanese consumer electronics companies of its time. Mr Morita was a brilliant leader and innovator. He was company chairman from 1946 to 1994. During this time, Sony produced its first magnetic tape recorder in 1950 and its first transistor radio in 1955. It followed this with the world's first transistor television set in 1960 and the first video tape recorder in 1965. Around the same period, it began to expand geographically with Sony America in 1960, Sony Hong Kong in 1962, Sony UK in 1968 and Sony France in 1973. It was not until the 1980s that it began to extend its business into music and film – CBS Records was acquired in 1988 and Columbia Pictures in 1989. Mr Morita was widely admired around the world for his vision, leadership and tenacity and won many international honours for his ability to build bridges between nations.

Mr Morita was followed as company chairman by Mr Nobuyuki Idei in 1995. Mr Idei led the company for ten years until 2005 and set up several new initiatives, including the beginning of Sony's first moves to cut costs. He then chose an American, Sir Howard Springer, as his successor in 2005. Hence, the Sony company has only had three chief executives since its foundation in 1946 – a remarkably stable relationship but one that, perhaps, can lead to a company being too inward-looking.

Reasons for the Sony profit problems

With any major worldwide company, there are always many and complex reasons for fluctuations in profitability. For the purposes of this case, we can identify at least three reasons for the drop in profits:

1. Shift away from innovative products

For Sony over many years, it was the innovative nature of its products that delivered its competitive advantage. Table 3.6 selects a few of the many Sony innovations. Importantly, many of them occurred before the 1990s – the list is selective but suggests that Sony may have lost its way in later years. Nevertheless, there is no denying the strong innovation record of Sony over the years. There were some smaller achievements since 1990 and these can be found on the Sony website. But many would regard its leading developments as being quite old. This is important for two reasons: first, because competitors are able to match most electronic

Table 3.6

Selected Sony innovations

Year	Product
1968	Trinitron Television – new high-quality and reliable TV picture for which Sony charged a premium price. [The writer of this case still has a working 23-year old Trinitron TV]
1971	Sony Walkman launched
1975	Home use video system – Betamax introduced. Subsequently overtaken as the industry recording standard by the rival VHS system
1982	World's first CD player
1985	8mm camcorder
1990	PlayStation games machine – still the market leader – see Case 6.4.

Source: Sony website – www.sony.net.

innovations over time; second, because rivals have attempted to source similar products from lower-cost sources as technology becomes mature.

Importantly, even during the innovative years, the Sony company's culture did not always support innovation. In 2004, the biggest profit earner was the Sony PlayStation. It is reliably reported that the Sony PlayStation was developed in 1990 by a *subsidiary* of the group without telling the headquarters: the subsidiary was afraid that HQ would halt the development as being a waste of Sony group resources!

The shift away from innovative products was deepened by the advent of digital technology in the late 1990s. Sony was simply not the market leader in this area and left this to rival companies. For example, Sony has recently completely lost the product initiative on liquid crystal display panels to rival companies such as Sharp from Japan and Samsung from Korea. It has managed to turn around its venture into the fast-growing market for mobile telephones, but only by a joint venture with the Swedish company Ericsson.

2. Involved in too many unprofitable businesses

Over many years, Sony has not cut back sufficiently on its unprofitable products. In the early years, Sony's innovatory consumer electronics were able to charge a price premium because they performed better than rivals. But in more recent years, competitors were able to match its product performance at lower costs. Sony was therefore forced to move production of some of its more standard electronic products to low-wage countries. Figure 3.8 shows where some of its plant was located in the late 1990s, with around 25,000 employees in Asian countries (out of a total of 135,000 employees at that time). Traditional consumer electronics goods like TVs and CD players were facing increasingly heavy competition, lower prices and lower profitability. Sony needed to make some major cuts in its extensive product range and/or outsource even more work to even cheaper locations. The vast majority

Figure 3.8

Sony's Asian manufacturing operations

	Facility	Start	Product
1	Taiwan Toyo Radio	1967	Radios, Walkmans, telephones, tape recorders
2	Sony Electronics of Korea	1973	Precision comp, CD Boomboxes, Headphones, TV tuners
3	Toyo Audio	1984	Radios, Walkmans, telephones
4	Sony Video Taiwan	1984	1/2″ VCR, multi-disc players
5	Sony Precision Eng. Center	1987	Precision components
6	Sony Electronics	1988	Hi-fi audio, Walkmans, CD Boomboxes, Discmans
7	Sony TV Industries	1988	CTV, TV tuners, deflection yokes
8	Sony Magnetic Products	1988	Audio tapes
9	Sony Siam Industries	1988	CTV, audio
10	Sony Semiconductor	1989	Bipolar ICs, MOS-ICs
11	Sony Mechatronic Products	1990	3.5″ MFDD
12	Sony Video	1990	1/2″ VCR, CD-Rom drive
13	PT Sony Electronics Indonesia	1992	Hi-fi audio, Boomboxes, CD Boomboxes
14	Sony Display Device	1992	CRT
15	Shanghai Suogang Electronics	1994	8mm VCR components, optical pick-ups
16	Sony Vietnam	1994	CTV, audio
17	Sony India	1995	CTV

Source: *Financial Times*, 15 November 1995.

▶ **CASE STUDY 3.4 continued**

of its employees in 2004 were still located in Japan, which is not a low-wage economy.

3. Large size and conflicting interests

When a company has over 100,000 employees worldwide, there are often conflicting interests between groups. In the case of Sony, the company became compartmentalised, with different parts wanting to pursue their own interests and being unwilling to co-operate for the good of the group. Some parts of the group also became overprotective of their short-term interests. For example, Sony Music was reluctant to develop a music downloading service over the internet in order to protect its existing business. The result was that Apple was able to take the initiative in this area – *see* Case 1.1. Subsequently, Sony Music was forced to engage in such activity by the bargaining power of companies like Apple and its revolutionary iPod. (Equally, this raises the important strategic question of why Apple developed the iPod and not Sony. This relates back to the reason discussed under heading 1 above.)

Both the new Sony appointees in 2005 recognised Sony's difficulties in terms of size and conflicting interests. The new Sony chairman, Sir Howard Stringer, gained his reputation with Sony over seven years in the US by overhauling Sony's US business. It was called 'Project USA' – the plan was for 9,000 job losses and US$700 million annual cost savings. The new Sony president, Mr Ryoji Chubachi, also gained a reputation in recent years for bringing down company barriers. For example, when he was appointed in June 2004 to head a new division that would oversee Sony's domestic electronics manufacturing, he set up a new production strategy headquarters. The prime purpose of this new HQ was to promote the sharing of technology and expertise across the whole company and reduce the separation that had developed over time. Importantly, compared to its rivals, Sony had large numbers of employees still employed in manufacturing and development operations in Japan, with all the implications that this has for high-wage production costs.

Sir Howard Stringer spoke about Sony's size and structure at an internal management conference some weeks before his appointment. According to a newspaper report, he warned that Sony was in danger of being slowed by its top-heavy management structure. According to one delegate, 'He said the whole edifice had become like a mushroom and the business was becoming more management than manufacturing and services'.

Sony's strategic challenge

In 2004, the Sony chairman, Mr Nobuyuki Idei, concluded: 'It has been 10 years since I became President and I decided that this was the best time [to make the changes.]' He therefore took the radical step of removing himself and nearly all his fellow board members from Sony. He then chose Sir Howard Springer as his successor.

Writing to all employees after his appointment Sir Howard acknowledged the considerable Sony legacy: 'But we cannot let that inhibit us – we need to take that legacy and reinvent it. We will accelerate cross-company collaboration . . . we will renew our focus on world-class technological innovation with customer-centric products and services. Growth cannot be achieved just through cost reductions. We need new ideas, new strategies and alliances and a shared vision.'

One senior colleague of the new Sony team summed up the situation: 'The challenge is to galvanise the Tokyo staff and harness their anger and pride, and redirect their energies in ways that will rebuild Sony.'

Sources: See reference[36].

Case questions

1 *What were the changes in the environment that led to the pressures in Sony?*

2 *Use the nine concepts explored in this chapter to analyse the company's competitive environment. What conclusions can you draw on Sony's competitive position?*

3 *What lessons, if any, can other companies learn about innovation strategy from Sony?*

STRATEGIC PROJECT
Will Sony recover?

This case was written in early 2005 at a time of great change for the company. By the time you read this, the Sony company will have moved on. It will have developed new strategies, new products and services. First, you might like to establish what precisely it has done – announcements about job cuts, product range changes and new product launches are areas worth researching.

In addition, the case above focuses on Sony alone and only refers in passing to rival companies. For a full strategic analysis, it is important to pick one or two companies – perhaps Sharp, Matsushita and Samsung are the obvious examples – and research the rival product ranges, profitability and new innovations. This would then allow you to develop a strong critical evaluation of the strategies of the new Sony Chairman. Will Sir Howard and his colleagues be able to rejuvenate Sony?

CRITICAL REFLECTION

What purpose is served by analysing the strategic environment?

There are two fundamental assumptions that underpin this chapter. First, strategic analysis assumes that it is possible to learn from past events. This assumption is important because strategy is essentially about future actions. Second, such a study implicitly assumes that the future is predictable in some way – otherwise, there would be little point in drawing any lessons from the analysis. Both these assumptions may rest on shaky foundations.

'Learning from the past' may examine a strategic environment with strategic perceptions and definitions that no longer apply: for example, the traditional market for air travel has been revolutionised by redefining it as being just like getting on a bus where aircraft seats are readily available without lengthy booking procedures. In the same way, 'Predicting the future' always runs the risk of making an incorrect prediction: for example, who would have predicted fifteen years ago how the internet would develop?

Perhaps, in developing new strategies, we cannot learn much from the past. Perhaps we cannot usefully predict the future. In which case, what purpose is served by PESTEL Analysis, Porter's Five Forces, etc?

SUMMARY

In analysing the environment surrounding the organisation, nine main factors were identified.

● *Environmental analysis can usefully begin with a basic assessment of the market definition and size, the market growth and the market share.* Market definition is important because it will determine the size and scope of the strategic opportunity. Market growth is commonly estimated early in any strategic analysis because of its importance with regard to the growth objectives of an organisation. A basic estimate of market share can be used to estimate whether an organisation has a significant share of a market as a starting point in exploring the strategic implications.

● *A general consideration of the nature of the environment and, in particular, the degree of turbulence.* When events are particularly uncertain and prone to sudden and significant change, corporate strategy needs to become more flexible and organise its procedures to cope with the situation.

● *A general analysis of the factors that will affect many industries.* This can be undertaken by two procedures: the PESTEL analysis and scenarios. The PESTEL analysis explores political, economic, socio-cultural, technological, environmental and legal influences on the organisation. It is important when undertaking such an analysis to develop a short list of only the most important items, not a long list under every heading. In developing scenarios, it should be recognised that they provide a different view of conceivable future events, rather than predict the future.

● *Growth characteristics* can be explored using the industry life cycle concept. Markets are divided into a series of development stages: introduction, growth, maturity and decline. In addition, the maturity stage may be subject to the cyclical variations associated with general economic or other factors over which the company has little control.

● Different stages of the life cycle demand different corporate strategies. The early stages probably require greater investment in R&D and marketing to develop and explain the product. The later stages should be more profitable on a conventional view of the life cycle. However, there is an argument that takes a more unconventional stance: it suggests that it is during the mature phase that investment should increase in order to restore growth.

● *The identification of key factors for success.* Moving towards an analysis of the environment surrounding the organisation itself, it is useful to establish the key factors for success in the industry (not the organisation). This requires a consideration of the resources of the organisation (*see* Chapter 6).

● *A Five Forces Analysis.* This will involve an examination of buyers, suppliers, new entrants, substitutes and the competition in the industry. The aim is to analyse the balance of power between each force and the organisation in the industry.

● *A Four Links Analysis* of the co-operators of the organisation. This will include a study of the complementors, networks and legal links that the organisation has with its environment. The purpose is to analyse the relative strengths of such links and their ability to enhance the competitive advantages of the organisation.

● *A study of selected direct competitors.* The purpose here is to identify the specific competitive advantages of rival companies and to highlight any strategic resources – unique possessions that will deliver competitive advantage to the rivals. Such a study needs to recognise the fluid and changing nature of competitors and their resources.

● *A study of customers.* The final area of analysis is concerned with actual and potential customers and their importance to the organisation. Segmentation of markets derives from customer analysis and plays an important role in corporate strategy development.

QUESTIONS

1 Using Case 3.3 and your judgement, determine the degree of turbulence in the European steel industry. Give reasons for your views.

2 Undertake a general environmental analysis of an industry of your choice, using both the PESTEL format and scenarios to draw out the major strategic issues.

3 Develop and compare the key factors for success in the following three industries: computer industry (Chapters 1 and 2), ice cream industry (Chapter 4) and steel industry (Chapter 3).

4 For the European steel industry, analyse the competitive forces within the industry using the Five Forces Model. Identify also any forms of co-operation in the industry using a Four Links Analysis.

5 Based on your answers to the previous questions, what strategic advice would you offer Arcelor and Corus? Use Section 3.7.6 to assist you.

6 Undertake a life cycle analysis of an industry of your choice. What strategic conclusions would

you draw for organisations in the industry, if any? Comment specifically on the difficulties of this approach.

7 Prepare a full environmental analysis for an industry of your choice and make recommendations on its future corporate strategy.

8 Undertake a customer analysis for your own organisation. What segments can you identify? What role is played by customer service and quality? What strategic conclusions can you draw?

9 Do you agree with the statement that stable environments favour prescriptive approaches to strategy whereas turbulent environments demand emergent strategies? Consider carefully the impact technology may have on a stable environment and the problem of long-term investment, even in turbulent industries.

10 To what extent can competitive analytical techniques be applied to the public sector and charitable institutions?

Further reading

M E Porter's *Competitive Strategy: Techniques for Analysing Industries and Competitors* (The Free Press, Harvard, MA, 1980) has careful and detailed studies for analysis of the immediate competitive environment. Mona Makhija's paper (2003) 'Comparing the resource-based and market-based views of the firm: empirical evidence from Czech privatisation', *Strategic Management Journal*, Vol 24, pp433–51

presents some useful comments on the Porter approach as well as a more general comparison relevant also to Chapter 6. R Rosen's *Strategic Management: an Introduction* (Pitman Publishing, London, 1995) has some useful strategic planning worksheets that will help to structure a study of the environment. However, it is important to treat them as a useful framework rather than a rigid format.

Notes and references

1 Porter, M E (1980) *Competitive Strategy*, The Free Press, New York.

2 Andrews, K (1987) *The Concept of Corporate Strategy*, Irwin, Homewood, IL.

3 Many strategy texts (including previous editions of this one!) set out in great depth various environmental concepts and forget that it is useful to begin with some basic data.

4 Levitt, T (1960) 'Marketing myopia', *Harvard Business Review*, July–Aug, pp45–56. Levitt's paper challenged the traditional definitions of the market.

5 There may be tautological problems here, but it is not appropriate to explore these at this early stage in strategy analysis. Suffice to say that it is possible to pursue this academic debate by starting with the well-known text by Buzzell, R D and Gale, B T (1987) *The PIMS Principles*, The Free Press, London. Follow this up with Baker, M (1993) *Marketing Strategy and Management*, 2nd edn, Macmillan, London.

6 Porter, M E (1980) Op. cit., Ch2.

7 The early part of this section is based on Ansoff, I and MacDonnell, E (1990) *Implementing Strategic Management*, 2nd edn, Prentice Hall, Englewood Cliffs, NJ.

8 D'Aveni, R (1994) *Hypercompetitive Rivalries*, Free Press, New York.

9 Note: In previous editions of this book, the term 'PEST' analysis has been used. This has now been extended to reflect the increased importance given to environmental and governmental/legal matters.

10 Simon, H 'The corporation: will it be managed by machine?', in Leavitt, H and Pondy, L (eds) (1964) *Readings in Managerial Psychology*, University of Chicago Press, Chicago, pp592–617.

11 Baden-Fuller, C and Stopford, J (1992) *Rejuvenating the Mature Business*, Routledge, Ch2.

12 Aaker, D R (1992) *Strategic Marketing Management*, 3rd edn, Wiley, New York, p236.

13 Smallwood, J E (1973) 'The product life cycle: a key to strategic marketing planning', *MSU Business Topics*, Winter, pp29–35.

14 Baker, M (1993) *Marketing Strategy and Management*, 2nd edn, Macmillan, London, p100 *et seq.* presents a short defence and interesting discussion of the main areas.

15 Dallah, N Y and Yuspeh, S (1976) 'Forget the product life cycle concept', *Harvard Business Review*, Jan–Feb, p101 *et seq.*

16 References for the European steel merger case: Usinor Annual Report and Accounts 1998, pp28, 29 and 30; British Steel Annual Report and Accounts 1998; Arcelor Annual Report and Accounts 2004; *Metal Bulletin*, 12 Mar 1998, p17; *Financial Times*, 19 Feb 1997, p30; 7 Jan 1998, p28; 23 April 1999, p32; 3 Jan 2002, p23; 19 February 2002, p26; 20 February 2002, p28; 24 January 1990; 10 Jan 1996, p23; 2 Aug 1996, p7; 15 Nov 1996, p27; 11 Dec 1996, p37; 20 Mar 1997, pp4, 31; 11 June 1997, p4; 24 July 1997, p30; 30 July 1997, p35; 23 Oct 1997, p4; 13 Nov 1997, p6; 15 Dec 1997, p23; 7 Feb 1998, p17; 9 Mar 1998, p24; 18 Mar 1998, p 43; 22 Apr 1998, p38; 27 May 1998, p27; 28 May 1998, p25; 4 June 1998, p23; 20 February 2001, p19; 16 March 2001, p24; 14 April 2001, p14; 26 November 2001, p12; 17 December 2001, p21; 7 February 2002, p7; 29 September 2004, p17; 24 February 2005, p27.

17 Porter, M E (1980) Op. cit. Note that Porter's work owes much to the writings of Professor Joel Bain and others in the 1950s on industrial economies. However, it was Porter who gave this earlier material its strategic focus. See also Porter's article, 'How competitive forces shape strategy' (1979) *Harvard Business Review*, Mar–Apr, pp136–45, which is a useful summary of the main points from the early part of his book.

18 Op. cit., p4.

19 Porter actually refers in his book to 'six' areas and then goes on to list seven!

20 Cusumano, M and Takeishi, A (1991) 'Supplier relations and management: a survey of Japanese, Japanese-transplant and US auto plants', *Strategic Management Journal*, 12, pp563–88.

21 Nielsen, A C (1988) *International Food and Drug Store Trends*, Nielsen, Oxford.

22 Aaker, D (1992) Op. cit.

23 Baker, M (1993) Op. cit.

24 Harvey-Jones, J (1991) *Getting it Together*, Heinemann, London, Ch14.

25 Porter (1980) Op. cit., Chs7 and 8.

26 Reve, T (1990) 'The firm as a nexus of internal and external contracts', *The Firm as a Nexus of Treaties*, Aoki, M, Gustafson, M and Williamson, O E (eds), Sage, London. See also Kay, J (1994) *The Foundations of Corporate Success*, Oxford University Press, Oxford, Ch5.

27 Kay, J (1994) Op. cit., p80.

28 Kay, J (1994) Op. cit.: Ch5 on architecture explores this topic in depth.

29 Nalebuff, B J and Brandenburger, A M (1997) *Co-opetition*, HarperCollins Business, London.

30 For example, Porter, M E (1980) Op. cit.

31 Levitt, T (1960) 'Marketing myopia', *Harvard Business Review*, Jul–Aug, p45.

32 Davidson, H (1987) *Offensive Marketing*, Penguin, Harmondsworth.

33 Adcock, D, Bradfield, R, Halborg, A and Ross, C (1995) *Marketing: Principles and Practice*, 2nd edn, Pitman Publishing, London, p386.

34 Porter, M E (1980) Op. cit., Ch2.

35 Egan, C (1995) *Creating Organisational Advantage*, Butterworth–Heinemann, Oxford, p83.

36 References for the Sony case: Sony Annual Report and Accounts 2004; website www.sony.net (note this is the global, Japan-based website but with English version); website www.sony.com (note this is the Sony US website); *Financial Times*: 15 November 1995; 8 March 2005, pp23, 30; 9 March 2005, p27.

Chapter 4

ANALYSING MARKETS, COMPETITION AND CO-OPERATION

 Learning outcomes

When you have worked through this chapter, you will be able to:

● understand the importance of sustainable competitive advantage;

● cope with the dynamics of competitive advantage;

● explore the intensity of competition and assess its strategic implications;

● outline the range of aggressive activities undertaken by competitors and assess their strategic significance;

● describe the main elements of product portfolio analysis and comment on its strategic usefulness;

● analyse individual competitors and their influence on strategy;

● develop co-operation strategies;

● explore and assess the importance of distributors;

● explain the role that governments play in the development of corporate strategy;

● identify the main international strategic competitive issues.

INTRODUCTION

A corporate strategy will only succeed in a competitive market place if it is based on a thorough analysis of the organisation's competitors. Any such analysis can usefully begin with a general consideration of competitive advantage in the market place. The intensity of competition and the aggressive strategies that may be employed should then be reviewed in detail.

In addition to these general considerations, it is important to examine three interrelated areas that may affect the *specific* immediate competitive environment of the organisation: product portfolios compared with rivals, the possibility of co-operation with other companies and the way that the product or service is distributed. The possibility of *co-operation* with other companies – through various forms of strategic alliance – has become an increasingly important way of competing against rivals. Market, competition and co-operation analysis are summarised in Figure 4.1. This chapter should be read in conjunction with the previous chapter, which explored other aspects of the topic.

Figure 4.1

Market and competitor analysis: the main considerations

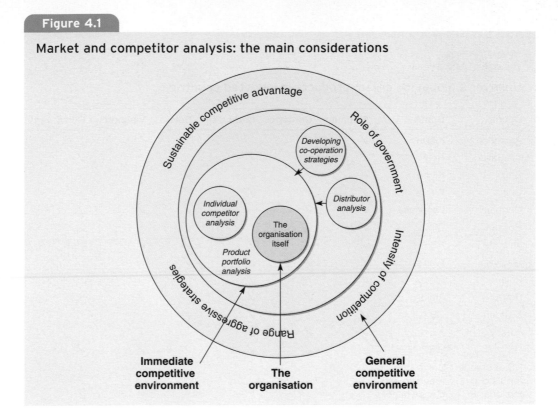

CASE STUDY 4.1

Unilever ice cream defends its global market share

With sales of US$6 billion and around 17 per cent of the world ice cream market, Unilever is the dominant global company. It has built its leading market position with innovation and acquisition strategies.

The major Dutch/British multinational, Unilever, operates across many countries of the world with well-known brand names like Dove soap, Hellman's mayonnaise, Flora margarine, Knorr soup and Fabergé personal products. Total sales amount to over US$60 billion – *see* Case 14.3 for more information.

In its ice cream operations, Unilever works through a series of local brand names but with a heart-shaped symbol that is the same everywhere around the world. It employs strategies in the ice cream market that combine both global and local activities. As well as the heart-shaped logo, global activities cover certain common products: Magnum ice cream, Cornetto wafer cone, Carte d'Or take-home packs of ice cream, etc. This product range has been developed in a highly innovative way over the last 15 years. In order to obtain economies of scale, such products are not necessarily manufactured in the country in which they are sold – transport costs are a sufficiently small part of total costs to justify regional manufacture. Products are chosen for a country, depending on local demand and the availability of freezer cabinet space. Table 4.1 identifies some of the leading global Unilever products in selected countries.

For Unilever, local ice cream products are also important. There are two reasons: first, to meet local ice cream tastes and price expectations – not every country likes a particular flavour and can afford expensive ingredients; second, to exploit the historic investment made in local brands over many years in some countries – there is much to be gained by building on local names. A simple example of local activity is South Africa where Unilever associates the heart symbol with the 'Ola' brand. It then sells various ice cream products like Magnum under the Ola brand name, but has also developed some local products for the South African market.

The most complex example of local activity is Unilever's involvement in the US, which is the largest ice cream market in the world – *see* Case 4.4 for more detail. Unilever operates four brands – Good Humor, Klondike, Breyers and Ben & Jerry's. Each of these four brands represents a part of the ▶

▶ **CASE STUDY 4.1 continued**

Table 4.1

Unilever's global ice cream products in selected countries

Country	Brand	Magnum	Cornetto	Carte d'Or	Solero	Viennetta	Ben & Jerry's	Local brands
Argentina	Kibon	✓	✓					✓
Australia	Heart	✓		✓			✓	✓
Brazil	Kibon	✓	✓	✓	✓			✓
China	Wall's	✓	✓	✓				✓
Germany	Langnese	✓	✓		✓	✓	✓	✓
Holland	Ola	✓	✓		✓		✓	✓
Ireland	HB	✓	✓	✓	✓	✓	✓	✓
Malaysia	Wall's	✓	✓	✓	✓			✓
Poland	Algida	✓		✓				✓
Russia	Algida	✓	✓	✓		✓		✓
Sweden	GB Glace	✓		✓	✓			✓
Turkey	Algida	✓	✓	✓		✓		✓
UK	Wall's	✓	✓	✓	✓	✓	✓	✓
US: 3 brands for historic reasons	Breyers, Klondike and Good Humor						✓	✓

Source: From Unilever world websites and *China Daily*.

Unilever has attempted to bring uniform branding, using a heart-shaped symbol, to its many different global ice cream companies.

history of the Unilever company in the United States – through acquisition, through local development and through regional strength. Geographically, the US is a large country with a history of the development of regional brands. Good Humor is the only brand – so far at least – using the heart-shaped logo from its global parent. However, some Breyers products are on sale in Unilever Australia. Another Unilever American example is Ben & Jerry's super-premium ice cream. Unilever only acquired the company in 1997 from the two original founders. As a result of its unique previous ownership and small-company philosophy, the Ben & Jerry's strategy at Unilever is to allow the company to continue as a semi-autonomous unit within Unilever – even developing its own activities worldwide outside the Unilever corporate umbrella and not using the heart-shaped logo. This is a genuinely innovative approach for a large multinational.

Unilever has been involved in ice cream markets for many years and this product category delivers around 10 per cent of its total profits. During the 1980s and 1990s, it faced an increasing threat from two competitors, Nestlé and Mars. In particular, Nestlé is the competitor that is catching Unilever in terms of worldwide market share through a different combination of acquisition and innovative strategies. This competitive activity is described in Case 4.4 at the end of the chapter.

Over the years, Unilever has developed strong distribution links with retailers, especially the smaller outlets that only have enough space for one freezer cabinet. A crucial factor in all ice cream strategy is that ice cream needs freezers for in-store storage. Unilever has been highly active in ensuring that its products gain the maximum amount of freezer space through frequent deliveries and, in the case of smaller stores, through renting its freezers to the store. It used this distribution strength to keep out Mars Ice Cream from smaller stores in Europe for many years. However, in 2003 the European Courts ruled that Unilever's strategy was uncompetitive and Unilever was forced to allow Mars products into its freezer cabinets.

Unilever's large market share has delivered economies of scale that newer entrants cannot match, preventing them from achieving the same low-cost structure. For this reason, Unilever has been the most consistently profitable of the major ice cream companies. Mars ice creams were launched in 1989 but were unprofitable for much of this time. Nestlé ice creams were also being developed over the last 15 years but they again were not major profit earners for the company – see Case 4.4.

Probably Unilever's greatest weakness is that the group has no involvement in the confectionery market, unlike Nestlé and Mars. Unilever thus had difficulty in responding to the 1990s' trend amongst rival companies to use confectionery brands in ice cream – like ice cream Mars. Eventually, Unilever developed its own global brands like Magnum and Cornetto.

But investing in these new brands has been an expensive strategy.

To counteract this weakness, Unilever began a new strategy in 2005. It licensed two global brands from other manufacturers. In the Carte D'Or range, the company launched Toblerone ice cream – the brand name being used under licence from Kraft Jacobs Suchard – and Lavazza coffee ice cream – with the brand name under licence from the Italian coffee company. The problem with a licence is that part of the profits is passed on to the owner of the brand rather than being retained by Unilever.

Case questions

1 *What is the source of Unilever's advantages over its competitors?*

2 *What are Unilever's main strengths? Where do its weaknesses lie? What, if anything, should Unilever do about its weaknesses?*

3 *Given Unilever's market dominance, what strategies would you adopt if you were entering the ice cream market? How do you attack a dominant competitor?*

4.1 SUSTAINABLE COMPETITIVE ADVANTAGE

4.1.1 The importance of sustainable competitive advantage

Definition ➤ Sustainable competitive advantage (SCA) is an advantage over competitors that cannot easily be imitated. The main reason for analysing competitors is to enable the organisation to develop *competitive advantages* against them, especially advantages that can be *sustained* over time. SCA involves every aspect of the way that the organisation competes in the market place – prices, product range, manufacturing quality, service levels and so on. However, some of these factors can easily be imitated: for example, prices can be changed virtually overnight or other companies can make ice cream just like Unilever.

The real benefits come from advantages that competitors cannot easily imitate, not from those that give only temporary relief from the competitive battle. To be *sustainable*, competitive advantage needs to be more deeply embedded in the organisation – its resources, skills, culture and investment over time. Unilever's advantages in ice cream come from its brand investment, its well-developed distribution service and its sheer size in the market place, which should deliver economies of scale.

More generally, the development of sustainable advantage can take many forms. Such activities may involve seeking something that is perhaps *unique* and certainly *different* from the competition, and so it follows that there will be a wide range of possibilities. Table 4.2 presents some possible sources of advantage for certain industries.

For many strategists, the development of sustainable competitive advantage lies at the core of corporate strategy development. Professor Michael Porter wrote persuasively about its importance in the 1980s in two classic strategy texts – *Competitive Strategy* (1980)[2] and *Competitive Advantage* (1985)[3] – which have influenced both academic and industry developments. For example, Stephen South, corporate planning director at Clark Equipment (US), commented:

Table 4.2

Some possible sustainable competitive advantages in different areas of business

High technology	Services	Small business	Manufacturing market leader
Technical excellence	Reputation for quality of service	Quality	Low costs
Reputation for quality	High quality and training of staff	Prompt service	Strong branding
Customer service	Customer service	Personalised service	Good distribution
Financial resources	Well-known name	Keen prices	Quality product
Low-cost manufacturing	Customer-oriented	Local availability	Good value for money

Sources: See reference[4].

The process of strategic management is coming to be defined, in fact, as the management of competitive advantage – that is, a process of identifying, developing and taking advantage of enclaves in which tangible and preservable business advantage can be achieved.[5]

There are other aspects to the development of corporate strategy – for example, those associated with the customers who buy the product and those linked with the strategy process and the purpose of an organisation. Hence, South's remark may overstate the importance of competitive advantage. Nevertheless, it is a vital aspect of corporate strategy development.

4.1.2 Public service and not-for-profit organisations

Most businesses face competitors, so the need for a sustainable advantage to help them compete is evident. It is more questionable, though, whether public service and not-for-profit organisations need SCA. In one sense, they may not because their services are often provided free to the consumer and without competition – for example, police services, hospitals, charitable institutions and so on.

However, many public services and charities depend for financial support either on government funds or on private donations. Such support is usually not unlimited, and so in this sense such organisations *compete for finance* from potential providers. Developing arguments and evidence to maintain and enhance the funds distributed will be important. Such organisations could usefully consider the decisions that have to be made by the fund providers and the *incremental advantages* that their service provides to the general public and which therefore justify extra funding. This is explored further in Chapter 18.

4.1.3 Prescriptive and emergent approaches to sustainable advantage

By definition, if an advantage is to be sustainable, then it cannot be quickly copied by others. It is likely that it will have taken some time, possibly years, for the organisation to have developed the advantage. A prescriptive approach, requiring a sustained period of development, is therefore likely to be required in principle at least. For example, it takes some years to develop and establish a new branded product such as Magnum ice cream.

Emergent approaches are not excluded, however. The development of SCA may well require a degree of experimentation, along with adjustments based on the developments by competitors. For example, the introduction of super-premium ice creams characterised by exotic ingredients and high prices, such as Häagen Dazs and Ben & Jerry's, will benefit from experimenting with new forms of distribution – such as the supply of freezer cabinets in pizza restaurants – in order to overcome the hold that the traditional ice cream suppliers have on more familiar outlets.

Hence, the development of SCA will probably require elements of both prescriptive and emergent strategic approaches. An extension of the emergent perspective on SCA is explored in the next section.

4.1.4 Developing sources of sustainable competitive advantage

In seeking the advantages that competitors cannot easily copy, it is necessary to examine not only the competitors, but also the organisation itself and its resources. Resources are explored in depth in Part 3 of this book, but it is appropriate here to identify some possible sources of advantage as a possible *starting point* for later study:

- *Differentiation.* This is the development of unique features or attributes in a product or service that position it to appeal especially to a part of the total market. Branding is an example of this source.

- *Low costs.* The development of low-cost production enables the firm to compete against other companies either on the basis of lower prices or possibly on the basis of the same prices as its competitors but with more services being added. For example, production in some South East Asian countries may involve lower labour costs that cannot be matched in the West.[6]

- *Niche marketing.* A company may select a small market segment and concentrate all its efforts on achieving advantages in this segment. Such a niche will need to be distinguished by special buyer needs. Fashion items such as those by Yves St Laurent or Dunhill are examples of products that are specifically targeted towards specialist niches.

- *High performance or technology.* Special levels of performance or service can be developed that simply cannot be matched by other companies – for example, through patented products or recruitment of especially talented individuals. The well-known global consulting companies and merchant banks operate in this way.

- *Quality.* Some companies offer a level of quality that others are unable to match. For example, some Japanese cars have, until recently, provided levels of reliability that Western companies have had difficulty in reaching.

- *Service.* Some companies have deliberately sought to provide superior levels of service that others have been unable or unwilling to match. For example, McDonald's set new levels of service in its fast food restaurants that were unmatched by others for many years.

- *Vertical integration.* The backward acquisition of raw material suppliers and/or the forward purchase of distributors may provide advantages that others cannot match. For example, in Chapter 3, the Arcelor steel company owned some steel distributors.

- *Synergy.* This is the combination of parts of a business such that the sum of them is worth more than the individual parts – that is, 2 + 2 = 5. This may occur because the parts share fixed overheads, transfer their technology or share the same salesforce, for example. Claims are often made for this approach when an acquisition is made, but this synergy is not necessarily achieved in reality. Nevertheless, it remains a valid area of exploration.

- *Culture, leadership and style of an organisation.* The way that an organisation leads, trains and supports its members may be a source of advantage that others cannot match. It will lead to innovative products, exceptional levels of service, fast responses to new market developments and so on. This area is more difficult to quantify than some of the other areas above, but this only adds to its unique appeal. It is unusual to find such an area listed in strategy texts, but it is a theme of this book.

Some organisations and strategists have become almost obsessed with the first three of these sources of sustainable competitive advantage – Porter's *generic strategies*, as they are often described – and these are discussed under this heading in Chapter 13. However, it is inappropriate to focus on three areas alone, because the others listed above (and many more not listed) are also important. In practice, Professor Porter's books explore many possible areas in considerable detail. It could also be argued that several of the sources in the list above involve some form of differentiation. To group these all under 'differentiation', however, would be to ignore the *specific nature* of the form of advantage and to deny the important individual areas of strategy opened up by such concepts.

More generally, Professor John Kay, the British strategy writer formerly at Oxford University Business School, has argued that competitive advantage is based on the *stability* and *continuity* in relationships between different parts of an organisation.[7] He argues that major advantages are not developed overnight or by some special acquisition or other miraculous strategy. Substantial advantages take many years to develop and involve the whole culture and style of an organisation. To this extent, it may even be misleading to see advantages as being summarised by the short list of items above. However, this does provide a starting point for further analysis.

Ultimately, there is no single route to achieving sustainable competitive advantage. The question that arises is therefore whether it is possible to test whether it has been achieved. Three possible tests for such advantages are shown in Exhibit 4.1.

Exhibit 4.1

Three tests for sustainable competitive advantage

The advantage should be:

- *Sufficiently significant to make a difference.* Modest advantages that hold no real benefits to the customer or the organisation are unlikely to be persuasive.

- *Sustainable against environmental change and competitor attack.* The market as a whole may move forward in terms of technology or tastes. Equally, competitors may be able to copy advantages developed by the organisation. In both cases, these advantages are not sustainable.

- *Recognisable and linked to customer benefits.* An advantage needs to be translated from a functional advantage inside the organisation – for example, low costs – into something that the customer will value – for example, low prices. Advantages that cannot be linked in this way may ultimately prove to have no persuasive and competitive edge.

Key strategic principles

- One of the main purposes of analysing competitors is to explore where and how sustainable competitive advantage (SCA) can be generated. The search for SCA will be wide and deep within the organisation.

- Public service and not-for-profit organisations may also wish to explore SCA as they may be in competition for finance from external bodies, such as the government, even if there is no competition for customers.

- SCA will probably require elements of both emergent and prescriptive strategy approaches to strategy development.

- There are numerous sources of SCA. These include: differentiation; low costs; niche marketing; high performance or technology; quality; service; vertical integration; synergy; and the culture, leadership and style of the organisation. Importantly, SCA develops slowly over time; such a list is only the starting point of a more detailed study.

4.2 DYNAMICS OF COMPETITIVE ADVANTAGE

Clearly, competitive advantage is unlikely to remain static forever: competitors, technology, managers, customers and many other factors are likely to change over time. Some strategists,[8] particularly those that have studied industries where advanced technology is involved, argue that the static identification of competitive advantage misses an important strategic opportunity. They suggest that competitive advantage should be seen as constantly evolving and that companies should be seeking to make this happen. In other words, competitive advantage is a *dynamic concept* that will provide a constant flow of new opportunities to the organisation.

4.2.1 Dynamic process – structured yet chaotic

According to such strategists, the key issue is for a company to strike a balance between supporting its long-term sustainable advantages and at the same time engaging in the process of constant change and renewal. Such a company will begin by identifying some sustainable competitive advantages that are structured, supported and clear – for example, Intel Corporation supports its 'Pentium' brand name and individual new computer chips as they are launched into the market place. However, at the same time, such a company will also deliberately have some other aspects of its activities that are disorganised and fall essentially outside its existing areas of advantage – for example, Intel Corporation might experiment with some totally new technology or computer software in one of its laboratories that has no obvious relation to its current competitive advantage but would be an interesting point of departure for the company. Thus, the strategy process is both *structured* – advertising the brand name – and *chaotic* – exploring a totally new and unproven technology – and, in this sense, dynamic.

4.2.2 Dynamic competitive advantage – some guidelines, not rules

Clearly such a dynamic strategic process has the potential to be both immensely beneficial and also totally unmanageable. Strategists therefore suggest that there should be some guidelines laid down to exploit the real benefits of such an approach. In the words of Brown and Eisenhardt:

> *Successful firms in fiercely competitive and unpredictably shifting industries pursue a competing on the edge strategy. The goal of this strategy is not efficiency or optimality in the usual sense. Rather, the goal is flexibility – that is, adaptation to current change and evolution over time, resilience to setbacks, and the ability to locate constantly changing sources of advantage. Ultimately, it means engaging in continual revolution.*[9]

In practice, for such organisations, this means striking a balance between structure and chaos – strong financial control systems are in place, but managers have significant free time to develop their own ideas. Thus the process may be inefficient and have failures. But it will be proactive in the sense of seeking positively after new initiatives and accept that there will inevitably be some failures. The process is often driven by a basic objective that the organisation will derive a significant percentage of its sales from totally new products over time – the 3M case in Chapter 11 will provide more detail.

Fundamentally, the process is guided by the concept of the organisation having a *continuous flow* of competitive advantages rather than a static list. Clearly this is an emergent rather than a prescriptive approach to strategy development.

4.2.3 Critical comment on the concept

There are some obvious flaws in such an approach:

● It may be possible in high-technology industries, but difficult to achieve and even irrelevant elsewhere – *see* Case 4.1, where Unilever's competitive advantage is real but does not depend on a technological advantage. The Unilever technology is available to competitors, who unfortunately may not necessarily have the economies of scale to justify the investment.

● There is a real difficulty in managing the difficult boundary between inspired development ideas and total chaos – *see* Case 4.2, where, arguably, the company went too far.

● Other important areas of competitive advantage, such as branding, appear to be largely discounted in the quest for technological benefits. This means that such advantages may be under-supported in a search for a totally new area of advantage.

Key strategic principles

● According to some strategists, competitive advantage should be seen as constantly evolving and companies should set out to make this happen, particularly in industries that involve advanced technology. In this sense, competitive advantage is dynamic rather than static.

● The process for developing such competitive advantage is both built around existing strengths – structured – and also exploits new and exciting areas – chaotic.

● The main rule for such a process is to strike a balance between structure and chaos.

● Criticism of the approach has centred on its relevance to more traditional industries outside high technology, on the difficulty of managing the chaotic part of the process, and on the possibility of ignoring existing competitive advantages in the pursuit of a new area of advantage.

CASE STUDY 4.2

Web strategy at Boo.com - to be booed? Or applauded?

With the wisdom of hindsight, it is easy to criticise the failed web strategy of the fashion and sportswear company Boo.com. This case outlines its brief history and explores whether it was right for investors to take the risk.

Background

In the late 1990s, many senior strategy consultants and well-known companies were enthusiastic about the potential of the worldwide web. It would revolutionise business and alter fundamentally the whole nature of competitive markets and the meaning of sustainable competitive advantage. For example in April 2000, the website of the well-known consultancy company Arthur Anderson made the following claims about the benefits of the web and the related concept of e-business:

eBusiness transforms the business landscape. New companies routinely challenge dominant market players. Unprecedented market efficiencies eliminate middlemen and create increased productivity by more closely matching supply and demand. eBusiness describes the way companies innovate and transform. It mandates rethinking, repositioning and retooling a company's entire value proposition. In a start up company, you basically throw out all assumptions every three weeks.

Thus, it was not only large companies that saw immense possibilities. Small entrepreneurial ventures were being started in every conceivable business area. And substantial funds were available: 'There was a view that raising money to fund a start-up was easy and any monkey could do it.' Venture capital funds were awash with cash and investors were scrambling to invest their money. One of these companies was Boo.com.

Boo.com - the beginnings

In January 1999, a new start-up company called Boo.com was seen as one with great potential. Its strategic purpose was to become the global leader in selling trendy sportswear over the web. Two of its three Swedish founders, Ernst Malmsten – entrepreneur; Kajsa Leander – fashion model; and Patrik Hedelin – investment banker, appeared on the cover of the leading US business magazine *Fortune* with the headline: 'Cool companies '99: 12 start-up companies – will one be the next Yahoo?' Malmsten was the original driving force, having previously founded a successful on-line book store. JP

Boo faces its critics but jury is still out on Net prospects

Internet retailer reveals figures but question is whether backers will wait for Europe to catch up with US

Source: Financial Times, 3rd February 2000

Boo's next?

The very public failure of the online fashion retailer is prompting investors to reassess the long-term viability of other European start-ups

Source: Financial Times, 19th May 2000

The rapid decline of Boo.com shows strategy at its most dynamic.

Morgan was the lead bank that helped them bring in some well-known blue-chip lawyers, technology providers and head-hunters.

Boo.com certainly had great ambitions. Its launch in June 1999 would be undertaken simultaneously in 18 countries. Its website was to be truly innovative, multilingual and offering high-class sportswear at premium prices. This last point was quite different from the usual website offer which advertised prices lower than those available in high street shops – for example, Amazon.com in books. In addition, Boo.com was proposing to set up a sales and distribution network in its 18 countries that would allow delivery in just a few days. By any standards, this was very ambitious – even more so for a company whose founders had never managed such a venture previously.

The company recruited some 400 people across its 18 countries. In addition, it spent substantial funds on advertising and software development. The money was spent on shooting television commercials in Los Angeles; spending US$10,000 on clothes at Barneys so that the founders would look good on the cover of *Fortune*; holding smart parties for staff; jetting around the world by Concord or private jet. As a result, the company was spending around US$1 million per week by the year 2000. The company launch was put back five times and US$30 million spent. During this time, it took six months to

appoint a chief financial officer and four months to find a good technology director. One investor explained: 'The lack of financial controls was excused because it was considered more important to spend money on promotion. The aim was to stay ahead of the pack.'

In August 1999, Malmsten took all the staff to an expensive lunch in London to announce that a new manager would be creating Project Launch in November 1999. At this time, a Lebanese investment company put in yet another US$15 million. The launch took place in November and pulled in 25,000 web hits – the business objective was 1 million. Sales were around U$4 million over the first six months. By this time, the company had spent over US$100 million on salaries, marketing costs, legal costs, office design costs and software development.

Boo.com goes bust

According to one investor in the company, 'If you looked at Boo in concept as potentially a global company, then spending US$100 million building it was not necessarily a lot of money. We were hoping to build a company worth US$1 billion.' Boo.com mainly sought funds from rich private investors rather than the public. For this reason, the company never made its trading figures public – except one day towards the end of its life when it was forced to reveal the sales figure mentioned above. In March 2000, investors were still debating over whether to put in another US$30 million. In May 2000, investors pulled the plug. The company simply ran out of cash.

Boo.com conclusions

Clearly the company had been too ambitious. It was too lax in financial controls and too unrealistic in wishing to break the rules. But it did attempt to break new ground. It was an important experiment that might have succeeded.

© Copyright Richard Lynch 2006. All rights reserved. This case was written by Richard Lynch from published sources only.[10]

Case questions

1 *What were the competitive advantages of Boo.com, if any?*

2 *Given that many investors in Boo.com were wealthy private individuals, were they right to invest their money? Would you personally invest money in such a company?*

3 *Boo.com claimed to be seizing the initiative and breaking the rules. Under what circumstances, if any, does it make sense to attempt this?*

4.3 THE NATURE AND INTENSITY OF COMPETITION IN AN INDUSTRY

Governments will set the basic degree of competitiveness that they wish to see in industries. Having established this, it is useful to start any analysis of competition with Porter's *Five Forces Analysis* (*see* Chapter 3). This will provide a basic starting point in any development of the major factors driving the dynamics of the industry. In addition to such an analysis, it is possible to examine two further areas:

1 the degree of concentration of companies in a market – examined here; and

2 the range of aggressive strategies of competitors in the market. (*See* Section 4.4.)

In microeconomic theory, the degree of concentration of companies in a market can be seen as being somewhere between two extremes, each of which will have strategic consequences for companies:

● perfect competition;

● pure monopoly.

In *perfect competition*, there are numerous buyers and sellers, with no single firm able to influence market prices: it is assumed that products are identical in every respect and that the firm accepts the price set by the market. The perfectly competitive firm sets its level of production output to maximise profits. From a strategic viewpoint, this leaves the firm at the mercy of market pressures and is therefore undesirable. It would be much better strategy for the firm to *differentiate* its product, dominate a sector of the market and thus influence that sector's market price – in other words, to gain sustainable competitive advantage.

At the other extreme from perfect competition, there exists the state of *pure monopoly*. In this case, there is no competition and the company has total control over its prices; it erects barriers to entry and maximises profits and value added. It does this at the expense of its customers, but from a corporate strategy viewpoint it might be argued that the corporation has no responsibility to such customers and should seek to maximise profit and value added regardless of their views: strategies would therefore include raising prices to the maximum that the market will bear and setting output accordingly.

In practice, for many companies the environment is neither one of perfect competition nor one of pure monopoly. For example, Boo.com had many competitors over the internet, but there were some that were more important than others. Corporate strategy needs to deal with a wide range of industrial structures in the middle. For some industries where there are economies of scale, it may actually be more efficient for the state and more profitable for individual companies to have a few large companies in an industry – that is, an *oligopoly*. Corporate strategy in such industries will therefore be directed towards obtaining and sustaining the oligopoly, if this is possible.

Industry structure and market characteristics have a significant impact on corporate strategy. However, the actions that companies take go well beyond the pricing activity often highlighted in microeconomic theory – for example, cost reduction, product differentiation, linkages with other companies through alliances and joint ventures. At Boo.com, pricing was clearly important but there were a whole range of factors associated with its fashion products that would also attract buyers. In the chapters that follow, these areas will be explored further.

The *concentration ratio* is often used to measure the degree to which value added or turnover is concentrated in the hands of a few or a large number of firms in an industry. It is usually defined as the percentage of industry value added or turnover controlled by the largest four, five or eight firms – the C4, C5 or C8 ratio respectively. Typically, C5 averages around 55 per cent in UK manufacturing industries and C4 averages around 34 per cent in US industries. After the ratio has been calculated, two areas of strategic significance can be analysed:

1 The *total number of firms in an industry* may influence their ability to exert buying power over suppliers. If there are few, then buying power may increase; if there are many, then their buying power will be lower.

2 The *mix of firms making up the industry* will also impact on profitability. If there are a few companies that are roughly equal in size, then there may be some tacit understanding between them to allow profits to grow. As the numbers increase and there is a likelihood

of some giants and some smaller companies, then there is a lower possibility of a tacit understanding, so profits will suffer.

Overall, it is likely that corporate strategy will vary with company size and the degree of market competition. Smaller companies, such as small shoe manufacturers, may have to adopt different strategies from larger organisations, such as the world's largest shoe chain, Bata. Large companies have the resources to set up retail chains to sell their products – unlike small companies. Highly competitive markets with few competing companies may therefore require different strategies from those with lower degrees of competition. This has profound significance because it suggests that corporate strategy will vary with industry.[11] There may be no single 'corporate strategy' that will suit all industries.

4.4 AGGRESSIVE COMPETITIVE STRATEGIES[12]

There is a whole range of aggressive strategies that competitors can undertake. These need to be analysed for two reasons:

1 to understand the strategies competitors may undertake;

2 to assist in planning appropriate counter-measures.

In practitioner literature and even some more academic articles in this area, the language and style are often *militaristic* in tone.[13] For example: 'Find a weakness in the leader's strength and attack at that point'; 'Strong competitive moves should always be blocked'. Professor Porter eschews some of the more colourful language but is in no doubt about the importance of this area. Professor Philip Kotler from North Western University, US, has developed the material in his well-known marketing text, *Marketing Management*[14] and has collaborated with Singh to write an influential article on the topic.[15] The analytical process is summarised in Figure 4.2.

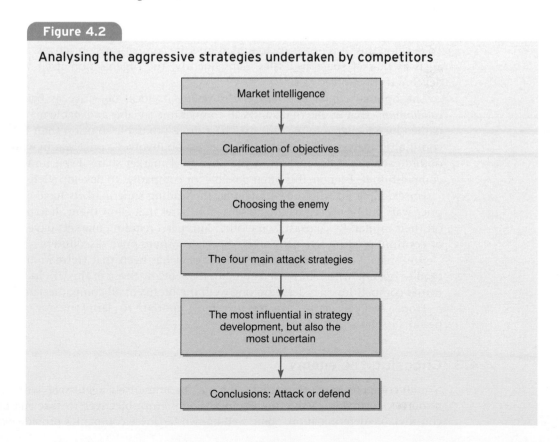

Figure 4.2

Analysing the aggressive strategies undertaken by competitors

Market intelligence

Clarification of objectives

Choosing the enemy

The four main attack strategies

The most influential in strategy development, but also the most uncertain

Conclusions: Attack or defend

4.4.1 Market intelligence

In accordance with the well-known saying 'knowledge is the basis of power', many companies monitor the activities of their competitors constantly. Occasionally, a few may undertake snooping or eavesdropping activities which may be illegal and are probably unethical. Although such behaviour cannot be condoned, it is entirely correct for companies to seek an understanding of their competitors' strategies. There are many entirely legitimate means for investigating this area. For example:

- company annual reports;
- newspaper articles;
- stockbroker analyses;
- exhibitions and trade fairs.

4.4.2 Clarification of the objectives of competitors

In military situations, the objective is often the total defeat of the enemy. This is rarely appropriate in corporate strategy for the following reasons:

- It may contravene monopoly legislation, certainly in the EU, the US and many other countries around the world.
- It often becomes increasingly costly to pursue the last remnant of share.
- A weakened opponent that is still in the market may be easier to handle than a new aggressive entrant.
- A defeated opponent may be acquired cheaply in a takeover by a new powerful entrant.

Even military strategists have recognised that the objectives of war may be better served by some form of stalemate or understanding. As Captain B H Liddell-Hart commented:

The objective of war is a better state of peace, even if only from your own viewpoint.[16]

To develop this, it is necessary to understand the competitor's objectives, especially in such areas as market share and sales. Subsequently, the organisation itself will also need to develop its own objectives.

The optimal corporate strategy may define its ideal objective as being a *new market equilibrium* – that is, one that allows all competitors a viable and stable market share accompanied by adequate profits. This may be a more profitable solution than the alternative of continuing aggression, especially if the aggression involves a price war in which competitors outbid each other downwards in the pursuit of market share. Even under strict national competition legislation, it is often possible for companies to develop such an equilibrium.[17]

For example, in UK grocery retailing, the leading supermarkets have engaged in minor price wars but have been willing to settle for shares that allow them all to make high returns on their capital. By contrast, some other European retailing markets have been the subject of continuing aggressive price wars, especially where price discounters – such as Aldi and Netto – have become major players. The result has been that German and other retailers tend to operate with returns on capital that are below those of the UK. In this context, cut-throat competition may serve no one well: the profits of all companies are then reduced.[18]

From a strategic perspective, it is therefore important to clarify the true objectives of competitors in the industry.

4.4.3 Choosing the enemy

Not all competitors are the same: some may be immensely aggressive, with large financial resources, relatively passive shareholders, long-term objectives to take market share and considerable determination. Some well-known Japanese companies provide examples here.

These are not the companies to choose to fight, although it may be inevitable that the organisation will compete with them.

Equally, attacking a market leader directly is a high-risk strategy because of the strength of such a competitor, even if the payoff appears to be attractive. Military strategists state that a superiority in people and machinery of 3:1 is needed before launching an attack, if the approach is to be successful. By definition, this is highly unlikely where the market leader is involved.

For these reasons, it may be better to analyse and target competitors of more equal size. Their weaknesses might then form the basis of an aggressive move. They might even be available for takeover.

4.4.4 The four main attack strategies

In any analysis of competitors, it is important to recognise the four main strategies that they may use against each other and any new entrant. It should also be noted that these represent a *checklist of strategy options* for use in Part 5 when it comes to further development of corporate strategy (*see* Chapter 13).

The four main attack strategies are shown in Exhibit 4.2. These are based on three main principles from military strategy:[19]

1 *the need to concentrate the attack on competition* so that it is overwhelming at that particular point and therefore more likely to be successful;

2 *the element of surprise* so that gains can be made while the competitor is still recovering (perhaps involving rewriting the rules of the game);

3 *the need to consolidate the attack* by continuing to invest for some period (except in the last option which is based on rapid withdrawal and limited losses).

Exhibit 4.2

The four main attack strategies

1 Head-on against the market leader

- Unless resources are sustained, the campaign is unlikely to be successful.
- Attack where the leader is weak.
- Pick a narrow front to open up the campaign.

2 Flanking or market segmentation

- Choose a flank that is relatively undefended.
- Aim to take a significant market share.
- Expect to invest in the flank for some years.
- Pricing and value for money are often distinguishing features of a successful flank.

3 Occupy totally new territory, i.e. where there is no existing product or service

- Innovate if possible.
- Seek market niches.

4 Guerrilla: that is, a rapid sortie to seize a short-term profitable opportunity

- Relies on good information to identify opportunities.
- Fast response needed and rapid withdrawal after success.
- Important not to stand and fight leaders on their own ground but pick new areas.

Again, as in military strategy, these principles

- involve a reliance on brute force to achieve an objective only when it is useful and achievable;
- recommend concentrating such force so that it will achieve maximum effect;
- suggest following up the use of force by longer-term strategies that will secure the position permanently.

For these reasons, the head-on strategy is rarely successful.

It should be emphasised that other strategies are also possible and, for the underdog, may be crucial. They often involve some form of *innovation* in the competitive environment (*see* Section 4.4.5).

4.4.5 Innovatory strategies

There are many forms of innovation but it is useful to identify four for our purposes:

1 rewriting the rules of the game;

2 technological innovation;

3 higher levels of service;

4 co-operation.

Many of these are particularly suited to smaller companies that do not have substantial resources.

Rewriting the rules of the game

In competitive strategy, the existing players in the market will work according to a mutual understanding of how competitors are engaged – the rules of the game. For example, life and household insurance was sold by agents who personally advised their customers on the best product for their circumstances. All the major companies invested vast sums in recruiting and training their people to undertake this task. Ultimately, their heavy investment meant that it was in the interests of such insurance companies not to offer any alternatives. Then along came smaller companies with telephone insurance selling. They changed the rules of the game and sold the product without the heavy overhead of a large salesforce, so that it was possible to offer much lower prices. The revolution has now largely happened across much of the European insurance industry. Rewriting the rules of the game is important in corporate strategy.

Technological innovation

Especially in the case of new, smaller players, it may be essential to introduce some form of innovation in order to take market share. This does not mean that this is the only way to enter a market and survive, but in certain types of industry it may represent a viable route. For example, the internet is set to revolutionise the distribution of recorded music – *see* Case study 20.2. Smaller companies will be able to distribute their music more readily.

Higher levels of service

In some industries, technology may not be a dominant feature but service levels may still be important. For example, in the shoe industry, there have been technical advances but some companies have survived because they have offered high levels of personalised service and shoe design. Even in retailing, small shops have been able to survive by staying open for long hours in their local communities.

Co-operation

Formal partnerships or some other form of joint activity have proved useful innovatory strategies in recent years. Joint ventures, alliances and other forms of co-operation have been used with success to beat larger rivals (*see* Section 4.6).

Key strategic principles

- In assessing the aggressive strategies of competitors, it is important to begin by monitoring competitive activity on a regular basis.

- Although total defeat may be appropriate as a military objective, it is rarely relevant in business. A new market equilibrium may be much more profitable, involving stable market shares, no price wars and viable levels of profitability.

- Some competitors may be naturally more aggressive than others and have more substantial resources. If it is possible to choose, then these may be the competitors to avoid.

- Choosing an enemy that can provide a successful outcome is important. Attacking the market leader is not usually wise.

- The four main attack strategies are: head-on, flanking, occupy totally new territory, and guerrilla.

- Innovatory strategies may prove particularly significant, especially for the underdog. These include rewriting the rules of the game, technological innovation, higher levels of service, and partnerships. (*See* further Chapter 11.)

4.4.6 Conclusions: attack or defend

In a static market, every company that identifies a market opportunity will present another company with a market problem. Attack strategies therefore invite defensive responses, but they are two sides of the same coin and need to be treated as such in corporate strategy.

The analysis of the range of aggressive strategies open to competitors is a useful starting point in the development of corporate strategy. However, Kay[20] has urged caution in the use of military analogies for two reasons:

1 *It may exaggerate the importance of size and scale.* The use of brute force is supported by the financial resources and market share that can be brought to bear. Kay points out that business success comes from *distinctive capabilities* rather than destroying the enemy. It is therefore important to recognise size and scale as useful but not conclusive devices in strategic terms.

2 *It invites excessive emphasis on leadership, vision and attack.* The generals plotting the strategy are the primary engines for successful military strategy. Kay observes that many successful companies rely on *teams*, rather than charismatic leaders – a theme that will be explored throughout this book.

In many respects, it is the *prescriptive* view of strategy that is best served by concepts of aggressive attack with plans that are carefully drawn up in advance. The more adaptive approach of *emergent* strategy does not lend itself so readily to such recipes, although the militarists would no doubt recognise the need for adaptation as the battle proceeds. Innovative strategies therefore have an important role.

4.5 ANALYSING AN ORGANISATION'S PORTFOLIO OF COMPETING PRODUCTS AND SERVICES

The majority of companies offer more than one product or service and many serve more than one customer – they have a *portfolio* of products. There are good strategic reasons for this: to be reliant on one product or customer clearly carries immense risks if, for any reason, that product or service should fail or the customer should go elsewhere. Decisions on strategy usually involve a range of products in a range of markets. This is the subject of portfolio analysis and strategy. It was originally suggested by the Boston Consulting Group (BCG) in the 1970s and, as a result, one version of the approach is known as the BCG

Definition ➤ or portfolio matrix. The portfolio matrix analyses the range of products possessed by an organisation (its portfolio) against two criteria: relative market share and market growth. It is sometimes called the growth–share matrix. Other versions were later developed to overcome weaknesses in the BCG approach – the *directional policy matrix* is also covered below in Section 4.5.3.

When an organisation has a number of products in its portfolio, it is quite likely that they will be in different stages of development: some will be relatively new and some much older. Many organisations will not wish to risk having all their products in the same markets and at the same stages of development. It is useful to have some products with limited growth but producing profits steadily, as well as having others that have real potential but may still be in the early stages of their growth. Indeed, the products that are earning steadily may be used to fund the development of those that will provide the growth and profits in the future.

According to this argument, the key strategy is to produce a *balanced portfolio of products* – some low-risk but dull growth, some higher-risk with future potential and rewards. The results can be measured in both *profit* and *cash* terms. (Cash is used as a measure here because, both in theory and in practice, it is possible for a company to be trading profitably and yet go bankrupt. This is because the company is earning insufficient *cash* as the profits are being reinvested in growth in the business. It is important to understand this distinction.)

4.5.1 The BCG growth–share matrix

This matrix is one means of analysing the balance of an organisation's product portfolio. According to this matrix, two basic factors define a product's strategic stance in the market place:

1 *relative market share* – for each product, the ratio of the share of the organisation's product divided by the share of the market leader;[21]

2 *market growth rate* – for each product, the market growth rate of the product category.

Relative market share is important because, in the competitive battle of the market place, it is advantageous to have a larger share than rivals: this gives room for manoeuvre, the scale to undertake investment and the ability to command distribution. Some researchers, such as Buzzell and Gale,[22] claim to have found empirical evidence to support these statements. For example, in a survey of major companies, the two researchers found that businesses with over 50 per cent share of their markets enjoy rates of return three times greater than businesses with small market shares. There are other empirical studies that also support this broad conclusion.[23] However, Jacobsen and Aaker[24] have questioned this relationship. They point out that such a close correlation will also derive from other differences in businesses. High market share companies do not just differ on market share but on other dimensions as well: for example, they may have better management and may have more luck. However, Aaker himself in a more recent work[25] has conceded that portfolios do have their uses, along with their limitations.

Figure 4.3	

The growth–share matrix – individual products or product groups categorised by market growth and share

	High relative market share	Low relative market share
High market growth rate	**Star** Cash neutral	**Problem child** Cash user
Low market growth rate	**Cash cow** Cash generator	**Dog** Cash neutral

Market growth rate is important because markets that are growing rapidly offer more opportunities for sales than lower growth markets. Rapid growth is less likely to involve stealing share from competition and more likely to come from new buyers entering the market. This gives many new opportunities for the right product. There are also difficulties, however – perhaps the chief being that growing markets are often not as profitable as those with low growth. Investment is usually needed to *promote* the rapid growth and this has to be funded out of profits.

Relative market share and market growth rate are combined in the growth–share matrix, as shown in Figure 4.3. It should be noted that the term 'matrix' is misleading. In reality, the diagram does not have four distinct boxes, but rather four areas which merge into one another. The four areas are given distinctive names to signify their strategic significance.

Definition ➤
- *Stars.* The upper-left quadrant contains the stars: products with high relative market shares operating in high-growth markets. The growth rate will mean that they will need heavy investment and will therefore be cash users. However, because they have high market shares, it is assumed that they will have economies of scale and be able to generate large amounts of cash. Overall, it is therefore asserted that they will be cash neutral – an assumption not necessarily supported in practice and not yet fully tested.

Definition ➤
- *Cash cows.* The lower-left quadrant shows the cash cows: product areas that have high relative market shares but exist in low-growth markets. The business is mature and it is assumed that lower levels of investment will be required. On this basis, it is therefore likely that they will be able to generate both cash and profits. Such profits could then be transferred to support the stars. However, there is a real strategic danger here that cash cows become under-supported and begin to lose their market share.[26]

Definition ➤
- *Problem children.* The upper-right quadrant contains the problem children: products with low relative market shares in high-growth markets. Such products have not yet obtained dominant positions in rapidly growing markets or, possibly, their market shares have become less dominant as competition has become more aggressive. The market growth means that it is likely that considerable investment will still be required and the low market share will mean that such products will have difficulty generating substantial cash. Hence, on this basis, these products are likely to be cash users.

Definition ➤
- *Dogs.* The lower-right quadrant contains the dogs: products that have low relative market shares in low-growth businesses. It is assumed that the products will need low investment

but that they are unlikely to be major profit earners. Hence, these two elements should balance each other and they should be cash neutral overall. In practice, they *may* actually absorb cash because of the investment required to hold their position. They are often regarded as unattractive for the long term and recommended for disposal.

Overall, the general strategy is to take cash from the *cash cows* to fund *stars* and invest in future new products that do not yet even appear on the matrix. Cash may also be invested selectively in some *problem children* to turn them into *stars*, with the others being milked or even sold to provide funds for elsewhere. Typically in many organisations, the *dogs* form the largest category and often represent the most difficult strategic decisions. Should they be sold? Could they be repositioned in a smaller market category that would allow them to dominate that category? Are they really cash neutral or possibly absorbing cash? If they are cash-absorbers, what strategies might be adopted?

Clearly the strategic questions raised by the approach have a useful function in the analysis and development of strategy. In Chapter 13, we will examine these further in the context of strategic options. Some care needs to be taken in calculating the positions of products on the matrix and Chapter 13 has a worked example to show how it can be done.

4.5.2 Difficulties with the BCG growth-share matrix

There are a number of problems associated with the matrix. The most obvious difficulty is that strategy is defined purely in terms of two simple factors and other issues are ignored. Further problems include:

- *The definition of market growth.* What is high market growth and what is low? Conventionally, this is often set above or below 5 per cent per annum, but there are no rules.

- *The definition of the market.* It is not always clear how the market should be defined. It is always possible to make a product dominate a market by defining the market narrowly enough. For example, do we consider the *entire* European steel market, where Usinor would have a small share, or do we take the *French segment* only, when the Usinor share would be much higher? This could radically alter the conclusions.

- *The definition of relative market share.* What constitutes a high relative share and a low share? Conventionally, the ratio is set at 1.5 (organisation's product to share of market leader's product) but why should this be so?

Hence, although the BCG matrix has the merit of simplicity, it has some significant weaknesses. As a result, other product portfolio approaches have been developed.

4.5.3 Other product portfolio approaches – the directional policy matrix

In order to overcome the obvious limitations of the BCG matrix, other product portfolio approaches have been developed. Essentially, rather than relying on the simplistic (but easily measurable) axes of market growth and market share, the further developments used rather more comprehensive measures of strategic success. In the case of the matrix developed by the well-known management consultants McKinsey, the two matrix axes were market attractiveness and business competitive strength.[27] In the case of strategy planners at the major oil company Royal Dutch/Shell, the matrix axes were called industry attractiveness and business competitive position:[28] Shell called its matrix development the *directional policy matrix* (DPM). Another very similar matrix was developed around the same time by the large US conglomerate General Electric, and called the *strategic business-planning grid*. Most of these matrices have much in common, so our exploration is confined to the DPM. The DPM axes are:

- *Industry attractiveness.* In addition to market growth, this axis includes market size, industry profitability, amount of competition, market concentration, seasonality, cycles of demand, industry profitability. Each of these factors is rated and then combined into a

Figure 4.4

Directional policy matrix

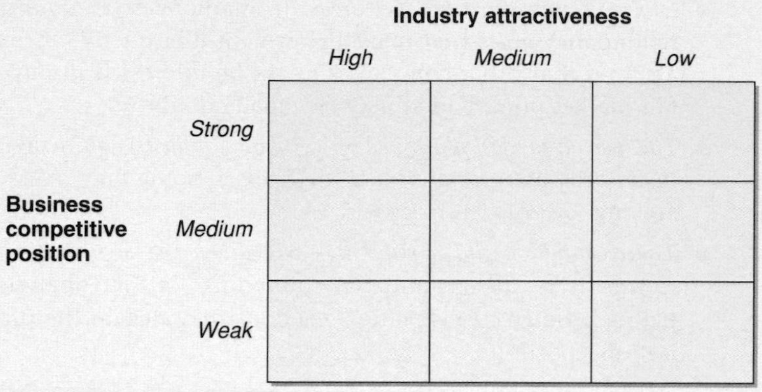

numerical index. The industry attractiveness of each part of a multiproduct business can be conveniently classified into high, medium or low.

- *Business competitive position.* In addition to market share, this axis includes the company's relative price competitiveness, its reputation, quality, geographic strengths, customer and market knowledge. Again, the factors are rated and classified into an index shown as strong, average or weak.

The complete matrix can then be plotted: *see* Figure 4.4. It will be evident that, where an organisation has a strong competitive position in an attractive industry, it should invest further. For example, Unilever has continued to invest worldwide in ice cream, with major acquisitions in the US, China and Brazil in recent years. Conversely, where a company has a weak competitive position in an industry with low attractiveness, it should strongly consider divesting itself of such a product area. For example, Unilever divested its Speciality Chemicals Division in 1997, where it was relatively weak compared with other companies and the market was subject to periodic downturns in profitability. Other positions in such matrices suggest other solutions. For example, a strong competitive position in an industry with low attractiveness might imply a strategy of cash generation, since there would be little point in investing further in such an unattractive industry but there would be important cash to be generated from such a strong competitive position. In Unilever's case, such a product group might be its oils and fats business, where it has a strong share in many countries, but the market prospects are not as attractive as in its consumer toiletries business.

All this may seem clear and highly valuable in strategy development. The first problem comes in developing the two axes: for example, exactly how do you develop an index that represents market growth, market size, industry profitability and so on? It can be done, but it is time-consuming and, partly at least, dependent on judgement. This means that it is open to management politics, influence and negotiation rather than the simple rational process of the BCG matrix. Beyond this, there are other problems associated with all product portfolio matrices – *see* Section 4.5.4.

4.5.4 Difficulties with all forms of product portfolio matrices

In spite of their advantages, all such matrices present a number of analytical problems:

- *Dubious recommendations.* Can we really afford to eliminate dogs when they may share common factory overheads with others? Are we in danger of underinvesting in valuable cash cows and diverting the funds into inherently weak problem children? Similar questions can be asked about the DPM.

- *Innovation.* Where do innovative new products fit onto the matrix? Do they have a small share of a tiny market and so deserve to be eliminated before they have even started? What meaning can be given to 'competitive position' in these circumstances?

- *Divesting unwanted product areas.* In many Western countries there may be substantial redundancy costs that make divestment unattractive. Even if there are not, divestment assumes that other companies might be interested in buying such a product range at a fair market price, which may be equally doubtful.

- *The perceived desirability of growth and industry attractiveness.* This assumption is not necessarily appropriate for all businesses. Some may make higher longer-term profits by seeking lower levels of growth.

- *The assumption that competitors will allow the organisation freedom to make its changes.* Competitors can also undertake a product portfolio analysis for both their own and competing products. Competitor reactions may negate the proposed changes in the organisation's portfolio.

Although the development of the product portfolio is useful in raising and exploring strategic issues, it is not a panacea for the development of corporate strategy. To overcome some of the issues raised above, various other formats for the product portfolio have been developed. Aaker[29] has provided a useful recent review of these. In 1977, Day[30] concluded that product portfolios were useful as a starting point in strategic analysis; such a comment still holds today.

Key strategic principles

- Portfolio analysis provides a means of analysing a company that has a range of products.

- The BCG portfolio analysis is undertaken using only two variables: relative market share and market growth. It is clearly a weakness that other variables are not included.

- The portfolio is then divided into four areas: stars, cash cows, problem children and dogs. These outline categories are then used as the basis for developing a balanced product portfolio. The technique is useful as a starting point only in the analytical process.

- Because of weaknesses in the BCG matrix, other matrices have been developed – for example, the *directional policy matrix* based on industry attractiveness and competitive position. But such dimensions remain vague and unsubstantiated.

CASE STUDY 4.3

The Galileo global satellite system – the result of European co-operation

In 1999, the 15 countries of the European Union finally agreed to co-operate in the development and launch of a new global satellite system to be called Galileo and launched in 2006. This case explores the consequences – both the threat to the existing American GPS system and the opportunity for China and other countries.

Background

Some years ago, the US government launched a global network of satellites aimed to assist navigation everywhere in the world. Essentially, the signals from the satellites allowed virtually anyone on the planet with the right equipment to obtain an accurate fix on a geographical location: the Global

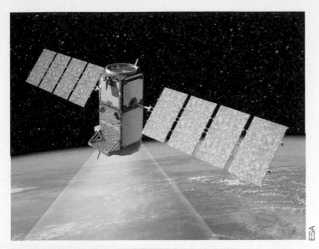

Europe's new Galileo satellite will compete directly against the American GPS satellite system.

Positioning System (GPS). In addition to its civilian use, the GPS is also used by the American military and its NATO allies for military purposes in time of conflict. There is also a Russian system, called GLONASS, that provides similar services.

There were three reasons why the European Union was not entirely happy with this arrangement:

- For some European countries, the reliance on American military technology was seen as a serious military weakness. President Chirac of France was reported as saying that Europe risked becoming a 'vassal' of the US.
- European countries realised that their national defence companies risked losing key technological knowhow and skills in satellite communications if they continued to rely on the US system and technology.
- Some European nations also identified a world commercial business opportunity to sell satellite receivers and related services. According to some estimates, there would be world market demand for around 3 billion receivers worth around US$250 billion by year 2020.

The problem for an individual European country and/or company was the heavy investment cost required to put up an alternative satellite system – around US$3.5 billion. This figure was beyond the resources of most individual European countries.

The Galileo joint venture

In 1999, the 15 countries (now 25) of the European Union agreed to the joint development of a pan-European satellite system to be called *Galileo*. The European Commission – the central administration of the EU – was granted a new frequency from the International Telecommunications Union to use with its proposed Galileo satellite system. Around the same time, each state within the EU agreed its share of the funding and design. Importantly, Galileo would use more sophisticated, new digital technology to deliver its positioning

signals. This meant that in addition to a free signal, like the American GPS system, there would also be another service called the Public Regulated Service (PRS): this latter service would *not* be free to the general public. The PRS would be encrypted so that it was available only on subscription from commercial organisations.

Galileo would also contain two other channel services: the first would only be available to Europe's military and defence establishments; the second would be used by its emergency services, such as the police and sea rescue. In summary, Galileo would be more accurate and have a wider range of services than the American GPS system as a result of using digital technology. In addition, the new European co-operative venture would make Europe independent of the American system. After the final agreement amongst European nations, experimental contracts were then prepared and a complete timetable developed for the European launch. Prototype satellites were planned for launch in 2005 and, depending on the testing, the full Galileo system would become operational in late in 2006.

Implications for the US

David Braunschwig is a senior member of the US Council of Foreign Relations: 'I believe Galileo is a place holder for European defence and security. The Galileo challenge raises the question as to whether the US will continue to enjoy its current dominance in providing the global standard for positioning, timing and navigation. That is why the Pentagon is so nervous.' Specifically, the US Government was seeking permission in 2003 to jam Galileo in the event of a major conflict. It argued that the European system was not sufficiently secure and could interfere with a planned upgrade of the American system due in 2012.

Perhaps not surprisingly, the Europeans took a different view. According to a senior EU diplomat, 'This is not about the Europeans competing as such with the US. It is about the Europeans establishing some degree of equality with the US so that we too can influence and set the international agenda.' Nevertheless, the EU has worked hard to reassure the US that its system will not interfere with the US system. The Europeans have used their technical experts to show that even though Galileo will 'overlay' the planned US expansion, the two systems can work together.

In fact, because Galileo will be more accurate than the GPS system, there is benefit in the two systems co-operating with each other. The view at the time of writing this case was that the two sides, Europe and America, would agree on co-operation.

Implications for China, India and other countries

The People's Republic of China covers a vast geographical area: parts remain underdeveloped with regard to technology and communications. In 2004, China approached the EU and suggested that it was willing to cooperate with the EU in the Galileo project, even offering US$300 million investment in the project. In January 2005, three Chinese officials were reported to be joining the Galileo joint undertaking committee that

▶ **CASE STUDY 4.3 continued**

was to manage the project. In addition, a Chinese satellite company was a small part of a consortium, led by the Franco–German company EADS, to bid for contracts for the Galileo system. The United States raised security objections to the involvement of China, but the EU explained that the agreement with China 'explicitly excluded' any confidential signals affecting Western security. The aim was to provide China with a more sophisticated system limited to civilian use. At the time of writing, the USA was still expressing reservations.

Importantly for Galileo, the EU was also pressing ahead with the involvement of other nations. In particular, negotiations were in progress with India – another country with a vast geographical territory that would benefit from a new satellite system. The EU was hoping to agree co-operation with India that might include an Indian investment of over US$400 million.

This would put India ahead of China as a key partner. Israel, Ukraine and Russia were also engaged in negotiations over possible co-operation with the Galileo project.

Case questions

1 *What are the benefits and problems of the Galileo co-operation project?*

2 *What lessons, if any, can companies and governments draw on co-operation strategy from the Galileo project?*

3 *Can you think of other examples where co-operation has proved to be a powerful strategy?*

4.6 DEVELOPING CO-OPERATION STRATEGIES

Definition ▶ Co-operation strategies involve organisations working with rivals or other related companies to the mutual benefit of both organisations. It is not essential to work with a competitor: the co-operation might be with another company offering a related product – for example, Dell Computers working with Microsoft to offer Windows software on Dell machines. A co-operation strategy is therefore a strategy in which at least two organisations work together to achieve an agreed objective.[32] Another example comes from the countries of the European Union who have agreed to co-operate with the agreed objective of launching the Galileo satellite system by 2006 – *see* Case 4.3. Recent business evidence suggests that co-operation strategy is becoming increasingly important when other forms of internal growth – such as those associated with portfolio matrices – become expensive.[33]

4.6.1 Types of co-operation

There are various forms of co-operation, amongst which are:

Definition ▶ ● *Strategic alliances*: co-operative strategies where organisations combine or share some of their resources.[34] For example, car companies like General Motors have developed purchasing alliances with Fiat and Suzuki to purchase car parts from suppliers. The benefit of such alliances is that GM, Fiat and Suzuki obtain lower prices from their suppliers than they would be able to obtain from individual negotiations.

Definition ▶ ● *Joint ventures*: co-operative strategies where two or more organisations set up a separate jointly-owned subsidiary to develop the cooperation.[35] For example, Cereal Partners has been set up as a 50/50 joint venture by Nestlé and General Mills to develop products for the worldwide breakfast cereal market – *see* Case 2.1.

Definition ▶ ● *Franchises*: co-operation strategies in which a master company (the franchisor) develops a business concept which it then shares with others (the franchisees) to their mutual benefit.[36] For example, Subway and McDonalds restaurants – *see* Cases 2.5 and 12.3.

Definition ▶ ● *Collusive alliances*: co-operative strategies in which firms seek to share information in order to reduce competition and/or raise prices. For example, the European Union has in the past investigated and heavily fined companies for colluding on price fixing in the organic peroxide market and in the PVC plastics market. Such forms of co-operation are illegal in many countries of the world because they are essentially anti-competitive. They are therefore not explored further in this chapter.

4.6.2 Benefits of co-operative strategies

In essence, co-operation strategy is used to create added value for the two or more co-operating organisations.[37] 'Value' means that the profits from the co-operation must exceed the costs involved in operating the form of co-operation. The benefits from co-operation can be generated in a number of ways, depending on the particular circumstances (sometimes called the 'strategic context') of the organisations involved and the markets in which they operate. In practice, this means that it is difficult to generalise about the specific benefits of an individual co-operative agreement. However, it is useful to identify two forms of strategic context that may influence the benefits of co-operation:[38]

- *Growth context* – where technological investment may still be heavy and risky, industry technical standards may still be under development and market opportunities still available. Benefits may include:
  - joint funding of technological investment;
  - development of industry standards;
  - access to new markets.

These three are explained in more detail below.

- *Mature context* – where competitive advantage may be more stable and cost reduction opportunities more attractive as a method of increasing profitability. Benefits may include:
  - competitive advantage;
  - cost reduction;
  - sharing of knowledge and prior investment.

These three benefits are also explained below.

Joint funding of technological investment: By combining individual resources, companies may be able to fund new research that would be beyond their available individual funds. In addition to sharing the costs, such co-operation also shares the risks and uncertainties of new technology development. For example, the Galileo satellite system described in Case 4.3 has this clear benefit to participants.

Development of industry standards: In some markets, particularly those associated with telecommunications and electronics, industry standards do not exist in the early years of development. This means that the manufacturing costs are higher because there are fewer economies of scale. For example, the early personal computers – before the IBM personal computer – were not standardised in design and therefore more expensive to produce: *see* Case 1.2. It is difficult for one company to develop an industry standard unless they dominate the industry, like IBM. An alternative strategy is therefore co-operation between companies to develop an industry standard. For example, at the time of writing, there is a major competitive battle to establish a new standard for DVD formatting for films in consumer electronics.[39] Rival companies are forming co-operative links. The benefits to the winning collaboration will come through royalty payments being paid by the losers.

Access to new markets: By combining the international resource of one competitor with the local knowledge resource of another competitor, it may be possible for the two companies to co-operate in the local market to mutual advantage.[40] In addition, such a co-operation may overcome trade barriers that would otherwise stop the international company entering the market. For example, a number of international car companies have entered the potentially large Chinese car market by setting up joint ventures with local, knowledgeable Chinese companies.

Competitive advantage: By combining resources, companies may be able to gain competitive advantages over rivals.[41] For example in the world airline market, Singapore Airlines, Lufthansa and North West have formed the Star Alliance network to be able to offer superior ticketing and air transfer services that offer superior benefits to passengers when compared to rivals.

Cost reduction: By combining resources, companies may be able to develop cost reduction opportunities jointly that would be difficult to find as separate companies.[42] For example, various purchasing companies have been set up by European Union farmers to buy agricultural supplies more cheaply than they would be able to obtain them individually.

Sharing of knowledge and prior investment: By co-operative agreements, companies may be able to achieve synergistic benefits form the cross-fertilisation of business activity.[43] For example, the franchise operation at Subway involves sharing Subway's knowledge of sandwich ingredients and preparation with its franchisees. Another example is Toyota's investment in developing its new Prius environmentally friendly car. The patents on its dual petrol-and-electric engine have been shared with rival companies like General Motors and Ford through licensing agreements, which are a form of co-operation.

4.6.3 Managing the risks of co-operative strategies

Co-operative strategies come with costs and risks that need to be managed. There are two broad approaches to this task:[44]

● *Cost minimisation* – a formal contract specifying how the co-operation is to be developed and monitored. The aim is to minimise the costs of co-operation and ensure that each partner adheres to the deal in a structured way.

● *Opportunity maximisation* – a more informal arrangement that allows the co-operators to exploit market opportunities as they are identified and also learn from each other as the co-operation progresses.

There are no clear guidelines for choosing between these two mutually exclusive approaches – they depend on the objectives of the parties involved, the nature of the opportunity and the risk-taking stance of each of the parties. Nevertheless, research has shown that there are two major factors that will determine the success or otherwise of many co-operative agreements:

● The *clarity* with which the objectives and expectations of the co-operation between the parties have been explored, agreed and understood at the outset of such an agreement.

● The *mutual trust* that has developed and persists between the co-operating parties.

Finally, it is sometimes said that, when the two parties have to resort to the detailed contract between them to resolve outstanding issues, then the co-operation agreement itself has run its course and should be terminated. In this context, it is worth noting that many co-operation agreements are fragile and need to evolve over time if they are to remain successful.[45]

Key strategic principles

● Co-operation strategies involve companies working with rivals or other related companies to the mutual benefits of both organisations.

● There are at least four types of co-operation: strategic alliances, joint ventures, franchises and collusive alliances. The last of these is illegal in most countries of the world.

● The benefits of co-operation depend on the strategic context within which the co-operation occurs. It is useful to make a distinction between growth and mature market contexts. Within growth, co-operation may deliver joint funding of projects, the establishment of industry standards and access to new markets. Within the market context, co-operation may deliver competitive advantage, cost reduction and the sharing of knowledge.

● Managing the risks of co-operative strategies involves two mutually exclusive mechanisms: cost reduction and opportunity maximisation. Cost reduction depends primarily on written contracts, careful negotiation and monitoring of developments. Opportunity maximisation is more informal, with the aim of identifying and exploiting business opportunities as they emerge. Trust is often a key factor in the success of co-operative agreements.

4.7 DISTRIBUTOR ANALYSIS

Definition ➤ An important area of strategy for many organisations is *distribution* or *channel strategy*: the strategies involved in delivering the product or service to the customer. Such strategies cover all the activities that happen beyond the factory gate, such as physical distribution, salesforce activity and customer service actions. To illustrate the strategic importance of distribution in certain markets, we have only to examine pharmaceutical industry strategy: in 1993–94, two US pharmaceutical companies spent over US$10 billion buying US drug distributors because of a fundamental reappraisal of their corporate strategies.[46] European car companies have also invested substantial sums in the distribution of their products and regard it as a vital part of overall company strategy.

With regard to distributor analysis, Lynch[47] has suggested that it is useful to distinguish between two types of customer to whom products are distributed:

1 *direct end-users* – who buy and consume the product that is purchased. They do not buy for stock and do not sell to third parties. They often buy in large quantities and usually obtain direct supplies from the manufacturer;

2 *distributors* – who buy a product for stock and then sell it to other customers. They may be agents, stockholders or other trade combinations. What distinguishes this group is that a 'sale' is not really made until they sell out their stock and reorder.

From a corporate strategy perspective, we are concerned not with the detail of such issues, but with the basic issue of how we distribute our product or service to the customer and the costs that are involved. The most striking opportunity in corporate strategy may well be to distribute the product differently. The most difficult problem in some industries has been to obtain any significant distribution for a product at all. Case study 4.4 mentions the problems that the well-resourced and skilled company, Mars, had in obtaining distribution for its highly popular ice cream products in the 1990s. Customer demand did not solve the distribution strategy problem.

Areas that the analysis will need to cover include:

- *Direct end-user or distributor objectives*. Many purchasers will be concerned not just with price but also with product quality, levels of service and technical support. At a more fundamental level, it will be important to deliver the levels of profitability or other objectives demanded by the end-user or distributor.

- *Service levels*. Important items under this heading include timetables for delivery but also levels of back-up service, order-taking policies and general after-sales service.

- *Technical and quality specifications*. For many end-users and distributors, specifications are vital. While the detail of such issues is not the subject of general strategy, the principles are important and their internal impact on the organisation will be explored further in Chapters 9 and 11. It should be noted here that international customers may well have more complex requirements than those from the home country.

- *Distributor pricing and discounts*. Competitor information is often just as important in this area as are basic data for the organisation itself.

- *Distributor support*. In many cases, the product or service has not really been 'sold' until the distributor has sold it from the warehouse, supermarket shelf or service centre. Promotional support to help the distributor may be a vital part of the organisation's strategy. In capital goods, design support, commissioning of the new machinery and continued technical advice are often required. The computer software company Microsoft recognised the importance and substantial costs of this when it launched its products Windows ME and XP in the early 2000s.

All these areas need careful analysis as part of the strategic development process. There are no strategic 'models' to consider: solid, careful study of the many complex factors and costs involved needs to be set against the sales to be gained. The main general principle to be followed is that of assessing the costs and benefits of each of the distribution options that have been identified.

Key strategic principles

● In distribution analysis, it is useful to distinguish between the use of distributors and delivery to direct end-users.

● Objectives for the two groups need to be established because they will have an important effect on the distribution that results.

● Service levels, quality, pricing and discounts and support from the distributor are all issues that then need to be investigated. There are few general models that govern these areas beyond that of an assessment of the costs and benefits that are available from the various options.

4.8 ANALYSING THE ROLE OF GOVERNMENT

At government policy level, politics and economics are inextricably linked. Corporate strategy is not concerned with forming such policies but does need to understand the implications of the decisions taken. Governments can stimulate national economies, encourage new research projects, impose new taxes and introduce many other initiatives that affect the organisation and its ability to develop corporate strategy. To analyse these influences, it is useful to identify three areas: the environment of the nation, its system of government and its policies. All these are summarised in the E–S–P paradigm – *see* Figure 4.5.

Figure 4.5

E-S-P paradigm: analysing the role of government

Components
- Human resources
- Natural resources
- Stage of economic development
- Culture and history

Environment (E): background characteristics of a country

Outcomes
- Level and structure of output: agriculture, industry, service
- Attitudes to wealth, work, etc

- Capitalist: laissez-faire
- Socialist: dirigiste
- Mixed

System (S): the country's system of government

- Structure of decision taking
- Role of free markets in allocating resources
- Desire for international commerce
- Nationalisation policy

- Macroeconomic
- Microeconomic
- Education, health, social
- FDI and competition

Policies (P): the main government policies

- Extent and type of government intervention
- Controls exerted
- Performance expected from industry

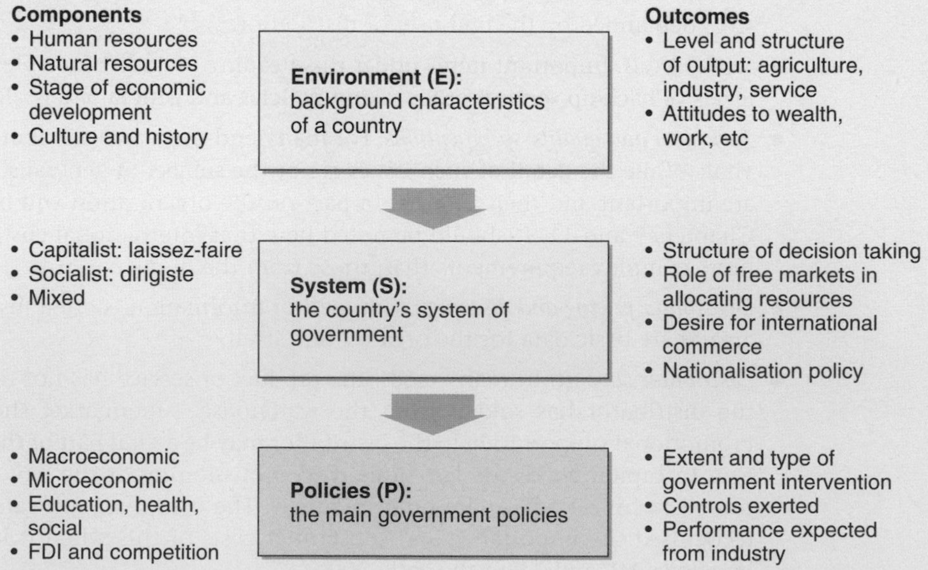

Source: Adapted from Koopman, K and Montias, J M (1971) 'On the description and comparison of economic systems', in Eckstein, A (ed) *Comparison of Economic Systems: Theoretical and Methodological Approaches*, University of California Press, Berkeley, CA. Copyright © The Regents of the University of California.

4.8.1 History and momentum in politics - the environment of the nation

Over the last four centuries, politics has been a great driver for industrial growth.[48] Much of this growth has come through a combination of wars, the search for power and the exploitation of resources. Corporate strategy will need to take into account the opportunities and the moral dilemmas that may arise. For example, the problems in China in the early 1990s did not stop major Western companies investing in that country in the years that followed; indeed, some may argue that such wealth creation is a contribution to overcoming the difficulties.

Any corporate strategy that does not take account of the history and momentum of politics is ignoring an essential element of the competitive environment. Looking back from the vantage point of the early twenty-first century, five political trends can be highlighted that are relevant to corporate strategy (*see* Exhibit 4.3).

Exhibit 4.3

Five political trends that have affected corporate strategy

1 *The decline of the centrally directed command economies of Eastern Europe and the move towards democracy and freer markets.* Even the great nation of China is now moving towards a larger element of laissez-faire, market-driven efficiency. This has provided major strategic opportunities for many companies, including those in China itself.

2 *The absence of world wars and the end of the Cold War.* This absence of global conflict has started to shift the balance away from defence industries and towards civilian activities – a development counterbalanced by the concentration of military forces and strongly held religious beliefs in the Middle East.

3 *The relative weakness of African and South/Central American economies.* This has resulted from their struggle with high inflation, weak currencies, low value-added industries and political instability. The recent changes in countries such as South Africa and Argentina hold out hope for stronger corporate strategic development opportunities in the future.

4 *The rise of international trade, global companies and new trading nations,* such as the 'Tiger' economies of South-East Asia.

5 *The emergence of supportive international finance and economic institutions,* such as the International Monetary Fund (IMF), the World Bank and European Bank for Reconstruction and Development (EBRD). Their research, guidance and influence have had a positive effect on international development.

4.8.2 The role of the state in industrial development - the system of government

In both the EU and the US, there are differing views on the extent to which the state should become involved in industrial development. In France, Italy and Greece, it has long been the tradition that state-owned companies and state intervention are important elements of the national economy. In the UK, Germany and the US, the opposing view has been taken. The approach adopted is essentially a *political* choice made by those in power. The two main

Definition ➤ approaches are often referred to as *laissez-faire* and *dirigiste*. *Laissez-faire* means a free market approach to management of the national economy. *Dirigiste* means a centrally directed state approach to the management of the national economy. Some countries offer a *balance* between the two approaches, with strong centralised support in some areas – for example, education, favoured industries (as in Singapore), investment in roads, power and water – coupled with a free-market approach in other areas – for example, privatisation of state monopolies or lower barriers to entry to encourage multinational enterprise (MNE) investment. (MNEs are the large global companies such as Ford, McDonald's and Unilever.) Each country will have its own approach so that any corporate environmental analysis will have to be conducted on a country-by-country basis.

At the beginning of the twenty-first century, it might be argued that state intervention is dead: the industrial chaos resulting from the collapse of communism in Eastern Europe certainly highlights the problems. The evidence from Eastern Europe only applies to the totalitarian state, however: it does not follow that all state intervention is useless. State involvement in the 'Tiger' economies of South-East Asia (Singapore, Malaysia, Hong Kong, Thailand, Korea) and selective intervention in Japan, the EU and the US suggest that some governmental policy can be beneficial.[49]

Corporate strategy should therefore anticipate that politics will continue to be a part of the equation. Companies may benefit from policies such as higher state subsidies, better education and international trade incentives, but may be hindered by measures such as new laws restricting competition, new taxes on profits, and limited investment in country infrastructure (e.g. roads, telecommunications).

Hence, corporate strategy needs to be acutely aware of the benefits and problems associated with government policies. It will certainly wish to press for policies that it regards as beneficial during the formation and implementation of strategic decisions. Influencing major political decisions is part of corporate strategy. As long as this is done openly and with integrity, there can be no objection by those with other interests. This means that lobbying of governments by companies, often using professional public relations advisers, is a legitimate part of corporate strategy.

4.8.3 Broader government policy and state institutions - policies of government

In addition to direct state intervention in industry, governments influence companies by a whole variety of other mechanisms:

- *Public expenditure.* In the EU, through the European Commission in Brussels, public expenditure is quite low as a percentage of GDP when compared with the expenditure concentrated at national government level. In the US, public expenditure is higher at federal (central) level in some areas, e.g. defence.

- *Competition policy.* This is strong at EU central level and likely to become stronger; it is similarly strong in the US at federal level.

- *Taxation policy.* This is weak at EU central level, with taxes largely left to individual nations; in the US, there are clear federal taxes, with further taxes raised at state level.

- *Regional policy.* There is clear EU support for weaker nations and parts of nations with infrastructure investment etc.; in the US, individual states are more likely to fulfil this role but federal support is still important in some industries.

All the above policies can have a major influence on where companies locate and whether they are profitable; in practice, organisations often make considerable efforts to obtain government grants and other forms of support as part of their corporate strategy.

At the international and global level, countries around the world have joined together in essentially politically inspired international institutions, trade agreements and trading blocks (*see* Chapter 19).

4.8.4 Strategic analysis of the national economy

Governments have some direct control over the economy of a country. It is easier for organisations to launch a growth or survival strategy when the national or international economy is showing steady growth with low inflation. Conversely, if economic decline is likely, the company might be well advised to take a more prudent view of strategic expansion. It follows that the *macroeconomic conditions* – that is, economic activity at the general level of the national or international economy – surrounding an organisation are an important element in the development of corporate strategy.

In practice, when exploring corporate strategy, many organisations, both large and small, use their own managers to make economic forecasts, buy in reputable forecasts or simply use published forecast material. The forecasts are usually made on key macroeconomic issues such as:

- gross domestic product (GDP), total and per head of the population;
- growth in GDP;
- retail and consumer price indices;
- trade flows in imports, exports and the balance of payments;
- private sector share of GDP; agricultural share of GDP;
- foreign direct investment (FDI), total and as a percentage of total investment.

Key strategic principles

- Politics has been an important driver of industrial growth. Corporate strategy needs to consider the opportunities and difficulties that derive from such policies.

- Government policies can have a general impact on corporate strategy: some countries have adopted a *laissez-faire*, free-market approach, while others have followed a *dirigiste*, more centrally directed approach to industrial development. Corporate strategy needs to be acutely aware of the benefits and problems of these areas.

- Other areas of government interest, such as public expenditure, competition policy and taxation issues, also need to be analysed. Influencing political decisions in these areas is an important part of corporate strategy.

- Macroeconomic conditions – that is, economic activity at the general level of the national economy – can have a significant impact on corporate strategy, which needs to be explored and assessed.

4.9 ANALYSING INTERNATIONAL COMPETITORS AND CO-OPERATORS

There is significant evidence that growth in world sales has considerably outstripped growth in manufacturing output over the last 20 years – *see* Chapter 19 for details. If this is the case, then it follows that international competition has increased. In addition and in order to access international markets, international co-operation has also increased, though the evidence is partly anecdotal. The key issue is whether international competitors pose similar or increased threats to those from the home country. There is good evidence that they present additional problems in at least three areas:[50]

1 *International ambitions* to deliver world sales volume will certainly pose an additional threat to domestic manufacturers. Global objectives of some companies have been well documented since the early 1980s.[51] Companies like Caterpillar (US) and Komatsu (Japan) in construction equipment, Ericsson (Sweden) in telecommunications equipment, Honda (Japan) in cars and motorcycles are all examples of companies that have taken share from domestic manufacturers.

2 *Lower costs* arise for a number of reasons. These include economies of scale from operating on a larger, international market and lower labour costs through sourcing some products in countries with this benefit.

3 *Global strategies* have been deliberately pursued in some industries to integrate world-wide strategy. Essentially, strategy is centralised for the whole world, with an integrated network of production and market positions in all the leading countries on a broadly similar platform. Not all industries are global, but those that hold this position present additional competition to domestic competitors.[52] Case 4.3 on the global satellite market is a clear example of the benefits of a global vision with regard to business activity.

International expansion and globalisation are explored in more depth in Chapter 19. As barriers to trade continue to be reduced, competition will increase. Equally, co-operation will increase in order to reduce the risks of international expansion. Because of the uncertainties surrounding the nature and pace of such change, emergent/experimental approaches to strategy development may prove particularly effective.

Key strategic principles

● International competition is increasing as a result of growth in international trade over the last 20 years: this means that corporate strategy needs to consider the opportunities and threats created by such a shift in strategic context.

● There are three special areas that require strategic analysis: the company's international vision and objectives, its lower cost opportunities and its global strategy ambitions.

CASE STUDY 4.4

Global ice cream: Nestlé goes on the attack

Unilever is the market leader in the global ice cream market. But it is under competitive attack from Nestlé along with a competitive threat from the multinational grocery chains. Will Unilever stay on top?

Global ice cream market: growing in some parts of the world

In 2005, the global market for ice cream was worth around US$60 billion at manufacturers' selling prices. There were major differences in consumption in different countries. For example, one estimate suggests that people in the US consume on average 19.8 quarts per year, Dutch people eat 7.2 quarts, Chinese only 0.9 quarts and Indians only 0.1 quarts. This is reflected in the geographical location of ice cream sales around the world – *see* Figure 4.6. Some world regions were therefore mature markets – particularly North America and Europe. It was for this reason that companies like Unilever and Nestlé were focusing their major growth strategies on developing Asian and other markets.

The global market for ice cream was growing around 3 per cent annually – an average of low growth in countries with high living standards coupled with higher growth in countries where wealth was still growing. Even up to the year 2010, the global market was still projected to grow at this level. Such growth is attractive both because the market is already large by comparison with other food markets and because such levels of

Nestlé regards its move into ice cream as a significant strategic opportunity

Figure 4.6

Location of ice cream sales 2005

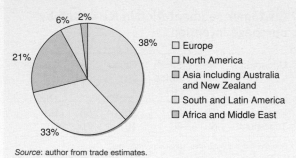

- Europe
- North America
- Asia including Australia and New Zealand
- South and Latin America
- Africa and Middle East

Source: author from trade estimates.

market growth are unusual in food. Food markets are mainly mature, with levels of growth largely in line with changes in the population. There are at least two reasons for the relatively high growth rate in ice cream:

- *increased wealth*: people consume more ice cream as their income rises;
- *increased convenience*: busier working lives and an increased desire for leisure time mean that customers like consuming products that are ready-to-eat like ice cream.

In northern countries, the cooler climates mean that ice cream consumption varies from year to year, depending on the temperature. More ice cream is consumed in hot weather. Such variations can have a significant impact on company profitability but do not deliver competitive advantage to one company, so they are not explored further in this case. However, it should be noted that some leading companies have been developing ice cream products that can be eaten throughout the year, e.g. take-home packs of dessert ice creams, so that there are opportunities regardless of the weather.

Global ice cream market: Unilever dominates but for how long?

In 2005, Unilever had around 17 per cent market share and was the largest player in this market – *see* Case 4.1. But mainly by a series of acquisitions, its main rival Nestlé was catching up and had amassed a market share of around 14 per cent – *see* Table 4.3.

The world market is highly fragmented beyond the market leaders. For example, there are over 4,000 ice cream companies in China and similar numbers in India. The many companies manufacture a wide range of products, including frozen water ice (sorbet) and frozen yogurt. There are companies with simple ingredients, production and overheads, leading to low costs and prices. There are also specialist companies with high-quality ingredients and premium prices.

Table 4.3

World market shares by value for leading companies

Company	World share (%) 2001	Strategies 2001–05	World share (%) 2005
Unilever	17	Focus on developing world brands – *see* Case 4.1	17
Nestlé	9	Acquisition and technical innovation – see text	
Dreyer – US	2	Dreyer is the market leader in US – the main source of its business: acquired by Nestlé 2002	
Häagen Dazs – US only	1	Acquired by Nestlé 2002	14
Scholler/Mövenpick	2	Major European ice cream company, previously owned by SüdZucker, a German sugar farming co-operative: acquired by Nestlé 2003	
Häagen Dazs – rest of world	1	Still controlled by General Mills (US) – came with GM acquisition of Pillsbury in 2001	1
Mars	1	Major independent family US company – see text	1
Baskin Robbins	1	Independent – US headquarters	1
Other	66	Highly fragmented – many national, regional and local brands along with supermarket own brands	62

Note: The market shares in Table 4.3 are defined by *value*: this raises the overall share of the leading global companies like Unilever and Nestlé. If the shares were defined by *volume*, they would show the 'other' category to be even higher because of the large volume of ice cream sold at low prices.

Source: author's best estimate from a variety of trade sources, not all of which are entirely consistent with each other.

► CASE STUDY 4.4 continued

Barriers to entry: branding, plant technology and retail distribution

It is not difficult to produce ice cream on a small scale: the ingredients need to be mixed and then frozen. However, there are significant barriers to entry if manufacturers are more ambitious. Some products, such as Unilever's Magnum and Nestlé's Extrême, require heavy investment in branding to become established in the market place. They also need sophisticated machinery for their manufacture. Unilever, Nestlé and Mars have all invested heavily in modern technology to produce significantly different products.

More generally, the barriers to entry are not high: smaller companies can easily develop simple mixing and freezing of ingredients. They can buy commercially available packaging and then sell their products from small kiosks. Even for the large supermarket chains such as Carrefour, Tesco and Aldi, there are plenty of national ice cream manufacturers able to manufacture and pack ice cream. For all these reasons, the 'other' category in Table 4.3 is quite high – there is plenty of fragmented competition in the ice cream market.

The differentiating feature that distinguishes ice cream from some other food markets, such as confectionery, is that it requires a special distribution infrastructure: ice cream needs low temperatures to survive. Thus a specialised distribution network involving cold stores, special vehicles and retailers with freezer cabinets is essential.

In the global ice cream market, distribution has proved the most difficult entry barrier for leading manufacturers to resolve. It is easy and cost-effective to hire vans to deliver ice cream in bulk to individual shops, but maintaining retail shop distribution is more difficult. There is no problem in larger grocery supermarkets with substantial freezer cabinet space. But smaller shops with only one small freezer can be a barrier to entry when your competitor (usually Unilever) owns the cabinet and insists that only the competitor's products are stocked. Building and maintaining distribution in such retail shops proved a strategic problem for Mars Ice Cream in the early years.

Customers and market segmentation: significant growth in the branded and luxury segments

Ice cream purchases can usefully be segmented into two areas – *impulse* and *take-home*: the former are bought for immediate consumption while the latter are usually taken home in bulk for consumption later. Impulse purchases typically take place in small shops such as beach kiosks and newsagents' stores whereas take-home products are normally bought in larger grocers and supermarkets. It would be wrong to draw a rigid distinction between the two segments: bulk packs are purchased by retailers to sell as scoops for impulse demand; impulse items such as chocolate bars are sold in multipacks and may then be consumed on impulse later at home.

In practice, detailed segment data is available for some national markets but no true global study has been published.

Table 4.4

Customer segmentation in ice cream by purchase intention

Occasion	US (%)	South Africa (%)	China (%)	UK (%)	Germany (%)
Impulse	40	80	90	30	50
Take-home	60	20	10	70	50

Source: author's estimates based on various trade articles

Best estimates from a variety of sources for some are shown in Table 4.4.

During recent years, there has been growth in ice creams using expensive ingredients, high prices and exotic flavours: some customers [but not necessarily all] have become more adventurous in taste, more wealthy and more demanding in terms of quality. There has been a new attempt to redefine customers by *price and quality*. Table 4.5 shows the main areas.

Nestlé ice cream objective: build a global business

Nestlé is one of Unilever's global rivals, but it came late to the European ice cream market: it had virtually no presence until the late 1980s. It has adopted four main growth strategies:

● the acquisition of existing national ice cream companies;
● the introduction of a heavily branded product range;
● the development of patented and proprietary products that are visibly different from rivals;
● the flexibility to develop and offer local flavour ice creams and target local ice cream price points.

Acquisition

In 1996, Nestlé had annual European ice cream sales around US$1 billion compared to its total turnover of over US$50 billion. By 2002, the company had ice cream sales of US$4.6 billion compared to a total turnover of US$60 billion. Much of this sales increase had been built from acquisitions of national companies. Between the early 1990s and the year 2000, Nestlé had acquired ice cream companies in over 30 countries. Major acquisitions then came in 2002. They were Dreyers, the US market leader, and Scholler, an important European ice cream company with involvement in a number of European markets.

Such a programme of acquisition will rest on the quality of companies that it is able to acquire. In the case of North America, it bought the market leader – Dreyers – and rolled its existing ice cream activities into Dreyers. Importantly, Nestlé allowed the Dreyers management to run Nestlé's US operations and claim that in many respects it was Dreyers that was the winner in terms of jobs, management and scope of business. The downside of this approach is that it makes the global integration of Dreyers into Nestlé more difficult over time.

Table 4.5

Customer segmentation by price and quality

Segment	Product and branding	Pricing	Market growth in around year 2000
Superpremium	High quality, exotic flavours, e.g. Häagen-Dazs Mint Chocolate Chip, Ben & Jerry's Fudge	Very high unit prices: very high value added	Up to 6% p.a. from a small market base – some countries only because of very high prices
Premium branded	Good quality ingredients with individual, well-known branded names such as Mars, Magnum and Extrême	Prices set above regular and economy categories but not as high as above: high value added	Up to 3% p.a. from a larger base than super-premium – leading brands available in many countries
Regular	Standard-quality ingredients with branding relying on manufacturer's name rather than individual product, e.g. Walls, Scholler	Standard prices: adequate value added but large-volume market	Static in developed countries from a large base – available in many countries – leading brands available in many countries
Economy	Manufactured by smaller manufacturers with standard-quality ingredients, possibly for supermarkets' own brands	Lower price, highly price-competitive: low value added but large market – perhaps high-quality ingredients	Static from a large base, particularly in some countries such as the UK – many local brands

Source: author's estimates from trade articles. The segments in Table 4.4 need to be treated with some caution since no precise information on the four market segments has been published.

Nestlé's acquisition strategy has not always been successful. In order to enter the mature UK ice cream market, Nestlé purchased the Clarkes Foods ice cream company in 1993. Clarkes traded under the brand name Lyons Maid and was the second largest ice cream manufacturer in the UK, after Unilever, with a dominant market share of around 40 per cent. By chance, Nestlé was able to buy Clarkes after the company had just invested in new production plant (and had gone bankrupt in the process). It had also purchased a useful share of the UK ice cream market: around 15 per cent of the total. Importantly for the future, Nestlé explained in 1993 that it had bought the distribution infrastructure and management expertise to build this share over the subsequent years.

In 2001, Nestlé sold its UK subsidiary, Clarkes, for US$10 million to a local UK ice cream manufacturer – Richmond Ice Cream. Nestlé commented that it had never made a profit since it bought the company: for example, it made a loss of US$18 million on sales of US$70 million in 2001. The new owner, Richmond, was a major manufacturer for the leading UK supermarket chains such as ASDA/Wal-Mart and Tesco. Richmond agreed to continue to make the Nestlé ice cream range under licence – but in this case, all Nestlé would receive from its continued UK market presence was a fee for the use of the licence.

Heavily branded product range

Like its major rival Unilever, Nestlé was determined to develop an international heavily branded range of products. It used a similar device to Unilever in that it made use of a local company name alongside the Nestlé logo. It then developed some global products – mainly the range of Extrême ice cream cones – to establish its position in individual markets. Importantly, such products were *labelled* with the national company name but were often *manufactured* at a central regional location. The purpose here was to gain economies of scale from central large-scale manufacture. Unilever also follows this strategy.

In addition to its own specialist branded range, Nestlé has also developed products under licence – such as Disney characters like Mickey Mouse – in order to appeal to specific market segments. Such a strategy reduces the profit margin because a royalty has to be paid to another company. But it does allow Nestlé to become associated with well-known characters and therefore become more established.

Patented and proprietary products

As an important part of its global strategy, Nestlé has set up two research laboratories – one in North America and the other in Europe – to develop new technologies in ice cream. They are mainly in the area of production technology – for example, introducing twists into frozen ice or biscuit layers between ice cream. The purpose is to develop a sustainable competitive advantage over rival companies with products that are both popular and unique to Nestlé. Examples include Nestlé's Maxibon ice cream biscuit sandwich and Itzakadoozie twisted fruit ice lollies. The weakness of such an ▶

▶ **CASE STUDY 4.4 continued**

approach is that it may not have the mass appeal of a basic vanilla or chocolate flavoured ice cream.

Flexibility for local flavours, costs and price points

In addition to offering the global products, Nestlé has followed the global/local strategy of allowing its individual national companies to develop local flavours for local tastes and levels of wealth. For example, Nestlé China has a product range that sells low-price ice creams starting at just 1 yuan (about 12 US cents) and flavours including red and green bean flavour ice creams especially for Shanghai. The problem faced by companies like Nestlé is that they compete – at least in part – against local companies with very low overhead costs. This is particularly important as the freezer distribution costs of ice cream make it risky to move outside certain major concentrations of population where it is economic to operate a freezer distribution network.

Nestlé strengths and weaknesses

After its acquisitions, Nestlé had become a strong player in the ice cream market. In addition, it was much stronger than the market leader, Unilever, in confectionery brands, having developed its chocolate products particularly over the last 20 years – Nestlé owns such brands as Kit Kat and Lion Bar. During the early 1990s, it then borrowed a strategy from Mars: it reformulated its confectionery brands as ice cream products and launched some as product extensions – for example, Nesquik Dairy Ice Cream and Dairy Crunch. As mentioned above, it has also licensed brands from companies like Disney and developed its own unique ice cream products, like the Extrême ice cream cones.

Importantly, Nestlé has long had a strong reputation for technical development. It has used its headquarters in Vevey, Switzerland, and two technical development units to develop a range of new technical innovations in ice cream. It has launched a series of patented ice cream products that rely on sophisticated manufacture beyond the scope of smaller, national manufacturers. To achieve economies of scale, Nestlé has chosen to limit the number of manufacturing sites around the world.

Despite these strengths, Nestlé has some major problems. The first is that it has developed its business by acquisition, with all the risks that this entails. In addition, it faces competition from local companies with much lower overheads in markets where the unit price is sometimes very low – this makes it difficult to build a profitable business. In addition, it faces competition in its more mature markets from the supermarket chains – see below.

Finally, where Nestlé has been able to acquire the market-leading company, it has developed a profitable business. But where it has only acquired a relatively small share of the market, it has struggled to achieve profitability. The reason is that the fixed costs of developing and distributing ice cream are high, meaning that high volumes are needed to achieve high profits: these are much more likely with a high market share.

Supermarkets – the new competitors

Supermarket chains – like Aldi and Tesco in much of Europe, Wal-Mart in North America and Carrefour in Europe and Asia – offer increased competition in the ice cream market through two mechanisms. First, they bargain with Nestlé and Unilever to gain good prices and promotions for their branded ice cream products. Second, they approach companies like Richmond Ice Cream in the UK to manufacture products that are very similar in quality and technology to those from Unilever and Nestlé but at much lower prices – the so-called supermarket own brands. The effect of such competitive activity is to reduce the profit margins of the major multinational ice cream manufacturers.

In the more mature markets of Europe and America, Unilever and Nestlé have therefore been forced to find alternative outlets for their products – like shopping malls, kiosks and cinemas – with all the distribution and other costs involved in such activities. In such markets, there is therefore a high fixed cost to ice cream strategy. There are also low barriers to entry for smaller companies. It is therefore advantageous to have built a high market share, like Unilever, and costly to develop market share in the early years.

Sources: See reference[1].

Case questions

1 *What are the main features of the Nestlé strategy in ice cream? How do they differ, if at all, from those of Unilever?*

2 *Why has Nestlé adopted the strategy of attempting to take a large market share? Do you think that this is viable? What alternative strategies could Nestlé have adopted? Use Section 4.3 to assist you.*

3 *What strategy lessons can we learn from a market where the barriers to entry are low and there are high fixed costs for the market leaders?*

STRATEGIC PROJECT
Branded ice cream markets

This chapter has explored the global ice cream market. You can take this further by examining the progress of Ben & Jerry's ice cream, Häagen Dazs and Mars Ice Cream. Given the strategic difficulties in operating in the global ice cream market described in the case, you could assess their chances of success. Such a project might begin by looking at the websites but it would also need to visit some individual outlets – such as supermarkets or Häagen Dazs' ice cream shops – in order to understand pricing issues, local competition, etc. Just how viable is a niche strategy in this market?

CRITICAL REFLECTION

Attack or co-operate?

Much of the strategic management literature emphasises the importance of gaining sustainable competitive advantage over other organisations. The assumption is that *competition* is vital to strategy development. However, some strategists have suggested in recent years that *co-operation* is far better as a strategy – less costly, more productive, more mutually beneficial – and the result has been a series of co-operative alliances of various kinds between organisations.

Perhaps it is better to co-operate with rivals rather than to attack them. There will be occasions when competition cannot be avoided and it is not suggested that an illegal collusion takes place. But are there strategic circumstances where co-operation is the superior strategy?

SUMMARY

- *Sustainable competitive advantage* has been placed at the centre of the development of corporate strategy. The real benefits of developing this area derive from those aspects of the organisation that cannot easily be imitated and can be sustained over time. Such advantages can take many forms: differentiation, low costs, niche marketing, high performance or technology, quality, service, vertical integration, synergy and the culture, leadership and style of the organisation.

- For some strategists, competitive advantage may also be *dynamic*. In this sense, it may be seen as constantly evolving and companies should set out to make this happen, particularly in industries that involve advanced technology. In this sense, competitive advantage is continuous and changing rather than static.

- The process for developing such dynamic competitive advantage is both built around existing strengths – *structured* – and also exploits new and exciting areas – *chaotic*. The main rule for such a process is to strike a balance between structure and chaos.

- In exploring the intensity of competition in an industry, it is useful to begin by exploring the *degree of concentration* in a market – ranging between the two extremes of perfect competition and pure monopoly. The concentration ratio itself can also be calculated – that is, the percentage of an industry turnover or value added controlled by the largest four, five or eight firms.

- Military language and concepts are often used to describe the *aggressive strategies* of competitors. The four main attack strategies are: head-on, flanking, totally new territory and guerrilla. In addition, *innovatory strategies* may be employed, especially those that rewrite the rules of the game in a market.

- *Product portfolio analysis* plots products or product groups in relation to market characteristics. The *BCG matrix* relates market growth to relative market share for the organisation's main group of products. It identifies four major categories of products: stars, cash cows, dogs and problem children. It permits some consideration of their contribution to the organisation and a comparison with competition. An alternative matrix, the *directional policy matrix*, plots industry attractiveness against industry competitive position. It attempts to overcome some of the weaknesses of the BCG matrix.

- *Co-operation strategies* involve companies working with rivals or other related companies to the mutual benefit of both organisations.

● There are at least four types of co-operation: strategic alliances, joint ventures, franchises and collusive alliances. The last of these is illegal in most countries of the world.

● The benefits of co-operation depend on the strategic context within which the co-operation occurs. It is useful to make a distinction between growth and mature market contexts. Within growth, co-operation may deliver joint funding of projects, the establishment of industry standards and access to new markets. Within the mature market context, co-operation may deliver competitive advantage, cost reduction and the sharing of knowledge.

● Managing the risks of co-operative strategies involves two mutually exclusive mechanisms: cost reduction and opportunity maximisation. Cost reduction depends primarily on written contracts, careful negotiation and monitoring of developments. Opportunity maximisation is more informal, with the aim of identifying and exploiting business opportunities as they emerge. Trust is often a key factor in the success of co-operative agreements.

● Another area of investigation is that concerning *distributors* – that is, those companies that purchase the product and then resell it to small end-consumers. In some markets, distributors are a vital part of the chain of sale and need to be analysed in detail. Service levels, quality, pricing and discounts and the support from the distributor are subjects for investigation.

● *Politics* has been an important driver of industrial growth. Corporate strategy needs to consider the opportunities and difficulties that derive from such policies. Government policies can have a general impact on corporate strategy: some countries have adopted a *laissez-faire*, free-market approach, while others have followed a *dirigiste*, more centrally directed approach to industrial development. Corporate strategy needs to be acutely aware of the benefits and problems of these areas.

● Other areas of government interest, such as public expenditure, competition policy and taxation issues, also need to be analysed. Influencing political decisions in these areas is an important part of corporate strategy. Macroeconomic conditions – that is, economic activity at the general level of the national economy – can have a significant impact on corporate strategy, which needs to be explored and assessed.

● *International competition* has increased over the last 20 years. This has taken many forms but three areas can be usefully highlighted: ambition of some companies for global expansion, low costs through careful sourcing of production, and global strategies to integrate worldwide strategy.

QUESTIONS

1 Consider the two case studies on web-based fashion (4.2) and global satellites (4.3) and identify where and how sustainable competitive advantages might be developed in each case.

2 Use the three tests for sustainable competitive advantage (SCA) in Exhibit 4.1 to analyse Nestlé ice cream and other products in the range. What are your conclusions for the Nestlé company?

3 Take an industry with which you are familiar and estimate its degree of concentration. For example,

you might pick the university and college of higher education market in a particular country. What strategic conclusions would you wish to draw from your analysis?

4 Analyse the aggressive strategies undertaken by competitors against Unilever in the European ice cream market. How would you classify their attack strategies?

5 Can you think of any examples of innovatory aggressive strategies? If you are having trouble, then you might like to skim through some of the

cases in this book to find those that fit this role. Give reasons for your selection.

6   *Military principles and strategies are not the whole answer to competitive strategy, but they do provide insight into what it takes for a company to succeed in attacking another company or in defending itself against an aggressor.* (Philip Kotler and Ravi Singh)

To what extent do you agree with this statement?

7   Choose an industry familiar to you and identify how it might use the concept of dynamic competitive advantage to develop its strategy. What are the benefits and risks of such an approach?

8   Using the procedures outlined in this chapter, prepare a competitive analysis of the European ice cream industry over the next five years from the viewpoint of Nestlé. *Or*, if you prefer, you can use a national ice cream manufacturer in your home country and consider the issues as global competition increases from Unilever and Nestlé in particular.

9   Bruce Henderson, founder of the Boston Consulting Group, commented:

Induce your competitors not to invest in those products, markets and services where you expect to invest most . . . that is the fundamental rule of strategy.

Briefly explain this statement and comment on its usefulness.

10 What general conclusions can you draw from the Unilever attack on Mars Ice Cream about the nature and importance of distributor strategy? What lessons does it imply for other companies, if any?

Further reading

Professor Porter's two books are the classic texts on competitive strategy – *Competitive Strategy* (1980) and *Competitive Advantage* (1985) – both published by The Free Press, New York. They are strongly recommended. In addition, the book by Professor David Aaker, *Strategic Market Management* (Wiley, 1992) has a well-argued exploration of the development of sustainable competitive advantage that merits careful reading.

In November 2003, the *Academy of Management Executive* ran a special issue on 'Building effective networks', Vol 17, pp6–94. It would be inappropriate to select particular papers from this strong group.

Notes and references

1   The two case studies of the global ice cream market in this chapter are based on data from published sources. These include: Unilever Annual Report and Accounts 2004, Nestlé Annual Report and Accounts 2004, General Mills Annual Report and Accounts 2004. Websites of these three companies plus individual country websites accessed from www.unilever.com. UK Monopolies and Mergers Commission (1994) *Report on the supply in the UK of ice cream for immediate consumption*, Mar, HMSO, London Cmd 2524; *European Court of First Instance Ruling* – Case T-65-98 R, Van den Bergh Foods Ltd. v Commission, Order of the President of the Court of First Instance, July 7 1998; Final ruling report in *Financial Times* on 24 October 2003, p8; *Financial Times*, 19 May 1993, p24; 17 Mar 1994 and 13 Jun 1995, p18; 23 November 1997, p10; 30 July 1998, p26; 31 July 1998, p23; 18 August 1998, p5; 15 February 1999, p6; May 1999, p9; 10 June 1999, p19; 20 July 1999, p12; 21 July 1999, p7; 24 February 2000, p3; 17 March 2000, p8; 17 August 2001, p17; 12 September 2001, p25; 18 June 2002, p30; 5 March 2003, p31; 7 March 2003, p23. *Dairy Industry International*, May 1994, p33; Aug 1994, p17 and Sep 1994, p19; *Food Manufacture*, June 1994, p24 and July 1994, p28; *Sunday Times*, 7 June 1992, pp1–8. Nestlé press release on acquisition of Dreyers – 'Strategic move to gain leadership in the US ice cream market' on the Nestlé website. http://app1chinadaily.com.cn/star 3 March 2005; www.checkout.ie/Market Profile on ice cream; Hindu Business Line – Hot battles on ice cream, 17 April 2003; *Beijing Youth Daily*, 19 March 2004; Competition Tribunal of the Republic of South Africa, Case no 61/LM/Nov01; 'Nestlé cutting back ice cream capacity,' *Quick Frozen Foods International* 1 October 2002.

2   Porter, M E (1980) *Competitive Strategy*, The Free Press, New York.

3   Porter, M E (1985) *Competitive Advantage*, The Free Press, New York.

4 High technology and services columns developed from Aaker, D (1992) *Strategic Marketing Management*, 3rd edn, Wiley, New York, p182; others from author.

5 Quoted in Aaker, D (1992) Ibid., p186.

6 For those obsessed with the generic strategies outlined in Professor Porter's two books, it should be noted that no mention has been made of a company being the lowest-cost producer. This book will argue that sustainable advantage may be achieved by having both low costs and other qualities that take the company beyond being merely the lowest-cost producer.

7 Kay, J (1993) *Foundations of Corporate Success*, Oxford University Press, Oxford, p367.

8 *See*, for example, Brown, S L and Eisenhardt, K M (1998) *Competing on the Edge*, Harvard Business School Press, Boston, MA and Hamel, G and Prahalad, C K (1994) *Competing For the Future*, Harvard Business School Press, Boston, MA.

9 Brown and Eisenhardt (1998) Op. cit.

10 Case references for Boo.com case: *Economist*, 17 March 2001, p85; *Financial Times*, 19 May 2000, p26 and website of Arthur Andersen. Also the fascinating book by Ernst Malmsten with Erik Portanger and Charles Drazin (2001) *Boo Hoo*, Random House, New York.

11 See Porter, M E (1980) Op. cit. for an extended discussion of this topic.

12 This section is based on the work of Professors Porter and Kotler (*see* refs 14 and 15) and on a lecture given by Professor Ken Simmons at the London Business School in 1988.

13 For example, *see* Ries, A and Trout, J (1986) *Marketing Warfare*, McGraw-Hill, New York.

14 Kotler, P (1994) *Marketing Management: Analysis, Planning, Implementation and Control*, 8th edn, Prentice Hall, New York.

15 Kotler, P and Singh, R (1981) 'Marketing warfare in the 1980s', *Journal of Business Strategy*, Winter, pp30–41.

16 Liddell-Hart, B H (1967) *Strategy*, Praeger, New York.

17 Kay, J (1993) Op. cit., pp236–8 provides an interesting discussion of the circumstances under which such an understanding can emerge without contravening monopoly legislation.

18 Lynch, R (1994) *European Business Strategies*, 2nd edn, Kogan Page, pp119–21 supplies some evidence here.

19 Liddell-Hart, B H (1967) Op. cit.

20 Kay, J (1994) Op. cit., p364.

21 Readers may care to note the wording used here. It is not the *absolute* market share that matters according to the BCG matrix. It is the market share relative to the market leader, i.e. relative market share is a *ratio* not an absolute percentage number. The appendix to Ch14 shows how to calculate relative market shares.

22 Buzzell, R D and Gale, B T (1987) *The PIMS Principles*, The Free Press, New York.

23 Aaker, D (1992) Op. cit., pp160–61.

24 Jacobsen, R and Aaker, D (1985) 'Is market share all that it's cracked up to be?', *Journal of Marketing*, Fall, pp11–22. A vigorous debate still continues in the academic press on the benefits of portfolio analysis. For example, a research paper from Armstong and Brodie in the *International Journal in Research in Marketing* (11(1),

Jan 1994, pp73 ff.) criticising such matrices produced a strong defence from Professor Robin Wensley in the same journal and a further reply from the two authors.

25 Aaker, D (1992) Op. cit., p176.

26 *See* McKiernan, P (1992) *Strategies for Growth*, Routledge, London. Ch1 has an excellent discussion of some of the problems that can arise.

27 Covered in many marketing strategy texts. For example, Kotler P, Armstrong G, Saunders J and Wong V, (1999), *Principles of Marketing*, 2nd European edn, Prentice Hall Europe, pp98–9.

28 Hussey, D E (1978) 'Portfolio analysis: Practical experience with the directional policy matrix', *Long Range Planning*, Aug, pp78–89.

29 Aaker, D (1992) Op. cit., p167 ff.

30 Day, G S (1977) 'Diagnosing the product portfolio', *Journal of Marketing*, April, pp29–38.

31 References for the Galileo Satellite Case: The European Union has an extensive website devoted to the basic details of the project at http://europa.eu.int/comm/ dgs/energy_transport/galileo/index_en.htm. *Financial Times*: 18 September 2003, p24; 24 January 2005, p20.

32 Barney, J B (2002) *Gaining and Sustaining Competitive Advantage*, 2nd edn, Prentice Hall, Saddle River, NJ, p339.

33 Hitt, M A, Ireland, R D, Camp, S M and Sexton, D L (2002) 'Strategic entrepreneurship: Integrating entrepreneurial and strategic management perspectives', In: Hitt, M A, Ireland, R D, Camp, S M and Sexton, D L (eds) *Strategic Entrepreneurship: Creating a New Mindset*, Blackwell, Oxford, Ch8.

34 Doz, Y L and Hamel, G (1998) *Alliance Advantage: The Art of Creating Value Through Partnering*, Harvard Business School Press, Boston, pxiii.

35 Inkpen, A C (2001) 'Strategic alliances', In: Hitt, M A, Freeman, R E and Harrison, J S (eds) *Handbook of Strategic Management*, Oxford University Press, Oxford.

36 Shane, S A (1996) 'Hybrid organizational arrangements and their implications for firm growth and survival: A study of new franchisers', *Academy of Management Journal*, Vol 39, pp216–34.

37 Inkpen, A C (2001) Op. cit.

38 Williams, J R (1998) *Renewable Advantage: Crafting Strategy Through Economic Time*, Free Press, NY.

39 Morrison, S (2005) 'Apple endorses Sony's Blu-Ray', *Financial Times*, 11 March, p27.

40 Lord, M D and Ranft, A L (2000) 'Organizational learning about new international markets: Exploring the internal transfer of local market knowledge', *Journal of International Business Studies*, Vol 31, pp573–89.

41 Harrison, J S, Hitt, M A, Hoskisson, R E and Ireland, R D (2001) 'Resource complementarity in business combinations: Extending the logic to organizational alliances', *Journal of Management*, Vol 27, pp679–99.

42 Dyer, J H (1997) 'Effective interfirm collaboration: How firms minimize transaction costs and maximize transaction value', *Strategic Management Journal*, Vol 18, pp535–56.

43 Doz, Y and Hamel, G (1998) Op. cit.

44 Dyer, J H (1997) Op. cit.

45 Inkpen, A C (2001) Op. cit.

46 Green, D (1995) 'Takeover fever', *Financial Times*, 22 Aug, p12.

47 Lynch, R (1994) Op. cit., Ch22.

48 Kennedy, P (1990) *The Rise and Fall of the Great Powers*, Fontana Press, London, pxvii.

49 World Bank (1994) *World Development Report 1994*, Oxford University Press, New York. Ch2 certainly supported selective state support and policies.

50 Dunning, J H (1993) *Multinational Enterprises and the Global Economy*, Addison Wesley, Wokingham.

51 Hout, T, Porter, M E and Rudden, E (1982) 'How global companies win out', *Harvard Business Review*, Sep–Oct, p98.

52 Porter, M E (ed) (1986) *Competition in Global Industries*, Harvard Business School Press, MA, Chs3, 4.

Chapter 5

DEVELOPING CUSTOMER-DRIVEN STRATEGY

Learning outcomes

When you have worked through this chapter, you will be able to:

- outline the main elements of customer-driven strategy and explain its importance;
- identify the relationship between customer profiling and sustainable competitive advantage;
- analyse the strategy implications of market segments;
- position the product or service against competitors;
- explain the strategy implications of branding and reputation;
- outline customer communication and its strategic implications;
- explain the main elements of pricing strategy;
- identify the main international issues in customer strategy.

INTRODUCTION

Customers are a vital part of corporate strategy development. Ultimately, customers provide either the revenue to generate the wealth of the organisation or the reason for the existence of a public service or charity. Moreover, part of the corporate strategy process will be to persuade customers of the competitive advantages of choosing the organisation's products or

Figure 5.1

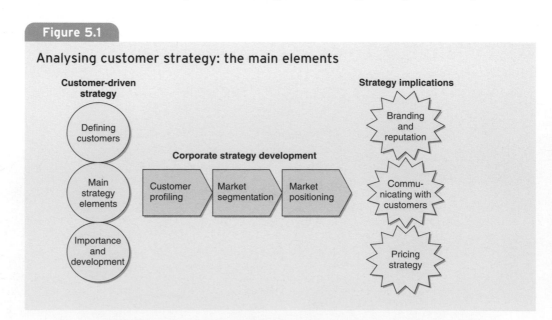

Analysing customer strategy: the main elements

services rather than those offered by a rival. For these two reasons, strategy analysis needs to explore its customers with the aim of developing customer-driven strategies.

This chapter considers the process of analysing customers as a part of strategy development. It begins by exploring why strategy should be driven by customers. Customer profiling is then explored in greater depth than the outline in Chapter 3. Market segmentation and competitive positioning are then analysed. The implications for the organisation in several key strategy areas are then investigated: branding and reputation, customer communications and pricing. Finally, the globalisation of markets from a customer perspective is examined. The main process of customer analysis is outlined in Figure 5.1.

CASE STUDY 5.1

Will Dyson remain successful?

By careful customer targeting, James Dyson was highly successful with a new domestic vacuum cleaner in the 1990s. However, his patents expired in 2002. Around the same time, he launched a new double-drum washing machine with the same premium-price customer strategy. Would the company be able to maintain its success?

Following his remarkable success worldwide with the revolutionary Dual Cyclone vacuum cleaner in the 1990s, James Dyson launched his company's Contrarotator washing machine in November 2000. The business strategy for the new machine was similar to that of his vacuum cleaner: high performance, premium-priced and aimed at the top market segment. However, it was unclear whether this strategy would be equally successful. In addition, the floor cleaner faced a new and major competitive threat from existing manufacturers in 2002 as a result of the expiry of patents on the bagless machine.

It would take a strong strategy and considerable determination for Dyson to hold its hard-won success. This case describes the company, its strategy in the European vacuum cleaner market and then its new strategy in the European washing machine market. In the face of these new competitive pressures, it raises the question of what strategies are needed at Dyson over the next ten years.

When the Dyson patent expired in 2002, it lost one of its main areas of competitive advantage.

Dyson Ltd

James Dyson and his company

Dyson's background
James Dyson is the founding owner and chief executive of Dyson Appliances Limited – a company based in the Wiltshire countryside in the West of England – with annual sales at over US$500 million in 2003. It is his leadership, design skills, persistence and imagination that have enabled his company to win against some of the world's leading domestic appliance manufacturers like Hoover (USA), Electrolux (Sweden) and Merloni (Italy).

In 1978, James Dyson accidentally had the idea of a bagless vacuum floor cleaner while renovating his country home

in the West of England. Over the period 1979–84, he made over 5,000 prototypes before developing what he called his Dual Cyclone vacuum cleaner, for which he applied for a trade mark and many special patents.

Dyson's new vacuum cleaner
During the years 1982–84, James Dyson visited many of the existing leading manufacturers of vacuum cleaners and attempted to interest them in licensing his new invention. But he was unsuccessful with the existing manufacturers. A unique feature of his invention was that his new machine did not need to have disposable bags for collecting dust. All ▶

existing machines used paper bags that were attached to the machine and then thrown away when full. Existing machine manufacturers made substantial sales and profits on these disposable bags – over £100 million in the UK alone, according to Dyson – and were therefore reluctant to lose these sales opportunities, even though such a change might be cheaper for their customers.

Dyson's reaction to rejection by the leading manufacturers – launch his own product

James Dyson produced his first prototype vacuum floor cleaner in 1983. Unable to interest any European manufacturer, Dyson went to Japan and found an importer of Western goods that was interested in selling the product. By 1991, it had become so well established that Dyson was able to claim that it had become a status symbol amongst Japanese households.

Encouraged by its Japanese success, James Dyson then decided that he would launch his own company to make the product. He set up his own factory in the West of England and launched his first model, the DC01, in May 1993. By 1995, the machine had become the best-selling vacuum cleaner in the UK. A new improved model, the DC02, was launched in 1995 and production moved to a new, larger factory in the same area to cope with increased demand. During the same year, the company began its overseas expansion, with its own sales and service subsidiaries in Australia and France. In subsequent years, offices were set up in many other European and Asia-Pacific countries to support sales expansion, including Japan itself in 1998. In 2001, fearing that his labour costs were too high, Dyson announced that the manufacture was being transferred to Malaysia, where the cost of labour was 75 per cent of UK costs. However, the design facility, which employed some 800 people, remained in the UK.

Importantly, the new machines had two other features beyond the innovative new technology. First, Dyson used his art design skills to develop machines that were different in colour combined with the use of plastic materials. His machines were to win design awards across Europe during the 1990s and be lodged in museums as examples of attractive, modern design. Second, Dyson charged a premium price for his product. For example in the UK, premium-performance vacuum cleaners were priced at the time of the Dyson launch at up to £150 each. Cheaper machines were priced at between £50 and £100. Dyson priced the DC01 at £200 and did not hesitate to price higher as he added more features with later models.

As a direct result of the move to Malaysia, profits at Dyson were reported to have doubled in 2003 to US$80 million compared to the previous year. But the company was beginning to lose market share in its traditional markets as a result of increased competition with Dyson's loss of its 'bagless' patent in 2002.

European vacuum cleaner markets – fiercely competitive

Market size, growth and share

The total European market for vacuum cleaners was worth around US$4 billion in 2003 and was growing at around 2–3 per cent per annum. Market trends reflect the fact that most vacuum cleaners were bought to satisfy replacement customer demand.

By 1999, Dyson claimed to be market leader in the UK, with a share by value of 52 per cent and by volume of 33 per cent. However, this was reported to have dropped to around 38 per cent by value and 20 per cent by volume in 2003 as competition increased. The company also claimed to be market leader across continental Europe, with a market share of around 20 per cent by value, reflecting in part at least its later launch into such countries. For example, it was only in January 1998 that the company set up a sales and service office in Germany.

Competition across the EU was fierce. The main competitors were Electrolux (headquartered in Sweden but with manufacturing across the EU), with around 20 per cent of the EU market by value; Hoover (owned in Europe by the Italian company Candy) with around 15 per cent of the EU market, and Miele (Germany) with around 7 per cent of the EU market.

Competition – strategies to counter the end of patent protection

Although James Dyson had originally attempted to license his product through one of the existing manufacturers, they had rejected his approaches. They were later to regret that decision, given the threat that they faced from the new Dual Cyclone. Once Dyson had become established, its patents provided significant protection against competitors during the 1990s.

After seeing the value of the patents, Hoover attempted to circumvent them with the development, prototyping and launch in year 2000 of its own new machine called the Hoover Triple Vortex. After its launch, Dyson accused Hoover of infringing its patents and brought an action in the UK High Court. Dyson won the action in late 2000, with Hoover being told to withdraw its machine at least until the Dyson patent had expired in June 2001. Nevertheless, after the patents expired, a number of companies launched bagless products across Europe. Inevitably, this had an impact on Dyson's sales and market share.

In 2003, Dyson responded by undertaking a major sales drive for the Dual Cyclone bagless machine in the US. The strategy was similar to that throughout Europe – premium-priced with a strong effort to obtain retail distribution in top-quality outlets. The strategy began with a modest US$20 million advertising, relying on word-of-mouth recommendations rather than a strong media campaign. 'We spend about 10 per cent of our money on research and 1 to 2 per cent on advertising; most of our US competitors do the opposite,' explained Mr Dyson. By early 2005, Dyson was claiming to be the top-selling vacuum cleaner by value in the US in the last quarter of the year 2004. However, the US market leader – Hoover – claimed market leadership in the US by both volume and value for the whole year 2004. But Dyson had made an impact in North America.

In early 2005, Dyson then launched a totally and patented new dual-cyclone model in the UK called The Ball: this was a vacuum cleaner mounted on a large plastic ball. The benefit was that the cleaner was much more manoeuvrable than other upright cleaners. James Dyson had high hopes for his new model: 'Until now you could only push a vacuum cleaner in two directions. This one for the first time moves when you want where you want, allowing you to get into tricky corners and not bump the furniture. We hope it will make up half our UK sales within six months.'

Certainly, new Dyson models were needed. Its existing range was under increased price pressure from cheaper bag-less machines with similar performance.

European automatic washing machine markets – again fiercely competitive

Market size, growth and share
The total European market for washing machines was worth around US$5.3 billion in 1999 and was growing at around 2–3 per cent each year. By 2003, the market was worth around US$5.7 billion. Like vacuum cleaners, washing machines were mainly bought to satisfy replacement demand.

Up to November 2000, Dyson was not involved in this market. Competition across the EU was fierce. Electrolux was the market leader in many European markets, with Merloni in second place. The UK market leader was a company called GDA. This was a joint venture with US and UK parents, trading under the well-known brand names Hotpoint and Creda. The company held around 35 per cent of the UK market by both volume and value. It also made own-branded products for some electrical retailers, giving it another 4 per cent share of the market. The position of GDA was much weaker in other European countries.

Dyson launch of its new Contrarotator washing machine in November 2000
It was into this market that Dyson launched its new automatic washing machine called the *Contrarotator*. There were three distinct segments in the European automatic washing machine market:

- *Budget-priced segment* – perhaps 35 per cent of the total market by volume and 30 per cent by value.
- *Mid-priced segment* – perhaps 55 per cent of the market by volume and the same by value.
- *Upper-priced segment* – perhaps 10 per cent of the market by volume and 15 per cent by value. It was into this latter

segment that the new Dyson machine was launched in November 2000.

Dyson's Contrarotator washing machine was different in that it had two drums as compared with all other machines, which had one drum. The two drums were constructed one inside the other and rotated in opposite directions to produce a turbulent washing action: Dyson claimed that this was much more like the more efficient hand-washing action that washing machines had replaced. Like his vacuum cleaners, the new Dyson machine was manufactured in strong primary colours and was premium-priced. For example, a typical UK price for the new Dyson machine was around £950, compared with £250–£500 for conventional competitors.

Clearly, this major launch would stretch the resources of Dyson Appliances to the limit. Initially, Dyson gained good distribution for the new model in many UK domestic appliance outlets. But its superior performance was not reflected in sales. By late 2003, the market share for the Dyson Contrarotator was less than 1 per cent of the British market. It had hardly made any impact and was losing retail space in some of the main domestic appliance retailers. However, it could still be bought on the internet.

Customers for vacuum cleaners and other domestic appliances
Around 85 per cent of EU homes had vacuum cleaners, refrigerators and washing machines. Level of ownership was higher in countries with higher per capita income and a little lower in other countries. Penetration was also lower for other appliances, such as dishwashers, microwave ovens and drying machines. With such a high level of penetration, sales were high across most income groups, with perhaps some skewing in favour of those with highest incomes. For example, vacuum cleaners were owned by over 70 per cent of households, even amongst the lower-income groups. Thus sales were prompted mainly by replacement demand and, until the Dyson machine, there was little differentiation beyond branding and the need to gain and hold distribution.

Retail distribution of domestic appliances
This was highly concentrated in most EU countries, with a few leading retail shop chains accounting for most sales.

Case questions

1 *What was the Dyson strategy? What were the main reasons for his success?*

2 *Will he continue to be successful? What changes, if any, does he need to make in his strategy?*

3 *Can other entrepreneurs learn from Dyson? If so, what lessons can be drawn from his example?*

5.1 CUSTOMERS AND CUSTOMER-DRIVEN STRATEGY - THE CONTRIBUTION OF THEODORE LEVITT[2]

Customers buy the organisation's products or receive its services and in this way realise the value that the company has added to its activities. Customers are thus vital to corporate strategy development. Indeed, the well-known marketing writer and former Marketing Professor at the Harvard Business School, Theodore Levitt, is on record as saying that: 'The purpose of an enterprise is to create and keep a customer.'

Definition ➤ If this is correct, then the prime focus of strategy becomes the development and retention of customers. In such a *customer-driven* strategy every function of an organisation is directed towards customer satisfaction. Levitt wrote clearly and with vision on the topic in the early 1960s and was instrumental in raising the profile of customers in the development of corporate strategy. He would have been delighted by the fact that Dyson chose to deliver a bagless cleaner that provided a new customer benefit.

Neverthless, Levitt accepted that, as long as customers have a choice, the development of corporate strategy will also need to consider the customer options available from competitors. Customer strategy therefore needs to be linked to competitor strategy. This is crystallised through the sustainable competitive advantages possessed by an organisation. Such advantages will attract customers and keep them, rather than allow them to move to competitors – the customer-driven strategy is designed to build such loyalty and customer satisfaction.[3]

5.1.1 Defining customers and competitors

The first task is to identify who the customers are now and who they might potentially be in the future. This might seem to be abundantly clear to many corporations, but nothing is ever obvious in corporate strategy. It was Levitt who pointed out in the 1960s that some large North American companies had made major strategic mistakes by incorrect identification of customers. If customers are not correctly identified, then it is quite possible that companies who are competing for the same customers will be left out of competitive analysis.

In identifying customers, a *broad view* of who they are should be taken initially in corporate strategy. Once this has been considered, a *narrower* view can then be adopted. Levitt[4] gave the example of the US railway industry, which identified its market during the 1950s as being that for *railway transport*. As a result, each company in the industry saw its environment as being largely a matter of competition between the railway companies. This was just around the time when the vast geographical distances in North America, coupled with the increasing cheapness and reliability of air transport, were allowing the new airlines to grow rapidly *at the expense of rail*. The corporate strategies of the railways were directed primarily at each other and ignored the threat of air travel. Levitt argued that the railway companies were not customer-oriented.

The importance of defining customers accurately lies in developing strategies that target them correctly and in ensuring that competitors have been properly identified. Ultimately, if the market environment is incorrectly defined, then competitors may creep up and steal customers without the company realising it until it is too late. However, there is a major difficulty with Levitt's approach. It may be unrealistically broad in its definition of customers. For example, while it is true that railways compete with airlines, buses and cars, it is unclear what practical significance this has: should railways start buying airlines? And car companies?

Professor Peter Doyle of Warwick University has proposed an alternative way of analysing customers based on three guidelines:[5]

1 *customer segmentation*: the number of segments to be served by the strategy;

2 *customer needs*: the range of needs to be met;

3 *technology*: which technologies to master in the pursuit of customers.

He argues that this will assist in narrowing down the customer definition in a way that is relevant for strategy development.

Comment

Such categorisation may prove useful in some industries, but is largely meaningless in others. The Doyle guidelines are justified with an example from the defence industry, where they work well. It is not at all clear how they might work in the aircraft industry, for example, where there is greater overlap between customer segmentation and customer needs and only one basic technology. In practice, organisations will be forced to use their judgement when identifying customers.

Hence, it is probably better, as a first step, to take a broad view of who the customers might be; this will ensure that the full range of potential competitors is identified. A narrower view might then be developed of the more immediate customers in order to establish in a manageable way the nature of the competitive advantage that the product or service has over others.

5.1.2 What are the main elements of customer-driven strategy?

As a deliberate part of their corporate strategy, some organisations have set out to become driven by the customer.[6] There are three main strands to this approach to strategy:

1 understanding the customer;

2 responsiveness by the organisation to customer needs;

3 provision of real value for money by the organisation.

The essence of such a strategy is that it goes way beyond the functional areas of the organisation that have traditionally had direct contact with the customer – that is, marketing and sales. The concept is that *everyone* – including, for example, finance and production – becomes involved. Some of the main areas are summarised in Exhibit 5.1.

Exhibit 5.1

Some examples of customer-driven strategy

Understanding the customer

● Direct customer contact at many levels

● Widely disseminated research on key customer findings, e.g. on segmentation

● Knowledge of why customers choose the organisation

Responsiveness of the organisation to customer needs

● Regularly receive and act upon customer satisfaction surveys compared with competitors

● Responsive to customer complaints and suggestions

● Track key customer data on company image compared with competition

Provision of real value for money

● Monitor quality relevant to the positioning of products in the market place

● Conduct comparative surveys of competitive prices and service offerings

● Rewards inside the organisation based on performance with customers

---

5.1.3 Why is customer-driven strategy important?[7]

Essentially, customer-driven strategy is concerned with meeting the needs of the organisation's actual and potential customers and, as a result, delivering the objectives of the organisation, such as profit or service in a public service organisation. The customer-driven concept argues that only by attracting and retaining customers will long-term profits be obtained. To quote Professor Doyle, 'Profit, growth and stability all depend upon management's ability to orientate the organisation to meeting the needs of customers . . . If a company does not attract and retain customers, it will not have a profitable business for long.'[8]

This view of the organisation is important because it suggests that simple financial measures of profitability will not be enough to ensure the growth and survival of a business: they need to be linked to customer satisfaction and customer loyalty. There is substantial empirical evidence to support this view:

● *Loyal customers are more profitable*: they tend to account for the majority of the sales of most organisations and their loyalty means that they are less sensitive to price increases and may even encourage new customers.

● *Attracting new customers costs organisations more than retaining loyal customers*: the extra cost may be three to five times as much.

● *Retaining existing customers can dramatically increase profits*: some 10 per cent of customers will leave an organisation every year. However, according to one study, increasing customer retention by 5 per cent produced an 85 per cent increase in profits.

Customer-driven strategy can therefore be expected to enhance company profitability and increase customer satisfaction; the latter advantage may be particularly important in public service organisations and is therefore a vital component of strategy.

5.1.4 How can customer-driven strategy be developed and improved?

Both emergent and prescriptive approaches are usually employed in the development and improvement of customer strategy.

An *emergent strategy* approach may be needed in the context of unmet customer needs or more general marketing research in difficult areas. It may also be required to ensure that customer service and quality are *continually* improved. It is likely to employ the innovative conceptual approaches explored in Chapter 11.

A *prescriptive approach* will be required in other contexts, especially where the customer is concerned. If the customer is to be assured of value for money, then it will be necessary to have a clear understanding of the product or service being sold at the price quoted: there can be no sense of trial and error. All this demands the greater clarity and precision of the prescriptive approach.

Key strategic principles

● Customers are vital to corporate strategy development. Demand needs to be estimated where possible. A broad view of likely levels of demand may be essential in order to identify possible competitors. However, a narrower definition will lead to identification of the attributes of the product or service that will persuade customers to choose a specific company rather than a rival.

● Some companies have set up customer-driven organisations as a deliberate part of strategy. This is a long-term task rather than a matter of short-term exhortation.

● Customer-driven strategy is important because it delivers the objectives of the organisation and helps increase customer loyalty.

● Both emergent and prescriptive approaches are needed in customer analysis and strategy development.

5.2 CUSTOMER PROFILING AND SUSTAINABLE COMPETITIVE ADVANTAGE

5.2.1 Importance of customer profiling

Definition ➤ To continue the strategy development process, it is essential to understand customers and their reasons for choosing particular products and services. Customer profiling describes the main characteristics of the customer and how customers make their purchasing decisions. Even those customers of public services and charities, who have no choice, may be better served by a deeper understanding of their needs. Moreover, such an analysis will explain why customers buy the products or services of the organisation rather than those of its competitors: it will help to identify the sustainable competitive advantages that the organisation possesses. This means profiling them and their purchase decisions using marketing research, as outlined in Chapter 3. In order to undertake this task, it is important to explore the customer buying decision further through customer profiling.

Customer profiles describe the main characteristics of the customers and how they make their purchase decisions. Exhibit 5.2 provides some examples of typical customer profiles using information that would normally be available in more depth from marketing research. The main features of the different categories are as follows:

Exhibit 5.2

Typical customer profiles

	Domestic consumer	Large industrial	Large private service	Not-for-profit charity	Public service	Small business	Strategic implications
Example	Unilever ice cream	Airbus aircraft	McDonald's restaurants	UNICEF	Health service hospital	Hairdresser or local builder	
Nature of demand	Primary	Derived or joint	Primary	Primary	Primary	Derived or joint	
Selling message	Immediate satisfaction: status can be important	Economic and non-economic needs	Immediate service: quality is part of service	Driven by belief in charity	As private service, but tempered by public service guidelines	As large industrial, but may place greater value on personal service	Major areas of difference may require industry-level strategies
Customer needs	Customers can be grouped into those with similar needs: segmentation	Each customer different	Customers grouped as in domestic	Customers may be grouped but individual service also important	Customers may be grouped but individual service also important	Customers may be grouped but many will be different	Strategies for segments and individual buyers
Purchase motivation	Individual or family	Buy for company	Will partly be driven by location, style	Receive for others and self	Receive for others and self	Local and national service	Major areas of difference may require industry-level strategies
Product	Branding, possibly low technical content	Perhaps technically sophisticated	People providing service are part of product	People providing services are part of product	People providing service are part of product. Also technical content	Possible technical content. Also possibly high and personal service	Technical sophistication in some areas. People as part service in others

- *Domestic customers* buy products or services for themselves or their families. This is called *primary demand*, since demand does not depend on any other group. Primary demand will be influenced mainly by factors from the industry itself. The customers seek immediate satisfaction from their purchases, e.g. eating ice cream. There are a large number of customers, each of whom makes a small purchase, so their individual bargaining power is low. Groups of customers can often be distinguished by some further feature of their lifestyle or consumption, e.g. family consumption of bulk packs of ice cream, giving a family segment. Domestic customers can often be persuaded to purchase products by pricing, branded goods and advertising, and by quality and service levels; these elements often form the basis of the sustainable competitive advantage of companies.

- *Large business customers* tend to buy for more rational and economic reasons, e.g. performance measures and cost are taken into consideration in purchasing aircraft from Airbus that meet particular travel specifications and criteria. Each business customer may be different, e.g. British Airways and Lufthansa (Germany) will have different requirements. Customers may not usefully be grouped together but often have large enough individual orders to justify the individual attention that they will receive. Demand is often *derived* demand, i.e. it is dependent on the demand from another industry. For example, the demand for aircraft will be derived from the demand for air travel. Derived demand requires the analysis of factors outside the immediate industry. Sustainable competitive advantage for companies in this group is often based on price, service and quality issues.

- *Small business customers* have many of the same characteristics as their larger counterparts. However, the size of their potential orders may not justify the same level of individual attention. Sustainable competitive advantage may be based on the greater levels of service and greater flexibility that a smaller company can offer.

- *Large service customers* often sell products to domestic customers for immediate consumption. Examples of such organisations are retail banks and major hotel chains. Importantly, the *product* includes the person providing the service, the ambience of the buildings and location of the service and the process by which the service is dispensed, e.g. with a friendly smile. Sustainable competitive advantages often relate to price, quality of service and branding.

- *Public service customers* may well exhibit considerable similarities to large service customers. However, commercial considerations may be less important. Sustainable competitive advantage may be less important if the service offered is a monopoly but, increasingly, such organisations have come under pressure to provide enhanced service at lower cost.

- *Not-for-profit charity customers* will also involve service, but may be driven by a stronger sense of beliefs and the need to keep voluntary workers interested. These may guide the charity's strategies towards a more co-operative approach. Sustainable competitive advantage may be inappropriate as a concept except in terms of seeking donations, where branding, focused benefits and value for money may be important.

In considering the strategy implications of typical customer profiles, it should be noted that some areas are specific to the industry and cannot be generalised across all strategic categories. Customer profiling is clearly related to the sustainable competitive advantage of the organisation, because it helps to identify why customers choose one product or service rather than another. For example, the product performance issues of the Dyson vacuum cleaner were clearly vital to choosing that particular model – *see* Case study 5.1. In addition, there are three other areas where customer profiling will support competitive advantage:

- Customer switching costs should be clearer.
- Customer bargaining power will be clarified by such a process.
- Customer co-operation can be identified.

5.2.2 Exploring future needs and breakthrough strategies

Beyond basic customer profiling, strategy is also about identifying future opportunities. To quote Hamel and Prahalad: 'Any company that can do no more than respond to the articulated needs of existing customers will quickly become a laggard.'[9] However, in turbulent markets, the exploration of future needs may be difficult: *see* for example the difficulty in forecasting demand for the new fast-growing broadband services described in Case 20.2. In this case, strategy will follow an emergent approach and move forward step by step without overexposing the organisation's resources.

It is easier to research reactions to existing products than to elicit responses to the largely unknown. For example, realistic research with passengers on a proposed new Airbus SuperJumbo in 1996 was difficult. This was because the proposed design involved the unfamiliar and totally new concept of a double-decker aircraft – that is, one with two complete passenger decks, one over the other. Potential customers will always have difficulty getting their minds around such totally novel approaches. Yet customer profiling may be vital in the category of the *revolutionary product* that may deliver the important, new, corporate strategy breakthrough.

Unmet customer needs are difficult to research and require close co-operation between technologists and strategists. Mock-ups, structured marketing research and trial products to test reactions may be beneficial.

5.2.3 The connection between customer profiling and strategy development: the customer/competitor matrix

Because of the infinite variety of customers and competitors, it can be difficult to structure the full strategic implications of customer profiling. However, by making some simple assumptions about the types of customer and competitor, it is possible to explore the strategies that

Definition ➤ might result. This can be shown in the *customer/competitor matrix*. The customer/competitor matrix links customer needs with competitive advantage to show the likely strategies required. The purpose of such an analysis is to explore the types of strategy that emerge from customer perceptions and the difficulties of entering or staying in such an industry.

The simplifying assumptions are:

● Customers either all have the same need or all have infinitely varying needs.

● Competitors are differentiated only on the basis of two factors: different economies of scale and product differentiation.

From the areas already explored in the chapter, it will be evident that these are useful but heroic assumptions with all the strengths and weaknesses of such simplicity. The resulting matrix is shown in Figure 5.2 and combines two main elements:

1 Customer needs – providing sources of competitive advantage:

● Some customers have essentially the *same needs* as others, e.g. when purchasing commodities such as sugar, cotton or electricity. The sources of competitive advantage will therefore be limited for such products: minor variations in the price and quality of cotton, for example.

● Some customers have *infinitely varied* needs – for example, in hairdressing and strategy consulting, where no two jobs are ever exactly the same. The sources of competitive advantage here are many and varied: type of service, quality of product, length of assignment, etc.

2 Competitor strategies – based on economies of scale and differentiation:

● Some companies will have small competitive advantages because either the scale is low or there is little differentiation possible. For example, coal mining and an average country hotel represent areas where the products are easily imitated.

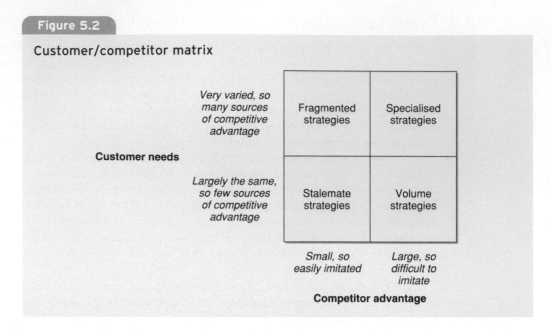

Figure 5.2

Customer/competitor matrix

Customer needs

Very varied, so many sources of competitive advantage — Fragmented strategies | Specialised strategies

Largely the same, so few sources of competitive advantage — Stalemate strategies | Volume strategies

Small, so easily imitated | Large, so difficult to imitate

Competitor advantage

- Some companies will have large competitive advantages because there are economies of scale and the product is well differentiated and difficult to imitate – for example, branded ice cream products at Unilever, and Boeing aircraft.

From the customer/competitor matrix, four types of strategic situation emerge:

1 *Fragmented strategies.* Customer needs are highly varied and provide sources of competitive advantage, but the advantages they deliver are easily imitated. Speciality retailing, hair-dressing and other small businesses are examples. Some accountancy companies fall into this category. However, the large, multinational accountancy companies have managed to break out and supply a service that relies on scale to audit their multinational clients: they fit into the specialised strategies below.

2 *Specialised strategies.* There are special or corporate skills, patents and proprietary products that are sold to many different customers who all have varied needs, often on a large scale. Examples are some of the major drug companies with varied endmarkets and strongly patented products, and international consulting companies.

3 *Volume strategies.* These are often based on economies of scale and branding but are sold to customers who basically want standard products with little individual variation. Examples include branded products and some types of basic industrial chemicals. Hospitals are increasingly offering services in this area, such as standard operations and medical checks.

4 *Stalemate strategies.* Here the products are easily imitated and most customer needs are essentially the same. The value added is therefore difficult to raise because customers can easily switch to another supplier. Examples are some staple food products and many commodities.

Key strategic principles

- Customer profiling will provide a basic understanding of the customer that is crucial to strategy development. Specifically, it will show why customers prefer one product or service to another and thus identify the sustainable competitive advantage possessed by the organisation. It may also clarify the organisation's strengths when faced with customers who wish to switch to rival products.

- Importantly, customers and their future needs may provide the breakthrough that will deliver a totally new strategic opportunity.

- The customer/competitor matrix links together two important aspects: the extent to which customers have common needs and the possibilities of achieving competitive advantage in the market place based on differentiation and economies of scale.

- The matrix identifies four main types of strategic situation: fragmented, specialised, volume and stalemate. The strategic significance of each can then be explored.

5.3 MARKET SEGMENTATION

For many markets, customer analysis needs to move beyond the consideration of basic markets to an analysis of specific parts of a market – *market segmentation* – and to the competitive stance of organisations within the segment – their *market positioning*, which is explored in the next section. Market segmentation is the identification of specific groups (or segments) of customers who respond to competitive strategies differently from other groups. The basic sequence for exploring the approach is shown in Figure 5.3. It employs a *prescriptive* approach as a first step in order to explore the elements. In practice, the sequence is likely to be more experimental and, in this sense, *emergent*, because it is often necessary to explore a number of positioning areas: this is also outlined in Figure 5.4.

Definition ➤

The three prescriptive stages are:

1 *Identify market segment(s)*. Identification of specialist needs of segments will lead to customer profiles of those in the segments.

2 *Evaluate segment(s)*. Some segments are likely to be more attractive than others. They need to be identified and targeted.

3 *Position within market segment*. Within the segment, companies will then need to develop a differential advantage over competitors.

In the development of customer strategy, customer analysis will often move rapidly to an examination of market segmentation.[10] Market segmentation may be defined as the

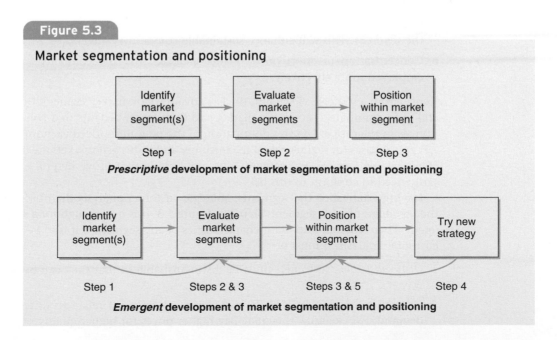

Figure 5.3

Market segmentation and positioning

Prescriptive development of market segmentation and positioning

Emergent development of market segmentation and positioning

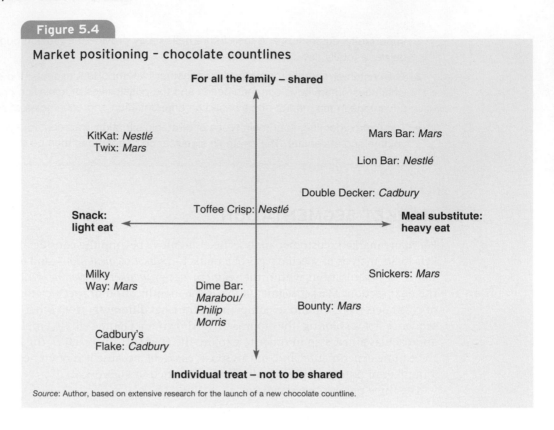

Figure 5.4

Market positioning – chocolate countlines

For all the family – shared

KitKat: *Nestlé*
Twix: *Mars*

Mars Bar: *Mars*

Lion Bar: *Nestlé*

Double Decker: *Cadbury*

Toffee Crisp: *Nestlé*

**Snack:
light eat**

**Meal substitute:
heavy eat**

Milky
Way: *Mars*

Dime Bar:
*Marabou/
Philip
Morris*

Bounty: *Mars*

Snickers: *Mars*

Cadbury's
Flake: *Cadbury*

Individual treat – not to be shared

Source: Author, based on extensive research for the launch of a new chocolate countline.

identification of specific groups (or segments) of customers who respond differently from other groups to competitive strategies. The advantages of identifying a market segment include:

● Strength in (and possibly dominance of) a group, even though the overall market is large. It may be more profitable to have a large share of a group than a small share of the main market. Thus competitive advantage may be stronger in a segment than in the broader market.

● Closer matching of customer needs and the organisation's resources through targeting the segment. This will enhance sustainable competitive advantage.

● Concentration of effort on a smaller area, so that the company's resources can be employed more effectively.

Hence, from a strategic viewpoint, the key advantage of market segmentation is probably the ability to dominate a sector of a market and then target benefits that will sustain this position, as in the case of Dyson's domination of the premium-priced vacuum cleaner segment.

Typical bases for segmentation in consumer and industrial markets are listed in Table 5.1. However, markets can be segmented by any criteria that prove helpful and do not necessarily need to conform to this list.

Having established the segments, strategic customer analysis then proceeds to evaluate the *usefulness* of each segment: Step 2 in Figure 5.3. It is not enough for a segment to be different. There are four important characteristics of any segment if it is to be useful in strategic customer analysis. It must be:

1 *Distinguishable.* Customers must be distinguishable so that they can be isolated in some way.

2 *Relevant to purchasing.* The distinguishing criteria must relate to differences in market demand. For example, they may pay higher prices for higher quality.

Table 5.1

Typical bases for market segmentation

Consumer products	Industrial products
• Geographic	• Geography
• Demographic (age, sex, education, etc.)	• End-use
• Socio-economic and income	• Customer business
• Ethnic group	• Buying situation
• Benefits sought	• Market served
• Usage rate and brand loyalty	• Value added by customer
• Attitudes	• Source of competitive advantage (price, service, etc.)
• Lifestyle	• Emphasis on R&D and innovation
• Situation (where the consumption takes place)	• Professional membership

3 *Sufficiently large.* If the segment is too small, then it will not justify the resources needed to reach it.

4 *Reachable.* It must be possible to direct the strategy to that segment.

It is also important to assess the future growth prospects of the segment. An example of market segmentation is explored in Case study 5.2.

CASE STUDY 5.2

Two methods of segmenting products in the European ice cream market

Method 1: purchase intention

European ice cream purchases can usefully be segmented into impulse and take-home: the former are bought for immediate consumption, while the latter are usually taken home in bulk for consumption later. Impulse purchases typically take place in small shops such as beach kiosks and newsagents' stores, whereas take-home products are normally bought in grocers' and supermarkets. It would be wrong to draw a rigid distinction between the two segments: bulk packs are purchased by retailers to sell as scoops for impulse demand; impulse items such as chocolate bars are sold in multipacks and may then be consumed on impulse later at home.

In practice, detailed segment data are available for some national markets but no true pan-European study has been published. Best estimates from a variety of sources for some leading European markets are shown in Table 5.2.

Interpreting the data in Table 5.2 is complex since there are several factors at work. In France, eating ice cream is sometimes regarded as a luxury and eating occasions may therefore be taken more seriously, rather than on impulse. In Italy, ice cream is also an expensive item, with many luxury ingredients, individual variants and local manufacturers, but it is bought more casually from cafés and gelaterias. In the UK, ice cream has traditionally been manufactured using lower-quality ingredients, e.g. vegetable oils in place of real cream. During the 1980s, there was substantial growth across Europe in the take-home trade of economy packs and, more recently, more expensive, higher-quality bulk packs. In Germany, ice cream has traditionally been bought on impulse, and more recently there has been substantial growth in the take-home market: in both market segments, expectations have remained high with regard to ingredients and taste.

Within each purchase intention, it is then possible to develop competitive positions for individual or groups of products. For example, the take-home product category will offer competitive positions ranging from the cheap, family category – such as supermarket own brands, to the luxury take-home products – such as Unilever's Carte d'Or. In the same way, impulse products might be positioned for children or grown-ups.

Table 5.2

Customer segmentation in ice cream by purchase intention

Occasion	France (%)	Italy (%)	UK (%)	Germany (%)
Impulse	30	40	30	50
Take-home	70	60	70	50

Source: Author's estimates based on various trade articles.

▶ CASE STUDY 5.2 continued

Method 2: price and quality

During the 1990s, Europe has seen a marked growth in ice creams using expensive ingredients, high prices and exotic flavours; some customers (but not necessarily all) have become more adventurous in taste, more wealthy and more demanding in terms of quality. There has been a new attempt to redefine customers by *price and quality*. Table 5.3 shows the main areas.

The segments in Table 5.3 need to be treated with some caution: no precise information on the four market segments has been published. The categories probably have too much overlap, with customers buying from several segments, depending on the meal occasion. In spite of the problem of accuracy, the above segments are certainly large enough to justify separate marketing and distribution activity. Many have been targeted accurately through appropriate media: for example, the use of up-market, young-profile colour magazines to reach potential Häagen-Dazs customers with a

sexually suggestive campaign, and the use of TV advertising to present the new Ice Cream Mars branded range to a wider TV audience. Thus some segments have real marketing potential in spite of difficulties in precise definition.

Case questions

1 *What other methods of segmenting the ice cream market are available?*

2 *Using the tests for segmentation, what conclusions do you draw on the usefulness of the two methods above?*

3 *If you were developing a new ice cream product, what segment would you judge to be particularly attractive for a small, new market entrant?*

Table 5.3

Customer segmentation by price and quality

Segment	Product and branding	Pricing	Market growth around year 2000
Superpremium	High-quality, exotic flavours, e.g. Häagen-Dazs Mint Chocolate Chip, Ben & Jerry's Fudge	Very high unit prices: very high value added	Up to 6% per annum from a small market base
Premium	Good-quality ingredients with individual, well-known branded names such as Mars and Magnum	Prices set above regular and economy categories but not as high as superpremium: high value added	Up to 3% per annum from a larger base than superpremium
Regular	Standard-quality ingredients with branding relying on manufacturer's name rather than individual product, e.g. Walls, Nestlé	Standard prices: adequate value added but large-volume market	Static in developed countries from a large base – available in many countries – leading brands available in many countries
Economy	Manufactured by smaller manufacturers with standard-quality ingredients, possibly for retailers' own brands	Lower price, highly price competitive: low value added but large market	Static from a large base, particularly in some countries such as the UK – many local brands

Source: Author's estimates from trade articles.

Key strategic principles

- There are three prescriptive stages in developing market segmentation and positioning: identify potential segments, evaluate and select segment(s), and position within segment(s).

- Market segmentation is the identification of specific groups of customers who respond differently from other groups to competitive strategies. They can be important in strategy development because they provide the opportunity to dominate part of the market.

- Identification of gaps in segment provision may provide the basis of new strategic opportunities.

5.4 COMPETITIVE POSITIONING[11]

Although a useful segment has been identified, this does not in itself resolve the organisation's strategy. The competitive position within the segment then needs to be explored, because only this will show how the organisation will compete within the segment.

Definition ➤ Competitive positioning is the choice of differential advantage possessed by an organisation that allows it to compete and survive in a market place or in a segment of a market place. For example, both the Mars Company (US) and Nestlé (Switzerland) compete in the market for chocolate products. However, the Mars' product Snickers is positioned as a 'meal substitute' – it can be eaten in place of a meal, whereas the Nestlé product KitKat is positioned as a 'snack' – it can be eaten as a break but is not substantial enough to be a substitute for a meal. Competitive positioning is thus the choice of differential advantage that the product or service will possess against its competitors. To develop positioning, it is useful to follow a two-stage process – first identify the segment gaps, second identify positioning within segments.

5.4.1 Identification of segmentation gaps and their competitive positioning implications

From a strategy viewpoint, the most useful strategic analysis often emerges by exploring where there are *gaps* in the segments of an industry: amongst others, Porter[12] and Ohmae[13] recommend this route. The starting point for such work is to map out the current segmentation position and then place companies and their products into the segments: it should then become clear where segments exist that are not served or are poorly served by current products. This is shown in Exhibit 5.3 using the European ice cream case as an example.

Exhibit 5.3

New or underutilised segment gaps: Unilever's presence in the European ice cream market, 1998

Market basis for possible segmentation

	Buyer type 1	Buyer type 2	Buyer type 3, etc.
Product variety 1 Product variety 2 Product variety 3, etc.			

Step 1: Existing segments with Unilever's European presence shown

	Grocery supermarkets	Small grocery stores	Restaurants and takeaways	Newsagents and leisure facilities
Superpremium Premium Regular Economy	✓ market test only ✓ ✓ ✓	 ✓ ✓ some		✓ few ✓ most

Step 2: Some possible new segments *in addition* to the above

	Garages	Temporary facilities at sporting and cultural events	Factory canteens and restaurants: contract catering
Superpremium Premium Regular Economy	 ✓	✓	 ✓ ✓

Note: For the sake of clarity, only Unilever's presence is shown in the above. Moreover, the example is *illustrative only* and may not represent the actual practice of the Unilever subsidiaries in each country. Further segmentation analyses based on criteria such as the geographical country might also produce some useful additional information.

Comment: It will be evident that there are some gaps in the existing coverage of the market. The segmentation criteria outlined in the text above could be used to assess whether it would be worthwhile filling the gaps. One obvious area where Unilever could take action was in the superpremium sector.

5.4.2 Identifying the positioning within the segment[14]

From a strategy perspective, some gaps may be more attractive than others. For example, they may have limited competition or poorly supported products. In addition, some gaps may possess a clear advantage in terms of competitive positioning. Others may not. To explore the development of positioning, we can return to our earlier example of two chocolate countlines from Nestlé and Mars. The full positioning map for the range of such products is shown in Figure 5.4.

The process of developing positioning of chocolate countlines runs as follows:

1 *Perceptual mapping*: in-depth qualitative research on actual and prospective customers on the way that they make their decisions in the market place, e.g. strong versus weak, cheap versus expensive, modern versus traditional. In the case of chocolate the dimensions of meal/snack and family/individual were established.

2 *Positioning*: brands or products are then placed on the map using the research dimensions. Figure 5.4 presents the existing configuration.

3 *Options development*: take existing and new products and use their existing strengths and weaknesses to devise possible new positions on the map. Figure 5.4 shows some gaps for some companies and some products that have an unclear position – Toffee Crisp at the time of the research.

4 *Testing*: first with simple statements with customers, then at a later stage in the market place.

It will be evident that this is essentially an emergent rather than a prescriptive process, involving experimentation with actual and potential customers.

Key strategic principles

- Competitive positioning is the choice of differential advantage that the product or service will possess against its competitors.

- The sequence for developing competitive positioning has four main steps: perceptual mapping, positioning, options development and testing. The process is essentially emergent rather than prescriptive.

5.5 STRATEGY IMPLICATIONS: ANALYSING BRANDING AND REPUTATION

Undoubtedly, customers will recognise the strength or weakness of an organisation's brands and its overall reputation: they will tend to make the customer more or less loyal. This is equally true for small companies as for large: branding may be limited, but reputation will be a key determinant of sustainable competitive advantage.

Definition ➤   It is important to draw a clear distinction between branding and reputation. *Branding is a specific name or symbol used to distinguish a seller's product or service.*[15] Its role is to allow a product or service to charge a higher price than a functionally equivalent non-branded version. In this sense, brands add value to products – for example, the higher price charged for *Magnum* ice cream over a similar product with no brand name or, more likely for a consumer product, the brand name of a supermarket such as Sainsbury or Carrefour.

Definition ➤   *Reputation is a broader concept: it is the sum of customer knowledge developed about an organisation over time. This will include branding, where relevant, but will also cover other areas:*

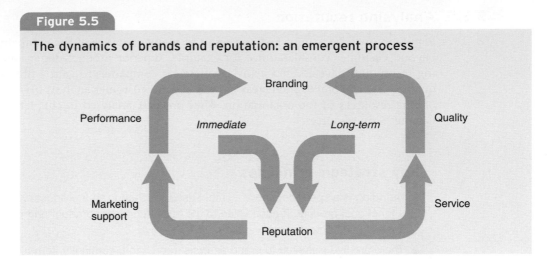

Figure 5.5

The dynamics of brands and reputation: an emergent process

- *product performance*: customers will use their experience to form judgements;
- *quality*: customers will expect certain levels, based on pricing, positioning, advertising and built-in performance levels;
- *service*: customers may be offered differing levels of delivery, installation, advice and other forms of customer experience with the organisation;
- *marketing support*: advertising, packaging, promotional activity.

Reputation may be an immediate result of some or all of these areas. In addition, the concept of time is important because reputation will also develop further over time, as well as being influenced by short-term events. The overall relationships are summarised in Figure 5.5 from an *emergent* perspective – the importance of the time relationships makes a prescriptive approach worthless. From a strategic perspective, reputation is important in delivering and maintaining sustainable competitive advantage. For example, the reputation of Boeing was dented in 1998 when it was unable to keep up with demand for its aircraft as a result of manufacturing delays at its factories; this had a clear impact in its competitive battle with Airbus. Reputation also adds value to the organisation and is therefore an important asset.

5.5.1 Analysing brands

Given the role and concept of a brand as adding value to a functional product, there are five areas that deserve analysis:[16]

1 Establish the *reputation* of a product (hence the circular nature of Figure 5.5): many have heard of the Disney name.

2 Provide *continuity* in the sense of an assurance that the product will continue to perform as it did in the past: Big Mac is the same everywhere.

3 Reflect a distinctive *formula* that is difficult for others to replicate: Sony's Trinitron television system is patented.

4 Communicate the company's position as an *established incumbent* in the market place: Intel and Microsoft signal their strengths in the computer hardware and software markets.

5 Provide a means for customers to *signal* information about themselves: Nike and Adidas fashion branding in sports shoes and clothing.

Different brands will have varying combinations of the above. From a strategic perspective, the analysis needs to concentrate on the degree of competitive advantage and added value provided by brands. It should be noted that financial measures and techniques have limited, if any, relevance here because they are unable to cope with these vital but vague concepts.

5.5.2 Analysing reputation

Reputation will be won or lost as a result of many activities of the company that go well beyond customer considerations: for example, superior product design and manufacturing techniques have assisted many Japanese car companies to gain a high reputation for quality – *see* Chapter 9. Such areas go well beyond customer analysis because they depend on the resources of the organisation. They are best analysed in this latter context – *see* Chapter 6 on resources.

Key strategic principles

- Branding is a specific name or symbol used to distinguish a product or service from a functional product. It adds value to the basic functional product and provides sustainable competitive advantage.

- There are five elements to brand analysis: reputation, continuity, formula, incumbency and information signalling.

- Reputation is a broader concept than branding. It is the sum of customer knowledge developed about an organisation over time. Reputation will include brands but may also cover other aspects such as quality and service levels. It also delivers sustainable competitive advantage and adds value to basic customer perceptions of the organisation.

5.6 STRATEGY IMPLICATIONS: COMMUNICATING WITH CUSTOMERS AND STAKEHOLDERS[17]

Organisations communicate with their customers in order to:

- inform them about their products;
- persuade them to purchase or continue buying products or services;
- establish and secure the sustainable competitive advantages of their product or service.

Definition ➤ In communicating with customers, the organisation also sends signals to the world at large: its stakeholders: the individuals and groups who have an interest in the organisation and, therefore, may wish to influence aspects of its mission, objectives and strategies. This group includes employees, shareholders, the government and many other bodies as well as customers.

Although the main emphasis of this chapter is on the customer, corporate analysis needs to consider the communications impact not only on customers but also on the *wider group of stakeholders*. This is considered separately below.

5.6.1 Cost-effectiveness in communication

In most situations, personal persuasion is the most effective method of communication because the message can be tailored to the individual customer. However, for many domestic consumer products, it is not cost-effective to call on each customer every time they fancy an ice cream. Mass marketing is required: advertising, branding and promotion.

The key criterion in measuring communication strategy proposals is *cost-effectiveness*, i.e. the cost of obtaining an effective communication with the customer, the effect usually being measured as the sale of the product or service. The difficulty is that it is usually substantially easier to estimate the *cost* of such items as operating a salesforce or telephone service team, or mounting a campaign on television or in the press, than it is to measure the *effects* on sales of such activity. For example, even if the sales go up, it is not always clear that it was the result of the specific communications activity.[18]

There are quantitative measures of the effects of such activity. They work well in some areas such as direct mail, i.e. promotions addressed and posted to individuals. However, they are incomplete in other areas, such as advertising and sponsorship, where there is often a time lag before the impact is fully realised. This means that there is an element of judgement involved in investment decisions in such areas but this does not usually inhibit strategic decisions to invest in brands, advertising and other communications areas.

Some commentators go further. Although communications are important for corporate strategy, advertising is essentially difficult to assess. As Professor John Kay says, 'This leads us to the conclusion that the effectiveness of modern advertising is fundamentally an irrational phenomenon.'[19] He then goes on to defend the role of advertising in building and supporting the *reputation* of the company, but still leaves the impression that it is essentially wayward and unquantifiable. Certainly, it is not easy to assess the effectiveness of advertising, but the empirical research evidence suggests that it can be done. Some other areas of communications *can* be assessed accurately in terms of cost-effectiveness, e.g. direct mail and personal selling.

5.6.2 Communications options available to reach customers

Within the requirement to communicate with customers, there are substantial differences of approach depending on the customer profile. These are shown in Exhibit 5.4.

Exhibit 5.4

Different customers require different types of communication

	Domestic consumer	Large industrial	Large private service	Not-for-profit charity	Public service	Small business	Strategic implications
Example	Unilever ice cream	Airbus aircraft	McDonald's restaurants	UNICEF	Health service hospital	Hairdresser or local builder	
Branding and advertising	Yes	Not usually beyond technical press	Yes	Possibly, but doubts about cost-effectiveness	Possible but unlikely	No, except local advertising	Mass market, scatter-gun effect but can be cost-effective
Personal selling	No, except to large distributors	Yes, important	Yes, in the sense of personal service	Unlikely: against the culture	Personal attention but no real selling	Important part of promotion	Targeted and personal but often expensive
Consumer promotions	Yes	Yes, possibly	Yes	Mailing letters important	Not usually	Simple cost-effective methods constantly being tried	Mass market but effect can often be carefully assessed
Technical promotions and exhibitions	No	Yes	No	No	No	Yes	Carefully targeted but some areas difficult to assess
Sponsorship, PR and other third-party events	Yes	Yes	Yes	Yes for fund raising	Possibly	Yes on small scale	One of the most difficult to assess impact, but can be vital

Essentially, from a corporate strategy perspective, the communications issues are related to the methods of persuading customers to remain with the organisation. They may include:

- *Branding*, i.e. the additional reassurance provided to the customer over the intrinsic value of the assets purchased by the customer. This can be a powerful method of retaining customer loyalty in mass market products.

- *Personal selling*, i.e. a personal relationship and individually tailored message for a single customer to purchase the product. Each selling occasion is expensive and can only be justified if the order that is placed is sufficiently large.

- *Technical promotions*, i.e. the use of the technical presentation of data on the product or service to persuade the potential customer of its merits. This may be conducted through research papers, magazines, technical advertising, exhibitions and trade conferences.

- *Consumer promotions*, i.e. devices that promote the product without building any fundamental relationship but may be effective where customer loyalty is low or a new product is being introduced.

- *Public relations and sponsorship*, i.e. the more general activities undertaken by the organisation that will have a customer and other stakeholders. These will include lobbying of governments and other public bodies, as mentioned in Chapter 4. They may also cover a broader range of corporate objectives, such as support for the community and charities, that take them beyond customer communications.

The key to distinguishing between the different communications methods is that they are likely to differ depending on the nature of the customer.

Key strategic principles

- Organisations communicate with their customers in order to inform and persuade them about the merits of their products and services. This will assist in establishing the sustainable competitive advantages of the product.

- Cost-effectiveness is the main criterion when assessing communications proposals. Costs are usually relatively easy to estimate but the effects of some promotional areas may be more difficult to assess.

- Different types of customers will need different forms of communication. Each will operate to communicate and secure the competitive advantages of the organisation.

5.7 STRATEGY IMPLICATIONS: STRATEGIC PRICING AND VALUE FOR MONEY

In the short term, pricing does not usually form the basis of sustainable competitive advantage because any price changes can be imitated very quickly by competitors. In the longer term, pricing strategy can be a major factor in competitive advantage because it will significantly alter the basis on which companies can compete. Pricing is therefore strategically important for several reasons:

- impact of price changes on profitability;

- positioning of products in the market place: the price can be used to signal more general forms of competitive advantage. There are no cheap Rolls-Royce or Porsche cars;

- value-for-money impression created about the organisation: price needs to be coupled with quality, after-sales service and other aspects of the product.

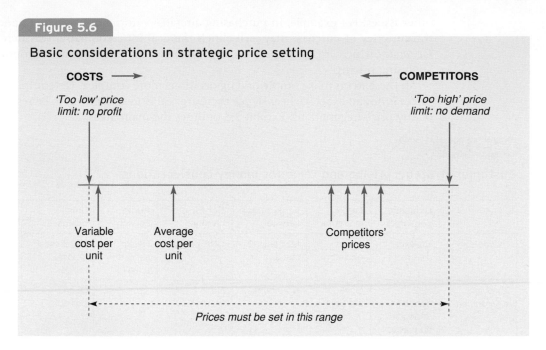

Figure 5.6

Basic considerations in strategic price setting

Prices must be set in this range

5.7.1 The pricing decision: the basic considerations

As a starting point for customer analysis, the pricing decision can be considered as a balance of two main factors:

1 *Costs*. Setting the market price below the marginal cost of production will certainly lose the company money.

2 *Competition*. Pitching the market price significantly above competition will result in minimal sales even if there is some product differentiation.

Figure 5.6 shows how these factors can be balanced out to provide some basic considerations in price setting. Beyond this basic structure, the factors that will then influence pricing include:

● price elasticity: the sensitivity of volume to changes in price;
● stage in the product life cycle: the early stages may need some special pricing strategies;
● strategic role of price.

It is this last element that will benefit particularly from further analysis. In some product categories and competitive situations, pricing forms a key part of overall company strategy. For example:

● *Price discounting* – where a company deliberately offers cut-price goods on a permanent basis, e.g. Aldi (Germany, UK and the Netherlands) and Morrisons (UK) in grocery retailing.

● *Premium pricing* – where a company sets out to price its goods at permanently high prices, e.g. Yves St Laurent, Dunhill and Gucci.

These are basic strategic decisions of the organisation that need careful analysis at an early stage. They will then form part of the *strategic options* considerations of Part 5 of this book.

5.7.2 Value for money

For many customers, other considerations beyond the quoted price also apply, such as quality, availability of stock, product performance, after-sales service, brand value and many other issues. For example, in purchasing aircraft, performance, special financing deals and the currency of purchase may well clinch the deal for a company. For such reasons, *value for money* which includes these broader elements may be a more appropriate method of analysing pricing.

All these items make simple pricing decisions more complex. Determination of costs and prices is not an exact science. Hence there are real issues that need to be resolved in advance of any price negotiations. Exhibit 5.5 outlines the main areas.

Exhibit 5.5

Customer strategy: pricing and value-for-money considerations

	Domestic consumer	Large industrial	Large private service	Not-for-profit charity	Public service	Small business	Strategic implications
Example	Unilever ice cream	Airbus aircraft	McDonald's restaurants	UNICEF	Health service hospital	Hairdresser or local builder	
Turbulent environment?	Not normally: depends on product	Quite possible	Not normally	No	No	Quite possible	When turbulent, then need for more flexibility and rapid reaction to events
Discounts and special terms?	No	Yes, many	No	Special deals being offered for annual contributions	Heavy negotiation with finance providers	Yes, many	Discounts need more initiative with individual managers, less centralised pricing
Negotiation	No	Yes	No	–	No	Yes	Bargaining power important in negotiation
Strategic role of price	Affects positioning and competition	Technical and complex negotiation	As domestic	Subscriptions used to smooth income across the year	Fixed, but financial providers may need evidence of value for money	Technical and personal negotiation	Can be complex and specific to industry

---

5.7.3 Target pricing

One major pricing technique that deserves careful analysis because of its strategic significance is *target pricing*. Target pricing sets the price for goods and services primarily on the basis of the competitive position of the company, almost regardless of the costs of producing the goods. Having established the target price, engineers, production workers, marketers, designers, suppliers and others are then given target costs that must be met so that profit targets can be achieved. This process contrasts sharply with the traditional practice of *cost-plus pricing*: all the costs are added up, a percentage profit margin is applied and the final price then determined. The two routes to pricing are shown in Figure 5.7.

Target pricing has been used for some years by Japanese car companies to achieve their profit and marketing objectives.[20] It has been highly successful but relies on close co-operation between all elements and the use of innovative ideas at the *design stage* to reduce costs. This aspect is explored further in Chapter 9. The detail of the procedures is not a matter of corporate strategy. However, the principle of target pricing is fundamental as an option for customer strategy analysis.

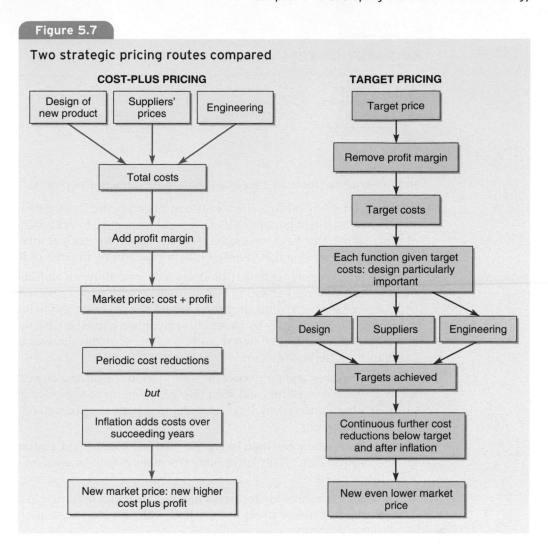

Figure 5.7

Two strategic pricing routes compared

Clearly, target pricing can put real pressure on competitors. It has actually been used by Airbus Industrie to compete against Boeing, though it is not entirely clear whether this was intentional or the only way that the company could operate. As Case study 5.3 explains, Airbus was until recently structured as a conglomerate GIE. This meant that Airbus had no production facilities of its own but used those of its shareholders: Dasa, Aerospatiale, BAe and Casa. Airbus therefore had only very limited information on its costs and simply negotiated a price with its customers. It then calculated the *target price* it was prepared to pay its shareholders for their components and told them. If the aircraft pricing fell, Airbus drove a harder bargain with its shareholder-suppliers, forcing them to cut costs if they wished to make a profit.[21] Although this changed when Airbus became a separate company in its own right in 2002, the underpinning principle of target pricing remained in Airbus's negotiations with its many outside suppliers – for example, aircraft engines from the major UK company, Rolls Royce. (This company has no connection with the car company of the same name.)

5.7.4 Pricing strategy analysis – the overall process

After analysing the various aspects of price setting, it is useful to consider the overall process; this is shown in Figure 5.8. A *prescriptive* approach is illustrated but it should be noted that a more experimental, *emergent* approach may in fact be used.

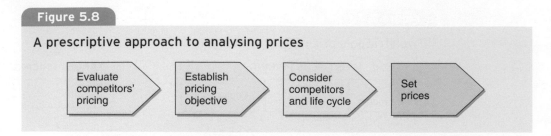

Figure 5.8

A prescriptive approach to analysing prices

Evaluate competitors' pricing → Establish pricing objective → Consider competitors and life cycle → Set prices

In price analysis, there are four main steps in the prescriptive process:

1 *Evaluate competitors' pricing.* The acquisition of competing price lists is an obvious first step. However, it is important to think beyond mere price towards customer perceptions of other factors that have influenced their buying choice, such as quality, performance, service levels. Factoring these matters into pricing will be a matter of judgement.

2 *Establish price objective.* Different products will have different objectives. These might include the following: harvesting mature products with higher prices; driving for growth by lowering prices; signalling quality by selling at a premium and maintaining the existing balance in the industry by matching competitive moves; establishing a new product at a special price. It will be important to analyse what the aim was in the specific circumstances of the organisation.

3 *Consider competitors and the product life cycle.* Within the pricing objective, it is then useful to consider competitors and their possible reactions to the pricing moves that have previously been undertaken. It is also useful to explore the position on the life cycle and its price implications.

4 *Set prices.* Price setting can then be analysed in the context of the customer and value-for-money considerations. This latter comment may include an element of service, design and other matters.

However, it should be noted that this is a highly prescriptive approach to the analytical process of pricing. It therefore needs to be treated with considerable caution because it treats price setting as a formula.

Key strategic principles

- In the short term, pricing does not usually form the basis of sustainable competitive advantage because any price changes can be imitated very quickly by competitors. In the longer term, pricing strategy can be a major factor in competitive advantage, because it will significantly alter the basis on which companies can compete.

- Pricing strategy can have strategic significance at three levels: rapid impact on profitability, positioning of the product and value for money.

- The price decision will be determined by a balance of factors under the general headings of costs and competitor analysis.

- Value for money, which includes quality, branding and other factors, represents the broader elements that will determine and condition pricing for many customers.

- It is possible to analyse prices using a four-stage process: evaluation of competitors' pricing; establishing pricing objectives; consideration of competitors and life cycle; the final process of establishing the price. However, this is a highly prescriptive approach and needs to be treated with caution because it treats price setting as a formula.

5.8 INTERNATIONAL CUSTOMER CONSIDERATIONS

Disney, Benetton, Sony, Heineken and Adidas are all examples of international brands that are instantly recognisable in many countries around the world. Products, tastes and markets are becoming increasingly international. In this sense, customer analysis also needs to become more international in its approach.

Probably the most famous article arguing for an international approach to strategy development was that of Theodore Levitt in 1983, entitled 'The globalisation of markets'.[22] He acknowledged that there were real differences in taste, culture and language around the world but argued that the pressures for globalisation would more than outweigh them. Everyone was developing global tastes: 'Cosmopolitanism is no longer the monopoly of the intellectual and leisured classes; it is becoming the established property and defining characteristic of all sectors everywhere in the world.'

To support his enthusiasm, Levitt quoted the evidence of a washing machine manufacturer who had *not* followed a global approach.[23] He also quotes some brief examples of companies that had successfully internationalised. His main arguments are summarised in Exhibit 5.6. The most significant point in developing international analysis is that it is *far more important to seek the similarities between nations* than to analyse the differences; this remains true at the beginning of the twenty-first century. Levitt also lays great emphasis on international economies of scale to deliver really low prices and thus overcome any differences in taste.

Exhibit 5.6

Levitt's main assertions about the reasons for increased internationalisation

- Price competition is important and persuasive for customers.
- It is possible to change national tastes if prices are low enough.
- Globalisation will emerge from a standardisation of products and services.
- Tariffs and quotas will not protect national industries against international attack.
- Major economies of scale are possible and will lead to increased international price competition.
- Global branding is meaningful and attractive to customers.

Comment

Levitt's article has certainly been influential. It is written in enthusiastic tones, bordering on the lyrical. However, the quality of evidence is poor, the assertions are inaccurate and the argument is open to question at several points. Several years later Douglas and Wind produced a critique that was both accurate and helpful.[24] They emphasised the importance of being sensitive to national (or local) customer variations as well as seeking the benefits of global scale outlined by Levitt. Nevertheless, the central argument that it is better to seek the similarities rather than the differences is still useful today. Chapter 19 explores these matters in more depth.

Key strategic principles

- Many business activities are becoming more international. Customer analysis from an international perspective needs to seek out the similarities rather than the differences between nations. However, it also needs to be sensitive to important national differences.
- There are numerous potential advantages from operating internationally. However, they depend on some assumptions about customers that need careful validation in reality.

Customer strategy at Airbus: competing in the SuperJumbo aircraft segment

During the late 1990s, Europe's leading company in the world civil aircraft market, Airbus Industrie, had to make an important strategic decision: whether to go ahead with a US$8 billion investment in a new SuperJumbo aircraft. The decision was made more difficult because its chief rival, the US company Boeing, had pulled out of a similar project, saying that there was insufficient demand. But, as Airbus knew only too well, customer strategy was more complex than simple estimates of market demand.

Background

In 1975, Airbus Industrie began as a special consortium called a Groupement d'Intérêt Economique (GIE). It had an advisory board and its own central management. However, it consisted essentially of the four European aircraft makers, who shared out its work and profits according to their shareholdings. The four were:

- Aerospatiale, France: 37.9 per cent share
- Dasa, Germany: 37.9 per cent share. This was part of Daimler-Benz Aerospace
- British Aerospace: 20 per cent share
- Casa, Spain: 4 per cent share.

By 2003, the company had built its share to over 50 per cent of the world civil aircraft market. Its corporate strategy had enabled four medium-sized European manufacturers to compete in the market for large civil aircraft against the US company Boeing, which had for many years been the market leader. The US company had tried to consolidate its lead in the market in 1997 when it acquired the world's third-largest civil aircraft company, McDonnell-Douglas, also located in the US. But Boeing was overtaken by the Airbus strategy of new aircraft designs, which were competitively priced and, in some cases, supported by European government grants. Boeing itself was also supported by the US government according to the European Union.

In the early years, the Airbus role was to assemble the parts supplied by its shareholders at the costs charged by the consortium members – the shareholding companies took the profits in the form of the prices they charged to Airbus. Thus

Airbus did not even know what profits were being earned by Aerospatiale, DASA, British Aerospace and Casa. Although this arrangement had been developed for good reasons, it carried real disadvantages in the 1990s. Airbus did not know whether it was being overcharged and it could not manage its inputs efficiently. In addition, it had only limited ability and possibly incentive to reduce its costs. As a result, the Airbus partners agreed to change the arrangement around the year 2001 and turn the company into a full commercial enterprise. Airbus was set up as a separate company with its French, German and Spanish parents owning the majority of the shares and with the British company, BAE as a 20 per minority shareholder. Its sustainable competitive advantages lay in its competitive prices, its reliable and modern designs and technology and its aggressive marketing team.

Competitive rivalry

From the earliest years, Airbus had been highly successful in taking sales from its great US rival, Boeing. For example, Airbus actually won roughly the same number of sales orders in 1997 as Boeing – 438 for Airbus and 432 for Boeing, according to Airbus figures. However, the US company disputed these figures, claiming that it had actually won 502 orders. Airbus then hit back by questioning the basis on which Boeing had made its estimates. Such a dispute says more about the high intensity of rivalry than about the accuracy of the detailed data. By 2005, Airbus was the undisputed market leader: it had outsold Boeing for five years out of six. It had an order backlog of 1,500 aircraft compared with only 1,097 at Boeing.

Airbus had been particularly successful with its widebodied mid-range aircraft, the A330 and the A340. Boeing had responded with its new 777 in 1994–95. But it was in the large, *long-range aircraft market segment* that Airbus was now seeking to expand. From its launch in 1974 to the present, Boeing had a monopoly of this market segment. But all this was about to change.

Aircraft market segments

Within the civil aircraft market, there were three main segments:

1 single-aisle, short/medium-range aircraft;
2 twin-aisle, short/medium-range aircraft;
3 long-range aircraft.

Major airline customers, including the large global transport carriers, are crucial to the strategy of both Airbus and Boeing

Figure 5.9

Market segmentation and co-operation in the aircraft market

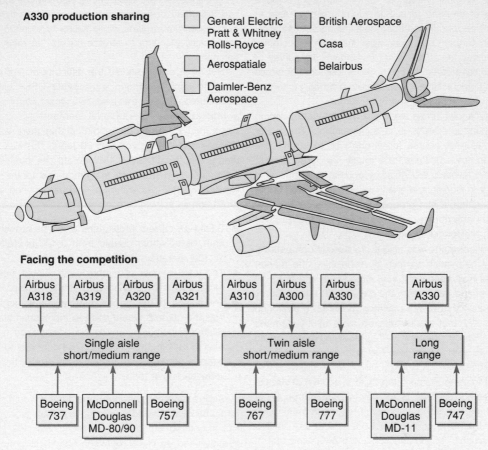

A330 production sharing

- General Electric
  Pratt & Whitney
  Rolls-Royce
- Aerospatiale
- Daimler-Benz
  Aerospace
- British Aerospace
- Casa
- Belairbus

Facing the competition

Airbus A318	Airbus A319	Airbus A320	Airbus A321
Single aisle short/medium range			
Boeing 737	McDonnell Douglas MD-80/90	Boeing 757	

Airbus A310	Airbus A300	Airbus A330
Twin aisle short/medium range		
Boeing 767	Boeing 777	

| Airbus A330 |
| Long range |
| McDonnell Douglas MD-11 | Boeing 747 |

Source: Courtesy of British Aerospace plc.

Airbus and Boeing were competing head-on in the first two sectors, but not in the long-range sector: *see* Figure 5.9. In this latter segment, Boeing had been selling for some years the 747–400 model. This was able to seat at least 400 people and was used on major intercontinental routes like London to Singapore and Los Angeles to Tokyo. The aircraft was originally designed in the 1960s as a smaller plane and then stretched. This meant that it used older technology, but the development costs of stretching this further were relatively low.

By contrast, Airbus's largest aircraft was a model called the A340–600: this was a stretched version of an earlier design and could just about carry 380 people. Its technology was newer and included 'fly-by-wire' hydraulics. But the lack of a really large aircraft put Airbus at a disadvantage in two respects:

1 For the world's leading airlines, their long-haul routes were more profitable if they were able to carry the maximum number of passengers in extra-large aircraft, like the 747–400. Airbus was not able to meet this customer demand.

2 Some airlines found it more profitable to buy from only one aircraft manufacturer. This saved on spare parts, training and servicing costs. Moreover, the company offering such a deal was also willing to offer special prices to secure a long-term contract on this basis – the so-called 'sole-supplier agreement'. But such airlines needed the supplier to be able to supply a *complete range* of aircraft, including the largest: only Boeing was able to offer this.

It was only as a result of an intervention by the European Commission in 1997 that Boeing was stopped from offering sole-supplier agreements to the world's two largest airlines, American Airlines and Delta. Airbus was given a breathing space with the A340–600, but it needed a new large aircraft – dubbed the 'SuperJumbo' – that would more than match Boeing's 747–400. The difficulty was that such a design would stretch Airbus's finances to the limit and therefore be a substantial risk. One possibility was to persuade Boeing to invest jointly with Airbus in a new large aircraft design.

▶ **CASE STUDY 5.3 continued**

SuperJumbo customer strategy at Boeing

In early 1997, Boeing announced that it had conducted a lengthy study of demand for a SuperJumbo aircraft able to carry 500–600 people. It had been considering stretching its 747–400 even further, but there was 'insufficient customer demand' to justify the US$7 billion investment. Its survey of the major airlines showed that only 480 SuperJumbos would be sold over 20 years. Boeing was therefore cancelling further development of its version of the SuperJumbo.

Even the *Financial Times* accepted this estimate, running an editorial headed 'Death of a superJumbo'. The paper argued that the best course for Airbus was to stretch the A340 and drop any ambitions for a totally new large aircraft. What the paper failed to recognise, according to Airbus, was that it was not in Boeing's interest to develop an even larger aircraft at this stage. It had production problems on its entire range and was attempting to integrate its recent acquisition of its US rival, McDonnell-Douglas.

But Boeing's strategy was also more directly competitive. The company had much to gain by rubbishing the market potential of its rival because it was already fulfilling much of the market demand, albeit with the old 747–400. In addition, Boeing also knew that it was planning to launch a stretched version of its 777 that would take up more of the demand from 2003 onwards: its new 777–300 would carry up to 479 passengers with a third less fuel and 40 per cent lower maintainance costs.

According to Jean Pierson, the chief executive of Airbus, in 1997, 'Boeing's strategy is to maintain its monopoly [of the long-haul market] without spending too much money. It's as simple as that. The strategy of Boeing is to say "this is my private garden".' M Pierson continued by saying that, if Airbus was able to prove demand for a SuperJumbo in the next few years, then he had no doubt that Boeing would change its view and rapidly develop its own version.

SuperJumbo customer strategy at Airbus

In the early 1990s, Airbus had co-operated with Boeing on a project called the 'Very Large Commercial Transport' – an attempt to develop jointly a new generation of large aircraft. But Boeing had wanted to think in terms of 600 seats, whereas Airbus wanted a 500-person aircraft. Airbus saw this different perspective as an attempt by Boeing to protect its monopoly of the 400-seat market. By setting up a lengthy project, Boeing was effectively delaying any separate market initiative by Airbus. This particular joint development failed in 1995 and Airbus was left to rethink its SuperJumbo strategy.

At the time, Airbus understood that it would cost Boeing only US$2 billion to stretch its 747–400. Over the next two years 1995–97, Boeing surveyed its customers, who said that they did not want such an old design to be stretched. Airlines wanted a totally new aircraft. The development costs of this approach were publicly estimated by Boeing at around US$7 billion. This was considered to be too high and led to Boeing's abandonment of the project in 1997, as described in the previous section. The Boeing rejection of the SuperJumbo had the effect of putting pressure on Airbus to abandon its own SuperJumbo plans, while failing to mention that Boeing was quietly planning to stretch the 777 to meet part of this demand.

But none of this solved the difficulty at Airbus in 1997 – could it justify spending a probable US$8 billion on the SuperJumbo? Over the next two years, Airbus conducted a market study of potential demand for a 550-seater SuperJumbo. The study estimated that there was a market demand for 1,442 aircraft over 20 years. This was rather larger than Boeing's estimate of 480 aircraft. The much larger Airbus estimate would make all the difference to the commercial viability of the SuperJumbo. Airbus justified its demand projection as follows:

● Based on current projections of airline growth, world aircraft fleets would double from 9,400 aircraft in 1997 to 17,100 aircraft in 2016.
● The total number of aircraft seats would increase rather more, from 1.7 million in 1997 to over 4 million in 2016.
● The reason for the proportionately greater increase in seats was that aircraft would need to increase in size. This was related to increasing government opposition in many countries to building new airports. The only way to use existing airports better was to increase the size of the aircraft that were landing at them.

Airbus accepted that the SuperJumbo would only be used on some relatively high-density, long-haul passenger routes. But it pointed out that the existing 747–400 aircraft were already used on flights between only 12 airports worldwide. Airbus concluded that there was sufficient demand to start designing a totally new SuperJumbo aircraft: 'Market studies have confirmed customer interest in a brand new advanced design, rather than a derivative of existing models.' In 2001, Airbus took the decision to commit by itself to develop the SuperJumbo. It would be called the A380 and would cost around US$10 billion to develop.

The position in 2005

By 2005, there were 149 firm orders for the Airbus A380, the SuperJumbo. The first aircraft was expected to be flying with Singapore Airlines in 2006. By 2005, the final capital cost estimate had risen to around US$18 billion, but part of this much higher figure was because of changes in currency rates between the US dollar and the Euro. In reality, there were some cost overruns but they were not impossible and the aircraft was expected to break even with sales of around 260 aircraft.

The design was complete for the world's biggest commercial airliner. There would be two full decks for passengers and a third deck for cargo, crew accommodation and perhaps entertainment. There were at least three different possible configurations of the seating with the most dense allowing the aircraft to carry 800 passengers. The experimental designs included new features like bars, casinos, and duty-free shops. The aircraft would only fly on the world's busiest routes – such as those between London and New York, Tokyo, Singapore, Dubai, Paris, Frankfurt, Los Angeles. Importantly, airline customers were attracted to its cost savings over existing aircraft. 'With operating costs 15 per cent below the B747–400, we believe the A380 [airline] operators will have an advantage on long-haul services in markets between Europe and Asia, across the Pacific and across the Atlantic.'

Boeing has responded by saying that it believes that there is insufficient demand for such a large aircraft: 'Is there any question that the A380 is a very expensive airplane for a very small market?' said Randy Baseler, Boeing's marketing vice president in early 2005. The US company has offered airlines a stretched version of its 747–400 but has received no firm orders.

Partly in response to the threat from the A380, Boeing identified a new market segment in 2004 – very long-haul medium-sized aircraft. It announced that it was developing a new model – the Boeing 7E7 – to fill this market niche. This model was subsequently renamed the Boeing 'Dreamliner' with the model number 787. In early 2005, Boeing said that it had firm orders for over 50 of this totally new design. The 787 would enter service in 2008.

Airbus was quick to respond to the new market challenge of the 787 Dreamliner. In mid-2004, Airbus announced that it was developing another new model – the A350 – which would compete directly with the new Boeing aircraft. The new Airbus A350 would enter service in 2010. More generally, Noël Forgeard, Airbus chief executive said that his company had made a 'successful metamorphosis to a world leader'. He said that Airbus was twice as profitable as Boeing's commercial aircraft division, assisted by a 'huge, relentless effort to reduce unit cost and grow our productivity: it is the reason why we can gain market share and grow profitably'.

From a customer perspective, Airbus is clearly in the ascendant at present. Tim Clark, president of *Emirates*, the Dubai airline, is one of the world's most important aircraft customers. He commented in 2005: 'Airbus has been braver, more brazen, more prepared to push the boat out. Boeing was more concerned with its shareholder returns. It lost its bravery about developing new lines.'

Case questions

1 *What reasons did Boeing give for cancelling its development of the SuperJumbo? Why were these open to another interpretation?*

2 *What strategic weaknesses did Airbus face in terms of its customer strategy?*

3 *Is the Airbus strategy driven by customers? Or rather more by a sense of rivalry with Boeing?*

4 *To what extent do you accept the Airbus demand estimates? What are the implications for customer-driven strategy?*

5 *Would you have supported the Airbus decision to proceed with the SuperJumbo?*

STRATEGIC PROJECT
The future of the SuperJumbo?

Boeing have now decided that the better strategy would be to produce smaller and more flexible aircraft than Airbus. But does this mean that they will no longer upgrade the 747–400? Does it mean that, even if the A380 is highly successful, they will ignore the large end of the market? What are the airline customers saying and doing? Have they all bought the A380? If not, why not? What do airline customers really want in this market? And what about the real pressures from rising fuel prices and 'green' environmental issues? Will they have any impact on what will happen in the future?

CRITICAL REFLECTION

Customers or competitors?

This chapter has focused on *customer-driven strategy* and related activities like positioning and pricing. But many strategists – such as those involved analysing markets (Chapters 3 and 4) and those concerned with analysing competitive resources (Chapter 6) – argue that the foundation of successful strategy development is *sustainable competitive advantage*.

In other words, such strategists put competitors *before* customers. Who is right?

SUMMARY

● Customers are a vital part of corporate strategy development. Ultimately, customers provide either the revenue to generate the wealth of the organisation or the reason for the existence of a public service or charity. Moreover, part of the corporate strategy process will be to persuade customers of the competitive advantages of choosing the organisation's products or services rather than those offered by a rival. For these two reasons, strategy analysis needs to explore its customers with the aim of developing customer-driven strategies.

● As a starting point, demand needs to be estimated where possible. A broad view of likely levels of demand may be essential in order to identify possible competitors. However, a narrower definition will lead to identification of the attributes of the product or service that will persuade customers to choose a specific company rather than a rival. Some companies have set up customer-driven organisations as a deliberate part of strategy. This is a long-term task rather than a matter of short-term exhortation.

● Customer profiling will provide a basic understanding of the customer that is crucial to strategy development. Specifically, it will show why customers prefer one product or service rather than another and thus identify the sustainable competitive advantage possessed by the organisation. It may also clarify the organisation's strengths when faced with customers who wish to switch to rival products. Importantly, customers and their future needs may provide the breakthrough that will deliver a totally new strategic opportunity.

● The customer/competitor matrix links together two important aspects: the extent to which customers have common needs and the possibilities of achieving competitive advantage in the market place based on differentiation and economies of scale. The matrix identifies four main types of strategic situation: fragmented, specialised, volume and stalemate. The strategic significance of each can then be explored.

● Market segmentation is the identification of specific groups of customers who respond differently from other groups to competitive strategies. They can be important in strategy development because they provide the opportunity to dominate part of the market.

● There are three prescriptive stages in developing market segmentation and positioning: identify potential segment(s); evaluate and select segment(s); position within segment(s). Identification of gaps in segment provision may provide the basis of new strategic opportunities.

● Competitive positioning is the choice of differential advantage that the product or service will possess against its competitors. Thus the advantages of segmentation in corporate strategy relate to the development of sustainable competitive advantage and to the ability to target products to that segment.

● When considering the implications of customer-driven strategy, there are three main areas: branding and reputation, communicating with customers and pricing strategy.

● Branding is a specific name or symbol used to distinguish a product or service from a functional product. It adds value to the basic functional product and provides sustainable competitive advantage. There are five elements to brand analysis: reputation, continuity, formula, incumbency and information signalling.

● Reputation is the sum of customer knowledge developed about an organisation over time. It will include brands but may also cover other aspects such as quality and service levels. It also delivers sustainable competitive advantage and adds value to basic customer perceptions of the organisation.

● Organisations communicate with their customers in order to inform and persuade them about the merits of their products and services. This will assist in establishing the sustainable competitive advantages of the product. Cost-effectiveness is the main criterion when assessing communications proposals. Costs are usually relatively easy to estimate but the effects of some promotional areas may be more difficult to assess.

● Different types of customers will need different forms of communication. Each will operate to communicate and secure the competitive advantages of the organisation. Communications policy may need an integrated approach across the organisation in the sense of considering other stakeholders as well as customers. It will be essential to examine the activities of competitors in order to identify the issues surrounding competitive advantage. It may also be necessary to consider innovative approaches to communications in order to adopt a fresh approach with customers and develop new areas of advantage.

● In the short term, pricing does not usually form the basis of sustainable competitive advantage because any price changes can be imitated very quickly by competitors. In the longer term, pricing strategy can be a major factor in competitive advantage, because it will significantly alter the basis on which companies can compete.

● Pricing strategy can have strategic significance at three levels: rapid impact on profitability, positioning of the product and value for money. The price decision will be determined by a balance of factors under the general headings of costs and competitor analysis.

● Value for money, which includes quality, branding and other factors, represents the broader elements that will determine and condition pricing for many customers. Target pricing places the main emphasis on competitors' prices and has proved an important element in the success of some companies over the last few years.

● Business is undoubtedly becoming more international. Customer analysis therefore needs to follow this trend. It has been argued that, although there are national differences in taste and culture, it is more important to seek out the similarities than to examine the differences. The greater economies of scale from operating internationally will be reflected in lower prices that will overcome any lingering problems over differences in taste.

QUESTIONS

1 Take the global market for large aircraft and explain the areas of customer analysis you would wish to consider in developing the corporate strategy for Airbus.

2 To what extent is it worthwhile estimating demand when a market is turbulent? What are the reasons for undertaking the task and what are the problems?

3 On the subject of customer needs, Professor G Hamel and Professor C K Prahalad comment:

   Any company that can do no more than respond to the articulated needs of existing customers will quickly become a laggard.

   Explain briefly the argument that is being used here and then comment on its validity. Are unmet needs so very important for strategy development?

4 Take a market with which you are familiar and explain the differences between immediate competitors and wider competitors. What implications does your distinction have for corporate strategy?

5 Compare and contrast the purchasing behaviour, communications strategy and pricing policies of the following three companies: a branded breakfast cereal manufacturer, a large retail bank and a national charitable institution of your choice.

6 What are the arguments in favour of cost-effectiveness in communicating with the customer? What are the difficulties? In view of your answer, what problems do you foresee in assessing the usefulness of such an approach in communications strategy for Unilever ice cream and for the Airbus SuperJumbo? Are they likely to be cost-effective?

7 Arguably Airbus over the last few years has followed a strategy of attempting to catch up with Boeing's initiatives. Is this the best approach to aircraft corporate strategy development? Or would Airbus have been better to seek out a new, unmet customer need?

8 What are the likely dangers of target pricing? Is it worthwhile? Are there any circumstances where it could not be used?

▶ Questions continued

9 *'A powerful force drives the world toward a converging commonality and that force is technology . . . the globalisation of markets is at hand.'* (Professor Theodore Levitt)

Discuss the implications for corporate strategy.

10 Identify where the following would fit on the customer/competitor matrix: a large hospital; a major league football team such as Real Madrid, Juventus or Manchester United; the Ford Motor Company; and Airbus. What are the strategy implications?

Further reading

There are two books that explore the subjects of this chapter in much greater detail: Philip Kotler (1994) *Marketing Management*, 8th edn, Prentice Hall, Englewood Cliffs, NJ; and Michael J Baker (1992) *Marketing Strategy and Management*, 2nd edn, Macmillan, London.

Notes and references

1 *Irish Independent* 2 March 2005: advertisement with pricing for Dyson vacuum cleaners; *Financial Times* (the first references are for articles on Merloni and Electrolux): 17 February 1999, p23; 5 February 2002, p30; 20 May 2001, p18; 19 June 2001, p20; 5 August 2002, p11; 14 November 2003, p13; 12 December 2003, pp1, 12; 8 March 2004, p23; 26 February 2005, p11; 15 March 2005, p3; Electrolux Annual Report and Accounts 2003.

2 Levitt, T (1960) 'Marketing myopia', *Harvard Business Review*, July–Aug, pp45–56. One of the classic marketing articles with important implications for strategy.

3 Note that loyalty and customer satisfaction are not necessarily the same thing. Piercy has argued convincingly that loyalty may be superficial and what is more fundamental for strategy development is long-term customer satisfaction: Piercy, N (1997) *Market-Led Strategic Change*, 2nd edn, Butterworth-Heinemann, Oxford, p40. See also Wirtz, B N and Lihotzky, N (2003) 'Customer retention management in the B2C electronic business', *Long Range Planning*, December, Vol 36, No 6, pp513–27.

4 Levitt, T (1960) Op. cit., p45.

5 Doyle, P (1997) *Marketing Management and Strategy*, 2nd edn, Prentice Hall Europe, Hemel Hempstead, p108.

6 Aaker, D (1992) *Strategic Marketing Management*, 3rd edn, Wiley, New York, p213.

7 This section is derived from Doyle, P (1997) Op. cit., Ch2.

8 Doyle, P (1997) Op. cit., p42.

9 Hamel, G and Prahalad, C K (1994) *Competing for the Future*, Harvard Business School Press, Cambridge, MA, p102.

10 Aaker, D (1992) Op. cit., p48.

11 It should be noted that, in theory at least, it is not necessary to segment a market before exploring its competitive positioning. However, it is usual and much easier to select part of a market before undertaking positioning. Many marketing strategy texts do not make this clear.

12 Porter, M E (1985) *Competitive Advantage*, The Free Press, New York, p233.

13 Ohmae, K (1983) *The Mind of the Strategist*, Penguin, Harmondsworth, p103.

14 Probably the best-known text exploring positioning issues in depth is: Hooley, G J and Saunders, J (1999) *Competitive Positioning*, Prentice Hall, Hemel Hempstead.

15 Doyle, P (1997) Op. cit., p166. See also Tollington, T (2001) 'UK brand asset recognition beyond "transactions and events"' *Long Range Planning*, Vol 34, No 4, pp463–88.

16 Kay, J (1994) *Foundations of Corporate Success*, Oxford University Press, Oxford, pp263–4.

17 This whole subject is relatively poorly discussed in corporate strategy literature. Professor J Kay is the only recent strategist to deal in any depth with the issues raised in this chapter: his *Foundations of Corporate Success* has two chapters but they treat the subject from an economics rather than a marketing perspective and are rather simplistic as a result.

18 Baker, M (1992) *Marketing Strategy and Management*, 2nd edn, Macmillan, London, Ch17.

19 Kay, J (1994) Op. cit., p252.

20 Cusumano, M A and Takeishi, A (1991) 'Supplier relations and management: a survey of Japanese, Japanese transplant and US Auto plants', *Strategic Management Journal*, 12, pp56–8.

21 Skapinker, M (1996) 'A struggle to fly to the top', *Financial Times*, 23 Feb, p15.

22 Levitt, T (1983) 'The globalisation of markets', *Harvard Business Review*, May–June, pp92–102.

23 Readers may care to note that some of this evidence is reduced in the shortened version of this article that appears in books such as that by R De Wit and B Meyer (1994) *Strategy: Content, Context and Process*, West Publishing, St Paul, MN. It is a pity that the flimsy nature of the empirical evidence has not been presented in full.

24 Douglas, S and Wind, Y (1987) 'The myth of globalisation', *Columbia Journal of World Business*, Winter. This is also reprinted in De Wit, R and Meyer, B (1994) Op. cit.

25 *See Financial Times*, 13 Sept 1990; 29 Jan 1993, p17; 3 Mar 1993, p19; 11 May 1994, p33; 19 Apr 1995, p17; 23 Feb 1996, p15; 14 Jan 1997, p17; 22 Jan 1997, pp1, 4, 21; 20 Feb 1997, p25; 7 Mar 1997, p6; 18 Apr 1997, p7; 14 Jan 1998, p4; 10 Aug 1998, p9; 3 December 1998, p21; 8 December 1998, p8; 25 February 1999, p38; 17 March 1999, p7; 15 October 1999, p22; 10 December 1999, p20; 23 December 1999, p19; 3 January 2000, p11; 14 March 2000, p3; 28 June 2000, p17; 30 August 2000, p22; 2 November 2000, p28; 20 December 2000, pp12, 24; 8 January 2001, p6; 2 April 2001, p29; 10 April 2001, p15; 27 April 2001, p38; 23 June 2001, p13; 21 September 2001, p33; 18 January 2002, p24; 5 February 2002, p16; 7 February 2002, p29; 16 April 2002, p32; 21 February 2003, p23; 2 May 2003, p21; 21 October 2003, p16; 14 November 2003, p31; 19 November 2003, p24; 25 November 2003, p28; 28 November 2003, p17; 8 December 2003, p19; 10 December 2003, p23 (John Kay); 16 December 2003, p15; 10 April 2004, pM3 Money and Business Section; 27 April 2004, pp21, 29; 15 July 2004, p29; 8 October 2004, p17; 20 October 2004, p26; 11 December 2004, pM6; 12 January 2005, p26; 13 January 2005, p29; 17 January 2005, p15; 21 January 2005, p20; 22 January 2005, pM3; 29 January 2005, pM6. Company Annual Reports of British Aerospace, UK; Aerospatiale, France; EADS France; Boeing, USA.

Chapter 6
Analysing resources – basics

- What key industry factors deliver the objectives of the organisation?
- How do resources add value to the organisation?
- How can value added be improved?
- Which resources are particularly important in adding value and competitive advantage?
- What are the main ways that resources deliver competitive advantage?
- How can competitive advantage be enhanced?

Chapter 7
Analysing human resources

- How do human resources add value? And how do they contribute to sustainable competitive advantage?
- What is the organisation's culture? How does it take decisions and develop its strategy?
- How does the organisation undertake change?
- How does the politics of the organisation affect change?

Chapter 8
Analysing financial resources

- How do financial resources add value? And how do they contribute to sustainable competitive advantage?
- What are the main sources and the cost of finance?
- What are the financial consequences of strategic expansion?
- What is the relationship between financial and corporate objectives?

Chapter 9
Analysing operations resources

- How do operations resources add value? And how do they contribute to sustainable competitive advantage?
- What impact do changes in technology have on corporate strategy?
- What areas of operations strategy make a major contribution to corporate strategy?
- What are the main elements of operations strategy?

ANALYSIS OF RESOURCES

Both the emergent and prescriptive strategy processes regard the organisation's resources as the foundation stone of strategy development.

The resources are the means by which the organisation generates *value*. It is this value that is then distributed to the employees as salaries, to government as taxes, to the shareholders as dividends or retained in the organisation to be reinvested for the future. Resources are also the means by which one organisation distinguishes itself from another. It is this aspect of resources that delivers and maintains *sustainable competitive advantage*. Part 3 introduces the concept of generating value and its fundamental importance to corporate strategy. It also explores how resources can and should generate advantages over the organisation's competitors. The three resources of the organisation – human, financial and operations – are then explored in turn.

The prescriptive strategic process

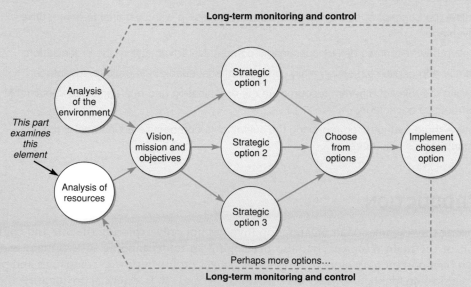

The emergent strategic process

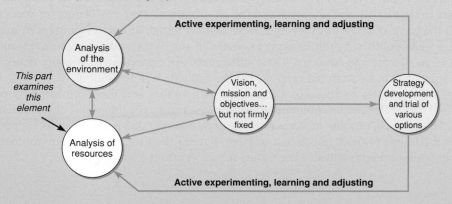

Chapter 6

ANALYSING RESOURCES - BASICS

INTRODUCTION

Analysing the resources of an organisation involves not only exploring the role and contribution of the main resources, but also developing an understanding of two main issues. First, it is important to explore how resources deliver profits in private companies and provide services in publicly owned organisations. Second, it is essential to identify those resources that enable an organisation to compete and survive against competition. In both cases, such an understanding will form the basis of future strategy development.

As a starting point, it is useful to consider the factors that deliver success in an industry as a whole, covering both the resources and the environment – the key factors for success.

Within the context of the industry, each organisation is then different – perhaps in small ways like a well-established product range, perhaps in major ways like exceptional leadership or a new, patented technology. These differences are important in strategy development, so they need to be analysed carefully for the individual organisation.

The resource analysis needs to proceed along two parallel and interconnected routes: value added and sustainable competitive advantage. Figure 6.1 identifies the elements involved. The *value-added* route explores how the organisation takes goods from its suppliers and turns them into finished goods and services that are then sold into the environment: how the organisation adds value to the inputs it receives from its suppliers.

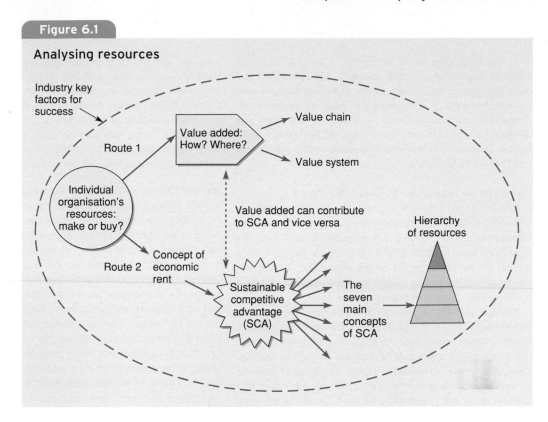

Figure 6.1

Analysing resources

The *competitive advantage* route examines the special resources that enable the organisation to compete: how and why some resources deliver sustainable competitive advantage is crucial to strategy development. This chapter analyses the organisation's resources from both these perspectives and considers how such resources might be improved.

Part 5a

CASE STUDY 6.1

Resource strategy at GSK: negotiating a merger and making it work

In the technically innovative and global market for pharmaceutical products, GlaxoSmithKline (GSK) is one of the world's largest drug companies – and size can matter in this industry. This case explores the competitive benefits of larger size and how GSK is using them to tackle the twin strategic challenges now facing the industry.

Background

Over the last 20 years, pharmaceuticals have become increasingly expensive to develop – typically, costing around US$500 million, spread over several years, for one major drug. After development, these drugs need to be marketed to customers such as doctors, hospitals and government health services – for example, several thousand specialist sales personnel may be required for such a task in the North American market alone. To support such activities, substantial cash resources are important. In addition, world alliances and other connections between manufacturers can also be highly beneficial: drug companies can use these to support areas where they are both weak geographically and have gaps in their product development programmes.

From the size perspective, it helps to have substantial resources. But this does not explain why even large companies have chosen to become larger over the last five years. For example, the Swedish company Astra merged with the UK company Zeneca and the French company Rhone-Poulenc joined together with part of the German company Hoechst to form Aventis during 1998/99. Over this time, half the world's largest drug companies announced either mergers or takeovers of fellow companies.

191

▶ **CASE STUDY 6.1 continued**

Some strategists would argue that if *all* the companies become larger then no drug company has developed any competitive advantage over another. The benefit cannot simply be size alone. It is necessary to examine the *individual* competitive resources of each company to see what size delivers. To explore this, we need to look separately at the two merger candidates in the case in question – Glaxo Wellcome and SmithKline Beecham.

Competitive resources at Glaxo Wellcome

During the period 1980–95, Glaxo (as it was then called) was highly dependent on its patented drug, Zantac, which is used for treating stomach ulcers. For example, in 1994 this one drug alone accounted for 44 per cent of the company's sales and 50 per cent of its profits. In the early 1990s, Zantac was the single biggest selling drug in the world and its ownership by Glaxo was a major strategic resource.

But this substantial strength faced two threats. First, the patents would begin to expire in 1997 and allow any company to manufacture and market the drug, thus reducing the profit margins that Glaxo was able to charge. Secondly, a new rival drug, Losec, was introduced to health authorities in 1993–94 by the Swedish company Astra Pharmaceuticals. Losec was claimed to be even more effective than Zantac. Glaxo knew the seriousness of such a competitive threat because its own drug, Zantac, had wiped the floor with an earlier rival in the mid-1980s, namely Tagamet, from the pharmaceutical company SmithKline Beecham.

Faced with these twin threats, Glaxo needed a new resource strategy. Given the time lag in developing new drugs, Glaxo used its existing resource strength – the profitability of Zantac – to acquire two existing drug companies. Wellcome (UK) was bought in 1995 for US$13.5 billion. This delivered a whole new range of patented drugs into the Glaxo portfolio, including the anti-AIDS drug Retrovir and the anti-viral drug Zovirax. In addition, the US company Affymax was bought for US$533 million. The latter company was developing a range of genetic products whose benefits would be truly revolutionary, if successful.

In addition to acquiring drugs from the two new companies, Glaxo gained other resource benefits from these purchases. The acquisition allowed Glaxo to combine its R&D team with that of Wellcome, saving 1,800 jobs and the labour costs associated with this. In addition, 3,000 jobs were lost in manufacturing by combining various plants and 2,600 jobs were lost in marketing and administration. In total, around US$1 billion cost savings were achieved. But it was not all good news: the patents on the top-selling drug Zovirax were due to expire from 1997 onwards (patents have roughly a ten-year life from first registration).

Competitive resources of SmithKline Beecham

It was the loss of profits from Tagamet mentioned above that forced its makers, the American company SmithKline, to seek a merger with the UK company Beecham in the late 1980s. Nevertheless, the new company had proceeded to develop many new, patented drugs over the succeeding ten years to the late 1990s. It had also exploited its range of branded medicines sold directly to the general public with higher profit margins than were available on many pharmaceuticals. By 1998, the company was particularly strong in anti-depressants, vaccines, antibiotics and diabetes medicines.

Merger failure in 1998 and success in 2000

In 1998, Glaxo Wellcome explored merging the company with SmithKline Beecham. This would have transformed the resource capability of the two companies because they both had different areas of product strength in the drugs market, and the duplication of some facilities and services could have been eliminated. But the merger did not take place. The two companies clashed over two matters: the styles of negotiation and the proposed new management structure. The cultures of the two companies were so different that the merger discussions themselves became difficult – for example, they were so bad that the participants never even had lunch together. In addition, there were differences between the two chief executives and other senior managers over their respective roles in the merged company. The result was that the merger never took place and the substantial resource benefits were never achieved.

In the face of increased competition and the cost of drug development, the pressure to consolidate remained. What made the difference was that the some of the senior managers involved in the abortive talks in 1998 decided to retire, allowing the two companies to merge in year 2000. As a result, the combined company was able to employ an enhanced research budget of over US$4 billion in 2002. Annual cost savings of US$750 million were achieved: this was ahead of earlier expectations. It had a sales team in North America alone of over 7,500 people. The two product ranges from the two companies complemented each other, with some minor overlap. The company had a global market share of over 7 per cent. This might appear small but the company dominated some segments of the world drug market. The combined picture of the group's activities is shown in Figure 6.2.

Twin strategy challenges of the new millennium

The increased size of the company delivered a diverse product range in terms of geographical spread and product portfolio. But the company faced two major strategic challenges in the new millennium:

● Some of its leading drugs would run out of patent protection, allowing generic varieties of the same drug to be made and sold much more cheaply. This was a major threat to companies like GSK that invested heavily in new drugs and then relied on a high profit margin stream to pay for the drug development costs. The generic drug

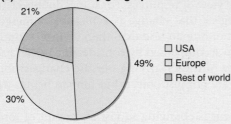

Figure 6.2

Turnover at GSK

(a) GSK turnover by geographical area 2004

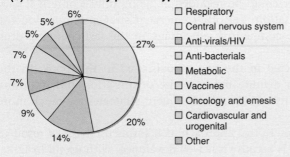

21%
49%
30%

☐ USA
☐ Europe
☐ Rest of world

(b) GSK turnover by product type 2004

6%
5%
5%
7%
7%
9%
14%
20%
27%

☐ Respiratory
☐ Central nervous system
☐ Anti-virals/HIV
☐ Anti-bacterials
☐ Metabolic
☐ Vaccines
☐ Oncology and emesis
☐ Cardiovascular and urogenital
☐ Other

danger for a large company like GSK was to make its research and development large and bureaucratic: the small bio-engineering companies had been more successful in recent years. Hence, with his new research director, Tachi Yamada, he set up seven 'centres of excellence for drug discovery' (CEDDs) in Europe and the USA.

'Size was getting in the way,' explained Mr Yamada. 'In the bureaucracy, traditional biotechnology expertise was forgotten. Very few companies believed that they were failing in the 1990s. Most are just beginning to realise how bad it is.' The GSK solution was to set up the seven CEDD teams, each no more than 300 strong and multidisciplinary in make-up. Each team had its own library, research facilities, even its own financial director. The smaller structure means that there were fewer reporting layers so that research can be started and stopped more quickly. One of Mr Yamada's colleagues explained: 'Before we could be stuck for years with a project that was not viable because the visibility was not there. . . . [Now] we can give a Go/No Go decision within six months. For many of our competitors, that takes two years.'

But the results of this massive re-organisation were not yet complete in early 2005. The company's turnover had continued to increase and it was making progress in terms of new product development: R&D productivity metrics were showing success in terms of drug developments in the pipeline. However, as the chief executive, Mr Garnier stressed at that time: 'We are not claiming victory yet.'

Case questions

1 *What are the key factors for success in this market? And what are the implications of your answer for large and generic drug manufacturers?*

2 *What was the nature of the competitive advantages held by Glaxo Wellcome? And SmithKline Beecham? Were they sustainable?*

3 *Do cost savings in themselves represent substantive competitive advantage?*

4 *What lesson, if any, on the development of sustainable competitive advantage can be drawn from the case for other companies outside pharmaceuticals?*

companies were picking off major drugs as they came out of patent and marketing cheap, reliable, copies at much lower prices.

● The new company had only a limited supply of new patented drugs in its pipeline. All drugs have to go through a period of rigorous testing procedure over several years. Inevitably, there would be failures during the tests, so it was essential to have a good pipeline of new drugs.

When the GSK chief executive took over in 2000, he made a detailed study of the company's drug pipeline. He concluded: 'We had an empty cupboard.' He therefore set about creating a new, vibrant research and development regime in the company. He regarded this as being crucial to the long-term future of any major pharmaceutical company. It would counteract the effects of the generic drug companies and would ensure continued growth at GSK. He recognised that the

---

6.1 PRESCRIPTIVE AND EMERGENT APPROACHES TO RESOURCE ISSUES

Both emergent and prescriptive approaches to strategy development regard resources as important. However, their perspectives are very different.

Prescriptive strategists take the view that it is important to use resources efficiently and build on resource strengths. Resources are to some extent regarded as inanimate objects without feeling. Hence it is possible for strategy to manipulate and mould resources in order to provide a more efficient organisation. For example, the GSK merger benefited from significant job cuts and the resultant annual savings of over US$750 million. Prescriptive strategists argue that the company will be stronger as a result.

Although there is not complete agreement among emergent strategists, they would certainly question the certainties of the prescriptive view of resources. For some, doubts centre on the assumption made by prescriptive strategists that change is achievable. Emergent strategists probably lay more stress on the impact of human resources than their prescriptive counterparts. For example, the GSK job cuts were accompanied by considerable uncertainty and worry, which must have affected the ability of those carrying out the changes: some emergent strategists argue that people resources are not just objects but human beings who can help or hinder strategic change.

For other emergent strategists, the environment is changing so fast as a result of forces beyond the control of the organisation that resources need to be flexible and aimed at survival. In this sense, the GSK merger could be regarded as being unwelcome if it produced a larger and less flexible organisation. Yet other emergent strategists question the value of patents to deliver sustainable competitive advantage in the fast-changing drug market.

These differences of views are reflected in the two models used in this book. In the prescriptive model, resources deliver a definite result to the organisation and its future strategies. In the emergent model, the resources and subsequent strategies are much more fluid and interrelated.

This chapter concentrates on the prescriptive approach as it forms the basis of resource analysis for strategy development. This is because it is well developed, with useful insights, and, in addition, even those who doubt its usefulness still need to understand it first.

In Chapter 7 and subsequent chapters, the emergent approach is explored further.

Key strategic principles

- Prescriptive approaches regard resources as objects to be moulded for maximum strategic benefit.

- Emergent approaches do not have a consistent theme with regard to resources. However, they tend to value the human element more highly: this is inherently less predictable. They also emphasise the need for a close relationship between the environment and the resources.

- This chapter concentrates on the prescriptive view because it is well developed and has useful strategy insights.

6.2 KEY FACTORS FOR SUCCESS IN AN INDUSTRY

Part 5b

By now, it will be evident that corporate strategy encompasses the whole organisation. Whether the strategic process is prescriptive or emergent, it needs to consider every part of the organisation and, most importantly, do so with limited resources.

Potentially, this raises a major strategic problem: corporate strategy analysis could be overwhelmed by the size of the task. An analytical process is needed that will examine the many factors that can potentially impact on strategy.

The Japanese strategist Kenichi Ohmae,[2] the former head of the management consultants McKinsey, in Japan, has suggested a way of tackling this matter by identifying *the key*

Definition ➤ *factors for success* that are *likely* to deliver the company's objectives. Key factors for success in an industry are those resources, skills and attributes of the organisations in an industry that are essential to deliver success in the market place. He argued that, when resources of capital, labour and time are scarce, it is important that they should be *concentrated* on the key activities of the business – that is, those most important to the delivery of whatever the organisation regards as success.

This concept of key factors for success is also consistent with Porter's view[3] that there are factors that determine the relative competitive positions of companies within an industry. Moreover, the foundation of Kay's approach[4] is that it is important to concentrate resources on the specific areas of the business that are most likely to prove successful. Amit and Schoemaker[5] provide a more extended theoretical framework for the same topic, but call their treatment 'Strategic Industry Factors'. All the above have said that identifying the key factors is not an easy task.

6.2.1 Identifying the key factors for success in the industry

Key factors concern not only the resources of organisations in the industry but also the *competitive environment* in which organisations operate. There are three principal areas that need to be analysed – Ohmae's *three Cs*.[6]

1 *Customers*. What do customers really want? What are the segments in the market place? Can we direct our strategy towards a group?

2 *Competition*. How can the organisation beat or at least survive against competition? What resources and customers does it have that make it particularly successful? How does the organisation compare on price, quality, etc? Does the organisation have a stronger distributive network than its competitors?

3 *Corporation*. What special resources does the company itself possess and how do they compare with those of competitors? How does the company compare on costs with its rivals? And on technologies? Skills? Organisational ability? Marketing?

Exhibit 6.1 sets out some key questions in more detail. No single area is more important than another. The *competition* and *customer* issues were examined in Chapters 4 and 5 and it is not proposed to repeat this analysis here. The *corporate* factors relate to the *resource* issues which are explored in detail in the remainder of this chapter.

6.2.2 Critical comment on the concept

Criticism of the key factors for success has concentrated on four issues:[7]

1 *Identification*. It is difficult to pick out the important factors.

2 *Causality of relationships*. Even though they have been identified, it may not be clear *how* they operate or interact.

3 *Dangers of generalising*. The competitive advantage of a single organisation, by definition, cannot be obtained by seeking what is commonly accepted as bringing success to all organisations in an industry.

4 *Disregard of emergent perspectives*. Success may come from change in an industry, rather than the identification of the current key factors for success.

Beyond these specific criticisms, some strategists have a more general concern about industry analysis (this is explored in the next section). Some of the criticisms can be countered if key factors for success are regarded as *guidelines* for directing strategy development, rather than rigid rules. But the criticisms suggest that key factors for success should be explored with caution. They are only a starting point in strategy analysis – the 'best' strategy may be to reject the key factors and do something completely different!

Exhibit 6.1

Identifying key factors for success in an industry

Note that key factors for success are directed at *all companies in an industry*, not just the target company for strategy development.

1 Customers

Who are the customers? Who are the potential customers? Are there any special segments? Why do customers buy from us? And from our competitors?

- *Price*. Is the market segmented by high, medium and economy pricing? For example, the market for European ice cream.

- *Service*. Do some customers value service while others simply want to buy the product? For example, top-class fashion retailers versus standard clothing shops.

- *Product or service reliability*. Is product performance crucial to the customer or is reliability useful but not really important? For example, heart pacemakers and pharmaceuticals.

- *Quality*. Some customers will pay higher prices for actual or perceived quality differences. Does this provide a route to success? For example, organic vegetables.

- *Technical specifications*. In some industrial and financial services, technical details will provide major attractions for some customers. Is this relevant in this industry? For example, specialist financial bond dealers.

- *Branding*. How important is branding for the customer? For example, Coca-Cola and Pepsi Cola.

2 Competition

Who are the main competitors? What are the main factors in the market that influence competition? How intense is competition? What is necessary to achieve market superiority? What resources do competitors possess that we lack and vice versa?

- *Cost comparisons*. Which companies have the lowest costs? Why? For example, Toyota until the mid-1990s.

- *Price comparisons*. Which companies have high prices? For example, Daimler-Benz does not make cheap cars.

- *Quality issues*. Which companies have the highest quality? Why? How? For example, Xerox (US) in the light of fierce competition from Japanese companies such as Canon.

- *Market dominance*. Which companies dominate the market? For example, Nestlé, with the strongest coffee product range in the world and the largest market share.

- *Service*. Are there companies in the industry that offer superior service levels? For example, industrial markets, such as those served by Asea Brown Boveri, which need high levels of service to operate and maintain sophisticated equipment.

- *Distributors*. Which companies have the best distributive network? Lowest costs? Fastest delivery? Competent distributors that really know the product or service? For example, major glass companies such as St Gobain (France) and Pilkington (UK).

3 Corporation

What are our key resources and those of our competitors? What do they deliver to customers? Where are the majority of the industry costs concentrated? A small percentage reduction to a large part of the total costs will deliver more than a large percentage reduction in an area of lower total costs.

- *Low-cost operations*. Are low-cost operations important for ourselves or our competitors? For example, Aldi (Germany) and Tesco (UK) are both low-cost supermarket operators.

- *Economies of scale*. Do these exist in the industry? How important are they? For example, large-scale petroleum chemical refinery operations such as those operated by Royal Dutch/Shell.

- *Labour costs*. Does our industry rely heavily on low labour costs for competitive operations? For example, Philips (Netherlands) has moved its production to Singapore and Malaysia to lower labour costs.

- *Production output levels*. Does our industry need full utilisation of plant capacity? For example, European paper and packaging companies.

- *Quality operations*. Do customers need consistent and reliable quality? How do we compare with others in the industry? For example, McDonald's has applied the same standards around the world in its restaurants.

- *Innovative ability*. Does our industry place a high reliance on our ability to produce a constant stream of new innovations? For example, computer hardware and software companies such as Apple, Epson and Microsoft.

- *Labour/management relations*. Is our industry heavily reliant on good relations? Are there real problems if disputes arise? For example, European large-scale steel production, at companies such as Usinor/Arbed.

- *Technologies and copyright*. Does the industry rely on specialist technologies, especially those that are patented and provide a real competitive advantage? For example, News International (Australia), which has exclusive global control over some forms of decoder cards for satellite television.

- *Skills*. Do organisations in the industry possess exceptional human skills and people? What are such skills? For example, advertising agencies and leading consultancy companies.

Key strategic principles

- Identifying the key factors for success shapes the key areas of strategic analysis.

- Such factors can conveniently be considered under three headings: customers, competition and corporation. By 'corporation' is meant the resources of the organisation.

- Key factors can be found in any area of the organisation and relate to skills, competitive advantage, competitive resources of an organisation in the industry, special technologies or customer contacts.

- Four criticisms of key factors have been made: identification, causality of relationships, dangers of generalising, and disregard of emergent perspectives. Caution is therefore needed in their application.

6.3 ANALYSING THE RESOURCES OF AN *INDIVIDUAL* ORGANISATION

6.3.1 The distinction between industry and *individual* companies in resource analysis

In Part 2, we explored environmental analysis extensively because it is essential for the development of two key strategic concepts: *competitive advantage* and *customer-led strategy*. Both have meaning only in the context of the environment within which the organisation operates. The previous section examined another aspect of environmental analysis: *key factors for success* in the industry. But these studies of the environment are fundamentally incomplete from a strategy perspective.

Organisations seeking competitive advantage over others need to make an offering to customers that is different from and more persuasive than those of its competitors. Therefore resource analysis needs to move beyond factors that apply to the industry as a whole. Each organisation needs to analyse and develop the *individual* resources that will allow it to survive and compete in the environment. For example, GSK is unlikely to survive because it has a powerful marketing and sales team – other companies also have this. GSK needs an effective and well-patented portfolio of its own exclusive drugs. Such products will deliver competitive advantage over others in the industry and high added value in the form of profits, cash and service to its customers.

Although it might seem clear now that industry resource analysis needs to be accompanied by an analysis of the individual organisation, this was not so obvious until recently.[8] For many years in the 1970s, 1980s and 1990s, the main emphasis in strategy development was laid on industry analysis – for example, the work of Porter[9] and others outlined in Chapter 3.[10] However, this stress on industry analysis in turn represented a shift from the 1950s and 1960s, which took a more inclusive approach – the work of Penrose[11] and others outlined at the end of Chapter 2. For our purposes, after analysing the resources of the industry and seeing how organisations add value in the early parts of this chapter, we will
Definition ➤ explore in the remainder the resources of the individual organisation. This emphasis on the importance of resources in delivering the competitive advantage of the organisation is called the resource-based view of strategy development.

6.3.2 Why does an organisation possess any resources at all?

The make-or-buy decision

As a starting point in identifying the strategic role of individual resources, it is useful to explore the reasons for an organisation to possess and use *any* resources beyond the minimum amount needed to stay in existence. Arguably, in an efficient market, there will be outside more specialised suppliers that will be able to sell some activities more cheaply to the organisation than it can make them for itself. For example, GSK does not produce its own advertising campaigns but employs an outside agency. Nor does the company manufacture its own cartons, boxes and foil in which to pack its drugs, but buys them in – why? Because it is cheaper to buy from an outside supplier than make them for itself. The decision to use the outside 'market' to buy in products or services rather than use the organisation's own resources to make them is known in strategic terms as outsourcing. However, there are also problems with buying in from outside – *see* Exhibit 6.2 – otherwise all organisations would buy everything and make nothing. Essentially, to resolve the problem of what an organisation should make rather than buy, the costs of using the market must be higher than the benefits.

Definition ➤

Exhibit 6.2

Benefits and costs of using the market

Benefits

● Outside suppliers can achieve economies of scale that in-house departments producing only for their own needs cannot.

● Outside suppliers are subject to the pressures of the market and must be efficient and innovative to survive. Overall corporate success may hide the inefficiencies and lack of innovativeness of in-house departments.

Costs

● Production flows need to be co-ordinated through the value chain of the organisation. This may be compromised when an activity is purchased from an independent market firm rather than performed in-house.

● Private information may be leaked when an activity is performed by an independent market firm – such information may be crucial to the competitive advantage held by the organisation.

● There may be costs of transacting with independent firms that can be avoided by performing the activity in-house.

Source: Adapted from Besanko, D, Dranove, D and Shenley, M (1996), *The Economics of Strategy*, p73. Copyright © 1996 John Wiley & Sons, Inc. This material is used by permission of John Wiley & Sons, Inc.

The make-or-buy decision is part of a broader strategic reappraisal of resources. Over the last 30 years, many organisations have come to redefine the boundaries of their resources – what they *make* is only part of the resources *owned* by the firm. For example, firms also have resources like brand names, which they do not manufacture on a production line but which are important contributors to value added. This profound rethink on the nature and role of resources by writers such as Coase, Penrose and Williamson has led to some important strategic resource decisions.[12]

Companies like Nike Sports (US) and Benetton Clothing (Italy) have achieved strategic success by buying in many of the activities that might previously have been undertaken in-house: both use networks of suppliers and, in the case of Benetton, distributors to make and sell their goods more cheaply. Nike designs and markets its new shoes but has them manufactured by outside suppliers in Asia – *see* Case 11.2. Benetton has a similar arrangement, using a group of local suppliers in northern Italy: this is called *outsourcing* supplies. Although it might appear that Benetton owns the resource of the shop chain that bears the company name, in fact most of the stores are not owned by the company. They are operated under the control of Benetton but owned by others outside the company: this is called *franchising*. The concepts of branded clothing, franchised clothing stores and out-sourced supplies formed the basis of Benetton's highly original new strategy in the 1970s. The starting point for such strategy development is an analysis of the resources of the organisation as they exist at present. We undertake this task during the rest of this chapter.

Key strategic principles

- Key factors for success in an industry represent a starting point for exploring the resources of the individual organisation. But the search for value added and sustainable competitive advantage must move beyond industry solutions. *Individual* resources must be identified for the organisation itself.

- The *make-or-buy decision* concerns the choice that every organisation has of either making its own products or services or buying them from outside. Every organisation needs to reappraise its activities regularly in this area.

CASE STUDY 6.2

How three European companies attempt to utilise their resources

In this case study, three totally different companies are explored to see how each utilises its resources and achieves its corporate objectives. The first two companies operate in the pharmaceutical and national railway service industries respectively; the third is a holding company with a range of activities mainly in construction, public services and television broadcasting.

The three companies under consideration are the UK-based pharmaceutical company GSK, the Dutch national railway company Nederlandse Spoorwegen, and the French services holding company Bouygues. Each has totally different resources, skills and methods of working, and each is involved in very different environments, including pharmaceuticals, transport services and the construction of roads. The purpose of this case is to identify the *key* strategic resources – that is, those that will make a difference to the company's corporate strategy.

Mission and objectives

As a starting point for any strategic analysis, it is important to consider *why* these three organisations are utilising the resources. What are they attempting to achieve? In principle, each is setting out to accomplish its *mission and objectives*. These need to be identified and explored.

Key resource analysis

Each of these companies brings totally different types of resources, skills and methods of operation to the achievement of its objectives. Figure 6.3 has used data taken from annual reports and other sources to construct the *cost profiles* for each of the three companies in this case study. The costs of each major item of company expenditure are expressed as a per-centage of sales, coupled with profits before tax and interest

as a percentage of sales. They are calculated by taking each cost item and dividing it by the sales figure and expressing this as a percentage. The profile demonstrates how each element of *resource* in the company contributes to profit and sales.

Resources for GSK

The information is identified in the GSK case study at the beginning of this chapter.

Resources for Nederlandse Spoorwegen

- *Increased utilisation of existing railway lines and rolling stock*. The investment in track and trains in most compan-ies is largely complete. The key is to obtain greater usage of what is already present.
- *Marketing, sales and special prices*. These are to encour-age customers to use the railways in preference to their competitors: road, air and bus traffic. This is particularly true in the Netherlands with its extensive and well-developed transport infrastructure.
- *High levels of service*. These involve the employees of the company and investment in new equipment on information and signalling to inform customers better of transport net-work problems.

Most national European railway companies are competing mainly within their national boundaries.[13] Resource analysis

Figure 6.3

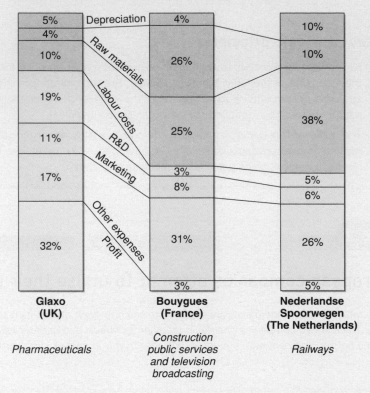

Cost profiles – costs as a percentage of sales

Glaxo (UK)	Bouygues (France)	Nederlandse Spoorwegen (The Netherlands)

Depreciation · Raw materials · Labour costs · R&D · Marketing · Other expenses · Profit

Pharmaceuticals — *Construction public services and television broadcasting* — *Railways*

therefore needs to concentrate on national transport competitors in the first instance.

With the high fixed investment already made in track, signalling and rolling stock, corporate strategy has relied largely on encouraging *greater utilisation of the existing facilities* – that is, the marketing and sales activities mentioned above.

Another aspect of strategy that is important for most railway companies is *the relationship with government*. During the period from which the data shown in Figure 6.3 were taken, the Dutch railway company was receiving grants from the Netherlands government that amounted to 9 per cent of its total revenue. These were used to subsidise train fares and freight passage so that railways would be used in preference to roads.

Resources for Bouygues

In this case, the resources will be dictated by the precise nature of each of the activities in which the company is engaged. In theory, it will be necessary to analyse each of the hundreds of companies in the group. In practice, three areas of the company accounted for over 90 per cent of sales:

Building and road construction	63%
Public utilities management	15%
Media and telecommunications	14%

For the purposes of *strategic analysis*, it is normally acceptable to ignore the remaining collection of areas. This is not a financial audit of the company, simply an overall judgement of the *main thrust* of the company's business. The comment on ignoring the remaining areas of the business would also be invalid if other areas were making huge losses or otherwise represented a significant potential shift in the company. We can identify the reasons involved in the three main areas of business:

1 Building and road construction resources include:
   ● raw materials for buildings and roads;
   ● labour construction costs coupled with skills and efficiency;
   ● design and engineering costs.
2 Public utilities management resources include:
   ● quality of services provided;
   ● management liaison with government owners;
   ● cost control and monitoring skills.
3 Media television station resources – French national channel TF1 and mobile telephone services:
   ● programme origination and purchasing;
   ● network management and costing;
   ● audience monitoring and assessment;
   ● mobile telephone service management and marketing.

It will be evident that analysing the resources in a diversified holding company is a major task. It has been simplified by concentrating on certain key areas of the business. However, this is a compromise.

Case questions

1 An examination of the cost profiles of the three companies reveals that research and development (R&D) feature more prominently in GSK than in the other two companies. Why

is this? What risks, if any, are associated with heavy R&D expenditure? What implications might this have for strategic decisions?

2 Marketing and related expenditures are much higher as a proportion of sales for GSK than for Nederlandse Spoorwegen. What are the reasons for this? Can you make out a strategic case for higher levels of marketing expenditure at the Dutch railway company?

3 The case study suggests that holding companies have a more complex task in managing their resources. Do you agree?

6.4 RESOURCE ANALYSIS AND ADDING VALUE

The fundamental role of resources in an organisation is to add value. All organisations need to ensure that they do not consistently lose value in the long term or they will not survive. For commercial organisations, adding value is essential for their future. For non-profit organisations, adding value may only be a minor part of the reason for their existence, other purposes being centred on social, charitable or other goals. Resources add value by working on the raw materials that enter the factory gate and turning them into a finished product.

Definition ➤ Added value can be defined as the difference between the market value of the output of an organisation and the cost of its inputs.

The concept is basically an economic one and is outlined, using GSK as an example, in Figure 6.4. For non-profit organisations, the concept of adding value can still be applied. The inputs to the organisation may be similar to those of commercial organisations – electricity, telephones, etc. – and may be very different, particularly voluntary labour, which has a zero cost. Equally, the outputs may be difficult to define and measure – service to the community, help for sick people, etc. But the *value added* is real enough, just difficult to quantify. To explore the basic concepts, commercial explanations *only* are examined in this section.

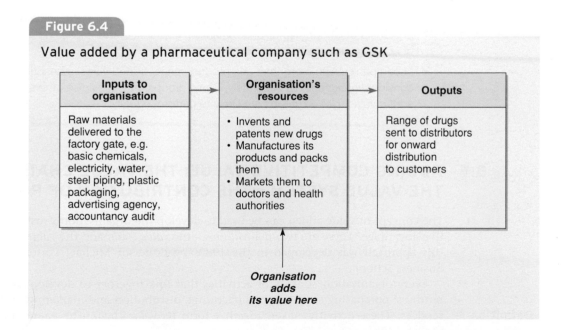

Figure 6.4

Value added by a pharmaceutical company such as GSK

Inputs to organisation	Organisation's resources	Outputs
Raw materials delivered to the factory gate, e.g. basic chemicals, electricity, water, steel piping, plastic packaging, advertising agency, accountancy audit	• Invents and patents new drugs • Manufactures its products and packs them • Markets them to doctors and health authorities	Range of drugs sent to distributors for onward distribution to customers

Organisation adds its value here

From the above definition of value added (i.e. outputs minus inputs), it follows that value can be added in an organisation:

● *either* by raising the value of outputs (sales) delivered to the customer;

● *or* by lowering the costs of its inputs (wages and salaries, capital and materials costs) into the company.

Alternatively, both routes could be used simultaneously. Strategies therefore need to address these two areas.

Raising the value of outputs may mean raising the level of sales, either by raising the volume of sales or by raising the unit price. Both these methods are easy to state and more difficult to achieve. Each will involve costs – for example, the cost of advertising to stimulate sales – which need to be set against the gains made. *Lowering the costs of inputs* may require investment – for example, in new machinery to replace workers – at the same time as seeking the cost reduction. These two strategic routes need to be examined in detail. *Outputs* have already been covered in Part 2; *inputs* are considered later in this chapter.

A strategic analysis of value added needs to take place at the market or industry level of the organisation, not at a corporate or holding company level. If this analysis were to be undertaken at the general level, the performance of individual parts of the business would be masked. Value added is therefore calculated at the level of individual product groups.[15]

Key strategic principles

● The added value of a commercial organisation is the difference between the market value of its output and the costs of its inputs.

● The value added of a not-for-profit organisation is the difference between the service provided and the costs of the inputs, some of which may be voluntary and have zero cost.

● All organisations need to ensure that they do not consistently lose value in the long term or they will not survive. For commercial organisations, adding value is essential for their future. For non-profit organisations, adding value may only be a minor part of the reason for their existence, other purposes being centred on social, charitable or other goals.

● In principle, there are only two strategies to raise value added in a commercial organisation: increase the value of its outputs (sales) or lower the value of its inputs (the costs of labour, capital and materials). In practice, this implies detailed analysis of every aspect of sales and costs.

● In companies with more than one product range, added value is best analysed by considering each group separately. Some groups may subsidise others in terms of added value. Not all groups are likely to perform equally.

6.5 ADDING COMPETITIVE VALUE: THE VALUE CHAIN AND THE VALUE SYSTEM – THE CONTRIBUTION OF PORTER

The concept of value added can be used to develop the organisation's sustainable competitive advantage. There are two main routes – the *value chain* and the *value system*. Much of this approach was developed in the 1980s by Professor Michael Porter of the Harvard Business School.

Every organisation consists of activities that link together to develop the value of the business: purchasing supplies, manufacturing, distribution and marketing of its goods and

Definition ➤ services. These activities taken together form its *value chain*. The value chain identifies where the value is added in an organisation and links the process with the main functional parts of the organisation. It is used for developing competitive advantage because such chains tend to be unique to an organisation.

When organisations supply, distribute, buy from or compete with each other, they form a broader group of value generation: the *value system*. The value system shows the wider routes in an industry that add value to incoming supplies and outgoing distributors and customers. It links the industry value chain to that of other industries. Again, it is used to identify and develop competitive advantage because such systems tend to be unique to companies.

The contributions of the value chain and value system to the development of competitive advantage, and the links between the two areas, which may also deliver competitive advantage, are explored in this section.

6.5.1 The value chain

The value chain links the value of the activities of an organisation with its main functional parts. It then attempts to make an assessment of the contribution that each part makes to the overall added value of the business. The concept was used in accounting analysis for some years before Professor Michael Porter[16] suggested that it could be applied to strategic analysis. Essentially, he linked two areas together:

1 the added value that each part of the organisation contributes to the whole organisation; and

2 the contribution to the competitive advantage of the whole organisation that each of these parts might then make.

In a company with more than one product area, he said that the analysis should be conducted at the level of product groups, not at corporate strategy level. The company is then split into the *primary activities* of production, such as the production process itself, and the *support activities*, such as human resources management, that give the necessary background to the running of the company but cannot be identified with any individual part. The analysis then examines how each part might be considered to contribute towards the generation of value in the company and how this differs from competitors.

Porter's outline process is shown in Figure 6.5. He used the word 'margin' in the diagram to indicate what we defined as *added value* in Section 6.4: 'margin is the difference between the total value and the collective cost of performing the value activities'.[17]

According to Porter, the *primary activities* of the company are:

- *Inbound logistics*. These are the areas concerned with receiving the goods from suppliers, storing them until required by operations, handling and transporting them within the company.

- *Operations*. This is the production area of the company. In some companies, this might be split into further departments – for example, paint spraying, engine assembly, etc., in a car company; reception, room service, restaurant, etc., in a hotel.

- *Outbound logistics*. These distribute the final product to the customer. They would clearly include transport and warehousing but might also include selecting and wrapping combinations of products in a multiproduct company. For a hotel or other service company, this activity would be reconfigured to cover the means of bringing customers to the hotel or service.

- *Marketing and sales*. This function analyses customers' wants and needs and brings to the attention of customers the products or services the company has for sale. Advertising and promotions fall within this area.

- *Service*. Before or after a product or service has been sold, there is often a need for pre-installation or after-sales service. There may also be a requirement for training, answering customer queries, etc.

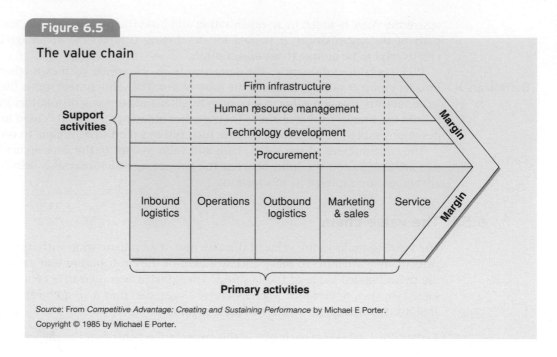

Figure 6.5

The value chain

Support activities {
- Firm infrastructure
- Human resource management
- Technology development
- Procurement

Margin

| Inbound logistics | Operations | Outbound logistics | Marketing & sales | Service |

Margin

Primary activities

Source: From *Competitive Advantage: Creating and Sustaining Performance* by Michael E Porter.
Copyright © 1985 by Michael E Porter.

Each of the above categories will add value to the organisation in its own way. They may undertake this task better or worse than competitors: for example, with higher standards of service, lower production costs, faster and cheaper outbound delivery and so on. By this means, they provide the areas of *competitive advantage* of the organisation.

The *support activities* are:

- *Procurement.* In many companies, there will be a separate department (or group of managers) responsible for purchasing goods and materials that are then used in the operations of the company. The department's function is to obtain the lowest prices and highest quality of goods for the activities of the company, but it is only responsible for purchasing, not for the subsequent production of the goods.

- *Technology development.* This may be an important area for new products in the company. Even in a more mature industry, it will cover the existing technology, training and knowledge that will allow a company to remain efficient.

- *Human resource management.* Recruitment, training, management development and the reward structures are vital elements in all companies.

- *Firm infrastructure.* This includes the background planning and control systems – for example, accounting, etc. – that allow companies to administer and direct their development. It includes corporate strategy.

These support activities add value, just as the primary activities do, but in a way that is more difficult to link with one particular part of the organisation. A worked example of the primary part of a value chain is shown in Case 6.3 on Louis Vuitton and Gucci later in this chapter.

Comment

The problem with the value chain in strategic development is that it is designed to explore the *existing* linkages and value-added areas of the business. By definition, it works within the existing structure. Real competitive strategy may require a revolution that moves *outside* the existing structure. Value chains may not be the means to achieve this.

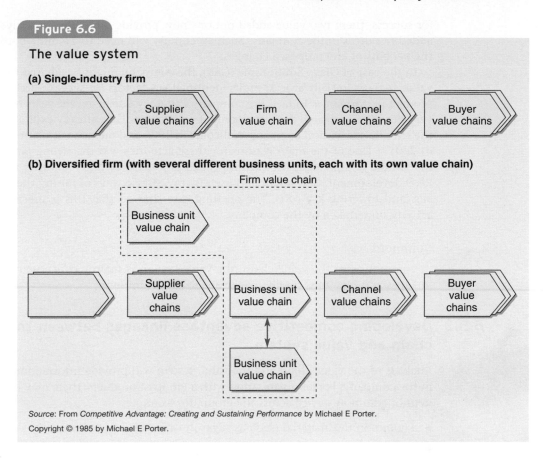

Figure 6.6

The value system

(a) Single-industry firm

Supplier value chains → Firm value chain → Channel value chains → Buyer value chains

(b) Diversified firm (with several different business units, each with its own value chain)

Firm value chain

Business unit value chain

Supplier value chains → Business unit value chain → Channel value chains → Buyer value chains

Business unit value chain

Source: From *Competitive Advantage: Creating and Sustaining Performance* by Michael E Porter. Copyright © 1985 by Michael E Porter.

6.5.2 The value system

In addition to the analysis of the company's own value chain, Porter argued that an additional analysis should also be undertaken. Organisations are part of a wider system of adding value involving the supply and distribution value chains and the value chains of customers. This is known as the *value system* and is illustrated in Figure 6.6.

Except in very rare circumstances, every organisation buys in some of its activities: advertising, product packaging design, management consultancy, electricity are all examples of items that are often acquired even by the largest companies. In the same way, many organisations do not distribute their products or services directly to the final consumer: travel agents, wholesalers, retail shops might all be involved in this role.

Competitors may or may not use the same value system: some suppliers and distributors will be better than others in the sense that they offer lower prices, faster service, more reliable products, etc. *Real* competitive advantage may come from using the *best* suppliers or distributors. New competitive advantage may be gained by using a new distribution system or obtaining a new relationship with a supplier. An analysis of this value system may also therefore be required. This will involve a resource analysis that extends beyond the organisation itself.

Value chain and value system analysis can be complex and time consuming for the organisation. This is where the *key factors for success* (*see* Section 6.2) can be used. If these have been correctly identified, then they will provide the focus for the analysis of added value that follows. Key factors may well be those factors that add value to the product or service.

In Section 6.4 we concluded that value added can only be raised by either increasing the outputs (sales) or by lowering the inputs (costs) of a company. Along with the key factors for success, these two value-added options now provide a method of analysing the value-added resources in the company. Such an enquiry will need to examine both the costs and the benefits of any proposed changes.

In the case of Glaxo Smith Kline (GSK), the company might be advised to concentrate its value analysis initially at least on its identified key factors for success: R&D, marketing and product performance. In fact, the company's strategy during recent years has been to invest very heavily in research and development – *see* Case 6.1. As already explored, GSK acquired the UK pharmaceutical company Wellcome in 1995 and merged with Smith Kline Beecham in 2001.[18] One of the main reasons for these activities was the strong range of new drugs that would complement the existing Glaxo product portfolio – another way of achieving R&D development. GSK might also usefully investigate ways of raising the value of key *outputs* and lowering key *costs*. The opening case showed that this is precisely the strategic activity undertaken by the company.

Comment

In common with the value chain, the value system is mainly concerned with the *existing* linkages and may miss totally new strategic opportunities.

6.5.3 Developing competitive advantage linkages between the value chain and value system

Analysis of the value chain and the value system will provide information on value added in the company. For an organisation with a group of products, there may be some common item or common service across the group, for example:

● a common raw material (such as sugar in various food products); or

● a common distributor (such as a car parts distributor for a group with subsidiary companies manufacturing various elements in a car).

Such common items may be *linked* to develop competitive advantage. Such possible linkages may be important to strategic development because they are often *unique* to that organisation. The linkages might therefore provide advantages over competitors who do not have such linkages, or who are unable to easily develop them.

It was Porter[19] who suggested that value chains and value systems may not be sufficient in themselves to provide the competitive advantage needed by companies in developing their strategies. He argued that competitors can often imitate the *individual* moves made by an organisation; what competitors have much more difficulty in doing is imitating the special and possibly unique *linkages* that exist between elements of the value chain and the value systems of the organisation.

In addition to analysing resources for value chains and value systems, therefore, competitive strategy suggests that there is a third element. It is necessary to search for special and possibly unique linkages that either exist or might be developed between elements of the value chain and between value systems associated with the company. Figure 6.7 illustrates this situation.

Examples of such linkages abound:

● Common raw materials used in a variety of end-products: for example, petrochemical feedstocks are used widely to produce various products.

● Common services, such as telecommunications or media buying, where a combined contract could be negotiated at a lower price than a series of individual local deals.

● Linkages between technology development and production to facilitate new production methods that might be used in various parts of a group – for example, direct telecommunications links between large retail store chains such as Marks & Spencer and their suppliers.

Figure 6.7

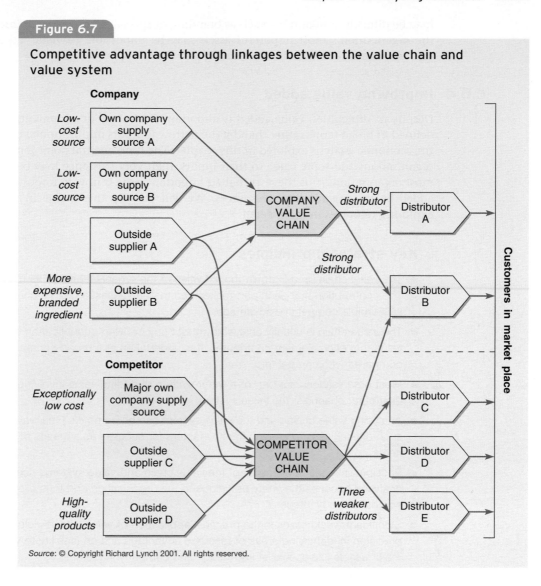

Competitive advantage through linkages between the value chain and value system

- Computer reservation systems that link airlines with travel ticket agents (proving to be so powerful that the European Commission has investigated their effects on airline competition).

- Joint ventures, alliances and partnerships that often rely on different members to the agreement bringing their special areas of expertise to the relationship (*see* Chapter 14).

All the above suggest that linkages that enhance value added may provide significant ways for companies to improve their resources.

Comment

One fundamental problem with the value chain, value system and its linkages is their broad perspective across the *range* of the company's resources. They are sometimes rather vague at identifying the *precise* nature and scope of the advantages such resources possess against competitors. Sustainable competitive advantage is not the primary target of the value-added analysis. The remaining sections of this chapter explore more direct ways of tackling this issue.

Another difficulty with value-added analysis is its focus on assets that can be clearly measured. This is a significant weakness because some of the organisation's most valuable assets may be difficult to quantify – such as branding or specialist knowledge. Moreover, some of the organisation's most important assets may be impossible to value, especially human resource assets like leadership and strong team building.

6.5.4 Improving value added

Despite its difficulties, value added is important in strategy development, especially when defined in broad terms rather than by the narrow (outputs minus inputs) definition used in the economic analysis explored in this chapter. The fundamental point remains that, unless organisations add some value to their inputs, their very existence may be in question. For most organisations, this suggests that an important issue is how to impose the value that is added by the organisation's resources. We will pick up this theme in Chapter 13 after exploring resources in more detail.

Key strategic principles

- The value chain breaks down the activities of the organisation into its main parts. The contribution that each part makes can then be assessed for its contribution to sustainable competitive advantage.

- The value chain is usually analysed without any detailed quantification of the added value that each element contributes. It is undertaken at a broad general level and is compared with competitors.

- Most organisations are part of a wider system of adding value involving supplier and distributor channels: the value system.

- Analysing value chains and the value system can be complex. One way of reducing such difficulties is to employ the key factors for success as a means of selecting the items.

- Possible linkages of elements of the value chain and value systems need to be analysed because they may be unique to the organisation and thus provide it with competitive advantage.

- Significant weaknesses in the practical application of value added include a lack of precision in identifying areas of resource advantage and an inability to value clearly major assets like specialist knowledge and company leadership.

6.6 RESOURCE ANALYSIS AND ECONOMIC RENT - THE CONTRIBUTION OF DAVID RICARDO

To understand the role of resources in competitive advantage, it is necessary to explore the concept of economic rent. This was first developed by David Ricardo (1772–1823), an English economist of the early nineteenth century. After making his fortune in stock-broking, Ricardo retired at the age of 42 and devoted his life to a consideration of economic and political issues.[20]

6.6.1 The concept of economic rent

Definition ➤ Economic rent is defined as any excess that a factor earns over the minimum amount needed to keep that factor in its present use. It was originally explored by Ricardo, who considered the rents earned by landlords from farmland that was used to grow corn. However, it is far more readily understood in the first half of the twenty-first century by examining the vast wages earned by pop stars, famous footballers and highly paid TV newscasters: typically, their annual salaries run to US$500,000 or more. Yet their ability to earn much beyond US$50,000 in other occupations is quite limited, so why pay them US$500,000 when they should be willing to play music, football and read the news for a mere US$50,000? Essentially, because such people are in short and fixed supply. They receive payments greatly in excess of the wages needed to stop them moving to other occupations: this excess of around US$450,000 (500,000 minus 50,000) is called *economic rent*.

6.6.2 Two main types of economic rent

In addition to some *resources* being in short supply, economic rent can also be derived from the market place – in strategic terms, opportunities in the organisation's *environment*. Ricardo never considered this latter form of rent. There are two main types of rent:[21]

Definition ➤ 1 *Ricardian rents* (after David Ricardo) derive from the *resources* of the organisation; they are rents generated from resources that possess some real competitive advantage, allowing the company to generate significant additional returns. For example, the advantage derived from a unique geographical location, like that of McDonald's outside the zoo in Berlin, or the possession of a special patent as in the case of the Dyson vacuum cleaner.

Definition ➤ 2 *Monopoly rents* derive from the *markets* in which the organisation operates. They are the rents associated with a company's unique position in the market place that allows it to earn exceptional returns. For example, a government-owned monopoly position in electricity or gas supply might generate exceptional returns. Equally, a privately owned position of market dominance can be built as a result of long and skilled investment in a market – Microsoft's possession of its Windows software with 90 per cent market share is an example here. It is important in this example to note that there is nothing special about Microsoft's resources – other companies have developed similar software but have been unable to dislodge the Microsoft dominance.

Definition ➤ There are other forms of economic rent, the most important from a strategic perspective being *Schumpeterian rents*. These are rents that derive from a new and innovatory product or service that allows the organisation to charge considerably above its costs of production. They will often involve risk-taking and entrepreneurial activity – as, for example, at the time of writing, in the case of some forms of digital video disc and digital computer cameras. Such rents are named after the famous US economist Joseph Schumpeter (1883–1950), who wrote extensively on the role of innovation in markets.[22] However, as Schumpeter himself recognised, such a position is inherently unstable because other organisations will enter a market place where high prices are being charged and high profits are being earned. New entrants will clearly need to find their way around any barriers to entry, but the result over time is that this form of rent will either disappear or become a subset of one of the two major types identified above. For example, Xerox (US) held patents on photocopying machinery in the 1960s and 1970s that included innovatory technology and allowed the company to earn exceptional profits. But in the period 1960–85, Canon (Japan) developed an alternative photocopying system that did not rely on the Xerox patents, thus negating the Xerox resource competitive advantage over time.

6.6.3 Implications of economic rent for resource analysis: scarcity and alternative use

Beyond its examination of the environment, the concept of economic rent has two significant implications for resource strategy:

1 *Scarcity of resource.* It identifies this concept and raises the possibility of developing resources that are so scarce that they can earn substantial economic rent.

2 *Alternative use for resources.* The concept explores other and more profitable uses for any resource beyond the one that is currently being pursued. Specifically, it considers the possibility that using the resource for another purpose might produce more rent.

Both these insights have considerable significance for the resource strategy of individual firms. Strategic development of the individual resources of an organisation can, at least in part, be directed at exploring these two issues – scarcity and alternative use. For example, GSK has developed a series of patented drugs that are sufficiently different for the company to charge a price premium – economic rent. Also, British Rail in the 1980s sold parts of the land that it was not using for its rail services to other manufacturing and retailing companies. The company increased its rent from the alternative use of some of its resources.

As far as the productive alternative use of resources is concerned, this is usually treated as an ongoing issue in strategy. In practice, some resources are more flexible than others in terms of alternative use. For example, once a factory has been built, it becomes difficult to make major changes because of its shape, design and layout (*see* Chapter 9). But companies that own their own fleet of transport may well find that they can sell it, invest the money in scarce resources and hire transport from outside companies more cheaply. At present, there is no substantive body of strategic resource theory that explores the alternative use of resources.

The characteristics of scarce resources that will generate high economic rent are explored in Section 6.7.

6.6.4 How does economic rent relate to accounting profit?

Accounting profit is the difference between total revenue and the *explicit* costs of generating this in a given time period – often over one year. Economic rent is different, because it is concerned with the difference between total revenue and the *opportunity cost* of the factors of production. The kernel of the concept of economic rent is that it is not concerned with the accounting profit that will arise from the current strategy, but the extra that might be earned beyond the current profit if the resources were to be used elsewhere. Accounting profit makes no attempt to measure this. More broadly, rent explores strategic concepts related to the organisation's possession and use of resources or its dominance in the market place. Accounting profit does not undertake this task. It is important in any strategic discussion of accounting profit to recognise its significant limitations – many strategies are evaluated in terms of their accounting profits and return on capital, so the problem cannot be dismissed lightly. Exhibit 6.3 compares the two concepts further.

Exhibit 6.3

Some differences between economic rent* and accounting profit

Economic rent*	Accounting profit
● Economic concept based on the alternative uses of resources	● Accounting concept based purely on artificial definitions of resources, etc.
● Time period unlimited	● Defined time period, e.g. one year
● Resources assessed for their value on the open market and for their ability to deliver future funds	● Quantification of resources based on historical costs rather than broader concept of their current usage
● Can be associated with specific resources and their ability to deliver unique sources of revenue	● No realistic possibility of identifying the quality of resources beyond simple numerical values
● Can also be associated with market dominance and its ability to deliver superior revenue	
● Important conceptually but difficult to calculate in practice	● Relatively easy to measure and calculate

* *Note*: Sometimes, economic rent is called economic profit. They are the same thing.

6.6.5 Comment on economic rent

Although economic rent is superior to accounting profit as a strategic concept and is widely used by economists, it has several difficulties:

- It is difficult to estimate because of the conceptual problem of ensuring that *all* alternative uses have been considered and accurately valued.

- It makes the simplistic assumption that every option can always be implemented, without regard for the human resource implications.

- It provides few insights on how to identify new Ricardian or monopoly rent opportunities at the commencement of strategy analysis. It is useful after the event (*ex post*) but is not so useful in advance when strategy is being formulated (*ex ante*).

Thus, its strategic benefits are mainly conceptual: Figure 6.8 provides a post-rationalised example from the world car industry of the strategic relationships between rents and resources.

Key strategic principles

- Economic rent is defined as any excess that a factor earns over the minimum amount needed to keep that factor in its present use.

- There are two main types of rent: *Ricardian* rents derive from the exceptional resources of the organisation and *monopoly* rents derive from the organisation's market position.

- Economic rent is important in strategy analysis because it highlights the scarcity of some resources and the possibility of alternative, more profitable uses for a resource.

- Economic rent is conceptually more relevant to strategic decision making than accounting profit because it is better at highlighting the main issues involved. However, economic rent is more difficult to calculate. Moreover, it oversimplifies some elements of strategy, such as human resource aspects and the strategic process itself.

Figure 6.8

Identifying the relationship between rent and resources – the global car industry

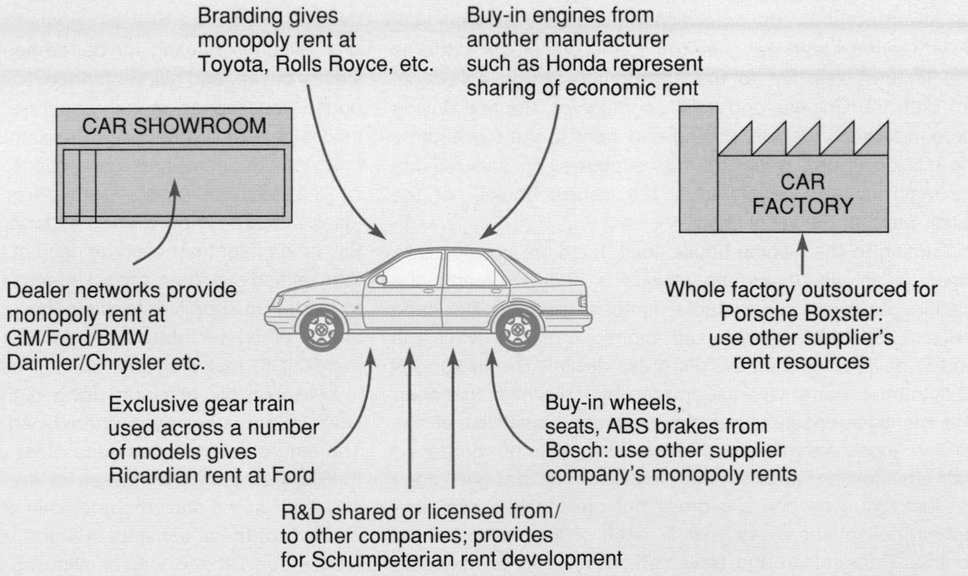

Branding gives monopoly rent at Toyota, Rolls Royce, etc.

Buy-in engines from another manufacturer such as Honda represent sharing of economic rent

CAR SHOWROOM

CAR FACTORY

Dealer networks provide monopoly rent at GM/Ford/BMW Daimler/Chrysler etc.

Whole factory outsourced for Porsche Boxster: use other supplier's rent resources

Exclusive gear train used across a number of models gives Ricardian rent at Ford

Buy-in wheels, seats, ABS brakes from Bosch: use other supplier company's monopoly rents

R&D shared or licensed from/ to other companies; provides for Schumpeterian rent development

CASE STUDY 6.3

Competitive advantage at Louis Vuitton and Gucci

With annual sales of over US$165 billion and gross profit margins of over 50 per cent, the major luxury goods companies rely on famous brands like Louis Vuitton and Gucci to deliver competitive advantage. But does the advantage come only from the brand name? Perhaps there are other advantages? This case explores competitive advantage in the world of high fashion luxury goods.

To explore competitive advantage in the industry, we begin by examining the *value chain* – where the profits are generated in the business. This is a useful starting point because it identifies those parts of the business that are particularly profitable and therefore likely to be linked with potential advantages. The second part of the case then uses the value chain to explore *competitive advantage* in luxury goods.

Value chain at a major fashion house

In practice in the luxury goods sector, the value chain is complex, with many interlocking parts. However, the key activity for most companies is the preparation and display of a new collection for its bi-annual fashion show. To explore this, we can take the example of a Paris fashion house, perhaps at the leading French company LVMH, which owns such brands as Louis Vuitton, Hennessy, Loewe, Kenzo, Givenchy and Thomas Pink. The lead designer at the fashion house has decided to make an embroidered silk *haute couture* dress as part of its next women's spring collection. This activity will generate profits through a value chain of business activities. The primary activities of the value chain are shown in Table 6.1. The support activities are not shown for reasons of simplicity, but the fashion designer, who oversees the whole process, is part of the firm infrastructure.

In order to make the dress, silk is supplied as thread mainly from China to a co-ordinating company, often in Northern Italy. The co-ordinating company has a network of associated companies in the geographical area to dye, spin and weave the silk. Importantly, the co-ordinating company will work very closely with the lead designer from LVMH on colours, patterns and textures relevant to the appropriate design collection. For both the Chinese and Italian companies, the real driving force in terms of design, pricing and sales to the customer is the fashion house, rather than its suppliers. For this reason, the main value is generated at the fashion house, not the earlier parts of the value chain.

Turning to the fashion house itself, there are considerable variations in where and how value is added. Clearly, the fashion designer – for example, famous designers like John Galliano, Stella McCartney and Giorgio Armani – takes the lead in developing the new silk dress design. The designer's work is often better when supported by a business manager. The manager ensures that the business objectives of the fashion house are met and that the designer is not burdened with unnecessary administrative matters. The designer does not just focus on one silk dress but creates two complete fashion collections every year in each of the major fashion centres: Paris, Milan and New York. The designer may also

Competitive advantage in the fashion industry includes brand reputation. But for the leading fashion houses, the lead fashion designer is probably more important.

© Royalty-Free/Corbis

develop men's as well as women's collections, arrange a pre-collection briefing for department stores and other subsidiary buyers and also contribute to the design of the fashion house accessories range – scarves, bags, shoes, etc. The embroidered silk dress of our example will probably appear only once in one of these collections.

The designer begins each dress collection with fashion ideas that are simply draped as fabric on a static mannequin. Silk fabric might not even be used at this stage. The ideas are then refined over time, the silk fabric chosen and the brief given to the Italian suppliers to make this specific fabric – described above. When the material arrives from the Italian supplier, it is then cut to make up the finished garment. The final stages involve invisible stitching using highly skilled seamstresses who are an extremely important part of a top fashion house. The embroidery too demands great expertise. The silk dress then appears on the catwalk of the fashion show and subsequently in the showroom for sale after public presentation.

Each of these activities will add value to the finished garment – see Table 6.1. Even allowing for the expense of hand

Table 6.1

Value chain of a *haute couture* silk dress

Position in chain	Activity	Amount and location of value added
Suppliers	Silk thread from China	Low – many suppliers
	Spinning, weaving and dyeing in Italy	Low/medium – several suppliers
	Design co-operation with fashion house on colours, patterns, styles and fabrics	High – specialist work requiring good contacts and co-operation with fashion house
Inbound logistics – the goods arrive at the fashion house	Variety of importers, direct purchases	Low – many methods available, none exclusive
Operations – the design and manufacture of each *haute couture* dress	Famous designer, e.g. John Galliano or Stella McCartney	High – crucial element – see text
	Draping and sculpting new design, cutting and sewing up finished dress	High but limited volume – see text
Outbound logistics – distributing the dresses to the shops and licensees	Mainly through the fashion house's own exclusive shops	Medium/high – need to keep control of brand
Marketing and sales	Fashion shows in Paris, Milan and New York	High
	Media coverage of show	Valuable – cost of show US$500,000 with value of media coverage into millions of dollars
	Special pre-collection briefing for department stores	Medium – useful for brand promotion and aspiration
	Brand-associated products like ready to wear and accessories like shoes, bags	Possibly highest value added here – see text
Service – exclusive and discreet levels of service to the wealthy clients	Through ownership of retail outlets	High, but small number of clients for *haute couture*
Additional and important service for clients wishing to purchase *prêt-à-porter*		Greater number of clients for *prêt-à-porter* (ready-to-wear)

Note: For reasons of simplicity, only the primary activities are identified in the value chain above. The fashion designer, who oversees the whole process, is arguably involved in every part of the primary activities and, in addition, is part of the firm infrastructure in the secondary activities.

Source: see references.

finishing, the resulting price of the silk dress may appear high – perhaps as much as US$30,000 – and the value added may therefore seem high. However, there are only a relatively few *haute couture* customers – perhaps only 2,000 around the world – who are able to afford such prices. Thus the 'value' generated from the embroidered silk dress in absolute terms is relatively small. The real value added at the fashion house comes in at least three other related areas:

1 *Off-the-peg dresses from the same design label*: many people may not be able to afford the $30,000 silk dress, but they will pay $2,000 for a *prêt-à-porter* (ready-to-wear) dress from the same designer.

2 *Shoes, scarves and other accessories*: many customers will also pay $500 for shoes and other items from the same fashion house. Some of these may be made inside the fashion house, but many will be subcontracted to outside suppliers and then sold through the retail outlets owned by the fashion house.

3 *Other related and licensed items*: customers will also pay $50–$100 for fragrances and other items related to the brand. Such items may not be manufactured by the fashion house but by licensees of the brand name.

The brand is therefore more than just a silk embroidered dress produced for a fashion show. Fashion houses license

► CASE STUDY 6.3 continued

their brand names to outside companies but also understand the real danger of diluting the brand. An example of 'brand dilution' is the Pierre Cardin brand, which used to be a major high fashion brand in the 1970s. During the 1980s, the brand was licensed to over 800 products, including toilet seat covers. The Pierre Cardin brand is still important and well respected, but it is no longer a part of the high fashion luxury market in the sense explored in this case.

High fashion houses guard their brands carefully and will even revoke licences if they judge that the brand is being diluted: examples of activities leading to brand dilution include selling the ends of lines below normal pricing or attaching the brand name to an unsuitable product. From a more positive perspective, brand licensing across a number of related products means that a fashion house has a range of activities to exploit its major brands. For example, the world's leading fragrance company, L'Oréal, has bought licences from fashion houses for several of the L'Oréal luxury fragrance ranges – including Giorgio Armani, Ralph Lauren and Cacherel – see Case 8.2.

There are two additional aspects to value generation at fashion houses that are not captured in the simple design and manufacture of a single silk dress:

- Most of the fashion houses have developed their *own retail outlets* to sell their products around the world. For example, the market leader in luxury goods is the French company LVMH: it has around 1,600 stores and derives around 80 per cent of its sales from these outlets.
- Fashion houses also operate a *range of brands*, each with its own designer and fashion activity. For example, LVMH owns at least 50 brands, though not all are involved in fashion clothing. The purpose of such a strategy is to spread the risk: if one fashion house brand within the group suffers a temporary downturn, then another brand can take over. In total, LVMH employs 56,000 people with two-thirds of them being located outside its home country, France.

Competitive advantage in the luxury goods industry

Although the value chain locates the high profit margin activities, it does not necessarily follow that all will deliver competitive advantage for a company. The high profit margin activities may be the same at all the fashion houses and therefore not deliver a competitive advantage to a particular fashion house. Nevertheless, the value chain is a useful starting point because competitive advantage is more likely to be

Table 6.2

The three leading high fashion houses

Company	Sales 2002	Main brands – some in accessories and fragrances	Extra activities
LVMH • Louis Vuitton Moët Hennessy • Based in France	• US$12 billion • 80 per cent of sales in own stores – around 1,600 stores • Advertising spend in 2004: US$220 million	• Loewe, Celine, Kenzo, Givenchy, Marc Jacobs, Fendi, StefanoBi, Emilio Pucci, Donna Karan, Thomas Pink	• 15 wine and spirit brands, including Hennessy cognac • 10 perfume and beauty brands, including Christian Dior and Guerlain • 6 watch and jewellery companies including TAG Heuer and Zenith • 7 retail accessory companies
Richemont • Based in Switzerland	• US$3.6 billion • 55 per cent of sales in own stores – around 3,500 stores • Advertising spend in 2004: US$75 million	• Chloé, Cartier, Piaget, Van Cleef & Arpels, Dunhill, Hackett • More than half sales come from Cartier, the jewellers. But the company plans to expand its Chloé high fashion brand	• 2 pen companies – Mont Blanc brand • 6 watch companies
Gucci Group • Controlled by Pinault Printemps Redoute (PPR), the French department store chain	• US$2.4 billion • 50 per cent of sales in own stores – around 1,500 stores • Advertising spend in 2004: US$55 million	• Gucci, Yves St Laurent, Alexander McQueen, Stella McCartney, Balenciaga, Sergio Rossi	• Retail shops, department stores, mail order catalogue

Source: see references.

associated with high profits. In the case of the luxury goods market, it will be immediately evident that the competitive advantage rests only partly with a *brand name* like Gucci or Louis Vuitton. Table 6.2 examines the three leading luxury goods companies and describes the main attributes that will then generate competitive advantage.

Taking the elements of the value chain, we can explore them to test whether they deliver competitive advantage for a leading fashion house:

● *Brand*. This is a key ingredient that sets one company apart from another. The leading company has some well-known brands but so do its rivals. Importantly in fashion, the brand needs to be constantly renewed with advertising to support this. Part of the competitive advantage is therefore in brand support, including two items:
  ● the amount of advertising spend – LVMH leads here;
  ● the fashion house designer as part of the brand: examples include Jean Paul Gaultier and Yves St Laurent. Competitive advantage is strong here.
● *Designer*. The name, flair, skills and creative ability of the designer is a crucial factor in developing and maintaining a top fashion house. Designers can revive fashion houses – for example, Tom Ford (designer) and Domenico de Sole (business partner) who transformed Gucci in the early 1990s. They have now left the company after it was sold to the French store group, PPR, but their reputation lives on. In March 2005, it was reported that the new designer in charge of women's wear at Gucci Group after Mr Ford, Alessandra Facchinetti, resigned as a result of 'commercial concerns ruling the fashion world'. Clearly, the designer is a crucial competitive advantage in high fashion but also needs to deliver the results.
● *Range of brands*. Both LVMH and PPR argue that one of their real strengths is that they have many brands. If one declines over time, then there are others to take its place. In addition, the range means that it can make a more comprehensive offering to a wide range of customers – perhaps classic designs for some, with avant-garde for others. However, it is not entirely clear whether the brand range at LVMH is *superior* to the ranges at other leading companies. This is not necessarily a competitive advantage.
● *Licensing and franchising*. This is a major source of revenue for all the high fashion houses. There are dangers, as outline above, but the benefits from controlled and

monitored business activity are significant. Again, although these activities are important, there is no evidence that one of the leading fashion houses has a competitive advantage here – they are all good.
● *Retail outlets*. The leading high fashion houses control at least half of their sales directly. There are several reasons for this: first, because they retain the profit margin; second, because they retain control over how the brand is presented; third, because they are able to present the right ambience and level of discreet and exclusive service for their leading clients. But there is no clear competitive advantage between the three leading companies in this area – they all have strong and well-located store chains.
● *Location*. Paris, Milan and New York are vital for a real impact in high fashion. (Berlin, London, Madrid and Singapore are good but not as important.) Part of the reason for this is the major industrial infrastructure developed near Paris, Milan and New York to support the fashion industry. For example, France has some 2,000 firms, 200,000 jobs and 5 per cent of total industrial production directly associated with the fashion industry. These figures do not include the textile industry and media-related activities also connected to high fashion. But location does not deliver competitive advantage for one leading company over another.

Case questions

1 *Do you agree with the above comments and conclusions on the competitive advantages of luxury goods companies? What are the competitive advantages of such companies?*

2 *Can the competitive advantages listed above be reclassified using the resource-based concepts developed by strategists like Hamel and Prahalad and Kay? You should consult the sections that follow to review possible areas and then use Figure 6.9 which summarises them.*

3 *Can companies outside the fashion industry draw any useful lessons from the strategies used in this industry? In exploring this question, you might like to consider such topics as branding, licensing, control of retail outlets and the levels of service.*

6.7 RESOURCE ANALYSIS AND COMPETITIVE ADVANTAGE – THE RESOURCE-BASED VIEW

If economic rent derives from exceptional resources, i.e. those that have sustainable competitive advantage, then the question arises as to what makes a resource exceptional. Over the years 1984–99, strategy writers developed a mainly prescriptive answer to this question. It did not happen all at once but emerged from various books and research papers over the period; some of the main contributors are summarised in Exhibit 6.4.[24] Hence, it is not appropriate to attribute the development to one person. The overall title of the

Definition ➤ approach is the *resource-based view* (RBV) of strategy development. The RBV stresses the importance of the *individual* resources of the organisation in delivering the competitive advantage of the organisation and represents a substantial shift in emphasis away from the market-based view that was emphasised in the 1980s and early 1990s through the work of Professor Michael Porter and others – *see* Chapter 3.

Exhibit 6.4

Some selected contributions to the development of the RBV[25]

Author(s)	Date	Summary
Wernerfelt	1984	Companies were seen as a collection of resources, rather than holding market positions in the development of strategy
Barney	1986, 1991	Competitive market imperfections, market entry barriers and other constraints require differing company resources and the immobility of resources for the development of successful strategy
Rumelt	1987	Importance of resources in strategy development
Dierickx and Cool	1989	Strategic assets are developed internally, not acquired. Such assets take time to develop
Schoemaker	1990	Identified factors important in determining useful assets. Some assets not readily tradable for reasons of specialist skills, know-how and reputation
Prahalad and Hamel	1990	Key resources: skills and technologies called core competencies – *see* text
Peteraf	1990	Identified four distinguishing features of resources
Grant	1991	Definition of resources, capabilities and competitive advantage
Connor	1991	Resources long-lived, difficult to imitate
Amit and Schoemaker	1993	Explored processes through which resources are developed, e.g. bounded rationality
Kay	1994	Identified the three most important resources as the firm's ability to innovate, its reputation and its network of relationships inside and outside (architecture) – *see* text
Teece, Pisano and Shuen	1997	Explored the changing nature of resources
Makadok	2001	Examined resource-based and dynamic capabilities with a view to developing a synthesis
Hoopes, Madsen and Walker	2003	Special edition of *Strategic Management Journal* on the RBV – 13 papers on the topic

6.7.1 The reasons for the development of the RBV

During the 1980s, strategists like Porter explored and emphasised the need to identify profitable markets and then find competitive advantage by industry solutions in those markets – for example, his 'generic strategies' are explored in Chapter 13. Even while these developments were receiving strong approval from some commentators, disturbing evidence was pointing in a different direction. For example, Rumelt[26] published a study in 1991 of the sources of profits in major US corporations in the 1970s. This suggested that the greatest contributor to overall company profitability was at the *individual company level* rather than at the higher, corporate level or at the level of the industry overall or the cyclicality of the industry. The results are shown in Table 6.3. For this North American sample, they indicate that what matters is the individual business area rather than the industry. Whether this finding is true for other countries and industry samples cannot easily be established. But it did suggest that industry solutions to resources are unlikely to be the main

Table 6.3

Contributions to the variance of profitability across business units

Source within corporation	Contribution to the total profitability of the corporation
Corporate ownership	0.8%
Industry effects	8.3%
Cyclical effects	7.8%
Business unit specific effects	46.4%
Unexplained factors	36.7%
Total across corporation	100%

Source: See reference 27.

source of profits, thus undermining the Porter approach. In fairness to Professor Porter, he produced similar evidence himself (with McGahan) in research published in 1997.[28] However, Porter's research suggested that the company effect was not quite as large as that found by Rumelt, possibly because Porter used a sample that included service industries as well as manufacturing.

Around the same time, other strategists were puzzled by the different long-term profit performance of companies in the same industry. They argued that, if industry was the main determinant of profits, then all companies in an industry should have similar levels of profitability. But this clearly was not the case. For example, Kellogg (US) had declining profits in its breakfast cereal business while General Mills (US) continued to grow – *see* Chapter 2. Toyota (Japan) and Honda (Japan) made massive strides worldwide in the car industry, often at the expense of General Motors (US), and Ford (US), who were losing profits, even in their home markets – *see* Chapters 9 and 19. Acer (Taiwan) and Dell (US) were growing in personal computers while companies like IBM (US) and Apple (US) were struggling to survive – *see* Chapters 1 and 2. Why did this happen? Industry analysis was certainly not wrong: it was needed to identify sustainable competitive advantage and customer needs. But it was clearly not enough.

The essence of the RBV development is its focus on the *individual* resources of the organisation, rather than the strategies that are common to all companies in an industry. It is important to understand the industry, but organisations should seek their own solutions within that context. Sustainable competitive advantage then comes by striving to exploit the *relevant* resources of the individual organisation when compared with other organisations. Relevance means the identification of resources that are better than those of competitors, persuasive to the customer and available from the range of strengths contained inside the organisation. For example, GSK's strategy on pharmaceutical development should concentrate on drugs that will be more effective than those of the competition, offer genuine benefits to the customer and fit with its existing areas of drug strength in treating asthma, viral drugs, etc. It should not move into an area involving technology that is new to the company but where potential competitors like Johnson & Johnson (US) are already well established, such as surgical equipment and dressings.

Within the context of industry analysis, the starting point for the RBV is a careful exploration of the resources of the organisation – this was explored in Section 6.3. But beyond this *general* analysis it is necessary to identify those attributes that give an individual organisation its *particular* strengths.

6.7.2 The seven elements of resource-based sustainable competitive advantage

Over time, various strategists have explored the advantages that an individual organisation might possess to obtain competitive advantage. There is no agreement amongst them on

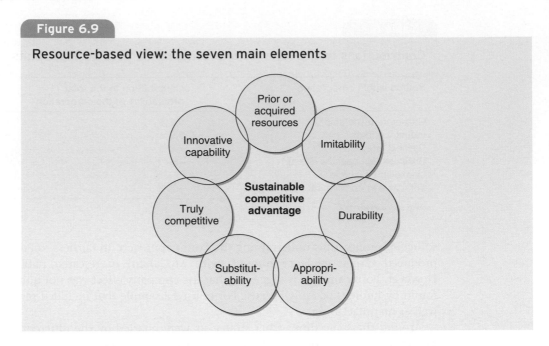

Figure 6.9

Resource-based view: the seven main elements

the precise source of such advantages. For example, Prahalad and Hamel highlighted one key resource,[29] Kay[30] has identified three main areas, Peteraf[31] suggested four areas, and Collis and Montgomery[32] have described five. Certainly, these and other writers have made significant contributions and all are agreed on the importance of individual company resources within an industry. Taking all these views into account, it is useful to identify seven elements that comprise the RBV: *see* Figure 6.9. In addition, it should be noted that several of these elements have *additional* clarifying subordinate aspects – perhaps this is where the disagreement has arisen.

- *Prior or acquired resources*. Value creation is more likely to be successful if it builds on the strengths that are already available to the organisation, rather than starting from scratch in a totally new area. It does not guarantee that the strategy will be successful but it is a major starting point. Moreover, building on existing strengths will exploit any real uniqueness that has been built as a result of the organisation's history and investment over many years – economists call this *path dependency*. It may be very difficult for competitors to develop the same complex resources. We explored this at the end of Chapter 2 in the section on strategy as history. Finally, one other prior strength that is of major importance in the development of future strategy is the existing reputation of the organisation. For example, the UK retailer Marks & Spencer has certain strengths in terms of *reputation* and quality that will form the basis of future strategy.

- *Innovative capability*. Some organisations are better able to innovate than others. Innovation is important because it is particularly likely to deliver a real breakthrough in competitive advantage that others will have difficulty in matching for a lengthy period. Innovation is explored at various points throughout this book, particularly in Chapter 11. For example, the Japanese consumer electronics company Sony has developed a consistent ability to produce new products over many years. We will return to innovation shortly.

- *Being truly competitive*. It is essential that any resource delivers a true advantage over the competition. This comes back partly to the test of *relevance* to customers, competitors and company strengths outlined in Section 6.7.1 above. But it emphasises that identifying the resource as being a real strength is not enough: the resource must be *comparatively* better than the competition. For example, it is not enough to have a 'low-cost, high-quality' factory – it must have lower costs and higher quality than that of competitors. For example, the US company Microsoft has developed a computer software package and market position that is superior to any other in the world.

- *Substitutability*. Resources are more likely to be competitive if they cannot be substituted. Sometimes unique resources can be replaced by totally new alternatives. This element was explored in Chapter 3 in Porter's Five Forces Model and is equally valid here in the RBV. For example, there is no substitute for the US Walt Disney company's Mickey Mouse character.

- *Appropriability*. Resources must deliver the results of their advantage to the individual company and not be forced to distribute at least part of it to others. Just because a resource has competitive advantage does not necessarily mean that its benefits will come to the owners. They could be forced to give up some profits to others by the bargaining power of the various stakeholders of the organisation – customers, employees, suppliers and so on. We will explore stakeholders in Chapter 12 and bargaining in Chapter 15, in the section on game theory. Another method of maintaining appropriability is through the company patenting its products and processes. Whatever method is used, the company must be able to keep the profits that the resource generates. For example, the Italian company Benetton has organised its business such that it owns both manufacturing and distribution outlets, thus ensuring that it retains the value added that has been generated throughout its value chain.

- *Durability*. Useful resources must have some longevity. There is no point in identifying a competitive resource whose advantage is not sustainable. At some future time, it is likely that all competitive resources will succumb to the fate described earlier in this chapter by Joseph Schumpeter and no longer deliver competitive advantage. But the longer a resource can keep its advantage, the better. Brand names like that owned by the US photographic company Kodak have that durability.

- *Imitability*. Resources must not be easy to imitate if they are to have competitive advantage. Although many resources can eventually be copied, such a process can be delayed by a number of devices:
  - *Tangible uniqueness*. Some form of specific differentiation, such as branding or a specific geographic location or patent protection, will delay imitability.
  - *Causal ambiguity*. It may not be obvious to competitors what gives a resource its competitive edge. There may be some complex organisational processes that have taken years to develop that are difficult for outside companies to learn or acquire.
  - *Investment deterrence*. When the market has limited or unknown growth prospects and it is difficult to make a small initial investment, a substantial investment by the organisation in the new strategy may well deter competitors from entering the market. This is particularly true where large capital plant or major advertising campaigns are essential to launch products and services.

For example, the Japanese car company Toyota has developed a manufacturing process that has many human resource elements like team working that cannot easily be observed. This has made it difficult for other car companies to copy the superior Toyota practices.

6.7.3 The relationship between the seven elements and the other resources of the organisation – the hierarchy of resources

Although seven RBV elements have been identified, it is unnecessary for an organisation to possess them all before it has competitive advantage over others. In practice, most successful strategies will involve only a few of the above. The precise combination that will deliver competitive advantage is totally dependent on the unique resource structure of each organisation – these can be considered as the *core resources* of the organisation.

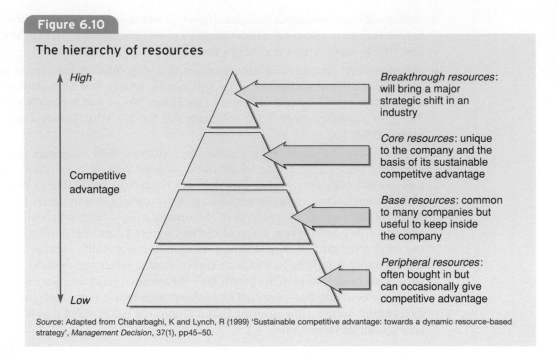

Figure 6.10

The hierarchy of resources

High

Breakthrough resources: will bring a major strategic shift in an industry

Core resources: unique to the company and the basis of its sustainable competitve advantage

Competitive advantage

Base resources: common to many companies but useful to keep inside the company

Peripheral resources: often bought in but can occasionally give competitive advantage

Low

Source: Adapted from Chaharbaghi, K and Lynch, R (1999) 'Sustainable competitive advantage: towards a dynamic resource-based strategy', *Management Decision*, 37(1), pp45–50.

One specific area of core resource deserves to be considered particularly carefully: innovative ability. It is very difficult to develop and is more likely to supply an advantage that competitors cannot possess in the short term. It will be in short supply, but any success will transform the competitive advantage of the organisation. Innovative ability can be considered as the *breakthrough resource* of the organisation. This topic is explored further in Chapter 11.

In addition to the special resources that have been identified as delivering sustainable competitive advantage, most organisations will have other resources that are cheaper and more convenient to own inside rather than purchase outside – perhaps company secretarial skills, information technology and other areas. They may not be unique but are important to the daily operation of the business. It should be noted that even these skills, knowledge and resources may also deliver some competitive advantage to an organisation, but such advantage is unlikely to be as substantive as the seven elements outlined above. They can be considered as the *base resources* of the business.

Finally, for reasons of convenience and history, many organisations also have other resources that they own or buy in as needed. These might include advertising, catering, transport, legal services, and so on. They are important for the business and can even deliver competitive advantage – perhaps by the *quality* of the outside knowledge or advice purchased. These can be considered for the most part as the *peripheral resources* of the organisation.

Together the above four areas make up the *hierarchy of resources* of the organisation – *see* Figure 6.10. The distinguishing feature of the levels of the hierarchy is an increased likelihood of sustainable competitive advantage in its higher levels.

6.7.4 The VRIO Framework – a mechanism for testing competitive resources

Even if the resource hierarchy is useful in providing an initial assessment of the resources possessed by an organisation, there is still the question of identifying those resources that are most likely to provide the return potential associated with exploiting the firm's resources or capabilities. We need a mechanism for testing the competitive resources.

Table 6.4

The VRIO Framework

Is a resource or capability . . .

Valuable?	Rare?	Costly to imitate?	Capable of being exploited by the organisation?	Competitive implications	Comparative economic performance to be expected from the resource
No	–	–	No	Competitive disadvantage	Below normal
Yes	No	–		Competitive parity	Normal
Yes	Yes	No		Temporary competitive advantage	Above normal
Yes	Yes	Yes	Yes	Sustained competitive advantage	Above normal

Source: Barney, Jay B, *Gaining and Sustaining Competitive Advantage*, 2nd Edition, © 2002, pp173, 174. Reprinted by permission of Pearson Education, Inc., Upper Saddle River, NJ.

Professor Jay Barney of Ohio State University has suggested the *VRIO Framework* to provide such a route – *see* Table 6.4. This is a sequential decision-making approach which starts by questioning each resource and asking if it is valuable. Having answered this question, the question then goes on to examine rarity, imitation and organisational capability as outlined below:

- *Valuable*. An organisation's resource needs to be valuable if it is to allow a firm to choose strategies that exploit environmental opportunities or neutralise a competitive threat.
- *Rare*. An organisation's resource needs to be rare. If the resource is available to competitors then exploiting the resource will not generate competitive advantage and economic performance will not be superior to rivals.
- *Cannot be imitated*. An organisation's resource needs to be costly to imitate. If it can be easily imitated then competitors will be able over time to take advantage of the profits generated in the market place to duplicate the rare resource.
- *Organising capability*. An organisation needs to be able to organise itself to exploit its valuable, rare and inimitable resource. In a sense, this is a balancing factor in relation to the three above.

These factors can then come together in the VRIO Framework as a series of cascading decisions. They start by asking whether a resources is valuable, then rare, then easy to imitate, then whether the organisation is well organised to exploit the opportunity. Table 6.4 shows the complete framework.

Key strategic principles

- The resource-based view (RBV) argues that the individual resources of an organisation provide a stronger basis for strategy development than industry analysis. The reason is that the RBV will identify those resources that are exceptional and have sustainable competitive advantage.

Key strategic principles *continued*

- There are seven elements of resource-based competitive advantage: prior or acquired resources, innovative ability, being truly competitive, substitutability, appropriability, durability and imitability.

- It is not necessary for an organisation to possess all of them before it has some competitive advantages. Each organisation will have a unique combination of resources, some of which will involve sustainable competitive advantage (SCA). These resources can be considered as a hierarchy with four areas defined by a decreasing likelihood of possessing SCA: breakthrough resources, core resources, basic resources and peripheral resources.

- The VRIO Framework – Valuable, Rare, Inimitable and Organisationally possible – can be used to test resources for their ability to contribute to competitive advantage.

6.8 IDENTIFYING WHICH RESOURCES DELIVER SUSTAINABLE COMPETITIVE ADVANTAGE

We are now in a position to identify those resources of the organisation that are most likely to deliver sustainable competitive advantage (SCA). However , it should be noted that this involves a degree of judgement. Moreover, strategic thinking is still developing in this area. The complete process related to SCA is summarised in Figure 6.11.

6.8.1 Analysing the resources of an individual organisation

In analysing how resources deliver SCA, it is essential to begin by analysing the complete range of resources of the organisation. This is not easy because some resources are difficult to measure or even define in an unambiguous way. For example, the patents of the pharmaceutical company GSK represent resources whose future value cannot simply be

Figure 6.11

Identifying the resources that deliver SCA

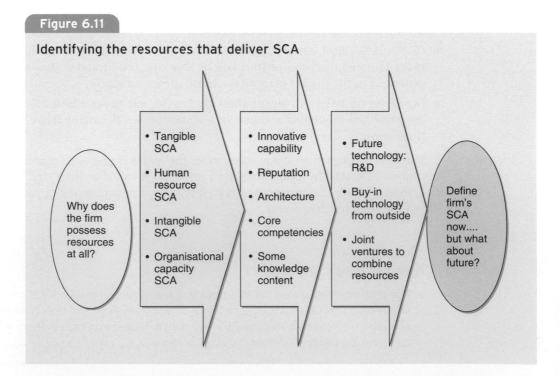

determined by examining the company's accounts. The reason is that such assets will decline in value as the patents expire, and may not be fully valued in the accounts in any event. Equally, the company's chief executive (Jean-Paul Garnier in 2002) provides an important resource called leadership, which is impossible to quantify but vital to strategy development. In strategy analysis, accounting and management systems data may represent a starting point, but little more.

Essentially, the resources of the organisation are those assets that contribute to the generation of value added. As a starting point, it is useful to divide them into three broad categories.[33]

Definition ➤ 1 *Tangible resources* are the physical resources of the organisation that contribute to its value added. Plant and equipment at the German chemical giant Bayer can clearly be identified and valued. The location of McDonald's restaurants on busy highways, rather than obscure secondary roads, is clearly a valuable and tangible resource.

Definition ➤ 2 *Intangible resources* are those resources that have no physical presence but represent real benefit to the organisation, like brand names, service levels and technology. The Mars Company (US) had a brand name that not only worked in chocolate but was extended into ice cream. The Sharp Corporation (Japan) has a knowledge of flatscreen technology that has allowed the company to develop a strong presence globally in the computer liquid crystal display market.

Definition ➤ 3 *Organisational capability* is the skills, routines, management and leadership of the organisation. The Toyota Motor Corporation (Japan) has become legendary for low-cost, lean manufacturing and also for developing new car models faster than its rivals. We examine this in Chapter 9. Such skills and routines take years to develop and represent an important resource for the organisation.

In practice, such an analysis will concentrate on the main resource areas of the organisation, especially those that deliver added value and competitive advantage. It may well employ the *key factors for success* in an industry as a starting point to make sense of what might otherwise be a time-consuming and unproductive task. An example of the main points of such an analysis is shown in Exhibit 6.5. We will return to these three areas of resource later in the chapter.

Exhibit 6.5

Resource analysis at the worldwide hotel chain Holiday Inns

	Resource
Tangible	● Physical locations at airports, city centres, holiday destinations, etc. ● Size and facilities of individual hotels: rooms, restaurants, swimming pool, etc.
Intangible	● Brand name of Holiday Inns ● Employees in management, reception, room cleaning, etc.
Organisational capability	● Suppliers of food, telephone services, etc. ● Management training to maintain and improve levels of service ● Management organisation and leadership ● Organisational routines that allow each hotel to run smoothly and efficiently

6.8.2 The particular importance of three distinctive capabilities: architecture, reputation and innovation

Part 5a

As outlined above, different researchers have approached the issue of the resources that will deliver sustainable competitive advantage in different ways. Two areas in particular deserve further exploration: distinctive capabilities and core competencies. Although they are contained within the framework outlined above, they represent particular areas of interest and insight. They also make the important point that different strategists lay the emphasis on different areas. For example, the distinctive capabilities approach treats 'innovative ability' as being no more important than any other core resources – in contrast to the approach in Section 6.7.3 above. This section explores distinctive capabilities in more depth and the next section examines core competencies.

In the analysis of resources, Professor John Kay argued that the distinctive capabilities of an organisation's resources are particularly important in delivering competitive advantage. *Distinctive capabilities* relate to three possible unique resource areas in an organisation: architecture, reputation and innovative ability.[34] They are complex and not necessarily capable of quantified analysis but they will undoubtedly contribute to the distinctive development of a company's strategy. He introduced and explored them by explaining that an organisation has a series of contracts and more informal relationships:

● with its employees inside the organisation;

● with its suppliers, distributors and customers outside in the environment and

● possibly between a group of collaborating firms inside and outside the immediate industry.

The relationships have been built over time. Some are formal and some informal. They are similar to, but more extended than, the linkages explored in the value system of Section 6.5.2 above. They provide the organisation with three major ways for their resources to be distinctive from competitors'.

Definition ➤ 1 *Architecture* is the network of relationships and contracts both inside and outside the firm. Its importance lies in its ability to create knowledge and routines, to respond to market changes and to exchange information both inside and outside the organisation. Long-term relationships with other organisations can lead to real strategy benefits that competitors cannot replicate. Examples include:

● the contacts between major construction companies such as Bouygues and government departments which place substantial contracts;

● negotiations between rail companies such as Nederlandse Spoorwegen and trade unions on new working practices to introduce new technologies and reduce costs;

● corporate negotiation between pharmaceutical companies such as GSK and Merck and governments on new drug price structures.

Definition ➤ 2 *Reputation* is the strategic standing of the organisation in the eyes of its customers and other stakeholders. This allows an organisation to communicate favourable information about itself to its customers. It is particularly concerned with long-term relationships and takes lengthy periods to build. Once gained, it provides a real distinctiveness that rivals cannot match. Examples include:

● Reputation for good-quality work, delivered on time and to budget. Construction companies can gain immensely over time as they perform consistently in this area.

● Reputation for a quality service that is usually punctual and reliable. Railway companies can gain or lose in this area, particularly when they are competing for business against alternative forms of public transport such as buses.

Definition ➤ 3 *Innovative capability* is the special talent possessed by some organisations for developing and exploiting innovative ideas. Some organisations find it easier to innovate than others because of their structures, culture, procedures and rewards. They may even innovate and then fail to take advantage of this against competitors. This is a highly important area of strategy that deserves careful study. It is therefore explored more fully in Chapter 11.

Comment

The above areas of resource will apply to a greater or lesser extent to most organisations. In themselves, they are important but uncontroversial.

All three areas usually require years of development. The first two are easier to define than they are to develop in terms of options: the *method* by which architecture and reputation are to be improved begs numerous questions about their nature that are difficult to explore. There is a tendency towards worthy, but largely meaningless, wish-fulfilment statements about the desirability of improving them. Kay offers no clear exposition in this area. The third element, innovation, will be explored in Chapter 11. Some strategists judge that there are so many other potential areas of resource-based advantage that it is not worth highlighting these areas, as appears in this text. The point is correct but fails to take into account the broad nature of the RBV and thus the difficulty of making it actionable.

The real point is how they are understood and used to gain competitive advantage. Resource analysis in these areas needs to take into account the changes that can occur over time and the need to explore not only the area itself but how it can be developed further. This is where the alternative viewpoint of the seven elements of the RBV can make a contribution.

6.8.3 The particular importance of core competencies

Definition ➤

Part 5a

In a related area of study, Hamel and Prahalad have explored the area of core skills and competencies.[35] Core competencies are a group of production skills and technologies that enable an organisation to provide a particular benefit to customers; they underpin the leadership that companies have built or wish to acquire over their competitors.

Core skills are a fundamental resource of the organisation. The two authors describe the example of Sharp (Japan) and Toshiba (Japan), both of which identified *flat-screen electronic technology* as an opportunity area that they expected to see grow in the future. Both companies invested hundreds of millions of dollars in developing their technology and skills in the market for flat screens that would then be used in miniature televisions, portable computers, digital watches, electronic video recorders and other areas. Importantly, this investment was made *before* it was possible to build a product-specific business case that would justify this level of investment. Core competencies form the basis of core products which, in turn, form the basis of the business areas of the company.

Core competencies cover an integration of skills, knowledge and technology. This combination can then lead to competitive advantage. The analysis of such areas is derived from a study of its components in an individual organisation. A skills analysis needs to be conducted at a level that is detailed enough to reveal useful strategic insights but not so detailed that it is unmanageable. The two authors suggest that if only three or four skills are identified this may be too broad, but if 40 or 50 are identified this may be too detailed. They suggest there are three areas that distinguish the major core competencies:

1 *Customer value.* Competencies must make a real impact on how the customer perceives the organisation and its products or services.

2 *Competitor differentiation.* This must be competitively unique. If the whole industry has the skill, then it is not core unless the organisation's skills in the area are really special.

3 *Extendable.* Core skills need to be capable of providing the basis of products or services that go beyond those currently available. The skill needs to be removed from the particular product group in which it currently rests. The organisation needs to imagine how it might be exploited in the whole area of its operations.

Importantly, core competencies are a vital *prerequisite* for the competitive battle that then takes place for market share: the development of key resources has to come before and not during market place activity. It should be noted that Hamel and Prahalad couple core competencies with the organisation's *vision of the future* – this is explained and explored in Chapter 12.

Examples of core skills will include:

- *GSK* – not just its ownership of its drug patents, but also the whole range of skills and contacts that the company has in the pharmaceutical market place with customers, distributors and health authorities.

- *Nederlandse Spoorwegen* will have core skills related to its operation of a rail network. But, more importantly from a competitive viewpoint, it will have skills in customer handling, timetabling, service scheduling and so on, as against those related to buses and aircraft.

- *Bouygues* has core skills in road building that relate to road design and construction. But many companies will have such skills. Its real competencies will relate to its ability to gain large contracts and manage such assignments once agreed. It will need to deliver on time to an agreed standard and within the agreed budget.

Comment

David Sainsbury, the chairman of the leading UK retailer, has said that he believes that the ideas contained in the above have real merit.[36] But he also comments that:

- Core skills may be easier to apply to larger rather than smaller companies, which may not have the depth of management talent. Certainly, the examples on core skills quoted in the text are all from large companies.

- The ideas have been most thoroughly developed for electronics and related markets. The concepts may need to be adapted for others, e.g. medium-sized engineering companies.

Beyond these comments, one of the practical problems with core competencies is that the developers never really offer any clear checklist of points for their development – they are all rather vague. Ten guidelines that explore resource-based competencies and capabilities are offered in Exhibit 13.3.

More fundamentally, core competencies ignore other areas highlighted by the RBV as contributing to resource analysis and development. Competitive advantage may be just as well served by a strong brand, an exclusive patent or a superior geographical location. These and other resources have little or no connection with core competencies.

6.8.4 Knowledge management as the main source of competitive advantage?

In recent years, some strategists have taken the view that the knowledge management of the organisation represents the main source of competitive advantage.[37] They argue that the retention, exploitation and sharing of knowledge are extremely important in the ability of companies to stay ahead of their rivals. In particular, the way in which knowledge is managed and disseminated throughout the organisation represents an important advantage, especially in international companies.[38]

Definition ➤ By knowledge is meant the accumulation over time of the skills, routines and capabilities that shape the organisation's ability to survive and compete in markets. In addition, as Leonard points out, 'Knowledge reservoirs in organisations are not static pools but wellsprings, constantly replenished with streams of new ideas and constituting an ever-flowing source of corporate renewal.'[39] We will explore the role of knowledge in the context of innovation in Chapter 11.

Comment

Clearly, it is conceivable that, in some types of organisation, knowledge is extremely important – for example, consulting companies, some accountancy and legal practices. But to raise the role of knowledge to be the prime source of advantage for *all* organisations may be to exaggerate its importance. For example, Nederlandse Spoorwegen possesses a unique collection of rail track in the Netherlands and McDonald's has employed branding of the Big Mac to deliver competitive advantage that is sustainable. Neither of these has any substantive connection with knowledge.

6.8.5 Resource-based view and SMEs

Although it might at first appear that the RBV is particularly suited to large companies with vast resources, it is also relevant for small and medium-size enterprises (SMEs). Such organisations tend to have a smaller number of resources but they can also be more flexible and entrepreneurial. Typically, organisations of this size often develop strategies that might include:

- higher levels of personal service;
- specialist expertise;
- design skills;
- regional knowledge;
- bespoke solutions.

All of these can be contained within the seven elements of the RBV. They suggest that core resources at SMEs need to be carefully developed to reflect these strategies – perhaps extra people, extra training, the use of local knowledge and so on. Some areas of the RBV may be difficult to develop in the early years, such as *tangible uniqueness* and *investment deterrence*. Microsoft was once an SME but now it has the ability to develop some of these more capital-intensive resource areas. In principle, the elements therefore provide useful guidance for SMEs.

6.8.6 Comment on the RBV

Although the RBV represents greater clarity in strategy development, it still harbours a number of important weaknesses:

- It is still just a list of factors to consider – there is no guiding logic between the elements. Probably there never will be because, by definition, such logic might imply an industry solution.

- Beyond the concept of innovation (and this is not present in many explorations of the RBV), there is little guidance on how resources develop and change over time. The dynamics of resource development are an important element in strategy and the RBV adds little insight to this.[40] We will explore this in Chapter 20.

- There is a complete lack of consideration of the human element in resource development. We will explore this in Chapter 7.

- Some recent critical comment suggests that the whole concept is a case of tautology.[41]

- There is little or no emphasis on emergent approaches to resource development and almost no recognition of the process aspects of strategy development. The simple assumption that each element just needs to be defined and then it will happen automatically is a gross oversimplification of the reality of strategy development.

Finally, some proponents of various aspects of the RBV hold exaggerated views of its role as the solution to most strategic issues. It is clearly an advance but it is no substitute for the comprehensive development of every aspect of strategy analysis.

Key strategic principles

- In identifying the SCA of an organisation, it is important to begin by analysing the complete range of resources of the organisation: tangible, intangible and organisational capability. Such resources go beyond the usual definitions of accounting and finance concepts into areas like the value of patents and leadership.

- Because of the potentially extensive nature of such an analysis, it should concentrate in practice on those areas that relate to the key factors for success in an industry and those that deliver value added.

- There is no general agreement on what constitutes the best single approach to the development of SCA. Two approaches have proved useful – *distinctive capabilities* from Kay and *core competencies* from Hamel and Prahalad.

- Distinctive capabilities identify three possible unique resource areas in an organisation: architecture, reputation and innovative ability.

- Core competencies are a group of production skills technologies that enable an organisation to provide a particular benefit to customers.

- The RBV has a number of weaknesses: it is simply a list of possible factors to consider; it ignores many aspects of human resource issues and it partially ignores the process aspects of strategy development.

6.9 RESOURCE ANALYSIS – IMPROVING COMPETITIVE ADVANTAGE

After analysing resources, organisations often find that they have few assets that are *truly* competitive. This is quite normal since most organisations will consist of a range of resources, many being similar to those of competitors, with just a few being exceptional. In this context, the long lists of 'core competencies' seen in some analyses suggest that the compiler has not been sufficiently rigorous rather than that the company is multitalented.[42] Regardless of the length of the list, the identification of the truly competitive resources based only on the analysis undertaken so far in this chapter may be misleading. The reason is that the approach so far has been largely static:

- the analysis of value added represents the picture at a point in time;
- the identification of the seven elements of RBV is usually based on current resources.

Although a static approach is useful, a resource analysis at a point in time is a distortion of reality. An organisation's capabilities will change over time, its competitors will invest in new assets and so on. For example, assets will be constantly consumed in an oil company and they will have a limited life in a fast-changing computer business. The real role of resource analysis is to act as the first step in improving resources.

Any enhancement of value added and competitive advantage will come about through a course of action over time. This is a strategic *process* with all that this implies in terms of the human resources of the organisation, its change of culture and its leadership. The process may be *emergent* as well as *prescriptive*. For example, it may involve experimental, trial-and-error approaches to resource development (emergent) just as much as the strict application of RBV analysis (prescriptive). Our main exploration of the ways of improving our resources must await a more detailed look at resources and a clarification of the purpose of the organisation in Chapters 7–12. But it is convenient and relevant to consider three elements now:

1 benchmarking;
2 exploiting existing resources – leveraging;
3 upgrading resources.

6.9.1 Benchmarking

Definition ➤ One approach to the task of assessing the comparative performance of parts of an organisation is *benchmarking* – the comparison of practice with that of other organisations in order to identify areas for improvement. The other organisation does not necessarily have to be in the same industry. The comparison simply has to be with another whose practices are recognised as leading the field in that particular aspect of the task or function.

For example, the Ford Motor Company (US) might wish to test the competitiveness of its supplier relationships. It might then identify a world leader in supplier relationships, such as the well-known UK retailer Marks & Spencer. Ford might then approach the retailer directly or indirectly through consultants or an industry association. Ford will ask to compare its performance against that of Marks & Spencer in this specific functional area. The differences in performance between Ford and the retailer in its chosen activity are then analysed to form the basis of improving the resource at Ford. The results are then used in the sequence shown in Exhibit 6.6.

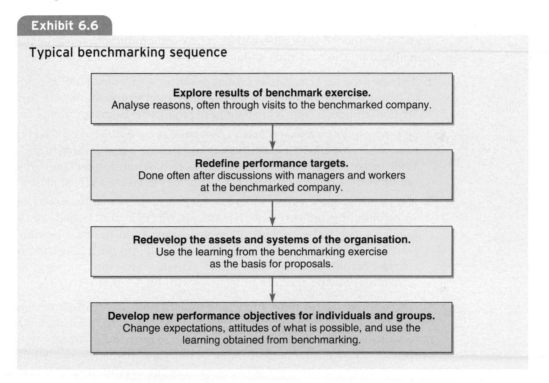

Exhibit 6.6

Typical benchmarking sequence

> **Explore results of benchmark exercise.**
> Analyse reasons, often through visits to the benchmarked company.

> **Redefine performance targets.**
> Done often after discussions with managers and workers
> at the benchmarked company.

> **Redevelop the assets and systems of the organisation.**
> Use the learning from the benchmarking exercise
> as the basis for proposals.

> **Develop new performance objectives for individuals and groups.**
> Change expectations, attitudes of what is possible, and use the
> learning obtained from benchmarking.

6.9.2 Exploiting existing resources – leveraging

Definition ➤ In any organisation, it is essential to exploit its existing resources to the full – this is sometimes called *leveraging resources*.[43] For example, for many years after Walt Disney died, his film company continued to make good films but made no attempt to exploit the many characters in any other medium. It took the arrival of Michael Eisner at the head of Disney in the 1980s to exploit the Disney resources and move the company into hotels, brand merchandising and publishing. More generally, existing resources can be exploited in five areas:

1 *Concentration* – focusing resources on the key objectives of the organisation and targeting, in particular, those that will have the largest influence on value added

2 *Conservation* – using every part of the resource, perhaps recycling where possible, with the aim of exploiting every aspect available to the organisation

3 *Accumulation* – digging deep into the resources of the organisation to discover every scrap of accumulated knowledge and skill, coupled with the acquisition of outside skills and experience, where appropriate

4 *Complementarity* – analysing resources from the perspective of blending new elements together, such as marketing and operations, and supporting stronger elements so that they do not suffer from weaknesses elsewhere in the organisation

5 *Recovery* – ensuring that resources generate cash quickly where possible, thus achieving the full benefit of new and existing resources sooner rather than later

These are all prescriptive routes towards exploiting existing resources and deserve careful study. A classic example in strategy development has been the way that News Corporation (Australia) used its existing strength in UK newspapers in the early 1990s to support and enhance its development of its new satellite television channels: they were heavily promoted in its leading UK newspapers the *Sun* and *The Times* – *see* Chapter 13.

6.9.3 Upgrading resources

Unfortunately, the results of a competitive analysis may show that an organisation has little or no competitive advantage, although it continues to add some value to its inputs. This situation is common in some industries, such as those involved with commodity products where there is little differentiation between products beyond the price – for example, agricultural products, mining and metals. There are three main ways to respond:

1 *Add new resources to support an existing product or service area.* Some organisations have tried to brand their commodities – for example, Intel Corporation with 'Intel Inside' and its Pentium computer chip. A programme of product development would also be relevant here.

2 *Enhance directly the resources that are threatened by competition.* This could be done by buying new, more cost-efficient machinery or negotiating a new joint venture – for example, the 1998 merger that formed DaimlerChrysler has transformed (potentially, at least) the resources of two medium-sized car companies to create a global player.

3 *Add complementary resources that will take the organisation beyond its current competition.* Sometimes the industry will remain unattractive and it may be better to develop resources that will eventually allow the organisation to move beyond its current competitors – for example, some farmers have moved into the leisure industry, setting up golf courses, accommodation and similar activities and thus moving out of reliance on agricultural pricing and into other areas with higher profit margins.

Upgrading resources raises the whole issue of how an organisation moves forward over time with regard to the resources at its disposal, the purpose of the organisation and the moves made by its competitors. Importantly, it relies on a strategic vision of where the organisation is headed – perhaps more of the same, perhaps moving into new areas. This requires a careful exploration of the purpose of the organisation – *see* Part 4.

Key strategic principles

- There are at least three ways to improve sustainable competitive advantage: benchmarking, exploiting existing resources and upgrading resources.

- *Benchmarking* is a comparison of practice with that of another organisation considered to display best practice in its field of operation. The aim of benchmarking is to identify areas of improvement in the resources of the organisation.

- *Exploiting existing resources – leveraging.* There are five main methods for undertaking this task. They are: concentration, conservation, accumulation, complementarity and recovery.

- *Upgrading resources.* There are three main methods: developing new resources, enhancing those threatened by competitors and adding complementary resources.

CASE STUDY 6.4

Xbox – the strategic battle for the home entertainment market has just begun

Microsoft's launch of its Xbox games console through 2001 into 2002 is only the beginning of a new strategic thrust. It is using its competitive resources to take a share of the market for home computer video gaming machines. In addition, it aims to establish itself as a leading player in the broader market of home entertainment. But it faces formidable opponents in two Japanese companies, Sony Corporation and Nintendo.

Background – the early years

There is nothing new in the home video game machine battle. The Californian firm Atari was the early leader back in the 1980s. However, it had no proprietary software or hardware – competitors could copy its machines and software games developers had unrestricted access to its games. As in the case of the IBM personal computer – *see* Chapter 1 – this was not a recipe for success.

Then along came the Japanese company Nintendo. It had learnt some important strategic lessons about competitive resources. First, it used a branded character called Mario. Second, it sold the games consoles at low prices and made its profits from its exclusive software games. Third, it made sure that the games consoles were unique and could not work with other games. Finally, it restricted the number of software houses that it licensed to develop its games, thus ensuring that it had some control over the quality of the games.

Game wars hot up in the 1980s and 1990s

Such success attracted another Japanese company, Sega. This company picked up some of the best ideas from Nintendo; for example, it developed its own branded character, Sonic the Hedgehog. In addition, it launched a more advanced machine and stole market share from Nintendo in a rapidly expanding market. By the early 1990s, Sega had become market leader, with around 50 per cent market share. Then Sony entered the market in the mid-1990s.

Sony gains market leadership in the late 1990s

Sony used its competitive resources well. As a result of its involvement in films, it had the use of branded characters from its entertainment business. In addition, it used its financial resources to acquire a software development company and its expertise in consumer electronics to develop a new generation of games machines based on CD-ROMs. In 1998, Sega responded with its Dreamcast machine, which had superior graphics. Sony then hit back with Playstation, which had even better graphics and was much faster than the Sega machine. Meanwhile, Nintendo was holding its own with Game Boy.

In 2001, Sega decided to throw in the towel on games machines – it had not made a profit for six years. Sony had invested US$500 million in Playstation and its successor, Playstation 2. It was reaping the rewards, with market

http://www.xbox.com/en-us/press/downloads.htm

leadership of around 80 per cent in a global market worth around US$20 billion per annum. Sony's games machine profits were the biggest contributor to its total business over this time. Then along came Microsoft in 2000.

Microsoft enters the home entertainment battle

Microsoft has been the market leader in personal computer software with its Windows system since the early 1980s. It has so dominated the global market that it has been the subject of anti-trust legal action in its home country, the US, and also in Europe. Microsoft would not deny that it dominated this market worldwide. But the Windows system was largely employed for home *work* rather than home *entertainment*.

Market opportunity 2001–2006

If you are an aggressive company like Microsoft, you can see an obvious opportunity to expand into entertainment – especially when the video-games console market is worth around US$20 billion and projected to grow at 15–20 per cent per annum up to 2008. Thus Bill Gates launched the new Microsoft games machine, the Xbox, in the US in late 2001

▶

▶ CASE STUDY 6.4 continued

Table 6.5

The rival products

Games machine	Maker	Launch prices	Typical 2005 prices	Facilities	Number of games available
Xbox – launched US Autumn 2001, Japan and Europe early 2002	Microsoft	UK price £299 subsequently reduced to £200	£99 plus extra for games, consoles and other add-ons	DVD ROM, 8GB hard drive, Ethernet port and broadband	20 games at launch Good range after four years
GameCube – launched May 2002 but able to play Game Boy games with an adaptor (launched 1998)	Nintendo	UK price £160–£170 subsequently reduced to £140	£80 including one game	Optional 56k modem, links with Game Boy Cannot play CDs or DVDs	At least 20 games at launch plus compatible with previous games
PlayStation 2 – launched November 2000	Sony	UK price £199	£100 plus extra for games, consoles, etc	DVD ROM, optional hard drive, optional broadband	Many games – still far superior to XBox

and in Japan and Europe in early 2002. Importantly, the new machine was in some respects more like a dedicated home computer, thus illustrating how the personal computer and the games machine may converge technically over the next few years. Arguably, this might threaten the Microsoft dominance of home PCs in the long term. Certainly, it also provided an opportunity for Microsoft to tackle a new and potentially lucrative market in the short term.

In the first years, Microsoft was not aiming to beat Sony's market share. Its machine was technically more sophisticated but was initially priced higher – see Table 6.5. Sony's Playstation 2 largely matched the Xbox performance. The Nintendo GameCube was simpler technically, but significantly cheaper. Both Sony and Nintendo had a wider range of software games in the early years than Microsoft. However, Microsoft claimed to have built into its new machine the technical ability for gamers to use the much faster broadband telecommunications system so that fast games could be played between homes. But, since broadband was only in 4 per cent of homes at the time of launch, this was not expected to be a major competitive advantage in the early years. More generally, after four years on the market, prices were settling down at levels substantially below those of the launch period – see Table 6.5.

In its first year, Microsoft was aiming to sell around 4–6 million machines, with sales of an estimated 25 million machines over the five-year life of the model to 2006. This can be compared with Nintendo, which also expected to sell around 25–30 million machines over the same five-year period, and Sony with 90–110 million over the period. The lengthy time period was important as typical launch costs of US$300–500 million would not be recovered for several years – rather like a

car manufacturer needing to recover the costs of developing a new model.

In May 2005, Microsoft launched the XBox 360 with a new generation of graphics capability and new software games. It would be in the shops by December 2005. Almost on the same day (what a coincidence!) Sony announced the launch of PlayStation 3. This would not reach the shops until early in 2006 but would include a new generation of significantly more powerful computer chips: judging by the early demonstrations, it would be take gaming to a totally new level and would be more powerful than XBox 360. But would customers wait for PlayStation 3? Would the XBox software persuade customers to invest in the Microsoft games machine? The competitive battle was entering a new phase.

Case questions

1 *What conclusions do you draw about the competitive advantages of Microsoft? Are its advantages sustainable over time?*

2 *What core competencies does Nintendo possess? Is it capable of leveraging them further? If so, how?*

3 *How does Sony score on Kay's three areas of distinctive capabilities? What conclusions can be drawn on future resource development?*

4 *What is the strategic significance, if any, of the efforts of games machine makers to establish their own special technical standards? What are the risks of such strategies?*

CRITICAL REFLECTION

How useful is the resource-based view?

At the present time, the resource-base view (RBV) of strategy development is the focus of a significant body of research and development. Some strategists believe that its insights lie at the core of strategy development. But the RBV also faces significant criticism in at least three areas:

● *Tautological*: the RBV is seeking truths that are part of the very definition of what is being sought. The RBV is supposed to identify the resources that lead to competitive advantage by identifying those resources that deliver value, rarity and inimitability. But competitive advantage itself is defined as something that is valuable, rare and inimitable. In this sense, the RBV only seeks to identify what it already knows or should know!

● *Vague generalisations*: the resource areas identified by the RBV – core competencies, innovative capability, etc. – are vague. Some suggest that they are so generalised as to be of little value. They need to be seen in the context in which they arise if they are to have any meaning. Otherwise, they are merely slogans or aspirations that everyone can seek.

● *Pathway to competitive resources*: the RBV is unclear on how organisations can develop and maintain their competitive resources. The destination of the superior, competitive resource is somewhat clearer than the path to develop it.

What is your view? Does the RBV have some useful insights? Or it over-rated as a meaningful concept?

SUMMARY

● For both prescriptive and emergent strategists, the resources of the organisation are an important element in strategy. Prescriptive approaches emphasise the need to build on strengths, whereas the emergent view favours flexibility and harnessing the more unpredictable human element. This chapter has concentrated on the prescriptive view.

● In seeking to understand the key factors for success in an industry, the three 'Cs' can be used as a basis for analysis: customers, competitors and company. The purpose of such an approach is to identify those strategic factors that are common to most companies in an industry and are essential to delivering the objectives of such companies. The key factors for success can be used to focus on other areas of strategy development.

● One basic resource decision facing every organisation is whether to make or buy, i.e. whether to make its own products or buy them from outside in the market place. Every organisation needs to reappraise its activities regularly in this area. The decision will be based not only on simple cost considerations but also on broader aspects related to the maintenance of sustainable competitive advantage.

● Resources are difficult to measure because many of them are intangible and cannot easily be captured in numerical data. It is important to go beyond accounting and management information systems in the measurement process.

● Resources add value to the organisation. They take the inputs from suppliers and transform them into finished goods or services. The value added is the difference between the market value of outputs of an organisation and the costs of its inputs. It is possible to calculate this accurately for an overall company but very difficult to do so for individual parts of the company. When used in developing competitive advantage for the individual parts of the company, the concept is therefore often left unquantified.

● In order to develop sustainable competitive advantage, it is necessary to consider the various parts of the organisation and the value that each part adds, where this takes place and how the contribution is made. The value chain undertakes this task. It identifies where value is added in different parts of the organisation and where the organisation may have competitive advantage.

● It may also be necessary to consider the *value system*, i.e. the way that the organisation is linked with other parts of a wider system of adding value involving suppliers, customers and distributors. Unique linkages between elements of the value system may also provide competitive advantage.

● Economic rent is defined as any excess that a factor earns over the minimum amount needed to keep that factor in its present use. Economic rent is important in strategy because it highlights the scarcity of some resources and the possibility of alternative, more profitable uses for a resource.

● In searching for sustainable competitive advantage, the resource-based view (RBV) argues that the individual resources of an organisation provide a stronger basis for strategy development than industry analysis. The reason is that RBV will identify those resources that are exceptional and deliver competitive advantage.

● There are seven elements that may be associated with resource-based competitive advantage: prior or acquired resources; innovative ability; being truly competitive; substitutability; appropriability; durability, and imitability. It is not necessary for an organisation to possess them all before it has some competitive advantages: each organisation will have some unique combination of resources, some of which will deliver sustainable competitive advantage.

● To begin identifying the truly competitive resources, there are three main areas of resource analysis that need to be undertaken – tangible: the physical resources; intangible: resources that have no physical presence but have real benefit; organisational capability: the skills, routines and management leadership of the organisation. Because of the extensive nature of such analysis, it should concentrate on those areas that are more likely to deliver value added and match with the key factors for success in an industry. The VRIO Framework – Valuable, Rare, Inimitable and Organisationally possible – can be used to test resources for their ability to contribute to competitive advantage.

● There is no general agreement on what constitutes the best single approach to the development of sustainable competitive advantage. Two approaches have proved useful: distinctive capability (architecture, reputation and innovation) and core competencies.

● There are at least three ways to improve competitive advantage: benchmarking, improving existing resources and upgrading resources.

QUESTIONS

1 Using your judgement, determine the key factors for success in the following industries: pharmaceuticals, fast food restaurants, charities helping homeless people, travel companies offering package tours.

2 Outline the value chain for an organisation you know. Explain the implications of your study for competitive advantage.

3 Take the value added and other data for Glaxo and outline the value chain for the company. Develop the value system within which the company operates. What strategy conclusions can you draw?

4 How do the seven elements of the resource-based view contribute to corporate strategy? What are their limitations?

5 Using the evidence from the case studies on IBM in Chapters 1 and 2, identify the main elements of IBM's competitive advantage. Use the seven elements of RBV to classify your answer and the hierarchy of resources to explain the relationship with the other resources possessed by the company.

6 Take an organisation with which you are familiar and identify its distinctive capabilities, using the key guidelines to assist the process. Compare the organisation with its competitors and comment on the strategy implications.

7 Identify the core competencies of pharmaceutical companies in general and GSK in particular. What

do your observations mean for corporate strategy development at GSK?

8 Can core competencies be bought in as a short-term strategic solution or do they have to be developed over the long term? Use an example to support your answer.

9 Could Microsoft's Xbox (see Case 6.4) use any of the three main ways to improve its competitive advantage? Which methods might be used? Why?

10 How would you rate human resources in relation to other aspects of resources in the development of corporate strategy? Do you think the value chain adequately captures your answer?

Further reading

For key factors for success: Ohmae, K (1983) *The Mind of the Strategist*, Penguin, Harmondsworth.

For the value chain and value system: Porter, M E (1985) *Competitive Advantage*, The Free Press, New York. An interesting more review of the value chain: Channon, D (2005) 'Value chain analysis', in McGee, J and Channon, D F (eds) *Encyclopedic Dictionary of Management*, 2nd edn, Blackwell Business, Oxford.

For core competencies: Hamel, G and Prahalad, C K (1994) *Competing for the Future*, Harvard Business School Press, Boston, MA.

For distinctive capabilities: Kay, J (1994) *Foundations of Corporate Success*, Oxford University Press, Oxford.

Two useful summaries of the resource-based view are contained in chapters in two major texts. The first is: Cool, K, Costa, L A and Dierickx, I (2002) 'Constructing competitive advantage', in Pettigrew, A, Thomas, H and Whittington, R (eds) (2002) *Handbook of Strategy and*

Management, Sage, London, pp55–71. The second chapter is: Barney, J B and Arikan, A M (2001) 'The resource-based view: origins and implications', pp124–88, in Hitt, M A, Freeman, R E and Harrison, J S (eds) *The Blackwell Handbook of Strategic Management*, Blackwell, Oxford.

For a more academic consideration of the problems with the RBV, see the critique by Priem and Butler in Priem, R L and Butler, J E (2001a), 'Is the resource-based view a useful "view" for strategic management research?', *Academy of Management Review*, January, Vol 26, no 1 and Priem, R L and Butler, J E (2001b), 'Tautology in the resource-based view and the implications of externally determined resource value: further comments', *Academy of Management Review*, January, Vol 26, no 1, pp1–45. Then read the response by Jay Barney in Barney, J B (2001) 'Is the resource-based "view" a useful perspective for strategic management research? Yes', *Academy of Management Review*, Vol 26, no 1, pp41–56.

Notes and references

1 *Financial Times*, 7 Dec 1993, p22; 16 July 1994, p10; 24 Jan 1995, p17; 27 Jan 1995; 9 Mar 1995, p33; 24 Mar 1995, p27; 24 Apr 1995, p11; 8 Sept 1995, p15; 9 Nov 1995, p25; 27 November 1995, pIV of Biotechnology Supplement; 17 June 1998, p25; 28 July 1998, p24; 14 April 1999, p14; 20 July 1999, p23; 17 January 2000, p18; 22 January 2000, p15; 16 February 2000, p25; 20 April 2000, p28; 23 February 2001, p26; 15 January 2002, p19; 12 March 2002, p28; 22 July 2002, p24; 24 July 2002, p16; 10 March 2005, p29; 18 March 2005, p15. Glaxo Wellcome Annual Report and Accounts 1997, pp2, 3, 8, 9, 86, 87. GSK Annual Report and Accounts 2004. Also GSK Analysts' Presentation in early

2005 – available on the web at www.gsk.com. The company also makes other presentations available on the same web site – useful source of company comment.

2 Ohmae, K (1983) *The Mind of the Strategist*, Penguin, Harmondsworth, Ch3.

3 Porter, M E (1985) *Competitive Advantage*, The Free Press, New York, Ch7.

4 Kay, J (1993) *Foundations of Corporate Success*, Oxford University Press, Oxford, Chs5 to 8.

5 Amit, R and Schoemaker, P (1993) 'Strategic assets and organizational rent', *Strategic Management Journal*, 14, pp33–46.

6 Ohmae, K (1983) Op. cit., p96.

7 Ghemawat, P (1991) *Commitment*, The Free Press, New York.

8 Some early articles on this shift in position include: Wernerfelt, B (1984) 'A resource-based view of the firm', *Strategic Management Journal*, Sept–Oct, p171; Barney J B (1986) 'Strategic factor markets: Expectations, luck and business strategy', *Management Science*, Oct, p1231; Rumelt, R 'Theory, strategy and entrepreneurship', in Teece, D J (ed) (1987), *The Competitive Challenge: Strategies for Industrial Innovation and Renewal*, Ballinger, Reading, MA.

9 Porter, M E (1980) *Competitive Strategy: Techniques for Analyzing Industries and Competitors*, The Free Press, New York. But note that this was based on earlier work, particularly that of Bain, J (1956) *Barriers to New Competition: Their Character and Consequences in Manfucturing Industries*, Harvard University Press, Cambridge, MA.

10 In particular, many marketing strategy texts make no mention of individual resource analysis. From this perspective, they should all be read with caution. However, many definitions of marketing have long recognised the importance of resources – one used at several universities in the UK makes explicit reference to the resources of the organisation.

11 For example: Penrose, E (1959) *The Theory of the Growth of the Firm*, Basil Blackwell, Oxford; Ansoff, I (1965) *Corporate Strategy*, McGraw-Hill, NY.

12 *See* the pioneering work of Coase, R (1937) 'The nature of the firm', *Economica*, 4, pp386–405. Also Penrose, E (1959) Op. cit., and Williamson, O (1975) *Markets and Hierarchies*, The Free Press, New York.

13 Lynch, R (1994) *European Business Strategies*, 2nd edn, Kogan Page, London, p43.

14 References for Case 6.2: Annual Reports and Accounts of GSK, Nederlandse Spoorwegen and Bouygues for various years.

15 For a more detailed example of value chain analysis, see Shepherd, A (1998) 'Understanding and using value chain analysis', in Ambrosini, V (ed) *Exploring Techniques of Analysis and Evaluation in Strategic Management*, Prentice Hall, Berkhamsted.

16 Porter, M E (1985) Op. cit., Ch2.

17 Porter, M E (1985) Ibid, p38.

18 Cookson, C and Luesby, J (1995) 'Glaxo Wellcome giant changes the drug mixture', *Financial Times*, 9 Mar, p33.

19 Porter, M E (1985) Op. cit., Chs9, 10 and 11.

20 Ricardo, D (1817) *Principles of Political Economy and Taxation*, J Murray, London. More detail on the origin of economic rent is contained in the following: Lipsey, R G and Chrystal, A (1995) *Positive Economics*, 8th edn, Oxford University Press, Oxford.

21 For a consideration of rent and its strategic implications, *see*: Mahoney, J and Pandian, J (1992) 'The resource-based view within the conversation of strategic management', *Strategic Management Journal*, 13, pp363–80. This gives a useful overall view. *See* also Schoemaker, P (1990), 'Strategy, complexity and economic rent', *Management Science*, 36, Oct, pp1178–92.

22 Schumpeter, J (1934) *The Theory of Economic Development*, Harvard University Press, Harvard, MA.

23 References for high fashion industry case: Three trips by the author with Middlesex MBA students to study the fashion industry in Como, Northern Italy. In particular, my thanks are due to Mantero SpA whose senior directors gave freely of their time. However, it should be noted that *no direct information* from Mantero is used in this case. All the data is from the publicly available sources listed below. The author also acknowledges the considerable guidance of his former colleague at Middlesex University, Mr Valeriano Lencioni, and two professors in the specialist fashion group at Bocchoni Business School in Milan, Professors Erica Corbellini and Stefania Saviolo, who also came to Como. The data used in this case comes from: LVMH Annual Report and Accounts 2003; PPR Annual Report and Accounts 2003; Gucci Annual Report and Accounts 2001 (the latest available); *Economist*, 'Rags and Riches – a survey of fashion', 6 March 2004; *Financial Times* Womenswear 'Business of Fashion' Supplement, Spring/Summer 2005, with newspaper in Feb 2005; *Financial Times* Menswear 'Business of Fashion' Supplement, Spring/Summer 2005, with newspaper in March 2005; *Financial Times* 9 March 2005, p30 – 'Designer quits as Gucci seeks results'. Fashion Business International: April–May 2002, pp52–53; Dec–Jan 2003, pp16, 45–46.

24 Many of these research papers are referenced elsewhere in this text. The remainder are: Dierickx, I and Cool, K (1989) 'Asset stock accumulation and sustainability of competitive advantage', *Management Science*, 35, pp1504–11; Connor, K (1991) 'A historical comparison of resource-based theory and five schools of thought within industrial organisation economics: Do we have a new theory of the firm?', *Journal of Management*, 17(1), pp121–54; Amit, R and Schoemaker, P (1993) 'Strategic assets and organizational rent', *Strategic Management Journal*, 14, pp33–46; Grant, R (1991) 'The resource-based theory of competitive advantage: implications for strategy formulation', *California Management Review*, 33, pp114–22. Makadok, R (2001) 'Towards a synthesis of the resource-based and dynamic capability views of rent creation', *Strategic Management Journal*, 22, pp387–401. Hoopes, D G, Madsen, T L and Walker, G (2003) 'Why is there a resource-based view? Toward a theory of competitive heterogeneity', *Strategic Management Journal*, 24, October, Special issue.

25 See also the special edition of the *Strategic Management Journal*, 24, October 2003 which has an extended discussion and review of the concept.

26 Rumelt, R (1991) 'How much does industry matter?', *Strategic Management Journal*, Mar, pp64–75.

27 Rumelt, R (1991) Op. cit.

28 McGahan, A and Porter, M E (1997) 'How much does industry matter, really?' *Strategic Management Journal*, 18, Summer special issue, pp15–30.

29 Prahalad, C and Hamel, G (1990) 'The core competence of the corporation', *Harvard Business Review*, May–June, pp79–91.

30 Kay, J (1994) Op. cit.

31 Peteraf, M (1993) 'The cornerstones of competitive advantage: a resource-based view', *Strategic Management Journal*, 14, pp179–91.

32 Collis, D and Montgomery, C (1995) 'Competing on resources: strategy in the 1990s', *Harvard Business Review*, July–Aug, pp119–128.

33 Collis, D and Montgomery, C (1995) Ibid., pp118–28.

34 Kay, J (1993) Op. cit., Chs5, 6 and 7.

35 Hamel, G and Prahalad, H K (1994) *Competing for the Future*, Harvard Business School Press, Boston, MA, Chs9 and 10.

36 Sainsbury, D (1994) 'Be a better builder', *Financial Times*, 2 Sept, p11.

37 Roos, J (1997) *Financial Times Mastering Management*, Pitman, London, Module 20.

38 Roos, J (1998) *Financial Times Mastering Global Business*, Pitman, London, Part 5, pp14–15.

39 Leonard, D (1998) *Wellsprings of Knowledge*, Harvard Business School Press, Boston, MA, p3.

40 *See* also Chaharbaghi, K and Lynch, R (1999) 'Sustainable competitive advantage: towards a dynamic resource-based strategy', *Management Decision*, 37(1), pp45–50.

41 Priem, R L and Butler, J E (2001) 'Is the resource-based view a useful perspective for strategic management research?', *Academy of Management Review*, 26, 1, pp22–40 and Lynch, R (2000) 'Resource-based view: paradigm or checklist?' *International Journal of Technology*, 3, 4, pp550–61. Professor Jay Barney is a strong supporter of the RBV. He responded to the Priem and Butler paper with the following: Barney, J (2001) 'Is the resource-based view a useful perspective for strategic management research? Yes', *Academy of Management Review*, Vol 26, no 1, pp41–56.

42 Collis, D and Montgomery, C (1995) Op. cit., p123, emphasise that lengthy lists of core competencies have sometimes become just a 'feelgood' factor.

43 Hamel, G and Prahalad, C K (1994) Op. cit., Ch7.

44 References for Xbox case: Brandenburger, A M and Nalebuff, B J (1997) *Co-opetition*, Harper-Collins, London; *The Economist*, 19 May 2001, p83; *Guardian Newspaper* 12 March 2002, p21; *Financial Times*, 14 Oct 1999, p31; 19 Jan 2000, p28; 28 Aug 2000, p9; 6 Sept 2000, p3; 25 Jan 2001, pp23, 29; 26 Jan 2001, p24; 1 Feb 2001, p32; 18 May 2001, p11; 19 May 2001, p12; 23 May 2001, p36; 7 July 2001, p14; 21 Sept 2001, p34; 6 Oct 2001, p18; 8 Jan 2002, p30; 7 Feb 2002, p28; 8 March 2002, p1; 12 March 2002, p36; 10 April 2002, p30; 23 April 2002, p30; 10 Sept 2002, p27; 4 Oct 2002, p30; 13 May 2003, p31; 14 May 2003, p32; 24 July 2003, pp11, 27; 25 July 2003, p27; 5 Nov 2003, p26; 14 Nov 2003, p29; 30 March 2004, p30; 5 May 2004, p13; 12 May 2004, p30; 17 Sept 2004, p28; 22 Sept 2004, p23; 18 Feb 2005, p25; 25 Feb 2005, p26; 8 March 2005, p5; 11 March 2005, p21.

Chapter 7

ANALYSING HUMAN RESOURCES

Learning outcomes

When you have worked through this chapter, you will be able to:

- conduct a human resource audit of an organisation and explore the strategic implications;
- outline the strategic issues involved in organisational culture and analyse the culture of the organisation;
- understand the impact of strategic change on strategy development;
- comment on the impact of downsizing and business process re-engineering in the context of human resources;
- analyse the political network of an organisation and assess its strategic implications;
- explain the strategic management implications of four major types of human resource approaches to strategy development;
- appraise the impact of international culture on strategy development.

INTRODUCTION

For many organisations, people are a vital resource. Their strategic significance extends beyond the resource context, however, because strategy development often involves change and some people may resist change to such an extent that it becomes impossible to implement the planned strategy. Human resource analysis is therefore essential during the development

> **Figure 7.1**
>
> ### The relationship between resources, culture, change and power
>
> Resource audit
>
> Organisational culture
>
> **Strategy implications**
>
> Power and politics
>
> Strategic change

of corporate strategy and cannot simply be left as a task to be undertaken after the strategy has been agreed.

One possible starting point for the analysis is an *audit* of the human resources of the organisation – the people, their skills, backgrounds and relationships with each other. An assessment of the *culture* of the organisation is also required – the style and learned ways that govern and shape the organisation's people relationships. *Strategic change* is analysed and its forces are explained (although covered in greater detail in Chapter 21). Finally, *power and politics* may guide and direct the organisation in its strategy development and therefore need careful assessment. The relationship between these subjects is circular – that is, no single area is dominant and all are interrelated – and is shown in Figure 7.1.

CASE STUDY 7.1

Ford Motors: strategy, leadership and strategic change

In 1994, Ford Motors was challenging its competitors with a new volume global strategy based on the Ford brand. By 1999, it had adopted a different strategy of acquiring major brands like Jaguar, Volvo and Land Rover. By 2001, it had sacked its chief executive and gone back to the basic business of delivering profits in its volume car business under Ford. By 2004, Ford had lost its second place in the world car market to Toyota. This case explores what happened, focusing particularly on the 'people' issues.

Ford's international operations

Ford was founded in the US around the turn of the twentieth century. After rapid and innovatory development in its home country, the company's founder, Henry Ford, set up the first overseas factory in the UK in the late 1920s. Seventy years later, the company had major production facilities in the UK, Germany, Belgium and Spain. But these operations were part of a European Division that worked semi-independently of its US headquarters. In addition, Ford had manufacturing and marketing operations in South America, India and Australasia that were also operated partly independently of the US. There was some central co-ordination but production and models were still largely confined to a particular continent. The reasons were the need to meet local customer demand in terms of style, price-points and performance. The next sections track Ford's more recent history and strategies.

In terms of organisational culture, the company had several strong characteristics. First, it was still controlled from Detroit by the founding family. The company followed a robust approach to markets and people and, for many years, was more likely to promote Americans into the most senior positions. Henry Ford himself had antagonised the unions in the 1930s. This memory remained into the 1980s with the labour force being strong and well organised. The white-collar office workers were highly dedicated and in a clear hierarchical structure with regard to promotion and work dedication. The company was results-driven and supported those who were high achievers. It was in this context that various stories circulated about the senior managers that are described later in the case, after exploring the history of the company. An analysis of the organisational culture of Ford is shown later in this chapter as Exhibit 7.2. It is an integral part of this case.

Ford 1994 – global strategy project called 'Ford 2000'

For many years, Ford had been attracted by the idea of a 'global' car. There were three good reasons for thinking that globalisation would deliver major benefits:

1 Major economies of scale and scope were expected in production.
2 Global manufacturers were able to negotiate global sourcing of car components, which would also deliver substantial additional cost savings.

Henry Ford was the founder of mass car manufacturing and his legacy remains with the controlling interest of the present generation of the Ford family.

From the Collections of the Henry Ford

3 Research and development on new models had become substantial, typically US$8 billion. Spreading this cost across more production would bring down the cost per vehicle and also save duplication costs.

However, this would require massive reorganisation and co-ordination across a company as large as Ford, so it was not a project to embark upon lightly. In 1994, the company therefore launched a totally new project called 'Ford 2000'. Its objective was to develop a fully integrated global company by the year 2000. It was expected that there would be annual cost savings of US$2–3 billion by the end of the decade and that this would present a serious challenge to Ford's competitors, like General Motors (US) and Toyota (Japan). The Ford plan was put into operation in early 1995 and involved integrating all its operations into one company. Core engineering and production were simplified in order to achieve considerable savings. New models were designed around a reduced number of platforms that would also save funds. Mr Jacques Nasser was put in charge of Ford's global automotive operations to implement the changes. He was so successful at killing off unprofitable vehicles, cutting costs and pressing suppliers and dealers for lower costs that he became known as 'Jack the Knife'. Substantial savings were made and Mr Nasser was promoted to chief executive officer of the worldwide Ford Motor Company in 1999.

Ford 1999 – global niche strategy

Mr Nasser then went on to oversee another major change in strategy in the company – the global niche strategy. He argued that there was a shift in car demand across the world towards *niche* car markets – 4-wheel drive off-road vehicles, people carriers, small luxury town cars, sports cars, etc. Moreover, such vehicles had higher profit margins than the traditional Ford business of volume cars – like the *Mondeo* and *Ka*. 'What you're seeing are niche cultures', explained Mr Nasser. Customers want more than a metal box that stops and starts and looks just like the neighbour's car. For Ford, the new trend in customer niche strategy is 'a marvellous business opportunity'.

To meet such demand variations, the company embarked on at least five further ventures that would not even use the Ford brand name:

1 *Acquisition and development of Jaguar Cars*. Ford had bought the luxury company in the late 1980s and then spent billions of dollars developing new models, refitting factories and other activities. It kept the marque separate from its Ford 2000 project in order to emphasise the special niche. By the late 1990s Jaguar had launched a series of models that were well received by the press and were attacking a market niche in which Ford had previously

hardly any representation, namely the luxury segment of Mercedes-Benz, Rolls-Royce and Toyota's *Lexus*.

2 *Development of the Lincoln*. Ford had some representation in the luxury segment in the US only under the Lincoln name. Another development under consideration was to introduce some of the leading Lincoln models to other parts of the world.

3 *Acquisition of Volvo Cars*. This Swedish company was acquired by Ford in 1999 for US$6.5 billion in order to increase its representation in the upper market segments, where it had previously been only partially successful. Again, this would tackle new market niches where its rivals were stronger – for example, BMW and Mercedes-Benz. But, in this case, it would also deliver major cost savings in purchasing and logistics.

4 *Acquisition of Land Rover*. The British 4-wheel drive company was also bought by Ford in 1999 for US$2.8 billion and used to develop its interests in this specialist car area. As with the other purchases above, Ford invested substantial new investment in people and machinery to modernise existing plant and develop new models over a number of years.

5 *Acquisition of KwikFit and consolidation of control of Hertz*. The European tyre, battery and exhaust-fitting company, KwikFit, was bought by Ford in the late 1990s for US$1 billion in order to offer customers a complete range of services. The company's link with the car rental company Hertz was also extended to take control of that company.

The new acquisitions were grouped together as a separate part of Ford, called the 'Premier Automotive Group'. The five-pronged global-niche strategy outlined above was expected to increase Ford's unit sales from 250,000 in 1998 to 750,000 in 2000. The new group was expected to deliver one-third of Ford's profits by 2005. Moreover, such sales would carry higher profit margins than those of its volume car range.

In practice, little of this was achieved:

● Jaguar took longer to turn around and needed further investment. Moreover, the Jaguar model policy was not wholly successful and its main production base in the UK meant that its American pricing suffered as the pound sterling gained against the US dollar.

● The company did not have the resources to move Lincoln outside North America.

● Volvo *was* a success after much investment and remains an important part of Ford's continuing international operations.

● Land Rover suffered from continued quality problems, cost issues and management upheaval: Ford was forced to make major cuts to restore profitability in 2003/4.

Table 7.1

Ford sales and profits for the period 1999-2003

Data in US$ millions

Sales	2003	2002	2001	2000	1999
Sales	164 196	162 256	160 504	168 930	160 053
Net income/(loss)*	495	(980)	(5 453)	3 467	7 237
Total assets	315 920	295 222	276 543	283 390	270 249

Note: *After tax and interest.

Source: Annual Report and Accounts.

Ford 2001 and after - 'back to basics' strategy

Importantly, the 'global niche' strategy took Ford's strategic focus away from its major activity of making profitable volume cars under the Ford brand name. The result was a profit disaster in 2001 – *see* Table 7.1. Although Mr Nasser had not been solely responsible for the strategy, he paid the price and was asked to leave suddenly in late 2001. 'The board had reached a conclusion and, in reaching that conclusion, the sooner we told Jac [Nasser] the better,' said Sir Nick Scheele, the former chairman of Ford Europe and new chief operating officer. 'What we need is to get back to basics. We have had a terrible year for a variety of unrelated circumstances, but we have to move on.'

The Ford family – still important minority shareholders in the Ford company – had become increasingly disenchanted with the strategy, which was simply not delivering the company's objectives. Mr Bill Ford, grandson of the founder Henry Ford, took over as chairman and chief executive of Ford. He then began an immediate drive to cut costs very substantially across every part of the Ford company. He focused on Ford's main business activities in North America and Europe:

- *Problems in North America*: A major cost-cutting exercise was begun in 2000 in North America to restore the profitability of this part of the company. Essentially, it was decided to axe five plants and 22,000 jobs in North America. Ford would also downsize activities at another 11 plants. In addition, it would also cut four low-profit models and sell US$1 billion of non-core assets and cut the company dividend by one-third. The new chairman, Bill Ford, explained with the benefit of hindsight: 'We pursued strategies that were either poorly conceived or poorly timed. We strayed from what got us to the top of the mountain and it cost us dearly.'
- *Problems in Europe*: For all the claims about the new global strategy, the reality was that Ford's European market share was dropping alarmingly – down from 12 per cent in 1994 to 8.7 per cent in 2000. Coupled with plant inefficiencies, this caused the company to show a US$1 billion loss in

Europe in 2000. Radical action was therefore taken to cut capacity, with plant closures in the UK, Portugal, Poland and Belarus and plant cutbacks in most of Ford's other European plants. Global strategy did not appear to form a significant part of the European cutbacks.

In addition, Ford suffered a major drain on profits as it coped with the Firestone tyre debacle: some Ford cars fitted with Firestone tyres were involved in accidents that were blamed on the tyres and both Ford and Firestone were sued for damages. Moreover, Ford also became engaged in a price war on a number of its basic volume models and its cost base was too high to respond and still make a profit. Then came the tragic events of September 11 and the economic downturn in the US. Over the next few years, Ford also faced increased pressure from its main US competitors, especially General Motors and Chrysler (part of DaimlerChrysler). In addition, Ford faced heavy competition from Toyota in Europe as the Japanese company began to build its market share in that continent. Toyota's *Camry* model was already the largest single-selling model in the US. By the end of 2004, Ford had lost its position as second largest car company in the world to Toyota – Case 19.3 picks up the story. Clearly this had a significant impact on the organisational culture and morale of the company around that time.

Case questions

1 *What were the main arguments in favour of the various Ford strategies over the last ten years?*

2 *How did the various changes impact on human resources at Ford?*

3 *When a company makes a major shift in strategy, such as plant closures in North America and Europe, how should it handle the people issues? For example, should it make an announcement in advance or should it just shut the plant and wait for the protests?*

7.1 HUMAN RESOURCE ANALYSIS AND CORPORATE STRATEGY

7.1.1 Prescriptive and emergent approaches

Definition ➤ Human-resource-based analysis emphasises the people element in corporate strategy. People are not machines: they respond to leadership, enthusiasm and shared decision making. Emergent strategy is more in tune with these issues because it encourages consensus and experimentation. Prescriptive stategy, with its emphasis on the rational solution, is less flexible and amenable to this stance.

Some prescriptive strategists have taken the view that human resources should be considered *only after the basic strategy has been derived*. Their view is based on two areas of evidence and thinking:

1 Alfred Chandler's highly influential research text, *Strategy and Structure*.[2] This book analysed strategy development at four leading US companies during the early twentieth century. Among its many conclusions, it said that it was necessary to formulate the strategy of the company *before* considering how the company should be organised to implement the strategy.

2 The focus on *important* strategy issues might be diluted by the consideration of other matters, such as human resource issues. For example, Porter's two books on *Competitive Strategy*[3] and *Competitive Advantage* certainly include human resource issues but lay the emphasis on competitive strategy development.

In fact, the Chandler text does not preclude the discussion of leadership and human resources in the formulation of strategy. On the contrary, it accurately describes their role in strategy development in some situations.[4] Moreover, Porter's concept of competitive strategy is consistent with the comparative analysis of human resources in an organisation as compared with those of its competitors. Nevertheless, the fact remains that some prescriptive strategists only consider human resource issues *after* the formulation of strategy.[5]

However, human resources need to be considered *during* the strategic resource analysis phase for four related reasons:

1 People-related strategies may form an integral part of the new strategy – for example, a change in the organisation's way of conducting its business. The purpose of such a change might be to achieve greater responsiveness and efficiency from people within the company, as at Ford Motor Company.

2 The increased technological skills required by, and the knowledge-based complexities of, many commercial processes have meant that an analysis of the existing human resources is essential for an accurate assessment of the options that are available.

3 Research and writings on organisational change and culture[6] have emphasised the importance of values and cultures in the *development* of organisational structure. These cannot simply be added on afterwards.

4 The resource-based view of strategy development (*see* Chapter 6) clearly identifies the role of the *network* of people in an organisation and their *relationships* with each other as a key element of strategy.

7.1.2 Sustainable competitive advantage

For most organisations, people are a vital resource. There are some industries where people are not just important but are the *key factor* for successful performance. For example:

● *Advertising and creative development*, where innovation through people is a crucial element in success;

- *Leisure and tourism*, where a company has a direct, intangible interface that relies on individual employees to give interest and enjoyment to customers;
- *Management consultancy and the advertising industry*, where client relationships are vital to successful outcomes;
- *Hospitals and the medical profession*, where people and personal relationships are essential to the delivery of quality services.

Even in organisations where there are other key factors for success, such as production plants at Ford Motor Company, human resources clearly play a major part in the process. The efficient and hard-working Ford executive is an essential feature of the company and close management co-ordination around the world is crucial to key strategic decisions.

In this context, the ability of people in some organisations to be more *adaptable to changes* in the environment is a real skill. It may even be a source of competitive advantage in fast-moving markets.[7] Arie De Geus, the former head of planning at Royal Dutch/Shell, has said:

The ability to learn faster than your competitors may be the only sustainable competitive advantage.[8]

Such skills are essentially people-related and the strategic approach is emergent.

7.1.3 Strategic change

The recognition that the threat posed to people by strategic change can be a significant barrier to the development of corporate strategy has come in the last 30 years. They fear that they may lose their jobs or their status: the Ford Motor Company reorganisation in 2000, which threatened several thousand jobs, took longer to implement and resulted in fewer cost savings than originally envisaged because of such fears.

To quote Whittington, writing about corporations in crisis:[9]

History is littered with managers apparently unable to adapt to new and threatening circumstances, and suffering the penalty of dismissal.

The Royal Dutch/Shell case later in this chapter captures the essence of that description. Even when companies are not in crisis, some writers take the view that the ability of people in the organisation to cope with change is a vital element in the development of strategy. This issue is explored later in this chapter and further in Chapter 21.

Key strategic principles

- Human-resource-based analysis emphasises the emergent approach to strategic development. It is essential to consider human resources during the development of corporate strategy because of the need to explore people-related strategies at an early stage.

- People are a vital competitive resource in most organisations. The adaptability of people in the organisation may be a source of real competitive advantage in fast-moving markets.

- The analysis of strategic change needs to be explored and built into the development of corporate strategy.

7.2 HUMAN RESOURCE AUDIT

7.2.1 Audit

Definition ➤ A human resource audit is an examination of the organisation's leadership, its people and their skills, backgrounds and relationships with each other. In undertaking the human

---

Exhibit 7.1

Human resource audit

People in the organisation

- Leadership in terms of people and style
- Employee numbers and turnover
- Organisation structure
- Structures for controlling the organisation
- Use of special teams, e.g. for innovation or cost reduction
- Level of skills and capabilities required
- Morale and rewards
- Employee and industrial relations
- Selection, training and development
- Staffing levels
- Capital investment/employee
- Role of quality and personal service in delivering the products or services of the organisation
- Role of professional advice in delivering the product or service

Role and contribution of human resource strategy

- Relationship with corporate strategy
- Key characteristics of human resource strategy
- Consistency of human resource strategy across an organisation with several divisions
- The responsiveness of human resource strategy to changes in business strategy and the environment
- The role of human resource strategy in leading change in the organisation
- The monitoring and review of human resource strategy
- The time frame for the operation of human resource strategy

---

resource audit of an organisation, it is important to give careful thought to a basic list of important areas in the business. Exhibit 7.1 shows a suggested list.[10] The main principles are:

- to obtain some basic information on the people and policies involved in the organisation;
- to explore in detail the role and contribution of the human resource management function in the development of corporate strategy.

7.2.2 Strategic implications

The difficulty is to move beyond a list to something of strategic significance. Three factors need to be added:

1. analysis of the list in Exhibit 7.1 using the *key factors for success*;
2. comparative data for a *leading competitor* or, in the case of a smaller company, several competitors of comparable size; and
3. consideration of the ownership shareholding and stakeholders of the organisation – *see* Chapter 12.

Using these additional factors, it should be possible to develop a human resource analysis that is rather more focused on the *key strategic issues* related to the company. Equally, it should be possible to define and explore the role of human resources in the development of *competitive advantage*. The development of such advantages is likely to derive both from:

- *Issues common to all organisations in the industry* – for example, levels of service expected in all organisations, such as the quality of cars for Ford customers.

- *Factors that are unique to the organisation itself* – for example, aspects of the service that only the organisation itself can provide, such as the local support for car servicing through the Ford dealer networks.

Key strategic principles

- The human resource audit will have two main elements: people in the organisation and the role and contribution of human resources to the development of corporate strategy.

- The development of sustainable competitive advantage will derive both from issues common to all organisations in the industry and to factors that are unique to the organisation itself.

- A basic analysis of human resources can be constructed for the company. However, from a strategy viewpoint, it would be more valuable if this were filtered using key factors for success, competitive comparisons and, if appropriate, international considerations.

7.3 ANALYSIS OF ORGANISATIONAL CULTURE

7.3.1 The elements of organisational culture

Definition ➤ Organisational culture is the set of beliefs, values and learned ways of managing of an organisation and this is reflected in its structures, systems and approach to the development of corporate strategy. Its culture derives from its past, its present, its current people, technology and physical resources and from the aims, objectives and values of those who work in the organisation.

Because each organisation has a different combination of the above, each will have a culture that is unique. Analysis is important because culture influences every aspect of the organisation and has an impact on its performance.[11] Specifically, it is the filter and shaper through which the leaders, managers and workers develop and implement their strategies. For these reasons, it will be one of the factors that influences the development of corporate strategy.

In spite of its importance, there is a significant problem in analysing culture. The difficulty is the lack of agreement amongst leading writers on its nature, structure and influence. As a starting point, this book explores the matter from a strategic perspective only and is therefore selective in its approach to this issue.[12]

The main elements of organisational culture are set out in Figure 7.2.

7.3.2 Environmental influences on organisational culture

Outside the organisation itself, there will be a whole series of influences on the organisational culture of the organisation.

People

We are concerned here with the impact on the organisation of people in the environment: such people will include customers and suppliers, along with government and professional advisors. The main areas are:

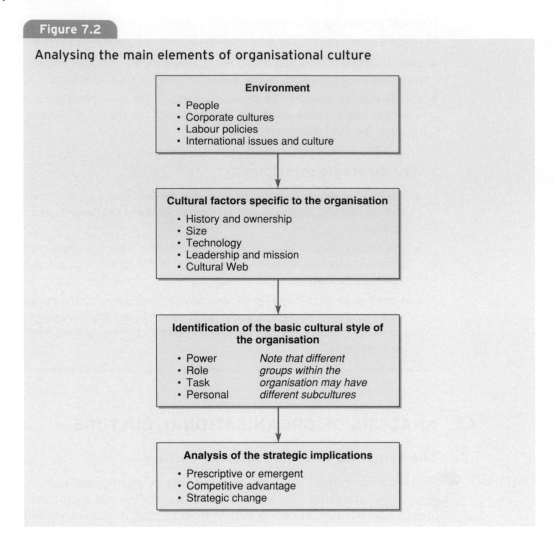

Figure 7.2

Analysing the main elements of organisational culture

Environment
- People
- Corporate cultures
- Labour policies
- International issues and culture

Cultural factors specific to the organisation
- History and ownership
- Size
- Technology
- Leadership and mission
- Cultural Web

Identification of the basic cultural style of the organisation
- Power
- Role
- Task
- Personal

Note that different groups within the organisation may have different subcultures

Analysis of the strategic implications
- Prescriptive or emergent
- Competitive advantage
- Strategic change

- *Age profile.* As the population grows older, so tastes change and recruitment changes.

- *Socio-economic group.* As people become richer, their needs and aspirations increase. Strategy will need to reflect these differences.

- *Male and female roles.* In some Western-based societies, females have not only extended their working lives but are asserting their right to equal status with males. In other societies, this has not happened. Strategy will need to be sensitive to such variations and be devised accordingly.

- *Language and communication.* Variations within and between countries represent real differences that need to be accommodated in strategy, both to control strategy better and to motivate those involved in the strategy process more effectively.

- *Religion and beliefs.* Strongly held beliefs must be respected and reflected in strategy development.

- *Government policy.* Policy on education, training, social welfare provisions, health and pensions provisions will have a significant influence on people development inside the organisation.

Corporate cultures[13]

The corporate cultural environment covers the *links* that the organisation has with *other similar organisations.* The connections may be both formal and informal in nature. The reasons for such links are varied but may stem from an aspect of national cultures: group goals matter more than the individual in some societies, such as those in Japan and Korea. They may also arise from the common interests that organisations share, such as petitioning governments for grants, laws and favourable economic status. There is also a tendency in many countries for like-minded companies to group together for reasons of history, common shareholdings, common customers, common enemies and so on.

Labour and employment policies

In some industrialised countries, trade unionism forms part of the environment that needs to be considered. However, the influence of organised labour has been declining over the last few years, with union membership declining around the world.[14]

International issues

International cultures may have a significant impact on corporate culture (*see* Section 7.6).

7.3.3 Cultural factors specific to the organisation

To understand the culture of an organisation, it is useful to consider the factors that have influenced its development.

History and ownership

A young company may have been founded by one individual or a small group who will continue to influence its development for some years. Centralised ownership will clearly concentrate power and therefore will concentrate influence and style. Family firms and owner-dominated firms will have clearly recognisable cultures.

Size

As firms expand, they may lose the tight ownership and control and therefore allow others to influence their style and culture. Even if ownership remains tight, larger companies are more difficult to control from the centre.

Technology

This will influence the culture of the company but its effects are not always predictable.[15] Those technologies that require economies of scale or involve high costs and expensive machinery usually require a formal and well-structured culture for success: examples might include large-scale chemical production or beer brewing. Conversely, in fast-changing technologies, such as those in telecommunications, a more flexible culture may be required.

Leadership and mission

Individuals and their values will reflect and change the culture of the organisation over time, especially the chief executive and immediate colleagues. These issues are vital to the organisation (*see* Chapters 10 and 12).

Cultural Web

Definition ➤ The Cultural Web consists of the factors that can be used to characterise some aspects of the culture of an organisation. It is a useful method of bringing together the basic elements that are helpful in analysing the culture of an organisation (*see* Figure 7.3).

The main elements are:

● *Stories*. What do people talk about in the organisation? What matters in the organisation? What constitutes success or failure?

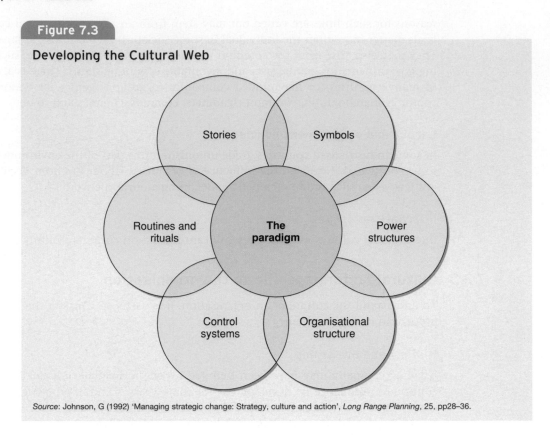

Figure 7.3

Developing the Cultural Web

Source: Johnson, G (1992) 'Managing strategic change: Strategy, culture and action', *Long Range Planning*, 25, pp28–36.

- *Routines*. What are the normal ways of doing things? What are the procedures (not always written down)?

- *Rituals*. Beyond the normal routine, what does the organisation highlight? For example, long service? Sales achievement? Innovation? Quality standards? How does it highlight and possibly reward such rituals?

- *Symbols*. What are the symbols of office? Office size? Company car size? Separate restaurants for different levels of managers and workers? Or the absence of these? How do employees travel: first, business or tourist class?

- *Control systems*. Bureaucratic? Well-documented? Oriented towards performance? Formal or informal? Haphazard? (*See* Part 6.)

- *Organisational structure*. Who reports to whom in the organisation on a formal basis and who has an informal relationship?

- *Power structures*. Who makes the decisions? Who influences the decisions? How? When? (*See* Section 7.3.4.)

The Cultural Web can usefully distinguish also between what is done *officially* in an organisation, such as press releases and post-project evaluation, and what is done *unofficially*, such as grapevine stories, office parties, e-mail messages and so on.

The paradigm not only links the elements but may also tend to *preserve* them as 'the way we do things here'. It summarises the culture of the organisation.

7.3.4 Identification of the basic cultural style of the organisation

Although each organisation has its own unique culture, Handy[16] has used the work of Harrison to suggest that there are four main types.

The power culture

The organisation revolves around and is dominated by one individual or a small group. *Examples*: small building companies; formerly, some newspapers with dominant proprietors. *Strategic change*: fast or slow depending on the management style of the leader.

The role culture

This organisation relies on committees, structures, logic and analysis. There is a small group of senior managers who make the final decisions, but they rely on procedures, systems and clearly defined rules of communication. *Examples*: civil service, retail banks. *Strategic change*: likely to be slow and methodical.

The task culture

The organisation is geared to tackling identified projects or tasks. Work is undertaken in teams that are flexible and tackle identified issues. The teams may be multidisciplinary and adaptable to each situation. *Examples*: advertising agencies, consultancies. *Strategic change*: will depend on the circumstances but may be fast where this is needed.

The personal culture

The individual works and exists purely for him/herself. The organisation is tolerated as the way to structure and order the environment for certain useful purposes, but the prime area of interest is the individual. *Examples*: co-operatives, communes and also individual professionals such as architects or engineers working as lone people in larger organisations such as health authorities. *Strategic change*: can be instant, where the individual decides that it is in his/her interests to make such a move.

In examining the four main types of organisational culture, there are three important qualifications:

1 *Organisations change over time*. The entrepreneur, represented by the *power culture*, may mature into a larger and more traditional business. The bureaucracy, personified by the *role culture*, may move towards the more flexible structure of the *task culture*. Hence, an analysis may need to be reassessed after some years.

2 *Several types of culture usually exist in the same organisation*. There may be small task-teams concentrating on developing new business or solving a specific problem and, in the same organisation, a more bureaucratic set-up handling large-volume production in a more formal structure and style. Corporate strategy may even need to consider whether different parts of the organisation should develop *different* cultures – for example, a team culture for a radical new venture, a personal culture for the specialist expertise required for a new computer network.

3 *Different cultures may predominate, depending on the headquarters and ownership of the company*. Hofstede's research[17] indicates that national culture will also have an influence and will interact with the above basic type (*see* Section 7.6).

For these reasons, strategic cultural analysis needs to be approached with caution. Nevertheless, there are many organisations, both large and small, where the mood, style and tone are clear enough as soon as you walk through the door. There is one prevailing culture that permeates the way in which business is done in that organisation. The implications for competitive advantage and strategic change follow from this.

An example of the analysis of organisational culture for the Ford Motor Company is shown in Exhibit 7.2.

7.3.5 Conclusions on organisational culture

Exhibit 7.3 lists ten guidelines for analysing cultural issues within an organisation. Both Brown[18] and Handy[19] have provided longer questionnaires than are shown in Exhibit 7.3.

Exhibit 7.2

Analysis of organisational culture at Ford Motor Company as it started to go 'Back to Basics' in 2001[20]

Environment:

- Highly competitive world market
- Legacy issues in the US as Ford coped with commitments to its former employees on health and pensions – profit pressures on the company
- 'Green' issues surrounding car emissions

Cultural factors specific to the organisation:

- History and ownership: highly significant – one of the founders of modern America – still strong family connections
- Size: worldwide, complex, many interlinking parts
- Technology: sophisticated but mature technology in petrol engines
- Leadership and mission: strong vision for the future, but stumbled as leader sacked and new chief executive took over
- Cultural Web:

  - *Stories*. Too early for clear development but the new chief executive, Bill Ford, was inexperienced and therefore supported by a chief operating officer from Europe, who was well known – Sir Nick Scheele. The story of the actual sacking of the former chief officer, Mr Nasser, was told in vivid detail around the company. Just a week before his sacking, stories were circulating that Mr Nasser was laughing off his reported demise: 'It would be like someone saying you're about to be moved, and you know nothing about it.'

  - *Routines*. New routines were introduced to turn around the business – special meetings were called for all senior executives at the company's head offices. They were totally non-routine to emphasise the seriousness of the situation.

  - *Rituals*. The announcement of the departure of Mr Nasser was announced at a special employee meeting. Mr Ford's announcement 'received a standing ovation from cheering and whooping employees at Ford headquarters'.

  - *Symbols*. The meeting rooms – called 'energy rooms' – to devise the new back-to-basics Ford strategy were not designed to be comfortable. Executives summoned to such meetings were told to make only brief presentations and given a simple agenda – 'Tell us how you are going to cut costs.'

  - *Organisation*. A totally new team was set up to develop a revised cost-cutting strategy between November 2001 and the announcement of the new strategy in January 2002. This would be followed by thousands of job losses, the closure of four US car plants and the sale of non-core activities like KwikFit.

  - *Control*. Some new controls were introduced but the Ford system already had substantial systems for the monitoring of performance.

  - *Rewards*. Given the nature of the crisis, the 'reward' was to keep your job. At the time of Mr Nasser's departure, 20 top managers 'decided to retire', were re-assigned to other jobs or were replaced.

  - *Power*. A major power battle took place in the run-up to the sacking of Mr Nasser. This was then followed by a period of stability that would see power concentrated such that the proposed changes could be made over the following three years to 2004–05.

Identification of the basic cultural style of the organisation

- Role culture: the large size of the Ford company makes this highly likely.
- But major new projects are sometimes conducted with task culture.

Strategic implications:

- Change likely to be slow, prescriptive and complex.
- Most decisions are taken under pressure as the company attempts to restore its profitability.
- Stakeholders such as managers, employees and union representatives will expect to be consulted.
- Shareholders and financial institutions will expect short-term action to halt the profit problems.

From a strategy viewpoint, they are useful but the danger with such an analysis is that it becomes another descriptive list of possible factors. The analytical process needs to be undertaken with reference to possible areas of strategic interest. For example, it is *interesting* to know that the organisation's culture is risk averse, but it is much more *relevant* to set this against a new corporate strategy that requires a higher degree of risk taking than was previously the case. Hence, Exhibit 7.3 also provides some possible criteria to test for relevance. This is sometimes referred to as *testing for strategic fit* with the current strategy.

Exhibit 7.3

Ten guidelines for analysing organisation culture and its strategy implications

1 How old is the organisation? Does it exist in a stable or fast-changing environment?

2 Who owns it? Shareholding structure? Small company owner-proprietor? Government shareholding? Large public company? What are the core beliefs of the leadership?

3 How is it organised? Central board? Divisions? Clear decision-making structure from the top? Are structures formal or informal? Is competition encouraged between people in the company or does the organisation regard collaboration as being more important?

4 How are results judged? Sympathetically? Rigorously? What elements are monitored? Is the emphasis on looking back to past events or forwards to future strategy?

5 How are decisions made? Individually? Collectively and by consensus? How is power distributed throughout the organisation? Who can stop change? And who can encourage it?

6 What qualities make a good boss? And a good subordinate?

7 How are people rewarded? Remuneration? Fear? Loyalty? Satisfaction in a job well done?

8 How are groups and individuals controlled? Personal or impersonal controls? Enthusiasm and interest? Or abstract rules and regulations?

9 How does the organisation cope with change? Easily or with difficulty?

10 Do people typically work in teams or as individuals? What does the company prefer?

Overall: Is the *whole* organisation being analysed or just a *part*?

Tests for strategic relevance might include:

- *Risk*. Does the organisation wish to change its level of risk?
- *Rewards*. What reward and job satisfaction?
- *Change*. High or low degree of change needed?
- *Cost reduction*. Is the organisation seeking major cost reductions?
- *Competitive advantage*. Are significant new advantages likely or will they be needed?

Key strategic principles

- Organisational culture is the set of beliefs, values and learned ways of managing that govern organisational behaviour. Each organisation has a culture that is unique.
- Culture influences performance and corporate strategy. It is the filter and shaper through which strategy is developed and implemented.
- Factors within the organisation influencing culture include: history and ownership, size, technology, leadership and mission, along with the Cultural Web of the organisation.

Key strategic principles *continued*

- The Cultural Web provides a method of summarising some of the cultural influences within an organisation: stories, routines and rituals, symbols, power structures, organisation structure, control systems.

- Factors external to the organisation influencing culture include: people, national cultures, corporate cultural environment, labour and employment policies.

- There are four main types of culture: power, role, task and personal. Their importance for corporate strategy lies particularly in their ability to encourage or cope with the *strategic change* that is likely to be needed with specific strategic initiatives and to deliver *competitive advantage*. Some types are better able to cope and manage strategic change than others.

- Guidelines can be developed for analysing organisational culture. For the purposes of strategy development, such an analysis needs to be assessed against the strategy in areas such as attitudes to risk, change, reward, cost reduction and competitive advantage.

CASE STUDY 7.2

Royal Dutch/Shell – what does it take to bring change?

In a bid to improve growth and profitability, the world's largest oil company Royal Dutch/Shell announced a radical reorganisation in 1995 that would sweep 'barons out of fiefdoms'. In 1999, the company's problems were unchanged and the barons – the managing directors of its national companies – were still there. In 2004, the company had major corporate problems, which at last forced the company into action. But would it be enough to bring real change?

Background

Royal Dutch/Shell is one of the world's great oil companies. It is based on a joint holding company set up in 1907 between the UK company Shell Transport and the Dutch oil company Royal Dutch. Over the years, the combined enterprise grew, becoming the largest oil company in the world in 1998, measured by turnover. However, global leadership was lost in 1999 – as we shall see later.

Unlike other oil companies, which had become more centralised, the delicate balance between the UK and Dutch interests was still preserved up to 1998. There was no overall holding company but two owners of all the subsidiaries: Royal Dutch owned 60 per cent of each subsidiary and Shell owned the other 40 per cent. This arrangement had originally been negotiated when the group was founded. There was no strong central core, nor any combined board of directors. The nearest that the company came to full co-ordination was a central management forum called 'the Conference'. This was a meeting of the management boards of the two operating companies but it had no legal existence. The obvious strategic weakness was that this massive oil company could never use its shares – since they did not exist – to acquire another company.

Although managers and employees referred to themselves as members of Royal Dutch/Shell, they were in fact members of one of its various subsidiaries. This meant that all decision making was slow, laborious and careful – not necessarily a bad thing in an industry where time horizons for oil investment are typically 30 years. 'There is a committee culture,' said Mr Enst van Mouvik-Boekman, one of the senior human resource managers in the company. The co-operative style extended around the world to the company's interests in North America,

Royal Dutch Shell had traditionally allowed its subsidiaries – like this one in Nagasaki, Japan – considerable freedom to take strategic decisions.

Australasia and many other areas. The company had been much admired over the years for 'breeding the right corporate types and fostering a co-operative atmosphere'. But by 1998 the structure 'has become part of the problem – reducing accountability, blurring responsibility and increasing costs', commented stockbrokers BT Alex Brown.

Proposed strategy and organisational changes in 1995

One result of the company's consultative style was that it had no chief executive to take final decisions. There was a committee of managing directors but its decisions were achieved by consensus and its chairman was simply the 'first amongst equals'. Decisions on capital expenditure were often decidedly odd. The national companies were legal entities and demanded a share of the capital budget, regardless of whether they could make the best strategic case. Until 1995, the collegiate style of the committee of managing directors had limited powers to resist such demands.

In practical terms, this meant that key strategic decisions either took lengthy periods to emerge or were taken lower down in the organisation by the powerful national companies that made up the Royal Dutch/Shell empire, namely the barons referred to above. It also meant that there were large numbers of staff in London and Rotterdam whose job it was to co-ordinate the national policies associated with the regional barons. For many years, this had served the company well. However, by the mid-1990s, the company's return on capital was stuck below 10 per cent and was set to decline further.

The 1995 reorganisation was supposed to sweep away such a decision-making structure and its consequences in terms of poor investment decisions based on national company interests rather than the global good of Royal Dutch/Shell. The national companies would report to a series of global operating companies and some 1,170 co-ordinating jobs would go at the centre. The aim was to save costs and focus decisions on the regional and global decision making. Figure 7.4 shows the change that was to be undertaken from 1995 onwards.

But the reorganisation quickly ran out of steam. Although some 900 staff jobs were cut, there was considerable resistance to the proposed changes. The consultation culture of the company led to 'laborious' negotiations with staff, especially in the Netherlands. Moreover, the barons were still in power through their membership of the new business committees and the company's profitability was declining – see Figure 7.5. According to many outside observers, much more drastic strategic change was required.

Figure 7.4

The 1995 reorganisation of Royal Dutch/Shell

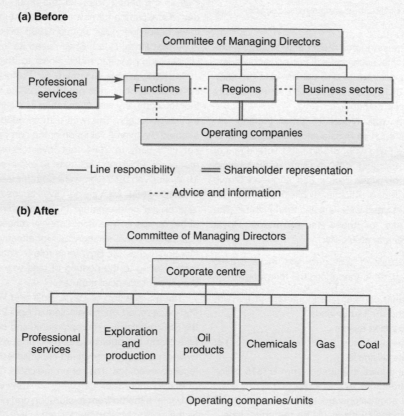

253

▶ CASE STUDY 7.2 continued

Figure 7.5

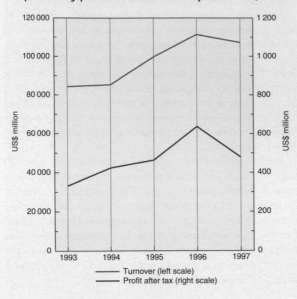

Operating performance at Royal Dutch/Shell

— Turnover (left scale)
— Profit after tax (right scale)

The 1998/99 strategic reorganisation

By the late 1990s, it was much more difficult for all the world's oil companies to make profits than earlier in the decade. There were four main reasons for this.

1 Higher environmental standards meant that capital investment in oil refineries was much higher than in earlier decades.
2 Oil prices had declined from US$15 per barrel in the early 1990s to around US$10 in the late 1990s because supply worldwide outstripped demand.
3 Political uncertainty was higher in some leading oil-producing countries such as Russia and Indonesia.
4 Rival companies like Esso (US), BP (UK) and Total (France) were acquiring or merging with rivals in order to gain further economies of scale: Exxon had acquired Mobil; BP had acquired Amoco, Atlantic Richfield and Castrol-Burmah; Total had merged with Fina and then with Elf. The subsequent success of these moves made Royal Dutch/Shell look weak strategically.

Royal Dutch/Shell realised that new and more drastic strategies were required, so it announced the following:

● Closure of its national company headquarters in the UK, Germany, France and the Netherlands
● Write-off of US$4.5 billion assets
● Sale of underperforming subsidiaries, especially 40 per cent of its chemicals business
● Cutbacks in annual capital investment from US$15 billion to US$11 billion per annum
● Several substantial acquisitions around the world that had been made earlier in the 1990s would be put up for sale

● The chairman of the committee of managing directors would be given new powers to take final decisions on capital expenditure. It was expected that, over time, his position would emerge as that of a dominant chief executive.

The annual cost savings from this reorganisation were projected by Royal Dutch/Shell as being US$2.5 billion by year 2001. 'I am absolutely clear that our group's reputation with investors is on the line', said the chairman of the committee, Mr (later Sir) Mark Moody-Stuart. He also used a phrase that in the past has been rarely heard at senior executive levels in Royal Dutch/Shell: he stressed the importance of 'executive accountability' when commenting on the 1998 reorganisation. He also said that the company had immense financial strength and flexibility to withstand further falls in the price of oil, even below US$10 per barrel.

The 2004 strategic problems

In 2004, the company's chairman resigned, the chief financial officer lost her job and Royal Dutch/Shell was the subject of a major investigation by the US Securities and Exchange Commission (SEC) – it is difficult to imagine a more serious situation in one of the world's largest companies. During 2004, the company had been forced to cut its proven oil and gas reserves by 23 per cent.

The seeds of the difficulty were sown in the years around the time of the 1998 reorganisation and its related cost savings. In the period 1996–99, the group invested US$6 billion per year exploring for new oil and gas deposits when it should have been spending around US$8 billion. It was not until 2000 that Royal Dutch/Shell raised its level of investment to US$9 billion per year, much closer to that of its rivals.

In 2001, a new chairman, Sir Philip Watts, took over at Royal Dutch/Shell. It is reported that he was warned in 2002 that the company was overstating its oil and gas reserves in its annual accounts. This was a most serious situation since it affected the overall valuation of the company. However, it was not until early in 2004 that investors were told about this matter. Sir Philip and his head of exploration and production, Mr Walter Van de Vijver, were both forced out of the company in March 2004. Mr Van de Vijver accused Sir Philip of being 'aggressive' or 'premature' in the recording of oil new reserves at the company. The chief financial officer, Judy Boynton also lost her job because she was 'not effective' in her compliance function. It was Ms Boynton's role to satisfy herself about the facts relating to the posting of reserves and compliance with the relevant financial statutes.

The US law firm of Davis, Polk and Wardwell produced a 450-page report on the problem in April 2004 at the request of the SEC regulators. The comments and direct quotes here are taken from the published parts of that report – at the time of writing, some parts remained unpublished because of possible legal proceedings. The report indicates that some employees of Royal Dutch/Shell were very unhappy with the situation. For example, a memo from exploration and production employees to their boss, Mr Van der Vijver in December 2003 concluded that the SEC filing in 2002 was 'materially wrong' and 'not to disclose it would constitute a violation of US securities law . . . and increase any potential exposure to liability within and outside the US'. Mr Van der Vijver immediately emailed back: 'This absolute dynamite, not all what I expected and needs to be destroyed.' The comments were not destroyed by the employees and were subsequently found by the US law firm.

The report also investigated the role of the chief financial officer, Ms Boyton, referred to above. In her case, the report concluded that she may have been in some difficulty precisely because of the confused organisational state of Royal Dutch/Shell during this period. The report pointed out that 'her ability to act effectively in a compliance function was somewhat impaired because, until recently, none of the business units' chief financial officers reported to her . . . on the issue of reserves, it may be that her responsibility exceeded her authority.' If this is correct, she was not told and had no authority to discover the situation because of the fragmented nature of the company – even in 2003/4.

Outcome in 2004/5

In March 2004, Mr Jeroen van der Veer was appointed to succeed Sir Philip as chairman of the committee of managing directors of Royal Dutch/Shell. He had two major tasks. The first was to repair the damage to the company's reputation as a result of the problems above. The second was to reorganise the company into a more manageable whole. In October 2004, Royal Dutch/Shell announced that it would be reformed into one company with its headquarters in the Netherlands. The dual HQ in London would be disbanded. In addition, both the chief executive and the chairman would be Dutch, but the understanding was that subsequent appointments would be made on merit, rather than nationality. The newly combined Royal Dutch Shell plc would be primarily listed in London and it would have a single board with executives and non-executives sitting together as one. At the time of writing, this new structure had not been approved by the shareholders. There were also legal and tax issues that remained unresolved. However, Mr van der Veer was enthusiastic: 'If you have a more simple structure, where you spend less time in lots of meetings, and with fewer executives, you make faster decisions.'

Perhaps the last word should be left to the employees. A year after the reserves crisis, less than one half of the company's employees were happy with the way that the company was managed. This was the finding of an internal survey undertaken in early 2005. When the survey was previously conducted in 2002, 67 per cent of employees felt the company was well led. This had dropped to 47 per cent by the time of the 2005 survey. Morale problems were particularly acute in the exploration and production part of the company that had been responsible for the overbooking of reserves. One employee was reported as saying: 'I am worried that far too little has visibly changed or happened. Those that are in charge of change are themselves tied to the old culture.'

In other words, it was still not clear whether the pressures on Royal Dutch/Shell would bring about the necessary strategic changes.

Case questions

1 *Why was the failure of the 1995 reorganisation and the changes in the late 1990s so predictable?*

2 *Do you think that the management changes of 2005 will be any more successful? Why? You may find it useful to use the Miles and Snow typology here to help you analyse the situation.*

3 *What lessons, if any, can we draw about the human resource aspects of strategy analysis from this case?*

7.4 ANALYSIS OF STRATEGIC CHANGE IN ORGANISATIONS

Definition ➤ Strategic change is the management of change in organisations in order to achieve clearly defined strategic objectives or to allow the company to experiment in areas where it is not possible to define strategic objectives precisely. Although some organisations may continue successfully with their current strategies, many will need to change. Any change brings uncertainty and some organisations and individuals are better able to cope with this than others. Some may even resist proposed new strategies and put at risk the new proposals – Royal Dutch/Shell being just one example. Strategic change can usefully be explored as the three interrelated topics shown in Figure 7.6.

7.4.1 Types of organisation and their ability to cope with strategic change – the contribution of Miles and Snow

Given the uncertainties that usually come with strategic change, organisations need to be analysed in advance for their ability to cope with this process. If they are likely to have difficulty, then there may be an argument for adjusting the proposed strategy to reflect this situation. There is no overall agreement on an analytical procedure for examining the link

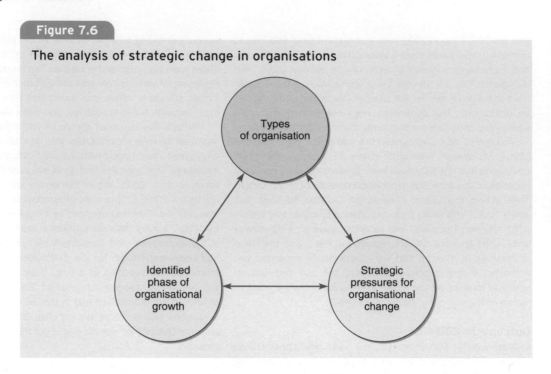

Figure 7.6

The analysis of strategic change in organisations

between organisation and strategic change. Commentators have proposed various ways of analysing the process.

Miles and Snow[22] proposed four main strategic types of organisation which can be analysed for their ability to cope with change:

1 *Defender organisations* produce products or services with the objective of obtaining market leadership. They may achieve their objectives by concentrating on a market niche through specialisation and cost reductions. The market may be mature and stable. The organisation is able to cope with sudden strategic change but would be more comfortable with steady strategic change.

2 *Prospector organisations* are involved in growing markets where they actively seek new opportunities through innovation. They are typically flexible and decentralised in their approach to the market and able to respond quickly to change. Their objectives are to seek new opportunities. Strategic change is no problem for such companies.

3 *Analyser organisations* seek to expand but also to protect what they already have. They may wait for others to innovate and delay while others prove new market opportunities before they enter. Large and small organisations can take this route, using mass production to reduce costs but also relying on some areas such as marketing to be more responsive and provide flexibility where required. Strategic change would need careful analysis and evaluation before it could be adopted.

4 *Reactor organisations* are those that respond inappropriately to competitors and to the more general environment. They rarely, if ever, take the initiative and, in a sense, may have no strategy: they always react to other strategies. Even if they have a strategy, it is entirely inappropriate to the environment and hence the resulting reactor organisation is bound to be inadequate. Strategic change will therefore be a problem.

In conclusion, the *prospector organisation* is probably the best able to cope with strategic change. The ability to cope is built into the culture, organisation and management style. Some markets are changing faster than previously, especially with new technologies and new international competition. The ability to cope and even enjoy change is a major competitive advantage.

Table 7.2

Four strategic types and their approaches to strategy

	Strategic environment	Strategic approach	Resource strategy	Simplified process approach
Defender	Stable	Protect market share Hold current position	Efficient production Tight control Centralised Manage via rules	Prescriptive
Analyser	Slow change	Hold market share but with some innovation Seek market opportunities but protect existing areas	Efficient production but some flexibility in new areas Tight control in existing areas but lower control in new products	Prescriptive
Prospector	Growing, even, dynamic	Find new opportunities Exploit and take risks	Flexible production Innovate with decentralised control	Emergent
Reactor	Growing or slow	Responding only to others Often late and inadequate	Muddled, centralised Slow	Prescriptive

Source: Adapted from *Academy of Management Review* by Miles, R E *et al*. Copyright 1987 by Academy of Management. Reproduced with permission of Academy of Management in the format Textbook via Copyright Clearance Center.

For strategy purposes, it will be essential to analyse the various parts of an organisation against their ability to cope with change. The above classification may oversimplify the real situation and needs to be treated with some caution. Nevertheless, it does provide real guidance on strategic change – *see* Table 7.2.

7.4.2 Phase of organisational growth

Whatever organisational classification is used in the analytical process, some changes may be more rapid and more dramatic than others. It is probably the case that the more intense the debate, the more difficult the change process and the more problems there are with the strategy. It is appropriate therefore to examine the *type of change* that might be expected. Greiner[23] identified two major determinants to clarify this process:

1 The *age of the organisation*. Young organisations are typically full of ideas, creative, perhaps a little chaotic but actively seeking change. As they grow older and achieve success, there is more to defend and more to co-ordinate. Royal Dutch/Shell was clearly at the older end of the spectrum.

2 The *size of the organisation*. Small organisations may be closer to the market place and have simpler administration. As the organisation becomes larger and acquires more people, it sets up systems and procedures to cope. Royal Dutch/Shell was clearly a large and complex organisation.

Greiner's five phases of growth are shown in Figure 7.7.[24] They are not meant to be taken literally – organisations can overcome their problems – but they are helpful in identifying the main issues to be met and the types of strategic change that may be needed.

Particular types of organisation will experience particular pressures for change.

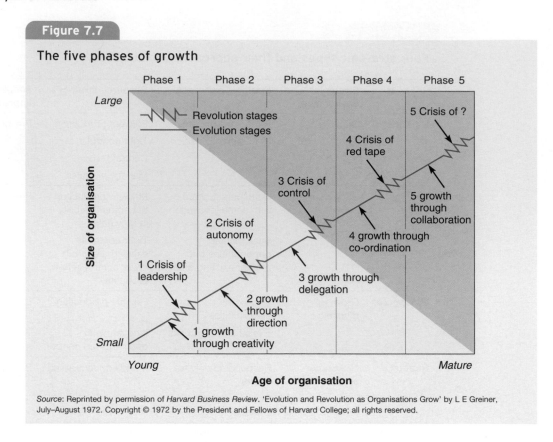

Figure 7.7

The five phases of growth

- *Small business.* As a small business expands, the owner-proprietor begins to lose control because s/he can no longer keep in contact with everyone personally. Moreover, the administration becomes more complex. Hence, it may become increasingly difficult to take rapid decisions and respond to changes in the environment. One strategic solution is to remain small and refuse to grow. Another solution is to sell out to a new group.

- *Large organisations that were formerly in government ownership.* Having previously relied on government funds, the organisation now needs to engage in marketing and other related business areas. However, it is large and has little experience of business pressures and culture. It is used to the bureaucracy that is demanded of government systems. Strategic change needs to be seen as a shift in *culture* just as much as new business-oriented *strategies*.

- *Not-for-profit institutions.* For an organisation which relies on public donations and voluntary help, there is an increasing problem as it grows older and expands in size. It needs to set up systems to manage its finances and services while at the same time keeping the personal touch and enthusiasm of its individual helpers. Change will present real problems.

- *Medium-sized business.* With expansion, it may no longer be possible to control every aspect of strategy from the centre. There will be a need for greater autonomy and delegation. Some managers are better able to delegate than others. The change strategy may involve not only new strategies but *new managers* recruited into the organisation.

7.4.3 Strategic pressures driving organisational change

As corporate strategy is analysed and developed, there are two main strategic pressures that may drive organisational change:

1 internal – desire for increased profitability, growth or some other objective, such as quality or innovation;

2 external – competitive pressures or other environmental change.

Such pressures need to be assessed for each organisation. For example, the pressures in the oil market and the need for proven oil reserves that eventually led to the beginnings of a major reorganisation at Royal Dutch/Shell.

Two specific strategies driving organisational change in the 1990s include *delayering*, which involves removing layers of management and administration, and *business process re-engineering*, which involves replacing people in administrative tasks by technology. Exhibit 7.4 explains the elements of these two techniques for driving change.

Exhibit 7.4

Examples of two strategic techniques to drive organisational change

Delayering

Definition ➤ Delayering is the removal of layers of management and administration in an organisation's structure.

Traditionally, big companies believed that one manager could only control a certain number of people – the *span of control* – often between seven and ten. Several layers of management were therefore needed to allow one senior person to control several hundred lower down in the organisation. With the new computer and telecommunications control systems, there is now a view that managers can control 30 people. This reduces the need to have so many managerial layers and thus opens the way for companies to cut costs – for example, the process undertaken by Shell to reduce its headquarters workforce by 1,170 employees.

To work properly, delayering needs to be undertaken with careful planning: this means examining the paperwork and bureaucracy that often accumulate in large companies and cutting these down at the same time. It also needs to be done radically once rather than in piecemeal fashion, because of the impact on morale every time cuts are made.

Business process re-engineering[25]

Definition ➤ Business process re-engineering is the replacement of people mainly in administrative tasks by computer technology, often accompanied by delayering and other organisational change.

It is more likely to occur in the lower levels of the company, rather than at managerial level. It is likely to involve combining departments such as customer handling, complaints, stock ordering, stock delivery and control. Typically, there will be a dismantling of demarcation between departments and a radical reduction in the number of employees. The human resource aspects of such a strategy are obvious. (*See* Case study 7.4.)

Strategic change will lead inevitably to organisational change. The starting point is careful *analysis* of the current situation. The subject of *managing* strategic change is explored in Chapter 21.

Key strategic principles

- Given the uncertainty that usually comes with strategic change, organisations need to be analysed for their ability to cope with this process.

- There are no agreed procedures for such an analysis but they usually involve categorising organisations into specific strategic types: four have been identified. The ability of each type to cope with change is then assessed.

- As strategies are developed in organisations, they may grow in size and certainly in age. In consequence, the nature of the strategic problems changes. Five stages of growth have been identified: creativity, direction, delegation, co-ordination and collaboration.

> **Key strategic principles** *continued*
>
> ● Change also needs to be assessed against the pressures that are on the organisation. These will be both internal and external. Strategies such as delayering and business process re-engineering are specific modern examples of such influences.

7.5 ANALYSIS OF POLITICS, POWER AND STRATEGIC CHANGE

When writing about his life in politics, the British politician Lord Butler called his book *The Art of the Possible*. Although certain changes in national life might be *desirable*, he argued that they were not always *possible*, given the electorate and the environment of that time. In politics, he believed that people needed to be persuaded and this was an art, not an exact science. Business and not-for-profit organisations also involve people. The early twentieth-century view of management pioneers such as F W Taylor and Henry Ford was that there was 'one best way' to achieve results and organisations were machines that could be directed to these ends. Views are now more sophisticated, especially where strategic change is concerned.

In organisations, there will be individuals and groups who are likely to have an interest in any strategic change. There may be pressure groups, rivalries, power barons and brokers, influencers, arguments, winners and losers. Some dispute may be disinterested and rational and some may be governed by strongly held views and interests. All these areas form the *politics* of the organisation. Politics is therefore concerned with the exercise of authority, leadership and management in organisations. Strategic change cannot be separated from such issues.

Definition ➤

Strategy too is about 'the art of the possible'. An analysis of the organisation's political situation is important in the early stages of strategic development. It may be highly desirable to alter radically a company's structure, but the cost in terms of management time may be too high in some circumstances, even with an imposed solution. Case study 7.2 explored the difficulties that faced the new chairman of Royal Dutch/Shell in 2004 as he attempted to achieve radical change and impose his preferred solutions on the organisation.

7.5.1 What are the main components of politics in organisations?

Taking an emergent strategy perspective, Handy points out[26] that it is wishful thinking to attempt to 'manage change' in the sense that it is possible not only to know where the organisation is heading but also to instruct everyone to take the same route. It is much more realistic and rewarding to 'cultivate change', suggesting that a positive attitude to change, coupled with learning and persuasion, is more likely to be productive.

There is nothing wrong with healthy competition between groups and individuals in an organisation. It can stretch performance and help groups to become more cohesive. It also helps to sort out the best. The difficulty arises when it gives rise to conflict and political manoeuvring. There are two principal reasons for organisational conflict:

1 *Differing goals and ideologies*. For example, different groups or individuals within an organisation may have different goals, make different value judgements, be given different and conflicting objectives, etc. There may also be a lack of clarity in the goals and objectives. It should be possible in the context of strategic change to ensure that conflict and confusion over goals are minimised.

2 *Threats to territory*. For example, some groups or individuals may feel threatened by others doing the same jobs, become jealous of other roles, be given instructions that cut across other responsibilities, etc. It is in this area that the greatest strategic difficulty is likely to arise. If savings are to be made or improved performance to be obtained, then it may be necessary to accept the conflict here.

Addressing the strategic change issue, Mintzberg[27] suggests that there are benefits from competition in organisations. It can be a force for achieving change. In this sense, politics is an inevitable consequence of strategic change and needs to be accepted and channelled for the best results.

7.5.2 How can strategic change be analysed in a political context?

It is important to clarify right at the start the organisation's objectives and the implications for individual parts of the organisation. If it is true that conflict arises as a result of confusion over objectives, then it follows that these need to be fully explored before other matters are raised.

In addition, five areas would benefit from analysis at this early stage:

1 *The extent to which the organisation has developed a culture of adaptation or experiment.* Such an approach will help when it comes to implementing agreed strategies later.

2 *The identification of major power groups or individuals* whose influence and support is essential for any major strategic change.

3 *The desirability or necessity of consultation rather than confrontation*, as the strategic analytical process continues.

4 *The role and traditions of leadership in the organisation* and the extent to which this may enhance the success and overcome problems associated with strategic change.

5 *The nature and scope of the external pressures on the organisation.*

These are the subjects that need to be analysed in the context of strategic change. They are interconnected as a network of relationships (*see* Figure 7.8). Once the main outline of strategies has been agreed, it will be necessary to return to the politics of strategic change again. We will do so in Chapter 21.

The political network of an organisation

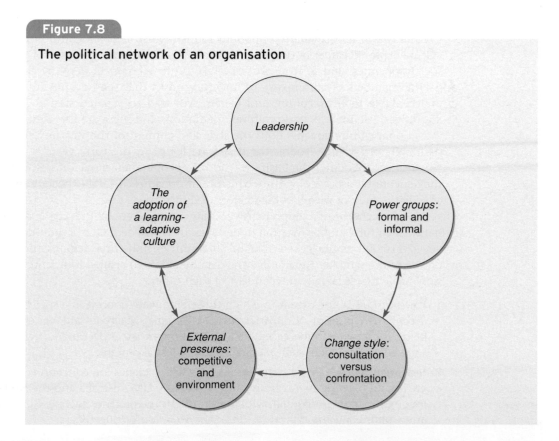

Key strategic principles

- Strategic change needs to take into account what is possible in terms of change, rather than what is desirable.

- Competition is healthy in organisations, except when it degenerates into unhealthy conflict and political manoeuvring.

- During the analysis phase of strategic development, there are political issues that can usefully be explored. In analysing the political network, it is necessary to survey power groups, leadership, the change style of the organisation, the adoption of a learning-adaptive culture and the nature of the external pressures.

7.6 INTERNATIONAL CULTURAL PERSPECTIVES

In one sense, *national culture* is just one of the organisational culture issues explored in Section 7.3. However, from a strategy viewpoint, it is important enough to be highlighted on its own. The reason is that some corporate strategies may be desirable in theory but extremely difficult to implement in practice, once national culture is considered. It would therefore be better to identify any national culture problems in the analysis phase and develop a different and more acceptable strategy.

There is no single agreed definition of national culture, but for our purposes we will use that of Hofstede:[28]

Definition ➤   *The collective programming of the mind which distinguishes the members of one human group from another . . . Culture, in this sense, includes systems of values; and values are among the building blocks of culture.*

Note that it is particularly important to distinguish *national* culture from *organisational* culture explored earlier in this chapter. National culture governs much of the way in which society operates, and so it needs to be taken into account in deriving corporate strategy. Asking members of a company to undertake tasks that they do not understand, or find unacceptable to their culture and beliefs, will lead to a failed strategy. Kluckhohn and Strodtbeck[29] defined six basic cultural orientations and these are listed in Table 7.3.

National culture governs both the style and content of the way business is done internationally. To a large extent, the basics are learnt in the early years of life, before individuals ever encounter the business world. As people then move into different companies, they encounter aspects of culture which their previous cultural expectations allow them to cope with easily or with varying degrees of difficulty.

Probably the most comprehensive study undertaken of the importance of different national cultural groups was that undertaken by Hofstede.[30] Over a number of years, he surveyed 116,000 employees at IBM in 50 countries and three regions (note the specialist nature of the sample). He grouped the data he obtained against four, and later five, dimensions which were largely independent of each other.

1 *Power distance* – the extent to which those who were poorest in a society were willing to accept their position. Countries such as Panama, Malaysia and Venezuela emerged as being those where such acceptance was common. Israel, Denmark, Ireland and Sweden were countries where such inequalities were less acceptable.

2 *Individualism/collectivism* – the extent to which societies are collections of individuals or are bound together in a cohesive whole. The US, UK, Australia and the Netherlands were among the more individual, with South American countries such as Guatemala, Panama and Columbia being typical of those who were more collectivist.

Table 7.3

Six basic national cultural orientations

Orientation	Range of variations
What is the nature of people?	• Optimistic or pessimistic in expectations about people? • Believing in people basically being good or evil or a mixture? • Suspicious or trusting of others?
What is the person's relationship to nature?	• Does s/he want to dominate and exploit nature or remain fatalistic about nature and what the future holds?
What is the person's relationship to other people?	• Individual or collective? • Does personal achievement matter or is the group's goal more important?
What is the modality of human activity?	• Are tangible reward and achievement important as a way of life? • Or are we born to a certain path with merit being rewarded in after-life or a future reincarnation?
What is the temporal focus of human activity?	• Is the future, present or past to be the focus of activity? • Can we plan and control society? • Or should we primarily look back to past events to guide the future?
What is the conception of space?	• Private, mixed or public? • Do meetings and events take place behind closed doors? Is it easy to visit colleagues without an invitation? • Or do most activities take place in public or semi-public areas?

3 *Masculinity versus femininity* – the extent to which a country is placed on a spectrum from masculine to feminine. In *male* cultures, there is a sharp distinction between the role the two sexes play in society and at work: males are expected to emphasise the importance of work, power and wealth. In *female* cultures, there is more equality between the two, with achievements being measured in terms of the environment and human contacts. Japan, Austria and Italy were typical masculine cultures and Sweden, the Netherlands and Finland typical feminine cultures.

4 *Uncertainty avoidance* – the extent to which members of a culture feel threatened by the unknown. Where uncertainty avoidance is *weak*, people are willing to embrace uncertainty and ambiguous situations: precision and punctuality for meetings were useful but not essential. In *strong* uncertainty avoidance countries, people need certainty, planning and order. Strong country cultures include Japan, Portugal, Greece and Belgium. Weak countries covered Singapore, Denmark, Jamaica and Hong Kong.

5 *Confucian versus dynamic* – Hofstede later added this category to those above. He discovered that different cultures have different time horizons – long-termism versus short-termism – which were also linked with the Confucian concept of 'virtue' versus the more Western concept of 'truth'. Thus *long-termism* emphasises the importance of taking a long view and adapting traditions to a modern context, while stressing perseverance. *Short-termism* seeks not only the short-term view but also the importance of status, social obligations and quick results. China, Hong Kong and South Korea typify the former, whereas the US, Nigeria, Canada and the UK were typical of the latter.

For a critique of the Hofstede research, *see* Meade.[31]

Such cultural variation will also be reflected in the corporate group cultures of various countries. These are explored in Case study 7.3.

CASE STUDY 7.3

Industry groups in Japan, Korea, Hong Kong and Italy

Companies often coalesce into informal industry groupings within a country. These can have a substantial influence on the strategy of group members, ranging from support in time of trouble to mutual benefits and co-operation on new strategic initiatives. Occasionally, such co-operation may be in danger of breaching anti-monopoly legislation.

For examples of such groupings, we can look at the Far East and Europe. In Japan, such groupings are called *Keiretsu* and in Korea *Chaebol*. (It should be noted that they are not quite the same in the two societies but they fulfil similar roles. The *Keiretsu* are more informal, while the *Chaebol* are effectively conglomerates.) From a strategy viewpoint, the links between the companies in the *Keiretsu* or *Chaebol* can be mutually supportive of new business initiatives. They can be used to help in difficult times and also to secure business deals that might otherwise prove difficult. The regular meetings of senior managers from such groupings can also be a source of useful business information. Competitors need to understand such groupings and to anticipate their mutual support in any negotiations.

Mitsubishi and Mitsui are examples of *Keiretsu* in Japan: they had 25 and 22 companies respectively in 1993 in their organisational orbit. The top six *Keiretsu* controlled 38 per cent of Japan's market capitalisation, 16 per cent of sales and 17 per cent of listed company profits in 1993.[32] In the same way, the three leading Korean *Chaebol* controlled over US$15 billion sales in 1993. Samsung, Hyundai and Lucky-Goldstar were the three biggest with sales of US$5.6, US$4.6 and US$3.5 billion respectively.[33] However, the Korean situation was not to last.

In spite of the Asian economic crisis of 1997–99 and the more general difficulties in the Japanese economy after this time, the *Keiretsu* groupings have proved remarkably resilient. However, the Fuyo *Keiretsu*, which includes the Fuji Bank and Nissan cars, was under pressure in Japan.[34] The Ssanyong *Chaebol* was being broken up in Korea. Most of the remaining Korean groups have subsequently disintegrated under political and economic pressure. However, a few Korean groups grew stronger as a result of acquiring weakened outside competitors.[35]

Such links are not confined to these two countries: networking has long been an important characteristic of Chinese families. The Riady family connections through their Lippo Group of companies in China, Hong Kong, the US and Indonesia are an example of a group that has now grown to a capitalised value of around US$2.5 billion.[36]

This should not be seen as a purely Eastern phenomenon. The Agnelli family in Italy have extensive interests that go well beyond Fiat cars into chemicals, aerospace and banking.[37] The Seagram family in the US in 1995 completed their purchase of MCA for US$2 billion. In 1998, the same family bought another entertainment group, Polygram, for around US$8 billion. They then sold all their media interests to the French company Vivendi in 2001. In both cases, there is a web of companies that have interconnections that extend across the corporate environment. They add to the complexity of the analysis of corporate strategy.

Case questions

1 *Compared with the other cultural areas outlined in this chapter, how important do you believe corporate cultures are for the companies above?*

2 *What are the main features of such a culture in terms of their influence and control over individual companies?*

3 *Can you identify a corporate culture close to your own organisation? For example, how about the student union? Or a trade association to which the company belongs? What are its chief distinguishing features? How does it influence the strategy of its members, if at all?*

From a national strategy perspective, the implications may be significant:

● For organisations engaged primarily in one national market, it will have some relevance if people from a number of cultural backgrounds are employed. For example, in South Africa, there are white and black communities with quite different cultural backgrounds working together.

● For organisations with a range of national companies in different countries, possibly across Europe, Africa or South-East Asia, the implications are equally important. There will be a need to devise a strategy that takes account of not only central HQ issues but also local cultures and styles, values and expectations. For example, a mission statement or a timetable for strategic change may need to reflect national cultural values and sense of urgency.

- For global companies, the cultural issue is more likely to be how to bring together the many cultures that exist. This may involve special integration programmes to break down cultural barriers.

Beyond these national-specific cultural issues, Olie[38] has pointed out that some management theories may be *culture-specific* – in other words, they may not 'work' outside the national culture in which they were invented. As an example, we might take Peters and Waterman's loose–tight principle:[39]

> *Organisations that live by the loose–tight principle are on the one hand rigidly controlled, yet at the same time allow (indeed, insist on) autonomy, entrepreneurship and innovation from the rank and file.*

This may operate well in the US but not in other cultures such as Korea, where there is a stronger need for certainty and collectivism. This is an important point that needs to be considered throughout this text.

Key strategic principles

- National culture is defined as the collective programming of the mind which distinguishes the members of one human group from another.

- National culture governs both the style and content of the way business is done internationally. It may therefore influence corporate strategy.

- Hofstede developed five dimensions that help to define and describe national cultures: power distance, individualism/collectivism, masculinity versus femininity, uncertainty avoidance, Confucian versus dynamic.

- The evidence from these national characteristics would suggest that they can have a profound effect on the human aspects of corporate strategy. They need to be taken into account during the development of strategy, not later.

- It may even be the case that *national* culture will influence some aspects of *organisational* culture.

CASE STUDY 7.4

How Xerox shifted its strategy and changed its organisation[40]

During the last ten years, Xerox has reduced the size of its workforce, reorganised its operating companies and introduced a new organisation and culture to the company. This case study examines the shift in its strategy and structure.

Background

For 30 years, the US company Xerox has been engaged in a major global battle with its Japanese rivals, especially Canon and Ricoh. From dominance of the photocopying market in the 1960s, Xerox's market share has slowly been reduced. Its sales have risen but not as fast as the market has grown. It has been the Japanese companies that have made all the running in terms of new products, higher quality, ease of use and maintenance-free equipment.

In 2004, Xerox Corporation had total sales of around US$15.7 billion and net income of US$859 million. In 2000, the company had made a loss of US$273 million. This case study examines the turnaround in strategy and organisation at Xerox during the period up to 2004.

Markets, competitors and customers

When Japanese companies decided to enter international photocopying markets in the 1960s, they had to find a way to overcome the dominance of Xerox. They chose to open up a new market segment: copiers for medium and small businesses that needed little maintenance and no regular service support. Xerox had a policy of always leasing its machines and then providing service engineers to maintain them: this was attractive to large companies with heavy printing demands, but smaller companies rapidly found the Japanese offerings more acceptable.

By 2000, Xerox had lost market share of the overall market. However, it still continued to maintain its market leadership in the high-end segment. Its competitive strengths still lay in its ability to provide a high level of service to customers. This was an area that the Japanese companies had never really attempted to match because of the high set-up costs and difficulty in obtaining minimum levels of business to make profits. Xerox had made several attempts to break into the lower end of the market. The last of these was in around 2000. However, its strengths and cost structures were still largely geared to large company customers.

In 1993, its European subsidiary, Xerox Europe, undertook a survey of its customers' photocopying requirements: it found that they were spending 8 per cent of their turnover creating and managing documents, including creating and developing printed material, photocopying it, and filing and recording the results. This compared with 3 per cent of turnover spent on information technology. Moreover, up to 60 per cent of their customers' time was regularly spent on various activities associated with documentation. In 2001, the parent company Xerox America undertook a similar study and confirmed that its customers were still spending considerable time on documentation but the nature of the work had changed – it was more concerned with electronic systems, the internet and accessing information electronically.

Problems in 2000

For a company with a strong range of products and some talented people, it may seem surprising that Xerox faced major problems in 2000. There were five main reasons:

- Increased competition from Japanese and American companies – photocopying and printing was becoming highly competitive.
- Failed reorganisation of its American salesforce had upset customers in its prime geographic area. The chief executive wanted Xerox to become more than a photocopier company. It needed to sell business solutions based on document work flows. This meant a major reorganisation of the company to provide industry specialists who would understand specific industries. It also involved drastically reducing the numbers of Xerox back office centres in order to lower the Xerox costs. The result of such a drastic change was little short of chaotic.
- Problems in some of its new growth markets – particularly Brazil and Thailand.

- Accounting problems in Mexico that eventually led to a Securities and Exchange Commission investigation with regard to equipment leasing in that country.
- High levels of debt from excessive borrowing.

The result was that the chief executive officer, Rick Thoman, resigned. The Xerox board then chose as the new chief executive someone who had worked for the company for 25 years – Anne Mulcahy. Her job was to turn around the Xerox company, which by this time was in real difficulties. She spent her first 90 days talking to customers and employees: 'There was such confusion and complexity in the company that I could have wasted a lot of time addressing symptoms that were not at the heart of what was wrong.'

Turnaround 2000 in business and organisational culture

Anne Mulcahy's turnaround plan was simplicity itself:

- The company would have to cut overheads by US$1 billion.
- It would have to close unprofitable activities.
- It would have to reduce its levels of debt finance by asset sales.

With colleagues, she then set about implementing these strategies. By 2002, the company had cut nearly 19,000 jobs. Costs were reduced by US$1.2 billion. The complete small office/home division of Xerox was closed down because it was unprofitable. The company sold its half-share in Fuji Xerox back to its Japanese associate, the Fuji Company in order to raise substantial finance. It also sold part of its customer financing business to GE Capital, again in order to raise finance and reduce its debts.

Importantly, Anne Mulcahy also started to change the company's culture. She had the dubious advantage that the company was clearly in trouble. This made it easier to explain to everyone that there was a real crisis and tough decisions would be needed. 'I used it as a vehicle to get things done that wouldn't have been possible in times of business as usual,' explains Ms Mulcahy. She used the crisis to obtain strategic change.

Her second step was to appoint a new management team. She was fortunate in that she knew her colleagues at Xerox well and wanted to promote from within where possible. 'I want to make sure someone feels ownership for every change initiative we have in place,' she said. 'Looking back, I think we had a lot of smart, articulate people – good presenters and good team players – who didn't necessarily like to take responsibility on their shoulders.' This meant that some of the people who were talented in other ways were not appropriate for the key management decisions that were now needed.

Beyond these changes, she did not alter the basic structure of committees and operations at Xerox. However, she did change the way that they were run. She herself describes an operations committee meeting: 'We were discussing customer satisfaction, an area where I think we should be doing better . . . The functional experts did a very nice job of presenting the process. We were all nodding and suddenly I had this feeling that this was the Xerox of the past. We were all going to go into conference rooms, we were all going to agree. . . . I just sat there and said: "Time out". If I were putting my money on the table right now, right out of my wallet, would I bet that any of this is going to make a hoot of difference in terms of results? The answer is that I wouldn't put a dime on the table. It looks good. Nice presentations. Nice process. But at the end of the day we are not confronting the tough issues. I can't let us sit there and lull ourselves into that kind of discussion any more.'

Anne Mulcahy wanted a change in style and thought processes at Xerox and she wanted a shift in strategy beyond the short-term activities of the turnaround.

Shift of basic strategy

Given the time spent by its customers and its own strengths in servicing large customers, Xerox decided to build on this but shift the emphasis of its basic business strategy. It would make three main offerings:

- *High-end copying*. It would continue to offer high-end copiers, printers and fax machines. This was its traditional area of strength and it had a highly skilled sales machine to undertake this task. This was the market where it competed against Hewlett-Packard, Canon and Ricoh.
- *High-end production printing*. It would expand its interests in large-scale printing presses, such as those involved in magazine printing. This was the area of industrial printing where its main competitor was the German company Heidelberg.
- *Document services and solutions*. It would offer consulting services and solutions for the archiving, documentation and printing problems of its client companies. It would help companies access archives containing 'millions of pages of R&D' or move millions of documents on to a company intranet in order to reduce costs. A new organisation, Xerox Global Services, was the result.

This implied higher degrees of service for all the document requirements of its customers, not just the photocopying part. The strategy shifted from simple photocopying towards offering a wider range of services and products to cater for the *document management* needs of its customers. Naturally, it continued to offer photocopying to those customers who preferred this.

In the early years, the company recognised that it would take time for customers to see the benefits of its broader range. It noted that its rivals soon picked up the same themes: 'document management' and the 'document solution' were soon appearing elsewhere. However, Xerox was convinced that its strategy was sound: it was built on its core skills and based on service. When done well, a service competitive advantage is immensely difficult for competitors to match because service is localised. However, the quality of that service is vital.

Table 7.4

Xerox – financial results

US$ (millions)

	2000	2001	2002	2003	2004
Total revenue	18 751	17 008	15 849	15 701	15 722
Net income (loss)	(273)	(94)	91	360	859
Employees at year-end	91 500	78 900	67 800	61 100	58 100

By 2004, the company had recovered its market position. The new strategies were beginning to pay off – *see* the results in Table 7.4.

Case questions

1 *How would you summarise the strategies adopted by Xerox in the face of strong Japanese competition? Do you think they will be successful?*

2 *Xerox laid great emphasis in its strategy initiatives on changing the organisational culture: what organisational, morale and human resource problems might arise as a result?*

3 *Given the success of Xerox in improving its profitability, what can other companies learn from the Xerox experience? Would other companies need to adopt the Xerox culture and strategic approach if they wished to emulate the success that was achieved?*

STRATEGIC PROJECT

The impact of new technology on such companies over the last ten years has made a substantial impact on human resource strategy. You might like to investigate other companies where there has been a similar change – for example, Kodak, which has been undermined by the collapse of the film business as cameras have become digital. You could consider the difficulties faced by national telephone companies as mobile telephones have gained in popularity and, in some countries like China and parts of Africa, come to dominate the market. You could first establish the basic situation by looking at the profit record of the companies themselves – often available on the web – and then follow this up by looking for public pronouncements, newspaper stories about changes in personnel and management.

CRITICAL REFLECTION

At what stage should organisational culture and power feature in the strategy process?

This chapter of the book rests on the assumption that it is appropriate to explore organisational culture and power *at this early stage* in strategy development. Many strategists (and textbook authors) disagree. They undertake an analysis of the organisation's environment and its competitive resources. They then define the purpose of the organisation and devise strategies to achieve that purpose. After this process, they consider organisational culture and power – it is often studied as the '*implementation*' of the strategic decision.

This book takes the view that it is necessary to explore culture, power and leadership *earlier* in strategy development. Perhaps the book is wrong? What are the arguments in favour of 'implementation' at the end of the strategy process? And what are the arguments in favour of exploring this topic earlier?

Why consider culture, leadership and power now?

SUMMARY

● The analysis of human resources is important for strategy development for two reasons. People are a vital resource. In addition, strategy development often involves change and some people may resist it. There are four areas to explore in the analysis of this area: resource audit, organisational culture, strategic change and its implications in terms of the power and politics of the organisation.

● Human-resource-based analysis emphasises the emergent approach to corporate strategy. Sustainable competitive advantage will often depend on human resources. In fast-moving markets, the adaptability of people inside the organisation becomes a special and important skill. Coping with strategic change is a vital element in the development of corporate strategy.

● The human resource audit will have two main elements: *people* in the organisation and the *contribution* of human resources to the development of corporate strategy. A basic analysis will reflect these two areas but also needs to consider key factors for success, competitive comparisons and possibly international issues.

● Culture is the set of beliefs, values and learned ways of managing the organisation. Each organisation has a culture that is unique. In analysing culture, there are four main areas: environment, cultural factors specific to the organisation, the basic cultural type of the organisation and the strategic implications.

● Factors within the organisation influencing culture include: history and ownership, size, technology and leadership. These can be coupled with the Cultural Web of the organisation to provide a method of summarising the main cultural influences. The Cultural Web includes stories, routines and rituals, symbols, power structures, organisation structure and control systems.

● The four main types of culture are power, role, task and personal. Their importance for corporate strategy lies in the ability of each type to cope with strategic change and to deliver competitive advantage.

● Analysis of strategic change needs to consider three areas: the type of organisation, the phase of organisation growth and the strategic pressures for organisational change. Four types of organisation have been identified, with each having a different response to strategic change. The age and size of an organisation will provide information on its phase of growth. The strategic pressures for organisational change need careful assessment. They may include such concepts as delayering – the reduction of the number of reporting layers in an organisation – and business process re-engineering – the use of new technology to reduce the administrative task and reduce costs.

● Strategic change needs to take into account what is possible in terms of change in the organisation, rather than what is theoretically desirable. Political issues in the organisation therefore need to be carefully explored – the political network.

● Four distinctive types of strategic decision makers have been identified: defender, analyser, prospector and reactor. Each is associated with a different approach to strategic decision making. In particular, the four approaches show different attitudes to risk and to the style of managing the business.

● International cultures may have a profound impact on corporate strategy. They may even make some strategy proposals very difficult to implement.

QUESTIONS

1 Use Exhibit 7.1 to audit the human resources of an organisation with which you are familiar. What conclusions can you draw with respect to corporate strategy?

2 You have been retained by a well-known fast-food restaurant chain to advise it on corporate strategy. You are aware that human resources are important in this work. What considerations would you wish to explore initially? How would you approach this task?

3 Analyse the culture of Royal Dutch/Shell over the period of Case study 7.2. Compare it with the Ford culture of Case 7.1.

4 'There is no robust, generalisable evidence that business process re-engineering has made any significant impact on business performance.' (Professor Colin Egan)[41]

If you were a senior manager at Xerox Europe, what would you make of this?

5 What are the general environmental influences on the culture of higher education at present? What are the strategic implications for institutions involved in this area?

6 Develop the Cultural Web for Xerox Europe from Case study 7.4 and identify the basic cultural style of the company. Give reasons for your views.

7 Use the criteria from Exhibit 7.2 to characterise the culture of the following four organisations: a multinational car company; a small, new computer software company; a recently privatised national telecommunications company (such as British Telecom or Deutsche Telekom); a local police station.

8 Analyse the strategic change implications of an organisation of your choice. Use the typology of Section 7.4 to explore the *type* of organisation, the *phase* of organisational growth, and the *pressure* for strategic change.

9 'An organisation's strategy makes visible its culture, expressing it in much the same way that speech creates meaning in language.' (Dr Andrew Brown)

How important is culture to strategy development when compared with other aspects of the analytical process?

10 Is *delayering* feasible in every national culture? Use Hofstede's analysis of culture to explain your answer.

Further reading

For a well-developed exposition of culture: Brown, A (1995) *Organisational Culture*, Pitman Publishing, London.

For some excellent and provocative reading on the relationship between human resources and strategy: Egan,

C (1995) *Creating Organisational Advantage*, Butterworth-Heinemann, Oxford.

For a well-developed survey of the international aspects of human resource management: Harzing, Anne-Wil and

Van Ruysseveldt, J (eds) (1995) *International Human Resource Management*, Sage, London, with the Open University of the Netherlands.

In November 2003, there was a major retrospective series of articles on the Miles and Snow typology in *Academy of Management Executive*, Vol 17, No 4, pp95–118. There was also an interesting paper in the previous issue: Gratton, L

and Truss, C (2003) 'The three-dimensional people strategy: Putting human resource policies into action', *Academy of Management Executive*, Vol 17, No 3, pp74–86.

There was also a retrospective on Geerd Hofstede's work in February 2004: *Academy of Management Executive*, Vol 18, No 1, 4 papers including an interview with Professor Hofstede, pp73–90.

Notes and references

1 Sources for the Ford globalisation strategy include: *Financial Times*, 22 Apr 1994 (reprinted in the first edition of this text); 16 Nov 1998, p12; 29 Jan 1999, p1; 3 Mar 1999, p14 (interesting article by Professor John Kay on globalisation in the car industry); 9 Mar 1999, p25.

2 Chandler, A (1962) *Strategy and Structure: Chapters in the History of the Industrial Enterprise*, MIT Press, Cambridge, MA, p14.

3 Porter M E (1980) *Competitive Strategy* and (1985) *Competitive Advantage*, The Free Press, New York.

4 Chandler, A (1962) Op. cit. *See*, for example, the roles of Durant, Du Pont and Sloan in Ch3 on General Motors.

5 There are several well-known strategic management texts that take this approach.

6 Handy, C (1989) *The Age of Unreason*, Business Books, London; Handy, C (1991) *The Gods of Management*, Business Books, London; Tyson, S (1995) *Human Resource Strategy*, Pitman Publishing, London, Chs4, 5 and 6; Brown, A (1995) *Organisational Culture*, Pitman Publishing, London, p198.

7 Pettigrew, A and Whipp, R (1991) *Managing Change for Competitive Success*, Blackwell, Oxford.

8 De Geus, A (1988) 'Planning as learning', *Harvard Business Review*, Mar–Apr, p71.

9 Whittington, R (1993) *What Is Strategy and Does It Matter?* Routledge, London, p122.

10 This exhibit has been derived from Tyson, S (1995) Op. cit., pp171–4 and Rosen, R (1995) *Strategic Management: an Introduction*, Pitman Publishing, London, p166.

11 Brown, A (1995) *Organisational Culture*, Pitman Publishing, London, p198.

12 Brown, A (1998) *Organisational Culture*, 2nd edn, Financial Times/Pitman Publishing, London.

13 This subject area does not seem to have been the subject of any major research study. It is included because of the practical experience of many companies.

14 International Labour Office (1993) *World Labour Report*, Geneva.

15 Handy, C (1993) *Understanding Organisations*, 4th edn, Penguin, Harmondsworth, pp193–4.

16 Handy, C (1993) Op. cit., p183. Handy uses the work of Harrison, R (1972) 'How to describe your organisation', *Harvard Business Review*, Sep–Oct. Handy uses Greek gods to typify the four cultural types: they make an interesting read, but mean rather less to those of us who studied *The Aeneid*.

17 Hofstede, G (1980) *Culture's Consequences: International Differences in Work-related Values*, Sage, Beverly Hills, CA.

18 Brown, A (1995) Op. cit., pp62–5.

19 Handy, C (1993) Op. cit., pp210–16.

20 *Financial Times*, 29 November 2001, and other articles in the same paper on 17 Feb 1992, p14; 29 Mar 1994, p30; 11 Apr 1994, p20; 23 Apr 1994, p11; 4 Oct 1994, pVII; 2 Dec 1994, p17; 6 Jan 1995, p17; 23 Jan 1995, p10.

21 Sources for the Royal Dutch/Shell case: Annual Report and Accounts 2004. *Financial Times*: 1 September 2003, p20; 14 January 2004, p12; 4 March 2004, p23; 20 April 2004, p25 (contains quotes from the explosive emails between Mr van de Vijver and Sir Philip); 30 July 2004, p23; 23 September 2004, p23; 29 October 2004, p21; 16 December 2004, p25; 2 February 2005, p19 (the employee survey).

22 Miles, R E and Snow, C C (1978) *Organisational Strategy, Structure and Process*, McGraw-Hill, New York. *See also* Miles, R, Snow, C, Meyer, A and Coleman (1978) 'A strategy typology of organisations', *Academy of Management Review*, July, and reprinted in De Wit, R and Meyer, R (1994) *Strategy: Content, Context and Process*, West Publishing, St Paul, MN. There is clearly some overlap here with the classification developed by Handy on types of culture. It is hardly surprising that the two areas are consistent; it would be alarming if they were not.

23 Greiner, L (1972) 'Evolution and revolution as organisations grow', *Harvard Business Review*, July–Aug.

24 *Source*: Greiner, L (1972) Ibid., p265.

25 Readers may care to note that there is a useful critique of this strategy in Egan, C (1995) *Creating Organisational Advantage*, Butterworth-Heinemann, Oxford, pp109–11.

26 Handy, C (1993) Op. cit., p292.

27 Mintzberg, H (1991) 'The effective organisation: forces and forms', *Sloan Management Review*, Winter.

28 Hofstede, G (1980) Op. cit.

29 Kluckhohn, C and Strodtbeck, F (1961) *Variations in Value Orientations*, Peterson, New York, quoted in Meade, R (1994) *International Management Cross Cultural Dimensions*, Blackwell, Oxford, p50.

30 Hofstede, G (1991) *Cultures and Organisations, Software of the Mind*, McGraw-Hill, Maidenhead, and *Images of Europe: Valedictory Address* given at the University of Limberg, 1993.

31 Meade, R (1994) Op. cit., pp73–6.

32 *Financial Times* (1994) 30 Nov, p15.

33 *Financial Times* (1994) 16 Sept, p26.

34 *Financial Times* (1998) 28 Oct, p24.

35 *Financial Times* (1998) 23 Nov, p23.

36 *Financial Times* (1993) 14 Apr, p30.

37 Friedman, A (1988) *Agnelli and the Italian Network of Power*, Mandarin, London.

38 Olie, R (1995) 'The culture factor in personnel and organisation policies', Ch6 in Harzing, A and Van Ruysseveldt (1995) *International Human Resource Management*, Sage, London, in association with Open University, Netherlands.

39 Peters, T and Waterman, R (1982) *In Search of Excellence*, Harper and Row, New York, p318.

40 References for Rank Xerox Case: *Financial Times*, 24 Sep 1991; 25 Aug 1992, p5; 13 Jan 1995, p19; 13 Feb 1995, p19; 28 Apr 1995, two-page advertisement; Lynch, R (1994) *European Business Strategies*, 2nd edn, Kogan Page, London, p87; Xerox *USA Annual Report 1992*.

41 Egan, C (1995) Op. cit., p109.

Chapter 8

ANALYSING FINANCIAL RESOURCES

Learning outcomes

When you have worked through this chapter, you will be able to:

- identify the sources of funds available to an organisation;
- carry out an analysis of an organisation's current financial resources;
- assess an organisation's potential for further funding and the costs and risks involved;
- identify and quantify the financial benefits of strategies and their cash flow implications;
- understand the role and importance of shareholder value-added concepts;
- understand the impact on the organisation of greater international activity;
- appreciate the importance of balancing the organisation's financial objectives with its other corporate objectives.

INTRODUCTION

Many corporate strategies involve the organisation's financial resources: investment in the organisation's activities now will be rewarded by profits or other benefits later. This chapter explores the *relationship* between the financial resources that are available for corporate strategy – their sources, costs and the risks involved – and the returns that may be achieved (*see* Figure 8.1). The financial risks and rewards can be fundamental to strategic success.

Financial analysis deals primarily with the precision of numbers, and therefore tends to be prescriptive rather than emergent in its approach. However, leading financiers are well

Figure 8.1

The relationship between financial resources and the resulting strategies

Financial resources		**Strategies**
Retained earnings		Reputation
Shareholder's equity		New customer services
Long-term debt	→ **Organisation** →	Research & development
Short-term funds		New plant
Leasing		Joint ventures
		Acquisitions

aware that in practice there is an element of judgement to the subject. This chapter considers both approaches and then goes on to explore the importance of maintaining the fine balance between the financial objectives of the organisation and those objectives involving more general issues, such as the public good, better pay and job satisfaction. The implications for those organisations engaged in international trade are also considered.

CASE STUDY 8.1

Heineken: how the company finances its global strategy

Over the last twenty years, the Dutch brewing company Heineken has built market leadership in many countries around the world. This case explores how it was achieved.

Global expansion through acquisition and brand building

With sales in over 170 countries, the Dutch family company of Heineken has achieved its major growth in recent years mainly through company acquisition. In the last two years, it has begun to supplement this with a strategy of brand building. This case describes the current company and examines the strategies of acquisition and brand building. The case then shows how Heineken has financed its international strategic expansion.

Heineken has three global brands: Heineken lager itself, Amstel lager and Murphy's Irish stout. It also has a series of regional and national beer brands, for example: Buckler (Western Europe), Paulaner Weiss (Germany), Tiger (Asia's leading beer), Cruzcampo (Spain). In terms of its total beer and lager sales, the company is particularly strong in Western and Eastern Europe. It is the second leading imported beer into the US but remains a specialist brand in that country, i.e. its total sales are small compared to the market leaders Budweiser, Miller and Coors. It has some important interests in a few

Although Heineken has made global acquisitions, it has been more cautious than its rivals. This has slowed its worldwide growth but its financial position remains sound.

African countries – market leadership in Nigeria, for example. Its total beer sales are shown in Table 8.1.

Heineken is the world's fourth largest brewer – the case at the end of the chapter explores this in more depth. The company is particularly strong in Europe – two thirds of all its sales are made in Western and Eastern Europe. It has built this position by acquiring local companies and therefore owns a series of *local* brands. This explains why its flagship *global* brand, Heineken, delivers less than 20 per cent of its total sales. Before examining future brand Heineken strategy, it is useful to examine how the company has arrived at its current position.

Heineken acquisition strategy

Founded in the nineteenth century by the Heineken family, the company has connections that extend far beyond its Dutch national roots. In the early 1980s, its dominant character from that time – Alfred 'Freddy' Heineken – took the view that the European market would consolidate over the succeeding 20 years. He excluded Germany from this, since its fragmented market was governed by a series of restrictive

Table 8.1

Worldwide source of Heineken sales 2004

	Heineken's *total* beer sales (million hectolitres)	Heineken *brand* beer sales within the total (million hectolitres)
Western Europe	43.5	11.0
Americas	23.7	7.2
Africa and Middle East	13.5	0.9
Central and Eastern Europe	31.6	0.9
Asia/Pacific	9.5	2.8
Total	121.8	22.8

Source: Annual Report and Accounts 2004.

▶ CASE STUDY 8.1 continued

practices that protected the German brewers – in spite of being judged illegal within the European Union. (He was right: it is only in the twenty-first century that the German market is opening up to non-Germans.) Freddy and his colleagues judged that either his company joined the worldwide consolidation process or it would find itself excluded from many markets. Heineken therefore took the strategic decision back in the 1980s to expand, mainly by acquisition since brand building was very slow.

During the 1980s and 1990s, Heineken bought up companies mainly in European Union countries. In the early 1990s, it began to move into Central and Eastern European markets – Poland, Hungary, Russia, etc. Since this was before some rival companies, it was able to build a strong market position that it maintains to the present. At the same time, it began exporting to the US and buying some small breweries in the rest of America. It also made its first moves into Asia, Africa and into countries like Lebanon and Egypt, where it makes a non-alcoholic beer for its Muslim customers. The outcome of its international expansion can be seen in sales and profits that have more than doubled over a ten-year period – see Table 8.2.

Heineken brand strategy

From a strategy perspective, the difficulties with acquisitions are the high integration costs in the short term and the 'legacy' issues in the longer term. Heineken has not published data on the short-term costs of integrating its new companies into the group. However, it has remained profitable during this process, suggesting that integration costs have been more than balanced by the integration benefits of economies of scale available in brewing and distribution.

The 'legacy' issues remain to be resolved. Legacy here means that Heineken has acquired a series of *national* brands that are valuable but do not support directly the *global* brand Heineken franchise. Hence, in 2004, the company developed a new strategy of investing and building its Heineken brand as a premium (high-price) beer. The company even went to the length of withdrawing Heineken from the UK in 2003 and then relaunching the brand into the UK in 2004 as a new, premium brand. Ironically, the only country in 2005 where Heineken remained a standard, non-premium beer was its home country, the Netherlands. The global investments in the Heineken brand franchise along with the earlier strategies of acquisition need to be financed.

Financing Heineken's international expansion and brand building

In examining the sources of Heineken's international expansion, the following sources are available:

● *Shareholders*. Heineken is a family-controlled company. Hence, the issuance of new shares would dilute the family's control over the firm and be unacceptable. Heineken made five *bonus share issues* in 1986, 1989, 1992, 1995 and 2004. These simply split existing shares into smaller amounts and made no attempt to raise fresh capital. By definition, bonus shares are issued in proportion to existing shareholdings and have no impact on the family interests. For many years, Freddy Heineken protected the family interests through a special controlling shareholding – 'Heineken, the Dutch brewer, came under pressure at the weekend to defend its ownership structure, amid accusations that this benefited the founding family at the expense of others,' reported the *Financial Times* in December 2000.

● *Retained profits*. In the early years, Heineken used this method more than any other to expand. More recently, it has relied on debt – see below and Table 8.3. Because it is family-controlled, it does not have the same pressures to pay a dividend each year. It was therefore able in 1997 to ignore any outside pressures, so long as the family members themselves continue to agree. However, the finance needed for international expansion is so large that there were unlikely to be sufficient retained profits. Long-term debt is also cheaper for a company.

● *Increased long-term debt*. Heineken used this method of financing in recent years as its main method of international expansion. In a similar way, SABMiller and Carlsberg have used long-term loans from banks or other lending institutions extensively to expand their worldwide interests – see Table 8.3. Note that Heineken's shift to long-term debt is no different from the shift at Carlsberg. Importantly, the cost of using long-term debt is cheaper than other forms of finance – see text.

● *Short-term funds*. If brewery companies can negotiate it, there is nothing to stop them paying their creditors

Table 8.2

Heineken's profit and sales performance

	1995	1996	1997	1998	1999	2000	2001	2002	2003	2004
Net turnover	3 830	4 646	5 174	5 347	5 973	6 766	7 637	8 482	9 255	10 005
Operating profit	457	459	546	659	799	921	1 125	1 282	1 222	1 248
Operating profit as % of total assets	10.4%	9.5%	10.7%	12.4%	13.3%	14.6%	15.6%	16.4%	12.2%	12.8%

Source: Company accounts 2004.

Table 8.3

Sources of capital in some leading brewers

Source of funds	Heineken % 1997	Heineken % 2004	And other brewers for comparison . . .		
			SAB Miller % 2004	Carlsberg % 1997	Carlsberg % 2004
Reserves and retained earnings	40	25	25	31	23
Shareholders	10	12	24	10	6
Provisions for tax, pensions, etc.	5	12	6	14	10
Debt: long-term	18	25	22	10	38
Debt: short-term	27	26	23	35	23
Total share of capital	100	100	100	100	100

Source: Company annual reports.

more slowly and insisting that those who owe them money pay faster.

Table 8.3 shows how Heineken raised its funds up to 1997 and 2004. For comparison, two other leading brewers are also shown. (It is important to point out that the companies do not have the same year end, and figures have been translated into a common currency (US$) at rates that may not be those used by the individual companies themselves. All this makes comparison only approximate.) An additional item in the table – *Provisions for tax, pensions, etc.* – relates to the need for companies to set aside funds that are owed to the government as tax and to their former employees as pensions. Because of the special purpose of such funds, they should not be used for financing the business and are therefore excluded from the above list of the sources of funds.

In terms of sources of finance, the financial resources of the three brewers shown in Table 8.3 need to be considered in the context of the *objectives* and *values* of the companies concerned.

Heineken is a family-controlled company and had only limited desire in the early years to raise funds from outside shareholders or the debt from banks. If this meant that it grew more slowly, then the company was willing to pay that price for family control until recently. With the strategic decision to expand globally, the company turned to the banks for long-term debt to fund its strategy.

Carlsberg is controlled by a Danish trust. Typically, such organisations do not have great ambitions for the future. However, Carlsberg has become more highly expansionist in recent years and has raised debt on a long-term basis.

SABMiller has its shares quoted on the London and Johannesberg stock exchanges and has wide share ownership. As explored in Case 8.4 later in this chapter, it has followed a vigorous and risky strategy of expansion over the last ten years, with a mix of acquisitions and internally generated growth activities. The company's ability to raise substantial finance, especially from the banks through long-term debt financing, has been crucial to its international expansion.

Case questions

1 *If you were Heineken, would you raise more finance through long-term debt and expand faster?*

2 *If you were Carlsberg or SABMiller, what limits would you put on international long-term debt financing? What are the risks and what are the rewards? From whom would you seek advice?*

3 *Can any company seeking strong expansion follow the long-term debt route used here? What are the benefits and costs?*

8.1 ANALYSING THE SOURCES OF FINANCE

Company ownership varies greatly around the world. In some countries, such as the UK and US, there is a strong tradition of private share ownership with public share quotation. In other countries, such as Germany, Italy and Spain, rather more companies may be at least part-owned by banks, private trusts, families and government institutions. As a starting point, we ignore these differences and simply identify the main *sources of finance* for strategic development or retrenchment. As an example, Figure 8.2 shows the sources of finance used by Heineken in 1997.

Figure 8.2

Sources of finance at Heineken (1997)

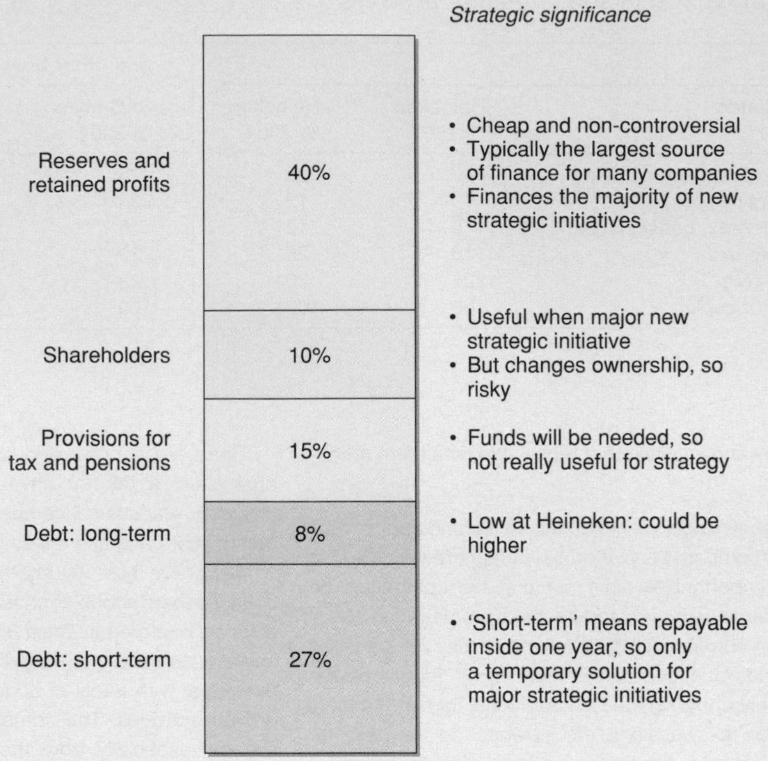

Strategic significance

Source	%	Strategic significance
Reserves and retained profits	40%	• Cheap and non-controversial • Typically the largest source of finance for many companies • Finances the majority of new strategic initiatives
Shareholders	10%	• Useful when major new strategic initiative • But changes ownership, so risky
Provisions for tax and pensions	15%	• Funds will be needed, so not really useful for strategy
Debt: long-term	8%	• Low at Heineken: could be higher
Debt: short-term	27%	• 'Short-term' means repayable inside one year, so only a temporary solution for major strategic initiatives

8.1.1 Sources of finance

Retained profits

Definition ➤ Retained profits are the profits that are kept by the organisation rather than distributed as dividends to shareholders. Hence, the profits earned from trading activities are kept back in the organisation and invested in new ventures. Although full evidence is not available,[2] this probably represents the most common source of finance for the organisation's strategies. However, strategies that demand a bold, new step – like a major acquisition – may need totally new sources of finance.

- *Advantages.* The company does not have to ask any outside group or individual. There are no issue costs involved in raising the funds and the company does not need to reveal its plans to outsiders such as banks in order to gain agreement. It is essentially non-controversial.

- *Disadvantages.* Profits that are retained and not distributed to shareholders represent dividends foregone to the owners. Owners may demand a regular dividend from the company. The company needs to be generating adequate profits, so this route is not suitable for those in financial difficulties.

Share issues or equity finance

Definition ➤ Share issues (or equity issues) are the issuance of new shares in an organisation to current and new shareholders in order to raise finance for new strategy activities. Share issues are frequently called the *equity capital* method of raising funds because they involve the 'equity' or shareholding of a company. It is often possible to seek further funds from existing share-holders through a *rights issue* – that is, the right to purchase new shares is issued to current shareholders in proportion to their existing voting rights in the company – although the success of such an issue clearly depends on how enthusiastic existing shareholders are about the company's prospects.

- *Advantages*. This method is useful when a large tranche of new capital is needed – for example, for an acquisition. Unlike a bank loan (*see* below), there is no automatic commitment to pay interest, nor repay the capital: dividends are paid only if the new funds earn profits. It rewards those shareholders who have stayed with the company.

- *Disadvantages*. It can clearly change the shareholding structure and allow predators to enter. Any share issue will have significant administrative costs, such as the cost of under-writing the issue.

Loans – for the short-term and the long-term

Loans from banks and financial institutions are a major source of funds in those countries where large and widespread shareholding is not a part of normal operations. It is also much more common in countries where banks have traditionally played a major role in the share-holding life of companies – for example, Germany and Japan. It is often called the *loan* or *debt capital* method of raising funds, for obvious reasons.

When a bank or other institution makes a loan, then interest is charged on that loan. However, in Muslim countries, interest charges are considered to be wrong and alternative arrangements are made.[3] Here loans can be given for short periods, usually defined as less than one year. *Short-term debt* is a loan to be repaid in less than one year; typically, it carries a high interest rate. *Long-term debt* is a loan to be repaid over a period of more than one year. Long-term debt is usually quite cheap, but carries the burden that it is usually secured on an asset of the organisation – for example an identified piece of land or a named building. If the debtor defaults on such a loan, then the person making the loan can seize ownership of the named asset.

Loans can be made in various ways to the organisation, with the rates of interest and the duration periods of the loan being either fixed or varied. Larger loans may carry exception-ally onerous terms, depending on how desperate the organisation is to obtain the funds. Such loans are usually secured on the assets of the organisation so, if there is a default, the lender can seize the asset. Because of this security, loan capital is often cheaper than equity capital. However, it carries the penalty that interest *must be paid* even if the company is earning little profit, whereas equity capital could forgo the dividend during that period. There are also limits on the amount of debt financing (*see* Section 8.2).

Risk assessment plays a large part in the lender's view of the loan and the company. Past company performance, the prospects for the new strategy, the quality of the secured assets and the long-term personal relationship between the parties will all have an influence on the source of funds.

- *Advantages*. Loans can be cheap, quick and retain the existing shareholding structure. This method of finance is also confidential and discreet. It may be essential where widespread public shareholding is not available.

- *Disadvantages*. This method can be painful, intrusive and involve increased risk for the company. The date of repayment and the need to pay interest in most circumstances can be a major burden if the strategy begins to show signs of weakness.

Leasing

Leasing is a form of debt where an organisation hires the asset for a period, possibly with the option of buying the asset at the end of the period. For example, a company might lease its fleet of delivery vehicles rather than own them. Leasing from specialist companies can be important in those countries where there are tax advantages and the company does not need to own the assets. The other advantage to the organisation taking out the lease is that it does not have to find the capital.

- *Advantages*. Leasing is clear, quick and perhaps tax-efficient. It is also a method for increasing the organisation's return on capital, because leasing reduces the capital employed by the organisation.
- *Disadvantages*. This method has limited scope and there is no ownership at the end of the period, unless this has been agreed in advance.

A reduction in short-term debt

Definition ➤ Short-term debt consists of all funds owed by the organisation that need to be repaid within one year. An organisation can reduce its short-term debt by introducing one of the following measures:

- *Paying creditors more slowly*. Taking longer to pay means that such funds are kept in the company for a longer period and are therefore available for investment.
- *Reducing stocks*. An organisation's *stock turn* – its ratio of turnover divided by stock – is a measure of its ability to operate with lower stocks. A lower level of funds invested in stocks will increase the organisation's ability to raise funds for use elsewhere.
- *Insisting on prompter payment by debtors*.
- *Advantages*. This method has many of the advantages of retained profits in the sense that it involves the more efficient use of the organisation's existing funds.
- *Disadvantages*. This method may be difficult for the organisation to achieve if it is already operating reasonably efficiently. There may need to be significant expenditure to achieve the saving – for example, a new computer system to control stocks will mean investment in the new system along with the subsequent stock reduction.

Sale of assets

Definition ➤ One way of raising finance is for an organisation to sell some of its valuable assets. Sale of some existing company assets to finance expansion elsewhere has proved to be a major strategy for some companies in the 1990s. The route clearly has merit when resources are limited and spread too thinly. Following from the logic of the *resource-based view* (*see* Chapter 6), it will be evident that this approach may have real benefits for some companies.

- *Advantages*. This method of finance is simple, clear, concentrates on core strengths, and clearly involves no dilution in shareholding interests.
- *Disadvantages*. This method is drastic, no going back, and forces choice when not essential. The sale of assets may have to be undertaken at less than their full value, depending on the timing of the sale.

Other methods

For large and global companies, there is an increasingly sophisticated and complex range of financial mechanisms for raising finances.

Key strategic principles

- There are six main sources of finance for strategic activities. Each has its merits and problems.
- *Retained profits*: the most common method of funding new strategy.

- *Equity finance*, i.e. the issuance of new shares to either existing or new shareholders, is one clear route but it has numerous disadvantages associated with the costs of issue and the possible loss of control in the company.

- *Long-term debt finance* is simpler and cheaper, but there are limits to the amount and major difficulties if the company defaults on paying the interest charges.

- *Leasing (renting) of plant and machinery* has some specialist uses and attractions: it can have tax benefits and lower costs. However, the equipment remains the property of the lessor at the end of the period.

- *Savings from reductions in short-term debt* can be a substantial source of funds to a company, but these can usually be made only once.

- *The sale of some existing assets* to fund development elsewhere is useful but drastic.

8.1.2 Constraints on sources of finance

After reviewing the main sources of finance for an organisation, we now need to consider two important constraints on the ability of the organisation to act:

1 difficulties with debt financing; and
2 difficulties with the dividend payout policy on equity shareholdings.

Difficulties with debt financing

As we saw in Section 8.1.1, debt financing means that the organisation agrees to pay interest on the debt it acquires. The rate of interest is usually fixed and has two constraints:

1 If there is a drop in profits, payment of interest *takes priority* over payment of dividends to shareholders.
2 The interest *must be paid*, regardless of how profits might fluctuate. (Clearly, if the company goes into loss then the interest cannot be paid and the company is technically bankrupt.)

It is, therefore, the *shareholders* who bear the risk of profit fluctuation, not the *debt lenders*, such as the banks. As a result, because the shareholders are bearing this greater risk, they look for a higher return on their funds than the debt lenders. Debt financing is therefore usually cheaper than equity financing and as a result some companies prefer a proportion of debt capital.

In spite of its lower cost in relation to equity financing, however, companies restrict their level of debt financing because, when debt capital is present, it causes any fluctuation in profits at the organisation to be reflected *disproportionately* in retained profits and dividends. Debt interest takes priority in payments from the organisation's profits. It is a simple mathematical task to show that the remainder, available as retained profits and dividends to shareholders, is bound to fluctuate more widely than if there had been no debt finance. Since retained earnings may well fund strategy, any fluctuation as a result of higher gearing – that is, the proportion of debt finance to total shareholders' funds (*see* Exhibit 8.1) – will impact disproportionately on corporate strategy.

Thus any company *with* debt is more exposed to fluctuations in dividends than one *without* debt – the higher the gearing, the more the exposure. Although debt finance is cheaper, there is therefore a limit to the amount of debt that a company can usually accept. Typically, companies with strong growth strategies and widespread public share ownership (such as SABMiller in Case study 8.4) will have a gearing ratio of up to 50 per cent. When

Exhibit 8.1

The gearing ratio

Definition ➤ The gearing ratio is the debt finance of the organisation divided by the total shareholders' funds. Most companies begin life with financing by shareholders – *equity financing*. They then generate some profits and retain part of those profits in the company, paying the rest out as dividends, tax, etc. The *total shareholders' funds* that then exist in the company are the original equity finance plus the retained profits.

At some stage in its life, the company may acquire significant amounts of long-term debt – *debt financing*. The ratio of debt finance to total shareholders' funds is called the *gearing ratio* of the company – often called *gearing* for short – and is usually expressed in percentage terms. For example, if a company with US$10 million of shareholder's funds raises US$5 million of debt finance, it has a gearing ratio of

$$\text{Gearing ratio} = \frac{\text{Debt finance}}{\text{Total shareholders' funds}} = \frac{\text{US\$5 million}}{\text{US\$10 million}} \times 100 = 50\%$$

the gearing of a company reaches 100 per cent, banks and other lenders become nervous because the company is so reliant on a steady, non-fluctuating stream of profits. It is for this reason that some companies are reluctant to *gear up* their company – that is, raise the proportion of debt to equity. Heineken is an example of a company that used to have low gearing in 1997 – *see* Case 8.1.

However, lower gearing means that fewer funds are available for growth strategies. Although Heineken did not have excessively low gearing, it was unable to grow at the same rate as other companies and take advantage of the international opportunities in brewing. Hence, Heinekein raised its gearing as a means of funding its expansion. As a result of the expansion, earnings per share at Heineken almost tripled over the ten years 1995–2004. These considerations reflect the risks over gearing that the company is willing to take and the value the company puts on growth as part of its objectives.

Difficulties with the dividend payout policy on equity shareholdings

In addition to constraints arising from gearing, it is also necessary to consider the *dividend payout policy* of the company on its ordinary shares. The higher the dividend, the lower the profit retained in the company and the more difficult it becomes to fund new strategies. In theory,[4] there is a balance to be struck between maximising the dividend payout and retaining profit for the company. In practice, companies usually prefer to keep the dividend payout *steadily and gently rising*. It is a reward for loyalty and is often reflected back in shareholder confidence and a stable share price. Moreover, retained profits are not lost to the shareholders but should themselves contribute to the capital appreciation of the shares. The data for Heineken in Table 8.4 show that dividends have not tracked profit, but have gone up in cautious stages.

Table 8.4

Heineken NV profits and dividends per share (€)

	2004	2003	2002	2001	2000	1999	1998	1997	1996	1995
Net profit per share	1.61	1.65	1.61	1.46	1.27	1.05	0.91	0.70	0.61	0.62
Dividend per share	0.40	0.32	0.32	0.32	0.26	0.26	0.20	0.16	0.16	0.16

Source: Annual Report and Accounts.

The implication of a stable dividend policy for retained earnings is clear: if dividends are steady, then any fluctuation in profits must be taken up by *retained earnings*. The reasons are just the same as those for debt capital interest above. Since it is retained earnings that fund corporate strategy, it is the *strategy area* that suffers disproportionately if there are major variations in profitability.

Overall, the choice between the funding methods for strategy will depend on a balance of the factors outlined above along with one other consideration – the cost of each route to the company – which we examine in Section 8.2.

Key strategic principles

- There are three main constraints on debt financing:
  1. the need to fund the interest payments regardless of profit fluctuations;
  2. the company with debt is more exposed to profit fluctuation than the one without;
  3. the reluctance of banks to offer finance that would gear companies above 100 per cent.

- The main constraint on equity financing is the need in many companies to establish a steady increase in dividend payouts, regardless of profit variations.

- As a result of the debt and equity payout constraints, fluctuations in profits impact disproportionately on the funding needed for strategic change.

8.2 COST OF CAPITAL AND THE OPTIMAL CAPITAL STRUCTURE

In order to assess alternative sources of capital, we need to start by considering their costs to the company. There are two principal sources of funds to the company: equity and debt. We will examine each of these separately and look at the problems, mainly in estimating the costs of equity capital. We then consider the factors surrounding the optimal combination of the two different sources and why calculating the cost of funds is important.[5]

8.2.1 Costing equity capital using the Capital Asset Pricing Model

It may seem slightly surprising to view *equity capital*, which includes the company's retained profits and its original share capital, as having a *cost*. The cost comes in the organisation's refusal to distribute profits to its shareholders, who could, in theory, have invested this money in shares in other companies. They might even have purchased a government bond in their home country. (Such bonds usually pay interest that is *guaranteed* and *virtually risk-free*, unless the state itself goes bankrupt. Naturally, the rate of interest on government bonds is lower than would be expected from commercial organisations that carry greater risks of failure.)

In both theory[6] and practice, it is often the case that the organisation invests part of its own funds *outside* the organisation, rather than in its own corporate strategies. Indeed, for reasons of high market risk and low profitability in an industry, companies occasionally find that their proposed new strategies are so unattractive that they actually invest some of their funds outside the company.[7] Investing in corporate strategies *inside* the organisation therefore has a *financial cost* associated with it. As a *minimum*, this cost would be the interest that might have been obtained from the alternative investment of the same funds *outside* the organisation. However, this still does not estimate the *actual* cost of the capital inside the company, only this *minimum* threshold.

The *Capital Asset Pricing Model*[8] is an attempt to estimate the actual cost of equity capital inside the company. The detail of the model is beyond the scope of this book. However, in essence, the model suggests that the cost of equity for a company is equal to the *risk-free cost of equity* plus a factor calculated as the average cost of equity in the *market* multiplied by a beta factor for the *company* concerned.

Definition ➤   To summarise, the cost of capital in an organisation is often measured by the cost of investing in a risk-free bond outside the organisation, coupled with some element for the extra risks, if any, of investing in the organisation itself.

8.2.2 Cost of equity capital using risk-free rates of interest

Where there is no widespread share ownership, a much simpler alternative to the Capital Asset Pricing Model has been used to estimate the cost of equity capital. It begins by estimating the value of the risk-free bond rate. This should be readily available in most countries. It then adds several percentage points to this rate to take into account the risks of dealing with shares where the returns are not guaranteed.

The difficulty with this method comes in estimating the additional rate of interest. It is usually derived from an examination of rates of return available on commercial bonds, other shares if available and other types of commercial contract. There are no clear rules and the method relies on judgement, but it does have the merits of simplicity and flexibility. With these problems, some will question whether it is important to calculate the cost of capital. We return to this issue once we have considered long-term debt capital.

8.2.3 Cost of long-term debt capital

The cost of debt capital is rather more straightforward. For existing funds, it is simply *the weighted average of the interest costs* of the individual loans already made to the company, after deducting the tax.

8.2.4 The weighted average cost of capital

Definition ➤   The *weighted average cost of capital* (WACC) is the combination of the cost of equity capital and the cost of long-term debt capital weighted in proportion to their part in the overall capital of the company. In practice, it is the average cost of raising additional funds for the company since the two elements are largely valued on the basis of their current and future interest rates. Hence, WACC is defined by the following formula:

$$\text{WACC} = \frac{(\text{cost of long-term debt}) \times (\text{long-term debt})}{(\text{total company capital})} + \frac{(\text{cost of equity}) \times (\text{equity})}{(\text{total company capital})}$$

8.2.5 The optimal capital structure

The overall aim of an analysis of the cost of capital will be to arrive at the optimal balance between equity and debt capital. In undertaking this task, it will be evident that each organisation has a unique set of circumstances that need to be taken into account. Financial strategy will wish to take the mathematical formulae shown above and adjust them for other factors that are more difficult to quantify. Factors that need to be considered include:

● the risk involved in the organisation's future strategies;

● company attitudes to risk (e.g. entrepreneurs might relish the risk whereas multinationals might be more dubious);

● the risk in the industry (some markets have greater uncertainty than others);

- competitors' costs of capital and capital structures (others may have good ideas, access to their own unique sources of funds, different attitudes to risk, etc.);
- possible trends in interest rates and factors that might substantially alter these, such as national economic performance.

Some of these considerations cannot easily be quantified but will have an important influence on the final choice of funding route. Having taken these considerations into account, it is now possible to address the questions:

- Can the organisations raise *more funds*?
- If so, *from what source* and *at what cost*?
- How does the cost of new funds *compare* with the cost of existing funds?
- What are the *risks involved* in tapping the new sources of funds?

The many sources of finance were discussed in Section 8.1, retained profits, equity and debt capital being the most common.

8.2.6 The importance of calculating the cost of funds

With all the complexities and uncertainties already mentioned, we may ask whether it is really necessary to calculate the cost of funds. Knowing the cost of funds is important for two reasons:

1 All the stakeholders need to be reassured that their efforts are worthwhile. There is no point in undertaking years of effort and investment if the financial resources could earn more in a lower-risk fund outside the organisation. The only rational way of approaching this is to start, however crudely, by estimating the cost of the funds being used inside the enterprise.

2 More specifically, the cost of funds is the starting point for the analysis of new strategies. If the return on the new proposals does not even match the cost of the funds that are required to undertake this task, then such projects should not be pursued. We consider this further in Section 8.3.

Key strategic principles

- The cost of equity capital can be calculated using the Capital Asset Pricing Model but it only really works where there is wide public shareholding.
- An alternative method starts with the cost of risk-free government bonds and then adds a factor for the risk of owning shares.
- The cost of long-term debt is calculated from the weighted average of the individual loans made to the company.
- For the company overall, the combined cost of debt and equity is called the weighted average cost of capital (WACC). It combines equity and debt in proportion to their use in the company.
- The optimal capital structure for a company will also involve the assessment of risks, in addition to the costs estimated above.
- Calculating the cost of capital matters because it reassures the stakeholders that their efforts are worthwhile and because it provides a benchmark for assessing the profitability of future strategies.

L'Oréal beauty products – using financial data to explore strategy

How does the world market leader, L'Oréal, compare with its rivals? How has the company built its beauty products business? What strategies are likely to prove successful in the cosmetics and fragrances business?

This case provides some answers: importantly, all the data is available from publicly available resources – Company Annual Reports, the world wide web and library-based surveys. For reasons of space, the case focuses on one part of L'Oréal and then one section within this part. In a more complete strategic analysis, it would be essential to explore every part of the company.

Comparison of L'Oréal with two competitors

We begin by comparing the financial performance of L'Oréal with two major national competitors – Estée Lauder and Shiseido – see Table 8.5. What does the data tell us? Clearly, L'Oréal has been consistently profitable over the last ten years. Moreover, it has been more profitable than the two rival companies. We can see this more clearly by calculating the net profit margins for each company – *see* Table 8.6. Net profit margin is calculated by dividing the annual net profit, i.e. profit after tax and interest, by the turnover of that year and expressing the result as a percentage.

How has L'Oréal managed to increase its net profit margin over a number of years to levels not achieved by its competitors? We would need to examine all three companies in depth to answer this question fully. For this case, we will simply focus on L'Oréal.

L'Oréal has three main branded lines – L'Oréal itself, Garnier and Maybelline. Each of these contributes to the overall financial success of the company.

More detailed examination of the L'Oréal Annual Report and Accounts

We can look further at the company accounts of L'Oréal to see the *geographic spread* of sales – *see* Figure 8.3. The data shows that the profit margin is higher in Western Europe than elsewhere. Moreover, Western Europe is the biggest contributor to sales and the most profitable part of the business. Perhaps L'Oréal derives more of its sales from Western Europe than the two rivals above? This is an important strategic question that is not answered in this case for reasons of space.

Table 8.5

Three companies in the world beauty business

All figures in US$ billion

Year	L'Oréal, France Sales	L'Oréal, France Net profit	Estée Lauder, US Sales	Estée Lauder, US Net profit	Shiseido, Japan Sales	Shiseido, Japan Net profit
2003	16.8	2.0	5.8	0.3	5.2	0.2
2002	15.0	1.5	5.1	0.3	4.5	(0.2)
2001	12.1	1.1	4.7	0.2	4.7	0.4
2000	11.9	1.0	4.6	0.3	5.6	0.1
1999	10.8	0.7	4.3	0.3	5.1	0.1
1998	13.4	0.8	4.0	0.3	4.7	0.1
1997	11.5	0.7	3.6	0.2	4.8	0.2
1996	11.5	0.7	3.4	0.2	5.2	0.2
1995	10.9	0.6	3.1	0.2	6.2	0.1
1994	8.9	0.6	2.9	0.1	5.3	0.1

Source: Annual Report and Accounts – note that the year-ends of the three companies are different so they are not strictly comparable year-by-year. In addition, financial figures for both L'Oréal and Shiseido have been converted into US$ and there will inevitably be some inaccuracies as a result. But strategy needs to look at the *broad picture* rather than the precise detail so this is unlikely to be a major problem.

Figure 8.3

L'Oréal: Geographic location of sales and profit margins 2004

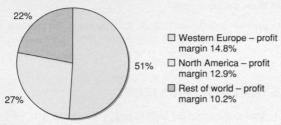

- ☐ Western Europe – profit margin 14.8%
- ☐ North America – profit margin 12.9%
- ■ Rest of world – profit margin 10.2%

Source: Company accounts for 2004 with graphic prepared by the author.

Figure 8.4

L'Oréal: Share of sales by product group 2004

Profit margins not published

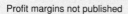

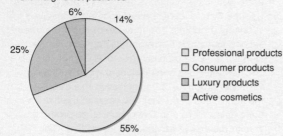

- ☐ Professional products
- ☐ Consumer products
- ☐ Luxury products
- ■ Active cosmetics

Source: Company accounts with graphic prepared by the author.

It would also be useful to examine in more depth which *products* have the highest product margins. The starting point is to examine the contribution that each product group makes to the overall sales of L'Oréal – see Figure 8.4.

Although the company accounts show the various products in L'Oréal's range, they do not show which products are the most profitable. Nevertheless, the annual report does give some further data on each product group. For our purposes, we will focus on the largest group – *consumer products*.

L'Oréal Consumer Products Division 2003

This product group uses mass-market retail channels to sell its products. Brand names included *L'Oréal Paris*, *Garnier Fructis*, *SoftSheen Carson* and *Maybelline*. The next two tables are taken from the web version of the annual report and accounts. They show sales by geographic zone and sales by business segment within the Consumer Products Division – see Tables 8.7 and 8.8.

Readers will see that some of the numbers appear to be inconsistent. For example, the sales appear to have *declined* between 2002 and 2003 whereas the web table claims that sales actually *grew* by 7.7 per cent on a like-for-like basis. We have to trust the accountants here – they will give the *actual* sales figures for 2002 and 2003. But in recording like-for-like

Table 8.6

Net income margins at three cosmetics companies: net income divided by sales revenue

Year	L'Oréal Net profit margin	Estée Lauder Net profit margin	Shiseido Net profit margin
2003	11.9%	5.2%	3.8%
2002	10.0%	5.9%	–
2001	9.1%	4.2%	8.5%
2000	8.4%	6.5%	1.8%
1999	6.5%	6.8%	2.0%
1998	6.0%	7.5%	2.1%
1997	6.1%	5.5%	4.2%
1996	6.1%	5.9%	3.8%
1995	5.5%	6.4%	1.6%
1994	6.7%	3.5%	1.9%

Source: Calculated by author from company accounts.

Table 8.7

L'Oréal: Consumer Products Division sales by geographic zone

Sales in € millions

	Sales 2002	Sales 2003	% of 2003 sales	Like-for-like sales growth 2003/2002 (%)
Western Europe	3 837	3 991	53.2	5.3*
North America	2 319	2 080	27.7	6.7*
Rest of world	1 445	1 434	19.1	16.4*
Total	7 601	7 506	100.0	7.7*

* See text for comment.
Source: Company accounts.

Table 8.8

L'Oréal: Consumer Products Division sales by business segment

Sales in € millions

	Sales 2002	Sales 2003	% of 2003 sales	Like-for-like growth 2003/2002 (%)
Haircare	4 048	3 957	52.7	6.2
Make-up	2 100	1 983	26.4	5.9
Skincare	1 020	1 179	15.7	23.7
Perfumes	151	128	1.7	–11.9
Other	282	259	3.5	–6.4
Total	7 601	7 506	100.0	7.7

Source: Company accounts.

▶ **CASE STUDY 8.2 continued**

comparisons, they will have adjusted for other events – for example, perhaps a product was discontinued or a subsidiary sold during the year and therefore removed from the accounting data.

L'Oréal Consumer Products Division was very satisfied with a +7.7 per cent sales growth, which it described as substantial. This growth is much higher than the market growth in ice cream, (for example – *see* Case 3.2 – so the conclusion is not unreasonable.) The company then goes on to explain how it achieved this growth by the following strategies:

- Operational teams in each country adapted the product mix provided by the centre – *local* strategy within a *global* base. 'Garnier's success with shampoo in the United States with skincare and colourants in Asia is a good example,' explains the company's report.
- Focusing on three flagship brands – L'Oréal Paris, Maybelline New York and Garnier – with each being targeted at a different customer segment. The report does not name the targets but looking at the products in-store would probably provide evidence for this.
- Launching new products patented by headquarters and then marketed globally.
- Targeting 'growth driver countries' like China with Maybelline make-up and the Russian Federation with Garnier skincare products in order to deliver growth objectives.
- Maintaining strong *co-operation* strategies with leading local country partners – the company comments that the 'point of sale' presentation is 'absolutely critical' to sales success and this can only be achieved with local partners and distributors.
- The skincare growth was exceptional at nearly 24 per cent. This was achieved using the L'Oréal Paris and Garnier brands along with new patented products in every part of the world.

The company claimed to outperform its competitors with such strategies. It also gives similar information on the other product areas. This information is available on the worldwide web at www.l'oreal.com.

STRATEGIC PROJECT

1 Use the world wide web to call up the remaining L'Oréal data and explore the strategies that it has adopted.
2 Make a comparison with rival companies like Estée Lauder and Shiseido. You will find that Estée Lauder's sales are stronger in the US and Shiseido in Japan. You might like to find the comment on the North American market by L'Oréal in its annual report 2003 that would then explain – at least in part – why Estée Lauder's sales were less profitable.
3 Use the web to identify other companies involved in beauty products. You may like to know that the second largest beauty products company in the world is the US company Procter & Gamble (P&G). The company has annual sales over US$30 billion in beauty products. It has achieved this through the acquisition in the last few years of the two companies Wella and Clairol as well as products acquired some years ago, including Oil of Olay and Panthene. You could look up P&G on the web but you may not find the full data – some large American companies choose to reveal only what is required by company law with regard to their trading performance and it may be that there is no such requirement to show such data.

8.3 FINANCIAL APPRAISAL OF STRATEGY PROPOSALS

When an organisation undertakes a new strategy, this essentially means that funds are invested today for benefits that will accrue in the future. In this section, we explore the *general concepts* of financial resource appraisal in relation to that initial investment (some of the more detailed aspects of this process are covered in Chapter 14, Section 14.2.4). Because of its implications for the survival of the organisation, we separate out the analysis of cash flow from more general financial analysis. In the next section, we explore recent developments that connect finance with the strategic concept of value added.

8.3.1 General concepts of strategic financial appraisal

Prescriptive strategists have a very clear view of financial appraisal for strategic decisions. They take the investment to be made and predict the financial returns in the future. They use forecasts of demand, resources, inflation and likely tax regimes in the country or countries in which the investment is being made. The whole process is often built using a computer spreadsheet and has a precision and consistency that is a model of rational decision making. To this is then added some evaluation of:

● the *risks* involved;

● the *financial exposure*, if the project were to fail;

● the *opportunity cost* of the strategy; that is, the benefits that would arise if the funds were used for an alternative investment.

This involves an element of judgement.

It was probably Joel Dean[10] in 1954 who introduced the concept of *discounting* future funds into financial analysis. He argued that the practice in government bonds of treating earnings several years away as worth less than money today should be extended to company analysis. He also pointed out that the *time pattern* of future flows must also be appraised – that is, the fact that future funds do not always accrue evenly over time but may be bunched. Hence, it was important to predict accurately the expected future cash flows and reduce them by a discounting factor based on the *cost of capital* of the company. In the 1960s, Merrett and Sykes[11] were among several writers who wrote persuasively in the UK and across Europe on this approach. For the last 30 years, *discounted cash flow* (DCF) techniques have been widely employed to reduce the future value of strategies to their present value (*see* Figure 8.5). Discounted cash flow is the sum of the projected cash flows from a future strategy, after revaluing each individual element of the future cash flow in terms of its present worth.

Definition ➤

More recently, among others, Grant[12] has argued that for international investment decision making it is essential to follow discounted cash flow procedures. Competitive pressure for excellence on a global basis is so intense that every strategy needs to be ruthlessly appraised for its contribution to long-term profit maximisation. Although there are some difficulties over the projection of future cash flows in uncertain fast-moving environments, it is essential to ensure that the post-tax rate of return for the strategy exceeds the company's cost of capital. These techniques are widely used in many institutions.

There are three difficulties with this approach.

Accurate prediction

There can be little doubt that, if markets are fast moving, then there are real difficulties in predicting future cash flows accurately. Even markets with steady growth will have real uncertainties as technology changes, government policies alter, social values and awareness evolve, wars occur and so on. This is the most difficult problem to overcome with discounted cash flow techniques.

By 1982, Hayes and Garvin[13] were pointing out that firms often coped with such uncertainties by setting tougher criteria. The net result of the need for accurate prediction, coupled with the increased uncertainty, was that many US companies were seeking extraordinarily high rates of return on strategic investments. Many investments were then mistakenly rejected because they did not meet these demanding criteria.

Arbitrariness of investment assumptions

Hayes and Garvin also pointed out[14] that investment decisions rely on three rather arbitrary assumptions:

● *The profitability of the project*. Arbitrary estimates are sometimes used regarding the funds that will be needed to undertake the strategy.

● *The deterioration of the assets employed*. Estimates that may be relevant for accounting and tax purposes may be arbitrary as far as the real life of the assets is concerned.

● *The external investment opportunities*. It may be somewhat arbitrary to assume that government bonds, alternative stocks and other investment possibilities are available.

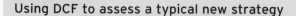

Figure 8.5

Using DCF to assess a typical new strategy

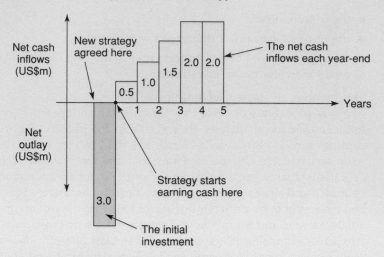

Cost of capital: Project needs to earn a minimum 10% so use 10% discount factor and discount tables

DCF calculation

End of year	Discount factor	×	Cash inflow		Present value (US$m)
1	0.9091	×	0.5	=	0.455
2	0.8264	×	1.0	=	0.826
3	0.7153	×	1.5	=	1.073
4	0.6831	×	2.0	=	1.366
5	0.6208	×	2.0	=	1.242
	Present value of cash inflows				4.962
	Less: net outlay initially				3.000
	Net present value				US$ 1.962 million

Note: In recent years, new techniques that claim to be better than DCF have been introduced. See Luerhman, T (1997) 'Using APV: A Better Tool for Valuing Operations', *Harvard Business Review*, May–June, p145. DCF is used in this book because of its wide acceptance, but this may change over time.

Source: Adapted from Glautier, MWE and Underdown, B (1994) *Accounting Theory and Practice*, 5th edn, Pitman Publishing, Ch28

Moreover, unless care is taken, *new* investments are treated on the same basis as the replacement of *existing* businesses.[15] This is highly dubious because new business is likely to be less well known and therefore have a higher degree of risk than existing business. This could perhaps be reflected in the calculation by using two different interest rates for new and existing business in the DCF calculations. However, the *choice* of the two interest rates will depend on individual judgement and be largely arbitrary.

Incorrect application of techniques

Even in those Western countries that strongly favour the DCF approach, there has been evidence that DCF techniques are incorrectly used or even ignored. Marsh *et al.*[16] showed in their survey of three UK companies that strategic decisions often ignored the formal guidelines laid down in their financial manuals. Whittington[17] describes other research that supports the contention that there are widespread problems in the use of DCF techniques in some UK companies. For example, one UK manufacturer adopted a segmentation strategy and proceeded to make the financial investment *before* the financial calculations had even been undertaken. According to these researchers, the idealised techniques described above do not accord with the reality of use.

The implications of these difficulties for strategy are explored in Section 8.3.3.

8.3.2 Basic cash flow analysis

Profit projections of the future strategy are the basis for DCF calculations. However, *profit* differs from *cash* in at least four ways:[18]

1 timing differences between when cash is paid or received and when transactions appear on the profit and loss (P&L) statement;

2 the effect of depreciation;

3 accounting transactions which are recorded on the balance sheet but do not go through the P&L account;

4 changes in working capital requirements.

Although there may be some debate over the use of financial appraisal techniques such as DCF, there can be no doubt that a basic cash flow analysis – that is, an analysis that does *not* involve discounting the future cash flows – of every strategic decision is essential. As Ellis and Williams[19] point out, without cash a business cannot survive. It is usually possible to adjust sales, costs and profits so that they fit whatever financial appraisal technique is being used and produce an acceptable return on capital, but 'creating *cash* is virtually impossible'. It is therefore vital to undertake some form of cash flow analysis for new strategies, however difficult the projections.

In strategic investment appraisal, the difficulties with cash flow usually arise in two areas:

1 in the initial period, where the project is likely to be a cash user rather than a cash generator; and

2 with projects that have a long payback, where there may be a major cash requirement some years into the venture before it starts to earn major revenues.

Cash flow analysis is particularly important in periods of uncertainty such as national economic decline or rapid currency fluctuation. The additional pressures from such events can worsen an already tight cash situation and cause real problems. Hence, in addition to conducting a normal cash flow analysis, it is usual to undertake a *sensitivity* or *worst-case analysis* for such events – that is, a cash flow analysis of the worst possible combination of events for that particular strategy.

8.3.3 Impact on corporate strategy

Whatever the problems, prescriptive strategists take the view that there is merit in conducting a thorough financial appraisal of the financial results against the costs of capital. It may be that some companies are incompetent in their approach but this does not invalidate the technique. Certainly, there are also genuine problems in projecting future profits and cash in some projects, as the Fiasco of the Channel Tunnel company between England and France financial appraisal has proved in recent years. However, there is no alternative.

Emergent strategists take the view that there are real uncertainties in the whole process: it is so difficult to predict the future that there is little point in trying. Moreover, there is evidence to support the view that corporate strategy decision making is not the rational process assumed by analytical formulae.

From the narrow viewpoint of strategic analysis, it is evident that there is little compromise between these views. This book takes the approach that there is merit in both arguments but that, ultimately, it is better to undertake some analysis, however flawed. What really matters is that the corporate strategy appraisal is undertaken with *imagination* and *vision*, *in addition to* the narrower financial criteria that have been explored in this chapter. We will explore this further in Chapters 10 and 11.

Moreover, judgement does play an important role in determining the sales, costs and profits on the one hand, and the risks and attractions, on the other, of a major new strategic initiative. This means that accurate projections are unlikely and some decisions will be wrong. For many companies, there is a need to accept the uncertainties that real life analysis will bring, while taking the positive decisions demanded of the highly original strategies that bring real competitive advantage.

Key strategic principles

- Strategic expansion is often analysed using discounting techniques to reduce future projected profits back to their value in today's monetary terms.

- Several difficulties have been identified with this approach. Probably the most substantial is the difficulty of producing accurate projections of future profitability.

- DCF is not to be confused with basic cash flow analysis, which is not discounted but projects net cash flows during the life of the project. Cash flow analysis is essential for project assessment in order to identify and avoid bankruptcy.

- Overall, while there are certain difficulties involved in the techniques, it is probably better to undertake these analyses rather than ignore them.

8.4 FINANCIAL MANAGEMENT AND ADDED VALUE: MAXIMISING SHAREHOLDER WEALTH[20]

One of the main purposes of strategy is to add value to the inputs of the organisation. In recent years, financial management has taken added value and combined it with the concepts explored earlier in this chapter to emphasise one purpose for the organisation – the maximisation of shareholder wealth. This section explores this approach and its consequences for financial analysis and corporate strategy. Because most shareholdings occur in business situations, the topic inevitably concentrates on *commercial business perspectives* and makes little or no reference to not-for-profit organisations.

8.4.1 Shareholder wealth and value added – the contribution of Alfred Rapaport

In his influential text on shareholder value Rapaport[21] argued, in the late 1980s, that the purpose of a business was essentially to increase the wealth of its owners – that is, its shareholders. All the activities of a business therefore need to be managed towards this approach to adding value:

> *Business strategies should be judged by the economic returns they generate for shareholders, as measured by dividends plus the increase in the company's share price . . . The shareholder value approach estimates the economic value of an investment (e.g. the shares of the company, strategies, mergers and acquisitions, capital expenditures) by discounting forecasted cash flows by the cost of capital. These cash flows, in turn, serve as the foundations for shareholder returns from dividends and share-price appreciation.*

Rapaport goes on to quote a financial journalist: 'Any management – no matter how powerful and independent – that flouts the financial objective of maximizing share value does so at its own peril.'

If the sole objective of a business is to increase the wealth of its owners, then all other activities must be judged against this criterion. Attempts to grow the business, provide service to the community, invest in environmentally friendly policies, deliver extra customer service and so on are implicitly rejected unless they also increase shareholder wealth. The clear merit of this approach is that it provides for simplicity in the analysis of strategy proposals. Such a theme was picked up enthusiastically by some members of the financial community in the 1990s – for example, the well-respected Lex Column in the *Financial Times*: 'Buybacks, demergers and the like are expressions of a single philosophy – shareholder value. The notion that companies should be run in the interest of shareholders, for long considered a weird Anglo-Saxon concept, is [now] taking root in Continental Europe.'[22]

Comment

We are entitled to view with suspicion such simplicities and certainties when they are applied to the real world. Full discussion of this important topic is pursued in Part 4 on the purpose of the organisation. However, others such as employees and government will also have an interest in the way that the business develops. To quote Charles Handy:[23]

> *The idea of a corporation as the property of the current holders of its shares is confusing because it does not make clear where the power lies. As such, the notion is an affront to natural justice because it gives inadequate recognition to the people who work in the corporation and who are, increasingly, its principal assets. To talk of owning other people, as shareholders implicitly do, might be considered immoral.*

Essentially, the importance of shareholders depends on the *values* of the organisation, the *power* of the stakeholders in the organisation, amongst whom will be the shareholders, and the other *external pressures* that impinge on every organisation. Nevertheless, the elevation of shareholder wealth represents an important pressure on many organisations today. For example, shareholders have been known to call successfully for the dismissal of senior executives whose strategies have turned out to be poor.

8.4.2 Calculating shareholder value added[24]

Definition ➤ Shareholder value added (SVA) is the difference between the return on capital and the cost of capital, multiplied by the investment made by the shareholders in the business. For example, referring back to the earlier case study in this chapter on Heineken and using the company accounts (www.heinekeninternational.com), we can estimate the 2004 return on capital at around 13 per cent, the cost of capital at around 9 per cent and the capital invested in the business at US$11,500 million: this gives an SVA in 2004 of US$460 million (0.13 minus 0.09, multiplied by 11,500). Measurement consists of estimating each of these three items. Three questions can be asked that will clarify the analysis:

1 What investment has been made by shareholders in the business?

2 What rate of return is currently being earned by such investment?

3 Is this sufficient to cover the cost of capital? What is the excess return over the cost of capital?

The excess return over the cost of capital can be multiplied by the investment to obtain the SVA. From the previous sections of this chapter, it should be possible to answer the three questions in outline. However, in practice, more detailed adjustments need to be undertaken. The consultants Stern Stewart of New York, who are leading exponents of this approach, claim that anything up to 164 changes may be required to the basic company accounts. They call their version of the concept *economic value added*™ and have successfully used it at the brewers SABMiller described in Case study 8.4.

To illustrate the difficulties in calculating SVA, we can consider the expenditures that companies make on research and development and marketing. By accounting convention, both these items are normally written off to the profit and loss account of the company in the year in which they are incurred. However, SVA argues that investment in these two items contributes to the *future value* of the business. These expenditure items should therefore be added to the balance sheet as assets and depreciated (amortised) over the years that the company will benefit from such investment, which is rather longer than the one year required by accounting convention. In the same way, by accounting convention, goodwill on acquisitions is normally written off to the profit and loss account. In SVA, it is both returned to profits and expressed as an asset, thus raising both profitability and also the invested capital.

The SVA adjustments raise a number of important issues. For example, over what period should marketing investment in a brand such as Heineken or Carlsberg be depreciated – since the brands were developed in the early nineteenth century or merely over the last ten years? And how far back should goodwill be adjusted – the last five years, or ten years, or when? The answers to these questions will depend on individual judgement, meaning that different analysts will arrive at different results in their calculations.[25]

In addition to the three questions above on calculating SVA, an additional question also arises. Using the concept of *economic rent* – *see* Chapter 6 – could the business increase its rate of return by redirecting the capital currently invested in the business towards other activities? Although redirecting the capital that is currently invested is more speculative and problematic, it can be usefully explored from a strategic perspective. Perhaps part of a business could be worth more if it was sold or simply closed down in the face of mounting losses. For example, Guinness (now part of Diageo) between 1991 and 1997 invested around US$1,400 million in acquiring and developing the Spanish brewing company Cruzcampo. Yet its investment was still only earning US$30 million annual profits in 1997 – a rate of return of just 0.2 per cent.[26] Perhaps not surprisingly, the company sold its Spanish subsidiary to Heineken in a bidding auction in 2000.

8.4.3 Future strategy and SVA: estimating risk

From a strategic perspective, the concept of SVA needs to be directed towards the returns from *future strategy*, rather than past events. This means that the rate of return for each proposed strategy needs to be estimated and assessed against the current and future cost of capital. But compared with the SVA calculation described above, there is one major difficulty: the problem of risk. Future strategy is not certain, unlike the balance sheet analysis of past events outlined in the previous section. Clearly, when Guinness invested in Cruzcampo in 1991, it was not projecting profit levels as low as those achieved, otherwise it would not have acquired the company. There is a strong element of judgement involved in assessing the degree of risk, which adds to the difficulties in estimating SVA.

8.4.4 Problems with SVA

There are seven problems with this approach to financial analysis:

1 *It uses accounting data from organisations*. Such data were often never designed to provide information on the current replacement value of assets, merely historic costs. Moreover, it ignores the strategic question of whether the company would replace the asset in any event.

2 *It totally ignores many of the company's best assets*. For example, its human resources, its networks, reputation and innovative ability – *see* Chapters 6 and 7 – never appear in the company accounts but are crucial to future strategic strength.

3 *It relies on an accurate measure of the cost of capital*. Professor Paul Marsh of the London Business School has pointed out that such estimates are at best within 3 percentage points either way.[27]

4 *It takes a defined time period for measurement – usually one year.* Measuring SVA over such a period privileges the short term over the full period of benefit from such an activity. Longer-term projects like basic R&D, brand building and telecommunications infrastructure are all disadvantaged.

5 *It is difficult to apply at the business unit level.* Although it may be calculated for a group of companies, it is more difficult to calculate for individual business units that *share costs*, benefit from *shared facilities* and so on. This matters because many strategic decisions cannot be taken at group level.

6 *It involves estimates of many key items – see* Section 8.4.2.

7 *It involves estimating the risk associated with future strategies – see* Section 8.4.3.

Comment

None of this would matter if companies were simply using SVA as a guide to future strategies. But it is being used to incentivise managers. There is a real danger that SVA short-termism, based on inadequate accounting data, will distort the fundamental strategic decisions that need to be taken by the organisation. To quote the principle in English law, *Caveat emptor!* (Let the buyer beware!)

Key strategic principles

- One view of the prime purpose of a company is to increase the wealth of its owners/ shareholders: this is often called the shareholder value added (SVA) approach.

- SVA is the difference between the return on capital and the cost of capital, multiplied by the investment made in the business.

- For use in strategy analysis, the SVA concept needs to be directed at estimating the profits from future strategic initiatives. The difficulty is that the future involves risk and therefore uncertain returns.

- There are seven problems with the SVA approach: use of accounting data; it ignores the company's best assets; it relies on an accurate measure of the cost of capital; it takes a defined time period; it is difficult to apply at the individual business level; it involves the use of judgement, and risk assessment is problematic.

8.5 RELATIONSHIP BETWEEN FINANCIAL AND CORPORATE OBJECTIVES

Without adequate financial performance, the survival of all commercial organisations would be put at risk. The same is also at least partially true of the many not-for-profit organisations that need to survive, if only to provide the services they offer. Much of this chapter has considered the analysis of financial resources against the background of maximising profits, retaining part of those profits, delivering attractive earnings per share, paying steadily increasing dividends and similar objectives. It has been argued that a basic criterion against which to judge strategy is the opportunity cost of capital.

All these matters have been judged in terms of the shareholder returns. For example, in Case study 8.3, SCA states that its main guideline is the profit delivered to shareholders, as represented by shareholder's equity after tax. Equally, the Capital Asset Pricing Model is essentially a quantification based on the primacy of shareholder interests. There are two reasons for suggesting that this view is oversimplistic and incomplete:

1 long-term *versus* short-term objectives; and

2 the importance of key stakeholders.

CASE STUDY 8.3

SCA's financial objectives[28]

This case study explores the relationship between group and financial objectives at the Swedish paper and packaging company, Svenska Cellulosa (SCA).

SCA is one of the world's largest pulp and paper companies with extensive interests in packaging and hygiene products as well as paper production. (www.sca.com)

Extract from SCA 1992 Report and Accounts	Comment
'The SCA Group's financial targets combine growth with financial balance. As a result of the divestment of the Energy business group, the capital structure changed substantially, reducing financial risk.'	A good example of the need to balance different business and financial requirements.
'Visible shareholders' equity almost doubled, at the same time as net debt decreased significantly. The objective is to sustain this enforced capital structure. Therefore, a certain downward adjustment of the return requirement on shareholders' equity is justified, from the current 15 per cent to 13 per cent.'	The company decreased its gearing substantially and reduced its reliance on heavy debt finance. Such a major change would reduce the risk to shareholders and allow a reduction in shareholder return targets.
'Profitability is the overriding guideline. Accordingly, expressed as return on shareholders' equity after tax, the requirement is 13 per cent, calculated as an average over an economic cycle.'	The company has chosen to define profitability in terms of its shareholders only. Other stakeholders are ignored. It has calculated this over the whole cycle because of the cyclicality of the iron and steel industry (see Case study 3.3). It means that in some years profitability needs to be above this level and in other years will be below it.
'This is based on yield on a risk-free, long-term investment in the European money market and a 3 per cent risk premium for share investments.'	The calculation of 13 per cent is clearly explained with a reference to the risk-free band rate. In order to calculate the actual cost of capital, the company simply added 3 per cent to the risk-free rate for the extra risks involved in raising funds where the return is not guaranteed, i.e. on the stock exchange. The company does not explain why it chose 3 per cent.
'Considering the current tax situation, interest and equity/assets ratio, this requires a consolidated return on capital employed of slightly less than 15 per cent.' 'The [15 per cent] requirement varies between the business groups.'	From the 13 per cent shareholder return, the company has then calculated the amount that it needs to earn on its assets to deliver this figure – that is, just below 15 per cent. Some markets are inherently more profitable than others, and so the company varies the 15 per cent for different business groups within the overall portfolio of its products. Some will be above 15 per cent and some below in order to average at 15 per cent overall.
'Individual operations within each business group are managed on the basis of the return required on its operating assets, as differentiated, taking into account local inflation rates and the age structure of the assets.'	Within each business group, further distinctions are then made for each operating asset. Where country inflation is high, this will inflate the profit figure, so the target is also set higher – a good example of country management. The comment on age structure is unclear. Old assets may perform worse and be less profitable. However, they may have been largely depreciated, in which case they would easily achieve the return on capital targets.

Case questions

1 *What were the main financial objectives of SCA in the early 1990s?*

2 *How do the financial objectives relate to the WACC? And to the return on capital required for strategy proposals?*

3 *If some workers are more profitable than others, why might the company maintain its involvement in less profitable areas? What are the implications for the financial objectives and for setting corporate objectives?*

8.5.1 Balancing long-term and short-term objectives

It is perfectly possible to maximise shareholder profits after tax by stopping research and development, cancelling all advertising and promotional expenditure, and by implementing such policies as a run-down of stocks and zero maintenance of the factory and so on. *In the short term*, profits and shareholder equity would rise substantially. *In the long term*, the organisation would die, which is clearly undesirable. The strategic issue is how to strike a *balance* between the short term and long term.

There is a subsidiary problem with the short-term approach to objectives. As soon as there are unfavourable variations in the external environment, the short-term view would suggest that longer-term investment should be cut back and the short term protected. For example, economic downturn might mean a major strategic capital project being delayed, even though its benefits were significant. Corporate strategy needs to consider how to manage the organisation so that this balance is not thrown off course at the first sign of difficulty.

8.5.2 Importance of key stakeholders

Some key stakeholders in a business – such as management and workers – seek rewards from the firm other than the maximisation of profit – job satisfaction and rewards, for example. A variety of research sources suggests that reasonable rather than maximum profits may be a more accurate reflection of their views. This is reflected in the Ford Motor Company mission and objectives statement (*see* Exhibit 12.4) which refers to its mission as 'allowing us to prosper as a business and to provide a reasonable return for our stockholders, the owners of the business'. The implication for financial evaluation is that there is a need to explore what 'reasonable' profit means and then to assess the organisation's financial resources in that context.

This does not mean that organisations should not raise new funds and explore the means of achieving this as cheaply as possible. It is perfectly rational to explore the cost of the capital that has been raised or is being sought. It is always desirable for the benefits of a strategy to be greater than the cost of capital, however calculated. It is nevertheless important for the benefits to be seen in a broader context than simply the maximisation of profit.

8.5.3 Distinction between strategic and financial objectives

It is important for a distinction to be drawn between an organisation's financial and strategic objectives. The starting point is to recognise the need to invest in the long-term future

---

Table 8.9

Financial and strategic objectives[29]

Financial objectives	Strategic objectives
• Faster revenue growth	• Bigger market share
• Faster earnings growth	• Higher, more secure industry rank
• Higher dividends	• Higher product quality
• Wider profit margins	• Lower costs relative to key competitors
• Higher returns on invested capital	• Broader or more attractive product line
• Stronger bond and credit ratings	• Stronger reputation with customers
• Bigger cash flows	• Superior customer service
• A rising stock price	• Recognition as a leader in technology and/or product innovation
• Recognition as a 'blue chip' company	• Increased ability to compete in international markets
• A more diversified revenue base	• Expanded growth opportunities
• Stable earnings during recessionary periods	• Higher salaries and other employee benefits

Source: Thompson A and Strickland A, *Strategic Management*, 9th edn.
© Richard D Irwin, a Times Mirror Higher Education Group, Inc. Company, Burr Ridge, IL, USA, p31. Adapted with permission of the publisher.

of the business and to establish the legitimate interests of other stakeholders in the business. Both of these aspects then need to be reflected in the organisation's objectives, which make up the organisation's broad strategies for the future. Essentially, this will lead to *strategic* rather than *financial* objectives. The distinction is shown in Table 8.9.

There can be little doubt that strategic objectives are essential for the long-term development of strategy.

Key strategic principles

- To define objectives purely in terms of the organisation's short-term financial profitability would be oversimplistic and incomplete.

- There are two principal reasons for this. First, it is often possible to sacrifice long-term profits to boost the short term at the expense of the survival of the organisation. Second, such an approach ignores the interests of other stakeholders in the organisation, such as employees.

- Hence, a distinction needs to be drawn between strategic and financial objectives.

8.6 INTERNATIONAL ASPECTS OF FINANCIAL RESOURCES

In examining international financial resources, there are many similarities with the techniques outlined in Sections 8.1 to 8.5. This section will therefore concentrate on the differences. There are five main areas to be considered:

1 capital structure of overseas holdings;

2 international fund remittances;

3 risk management, including currency;

4 taxation considerations;

5 cost of capital variations across countries.

8.6.1 Capital structure of overseas holdings

In principle, the same mixture of equity, debt and other forms of finance is available in overseas companies as in the home country. Retained earnings are often the main method of financing overseas subsidiaries, but debt capital can also sometimes be high.[30] Special considerations that might be applied to overseas companies include:

- Where the company is located in a country with widely fluctuating exchange rates, there is a case for using as much *local* debt finance as possible. This allows the company to avoid the uncertainties of using its own funds.

- Special grants and investment loans from sources such as the EU and World Bank may make a substantial difference to strategy profitability.

8.6.2 International fund remittances

Paying funds to and obtaining dividends from foreign subsidiaries will almost certainly need careful thought. For example, some years ago a South American government had a policy that allowed only limited repatriation of company profits back to Europe from activities in that country. There was no point in evaluating the cost of capital without taking this into account. One way round the problem was to seek payment from foreign subsidiaries for other services beyond dividends on shares – for example, royalties on the use of brand names, patents, management services, goods supplied from the home country and so on. Naturally, these other payments were all agreed with the government authorities of the country concerned, but they did make the financial resource evaluation task more complex and hence the strategic analysis more difficult.

8.6.3 Risk management

When companies are forced to rely on payments from countries with weak currencies, they always face the risk that their earnings will decline from the projections made at the time when the strategy was devised. There are a number of mechanisms for reducing such risks, but none is without its problems. Essentially, they all amount to some form of insurance and have a cost that needs to be built into the analysis of financial resources. Judging by some major corporate disasters of the last few years, probably the most important area of risk is that of *currency management*.

8.6.4 Taxation considerations

Among the many matters to be evaluated, there are the issues of:

- the choice of the country in which to take any profits earned;
- the possibility of moving funds to countries that have no corporation tax;
- the complexities of different national tax systems on profits.

Even within the EU, there has been no real harmonisation of the important tax rates, nor is there likely to be in the near future.[31] Tax matters make the evaluation of financial resources for overseas companies sufficiently complex to require specialist advice and consultation.

8.6.5 Cost of capital variations across countries

For reasons associated with levels of inflation, currency and national resources, different countries have differing costs of capital. In practice, this important issue can be explored both within large companies and, using outside financial advisers, with smaller companies. The important point from a strategy perspective is to know that this is a question that must be properly investigated.

Key strategic principles

- When international operations are involved, financial resource analysis becomes more complex.
- The capital structure of equity and debt is broadly similar, but sending funds to and obtaining dividends from overseas companies is more difficult because of barriers to trade, country differences on tax and economies' growth and currency uncertainties.
- Probably the greatest single area of risk in many overseas operations is currency fluctuation.
- Taxation and cost of capital are both subjects that require in-depth and possibly specialist financial analysis.
- For a variety of reasons, the cost of capital will vary between countries. This means that the financial analysis of strategic projects will need to be conducted on an individual country basis.

SABMiller: South Africa goes global

Over the last 15 years, South African Breweries (SAB) has transformed itself from a local South African holding company into the world's second-largest brewer of beer and lager. This case examines how it went global, focusing particularly on the financial activities that funded the strategy.

Overview of world beer markets – size, growth and share

The world market for beers and lagers amounted to around 1,400 million hectolitres in 2002. The leading markets by size are shown in Figure 8.6. It will be self-evident why the world's largest brewers have all been targeting the Chinese market over the last five years.

Growth varied between countries – low growth (1–3 per cent per annum) in the mature North American, Australia/New Zealand and Western European markets; higher growth (5–15 per cent per annum) in the Chinese, other Asian and central European markets; variable growth in African markets – some were relatively mature like South Africa and Nigeria, some recovering like Angola; South American markets were relatively mature (3–7 per cent per annum); the Middle East market was a special case with respect to Muslim views on the consumption of alcohol and the growth of non-alcoholic beers; India was a growth market but highly regulated.

In terms of market share in 2002, the world's five largest brewers accounted for 17 per cent of world sales. By 2004, it was estimated that the world's five leading brewers had grown to take 40 per cent of world share, with this rising to 50 per cent by 2010. Essentially, consolidation was taking place in the world brewing industry through a combination of acquisitions and mergers. Table 8.10 shows the most active players:

Beginning with Castle Lager in South Africa, SABMiller has built a worldwide group of brands over the last ten years.

- *InBev* – formed from the European brewing company InterBrew and the South American company AmBev. InterBrew owns Stella Artois (Belgium) Labatts (Canada) Beck's (Germany) and Whitbread (UK) as a result of a series of takeovers in the 1990s. Brazil's *AmBev* – the market leader in South America – dominates the Brazilian market and is also strong in other South American markets: its

Table 8.10

Annual sales of the world's leading brewers in 2000 and 2004

Company	Home country	World beer sales 2000 (million hectolitres)	Company	World beer sales 2004 (million hectolitres)
Anheuser Busch	US	120	InBev – see text	190
Interbrew	Belgium	76	SABMiller – see text	136
Heineken	Netherlands	74	Anheuser-Busch	132
South African Breweries	South Africa	56	Heineken	122
AmBev	Brazil	56	Carlsberg	92
Miller Brewing	US	54	Scottish & Newcastle	50
Carlsberg	Denmark	47	Asahi	35
Scottish & Newcastle	UK	36	Kirin	33
Asahi	Japan	35		
Kirin	Japan	33		

Source: Author, from trade estimates and company annual reports.

Figure 8.6

World beer – the ten largest markets 2002

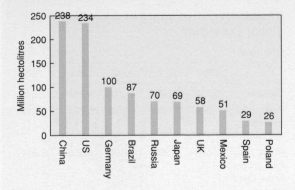

savings were those quoted by the merged company and remained to be proven in practice at the time of writing.

Background to South African Breweries

During the apartheid years, political sanctions made it impossible for SAB to move outside its home country, in spite of the profits from its dominant home market position. SAB therefore ploughed its profits back into a wide range of home businesses: clothing, retailing, textiles, plate glass and fruit juice were all investment targets. After sanctions were lifted, it began to move overseas. To fund the overseas expansion described below, SAB sold virtually all its non-beer South African activities around 2001.

Even in the early 1990s, SAB made the important strategic decision that it needed to build from what it knew best – the brewing of beer and lager. The company already had the major share of its home market for beer with brands like Castle Lager. The company had been founded in 1895 as a brewer and was one of South Africa's leading companies. Not only did it know how to brew beer, but it also had expertise to exploit the substantial economies of scale available in the brewing industry in brewing, bottling and distribution. Over time, SAB had also become the largest bottler and distributor of Coca-Cola carbonated drinks in South Africa. In the early 1990s, there was little further scope in South Africa for SAB but it could see opportunities worldwide, where the brewing industry was still fragmented.

First international steps

Back in 1993, SAB made its first international acquisition. The brand was Dreher, Hungary's largest brewer. This was at the time when central Europe was moving away from domination by Russia and was beginning to privatise its former state enterprises. The opportunity was there for SAB to seize and was financed from retained profits. SAB subsequently admitted that it learnt some lessons from this acquisition. 'We made some mistakes when we first went in. You could argue that with our first acquisition in Europe, which was Hungary, we made serial mistakes. By the time we had got through a few of them, we knew what approach to take, what things to look out for, what things to do quickly and how to prioritise,' commented Graham Mackay, chief executive of SAB some years later.

Consistent with the vision, SAB's next step in 1994 was to move into the People's Republic of China in a joint venture with a Chinese government-owned brewery company. SAB took a 49 per cent stake and carefully and quietly began building its presence in that important country long before it became a target for Western companies. In the same year, SAB used its regional strengths and network contacts in Africa to begin moves into Tanzania, Mozambique and Zambia. All these moves were relatively modest and funded essentially from retained earnings.

In spite of its early problems in Hungary, SAB saw further opportunities in central Europe. In the period 1995–99, it acquired leading breweries in Poland, Romania, Slovakia and Russia itself. Towards the end of this period, SAB had some luck. The major investment bank, Nomura, had acquired the

main brand is Brahma. There are plans to launch Brahma worldwide as a result of the merger. The claimed financial benefits of this merger are considered later in this section.

- *SABMiller* – whose activities are described in more detail in this case.

- *Anheuser-Busch* – the American producer and world's largest brewer in 2000. It stayed away from world markets until recent years. American home sales still account for 90 per cent of its total by volume. It has now moved aggressively into China with various acquisitions. Budweiser remains its key brand.

- *Heineken* – a family company from the Netherlands that has moved onto the world stage. Its main brands are Heineken, Amstel and Murphys. It is now beginning to build these into world, premium brands. Its activities were explored in Case 8.1.

- *Carlsberg* – controlled by a Danish charitable trust that has also been highly active in terms of acquisitions. The company has strong interests in some Western European countries, particularly Scandinavia. It has also developed its interests in some Eastern European countries. Much of this development has again been through acquisition.

To an extent, company size does matter in brewing. There are economies of scale in production and distribution. There are scale benefits from building and promoting global brands, especially those that lend themselves to a premium price positioning – higher profit margins, customer loyalty. For these reasons, InterBrew and AmBev estimated substantial benefits from their merger, announced in 2004. The company claimed that the combined group would be able to generate US$350 million of annual synergies per annum 'through a combination of technical, procurement and other general and administrative *cost savings*'. There would also be commercial synergies of US$175 million per annum through two methods: first, 'applying AmBev's best practices in point of connection management to InterBrew's operations, particularly those in developing markets'; second, 'through cross licensing of Beck's and Stella Artois in Brazil and Argentina, and of Brahma through the existing InterBrew platform'. The claimed

▶

▶ CASE STUDY 8.4 continued

dominant Czech brewery brand Pilsner Urquell as part of a complicated deal involving other aspects of privatisation in what was then Czechoslovakia. Nomura decided to auction its Czech beer brand. Pilsner Urquell had 44 per cent of the Czech market and was well known throughout central Europe. The auction drew interest from Anheuser-Busch of the US, InterBrew of Belgium (now merged to form InBev) and Heineken of the Netherlands. But it was SAB that bid the highest – US$629 million – and was successful. The bid was financed from SAB's own resources – retained profits and debt. The real issue was that the Czech brewer only made US$17.2 million profit in 1998. Such low profitability would not support the purchase price without drastic action being taken. SAB planned to take Pilsner Urquell back to its former brand glory in central Europe. It would modernise the plant, raise prices to position the product as a premium beer and use the central location of the Czech Republic as the springboard of all its central European operations. 'This is right on strategy,' said the chief executive, Graham Mackay. 'But not the end of the story. Czech brewing has a great reputation in eastern and central Europe and Pilsner Urquell the greatest of all. But there is still room for further consolidation [in the brewing industry] and we are here to participate.'

SAB completed their plans in the late 1990s by moving their primary share listing to London to be able to raise capital to finance more acquisitions. Most of the leading managers remain South African to the present, including the distinguished South African politician Mr Cyril Ramophosa, who is a non-executive member of the SABMiller board. The move to London also had problems: 'We suffer from the fact that we are listed in London but do not have a business presence there,' explained Mr Mackay. Because the shareholder base is very thin in London, the shares have not been easy to trade on the London market. The cost of capital at around 11 per cent was also higher than for equivalent world brewers because it included a risk element for the South African currency, the Rand, where much of the business was located.

SAB becomes a world company

By 2000, SAB had played its strategy well. It had picked up dominant brands in central Europe, where it could exploit its core competencies. It had moved into markets with great growth potential – other parts of Africa and China. It had even bought a regional brewer in another country with great long-term protential – India. SAB acquired the Narang brewery, even though it regarded the Indian market as highly regulated and immature. At the time of writing, SABMiller is in the process of revising its relationship with the local Indian company, Shaw Wallace Breweries. The combined joint venture will be the second-largest company in the Indian market, behind Heineken.

Although the company was building for the future, SAB was having difficulty in completing its global ambitions. Its rivals – Heineken, InterBrew and Carlsberg – dominated much of Western Europe. Anheuser-Busch with its Budweiser brand was steadily building its global status. Then, over the period 2001–2003, SAB made three major strategic moves:

Table 8.11

Results over five years of SABMiller's global expansion

US$ million

	2000	2001	2002	2003	2004
Turnover	5 425	4 184.	4 363	8 984	12 645
Profit before interest and tax	844	700*	704	933	1 579
Net assets: total assets less current liabilities	2 559	2 292*	3 054	6 350	6 984
Earnings per share (US cents (adjusted))	56.6	53.3	48.7	54.0	77.6

* *Note*: The decline in the various figures in 2001 was due to the removal from that year of non-brewing activities from the accounts. This was because they were no longer part of SABMiller. They were sold or merged with other companies outside the brewer's trading activities and therefore no longer appeared in the SABMiller accounts.
Source: Annual Report and Accounts.

● *Central America*: in 2001 it acquired a 58 per cent interest in breweries in Honduras and El Salvador at a cost of US$500 million.
● *North America*: it spent US$5.6 billion in 2002 to acquire the US brewer Miller from Altria (the former Philip Morris tobacco conglomerate). Miller was the second-largest brand in the US. But its share was only 17 per cent against the market leader, Budweiser, which had 49 per cent. The market was described as being 'crowded and low-growth' and the Miller brand was described as 'ailing'. SAB was not buying success.
● *Western Europe*: it spent US$270 million to acquire the Italian lager company Peroni. This was the first time that SAB had moved into the more mature markets of Western Europe.

The largest of these acquisitions was the purchase of Miller. The company recognised this by changing its name to *SABMiller*. It had made the purchase partly to move into the largest beer market in the world – the US. The acquisition also reduced its exposure to the Rand, thereby reducing its cost of capital from 11 per cent to 9 per cent. However, the company was forced to admit after six months that the problems were worse than it had anticipated on the purchase. The existing Miller chief executive who had been allowed to remain was sacked and a SAB executive moved in. 'We went into Miller with our eyes open. It will be a long turnaround, but we have no doubt we will fix the problems,' commented Mr Mackay one year later.

The acquisition of Miller was funded by a share issue for the first time. The shares were taken up by Altria, the previous owner of Miller. Altria is an American company, possibly better known as the tobacco company Philip Morris, the makers of the Marlboro brand. Altria then had 23 per cent of the shares of SABMiller, the largest single shareholding in the company. Did SAB pay too much for Miller? Its chief executive, Graham Mackay commented: 'That is a somewhat futile debate . . . I think that in the medium and long term we will cover the cost of capital. The business has strategically transformed our company and I think will deliver value on its own account.'

The outcome of SABMiller's strategic decision to become a global company is shown in Table 8.11. As a result of its strategies, the company more than doubled turnover and nearly doubled profit before interest and tax.

SABMiller outlook

At the time of writing, there was some hint in the press that SABMiller might be about to make another major international move. Columbia's largest brewer, Grupo Empresarial Bavaria, was reported to be seeking an international buyer. Bavaria also had leading market positions in Ecuador, Peru and Panama and was particularly interested in a merger. 'Bavaria is going ahead with a process of globalisation and consolidation,' said a Bavraria spokesman. 'We remain interested in strengthening that process, always looking towards the future and following the business cycles of the industry. So far, that strategy does not include a sale of the company.' SABMiller would be well placed to undertake a merger – its rival InBev was still in the process of merging; Anheuser-Busch strategy was largely organic growth and the fourth company, Heineken, was pursuing a strategy of investing in its leading premium brands, Heineken and Amstel, rather than seeking acquisitions.

By 2004, SABMiller itself was beginning to turn around its Miller brewing interests. Trading profit had risen substantially over the two years since the acquisition. Its Miller brewing interests in North America were beginning to make a contribution, though still weak relative to other parts of the business: 38 per cent of turnover but only 12 per cent of trading profits – *see* Figure 8.7. The South African brewery interests were still the largest contributor to overall profits and an important source of funds for international expansion.

SABMiller's other businesses were also doing well, with substantial increases in sales, particularly in the premium brands where the profit margins were highest. 'There will only be three or four top-tier global companies. My ambition is to stay there and offer a superior growth profile as a result of our acquisitions. We have never pursued size for the sake of size,' commented Mr Mackay. But, even now, he can take satisfaction from the way that SABMiller has been transformed over 15 years from a local South African holding company into a major global brewer.

Case questions

1 What were the main strategic moves made by SABMiller over the last few years and how were they financed? What was the impact on cost of capital?

2 *What were the risks of its strategic moves from a financial perspective? And what from a strategy perspective? What are the implications of failure to deliver on the benefits of the Miller and Peroni acquisitions?*

3 *What lessons, if any, can other companies learn from the SAB strategy for growth?*

Figure 8.7

SABMiller – contribution to sales and trading profit 2004

(a) Share of turnover 2004

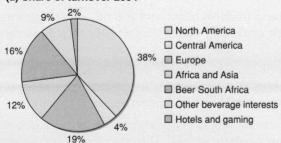

- ☐ North America
- ☐ Central America
- ☐ Europe
- ☐ Africa and Asia
- ☐ Beer South Africa
- ☐ Other beverage interests
- ☐ Hotels and gaming

(b) Share of operating profit 2004

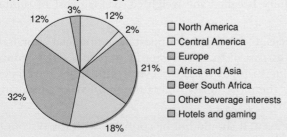

- ☐ North America
- ☐ Central America
- ☐ Europe
- ☐ Africa and Asia
- ☐ Beer South Africa
- ☐ Other beverage interests
- ☐ Hotels and gaming

STRATEGIC PROJECT

This case focuses on SABMiller. The other leading brewery companies would all lend themselves to similar research from a strategy perspective. The starting point could easily be the websites of the various companies, which are readily accessible. One interesting approach would be to compare the international growth strategies of the leading companies – for example, the late entry of Anheuser-Busch (why were they late?); the early acquisition moves of Heineken, switching more recently to brand building (why switch?); one of the companies that appears to have been left behind – Scottish and Newcastle (why?). There is plenty of scope for interesting projects here in international brewing.

CRITICAL REFLECTION

Shareholders or stakeholders?

Modern finance argues that the only people who matter in organisations are the shareholders, who are the owners of the organisation. Thus all of strategy needs to be directed to maximising *shareholder* wealth. Essentially, this is the argument of Alfred Rapaport outlined earlier in the chapter.

Equally, there are others who argue that, beyond an adequate level of compensation to the shareholders, any organisation has a greater responsibility to its *stakeholders* – management, employees, government and others in society. Such arguments have become particularly strong as organisations have accepted the implications of the organisation's *corporate social responsibility*. Saving the natural environment, caring for the underprivileged and conserving energy are among the many responsibilities of all organisations. Strategy needs to be directed, at least in part, to achieving these aims.

These views would seem to be in direct conflict, but they need to be resolved if corporate strategy is to be developed. How? Who is right?

SUMMARY

● Organisations need to finance their existing and proposed new strategies. There are six main sources of funds for such activities, each with its own merits and problems. Retained profits are the first source of finance for most organisations, probably the largest and cheapest source of funds. Equity finance – that is, the issuance of new shares to either existing or new shareholders – is another way of raising funds. Long-term debt finance is simpler and cheaper than equity but there are limits to the amount that can be raised. There are also major constraints on debt finance. These relate to the need to pay interest on the debt regardless of the profit fluctuations in the business.

● Other sources of finance include leasing (renting) plant and machinery, savings from reductions in short-term debt and the sale of existing assets. They all have their advantages and problems.

● All capital raised by the organisation has a cost associated with it. Calculating the cost matters because it reassures the stakeholders that their efforts are worthwhile and because it provides a benchmark for assessing the profitability of future strategies.

● The cost of equity capital can be calculated using the Capital Asset Pricing Model, but it really only works where there is wide public shareholding. The cost of debt is calculated from the weighted average of the individual loans to the company. For the company overall, the combined cost of debt and equity is called the weighted average cost of capital (WACC).

● When assessing new strategic proposals, it is normal to undertake a financial appraisal. Discounting techniques are often used as part of this in Western companies. They reduce future net cash flows back to their value in today's terms. Several difficulties have been identified with this approach. Probably the most substantial is the problem of producing accurate projections of future profitability.

● Basic cash flow analysis is also undertaken. It should not be confused with the discounting techniques above. Analysing cash flow is essential to ensure that the company avoids bankruptcy.

- One view of the prime purpose of a company is to increase the wealth of its owners/shareholders. This is often called the shareholder value added (SVA) approach. SVA is the difference between the return on capital and the cost of capital, multiplied by the investment made in the business. From a strategic perspective, SVA has a number of difficulties, including that of estimating the uncertain future returns from new strategy initiatives.

- To define objectives purely in terms of the organisation's short-term financial profitability would be oversimplistic and incomplete. A distinction needs to be drawn between strategic and financial objectives.

- When international operations are involved, financial resource analysis becomes more complex. Probably the greatest source of risk for many companies is currency fluctuation. Taxation and the cost of capital are both subjects that require in-depth and possibly specialist financial analysis.

QUESTIONS

1 You have been commissioned to comment upon a proposal to invest US$100 million in a new mobile telephone service. The company already operates such a facility but it has seen opportunities for expansion into new geographical areas. Competition is strong and the market is growing at around 12 per cent per annum. The company currently has gearing of around 90 per cent and a WACC of 12 per cent. The new funds would double the total already invested in the company. What would you advise?

2 Use Section 8.1 to analyse the financial resources of an organisation with which you are familiar. Comment particularly on the strategic implications.

3 Explain the constraints on sources of finance likely to be experienced by Heineken, Carlsberg and Danone. To what extent can these constraints be overcome?

4 'Marketers and finance people seldom see eye to eye. The marketers say, "This product will open up a whole new market segment." Finance people respond, "It's a bad investment. The discounted rate of return is only 8 per cent." Why are they so often in opposition?' (Professors Patrick Barwise, Paul Marsh and Robin Wensley)

How would you approach this issue?

5 Investigate the cost of capital for an organisation of your choice. How would you calculate it? With what result? What are the implications for the development of corporate strategy?

6 Compare the shareholding structures of the brewery companies named in the chapter and comment on the financial and strategic implications.

7 There appears to be a conflict in companies between financial and strategic objectives. Do you agree? How can any such conflict be resolved?

8 'Capital investment represents an act of faith, a belief that the future will be as promising as the present, together with a commitment to making the future happen.' (Professor Robert Hayes)

Discuss the implications for financial and strategic appraisal of new corporate strategies.

9 Why has SVA grown in importance over the last ten years? What implications does this have for corporate strategy?

APPENDIX 1: CHECKLIST OF THE MAIN FINANCIAL RATIOS

Note: It is important to obtain comparative data for competitors and to analyse the trends over several years. It is also valuable, where possible, to make comparisons with the norms across an industry.

Liquidity – measures the ability to survive and avoid default

$$\text{Current ratio} = \frac{\text{Current assets}}{\text{Current liabilities}}$$

$$\text{Acid test} = \frac{\text{Current assets} - \text{Stocks}}{\text{Current liabilities}}$$

Gearing – examines the financial strength and the different forms of finance

$$\text{Gearing} = \frac{\text{Long-term borrowing}}{\text{Capital and reserves}}$$

$$\text{Interest cover} = \frac{\text{Earnings before interest and tax (EBIT)}}{\text{Interest}}$$

Profitability

$$\text{Profit margin} = \frac{\text{EBIT}}{\text{Sales}}$$

$$\text{Return on capital employed} = \frac{\text{EBIT}}{\text{Capital employed}}$$

Investor ratios – measures the earnings available to those who own the company

Usually uses profit after tax and interest, i.e. *net profit*.

$$\text{Net profit margin} = \frac{\text{Net profit}}{\text{Sales}}$$

$$\text{Earnings per share} = \frac{\text{Net profit margin}}{\text{number of shares}}$$

$$\text{P/E ratio} = \frac{\text{Price per share}}{\text{Number of shares}}$$

$$\text{Earnings yield} = \frac{\text{Earnings per share}}{\text{Price per share}}$$

$$\text{Dividend per share} = \frac{\text{Dividends}}{\text{Number of shares}}$$

Trading activity

$$\text{Stock cover} = \frac{\text{Cost of sales}}{\text{Stock}}$$

$$\text{Debtor days} = \frac{\text{Debtors} \times 365}{\text{Sales}}$$

$$\text{Creditor days} = \frac{\text{Other creditors} \times 365}{\text{Sales}}$$

$$\text{Fixed asset turnover} = \frac{\text{Sales}}{\text{Fixed assets}}$$

APPENDIX 2: CORPORATE STRATEGY BECOMES LEGAL REQUIREMENT FOR BRITISH COMPANIES

As this edition was going to press, all large and medium-sized British companies were being forced by new laws to publish their 'objectives, strategies and the key drivers of the business' in their Annual Report and Accounts.

From 1st April 2005, all such companies were required to include an *Operating and Financial Review* (OFR) alongside the annual company financial report. The aim was to allow shareholders – and to a lesser extent other stakeholders – to form a judgement about the future prospects of the company. The reasons for the new OFR were:

1 To overcome the problem of financial results that report essentially on past events: both the *Balance Sheet* and the *Profit and Loss Statement* look back, not forward.

2 To provide more evidence on the intangible assets of a company: for example, its reputation, brands, intellectual capital, patents, customer/supplier relationships, market position and dominance.

3 To help shareholders reconcile high share prices with relatively low accounting or book asset values.

The OFR will necessarily contain much of the strategic content explored in this book. It will be a legal requirement to provide this. However, the directors of the company will decide precisely what information will appear in the OFR. Importantly, they will need to distinguish between what is declared to *shareholders* and what is revealed to *competitors* as a result of the OFR. There is a danger that commercially sensitive information – better kept secret – will be published.

More generally, corporate strategy will become an important feature of the annual reports of larger companies. It may also provide useful extra data for strategy research as time passes. For more information: www.dti.gov.uk/cld/OFR_Guidance.pdf.

Further reading

For a general survey of financial issues: Glautier, M W E and Underdown, B (1997) *Accounting Theory and Practice*, 6th edn, Pitman Publishing, London.

For a critical look at DCF techniques: Hayes, R (1982) 'Managing as if tomorrow mattered', *Harvard Business Review*, May–June.

For the link between finance and strategy: Barwise, P, Marsh, P and Wensley, R (1989) 'Must finance and strategy clash?' *Harvard Business Review*, Sep–Oct.

For a discussion of cost of capital and financial issues: Watson, D and Head, T (1998) *Corporate Finance: Principles and Practice*, Financial Times Management, London, Chs8 and 9 – an admirably clear text, as is Arnold, G (1998) *Corporate Financial Management*, Financial Times Management, London, Chs15 and 16.

Notes and references

1 References for the Heineken case: Carlsberg Annual Report and Accounts 2004; SABMiller Annual Report and Accounts 2004; Annual Report and Accounts 2004 coupled with the Heineken website which has a history of Heineken – www.heineken.com. *Financial Times*: 16 April 1999, p19; 30 November 1999, p34; 11 December 2000, p28; 14 December 2000, p30; 27 April 2001, p33; 5 January 2002, p15; 28 February 2003, p30; 9 July 2003, p29.

2 There is evidence for the UK which showed that in 1990 it accounted for around 50 per cent of the total source of funds: *Annual Abstract of Statistics*, HMSO, London,

1993. Such data do not appear to have been researched for a broader range of countries. However, sampling of company accounts would appear to confirm this at least for Europe and the US.

3 Bokhari, F. (2000) 'Islam's interest and principles', *Financial Times*, 31 August, p19.

4 Gitman, L J (1982) *Principles of Managerial Finance*, 3rd edn, Harper and Row, NY.

5 This section makes no attempt to explore the Modigliani/Miller argument that there is no difference between the cost of equity and the cost of debt. It is beyond the scope of this text. For a full and admirably

clear exposition, *see* Watson, D and Head, T (1998) *Corporate Finance: Principles and Practice*, Financial Times Management, London, Ch8.

6 Franks, J R and Broyles, J E (1979) *Modern Managerial Finance*, Wiley, Chichester, Ch2.

7 For example, the UK company General Electric has held large cash balances for many years rather than invest these in company projects.

8 Franks, J R and Broyles, J E B (1979) Op. cit., pp106 *et seq*.

9 Sources for L'Oréal case: L'Oréal Annual Report and Accounts; Estée Lauder Annual Report and Accounts; Shiseido Annual Report and Accounts; Much of the detailed L'Oréal market commentary is available on www.loreal.com/enww/press-room; the L'Oréal financial data is available on www.loreal-finance.com.

10 Dean, J (1954) 'Measuring the productivity of capital', *Harvard Business Review*, Jan–Feb, p21.

11 Merrett, A J and Sykes, A (1966) *Capital Budgeting and Company Finance*, Longman, Harlow.

12 Grant, R M (1991) *Contemporary Strategy Analysis*, Blackwell, Oxford.

13 Hayes, W and Garvin, J (1982) 'Managing as if tomorrow mattered', *Harvard Business Review*, May–June, p71.

14 Hayes, W and Garvin, J (1982) Ibid., p75.

15 Hayes, W and Garvin, J (1982) Ibid., p76.

16 Marsh, P, Barwise, P, Thomas, K and Wensley, R (1989) *Managing Strategic Investment Decisions in Large Diversified Companies*, London Business School Centre for Business Strategy, London.

17 Whittington, R (1993) *What Is Strategy and Does It Matter?*, Routledge, London, pp64–5. The comments in this reference include a much more extensive discussion of the problems than is possible in this text.

18 Ellis, J and Williams, D (1993) *Corporate Strategy and Financial Analysis*, Pitman Publishing, London, p172.

19 Ellis, J and Williams, D (1993) Ibid., p168.

20 This section has benefited from Chapters 15 and 16 of Glen Arnold's book *Corporate Financial Management*, Financial Times Management, London, 1998.

21 Rapaport, A (1986) *Creating Shareholder Value: The new standard for business performance*, The Free Press, New York, Ch1. An extract from the opening chapter of this book is also contained in De Wit, R and Meyer, R (1998) *Strategy: Process, Content and Context*, 2nd edn, International Thompson Business Press, London.

22 Lex Column, *Financial Times*, 28–29 Dec 1996.

23 Handy, C (1997) 'The citizen corporation', *Harvard Business Review*, Sept–Oct, pp26–28.

24 For a review of SVA techniques as used in economic value added (EVA), *see* Young, D (1997) 'Economic value: A primer for European managers', *European Management Journal*, 15, Aug, pp335–43.

25 Arnold, G (1998) Op. cit., pp704–5.

26 Oram, R (1997) *Financial Times*, 4 Feb, p25.

27 Quoted in the *Financial Times*, 7 Oct 1997, p12.

28 Extracts from 1992 Report and Accounts.

29 Adapted from Thompson, A and Strickland, A (1993) *Strategic Management*, 9th edn, Irwin, Homewood, IL, p31.

30 Brooke, M Z (1992) *International Management*, 2nd edn, Stanley Thornes, Cheltenham, Ch8.

31 *See* Citron, R (1991) *Getting into Europe*, Kogan Page, London, for a more detailed discussion of this area.

32 References for SABMiller Case: SABMiller Annual Report and Accounts 2004; InBev Annual Report and Accounts 2004; Anheuser-Busch Annual Report and Accounts 2004; Heineken Annual Report and Accounts 2004; Carlsberg Annual Report and Accounts 2004; Scottish and Newcastle Annual Report and Accounts 2004. All these companies have extensive websites which can be accessed quickly via any web search engine. *Financial Times*: 8 Oct 1999, p26; 31 May 2002, p27; 15 May 2003, p23; 21 Nov 2003, p25; 6 Oct 2003, p6 Special Report on Investing in South Africa; 4 May 2004, p23; 5 May 2004, p21; 21 Jan 2005. Plus other *Financial Times* news items on the brewing industry and competition: 21 June 1999, p23; 27 Sept 2000, p31; 9 Nov 2000, p33; 4 Jan 2001, p22; 23 June 2001, p18; 29 Nov 2001, p25; 15 Feb 2002, p20; 15 Feb 2002, p26; 28 Feb 2002, p30; 8 July 2002, p4; 12 July 2002, p3; 13 May 2003, p31; 9 July 2003, p29; 23 Sept 2003, p37; 2 Dec 2003, p24; 13 Dec 2003, pM12; 9 Jan 2004, p33; 4 March 2004, p27; 5 March 2004, p25 (advertisement announcing InBev) 21 July 2004, p15; 28 Aug 2004, pM5; 4 Jan 2005, p20.

Chapter 9

ANALYSING OPERATIONS RESOURCES

Learning outcomes

When you have worked through this chapter, you will be able to:

- assess the contribution of operations strategy to the corporate strategy process;
- identify the competitive advantage and value-added contributions that the operations function makes to the organisation;
- analyse the operations environment for relevant trends, especially major changes in technology;
- identify how and where operations strategies contribute to value added;
- analyse operations in organisations for the specific areas that are most likely to impact on corporate strategy;
- understand the importance of the main elements of operations strategy;
- explore the differences that exist between operations in manufacturing and in service industries.

INTRODUCTION

Operations management covers all manufacturing processes in an organisation and includes raw material sourcing, purchasing, production and manufacturing, distribution and logistics – in other words, the contribution of the production function to the organisation's ability to add value to its goods or services. Importantly, human resource aspects of the function are just as significant as machinery. In many corporate strategy texts, operations management

Figure 9.1

Analysing operations resources

Organisation

Environment	Operations value chain (Section 9.3)	leading to	Results
• Technology change			Value-added and sustainable competitive advantage
• Discontinuities			
• Global issues			
(Sections 9.1 and 9.2)			

Operations strategies
- Specific contributions
- Analysis of operations processes
- Impact on corporate strategy
  (Section 9.4)

Operations activities in service industries (Section 9.5)

barely rates a mention, and yet it has delivered real benefits to organisations in both the commercial and public sectors over the last 25 years.

There are four main topics in this chapter: the environmental forces that have been a powerful influence on operations development; the contribution of operations to value and sustainable competitive advantage; operations activities and corporate strategy; and the application of operations concepts to the service industry (*see* Figure 9.1).

CASE STUDY 9.1

Dell – competitive advantage through low-cost manufacturing

When Michael Dell first thought of selling computers by mail in his student room at Texas University in 1987, he could hardly have foreseen the consequences. Today, Dell claims to be the market leader in the worldwide personal computer (PC) market, with sales around US$41 billion. And Michael Dell, still aged only 40, was the eighteenth richest person in the US. The company's main competitive advantage is that it has lower manufacturing costs than most of its competitors. But this case identifies a new competitive threat to that position.

Dell history

Michael Dell was 19 when he first had the idea of using mail order to cut the costs of selling PCs – no distributor profit margins, no inventory held to meet future customer demand, one centralised customer supply-base per country or region. Within two years, he had launched into Europe. 'We had 22 journalists turn up [for the launch] and 21 said it was a horrible idea,' says Mr Dell. 'It wouldn't work. It was an American concept. I've been underestimated, rejected, describe it any which way you want, but every time we opened new offices round the world, people said it wouldn't work.'

Perhaps journalists do have a point with regard to customer demand. Even today, some 60 per cent of European PCs are bought through shops and other distributors. Only 40 per cent are bought through mail order, though the percentage is higher in the US, where over half are sold by this method. Yet PCs bought by mail order have lower prices than shop PCs. And, at least in the case of Dell, the lower price comes from Dell's lower manufacturing costs.

Dell's strategy of low-cost leadership in the personal computing industry has relied heavily on its operations and manufacturing skills over the last ten years.

Dell's competitive advantage

Dell's advantage is much deeper than the costs it saves by selling via mail order: some rivals, like Gateway Computers, also sell using this method. What sets Dell Computers apart is its manufacturing system. Most of its leading rivals, like Hewlett-Packard/Compaq and IBM, have their PCs made for them in low-cost labour in countries like Taiwan. Dell assembles virtually all its own PCs in-house, thus retaining all the

manufacturing profits. And Dell claims to have the lowest manufacturing costs in the world.

How does it achieve such low costs? By borrowing manufacturing concepts from the car industry and applying them rigorously, with strict monitoring of results.

The Dell value chain

Unlike competitors who may have four *weeks'* stock of component supplies, Dell has only two *hours'* supply. It uses just-in-time delivery to call off components from stocks held locally to its massive Round Rock factory in Texas: the cost of these stocks is borne by its suppliers, not by Dell. It uses similar systems at its main European factory in Limerick, Ireland. This all means that if a supplier, like Intel, launches a new computer chip, then Dell is not caught with high stocks of the old chip. Dell can introduce the new chip immediately and deliver an enhanced product to its customers.

In the Dell manufacturing system, parts come into the factory to fulfil actual customer orders – no PCs are made for stock, so there is no cost of holding stock. The detail of each customer order – RAM size, hard disc storage, CD-format, etc. – is turned into a white bar code label. Each label is then scanned and the relevant parts selected automatically by machine and placed in a box. Workers then assemble the parts, often using clips to fix them rather than screws because clips are faster. In many cases, the parts are colour-coded with the PC frame to make it easier to see where and how to fit them. This *attention to detail* is essential to produce efficient, quality products.

PCs are then individually boxed, addressed and shipped immediately to customers, who can then be billed. There is direct telephone and computer tracking between the placing of the customer order and the factory floor – all the way through to final delivery.

Dell monitoring

Importantly, such a system lends itself to very detailed and constant monitoring of order-taking, supplier delivery, factory production, customer delivery and so on. This highly analytical approach means that *every* worker has detailed targets. These will include sales and profit targets for senior managers, quality and production targets for factory floor workers, ordertaking for sales personnel. Every quarter, every employee is assessed against profit, cost, quality and productivity targets.

This means first that Dell knows where it stands in relation to its annual plan. But it also allows Dell to lay off workers rapidly if demand falls – for example, the company said that it would eliminate 3,000 to 4,000 positions over two quarters after the IT spending slowdown in 2001. It also means that if suppliers, like Intel Corporation, lower the price of computer chips then Dell can lower its PC prices quickly and announce them over the internet: Dell takes over 50 per cent of its orders from the internet in the US and finds that customers compare prices before making decisions.

Employees find the system more interesting because they see the product from start-to-finish. They are not merely a small part of an assembly line. Dell supports this by encouraging those assembling PCs to come up with ideas for better, lower cost ways of assembly.

Dell's competitive advantage – the results

In 2001, Dell reported its operating expenses at 10.2 per cent of sales. This can be compared with 18.3 per cent at Compaq and 20.6 per cent at Hewlett-Packard. This impressive performance has been repeated in more recent years. Essentially, Dell operates a *lean manufacturing system* – see Section 9.4.7.

Figure 9.2

Dell: ten years of profitable growth

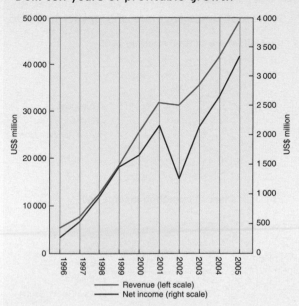

Source: Dell Annual Report and Accounts.

It concentrates on standardised technologies for high-volume production. It does not focus on product innovation. John Mendica, Dell's vice president of client products, formerly worked for Apple Computers. 'At Apple, demand is created through innovative products. At Dell, our innovation is around the business [production] model.'

During 2004, the world PC market grew by around 14 per cent while Dell's sales rose by 21 per cent. Dell's share of the market had grown every year for ten years and stood at 17.8 per cent in 2004. It had taken back market leadership from the merged Hewlett-Packard/Compaq company – see Case 21.4. Essentially, the PC market was price-sensitive and Dell was able to cut its prices because it had a lower manufacturing cost base than its rivals. Thus Dell was able to deliver better value for money to its customers and profits for its shareholders – see Figure 9.2.

New competitive threat for Dell?

In 2004, Dell was still focused particularly on its businesses in the Americas, particularly the US, and in Europe. These two areas accounted for over 80 per cent of its sales and profits – see Figure 9.3. However, there was a possible future problem for Dell, evidenced by its more limited success in the Asia/Pacific region. Dell was only fourth in the Japanese market and was having even more difficulties in another country: China. The company had been forced to stop selling some of its low-end PCs in China. The reason was that Dell's costs and prices in the local Chinese market could not compete with the *very* low costs and prices of local Chinese PC manufacturers.

▶ **CASE STUDY 9.1 continued**

Figure 9.3

Source of Dell's revenue and profits in 2005

(a) Dell: share of total revenue 2005

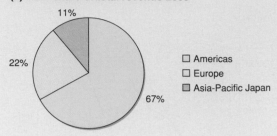

☐ Americas
☐ Europe
☐ Asia-Pacific Japan

(b) Dell: share of operating income 2005

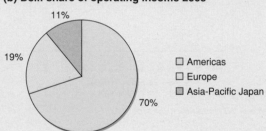

☐ Americas
☐ Europe
☐ Asia-Pacific Japan

Some commentators were wondering what would happen if such Chinese companies began to market their low-priced products worldwide. One analyst said: 'It pierces the aura of invincibility [of the lowest possible costs] that Dell has – [the competitive claim] that it is so efficient that nobody can under-cut Dell.' One Chinese company – called Lenovo – was even bidding to buy the IBM PC brand name in 2005 and expand beyond China – see Case 2.6.

Case questions

1 *What is the competitive advantage of Dell Computers? Is it sustainable? If so, how? How can it compete against Chinese manufacturers?*

2 *What competitive advantages do rival PC companies have? Could they go down the same route as Dell? Why have they avoided this up to the present time? Would you advise companies like Compaq and HP to follow the Dell route? What are the problems, if any?*

3 *In what way is new technology a risk to Dell? Is it the main risk? How can it be overcome, if at all? (See Section 9.2.2 if you want to know more about the significance of this question.)*

9.1 OPERATIONS AND CORPORATE STRATEGY

9.1.1 Why operations matters to corporate strategy

Operations management is an important element of corporate strategy for three reasons:

1 *The rewards from the successful implementation of such strategies can be very high* – for example, *see* Case study 9.1 on Dell and its gains in terms of market leadership and Case study 9.2 on Toyota and the resulting delivery of US$2.2 billion annually to that company.

2 *Major investment in physical and human resources is necessary to achieve the identified results* – for example, *see* the large investments needed in production plant in European steel companies described in Chapter 3.

3 *Fundamental changes in both people and machines need to be addressed by every company* – for example, the Dell Computer case also shows the importance of major changes in these areas if improvement is to be obtained.

As Hill comments,[2] operations strategy has two major contributions to make to corporate strategy:

1 It aims to provide manufacturing and related processes that will give the organisation competitive advantage over competition.

2 It supplies co-ordinated support for products so that they will win sales orders in a competitive market place.

As a result, operations resource analysis is important to strategic development because it can lead to *competitive advantage* in areas such as:

- *adaptable production* to make products that are more precisely tailored to individual customer requirements – *see* Toyota's new flexible manufacturing in Case study 9.2;

- *lower costs* than competitors for the same product performance – *see* Dell Case study 9.1;

- *product quality* that is superior to that of the competition – *see* Case study 9.2;

- *enhanced services and delivery* associated with the product that is superior to rivals – *see* the SuperJumbo Airbus Case study 5.3.

For small companies in particular, operations strategies have sometimes provided a means to tackle larger, more established competitors. Small companies often lack size, market position and proprietary technology. But they can benefit from greater flexibility and operational knowledge gained over time.[3]

9.1.2 Prescriptive and emergent approaches

Traditionally, the operations function has seen itself as using machines to undertake tasks as efficiently as possible. Professionally, it has an engineering and science background and has viewed its tasks as essentially oriented towards the same goal. Its management roots go back to Taylor, Gantt, the Gilbreths and Knoeppel – all pioneers in the field of 'scientific management'.[4] In keeping with these traditions, operations management has often been *prescriptive* in its solutions to strategy issues.

The one-sidedness of this approach has been recognised for many years. In 1945 a number of psychologists formed groups to redress the balance – the Tavistock Institute in London and the Socio-Technical Round Table in the US, for example.[5] The *emergent* strategy approaches of team working and empowerment, as described in the Toyota case study, were pioneered during that period. At the same time, similar Japanese developments were being initiated by people such as Ohno (*see* Case study 9.2) and others. In a similar way German and French social reconstruction was also being initiated that took the same broader view of the nature of work and its social role.

Corporate strategy needs to take both this broader emergent perspective and the important prescriptive approaches. All the topics in this chapter therefore need to be explored from both emergent and prescriptive perspectives.

Key strategic principles

- Operations needs to be considered as part of corporate strategy because of the sustainable competitive advantage it brings, the major investments that may be required and the fundamental changes that may be needed.

- Traditionally, operations has taken a prescriptive approach to strategy issues. It is becoming increasingly recognised that emergent perspectives are also required.

9.2 ANALYSIS OF THE OPERATIONS ENVIRONMENT

Over the last 30 years, there have been many fundamental changes in the environment surrounding operations at the strategic level. Although factors are specific to the organisation itself, three general trends deserve investigation:

1 technological environment;

2 discontinuities in technology;

3 global activity and cost reductions.

9.2.1 Technological environment

Owing to the impact of technology, the world has changed more dramatically over the last 150 years than it did in the previous 2,000 years.[6] Arguably, the pace is increasing: this will have an even greater effect on the corporate environment. Hill[7] identifies five factors that have allowed Far Eastern countries to move ahead of the West, although it should be noted that Germany and France are perhaps less guilty than the others of lagging behind. More recently, it is China in particular that has been setting the pace. But the five strategic opportunities listed below remain substantial in countries like Singapore and Taiwan:

1 the increased pace of technological change;
2 the failure to appreciate the impact of increased world manufacturing capacity. In some markets, there is now substantial excess capacity, which impacts particularly during a downward trade cycle. Shipbuilding is an example. Competition is inevitably keener;
3 lack of willingness to invest in research and development in some countries;
4 top management lack of experience in manufacturing;
5 the production manager's obsession with short-term output, rather than the longer-term strategic viewpoint.

In analysing technological change, the pervasiveness of electronics and the rapid pace of electronic development have led to shorter life cycles in some industries, particularly industrial markets.[8] In addition, better communications have meant that any technological advance is now shared much more quickly around the world, so that it is difficult to sustain technological advantage without patents. At the same time, research and development is becoming more expensive. Analysis of technology will need to examine both the life cycle of the organisation's major products and, at a more fundamental level, the technological resources available to the company.

When the Swiss pharmaceutical company Roche lost its exclusive patents to the tranquilliser Valium in the 1960s, it faced the real problem of how to generate the same profitability from new drug sources. It invested heavily in research for many years and achieved some success. The real breakthrough in technology, however, was its acquisition of 60 per cent of the shares in the US biotechnology company Genentech in 1990 for US$2 billion. This was a company with sales of US$500 million and hardly any profit, but its acquisition opened up a window of new technology opportunity for Roche.

However, not all organisations are at the cutting edge of technological development: many parts of the poorer nations and many markets in richer nations rely on more mundane activities for the production of their goods. For example, technology is unlikely to be the main strategy in some of the more traditional parts of the food industry. While some markets may see rapid technological change, others are better seen as being more mature. Technology strategies need to be seen in the context of industry life cycles (*see* Chapter 3).

9.2.2 Discontinuities in technology

Many students will be aware of the latest powerful, laptop computers with full-colour liquid-crystal displays used to undertake complex calculations. They are battery-driven and cost under US$1000. Compare them with the 'calculating aids' that have been available over the last 40 years:

1950s Slide rules and logarithm tables (and this author is old enough to remember using them at school!)
1960s Mechanical calculating machines, each with a turning lever that was cranked around to undertake the calculations (which this author used as a university undergraduate)
1970s Large, simple electronic calculators with an electronically lit display
1980s The first liquid-crystal displays, but the calculations were still simple.

What is striking is not just the change of technology but the *strategic implications* for those businesses still producing the older versions of the above equipment – for example, the slide rule manufacturers. These companies changed or went out of business many years ago because of a discrete change in the technology – a *discontinuity*.

For shareholders, managers and employees, the impact of a discontinuity on an organisation is significant. It may be caused by anything from a change in fashion to a radically new technology. Essentially, it is a change in the organisation's environment that makes a radical difference to its strategy. One of the more likely reasons for this in the new millennium is a change in technology and its consequent impact on manufacturing. Owing to its radical nature, it is often not possible to predict such a change. It is therefore important not to predict, but rather to develop, a strategy that needs to be followed once a discontinuity has occurred. According to Strebel,[9] there are two distinct phases after such an event has taken place:

1 *Development phase.* Competitors attempt to develop the value of the product, its functionality, uses and benefits. The phase is often characterised by product innovation, new technologies, new suppliers and new entrants. At the *end* of this phase, an industry standard of performance is developed. Strebel points to the example of the IBM personal computer which set a standard in that market. Case 9.1 showed that it is not IBM that has benefited from this standard but Dell Computers.

2 *Consolidation or cost reduction phase.* Having established an industry standard, competition then moves on to produce this at increasingly lower costs. For example, in personal computers, Dell Computers successfully reduced the cost of personal computer components *once the standard was set*. The phase will typically include price wars and similar products. The bargaining power may shift from manufacturers to distributors. Dell has maintained its bargaining power by setting up its *own distribution system* – its computer-by-mail-order operations.

At a later stage, Strebel suggests that there may well be another phase that links back towards development again, as technology makes another breakthrough. The cycle may then repeat itself with periods of *divergence* (the development phase) followed by periods of *convergence* (the consolidation or cost reduction phase). It is important for organisations to understand what phase of the industry development they are engaged in and develop appropriate operations and other strategies.

Naturally, companies will attempt to analyse or, at least, be sensitive to discontinuities as they begin to occur. But in corporate strategy, companies may want to be more *proactive* in forcing the pace of change. Listen to the president of Toyota, Mr Fujio Cho: 'Steady success is good but it can foster serious weakness. Complacency sets in, customer focus declines, creative ideas dry up and, before you know it, you are in trouble.'[10] Toyota leads car industry profitability worldwide.

9.2.3 Global activity and cost reductions

During the 1970s and 1980s, the Italian sportswear company Fila slowly transferred its production from Italy to a range of subcontract manufacturers in the Far East, in countries such as China and Indonesia. Its workforce in Italy declined from 2,500 employees in the 1950s, through 1,800 in the 1960s to around 250 in the mid-1990s. In 1994, a further 670 employees, spread worldwide, were working on design, distribution, marketing and liaising with their manufacturing operations.

The reason for this shift was that it was the only way for Fila to survive. By 1994, it was around eight times more expensive to produce the goods in Italy than in China. The company faced low-priced competition using low-cost labour and could only respond by moving its own operation onto a global basis.

To take another example from the textile trade, Great Future Textiles Ltd of Taipei was described by the World Bank[11] as an important supplier to Modern Fashions GmbH in

Düsseldorf, Germany. Fashions are designed in Taipei, but are made up in a factory near Bangkok, Thailand. The factory imports cloth from Rajasthan, India, cotton from Texas, US, and yarn from Java, Indonesia. The finished product is air-freighted directly from Bangkok to Düsseldorf. This system is operated to take advantage of the *comparative advantages* of the various nations involved and the low barriers to trade that exist in the world textile industry.

In practice, the world is beginning to return to the policies of free trade of the early twentieth century.[12]

There are two main implications for operations strategy:

1 *World trade barriers have been reduced.* These will come down further as the 1993 GATT Uruguay Round of tariff cuts is implemented into the new millennium.

2 *World manufacturing has become more complex.* Some companies now source products in one country and market in another.

More generally, markets around the world have been subject to slower growth and to the attack of new industrial competitor nations, such as China, Vietnam and Malaysia. This has led to pressure on costs, fragmentation in market share, rapid copying of competitors' products and increasing globalisation of market demand. Customers have also become more demanding, especially in terms of quality and value for money. The implication is that production machinery has needed to be more flexible and workers have either been forced to adapt or face the possibility that their company will not survive. Western manufacturers have had to reduce costs and increase quality to remain competitive.

In the consumer electronics market, the two factors identified above have both been at work. Japanese companies such as Sony and Matsushita dominate the world industry. Key components are made in Japan but much of the basic assembly now takes place in the Asian 'Tiger' economies – Singapore, Malaysia, Thailand, Korea and Hong Kong.[13] Components and parts are imported into such countries, assembled using low-cost labour, and exported again. This is done inside the countries, using free-trade zones which do not attract import and export tariffs and controls. As the Japanese yen increased in value against world currencies in the 1980s, such manufacturing strategies became even more important. If the companies had kept their production in Japan, their products would probably have been priced out of world markets. Even at the beginning of the twenty-first century, such differences remain.

The implications for the operations of companies all around the world need to be carefully explored. Importantly, it does not automatically follow that all production should be shifted to countries with low labour costs. Higher-labour-cost countries may have other advantages in terms of higher productivity through better training and knowledge that can offset their labour cost disadvantages. However, such skills are most likely to be best used in the more sophisticated manufacturing operations. In turn, these are likely to be those with higher value added that can support higher labour costs.

Moreover, global activities are only possible for some goods and for services. Other important conditions might include:

- high value-added consumer products that can support the transport costs;
- long shelf-life items that will not perish during transport;
- industrial goods with a high-labour-cost content.

Other considerations apply to *service products*, such as consultancy, restaurants and hotels. If these services require various forms of direct and ongoing contact with the customer, then they are often wholly unsuited to production on the other side of the globe, although they may still be part of a *global services network*.

When considering global manufacturing, operations strategy will need to consider where the balance of cost, services, feasibility and skill is likely to rest over the coming years.

Key strategic principles

● Particularly in the area of operations, new technology can shape future strategy. The pace of change is growing. There are other environmental difficulties facing some companies, especially a lack of awareness of the implications of new manufacturing capacity and the impact of new production techniques.

● Discontinuities, i.e. major changes in technology and markets, can have a substantial impact on strategy. By definition, they are difficult to predict, so organisations should sensitise themselves to the environment in these circumstances. Typically, after a discontinuity, industries go through two phases: divergence, which is a development phase, then convergence, which is a cost reduction or consolidation phase.

● The lowering of trade barriers around the world and the movement of some company production to low-labour-cost countries have had a significant impact on operations strategy in some industries. However, not all industries are affected by such trends.

CASE STUDY 9.2

Toyota: taking out costs and adding value

Over the last 30 years, Toyota Motor Corporation has become one of the top three global car companies, alongside General Motors (US) and Ford (US). Its rise centres on twin strategies related to operations and marketing. This case study concentrates mainly on its operations successes but also touches briefly on marketing, since the two areas are interlinked. The Toyota operations strategies have been copied around the world, though rarely with the same success.

Background

In the year to end-June 2004, Toyota produced and sold over 6.5 million vehicles around the world.[14] The company had only started car production in the 1930s. Even in the early 1950s, it was still only averaging 18,000 vehicles per annum.[15] The increase in production and sales between 1950 and 2004 was, by any standards, remarkable – Figure 9.4 shows the recent

Figure 9.4

Toyota's annual production and sales 2004

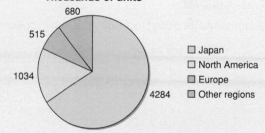

(a) Vehicle production by region 2004
Thousands of units

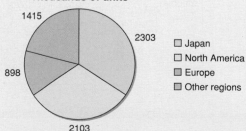

(b) Vehicle sales by region 2004
Thousands of units

Toyota has led the world over the last twenty years in innovative operations strategy and this has produced outstanding company results.

► **CASE STUDY 9.2 continued**

data for 2004. Toyota's strategic problem was that it was a tiny company competing against large competitors. The only way that it could survive was by finding new, flexible production methods that could be used by smaller companies. 'The Toyota Production System originated as a means of achieving mass production efficiencies with small production volumes' (Toyota Annual Report and Accounts 1998). Importantly, even in 2004, the major Toyota production location was Japan – from a strategy perspective, this raises important questions about how long its Japanese factories can remain low-cost centres of production.

Many of the production successes between 1950 and 1980 have been accredited to the Toyota Production System and its chief engineer during that time, Taiichi Ohno. He started experimenting to improve production in the late 1940s, but it took many years to develop the systems described below, such as *kaizen* and *kanban*, and to have them widely adopted across the company. Even in the 1990s, experimentation and change were still taking place to improve production. Indeed, such change was by definition an *integral* part of the process of achieving production improvements: it was called 'continual improvement'[16] or *kaizen* in Japanese.

During the same period of time, Toyota operated a separate marketing company that essentially sold Toyota production. It was headed by Shotaro Kimaya, who had trained in US marketing methods after the Second World War. He is credited with many marketing innovations in the company during the 1960s and 1970s. They slowly propelled Toyota to market leadership in Japan, with over 40 per cent of the market. Among other initiatives, he set up dealer networks, cheap car finance for customers and a strong, dedicated salesforce. He also developed Toyota exports so that by the 1970s around 40 per cent of all production was being sold outside Japan, especially in the US.[17] Toyota's Camry model is today the biggest single-selling car in the US.

Operations initiatives at Toyota between 1950 and 1980

During this period, Toyota introduced a whole series of operations initiatives that assisted car and truck production – essentially a repetitive, mass-manufacturing process. The new procedures were designed to achieve three main objectives:

1 to reduce costs;
2 to increase quality;
3 to control the production process more tightly, thus reducing the inputs needed and making the company more responsive to market demand.

The first two objectives had an immediate impact on added value in the plant; the last had an indirect influence on added value. To achieve these objectives, Toyota had a number of key operations strategies:

● *Design*. More costs can be taken out at the design phase of operations than at any other stage. For example, Toyota has consistently used research and development to undertake such tasks as combining components so that they can be produced by one process rather than two.
● *Kaizen*. This means 'continuous improvement' across every aspect of production. Toyota's engineers invented this approach to operations strategy.[18] It is reflected in Toyota's attention to detail, which is legendary.[19] The result of one stage in *kaizen* is shown in Figure 9.5.
● *Kanban system*. This was originally a system of coloured cards on the factory floor that were associated with the

Figure 9.5

Axle-stand production line at a car accessory factory

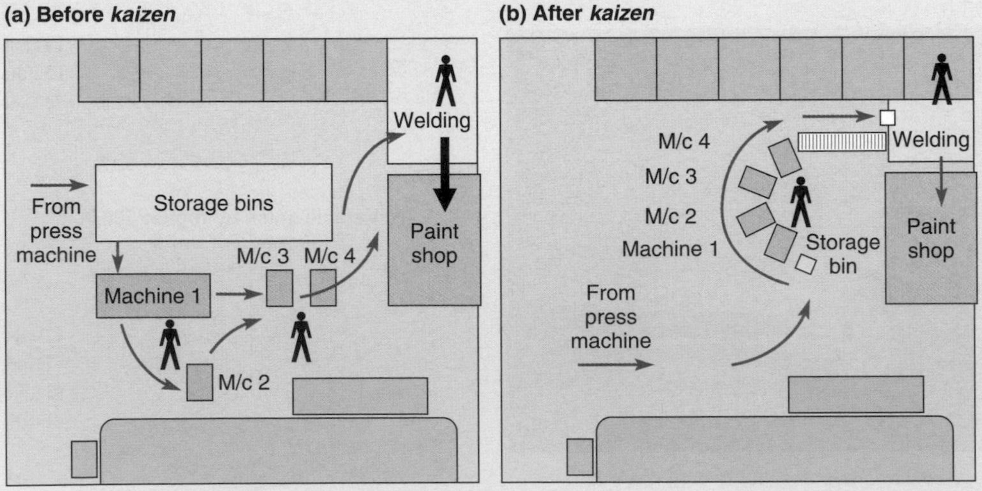

Source: *Financial Times*, 4 Jan 1994.

amount of stock available for production. These were used to signal when stock needed to be replenished and provided a simple but extremely effective visual system, both to tell operatives when to reorder and to keep stocks controlled and low up to that time.

- *Layout*. Instead of long, linear layouts for production lines, cellular layout arrangements of plant machinery were designed. They allowed workers to operate a number of machines and allowed them to work in teams to provide support and back-up more effectively. The teams had to be flexible in their willingness to operate any machinery in the layout and needed to be highly trained to complete the varied range of tasks. Some other Japanese companies, such as Nissan, have had difficulty in achieving the same results,[20] probably because of the sophistication needed to operate this system.

- *Supplier relationships*. Close co-operation was obtained and maintained with a small group of leading suppliers to Toyota. It was used to work jointly on cost reduction schemes and seek higher quality from bought-in components. This was particularly important in the value-added process at Toyota because the company had a higher proportion of bought-in items from suppliers than its main international rivals. This arrangement applied to other companies in Japan but was extended when Toyota opened its plants overseas – for example, in 1993 at Burnasten in the UK.[21]

- *Just-in-time systems*. Toyota pioneered the arrival of stock from suppliers using methods which involve close contacts with suppliers. When stocks in the factory run low, they are replaced by stocks from suppliers very rapidly, using computer linkages and daily or even more frequent deliveries – *just in time for production*. The clear advantage to companies such as Toyota is that their capital investment in stock is permanently kept lower than otherwise. The company is not unique in the use of such systems.

Each of these developments was equally important at Toyota. All contributed to the general improvement in the production efficiency of the company.

By the early 1980s, the Toyota Production System was being described and recommended for introduction into Western companies.[22] Japanese rivals such as Nissan and Honda also attempted to introduce the same or similar schemes. During the 1990s, the Toyota plant at Takaoda was compared as a model of production with the worst North American plant.[23] Toyota was used as a pointer to the changes required in the US. However, there are cultural and industry structure problems that make complete adoption of the Toyota system difficult: for example, team working and flexibility may be closer to the Japanese model of society than to Western cultures.[24] Toyota itself saw the techniques it had developed as being a set of evolving production strategies with no single ideal solution: *kaizen* meant what it said.[25]

Production at Toyota into the new millennium

Over the last ten years, Toyota experienced real problems in the macroeconomic environment. They were:

- Downturn in worldwide demand for cars, including for the first time ever a drop in demand in its key Japanese home market;

- Significant rise in the value of the Japanese yen, making exports from Japan more expensive.

These developments prompted a major reappraisal of its production methods at the company and a redoubling of efforts to achieve new, lower costs. All Japanese car manufacturers, including Toyota, were forced to shift in a major way the focus of their operations strategy from rapid model changes to cost reductions.[26] Toyota responded to the pressures by setting up a major cost reduction programme.

By 1994, the company was claiming that it had found savings at an annual rate of US$1.5 billion.[27] But it was still not satisfied. By 2004, this had risen to US$ 2.1 billion.[28] Two recent examples of Toyota's production strategy:

- In 2001, Toyota announced a totally new programme called 'Construction of Cost Competitiveness for the 21st Century' or *CCC21*, for short. The relentless drive for improvement would be renewed. The company was looking again at every aspect of design, manufacturing, procurement and fixed costs. This was expected to lead to better utilisation rates for manufacturing equipment and less 'expenditure on human resources'. But this will not necessarily mean sacking workers, which is against the Toyota tradition. It may mean that some of the workers on temporary contracts will not have their contracts renewed, but the company was keen to avoid even this, if possible.

- In 2004, Toyota began its new UMR (Unit & Material Manufacturing Reform) Strategy. 'This project sets and innovates toward production engineering targets on a different order of magnitude from anything tried before,' claimed Toyota. The company gave the example of the simplification of the moulds used in manufacturing car parts. All car production is centred on moulding – die-casting moulds, forging moulds, plastic injection moulds, etc. If it is possible to simplify moulding techniques, then it is possible to simply the entire production process. Toyota was able to re-engineer its moulding techniques so that moulds were reduced to between one-third and one-tenth their former sizes. UMR was also used to shorten the machining and assembly lines for some of the Toyota engines. UMR also had benefits for overseas plants. 'Through UMR, we are creating a production system for overseas plants that overcomes differences in experience, location and language and enables highly efficient production of in-house components of the same quality the world over. By implementing the UMR initiative, we aim to strengthen our global competitiveness.'

Some would question how Toyota could have been so efficient during the 1990s if it was still able to generate such massive savings in recent years. Toyota has always had problems transferring its production system beyond its factories to other areas of the value chain. It had some success with its immediate suppliers but struggled both with raw material suppliers and with the marketing/selling end of the value chain.[29] These difficulties were then compounded as the Toyota Production System was subjected to the pressures of worldwide demand, the implications for production at its factories and a slump in Japanese domestic demand in the late 1990s.

▶ **CASE STUDY 9.2 continued**

Nevertheless, personal and team motivation remain an important part of the Toyota system.

Toyota's global vision on production and vehicle development

According to the *2010 Global Vision* Toyota document released in April 2002,[30] the company aimed to increase its production by 50 per cent over the next nine years. It was also seeking to increase its market share by the same percentage. If it was successful, it would increase its market share from 10 to 15 per cent and would challenge General Motors for the title of the largest car company in the world. The company would seek to grow its share, particularly in North America, while retaining its dominance in Japan. It was also seeking major growth in India and China, possibly through joint ventures. It had already entered into technical co-operation alliances with rival companies such as PSA Peugeot Citroën to produce a new small car in the Czech Republic. It had also made a similar agreement with two local car companies in China, FAW Group Corporation on cars and Guangzhou Automobiles on car engines.[31]

In 2005, Toyota's president became concerned that 'the real meaning of Global Vision 2010 is often not fully understood . . . I originally put the 15% target forward as a common ambition that would unite employees worldwide as they pursued it and give them the impetus to win out in fiercely competitive markets. In my view, companies that lose their appetite for growth stagnate.'[32]

One production and marketing strategy that Toyota has embraced is the development of more environmentally friendly vehicles. Its Hybrid-Vehicle Strategy over the last ten years has led to the Prius, one of the first cars to have an engine that switches between petrol and electric power depending on the road situation. In its first year 1998, the Prius sold 50,000 units. By 2004, this had risen to 300,000 units per year and sales were still growing fast. To encourage wider use of the technology (and arguably to establish it as the industry standard), Toyota was offering its patented hybrid systems to rival car manufacturers. It claimed to be a world leader in environmental engine technology: 'We are convinced that hybrid technology will become the core technology in the creation of the ultimate eco car.'

The one strategy that Toyota remained totally against was acquisition of a rival car company.[33] The reason was simple:

it would be impossible to introduce and gain the benefits of the Toyota Production System that was the main competitive advantage of the company.

Case questions

1 *Using the definition of corporate strategy in Chapter 1, identify which of the operations strategies undertaken by Toyota (kaizen, kanban, design, etc.) have a corporate strategy perspective and which are mainly the concern of operations management alone.*

2 *Examining the Toyota Production System overall, to what extent do you judge this to be critical to the company's strategic success? If you believe it to be critical, then how does this fit with strategy theories that lay stress on the market aspects of corporate strategy, such as Porter's Five Forces Model? If you believe operations to be relatively unimportant, then how do you explain the remarkable success of Toyota globally since the 1950s?*

3 *Some commentators argue that it is relatively easy for market leaders such as Toyota to undertake the investment in machinery and training programmes to achieve strategic success but more difficult for smaller organisations. Do small companies have anything to learn from Toyota? If so, what?*

4 *The case describes how Toyota remains ambitious to take global market leadership by 2010. Do you believe that the company will really overtake Ford and General Motors by this time?*

STRATEGIC PROJECT

Although Toyota has led the way, others have followed. Toyota is not the most efficient manufacturing plant in Europe – that honour goes to the Nissan plant in Sunderland, UK. You can follow this up by investigating why and how Nissan was able to be so successful in the UK. There are some relevant websites listed in the companion case to this: Cases 19.3 and 19.4 about global car manufacturing.

9.3 **THE ROLE OF OPERATIONS IN ADDING VALUE AND ACHIEVING SUSTAINABLE COMPETITIVE ADVANTAGE**

9.3.1 Value added, competitive advantage and operations strategy

Operations strategy has two major structural constraints:

1 Operations resources take time to plan and build: for example, many factories take years.

2 Once installed, they are difficult and expensive to change: for example, bulldozing the completed factory is not an easy option.

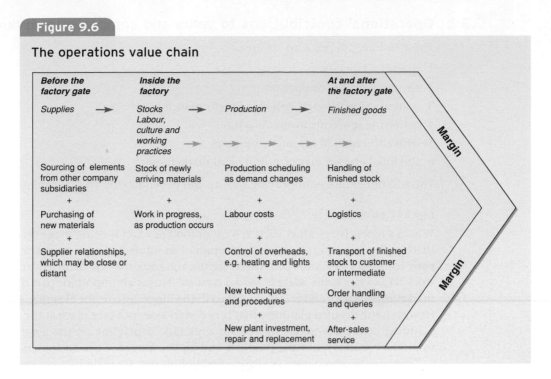

Figure 9.6

The operations value chain

Before the factory gate	Inside the factory	Production	At and after the factory gate
Supplies	Stocks Labour, culture and working practices	Production	Finished goods
Sourcing of elements from other company subsidiaries	Stock of newly arriving materials	Production scheduling as demand changes	Handling of finished stock
+	+	+	+
Purchasing of new materials	Work in progress, as production occurs	Labour costs	Logistics
+		+	+
Supplier relationships, which may be close or distant		Control of overheads, e.g. heating and lights	Transport of finished stock to customer or intermediate
		+	+
		New techniques and procedures	Order handling and queries
		+	+
		New plant investment, repair and replacement	After-sales service

Margin / Margin

Moreover, resource analysis in the operations area is *complex* because it often involves the bulk of the organisation's assets and employees.

Ideally, operations strategy needs to be split into a series of separate, but interlinked, analyses. Each of these would cover the different parts of the operations process and would be different for each organisation. Porter's *value chain* from Chapter 6 can be used as a starting point for such studies (*see* Case 9.1 and Figure 9.6). Importantly, much of this is *not* corporate strategy, in the sense that the detailed day-to-day operations are outside the definition of corporate strategy. Nevertheless, corporate strategy will set the *focus*, *agenda* and *priorities* in these areas – for example, on issues such as which customers take priority, how quality is improved, the relationships between subsidiaries of the same company. The strategies are then translated into decisions that are subsequently followed in detail by the managers concerned. The remarks of the president of Toyota are an excellent example of strategic thinking here – *see* Case 9.2.

When dealing with strategy in such tangible areas as building a new factory or producing an existing product, corporate strategy might be primarily *prescriptive* rather than *emergent* in its approach: after all, the factory or product is a physical entity. In practice, the corporate strategy of operations resources has elements of *both*.

- After the strategic decision has been taken to build a new factory, the actual building process will typically be lengthy. The decision to embark on this process can only be based on assumptions and predictions about the future. Moreover, in existing factories, sales estimates are often required in advance of the sales order actually being taken, so that production can be scheduled smoothly and at the lowest costs. This is essentially *prescriptive* in its strategic approach.

- However, after the new factory has been built, and certainly in existing sites, many aspects of the production process rely heavily on worker attitudes, culture and motivation. Typically, change is undertaken in small steps. Some companies even refer to this process as 'continuous improvement', with no specified final end-point. This is essentially *emergent* in its strategic direction.

9.3.2 Operations' contributions to value and competitive advantage

These can be grouped into six areas:

1 market adaptability;
2 winning against competition;
3 adding value through enhanced performance or service;
4 achieving low costs in manufacture;
5 delivering human resource objectives;
6 the link between manufacturing and marketing.

The additional task of improving quality and dependability will be explored in Chapter 12.

Market adaptability

Where a repetitive product such as a car or food product is being made by mass production, there is usually a need to match production of an individual type, brand, model, colour, etc., with consumer demand. Otherwise, significant costs may be incurred in holding finished stock. *Production needs adapt to market demand.* This is an important part of the production/marketing interface and is well described in the literature (*see*, for example, Hill[34] and Wild[35]). However, the detailed planning that is necessary does not take place at the level of corporate planning. It is a day-to-day or week-to-week task, depending on the length of time it takes to produce variations in the products and on the nature of the customers.

There are two corporate strategy aspects of market adaptability:

1 *The extent to which an organisation will wish to respond to individual customer needs.* In essence, this will depend on two balancing factors:

- the size of the customer's individual order – whether it is sufficiently large to justify the time and costs of producing a product that is specialised to that customer; and

- the capacity and adaptability of the production machinery to reduce the costs involved.

2 *The contribution that market adaptability might make to beating competition.* Some customers may find the option of customised production highly attractive. Companies, like Toyota, that have been able to achieve this possess highly valuable resources that deliver sustainable competitive advantage.

Importantly, the technology of market adaptability is becoming one of the most important factors in car industry strategy in recent years. A major method of developing competitive advantage – especially if the company is one of the smaller car companies – is the use of *flexible manufacturing techniques*, i.e. to adapt the car production line to adapt to changes in the market. Honda car factories in Japan and the UK have become particularly skilled at such production processes.[36]

Winning against competition

The development of manufacturing strategy to win orders against competition is an important aspect of operations resource analysis. Hill[37] explains that this process may be market-led but manufacturing has a major role in two areas: contributing to the debate and delivering the successful products that beat competitors. The resource-based view recognises the importance of operations resources in this task.

Adding value through enhanced performance or service

We explored this in Chapter 6. Many of the operations areas are directly concerned with adding value to the supplies that are brought into the company. Although the detail of such matters does not come within corporate strategy, the basic arrangements made by the organisation are at the centre of the strategy process.

Value can be added to a product not just by physical production but also by the performance or the quality of the service that is related to the product. Technology can also contribute to product added value by providing new opportunities and variations from competition. The resource-based view lays special emphasis on the uniqueness of operations' core resources.

Achieving low costs in manufacture

As the Toyota case showed, many of the strategies in the operations area have the basic objective of achieving low costs. For the sake of clarity, it is important to distinguish here between the *objective* of cutting costs – for example, in order to raise profits at Toyota – and the *strategy* by which this is achieved – for example, by redeploying labour in the Toyota plant. The resource-based view supports this approach but lays greater emphasis on finding ways of doing this that are owned by the company and not easily available to competitors.

Delivering human resources objectives

This objective is naturally a part of the human resource analysis of the company. In addition, it appears here for two reasons:

1 the large number of people often employed in the operations function;
2 the crucial need, in many instances, to obtain the co-operation of such people in order to deliver the other objectives.

The resource-based view also highlights this area for its contribution to the special *knowledge and skills* often possessed by those working in the company. These may form the basis of competitive advantage, as well as providing job satisfaction.

The link between manufacturing and marketing

From the above factors, it will be evident that successful operations strategy demands that there is a strong link between these two functional areas. Hill[38] lists five steps to achieving this:

Step 1   Define corporate objectives.

Step 2   Determine marketing strategies to meet these objectives.

Step 3   Assess how different products win orders against competitors.

Step 4   Establish the most appropriate mode to manufacture these sets of products – *process choice*.

Step 5   Provide the manufacturing infrastructure required to support production.

It is essential to see the steps as *sequential*, but also *interactive*, with feedback loops connecting the first three in particular.[39]

Key strategic principles

- Operations faces two structural constraints: the length of time to build new resources and the difficulty of altering them once they are installed. For these reasons, it is useful to apply the value chain concept to the process and analyse every element individually.

- It is essential to clarify the purposes to be served by operations and technologies strategies, because they are complex and may need to be prioritised.

- Market adaptability, winning against competition, added value through enhanced performance or service, cutting the costs of manufacture, improved quality and human resource objectives are the main elements that need to be considered. Many of these will contribute to the sustainable competitive advantage of the organisation, according to the resource-based view.

- The five steps that enable marketing and manufacturing strategy to link together are a vital part of the development of operations analysis. They will determine the manufacturing processes and infrastructure required for the corporate strategy.

9.4 OPERATIONS ACTIVITIES AND CORPORATE STRATEGY

In examining this area from a corporate strategy perspective, the difficulty is the large number of possible strategies that are available. There are dangers for the analytical process from:

- becoming immersed in the detail that is important to those undertaking the strategy but largely irrelevant to the corporate strategist;
- failing to identify those strategies that will have a *real* impact on the future direction of the business, as against those that are useful but not crucial.

Corporate strategy really needs to confine itself to an awareness of the areas to be probed and a sense of priority regarding the areas that will deliver the organisation's objectives. A strong analysis will start by considering this matter rather than plunging into long lists of specific strategies. As guidance, the criteria shown in Table 9.1 are suggested. With these words of caution, we can now turn to consider the areas that may need to be analysed in more detail. We tackle this under several headings that broadly follow the way that value is added during the manufacturing process and link with basic texts in this area:[40]

- Make or buy?
- Supplier relationships
- Manufacturing strategy
- Product design prior to manufacture
- Factory layout and processes
- Logistics and transport
- Lean thinking
- Human resource implications
- International manufacturing
- Conclusions

Table 9.1

Criteria for the relevance of manufacturing strategy to corporate strategy

Strategic area	Issues to be explored
Organisation objectives	Possible impact? Some strategies may be more important than others
Added value	To what extent does the strategy add significant value?
'What if?' questions	Explore what would happen if certain conditions were changed and assess the impact on objectives, e.g. what would happen if we were able to reduce supply prices by 10 per cent? Would this have a substantial impact or not make much difference?
Key factors for success	In Chapter 6, we explored this area. These factors may well guide the selection of the most appropriate manufacturing strategies
Human resource implications	Operations strategy often involves change in working practices, responsibilities and reporting relationships. Some strategies may be difficult to operate unless these human factors are explored against the organisation's human resource objectives

9.4.1 Make or buy?

Instead of buying products from suppliers, some manufacturers will choose to make the products themselves. The strategic decision on the best route to take is complex but can be summarised as:

Make, when:

- the company has specialised needs;
- it needs to have a really secure source of supply; or
- the cost of supply is a high part of the total costs.

Buy, when:

- the company wants to maintain flexibility in its sources of supply;
- the company has only limited skills and resources in the supplier's area.

The decision is clearly related to *vertical integration* of the organisation back into its suppliers. However, in the case of such integration, the company would actively market the products that formerly came from its supplier, as against merely supplying its own factories.

Analysis will clearly need to examine not just the costs of each alternative make-or-buy decision but also the skills, resources needed and broader strategic direction of the company. It will also look at what competitors do and explore the reasons for any differences.

9.4.2 Supplier relationships

Two different and opposing trends[41] can be observed in the strategies adopted by manufacturing companies:

1 *Closer relationships with suppliers*. As used by Toyota, this will involve sharing technical and development information in order to lower the cost of the finished product. It implies closer co-operation over many years, often with a small number of key suppliers. Inevitably, some of the value added is passed from the manufacturer to the supplier. However, it can help to drive down costs overall and raise quality.

2 *More distant relationships with suppliers*. This will involve aggressive negotiating to obtain the lowest possible price for an agreed specification. For example, Saab Cars (part-owned by General Motors) actually telephoned its suppliers of car mirrors twice a day for two weeks requesting lower quotes before deciding.[42] In this case, supplier relationships are at arm's length and obtain the lowest prices. However, there may be only limited involvement in the development process and the contributions to quality improvement are strictly defined rather than a joint ideas process. This supplier system is used by General Motors and Volkswagen, Germany (who recruited the GM purchasing director in 1994).

There is some recent evidence that the first of the two options above is becoming the preferred strategy.[43] As described in Section 9.2.3, there is also increasing *globalisation* in the sourcing of supplies. This makes the purchasing task more complex and demanding.

9.4.3 Manufacturing strategy

To analyse this area, it is useful to examine the six basic areas of manufacturing strategy. In addition to the make-or-buy decision above, there are five other key areas:[44]

1 *Factory location and size*. Most organisations start with an existing configuration, from one site to several. For example, Ford Motors has a number of plants in several different European countries; each has different products and capacities and many are linked together in the production chain.

2 *Processes.* Each factory will have certain types of equipment and procedures for making products, dealing with variations in demand and so on. For example, Toyota makes different models at different plants; each plant has different production equipment relevant to the models at that location. Each factory has links with sales to vary demand accordingly.

3 *Production capacity.* From a strategic perspective, the capacity of the plant to meet customer demand is an important consideration. Clearly, in the long term this will change as markets grow and decline. In addition, there are short-term plant capacity scheduling issues which are largely outside the interest of corporate strategy. For example, Chapter 3 explored the strategic implications of excess production capacity in the European steel industry.

4 *Manufacturing infrastructure.* Planning and control of stocks, quality, work-in-progress inventories and the flow of goods are vital to factories. The overall principles by which this is done are part of corporate strategy but the detail is not. For example, Case study 9.1 on Dell showed how the company introduced the principles and then allowed the factory floor to follow them up.

5 *Links with other functions.* Manufacturing has started to move towards production that meets *precise* customer demand through *flexible manufacturing*. This is only possible from close links with sales. The *range of the products* that are manufactured will also depend on such links. In both cases, there are often economies of scale from manufacturing a limited range in large quantities, but this may not match market demand. With new modern flexible equipment and telecommunications links, a new strategy may be to introduce shorter production runs and rapid changeover to other products. For older plant and some manufacturing processes, a *compromise* is needed and this is a strategic decision. For example, the prime objective of a factory which regularly produces six months' supply of some confectionery lines, such as Hazelnut Brittle, is to reduce the cost of its production, rather than the cost of its finished goods stock and the fresh quality of its finished product.

Overall, Skinner[45] comments that:

● It is not necessary to be the lowest-cost producer – quality and service being more important for some customers – but this implies an understanding of competitors and how they compete on costs, quality and service.

● Factories need to *compromise* regarding a number of variables. For example, the flexible, low-volume product with frequent model changes needs to be balanced by the lower costs of large-volume production runs and the stockholding that may result. Another example is the need for investment to increase plant capacity against the need to house it in a new building because existing ones are full.

● Simple repetitive tasks in mass manufacturing are more likely to lead factories down the cost experience curve (*see* Chapter 13).

9.4.4 Product design prior to manufacturing

In some cases, up to 70 per cent of the cost of manufacturing a product is determined at the design stage – that is, before the product ever reaches the factory.[46] The reason is that it is at the design stage that major savings can be made on components, plant and procedures. It is more difficult to make them once products have reached the factory floor because of the inflexibility of installed machinery and the high cost of changing over time.

Design procedures might include analysing the product for the *number of parts* it contains: the smaller the number, the quicker it will be to assemble. Procedures might also cover *methods of assembling the product.* For example, by careful design, it may be possible to put the product together without using a machine to grip or hold the product (commonly called a *jig*). The advantage of such a procedure is that any variation in the product might otherwise involve resetting the jig, which takes unproductive time and adds no value to the product. Clearly, the detail of such procedures is not part of corporate strategy but the *principle* of careful and adequate expenditure on design is vital.

In addition, efficiency in the design procedures themselves has become an important element in the process. It can take years to design some products, with all the consequent costs involved. If time can be saved, this reduces the cost of the process. For example, Renault Cars (France) announced a new design and development facility in 1995 costing US$1.22 billion.[47] The aim was to reduce design time from 58 months to 38 months for a new car launch in the year 2000. The facility's current cost per car was between US$1 billion and US$5 billion, depending on the model: this would be reduced by US$200 million per model simply by producing each design more quickly.

Again, analysis of this topic needs a study of *competition*. For example, Renault may have invested a large absolute amount in design but comparison with the amounts invested by other car companies would:

● show whether it would improve the French company's competitive position; or

● simply mean that Renault was catching up with others, especially some Japanese car companies.

9.4.5 Factory layout and procedures

Within an existing factory installation, it is possible to make substantial cost savings and other improvements by changes in the factory layout. For example, Case study 9.2 showed how changes in factory procedures at Toyota could have a dramatic effect on production costs.

9.4.6 Logistics and transport

Once the product is ready to leave the factory, there are further decisions on two areas:

1 *Logistics* – where to hold the finished product, in what quantity and with what delivery schedule to customers.

2 *Transport* – what product to send, in what economic delivery quantity, by what transport method and from what location.

Essentially, these decisions involve a balance between the customers, who might like small amounts of the product frequently, and the costs involved in such lengthy and detailed procedures. According to Christopher,[48] there are five basic elements to balance in the analytical process:

1 *Facility decisions*. These involve deciding where warehouses and factories are to be located. Clearly, this is a long-term issue.

2 *Inventory decisions*. Stockholding has a cost but may be necessary to provide adequate customer service.

3 *Communications decisions*. Information is essential to deliver the correct goods to the customer. Thus, ordering, processing and invoicing goods all form part of the essential information. A system for handling normal customer queries and complaints is also needed.

4 *Utilisation decisions*. Pallets, containers and other means of transporting the goods need to be resolved.

5 *Transport decisions*. The method of transport, ownership, leasing or hiring of vehicles all need resolution; the choice of road, rail, ship and air may all be key decisions.

As Lynch comments,[49] the balance of these issues will vary with the type of industry, as well as with the customer. It will also depend on competitors and the level of service that they are offering. Industry distribution costs for the above have been published and provide a basis for comparison for national and international expansion.

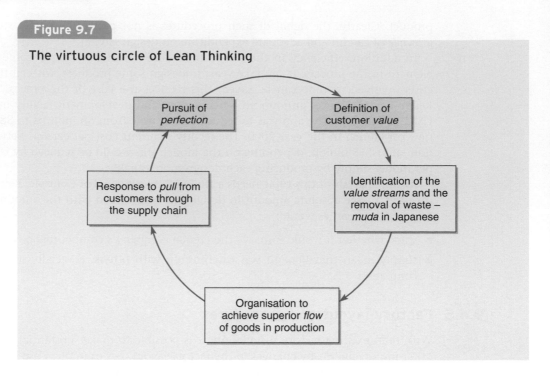

Figure 9.7

The virtuous circle of Lean Thinking

9.4.7 Lean Thinking[50]

Deriving many of its principles from studies of car companies like Toyota, *Lean Thinking* has become a well-established part of operations strategy. The underlying concept is one of *value*, as perceived by the customer and defined by the performance of the product. Competitive advantage derives from the application by managers of the five Lean Thinking principles (*see* Figure 9.7) which will deliver superior value to customers and superior profits to companies. The word 'lean' is used to emphasise the rational concentration on the essentials and the trimming of all waste in the development of operations strategy. The concepts of value and the value chain were explored in Chapter 6, but need to be reconsidered here from the perspective of the value delivered to the *customer*. The other concepts are explored elsewhere in this chapter.

9.4.8 Human resource implications

When the Norwegian engineering company Kvaerner acquired the Govan shipyard in Scotland in 1988, it needed to boost productivity dramatically.[51] Part of the change came through the investment of US$52 million in the yard by the new owners. However, just as important, the company introduced new procedures for working that involved many of the concepts described above. They involved:

- devolved responsibility;
- frequent progress reports to management;
- improved internal communications;
- changed staff attitudes;
- shared responsibility and commitment;
- joint management and workers' committee to monitor progress.

In each of the cases, there was a significant human resource element that needed to be analysed during the formative phase of the corporate strategy process. The impact on workers, their attitudes and the degree of co-operation required are all important elements to be estimated in assessing the feasibility of strategy. Specifically, worker participation is a key element in many aspects of manufacturing strategy.

9.4.9 International manufacturing

Manufacturing strategies have been developed that cover *regions* of the world, such as the North American Free Trade Area, Association of South-East Asian Nations and the European Union. As an example of pan-regional activity, the *European single market* was designed to help deliver economies of scale, reduce excess production capacity, integrate operations across the EU and deliver significant cost savings to companies.

9.4.10 Conclusions

There are some broader lessons to be learned from the research. The increased standardisation has allowed some companies to tackle such problems as:

- overcapacity in production;
- stock reduction;
- critical production mass from fewer locations;
- more efficient transport and logistics operations;
- better planning, processes and procedures.

To summarise operations strategy, there are ten guidelines for analysing the operations and technology manufacturing strategies of organisations. These are shown in Exhibit 9.1.

Exhibit 9.1

Ten guidelines for analysing operations and technology manufacturing strategy

1 Does the company buy or make all its supplies? How do competitors handle this decision?

2 What relationship does the company have with its suppliers? Distant or close? Why?

3 Where is value added in the production process? What stage of the production process is really important? How does this compare with competition?

4 What is the role of technology? High? Low? What investment normally takes place in R&D? How does this compare with competition?

5 How does at least one competitor organise its production? What factories? Stock levels? Age of factories, plant and machinery? Investment programmes? Comparative costs?

6 How is production organised in our own factories? What factories and departments are involved? What machines and workflow? How old are the machines and what is their capacity? What are the costs of production? How do the organisation, its machinery and costs compare with competition?

7 How are stocks organised and controlled before, during and after production? How does competition organise this area?

8 What is the style of operation? Centre-dominated? Co-operative with workforce?

9 How are links organised with other departments? Are they good or poor?

10 Is there organised labour? And what is it role and style? Co-operation or conflict?

Key strategic principles

- Before starting on a detailed analysis of manufacturing strategy, it is useful to establish what areas are particularly important. Six tests can be employed to assist this process but it is essentially a question of judgement.

- Whether a company makes or buys in its products will depend on the balance between the costs and benefits of the two routes. It is useful to explore what competitors do in this area.

- Supplier relationships can be close or distant. This will depend on the company's basic management style and culture. There are no conclusive reasons for choosing one approach.

- Manufacturing strategy is complex and depends on a number of interrelated factors: factory location, size, production capacity and infrastructure. In addition, links with other functions such as sales are important in determining both efficiencies and customer service. Comparison with competition is an important element in the analysis.

- With many products, greater cost savings are achieved during the design stage of the process than during the subsequent procedures. Expenditure in this area usually has a clear positive payback. Competitor expenditure and effort in this area needs also to be analysed.

- Factory layout and procedures need to be governed by attention to detail and co-operation with the workforce. Coupled with specific techniques, the corporate strategy interest lies mainly in initiating the task rather than in the detail that follows.

- Logistics and transport need careful planning, both to reduce costs and to provide adequate service to customers. The level of service that competitors offer will be a factor in deciding the optimal configuration.

- The human resource implications of all the above need to be considered during the analysis phase of corporate strategy, not later.

CASE STUDY 9.3

Cost reduction strategy at Bajaj, the India-based motorcycle maker

Bajaj Auto is India's biggest scooter and motorcycle manufacturer, yet it faces intense competition from some of the world's leading scooter and motorcyle manufacturers. This case explores how it was using supplier strategies originally developed by General Motors (US) to reduce its costs and remain competitive.

In 1998, Bajaj Auto – India's biggest scooter and motorcycle manufacturer – was struggling to shake off a strong challenge from Honda, Suzuki and Piaggio in its home market. The family-owned company, which lacks the technological resources of its competitors, had to compensate by watching its expenses. 'We must remain the lowest cost producer in the world,' says Rahul Bajaj, the chairman.

But no matter how hard Bajaj tries to control costs and improve productivity at its plants near Pune, in West India, the incremental savings are a sliver of the sale price of its bikes. This is because most of the costs are incurred before the components enter Bajaj's factory gates. 'In-house costs make up about 10 to 12 per cent of the sales price,' says

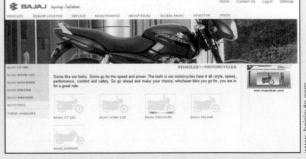

Bajaj has led Indian operations strategy over the last ten years and is now exporting this to other parts of Asia.

Sangiv Bajaj, Rahul Bajaj's younger son and general manager of corporate finance. Advertising and distribution costs account for a further 3 to 4 per cent. By contrast, 'about 65 per cent of the sales price comes from costs outside our direct control'. This can rise to 75 per cent for new models. Bajaj has recently realised that further big cost savings are more likely to come from its suppliers than from the manufacturing process.

GM-style supplier management

Sangiv Bajaj is heading an effort to introduce US-style supply chain management, using General Motors as a model. It is a task for which he is well suited. A trained engineer, he went into the finance department because his elder brother, Rajiv, had already been groomed to take over the core manufacturing responsibilities. 'I am in the wrong job,' he jokes. But in this instance, engineering expertise helps him to understand where costs can be trimmed.

Bajaj, which produces 1.3 million vehicles a year, has about 900 direct tier-1 suppliers. According to the GM model, it should have 80. Many of them are small, low-technology, family-run businesses with poor productivity and slack quality control.

'We need to identify who the good vendors are, reduce the number of vendors and give them a bigger share of the pie,' says Sangiv Bajaj. Then, he adds, the company will try to negotiate lower prices for higher volumes. As in the case of GM, Bajaj hopes to work with its suppliers to improve 'quality and reliability'. The company aims to help its chosen suppliers invest in new equipment and improve productivity over the long term, bearing in mind 'our future requirements'.

Bajaj has followed GM principles by dividing its suppliers into different categories: those that own specialist knowledge and provide it in the form of proprietary items such as headlamps; those that provide model design parts on the basis of knowledge passed on by Bajaj; those that provide basic nuts and bolts hardware; and non-core product suppliers.

It has also set out four issues to be looked at with its suppliers: the 'make-or-buy' decisions that determine which products a customer buys; issues pertinent to each component sector; a vendor rating system; a vendor integration programme to introduce quality control systems used by Bajaj to its suppliers.

Difficulties with applying US-style strategy

But this is where the similarity with GM ends. 'You can't use textbook theories,' says Sangiv Bajaj. 'In India you have to consider questions like labour and power supply.' Unlike GM, Bajaj cannot afford to rely on only one supplier for a particular part because its operations would be paralysed if that supplier's workers went on strike – a common occurrence in India's highly unionised manufacturing industry. Similarly, having just one supplier would be risky because its output could be disrupted by power shortages, another regular occurrence. It makes sense to have suppliers in different areas, since simultaneous power failures are less likely.

Bajaj also has to wrestle with problems such as India's poor road system, which affects distribution and makes location important. Few Indian suppliers could shoulder the responsibilities GM puts on its US suppliers. There are also issues that relate specifically to components. 'Two of our three suppliers of shock absorbers are subsidiaries of competitors,' says Sangiv Bajaj. 'Long term this is questionable.' The company may opt to build up a third supplier in a relationship of 'interdependence'.

Rationalising the supply chain will take several years. When it is completed, Bajaj will still have far more suppliers than the GM model suggests it should. Sangiv Bajaj talks of '200, 300 or 400', though he says the company will decide the final figure 'from the bottom up'.

Bajaj hopes this will produce cost savings and quality improvements that will help compete against world-class products in an increasingly discerning market. It remains to be seen whether this will be enough. Bajaj will also have to match Honda and its other rivals in design, engine technology and marketing. But better management of its suppliers, while not guaranteeing success, is likely to be a necessary requirement for it.

Progress to 2005

By 2005, Bajaj Auto was well established as a major motorcycle manufacturer in India. It had created a major manufacturing facility at its base in Pune. It had developed a strong distribution and service network and an important R&D facility, which had led to the introduction of new Digital Twin Spark Ignition Technology. The company had also become a major exporter of motorcycles in the Asian region and was negotiating to set up a manufacturing facility in Indonesia. Although not mentioned in the case above, the company had an important line of vehicles – Bajaj was the leading company in the Indian three-wheeler market and had a profitable revenue stream from this market segment.

However, Bajaj Auto had lost its market leadership in motor cycles to a rival company, Hero Honda. This was partly as a result of having little success in launching successful models into the fast-growing executive segment of the Indian motor cycle market, where Hero Honda was the market leader. Bajaj was still engaged in a fierce price war with Hero Honda in the standard market segment where low production costs were crucial to profitability. In addition, the original Japanese motorcycle company, Honda, had entered the Indian market in 2004 as a new threat to both Hero Honda and Bajaj.

Finally, Bajaj was so pleased with the overall performance of Mr Rajiv Bajaj that it appointed him as managing director of the group in 2005. He had delivered a major transformation in the group's fortunes over the period from 1998 and was well positioned to take the group forward.

Source: This case has been adapted from Krishna, G (1998), 'India's scooter giant seeks US style kickstart', *Financial Times*, 6 July, p15. © *Financial Times* 1998. Used with permission. The update to 2005 was written by Professor Richard Lynch from data on the world wide web.[52]

▶ **CASE STUDY 9.3 continued**

Case questions

1 What are the main problems facing Bajaj Auto? To what extent are they related to operations issues?

2 Is it possible or even realistic to employ US-style operations strategies in a country where the suppliers present rather different problems from those experienced in the US?

3 Can you think of any other options to assist Bajaj develop its strategy beyond supply chain issues? What are the problems and opportunities with such options?

4 What lessons can companies draw from the experience of Bajaj on the application of the strategic issues outlined in this chapter?

9.5 SERVICE OPERATIONS STRATEGY

A survey of research published in the area of operations strategy[53] seemed to show that most of the research has concentrated on *manufacturing* strategy – that is, strategy concerned with making products in factories – and yet, in 1989, *services* such as telecommunications, travel and banking accounted for almost 50 per cent of the gross domestic product of Japan and the EU and 54 per cent in the US.[54] Moreover, the services sector continued to grow faster than manufacturing.

From an operations strategy perspective, the difficulty is that services have a number of major differences from products. For example:

● *Retail banking counter services* depend heavily on the performance of the employees behind the counter at the time of the service. The employees are part of the product.

● *Rail commuter services* cannot be stored as finished goods in a warehouse.

Service operations involve people and immediate responses that need special consideration when it comes to operations strategy development.

9.5.1 Services and products compared

Although there are differences in *nature* between products and services, it is important to keep this in perspective, since there are likely to be service elements in the supply of most products. The service content might range from a pre-sales personalised training course to an after-sales maintenance contract. From the extensive research on services marketing, five main differences between services and products have been identified and these are outlined in Table 9.2.[55] In addition to the five distinguishing features at the point of service, there will also be various *tangible* elements that are clearly product-oriented. For example, telephone lines, hotel beds, hospital reception areas and advertising agency studios are physical areas that are part of the service. These areas are part of the operation. They can be quantified and be the subject of a normal manufacturing-type analysis – for example, a stock analysis.

9.5.2 The value chain in operations services

It is now possible to examine how the value chain will change for services operations (*see* Figure 9.8). Many of the early operations aspects do not change radically. For example, there is still a need to obtain raw materials and also likely to be a requirement for after-sales service, albeit of a different kind. In truth, many service businesses rely heavily on *repeat business*, in just the same way as many products. This directs the operations task closer to that of products than might otherwise be the case.

9.5.3 Implications for the analysis of service operations strategy

With the growing importance of service industries, the detail of their operations strategy needs careful analysis. It will be evident that many of the early aspects of the analysis are not significantly different from manufacturing: at least the same elements apply in principle.

Table 9.2

The five main differences between services and products

Distinguishing features at the point of service	Description	Example	Impact on operations strategic analysis
Intangibility	• Cannot be seen or tasted like a product	• Bank counter service • Airline booking	• More difficult to define but important for setting standards. Hence, difficult to analyse
Inseparability	• Cannot be separated from the person of the seller • Consuming and selling may be undertaken at virtually the same time	• Telephone selling of car insurance • McDonald's 'Big Mac'	• High reliance on the people delivering the service • Need for careful selection and training
Heterogeneity	• Difficult to standardise service output • Reliant on human element	• Hospital in-patient care • Reception welcome at Holiday Inns Hotel	• Decision on whether it is necessary, desirable or even possible to standardise service
Perishability	• Services cannot be stored	• Empty hotel room • Telephone call not made	• Concept of stock may be irrelevant • Strategy needs to address issue of immediate utilisation of service
Ownership	• Customer may not own what is being consumed	• Cinema, night club, football stadium	• No physical need for logistics and transport

Figure 9.8

The operations value chain in a service industry (the areas that have changed from manufacturing are highlighted in coloured type)

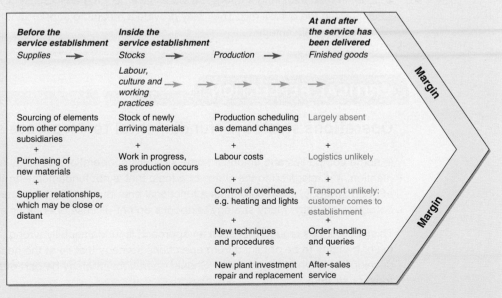

Where services differ is in the *direct customer interface*. It is here that operations need to be redefined.

From a competitive strategy perspective, we should also note that service has become an increasingly strong element in manufacturing strategy. This is not a new idea. As Levitt[56] observed in 1972:

There is no such thing as service industries. There are only industries whose service components are greater or less than those of other industries. Everybody is in service.

This has important implications for corporate strategy for three reasons:

1 Operations needs to consider carefully the service requirements of its customers. If the service is to run smoothly, there needs to be a direct link connecting production to the customer. Such an arrangement has to be part of the organisation's strategy.

2 One way of enhancing sustainable competitive advantage might be to strengthen the service element associated with a product – for example, more comprehensive after-sales and follow-up.

3 In those markets that have become increasingly global, one defence strategy is to offer higher levels of service. The reason is that, almost by definition, services are difficult to offer from a distance. They are best delivered locally. The cost and local knowledge required to set up and maintain such services will benefit the national operator against the global organisation.

Overall, the whole approach to service is likely to need an increased reliance on human resources and investment in training and education if it is to be successful.

Key strategic principles

- The people element and the need for immediate responses mean that services need special consideration from operations.

- There are five main points of difference between products and services that have implications for operations analysis: intangibility, inseparability, heterogeneity, perishability, ownership.

- Nevertheless, there are many points of similarity along the value chain for both products and services, so many of the same basic principles apply to both areas.

- Even in manufacturing strategy, services have become an increasingly strong element in the overall mix. They may provide a means to support and enhance competitive advantage.

CRITICAL REFLECTION

Operations strategy – fundamental to corporate strategy?

In some companies and amongst some strategists, operations strategy never gets a mention. It is relegated to the status of a topic that is not fundamental to the development of good strategy. It is regarded as a functional area that is not at the foundation of corporate strategy. Many strategy textbooks do not discuss operations strategy.

This chapter has argued that such an approach is fundamentally wrong. There are major benefits to be obtained from operations strategy that lie at the heart of strategy development. What do you think? Should operations strategy be part of the fundamental topic of strategy?

SUMMARY

● Operations includes raw materials sourcing, purchasing, production and manufacturing, distribution and logistics. Its coverage of the organisation's resources is therefore wide and comprehensive. Its importance in the strategic process is in delivering sustainable competitive advantage and in providing co-ordinated support for products – that is, every aspect of order handling, delivery and service to the customer – so that sales orders can be won by the organisation.

● There are two major constraints on operations:

1 they take time to plan and build; and

2 once installed, they are expensive to change.

These constraints mean that great care needs to be taken in arriving at the optimal strategy.

● The analytical process that accompanies such considerations will need to examine *where* and *how value is added* in the operations process from raw materials arriving at the factory gate through to finished goods being shipped to the final customer.

● It is evident from any analysis of the operations environment that the pace of technological change has clearly increased. Major changes in technology, often called *discontinuities*, also deserve careful analysis, as does global activity, particularly where it is aimed at cost reduction through the use of low-cost labour.

● Value added is an important part of the analytical process. It is likely to occur in the following areas:

1 adapting products to meet customer needs;

2 delivering better products than competitors;

3 adding value through enhanced performance or quality;

4 cutting the costs of manufacture.

● The methods of achieving operations strategy involve both human resource considerations and the link between manufacturing and marketing. Such approaches are major contributors to the sustainable competitive advantage of the organisation.

● In any detailed analysis of operations strategies, part of the problem is the size and complexity of the resources under consideration. Tests can be applied to identify the major factors affecting the achievement of corporate objectives, adding value and the critical success factors identified for an industry. In addition to these basic procedures, operations strategy needs to examine nine strategy areas:

1 make-or-buy decisions

2 supplier relationships

3 manufacturing strategy

4 product design prior to manufacture

5 factory layout and procedures

6 logistics and transport

7 Lean Thinking

8 human resources implications

9 international manufacturing.

● When analysing organisations involved primarily in services, such as banking or travel, some special considerations apply. Services are different in five areas: intangibility, inseparability, heterogeneity, perishability and ownership. However, they still cover areas that have much in common with manufacturing – for example, raw materials, supplier relationships, stocks and work in progress.

● In practice, service has become an increasingly strong element in manufacturing strategy. Service usually needs to be delivered locally, and as a result this has provided some protection against increased globalisation of manufacturing. More generally, service is heavily reliant on human resources and investment in training and education.

QUESTIONS

1 Operations strategy has made major contributions to corporate profitability over the last 20 years, yet has not always featured in some descriptions of corporate strategy. What are the reasons given in the chapter for this? Do you think that they are likely to continue to apply over the next few years?

2 Hill contends that manufacturing strategy needs to be led by changes in customer demand. If this is the case, how is it possible to develop products that are revolutionary in their technology and essentially unknown to the customer?

3 The chapter argues that the low-cost-labour strategies of some developing countries can be offset by more sophisticated operations strategies in Western countries. If you were managing a Western company, what type of manufacturing would you seek to keep in the West and what would you move to a developing country?

4 In Section 9.4, the comment is made that some detailed operations decisions are more likely to be outside the scope of corporate strategy. For each *element* of Section 9.4, explain the extent to which corporate strategy is involved and the extent to which it is not.

5 Analyse the world car industry for the contribution that operations strategy has made to the corporate strategies of companies in these industries.

Comment also on the future potential of operations strategy in these industries. Use the references at the end of this chapter to assist the process.

6 Operations strategy has become more international over the last 20 years. Do you think this trend will be reflected in services? What are the problems in the services area?

7 Apply the ten guidelines for analysing operations to an organisation of your choice. What are the implications of your analysis for corporate strategy?

8 *'Design is a strategic activity whether by intention or default.'* (Daniel Whitney) Discuss.

Further reading

Slack, N, Chambers, S, Harland, C, Harrison, A and Johnston, R (1998) *Operations Management*, 2nd edn, Pitman Publishing, London, is a comprehensive text, clearly written and presented. This book explores manufacturing issues in further detail.

Hill, T (1993) *Manufacturing strategy*, 2nd edn, Macmillan, Basingstoke. This is a clear, basic text that is well referenced and directed at exploring corporate strategy issues.

For an exploration of the future of manufacturing strategy in the car industry, read: Special Report – Car Manufacturing, *The Economist*, 23 February 2002, pp99–101, which contains many useful insights and is clearly written.

Harrison, M (1993) *Operations Management Strategy*, Pitman Publishing, London. This is thoughtful and has useful academic references.

Whitney, D (1988) 'Manufacturing by design', *Harvard Business Review*, July–Aug. This explores some of the areas outlined in the chapter, especially concentrating on the strategic implications of design and technology.

Womack, J P and Jones, D T (1996) *Lean Thinking*, Simon & Schuster, New York. This is an excellent text on exploring the strategic shift required in operations (much better than the earlier text involving these authors, *The Machine that Changed the World*). If you read this, then you should also consider reading the critical appraisal of the approach: Piercy, N F and Morgan, N A (1997) 'The impact of Lean Thinking and the Lean Enterprise on marketing', *Journal of Marketing Management*, 7, Oct, pp679–94.

Notes and references

1 Sources for Dell Computer Case 9.1: *Dell Computer Company Annual Report and Accounts 2004* and previous data all on the Dell website – www.dell.com and look up the 'investors' drop-down menu; *Financial Times*, 16 February 2001, p13; 2 April 2002, p22; 20 March 2003, p14; 9 October 2003, p34; 5 March 2004, p33; 1 June 2004, p10; 17 August 2004, p25; 19 October 2004, p29.

2 Hill, T (1993) *Manufacturing Strategy*, 2nd edn, Macmillan, Basingstoke, p18.

3 Hayes, R H and Upton, D (1998) 'Operations-based strategy', *California Management Review*, 40(4), pp8–25. This article provides further extensive examples, particularly of smaller companies that have been successful.

4 Urwick, L (1956) *The Golden Book of Management*, Newman Neame, London.

5 Mumford, E (1996) 'Restructuring: values, visions, viability', *Financial Times*, 9 Apr, p12. A really interesting article on the history of this subject.

6 Kennedy, P (1989) *The Rise and Fall of the Great Powers*, Fontana, London, p259.

7 Hill, T (1993) Op. cit., Ch1.

8 Lorenz, C (1991) 'Competition intensifies in the fast track', *Financial Times*, 28 June.

9 Strebel, P (1992) *Breakpoints*, Harvard Business School Press, Boston, MA, Chs1 and 2.

10 Ibison, D. (2004) Toyota seeks to re-invent itself, *Financial Times*, 6 August, p25.

11 World Bank Report (1991), *Trade and Industry Logistics in Developing Countries*, H J Peter.

12 Kennedy, P (1989) Op. cit., p535.

13 Wong Poh Kam (1991) *ASEAN and the EC*, ASEAN Economic Research Unit, Singapore, pp170 ff.

14 Three useful articles here from Tim Burt and David Ibison on *Toyota, Parts 1, 2 and 3*: *Financial Times*, 12 December 2001, p16, 13 December 2001, p13 and 14 December 2001, p15. The 2004 data on car production is taken from the Toyota Annual Report and Accounts 2004 published in English.

15 Williams, K, Haslam, C, Johal, S and Williams, J (1994) *Cars: Analysis, History and Cases*, Berghahn, Providence, RI, p108. *See also* the graphic account of the early Toyota years in Womack, J P and Jones, D T (1996) *Lean Thinking*, Simon & Schuster, New York, Ch10. Riveting story, well told.

16 Toyota (1994) *Annual Report and Accounts*, p11 (English language version).

17 Williams, K *et al* (1994) Op. cit., p118.

18 Gourlay, J (1994) 'Back to basics on the factory floor', *Financial Times*, 4 Jan, p7.

19 Griffiths, J (1993) 'Driving out the old regime', *Financial Times*, 20 Aug, p8.

20 Williams, K *et al* (1994) Op. cit., p115.

21 Griffiths, J (1995) '£200m Toyota expansion may create 3,000 jobs', *Financial Times*, 17 Mar, p9.

22 Hartley, J (1981) *The Management of Vehicle Production*, Butterworth, London.

23 Womack, J, Jones, D and Roos, D (1990) *The Machine that Changed the World*, Rawson Associates, New York.

24 Williams, K *et al* (1994) Op. cit., p115.

25 Sobek, D K, Liker, J K and Ward, A K (1998) 'Another look at how Toyota integrates product development', *Harvard Business Review*, July–Aug, pp36–50. A good description of the importance of management and human resource strengths that make Toyota so difficult for other companies to copy.

26 Butler, S (1992) 'Driven back to basics', *Financial Times*, 16 July, p16.

27 Toyota (1994) *Annual Report and Accounts*, p1 (English language version).

28 Toyota (2004) *Annual Report and Accounts*, p27 (English language version)

29 Womack, J P and Jones, D T (1996) Op. cit., p241.

30 Ibison, D (2002), 'Toyota plans to challenge US dominance', *Financial Times*, 2 April, p24.

31 Burt, T and Ibison, D (2001) 'PSA welcomes Toyota as latest co-driver', *Financial Times*, 9 July, p29. Toyota (2004) *Annual Report and Accounts*, pp29 and 119.

32 Toyota (2004) *Annual Report and Accounts*, p13.

33 Burt, T (2001) 'A pace-setter gears up for growth', *Financial Times*, 24 September, p15. Interview with Toyota company chairman, Hiroshi Okuda.

34 Hill, T (1991) *Production and Operations Management*, 2nd edn, Prentice Hall, Hemel Hempstead.

35 Wild, R (1984) *Production and Operations Management*, 3rd edn, Holt, Reinhart and Winston, New York.

36 *Economist* (2002) 'Incredible shrinking plants', Special Report on Car Manufacturing, 23 February, pp99–101.

37 Hill, T (1993) Op. cit., Ch2.

38 Hill, T (1993) Op. cit., p36. (*See also* pp55 and 56 for further clarification of these matters.)

39 *See also* Hill, T and Westbrook, R (1997) 'The strategic development of manufacturing: market analysis for investment priorities', *European Management Journal*, 15(3), pp296–302.

40 Hill, T (1991) Op. cit.

41 *See*, for example, Cusumano, M and Takeishi, A (1991) 'Supplier relations and management; a survey of Japanese, Japanese-transplant and US auto plants', *Strategic Management Journal*, 12, pp563–88. Also Macduff, J P and Helper, S (1997) 'Creating lean suppliers: diffusing lean production throughout the supply chain', *California Management Review*, 39(4) pp118–51.

42 Marsh, P (1995) 'Car mirror rivalry turns cut-throat', *Financial Times*, 14 June, p10.

43 *Economist* (2002) 'Incredible shrinking plants', *Special Report on Car Manufacturing*, 23 February, pp99–101.

44 Hill, T (1991) Op. cit.

45 Skinner, W (1974) 'The focused factory', *Harvard Business Review*, May–June.

46 Whitney, D (1988) 'Manufacturing by design', *Harvard Business Review*, July–Aug, p83.

47 Ridding, J (1995) 'Renault unveils plant to speed launches', *Financial Times*, 17 Feb, p24.

48 Christopher, M (1992) *Logistics and Supply Chain Management*, Pitman, London. (*See also* Christopher, M (1993) 'Logistics and competitive strategy', *European Management Journal*, June, pp258–61.)

49 Lynch, R (1992) *European Marketing*, Kogan Page, London, p214.

50 Womack, J P and Jones, D T (1996) *Lean Thinking*, Simon & Schuster, New York. This section largely derives from this text. But note that most of the examples come from slowly growing markets – prescriptive approaches. An excellent critique of the 'Lean Thinking' approach is contained in Piercy, N F and Morgan, N A (1997) referenced in the Further Reading section above.

51 Carnegy, H (1995) 'Time to chart a different course', *Financial Times*, 7 Aug, p9.

52 Sources for the Bajaj update: www.domain-B.com/ Bajajauto – articles dated 15 January 2004, 16 June 2004, 20 July 2004, 10 March 2005.

53 Adam, E A and Swamidass, P M (1989) 'Assessing operations management from the strategic perspective', reprinted as Ch19 in Voss, C (1992) *Manufacturing Strategy – Process and Content*, Chapman and Hall, London.

54 *See* 'Can Europe compete?', *Financial Times*, 1 Mar 1994, p14.

55 *See*, for example, Cowell, D (1984) *The Marketing of Services*, Heinemann Professional, Oxford, Ch2.

56 Levitt, T (1972) 'Production line approach to service', *Harvard Business Review*, Sept–Oct, pp41–52.

Chapter 10
Purpose shaped by vision, leadership and ethics

- How is purpose shaped by the organisation?
- What vision does the organisation have for its future? What does this mean for purpose?
- How does leadership shape purpose?
- What is the relationship between purpose and the corporate governance of the organisation?
- What are the organisation's views on corporate social responsibility? How will they affect purpose?

Chapter 11
Purpose emerging from knowledge, technology and innovation

- What knowledge does the organisation possess? How can it create and share new knowledge? What will be the impact on the organisation's purpose?
- What are the strategic implications of new technologies? How can technology be used to develop competitive advantage?
- Can innovation contribute to the organisation's purpose? If so, how?

Chapter 12
Purpose delivered through corporate and business objectives

- What is the purpose of the organisation?
- What is the difference between purpose in a diversified company and a single business? What are the main elements of corporate-level strategy?
- Who are the stakeholders in the organisation and what do they want from it?
- What is the organisation's mission? How is a mission statement developed?
- What are the objectives of the organisation? How are they developed?
- What is the organisation's policy on quality?

Part 4

THE PURPOSE OF THE ORGANISATION

It is impossible to develop corporate strategy without first establishing the general direction of the organisation. Building on the analyses of the organisation's environment and resources, this part of the book now explores the purpose of the organisation. The next three chapters explore the topic from three perspectives: how purpose is shaped by vision, leadership and governance; how purpose emerges from knowledge, technology and innovation; and how purpose is delivered through the organisation's mission and objectives.

The mission and objectives of the organisation are developed in the context of the organisation's stakeholders. In a prescriptive approach, they are likely to be defined in general terms for some years to come. In an emergent approach and in turbulent markets, they will be more fluid and contingent upon unfolding events.

The prescriptive strategic process

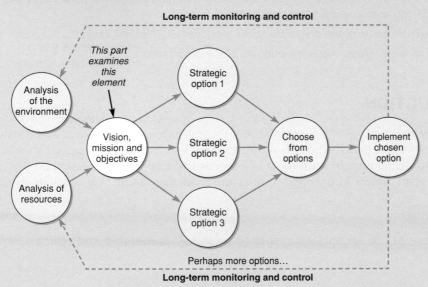

The emergent strategic process

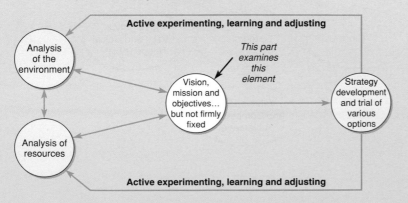

Chapter 10

PURPOSE SHAPED BY VISION, LEADERSHIP AND ETHICS

Learning outcomes

When you have worked through this chapter, you will be able to:

- outline the main considerations in the development of purpose;
- explore the organisation's vision for the future and its strategic implications;
- explain the contribution of leadership to the development of corporate strategy;
- identify the three main approaches to leadership analysis and explain why the contingency approach is the most useful from a corporate strategy perspective;
- outline the chief areas of corporate governance that will influence corporate strategy and decision making at the centre of the organisation;
- identify the main areas of the corporate social responsibility that will influence purpose;
- show how all these areas shape the purpose of the organisation.

INTRODUCTION

In developing the purpose of the organisation, there is a need to stand back and consider why the organisation exists, who it is meant to serve and how its value added should be generated and distributed. In addition, it is important to take the process beyond the current horizons and explore future opportunities and challenges. Some may conclude that the

Figure 10.1

The purpose of the organisation: shaped by vision, leadership and ethics

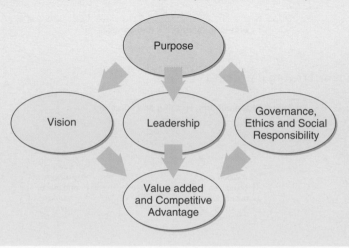

future is too turbulent to predict and therefore the result is worthless. However, in many strategic situations, this will not be the case, even in turbulent markets. The purpose of the organisation and its vision for the future will set the boundaries and stretch the organisation as it develops its mission and objectives.

There are three additional areas that will help shape the purpose of the organisation and deserve early examination in its development. These are: the leadership of the organisation, the way that the directors govern the organisation and the social responsibility policies that it will pursue. Corporate governance has become an important issue over the last few years because of new stricter rules and legislation after the failure of a few companies in this area. Corporate social responsibility explores the policies that organisations will adopt on such matters as 'green' issues, poverty, AIDS and working conditions. These are considered in this chapter before we return to the issues of value added and competitive advantage and examine their relationships with purpose. These areas are shown in Figure 10.1.

CASE STUDY 10.1

Starbucks – sacrificing dividends for global growth

Most companies with annual sales over US$5 billion would wish to pay an annual dividend to their shareholders. But not the coffee restaurant chain Starbucks. Its purpose is to grow the company and it retains all its profits to achieve this. The case explains the background and explores the implications.

Starbucks history

Originally a coffee roasting company, Starbucks opened its first coffee bar in Seattle, US, in 1985. The young Howard Schulz, who had joined the company in 1982 as marketing executive, persuaded the original owners to use the company's roasted beans to experiment with an 'Italian coffee bar' concept. The early bars were successful, so Mr Schulz persuaded some local backers to help him buy the company in 1987. Starbucks then expanded into new cafes in Chicago and Vancouver, Canada. It was not long before there were some 17 bars. The numbers then expanded and numbered 165 at the time the company made a public offering of its shares in 1992.

Starbucks operations

Essentially, Starbucks sells fresh coffee, tea and other beverages, along with a range of snacks and light refreshments. It operates mainly in high-traffic, high-visibility locations and, in North America, it usually owns the shops. The company's American stores dominated the total worldwide business in 2004, with almost 4,300 coffee shops. There were also another 1,800 Starbucks in the US that were licensed to other operators to sell Starbucks coffee products in areas where the company was not otherwise represented, such as smaller neighbourhoods, off highways and in rural locations. Starbucks' strategy was to seek out innovative new flavours, products and even music to enhance its stores: 'The Starbucks Experience has a rich emotional connection for people everywhere and we are creating a "third place" [in addition to home and work] for an ever-broadening audience around the world.'

Internationally, the company opened its first Starbucks outside North America in 1997. By the end of 2004, there were

Starbucks in Kyoto, Japan, follows the same vision as its founders – with the same quality and standards of service everywhere around the world.

almost 1,000 company-owned stores and another 1,500 licensed stores in over 40 countries. For example, there were over 500 stores in Japan, 150 in China, 100 in South Korea and 35 in Singapore; there were over 400 stores in the UK, 35 in Germany but only 4 in France; there were also substantial licensing operations in the Middle East and South America but none in Africa at the time of writing. The company was continuing to expand rapidly and estimated that it was serving 30 million customers every week. The company commented in 2004: 'Given our sustained success to date, we believe that we previously underestimated the scope of the long-term opportunity for Starbucks. Accordingly, we recently increased our ultimate projected growth from 25,000 to at least 30,000 stores worldwide, with at least 15,000 locations outside the United States.'

Starbucks' financial results

The rapid increase in stores is reflected in similar increases in annual revenue and net profits – see Figure 10.2. The company has increased its sales profit margin over the years by buying centrally and by operating tightly controlled costs procedures. Conscious of its responsibility to local coffee producers, the company runs a Farmer Support Centre in Costa Rica to support its local coffee suppliers and it also operates third-party verification procedures with regard to the social and economic practices of its many agricultural and other suppliers.

A number of the company's senior employees were also shareholders in the company, including Howard Schulz, who was 'chairman and chief global strategist'. Employee-shareholding was part of Starbucks' company policy since the shares were first offered for sale to the public in 1992. With such rapid growth, there was a related need to increase working capital and capital investment at the company. It was therefore not surprising that the company had never paid a dividend to its shareholders up to 2004, though there were other methods of raising finance for such expansion – see Chapter 8. Although no share dividend was paid, shareholders clearly had the benefit of the underpinning increase in the capital value of their shares.

Even though the company had performed exceptionally up to 2004, some strategists would argue that there would come a time when the share dividend policy would need to change: shareholders would demand an annual income rather than waiting for capital growth. Such a change might arise especially if the growth began to slow substantially and there was then no longer an immediate need to finance such growth. The reasons for slower growth were unclear at the time of examining the company. However, if the McDonalds Restaurants example was any guide – see Case 12.3 – then increased competition would slow growth and decreased demand for the Italian coffee bar concept would also lead to slower growth.

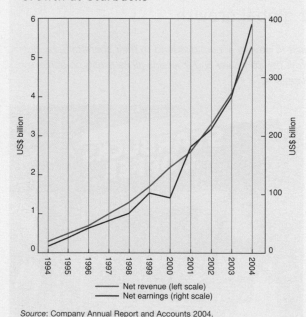

Figure 10.2

Growth at Starbucks

Net revenue (left scale)
Net earnings (right scale)

Source: Company Annual Report and Accounts 2004.

Case questions

1 *What are the benefits and dangers of focusing strongly on growth as the only purpose of an organisation?*

2 *Can other companies learn anything from Starbucks or is the company unique?*

10.1 SHAPING THE PURPOSE OF THE ORGANISATION

Part 9a

In Chapter 1, the topic of corporate strategy was defined in the context of the purpose of the organisation – strategy is only a means to an end, that end being the purpose of the organisation. It follows that it is impossible to develop strategy if the organisation's purpose remains unclear. It is perhaps surprising therefore that there has been so little exploration of purpose in the strategy literature; purpose is often simplified to 'profit maximisation' by writers such as Professor Michael Porter[2] or 'survival' by Professor Oliver Williamson[3] or some other simplifying assumption. For example, the purpose at Starbucks was to grow the business profitably.

The reason for such a simplification in the definition is that purpose is *complex and multifaceted*, involving not only profit and survival but also the motivations of the people involved and the relationship of the organisation with society and the community. Starbucks is an example of a company where the original owners are still the driving force in building a large and successful company that is more than a simple profit-maximising enterprise. Moreover, purpose will be *unique* to each organisation. Yet, however complex and singular, the general principles underlying the development of purpose need to be understood and clarified if the subsequent development of strategy is to be meaningful.

For many writers,[4] purpose is explored or defined solely in terms of business organisations, with profit featuring somewhere in its definition. But many other not-for-profit organisations, such as government institutions, charities and public services, also generate value-adding activities that have a clear purpose and need strategies to attain that purpose. An exploration of purpose therefore needs to be broad enough to include such bodies.

Whether private company or public body, every organisation needs to develop its purpose and develop a common understanding of the main elements. The potential complexity of this approach is usually overcome by identifying and concentrating on the essentials for that organisation. Such a process takes time and is best described as a process of *shaping* the purpose of the organisation. There are five main areas to be considered:

1 What is our area of activity – and what should it be?
2 What kind of organisation do we wish to be?
3 What is the relative importance of shareholders and stakeholders?
4 Do we want to grow the organisation?
5 What is our relationship with our immediate environment and with society in general?

However, such questions are somewhat *prescriptive* in their approach: they assume that clear answers can be given and that the actions that might follow are within the power of those people shaping the purpose of the organisation.[5] Neither of these assumptions is necessarily correct. For example, it may be difficult and unwise to define too clearly the area of activity because it may preclude opportunistic alternatives. Moreover, decisions on the type of organisation, growth and society depend on external forces, like governments and economic growth, that are not within the control of those asking the questions. *Emergent* approaches will also be needed if the organisation is to develop its purpose successfully. However, as a starting point in the development of purpose, it is useful to explore the questions.

10.1.1 What is our area of activity – and what should it be?

Fundamental to purpose is an examination of the area of activity that is undertaken – the business in which a company is engaged or the service offered by a non-profit organisation. This is at the heart of the definition of corporate strategy explored in Chapter 1.

With all the certainty of hindsight, we can conclude that Howard Schulz was probably right to concentrate the purpose of Starbucks on growth of the Italian coffee bar concept. Many other successful companies, like Microsoft and Intel, also focus purpose on a narrow business. But the Starbucks concept of focusing on growth does carry the danger that it may become difficult to sustain over time. In contrast to a concentrated purpose, some companies have successfully adopted broad roles for purpose: for example, the US conglomerate General Electric is involved in a range of industries from electric turbines to television broadcasting. The first issue in purpose is therefore one of *focus* – should we concentrate the purpose or allow it to range broadly? From an examination of the evidence on the profitability of focused versus diversified organisations,[6] there is no clear answer to this question – purpose can be broad or narrow. However, smaller companies will probably benefit from focus or they risk possessing insufficient competitive advantage in one area as a result of becoming merely competent in a number of areas. More generally, purpose needs to be narrow enough to be actionable and broad enough to allow scope for development.

Excluding start-up organisations, the strategy writer Professor Peter Drucker explored the issue of the area of activity from a different perspective. He recommended that the area of activity is examined by a consideration of *customers*.[7] He argued that it was the organisation's customers that defined the nature of the organisation and therefore shaped the breadth of its purpose.

More recently, strategists would add to his answer by suggesting that the *competitive resources* of an organisation will also define its purpose.[8] For example, the coffee shops and skill resources at Starbucks would make it difficult for the company to define its purpose as being engaged in car manufacturing. The resource-based view – *see* Chapter 6 – certainly suggests that the chosen area of activity should be related to the competitive advantage of the organisation. In practice, there needs to be a *balance* between customers and resources.

Neither of these customer/resource considerations explores where the organisation *should* locate its activities. Purpose is about the future direction of the organisation just as much as the present. All organisations have the opportunity to redefine and redirect their activities in the future. This may be particularly important if their survival is threatened in the present or if they see unique and attractive opportunities that would require a redefinition of purpose.

10.1.2 What kind of organisation do we wish to be?

Given the amount of time and effort that individuals devote to organisations, it is arguable that the purpose of the organisation is, at least in part, to provide living space for those engaged in its activities. All organisations have some choice to develop in two related areas:

1 culture and style – their *organisational culture*;
2 challenges to be posed to the members of the organisation.

For example, some may choose to be hard-nosed and competitive, while others may choose to be caring, considerate and co-operative. It should be acknowledged that complete freedom of choice in organisational culture is unlikely for two reasons: it is highly dependent on the previous history of the organisation and, in most cases, can only be changed slowly.[9] Nevertheless, it would be equally misleading to suggest that organisations are unable to make any change in their culture and it is therefore appropriate to explore this matter in the context of purpose.

To some extent, the kind of organisation will be dictated by the environment in which it operates:[10] for example, a fast-moving, buccaneering market like that for third-generation mobile telephones may not be well served by an organisation that chooses to be staid and sober in its purpose and culture. However, there are other aspects of choice in relation to purpose and culture that deserve consideration. The four types of organisational culture explored in Chapter 7 – power, role, task and personal – are to some extent matters of choice by the organisation.[11] The purpose of the organisation might therefore range from the *personal satisfaction* provided to someone involved in charity work to the *group goals* involved in meeting a challenging new product launch.

In addition to culture, organisational purpose may also be defined in terms of the *challenge* that purpose should pose to the organisation's members.[12] This approach will have an additional impact on the working style of the organisation.

> *No organisation can depend on genius; the supply is scarce and always unpredictable. But it is the test of an organisation that it can make ordinary human beings perform better than they are capable of, that it brings out whatever strength there is in its members and uses it to make all the other members perform more and better.*

Clearly, organisations have a choice here to offer no challenge. But some strategists would argue that those organisations which offer a challenge are more successful because they 'make common people do uncommon things', to paraphrase Lord Beveridge.

10.1.3 What is the relative importance of shareholders and stakeholders?[13]

For some companies, the purpose of the organisation is ultimately to advance the interests of its owners, usually the shareholders. Typically, this means that purpose is defined in terms of increasing the wealth of the shareholders. One example is the SVA concept explored in Chapter 8. Other ways of pursuing increased shareholder wealth include encouraging higher share prices and larger dividends in the short term and, for those strategies concerned with the longer term, including some measure of long-term profit growth. This approach to purpose is called the *shareholder perspective* on purpose.

With such an approach to purpose, the problem is often the separation between ownership by the shareholders and control of the enterprise by its senior managers. Since the 1930s, it has been recognised that, as companies grow larger, two trends emerge.[14] Shareholdings become more widespread and diffuse, so giving individual shareholders less power. At the same time, managers gain control over a larger range of assets and acquire increasingly greater remuneration and power. Thus purpose, according to this view, tends to drift from a clear focus on owners, who have lost the power to influence events, towards the senior management, who may pursue other interests as long as they keep the shareholders happy with steady increases in dividends and a generally rising share price.

Another wholly different view of purpose views the ownership of the organisation merely as one input to its continued existence.[15] In this view, shareholders supply the financial capital to which is added the managerial expertise of the organisation's senior managers, the labour input of other workers, the expertise and skills of its suppliers and so on. In this sense, the organisation is a joint venture between a number of its participants, each of whom has a stake in the purpose of the organisation. This is called the *stakeholder perspective* on purpose.

Clearly, the shareholder and stakeholder perspectives have considerable potential for conflict. For example, shareholders' higher dividends might need to come at the expense of paying managers and workers lower salaries. This matter is explored further in Chapter 12 in the context of the specific proposals on purpose summarised in the mission and objectives of the organisation.

10.1.4 Do we want to grow the organisation?

Some writers have argued that organisations need to see growth as at least part of their purpose. For example, the management guru Tom Peters argued that 'A firm is never static – it is either growing or stagnating',[16] and the strategy writers Gertz and Baptista claimed that 'No company ever shrank to greatness.'[17] For some people, such phrases are vapid sloganising, but there is an established tradition in economic writing that assumes that organisations will wish to grow. For example, the well-respected work of the economist Edith Penrose – *see* Chapter 2 – is based on the assumption that firms will wish to grow.[18] Yet organisations may have a choice on growth and not all organisations will wish to grow – they may be perfectly satisfied to continue on their present course. The decision on growth is an important one but entirely dependent on the organisation and its environment – the choice is not automatic.

10.1.5 What is our relationship with the immediate environment and with society in general?

Purpose cannot be set without some consideration of the environment within which the organisation operates. This can conveniently be considered from the twin perspectives of the immediate environment and the wider context of society in general, though there may in practice be other approaches.

In the immediate environment, the main problems affecting purpose are likely to be general turbulence and strong competitive activity. There may be occasions when the environment is so chaotic or competition so powerful that survival is the only sensible purpose. All other aspects of purpose will need to be subordinated to this. It may even be that survival is not possible, in which case an orderly exit should be the purpose.

In the wider environment of society in general, there may be some need to define purpose in the context of the pressures and demands of that society. For example, government policy may dictate an adjustment in purpose. Equally, society may put pressure on a company to alter its purpose, such as the campaign to have responsible environmental 'green' policies written into the purpose of organisations. Increasingly, such considerations have become important and are discussed further under the heading of *Corporate Social Responsibility* later in this chapter.

More generally, from the perspective of the environment within which the organisation operates, some strategists argue that all organisations will adapt their purpose to reflect the values and pressures of such societies. The socio-cultural theories of strategy stress the contingent nature of every aspect of strategy development, starting with purpose – *see* Chapter 2.

10.1.6 Conclusions: the Purpose-Process-Outcome (P-P-O) Paradigm

With so many divergent views and little coherent thread, what are we to make of purpose? How can it be developed? As mentioned earlier, one response has been to simplify purpose down to a single, leading role such as:

1 growth; or

2 survival; or

3 profit maximisation.

In the development of strategy theory, such definitions play an important role in clarifying the logic of the strategies that should then be followed. However, they inevitably oversimplify the development of purpose, as the above sections have demonstrated. The purpose of the organisation is multidimensional and not just a simple matter of defining a single specific purpose, such as the three areas listed above. Morgan best captures the fullness of purpose in his comments on the different ways of exploring organisations: 'There can be no single theory or metaphor that gives an all-purpose point of view and there can be no one "correct theory" for structuring everything we do.'[19] It follows that a simple definition of purpose may fail to capture the full range of roles of the organisation.

In spite of this, most organisations have found some simplified definition of their purpose to be helpful because it provides a method of communicating the basis of the organisation's values and a forum for focusing on its future direction. Given this stance, three general guidelines on purpose can be developed:

1 *The importance of value added*: every organisation, including those in the public and not-for-profit sectors, needs to consider where and how it adds value to its inputs.[20,21]

2 *The balance between shaping and being shaped by the environment*: some organisations may choose to shape the environment in which they operate, as well as passively coping with changes in the environment.[22]

3 *The changing nature of purpose over time – the P–P–O Paradigm*: the organisational *purpose* will be delivered by the *process* of strategy development. This will then provide an *outcome* (often as a profit or a service) that will then feed back into purpose at a later stage. These three elements make up the P(urpose)–P(rocess)–O(utcome) Paradigm – *see* Figure 10.3.

Comment

One final cautionary note on purpose is essential in relation to this section. The whole concept of purpose above is built on the assumption that it is useful and desirable to develop a

Figure 10.3

The P-P-O Paradigm

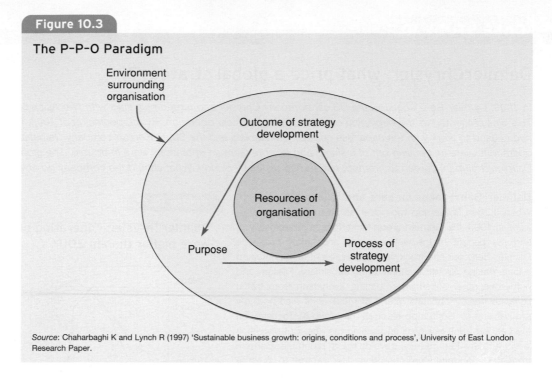

Source: Chaharbaghi K and Lynch R (1997) 'Sustainable business growth: origins, conditions and process', University of East London Research Paper.

clearly defined purpose for the organisation. Chapter 11 will explore the important strategic areas of knowledge, technology and innovation, where it may be better to leave some aspects of purpose much more open and flexible.

Key strategic principles

- Fundamental to the exploration of purpose is the definition of the organisation's activities. It needs to be narrow enough to be actionable and broad enough to allow scope for development. It will develop from a consideration of the organisation's customers and its competitive resources.

- Organisations have some opportunity to influence the type of organisation that they wish to be. This will be reflected and defined in the organisation's culture. However, culture is confined by its past and is difficult to change, so this will restrict the choices available in the context of purpose.

- Different stakeholders – shareholders, employees, etc. – will have different perspectives on the purpose of the organisation. These need to be recognised and explored in the context of purpose.

- Purpose will also be defined by any specific desire to grow the organisation and by an exploration of the demands of the environment in which the organisation exists.

- Organisations are multidimensional and unlikely to have a single purpose. However, for reasons of focusing on specific objectives and communicating with those in the organisation, a simplified definition of purpose is often developed.

- The P–P–O Paradigm captures the developing relationship between the future purpose of the organisation and its past performance. It does this by highlighting three consecutive elements – P(urpose), P(rocess) and O(utcome) – in the context of the organisation's resources and its environment.

DaimlerChrysler: what price a global strategy?

In 1998, Daimler-Benz acquired the US car company Chrysler and forged new links with two Asian car companies. This was presented as the beginning of a new, truly global car operation. By the beginning of 2005, DaimlerChrysler had ceased to work with the Japanese company Mitsubishi and the South Korean company Daihatsu. The Chrysler operations were just pulling out of a slump and its core German operations were in trouble. The global vision of the Daimler chairman, Jürgen Schrempp, had turned distinctly cloudy. What should the company do now?

Daimler-Benz: focus on cars and trucks

When Jürgen Schrempp took over as chairman of Daimler-Benz in 1995, the German group lacked focus strategically. It had the benefit of the well-regarded and highly profitable Daimler-Benz car and truck range. However, it also contained a loss-making aircraft manufacturing subsidiary, Fokker, and numerous other subsidiaries making everything from traffic lights to freezer cabinets; many of these units also had low profitability. Mr Schrempp rescued the group by focusing on the car and truck business and selling the rest. But his vision went further than merely developing a profitable German transport manufacturing operation. He wanted to build a *global* car and truck company. After considering various possibilities (including the acquisition of the car company Nissan), Mr Schrempp did the deal in 1998 that would in his words 'change the face of the industry forever'. Daimler-Benz bought the company that was third in the American market, Chrysler, for US$38 billion. He went on to build links with Japan and South Korea with the objective of building a global business. The results over the ten years to 2004 suggested that the company's strategy was unsuccessful up to that time – *see* Figure 10.4.

Global vision of 1998

To be a global car company, the German car company, Daimler-Benz, judged that it was essential to have a substantial presence in the world's largest car market – the US. The acquisition of Chrysler was the quickest route to achieving this: the other two main US companies, General Motors and Ford, were not available. During the 1990s, the chairman of Chrysler, Bob Eaton, and his team had turned Chrysler from being the sick man of the US car industry into one of its most profitable companies. This was done by focusing on niche markets, like those for sports utility vehicles and minivans, and avoiding the low-profit mass car manufacture of its rivals, General Motors and Ford. The result was that the company was highly valued on the US stock exchange when Daimler-Benz began negotiations in 1998. Chrysler was sold to Daimler-Benz for US$38 billion: arguably, Chrysler did a good deal by selling at what turned out to be the peak of Chrysler's profitability up to that time.

Daimler-Benz was very happy with the price of its North American purchase. The chairman, Jürgen Schrempp, commented: 'We'll have the size, profitability and the reach to take on everyone.' Daimler also continued to pursue its global

Figure 10.4

DaimlerChrysler – operating profits in 1996 were higher than in 2004

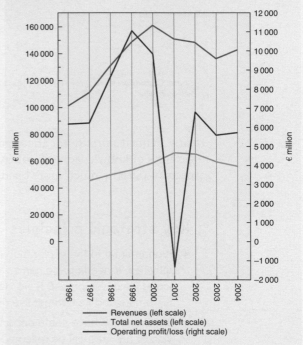

Revenues (left scale)
Total net assets (left scale)
Operating profit/loss (right scale)

Source: Annual Report and Accounts 2004.

ambitions by buying 34 per cent of the Japanese car company Mitsubishi and taking a 10 per cent stake in the Korean car company Hyundai. In addition, Daimler acquired further companies to support its truck interests in North America and elsewhere. The company also continued its programme of new models for its Mercedes flagship brand. Finally, it launched in Europe and America a new small car with the brand name Smart using a totally new dealer network.

Turnaround at Chrysler

Unfortunately, although the German Daimler operation remained highly profitable, the Chrysler acquisition started to go wrong. In 2000, Chrysler was forced to lower its prices to clear old models; new sports utility and minivans were launched by rival companies; new Chrysler models were slow to appear and expensive to launch. At the same time, Daimler-Benz realised that the benefits of globalisation – greater economies of scale, shared research and development costs – could not be achieved if Chrysler was allowed to operate completely on its own. Integration was needed. In addition, the company culture of the German parent – technocratic, planned and precise – was at odds with the Chrysler culture – free wheeling, opportunistic and informal.

The acquisition, which had originally been presented as a 'merger between equals', rapidly became a straight take-over. Eaton and other senior colleagues left the company and Daimler-Benz put in its own top management team. The German company was determined to combine operations, cut costs and return to high profits. One of the parent company's top managers, Dieter Zetsche, was made managing director at Chrysler. He decided to introduce what he described as a new culture of 'disciplined pizazz' into the Chrysler company over the next three years. He explained that this phrase was meant to capture two things: the German attention to the detailed job of improving quality and cutting costs, coupled with the American flair that had produced innovative new designs in

Chrysler cars during the 1990s. The new approach did not produce instant results – even in 2003, the company was reporting a 12 per cent drop in sales and a US$1.1 billion operating loss as new models were late coming to market and competition was increasing.

But business was beginning to change. The entire 1998 Chrysler board was gone. The workforce was reduced by one-third to 87,000. Capital spending was reduced drastically and new model launches were increased by 50 per cent in late 2003. Importantly, the new models included attractive new designs like the Chrysler 300 luxury saloon and the Dodge Magnum wagon. In addition, Chrysler began to exchange design technologies with other parts of Daimler – notably, the rear-wheel drive platform from the Mercedes E-class was used on one of the Dodge vehicles. Cars from rival companies – like the Toyota Tundra and the Chevrolet Silverado – were benchmarked and Chrysler manufacturing was made increasingly flexible. The result was a major turnaround at Chrysler – see Table 10.1. As it turned out, this improvement was greatly appreciated by the parent company, Daimler, which was in major trouble in Asia and had declining profits in its home country, Germany.

Table 10.1

Turnaround at Chrysler but problems at Mercedes

All figures in US$ millions

	Major activity base	2004		2003		Comment
		Sales	Operating profit (loss)	Sales	Operating profit (loss)	
Mercedes Car Group	Mainly German manufacturing but global sales of luxury models	67 189	2 255	69 647	4 232	Sales lower coupled with sharp decline in profits
Chrysler Group	US manufacturing with some sales outside North America	67 010	1 932	66 770	(685)	Major turnaround – see case
Commercial Vehicle Group	German manufacturing of buses, trucks, etc.	47 064	1 803	36 290	1 100	Reliable steady profit earner
Services	Worldwide financial support – leasing and financing	18 871	1 692	19 003	1 700	Car companies usually earn profits from such activities
Other	Other activities of group, e.g. traffic signalling equipment in Germany	2 978	617	5 529	1 800	Traffic signalling proved major problem – see text
Eliminations and adjustments to operating profit			(509)		(425)	Normal adjustments for inter-group trading
Total		192 319	7 790	197 239	7 722	

Source: Company Annual Accounts 2004. Note that 2003 figures have been converted by the author from Euros at the 2004 US Dollar rate and are therefore only approximations. For strategic purposes, they give an adequate indicator of the underlying changes.

► CASE STUDY 10.2 continued

Problems at Mitsubishi and Hyundai

Although it was not the market leader, Mitsubishi was a significant Japanese car company, with interests in many Asian markets. In the late 1990s, DaimlerChrysler identified Mitsubishi as an important partner in its global strategy and paid US$3 billion for a 37 per cent share of the Japanese company. Unfortunately for Daimler, its Japanese partner then ran into trouble with the Japanese authorities and customers. This included police raids on the Mitsubishi headquarters, the cover-up by Mitsubishi executives of fatal vehicle flaws and major bad debts in the North American market.[23] By 2004, the Mitsubishi company needed a major injection of capital of around US$6 billion to continue trading. It turned to DaimlerChrysler as part of this process. After considering the matter, Daimler decided to end its relationship with the Japanese company, despite the hole that this would leave in the German company's global strategy. It simply did not believe that it would get the returns it required, according to Manfred Gentz, finance director at Daimler.

Around one month later, DaimlerChrysler ended its broad alliance with the South Korean car manufacturer Hyundai. The German company had acquired a 10 per cent share of the Korean company in 2000 for around US$400 million. Daimler was able to sell for around US$1 billion so it made a good profit. The problem was that Hyundai and DaimlerChrysler were unable to complete plans for a joint venture to manufacture commercial vehicles in South Korea. In addition, Hyundai had ambitions for its Chinese operations that were in conflict with those of the German company – essentially, they were competing in the Chinese market and this was unacceptable to Daimler. Again, this meant that another part of the DaimlerChrysler global strategy had ended.

Problems in Germany

Even in 2002, DaimlerChrysler was in trouble. The problems were so bad that the company was forced to declare a loss after taking into account exceptional items. It had to reduce its dividend for the first time for many years and said that it would take much longer to turn around its North American and other operations: 'The first year almost was tremendous hype. We were the heroes,' explained Mr Schrempp. 'This was a spectacular deal, we were lifted to the heights where we didn't belong. Then came reality day, that is what we are experiencing.' But in 2002, the basic Mercedes operations in Germany were still highly profitable.

Unfortunately for the company, its German operations ran into difficulties over the next three years. In summary, these were:

● German manufacturing costs were too high. Negotiations with the unions over job cuts were begun but were making only slow progress. DaimlerChrysler threatened to switch some manufacturing to South Africa unless the German unions relented. More generally, a US$5 billion cost-cutting programme, including major investment in new plant, was under way in Germany. But it would be several years before any major turnaround was seen.

● The Smart car was in major trouble – 'disaster' was the word used by the chief executive of the Mercedes car group, the German subsidiary of DaimlerChrysler. It had been launched in 2000 as a revolutionary small car to complete the model range offered by the Mercedes car group. It was supposed to break even by 2004 but the company was still losing US$6,000 on each car sold up to that point. In 2005, DaimlerChrysler announced that it would cut 700 jobs, reduce the number of models and reorganise the distribution of the Smart to bring it into profit by 2007.

● Mercedes models, especially the E-class, were subject to significant quality problems. The electronics in particular were causing enough difficulties for the company to recall 1.3 million cars in early 2005. Breakdowns were estimated to have cost the company US$600 million alone in 2004. Even Mr Schrempp had encountered trouble when attempting to use the Mercedes navigation computer in one of his company cars in late 2004. The company was optimistic that its difficulties were now over and that there were no longer quality problems with new vehicles being assembled in 2005.

Understandably, some commentators were concerned that sorting out the Smart car model would divert attention away from the more important task of resolving problems with the Mercedes models and the basic task of cost-cutting. The Smart model was not a major part of the Mercedes activity base – *see* Figure 10.5. After the acquisition of Chrysler, the Daimler shares rose to a post-merger peak value of US$110 billion in 1999. By 2005, the group's shares were worth around US$50 billion. Some of this drop can be explained by overall changes in the German and world stock markets. But there was no doubt that the company itself had also run into major difficulties, including implementing its global vision. The *Financial Times* commented: 'Mr Schrempp

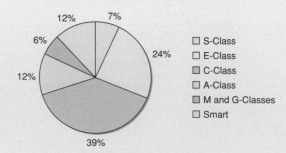

Figure 10.5

Mercedes Group sales by class of car 2004

- □ S-Class
- □ E-Class
- □ C-Class
- □ A-Class
- ▤ M and G-Classes
- □ Smart

Source: Company Annual Report and Accounts 2004.

will stay on. We must hope his grandiose vision [of a global strategy] will not.'

When interviewed in 2003, Mr Schrempp had no doubts about the original merger with Chrysler: 'I still believe that our merger of equals was fantastic . . . we are making tremendous progress,' he said. The chief executive continued to receive the full backing of his executive board, in spite of the difficulties that had arisen. He also received in 2004 a pledge of loyalty from his top managers, in spite of the failure of the Asian strategy. In 2005, Mr Schrempp again re-affirmed his belief in the broad global strategy of the group. He pointed out that the company had clear plans to resolve its difficulties. In addition, he commented that the company's global strategy was good for the company's home country, Germany: 'The ultimate way of how someone is judged having run a company is not only the bottom line . . . It is whether we have made a contribution to society. This point is close to my heart.'

Note: Just as this book was going to press, it was announced by DaimlerChrysler that Mr Schrempp was to step down as Chief Executive in late 2005 – almost two years early. He would be replaced by Mr Dieter Zetsche, who was previously responsible for the turn-around at the company's US Chrysler Division.

Case questions

1 *What was the vision of Daimler-Benz when it made its strategic moves outside Germany? What were the benefits? To what extent were such benefits achieved?*

2 *Should the company continue to pursue its global vision? Or should it accept the reality of its present position? What are its priorities?*

10.2 DEVELOPING A STRATEGIC VISION FOR THE FUTURE

Vision can be defined as 'a mental image of a possible and desirable future state of the organisation'.[25] In developing the purpose of the organisation, there are two views on the value of developing a strategic vision for the future of an organisation: first, that it is irrelevant; second, that it has value. We deal with these in turn.

10.2.1 The irrelevance of strategic vision

Where the short-term needs to take priority, it may not be appropriate to develop a strategic vision for an organisation. A famous example comes from the major computer company IBM in 1993 – *see* Case 2.6. The company had just appointed a new chief executive, Mr Lou Gerstner, to tackle its major profit problems. He commented: 'The last thing IBM needs right now is a vision.' What he meant was that the strategic context of the circumstances surrounding IBM made any strategy beyond an *immediate focus on turnaround* irrelevant. In this sense, strategic vision may be inappropriate in a strategic context where the short-term needs to take priority.

Given that a vision of the future is not always appropriate, the difficulty then comes in the correct definition of the strategic problem facing the organisation. There are no simple methods of undertaking this difficult task, which remains one of the most difficult facing any strategist. For example, DaimlerChrysler – *see* Case 10.2 – shows the company's difficulty in 2005 in identifying what should be the focus of the strategy at the company – is it Mercedes? Is it Smart? Is it the North American recovery? Is it rebuilding an Asian presence? Is Mr Schrempp himself part of the problem rather than the solution?

10.2.2 The value of strategic vision

Vision can be defined in more complete terms than the opening statement of this section.

Definition ➤ Vision is a challenging and imaginative picture of the future role and objectives of an organisation, significantly going beyond its current environment and competitive position. In spite of such difficulties, some strategists are convinced that there are at least five reasons to develop a strategic vision:[26]

1 Most organisations will compete for business and resources. They will have ambitions that go well beyond the immediate future and *any full investigation of purpose needs to explore this vision*. Even not-for-profit organisations or those in the public sector usually need to compete for charitable or government funds and often desire to increase the range of services that they offer; such organisations will also benefit from a picture of where they expect to be in the future.

2 The organisation's *mission and objectives may be stimulated* in a positive way by the strategic options that are available from a new vision.

3 There may be major strategic opportunities from exploring new development areas that go *beyond the existing market boundaries and organisational resources*.[27] These require a vision that deserves careful exploration and development.

4 Simple market and resource projections for the next few years will miss the opportunities opened up by a whole new range of possibilities, such as new information technologies, biogenetics, environmental issues, new materials and lifestyle changes. Virtually every organisation will feel the impact of these significant developments. *Extrapolating the current picture is unlikely to be sufficient*.[28]

5 Vision provides a desirable *challenge* for both senior and junior managers.

Vision is therefore a backdrop for the development of the purpose and strategy of the organisation.

To be clear, vision is not the same as purpose: vision is the *future* picture, with purpose being the more immediate and broader role and tasks that the organisation chooses to define based on the current situation. However, it may be that the vision will lead to the purpose: for example, the Daimler-Benz vision of a global car company led directly to its acquisitions of Chrysler and its minority shares in Mitsubishi and Hyundai.

Vision may also lead to a change in purpose. For example, a small grocery store competing against a new hypermarket might see its *vision* as being increased competition from a newly opened hypermarket. It might then change its purpose to that of moving from that geographical area, rather than be driven out by the larger store in two years' time.

Hamel and Prahalad[29] have suggested five criteria for judging the relevance and appropriateness of a vision statement. These are shown in Table 10.2. They are important because it would be all too easy to develop some wild and worthy vision that bore no relationship to the organisation, its resources and the likely market and competitive developments. Daimler-Benz was in this category during the period 1995–2000.

Table 10.2

Five criteria for judging the organisation's investigation of its vision

Criterion	Indicative area to be investigated
Foresight	What imagination and real vision is shown? Over what time frame?
Breadth	How broad is the vision of the changes likely to take place in the industry? And of the forces that will lead to the changes?
Uniqueness	Is there an element of uniqueness about the future? Will it cause our competitors to be surprised?
Consensus	Is there some consensus within the organisation about the future? If not, there may be a problem if too many different visions are pursued at once.
Actionability	Have the implications for current activity been considered? Is there basic agreement on the immediate steps required? Have the necessary core competencies and future market opportunities been identified?

The important action points that arise from the investigation of vision are connected with:

- *special resources*: do we have the technology and skills to meet this vision?
- *market opportunities*: what will this mean for market development? How can we take the opportunities as they arise?

It is also necessary to consider *how* the vision of the organisation is to be developed. It is likely that this will be guided by the chief executive officer. To quote Warren Bennis and Burt Nanus in their well-known text on leadership:

> *To choose a direction, a leader must first have developed a mental image of a possible and desirable future state of the organisation . . . The critical point is that a vision articulates a view of a realistic, credible, attractive future for the organisation, a condition that is better in some important ways than what now exists.*[30]

However, other strategists would argue that this should not be a task just for the leader but should involve many in the organisation. There is a strong case for using multifunctional teams that are brought together to investigate an area of the business. However, the precise format will depend on the prevailing culture of the organisation – *see* Chapter 12 for a further exploration of this important area.

Critical comment

Although the idea of vision is widely accepted as a useful addition to the general development of purpose, there is a problem. Vision has little meaning unless it can be successfully communicated to those working in the organisation, since these are the people that will have to realise it. The usual assumption is that such vision will be widely welcomed throughout the organisation. However, Hunt has questioned this and suggested that there will be groups of workers associated with many companies that do not have this degree of commitment.[31] He cites part-time workers, contracted suppliers and other flexible workers who may not feel committed to such a vision. 'This raises the question about the value of attempting to establish shared visions and values amongst different contributors. It highlights the fallacy of many human resources policies and practices based on some average employee.' As an example, Royal Dutch/Shell – *see* Chapter 7 – shows the difficulties that can arise from a senior management vision of a global company and a middle management view which was rather different.

Key strategic principles

- Strategic vision may be inappropriate in a strategic context where the short-term needs to take priority. The difficulty then becomes defining correctly the strategic problem facing the organisation. There are no simple methods of undertaking this difficult task.
- When developing purpose, there is a need to develop a vision of the future within which the organisation will operate. The main reason is to ensure that every opportunity is examined.
- Vision is not the same as the organisation's purpose, though the two may be related.
- There are five criteria that may assist in developing the organisation's vision: foresight, breadth, uniqueness, consensus and actionability.

Leadership in action: Jürgen Schrempp of Daimler-Benz

In 1995, Mr Jürgen Schrempp became the new chairman of the famous German car and truck company. He took over at a difficult time and steered the company towards building a global car and truck company. This case describes his leadership style and strategic decisions over the first few difficult years up to 2001. Commenting on his leadership style, the Financial Times *described him as 'a corporate animal driven by an insatiable appetite for power'.*

In spite of the many difficulties – *see* Case 10.2 – Jürgen Schrempp was still upbeat in 2001: 'DaimlerChrysler is on the way up and I have no doubt that what we have in mind will bring us to a new plateau. All the pillars are in place.'

Sitting on the 11th floor of the DaimlerChrysler Stuttgart headquarters, the chairman insists that he will not be deflected from his mission. 'We have done basically all the acquisitions we need and the divestments; we are 90 per cent automotive,' he says. 'Now the concentration is to have the right people and to have the right execution of our strategy.'

That grand perspective seems a long way from Mr Schrempp's humble origins at Daimler, where he began work as an apprentice mechanic at his local Mercedes dealership. In the intervening 40 years, the engineering graduate has emerged as the most powerful industrialist in Germany, with a global reputation as a turnaround expert. That record was honed in South Africa and the US, where he ran Mercedes' car operations and Euclid's heavy truck business, respectively. It culminated in a brutal overhaul of Daimler's European aerospace activities in the mid-1990s.

His attempt to repeat the exercise at Chrysler has won him few friends at the US carmaker. His reputation at the company's Auburn Hills headquarters has been scarred by a management exodus. Two successive Chrysler presidents, Tom Skallkamp and Jim Holden, have been fired. And the group has actioned six plant closures and 26,000 job losses. But Mr Schrempp is ready to defend his action. 'I deal with criticism by facing the music. I go to see the people,' he says. 'I listen and often go away with additional input, and sometimes think maybe we should address this or that point.'

In the end, however, he usually gets his way. In 1995 he wrested control of Daimler-Benz from Edzard Reuter, his previous boss, and set about refashioning the business from a diversified industrial group into a focused automotive business. He also engineered the departure of other executives, including Helmut Werner, former head of Mercedes car and truck businesses. 'Over the last five years, there have been a lot of management changes, notably more on the German side than the US. The job of the chief executive is to analyse, find weaknesses and to decide on change.'

His detractors argue that he has abandoned German-style social contracts in favour of US business values. Claiming DaimlerChrysler attaches more importance to its share price than workers' rights, they point to his dismemberment of Fokker, the Dutch aircraft maker, in the mid-1990s and the closure of Dornier factories in Germany.

He maintains that these are not 'lonesome decisions' but part of a long process, fully endorsed by the supervisory board and its labour representatives. In spite of his reputation as a

Jürgen Schrempp has been chief executive during a difficult period for the company's strategy.

tough cost-cutter, Mr Schrempp is said to be passionate about union representation in the supervisory board. He insists that restructuring is easier with union–management consensus, and he is not about to abandon co-determination at DaimlerChrysler. He says his record in South Africa, where he challenged apartheid policies, shows his commitment to corporate citizenship. He is still attached to the country and serves as South Africa's honorary consul general to Germany. To unwind, he likes to return to South Africa where he owns a game farm. 'I like the bush, I relax extremely well in the bush,' he says.

Not that the man described by friends as 'stateless, not rootless' gets a lot of time to watch game. 'I know what my priorities are at the moment. I so much believe in what we're doing and I put all my life and heart into proving the point.' As on most other matters, Mr Schrempp details those priorities at breakneck speed. Indeed, he is in such a rush that he has pulled on the wrong jacket as he runs between offices. Aides say his speed at work owes much to a personal fitness regime. Hotels on his itinerary are chosen according to gym facilities, with time reserved three or four times a week for hard exercise.

The DaimlerChrysler chairman also hints that fitness proves a useful antidote to his habit of living life to the full. 'I believe that where there's a healthy body there's a healthy brain,' he says. 'I like my wine; I like to live. But I have to do it in a disciplined way. I have weaknesses, as everybody knows. But I try to get people around me who have strengths where I have weaknesses.' What these weaknesses are he does not make clear. But a lack of willpower is not one of them. If a company could be driven to greater profits and shareholder value by force of personality, DaimlerChrysler would be one of the world's highest performing carmakers.

Overall, the effort to transform the company and build the global base is led by a group chairman who is reluctant to slow down. 'Sometimes friends ask: "Can you sustain that?" You can only do that if your life is in balance. I have a very happy private life,' he says. 'But there are people saying, "Shift one gear back" but there is no way – right or wrong – and I stand on the accelerator pedal to do it.'

Situation in 2005

By 2005, the company's situation still remained difficult. Mr Schrempp remained the chief executive and had been given the full support of the advisory board in 2004. However, he faced hostile criticism from shareholders at the Annual General Meeting of the company in April 2005: 'For seven years [since the merger of Daimler-Benz and Chrysler] management has said we should trust DaimlerChrysler and every year there is a disappointment . . . Schrempp has not kept his promises. Why should we trust him now?' commented Klaus Kaldemorgen, head of equities at DWS, a leading investment firm. Mr Schrempp responded that he found the Smart's results 'totally unacceptable' and he was 'unsatisfied' with the share price, which had underperformed its rivals since the merger. 'Each year he says he is unsatisfied with something,' said Thomas Körfgen head of equities at SEB Invest, another leading investment firm. 'When is he actually going to do something about it?'[32]

Case adapted by Richard Lynch from an article by Tim Burt, *Financial Times*, 26 February 2001, p12. Copyright *Financial Times*. Used with permission. Update by Richard Lynch.

Case questions

1 *How would you characterise the leadership style of Mr Schrempp?*

2 *To what extent has the purpose of the company changed under the chairmanship of Mr Schrempp? How important was leadership here?*

3 *Are there any dangers in leaders dominating their organisations? What are they? How might they affect the development of strategy? How should strong leaders cope with such dangers?*

10.3 PURPOSE AND THE ROLE OF LEADERSHIP

Definition ➤ Leadership is the art or process of influencing people so that they will strive willingly and enthusiastically towards the achievement of the organisation's purpose. As the case study on Jürgen Schrempp of DaimlerChrysler demonstrates, leadership will have a significant influence on the performance of the organisation. However, the basic argument of this section is that the precise relationships between leadership and purpose are complex and depend on the specific circumstances. This means that it is difficult to provide prescriptive general principles on the relationship between the two topics. Two ways are suggested in this section. One relies on the notion that leadership needs to avoid lasting conflict with subordinates. The other suggests that specific styles of leadership are likely to be associated with specific approaches to the development of purpose. Finally, it is suggested that the most successful leadership needs not just to define purpose in a cold, abstract manner but also to communicate trust, enthusiasm and commitment to the organisation.

10.3.1 Understanding the influence of leadership

Jürgen Schrempp of DaimlerChrysler, François Michelin of Michelin Rubber, Bill Gates of Microsoft, Akio Morita of Sony, Gianni Agnelli of Fiat are all examples of leaders who have guided and shaped the direction of their companies. *Leadership* is defined as 'influence, that is the art or process of influencing people so that they will strive willingly and enthusiastically toward the achievement of the group's mission'.[33]

The organisation's purpose and strategy do not just drop out of a process of discussion, but may be actively directed by an individual with strategic vision.

Visionary leadership inspires the impossible: fiction becomes truth.[34]

Leadership is a vital ingredient in developing the purpose and strategy of organisations. The potential that leaders have for influencing the overall direction of the company is arguably considerable. There is substantial anecdotal evidence to support this observation, though it is important to be aware of the hagiography (sainthood) that sometimes surrounds leaders – for example, the description of Jürgen Schrempp in Case study 10.3 portrays him in a generally favourable, if dominant, way. Nevertheless, in drawing up purpose and related strategy, it would be wise to consider carefully the personality, role and power of the leading person or group in the organisation.

Given the evident power that leaders may have in developing the company's mission and strategy, it is important to note some areas of caution based on research:

- Leaders should to some extent *reflect* their followers[35] and, in some company cultures may need to be good team players if they are to effect change. Otherwise, they will not be followed.

- Vision can be eccentric, obsessed and not always logical.[36]

- It is certainly possible to exaggerate the importance of individuals when they are leading large and diverse groups that have strong company–political instincts.[37]

Certainly, these latter features are important in the modern, complex consideration of corporate strategy. Companies such as Philip Morris (US), Royal Dutch/Shell (UK/Netherlands) and Toyota (Japan) may all be more comfortable with a corporate leader who is inclined to be evolutionary rather than revolutionary. To this extent, we may be suspicious of the hero worship of management saviours who have ridden with vision and purpose to the rescue of failing businesses. The same variations can be found in small business, not-for-profit and government organisations. In every case, leadership can have a profound effect on purpose.

10.3.2 Analysing leadership in the context of purpose

In order to understand the way that purpose and strategy interrelate with leadership, it is useful to analyse the leadership role. However, in spite of extensive study reaching back to the 1950s, there is no general agreement on leadership analysis.[38] There are three main approaches:

Definition ➤ 1 *Trait theories* argue that individuals with certain characteristics (traits) can be identified who will provide leadership in virtually any situation. According to the research that has been done, such individuals will be intelligent, self-assured, able to see beyond the immediate issues and come from higher socio-economic groups. In recent times, such theories have been discredited because the evidence to support them is inconsistent and clearly incomplete in its explanation of leadership. *Purpose* here would be decided largely by the individual leader.

Definition ➤ 2 *Style theories* suggest that individuals can be identified who possess a general style of leadership that is appropriate to the organisation. For example, two contrasting styles would be the authoritarian and the democratic: the former imposes the leader's will from the centre and the latter allows free debate before developing a solution. According to the research, this has some validity, but leadership is much more complex than the simplicities of style. For example, it needs to take into account the varied relationships between leaders and subordinates, the politics of decision making and the culture of the organisation. Such theories have therefore been downplayed in recent years. *Purpose* here would be defined by the leadership style.

Definition ➤ 3 *Contingency theories* explore the concept that leaders should be promoted or recruited according to the needs of the organisation at a particular point in time. The choice is *contingent* on the strategic issues facing the organisation at that time and leaders need to be changed as the situation itself changes. Thus the leader needs to be seen in relation to the group whom s/he will lead and the nature of the task to be undertaken. For example, recovery-from-disaster strategies will require a different type of leader from the steady development type of strategy. There is some evidence to support this approach but it is

Figure 10.6

An example of the best-fit approach to leadership analysis

Rigid ←——————————————————————————→ *Relaxed*

Chief executive officer

Senior/middle managers

Chosen purpose and strategies

- **Chief executive officer** prefers a structured style, possibly even dominant.
- **Senior/middle** managers like to be given more personal initiative and responsibility.
- **Chosen strategies** are tightly defined in some areas, but allow some managerial initiative.
- **Conclusion:** In the above case, the three areas do not 'fit' – change and compromise are needed. Purpose here may not be achieved with such contrasting styles and disagreements

still anecdotal and oversimplifies the leadership task. *Purpose* here would clearly depend on the strategic situation.

From a strategic perspective, the contingency theory approach holds the most promise for two reasons. It is the one that best captures both the leader and the relationship with others in the organisation, and it also identifies clearly the importance of the strategic situation as being relevant to the analysis of leadership.

Within contingency theory, there is one approach that is particularly used: it is called the *best-fit* analytical approach. This is essentially based on the notion that leaders, subordinates and strategies must reach some compromise if they are to be successfully carried forward. There may be some difference of views but, ultimately, purpose will best be developed by some agreement between them. This is useful in corporate strategy because it allows each situation to be treated differently and it identifies three key analytical elements:

1 the chief executive officer or leader;

2 the senior/middle managers who carry out the tasks; and

3 the nature of the purpose and strategies that will be undertaken.

Each of these is then plotted on a common scale, ranging from rigid (or heavily structured) to relaxed (or supportive and flexible). The best fit is then sought between these three elements. An example is shown in Figure 10.6. The result is inevitably vague but may prove useful in identifying the balance of style and its influence on people, strategies and purpose.

10.3.3 Leadership style and its relationship with the development of purpose

Leadership style can vary from the *shared vision* approach of Senge to the *dominance* of individuals like the first Henry Ford or Margaret Thatcher in the UK in the late 1980s. Each style will influence the way that purpose is developed and the content that results.

Shared vision approach

Senge had a useful perspective on the relationship between the organisation and its leadership.[39] It is the *leaders* of the organisation who can show the way. However, he argued that, in well-managed development, the *whole organisation* is involved in developing the purpose and strategy. The way an organisation evolves is a function of its leadership as much as its strategy. However, the leader does not dominate and decide for the organisation; rather s/he helps the organisation to develop a *shared purpose* of its future and the changes required to achieve it. It is the leader who focuses on the underlying trends, forces for change and their impact on the organisation. To explain his view, Senge quotes an age-old vision of leadership that expresses this relationship between the leader and the organisation:

> *The wicked leader is he who people despise.*
> *The good leader is he who people revere*
> *The great leader is he who the people say, 'We did it ourselves.'*
>
> Lao Tsu

Thus, purpose here is developed by co-operation, discussion and broad agreement. The outcome may be slow, complicated and a compromise but it is likely to be well understood by everyone and to generate strong commitment from those involved in developing it.

Dominance approach

The words of Lao Tsu read well, but they may not be appropriate in some strategic situations. If a company is in crisis, then it may need strong and firm central leadership to enable it to survive. When a company is in the early stages of development, with a new vision about its future, it may also benefit from a strong, entrepreneurial leader with a quite different style and approach to the purpose.

In this case, purpose is developed mainly by the choice of the leader and, possibly, the immediate subordinates. It will be largely imposed on others in the organisation and will not engender the same degree of commitment.

Contrasting the two basic approaches: other styles of leadership

The leadership system that best describes the management style of the leader needs to be taken into account in devising the purpose and strategy. Where the leader is dominant then s/he will be involved early. Where the leader is more consultative then early involvement will be on a more participative basis. In addition, the style of the leader will be conditioned by the style and culture of the organisation and the development of purpose and strategy will also need to take this into account in devising its procedures.

In order to explore the main elements, the above discussion has relied on two basic leadership styles in the exploration of purpose. Other styles can be identified – some are shown in Exhibit 16.7.

Choice of leadership style

Leaders and their organisations will wish to consider how they should be led. The choice of leadership style will ultimately depend on a number of factors that go beyond the personality and personal wishes of the individual. Some factors that will influence leadership style are shown in Exhibit 10.1.[40]

Exhibit 10.1

Factors influencing the leadership style of organisations

- Personality and skills of leader
- Size of company
- Degree of geographical dispersion
- Stability of organisation's environment
- Current management style of the organisation's culture
- Organisation's current profitability and its desire and need for change

10.3.4 The importance of trust, enthusiasm and commitment – the contribution of Bennis and Nanus

In developing the purpose of the organisation, it is important to recognise that such a process will affect many parts of the organisation in terms of its impact. Thus, if leadership is to be successful, it cannot be regarded as just a cold and abstract analytical statement. The leader needs to generate trust, enthusiasm and commitment amongst key members of the organisation for the chosen purpose.

Amongst the most widely read writers on leadership in relation to the tasks of the organisation are Warren Bennis and Burt Nanus. These two US authors researched leadership amongst US organisations in the 1980s. They included failure as well as success and wrote a highly successful book full of short anecdotes and pithy conclusions on leadership and especially its people aspects.[41]

With regard to purpose only, their conclusions on successful leadership suggest that:

- Leaders need to generate and sustain *trust* in the strategy process and the general integrity of the organisation while developing its purpose.

- Leaders will deliver a more robust statement of purpose if they have generated and used the *intellectual capital* of the many people involved in the organisation. This means that leaders have tapped the knowledge, interest and experience of those below them in the organisation.

- Leaders need to demonstrate a *passion and determination* to seek out and then achieve the purpose that has been identified by the process.

As was clearly demonstrated with Mr Jürgen Schrempp in Case study 10.3, leadership is not just a matter of identifying purpose in a cold and abstract manner. Leadership needs to demonstrate commitment, develop understanding and fire enthusiasm for the purpose if it is to be successful. Another example of leadership is that of Mr Andy Grove, the highly successful leader of Intel, the US computer chip manufacturer. He also needed to go beyond the cold, clinical definition of purpose to redirect his company's purpose at several crucial points during the 1990s when his company was in trouble.

10.3.5 Prescriptive and emergent approaches to leadership

Airport bookshops are full of leadership texts that claim to identify good leaders and the characteristics that are essential to fulfil such a role. These are usually prescriptive approaches to the leadership task and imply that all good leaders have particular attributes. But such books need to be treated with caution if contingent theories are correct, because such theories suggest that leadership depends on the strategic circumstances of the organisation. There is no one best way.

There is an additional reason for caution. The act of identifying leadership as a prime mover in the development of strategy reduces the role of other elements that are important. For example, team building and family ownership of the company can be equally important factors in certain types of organisation.

> ### Key strategic principles
>
> - Leaders can have a profound influence on mission and objectives. They may be particularly important in moving the organisation forward to new challenges. However, in large and complex organisations their role is more likely to be evolutionary than revolutionary.
>
> - There is no agreement on how to analyse leadership. Contingency theories are probably the most useful approach. They state that the choice and style of

Key strategic principles *continued*

leadership is *contingent* on the strategic issues facing the organisation at that point in time.

● Within the context of contingency theory, the best-fit analytical approach can be used. It is useful in strategy because it allows each situation to be treated differently.

● Leadership style can vary from shared vision to dominance. The style needs to be modified to suit the strategic situation, with other styles being possible depending on the organisation and its environment.

● With regard to purpose, leaders need to generate trust in the strategic process. They need to draw upon the intellectual capital of the organisation and to demonstrate passion and determination.

● In some circumstances, leadership may be better served by allowing the purpose to emerge from the group working on a strategic task, rather than be imposed by the leader from the centre.

CASE STUDY 10.4

Citigroup – rebuilding its corporate governance

Citigroup is the world's largest financial institution, dealing every day in billions of dollars of banking instruments such as currencies, shares and bonds. It is a lead-bank in the financing of major world capital projects as well as handling over 200 million customers worldwide. Yet it has recently been involved in a series of financial scandals that have led the company to rebuild its corporate governance. This case explains how this came about and what is now being done.

Citigroup's growth

Starting as a bank around 200 years ago in New York City, Citigroup has grown over the last 20 years by a series of aggressive acquisitions and mergers in many parts of the world. The major change took place in 1998 when Citigroup itself merged with Travelers to 'create a new model of financial services to serve its clients' financial needs'. In addition, there were large numbers of smaller firms acquired over the period 1995–2003. By 2004, the company was the world's largest financial institution, with dealings in over 100 countries around the world and major activities in all the leading financial centres.

In the period 1998–2004, Citigroup's net revenue almost doubled and its net income went up even faster – see Table 10.3 – and this all happened in a company that was already large by international standards. Importantly, its employee numbers never increased as fast, implying that each employee delivered increasing amounts of business and profits over that time. In practice, what happened was that each of the acquisitions added to turnover but the 'back office' of most of the takeover candidates – the administration, systems, financial compliance, the IT support – was substantially reduced by Citigroup and replaced by Citigroup's own systems. This

Table 10.3

Citigroup: major growth in revenue and net income, but not in employees

	1998	1999	2000	2001	2002	2003	2004
Total net revenues US$ billions	45.00	54.80	63.60	67.40	71.30	77.40	86.20
Net income US$ millions	6 950	11 243	13 519	14 126	15 276	17 853	17 046
Employees	202 400	212 500	233 000	268 000	250 000	253 000	287 000

Source: Company Annual Report and Accounts 2004.

Citibank became the world's largest bank by a series of acquisitions and mergers that eventually led the company itself to redefine its ethics and corporate governance.

produced substantial cost savings and justified the company purchases but it had two other effects:

1 It reduced the people available for undertaking governance activities in the new subsidiaries.

2 It made central monitoring of a large group even more complex – there were not enough people.

The new, much-enlarged Citigroup of 2003 was a mixture of many different types of financial operations. It included investment banking, credit card operations, retail banking and lending to poorer people. Importantly, this vast range of banking activity resulted in two further issues:

● It meant that there were possible conflicts of interest between these different operations which would impact on governance. For example, the investment banking business might be advising on a new takeover at the same time as the private banking part of Citigroup was considering investing in the takeover candidate.

● The knowledge and skills needed in the various parts of the bank are quite varied – for example, investment banking is quite different from credit card handling. This made it difficult for Citigroup to transfer people between parts of the company – useful if Citigroup wanted to develop a new company organisational culture.

Citigroup's rule breaking

Over the period 1998–2003, Citigroup was governed by the style of its chief executive, Sanford Weill. It was Mr Weill who prompted many of the deals and mergers that doubled the size of Citigroup. Specifically, Mr Weill put pressure on his colleagues to make such deals work financially – he set tough profit targets for the operating subsidiaries and they were then given considerable autonomy to achieve them. According to the *Financial Times* commenting on Citigroup, 'Executives who cut corners to hit quarterly profit targets could earn large performance bonuses.'[42] Ms Amey Stone, a journalist with the financial magazine *Business Week*, co-authored a book on

Mr Weill: '[He] was a very hands on and controlling manager who oversaw a lot of operations. He did have an aggressive style, he emphasised profits, he was very strict about divisions delivering profits. I think questions of ethics really took a back seat.'[43]

Whatever the pressures on its employees, Citigroup became involved in a series of financial rule-breaking deals:

● Citigroup is expecting to have to pay nearly US$5 billion to cover legal actions arising from its relationship with the bankrupt telecoms company Worldcom – *see* Exhibit 10.2 at the end of this chapter.[44] It also faces similar difficulties with regard to Enron – see Exhibit 10.2.[45]

● Citigroup will pay US$20 million in fines to resolve US federal regulators' allegations that it kept from customers the fact that brokers were paid to recommend certain mutual funds, creating a conflict of interest. In a related action, the US National Association of Securities Dealers disclosed that Citigroup, American Express Co and JPMorgan Chase and Co had agreed to pay a total of US$21.25 million for alleged violations in sales of mutual funds – within this, Citigroup itself agreed to pay US$6.25 million.[46]

● Citigroup was scheduled to pay the American Securities and Exchange Commission almost US$200 million after an investigation into commission payments.[47]

● Citigroup agreed to pay US$75 million to settle a class action suit over its role in the collapse of the telecom network provider Global Crossing.[48]

● Citigroup was forced to close its Japanese private bank after 'repeatedly breaking local rules'.[49]

In addition at the time of writing, Citigroup was facing legal action by the administrators of the Italian food group Parmalat – *see* Exhibit 10.2. However, it is important to note that Citigroup denied any wrongdoing with regard to this activity. Citigroup had also been cleared by the German financial market regulator of criminal wrongdoing with regard to bond trading in European government bonds in August 2004: 'Like in cases of fraud, there must be evidence of deception in order to press charges,' the German federal prosecutors explained. The bank allegedly made a profit of US$17.5 million on the trade.[50] Importantly, when Citigroup was given permission by the US central reserve bank – the US Federal Reserve – to take over a privately held Texas bank in 2005, the Fed was prompted to advise Citigroup to delay big takeover plans 'until it tightens internal controls and addresses many regulatory problems inside and outside the United States.'[51]

In practice, Citigroup had already decided that it needed to make a major change in its practices: '2004 was not a good year for us. There are places where we have done some things we should not have done. We need to make things right and express our regret. We need to move on and make sure we're learning form it,' explained Sallie Krawcheck, Citigroup's chief financial officer.

Citigroup's new corporate governance approach

In 2003, Citigroup appointed a new chief executive, Charles (Chuck) Prince. He undertook a major survey of the company ▶

during 2004 and formed the view that radical change was required. In a message to employees in February 2005, he said: 'Let me be very clear: to be the most respected company does not require a sea change in our culture. Citigroup already has one of the world's most respected names in financial services with a legacy and record of accomplishment few companies could even dream to match. Yet at times our actions have put at risk our most precious commodity – the trust of our clients, the patience of our employees, and the faith of our shareholders.'

The company developed a five point plan to enhance corporate governance at Citibank:

1 *Expanded training*: annual franchise training for all employees, with special training for the top 3,000 managers.
2 *Improved communications*: bimonthly dialogue between the chief executive and senior managers; broad communications with all employees, including an 'ethics hotline'.
3 *Enhanced focus on talent and development*: executive coaching; anonymous feedback on senior managers; expansion of development programmes.
4 *Balanced performance appraisal and compensation*: consistent appraisal and goal setting for senior managers; evaluation of middle-level managers; compensation on the basis of Citigroup performance – not how an individual performs. This latter point was important – performance pay was to be based on the group's results, not on whether an individual had achieved a particular profit target.
5 *Strengthened controls*: independent global compliance function; risk control assessments; expanded audit coverage; continuing education for control function managers such as financial audit personnel. There was almost a

threat: 'Unsatisfactory results in Risk Control Assessments, audits or regulatory exams will be reviewed personally with Chuck Prince and Bob Willumstad.'

In addition to its five-point plan, Citigroup also developed a 13-page set of guidelines on corporate governance especially for its board of directors. These covered such issues as the directorial independence of two-thirds of the board; qualifications to ensure board directors were adequately skilled and experienced; insistence that board directors should offer to resign if they were given major new responsibilities in other organisations; annual reviews of directors' performance; regular attendance at board meetings; direct access to senior managers to review important issues; rules on insider transactions and other business relationships.[52]

Commenting on the changes, the British newspaper, the *Financial Times* concluded: 'Focused financial services companies find themselves involved in scandals from time to time. It will be much harder for a diversified group to avoid such lapses, given the nature of the industry. Mr Prince's plans are welcome, but it will require laser-like execution to make them effective.'[53]

© Copyright Richard Lynch 2006. All rights reserved. This case was written from published information only.

Case questions

1 *How do you assess the changes in corporate governance at Citigroup? Will they be successful?*

2 *Can other companies learn anything from Citigroup or is the company so different from others that no useful conclusions can be drawn?*

10.4 CORPORATE GOVERNANCE AND THE PURPOSE OF THE ORGANISATION

As the Citigroup case shows, corporate governance has become increasingly important in corporate strategy. The chief executive can influence every aspect of an organisation, including the way that it treats its employees, its customers, its shareholders and other stakeholders. But it is the chief executive and other executive directors that take strategic decisions on behalf of the stakeholders. Corporate governance refers to the influence and power of the stakeholders to control the strategic direction of the organisation in general and, more specifically, the chief executive and other senior officers of the organisation.

Definition ➤

The corporate governance relationship with strategy arises from the opportunities given to senior managers to influence the future purpose of the organisation. The senior officers are usually the directors of the organisation. However, they may also include senior representatives of workers and senior outside advisers with no daily responsibility for strategy development. In some European countries such as Germany, Sweden and the Netherlands, this latter group would constitute a supervisory board that oversaw the work of the directors.

Many public bodies will also have corporate governance structures. These are likely to cover the major issues of the not-for-profit sector, including the monitoring of the quality of public services and the value-for-money obtained by taxpayers and charity givers.

For most organisations, corporate governance goes beyond selecting, remunerating and reviewing the conduct of the senior officers. It will also include a review and approval process for the main corporate strategies that have been developed by the officers. Typically, such a procedure might take place on an annual basis. In addition, to quote the corporate governance statement of the major international oil company British Petroleum,[54] there may be additional monitoring during the year to test 'the confidence in or risks to the achievement of the performance objectives and the observance of the strategy and policies'. Such policies have been tightened up in the wake of a number of corporate scandals in recent years – *see* Exhibit 10.2.

Exhibit 10.2	

Some examples of extreme problems in corporate governance

Company	Situation
Enron – an American company trading in energy futures	Enron was valued at US$60 billion in 2000 but filed for bankruptcy in 2001. In late 2001, the company admitted inflating its profits. Various senior executives were prosecuted for corrupt practice – at the time of writing, not all had been found guilty. The company's accounting auditors – Andersen – were at that time one of the world's Big Five: their financial audits did not identify the Enron problems and they collapsed in the wake of the scandal.
WorldCom – an American company involved in telecommunications services	WorldCom's chief executive officer, Bernie Ebbers, was found guilty in 2005 of engineering an US$11 billion accounting fraud in order to keep WorldCom's share price high and prevent margin calls on his personal outstanding loans totalling US$400 million. At the time of writing, Mr Ebbers was expected to receive a 25-year prison sentence.
Vivendi – a French company that acquired one of the world's largest entertainment companies – Universal	In December 2003, the chief executive of Vivendi Universal, M. Jean-Marie Messier, was fined US$1 million by the US Securities and Exchange Commission. He was denied a US$25 million golden payout and barred from being an officer in a publicly listed US company for ten years. He was accused of fraudulently disguising cash flow and liquidity problems by improperly accounting to meet earnings targets and by failing to disclose huge off-balance sheet financial commitments.
Skandia – a Swedish company engaged in offering insurance services in Scandinavia and the US	In 2002, the company was forced to sell its flagship US operation with a loss of US$600 million because of a collapse in profitability through inflated share prices. It was also suggested that a small group of senior executives extracted around US$100 million as bonuses from the company in the period 1997–2000 and gained the benefit of luxurious residences in the centre of Stockholm. There was particularly strong criticism of the way that Skandia used the funds of its insurance policy holders to prop up such plans: 'Skandia's troubles provide an example of what can happen when strong management is left unchecked by a weak board.' (*Financial Times*, 2 December 2003, p31)
Parmalat – an Italian company involved in milk processing, dairies and related agricultural products in over 40 countries around the world	In January 2004, it had been established that at least US$13 billion was missing from the balance sheet of Parmalat. At the time of writing, the full investigation was still in progress but it would seem that a fraud involving US$10 billion had been perpetrated, with Sig. Calisto Tanzi, the company's founder and chairman, being under investigation and house arrest.

STRATEGIC PROJECT

You might like to follow up the examples of malpractice given in Exhibit 10.2, along with some others: there are references on the *Corporate Strategy* website to assist you. Are such offences rare? What actions have companies taken to stop them happening again? What has been the impact on the purpose, costs and strategies of other companies?

It should be emphasised that the majority of companies do not behave corruptly. However, the serious consequences of major scandals in this area have led to considerable tightening of corporate governance in recent years. These are described in the sections that follow.

10.4.1 Separation of ownership and control

Because the senior officers are responsible for taking strategic decisions and then acting upon them, they act as *agents* for the stakeholders. In this sense, there is a separation of the *interests* of the organisation represented by the stakeholders and the *control* of the organisation vested in the directors. Corporate governance has become important because the interests of the stakeholders in recent years have not always coincided with the interests of the directors. For example at Citibank, the directors appear on occasions to have been willing to cut corners in order to grow the company, but have incurred significant penalties that have then to be deducted from shareholder dividends.

Larger companies now separate ownership and control. For example at BP Oil – *see* Exhibit 10.4 later in this chapter – the company has a clear separation between the *executive* directors who manage the business affairs of the company and the *non-executive* directors whose task is to monitor this management activity.

10.4.2 The power of corporate governance

The importance of corporate governance lies in the *power* that is given to the senior officers to run the affairs of the organisation. In recent times, this power has not always been used in the best interests of the shareholders, employees or society in general. Examples of the abuse of this power abound, but are illustrated by a consideration of the UK company magnate Robert Maxwell. This man was chairman of a major international publishing and media group in the late twentieth century. By all accounts, he was corrupt, yet continued to operate with impunity for some years; the situation was only discovered after he died in a boating accident in 1993. Some other examples are shown in Exhibit 10.2.

More recent governance incidents may not be so extreme. They have often related to the pay and other privileges that board members have awarded themselves to the detriment of others inside and outside the organisation – for example, the 'fat cat' company directors of the UK gas and electricity companies who gave themselves large share options at the time of privatisation and ended up with vast fortunes at the expense of the nation.

As a result of these and other matters, professional bodies (especially those in the accounting profession) have set up standards to govern the ethical and professional conduct of the senior officers of organisations. Several commissions on such standards have also produced reports: for example, the Cadbury, Greenbury and Hampel committees in the UK, the Vienot report in France and the Dutch Governance Commission. In the US, the corrupt behaviour at some companies led to the passing in 2002 of the Sarbanes-Oxley Act. This act made it essential for all companies operating in the US (including foreign companies) to keep an *audit trail* of all decisions taken by the company. For many companies, this has involved totally new procedures that have been lengthy, costly and time-consuming.

10.4.3 Governance and information flows

The problem with so much power concentrated into the central management of the organisation is that it needs to be used with responsibility. This difficulty is made worse if poor-quality information about the organisation's performance is given to other stakeholders in the organisation – wrongdoing will go unchecked as long as it remains unknown or unreported. Thus one of the key aspects of corporate governance is that of information and its availability – good-quality information will encourage responsible conduct. Sarbanes-Oxley was designed precisely to achieve this.

It might be thought that the easy way to ensure governance would be to require that information should be freely available on all the main activities of the organisation. The difficulty here is that some information will be commercially sensitive, so cannot easily be sent outside the organisation or even circulated fully inside it. However, the danger of not circulating the full information is that commercial sensitivity can be used as an excuse to hide what is going on by those who do not wish to reveal it.

The starting point in resolving such a conflict is to identify the normal flows of information that exist between the organisation and those inside and outside it. Exhibit 10.3 lists some of the typical flows of information that will be regularly available to different stakeholder groups. Ultimately, stakeholders are often reliant on independent professional advisers to inspect the information on a confidential basis – as accountants do in an annual audit – to confirm responsible conduct.

Exhibit 10.3

Typical information available to different stakeholders in a company

Stakeholder	Information regularly obtained	Comment
Shareholders	Annual report and accounts	Limited to what the organisation wants its shareholders to know
Investment analysts, e.g. in stock-broking companies; also journalists	Regular updates of progress, sometimes face-to-face meetings	Better informed but still possible for the organisation to mislead
Main company board	Relatively full information but possible to mislead; legal obligation to be properly informed and to inform	Full disclosure of all issues is assisted by the character and independence of any non-executive directors
Senior managers	Detailed information in some areas but rely on managers to bring issues to their notice – remember Nick Leeson of Barings Bank	Likely to be without the full picture available to the main board; can be the 'whistleblower' on unethical, illegal or improper conduct but may also engage in such conduct
Managers	Some information but often incomplete	Can sometimes be the 'whistleblower' but under considerable pressure to conform to company rules
Employees	Usually only limited information unless the workers have representatives on a supervising board	New EU directives make senior representation more likely and offer some protection here

Another important check can be provided if some of the main board members have semi-independent status, i.e. their main responsibilities and experience rest elsewhere. They are usually associated with organisations that have no commercial or other interest whatsoever in the organisation but have sufficient senior experience to comment on its affairs. These people are usually called *non-executive directors*, meaning that they have no day-to-day management responsibility for the operation of the organisation. In recent years, the appointment of these independent directors has been seen as a means of ensuring that the conduct of the organisation is beyond reproach. The danger of such a system is that the choice of who to appoint to non-executive positions remains with the company being monitored. However, if non-executives are of sufficient prominence in their own fields, then other stakeholders can have confidence in their independence of judgement. The Citigroup case earlier in the chapter shows how that company was willing to set out procedures to ensure the non-executive directors would remain independent.

10.4.4 Governance and corporate conduct

Beyond the matter of information availability, corporate governance is more a matter of the principles for conducting the organisation's affairs than of hard and fast rules. It is concerned with ensuring that the value added generated by the assets of the organisation is distributed equitably among the stakeholders. The principal officers of the organisation bear prime responsibility for this task, under the supervision of the main or supervisory board. Importantly, corporate governance often insists on a separation between the roles of chairman and chief executive of the organisation:

- *Chairman.* The most senior person in the organisation but without day-to-day responsibility for its operation. The chairman often concentrates relations *outside* the organisation, such as those with banks, government and shareholders.
- *Chief executive.* The most senior manager with responsibility for day-to-day operations, including the preparation and implementation of strategy. All directors, apart from the non-executive directors, would report to this person. The chief executive often concentrates on relations *within* the organisation.

Exhibit 10.4

Corporate governance at BP Oil: the principal committees of its board of directors

BP Oil is one of the world's largest oil companies, with interests in every continent. The BP committees are responsible not only for governance matters but also for the ethics and social responsibility issues explored in the next section. Membership of each committee includes a number of non-executive directors, who have no day-to-day responsibility for the development and execution of the affairs and strategies of the organisation. However, they will have relevant outside experience and knowledge of other similar organisations – in this case, the oil industry and financial reporting – so that they can ask difficult but appropriate questions.

Committee	Responsibility
Chairman's committee	Considers broad issues of governance, including the performances of the chairman and group chief executive. It is also concerned with succession planning and how the group is organised.
Audit committee	Systematic monitoring and obtaining assurance that the legally required standards of disclosure are met and that the executive limitations with regard to financial matters are being observed. Also reviewed implementation of Sarbanes-Oxley. This committee has a heavy workload.
Ethics and environment committee	Monitors matters relating to the executive's management processes to address environmental, health and safety, security and ethical behaviour.
Remuneration committee	Determines on behalf of the board the terms of engagement and remuneration of the executive directors.
Nominations committee	Identifies and evaluates candidates for appointment and re-appointment as directors or company secretary, especially in relation to coming work programmes and retirements.

Source: BP Annual Report and Accounts, 2004. Available on the web at: www.bp.com/investors.

Some organisations combine the two roles but this has been actively discouraged in recent reviews of corporate governance, such as those by Hampel and Higgs. However, such a separation may be too elaborate for small companies. The main way of monitoring the corporate governance task is typically through a series of committees that have responsibility for specific areas of the organisation – an example is shown in Exhibit 10.4. Many of these committees will have decision-making influence in areas that are directly related to corporate strategy – for example, those responsible for the effectiveness of the organisation and for considering attitudes to business risk.

Key strategic principles

- Corporate governance refers to the influence and power of the stakeholders to control the strategic direction of the organisation in general and, more specifically, the chief executive and other senior officers of the organisation.

- Corporate governance relates primarily to the selection, remuneration and conduct of the senior officers of the organisation. It is also concerned about their relationships with the owners, employees and other stakeholders of the organisation. The senior officers act as agents on behalf of the stakeholders in the organisation.

- The importance of corporate governance lies in the power that it gives the senior officers to run the affairs of the organisation. The problem with power is that it needs to be used responsibly.

- One check on the responsible conduct of the organisation is the information relayed to all the stakeholders – good-quality information will encourage responsible conduct. The problem is that such information may be commercially sensitive. Confidential independent advisers, such as accountants in an audit, may be the means of keeping check on corporate conduct.

- Another way of checking on the conduct of the company is by the appointment of non-executive directors who have no other commercial connection with the company.

- Beyond the matter of information availability, corporate governance is more a matter of the principles of conduct than simple rules. The main aim is to ensure that the value generated by the assets of the organisation is distributed equitably amongst the stakeholders.

10.5 PURPOSE SHAPED BY ETHICS AND CORPORATE SOCIAL RESPONSIBILITY

Definition ➤

Decisions on ethics and corporate social responsibility are at the heart of corporate strategy. They particularly influence the purpose of the organisation. By ethics and corporate social responsibility is meant the standards and conduct that an organisation sets itself in its dealings within the organisation and outside with its environment.

- *Ethics* is particularly concerned with the *basic* standards for the conduct of business affairs – for example, policy with regard to honesty, health and safety and corrupt practice.

- *Corporate social responsibility* has a *wider remit* to include the organisation's responsibility beyond the minimum to its employees and those outside the organisation. Topics will vary with each organisation but may include environmental 'green' issues, treatment of employees and suppliers, charitable work and other matters related to the local or national community.

In practice, both ethics and corporate responsibility are interrelated and are therefore treated as one topic in this section. Such issues concern not only business organisations like BP Oil and Citigroup but also public and not-for-profit organisations. In the new millennium, both businesses and not-for-profit organisations can wield significant power both inside and outside their organisations. Most therefore now accept that some form of ethical standards and governance should govern and guide their activities. There are plenty of examples of the significance of such issues: for example, the *Exxon Valdez*; disposal of a Royal Dutch/Shell North Sea oil platform; the international ivory trade; the case of the American company Enron.[55] There is no one appropriate time to introduce a consideration of such standards but it is appropriate to examine them in the development of the organisation's purpose.

10.5.1 Ethics and corporate social responsibility: basic issues[56]

To study such issues is to try to identify what is morally correct behaviour for the organisation. There are four main reasons for considering the ethical conduct of organisations:

1 In every society, such considerations are sometimes *inescapable*, e.g. legal limits on conduct.[57]

2 They may be *important* to conduct in that society, e.g. respect for 'green issues' in the environment that go beyond legal limits.[58]

3 A consideration of ethics is part of the *professionalisation* of business, e.g. the treatment of workers and ethnic groups.[59]

4 The *self-interest* of organisations is often best served by developing attitudes to ethical issues before they become acute, e.g. bad publicity as a result of accusations of incorrect behaviour.

Exhibit 10.5 shows some examples of the type of issues that can readily arise. Any one of these would justify the exploration of ethics and corporate social responsibility issues. They raise three basic areas that need to be explored in the context of purpose and strategy development:

1 the extent and scope of ethical and social responsibility considerations;

2 the cost of such considerations;

3 the recipient of the responsibility.

In more detail:

● *Extent and scope*. Beyond the legal minimum, to what extent does the organisation wish to consider the ethical and social responsibility issues that could arise in its conduct of its business? Does it wish to be involved in every area or lay down some basic principles and then leave parts of the organisation or individuals to conduct themselves appropriately?

● *Cost*. Some actions will have a cost to the organisation. Many of the real conflicts arise here because if the actions were without cost then they would be easily undertaken. There are no abstract rules but each organisation will need to consider this area.

● *Recipient*. Is it considered that the organisation has a responsibility to the state? To the local community? To individuals? To special interest groups? These matters will need careful consideration in the light of the particular circumstances of the organisation.

Beyond these matters, ethical and social responsibility considerations may influence corporate strategy at a number of levels – these are shown in Exhibit 10.6. The values of the organisation will then need to be reflected in its purpose and possibly its mission statement; even the *absence* of values in the mission is itself a statement about the organisation and its view about its role in society. Such matters may well reflect the role that the organisation sees itself playing in society, if any, and the responsibilities that flow from this.

Exhibit 10.5

Ethical and corporate social responsibility issues

Some basic examples of ethical issues that might impact on purpose

- *Espionage.* How does a company find out about competition? Where does reasonable enquiry finish and aggressive search for additional data commence? Perhaps anything goes?

- *Tyrannical regimes.* Does a company sell weapons or even life-saving equipment to a country that is run by regimes retaining power by unjustified use of force and human rights abuses? After all, the argument might be that lives might be saved in that country and jobs could be preserved in the selling company.

- *Bribery and corruption.* Should all organisations refuse to engage in such activity in every circumstance? Jobs may be saved and contracts won for only limited sums to a small number of people. On the other hand, the organisation itself would not wish to be on the receiving end of such conduct so why should it encourage it in others? Moreover, might it be profoundly unacceptable in society?

- *Telling half-truths and operating misleading negotiating tactics.* If such practices are unacceptable in general society, are they also unacceptable in business negotiations? Or does business operate by a different set of rules?

Some basic examples of corporate responsibility issues that might impact on purpose

- *Treatment of suppliers.* Some global clothing companies have been criticised for allowing the workers in Asian and African companies who make up their clothes to employ very young workers and also pay them very low wages in relation to the price paid by the final customer.

- *'Green issues':* some companies have been criticised for failing to stop the destruction of the world's forests in order to feed customer demand for quality wood like mahogany. Other companies have been criticised for over-fishing some of the world's oceans in order to satisfy customer demand for fish products, regardless of the long-term impact on the environment.

- *Education:* on a more positive note, some companies judge that they have a role to help educate and inform the community in which they live, thereby contributing to the social development of society.

Exhibit 10.6

Ethical and social responsibility considerations: some connections with corporate strategy

- *The national and international level* – the role of the organisation in society and the country. Political, economic and social issues such as those explored in Chapter 3 will impact here: *laissez-faire* versus *dirigiste*, the role and power of trade blocks and state social policies. The organisation is entitled to have a view on these matters and seek to influence society, if it so desires.

- *The corporate level* – ethical and corporate issues over which the organisation has some direct control. Such matters as the preservation of the environment, contributions to political parties, representations to the country's legislative parliament are all examples of direct corporate activities that need to be resolved.

- *The individual manager and employee level* – standards of behaviour which organisations will wish to set for individual managers and workers. Some of these matters may not be strategic in nature in the sense that they are unlikely to affect the future direction of the organisation overall but rather the future of individuals. However, there may well be some general policies on, for example, *religious, ethnic and equality issues* that involve both the individual and fundamental matters relating to the direction of the organisation. These general matters of policy deserve to be treated at the highest possible level and therefore come within the ambit of corporate strategy.

10.5.2 Corporate social responsibility: shareholder and stakeholder perspectives[60]

It should be noted that not all commercial organisations believe that they have a role beyond their own business. They take the view that society is perfectly capable of looking after itself and the prime responsibility of the enterprise is to care for its shareholders: this view was particularly prevalent during the stock market boom of the late 1990s. It was captured in the film *Wall Street* in which Michael Douglas played the crooked financier Gordon Gecko, who infamously believed that 'greed is good'. Such a view would probably mean that the company's purpose is unlikely to include any explicit comment on business ethics. It should be emphasised that this does *not* mean that such a company would behave unethically: simply that there is no need to reflect this in its purpose; its responsibilities are limited to the interests of the company. This is related to the *shareholder perspective* explored earlier in the chapter.

There are other companies which take the view that it is in the long-term benefit of both the company and the shareholders for the company to play a role in society beyond the minimum described by law. Sponsorship of outside initiatives, welfare provisions for workers, strong ethical beliefs and standards may all follow from such a view and be reflected in comments *associated with* the purpose and possibly the mission statement. This is the *stakeholder perspective* explored earlier in the chapter.

Beyond this again, there are organisations that exist primarily or wholly for their social functions in society, e.g. those engaged in providing social services. Clearly, for these latter groups, it will be vital to specify the relationship with society. This group may well wish to include some statement of its beliefs and values in its overall purpose and also in its mission statement.

As an example of how business can both work within the community and at the same time focus on its more obvious commercial concerns, the UK charity *Business in the Community* provides a useful model. Essentially, it allows those businesses that believe that they should have a role in the community to *channel their efforts* while at the same time focusing on what they do commercially. No doubt similar organisations exist in other countries, ranging from Chambers of Commerce to some specific industry initiatives.

Comment

While this book needs to reflect a *broad range* of views on ethics and corporate social responsibility, this does not mean that the book has no opinion on such matters. Companies do have a clear responsibility that goes beyond their immediate shareholders because they live in society, serve customers in one or more countries and interact with every aspect of the nation or nations in which they exist. The idea that the organisation's purpose is to serve *only* the selfish interests of the owners and the senior directors is morally and ethically wrong. This does make purpose more complex to develop in corporate strategy. But that is the price we pay for co-existing with others in society and contributing to its welfare. Readers are naturally entitled to disagree with this view.

Key strategic principles

- By ethics and corporate social responsibility is meant the standards and conduct that an organisation sets itself in its dealings within the organisation and outside with its environment. These need to be reflected in the mission statement.

- There are three prime considerations in developing ethics and social responsibility: the extent and scope of such considerations, their cost and the recipient of the responsibility.

- There are numerous differences between organisations over what should be covered under ethics and social responsibility, reflecting fundamentally different approaches to doing business.

CRITICAL REFLECTION

Is purpose over-complicated?

This chapter has argued that strategic purpose is complex and multifaceted. It needs to take into account such matters as leadership, corporate governance, ethics and corporate social responsibility. The problem is that all this makes purpose difficult to analyse, define and communicate to employees, managers, shareholders and other stakeholders. Moreover, there is no clear logical path to the development of purpose, with vague areas like 'managerial judgement' being used to justify particular goals.

Given these definitional and logical difficulties, perhaps it would be much better to simplify matters and focus on one area such as maximising profits? Or maximising shareholder wealth? Or even maximising the organisation's contribution to society after paying shareholders a minimum dividend?

Is there any merit in purpose being complex and multifaceted?

SUMMARY

● The definition of the organisation's activities is fundamental to the exploration of its purpose. It needs to be narrow enough to be actionable and broad enough to allow scope for development. In addition, organisations also have some opportunity to influence the type of organisation that they wish to be. This will be reflected and defined in the organisation's culture. However, culture is confined by its past and is difficult to change, so this will restrict the choices available in the context of purpose.

● Different stakeholders – shareholders, employees, etc – will have different perspectives on the purpose of the organisation. These need to be recognised and explored in the context of purpose. Purpose will also be defined by any specific desire to grow the organisation and by an exploration of the demands of the environment in which the organisation exists. Although organisations are multidimensional and unlikely to have a single purpose, a simplified definition of purpose is often developed. This allows the organisation to focus on specific objectives and communicate the definition to those within it.

● The P–P–O Paradigm captures the developing relationship between the future purpose of the organisation and its past performance. It does this by highlighting three consecutive elements – P(urpose), P(rocess) and O(utcome) – in the context of the organisation's resources and its environment.

● When developing purpose, there is a need to develop a vision of the future within which the organisation will operate. The main reason is to ensure that every opportunity is examined. Vision is not the same as the organisation's purpose, though the two may be related. There are five criteria that may assist in developing the organisation's vision: foresight, breadth, uniqueness, consensus and actionability.

● Leaders can have a profound influence on the organisation's purpose, especially through the development of its mission and objectives. Leaders may be particularly important in moving the organisation forward to new challenges. However, in large and complex organisations their role is likely to be evolutionary rather than revolutionary.

● Because leadership is so important, it is necessary to analyse it. However, there is no agreement on the analytical process. Contingency theories are probably the most useful approach. They state that the choice and style of leadership are *contingent* on the strategic issues facing the organisation at that point in time. Within the context of contingency theory, the best-fit analytical approach can be used. It is useful in strategy because it allows each situation to be treated differently.

● Leadership style can vary from shared vision to dominance. The style needs to be modified to suit the strategic situation, with other styles being possible, depending on the organisation itself and its environment. With regard to purpose, leaders need to generate trust in the strategic process. They need to draw upon the intellectual capital of the organisation and to demonstrate passion and determination. In some circumstances, leadership may be better served by allowing the purpose to emerge from the group working on a strategic task, rather than be imposed by the leader from the centre.

● Corporate governance refers to the influence and power of the stakeholders to control the strategic direction of the organisation in general and, more specifically, the chief executive and other senior officers of the organisation. Corporate governance relates primarily to the selection, remuneration and conduct of the senior officers of the organisation. It is also concerned about their relationships with the owners, employees and other stakeholders of the organisation. The senior officers act as agents on behalf of the stakeholders in the organisation.

● The importance of corporate governance lies in the power that it gives the senior officers to run the affairs of the organisation. The problem with power is that it needs to be used responsibly. One check on the responsible conduct of the organisation is the information relayed to all the stakeholders – good-quality information will encourage responsible conduct. The problem is that such information may be commercially sensitive. Confidential independent advisers, such as accountants in an audit, may be the means of keeping check on corporate conduct.

● Another way of checking on the conduct of the company is by the appointment of non-executive directors who have no other commercial connection with the company. Beyond the matter of information availability, corporate governance is more a matter of the principles of conduct than simple rules. The main aim is to ensure that the value generated by the assets of the organisation is distributed equitably amongst the stakeholders.

● By corporate social responsibility is meant the standards and conduct that an organisation sets itself in its dealings within the organisation and outside with its environment. These need to be reflected in the mission statement. There are three prime considerations in developing business ethics: the extent and scope of ethical considerations, their cost, and the recipient of the responsibility. There are numerous differences between organisations over what should be covered under the topic, reflecting fundamentally different approaches to doing business.

QUESTIONS

1 Take an organisation with which you are familiar and attempt to define its purpose: how has this been influenced by the factors outlined in Section 10.1, including its environment, resources, culture and stakeholders? How has the purpose changed over time? Why have these changes occurred?

2 In around 2000, Starbucks claimed that its vision of the future was that of a global Italian coffee bar chain. Use the classification developed by Hamel and Prahalad to evaluate this vision critically (see Section 10.2).

3 Can *organisations* have vision or is it the *managers* inside the organisation who have the vision? What are the implications of your answer for the development of strategy, especially in terms of communication within the organisation?

4 In what strategic circumstances should a leader be dominant? And in what circumstances should a leader work with a shared vision? Give examples to support your views and show how other factors can also influence leadership style.

5 Do companies always need to behave ethically, regardless of the costs?

6 Should 'green' environmental issues form part of the corporate social responsibility of a business? How, if at all, will your answer impact on the strategy of the business?

7 How is corporate governance related to corporate strategy? What systems, if any, does DaimlerChrysler need to put in place to ensure compliance with corporate governance issues? Use the example of Citibank to assist you.

8 Take an organisation with which you are familiar and assess the information that it supplies to its stakeholders in terms of corporate governance issues. Is it doing a good job by its own standards and by the likely standards of its stakeholders?

9 Can the concept of purpose and competitive advantage be applied to the whole of DaimlerChrysler? Compare your answers with the statements in the text from the company and comment on any differences.

Further reading

On purpose: read Drucker, P (1961) *Practice of Management*, Mercury, London.

On vision: see Tregoe, B B *et al.* (1989) *Vision in Action*, Simon & Schuster, London. See also Hamel, G and Prahalad, C K (1994) *Competing for the Future*, Harvard Business School Press, Boston, MA. Both books are at the practical end of the subject.

On leadership: Bennis, W and Nanus, B (1997) *Leaders: Strategies for Taking Charge*, HarperCollins, New York is a readable text with some useful insights. See also the special issue of *Academy of Management Executive* (2004) Vol 18, No 3, pp118–42, on leadership including: Conger, J A, 'Developing leadership capability: What's inside the black box?'

On ethical issues: a good basic text is Chryssides, G D and Kaler, J H (1993) *An Introduction to Business Ethics*, International Thomson Business Press, London. The special issue of *Academy of Management Executive*, (2004) Ethical Behavior in Management, pp37–91 with guest editor, John F Veign constitutes a substantial review with thoughtful papers on various current topics.

Notes and references

1 Starbucks Annual Report and Accounts 2004; www.starbucks.com; Rubinfeld, A and Hemmingway, C (2005) *Expanding Your Business around the Corner or across the Globe*, Wharton School Publishing, PA.

2 Porter, M E (1980) *Competitive Strategy*, The Free Press, New York.

3 Williamson, O (1991) 'Strategizing, economizing and economic organization', *Strategic Management Journal*, 12, pp75–94.

4 For example, *see* Drucker, P (1961) *Practice of Management*, Mercury, London, p5.

5 The comments of one of the anonymous reviewers of the 2nd edition are acknowledged in this section of the text.

6 Whittington, R (1991) *What Is Strategy and Does It Matter?*, Routledge, London, p99.

7 Drucker, P (1961) Op. cit., Ch6.

8 For example, see Prahalad, C K and Hamel, G (1990) 'The core competence of the corporation', *Harvard Business Review*, May–June, pp79–91.

9 Handy, C (1993) *Understanding Organisations*, 4th edn, Penguin, Harmondsworth, Ch4.

10 Lawrence, P R and Lorsch, J W (1967) *Organisation and Environment*, Harvard University Press, Cambridge, MA.

11 Handy, C (1993) Op. cit., Ch4.

12 Drucker, P (1961) Op. cit., Ch13.

13 For an extended exploration of this area, *see* De Wit, B and Meyer, R (1998) *Strategy: Process, Context and Content*, 2nd edn, International Thompson, London, Part V, pp805–86. But note that the purpose of the organisation is a much broader concept than that explored in this text.

14 Berle, A A and Means, G (1932) *The Modern Corporation and Private Property*, Macmillan, New York.

15 Handy, C (1993) Op. cit., Ch4.

16 Peters, T (1987) *Thriving on Chaos*, Pan Books, London.

17 Gertz, D and Baptista, J P (1995) *Grow to be Great*, The Free Press, New York.

18 Penrose, E (1959) *The Theory of the Growth of the Firm*, Oxford University Press, Oxford.

19 Morgan, G (1998) *Images of Organization*, Sage, Thousand Oaks, CA, p10.

20 Drucker, P (1961) Op. cit., p5.

21 Kay, J (1994) *The Foundations of Corporate Success*, Oxford University Press, Oxford, Ch2.

22 Drucker, P (1961) Op. cit., p9. He was thinking of the work that started with Adam Smith, David Ricardo, Alfred Marshall and others.

23 *Financial Times*: 24 April 2004, p1.

24 References for Daimler-Benz: DaimlerChrysler Annual Report and Accounts 2004 available on the web. *Economist* 27 Apr 1991, p87; 26 June 1993, p77; *Financial Times* 7 Apr 1993, p26; 23 Sept 1993, p24; 1 Dec 1993, p49; 16 Dec 1993, p21; 20 Dec 1993, p13; 21 Dec 1993, p3; 11 July 1995, p24; 8 Aug 1995, p13; 20 Dec 1995, p25; 18 Jan 1996, p27; 14 Feb 1996, p23; 7 Mar 1996, p28; 12 Apr 1996, p23; 4 May 1999, p26; 10 October 2000, p24; 30 October 2000, p26; 15 November 2000, p46; 24 January 2001, p37; 21 February 2001, p30; 27 February 2001, p20; 8 February 2002, p28; 22 May 2002, p16; 9 August 2002, p27; 17 March 2003, p28; 25 July 2003, p25; 3 September 2003, p31; 6 October 2003, p28; 12 December 2003, p30; 21 December 2003, p32; 24 March 2004, p26; 30 March 2004, p23; 6 April 2004, p21; 19 April 2004, p28; 23 April 2004, p19; 24 April 2004, pM1; 26 April 2004, pp18 (Editorial) and 26; 30 April 2004, 22 (Lex); 4 May 2004, p23; 11 May 2004, p26; 18 August 2004, p24; 29 October 2004, p1; 11 January 2005, p29; 3 March 2005, p21; 21 March 2005, p11; 1 April 2005, p21; 2 April 2005, ppM1 and M6; 4 April 2005, p26; 14 April 2005, p15.

25 Bennis, W and Nanus, B (1997) *Leaders: Strategies for Taking Charge*, HarperCollins, New York, p82.

26 Bennis, W and Nanus, B (1997) Op. cit.

27 Hamel, G and Prahalad, C K (1994) *Competing for the Future*, Harvard Business School Press, Boston, MA, p31.

28 Hamel, G and Prahalad, C K (1994) Ibid, p29.

29 Hamel, G and Prahalad, C K (1994) Ibid, p122.

30 Bennis, W and Nanus, B (1997) *Leaders: the Strategies for Taking Charge*, Harper and Row, New York.

31 Hunt, J (1998) 'Questions of commitment', *Financial Times*, 20 May, p18.

32 Comments from DaimlerChrysler AGM reported in *Financial Times*, 7 April 2005, p27.

33 Weihrich, H and Koontz, H (1993) *Management: Global Perspective*, 10th edn, McGraw-Hill, New York, p490.

34 Westley, F and Mintzberg, H (1989) 'Visionary leadership and strategic management', *Strategic Management Journal*, 10, pp17–32.

35 Homans, G (1965) *The Human Group*, Routledge and Kegan Paul, London. Ch7 on the 'Norton Street Gang' is illuminating and reflects research by Whyte in 1943.

36 Whittington, R (1991) Op. cit., pp47–9.

37 Miles, R E and Snow, C C (1978) *Organisation Strategy, Structure and Process*, McGraw-Hill, New York.

38 Handy, C (1993) Op. cit., Ch4. This whole section has benefited from this excellent text.

39 Senge, P (1990) 'The leader's new work: building learning organisations', *Sloan Management Review*, Fall. Reprinted in De Wit, R and Meyer, R (1994) *Strategy: Process, Content, Context*, West Publishing, St Paul, MN, pp132–41.

40 Developed from the work of Bourgeois, L J and Brodwin, D (1983) 'Putting your strategy into action', *Strategic Management Planning*, Mar/May. The complete paper is reprinted in De Wit, B and Meyer, R (1998) Op. cit., pp682–90.

41 Bennis, W and Nanus, B (1997) Op. cit.

42 Editorial (2005) *Financial Times*, 18 February, p16.

43 Cooper, L. (2005) Scandal-hit Citigroup rebuilds its image, *BBC World Service Report* on the worldwide web, 14 March.

44 Cooper, L. (2005) Ibid.

45 Reuters (2005) 'Citigroup completes Texas deal that alerted Fed', 31 March.

46 Associated Press (2005) 'Citigroup, Putnam pay SEC fines over funds', 23 March.

47 Cooper, L. (2005) Op. cit.

48 Cooper, L. (2005) Op. cit.

49 Cooper, L. (2005) Op. cit.

50 Associated Press (2005) 'German prosecutors won't probe Citigroup', 21 March.

51 Reuters (2005) Op. cit.

52 Available on the web at www.citi.com/citigroup/

53 Ibid. Editorial (2005).

54 British Petroleum (2004) *Annual Report and Accounts*.

55 Useful survey of Enron ethics: Chaffin, J and Fidler, S (2002) *Financial Times*, 9 April, p30.

56 This section has benefited from Chryssides, G D and Kaler, J H (1993) *An Introduction to Business Ethics*, International Thomson Business Press, London.

57 Dickson, T (1995) 'The twelve corporate commandments', *Financial Times*, 11 Oct, p18.

58 *Financial Times* (1998) *Visions of Ethical Business*, Volume 1, October. Various authors.

59 Dickson, T (1994) 'The search for universal ethics', *Financial Times*, 22 July, p11.

60 For a fuller discussion, *see* Chryssides, G D and Kaler, J H (1993) Op. cit., Ch5. *See also* Badaracco, J L and Webb, A (1995) 'Business ethics: a view from the trenches', *California Management Review*, 37, Winter, pp8–29, and reply in *California Management Review*, 39 Spring 1997, Letter to the Editor, p135. *See also* Reich, R B (1998) 'The new meaning of corporate social responsibility', *California Management Review*, 40, Winter, pp8–17.

Chapter 11

PURPOSE EMERGING FROM KNOWLEDGE, TECHNOLOGY AND INNOVATION

Learning outcomes

When you have worked through this chapter, you will be able to:

- define and explore the implications of tacit and explicit knowledge;
- explain how purpose emerges from knowledge creation;
- examine the implications of developments in technology for the organisation's purpose and strategy;
- identify the main innovation processes relevant to purpose;
- show how purpose changes with innovation;
- explain why an organisation's purpose may sometimes be emergent rather than prescriptive.

INTRODUCTION

Chapter 10 concentrated on shaping purpose in a defined and explicit way. Essentially, it adopted a *prescriptive* approach. Typically, many organisations seek to define purpose in such terms – for example, they might develop a defined code of ethical conduct, a target for earnings per share, a specific increase in the return on capital employed, a gain in market share and so on. One of the consequences of shaping purpose explicitly in this way is that it will exclude, by definition, alternative purposes and strategies whose outcomes are unknown and non-specific or whose outcomes are predicted to fail to meet the defined

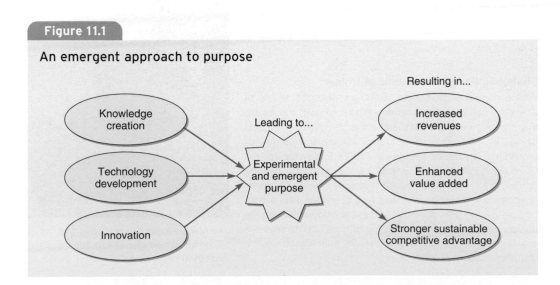

Figure 11.1

An emergent approach to purpose

Knowledge creation · Technology development · Innovation → Leading to... Experimental and emergent purpose → Resulting in... Increased revenues · Enhanced value added · Stronger sustainable competitive advantage

prescriptive criteria. The danger of such approaches is that they may exclude purposes and strategies that may be more rewarding in the long term and deserve some early exploration as part of strategy development. The objective of this chapter is to redress the balance.

In open-ended investigations, purpose might be allowed to be more experimental and developed from the process itself – an *emergent* approach to purpose. The issue is how to set about this task. There are many routes, three of which are explored in this chapter: knowledge creation, technology development and innovation. Ultimately, all three processes need to be related back to the organisation, especially with regard to their ability to contribute to value added and to sustainable competitive advantage. These two areas are useful criteria for this more open-ended approach to the development of purpose – *see* Figure 11.1.

CASE STUDY 11.1

Maglev – Shanghai's innovative new transport system

Opened in December 2002 in the presence of the Chinese premier and the German chancellor, the Maglev railway is the fastest public transport system in the world. It runs between Pudong Airport and the city of Shanghai but, unfortunately, has not carried as many passengers as expected. Just what are the implications for innovation?

Maglev background

'Maglev' means *electromagnetic levitation* and refers to a system whereby a public transport carriage runs on railway-like tracks. Magnetism holds the carriage in the air just above the track itself so that there is very little friction between the track and the carriage – unlike a normal carriage that sits on the track itself. The power for the system is in the track rather than carried on board, so that the carriages are also lighter than normal. The resulting low friction means much greater acceleration, higher speeds and very smooth rides are possible. Maglev is faster than the Japanese 'Bullet Train' – the *Shinkansen* – and faster than the French and German high speed trains, *TGV* and *ICE* respectively. But the system does require a special track and carriages and, until the Shanghai development, had not been used commercially anywhere else in the world. It was originally a British patent, but was developed commercially by a German company who persuaded the Chinese authorities to experiment with the new system in 2000.

Shanghai, People's Republic of China

With a population of around 15 million, Shanghai is one of China's great cities, both as a commercial port and as the major centre of commercial and financial activity in Eastern China. In order to provide room for substantial further growth, the city decided in the early 1990s to develop an area of muddy agricultural land east of the existing city. The *Pudong* area – with its massive skyscrapers, television tower, apartments and hotels – was then built over a ten-year period. Unquestionably, this development took considerable imagination on the part of the city's leading officials and its developers, but it paid off in terms of the city's increased wealth, status and urban renewal.

Shanghai's existing airport was located south west of the city and could not cope with the resulting increased demand for both internal and international air travel. It was therefore decided to build a completely new airport on the other side of the city, beyond Pudong, and 30 km (19 miles) from the city centre. The new airport would be connected to the city with a new rapid transit system. Maglev was chosen and built at a cost of US$1.2 billion in the relatively short time of two and a half years for a complex project. In addition to the Maglev, the authorities also built motorways to allow taxis and buses to carry passengers and visitors to the airport. A single journey to the airport by taxi costs around US$10–15 and takes at least one hour, depending on the time of day – Shanghai's tunnels

The Maglev looks like any other train as it arrives in Shanghai Airport station but this hides the new and innovative technology.

and flyovers under and over the river system can be very crowded at peak periods.

Maglev trains run on specially built overhead double tracks. They run every 20 minutes between 08.30 and 17.30 and can carry 440 people in modern comfortable carriages. The journey takes around 8 minutes to cover a distance of 30 kilometres at speeds up to 430 km/hour (270 miles/hour). Unfortunately for planning reasons, the track does not end in the centre of Shanghai but finishes several kilometres outside. It stops next to one of Shanghai's busy subway stations, Longyang Road. Passengers therefore have to leave the Maglev and carry their bags and cases down into the subway before buying a ticket for the rest of the short journey into the centre of town.

Maglev prices and financial situation

For the first experimental year 2003, the Maglev tickets were priced at 75 yuan (about US$9) for a single journey. The final subway ride was a small, additional cost for those wishing to continue into the city centre. Unfortunately, the trains were running with an average of only 73 passengers per trip for the first year, so it was decided to reduce the fare to 50 yuan in Spring 2004. Even with this reduction, the Maglev was still only carrying around 8,000 passengers per day during 2004. This brought revenues of around 130 million yuan annually – 'less than half the yearly bank loan interest at over 300 million yuan'. Essentially, this meant that the Maglev was not covering its cost of capital and needed to be subsidised by the city's transport authority.

What of the future?

With the Summer Olympic Games coming to Beijing in 2008, the authorities were exploring upgrading the existing rail track between Beijing and Shanghai. Initially, it was thought that the Maglev system might be used because it would shorten the 14-hour journey time dramatically. But other systems – including the Shinkansen, the TGV and ICE – were also under consideration. At the time of writing, no final decision had been made, but it was unlikely that the Maglev would be chosen: the technology was still only proven over relatively short distances and the capital costs were high at US$30 billion. However, Shanghai was planning a new international open-air exhibition site in 2010 near the centre of the city. It was thought that the Maglev Public Transport System might be extended to serve the exhibition ground by that time.

Case questions

1 *Maglev was an innovative new transport system: what are the risks and rewards of undertaking such an innovation?*

2 *Can other companies learn anything from the city of Shanghai's decision to experiment with the Maglev transport system or is the situation unique?*

11.1 THE NATURE OF KNOWLEDGE

Over time city authorities like those in Shanghai can develop considerable knowledge about new technologies, customers and their preferences: that is why they invest in experimental systems like the Maglev. In the same way commercial companies can develop knowledge about existing and new technologies, customers, suppliers and other aspects of the various manufacturing processes that are important to the company's purpose. In this sense, knowledge is a *resource* of the organisation and deserves to be analysed along with other resources in Part 3 – *see* Chapter 6. However, knowledge can also be explored from another perspective – that of *creating future knowledge* – and it is this approach that opens up new opportunities. It is this second perspective that we will concentrate on in this chapter. Clearly, such a viewpoint could have a considerable impact on the future purpose of the organisation.[2]

In order to clarify knowledge creation, it is helpful to begin by exploring the nature of the knowledge of an organisation and by assessing its existing knowledge resources. Having explored these two areas, we can then move on to consider the issue of knowledge development, essentially an *emergent* process. Finally, we can relate knowledge development to the purpose of the organisation and explore the implications of this approach.

11.1.1 Knowledge: its strategic origins and definition

For many years in strategy development, the topic of knowledge never received any substantive or explicit attention.[3] Some early writers on strategy recognised its importance but only Drucker made any significant attempt to explore its significance. He wrote in 1964:

> *Knowledge is the business fully as much as the customer is the business. Physical goods or services are only the vehicle for the exchange of customer purchasing – power against business knowledge.*[4]

However, beyond pointing out that each business is likely to have areas of distinctive knowledge, Drucker offered no clear definition of the topic. Even in the new millennium, there is no widely agreed definition of the main aspects of knowledge from a strategic perspective. But if we are to use knowledge in strategy development then we need to be able to recognise it, so some form of definition is important. For our purposes, we will adopt the definition of knowledge proposed by Davenport and Prusack:[5]

> *Knowledge is a fluid mix of framed experience, values, contextual information and expert insight that provides a framework for evaluating and incorporating new experiences and information. It originates and is applied in the minds of knowers. In organisations, it often becomes embedded not only in documents or repositories but also in organisational routines, processes, practices and norms.*[6]

The keys to this lengthy but helpful definition lie in such words as 'fluid mix . . . embedded . . . practices'. The most useful knowledge in many organisations is often the most difficult to understand, codify and replicate. Just as it is difficult to pin down a simple definition of knowledge, it is also problematic to identify the knowledge of an organisation. To explore this point, we will use the example of the Nike company, which is described in Case 11.2 later in this chapter. Importantly, the above definition also tells us what knowledge is not:

● Knowledge is not just *data* – a set of discrete, observable facts about events, e.g. the market share data on Nike quoted in the earlier case. The weakness with such data is that it only describes a small part of what happened at Nike and gives little idea of what made the company so successful.

● Knowledge is not just *information* – the information message, often in a document or some other form of communication, certainly has meaning but it has little depth. And knowledge requires depth from a strategy perspective. For example, it is useful to know that Nike's positioning was summarised in the phrase 'just do it'. But the meaningful part is to understand why such wording was chosen and how it was developed.

More generally, Nike's experience of dealing with its customers and suppliers cannot be usefully summarised in statistical data and information, although this might form part of a broader whole. Nike's knowledge will have two main parts:

1 a range of manufacturing contracts, procedures and practices built up over time – the 'routines and processes' part of its knowledge;

2 a whole series of working experiences, personal friendships and other activities also developed over time that are much more difficult to summarise – the 'framed experiences, values' part of the definition above.

Because it is difficult to define knowledge, most organisations have taken a broad view on what should be included. This has the disadvantage of possible information overload but avoids pre-judging what will be important for individuals in developing new areas of purpose.

Whatever view is taken of knowledge, the information age will certainly mean that it will be central to corporate strategy. Knowledge will go well beyond basic market share, financial data and management accounting information and involve people and unquantifiable assets. To paraphrase Professor Gary Hamel,[7] Madonna may have been the material girl but what sets her apart are her immaterial assets – her knowledge-based copyrights, recording deals, television and film contracts and so on. In addition, her reputation, her life and her relationship with her audience will also represent important assets. Many of these items are less easy to measure, but represent the real wealth and knowledge at the centre of the global information environment. They are Madonna's sustainable competitive advantage.

11.1.2 Knowledge: the distinction between tacit and explicit knowledge

With hindsight, some knowledge assets are clear enough. But the company itself may be unclear on what knowlege is needed for future product developments. Moreover, some knowledge – called *explicit knowledge* – may be clearer than other, rather more vague but equally valuable, knowledge – *called tacit knowledge.*

This useful distinction between two types of knowledge was first drawn by Nonaka and Takeuchi.[8] They researched the experiences of the Japanese domestic appliance company Matsushita Electric in 1985. The company was attempting to develop a new home bread-baking machine. For months, dough was analysed and X-rayed and prototype machines were built. But none produced a decent loaf. They were all undercooked, burnt, unevenly cooked or simply dried out. Finally, a software developer, Ikuko Tanaka, proposed a practical solution: find the best bread maker in the local town and watch how bread was made. She discovered that it was made in a distinctive way, involving stretching and kneading the dough. After a year of study and experimentation, Matsushita was able to launch its bread-making machine, which made good bread and achieved high sales. Nonaka and Takeuchi drew two specific conclusions on the nature of knowledge from this and other studies:[9]

1 Some knowledge is difficult to specify. It is fuzzy, often complex and unrecorded; they called this *tacit* knowledge.

2 After such knowledge has been carefully analysed, it is often possible to define it more precisely; they called this *explicit* knowledge.

All organisations have tacit and explicit knowledge, including Nike. It is the tacit knowledge that often delivers the sustainable competitive advantage because it is this part that competitors have trouble in replicating. For example, the managing director of one of Toyota's car manufacturing plants in the US never had any doubts about inviting competitors to tour his plant. He knew that they would never discover the real secrets of the Toyota Production System because much of the knowledge was tacit and impossible to observe on one quick visit.

However, explicit knowledge may also provide sustainable competitive advantage – for example, a company's patents will be recorded for other companies to examine, but remain exclusively owned by the originating company. Although both types may contribute to the sustainable competitive advantage of the organisation, tacit knowledge may be particularly important because it is less easy for competitors to comprehend and therefore copy. Exhibit 11.1 shows examples of tacit and explicit knowledge in a company.

Exhibit 11.1

Examples of tacit and explicit knowledge in a company

Tacit knowledge	Explicit knowledge
● Practical and unwritten procedures for unblocking production stoppages	● Costing procedures codified in company accounting manuals
● Informal networks and procedures for sales order processing	● New product development through formal company review procedures
● Multifunctional team working on new projects that rely on informal contacts	● Company patents and legal contracts
● Experience of what has worked in practice in branding development over a number of years	● A company's written history of its past events and experiences, successes and failures – often very limited
● Specific company treatments of some detailed aspects of management accounting	● Training schemes and apprenticeship programmes that develop and teach best practice

Importantly, the description of the interrelationship between tacit and explicit knowledge shows that one can lead to the other. Thus a mechanism is provided for emergent strategy development.

11.1.3 Knowledge audit and management

If knowledge creation is important for purpose, the question arises as to whether it is possible to draw up an inventory of existing knowledge and renewal capacity as a starting point for future development. In the phrase of the Swedish insurance company Skandia, can we assess the *intellectual capital* of an organisation? It is this company that has provided a lead in this area. In the early 1990s, it argued that many of the accounting laws and rules developed after the Second World War were outmoded because they did not measure a company's intellectual assets, only its physical assets such as land, plant and raw materials.

Skandia defined the intellectual capital of its operations as its:

future earnings capacity from a deeper, broader and more human perspective than that described in [its financial reports]. It comprises employees as well as customers, business relations, organisational structures and the power of renewal in organisations. Visualising and interpreting these contexts can provide better insight into future development at an earlier stage.[10]

The company then divided the basic concept of intellectual capital into a number of components, each of which contributes to the creation of market value. It pointed out that in traditional economics only one of these aspects is measured – the financial capital – but, in reality, there are many other contributors to a company's future profits summarised in its intellectual capital. These elements are shown in Exhibit 11.2.

Exhibit 11.2

Skandia value scheme

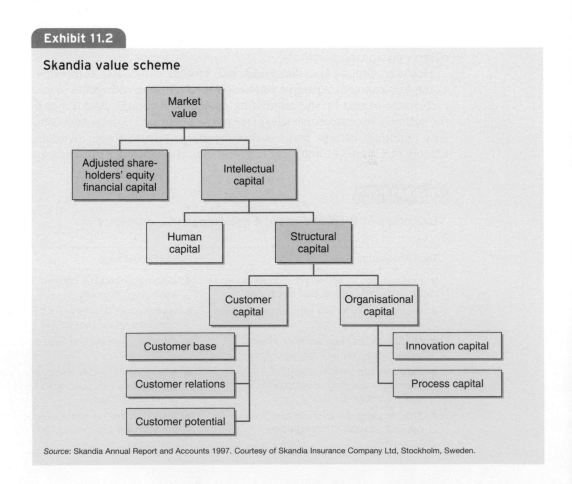

Source: Skandia Annual Report and Accounts 1997. Courtesy of Skandia Insurance Company Ltd, Stockholm, Sweden.

Intellectual capital has two main components: *human capital*, which is similar to the tacit knowledge outlined in the previous section, and *structural capital*, which is similar to the explicit knowledge also covered. Structural capital can then be divided into two further elements related to the *customer capital* and the *organisational capital* of a company. The organisational capital includes information systems, databases, information technology solutions and other related knowledge areas. The company has then developed a method of exploring the implications of this knowledge valuation exercise that lays particular emphasis on the future value of knowledge.

Over the last few years, similar approaches to knowledge assessment and its transferral around the organisation have been adopted in varying ways by many other organisations.[11] Rather than concentrating on the calculation of the total sum of knowledge in an organisation – the intellectual capital approach – such efforts have focused on the gathering and sharing of knowledge around an organisation – the *knowledge management* approach. But they cover similar areas.

Particularly in service and consultancy organisations, knowledge management has come to be regarded as the prime source of competitive advantage. Hence, the collection and dissemination of knowledge around the organisation has become a top strategic priority. Assessments have been made of the factors that are most likely to contribute to the success of knowledge management.[12] These are shown in Exhibit 11.3. The first point is particularly important because, for some groups in an organisation, 'knowledge is power'.[13] These groups may not be willing to share such knowledge and may regard knowledge networks as a threat. Care therefore needs to be taken when introducing such new initiatives.

Exhibit 11.3

Factors contributing to success in knowledge management

- Building a knowledge-sharing community inside the organisation, both in technical terms and in terms of a willingness to share knowledge
- Contribution of knowledge to economic performance and value, e.g. profits and cost savings
- Technical and organisational infrastructures, which need to be wide-ranging to succeed
- The need to gather both the tacit knowledge, which is difficult to record, and the explicit knowledge, which is easier to record and circulate
- Clarity on the background history of how the knowledge was derived, its context in relation to other areas and the learning that has resulted
- Recognition that many channels are needed for knowledge gathering and transfer
- Senior management support and encouragement

In recent years, knowledge management has been used to share best practice across organisations. For example, Unilever's subsidiaries in South America had considerable knowledge of the management of companies in high-inflation economies, after the experiences in the continent in the 1980s. The company used its knowledge management intranet to transfer management practices to some Asian subsidiaries when they were faced with similar problems in the late 1990s.

Comment

From a strategic perspective, knowledge management has become important. However, no single concept or process has yet been devised that will capture all the main elements.[14] The audit and its implications remain to be fully developed. Moreover, in spite of the enthusiastic reception for auditing knowledge, it has three disadvantages in strategy development:

1 The approach may lend itself to what can be easily audited and circulated – *explicit* knowledge – rather than the *tacit* knowledge that will also deliver competitive advantage but remains, by definition, less easily defined and audited.

2 An audit makes little attempt to distinguish between what is merely interesting and what is vital to strategy and purpose. Companies run the risk of being swamped by the irrelevant in the name of knowledge management.

3 The knowledge audit is backward-looking while strategy development is forward-looking. Its value may therefore be somewhat limited.

Key strategic principles

- The knowledge of an organisation is hard to define precisely. Essentially, it is a constantly changing mixture of experience, values, contextual information and expert insight. Importantly, knowledge is not just data and information.

- The distinction between explicit and tacit knowledge is important. Explicit knowledge is recorded and structured. Tacit knowledge is fuzzy and difficult to set out. Both types may contribute to the sustainable competitive advantage of the organisation, but tacit knowledge may be particularly important because it is less easy for competitors to comprehend and therefore copy.

- An organisation's knowledge can be audited but the process is easier with explicit than tacit knowledge. The audit might form the basis of strategy development but suffers from several disadvantages.

CASE STUDY 11.2

Developing new knowledge at Nike

When Phil Knight founded Nike with US$500 in 1964, he could hardly have seen his purpose as building the biggest sports company in the world. Yet this is what Nike had become by 2005. This case examines the foundations of the company's growth, especially the knowledge developed and retained within the company over the years.

Early learning years: the 1960s and 1970s

Back in 1958, Phil Knight was a middle-distance runner in the University of Oregon's track team, where his coach was Bill Bowerman, who later trained the US Olympic team. It was Bowerman who considered the existing running shoes were too heavy and designed and made his own lighter version. After graduating from Oregon, Knight studied for an MBA at Stanford University, where he was inspired by Bowerman to write a thesis on trainer manufacture. Knight then went on a world tour that included a visit to Japan, where he found the leading shoe brand called Tiger. He decided that this was a superior product and set up an importing company to bring Tiger running shoes to the US while still continuing to work as an accountant. Then in 1964, he and Bowerman each put up US$500 to found the *Nike* shoe company, named after the Greek goddess of victory. Its first 'office' was the laundry room at Knight's family home.

To start the company, Knight used his athletics contacts to sell Tiger running shoes from a station wagon at track and field events. He bought the shoes from Japan but both he and Bowerman always felt that there was potential for a US-designed shoe. This led Bowerman to invent the 'waffle' trainer. In the early 1970s, demand for Nike shoes was sufficient for the company to consider developing its own shoe manufacture. However, he was concerned to use Japanese experience of shoe production. In 1972, he placed his first contract in Japan to begin shoe manufacture to a Nike all-American design.

Over the next couple of years, the yen moved up against the dollar and Japanese labour costs continued to rise. This made Japanese shoe production more expensive. In addition, Nike itself was gaining more experience of international manufacture and making more contacts with overseas shoe manufacturers. In order to cut production costs, Nike switched its operations in 1975 from Japan to two newly industrialised nations, Korea and Taiwan, whose wage costs were exceptionally low at that time. Nike's costs came down dramatically, allowing the company more scope for funding further product development and marketing.

In sourcing production internationally from low-wage countries, Nike's approach to shoe manufacture was revolutionary for its time. The company realised that sports shoe manufacture required substantial labour input, so labour costs were potentially high and justified manufacture in countries where workers were paid much lower wages. However, there were real risks in manufacturing overseas because the greater geographical distance and different national cultures made it more difficult to control production and quality. Thus the company only switched contracts for large-scale production when it could be sure that a new manufacturing contractor was able to meet its quality standards. In this context, the company had to learn how to handle overseas production, how to brief manufacturers on new designs and models, and how to set and maintain quality standards.

The decade of difficulty and renewal: the 1980s

By the early 1980s, Nike was profitable and continuing to develop its role as a specialist US sports shoe manufacturer with no production facilities in its home country. It became the leading brand of sports trainers in the US. Then along came competition in the form of a new sports shoe manufacturer, *Reebok*. From a start-up company in 1981, Reebok went into battle against Nike under its founder and chief executive, Paul Fireman. Reebok launched a strong and well-designed range of sports shoes with great success. By the mid-1980s, Reebok had equalled Nike's annual sales in a fierce competitive battle. In 1987, Reebok was clear market leader with sales of US$991 million and a market share of 30 per cent, compared with Nike sales of US$597 million and a share of 18 per cent.

To hit back against Reebok, Nike then began to invest considerable sums on developing new and innovative sports shoe designs. The most successful of these was begun in the late 1980s, the Nike Air shoe. 'It was an intuitively simple technology to understand,' said John Horan, publisher of *Sports Goods Intelligence*, a US industry newsletter. 'It's obvious to consumers that if you put an airbag under the foot, it will cushion it.' But it was not until 1990 that the Nike Air shoe was launched and began to deliver success for Nike. Thus the 1980s were both the decade of difficulty and the time for renewal. Nike had learned about the heat of competition and the need for innovation and continual R&D in its shoe designs.

The new heights of the 1990s – sponsorship and brand building

Coupling the new Nike Air shoe with advertising featuring Michael Jordan was a touch of marketing inspiration. The US basketball star, top of his chosen sport, was signed up to promote the new product in a multimillion-dollar deal that added a new dimension to sports sponsorship. The marketing campaign developed links between Nike and Jordan's athletic ability and image. Reebok hit back with its own design, the Reebok Pump shoe, but it was forced to use Shaquille O'Neal, who, though a major basketball star, was second to Michael Jordan. Thus around the turn of the decade, Nike's market share rose from 25 per cent in 1989 to 28 per cent in 1990 while Reebok's share dropped from 24 per cent to 21 per cent.

Building on this success, Nike realised that such promotion provided powerful support for the brand. Over the next few years, this was enhanced by the heavy funds Nike was prepared to invest. For example, in 1995 Nike invested almost US$1 billion in sports marketing, compared with Reebok's spending at around US$400 million.

In addition, Nike began sports sponsorship deals. These included the golf star Tiger Woods and, for a previously unheard-of sum, the whole Brazilian football team. By signing a ten-year deal in 1996 worth between US$200 million and US$400 million, Nike broke new ground in football sponsorship. Importantly, this moved the company into totally new areas of sports goods. Tiger Woods brought Nike into the lucrative world of golf shoes and clothing where it competed with the existing companies. In the same way, the Brazilian football team sponsorship moved Nike into competition with manufacturers in another new market – football boots and other kit. The sponsorship gave Nike credibility in a new market area along with knowledge of that area. For example, the technology of a football boot is not the same as that of an athletic running shoe.

But it was not just the Nike sports sponsorship that was important. The brand and the message were also important. During the 1980s and 1990s, the company had come to understand its target market well – young, cool and competitive teenagers. The 'swoosh' logo was highlighted on all its goods to help brand the product and the main message, 'just do it',

Figure 11.2

Nike's global sales 2004 (US$ millions)

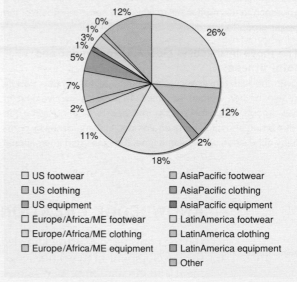

- ☐ US footwear
- ☐ US clothing
- ☐ US equipment
- ☐ Europe/Africa/ME footwear
- ☐ Europe/Africa/ME clothing
- ☐ Europe/Africa/ME equipment
- ☐ AsiaPacific footwear
- ☐ AsiaPacific clothing
- ☐ AsiaPacific equipment
- ☐ LatinAmerica footwear
- ☐ LatinAmerica clothing
- ☐ LatinAmerica equipment
- ☐ Other

▶ **CASE STUDY 11.2 continued**

Figure 11.3

Nike more than doubles revenue and net profits over ten years

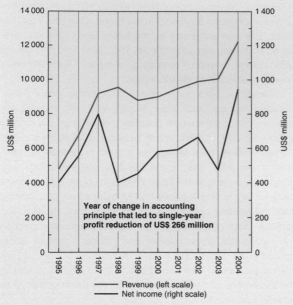

Revenue (left scale)
Net income (right scale)

* Year of change in accounting principle that led to single-year profit reduction of US$266 million.

Source: Company Annual Report and Accounts 2004.

was developed to express the individuality of the target group. The accompanying slogan of 'winning your own way' captured the aggression, competition and individual success epitomised by the sports stars who were signed up. However, Nike was criticised for its use of cheap labour in some countries and was forced to take steps to deal with this. The company's approach to this matter still rankles with some members of the target group to this day.

The move into sports clothing, equipment and total fitness

Over the last ten years, Nike continued to develop rapidly in two further, related activities. It used its involvement in new sports areas to develop into sports clothing using the Nike brand and into sports equipment, in some cases by company acquisition. At the same time, it began rapid international

expansion, for example using its sponsorship in Brazil to expand in Latin America and its sponsorship of Arsenal Football Club to expand its position in Europe. It was using its resource-based competitive advantages to build into related markets.

By the year 2004, Nike was the biggest sports and fitness company in the world, with a truly global spread of sales – see Figure 11.2. Note that the 'other' figure in the total turnover relates to several Nike acquisitions of related sports branded clothing and goods companies in years 2002–2004.

In the late 1990s, the Asian economic downturn hit the company hard. There was also heavy overstocking of its products in the US retail trade that hit the company in 2000 – see Figure 11.3. Trading profits soon recovered but they were affected by an 'accounting change' in 2003 that reduced profits in that year. They then recovered to record levels in 2004. Phil Knight became the chairman and Tom Clarke took over as chief executive. Mr Clarke was quite clear:

> You grow a lot, then you need a period when things aren't booming to ask what works and what doesn't . . . Remember, we're a fairly self-critical bunch. We're running the company for the long term, not to keep people happy for the next couple of quarters.

In early 2005, Phil Knight announced that he would retire from Nike. It was just over 40 years since he and his friend Bill Bowerman had started selling trainers from the back of a station wagon in 1964. The purpose of Nike changed over time as a result of building competitive resources, taking risks, achieving business success and employing the knowledge built up and shared in the company.

Source: See reference.[15]

Case questions

1 *What knowledge has Nike acquired over the years? Use the definitions of knowledge contained in this chapter to help you move beyond the obvious.*

2 *What other resources beyond knowledge does the company possess that offer clear sustainable competitive advantage?*

3 *From a consideration of this case, what conclusions can you draw on the emergent purpose of Nike in relation to its knowledge?*

11.2 KNOWLEDGE CREATION AND PURPOSE

Definition ➤ Having considered existing knowledge in the last section, we can now move on to consider the development of new knowledge. Knowledge creation can be considered as the development and circulation of new knowledge within the organisation. Although the knowledge audit helps to define the starting point, its role is essentially static. Knowledge creation arguably requires a more dynamic approach and offers a new strategic opportunity. The full mechanisms for knowledge creation remain to be resolved but some key elements can be distinguished:

● conversion and communication of existing knowledge;

● knowledge creation and acquisition processes;

● knowledge transfer processes.

11.2.1 Conversion and communication of existing knowledge

The creation of new knowledge in an organisation can usefully start from an exploration of the existing knowledge base of the organisation, especially how this is converted and communicated within the organisation. One useful method is to structure this using Takeuchi and Nonaka's Model of Knowledge Conversion – *see* Figure 11.4. This concept starts from the assumption that there are two main types of knowledge in any organisation – tacit and explicit – as explored in the previous section. If this is the case, then it follows that there are only four ways that these two types can be communicated and shared within the existing knowledge base:

1 *From tacit knowledge to tacit knowledge: socialisation.* One way that companies can share unwritten knowledge across the firm is to socialise, sharing unwritten experiences and information, perhaps in informal meetings or working together. For example, the Nike company will have informal contacts between their sponsored sports stars and the Nike marketing and advertising agencies that can be used to develop specific sponsorship timing opportunities, work on topical campaigns, etc. None of this is necessarily written down but may be helpful in increasing Nike brand awareness and loyalty.

2 *From tacit knowledge to explicit knowledge: externalisation.* Companies can also exchange unrecorded knowledge and other vague concepts by making them more formal. This may mean conceptualising and modelling vague ideas – perhaps again in meetings, but this time attempting to record and structure what was previously hidden. For example at

---

Figure 11.4

Four modes of knowledge conversion

	To tacit knowledge	To explicit knowledge
From tacit knowledge	Socialisation	Externalisation
From explicit knowledge	Internalisation	Combination

Source: 'Fig 3-2: Four Modes of Knowledge Conversion', from *The Knowledge-Creating Company: How Japanese Companies Create the Dynamics of Innovation* by Ikujiro Nonaka and Hirotaka Takeuchi, copyright © 1995 by Oxford University Press, Inc. Used by permission of Oxford University Press, Inc.

Nike, this approach might involve a new unwritten idea for a training shoe, which is then turned into an experimental model or drawing for market research.

3 *From explicit knowledge to explicit knowledge: combination.* Companies can also take previously recorded explicit knowledge and share this more widely within a company – perhaps using an intranet system or some other company-wide means of communication. For example at Nike, the company could use its web-based communications to distribute Nike customer data between different parts of the world.

4 *From explicit knowledge to tacit knowledge: internalisation.* Companies can also take written and recorded information and use this as a starting point for further shared experiences which are not necessarily written down. For example at Nike, this could involve taking a general training manual on in-store merchandising at a Nike shop and using this to examine what informal lessons need to be applied in an individual Nike retail store.

Comment

While the above four areas are helpful, they do rely on a rather simplistic assumption about the tacit/explicit nature of existing knowledge in an organisation. There will be many variations in the range and type of information and knowledge. Yet they need to be forced into only one of the four boxes of the matrix. Such knowledge may benefit from a broader view of their usage. However, the underpinning concepts of sharing, conceptualising and communicating both unwritten and recorded knowledge more widely are useful when it comes to knowledge creation.

11.2.2 Knowledge creation and acquisition processes

Beyond exploring and sharing the knowledge already in the organisation, there are also processes for creating new knowledge. Davenport and Prusak recommend six mechanisms that will assist in knowledge creation.[16] They are:

1 *Acquisition.* New knowledge does not necessarily come from inside the organisation. British Petroleum is reported by Davenport and Prusak to award a 'Thief of the Year' award to the employee who has 'stolen' the best ideas in applications development from other companies.

2 *Rental.* Knowledge can also be rented or leased in the sense that it can be sponsored and developed by an outside institution such as a university or a consultant. It is important in this case for the sponsoring organisation to retain the ownership of its use.

3 *Dedicated resources.* Typically in many organisations, special groups or task forces are set up with the objective of generating new knowledge in a specific area. For example, a task force might be used by Nike to develop new areas of sponsorship.

4 *Fusion.* For certain complex problems, some organisations bring together people from different functional backgrounds and with differing personalities. They are *fused* together in the sense of forcing interaction in order to develop totally new approaches to a task. For example, the Matsushita bread machine required bakers, engineers and software developers. This is a well-proven method of knowledge development.[17]

5 *Adaptation.* Many external pressures will force organisations to adapt to new realities or they will not survive. Case study 11.3 later in this chapter describes the new knowledge that will be needed in the banking market if traditional banks are to survive.

6 *Networks.* Formal and informal communities of knowledge sharing exist in many organisations. Such networks of knowledge are now being supplemented by such electronic mechanisms as the intranet, a formal computer network inside an organisation for the exchange of knowledge. For example, Heineken set up a new company-wide intranet site in 1998 under the heading 'Knowledge is Power'.[18]

11.2.3 Knowledge transfer processes

New knowledge is unlikely to deliver its full potential if it remains with the originators in an organisation – it needs to be transferred to others. Knowledge transfer is related to the areas explored in the first section above on knowledge conversion and communication but the process is taken further by the *proactive decision* to share knowledge.

Knowledge transfer is not a simple task because such a process involves people and groups. People may not understand each other, may feel threatened by new developments and may be unwilling to tolerate the mistakes or ambiguity that will surely occur during the process of transferral. In addition, groups of people may judge themselves to be the main owners of certain types of knowledge and also judge that their status will be lowered if such knowledge is shared.[19] These matters need to be addressed if the knowledge transfer process is to be successful. They may involve changes in the culture of the organisation, which cannot be achieved quickly.

Beyond these difficulties, there are some mechanisms that will assist in the transfer of knowledge. The 3M company is a well-known and successful exponent of them. The reader is therefore referred to the description of these mechanisms in Case study 11.4 later in the chapter.

11.2.4 Conclusion – Knowledge creation and purpose

If new knowledge is significant in its impact, then it may well change the purpose of the organisation, perhaps providing the opportunity for global market leadership, as happened at Nike, perhaps threatening the survival of a business, as occurred with the mechanical calculator companies described in Chapter 9, which were overwhelmed by the new electronic machines.

The important point here is that the purpose of the business will only be changed *after* the new knowledge has been developed and made explicit. In this sense, a new definition of purpose *emerges* from the new acquisition of knowledge and cannot be easily defined in advance. This has not stopped companies attempting to define purpose in advance of a specific breakthrough in their knowledge: Hewlett-Packard (US), 3M (US) and Glaxo Wellcome (UK) are examples. But the attempt is usually made to focus minds and energy inside the company, rather than anything more explicit. It follows that the success rate is mixed – just look at the poor growth in the 3M case study later in this chapter for the years 2000–2002 from a company that had consistently set innovative growth targets and then struggled to meet them.

Within this caution about the emergent nature of purpose, it is possible to be more explicit about the way that knowledge management will contribute to the purpose of the organisation. This book has argued that, fundamentally, the purpose of an organisation is to *add value* and that this is assisted by the development of *sustainable competitive advantage*. It is therefore appropriate to explore how knowledge contributes to these two areas. Knowledge is essentially a resource of the organisation, so these two issues can be explored by considering the *resource-based view* of the organisation, outlined in Chapter 6. Teece has argued that knowledge can contribute to competitive advantage through two related mechanisms:[20]

1 *Replicabililty*. As outlined above, knowledge is often only useful when it is transferred and replicated in other parts of an organisation. This is particularly difficult where tacit knowledge is the main asset. Even where knowledge is explicit, organisations may have difficulty in replicating it where such knowledge is complex, relies on local cultures and faces other impediments.

2 *Imitability*. This simply means the ability of competitors to replicate the knowledge of the first organisation. If replication is difficult for the original owner, then it will surely be more difficult for competitors. However, when knowledge becomes explicit and

Figure 11.5

Creation and diffusion of knowledge

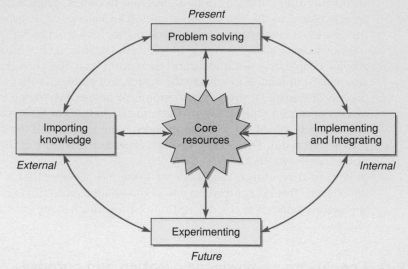

Note: 'Core resources' refers to those resources that are particularly likely to possess sustainable competitive advantage – *see* Chapter 6.

Source: Adapted from Leonard, D (1995) *Wellsprings of Knowledge*, Harvard Business School Press, Barton, MA. © Copyright 1995 by the President and Fellows of Harvard College. Reprinted with permission.

published, then it is more likely to be imitated. This is particularly possible where an organisation has failed to defend its knowledge through the acquisition of intellectual property rights, such as patenting.

Finally, knowledge adds value through a circular mechanism that will impact on purpose at various stages of development. This is best seen in Dorothy Leonard-Barton's model of the creation and diffusion of knowledge – *see* Figure 11.5. This makes a clear distinction between the current and future tasks of an organisation: *in the present*, the organisation can problem-solve, whereas *in the future* it can experiment without being clear about the outcome. The model also separates two mechanisms for the acquisition of knowledge: *internally* through discussion, implementation and integrating mechanisms, and *externally* through the knowledge acquisition.

Key strategic principles

- Conversion and communication of existing knowledge can take place through four mechanisms: socialisation, externalisation, combination and internalisation. All four processes relate to the basic distinction between tacit and explicit knowledge existing in any organisation.

- Knowledge creation – the development and circulation of new knowledge – offers a dynamic strategic opportunity. There are three mechanisms: organisational learning, knowledge creation and acquisition, and knowledge transfer.

- If new knowledge is significant in its impact on the organisation, then it may well change the purpose of the organisation. Importantly, the purpose will only change after new knowledge has been developed. In this sense, the purpose of the organisation *emerges* from knowledge creation.

CASE STUDY 11.3

Will traditional retail banks survive the threat of the new technologies – the internet and telephone banking?

In the new millennium, retail banks around the world are under two related strategic threats from a totally new technology: banking on the internet and banking by telephone. This case study examines this competitive problem. Some adaptation is clearly required, but might the threat be exaggerated? Or will traditional retail banks largely disappear?[21]

Back in 1994, Bill Gates, the chief executive of Microsoft (US), upset the banking community by deriding them for being 'dinosaurs' and claiming that his company could 'bypass them'. Subsequently, he explained that what he meant was that banking software systems were old-fashioned, rather than the whole banking infrastructure. But the jibe hit home, with some banks reconsidering how they handled customer transactions. The need to adapt has become particularly acute as computer usage has grown, telephone messaging has become cheaper and more reliable, and the internet World Wide Web network has shown explosive growth.

Traditionally, retail banks asked their customers to come into their marble-clad banking halls to receive their cheque books, pay in their cash and negotiate their loans with their friendly but often rather distant bank managers. Now such transactions are increasingly being done on the telephone to call operators at central locations or on the internet without human intervention. There are still some security problems but these will be overcome. The pace of modern life, the lower loyalty of newer customers and the increased competition from many new lenders are beginning to transform the nature of banking transactions. To what extent should banks therefore embrace the new technologies? The easy option would be to move onto the World Wide Web. The much more difficult problem would be whether to close many branches and provide a service mainly through the web and through telephone banking.

Some suggest that there is no fundamental strategic issue. Essentially, they argue that telephone and internet banking will shortly be offered by all the major banks, so there will be no competitive advantage in it. Moreover, bank branches are still important for paying in cash, raising loans and many other more complex transactions that require the personal touch. Finally, they point out that the real benefit for customers would only come if they changed their account, and this is a long and tedious procedure that deters many people.

Others argue that the revolution is coming. New customers are computer-literate, the internet provides the possibility of a 'financial supermarket' of choice for a wide range of financial services and a one-stop shop. Moreover, the rapid acceptance of the new services shows that there is substantial customer demand. Professor Gary Hamel has dismissed traditional retail banks as 'mausoleums-in-the-making' and suggested that they will largely disappear within ten years. For *new* providers of financial services, there would be a clear case for using the new technology. But for the *existing* retail banks, their substantial investment in a branch network makes the strategic decision more difficult.

Case questions

1 *What strategy would you recommend if you were managing a large retail banking network?*

2 *Can you think of other industries and markets that might also be affected by the new technology of telephone service and the internet? What are the strategy implications?*

11.3 USING TECHNOLOGY TO DEVELOP PURPOSE AND COMPETITIVE ADVANTAGE

11.3.1 Technology and competitive advantage[22]

Given the pace of change over the last 20 years, technology has come to play an important role in the development of sustainable competitive advantage. Even in mature industries, not-for-profit organisations and small businesses, it is technology that has on occasions added the extra element to differentiate the organisation. For these reasons, technology strategy deserves careful investigation.

New technology developments are just as likely to alter the vision and purpose of the organisation as any other area. They can extend and enhance the existing position of the company. However, it should be noted that this will take time and resources – there may be no short-term impact on strategy. There are two main phases to this task:

Phase 1 Survey of existing technologies

Phase 2 Development of technology strategy

Phase 1 Survey of existing technologies

This phase has four elements:

1 *An organisation-wide survey of existing technologies.* This should examine areas in detail rather than making broad generalisations, in order to ensure that no opportunities are missed. The result will be an audit of which technologies are used and where in the organisation they are used. The *audit* data are then classified into three areas:

- *base technologies* that are common to many companies;
- *core technologies* that are exclusive to the organisation itself, possibly delivering real competitive advantage;
- *peripheral technologies* that are useful but not central to the organisation.

2 *An examination of related areas inside the organisation.* For example, patents and intellectual property may form the basis of important areas of competitive advantage. Some companies have special skills that have never been patented but come from years of experience and training; these may also present real advantages over competitors.

3 *A technology scan external to the organisation.* This will identify opportunities that are available for later consideration.

4 *A technology/product portfolio.* A matrix can be constructed relating products and technologies (*see* Figure 11.6).

Phase 2 Development of technology strategy

To develop technology strategy, it is important to take one technology at a time or risk muddle and confusion. It may also be important to develop both the technology and the *operations* (manufacturing) processes at the same time because the two areas are interrelated and because lead times need to be shortened.

Figure 11.6

Technology/product portfolio matrix

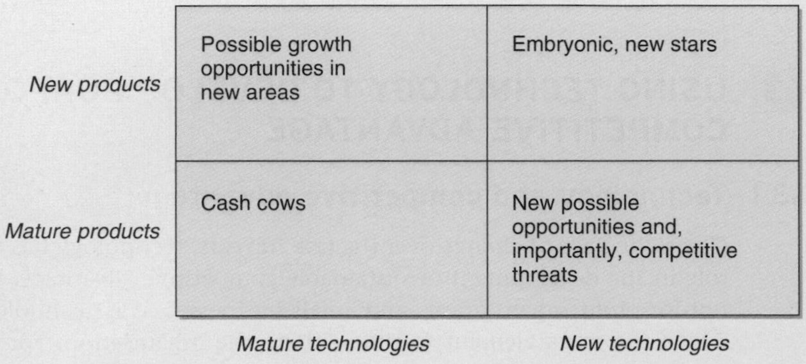

	Mature technologies	New technologies
New products	Possible growth opportunities in new areas	Embryonic, new stars
Mature products	Cash cows	New possible opportunities and, importantly, competitive threats

The technology development initiative then needs to be analysed in two ways:

1 the technological developments of the organisation compared with those of competitors; and

2 the costs of further development compared with the time that this will take. (There is always a trade-off here.)

In addition to these two tasks, it is important to consider the possibilities of *acquiring* new technology – possibly through company acquisition, joint ventures or the purchase of a licence to use technology, probably from a company outside the home market.

Two final issues then need to be considered:

1 *the speed of imitation.* It is important to estimate how quickly any technology development could be imitated by competitors;

2 *issues of globalisation.* It may be possible to exploit the new area on a worldwide scale and thus alter the attractiveness of the business proposition.

The above procedure may be too elaborate for some small companies and for not-for-profit organisations. However, small companies often gain their initial advantage from a technology edge. Larger companies may fail to consider the benefits of a clear drive on technology development, especially when they are operating in mature industries. The area has considerable potential strategic importance.

Technology developments are probably prescriptive in their overall approach in the sense that there needs to be a definite objective. However, they may be emergent in their detailed processes and by the nature of the experimental process.

11.3.2 Technology and innovation strategy

Given that companies and industrial sectors differ so much, it is extraordinarily difficult to develop a single framework that embraces all technology and all innovation strategy. For example, ethical drugs require *product innovation* through new patented drugs, whereas retailing services in recent years have relied largely on *process innovation* through new IT systems to improve such areas as stock delivery and stock control. In spite of such difficulties, there are two underpinning principles for technology and innovation strategy:

● core competencies;
● five major technological trajectories.

Core competencies

As identified by Prahalad and Hamel, core competencies focus on an individual company's competitive technological resources that deliver competitive advantage: 'The real sources of advantage are to be found in management's ability to consolidate corporate-wide technologies and production skills into competencies that empower individual businesses to adapt quickly to changing opportunities.'[23] Core competencies need to be identified and harnessed in the development of technology strategy. They go deeper than the immediate technologies employed by organisations – examples of core competence include Sony in miniaturisation, Philips in optical media and 3M in coatings and adhesives. Having identified core competencies, it is then possible to consider the implications for R&D and for the way that the company's funds are allocated – perhaps more money and people need to be invested in core competencies. However, it is important to recall the words of caution from Chapter 6 on the problems with core competencies.

Five major technological trajectories

Most organisations are constrained by their existing range or products or services, their past histories and the organisational culture and leadership that permits and supports innovation.

In short, they are *path-constrained*:[24] this was explored in Section 2.6. From a technology and innovation perspective, it means that companies rarely start from scratch when it comes to innovation because of:

● *their positions*: their market positions against competing firms;

● *their paths*: their current products or services and the specific opportunities now open;

● *their processes*: their current methods by which they achieve innovation.

These three will guide and limit the innovation process. Within these constraints, recent research[25] suggests that there are *five major technological trajectories* that will guide specific types of industry. They are:

1 *Supplier-dominated firms*: examples are agricultural companies, traditional manufacturers like textiles and some services. Technical change comes mainly from the suppliers to these companies. Hence such companies need to develop close links with their suppliers when seeking technology innovation.

2 *Scale-intensive firms*: examples are consumer durables, automobiles and bulk chemicals. Technical innovation will come from the building of complex plant and products. Given the high cost of such plant and consequent risks of failure, innovation tends to come in stages. Hence, technological innovation is concerned with small, frequent improvements in plant efficiencies – Toyota in Chapter 9 is a good example.

3 *Science-based firms*: examples include pharmaceutical and electronics companies. Technological innovation will often come from a central R&D facility or from a university special incubator. Innovation is often associated with new discoveries and new patents. Hence the task of innovation is to find and exploit such new technologies – perhaps by looking outside the company.

4 *Information-intensive firms*: examples include publishing, banking, telecommunications and travel booking. Technological innovation will come both from in-house systems in the large companies and bought-in systems in both large and small companies. In both cases, the aim is to develop large and often complex systems for handling large quantities of data processing and also making such systems user- and customer-friendly. Totally new services may also result.

5 *Specialised supplier firms*: examples are small specialist companies that supply specialised, high-performance machinery, instruments and specialist software. Technology innovation comes from such firms understanding their customers' needs, their competitors' activities and new developments in their specialised areas of operation. Such companies will innovate by constantly searching for new technologies – perhaps internationally – and from keeping close to their customers.

11.3.3 Three specific technologies and their implications for corporate strategy

Three fundamental developments in technology may have implications for innovative developments over the next ten years.[26] They are:

● *Biotechnology and healthcare developments* – mapping of the human genome and developments in medical technology promise a revolution in healthcare over the next 20 years. Such changes have already led companies like Philips and 3M – *see* Case studies 11.4 and 11.5 – to redefine their company purpose in terms of such new opportunities in healthcare. Not every company will be interested or able to benefit from such technological advances but they have the potential to deliver some revolutionary strategies.

● *Developments in microchip technology* – the increased miniaturisation and extra controls that come from embedded microchips in some products. Many companies produce products that require delivery to customers – an embedded microchip could keep such companies and their customers informed of the status of delivery. Increased chip miniaturisation will also change fundamentally some manufacturing processes and some domestic products. Mobile telephones are one example of technological innovation that has changed the lives of millions. The potential changes here remain to be fully exploited.

● *Improvements in information technology* – the increased information that comes from the adoption of new IT systems, especially in a global context. We are in the middle of what has been called the third industrial revolution – *the information age*. Moreover, the information is global, not just local or national. For example, a major UK company now has a permanent *three-way* telecommunications link between its engineering design teams in the US, UK and India. The communications use the specialist engineering knowledge of the US team, the skills but low labour costs of their Indian colleagues, and the overall co-ordination and marketing skills of the UK headquarters. Such activity was simply not possible some years ago. New information technology has also opened up the possibility of greater strategic control in companies. Again, the possibilities from such technological innovations will provide continued strategic opportunities for companiees.

Critical comment

With regard to all the above, it is important to note that all such competitive advantages last only for a limited period of time – for example, traditional banks and insurance companies have begun telephone selling, where required. It is conceivable that technology advantages are not sustainable unless they involve some form of patent and, even then, the patent expires after a set time.

Key strategic principles

● An internal and external scan of technologies is vital to corporate strategy development. It may alter the purpose of the organisation over time.

● Technologies should be classified into base, core and peripheral. Base areas are common to many companies. Peripheral areas are not mainstream to the organisation. The core areas are most likely to deliver competitive advantage, along with patenting and special skills.

● Each technology should be assessed separately against competition along with the costs of further development against the time taken. The speed of imitation and possible global exploitation also deserve examination.

● Core competencies – corporate-wide technologies and production skills – can form the basis of new areas of technology innovation.

● Organisations are constrained by their current products, competitors and organisational culture. Five main technology *path constraints* have been identified – supplier-dominated, scale-intensive, science-based, information-intensive, specialised suppliers.

● Three new areas of technology may provide major opportunities for companies in innovation technology over the next ten years: biotechnology and healthcare improvements, developments in microchip technology, improvements in information technology.

CASE STUDY 11.4

Revitalising innovation at 3M

Ever since the US multinational 3M invented Scotch tape and Post-it notes in the mid-twentieth century, the company has been held up as an example of innovative growth. Yet 3M had a problem when growth stalled in recent years. This case examines its famed innovation processes and how 3M came back to growth.

Early years

To give the company its full title is to reveal its early origins. The Minnesota Mining and Manufacturing Company – commonly known as *3M* – started when a group of investors bought a mine in 1902 that was understood to contain the valuable and highly abrasive mineral corundum. When they discovered that only low-grade minerals were present, they decided to branch out into other products that would be more profitable. This approach typifies some of the spirit of the present company, which has made its purpose to seek out high profitability from a wide range of products.

Wide product range in the year 2000

By 2000, the 3M turnover was US$16.7 billion and its wide product range included Scotch tape (clear adhesive tape), scrub sponges, tooth-filling materials, microflex electrical circuits and replacement CFC chemicals. Figure 11.7 shows the broad product areas in which the company was involved.

The reasons for this breadth of product range relate to the development style and investment criteria of the company:

● Does a proposed new product deliver high profit margins?
● Does a proposed new product provide innovative growth opportunities?

Importantly, there is no requirement for the product range to stay within the existing core markets of the company – the strategic concept of the resource-based view is interpreted broadly. New products can come from any part of the company. Some outsiders regarded the company as a conglomerate, which is rather unfashionable in the context of 'core competencies' – *see* Chapter 6. However, the 3M's former chief executive, Mr Livio DeSimone stoutly defends its range of 50,000 products: 'A very large part of what this company

3M prides itself with justification on its innovative record which it has written into its company description in Canada.

does has sticky stuff on it. Whether you talk about Post-it notes, or office tape, or bonding tape for industry, they're clearly sticky,' explained Mr DeSimone. 'The knowledge we have [allows us] to make those [basic products] valuable.' In practice, the core competencies of 3M probably lie in its deep knowledge of coatings and adhesives, which it then applies across a broad range of products.

3M's innovative process: two examples

The company is famed for its innovative processes. Its Annual Report for 2000 comments: 'In 2000, the company experienced one of the highest levels of innovation in our history, generating US$5.6bn – nearly 35 per cent of total sales – from products introduced in the past four years, with over US$1.2bn of sales coming from products introduced in 2000.' Innovation is at the essence of its business strategy and this is stimulated and supported throughout the organisation.

To illustrate the 3M approach to innovation, it is useful to consider two famous 3M examples – Scotch tape and Post-it notes. These two major products came about as a result of the company's support for the personal initiatives of two of its managers, Dick Drew and Art Fry. Mr Drew developed the former product and Mr Fry invented the latter. The way that these developments happened is important in exploring innovation at 3M.

Dick Drew was a 3M sandpaper salesman who had customers in the automobile industry. He noticed one day that they were having difficulty painting two-tone cars: it was difficult to stop the paint spreading from one area to the other. He had an idea for a sticky tape that would protect and separate the areas. He approached his company, which at that time did not make sticky tape, and was allowed to work on the project over the ensuing months. At one stage, he had so little success that he was told by the president of his division at 3M to stop work on the project, but after some persuasion, he was allowed to continue. The product was eventually perfected and was used five years later as the basis of Scotch tape, which became market leader in North America.

Figure 11.7

The wide range of 3M products in 2004

Turnover by business area – 2004 (US$ millions)

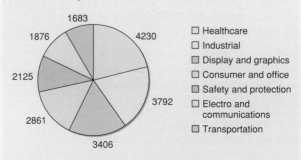

□	Healthcare
□	Industrial
□	Display and graphics
□	Consumer and office
□	Safety and protection
□	Electro and communications
□	Transportation

Source: 3M Annual Report and Accounts 2004.

Art Fry sang in his local church choir and needed some markers for his hymn book that would not fall out. He had the idea of taking a peelable adhesive that had been developed some years earlier at the 3M research laboratories and spreading it on the markers. It worked well and he asked if he could develop the product commercially. He was given permission and, after some persistence, developed a manufacturing process. But the marketing team was discouraging, pointing out that customer research suggested that a weak adhesive would not sell. Mr Fry then decided to make some markers anyway and distributed them to colleagues to try in the company. The result was a highly successful product, which became known as Post-it notes.

3M's innovative company culture

The stories above are important because they illustrate the style of 3M: 'Pursue your dream with freedom'. Employees can spend up to 15 per cent of their total time developing their own ideas. They are given extensive support, especially from their superiors, who act as coaches and mentors, rather than judges and leaders. Failure is accepted without criticism as part of the process and there is an obsession right across the company with new ideas that have no boundaries. Regular meetings and knowledge fairs are held to allow researchers to exchange ideas. The company on-line knowledge base is extensive and widely used. The whole company culture is supportive of new ideas. This style of innovation management has led to 3M being held up as a classic example of the best practice in the area. The company has often been in the top ten of *Fortune* magazine's most admired US companies.

Slower growth, then recovery – how?

For all the innovation practices at 3M, the company has failed to maintain its growth rate: sales growth in 1994–95 was around 11 per cent per annum. By 2000, this had dropped to 6 per cent per annum – see Figure 11.8. Profits followed a similar pattern. Part of the reason for the slower growth was the Asian crisis of the late 1990s: around 25 per cent of the company's sales were in this region and its profit margins were also under pressure here. This was then followed by a slowdown in its home country economy – the US – which accounted for 45 per cent of turnover. Nevertheless, in the years to 2004, the situation recovered in both sales and profits. But if a company has a growth objective, then it should be able to overcome these problems.

How did 3M turn around the situation by 2004? The company answered its critics by progressively introducing a new approach to growth. It was called the *Six Sigma* initiative. The *Six Sigma* name comes from total quality management (TQM) statistical concepts about the number of acceptable defects in any production process: these are beyond the scope of this book to detail. In any event, it is not necessary to understand such concepts in depth in order to see their contribution to 3M's innovation. Moreover, the company appears to use Six Sigma as a name for two broad concepts, the second of which has little connection with TQM:

- DMAIC – Define, Measure, Analyse, Improve, Control – a structured method for directing project teams at 3M to improve the quality of their products in the production process. (In other words, a form of TQM.)

Figure 11.8

Ten-year revenue growth at 3M

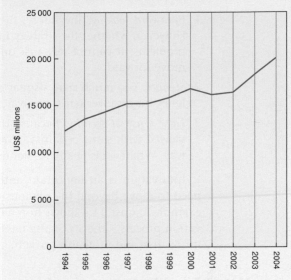

Source: Annual Report and Accounts 2004.

- DFSS – Design for Six Sigma – a standardised methodology for creating and accelerating new products into the market place. (Not necessarily related to TQM.)

3M began with the two Six Sigma concepts in early 2001 by introducing them to the senior leaders of the company. By 2004, all employees had been trained in the two methodologies and processes. The structure introduced by 3M contained a detailed Six Sigma hierarchy of 'directors, champions, master black belts, black belts, green belts and six sigma coaches' to implement the system. Six Sigma is fast becoming a basic component of our corporate culture.

According to 3M, the advantages of this approach to analysing and structuring innovation were that it provided a common approach throughout the company and a common language globally – important for a company with operations in many countries. It also developed leadership skills, encouraged tangible, measurable results and focused on customer satisfaction, especially DFSS. Ultimately, according to 3M, it 'provides better products faster.' Although some of the increase in sales and profitability 2002 to 2004 may be due to external factors, the results suggest that the Six Sigma approach had a positive impact on the company.

Case questions

1 *What are the main elements of the innovative process at 3M? Is it possible and desirable for other companies to emulate them?*

2 *What do you think of Six Sigma? Can other companies do the same?*

3 *To what extent, if at all, does innovation matter in setting the purpose of an organisation?*

11.4 INNOVATION AND PURPOSE

The analytical process described in earlier Parts 2 and 3 (Chapters 3 to 9) of this book brings three potential dangers:

1 *Backward looking.* Inevitably, historical data form the starting point for future action. However, whether the strategy intends to build on past success or to fight its way out of problems, it cannot rely just on the past. There needs to be a determined attempt to move forward.

2 *Sterility.* Too much analysis may stifle creativity. New ideas, new approaches to old problems, may be weakened by overemphasis on analysis and data collection.[28]

3 *False sense of security.* Because they have already happened, events in the past can be viewed with some certainty. However, it would be wrong to see the future in the same way. Whatever is predicted stands a high probability of being at least partially incorrect.[29]

Innovation is an important antidote to these real problems. In corporate strategy, we need to move beyond the obvious and comfortable into the new and interesting. The 3M example in Case 11.4 shows how a company has attempted to use a highly structured innovation process – the Six Sigma methodology – to achieve its stated organisational purpose: innovative and profitable growth.

11.4.1 The strategic role of innovation

Definition ➤ By definition, innovation moves products, markets and production processes beyond their current boundaries and capabilities. Innovation is the generation and exploitation of new ideas. It also provides organisations with the ammunition to move ahead of the competition. Hence, innovation can deliver three priceless assets to corporate strategy:

1 substantial future growth;

2 competitive advantage;

3 ability to leapfrog major competition, even dominant competitors.

However, none of the three above areas will automatically deliver future profitability to innovating companies – *see* Figure 11.9. Consider the cases of Canon (Japan) and EMI (UK). Both companies developed major new innovations during the 1970s.

Figure 11.9

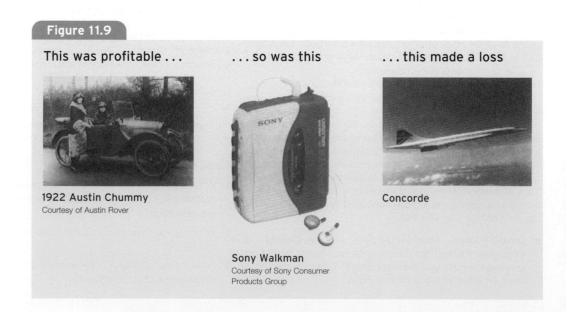

This was profitable . . .   . . . so was this   . . . this made a loss

1922 Austin Chummy
Courtesy of Austin Rover

Sony Walkman
Courtesy of Sony Consumer
Products Group

Concorde

- *Canon* set out to compete with and beat Xerox (US) in world photocopying markets. It developed a series of new processes that did not infringe the Xerox patents yet produced products that turned Canon into one of the world's leading photocopying and printing companies. By the mid-1990s, it had a larger market share than Xerox.[30]

- *EMI* was so badly wounded by its foray into medical electronics that its scanner business had to be sold off at a knock-down price. This happened despite the fact that its product was truly innovative and was the first in the market place by a significant period.[31]

Innovation is not without risk. Yet, if it is successful, the payoff is significant. There are two principal sources of innovation to be examined, neither of which is sufficient in itself:

- customer needs analysis – *market pull*
- technology development analysis – *technology push*.

11.4.2 Customer needs analysis: market pull

Baker[32] suggests that innovation occurs when companies identify new market opportunities or a segment of an existing market that has been neglected. Essentially, it is important to develop such opportunities in terms of the *customer need served* in broad general terms – for example, transport, convenience – rather than by examining current products and how they meet demand. For example, Canon photocopiers were innovatory in meeting the general demand for photocopying rather than the needs of the existing customer base, which was biased towards large companies. The company developed new machines requiring little maintenance or repair, which were sold to a much broader range of customers – the medium-sized and small businesses. This process is known as *market pull – see* Figure 11.10.

As Whittington points out,[33] the importance of market pull in successful innovation has been well validated by research. It relies on identifying a market need that needs to be satisfied by a technological advance – essentially a *prescriptive* approach to corporate strategy. It is used in research and development of some new pharmaceuticals, consumer electronics and other areas of technology that are market-driven.

However, prescriptive approaches to the study of market demand carry the danger that customers are often constrained in their vision by their current experience and knowledge. More experienced approaches to market need may also be worthwhile.

11.4.3 Technology development analysis: technology push

Market pull procedures do not fully describe the way that many real innovations happen, however.[34] Innovation may be born out of developments at small companies, often in a two-way process with their customers, who may be larger companies. Alternatively, innovations

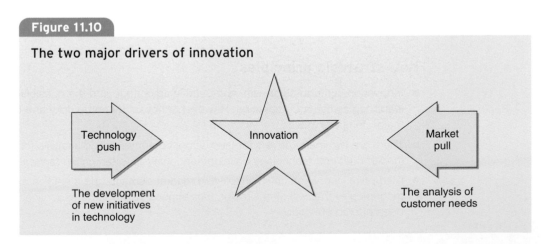

Figure 11.10

The two major drivers of innovation

Technology push

Innovation

Market pull

The development of new initiatives in technology

The analysis of customer needs

may start as narrow solutions to particular problems. For example, Thomas Watson, President of IBM, said that a new calculator built by his company in 1947 (the Selective Sequence Electronic Calculator) would be able to solve many of the world's major scientific problems but had no commercial applications. It proved to be one of the first IBM computers.

Successful technology often takes time to diffuse through to other industries. It follows that, in addition to monitoring customer needs, an innovatory company should also survey other industries for their technology developments and assess their relevance to its own – essentially an emergent approach to corporate strategy. This process is sometimes known as *technology push – see* Figure 11.10.

Case 11.5 describes how technology push works at the Dutch electronics company Philips. Importantly, it shows that how the company is organised and how it handles the human side of technology are just as important as the new product derived from technology push.

11.4.4 Disruptive innovation – a variation of customer pull and technology push

In the mid-1990s, Professor Clayton Christensen of Harvard University Business School suggested that there was another form of innovation, which he called 'disruptive innovation'.[35]

Definition ➤ Disruptive innovation takes an existing market and identifies existing technologies that will offer simpler, less expensive products or services than have been offered previously. This may result in some existing customers switching to the cheaper product or the lower costs and prices of the new product may attract new customers to that market. Disruptive innovation may not involve breakthrough technology but rather the re-packaging of existing technology in a way that brings a new and possibly cheaper offering to the market place. The customers for such an offering might be those who would not previously have bought the product or those who would be happy with a low-performing version of the product. For example, customers who had not previously acquired an expensive hi-fi sound system might be attracted to purchase a lower-priced system that worked adequately, but was produced using mature technology, cheaper standardised components and was assembled labour from low wage-cost countries like China. The importance of this approach is that the existing companies may not regard such a new segment as having much attraction. This therefore allows the disruptive company to enter the new market segment.

Disruptive innovation differs from the main thrust of technology push in so far as the latter involves the development of leading-edge new technology. It also differs from customer pull in the sense that disruptive innovation does not seek to identify a totally new area of consumer demand, but to attract those who currently are not part of an existing market demand. One way to identify where disruptive technology might operate is to analyse the *value chain* of a product or service – *see* Chapter 6. The location of highest value within the chain might suggest the area to attack.

> ### Key strategic principles
>
> - Innovation contributes growth, competitive advantage and the possibility of leapfrogging major competition. However, innovation can be risky and can result in major company losses.
>
> - There are two major drivers for innovation: customer needs analysis (often called *market pull*) and technology development analysis (often called *technology push*).
>
> - Disruptive innovation takes an existing market demand and identifies existing technologies that will offer simpler, less expensive products or services than have been offered previously.

CASE STUDY 11.5

How Philips exploits its technology edge

The Dutch-based electronics giant, Philips, has a poor record of turning its scientific brilliance into revenues and profits. This case explores how the company is changing.

Background – global from its Dutch base

In 2000, Philips had over 250,000 employees and US$36 billion sales. By year 2004, the company had 160,000 employees and sales around US$33 billion. Importantly, after several years of losses, it reported a profit of US$3 billion in 2004. Philips had a wide geographic spread of sales but its profits were mainly generated from its European operations – see Figure 11.11. The company's strategy was to use its technology base to develop worldwide profitability.

Philips is one of Holland's best-known global companies with a wide product range including lighting, consumer electronics, small domestic appliances, semiconductor components, medical technology, optical storage and displays. The company has its headquarters in Eindhoven, Holland, from which it directs its worldwide activities. The Philip's strategic problem for some years has been that it was particularly strong in mature and highly competitive industries like lighting and television manufacture. It had strong European sales, particularly in these product areas. Philip's undoubted competitive strength was its strong research foundation and

Philips is an important company in India for its new technology and leading edge consumer electronics.

Figure 11.11

Philips – global sales but most of the profits from Europe

(a) Philips location of sales 2004

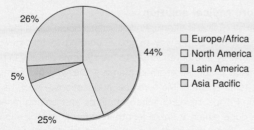

- ☐ Europe/Africa
- ☐ North America
- ☐ Latin America
- ☐ Asia Pacific

(b) Philips location of profits 2004

- ☐ Europe/Africa
- ☐ North America
- ☐ Latin America
- ☐ Asia Pacific

Source: Company Report and Accounts 2004.

research record. Its strategic opportunity was to exploit and direct this competitive and innovative resource more profitably in every part of the world. In order to undertake this task, it needed to move beyond its mature products into areas that would have a leading technological edge and therefore offer sales opportunities in other parts of the world as well as Europe.

Philips' technology base

Philips has around 1,500 'creative' research staff, mainly scientists in 13 laboratories, who are funded by a research budget of US$250 million. It owns 65,000 patents and claims an illustrious list of inventions – see Table 11.1. About two-fifths of its researchers are based in Eindhoven. But there are others in the UK, France, Germany, Taiwan and China. In addition, the company spends about six times its research budget on product development – primarily in the company's six product divisions.

Research record – inventive but not yet sufficiently exploitative

In spite of its record of invention, many observers think that Philips has failed to make the most of its research in fields such as medical equipment, home video recorders and disc-drive technology. One technology consultant says that the company has not done enough to link its researchers with

▶ **CASE STUDY 11.5 continued**

Table 11.1

Philips' inventions

1926	Pentode radio tube
1934	High-pressure mercury lamp
1968	Charge-coupled devices for sensing
1968	Spiral groove bearings for mechanical engineering
1972	Video long-play systems
1976	Nickel-metal-hydride batteries
1980	Modulation systems for compact discs
1980s	Low-frequency lasers for telecommunications
1995	High-speed transistors for cell phones
1997	Plastic semiconductors

outsiders, preventing it from making the most of good ideas. 'The company's research establishment has been inward-looking and arrogant,' he says. While not necessarily accepting the direct criticism, Philips' worldwide head of research, Mr Ad Huijser, recognises that there has been a problem. He has set himself the task of increasing the rate at which Philips' scientific ideas turn into profits. 'When a venture capitalist invests in new ideas, he wants to make a return,' says Mr Huijser. 'We must try to develop the same mindset.'

By 2004, Philips was developing five collaborative alliances with other major corporations:

● Healthcare software with Epic Systems Corporation;
● Home brewing machine with InBev – see Chapter 8 for this company;
● Coffee brewing machine with Douwe Egberts Coffee company (part of Sara Lee Corporation);
● Chip technology for credit cards with Visa International;
● Internet home entertainment content and devices with Yahoo!

Organising the links for invention

In such a large company, managing the research effort is a complex task. Yet it is vital if the benefits of new inventions are to be exploited commercially. Linking the company's scientists to the six divisions of the company is one aspect of Mr Huijser's approach. This is partly accomplished by making the divisions pay for the research: two-thirds of the research bill is covered by contracts that they have instituted. The divisions pay for directed research areas such as software, materials, integrated circuit design, electronic storage and communications technologies. The other third of the money is accounted for by 'blue sky' research authorised by Philips' research staff. An essential part of the link between product divisions and scientists is the chief technology officers who work in each

division. Their job is to scout for new technologies, devised either in Philips or outside, that could help commercial efforts.

In a second part of Mr Huijser's efforts to institute 'market pull' Philips has recruited ten business development officers. They are based in the company's worldwide research laboratories and their role is to provide a critical view of the ideas coming from the research. They may also suggest ways to commercialise them. These people, says Mr Huijser, tend to have more of a business background than the research scientists. 'They provide a different perspective. They set targets for the ideas being pursued inside laboratories and a timetable for potential commercialisation.'

The business development officers also provide a potential conduit between Philips' research staff and other businesses with which the company might want to form a partnership to commercialise particular ideas. According to Mr Huijser, such links are growing and now number several dozen. Mr Huijser says that Philips has to be 'more alive' to the idea that sometimes other companies are in a better position to take on its scientific ideas than Philips itself.

The third Huijser initiative consists of attempts to quantify the output of Philips' research employees. This is controversial, because measurement of the results from research involves difficult questions of what constitutes success. Even so, many think such efforts worthwhile as part of the interest in getting away from valuing research solely in terms of how much has been spent. Mr Huijser treads carefully, looking at factors such as licensing income, patent registrations and publication of scientific papers. More unusually, every year he asks Philips' product divisions how much of their revenues in the previous 12 months has come from new scientific ideas devised by research staff. The exercise is imperfect and subjective, Mr Huijser admits, and for this reason the results are never published.

A more radical solution

For all Mr Huijser's efforts, Philips' critics could claim the company still has some way to go. According to this view, his ideas merely add bureaucracy to the systems already in place to govern – and sometimes cramp – the way the company exploits its science. More radical suggestions – such as dissolving Philips' research establishments and leaving research to be done either at arm's length in external organisations or directly under the control of the product divisions – seem unlikely to be taken up by the company's senior executives, who have built up a reputation over the years for conservatism. Mr Huijser believes that his moderate efforts are paying off. The company is progressing towards the goal of making the research effort sharper. 'We are better structured and there is less waste,' he says. 'I believe we are at least as good as other companies around the world.'

Adapted by Richard Lynch from an article by Peter Marsh, *Financial Times*, 22 March 2001, p12. Copyright *Financial Times*. Used with permission. The opening sections and updated information were written by Richard Lynch.

Case questions

1 *What three methods has the company introduced to exploit its research base? How successful has it been so far?*

2 *How does Philips attempt to employ what it calls 'market pull'? Is this really market pull, as defined in the chapter, or is it, in reality, 'technology push' with a more commercial bias?*

3 *What are the problems, if any, with seeking links with other companies when attempting to exploit technology innovation?*

4 *Given the difficulties of quantifying research output, would you look for a more radical solution as suggested by some in the case? What are the benefits and problems of such an approach?*

STRATEGIC PROJECT

Philips is a very interesting company from a strategy perspective because it is beginning to change. For many years, it produced exceptionally innovative solutions from a technical perspective but was less successful at marketing them. It is now changing and there is a good presentation on the web at www.philips.com which explains the company's progress. An interesting project would be to re-evaluate Philips one year on from the original presentation – just how much progress has it made? What principles has it used to develop its technology strategy? Do you think that it will be successful?

11.5 HOW TO INNOVATE: THE 'IDEAS' PROCESS

11.5.1 The phases of innovation

Innovation often occurs through a diffusion process.[36] It may well be adopted slowly at first, then the pace quickens until finally there are just a few late-adopters left to take up the process. Diffusion thus follows the S-shaped curve shown in Figure 11.12.

Sometimes the early pioneering companies fail to make profits because there are still few purchasers and large sums have been invested in developing the process. It is at this stage that business failures like that of the EMI scanner occur. The real profits are made during the rising part of the curve when there is major demand, pricing is still high to reflect the genuine innovation or costs have been dramatically reduced as a result of a technological breakthrough.

In some respects, corporate strategy may therefore be better served by those who are 'fast seconds' into the market place: the curve is still rising and the original innovator has still not come to dominate the market. For example, the anti-ulcer drug Zantac (Glaxo Wellcome, UK) was second into the market after Tagamet (SmithKline Beecham, UK/US) yet came to dominate the market eventually and make a substantial contribution to Glaxo profitability. The inventions at Philips – *see* Table 11.1 – also support the point that being first does not necessarily deliver profit.

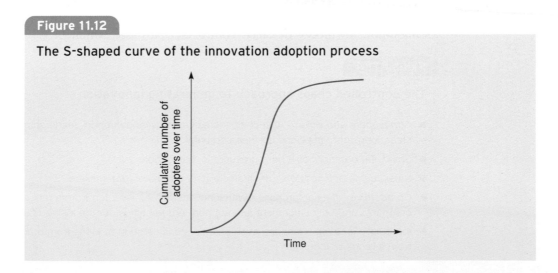

Figure 11.12

The S-shaped curve of the innovation adoption process

This finding is supported by the research of Mansfield,[37] who tracked innovations over a 30-year period. He estimated that on average those who were second into a market could make a new product for two-thirds of the cost and time of the original innovating company. The strategic problem is how to identify correctly and react quickly to the truly new innovation – not an easy task. Utterback[38] has identified three phases in individual innovation that may help in this identification process:

1 *Fluid phase*. In the early days of an innovation, the market is in a state of flux. The products are not standardised. There are often very few small-scale producers and the manufacturing equipment is general-purpose and small-scale. Competition is limited, with heavy reliance on further product development initiatives. Innovation comes from new product development.

2 *Transitional phase*. After a period, demand has risen sufficiently to justify dedicated production machinery. At least one product design has established itself to deliver volume sales. More competitors have entered the market but the rate of entry is beginning to decline as a dominant design emerges and some companies adopt this and get ahead of competition. The competitive threat is likely to come, for the first time, from producers with lower costs and higher quality. Innovation is more likely to come from developments in the manufacturing process.

3 *Specific phase*. Over time, innovation slows down and becomes small and incremented. A few large-scale manufacturers dominate the market. They produce their goods on a relatively large scale, using specialist and dedicated machinery. Competition is more likely to be based on price and branding, until a new and genuine innovation is again developed.

We return to the dynamics of innovation in Chapter 20. For now, we should note that the above description is based on two basic assumptions and empirical observations:

1 that economies of scale and scope are possible in an industry and remain the chief means of reducing costs;

2 that custom demand can be satisfied by standardised products.

These may not be true in all industries – *see* the customer/competitor matrix in Chapter 5 and flexible manufacturing in Chapter 9.

11.5.2 The routes to delivering innovation

Given its value to the organisation, the real issue is how to deliver innovation.

For the original innovators, the payoff can be substantial with the right product. Professor James Quinn[39] of Dartmouth College, US, investigated the innovation process of a variety of companies and concluded that large companies need to behave like small entrepreneurial ventures to be truly successful. He suggested that innovatory companies should ideally follow the process he called 'controlled chaos' (*see* Exhibit 11.4) – not an easy task.

Exhibit 11.4

The controlled chaos approach to generating innovation

● *Atmosphere and vision* – with chief executives providing support, leadership and projecting clear, long-term ambitions for their company

● *Small, flat organisation* – not bureaucratic, but flexible

● *Small teams of innovators* – multidisciplinary groups of idea makers

● *Competitive selection process* – with innovatory ideas selected from a range in the company, and encouragement and support, not penalties, for the losing team

● *Interactive learning* – random, even chaotic, consideration of ideas from many sources and from a range of industries

Quinn believed strongly in the *emergent process* for innovation strategy. Writing around the same time, Fred Gluck[40] of the consulting company McKinsey took largely the opposite view. He argued that the really innovatory achievements needed a *'big bang'* approach. They need masses of information, a decision-making process that can discern patterns in these undigested data and the functional skills to implement the decisions once they were made. He urged the larger corporations, to which he was addressing his remarks, to become more sensitive to major environmental changes and to create a better climate to explore *big bang* ideas.

This conflict of views as to the best way forward for innovation would appear to be equally true for Japanese researchers. One study[41] describing Japanese practice was based on a survey of products in eight major companies including Honda, NEC, Epson and Canon. It found that the process was informal, multifunctional and involved excess information over that initially identified to solve the problem. The conclusion was that the most successful innovation processes often involved redundant information that interacted through chance, even chaotic, processes to produce the innovatory result. By contrast, another study[42] of Japanese innovation processes concluded that a more analytical approach can also be employed in some circumstances.

The overall conclusion is probably that there is no one route to innovation: both prescriptive and emergent approaches have been successfully used. There are, however, seven general guidelines that might be used to encourage the innovation process.[43]

1 *Question the present business strategies and market definitions.* Once the present strategy has been defined, there is a clear case for questioning every aspect of it. There are bound to be areas that would benefit from new definitions and approaches. A real problem for many organisations is that they live with their existing preconceptions for many years and have real problems in raising their sights to new perspectives.

   For example, the market and its customers might be redefined either more broadly or more narrowly. This might lead to a redefinition of the competitors and the threats and opportunities that arise. In turn, this might suggest new insights into areas where the organisation has a competitive advantage – some real leverage over others in the market. The Walt Disney Corporation redefined its market in the 1970s as one of providing pleasure using themed characters such as Mickey Mouse and Donald Duck: it used these ideas to develop another way of delivering such entertainment with the first of its Disney theme parks in Anaheim, California.

2 *Consider carefully the purpose served by the current products or services.* Exploring carefully the purpose served by the current offerings may lead to ideas about the future. It may be possible to reach the same end by new and more rewarding means. While some piano manufacturers were unable to compete for the attention of youngsters against the attractions of computer games such as Nintendo and Sega, Yamaha had other ideas. It redefined its piano as a keyboard and added new designs, sizes and technology to provide as much fun as a game.

3 *Explore external timing and market opportunities.* There are often strategic windows of opportunity that may provide real benefits if they can be tackled. Resources then need to be concentrated on such areas to ensure progress is quick, but the rewards are significant. Timing is vital, however. For example, Asea Brown Boveri (Switzerland/Sweden) and Deutsche Babcock (Germany) have seized opportunities to develop products in the area of environmental control engineering over the last few years, building on the new concerns of some governments, especially those in Northern Europe and the US.

4 *Seek out competitors' weaknesses.* Most organisations have areas in which they are weak. These might provide opportunities for others to expand. However, such an approach does invite competitive retaliation and so needs to be considered carefully. For example, Microsoft has dominated world markets for computer software for years with its Windows system. The company did not notice that Netscape Communications had quietly developed software for the internet 'browser' market and by 1995 had come to

dominate this segment. Microsoft was then involved in some expensive joint deals to recover the situation in this area.

5 *Deliver new and better value for money.* Companies sometimes become locked into assumptions about the possibilities of further reductions in costs and improvements in quality. However, design and technology development is moving at such a pace in some markets that new opportunities have arisen. For example, all the Japanese car manufacturers were able to make real share gains in the 1970s and 1980s not only by competitive prices but also by offering superior quality and performance standards.

6 *Search wide and far.* Examining areas such as lifestyles, technology, regulatory regimes and demographics can generate significant opportunities. For example, Motorola (US) and Nokia (Finland) have both benefited from the rise of the mobile telephone, having developed expertise in this market over the last ten years. In the same way, Sharp (Japan) was the leading company in the launch of pocket computer organisers because it recognised trends to busier and more complex lives that needed to be managed.

7 *Seek to challenge conventional wisdom.* Acceptance of the current market and resource status is unlikely to lead to major new developments. There is a need to challenge every aspect of what is believed to be the generally held view in markets. This might include a challenge to areas such as *key factors for success*, perhaps by finding a totally new method of delivering a product or service. Some managers are better at the challenge process than others and need to be encouraged and supported as they engage in this task. For example, as late as the 1980s it was considered impossible for personal car insurance to be sold over the telephone: it was far too complicated and customers would not accept it. This has proved to be totally false. By the mid-1990s, telephone selling had become the dominant mode of selling in several of Europe's largest markets. As a result, the new companies such as Direct Line (now a subsidiary of the Royal Bank of Scotland) have taken over market leadership in the UK.

It will be evident that there is no one piece of conventional strategic theory that will prompt innovative developments, but the strategic payoff from such processes can be substantial.

11.5.3 International perspectives on innovation

International country comparisons on innovation pose significant problems. This is because innovation is dependent on the *product group*: for example, innovation is likely to be higher in biotechnology and lower in food products because of the state of technological development in these two categories. Different countries have different strengths in different product groups (*see* Chapter 19 for an exploration of this area). Hence, it is difficult to make generalisations about countries without assessing the product groups with which they are involved.

Nevertheless, the reasons why the pace of innovation seemed to be higher in some countries than in others were explored in the 1980s.[44] Three interrelated groups of factors were identified:

1 factors that influence *inputs* to the innovation process, such as the quality of the country's scientific community, especially its educational institutions;

2 factors that influence *demand*, such as receptive and interested customers;

3 an *industrial structure* that favours intense competition to stimulate growth and provides some method for companies to spread the cost and results of scientific research, such as through a government agency.

These conclusions are similar to those of Porter when exploring the competitive advantage of nations (*see* Chapter 19).

The role of government may also be important. In France, the UK and the US, it was 'top down', directed at specific industries, such as defence, and with specific measurable objectives. In other countries, such as Sweden, Switzerland and Germany, government acted in a more 'diffusion-oriented' way. It responded to market signals and provided education and training and set industry standards that raised quality and diffused technology.

In terms of competitive advantage, over the centuries nations have come to rely less on the possession of raw material wealth, which can be bought through international trade. They also place less emphasis on being close to markets, since transport costs have come down dramatically. Countries now rely heavily on scientific skills, not only to invent products but also to manufacture those that have been developed. In turn, such developments require a highly skilled workforce and investment by the state in education. In seeking sources of innovation, organisations will wish to consider the role that the state has played and is continuing to play in investing in its future workpeople. Countries such as Singapore and Malaysia have recognised the importance of investment in education to provide the structural basis for the innovatory process.

11.5.4 How purpose can emerge from innovation

If the purpose of the organisation is defined in terms mainly of survival, then it can be argued that such a purpose is present in most organisations in advance of any process of innovation. In this sense, purpose cannot be said to emerge from innovation but, rather, to precede it. However, if the purpose of the organisation is defined in some broader way to include, for example, the delivery of additional value, quality or service, then innovation can take on a very different role.

Given the right circumstances and people, innovation can occur anywhere in an organisation. It is not confined to corporate technologists or marketing managers. Innovation can thus provide new opportunities to move beyond the current position in an industry. But until the full extent and implications of an innovation have been explored, its true potential cannot meaningfully be assessed. In this sense, the new purpose that will be presented by a radical innovation – such as some aspect of bioengineering or the internet – cannot be defined in advance but must be left to *emerge* as the innovation proceeds. Corporate strategy may be better served if at least some part of it is free from the straitjacket of a tightly defined purpose.

Key strategic principles

- The innovation process is complex and risky – early innovation pioneers did not always gain the full financial benefit from their work.

- Innovation development often follows an S-shaped curve, with the real profit being made during the growth phase, after the initial development.

- There are three phases in industrial innovation: fluid, transitional and specific. Change from the first to the second phase occurs when a product design becomes dominant. Change from the second to the third phase occurs through large-scale production.

- The innovation process can be *emergent*, with ideas freely generated from many sources. It can also be *prescriptive*, with a more analytical and directed approach to the task.

- The seven guidelines offered on innovation to start this process do not claim to be comprehensive. They have as their central theme the need to challenge conventional understanding and wisdom.

- International perspectives in innovation suggest that a strong national education structure is useful.

- If the purpose of the organisation includes an element of growth, then it may be better to allow such a purpose to *emerge* from an innovative opportunity, whose full potential cannot be known in advance.

CRITICAL REFLECTION

Innovation: emergent or prescriptive?

This chapter has argued for an experimental, emergent approach to purpose, based on knowledge, new technologies and seeking out innovation in every area of an organisation. Crucially, the purpose of an organisation to develop this approach needs to be left open and undefined.

The difficulty is that this open-ended approach to purpose is completely contrary to the way that many organisations like to work. They make commitments to their shareholders about growth targets; they allocate funds for research on the basis of the likely benefits from such activities; they manage their employees on the basis of sales and profit development targets. In other words, they adopt highly prescriptive approaches to innovation and research.

Should these two approaches be reconciled? Can they be reconciled? If so, how?

SUMMARY

● The knowledge of the organisation can be used to deliver and maintain sustainable competitive advantage. Knowledge is hard to define precisely but can be considered as a constantly changing mixture of experience, values, contextual information and expert insight. It will be evident that such areas might well be exclusive to the organisation and provide distinctiveness from competition.

● Knowledge needs to be divided between its tacit and explicit forms. Explicit knowledge is recorded and structured. Tacit knowledge is fuzzy and difficult to set out. Both can lead to competitive advantage but tacit knowledge may be particularly important because it is less easy for competitors to comprehend and copy. An organisation's knowledge can be audited as the basis for strategy development, but the audit has several disadvantages.

● Conversion and communication of existing knowledge can take place through four mechanisms: socialisation, externalisation, combination and internalisation. All four processes relate to the basic distinction between tacit and explicit knowledge existing in any organisation.

● Knowledge creation – the development and circulation of new knowledge – offers a dynamic strategic opportunity. There are three mechanisms: organisational learning, knowledge creation and acquisition, and knowledge transfer.

● If new knowledge is significant in its impact on the organisation, then it may well change the purpose of the organisation. Importantly, the purpose will only change after new knowledge has been developed. In this sense, the purpose of the organisation *emerges* from knowledge creation.

● An internal and external scan of technologies is vital to the development of corporate strategy. It may alter the purpose of the organisation over time. Technologies need to be classified into base, core and peripheral. It is the core area that is most likely to deliver sustainable competitive advantage. Each technology then needs to be assessed against its competitors and for time and costs of development estimated.

● New information technology (IT) has opened up the possibility of greater strategic control in organisations. The control that can be exercised needs to go beyond basic financial data into people aspects of the organisation. At the same time, IT may present new opportunities to develop sustainable competitive advantage, but they are likely to be short-lived unless backed by patents.

● Innovation contributes growth, competitive advantage and the possibility of leapfrogging competition. However, it can also be risky and result in major losses to the organisation. There are two major drivers for innovation: customer needs analysis (market pull) and technology development analysis (technology push). The innovation process can be both prescriptive and emergent.

● There are three phases in industrial innovation: fluid, transitional and specific. Change from the first to the second phase occurs when a product design becomes dominant. Change from the second to the third phase occurs through large-scale production. The first of these is primarily concerned with product innovation. The second and third phases are more likely to be associated with manufacturing process innovation.

● If the purpose of the organisation includes an element of growth, then it may be better to allow such a purpose to *emerge* from an innovative opportunity, whose full potential cannot be known in advance.

QUESTIONS

1 Take an organisation with which you are familiar and identify its areas of explicit and tacit knowledge. To what extent, if at all, does the process assist in identifying the sustainable competitive advantage of the company?

2 In what ways might a company like Nike use a 'knowledge audit' as part of its strategy development process? What are the problems with this approach? Would you recommend it?

3 *'In an economy where the only certainty is uncertainty, one sure source of lasting competitive advantage is knowledge'* (Ikijuro Nonaka).

   Do you agree with Professor Nonaka about the unique importance of knowledge?

4 Take an organisation with which you are familiar and classify its technologies into basic, core and peripheral. What conclusions can you draw on sustainable competitive advantage for the organisation's strategy?

5 With the introduction of the World Wide Web, it has been argued that this: *'will give consumers increased access to a vast selection of goods but will cause a restructuring and redistribution of profits amongst stakeholders along the [value] chain'* (Robert Benjamin and Rolf Wigand).

Discuss the strategic implications of this comment from the viewpoint of (a) a major retailer and (b) a small to medium-sized supplier of local building services.

6 Do you think that the increased use of IT will affect all organisations equally? Will some remain relatively unaffected apart from the introduction of a few computers and a link to the internet? What are the strategic implications of your answer?

7 Identify some recent innovations and classify them into market pull and technology push. Explain how each innovation has been delivered into the market, using the S-shaped curve to show the process.

8 Quinn argues that large companies need to behave like small entrepreneurial ventures to be truly innovative. Gluck suggests that major innovations only come from a 'big-bang' push that needs major resources. Can these two views of the innovative process be reconciled? (*See* references 38 and 40.)

9 *'Innovate or fall behind: the competitive imperative for virtually all businesses today is that simple'* (Professors Dorothy Leonard and Susan Straus).

   Is this true? Is innovation fundamental to all business strategy?

Further reading

On knowledge: Davenport, Thomas and Prusack, Lawrence (1998) *Working Knowledge*, Harvard Business School Press, Boston, MA, is comprehensive and insightful. Nonaka, I and Takeuchi, H (1995) *The Knowledge-Creating Company*, Oxford University Press, Oxford, is one of the leading texts. Leonard, Dorothy (1995) *Wellsprings of Knowledge*, Harvard Business School Press, Boston, MA, is also about

innovation. A good compendium of interesting papers is Morey, D, Maybury, M and Thuraisingham, B (eds) (2002) *Knowledge Management: Classic and Contemporary Works*, The MIT Press, Cambridge, Mass. *See also* Krogh, G, Nonaka, I and Aben, M (2001) 'Making the most of your company's knowledge', *Long Range Planning*, Vol 34, No 4, pp421–40.

On technology and corporate strategy: Contractor, F-J and Narayanan, V K (1990) 'Technology development in the multinational firm', *R&D Management*, Basil Blackwell, Oxford, republished in Root, F R and Visudtibhan (eds) (1992) *International Strategic Management*, Taylor and Francis, London, pp163–83, is well developed, thoughtful and comprehensive.

On IT and corporate strategy: Porter, M E and Millar, V E (1985) 'How information gives you a competitive advantage', *Harvard Business Review*, July–Aug is useful. *See also* Benjamin, R and Wigand, R (1995) 'Electronic markets and virtual value chains on the information superhighway', *Sloan Management Review*, Winter, p62.

On innovation: Tidd, Joe, Bessant, John and Pavitt, Keith (2001) *Managing Innovation*, 2nd edn, John Wiley, Chichester, is comprehensive, with a useful academic foundation. Trott, Paul (1998) *Innovation Management & New Product Development*, Financial Times Management, London, is also a useful and insightful text, including knowledge. Utterback, James (1996) *Mastering the Dynamics of Innovation*, Harvard Business School Press, Boston, MA, is an excellent text with strong empirical research base.

Notes and references

1 Sources for Maglev case: Visit by author to Shanghai, June 2004. *Financial Times*: 28 June 2003, p8; 5 July 2003, p M5; 7 August 2003, p7. www.shairport.com/en. *China People's Daily* 31 December 2002 'World's first commercial Maglev line debuts in Shanghai'. *Shenzen Daily*: 15 April 2004 'Shanghai Maglev ticket prices cut by 1/3'. See also http://englishpeople.com.cn 'Rail track beats Maglev in Beijing-Shanghai high speed railway.' www.cnn.com/2004/TRAVEL/Shanghai Maglev – 30 November 2004 'Shanghai to extend Maglev rail.' http://en.ce.cn/Industries/Transport/200412/15/ 'German Maglev technology abandoned?'

2 Nonaka, I (1991) 'The knowledge-creating company', *Harvard Business Review*, Nov–Dec.

3 Nonaka, I and Takeuchi, H (1995) *The Knowledge-Creating Company*, Oxford University Press, Oxford, Ch1. This chapter traces the development of knowledge as a topic area and clearly demonstrates that it was tangential to strategy development for many strategy writers. It should also be noted that many strategy texts make no significant reference to the subject even to the present time.

4 Drucker, P (1964) *Managing for Results*, William Heinemann, London, Ch6.

5 Davenport, T H and Prusack, L (1998) *Working Knowledge: How Organizations Manage What They Know*, Harvard Business School Press, Boston, MA, pp2, 3.

6 Davenport, T H and Prusack, L (1998) Ibid., p5.

7 Hamel, G (1995) Foreword, *FT Handbook of Management*, Financial Times, London. *See* also his article in *Financial Times*, 5 June 1995, p9, for an abridged version of the article (highly entertaining phraseology but somewhat confused argument).

8 Nonaka, I and Takeuchi, H (1995) Op. cit., pp109–11.

9 Nonaka, I and Takeuchi, H (1995) Op. cit., p27.

10 Skandia, Annual Report and Accounts 1997, p62. *See* also Edvinsson, L (1997) 'Developing intellectual capital at Skandia', *Long Range Planning*, 30(3), pp366–73. Mr Edvinsson has made a significant contribution in this area at Skandia.

11 For example, *see* Davenport, T H and Prusack, L (1998) Op. cit., pxv.

12 Davenport, T H, De Long, D W and Beers, M C (1998) 'Successful knowledge management projects', *California Management Review*, 39(2), pp43–57. *See* also Norman, R and Ramirez, R (1993) 'From value chain to value constellation', *Harvard Business Review*, July–Aug, p65 (which explores knowledge and elements of key resources). Chan, Kim W and Maurborgue, R (1997) 'Fair process: managing in the knowledge economy', *Harvard Business Review*, July–Aug, p65 (which explores the impact on employees). Evans, P B and Wurster, T S (1997) 'Strategy and the new economics of information', *Harvard Business Review*, Sept–Oct, p70 (which discusses the internet).

13 This is actually the headline in the 1998 Annual Report and Accounts of Heineken NV (*see* Chapter 8) introducing its new knowledge management world network. It is not clear whether the company was aware of the political significance of this phrase and its impact on some groups within the company.

14 Boshyk, Y (1999) 'Beyond knowledge managment', *Financial Times Mastering Information Management*, 8 Feb, pp12–13.

15 References for the Nike case: Nike Annual Report and Accounts 2004 available on the web www.nike.com *Financial Time*s, 15 July 1996, p9; 15 Dec 1996, p9; 22 Dec 1996, p18; 2 Apr 1997, p22; 11 Oct 1997, p17; 17 Jan 1998, p6; 16 July 1998; 20 March 1999, p19; 20 March 2001, p6 of Creative Business Supplement; 4 November 2003, p19; 19 August 2004, pp10, 25; Seth, A (1998) *Marketing Business*, Feb. *Guardian*, 17 June 2003, p15 – interesting interview with Phil Knight.

16 Davenport, T H and Prusack, L (1998) Op. cit., Ch3.

17 For example, *see* case studies quoted in Davenport and Prusak, and Nonaka and Takeuchi above. But also *see* researchers like Kanter R (Changemasters) and Quinn explored in Chapter 16.

18 Heineken Annual Report and Accounts 1998.

19 For an extended discussion of this important area, *see* Davenport, T H and Prusack, L (1998) Op. cit., Ch5. The author (RL) will never forget the months of negotiation with his fellow finance director on one such knowledge issue.

20 Teece, D (1998) 'Capturing value from knowledge assets', *California Management Review*, 40(3), pp55–79.

21 References for the internet retail banking case study: *Financial Times*, 2 Oct 1996, Information Technology Supplement, p1; 15 Oct 1996, p18; 14 Mar 1997, p21; 30 Apr 1997, p27; 15 Sept 1997, p15; 7 Apr 1998, p29; 9 Apr 1998, p32; 15 Apr 1998, p19.

22 This section has benefited from Contractor, F J and Narayanan, V K (1990) 'Technology development in the

multinational firm', *R&D Management*, Basil Blackwell, Oxford, republished in Root, F R and Visudtibhan (eds) (1992) *International Strategic Management*, Taylor and Francis, London, pp163–83. Well developed, thoughtful and comprehensive.

23 Prahalad, C K and Hamel, G (1990) 'The core competencies of the corporation', *Harvard Business Review*, May–June, pp79–91. Prahalad, C K and Hamel, G (1994) *Competing for the Future*, Harvard Business School Press, Cambridge, Mass.

24 Teece, D, Pisano, G and Shuen, A (1997) 'Dynamic capabilities and strategic management', *Strategic Management Journal*, 18 (7) pp509–33.

25 This section has benefited from Tidd J, Bessant, J and Pavitt, K (2001) *Managing Innovation*, 2nd edn, Wiley, Chichester, Ch5.

26 Ibid. Tidd J, *et al.* (2001)

27 Sources for the 3M case study: Annual Report and Accounts 1997 and 2000; Takeuchi, I and Nonaka, H (1995) Op. cit., pp135–40; Davenport, T H and Prusak, L (1998) Op. cit., pp104–6; *Financial Times*, 7 Sept 1998, p14.

28 Hamel, G and Prahalad, C K (1994) Op. cit., p274.

29 Stacey, R (1993) *Strategic Management and Organisation Dynamics*, Pitman Publishing, London, p115.

30 Harvard Business School (1983) *Canon (B)*, Case 9–384–151 plus note on world photocopying industry.

31 Harvard Business School (1984) *EMI and the CT Scanner (A) and (B)*, Case 383–194 and the *Economist Survey on Innovation*, 11 Jan 1992, p21.

32 Baker, M (1992) *Marketing Strategy and Management*, 2nd edn, Macmillan, London, p28.

33 Whittington, R (1993) *What is Strategy and Does it Matter?*, Routledge, London, p82.

34 *The Economist* (1992) Loc. cit., p21.

35 Christensen, C. (1997) *The Innovator's Dilemma*, Harvard Business School Press, Boston, Mass.

36 Baker, M (1992) Op. cit., p110, and *The Economist* (1992) Loc. cit., p22.

37 *The Economist* (1992) Loc. cit., p22.

38 Utterback, J M (1996) *Mastering the Dynamics of Innovation*, Harvard Business School Press, Boston, MA, pp94–5.

39 Quinn, J B (1985) 'Managing innovation: controlled chaos', *Harvard Business Review*, May–June, p73.

40 Gluck, F (1985) 'Eight big makers of innovation', *McKinsey Quarterly*, Winter, p49.

41 Nonaka, I (1990) 'Redundant, overlapping organisations: a Japanese approach to managing the innovation process', *California Management Review*, Spring, p27.

42 Kawaii, T (1992) 'Generating innovation through strategic action programmes', *Long Range Planning*, 25, June, p42.

43 Developed principally from two sources: Hamel, G and Prahalad, C K (1994) Ibid., Ch4, and Day, G S (1987) *Strategic Marketing Planning*, West Publishing, St Paul, MN, Ch6.

44 Ergas, S, quoted in *The Economist* (1992) Survey on Innovation, 11 Jan, p23.

Chapter 12

PURPOSE DELIVERED THROUGH CORPORATE AND BUSINESS OBJECTIVES

Learning outcomes

When you have worked through this chapter, you will be able to:

- define the main factors that form the purpose of the organisation;
- explain how purpose can be defined for diversified companies;
- outline the main elements of corporate-level strategy;
- identify the main stakeholders and conduct a stakeholder power analysis;
- develop a mission statement for the organisation;
- develop the objectives consistent with this mission statement;
- understand and develop the organisation's policy on strategic quality issues.

INTRODUCTION

Having explored the main issues surrounding the purpose of the organisation, it is now time to define the purpose more precisely. This chapter begins by distinguishing between purpose in individual businesses and purpose in diversified groups of businesses. It also draws together the many diffuse elements that make up the polygon of purpose. The chapter then explores purpose and strategy at the corporate level in more depth before

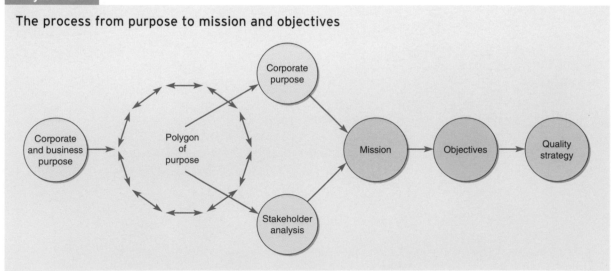

Figure 12.1

The process from purpose to mission and objectives

examining stakeholders and their influence on purpose. After these general influences, the chapter then focuses on the development of the *mission and objectives* of the individual organisation. Such a definition is crucial to the development of the strategy that follows later. As part of this definition, the particular problems posed by the issue of quality are explored. The process is shown in Figure 12.1.

Purpose at two conglomerates – General Electric, USA, and Siemens, Germany

Conglomerates are supposed to make superior profits from their internal resources and from their external market positions. But a comparison of two leading conglomerates suggests that pursuing profitability is more complex in practice.

General Electric

One of the world's largest companies, GE has a wide range of commercial activities, ranging from financial services to media companies and heavy engineering – *see* Figure 12.2. The company's twin purpose for many years has been to achieve high cash flow and drive down costs. Jack Welch, who retired as chief executive officer from GE in 2001, was regarded as one of America's leading managers. He guided the group towards its current high profitability through mergers, acquisitions and divestments. Importantly, he also had a robust view of the performance of his senior managers and sanctioned employment cuts where necessary to achieve the company's purpose.

Siemens

Siemens is one of Germany's largest companies, with a long and distinguished history of invention, especially in engineering. In fact, the company has a reputation of being dominated for many years by engineers in senior management positions, with a consequent focus on the engineering excellence of its products. According to the *Financial Times*, '[It] had management methods rooted in the 19th century and financial returns to match. Much of its manufacturing was based on rigid production processes that could not be easily adapted to new products.'[1] But Siemens' chief executive officer for the period 1992–2004, Hienrich von Pierer, guided the company towards

GE and Siemens – both massive conglomerates

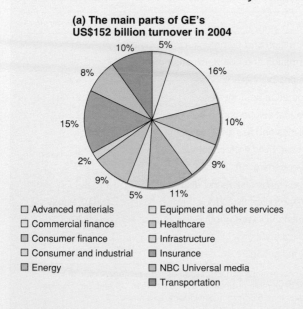

(a) The main parts of GE's US$152 billion turnover in 2004

☐ Advanced materials
☐ Commercial finance
☐ Consumer finance
☐ Consumer and industrial
☐ Energy
☐ Equipment and other services
☐ Healthcare
☐ Infrastructure
☐ Insurance
☐ NBC Universal media
☐ Transportation

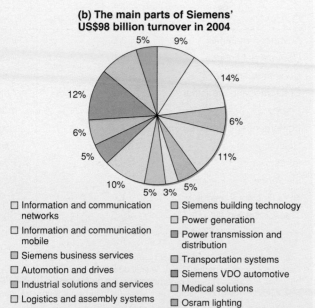

(b) The main parts of Siemens' US$98 billion turnover in 2004

☐ Information and communication networks
☐ Information and communication mobile
☐ Siemens business services
☐ Automotion and drives
☐ Industrial solutions and services
☐ Logistics and assembly systems
☐ Siemens building technology
☐ Power generation
☐ Power transmission and distribution
☐ Transportation systems
☐ Siemens VDO automotive
☐ Medical solutions
☐ Osram lighting

▶ **CASE STUDY 12.1 continued**

An intriguing strategic question is why the German conglomerate Siemens has lower profitability than its comparable American rival, General Electric.

a more market-oriented approach – now continued by his successor, Klaus Kleinfeld.

Siemens appears to have been in a constant state of re-organisation since the mid-1990s, when it had a major downturn in its profits. Siemens sold a range of poorly performing businesses in the late 1990s and around 1999 introduced a new three-part concept to improve its performance called *Top*. It had three main pillars – cost-reduction, growth and innovation – directed at increasing the long-term profitability of the company. Cost-reduction was particularly important as Siemens' costs in many product areas were 20 to 30 per cent higher than competitors. Growth was set as an additional target – 'Managers did not set themselves a static target, but one that was dynamic and took into account changes that competitors were likely to make,' explained the main board member responsible for *Top*, Mr Edward Krubasik. Although the senior managers of Siemens' various divisions grumbled, this meant that they had to benchmark themselves against competitors. The third part was innovation through the introduction of new products that would compete better on world markets.

Table 12.1

Comparison of sales margins for 2004

General Electric		Siemens	
• Total 2004 turnover across all divisions: US$152 billion • Total number of employees in 2004 across all divisions: 227 000		• Total 2004 turnover across all divisions: US$98 billion • Total number of employees in 2004 across all divisions: 430 000	
Division	*Sales margin %*	*Division*	*Sales margin %*
Advanced materials	8.6	Information and communication networks	3.2
Commercial finance	19.0	Information and communication mobile	3.1
Consumer finance	4.6	Siemens business services	0.8
Consumer and industrial	20.7	Automation and drives	12.2
Energy	16.4	Industrial solutions and services	2.2
Equipment and other services	7.1	Logistics and assembly systems	0.1
Healthcare	16.9	Siemens building technology	2.5
Infrastructure	16.3	Power generation	12.8
Insurance	2.5	Power transmission and distribution	6.6
NBC Universal media	1.8	Transportation systems	(10.1) loss
Transportation	20.6	Siemens VDO automotive	6.2
		Medical solutions	14.8
		Osram lighting	10.5

Note: Sales margin defined as divisional operating profit divided by divisional revenue and expressed as a percentage. Some of the business activities of the two companies are different. However, directly comparable business activities between GE and Siemens are highlighted in the above table. They show that GE has higher sales margins than Siemens in similar business areas.

Source: Annual Report and Accounts with sales margins calculated by author.

Even after five years of *Top* and similar initiatives, Siemens still remained a distant second to GE in fields where a comparison can be made – *see* Table 12.1. While the overall product mix is different for the two companies, they do have some similar products, particularly in heavy engineering: compare the profit margins at GE's energy and transportation divisions with the similar product ranges of Siemens' power generation, power transmission and transportation systems businesses.

GE and Siemens

In some senses, the product ranges of the two companies are so different that it is not appropriate to make comparisons of performance. However, it might be argued that they are both diversified groups (sometimes called *conglomerates*) and therefore able to work with the special strategies associated with such groups – for example, the ability to seek economies of scope and the possibility of employing core competencies across the divisions of the conglomerate. In practice, Siemens has a range of companies that include those built on its earlier engineering tradition rather than modern areas of market growth. In addition, the company has other modern divisions where it struggles to compete because it is smaller than its rivals and competition is fierce – for example, its business in mobile telephones and telecommunications equipment. For some years, Siemens had been divesting itself of poorly performing parts of the group but it still compared poorly against GE in 2005

Case questions

1 *Can Siemens ever achieve the profit margins of GE? What should it do now – continue to divest under-performing parts and invest in the profitable parts? Or is something more radical required – perhaps to break itself up and cease to be a conglomerate?*

2 *What conclusions do you draw on the strategic benefits of operating a conglomerate? Does the theory outlined in Sections 12.1 and 12.2 help?*

12.1 CLARIFYING THE PURPOSE OF THE ORGANISATION

Part 6a

Clarifying the organisation's purpose is crucial to strategy development – it is difficult to develop strategies to achieve a purpose that remains unclear. The problem is that there is no simple formula that can be applied to define the purpose of an organisation. Moreover, as the Siemens case demonstrates, the definition of a purpose for an organisation is no guarantee that it will be achieved. This chapter is concerned with the task of clarifying the purpose and developing the mission and objectives of the organisation that arise from purpose. This task is an essential prelude to the strategy development of the rest of this book.

As a starting point, it is important to bring together the influences on purpose explored in Chapters 10 and 11. In addition, several other factors will influence purpose, especially those relating to the underlying ambitions of the organisation and those linked with the timing of new strategy initiatives – the latter may be particularly important when the underlying environment is changing significantly. The stakeholder dimension mentioned below was explored briefly in Chapter 10 and is further covered in a later section of this chapter. However, we begin with two fundamental considerations – the distinction between purpose at the corporate and business level and the complexity of purpose.

12.1.1 The distinction between corporate and business purpose

When a firm decides to move beyond one main market or industry and operate in several, its purpose and strategy change fundamentally. The firm's corporate purpose becomes the management of a diversified set of businesses. The examples of GE and Siemens in the opening case show how purpose in such companies moves beyond single-business issues – for example, Siemens' market share in the mobile telephone business – to broader issues like acquiring and divesting a range of businesses – for example, whether Siemens should remain in transportation given its low profitability. Essentially, there is a corporate purpose for the group of diversified businesses above the business purpose of each individual part of the diversified group. Corporate purpose and strategy are explored in the next section.

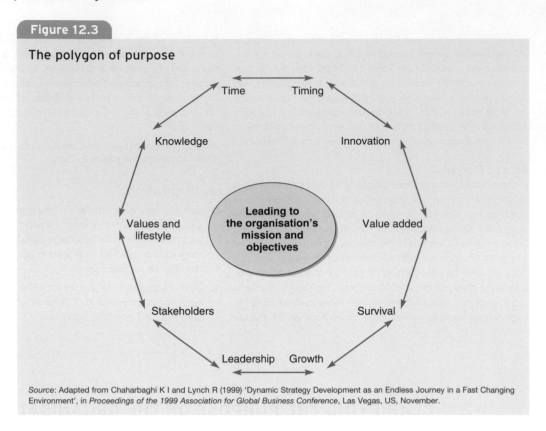

Figure 12.3

The polygon of purpose

Source: Adapted from Chaharbaghi K I and Lynch R (1999) 'Dynamic Strategy Development as an Endless Journey in a Fast Changing Environment', in *Proceedings of the 1999 Association for Global Business Conference*, Las Vegas, US, November.

12.1.2 The complexity of purpose

There is a tendency for organisations to summarise their purpose in a few sentences. Typically, an organisation will summarise its purpose as the maximisation of shareholder wealth, the achievement of growth targets, the delivery of market share and similar statements. In practice, purpose is more complex and multifaceted, with a number of important elements. To bring all the elements together, it is possible to construct the *polygon of purpose* shown in Figure 12.3.[3] *Polygon* means a many-sided figure with no obvious dominant side. This is precisely the situation with the development of purpose, where there are a number of factors, none of which is usually crucial. The main elements of the polygon are shown below with examples from the Siemens case:

● *Time dimension* – long- and short-term perspectives will have a substantive impact on the purpose.[4] Siemens had a five-year strategy for each of its major businesses in addition to annual targets that needed to be met.

● *Timing* – when to begin or end a new period of change. This will, in turn, depend on such issues as the cyclicality and the static or dynamic nature of the environmental forces.[5] After Siemens moved into mobile telephones in the late 1990s, the market declined and necessitated a change in purpose and strategy at the company.

● *Innovation* – the generation and exploitation of new ideas. These may have a profound impact on the purpose of the organisation – *see* Chapter 10. One of the major elements of the *Top* programme at Siemens was directly concerned with innovation.

● *Value-added dimension* – for every organisation, it is axiomatic that some value needs to be added for the organisation to continue to exist.[6] Value here does not necessarily mean economic rent. It could mean service or some other concept associated with other aspects of purpose. For business organisations, it means *profits* and related issues. Parts of Siemens forgot that value added has a short-term time dimension.

- *Survival dimension* – the desire to survive. This is particularly important in some environments, perhaps all in the long term.[7] Siemens' existence was threatened in the mid-1990s when it suffered a major downturn in profitability.

- *Growth dimension* – the desire for sustained growth. This will not apply to all organisations, but certainly needs to be considered as an objective for some.[8] Siemens clearly set growth as part of its *Top* programme.

- *Leadership* – the style and substance of the way the organisation is led. The impact of this on purpose may be substantial – *see* Chapter 10.[9] The judgement of Heinrich von Peirer and Klaus Kleinfeld at Siemens and Jack Welch at GE was crucial to the development of company purpose in these two companies.

- *Stakeholder dimension* – definition and delivery of value added to the various interested parties, especially those with the most power.[10] At Siemens, the stakeholders influenced the company through the supervisory board, which included employees as well as directors. This was particularly important when it came to decisions with regard to reducing employment numbers at the company.

- *Values and lifestyle* – different organisations will hold different principles on what is important about the quality of life and the way that their activities should be conducted – *see* Chapter 10.[11] Ethics and corporate governance will form part of the considerations here – *see* Chapter 10. Siemens' values are reflected in the way that it approached the business of integration and people issues.

- *Knowledge* – the constantly changing mixture of experience, values, contextual information and expert insight – *see* Chapter 10. Knowledge has the ability to create new elements of purpose. At Siemens, the use of the *Top* programme allowed the various parts of the organisation to share knowledge on the three dimensions of the programme.

The polygon is useful as one way of summarising the nature of purpose. But it is not conclusive and other factors not covered in the list may be more important for some organisations – for example, aspects of service delivery in the public services and power and wealth creation for some entrepreneurs. It is for this reason that it has been called a many-sided polygon rather than the ten-sided polygon that is actually drawn in Figure 12.3.

Key strategic principles

- In developing the purpose of a diversified organisation, it is essential to distinguish between corporate-level purpose and business-level purpose. Corporate purpose is concerned with the role and contribution of the headquarters of the diversified organisation, whereas business purpose relates to the targets in one individual business area.

- It is essential to clarify the purpose of the organisation at the outset of strategy development. Many different aspects are potentially involved. In most cases, no single element is dominant.

- The polygon of purpose is one way of drawing the elements together. Although ten specific elements can be identified in the polygon, other elements may be more important and some of those highlighted may have little relevance in particular organisations.

- The ten identified elements are: time dimension, timing, innovation, value added (including profitability), survival, growth, leadership, stakeholders, values and lifestyle, and knowledge.

12.2 CORPORATE PURPOSE AND CORPORATE-LEVEL STRATEGY

Definition ➤ Corporate purpose is the purpose and contribution of the central headquarters of a diversified group of companies. Over the last 30 years, opinion on the strategic purpose in diversified groups has changed quite markedly. It used to be said that being involved in a series of unrelated industries meant that the risks of overall failure were lower because the upswing in one market, such as health, would counterbalance any downswing in another market, such as transportation products.[12] In addition, it was also argued that basic technological linkages between companies meant that they could provide mutual technical support – *see* the 3M Case in Chapter 11 for an example of this approach. Some recent thinking on strategic purpose in conglomerates has tended to emphasise core competencies.[13] It is also argued that it is beneficial for a group of companies to have a range of knowledge, technical skills and technologies around which to learn and build the company's resources.[14] Finally, it is the role of the group headquarters to identify and manage the financial and other capital resources of the firm.[15] We examine each of these areas in this section.

12.2.1 Levels of diversification[16]

Before exploring the benefits of the corporate headquarters, it is useful to begin by examining the nature of diversification in groups of companies. Some diversified groups seem to have very little connection across parts of the group – for example, at GE, its healthcare division does not appear to have much connection with its commercial finance division. Equally, other diversified groups have a clear connection between the various parts – for example, at Unilever, the ice cream business has connections with its haircare business because both companies call on the same supermarket customers. For the purposes of strategy development, it is useful to identify three main levels of diversification:

1 *Close-related diversification*: in this case, the different companies within the group may have different products or services but have some form of close affinity such as common customers, common suppliers or common overheads. For example, the Unilever group includes separate companies in such businesses as Magnum ice cream, Flora margarine, Hellmans mayonnaise and Knorr soups – *see* Case 14.3. Each of these businesses has its own competitors, markets and brands. But each company shares similar supermarket customers, some common suppliers and some common competitors. It makes commercial sense for such companies to seek the benefits of co-operation where appropriate.

2 *Distant-related diversification*: in this case, the different companies in the group are more diversified, with quite different products or services, possibly using wholly different technologies. However, they may share the same underpinning core competencies or some other area of technology or service that would benefit from co-ordination by a central headquarters. For example, 3M has many diversified businesses but its underpinning core competencies in adhesives and coatings are used widely throughout the group – *see* Case 11.4. Another example is the Japanese company Canon, whose underpinning core competencies in optics are used in a range of applications from cameras to photocopiers – *see* Case 17.2.

3 *Unrelated diversification*: in this case, the different companies in the group have little in common with regard to products, customers or technologies. However, they benefit from the resources of the headquarters with regard to the availability of lower-cost finance, quality of management direction and other related matters – for example, GE and Siemens in Case 12.1.

We can use these distinctions with regard to the level of diversification to explore the benefits of a corporate-level strategy.

12.2.2 Benefits of a corporate-level strategy

In a diversified group of companies, each of the subsidiaries may have a large or a limited trading connection with another part of the group, and each of them will have its own resources. In addition, the whole enterprise will have a corporate headquarters. Definition ➤ Corporate-level strategy is the value added contribution of the central headquarters of a group of diversified businesses, each with its own strategy.[17] It is delivered by the headquarters' decisions on the selection of businesses to be in the group, their management in the group and the resources allocated by the centre to individual companies. Corporate purpose is therefore the maximisation of value added and the additional competitive advantage contributed by the central headquarters of the group of companies.

The diversified group should earn above-average profits by the special contribution of the group's headquarters over and above the contribution of the individual companies. This means that the diversified firms that make up the diversified group are worth more as part of that group than they would be worth individually. For example at GE, the theory suggests that the commercial finance division is worth more because it is located in the same group as the divisions making steam turbines and broadcasting NBC national television programmes across the US. Some may find it difficult to understand what conceivable benefit could possibly be gained by combining such diversified elements. But according to corporate strategy theory, benefits are possible – for example at GE, the corporate headquarters is able to provide access to cheaper finance and lower capital costs than would be available to individual companies – such as GE's subsidiaries in commercial finance, steam turbines and television stations.

More generally, the benefits of such a central headquarters relate to the degree of diversification with the group. Such benefits can be delivered in three main areas: internal, external and financial.

Internal to the group

- *Economies of scope*: for a close-related diversified group, it is possible that there may be Definition ➤ economies of scope within the group.[18] Economies of scope are cost savings developed by a group when it shares activities or transfers capabilities and competencies from one part of a group to another. For example, two different companies might share a common sales team or share similar technologies.

- *Core competencies*: for close-related and distant-related groups, it may be possible to transfer core competencies between companies internally within the group.

- *Shared activities*: for distant-related groups, it may be possible to share activities. For example, companies might share purchasing activities because they have similar raw materials or distribution activities because they have similar customers. Such activity occurs regularly in many consumer product companies like Unilever where sugar and supermarkets apply respectively.

External to the group

Definition ➤
- *Vertical integration*: this occurs when a company produces its own inputs (backward integration) or when a company owns the outlets through which it sells its products (forward integration). This may deliver cost savings through not having to pay distributors, or market power through direct access to customers.[19] A company like the natural cosmetics retail shop chain *Body Shop* produces many of its products and then sells them in its own stores. This means that it has more control over its special product range and is able to respond quickly to market trends without having to negotiate with other retailers to stock its products. The Dell company is another example of a company that has taken control of the outlets through which it sells its computers – the telephone and the internet.

- *Market power*: some co-operation between close-related diversified firms in a group may have external benefits in terms of increased negotiating power with customers or lower costs with regard to distribution. Market power exists when a company has lower costs or a superior competitive position as a result of such co-operation.[20]

● *Competitor blocking*: another result of market power may be to support the blocking of competitive activity through the ability to offer a wider range of products from within a closely-related diversified group. This may have the effect of blocking competitors from offering such products or, more likely, being able to offer even lower costs.

Financial benefits – often apply even for an unrelated diversification[21]

● *Lower cost of capital*: the central headquarters may be able to use its greater negotiating power to obtain finance for individual companies than they would obtain independently of the group.

● *Business restructuring*: the central HQ may be able to facilitate and finance essential restructuring of a business in the face of competitive pressure beyond the resources of an individual company.

● *Efficient capital allocation*: central HQ should allocate finance across the group more efficiently as a result of its central viewpoint of the needs and returns of individual companies.

12.2.3 Corporate strategy and the role of the centre

In some texts,[22] the words 'corporate strategy' refer *exclusively* to strategies pursued by such a corporate headquarters. In this book, the term 'corporate strategy' has been used more **Definition ➤** freely, as explained in Chapter 1. In this chapter, corporate strategy or *parenting* means the special relationships and strategies pursued by the headquarters of a diversified group of companies. The corporate headquarters can offer:

● *corporate functions and services* such as international treasury management and central human resource management;

● *corporate development initiatives*, such as centralised R&D and new acquisitions;

● *additional finance for growth or problem areas*, on the principle of the product portfolio outline in Chapter 3;

● *development of formal linkages between businesses* such as the transfer of technology or core competencies between subsidiaries.

For example at News Corporation, the film library of its subsidiary company Twentieth Century Fox is available to its other subsidiaries, including its TV stations in both the US and the UK, even though they are operating totally independent schedules and are completely independent companies. In addition, the News Corporation centre is the major provider of funds for the main growth areas such as its Far Eastern satellite ventures – Star TV – and the new, exclusive sports channels and contracts – Fox TV, etc.

Clearly, such parenting resources are formidable if carefully developed. Each group will have its own combination of resources, depending on its mix of businesses and the relevant strategic issues. However, corporate headquarters have a cost. The purpose of parenting is to add value to the subsidiaries that are served, otherwise the parental cost cannot be justified.[23] Subsidiaries need to perform better with the parent than they would independently.

12.2.4 Corporate headquarters characteristics

For the full benefits of corporate strategy, it is not enough for the headquarters to provide a few add-on services. It means developing the core skills of the parent itself; these are called the corporate or *parenting characteristics* of the headquarters.[24]

The parent needs two attributes:

1 an understanding of or familiarity with the *key factors for success* relevant for all of the diverse industries in which each of its subsidiaries is engaged;

2 an ability to *contribute something extra* beyond the subsidiaries that it manages. These might be from any of the four areas listed earlier in this section, e.g. R&D, finance.

Key strategic principles

- Corporate purpose is the purpose and contribution of the *central headquarters* of a diversified group of companies. Corporate-level strategy is the value added contribution of the central headquarters of a group of diversified businesses, each with its own strategy.

- There are three levels of diversification in such companies: close-related, distant-related and unrelated. Each is important in assessing the benefits from operating a corporate-level strategy.

- The benefits of a central headquarters and its related corporate strategy can be delivered in three main areas: internal, external and financial. Internal relates to the cost savings from shared resources and shared activities. External benefits can derive from vertical integration, increased market power and the ability to block competitive activity. Financial benefits come from the ability of the headquarters to be able to lower the cost of capital, provide resources for business restructuring and allocate funds more efficiently across the group.

- Parenting concerns the corporate headquarters of a group of subsidiaries, whose areas of business may be unrelated to each other. Such a business still needs to define its purpose and develop its mission and objectives. This may be difficult where the activities are widely spread.

- The role of the corporate headquarters is to add value to the subsidiaries that are associated with the organisation, otherwise the cost of running a corporate headquarters cannot be justified.

- The corporate headquarters can make offerings in four areas: corporate functions; corporate development initiatives; additional finance for growth or problem areas; the development of formal linkages between parts of the group.

- Corporate headquarters need two special attributes to operate effectively: an understanding of the key factors for success in the diverse industries of their subsidiaries and an ability to make a special contribution.

12.3 STAKEHOLDER ANALYSIS

12.3.1 Identifying the stakeholders

Definition ➤ Stakeholders are the individuals and groups who have an interest in the organisation and, therefore, may wish to influence aspects of its mission, objectives and strategies. An organisation's mission and objectives need to be developed bearing in mind two sets of interests:

1 the interests of those who have to carry them out – for example, the managers and employees; and

2 the interests of those who have a stake in the outcome – for example, the shareholders, government, customers, suppliers and other interested parties.

Together these groups form the *stakeholders*.

Given this situation, it is perhaps not surprising that the organisation's mission is not formulated overnight. It can take months of debate and consultation within the organisation. When its implications are clearly set out for the directors, managers and employees, they may not necessarily accept the mission without question: there may be objections as it is realised that individuals will have to work harder, undertake new tasks, or face the prospect of leaving the company. The individuals and groups affected may want to debate the matter further. Such individuals and groups have a *stakeholding* in the organisation and therefore wish to influence its mission. For example, the German company Siemens explored earlier in this chapter has a supervisory board, which contains representatives not only of the managers and shareholders but also the employees – all stakeholders in Siemens.

This concept of stakeholding extends *beyond* those working in the organisation. Shareholders in a public company, banks which have loaned the organisation money, governments concerned about employment, investment and trade may also have legitimate stakeholdings in the company. Customers and suppliers will also have an interest in the organisation. They may be informal, such as government involvement in a private company, or formal, such as through a shareholding in the company. All can be expected to be interested in and possibly wish to influence the future direction of the organisation. It is not necessary to have a *shareholding* in order to have a *stakeholding*.

12.3.2 Conflict of interest amongst stakeholders

The key issue with regard to stakeholders is that the organisation needs to take them into account in formulating its mission and objectives. If it does not, they may object and cause real problems for the organisation: for example, major shareholders may sell their shares and key employees may leave.

The difficulty is that their interests may be in conflict. For example, workers may want more pay at the expense of profits and dividends for the shareholders. There are other areas where interests may also conflict. Some of these are summarised in Table 12.2. Consequently, the organisation will need to resolve which stakeholders have priority: *stakeholder power* needs to be analysed.

Importantly in many organisations, it is no longer the case that the shareholders who own the organisation automatically have absolute power. Ever since the 1930s, there has been evidence of an increasing gap between shareholders and senior managers in large companies. Berle and Means[25] surveyed top management in the US and produced evidence that there was an increasing gap between senior managers and shareholders. In about half of the 2000 US companies studied, 'ownership' had become separated from 'control'. Stakeholder *managers* did not necessarily have the same interests as stakeholder *shareholders*.

Table 12.2

Stakeholders and their expectations

Stakeholder	Expectations	
	Primary	Secondary
Owners	Financial return	Added value
Employees	Pay	Work satisfaction, training
Customers	Supply of goods and services	Quality
Creditors	Creditworthiness	Payment on time
Suppliers	Payment	Long-term relationships
Community	Safety and security	Contribution to community
Government	Compliance	Improved competitiveness

Source: Adapted from Cannon, T (1994) *Corporate Responsibility*, Pitman Publishing.

Managers may be more interested in size than profits: as companies grow, they are more protected from takeover and can afford to offer larger and more prestigious rewards to their leading managers.[26] By contrast, owners are more likely to be concerned with maximising profits and seeking only moderate growth. Unless managers in large organisations are threatened by takeover or incentivised financially, they may take a broader view of the purpose of the organisation than shareholders:[27,28,29] for example, shareholder dividends may be less important to senior managers than power and prestige. Because shareholding is fragmented in large companies, such managers have considerable power.

12.3.3 Analysing and applying stakeholder power

From a corporate strategy viewpoint, the major issue is to identify the influence of *stakeholder power* on the direction of the organisation, typically its mission and objectives. Importantly, this can be positive as well as negative – many organisations will welcome the contributions of and discussions with those who have power. Ford shareholders ultimately used their power in 2001 to force a change in leadership at the company – *see* Case 7.1.

Some of the major possible stakeholders are shown in Figure 12.4. The analysis of their relative power is likely to vary country by country. In addition, there is likely to be variation by industry: the volume car industry may well have a different profile from a more fragmented industry such as the textile garment industry with its smaller companies and family shareholdings. It is difficult to generalise but the checklist in Exhibit 12.1 may provide a useful guide on analysis for a particular organisation.

Exhibit 12.1

Checklist for the analysis of stakeholder power

Managers

- Large or small company? Relative remuneration versus employees?
- Power of middle managers to support or disrupt any chosen purpose?
- Style of company on hiring and firing?
- Company profitability versus that of the industry?

Employees

- Trade union legislation?
- Presence of workers' representation on supervisory board?
- Widespread presence and acceptance across company?
- Presence of workers' co-operative?
- National traditions on unionisation and influence?

Government

- Laissez-faire or dirigiste?
- Shareholding and ownership policy beyond national institutions?

- Support for favoured industries? Encourages registration of shares in companies?
- Favours world trade or protectionist?

Banking institutions

- Shareholding or just loan involvement?
- Presence on supervisory board?

Shareholders

- Have full voting shares?
- Elect management to supervisory board?
- Have blocking or cross-shareholdings that make external pressure difficult?
- Family influence (still) strong?
- Can they sue the company for poor performance? (They can in the US.)

Customers and suppliers

- *See* the Five Forces Analysis in Chapter 3.

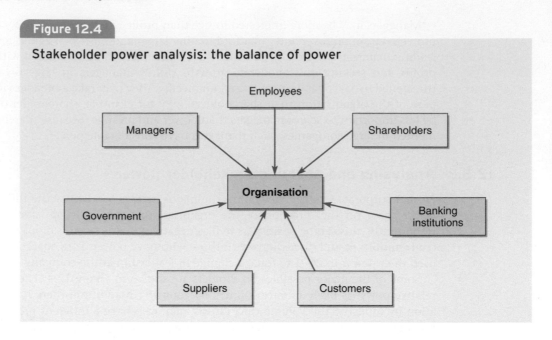

Figure 12.4

Stakeholder power analysis: the balance of power

However welcome contributions may be to the development process, the fact remains that there are likely to be conflicts of interest. Those with the most power therefore need to be considered most carefully. A *stakeholder power study* needs to be undertaken. This is shown in Exhibit 12.2.

Exhibit 12.2

Stakeholder power study

There are six major steps:

1 Identify the major stakeholders.

2 Establish their interests and claims on the organisation, especially as new strategy initiatives are developed.

3 Determine the degree of power that each group holds through its ability to force or influence change as new strategies are developed.

4 Development of mission, objectives and strategy, possibly prioritised to minimise power clashes.

5 Consider how to divert trouble before it starts, possibly by negotiating with key groups.

6 Identify the sanctions available and, if necessary, apply them to ensure that the purpose is formulated and any compromise reached.

As part of the analysis of stakeholder power, some explicit investigation needs to be undertaken of the *sanctions* available against specific stakeholder groups. These might be used to ensure that, where conflict exists between stakeholder groups, some resolution is achieved. Such an analysis may be the beginning of a *bargaining process* between the various groups. This is likely to involve compromise, depending on the power of groups of stakeholders and their willingness to agree. However, it may also involve the use of sanctions to bring pressure to bear on particularly difficult groups. Such a negotiation process can involve the game theory outlined in Chapter 15.

Key strategic principles

- Stakeholders are the individuals and groups who have an interest in the organisation. Consequently, they may wish to influence its mission and objectives.

- The key issue with regard to stakeholders is that the organisation needs to take them into account in formulating its mission and objectives.

- The difficulty is that stakeholder interests may conflict. Consequently, the organisation will need to resolve which stakeholders have priority: *stakeholder power* needs to be analysed. Where conflict exists, negotiations are undertaken to reach a compromise. Sanctions may form part of this process.

- A stakeholder power study covers six stages: identification of stakeholders; establishment of their interests and claims; estimation of their degree of power; prioritised mission development; negotiation with key groups; sanctions application where relevant.

CASE STUDY 12.2

Coca-Cola: lowering the fizz in its objectives

Coca-Cola, the world's largest soft drinks company, reduced its key earnings objective in 2002 and again in 2005. This case examines the reasons for the downgrade and questions whether the company has gone far enough.

Objective setting at Coca-Cola

For most companies in relatively mature markets like soft drinks, the starting point in setting the future objective of the company is what has happened in the past. Coca-Cola achieved annual growth in its earnings for shareholders of between 15 and 20 per cent in the years 1991 to 1997. There then followed three years of sharply declining earnings before a rebound in 2001. The company's operating income hardly moved ahead in the years to 2004 – *see* Figure 12.5. There were some one-off gains in net income (not shown in Figure 12.5) but these were exceptional and would not be repeated.

It was against this background that the company needed to define its purpose and then set its sales and operating profit objectives. In 2001, the company's chief executive – Mr Douglas Daft – set what he regarded as a more realistic objective for the next few years of 11–12 per cent per annum operating income growth. This target was reduced to 10 per cent in 2003 as the company clearly was unable to meet the target. A new chief executive, Mr Noel Isdell, then reduced it even further to 6–8 per cent in late 2004. Yet, there are at least four reasons to question whether even this new, lower objective will be achieved.

Coca-Cola is one of the world's leading global brands – an Indian delivery vehicle and a Mexican shoeshine stall.

▶ **CASE STUDY 12.2 continued**

Figure 12.5

Coca-Cola's sales and profits record

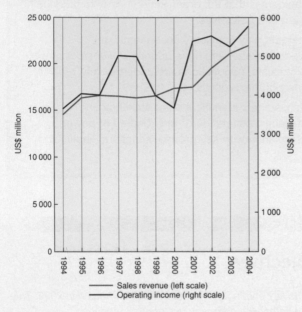

Sales revenue (left scale)
Operating income (right scale)

Soft drink market growth

The first problem is the low growth in the market. Carbonated soft drink markets grew by only 2 per cent by volume worldwide during 2001. By 2004, the growth was only 1 per cent in Coca-Cola's leading market, North America. Coca-Cola dominates the carbonated soft drink market, from which it derives 87 per cent of its total sales. If the market is growing so slowly and the company is heavily reliant on the market, it is difficult to see how the company can outpace market growth without other measures.

Drinks markets that were growing faster include bottled water, fruit juices and sports drinks. Coca-Cola's chief rival, Pepsi, was much stronger in these markets, having spotted the trends to higher growth in these markets earlier than Coke. Coca-Cola's own attempt to enter the bottled water market in 2002 included the launch of the *Dasani* brand, which had success in some countries but was bungled and eventually withdrawn in the UK. Hence, the fact remains that Coca Cola is underrepresented in some soft drink market sectors.

Coca-Cola and its bottling companies

The second problem is the way that Coca-Cola earns its profits. The company does not just sell products in the market place. It works around the world through local bottling companies, some of which it owns and some of which it does not. Essentially, the company makes part of its profits by charging its local bottlers for the concentrates and syrups supplied from its headquarters – the bottlers add carbonated water, bottle

and distribute the finished product. During the 1990s, Coca-Cola was reported to be buying up small bottling companies around the world and then selling them at a higher price to larger regional bottling companies, putting the profits from the sale into the Coca-Cola profit line.[30] The company was also charging ever-higher prices for its concentrates, again taking the profits.

Such strategies did not necessarily result in losses at its bottling companies or higher prices for bottles of Coke. The reason is that the consolidation from smaller to larger regional bottlers produced economies of scale that cut costs. But Coca-Cola has now recognised that this process could not continue indefinitely and that it must share more of its profits with the bottlers, some of which were owned by the company anyway. For this reason, it reduced its earnings growth objective for the latest period.

New product development

The third reason for doubt about the earnings growth objective relates to the successful introduction of new products. Coca-Cola's record here is disappointing. Its great rival, Pepsi, has a significantly smaller market share in most countries than Coke. But it has a good, possibly even superior, record on new product introductions – Pepsi was first to launch a diet cola and first to introduce cola with a lemon twist in 2001. Coke beat Pepsi to the launch of cherry Coke but this was back in 1985 and the variety still only accounts for 3 per cent of the volume generated by classic Coke. In addition, customers, employees and bottlers still remember the major protests generated when Coca-Cola attempted to replace classic Coke with a more modern version in the early 1990s and eventually had to bring back the original variety.

In the years up to 2005, Coca-Cola has undertaken some new product launches and they have been moderately successful. But there had been no dramatic breakthrough and none was likely. The company's strategy was to focus on marketing its main brand, Coke: 'Unless we have a healthy Coca-Cola [brand], we will not have a healthy Coca-Cola company,' explained the new chief executive, Mr Neville Isdell.

Earnings growth through acquisition

The fourth problem is the reluctance of the company to make acquisitions that might enhance earnings growth. Coca-Cola bought the Schweppes mixer drink brand from Cadbury Schweppes (UK) in some parts of the world in 1999 and it has made a series of bottling plant acquisitions in recent years. Yet the Coca-Cola board failed to support the recommendation of its then chief executive, Mr Daft, to acquire the Quaker Oats company in 2001. The attraction of the purchase was the Quaker sports drink brand called Gatorade. This would have moved Coca-Cola firmly into a new market segment in which it is currently unrepresented and which is growing fast. However, the board felt that the price of US$16 billion was too high. Pepsi bought Quaker in 2001.

Situation in 2005 - still struggling

After another three years of management upheaval – including a chief executive officer, Mr Neville Isdell, brought back out of retirement – the company was still struggling to grow. The revised earnings growth objective of 11–12 per cent per annum over the next three years was quietly reduced to 5–6 per cent volume *sales* growth sometime in 2003. It was then reduced further in 2004 to 3–4 per cent late in 2004 after the arrival of a new chief executive. The sales growth objective was accompanied by the *operating income* growth of 6–8 per cent mentioned earlier in this case. According to Mr Isdell, the operating income target would be achieved by a focus on the 'thousands of little things' that go into managing and promoting the world's biggest brand. For example, the company was beginning to explore global advertising rather than rely on national advertising, to develop more sophisticated pricing structures and to identify more product development in its core carbonated soft drink products.

Case questions

1 *What is your view of the earnings growth objective? Is it set too high? If you would lower it, what figure would you pick? You should read the next section about challenging but achievable objectives in arriving at your conclusion.*

2 *How should organisations set objectives? Past experience? Current market performance? Challenging objectives? Or what?*

12.4 DEVELOPING THE MISSION

Definition ➤ The *mission* of an organisation outlines the broad directions that it should and will follow and briefly summarises the reasoning and values that lie behind it. Such a mission needs to be defined in the context of the purpose explored earlier. The *objectives* are then a more specific commitment consistent with the mission over a specified time period. They may be quantified, but this may be inappropriate in some circumstances.

As explored in Chapter 1, the strategies that will achieve the objectives then follow from this. The mission and objectives define the whole strategic process and are therefore important in the development of corporate strategy.

12.4.1 Prescriptive approach to mission development

Under prescriptive theories of strategy, the organisation will set out its mission and objectives for the next few years. It then develops strategies consistent with the mission and aimed at achieving the objectives – for example, Ford's global ambitions fit here.

The analysis of the environment and resources is used to develop the mission and objectives of the organisation. A prescriptive *mission statement* is then developed, setting out the organisation's purpose over a period of time. Several examples are given later in the chapter.

12.4.2 Emergent approaches to mission development

In contrast to the prescriptive approach, some emergent strategists argue that it is a contradiction in terms to couple the concept of purposeful planning with the idea of a strategy emerging in the organisation. They would argue that, by definition, purposes do not emerge.

For other emergent strategists – the *uncertainty-based* strategy theorists of Chapter 2 – the whole idea of purpose for an organisation is largely incomprehensible. For example, they would argue that Siemens' ambitions to increase its profitability outlined at the beginning of the chapter are a waste of time; too many chance events may blow the company off its chosen route. They would reject those parts of this chapter concerning mission and objectives. They would probably accept the stakeholder section of the chapter but would see it as supporting their view that the uncertainties they introduce only make it more difficult to set out clearly an organisation's purpose.

For yet other emergent strategists – the *survival-based* theorists and the *human-resource-based* theorists of Chapter 2 – the situation is less clear. Certainly, they would have doubts about a mission that was developed without consideration of the external forces and without careful discussion between the interested parties in the organisation. But they would not reject the concept of purpose completely – they would accept it with reservations. Siemens' profit ambitions would probably meet their criteria for acceptance since they were developed out of the company's views on the way that external forces were moving and were discussed among senior managers before being introduced.

Some emergent strategists would want the complexity of the interests of the *stakeholders* in the business to become part of the purpose – that is, the interests not only of the shareholders but also of the senior managers and the employees, who all have a share in the success of the organisation. They would be impressed by Siemens' attempts to communicate the profitability purpose to all employees.

As we saw in Section 12.3, stakeholders may well have conflicting interests – for example, shareholders' desire for profits versus the employees' desire for continued employment even when that may not be profitable. The organisation's purpose for the human resource theorist may thus need to be tempered by *compromise* between the various interested parties.

12.4.3 What is the role of a mission statement?

The mission statement outlines the broad directions that the organisation will follow and briefly summarises the reasoning and values that lie behind it. The role of the mission statement is to *communicate* to all the stakeholders inside and outside the organisation what the company stands for and where it is headed. It therefore needs to be expressed in a language and with a commitment that all of those involved can understand and feel relevant to their own circumstances.[32] Importantly, mission statements must reflect the areas of purpose developed above and in previous chapters.

Amongst strategists, there is some dispute over the definition of a mission statement.[33,34] There is really no agreed definition. There has been a high degree of interest by companies and other practitioners but relatively limited definition and research of a more academic nature. In addition, some researchers have questioned the lengthy nature and content of such statements: some[35,36] have even suggested that companies should concentrate on short and concise statements of their 'strategic intent'.

There are considerable differences of view on the form, purpose and content of such statements. At the same time, many leading companies in Europe and North America have developed and quoted their mission statements in their annual reports and accounts. Even if there is no agreed definition, companies still find the process of developing their mission statement useful.

12.4.4 How to formulate a mission statement

Because no two organisations are exactly the same in terms of ownership, resources or environmental circumstances, the mission statement is specific to each organisation.

Essentially, there are five elements:

1 Consideration of the *nature* of the organisation's business. Typical questions include: 'What business are we in? What business *should* we be in?'

2 The responses need to be considered from the *customer* perspective, rather than the organisation itself: 'We are in the business of developing books that will inform and educate our readers about strategy', *rather than* 'We are in the business of developing textbooks on strategic issues.'

3 The mission needs to reflect the basic *values and beliefs* of the organisation:[37] 'We believe it is important to respect the environment and offer employment that is free from any prejudices associated with culture, race or religion.'

4 Where possible, the mission needs to reflect the element of the *sustainable competitive advantage*:[38] 'It is our aim to be a leader in this field.' This may not be possible in a diversified group of companies. It may also be more appropriate to adjust this to reflect *distinctiveness* in an organisation which has no direct competitors, e.g. a charity.

5 The mission needs to summarise the *main reasons* for its choice of approach: 'We are a team. We must treat each other with trust and respect' is a good example from the Ford mission statement presented in Exhibit 12.4.

All the above will rely on *business judgement*, which is imprecise and difficult to define by its very nature. Business judgements are usually made by senior managers in the company.

Because a mission statement needs to be communicated as well as to summarise the organisation's purposes, it needs to be worded carefully. It needs to be written in language that is commonly understood. Some criteria for judging the results of attempting to draft a mission statement are shown in Exhibit 12.3.[39]

Exhibit 12.3

Some criteria for judging mission statements

Mission statements should:

- be specific enough to have an impact upon the behaviour of individuals throughout the business;
- reflect the distinctive advantages of the organisation and be based upon an objective recognition of its strengths and weaknesses;
- be realistic and attainable;
- be flexible enough to take account of shifts in the environment.

The need for precision and care is an important part of the analysis and development of mission statements. As an example of a complete mission statement, Exhibit 12.4 returns to the Ford Motor Company of Case 7.1 and gives the material circulated within the company on this matter.

Exhibit 12.4

Ford Motor Company – Company mission, values and guiding principles

MISSION

Ford Motor Company is a worldwide leader in automotive and financial products and services. Our mission is to improve continually our products and services to meet our customers' needs, allowing us to prosper as a business and to provide a reasonable return for our stockholders, the owners of our business.

VALUES

How we accomplish our mission is as important as the mission itself. Fundamental to success for the Company are these basic values:

- **People** – Our people are the source of our strength. They provide our corporate intelligence and determine our reputation and vitality. Involvement and teamwork are our core human values.
- **Products** – Our products are the end result of our efforts, and they should be the best in serving customers worldwide. As our products are viewed, so are we viewed.

Exhibit 12.4 *continued*

● **Profits** – Profits are the ultimate measure of how efficiently we provide customers with the best products for their needs. Profits are required to survive and grow.

GUIDING PRINCIPLES

● **Quality Comes First** – To achieve customer satisfaction, the quality of our products and services must be our number one priority.

● **Customers are the Focus of Everything We Do** – Our work must be done with our customers in mind, providing better products and services than our competition.

● **Continuous Improvement is Essential to Our Success** – We must strive for excellence in everything we do: in our products, in their safety and value – and in our services, our human relations, our competitiveness, and our profitability.

● **Employee Involvement is Our Way of Life** – We are a team. We must treat each other with trust and respect.

● **Dealers and Suppliers are our Partners** – The Company must maintain mutually beneficial relationships with dealers, suppliers and our other business associates.

● **Integrity is Never Compromised** – The conduct of our Company worldwide must be pursued in a manner that is socially responsible and commands respect for its integrity and for its positive contributions to society. Our doors are open to men and women alike without discrimination and without regard to ethnic origin or personal beliefs.

Source: Copyright © Ford Motor Company 1996. Reprinted with permission.

Key strategic principles

● The *mission* of an organisation outlines the broad directions that it should and will follow and briefly summarises the reasoning and values that lie behind it.

● The *objectives* are then a more specific commitment consistent with the mission over a specified time period. They may be quantified, but this may be inappropriate in some circumstances.

● Prescriptive approaches emphasise the need to set out a mission and objectives for the organisation for the next few years.

● Some emergent approaches doubt the usefulness of a mission and objectives because the future is so uncertain. Other emergent approaches accept the need for a mission and objectives but place great emphasis on the need to include the managers and employees in their development.

● The purpose of the mission statement is to *communicate* to all the stakeholders inside and outside the organisation what the company stands for and where it is headed.

● There are five elements in formulating a mission statement: nature of the organisation; customer perspective; values and beliefs; competitive advantage or distinctiveness; main reasons for the approach.

● Mission statements rely on business judgement but criteria can be developed to assess the results.

12.5 DEVELOPING THE OBJECTIVES

Definition ➤ Objectives take the generalities of the mission statement and turn them into more *specific* commitments: usually, this will cover *what* is to be done and *when* the objective is to be completed. Objectives may include a *quantified* objective – for example, a specific increase in market share or an improvement in some measure of product quality. But the objective will not necessarily be quantified.

The purposes of objectives therefore are:

● to focus the management task on a specific outcome;

● to provide a means of assessing whether that outcome has been achieved after the event.

12.5.1 Different kinds of objectives

In the 1960s and 1970s, several writers were keen to make the objectives quantified and thus measurable.[40] It is now generally recognised that some objectives cannot easily be quantified, e.g. those associated with business ethics and employee job satisfaction, yet they may represent extremely important parts of the activities of companies.

Nevertheless, a company that has a mission but no quantified objectives at all would be in danger of engaging in meaningless jargon. As we saw in Chapter 8, it is usual for companies to set objectives in two types of areas, the first of which is likely to be quantified and the second only partially:

1 *financial objectives*, e.g. earnings per share, return on shareholders' funds, cash flow.

2 *strategic objectives*; e.g. market share increase (quantified); higher product quality (quantified); greater customer satisfaction (partially quantified); employee job satisfaction (supported by research survey but not necessarily quantified).

None of the areas above is necessarily more important than any other. Individual organisations will devise their own lists depending on their stakeholders, culture, leadership, mission and future direction.

12.5.2 Conflict between objectives

There are some objectives that ensure the *survival* of the organisation, e.g. adequate cash flow, basic financial performance. These need to come early in the process. But for many organisations, survival is not really the main issue for the future: for example, companies like General Electric and Coca-Cola are not about to disappear tomorrow. A major issue for these organisations concerns *development and growth* – for example, the Ford statement in Exhibit 12.4 contains the phrase 'survive and grow'. Equally, the McDonald's case later in this chapter revolves around the issue of delivering growth objectives.

Development and growth take time and require investment funds. Money invested in growth is not available for distribution now to shareholders. Growth objectives are therefore potentially in conflict with the short-term requirement to provide returns to shareholders, the owners of the company. Taking money out of the business today will not provide the investment for the future. Objectives therefore need to reach a *compromise* between the short and long term. It is for this reason that the Ford mission statement refers to providing a '*reasonable* return for our stockholders, the owners of our business'. This comment will then be translated into a numerical objective in terms of a dividend payout at General Electric and Siemens that reflects the need to invest as well as satisfy the shareholders.

Where a *competitive environment* exists, as in the global car industry, it is particularly important to recognise that any funds distributed now make it much more difficult to maintain performance against competitors in the future. For any organisation that needs to distribute the value that it adds, there will always be a potential conflict between the short and long term.

12.5.3 Implications of shareholder structure

The conflict between the long and short term becomes even more acute in some national markets where *shareholder power* is particularly demanding. The North American and UK stock markets have a reputation for *short-termism*:[41] that is, companies need to maintain their dividend record or face the threat of being acquired. Other European, Japanese and South-East Asian companies have had less pressure here because their shares are often held by governments and banking institutions, which have been able to take a longer-term view. For example, German car companies such as Volkswagen and DaimlerChrysler have had large share interests held by leading German banks. By contrast, Ford and General Motors have had their shares largely held on the open stock exchanges of Europe and North America. Thus the US companies have faced more acute shareholder pressures than the German companies. These priorities are bound to be reflected in how the objectives for the company are devised initially and monitored later.

12.5.4 Challenging but achievable objectives

When developing objectives, one of the real issues that arises is just how *challenging* the objectives should be. Do we merely set objectives that are easy to achieve so that we can then show real success beyond this? Or do we set objectives that are more challenging but still achievable? If we set the latter, to what extent are these open to negotiation with those who will be responsible for delivering them? Do we need a contract? And a reward?

These are difficult questions to resolve and will depend on the culture and style of the organisation and its senior managers, along with the nature of the organisation's mission and its competition, if any. Some will set demanding objectives and assess performance accordingly; others will discuss and agree (rather than set) a balance between demanding and easy objectives. In spite of Peter Drucker's optimism that this might be done more scientifically by the late 1990s,[42] this aspect of objective setting still requires great business judgement.

12.5.5 Developing objectives in larger organisations

In larger organisations and those with scarce resources, the situation may be more complicated. Very often such organisations are split up by the type of business: in the Siemens example at the beginning of the chapter, there were 13 groups, each responsible for a different group of products. Such groups are often called *divisions* or *strategic business units* (*SBUs*): each may be so large that it has its own CEO and functional managers. In these circumstances, the corporate objectives need to be examined by each of the SBUs. In addition, the corporation may not have unlimited funds and will need to allocate those that it has. Where an SBU has received less than the funds it requested, it may be inappropriate for the headquarters to set an objective as demanding as it might otherwise have been.

For these reasons, corporate objectives will not necessarily translate into the same objective for each SBU. For example:

- There may be limited financial resources which are *rationed* between the SBUs, so it would not be realistic to expect them all to perform against the group objectives.
- Some divisions may be in rapidly growing markets that will need substantial funds but will deliver well above any standardised group-wide objective; other divisions may be in decline and struggle to perform against any averaged corporate objective, regardless of the resources they are given.

In larger organisations, a distinction needs to be drawn between what the overall corporation will achieve and what each of the divisions will be expected to achieve. The *corporate objectives will need to be translated into divisional or SBU objectives*. The divisional objectives will also be subordinate to the corporate objectives – *see* Figure 12.6.

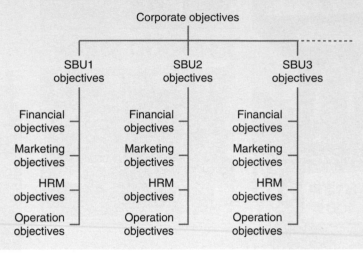

Figure 12.6

Translating corporate objectives into SBU and functional objectives

Key strategic principles

- Objectives take the generalities of the mission statement and turn them into more *specific* commitments: usually, this will cover *what* is to be done and *when* the objective is to be completed.

- Different kinds of objectives are possible. Some will be quantified and some not.

- There may be conflict between objectives, particularly between the long- and short-term interests of the organisation.

- Shareholding structures will impact on objectives. UK and US companies are under greater pressure for short-term performance.

- Objectives need to be challenging but achievable.

- In larger organisations and those with scarce resources, the objectives may need to be adjusted to take into account the circumstances and trading situation of different parts of the organisation.

CASE STUDY 12.3

McDonald's restaurants: how to maintain momentum?

After growth problems in the late 1990s, McDonald's was firmly set on a growth path in 2005 in terms of sales revenue and profits. But this success has brought a new strategic problem: how to maintain the momentum. Perhaps the company should even consider reducing its growth targets?

1990s: International expansion followed by acquisitions

In spite of its dominant market position in the US$60 billion global fast food market, McDonald's faced a serious problem with regard to sales and profit targets in the late 1990s. It was struggling to achieve the double-digit growth target of 10–15 per cent increase in annual profits that it had previously announced to its shareholders. This was not surprising since a 10 per cent increase in annual profits might need a rise of up to US$1.4 billion in annual sales – a challenging increase in the mature market for fast food.

In the early 1990s, McDonald's had achieved its strong growth targets by moving from the saturated North American market into Europe and Asia Pacific. Essentially, there had ▶

431

▶ CASE STUDY 12.3 continued

  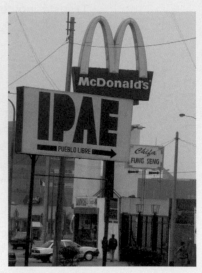

McDonald's has developed into the world's largest restaurant chain – Tokyo in Japan, Shanghai in China and Lima in Peru. But where does it go from here?

been a rapid expansion of new outlets around the world. By 1998, this growth strategy had taken its course. There had even been some cutbacks in the number of openings because some new stores were not profitable.

For the period 1999–2001, McDonald's judged that further growth in its existing restaurant chain was so difficult that it would need to look elsewhere. The traditional burger and fries market was mature in North America in terms of growth and there was strong competition from companies like Burger King and Wendy's. McDonald's therefore began a new strategy of acquiring what it called 'partner brands'. Essentially, it bought companies engaged in other parts of the restaurant business – for example, it acquired the Chipotle Mexican grill restaurants, the Donato's pizza chain and the Pret à Manger sandwich shop chain.

2002: 'We took our eyes off the fries'
Unfortunately, the new acquisition strategy did not produce the required growth over the period 1999–2002. The chief executive officer (CEO) who had introduced this shift in policy, Mr Jack Greenburg, was ousted from his job in late 2002 and a new, experienced 59-year old CEO was appointed – Mr James Cantalupo. He was assisted by a new younger chief operating officer, Mr Charlie Bell, who had previously been the head of European operations for McDonald's and, before that, the CEO in his native Australia. The new executive team undertook a thorough review of the strategy. They concluded that the strategy itself was flawed, not only because of the lack of profitable growth from the new outlets, but from its impact on the traditional McDonald's Restaurants business. There was even some evidence that the basic McDonald's service, quality and cleanliness had declined during this period because the company was focused too strongly on the new expansion strategy. In Mr Cantalupo's memorable phrase: 'We took our eyes off the fries.' Thus around the year 2002, McDonald's decided that it needed to return to its core restaurant strengths.

2003: Back to basics with a healthy twist
Because of difficulties in meeting its targets from the 1990s, McDonald's began by reconsidering its earlier sales growth targets of 10–15 per cent per annum. The company considered that they were not realistic, so produced much lower targets of 1–2 per cent sales increase in mature fast food markets – like the US and Western Europe – coupled with 2–3 per cent sales increase in the faster growing markets – like Asia and Eastern Europe. These very low sales growth figures would nevertheless translate into profit increase targets of 6–8 per cent. The more challenging profit targets would be achieved through new strategies of cutting costs, working more efficiently and more productively. However, although the company recognised that it needed to focus on its basic restaurants, simply doing more of the same was not enough. It also needed to revise its strategy.

McDonald's largest business and biggest profits were generated in the US: 34 per cent of sales and 54 per cent of profits came from this one country in 2004 – see Figure 12.7. The difficulty was that the fast food market in the US was without any significant growth. In addition, it remained a highly competitive market, with aggressive competitors such as Burger King and Wendy's. In addition, there were *some* customers – but by no means all – who criticised McDonald's for its high-calorie, high-saturated-fat menu with items like the *Big Mac* and the milk shake. In the years 2002–04, McDonald's responded by launching new salad main meals and fruit ranges to all its stores. Moreover, the company promoted these products heavily to a new, health-conscious target group outside its traditional customer base. Such a switch in menu strategy was not quite as simple as it might seem. In order to launch the new range, McDonald's needed to restructure its supplies, its packaging and, importantly, to cut its existing in-store menu range. Fast food is only possible if the menu range is limited. Introducing new items meant that some part of the existing range had to be cut, thus losing the sales and profits from the deleted items.

Figure 12.7

McDonald's source of sales and profits 2004

(a) McDonalds revenue 2004 by geographic area

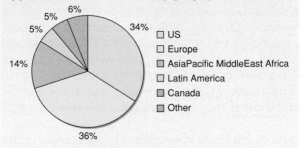

- □ US
- □ Europe
- ■ AsiaPacific MiddleEast Africa
- □ Latin America
- ■ Canada
- ■ Other

(b) McDonalds profit 2004 by geographic area

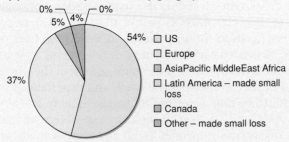

- □ US
- □ Europe
- ■ AsiaPacific MiddleEast Africa
- □ Latin America – made small loss
- ■ Canada
- ■ Other – made small loss

Figure 12.8

McDonald's ten-year record

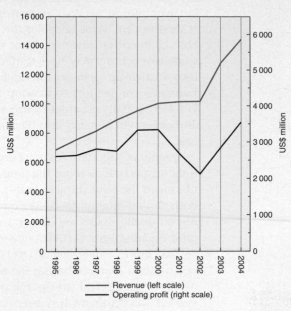

— Revenue (left scale)
— Operating profit (right scale)

Source: Annual Report and Accounts 2004.

In spite of the difficulties, the new strategy was successful, as shown by the results to 2004 – see Figure 12.8. Unfortunately, Mr Cantalupo was taken ill with a heart attack later in 2004. He was replaced by his assistant, Mr Bell. Sadly, Mr Bell was diagnosed with cancer five weeks into taking up the post and died in early 2005. In a sense, the financial results are their legacy to the company. Together, the two men had refocused McDonald's on its growth purpose. They had produced major growth in its traditional North American markets by introducing the new main course salad range. They had tightened up the basic standards of food service and cleanliness by a new system of inspectors who visited individual franchise restaurants. They also prompted the launch for the first time of a global McDonald's marketing programme with a common worldwide payoff line: 'I'm Lovin' It'.

As both executives would acknowledge, the company has to continue in spite of the pressures on its senior managers. There was a hint in early 2005 that the company might sell its Chipotle Mexican chain. The new chief executive, Mr Jim Skinner explained: 'We believe Chipotle's value and potential might be maximised through alternative strategies that could include raising additional equity capital in the public or private markets.' The company was also planning a further new advertising campaign for its main restaurants and more health-oriented food menu items.

At the same time, the company was faced with new demands from its shareholders for continuing growth. China and India were regarded as countries with more scope for sales, assuming that the core markets in the US, Canada and Europe could be stabilised. But there was further pressure for a reconsideration of its growth targets – perhaps the company would be unable to keep up the pace? Perhaps it would be better to modify the targets further?

Case questions

1 *Clearly the shift to new restaurants did not work in the period 1999–2002: would you have persisted for longer?*

2 *Does McDonald's need to redefine its purpose in 2004? If so, in what way? If not, how will it meet its growth targets?*

3 *McDonald's solved its strategic problem in the early 2000s by going 'back to basics' and introducing new healthy products. Can other companies use the same approach? What are the limits to such a strategy, if any?*

STRATEGIC PROJECT

McDonald's has gained some growth from its new range of salad meals. But where does it go from here? Should it revert to its previous strategy of acquiring alternative restaurant chains? If so, which chains? If not, then just how much further growth is there in the concept of fast food? This is a real strategic problem for a company whose shareholders demand continued profitable growth. Perhaps the company should try a completely new approach? In addition to looking in greater depth at McDonald's, it would be interesting to look at some alternatives such as Subway, described earlier. There are websites for both these companies.

12.6 QUALITY OBJECTIVES AND STRATEGIC PURPOSE

Over the last 30 years, organisations have increasingly highlighted quality as a fundamental part of their purpose: the McDonald's example shows the problems that can arise when attention is taken away from this fundamental strategic issue. The reason is that it increases the value added of the organisation. In addition, it often provides the sustainable competitive advantage that competitors have real difficulty in matching. Equally, some competitors may have started to emphasise their quality and force their competitors into a catch-up strategy. For example, Japanese car companies have forced their US and European competitors to develop major quality performance objectives over the last ten years. Essentially, in order to stress its importance, quality has become part of the purpose and objectives of many leading companies, rather than being relegated to a lesser strategic role.

Quality is important for most organisations but needs to be defined in the context of customer expectations about the product, its price and other issues. For example, quality does not mean the same thing to Rolls-Royce or Mercedes as it does to a market trader. Although both should attempt to deliver quality to their customers as part of their overall strategy, not all quality issues are strategic. Quality needs to form part of the defined objectives of most organisations. It therefore needs to be tackled early in strategy development.

Definition ➤ *Total quality management (TQM)* is the modern approach to the management of the whole organisation that emphasises the role of quality in meeting the needs and expectations of its customers.[44] TQM stresses the need for the whole company to manage quality at every stage of the company. It is essential to operate this as part of the corporate objectives and strategy of the organisation. Not every organisation operates TQM, although virtually all have some form of *quality control*, i.e. the regular inspection of goods and services to ensure that they meet minimum standards. Quality control is involved with day-to-day detail and is *not* strategic in its approach.

TQM is strategic for three reasons:

1 the TQM emphasis on the *whole* organisation;

2 the TQM requirement for active support from *senior* management;

3 the significant contribution that TQM can make to competitive advantage.

Quality procedures in general and TQM in particular can be considered as having an influence on corporate objectives, such as profitability, by a series of interconnected routes. These are shown in Figure 12.9 and backed by empirical research. The PIMS database of 3,000 companies showed a strong correlation between quality and profitability – *see* Chapter 14.[45]

TQM has a strategic role because of the success of some companies in developing quality and reliability as competitive weapons in the international market place. Thus quality itself has become a sustainable competitive advantage. Although quality was first conceived in the US in the mid-1950s, it was Japanese interest and persistence that really developed this area during the period between 1955 and 1985. Pioneers worked mainly in Japan and included Deming, Juran, Ishikawa, Taguchi and Crosby.[46]

After the proven success of Japanese companies in slowly and painfully developing new procedures over 30 years,[47] TQM was picked up by Western companies. This does not mean that Western companies had no quality procedures prior to this time – they simply used more limited and different methods. With the benefit of hindsight, some would argue that such Western procedures were less successful but this has not been conclusively proved. Many Western companies do not operate TQM procedures at the present time but do place significant and successful emphasis on quality control. The detail of this area is beyond the scope of this book and is not strategic as such.[48] However, there are two aspects that have strategic relevance:

Figure 12.9

The relationship between quality and profit

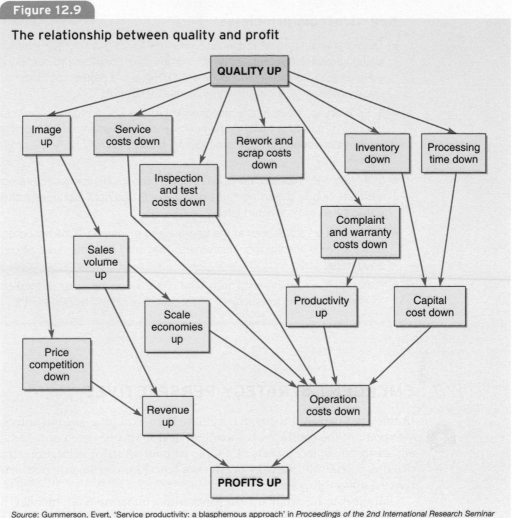

Source: Gummerson, Evert, 'Service productivity: a blasphemous approach' in *Proceedings of the 2nd International Research Seminar in Service Management*, Institut d'Administration des Entreprises (IAE), Université d'Aix-Marseille, France, June 1992. Reproduced with permission.

1 *Differences in management approach.* A TQM business is more co-operative, less Taylorist in its style.

2 *Results in terms of customer relationships with the organisation.* A TQM business is likely to have a deeper, more quality-based relationship with its customers.

Both of these might possibly form the basis of competitive advantage. However, TQM is not without its costs and difficulties. Japanese companies such as Honda, Nissan, Toyota and Matsushita have been working on TQM for over 35 years. Among the earlier Western companies to adopt the approach are Motorola (US) and Texas Instruments (US), which began operating TQM procedures in the early 1980s.[49] One of the real problems found by all the companies, including the Japanese ones, is that the benefits take time to emerge but the costs are only too obvious from an early stage. In some cases, some benefits emerge quickly as early procedures tighten and then the rest come slowly over a period of years. To this extent, TQM is probably best seen as an *emergent* rather than a *prescriptive* process, in spite of the clear decision needed to undertake the task at the outset.

Key strategic principles

- Quality is vital for most organisations and will form part of their strategic purpose and objectives. It delivers value added and may contribute to sustainable competitive advantage. Total quality management (TQM) is the modern strategic approach to quality delivery. It is not the same as quality control.

- TQM is an approach to the management of the whole organisation that emphasises the role of quality in meeting the needs and expectations of its customers. Not every organisation operates TQM procedures, though virtually all have some form of quality control.

- TQM lays the emphasis on workers being responsible for quality, rather than using a separate quality department. It aims to 'get things right first time' rather than have defects that are corrected later.

- There are real differences in the approach to managing TQM-based organisations and their relationships with customers. They may form the basis of competitive advantage.

- Although there are benefits from TQM, there are many costs. It frequently takes years for the full benefits to emerge but the costs are often obvious from an early stage.

12.7 EMERGENT STRATEGY PERSPECTIVES

Part 7a

In the latter part of this chapter, we have been exploring mission and objectives from the viewpoint of the *prescriptive* corporate strategist. This has been done because it is occasionally easier to explore aspects of a topic without all the qualifications that might apply in practice. Specifically, the work of Professor J. B. Quinn on 'logical incrementalism'[50] has been ignored up to this point.

Quinn began his seminal 1978 paper with a quote from an interview he undertook:

When I was younger, I always conceived of a room where all these [strategic] concepts were worked out for the whole company. Later I didn't find any such room . . . The strategy [of the company] may not even exist in the mind of one man. I certainly don't know where it is written down. It is simply transmitted in the series of decisions made.

Quinn went on to comment that, when well-managed major organisations make significant changes in strategy, the approaches they use frequently bear little resemblance to the rational-analytical systems so often touted in the planning literature. He was reacting (with justification, in my view) to the formalised planning systems that were being recommended in the 1970s: strategy was seen almost to be a mathematical formula rather than the craft it actually is. An important issue is whether his comments should still be applied to some of the processes described during this chapter, especially in the later sections.

Stakeholder analysis and company culture analysis would probably not cause a problem. Business ethics might also be acceptable. However, Quinn might have difficulty with the mission statement. It was for this reason that Campbell and Yeung commented on the need to see a mission statement not just as a statement of purpose but also as expressing the *values of the organisation*. Nevertheless, the practice of producing mission statements might cause Quinn some concern. But, as we have seen, they are extensively used by companies in the early twenty-first century. Translating these into objectives involves such an element of business judgement that Quinn might judge that his original research was still valid.

Key strategic principles

- There is a danger in being too rational in the development of mission and objectives.
- Mission statements need to reflect the *values* of the organisation as well as a statement of its purpose.

12.8 STAKEHOLDER POWER AROUND THE WORLD AND ITS INFLUENCE ON MISSION AND OBJECTIVES

From the earlier discussion of stakeholders, it will be evident that they have a substantial influence on the mission and objectives of an organisation. However, the roles and power of owners, shareholders, financing banks and worker-owners will differ around the world as a result of different ownership structures, national government policies and other matters. In particular, *shareholding structures* can vary significantly. Thus the mission and objectives may also change and this needs to be considered in international strategy development.

Much of the shareholder research appears to have been conducted in an Anglo-American context. In the UK and North America, stock markets have been described as demanding short-term results from quoted companies. Shares are widely held and many larger companies have *public share quotations*. This does not imply that shareholders always put direct pressure on senior company managers, but company shares can always be sold as a means of applying pressure. Privatisation has largely taken place so that most companies are influenced only indirectly by governments. Some unions are still powerful in the US in certain industries, but in the UK unions lost their substantial power base through the Thatcher labour law reforms of the 1980s.

Owner–stakeholder interests across other parts of Europe are not necessarily the same. Specifically, *large commercial banks* have much larger shareholdings in major companies in Germany,[51] France,[52] Italy[53] and Spain.[54] For example, in Germany, the large German banks have traditionally held large share blocks in leading German companies: Deutsche Bank in 1994 owned 28 per cent of DaimlerChrysler, 10 per cent of Allianz and 25 per cent of Karstadt – Germany's largest car, insurance and department store chain respectively. Such banks will certainly be interested in the long-term profitability of their investments but do not have the short-term profit horizons of the Anglo-American model. The banks can afford to wait for years because each shareholding is only a small part of their total portfolio and because they are able to spread the risk. Banking power has usually been benign and supportive.

Across Europe, it is not just a question of bank shareholding. For example, it was estimated in 1991 that only seven of the top 200 companies listed in Milan had over half their shares in public hands.[55] There has been some resistance to the widespread ownership of shares in Germany. In France, the state has been the traditional owner of companies, some of which were privatised in the 1980s, with more in the mid-1990s.

We must also not forget the strong tradition in some European countries of *worker co-operatives* and other mutual and non-profit organisations, where the workers and others own the shares of the enterprise. These are shown in Exhibit 12.5. In these organisations, power will be distributed differently. There will be more worker involvement, open discussion and employee representation on senior company councils.

In addition to all the above, there is also a range of *mutual* companies whose shares are essentially owned by their members. The UK has a particularly strong tradition in this area. These include, for example, some of the larger insurance companies in Europe. In all these cases, it would be quite correct to envisage co-operative organisations having a rather broader perspective on the purposes of the organisation.

Moving beyond Europe, Japanese share ownership is widespread but the structure of industry is different, with strong groupings and interlocking shares of companies.[60] Hostile

---

Exhibit 12.5

Worker co-operatives and similar forms of power

They are particularly strong in the following:[56]

- Co-operative banks
- Production co-operatives such as farmers' agricultural organisations, including, for example, the largest milk producer in the EU, the Dutch company Campina MelkUnie[57]
- Consumer co-operatives such as retail and wholesale shops, including the CWS in the UK and Migros in Switzerland[58]
- Social pharmacies where legislation permits
- Social tourism organisations: for example, in France they represent 12 per cent of the overall tourist activity of the country[59]
- Housing and social accommodation co-operatives

---

takeovers are almost unheard of: the Japanese word for takeover is the same as that for hijack and indicates the same degree of enthusiasm. The threat of hostile shareholder activity is muted. Union membership is low and has been in decline,[61] so stakeholder power from this source is not high either. Government involvement in industry development has traditionally been high in certain industries.[62] Power relationships are therefore more complex. The same considerations apply in other Asian countries such as Korea, Malaysia and Singapore.

Although the same depth of research has not been conducted on employee influence on the mission of the organisation, the history of twentieth-century labour relations would suggest that there have periodically been conflicts in some Western countries (but not all) between managers and workers. Stakeholder interests may not be the same.

Around the world, it is not at all clear how the balance of stakeholder interests will develop. What is certainly evident is the need to conduct a thorough analysis of stakeholders early in the process of developing corporate strategy.

Key strategic principles

- In developing mission statements, recognition needs to be given to the different power of shareholders in different countries around the world. There are greater pressures on companies in the UK and US for short-term results.
- Mutual and non-profit co-operatives will approach power issues in the development of mission statements in a different way from other more commercial institutions.

CRITICAL REFLECTION

How useful are mission statements?

How useful are 'Mission Statements'? Their benefits are that they capture the main thinking, logic and culture of organisations in both the private and public sectors. They allow these to be communicated to all stakeholders, including shareholders.

But some organisations regard mission statements as being full of worthy statements that bear no relationship to the reality of business life. Their logic is limited and full of generalised statements. Some strategy textbooks make almost no mention of them.

What do you think? Are they a useful contribution to the company or not worth the paper that they are written on?

SUMMARY

● In developing the purpose of a diversified organisation, it is essential to distinguish between corporate-level purpose and business-level purpose. Corporate purpose is concerned with the role and contribution of the headquarters of the diversified organisation, whereas business purpose relates to the targets in one individual business area.

● The purpose of the organisation needs to be clarified at the outset of strategy development. Many different aspects are potentially involved. In most cases, no single element is usually dominant.

● The polygon of purpose is one way of drawing the elements together. Although ten specific elements can be identified in the polygon, other elements may be more important and some of those highlighted may have little relevance in particular organisations. The ten identified elements are: time dimension, timing, innovation, value added (including profitability), survival, growth, leadership, stakeholders, values and lifestyle, and knowledge.

● Corporate purpose is the purpose and contribution of the *central headquarters* of a diversified group of companies. Corporate-level strategy is the value added contribution of the central headquarters of a group of diversified businesses, each with its own strategy.

● There are three levels of diversification in such companies: close-related, distant-related and unrelated. Each is important in assessing the benefits from operating a corporate-level strategy.

● The benefits of a central headquarters and its related corporate strategy can be delivered in three main areas: internal, external and financial. Internal relates to the cost savings from shared resources and shared activities. External benefits can derive from vertical integration, increased market power and the ability to block competitive activity. Financial benefits come from the ability of the headquarters to be able to lower the cost of capital, provide resources for business restructuring and allocate funds more efficiently across the group.

● Parenting concerns the corporate headquarters of a group of subsidiaries, whose areas of business may be unrelated to each other. Such a business still needs to define its purpose and develop its mission and objectives. This may be difficult where the activities are widely spread.

● The role of the corporate headquarters is to add value to the subsidiaries that are associated with the organisation, otherwise the cost of running a corporate headquarters cannot be justified.

● The corporate headquarters can make offerings in four areas: corporate functions; corporate development initiatives; additional finance for growth or problem areas; the development of formal linkages between parts of the group.

● Corporate headquarters need two special attributes to operate effectively: an understanding of the key factors for success in the diverse industries of their subsidiaries and an ability to make a special contribution.

● The mission of an organisation outlines the broad directions that it should and will follow and briefly summarises the reasoning and values that lie behind it. The objectives are then a more specific commitment consistent with the mission over a specified time period. They may be quantified, but this may be inappropriate in some circumstances. Prescriptive approaches emphasise the need to set out a mission and objectives for the next few years for the organisation. Both mission and objectives must be connected with the defined purpose of the organisation.

● Some emergent approaches doubt the usefulness of a mission and objectives because the future is so uncertain. Other emergent approaches accept the need for a mission and objectives but place great emphasis on the need to include the managers and employees in their development.

● Stakeholders are the individuals and groups who have an interest in the organisation. Consequently, they may wish to influence its mission and objectives. The key issue with regard to stakeholders is that the organisation needs to take them into account in formulating its mission and objectives.

● The difficulty is that stakeholder interests may conflict. Consequently, the organisation will need to resolve which stakeholders have priority. Stakeholder power needs to be analysed. Stakeholder power analysis covers five stages: identification of stakeholders; establishment of their interests and claims; estimation of their degree of power; prioritised mission development; negotiation with key groups.

● The purpose of the mission statement is to communicate to all the stakeholders inside and outside the organisation what the company stands for and where it is headed.

● There are five elements in formulating a mission statement: nature of the organisation; customer perspective; values and beliefs; competitive advantage or distinctiveness; main reasons for the approach. Mission statements rely on business judgement but criteria can be developed to assess the results.

● Objectives take the generalities of the mission statement and turn them into more specific commitments. Usually, this will cover what is to be done and when the objective is to be completed. Different kinds of objectives are possible. Some will be quantified and some not. There may be conflict between objectives, particularly between the long- and short-term interests of the organisation. Shareholding structures will impact on objectives. UK and US companies are under greater pressure for short-term performance. Objectives need to be challenging but achievable.

● There is a danger in being too rational in the development of mission and objectives. Mission statements need to reflect the values of the organisation as well as a statement of its purpose.

● Quality is vital for most organisations and will form part of their strategic purpose and objectives. It delivers value added and may contribute to sustainable competitive advantage. Total quality management (TQM) is the modern strategic approach to quality delivery. Not every organisation operates TQM procedures, but every organisation needs to place quality high in priority with regard to corporate strategy. Although there are benefits from TQM, there are many costs. It often takes years for the full benefits to emerge but the costs are often obvious from an early stage.

QUESTIONS

1 Considering the McDonald's case earlier in the chapter, is 'back-to-basics' an objective or a strategy to achieve an objective?

2 Critically evaluate the form and content of the Ford mission and values in this chapter against its strategy approach, which is set out in Case 7.1 at the beginning of Chapter 7 of this book.

3 The chapter suggests that developing mission statements should be conducted from a customer viewpoint. Do you agree with this? What are the difficulties of this approach?

4 Choose two organisations with which you are familiar, one from the commercial sector (perhaps from work or from your place of study) and one

voluntary body (perhaps from a hobby, sport or society to which you belong). Analyse their leadership and culture and show how these relate to their objectives.

5 Do small companies really need mission statements and objectives? What might be the problems of setting these in small companies? Do smaller companies like Bajaj Auto in Chapter 9 need a mission and objectives?

6 What are the benefits and problems of short-termism, i.e. the concentration on delivering short-term objectives such as immediate shareholder dividends? How might this affect the development of the mission and objectives of an organisation?

7 Take an organisation with which you are familiar and suggest some areas where it has both quantified and unquantified objectives. Is it important that some are unquantified?

8 *'Good corporate parents constantly search for ways in which they can improve the performance of their businesses.'* (Michael Goold)

Is it wise for corporate parents to interfere in the strategies of diversified groups of companies?

9 Take an organisation with which you are familiar and assess the importance of quality in the organisation's strategy. How is quality defined? How is it monitored? Are competitors also monitored? In your view, is the process useful?

10 If emergent approaches to corporate strategy have any significance, then why do companies insist on defining and sticking rigidly to prescriptive corporate objectives?

Further reading

On corporate strategy see Markides, C (2002) 'Corporate strategy: the role of the centre', Chapter 5, in: Pettigrew, A, Thomas, H and Whittington, R (eds) *Handbook of Strategy and Management*, Sage, London. This is a very useful summary of the background theory with useful references.

On parenting strategy read Campbell, A, Goold, M and Alexander, M (1995) 'Corporate strategy: the quest for parenting advantage', *Harvard Business Review*, Mar–Apr. See also their book: *Corporate-level Strategy: Creating Value in the Multibusiness Company*, Wiley, New York, 1994. Michael

Goold has also written a useful article: Goold, M (1996) 'Parenting strategies for the mature business', *Long Range Planning*, June, p359.

On mission statements see Andrew Campbell and Sally Yeung (1991) 'Creating a sense of mission', *Long Range Planning*, Aug.

On quality and TQM, read the chapters in Slack, N, Chambers, S, Harland, C, Harrison, A and Johnson, R, *Operations Management*, Pitman Publishing, London, 1995. These are a good starting point.

Notes and references

1 Marsh, P (2000) 'Engineering a recovery', *Financial Times*, August, p10.

2 Sources for GE/Siemens Case: GE Annual Report and Accounts 2004 – available on the web at www.ge.com. Siemens Annual Report and Accounts 2004 – available on the web at www.siemens.com. *Financial Times*: 21 September 1998, p28; 13 October 1998, p27; 18 June 1999, p33; 5 November 1999, p32; 8 August 2000, p10; 27 November 2000, p18; 12 July 2001, p9; 18 October 2001, p28; 21 January 2002, p10; 30 June 2003, p26; 9 August 2004, p24; 19 August 2003, p10; 2 March 2004, p9; 8 July 2004, p29; 3 August 2004, p10; 8 November 2004, p26; 26 January 2005, p28; 25 March 2005, p26.

3 A fuller discussion of this depiction of purpose is contained in Chaharbaghi, K and Lynch, R (1999) 'Dynamic strategy development as an endless journey in a fast changing environment', *Proceedings of the 1999 Association for Global Business Conference*, Las Vegas, US, November.

4 Stalk Jr, G and Hout, T (1990) *Competing Against Time: How Time Based Competition is Reshaping Global Markets*, The Free Press, New York.

5 Grinyer, P, Mayes, D and McKiernan, P (1988) *Sharpenders: the Secrets of Unleashing Corporate Potential*, Blackwell, Oxford.

6 Kay, J (1994) *Foundations of Corporate Success*, Oxford University Press, Oxford.

7 Williamson, O (1991) 'Strategizing, economizing and economic organization', *Strategic Management Journal*, 12, pp75–94.

8 Penrose, E T (1959) *The Theory of the Growth of the Firm*, Basil Blackwell, Oxford.

9 Harrison, J and Caron, H (1993) *Strategic Management of Organizations and Stakeholders: Concepts*, West Publishing, St Paul, MN.

10 Berle, A A and Means, G (1932) *The Modern Corporation and Private Property*, Macmillan, New York; Rappaport, A (1986) *Creating Shareholder Value: the New Standard for Business Performance*, The Free Press, New York; Kay, J (1994) Op. cit.

11 Bennis, W and Nanus, B (1997) *Leaders: Strategies for Taking Charge*, Harper and Row, New York.

12 *See*, for example, Heller, R (1967) 'The legend of Litton', *Management Today*, Oct, pp60–7. But note that the claim is made in the article that subsidiaries were interconnected. It was only later that this proved to be overstated and Litton was broken up.

13 Hamel, G and Prahalad, H K (1994) *Competing for the Future*, Harvard Business School Press, Boston, MA.

14 Markides, C C and Williamson, P J (1994) 'Related diversification, core competencies and corporate performance', *Strategic Management Journal*, 15, Special issue: pp149–65.

15 Williamson, O E (1975) *Markets and Hierarchies: Analysis and Antitrust Implications*, Free Press, NY.

16 Rumelt, R P (1974) *Strategy, Structure and Economic Performance*, Harvard Business School Press, Boston, MA.

17 Markides, C (2002) 'Corporate strategy: the role of the centre', Ch5, in Pettigrew, A, Thomas, H and

Whittington, R (eds) *Handbook of Strategy and Management*, Sage, London. Many reasons are given for corporate-level strategy: Markides provides a useful and structured argument of the main areas in this summary chapter. *See* also: Chatterjee, S and Wernerfelt, B (1991) 'The link between resources and type of diversification', *Strategic Management Journal*, 12, pp33–48. Farjoun, M (1998) 'The independent and joint effects of relatedness in diversification', *Strategic Management Journal*, 19, pp611–30.

18 Williamson, O E (1975) Op. cit.

19 Williamson, O E (1996) 'Economics and organization: a primer', *California Management Review*, 38, No 2, pp131–46.

20 Shepherd, W G (1986) 'On the core concepts of industrial economics', in deJong, H W and Shepherd, W G (eds) *Mainstreams in Industrial Organization*, Kluwer, Boston, MA.

21 Williamson, O E (1975) Op. cit.

22 *See*, for example, Porter, M E (1987) 'From competitive advantage to corporate strategy', *Harvard Business Review*, May–June.

23 Goold, M (1996) 'Parenting strategies for the mature business', *Long Range Planning*, June, p359.

24 Campbell, A, Goold, M and Alexander, M (1995) 'Corporate strategy: the quest for parenting advantage', *Harvard Business Review*, Mar–Apr.

25 Berle, A A and Means, G C (1967) *The Modern Corporation and Private Property*, Harvest, New York (originally published in 1932).

26 Marris, R (1964) *The Economic Theory of Managerial Capitalism*, Macmillan, London.

27 Holl, P (1977) 'Control type and the market for corporate control in large US corporations', *Journal of Industrial Economics*, 25, pp259–73.

28 Lawriwsky, M L (1984) *Corporate Structure and Performance*, Croom Helm, London.

29 Whittington, R (1993) *What is Strategy and Does it Matter?* Routledge, London.

30 Tomkins, R (2002) 'Added spice', *Financial Times*, 5 April, p16 and Hope, K (2002) 'A worldwide bottling empire looks to Athens', *Financial Times*, 19 April, p13. The first article quotes a financial analyst, Andrew Conway of Crédit Suisse First Boston, who describes this approach to profit taking. The second article quotes company managers from one of the company's leading bottlers, showing how profits are generated partly from the acquisition and rationalisation of bottling companies.

31 Sources for Coca-Cola Case: *Financial Times*: 19 June 1999, p11; 22 July 1999, p2; 29 January 2000, p15; 27 March 2000, p20; 1 August 2000, p15; 15 March 2001, p20; 15 March 2001, p20; 5 April 2002, p16; 17 April 2002, p29; 19 April 2002, p13; 15 May 2002, p25; 17 April 2003, p24; 18 June 2003, p31; 11 December 2003, p18; 24 February 2004, p32; 10 March 2004, p17; 25 March 2004, p1; 20 April 2004, p27; 5 May 2004, p21; 11 May 2004, p31; 23 June 2004, p31; 16 September 2004, p33; 28 September 2004, p28; 12 November 2004, p1; 6 January 2005, p20; 12 February 2005, p19. Coca-Cola Annual Report and Accounts for 2001 and 2004, available on the web at www.coca-cola.com.

32 Christopher, M, Majaro, S and McDonald, M (1989) *Strategy: a Guide for Senior Executives*, Wildwood House, Aldershot, Ch1.

33 Bart, C K and Baetz, M C (1998) 'The relationship between mission statements and firm performance: an explanatory study', *Journal of Management Studies*, 35, No 6, pp823–54.

34 Hooley, G, Cox, A and Adams, A (1991) 'Our five year mission to boldly go where no man has been before', *Proceedings, Marketing Education Group Annual Conference*, Cardiff, pp559–77.

35 Prahalad, C and Doz, Y (1987) *The Multinational Mission*, The Free Press, New York.

36 Hamel, G and Prahalad, C (1989) 'Strategic intent', *Harvard Business Review*, May–June, pp79–91.

37 Campbell, A and Nash, L (1992) *A Sense of Mission: Defining Direction for the Large Corporation*, Addison-Wesley, Workingham.

38 Christopher, M *et al.* (1989) Op. cit.

39 Adapted from Christopher, M *et al.* (1989) Op. cit., p8.

40 Ansoff, I (1968) *Corporate Strategy*, Penguin, Harmondsworth, p44.

41 There are many papers on this controversial topic: *see*, for example, Williams, K, Williams, J and Haslam, C (1995) 'The hollowing out of British manufacturing and its implications for policy', *Economy and Society*, 19(4).

42 Drucker, P (1961) *The Practice of Management*, Mercury Books, London, p54.

43 Sources for McDonalds Case: McDonalds Annual Report and Accounts 2004. *Financial Times*: 3 September 1998, p20; 13 December 2000, p14; 15 April 2002, p13; 26 April 2002, p21 (Burger King); 23 October 2002, p21; 1 March 2003, p3; 29 August 2003, p15; 26 November 2003, p7; 5 February 2004, p11; 9 March 2004, p31; 9 January 2005, pM6; 18 January 2005, p29.

44 Slack, N, Chambers, S, Harland C, Harrison, A and Johnston, R (1995) *Operations Management*, Pitman Publishing, London, p684.

45 Buzzell, R D and Gale, B T (1987) *The PIMS Principles*, The Free Press, New York, Ch6.

46 Slack, N *et al.* (1995) Op. cit., pp812–14.

47 *The Economist*, (1992) 'The cracks in quality', 18 Apr, p85.

48 Slack, N *et al.* (1995) Op. cit., p824

49 *The Economist* (1992) Loc. cit., p86.

50 Quinn, J B (1978) 'Strategic change: logical incrementalism', *Sloan Management Review*, Fall.

51 For example, in Germany Deutsche Bank has major shareholdings in some of Germany's leading companies: Simonian, *Financial Times*, 27 Oct 1989; *The Economist*, 30 Nov 1991, p81; Waller, 'German group's reluctant to list', *Financial Times*, 21 Feb 1994, p21, takes this into Germany's family-owned *Mittelstand*, the middle-rank private companies; Waller, 'Resisting the bait of equity ownership', *Financial Times*, 14 July 1994, p27, takes this further.

52 For example, banks such as Indo-Suez and Crédit Lyonnais have been much criticised for their extensive, relatively non-productive shareholdings in French companies during 1995.

53 For example, *see* the labyrinthine bank sharehold-ings controlled by Italy's largest merchant bank, Mediobanca, and described in Friedman, A (1988) *Agnelli and the Network of Power*, Mandarin, London.

54 For example, *see* Bruce, P (1991) 'Climate control in cor-porate Spain', *Financial Times*, 16 July.

55 *The Economist* (1991) 30 Nov, p81.

56 Panorama of EC Industry 1991–92, *Cooperative, Mutual and Non-profit Organisations in the EC*, Luxembourg: OPOCE, pp121–41. Note that, because they were not members of the EU at the time, Sweden and Finland, which have some very large co-operative organisations, are not included in this survey.

57 *See* Lynch, R (1994) *European Business Strategies*, 2nd edn, Kogan Page, London, p62.

58 Lynch, R (1994) Ibid, pp119, 120.

59 Panorama of EC Industry 1991–92, Loc. cit., p129.

60 Tasker, P (1987) *Inside Japan*, Penguin, London, p307.

61 Jetro, (1990) *Nippon 1990: Business Facts and Figures*, p131.

62 Tasker P (1987) Op. cit., p68.

**Chapter 13
Developing strategic options: the prescriptive process**

- What are the main environment-based opportunities available to the organisation?
- What are the main resource-based opportunities available to the organisation?
- What strategy options arise from these opportunities?

**Chapter 14
Strategy evaluation and development: the prescriptive process**

- What is the important distinction between strategic content and strategic process?
- Which options are consistent with the purpose of the organisation?
- Which options are particularly suitable for the environmental and resource conditions facing the organisation?
- Which options make a valid assumption about the future?
- Which options are feasible?
- Which options contain acceptable business risk?
- Which options are attractive to stakeholders?

**Chapter 15
Finding the strategic route forward: emergent and prescriptive approaches**

- What is the distinction between strategic context and the other two elements – content and process?
- How do emergent strategic considerations alter the decisions?
- What are the main features of alternative strategic approaches?
- What are the consequences for the chosen strategies?

**Chapter 16
Organisational structure, style and people issues**

- What are the main principles involved in designing an organisation's structure to implement its strategy?
- What special considerations apply when seeking innovatory strategies?
- How are managers selected and motivated to implement strategies?

Part 5

DEVELOPING THE STRATEGY

Having explored and defined the purpose of the organisation, it is now possible to develop the strategy. With no single process agreed by all strategists, in this part of the book we first introduce the *prescriptive* approach to the development process – the generation of a number of strategic *options*, followed by a *rational selection* between them, using agreed strategic criteria – and then in later chapters we apply the *emergent* approach to adjust the basic recommendations.

The routes suggested by the prescriptive approach may need to be re-examined. Some strategists may choose to introduce the emergent approach at an earlier stage.

Finally, the organisation structure and the style of the company are explored as these elements may have an important influence on the strategy, possibly even entailing a further reworking of it. It should be noted, however, that some strategy writers regard the structure as something to be resolved *after* the strategy has been agreed and would therefore not include a consideration of the organisation structure at this stage in the development process. For the reasons explained in Chapter 16, this book takes the view that it is better to consider strategy, organisation structure and style together.

The prescriptive strategic process

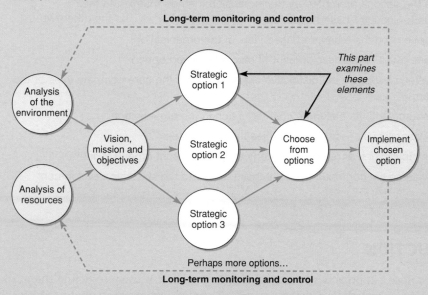

Using the emergent strategic process

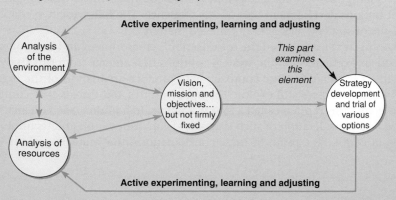

Chapter 13

DEVELOPING STRATEGIC OPTIONS: THE PRESCRIPTIVE PROCESS

Learning outcomes

After working through this chapter, you will be able to:

- undertake a SWOT analysis;
- develop options at the corporate level;
- generate options on the environment-based view of the organisation;
- explore generic strategy options and evaluate their potential;
- outline the market options matrix and its contribution to developing industry-based options;
- investigate the options prompted by the expansion method matrix and their implications for industry-based options;
- generate options on the resource-based view of the organisation;
- use the value chain in the development of resource-based options;
- develop options based on the distinctive capabilities and the core competencies of the organisation;
- identify resource options based on cost reduction in the organisation;
- explain how small businesses can organise their resources;
- outline the implications of resource strategy for not-for-profit organisations;
- critically evaluate the contributions of all these routes to the strategic development process.

INTRODUCTION

In many prescriptive approaches to strategy development, it is usual to define the purpose of the organisation and then develop a range of *strategy options* that might achieve that purpose.[1] After developing the options, a selection is made between them. This chapter is concerned with the options development part of this sequence. The following two chapters then explore the issue of strategy selection and related matters.

In Parts 2 and 3 of this text we analysed the organisation's environment and its resources. Before embarking on an exploration of the strategic options that emerge from this study, it is useful to summarise the situation. One approach is to produce an analysis of the organisation's strengths and weaknesses and explore the opportunities and threats that connect it with the environment – this is often called a SWOT analysis. In addition, such an analysis might be supported by a consideration of such issues as vision, innovation and technology, which are outlined in Part 4. As a result of these considerations, the strategic options will then focus on *achieving the mission and objectives* agreed as a result of Part 4. In addition to the SWOT analysis, most organisations would also draw up a summary of the main elements of the organisation's purpose as a starting point for options development.

To develop the strategic options, both rational and more imaginative processes can be used. Inevitably, because of the difficulty of modelling imagination, strategic research papers and books tend to concentrate on the more rational aspects, which are easier to outline, structure and study. Thus this chapter concentrates on the more rational approaches, but it acknowledges the importance of the creative process in options generation – *see* Figure 13.1.

The options development process begins by exploring the *competitive environment* through three rational strategic routes: generic strategies, market options and expansion methods. It then turns to the organisation's *own resources* and explores another three rational areas: the value chain, the resource-based view and cost-cutting options. Importantly, it should be noted that there are considerable *cross-linkages* between these two routes: for example, the market environment considers the resources of competitors and the company's own resources need to be considered in the context of its competitors.

Part 6a

In theory, there are a very large number of options available to any organisation, probably more than it can cope with. Some final comments are therefore offered on how to reduce these to a more manageable size. The structure of the chapter is summarised in Figure 13.1.

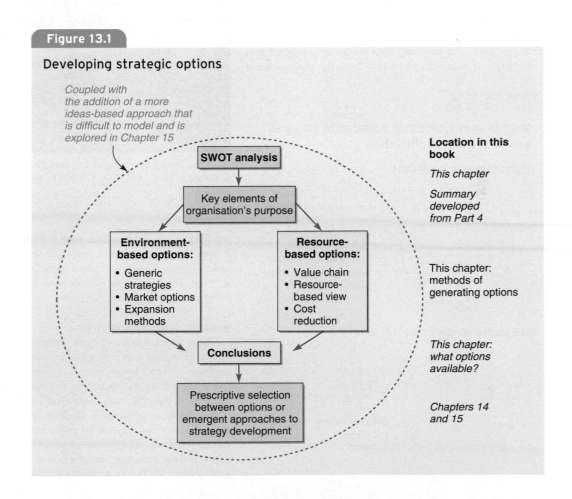

Figure 13.1

Developing strategic options

Coupled with the addition of a more ideas-based approach that is difficult to model and is explored in Chapter 15

SWOT analysis

Key elements of organisation's purpose

Environment-based options:
- Generic strategies
- Market options
- Expansion methods

Resource-based options:
- Value chain
- Resource-based view
- Cost reduction

Conclusions

Prescriptive selection between options or emergent approaches to strategy development

Location in this book

This chapter

Summary developed from Part 4

This chapter: methods of generating options

This chapter: what options available?

Chapters 14 and 15

CASE STUDY 13.1

Walt Disney: building options for Mickey Mouse

In spite of its considerable competitive strengths, the Walt Disney Company was under pressure in the mid-2000s to deliver further growth. Its best-known character, Mickey Mouse, represented one way forward. This case explores some strategic options for the company.

The Walt Disney Company

Founded by Walt and his brother Roy, the Walt Disney Company first made its name with brilliant and innovatory animated cartoons in the early 1920s and 1930s. In addition to characters such as Mickey and Minnie Mouse there were famous cartoons such as *Snow White and the Seven Dwarfs*, *Fantasia* and *Bambi*. The first theme park using such characters was opened in California in 1952. Subsequently, the company branched out into other types of filmed entertainment and into the ownership of one of America's major television broadcasters – the ABC television network. By the year 2005, the company was the second-largest media conglomerate in the world. Its interests included 70 radio stations, several cable TV channels such as ESPN (80 per cent owned), A&E television (38 per cent owned), Walt Disney Pictures, Touchstone, Miramax. It also operated Walt Disney Parks and Resorts in the US, in Japan (under licence), in Europe (majority share) and also a new resort in Hong Kong from October 2005. The company also owned an important and valuable range of brands, particularly those like Mickey Mouse

The Walt Disney Corporation has skilfully exploited the potential of Micky Mouse but needs to find new growth options.

Figure 13.2

Walt Disney Company: sources of revenue and operating profit 2004

(a) Sources of revenue 2004

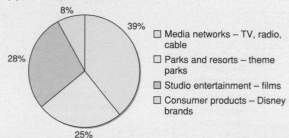

- 39%
- 8%
- 28%
- 25%

□ Media networks – TV, radio, cable
□ Parks and resorts – theme parks
□ Studio entertainment – films
□ Consumer products – Disney brands

(b) Sources of operating profit 2004

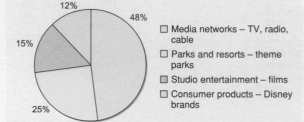

- 48%
- 12%
- 15%
- 25%

□ Media networks – TV, radio, cable
□ Parks and resorts – theme parks
□ Studio entertainment – films
□ Consumer products – Disney brands

and Winnie the Pooh, which were linked with children and it used these to develop merchandise sold in its theme parks, Disney Shops and other direct marketing business activities. The main elements of its sales and profits are shown in Figure 13.2.

Need for profitable growth

For many years, the Walt Disney Company had been able to deliver consistent and profitable growth to its shareholders. However, in recent years, various problems arose and profits began to stagnate. Its media networks suffered from competition from all the other major television stations in the US and its income from advertising declined, though there was a major recovery here in 2004. Its parks and resorts were hit by various problems – the Florida parks were hit by several hurricanes in 2004, resulting not so much in damage but people staying away; its European theme park had rarely made any

Table 13.1

The Walt Disney Company: five-year record

US$ millions

	2000	2001	2002	2003	2004
Revenues					
Media networks	9 836	9 569	9 733	10 941	11 778
Parks and resorts	6 809	7 004	6 465	6 412	7 750
Studio entertainment	5 918	6 009	6 691	7 364	8 713
Consumer products	2 762	2 590	2 440	2 344	2 511
Total revenue	25 325	25 172	25 329	27 061	30 752
Operating income					
Media networks	1 985	1 758	986	1 213	2 169
Parks and resorts	1 615	1 586	1 169	957	1 123
Studio entertainment	126	260	273	620	662
Consumer products	386	401	394	384	534
Total operating income	4 112	4 005	2 822	3 174	4 488

Source: Annual Report and Accounts 2004.

profits since its launch in 1992: it was too far north for year-round sun and also competed with the company's own parks in Florida; the Japanese theme park was profitable but Disney was only a minority shareholder. However, Disney had successfully begun a new venture – family cruise ships to a Caribbean holiday location – as the part of a holiday resort complex. Probably the biggest turnaround in 2004 was in filmed entertainment: the company had major successes in 2003 with *Finding Nemo* (co-production with Pixar) and *Pirates of the Caribbean*. But 2004 included the film *The Alamo*, which cost US$100 million and was unsuccessful at the box office. The branded consumer products increased steadily but would never be the major part of the business. Table 13.1 shows how sales and profits developed 2000–2004.

New growth at Disney: what resources and what options?

Having survived a takeover attempt by a rival American media company – Comcast – in 2004, the Walt Disney Company was seeking new growth opportunities. It was hampered in recent years by a considerable disagreement over strategy between some of the shareholders led by Roy E. Disney, son of one of the company's founders. He was in dispute with the company's dominant chief executive, Michael Eisner. Mr Eisner had been with the company for 20 years and had been behind

many of its recent major strategic moves. But he had fallen out with some major shareholders who felt that he had become an obstacle to growth and did not recognise some of the major strengths of the Disney Company. For example, it was Eisner who decided that the remaining highly skilled studio animators should be asked to leave. He was criticised by Mr Disney, who commented: 'It is not cost-effective to fire a lot of talented artists and make mediocre movies. The safe decision is always the most dangerous one.' Mr Disney even set up a website to fight the company's management – www.SaveDisney.com. The outcome of this was that Mr Eisner was stripped of his Disney chairmanship in 2004: he announced that he would be leaving the company in September 2005.

The competitive resources of the Disney company were formidable: its library of filmed material, its branded characters, its ownership of the method of delivering media, its theme parks and its experience in studio entertainment. It was particularly strong in family entertainment, with the Disney brand itself being particularly powerful in this area. For several years, it had also combined with the animation company Pixar to distribute its films – *Finding Nemo*, etc. – but Pixar decided that it would look for an alternative distributor from 2006.

Disney's future strategic options included the following:

- *Further development of its theme parks*: it was negotiating a possible site in Shanghai, China. The problem with theme parks is that they are capital-intensive and take a lengthy period to develop: for example, the Hong Kong park on Lantau Island was first agreed in 1999.
- *Media network development*: this would be difficult in the saturated US market, but the company was looking to the increasingly fragmented European market, especially the UK.
- *Studio filmed entertainment*: this was essentially a risky business. There are good payoffs if the judgement is right but a strong downside if the film is unsuccessful.

Arguably, this was the time for Disney to look more broadly at its strategic options – perhaps the new media would present further scope for business development? Perhaps it should use its brand strength to develop new products for the tourism and travel industry?

Case questions

1 *What are the competitive advantages of the Disney group? Which, if any, are sustainable over time?*

2 *Using concepts from this chapter, what are the options available to Disney over the next five years?*

3 *Can companies in the media and travel industries, like television stations and theme parks, gain and retain competitive advantage simply by offering new products? Or do they need to rethink other aspects of their strategy? If so, which aspects?*

13.1 PURPOSE AND THE SWOT ANALYSIS – THE CONTRIBUTION OF ANDREWS

As a starting point for the development of strategic options, Professor Kenneth Andrews first identified the importance of connecting the organisation's purpose – its mission and objectives – with its strategic options and subsequent activities. 'The interdependence of purposes, policies, and organised action is crucial to the particularity of an individual strategy and its opportunity to identify competitive advantage.'[3] We explored purpose in Part 4 of this book, so we will assume here that we have some agreed definition against which to develop some options.

Andrews went on to argue persuasively that the rational analysis of the possibilities open to organisations was an essential part of strategy development. As a starting point in developing options, it is useful to summarise the current position. A useful way of capturing this

Definition ➤ is a SWOT analysis of the organisation. This is an analysis of the Strengths and Weaknesses present internally in the organisation, coupled with the Opportunities and Threats that the organisation faces externally. This approach follows from the distinction drawn by Andrews between two aspects of the organisation:

1 Strengths and weaknesses – explored in the *resource-based* analysis of Part 3 of this book;

2 Opportunities and threats – explored in the *environment-based* analysis of Part 2 of this book.

Each analysis will be unique to the organisation for which it is being devised, but some general pointers and issues can be drawn up. These are indicated in Table 13.2, which provides a checklist of some possible factors.

Table 13.2

Some possible factors in a SWOT analysis

INTERNAL

Strengths	Weaknesses
• Market dominance	• Share weakness
• Core strengths	• Few core strengths and low on key skills
• Economies of scale	• Old plant with higher costs than competition
• Low-cost position	• Weak finances and poor cash flow
• Leadership and management skills	• Management skills and leadership lacking
• Financial and cash resource	• Poor record on innovation and new ideas
• Manufacturing ability and age of equipment	• Weak organisation with poor architecture
• Innovation processes and results	• Low quality and reputation
• Architecture network	• Products not differentiated and dependent on few products
• Differentiated products	
• Product or service quality	

EXTERNAL

Opportunities	Threats
• New markets and segments	• New market entrants
• New products	• Increased competition
• Diversification opportunities	• Increased pressure from customers and suppliers
• Market growth	• Substitutes
• Competitor weakness	• Low market growth
• Strategic space	• Economic cycle downturn
• Demographic and social change	• Technological threat
• Change in political or economic environment	• Change in political or economic environment
• New takeover or partnership opportunities	• Demographic change
• Economic upturn	• New international barriers to trade
• International growth	

Note: See text for dangers of lists and bullet points!

In devising a SWOT analysis, there are several factors that will enhance the quality of the material:

- Keep it brief – pages of analysis are usually not required.
- Relate strengths and weaknesses, wherever possible, to industry key factors for success.
- Strengths and weaknesses should also be stated in competitive terms, if possible. It is reassuring to be 'good' at something, but it is more relevant to be 'better than the competition'.
- Statements should be specific and avoid blandness – there is little point in stating ideas that everyone believes in.
- Analysis should distinguish between where the company *wishes to be* and where it is *now*. The gap should be realistic.
- It is important to be realistic about the strengths and weaknesses of one's own and competitive organisations.

Probably the biggest mistake that is commonly made in SWOT analysis is to assume that it is certain to be 'correct' because it contains every conceivable issue and is truly comprehensive. Nothing could be further from the truth. This merely demonstrates a paucity of real thought and a lack of strategic judgement about what is really important for that organisation.

Another common error is to provide a long list of points but little logic, argument and evidence. A short list with each point well argued is more likely to be convincing. Arguably, Table 13.2 with its bullet points and lack of any explanation is thoroughly misleading on this point. Whittington has a useful summary of some more general criticisms of SWOT analysis.[4]

13.2 ENVIRONMENT-BASED OPTIONS: GENERIC STRATEGIES – THE CONTRIBUTION OF PORTER

Definition ➤ We begin our exploration of environment-based options by considering the *generic strategies* first outlined by Professor Michael Porter of Harvard Business School. Generic strategies are the three basic strategies of cost leadership, differentiation and focus (sometimes called niche) open to any business. Porter's contribution was based on earlier work in industrial economics, exploring how firms compete.[5] Porter made the bold claim that there were only three fundamental strategies that any business could undertake – that is why he called them *generic*. During the 1980s, they were regarded as being at the forefront of strategic thinking. Arguably, they still have a contribution to make in the new century in the development of strategic options. However, strategists concentrating on the resource-based view now regard generic strategies as being largely historic. We return to a consideration of their merits at the end of this section.

Generic strategies were first outlined in two books from Professor Porter, *Competitive Strategy*[6] in 1980 and *Competitive Advantage*[7] in 1985. The second book contained a small modification of the concept. The original version is explored here. After exploring the basic elements, a case example is considered and some comments on their theoretical validity and practical usefulness are offered. Professor Porter confined his books to business situations and did not explore not-for-profit organisations.

13.2.1 The three generic competitive strategies: the three options

Professor Porter argued that there were three basic, i.e. *generic*, strategies open to any business:

1 cost leadership
2 differentiation
3 focus.

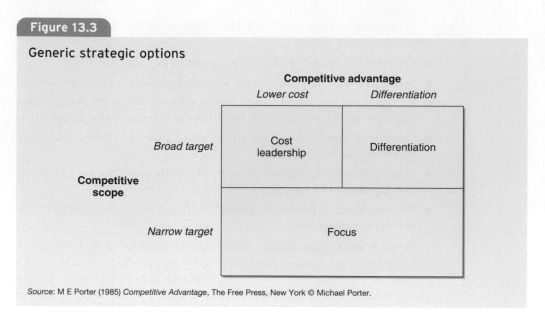

Figure 13.3

Generic strategic options

Competitive advantage

	Lower cost	Differentiation
Broad target	Cost leadership	Differentiation
Narrow target	Focus	

Competitive scope

Source: M E Porter (1985) *Competitive Advantage*, The Free Press, New York © Michael Porter.

According to the theory, every business needs to choose one of these in order to compete in the market place and gain sustainable competitive advantage. Each of these three strategic options represents an area that every business and many not-for-profit organisations can usefully explore. The three options can be explained by considering two aspects of the competitive environment:

1 *The source of competitive advantage*. There are fundamentally only two sources of competitive advantage. These are *differentiation* of products from competitors and *low costs*. We explore these two areas below.

2 *The competitive scope of the target customers*. It is possible to target the organisation's products as a *broad target* covering most of the market place or to pick a *narrow target* and focus on a niche within the market.

Porter then brought these two elements together in the well-known diagram shown as Figure 13.3.

In his second book, Porter modified the concept to split the niche sector into:

● niche differentiation

● niche low-cost leadership.

The figure is sometimes shown in this modified form.

13.2.2 Low-cost leadership

Definition ➤ The low-cost leader in an industry has built and maintains plant, equipment, labour costs and working practices that deliver the lowest costs in that industry.

Later in this chapter, we will explore a number of options that organisations can follow for reducing costs – *see* Section 13.7. The essential point is that the firm with the lowest costs has a clear and possibly sustainable competitive advantage. However, in order to cut costs, a low-cost producer must find and exploit *all* the sources of cost advantage. Low-cost producers typically sell a standard, or no-frills, product and place considerable strategic emphasis on reaping scale or absolute cost advantages from all sources. In practice, low-cost leaders achieve their position by shaving costs off every element of the value chain – the strategy

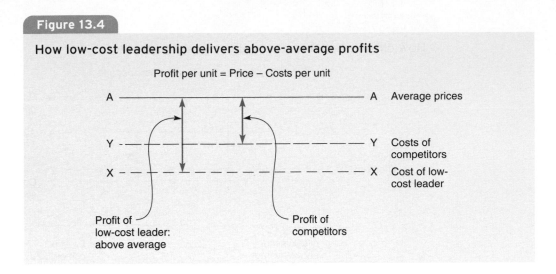

Figure 13.4

How low-cost leadership delivers above-average profits

Profit per unit = Price – Costs per unit

A ———————————————————————— A   Average prices

Y – – – – – – – – – – – – – – – – – – Y   Costs of
competitors

X – – – – – – – – – – – – – – – – – – X   Cost of low-
cost leader

Profit of
low-cost leader:
above average

Profit of
competitors

comes from attention to detail. McDonald's Restaurants achieves its low costs through stand-ardised products, centralised buying of supplies for a whole country and so on.

The profit advantage gained from low-cost leadership derives from the assertion that low-cost leaders should be able to sell their products in the market place at around the aver-age price of the market – *see* line A–A in Figure 13.4. If such products are not perceived as comparable or their performance is not acceptable to buyers, a cost leader will be forced to discount prices below competition in order to gain sales.

Compared with the low-cost leader, competitors will have higher costs – *see* line Y–Y in the figure. After successful completion of this strategy option, the costs of the lowest-cost producer will be lower by definition than those of other competitors – *see* line X–X in Figure 13.4. This will deliver *above-average profits* to the low-cost leader.

To follow this strategy option, an organisation will place the emphasis on cost reduction at every point in its processes. It should be noted that *cost leadership does not necessarily imply a low price*: the company could charge an average price and reinvest the extra profits gener-ated. Referring back to Chapter 5, an example of cost leadership in the European ice cream market would be Unilever's product range across Europe. The company enjoys the advant-age of the substantial cost benefits of being market leader in a high fixed cost industry.

13.2.3 Differentiation

Definition ➤ Differentiation occurs when the products of an organisation meet the needs of some cus-tomers in the market place better than others. When the organisation is able to differenti-ate its products, it is able to charge a price that is higher than the average price in the market place.

Underlying differentiation is the concept of *market segmentation*, which was explored in Chapter 5 – the identification of specific groups who respond differently from other groups to competitive strategies. Essentially, they will pay more for a differentiated product that is targeted towards them. Examples of differentiation include better levels of service, more luxurious materials and better performance. McDonald's is differentiated by its brand name and its 'Big Mac' and 'Ronald McDonald' products and imagery. Another example can be taken from the European ice cream industry. The Mars Ice Cream range is clearly differ-entiated by its branding and its consequent ability to charge a premium price.

In order to differentiate a product, Porter argued that it is necessary for the pro-ducer to incur *extra costs*, for example, to advertise a brand and thus differentiate it. The

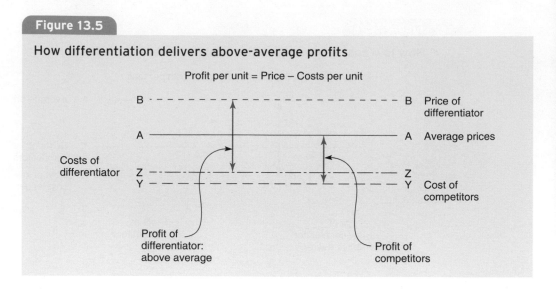

Figure 13.5

How differentiation delivers above-average profits

Profit per unit = Price – Costs per unit

differentiated product costs will therefore be higher than those of competitors – *see* line Z–Z in Figure 13.5. The producer of the differentiated product then derives an advantage from its pricing: with its uniquely differentiated product it is able to charge a premium price, i.e. one that is higher than its competitors – *see* line B–B in Figure 13.5.

There are two problems associated with differentiation strategies:

1 It is difficult to estimate whether the extra costs incurred in differentiation can be recovered from the customer by charging a higher price.

2 The successful differentiation may attract competitors to copy the differentiated product and enter the market segment. There are often costs associated with being first into a market, so there may be additional cost advantages from moving in second – for example, other companies have followed McDonald's and Mars Ice Cream.

Neither of the above problems is insurmountable but they do weaken the attractiveness of this option.

13.2.4 Focus strategy (sometimes called niche strategy)

Sometimes, according to Porter, neither a low-cost leadership strategy nor a differentiation strategy is possible for an organisation across the broad range of the market. For example, the costs of achieving low-cost leadership may require substantial funds which are not available. Equally, the costs of differentiation, while serving the mass market of customers, may be too high: if the differentiation involves quality, it may not be credible to offer high-quality and cheap products under the same brand name, so a new brand name has to be developed and supported. For these and related reasons, it may be better to adopt a *focus* strategy.

Definition ➤   A focus strategy occurs when the organisation focuses on a specific niche in the market place and develops its competitive advantage by offering products especially developed for that niche.

Hence the focused strategy selects a segment or group of segments in the industry and tailors its strategy to serve them to the *exclusion* of others. By optimising its strategy for the targets, the focuser seeks to achieve a competitive advantage in its target segments, even though it does not possess a competitive advantage overall. In a later development of his theory, Porter argued that the company may undertake this process either by using a cost leadership approach or by differentiation:

- In a *cost focus* approach a firm seeks a cost advantage in its target segment only.
- In a *differentiation focus* approach a firm seeks differentiation in its target segment only.

The essence of focus is the exploitation of a narrow target's differences from the balance of the industry.

By targeting a small, specialised group of buyers it should be possible to earn higher than average profits, either by charging a premium price for exceptional quality or by a cheap and cheerful low-price product. For the European ice cream market, examples would be:

- *differentiation focus* – superpremium ice cream segment;
- *cost focus* – economy ice cream segment.

In the global car market, Rolls-Royce and Ferrari are clearly niche players – they have only a minute percentage of the market worldwide. Their niche is premium product and premium price.

There are some problems with the focus strategy, as follows:

- By definition, the niche is small and may not be large enough to justify attention.
- Cost focus may be difficult if economies of scale are important in an industry such as the car industry.
- The niche is clearly specialist in nature and may disappear over time.

None of these problems is insurmountable. Many small and medium-sized companies have found that this is the most useful strategic area to explore.

13.2.5 The danger of being stuck in the middle

Professor Porter concluded his analysis of what he termed the main generic strategies by suggesting that there are real dangers for the firm that engages in each generic strategy but fails to achieve any of them – it is stuck in the middle. A firm in this position

> *will compete at a disadvantage because the cost leader, differentiators, or focuser will be better positioned to compete in any segment . . . Such a firm will be much less profitable than rivals achieving one of the generic strategies.*

Several commentators, such as Kay,[8] Stopford and Baden-Fuller[9] and Miller[10] now reject this aspect of the analysis. They point to several empirical examples of successful firms that have adopted more than one generic strategy: for example, Toyota cars and Benetton clothing manufacturing and shops, both of which are differentiated yet have low costs.

13.2.6 Comment on Porter's generic strategies

Hendry[11] and others have set out the problems of the logic and the empirical evidence associated with generic strategies that limit its absolute value. We can summarise them as follows:

Low-cost leadership

- If the option is to seek low-cost leadership, then how can more than one company be *the* low-cost leader? It may be a contradiction in terms to have an *option* of low-cost leadership.
- Competitors also have the option to reduce their costs in the long term, so how can one company hope to maintain its competitive advantage without risk?
- Low-cost leadership should be associated with cutting costs per unit of production. However, there are limitations to the usefulness of this concept, which are described in Section 13.7. They will also apply here.

Generic strategy options analysis: global ice cream

It is useful to explore some of the benefits and problems of options that have been developed from generic strategies. To undertake this, we can use the data from Chapter 4 to analyse the possible strategy options in this industry in the mid-2000s. The generic strategies are set out in Figure 13.6.

Although the market is still growing, it is relatively easy to position the basic companies in the global ice cream market. The positions of Nestlé and Mars are important. Whereas Nestlé has developed global scale it is still considerably

To develop new options, ice cream companies can move into niche strategic areas like ready-to-serve ice cream at Ben & Jerry's.

Figure 13.6

Generic strategies in European ice cream

		Competitive advantage	
		Lower cost	Differentiation
Competitive scope	Broad target	**Cost leadership** Unilever	**Differentiation** • Nestlé • Mars Ice Cream?
	Narrow target	**Cost focus** Economy ice cream made by small, local ice cream companies with low overheads	**Differentiation focus** Superpremium, e.g. Häagen-Dazs, Ben & Jerry's

smaller than the low-cost leader, Unilever. However, Nestlé does have a strong range of existing ice cream brands that will allow a premium price to be charged. Mars has differentiated products by the nature of its strong brands, but still remains a relatively small player: arguably it should be repositioned in the 'differentiated niche' category.

Case questions

1 *If you were Nestlé in the global ice cream market, what strategy options would you pursue?*

2 *If you were Häagen-Dazs and someone recommended a low-cost option, what would your reaction be?*

3 *Are there any weaknesses in using Porter's generic strategies to generate market-based options in the European ice cream market? Make sure that you have read and understood the text before answering this question.*

- Low-cost leadership assumes that technology is relatively predictable, if changing. Radical change can so alter the cost positions of actual and potential competitors that the concept may have only limited relevance in fast-changing, high-technology markets.
- Cost reductions only lead to competitive advantage when *customers* are able to make comparisons. This means that the low-cost leader must also lead *price* reductions or competitors will be able to catch up, even if this takes some years and is at lower profit margins. But permanent price reductions by the cost leader may have a damaging impact on the market positioning of its product or service that will limit its usefulness.

Differentiation

- Differentiated products are assumed to be higher priced. This is probably too simplistic. The form of differentiation may not lend itself to higher prices.
- The company may have the objective of increasing its market share, in which case it may use differentiation for this purpose and match the lower prices of competitors.
- Porter discusses differentiation as if the *form* this will take in any market will be immediately obvious. The real problem for strategy options is not to identify the *need* for differentiation but to work out what *form* this should take that will be attractive to the customer. Generic strategy options throw no light on this issue whatsoever. They simply make the dubious assumption that once differentiation has been decided on it is obvious how the product should be differentiated.

Competitive scope

- The distinction between broad and narrow targets is sometimes unclear. Are they distinguished by size of market? Or by customer type? If the distinction between them is unclear then what benefit is served by the distinction?
- For many companies, it is certainly useful to recognise that it would be more productive to pursue a niche strategy, away from the broad markets of the market leaders. That is the easy part of the logic. The difficult part is to identify *which* niche is likely to prove worthwhile. Generic strategies provide no useful guidance on this at all.
- As markets fragment and product life cycles become shorter, the concept of broad targets may become increasingly redundant.

Stuck in the middle

As was pointed out above, there is now useful empirical evidence that some companies do pursue differentiation *and* low-cost strategies at the same time. They use their low costs to provide greater differentiation and then reinvest the profits to lower their costs even further. Companies such as Benetton (Italy), Toyota (Japan) and BMW (Germany) have been cited as examples.

Resource-based view

In Chapter 6, we explored the arguments supporting this view of strategic analysis. They also apply to strategy options and suggest that options based on the uniqueness of the *company* rather than the characteristics of the *industry* are likely to prove more useful in developing competitive strategy. We return to these issues later in this chapter, but comment now that the resource-based view does undermine much of Porter's approach.

Fast-moving markets

In dynamic markets such as those driven by new internet technology, the application of generic strategies will almost certainly miss major new market opportunities. They cannot be identified by the generic strategies approach.

Conclusions

Faced with this veritable onslaught on generic strategies, it might be thought that Professor Porter would gracefully concede that there might be some weaknesses in the concept. However, he hit back in 1996 by drawing a distinction between basic strategy and what he called 'operational effectiveness' – the former concerned the key strategic decisions facing any organisation while the latter are more concerned with such issues as TQM, outsourcing, re-engineering and the like.[13] He did not concede any ground but rather extended his approach to explore how companies might use *market positioning* within the concept of generic strategies – this topic was explored in Chapter 5.

Given these criticisms, it might be concluded that the concept of generic strategies has no merit. However, as long as it is treated only as part of a broader analysis, it can be a useful tool for generating basic *options* in strategic analysis. It forces exploration of two important aspects of corporate strategy: the role of *cost reduction* and the use of *differentiated products* in relation to customers and competitors. But it is only a starting point in the development of such options. When the market is growing fast, it may provide no useful routes at all. More generally, the whole approach takes a highly *prescriptive* view of strategic action. We will leave our consideration of this issue until Chapter 15.

Key strategic principles

- Generic strategies are a means of generating basic strategy options in an organisation. They are based on seeking competitive advantage in the market place.

- There are three main generic options: cost leadership, differentiation and focus.

- Cost leadership aims to place the organisation amongst the lowest-cost producers in the market. It does not necessarily mean having low prices. Higher than average profits come from charging average prices.

- Differentiation is aimed at developing and targeting a product against a major market segment. Because the product is especially developed, it should be possible to add a small premium to the average price. Differentiation has a cost but this should be more than compensated for in the higher price charged.

- Focus involves targeting a small segment of the market. It may operate by using a low-cost focus or differentiated focus approach.

- According to the theory, it is important to select between the options and not to be 'stuck in the middle'. Some influential strategists have produced evidence that has cast doubt on this point.

- There have been numerous criticisms of the approach based on logic and empirical evidence of actual industry practice. Undoubtedly these comments have validity, but generic strategies still represent a useful starting point in developing strategy options.

CASE STUDY 13.3

Market-based strategies in global TV: exciting opportunities in a fast-expanding market

Over the last 15 years, global television has become a major business opportunity. This case explores how such opportunities have arisen and been exploited by some of the leading companies. It also outlines some further market possibilities for both national and global companies in the new millennium.

Industry-based change: technology and politics bring new opportunities

Until recently, newspapers have been highly competitive in many countries of the world, but TV has not. Because of technical limitations on the numbers of TV channels that could be broadcast and the deep influence of TV on its audience, TV companies were often controlled by the state or by a small number of commercial interests. However, by the late 1990s, the global media market was growing rapidly. Major new profit opportunities came from two new sources: technology and politics.

- *Technology* – via new satellite channels and the greater availability of cable TV broadcasting. At the beginning of the twenty-first century, technology will be augmented by the advent of digital broadcasting, the essential effect here being to allow many more TV channels to appear on air.

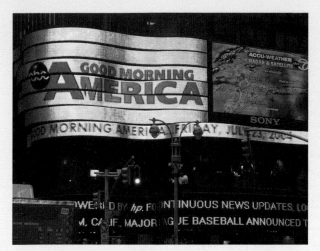

ABC television's Good Morning America *is broadcast from New York but often takes live pictures from every part of the world – a total change over the last ten years.*

- *Politics* – through national governments either privatising government-owned channels or simply allowing new, private, commercial TV channels to broadcast.

The two main profit streams of global media: production and broadcasting

Media companies can generate revenue and profits in TV in two main ways: TV production and network broadcasting.

- *TV production* – the manufacture of programmes for broadcast. Creative ideas, popular stars and strong entertainment values can deliver competitive advantage. TV production facilities, such as studios, can be hired and are relatively inexpensive. Production costs can range from cheap game shows to expensive TV drama. Revenue then comes from the sale of such programmes to the TV broadcasters.
- *Network broadcasting*. Traditionally, this has involved competition between a limited number of companies broadcasting across the airwaves. In recent years, new forms of transmission using cable and satellite and new technology are extending dramatically the number of channels available. But the capital cost of such developments is high, especially for cabling to homes. Revenues are then derived from advertising or from subscription revenues to the cable (or satellite) channel or both.

Many companies are engaged in both production and broadcasting. However, there are also a large number of independent production companies because the barriers to entry are much lower than for broadcasting. The costs of setting up a production company to make TV programmes might typically be US$1 million, but these are much smaller than the costs of developing a broadcasting station – typically US$10–100 million. Strategically, the broadcasters have the greater bargaining power because they control access to large numbers of viewers, whose only bargaining power is to turn off the TV.

In practice, many of the leading companies have other related sources of entertainment revenue – for example, Disney's theme parks and Time Warner's AOL computer on-line service provision.

International TV markets: still not truly global

Although some programmes are regularly broadcast around the world – ranging from *Star Trek* to World Cup football – both customer tastes and the various competitors vary from one continent to another. Some specialist niche categories such as coverage of the *Olympics* and *Formula 1 Motor Racing* may be considered global. However, in many respects, there is no single global market. In terms of size, three main areas are currently important:

1 North America: US and Canada
2 Europe: the European Union
3 Asia–Pacific: China and India are the largest.

Other important and sizeable markets also exist, such as those in Latin America, the Middle East and Southern Africa. For our purposes, we will focus on the first three above.

The US: market fragmentation produces new industry linkages

In the US, TV broadcasts by the three main traditional channels – ABC, NBC and CBS – are available free across the airwaves – the programmes are paid for by advertising. In strategic terms, the battle between these channels has become fiercer as a new national network station has been developed, namely Fox TV from News Corporation, which is described in Case study 13.4. The traditional networks have also been fighting increased *market fragmentation* of their audience. This has derived mainly from the large numbers of cable and satellite channels which have been launched, offering news, live sport, new films and specialist music to their subscribers, who traditionally watched one of the national channels.

To fight this competition, strong links have developed between the main traditional network broadcasters and six leading film companies – *see* Table 13.3. The sustainable competitive advantage is strong when a company owns exclusive rights to popular films, such as the James Bond series or Disney cartoons. Essentially, film and other entertainment companies acquired all the main network broadcasters during the last few years.

To pursue the battle further, some of the main film companies have also acquired the other enemy: cable and satellite channels. Warner Brothers, Disney, Twentieth Century Fox and Paramount all have access to the new media. Table 13.3 outlines some of the linkages.

Competition in European network broadcasting: cable and satellite represent the major threat

In Europe, the dominant broadcasters for many years have been the limited number of national broadcasters, such as the BBC and ITV (UK), TF1 and Antenne 2 (France), ZDF and NDR (Germany), RAI (Italy). There have not been the same links between TV production and film companies because film is

▶

▶ CASE STUDY 13.3 continued

Table 13.3

Leading film and television companies in the US

Holding company	Film company	Television: broadcast, cable and satellite
Time Warner	Warner Brothers	Turner Broadcasting; Cable News Network: extensive cable service
Walt Disney	Disney	ABC national TV network – see Case 13.1
News Corporation	Twentieth Century Fox	Fox national TV network; also owns a major stakes in other networks – see Case 13.4
Sony	Sony	None, but sells programmes and films to broadcasters – has acquired the MGM film library
Viacom	Paramount	MTV, Nickelodeon, extensive cable network CBS national broadcast TV network plus extensive cable network and largest radio network in US
General Electric	MCA/Universal Studios	NBC national broadcast TV network plus Universal films and theme parks

Source: Author from various studies.

largely dominated by the major US studios. Much of the European production has therefore been undertaken by the broadcasters, though there has been a recent trend to employ independent TV production companies.

In addition to the national European broadcasters, recent years have seen the rise of a series of cable channels, mostly based on subscription. Some of these rely purely on cable delivery, but some use satellite direct broadcast into people's homes with a set-top box decoder. During the last five years, these have developed extensively and the national broadcasters have become increasingly marginalised. In other words, *market fragmentation* is now taking place across European markets.

Asian and Far Eastern markets: national broadcasters threatened by satellite channels

In Asia and Far Eastern markets, the dominant broadcasters are still the national TV networks – satellite and cable are still in the early stages of development. However, satellite transmission does have real potential for growth because it is cheaper to put up one satellite for a large geographic area, rather than build an extensive network of small transmitters each serving a small geographic area. This principle has been used extensively in India by the national TV broadcaster Doordarshan, for instance. However, in many parts of Asia the traditional broadcasters still hold the majority of the audience: Hong Kong TV, Malaysian TV and Singapore TV are examples of such dominance.

Some of the new satellite owners are local companies, such as those operating in the Australia, Hong Kong, the Philippines and Zee TV in India. However, News Corporation has also been active, with new satellite channels launched in Hong Kong (Star TV), Japan (JSkyB) and India (Star India). The new channels have not always been welcomed by the relevant national governments and local rival media channels. For example, the Chinese government was still cautious about Star TV, but had

agreed to News Corporation broadcasts in southern China. The company was pursuing the opportunity because of the very large potential audience in the area.

TV business strategies: the choice between software and hardware and the need for innovation and negotiation skills

There is some disagreement between the leading companies about the most effective business strategies for the 2000s. Sony believes the best approach is through 'software', i.e. the purchase of exclusive rights to films, TV programmes and books. Other companies such as Viacom, News Corporation and Disney have spent at least part of their efforts on 'hardware' – i.e. the devices that deliver the TV signal to the final customer – through ownership of TV stations in some countries, satellite or cable channels. Both these routes can produce high barriers to entry in terms of the substantial investment required.

Other strategies in the TV market include:

● delivery of *attractive programmes* such as live and exclusive TV sport or recent films;
● *restrictive access*, meaning that the viewer has no choice but to buy into the network. Supply is via cable or an encrypted TV signal that takes a special box to decode;
● *outright acquisition of old films*, delivering unique competitive advantage here;
● *heavy investment in new cable and satellite channels* – for example, cable companies are investing around US$10 billion in the US and a similar amount in the UK;
● *company acquisitions and joint ventures* – for example, Disney acquired the ABC TV network and other assets for US$19 billion; Viacom acquired CBS for US$35 billion.
● *cross-promotion deals* across the different media, e.g. from book to film or video to satellite.

Because the necessary investment often amounts to billions of dollars, companies may not have the resources to pursue *both* strategies and need to make a choice. More generally, it will be evident that the fast-moving environment has required two strategies above all others:

1 *Innovation* – seizing opportunities in film and sports deals, new channels, new technologies, etc.
2 *Negotiation skills* – many of the new strategies needed deals to be struck with governments, competitors, sports bodies, technology companies, etc.

Key factors for success in TV: how to build sustainable competitive advantage and value added

Because there is some disagreement on corporate strategy across the industry, the key factors cannot be identified with certainty. However, it is likely that on a global basis they would include the following:

● highly creative and innovative people to create programme content;
● strong financial base in order to fund the high market growth;
● real strengths in selected markets in terms of market share, at least in some market segments. This might be built using sports contracts, media contracts, a strong film library and even total control over subscribers to their channels;
● means of overcoming barriers to entry – either access to programmes or channels of distribution;
● commercial acumen and deal-making skills.

© Copyright Richard Lynch 2006. All rights reserved. This case was written by Richard Lynch from published information.[14]

Case questions

1 *Do Porter's generic strategies provide any useful insights in structuring the strategic opportunities in global TV? Think carefully about the criticisms before you answer this question.*

2 *If you were developing strategy options for a small company, what strategy options would you consider? What problems might you encounter?*

3 *What strategy options would you consider if you were given the task of developing a truly global TV network? Would it be profitable?*

4 *What lessons, if any, can be drawn from the global TV market on the broad task of developing strategic options?*

STRATEGIC PROJECT

This case only touches on the many media changes that have occurred in every part of the world over the last ten years. A more detailed study of the potential in one country would be both challenging and interesting. It needs to start with the national broadcaster and then expand to cover the competition, how the market is becoming increasingly fragmented and which channels are particularly popular. Much of this can be gained from websites and broadcast magazines. It would be particularly interesting to explore strategy over the next five years as further change is highly likely.

13.3 ENVIRONMENT-BASED STRATEGIC OPTIONS: THE MARKET OPTIONS MATRIX

Definition ➤ The market options matrix identifies the product and market options available to the organisation, including the possibility of withdrawal and movement into unrelated markets. The distinction is drawn between *markets*, which are defined as customers, and *products*, which are defined as the items sold to customers. Thus, for example, one customer could buy several different products, depending on need.

The market options matrix examines the options available to the organisation from a broader strategic perspective than the simple market/product matrix (called in some texts the *Ansoff matrix*). Thus the market options matrix not only considers the possibility of launching new products and moving into new markets, but explores the possibility of *withdrawing* from markets and moving into *unrelated* markets. Nevertheless, the format is based on product/market options. It is shown in Figure 13.7. The foundation in 'product/market options' suggests that such options are primarily at the *business* level of the organisation. In practice, some options may need to be considered at the *corporate* level in an organisation: the reason is that some decisions like withdrawal or diversification may impact on other areas of the business and also make it more difficult for the group in total to employ core

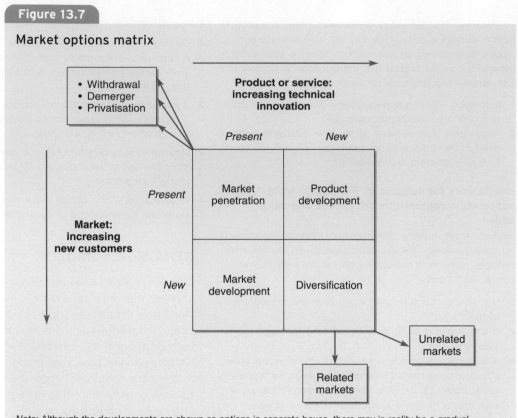

Figure 13.7

Market options matrix

Note: Although the developments are shown as *options* in separate boxes, there may in reality be a *gradual* movement from one area to another. They are not absolutes. To avoid confusion, it should be noted that market *penetration* differs from market *development* because penetration concentrates on existing or potential customers, whereas development seeks totally new segments of customers or totally new customer groups.

Source: Author based on Ansoff, I (1989) *Corporate Strategy*, rev. edn, Penguin, Harmondsworth. The matrix also uses concepts outlined by Day, G S (1987) *Strategic Market Planning*, West Publishing, St Paul, MN.

competencies, block competitive moves, etc. Such decisions will need to be decided on a case-by-case basis.

Each of the strategic options is now considered in turn.

13.3.1 Withdrawal

It may seem perverse to begin the consideration of market options with the possible strategy of withdrawing from them. But strategy must always consider the unpredictable if it is to develop competitive advantage. There are a number of circumstances where this option may have merit, for example:

● *Product life cycle in decline phase with little possibility of retrenchment.* In the context of global TV, the time will come in the next 20 years (or sooner) when digital TV channels will take over from analogue broadcasts and all the old products will simply be scrapped.

● *Overextension of product range which can only be resolved by withdrawing some products.* In television, some of the many channels now being offered may have such small audiences that they do not justify even the minimal expense of keeping them operating.

● *Holding company sales of subsidiaries.* Such companies often see their subsidiary companies, perhaps in diverse industries, as being little more than assets to be bought and sold if the price is attractive. US TV companies regularly sell local TV stations and withdraw from that market for reasons associated with finance, ability to link with other stations, change of corporate objectives, etc.

● *Raise funds for investment elsewhere.* Organisations may be able to *sell* the asset they are planning to withdraw from the market. Even without a sale, the working capital and management time devoted to the asset might be redeployed to other more productive uses. Government-owned companies faced with restrictions on outside funds might regard withdrawal and sale as a useful strategy here.

13.3.2 Demerger

In a sense, this is a form of withdrawal from the market, but it has a rather specialist meaning with some attractive implications. For some companies whose shares are openly traded on the stock exchange, the value of the *underlying assets* may be rather larger than the value implied by the *share price*. For example, the UK-based chemical company ICI was split into two companies in 1993 by issuing two sets of shares to its existing shareholders. The shares of the two companies were then separately traded on the London Stock Exchange at a greater value than when they had been combined. The reason was that part of the company's product range was in basic and specialist chemicals. A separate part was in agrochemicals and pharmaceuticals, the latter being highly attractive to stockholders. ICI was *demerged*, with the first part keeping the name ICI and the second part taking the name Zeneca. Subsequently, other chemical companies – such as the major German chemical company Hoechst – have followed a similar strategy.

This strategy has been used increasingly to realise the underlying asset values in publicly quoted companies. It also has the benefit that companies with totally unrelated market activities allow each part to focus on its own activities without competing for scarce resources. It has the disadvantage that it may destroy the benefits of size, cross-trading and uniqueness of a larger company.

13.3.3 Privatisation

In many countries around the world, there has been a trend to privatise government-owned companies – that is, to sell the company's shares into private ownership. This has become a major option for some institutions. For example, many national telecommunications companies have now been privatised, except in the US, where they have always been in the private sector. The results in terms of management style, public accountability, ownership and strategy changes have been substantial. The changes in the product range, levels of service and public perceptions have also been significant.

13.3.4 Market penetration in the existing market

Without moving outside the organisation's current range of products or services, it may be possible to attract customers from directly competing products by penetrating the market. Market penetration strategy should begin[15] with *existing* customers. A direct attack on *competing* customers invites retaliation that can nullify the initial gains and erode the company's profit margins. Retaining an existing customer is usually cheaper, especially in consumer goods markets. Car companies such as Toyota and BMW make great efforts to retain customers when they change cars.

If a direct attack is to be mounted on a competitor in order to penetrate the market, it is likely to be more effective[16] if a *combination* of activities is mounted – for example, an improvement in product quality and levels of service along with promotional activity. Clearly, this is likely to be more expensive in the short term but should have benefits in the long run in terms of increased market share. News Corporation satellite operations regularly combine new TV channels with advertising and special deals on decoders as part of its strategy to penetrate the market.

Market penetration may be easier if the market is *growing*. The reason is that existing customer loyalties may be less secure and new customers entering the market may still be searching for the most acceptable product. The most attractive strategy in these circumstances will vary with the company's market share position:

- Existing companies with *low relative market share* in a growing market have little to lose from aggressively attacking the market or a segment of it. For example, the smaller Burger King (Grand Metropolitan, UK) has attacked McDonald's hard over the last few years with some success.

- Existing companies with a *high relative market share* in a growing market have potentially an attractive position which might be lost. Predatory price cutting is a strategy sometimes employed to keep out the smaller new entrants. It will work well and move the company down the experience curve, as long as it has the production capacity. This strategy has been employed by Intel to launch new-generation computer chips and hold off the smaller new entrants such as Cyrix and AMD (all US companies).

13.3.5 Market development using existing products

For this strategic route, the organisation moves beyond its immediate customer focus into attracting new customers for its existing product range. It may seek new *segments* of the market, new *geographical areas* or new *uses* for its products or services that will bring in new customers.

Expansion to bring totally new customers to the company for its existing products could easily involve some slight repackaging and then promotion to a new market segment. It will often involve selling the same product in new international markets – there are many examples of such a strategy throughout this book. Using core competencies and a little ingenuity, it may be possible to find new uses for existing products. For example, the pharmaceutical company Glaxo (UK) has sought to develop the markets for its anti-ulcer drug Zantac as markets have matured in Western Europe and North America. Thus it has marketed the product to an increasing range of countries and it has also developed a lower-strength version to be sold without prescription as a stomach remedy in place of antacid remedies.

We explore the methods by which organisations can undertake such expansion in the next section.

13.3.6 Product development for the existing market

We refer here to significant new product developments, not a minor variation on an existing product. There are a number of reasons that might justify such a strategy:[17]

- to utilise excess production capacity;
- to counter competitive entry;
- to exploit new technology;
- to maintain the company's stance as a product innovator;
- to protect overall market share.

Understanding the reason is key to selecting the route that product development will then follow. Probably the area with the most potential is that associated with innovation: it may represent a threat to an existing product line or an opportunity to take market share from competition. Sometimes product development strategies do not always fall neatly into an existing market. They often move the company into markets and towards customers that are not currently being served. This is part of the natural growth of many organisations.

13.3.7 Diversification: related markets

When an organisation diversifies, it moves out of its current products and markets into new areas. Clearly, this will involve a step into the unknown and will carry a higher degree of business risk. However, the organisation may minimise this risk if it moves into related markets. (*Related* here means a market that has some existing connection with its existing value chain.) It is usual to distinguish three types of relationship based on the value chain of Chapter 6 and explored in the section on corporate strategy in Chapter 12:

1 *Forward integration.* A manufacturer becomes involved in the activities of the organisation's *outputs* such as distribution, transport, logistics – for example, the purchase of glass distributors by Europe's two leading glass manufacturers, St Gobain (France) and Pilkington (UK).[18]

2 *Backward integration.* The organisation extends its activities to those of its *inputs* such as its suppliers of raw materials, plant and machinery – for example, the purchase by the oil company Elf (France) of oil drilling interests in the North Sea.[19]

3 *Horizontal integration.* The organisation moves into areas immediately related to its existing activities because either they compete or they are complementary – for example, the acquisition by BMW (Germany) of the UK car company Rover in 1994.

News Corporation has engaged in forward integration by purchasing cable and satellite channels to deliver TV programmes directly to customers. It has integrated backwards into film production companies. It has undertaken horizontal integration by extending the range of its activities from newspapers to books, TV and electronic media.

Synergy is the main reason given for such activities.[20] It means essentially that the whole is worth more than the sum of the parts: the value to be generated from owning and controlling more of the value chain is greater because the various elements support each other. This concept is relatively easy to understand but rather more difficult to analyse precisely. This means that it is difficult to assess its specific contribution to corporate strategy. It is related to the concept of *linkages* in the value chain that were explored in Chapter 6 and is probably best assessed using these concepts.

13.3.8 Diversification: unrelated markets

When an organisation moves into unrelated markets, it runs the risk of operating in areas where its detailed knowledge of the key factors for success is limited. Essentially, it acts as if it were a *holding company*. Some companies have operated such a strategy with success, probably the best known being Hanson plc (UK, but with strong interests in the US) and General Electric (US). The logic of such an expansion is unlikely to be market-related, by definition, since the target market has no connection with the organisation's current areas of interest. There are two reasons why the strategy may have some merit:

1 There could be other connections in finance with the existing business that would justify such expansion.

2 There may be no connection but the diversification could still be operated successfully if the holding company managed such a venture using tight but clear financial controls.

Clearly, such strategies are directly related to the discussion on strategic parenting in Chapter 12. However, it should be pointed out that unrelated diversification is not popular at present: it flies against the evidence and logic of the resource-based view.

Comment

The market options matrix is a useful way of structuring the options available. However, it does not in itself provide many useful indicators of which option to choose in what circumstances. Thus its value lies in *structuring* the problem rather than *solving it*. The main strategic insights come from the possibilities that it raises to challenge current thinking by opening up the debate.

Such routes may involve the expenditure of some funds on new product development, research, advertising and related matters. Hence, the options are more likely to be favoured by those organisations with significant financial resources. Many of the options are more likely to be considered by profitable companies, rather than those attempting to recover from substantial losses. However, by disposing of some assets, market-based options may actually raise funds and provide greater freedom of action for those remaining in the organisation. Typically, these might include the sale of parts of companies.

The market options matrix may be more appropriate in the commercial, non-government-owned sector because state companies are usually set up to fill a specific role with little room for development beyond this definition.

Key strategic principles

- By examining the market place and the products available, it is possible to structure options that organisations may be able to adopt: the overall structure is called the *market options matrix*.

- Options include moving to new customers and new products. As these are developed further, they may involve the organisation in diversifying away from its original markets.

- Synergy is the main reason behind diversification into related markets: the whole being more than the sum of the parts. This concept is associated with linkages in the value chain.

- The market options matrix is a method of generating options but provides no guidance on choosing between them. The main strategic insights come from the possibilities that it raises to challenge the current thinking by opening up the debate.

13.4 ENVIRONMENT-BASED STRATEGIC OPTIONS: THE EXPANSION METHOD MATRIX

Definition ➤ The expansion method matrix explores in a structured way the methods by which the market opportunities associated with strategy options might be achieved. By examining the organisation's internal and external expansion opportunities and its geographical spread of activity, it is possible to structure the various methods that are available.

In addition to exploring the routes to develop strategy options, it is also important to explore the methods by which these can be achieved. For example, launching a new product could be done using an existing company or an acquisition, merger or joint venture with another firm. As companies have moved outside their home countries, the methods used for such development have also increased. We have already seen how News Corporation has used a variety of contractual arrangements in different countries in the world to develop its global presence. The full list of options is set out in Figure 13.8.

13.4.1 Acquisitions

Probably the most important reason for this method of market expansion is that associated with the particular assets of the company: brands, market share, core competencies and special technologies may all represent reasons for purchase. News Corporation acquired its encryption technology by buying a company in 1990. The obvious disadvantage is that, if a company really has an asset, there may be a substantial premium to pay over the asset value of the company. For example, Nestlé paid double the value at which the shares of Rowntree had previously been quoted on the stock exchange when it bought the chocolate company in 1989.

Acquisitions may also be made for competitive reasons. In a static market, it may be expensive and slow to enter by building from the beginning. For example, in the slow-

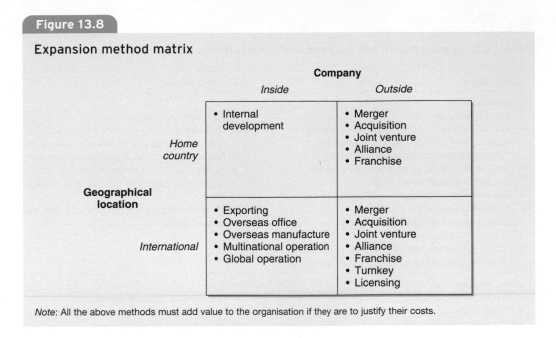

Figure 13.8

Expansion method matrix

Note: All the above methods must add value to the organisation if they are to justify their costs.

growing coffee market, Philip Morris/Kraft General Foods has made a series of company purchases to add to its Maxwell House brand: Café Hag and Jacobs Coffee. In fast-growing markets, acquisitions may be the means to acquire presence more rapidly. For example, the purchase of the Biogen Company by Roche (Switzerland) moved the Swiss company at a stroke from its traditional drugs market into the totally new area of biomedical sciences.

13.4.2 Mergers

Mergers are similar to acquisitions in the sense of two companies combining. However, mergers usually arise because neither company has the scale to acquire the other on its own. This has the potential benefit of being more friendly but requires special handling if the benefits are to be realised. In other respects, it is similar to an acquisition in terms of the main strategic issues.

13.4.3 Joint ventures and alliances

A *joint venture* is the formation of a company whose shares are owned jointly by two parent companies. It usually shares some of the assets and skills of both parents. Cereal Partners Inc. is a 50/50 joint venture between Nestlé and General Mills (US) whose purpose is to attack Kellogg's breakfast cereals around the world except in North America – *see* the case in Chapter 2.

An *alliance* is some form of weaker contractual agreement or even minority shareholding between two parent companies. It usually falls short of the formation of a separate subsidiary. Several of the European telecommunications companies have built alliances as the basis for international expansion.

13.4.4 Franchise

A franchise is a form of licensing agreement in which the contractor provides the licensee with a pre-formed package of activity. It may include a brand name, technical service expertise and some advertising assistance. Payment is usually a percentage of turnover. McDonald's Restaurants are among the best-known franchises.

The main advantages and disadvantages of the various methods of market expansion are summarised in Table 13.4.

Table 13.4

Methods of expansion: advantages and disadvantages

Advantages	Disadvantages
Acquisition	
• Can be relatively fast	• Premium paid: expensive
• May reduce competition from a rival, although such a move usually has to be sanctioned by government competition authorities	• High risk if wrong company targeted
	• Best targets may have already been acquired
• Cost savings from economies of scale or savings in shared overheads	• Not always easy to dispose of unwanted parts of company
• Maintenance of company exclusivity in technical expertise	• Human relations problems that can arise *after* the acquisition: probably the cause of more failures than any other
• Extend to new geographical area	
• Buy market size and share	• Problems of clash of national cultures, particularly where target 'foreign'
• Financial reasons associated with purchase of undervalued assets that may then be resold	
Joint venture	
• Builds scale quickly	• Control lost to some extent
• Obtains special expertise quickly	• Works best where both parties contribute something different to the mix
• Cheaper than acquisition	
• Can be used where outright acquisition not feasible	• Can be difficult to manage because of need to share and because parent companies may interfere
• Can be used where similar product available	• Share profits with partner
Alliance	
• Can build close contacts with partner	• Slow and plodding approach
• Uses joint expertise and commitment	• Needs constant work to keep relationship sound
• Allows potential partners to learn about each other	• Partners may only have a limited joint commitment to make alliance a success
• Locks out other competitors	• Unlikely to build economies of scale
Franchise	
• Lower investment than outright purchase	• Depends on quality of franchise
• Some of basic testing of business proposition undertaken by franchise holder: lower risk	• Part of profits paid over to franchise holder
• Exclusive territory usually granted	• Risk that business built and franchise withdrawn

Source: Adapted from Lynch, R (1994) *European Business Strategies*, 2nd edn, Kogan Page, London. © Richard Lynch 2000. All rights reserved.

13.4.5 International options

In spite of the publicity on some occasions across Europe, acquisitions are relatively infrequent outside the UK and North America.[21] They are also used sparingly in many countries of South-East Asia and in Japan. There are two main reasons: shares are more openly traded in Anglo-Saxon countries than in parts of Europe and Asia, where bank and government holdings are more important; and there is a stronger tradition in some countries of interlocking shareholdings that makes outright acquisition difficult, if not impossible.

Beyond this basic issue, the greater degree of global trading has made options that might have applied in a few Western countries now available around the world. There are two that have some importance for overseas operations:

1 *Turnkey*. A contractor who has total responsibility for building and possibly commissioning large-scale plant. Payment can take many forms.

2 *Licensing*. Technology or other assets are provided under licence from the home country. Payment is usually by royalty or some other percentage of turnover arrangement.

More generally, overseas expansion for many companies may take the form of the following sequence:[22]

- *Exporting* as a possible first expansion step.

- An *overseas office* may then be set up to provide a permanent presence.

- *Overseas manufacture* can take place, but this clearly increases the risk and exposure to international risks such as currency.

- *Multinational operations* may be set up to provide major international activity.

- *Global operations* may be introduced. The distinction from multinational operations lies in the degree of international commitment and, importantly, in the ability to source production and raw materials from the most favourable location anywhere in the world.

There are various risks and opportunities associated with all the above operations. Probably the most important of these is currency variation – that is, the difficulty of trading in currencies that are volatile and may cause significant and unexpected losses.

Comment

The expansion method matrix suffers from the same disadvantage as the previous matrix – i.e. it is useful at structuring the options but offers only limited guidance on choosing between them.

Key strategic principles

- The *expansion method matrix* explores in a structured way the methods by which market options might be achieved. By examining the organisation's internal and external expansion opportunities and its geographical spread of activity, it is possible to structure the various methods that are available.

- Within the home country, the four main methods of expansion are: acquisition, joint venture, alliance and franchise. Each has its advantages and problems.

- Beyond the home country, there are additional means of international expansion, including exporting, setting up overseas offices and undertaking full manufacturing. The most important risk associated with international expansion is probably currency fluctuation.

CASE STUDY 13.4

Building a global media company at News Corporation

From a small Australian/UK newspaper operation, News Corporation has been built into a global force in media over the last 20 years. This case outlines the strategies that have proved so successful, including those that challenge the conventional 'strategic options' approaches.

Company background: newspapers developed by risk taking and innovation

Over the last 20 years, News Corporation has been shaped by its chairman and chief executive, Rupert Murdoch. He had the reputation as a young man of being something of a rebel. However, he was born into a wealthy family and inherited his father's chain of newspapers in Australia at the age of 21. He then used these as the starting point for his ambitions.

Murdoch radically repositioned his Australian newspapers by taking some downmarket and others upmarket. Building on this success, he moved from Australia to the UK and acquired control of a similar range there during the 1960s and 1970s. The newspapers included the brash and breezy *Sun* and the prestigious *Times*. Murdoch had the reputation of being aggressive, plain speaking and a good judge of managers. He knew what he wanted and controlled the main elements of his

▶

Louie Psihoyos/Corbis

Rupert Murdoch has built News Corporation into a global media organisation over the last 30 years from his origins in Australia.

company with clarity and vision. He did not hesitate to plan and pick a fight with the UK print trade unions in the 1970s in order to break their power over the industry – he won and added to his reputation for ruthless efficiency. His companies were prepared to take risks and innovate in order to advance strategically, but they were still small by international standards and had no significant TV interests.

News Corporation: innovation in TV nearly brought down the company

In the 1980s, News Corporation was one of the earliest companies to see the potential for satellite broadcasting. By a series of bold moves in the UK, it launched a TV service 18 months ahead of the official government-sponsored rival. The early days were difficult, with the new venture being a major drain on cash across the group. At one stage in 1990, the whole News Corporation group was within hours of bankruptcy. Eventually, Murdoch's own and the rival channel were merged to form British Sky Broadcasting (BSkyB), in which News Corporation held a 50 per cent share (subsequently reduced to 35 per cent). When BSkyB was floated on the stock exchange in 1994, it had a valuation of US$8.7 billion.

In the late 1980s, Murdoch also identified the US as having major TV potential. His company acquired the film company Twentieth Century Fox in 1985. He then made a typically bold move and announced that he was going to build a fourth national US TV channel to rival the existing three networks, ABC, CBS and NBC. He used the Fox Studios as a base for four years of expansion by buying or setting up cable, satellite and terrestrial broadcast stations across the US. When it was pointed out to him that only US citizens could own TV stations

in the US, he renounced his Australian nationality and became a US citizen. The whole TV strategy had never been undertaken before and was highly innovative.

During the 1990s, News Corporation began building TV networks in the Far East. The company acquired Star TV in Hong Kong as a basis for expansion into China. It also acquired TV channels on several Far Eastern satellites in order to broadcast over much of Asia. By year 2004, News Corporation had built an international media group with a strong record of growth in both revenue and net profit – *see* Figure 13.9.

News Corporation: competition is fierce and well financed

In the rapidly changing global media market, it is difficult to keep track of competitors and their particular strengths. In every area of its operations, News Corporation faces aggressive rivals. This is partly because it is competing against North American companies where this is part of the culture. It has also arisen because of the world opportunities that leading companies have identified over the next five years: they all judge that now is the time to establish their positions and many have access to substantial funds. Major US and European companies like Viacom (US), Disney (US), Bertelsmann (Germany) and Mediaset (Italy) have put considerable competitive obstacles in the expansion path of News Corporation. Some governments also have made it difficult for the company to expand, mainly through insisting on some form of national media ownership.

News Corporation: its future vision and core resources

The key to understanding the News Corporation TV strategy is its vision of the future: 'Our evolution from primarily a newspaper publisher to an electronic media powerhouse' sums up the company's intentions. It also envisaged only four or five leading global TV companies by the end of the decade and News Corporation would be one of them.

Over the 20 years to 2005, the company had enhanced its core resources in the development and management of global TV operations. Specifically, these have included:

- entertainment and news-gathering skills coupled with TV production knowledge;
- an adequate library of entertainment programmes, though it was weaker in the Far East and Latin America and Africa. It was not really comparable to the library of the very large US companies such as Disney, Viacom (Paramount Films) and Time Warner (Warner Brothers Films);
- management skills to produce programmes on time and to budget;
- a range of satellite and cable channels for global coverage (explained below);
- the ability to negotiate useful deals with other broadcasters and owners of attractive media opportunities such as sport;
- skill in identifying revolutionary and imaginative new media opportunities;
- satellite encryption technology (explained below).

Figure 13.9

News Corporation's major business activities 2004

(a) Source of revenue 2004

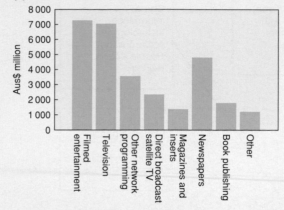

(b) Source of profit and loss 2004

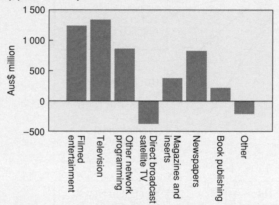

Note: The above data does not fully reflect the business interests of News Corporation: for example, the company has minority shareholdings in two satellite broadcasters, BskyB in the UK and Directv in the US, and the business activities of these two companies are therefore not included in the above figures. Nevertheless, News Corporation effectively controls these two companies.

Source: Annual Report and Accounts 2004.

Back in the late 1980s, News Corporation pioneered the development of satellite television delivery in the UK. Its breakthrough came when it secured exclusive rights to the broadcasting of the UK Premier Football (Soccer) League. It used this to drive the take-up of satellite TV in the UK, but did not stop with a single offering. It has become particularly skilled at gaining and maintaining its subscriber base through a variety of deals and incentives to its customers: 'The Sky marketing machine is awesome', according to the *Financial Times*. In addition, News Corporation pioneered the development of enhanced, digital set-top box technology in the early 2000s. It spent millions of pounds to exchange old technology

boxes for free. News Corporation now had a highly sophisticated, world-beating system for satellite broadcasting, which it was then determined to apply in North America.

In 2003, News Corporation finally acquired a controlling interest in the American satellite broadcaster, Directv. Rupert Murdoch commented after the acquisition, 'Directv is about changing the whole model of News Corp's output in the US.' By 2004, it was introducing the same technology to North America as it had developed in the UK. The website of Directv in 2005 showed the new interactive offerings that were being made to its American customers – www.directv.com. 'The nation's leading and fastest growing digital multichannel television service provider' was threatening to provide strong competition to the existing American and Canadian cable channels.

News Corporation was also the first company to identify satellite encryption technology as an important aspect of business strategy. The TV signal from its satellite channels is scrambled on broadcast and then decoded using a special machine and smart card in the individual home. Smart cards are purchased from News Corporation on a monthly or annual subscription. The company owns the exclusive world rights to the technology. By 1995 in developed world markets such as the UK and the US, News Corporation was receiving about five times more revenue from subscription to the smart cards than it was from advertising on its channels. However, News Corporation's encryption itself is not exclusive as a route to sustainable competitive advantage. Other forms of encryption exist. In addition, cable companies have a similar ability to control the signal that is delivered to individual homes. They do not need encryption but simply disconnect homes that do not pay.

News Corporation: corporate strategies are opportunistic, innovative and deal making

From a standing start in the mid-1980s, News Corporation has built one of the world's largest television networks. Many of its strategies are *negotiation-based* and derive from the rapid growth in world electronic media. In some respects, News Corporation's main strategy has been opportunistic. It has seized the market and technical opportunities that have emerged over the last few years. For example:

- the acquisition of Star TV was clearly dependent on the Chinese owners being willing to sell;
- the arrival of new satellite digital technology provided opportunities for enhanced services;
- the encryption technology relied on the availability of this technical development at that time.

News Corporation has also attempted to negotiate an interest in the major media around the world. In addition to the examples already discussed, another deal was attempted with the German TV companies controlled by the Kirch Gruppe. By 2002, the German group was in liquidation and News Corporation had lost over US$800 million on this deal – News Corporation accepted that risks had to be taken if new deals were to be obtained. However, the company was more

▶ CASE STUDY 13.4 continued

Figure 13.10

News Corporation: examples of joint ventures and alliances in 2004

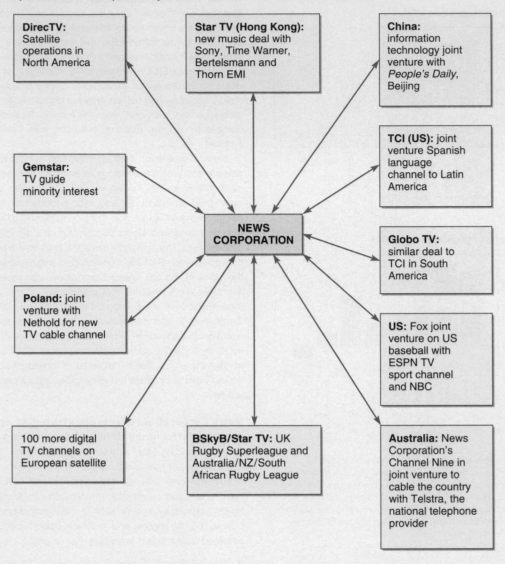

successful in Italy, where it acquired the television station TelePiu in 2002 and used this to become the monopoly supplier of Italian satellite pay-TV. However, the new Sky Italia was heavily loss-making and not expected to break even for some years.

News Corporation has itself identified four basic strategies underlying these emerging business opportunities:

1 *Vertical integration* from film making through to delivery of the electronic signal to the final customer. Thus it acquired the film company, Twentieth Century Fox, as well as having an interest in the satellite broadcaster BSkyB.

2 *Content creation*, not only through creative skills but also by negotiating exclusive new sports deals that buy up the media rights to world sporting events. For example, the company's deals for Southern Hemisphere Rugby, exclusive live coverage of Premier League football in the UK, and the US TV rights to American football were all dramatic ways to build a new, loyal audience. They delivered real sustainable competitive advantage to the company while the contract lasted.

3 *Globalisation* to give world coverage of electronic media. This is particularly important for news and sports events. It is less important for entertainment, which is more culture-

specific. For example, News Corporation announced in late 1995 that it would use its UK-based TV news channel to develop a world news network to rival CNN. There are competitive risks from such a strategy – *see* below.

4 *Convergence* of newspapers, books and TV so that they all support each other and promote each other's interests. For example, the cross-promotion of News Corporation's TV channels in the company's newspapers, which had a much wider audience in the early days, was an important contributor to their success.

In practice, News Corporation has also chosen to add two more strategies that are important in delivering competitive advantage:

1 *Digital satellite technology.* The company is a world-leader in this technology.
2 *Alliances and joint ventures.* To extend its global network, the company has entered into a number of deals with companies in individual countries or regions of the world – *see* Figure 13.10.

Finally, it should be noted that Rupert Murdoch himself did not believe in economies of scale in the industry: 'There may be diminishing returns to being bigger.' But this had not stopped both his company and his competitors' from growing even bigger.

Case questions

1 *Among the media companies, there is disagreement on the best route forward for corporate strategy: the software route versus the hardware route. Where does News Corporation stand in this debate? Do you judge that News Corporation has chosen the most successful long-term strategies?*

2 *How and where does News Corporation add value to its services? And where does it obtain its competitive advantage? What strategies has it adopted on barriers to entry?*

3 *In such a fast-changing market, is it possible to follow the prescriptive approach of options development and selection? Would News Corporation perhaps be better advised to have a general vision and then grab business opportunities as they arise?*

4 *Why has News Corporation been so successful? Where does it go from here?*

13.5 RESOURCE-BASED STRATEGIC OPTIONS: THE VALUE CHAIN[24]

From Penrose[25] to Hamel and Prahalad[26] the development of strategy options based on resource considerations is reasonably well established. This section is concerned only with the *value chain*. The following two sections explore two other resource-based options.

Resource-based options are those that arise from the analysis of the organisation examined in Part 2. There was a period in the 1970s and 1980s when the focus shifted to environment-based opportunities (these were explored earlier in this chapter), but the resource-based approach has now regained its deserved role as a means of generating options. It is particularly relevant when market opportunities are limited, either because the market is only growing slowly or because the organisation itself has very limited resources. For example, public sector organisations with limitations placed on their resources by government may find that resource-based options provide more scope than environment-based opportunities.

13.5.1 Identifying sources of value added: upstream and downstream

Value can be added early in the value chain, i.e. *upstream*, and later in the value chain, i.e. *downstream*. Examining where and how value can be added by the resources of the organisation will generate strategic options.

● *Upstream* activities are those that add value early in the value chain. Such activities might include procurement of raw materials and the production processes. To add value here, it is useful to buy in bulk and make few changes to the production process, thus keeping costs low and throughput constant. This is assisted if the organisation produces

Figure 13.11

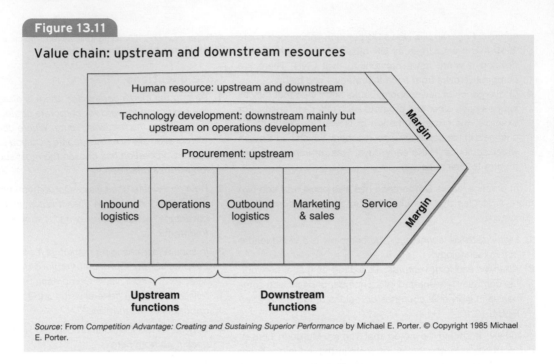

Value chain: upstream and downstream resources

Source: From *Competition Advantage: Creating and Sustaining Superior Performance* by Michael E. Porter. © Copyright 1985 Michael E. Porter.

standardised items. Upstream value is added by low-cost efficient production processes and process innovations, such as those described in Chapter 11. Value is also added by the efficient purchase of raw materials and other forms of procurement.

● *Downstream* activities are those that add value later in the value chain. These activities may rely on *differentiated* products for which higher prices can be charged. Such product variations may mean stopping the production line and making changes, which incurs extra costs. The resources may also involve elements of advertising or specialised services to promote the differentiated items. Downstream value is also added by research and development, patenting, advertising and market positioning.

The value chain can itself be associated with upstream and downstream activities – *see* Figure 13.11.

Table 13.5

The location of the main source of value added in different single-product industries

Main resources	Examples of industries	Location: primarily upstream or downstream?
Raw material extraction	Coal, oil, iron ore	Upstream
Primary manufacture to produce standardised output	Paper and pulp, iron and steel, basic chemicals	Upstream
Fabrication of primary manufacture	Paper cartons, steel piping, simple plastics	Upstream
Further added value through more complex manufacture, patents and special processes	Branded packaging, cars, specialist plastic products	Downstream
Marketing and advertising	Branded products	Downstream

Possible resource options associated with upstream and downstream activities

Upstream resource options might include:

● Increased standardisation of products

● Investment to lower the costs of production

● Operations innovation to lower the costs of production or improve the quality

● Capital investments that add value

● Seeking many customers from a wide range of industries that require a common product without variation.

Downstream resource options might include:

● Varied products targeted at particular market segments

● R&D and product innovation to add more value

● Advertising investment and branding

● New increased services to add value.

Many organisations are, of course, involved in adding value both upstream and downstream. For example, News Corporation would clearly have resources in the downstream part because its magazines and books are targeted at specific groups of customers. However, it would also use largely undifferentiated newspaper and printing inks to produce its products, which would be located upstream.

Nevertheless, some organisations are *primarily* located either upstream or downstream. Some examples for different industries engaged in one main business are shown in Table 13.5.

13.5.2 Resource implications of upstream and downstream value added

Using the concept of upstream and downstream value added, it is possible to develop resource options. For example, if *standard* products are required, then economies of scale may be possible. Other resource options that might produce standardised products more cheaply will also deserve investigation – the upstream activities of Exhibit 13.1.

For *differentiated* products that are carefully targeted at niche markets, it will be necessary to promote them carefully, with resources based on downstream activity. The resource options more likely to be associated with downstream activities are also shown in Exhibit 13.1.

Key strategic principles

● Resource options can be developed by considering the value chain of the organisation. This is particularly important because the chain will help to identify competitive advantage.

● Value can be added early in the value chain, *upstream*, or later in the value chain, *downstream*. Examining where and how value can be added will generate strategic resource options.

● Upstream activities add value by processing raw materials into standardised products. Resource options concentrate on lower costs.

● Downstream activities use intermediate products to manufacture differentiated items targeted at specific customer needs. Resource options focus on R&D and marketing areas.

13.6 RESOURCE-BASED STRATEGIC OPTIONS: THE RESOURCE-BASED VIEW

As explored in Chapter 6, resource-based strategies need to consider the opportunities presented by the resource-based view. The identification of those resources that are particularly important in delivering sustainable competitive advantage will represent an important starting point in the development of strategic options – for example, the brands of the organisation, its special and unique locations, its patents and its technologies. New resources might also be licensed from other companies or obtained through acquisition.[27]

13.6.1 Finding resource-based options: architecture, reputation and innovation

Essentially the resource-based view argues that organisations need some form of *distinctiveness* over competitors. In seeking out options, one method would be to test our resources against the criteria of architecture, reputation and innovation.[28] This would focus the process in terms of both current resources and those needed for the future. For example, using these three concepts, we can specify the ways in which News Corporation has been developing in this area:

● The network of relationships and contracts both within and around the organisation: the *architecture*. News Corporation has built a range of companies that are all focused in the areas of news, sport and entertainment. They make the company quite distinctive from Disney or Time Warner. This is clearly an asset that the company has developed.

● The favourable impression that News Corporation has generated with its customers: *reputation*. Again, News Corporation has developed a clear image in this area, based on its newspapers in particular. Its aggressive, open and iconoclastic style has set it apart from its rivals. This is clearly an asset of the organisation.

● The organisation's capacity to develop new products or services: *innovation*. Several examples of the innovative ability of News Corporation are recorded in Case study 13.4. This may well cover core competencies as well as resource assets at the company.

13.6.2 Finding resource-based options – core competencies

Core competencies are defined as a group of skills and technologies that enable an organisation to provide a particular benefit to customers.[29] We explored them in Chapter 6 and can use them again here to guide the development of strategy options. Options that do not address core competencies are less likely to contribute to strategy than those that do. This suggests that a careful exploration of core competencies in the context of strategy development is desirable. (Readers are referred to the earlier chapter for an exploration of this area.)

One way of generating options based on core competencies is to consider them as a *hierarchy of competencies*, starting with low-level individual skills and rising through the organisation to higher-level combined knowledge and skills. The basic assumption behind such an approach is that some competencies are formed from the integration of more specialised competencies.[30] Exhibit 13.2 shows the basic hierarchy of competencies, which might be used to identify and structure new areas.

13.6.3 Strategic options based on the resource-based view

Beyond the two areas outlined above, there are no detailed structures to conduct such an examination because every organisation is different. It will be necessary to survey each of the functional areas of the organisation for their resources. The aim of such an exercise is to explore those areas for their contribution to value added and competitive advantage.

Exhibit 13.2

The hierarchy of competencies

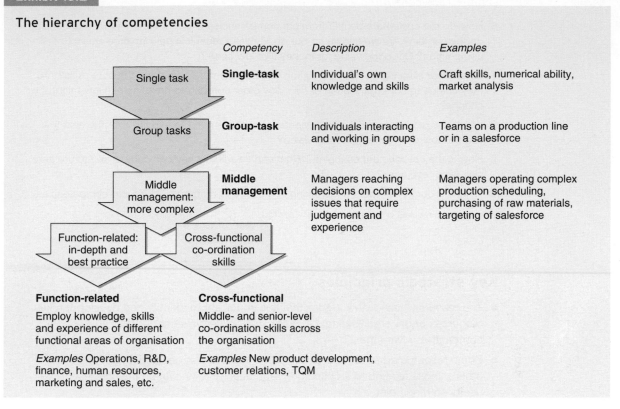

	Competency	Description	Examples
Single task	**Single-task**	Individual's own knowledge and skills	Craft skills, numerical ability, market analysis
Group tasks	**Group-task**	Individuals interacting and working in groups	Teams on a production line or in a salesforce
Middle management: more complex	**Middle management**	Managers reaching decisions on complex issues that require judgement and experience	Managers operating complex production scheduling, purchasing of raw materials, targeting of salesforce

Function-related: in-depth and best practice

Cross-functional co-ordination skills

Function-related

Employ knowledge, skills and experience of different functional areas of organisation

Examples Operations, R&D, finance, human resources, marketing and sales, etc.

Cross-functional

Middle- and senior-level co-ordination skills across the organisation

Examples New product development, customer relations, TQM

The checklist presented in Exhibit 13.3 has been prepared to assist the search for key resource options. However, such a list is not without its strategic dangers – readers are referred to the comments on SWOT analysis at the beginning of the chapter for a discussion. Moreover, a mechanistic combination of resources would miss the important issue that unique resources may derive from the *tacit knowledge* of the organisation. Such knowledge is unlikely to be discovered by a checklist.[31]

Exhibit 13.3

Ten guidelines for the options based on the resource-based view

1 What *technology* do we have? Is it exclusive? Is it at least as good as the competition? Is it better?

2 What *links* are there between the products that we manufacture or services that we operate? What common ground is there?

3 How do we generate *value added*? Is there anything different from our competitors? Looking at the main areas, what skills are involved in adding value?

4 What *people skills* do we have? How important is their contribution to our competencies? How vital are they to our resources? Are there any key workers? How difficult would they be to replace? Do we have any special values? What is our geographical spread?

5 What *financial resources* do we have? Are they sufficient to fulfil our vision? What is our profit record (or financial record in not-for-profit organisations)? Is the record sufficiently good to raise new funds? Do we have new funding arrangements, tax issues or currency matters?

Exhibit 13.3 *continued*

6 How do our *customers* benefit from our competencies and resources? What real benefits do they obtain? Are we known for our quality? Our technical performance against competition? Our good value for money (*not* low cost)?

7 What *other skills* do we have in relation to our customers? What are the core skills? Are they unique to our organisation or do many other companies have them? How might they change?

8 What *new resources*, *skills and competencies* do we need to acquire over the next few years? How do they relate to our vision?

9 How is the *environment* changing? What impact will this have on current and future core skills and resources?

10 What are our *competitors* undertaking in the area of resources, skills and competencies?

Note: Caution is required in using this checklist – *see* text.

Key strategic principles

- The resource-based view argues that it is important to identify and develop the key resources of the organisation, i.e. those that deliver value added and sustainable competitive advantage.

- Some resource areas are more likely to be important in developing options than others; those relating to architecture, reputation and innovation may represent one useful starting point.

- Core competencies explore options deriving from such areas as the basic skills, knowledge and technology of the organisation. They may also represent a way of structuring new strategic options in an organisation. A hierarchy of competencies can be built to explore the potential for new options.

- Because such resources are unique to each organisation, it is not possible to develop a general formula that will generate new options. However, a general checklist of some key areas can be developed, though caution is required in using it.

13.7 RESOURCE-BASED STRATEGIC OPTIONS: COST REDUCTION

Strategic options are not only concerned with expansion into new resource capabilities and core competencies. The organisation may also need to consider cutting back its current operations in order to reduce costs. Given the increasingly global nature of competition in some markets, it is quite possible that low-wage-settlement countries such as Thailand, Malaysia and the Philippines will provide real competition. This will mean that companies are unable to survive in Western countries unless they can cut costs drastically (e.g. *see* the Fila example in Section 9.2.3). Cost reduction strategy options therefore need to be considered. The main routes to cost reduction are:

1 *Designing in cost reduction*. In some industries, large cost reductions come not from activity in the production plant, but *before* the product ever reaches the factory. By carefully designing the product – for instance, so that it has fewer parts or is simpler to manufacture – real reductions in costs can be achieved.

2 *Supplier relationships*. If a supplier is willing and able to maintain quality and reduce costs, then the organisation will achieve a cost reduction.

3 *Economies of scale and scope*. For a large plant, unit costs may fall as the size of the plant increases. It may also be possible for different products to share some functional costs.

4 *The experience curve*. As a company becomes more experienced at production, it may be able to reduce its costs.

5 *Capacity utilisation*. Where plant has a high fixed cost, there may be cost reductions to be obtained by running production as close to capacity as possible.

The first two areas deserve detailed consideration and are explored under the subject of operations (production) in Chapter 9. They are headlined here because it is important to have a comprehensive view of the options available and these two areas can be major contributors to the process. The discussion here is therefore confined to the last three areas.

13.7.1 Economies of scale and scope

Definition ➤ Economies of scale are the extra cost savings that occur when higher volume production allows unit costs to be reduced. When it is possible to perform an operation more efficiently or differently at large volumes, then the increased efficiency may result in lower costs. Economies of scale can lead to lower costs – for example, in major petrochemical plants and in pulp and paper production.

Economies of scale need to be distinguished from capacity utilisation of plant. In the latter case, costs fall as the plant reaches capacity but would not fall any further if an even larger plant were to be built. With economies of scale, the larger plant would lead to a further cost reduction.

Definition ➤ Economies of scope are the extra cost savings that are available as a result of separate products sharing some facilities. An example might be those products that share the same retail outlets and can be delivered by the same transport.

Economies of scale are also available in areas outside production. They may occur in areas such as:

● *Research and development*. On some occasions, only a large-scale operation can justify special services or items of testing equipment.

● *Marketing*. Really large companies are able to aggregate separate advertising budgets into one massive fund and negotiate extra media discounts that are simply not available to smaller companies.

● *Distribution*. Loads can be grouped and selected to maximise the use of carrying capacity on transport vehicles travelling between fixed destinations.

In the analysis of resources, economies of scale are a relevant area for analysis. It is important to make an assessment for at least one leading competitor if possible. Factors to search for will include not only size of plant, but also age and efficiency of equipment.

Although writers such as Porter[32] are clear about the basic benefits of economies of scale and scope, real doubts have been expressed about the true reductions in costs to be derived from them – *see* for example, Kay.[33] The doubts centre on the argument that larger plant will have lower costs. When Henry Ford built his massive new Baton Rouge car plant in the 1930s, he was driven by this view. In practice, he encountered a number of problems.[34] They included:

● *Machine-related issues* – the increased complexity and inflexibility of very large plant

● *Human-related issues* – the increasingly depersonalised and mechanistic nature of work in such plant, which made it less attractive or interesting for workers to perform to their best ability.

Although there were other management problems associated with the relative failure of this plant, some of the major reasons lay in the above areas. In the 1990s, large-scale steel plant was held up as providing lower costs, but new technologies have now allowed much smaller-scale operations to make the same profits.

The competitive advantage of large plant is lost if the market breaks into segments that are better served by higher-cost plants that produce variations on the basic item which more directly meet customers' needs. Car markets and consumer electronics markets are examples where, respectively, four-wheel-drive vehicles and specialist hi-fi systems are not the cheapest in terms of production but meet real customer demand.

The conclusion has to be that economies of scale have their place but are only part of a broader drive for competitive advantage.

13.7.2 Using the experience curve effect

Definition ➤ The experience curve is the relationship between the unit costs of a product and the total units *ever produced* of that product, plotted in graphical form, with the units being cumulative from the first day of production.

In the 1960s, a large number of unrelated industries were surveyed in terms of their costs and the cumulative production *ever achieved*: it is important to understand that this is cumulative production ever achieved, not just the production in one year. It was shown that an empirical relationship could be drawn between a cost reduction and cumulative output. Moreover, this relationship appeared to hold over a number of industries, from insurance to steel production. It appeared to show dramatic reductions in costs: typically, costs fall by 15 per cent every time overall output doubles. It is shown in Figure 13.12. The relationship was explained by suggesting that, in addition to economies of scale, there were other cost savings to be gained – for example through:

● technical progress;
● greater learning about the processes;
● greater skills from having undertaken the process over time.

The cost experience concept can be seen at both the *company* level and the *industry* level.

● At the company level, the market leader will, by definition, have produced cumulatively more product than any other company. The leader should have the lowest costs and other companies should be at a disadvantage.

● At the industry level, costs should fall as the industry overall produces more. Every company should benefit from knowledge that is circulated within its industries.

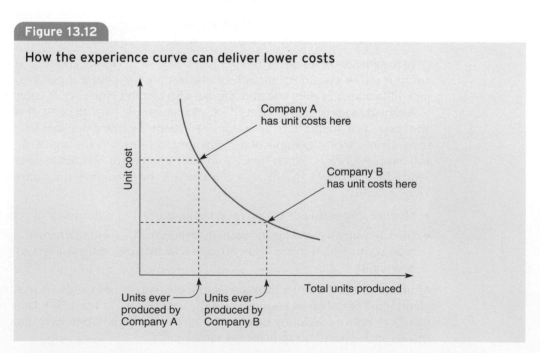

Figure 13.12

How the experience curve can deliver lower costs

When comparisons are drawn across different and unrelated industries, the similarities in the cost-curve relationship are remarkable for industries as far apart as aircraft manufacture and chicken broiler production. But there are few, if any, broad lessons for corporate strategy. As Kay points out,[35] the only similarity between aircraft and chickens is that they both have wings. There may be an *apparent relationship* in that the cost-curves look similar, but the *causes* are entirely different. Hence, the strategy implications are entirely different. Aircraft production is essentially global – *see* Case study 5.3. Chicken production relies largely on national markets and requires somewhat less sophisticated technology and totally different forms of investment from aircraft manufacture and assembly. It is essential to consider the concept of experience curves *within an industry* only.

Even within an industry, there are ways of overcoming experience curve effects, the most obvious being by new technology. Another way would be to entice an employee of a more experienced company to join the organisation. As Abernathy and Wayne[36] point out, there are real limits to the benefits of the experience curve:

● Market demand in market segments for a special product change or variation cannot easily be met: to achieve scale, production flexibility may have to be sacrificed.

● Technical innovation can overtake learning in a more fundamental way: a new invention may radically alter the cost profile of an existing operation.

● Demand needs to double for every significant proportionate cost reduction. In markets where growth is still present but slowing down, this is only possible if an ever-larger market share is obtained. As market share becomes larger, this becomes progressively more difficult and expensive to achieve. In a static market where a company already has 51 per cent market share, this becomes logically impossible.

Within a defined market, the experience curve may suggest a significant route to cost reduction, but it is not always a key source of cost advantage.

13.7.3 Capacity utilisation

Definition ➤ Capacity utilisation is the level of plant in operation at any time, usually expressed as a percentage of total production capacity of that plant. In the European iron and steel industry discussed in Chapter 3, we saw an example of the cost benefits to be gained by full utilisation of plant capacity. But we also saw how companies cut their prices as they scrambled to fill their plant, thus reducing their profit margins. High-capacity utilisation is useful but relies on competitors allowing such activity to take place, which may weaken its effect.

13.7.4 Structured process to achieve cost reduction options

We explored the basic issue of cost reduction above. However, Ohmae has suggested a model which structures this process in a logical and cross-functional way. It deserves to be examined for its implications in this area, and is shown in Figure 13.13. Overall, the model does not pretend to be comprehensive but rather to show the options that are possible, their logical flow and the interconnections between the various elements. For example, News Corporation over the last five years has emphasised the need to cut costs in order to remain competitive. It has introduced various programmes to achieve this.

> **Key strategic principles**
>
> ● There are *at least* six routes to cost reduction: design, supplier relationships, economies of scale and scope, the experience curve, capacity utilisation and synergistic effects.
>
> ● Economies of scale and scope are generally seen to reduce costs and raise value added, but the lack of production flexibility and the depersonalised nature of the work may be significant drawbacks.

Key strategic principles *continued*

- The experience curve suggests that significant reductions in costs are achieved as companies and the whole industry produce more product. The cost reductions relate to the cumulative production ever achieved, not just in one year.
- Experience curve cost reductions arise from a whole series of sources. They need to be sought and do not just happen automatically.
- Comparisons of experience curves across industries have little meaning, if any, in terms of the strategy lessons to be drawn.
- Utilising existing plant capacity is an important consideration in cost reduction.
- In exploring cost-cutting options, it is possible to develop a model which examines this in a structured and cross-functional way.

Figure 13.13

Structured approach to cost reduction options

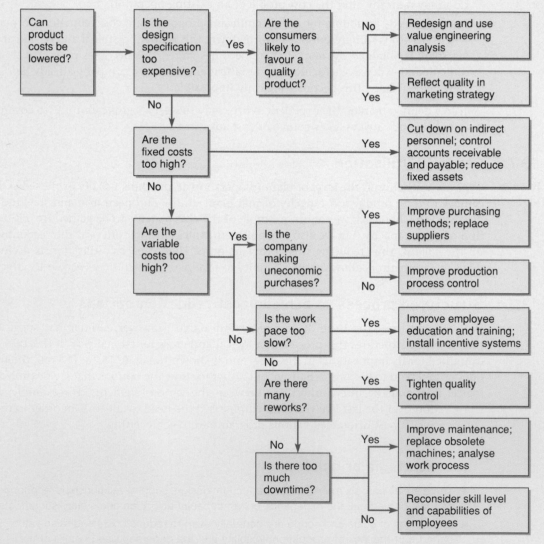

Source: Ohmae, K (1983) *The Mind of the Strategist*, McGraw-Hill, pp24–25.

© Copyright 1983 McGraw-Hill. Reproduced with the kind permission of the McGraw-Hill Publishing Company.

13.8 RESOURCE-BASED OPTIONS IN SOME SPECIAL TYPES OF ORGANISATION

In addition to a consideration of general resource options, some specific types of organisation present special opportunities and problems in terms of managing resources. It is useful to identify two situations:

1 small businesses

2 not-for-profit organisations.

13.8.1 Small business resources

By definition, small businesses are unlikely to contain the range of resources available to the larger companies. There will be fewer people, more limited finance and so on. The strategic issue is how to manage this special resource situation. There are three main methods:

1 *Employ outside advisers such as consultants.* This can be expensive but is probably appropriate where particular specialist skills are needed. Outside resources are hired temporarily.

2 *Concentrate resources on particular tasks that are more likely to yield added value and competitive advantage.* The problem here is that other areas of the organisation are inevitably neglected. Correct choice of the selected area is therefore vital. For these reasons, resources are often concentrated on a segment or niche of the market that is likely to bring long-term benefit. The limited resources are focused.

3 *Offer superior service.* This can be an area where smaller companies can win against larger competitors. By being unencumbered by the slow decision making of large companies, smaller organisations can react faster and more flexibly to customers. This may even justify slightly higher prices than the larger competitors. Resource strategies here may involve extra training and possibly even the hiring of extra service staff in some cases.

13.8.2 Resources in not-for-profit organisations

These vary from the small charitable organisation to large government-funded institutions. They need to be considered separately.

Charitable organisations

These have two unique areas of resource:

1 *Beliefs.* These drive the organisation forward in terms of the charitable purpose. This means that everyone is likely to be highly motivated. It is a real resource in terms of extra work that people are prepared to undertake on occasions.

2 *Voluntary workers.* These people can put exceptional effort into the enterprise and undertake major tasks. However, because of the voluntary nature, such a resource needs to be handled with care. People can become demotivated. Some need to be given a greater degree of freedom than would be appropriate in a commercial organisation.

Government-funded institutions

These often have highly professional resources but may be strongly bureaucratic. The culture of such organisations needs to be taken into account in devising resource options. Resources may be large and unwieldy and slow to respond to outside events.

Key strategic principles

- Some specific types of organisation present special opportunities and problems in the management of resources.

- Small businesses are unlikely to contain the range of resources of larger enterprises. However, this problem can be overcome by employing outside advisers and concentrating resources. More flexible service may provide a real competitive advantage.

- Charitable organisations benefit from exceptional resources: the beliefs that drive the society and the use of voluntary workers. However, they may need to give such people extra freedom to keep them motivated.

- Government institutions have highly professional resources but may be bureaucratic in their approach. Resources may be unwieldy and slow to respond to events.

CRITICAL REFLECTION

Is the strategic options process too comprehensive? Too lacking in creativity?

This chapter has focused on two main approaches to developing strategic options – one related to the strategic environment and the other related to strategic resources. Some strategists place particular emphasis on the environment – Porter's *generic strategies*, for example – while others place more importance on resources – Hamel and Prahalad's *core competencies*, for example. More generally, the chapter reviews a whole range of other approaches under these two general headings.

While such an approach clearly has merit in that it is comprehensive, some strategists would regard this as a significant weakness. They argue the whole concept is too rigid, too wide-ranging in considering all possible options. They suggest that its very comprehensive nature makes it difficult to identify what is really important. In this sense, it is unhelpful to the company. Moreover, the generation of options may become a rigid exercise that lacks the real creativity to deliver new ideas.

What is your view? Is the strategic options process too comprehensive and lacking in creativity?

SUMMARY

- In the prescriptive strategy process, the development of strategic options is an important part of the strategic process. Essentially, it explores the issue of what options are available to the organisation to meet its defined purpose. Although rational techniques are usually employed to develop the options, there is a need in practice to consider generating creative options from many sources. This chapter has concentrated on the more rational techniques because they are more suited to analysis and development.

- There are two main routes to options development: market-based and resource-based approaches. These correspond to the analytical structure of the earlier part of the text. Within the market-based approach, there are three main routes: generic strategies, market options and expansion methods. Each of these can usefully be considered in turn.

● According to Professor Michael Porter, there are only three fundamental strategic options available to any organisation – he called them generic strategies. The three options are:

1 *cost leadership*, which aims to place the organisation amongst the lowest-cost producers in the market;

2 *differentiation*, which is aimed at developing and targeting a product that is different in some significant way from its competitors in the market place;

3 *focus*, which involves targeting a small segment of the market. It may operate by using a low-cost focus or differentiated focus approach.

According to the theory, it is important to select between the options and not to be 'stuck in the middle'. Some influential strategists have produced evidence that has cast doubt on this point. There have been numerous criticisms of the approach based on logic and empirical evidence of actual industry practice. Undoubtedly, these comments have validity, but generic strategies may represent a useful starting point in developing strategy options.

● By examining the market place and the products available, it is possible to structure options that may be possible for organisations to adopt: the overall structure is called the *market options matrix*. The matrix represents a method of generating options but provides no guidance on choosing between them. The main strategic insights come from the possibilities that it raises to challenge the current thinking by opening up the debate.

● The *expansion method matrix* explores in a structured way the methods by which market options might be achieved. By examining the organisation's internal and external expansion opportunities and its geographical spread of activity, it is possible to structure the various methods that are available.

● In addition to the market-based options, there is a range of options based on the resources of the organisation. There are three main approaches to the development of such options: the value chain, the resource-based view and cost reduction. Each of these approaches may be useful in options development.

1 Value can be added early in the value chain, *upstream*, or later in the value chain, *downstream*. Upstream activities add value by processing raw materials into standardised products. Downstream strategies concentrate on differentiated products, targeted towards specific market segments.

2 The resource-based view argues that each organisation is unique in terms of its resources. This means that there can be no formula that will identify the strategic options. However, the criteria developed by Kay – architecture, reputation and innovation – may provide some guidance. In addition, Hamel and Prahalad's core competencies may also provide some strategic options. A hierarchy of competencies may be developed to identify and develop new competencies in the organisation.

3 Cost reduction options also deserve to be explored. Opportunities exist in many organisations to reduce the costs incurred by the resources of the organisation. There are five main opportunity areas for cost reduction: designing in cost reductions, supplier relationships, economies of scale and scope, the experience curve and capacity utilisation.

● Some specific types of organisation need special consideration in the development of options:

1 *Small businesses* are unlikely to contain the range of resources of larger enterprises. However, this problem can be overcome by employing outside advisers and concentrating resources. More flexible service may provide a real competitive advantage.

2 *Charitable organisations* benefit from exceptional resources: the beliefs that drive the society and the use of voluntary workers. However, they may need to give such people extra freedom to keep them motivated.

3 *Government institutions* have highly professional resources but may be bureaucratic in their approach. Resources may be unwieldy and slow to respond to events.

QUESTIONS

1 Do small firms have anything useful to learn from a consideration of the options available from generic strategies?

2 Plot the position of News Corporation on the generic strategies matrix. What conclusions, if any, can you draw from this about future strategies for the company? (Note the hint in the 'if any' phrase.)

3 *'Generic strategies are a fallacy. The best firms are striving all the time to reconcile opposites.'* (Professors Charles Baden-Fuller and John Stopford)

Discuss.

4 Take an organisation with which you are familiar, such as a small voluntary group, and consider the possibilities of expansion: apply the market options matrix and expansion method matrix to your choice. What conclusions can you draw about future expansion strategy?

5 *'A recurring theme to criticisms of strategic planning practice is the pedestrian quality of the strategic options that are considered.'* (Professor George Day)

By what methods might this legitimate concern be overcome, if at all?

6 Choose an organisation with which you are familiar and identify the upstream and downstream parts of the value chain for that organisation. Which is the most important for that organisation or do they contribute equally?

7 Identify the probable key competitive resources of the following: a charity like UNICEF; a major consumer electronics company; a holiday travel tour operator; a multinational fast-moving consumer goods company.

8 *'During the 1990s, top executives will be judged on their ability to identify, cultivate and exploit the core competencies that make growth possible.'* (Professors Gary Hamel and C K Prahalad)

Discuss whether this is still relevant in the twenty-first century. Was it appropriate in the last century?

9 If key competitive resources are important, can they be acquired in the space of a few months or do they take years to develop? What are the implications of your response for the development of competitive advantage?

10 Take a small student society or charitable institution with which you are familiar. What strategic options based on its resources does it have for development?

11 It has been argued in this chapter that small businesses can develop competitive advantage over larger companies by offering higher degrees of service. What are the possible problems with this approach?

Further reading

The two books that need to be read on environment-based options are Porter, M E (1980) *Competitive Strategy*, The Free Press, New York, and Porter, M E (1985) *Competitive Advantage*, The Free Press, New York. It should be noted that they also provide a much broader view of strategy than this single topic.

The market options matrix and expansion method matrix are covered in many marketing texts in a more limited form. Professor George Day's book is probably the best at providing a breadth of viewpoint beyond the marketing function: Day, G S (1984) *Strategic Marketing Planning*, West Publishing, St Paul, MN.

On distinctive capabilities, the book by Professor John Kay represents an important, well-referenced text on the topic: Kay, J (1993) *Foundations of Corporate Success*, Oxford University Press, Oxford.

On core competencies, you should read Hamel, G and Prahalad, C K (1994) *Competing for the Future*, Harvard Business School Press, Boston, MA. *See* also by the same authors, 'The core competence of the corporation', *Harvard Business Review*, May–June, 1990.

Notes and references

1 Many of the popular texts take this approach.
2 References for the Walt Disney Company case: Annual Report and Accounts 2004. Available at http://corporate.disney.co.com. *Financial Times*: 28 October 1998, p26; 3 November 1999, pp14, 35; 16 March 2002, p18; 2 August 2003, pM4; 9 October 2003, p16; 30 October 2003, p14; 29 April 2004, pp21, 27; 21 January 2005, p18; 27 January 2005, p30; 19 February 2005, pM6. BBC

News Website – 15 March 2005 – 'How Mickey Mouse made Disney a giant.'

3 Andrews, K (1987) *The Concept of Corporate Strategy*, Irwin, Homewood, IL.

4 Whittington, R (1993) *What is Strategy and Does it Matter?*, Routledge, London, pp73–4.

5 Bain, J (1956) *Barriers to New Competition: Their Character and Consequences in Manufacturing Industries*, Harvard University Press, Cambridge, MA.

6 Porter, M E (1980) *Competitive Strategy*, The Free Press, New York.

7 Porter, M E (1985) *Competitive Advantage*, The Free Press, New York.

8 Kay, J (1993) *Foundations of Corporate Success*, Oxford University Press, Oxford, Ch1.

9 Stopford, J and Baden-Fuller, C (1992) *Rejuvenating the Mature Business*, Routledge, London.

10 Miller, D (1992) 'The generic strategy trap', *Journal of Business Strategy*, 13(1), pp37–42.

11 Hendry, J (1990) 'The problem with Porter's generic strategies', *European Management Journal*, Dec, pp443–50.

12 References for global ice cream case: *see* data sources for Cases 4.1 and 4.4.

13 Porter, M E (1996) 'What is strategy?', *Harvard Business Review*, Nov–Dec, pp61–78.

14 References for Case study 13.3: *Financial Times*, 16 Feb 1994, p32; 20 Feb 1995, p16; 28 Mar 1995, p21; 21 Apr 1995, p27; 1 Aug 1995, p17; 3 Aug 1995, p19; 31 Aug 1995, p11; 11 January 2000, p1; 7 October 2000, p18; 8 January 2001, p31;17 January 2002, p19; 28 March 2002, p25; 27 April 2002, p10; 30 July 2002, pp14, 22; 16 September 2002, p30; 12 April 2003, p26; 30 April 2003, p19; 15 May 2003, p16; 6 June 2003, p31; 3 July 2003, p27; 8 July 2003, p10 Creative Business Supplement; 6 September 2003, p13; 9 October 2003, p34; 11 December 2003, p23; 14 February 2004, p13; 23 April 2004, p28; 2 June 2004, p30; 30 November 2004, p17; 11 January 2005, p26; *Sunday Times* (UK), 6 Aug 1995, p2.3.; News Corporation Annual Report and Accounts for 1995 and 1997. The direct quote comes from the 1995 document.

15 Day, G S (1987) *Strategic Market Planning*, West Publishing, St Paul, MN, p104.

16 Buzzell, R and Wiersema, F (1981) 'Successful share-building strategies', *Harvard Business Review*, Jan–Feb, pp135–44.

17 Kuczmarski, T and Silver, S (1982) 'Strategy: the key to successful product development', *Management Review*, July, pp26–40.

18 Lynch, R (1994) *European Business Strategies*, 2nd edn, Kogan Page, London, p208.

19 Lynch, R (1993) *Cases in European Marketing*, Kogan Page, London, p31.

20 Synergy is explored in Ansoff, I (1989) *Corporate Strategy*, rev. edn, Penguin, Harmondsworth, Ch1, p22.

21 Kay, J (1993) Op. cit., p146.

22 More information on international expansion is available in Lynch, R (1992) *European Marketing*, Kogan Page, London, Ch8.

23 References for Case study 13.4: News Corporation Annual Report and Accounts 2004 plus webcast for financial analysts all available on the web: www.newscorp.com There are hundreds of articles on this company so the following list reflects only some of the sources used to develop the case. *Financial Times*, 4 Sept 1993, p6; 5 Mar 1994, p11; 3 Aug 1994, p22; 10 Aug 1994, p14; 6 Jan 1995, p15; 24 Jan 1995, p23; 13 Feb 1995, p3; 14 Feb 1995, p25; 3 Apr 1995, p13; 7 Apr 1995, p1; 11 Apr 1995, p17; 27 May 1995, p8; 14 June 1995, p1; 18 June 1995, p9; 27 July 1995, p25; 2 Aug 1995, p15; 19 Aug 1995, p17; 30 Aug 1995, p15; 8 Nov 1995, p33; 30 Nov 1995, p8; 5 July 1999, p21; 16 January 2001, p24; 31 May 2001, p35; 19 March 2002, p18; 11 June 2002, p30; 2 October 2002, pp25, 30; 9 January 2003, p27; 12 February 2003, pp15, 23; 11 April 2003, p27; 12 April 2003, p5; 22 April 2003, p11 Creative Business Supplement; 20 May 2003, p9 Creative Business Supplement; 22 July 2003, p18; 25 August 2003, p25 (Star India restrictions); 8 November 2003, pM3; 7 April 2004, p24; 7 May 2004, p21; 19 May 2004, p20: 27 October 2004, p18; 4 November 2004, p30; 12 November 2004, p32; 25 January 2005, p28; 16 February 2005, p1; 18 February 2005, p25 (Company moving into new internet areas – not discussed in the case).

24 This section has benefited from the paper by Galbraith, J R (1983) 'Strategy and organisational planning', *Human Resource Management*, Spring–Summer, republished in Mintzberg, H and Quinn, J (1991) *The Strategy Process*, Prentice Hall, Englewood Cliffs, NJ, pp315–24. Galbraith's concept has been applied to the value chain, although he did not use this terminology.

25 Penrose, E (1959) *The Theory of the Growth of the Firm*, Oxford University Press, Oxford.

26 Hamel, G and Prahalad, C K (1994) *Competing for the Future*, Harvard Business School Press, Boston, MA, Ch1.

27 Stalk, G, Evans, P and Shulman, L (1992) 'Competing on capabilities', *Harvard Business Review*, April–May. Hamel and Prahalad make no reference to this paper and its criticism of core competencies in their book published in 1994. However, their letter to the *Harvard Business Review* in 1996 stated that they could see no essential difference between core competencies and core capabilities.

28 Kay, J (1993) Op. cit., p64.

29 Hamel, G and Prahalad, C K (1994) Op. cit., p221 and Ch10 that follows.

30 Grant, R M (1998) *Contemporary Strategy Analysis*, 3rd edn, Blackwell, Oxford, pp122–3. I am grateful to one of the reviewers of the second edition for suggesting this approach to options generation.

31 I am grateful to one of the reviewers of the second edition for making these important points.

32 Porter, M (1985) Op. cit., Ch3.

33 Kay, J (1993) Op. cit., pp170–5. It is difficult to convey fully the interesting data that Kay brings to this discussion in summary format in the text.

34 Abernathy, W and Wayne, K (1974) 'Limits of the learning curve', *Harvard Business Review*, Sept–Oct, p108.

35 Kay, J (1993) Op. cit., p116, where he reproduces the two charts.

36 Abernathy, W and Wayne, K (1974) Op. cit., p128.

Chapter 14

STRATEGY EVALUATION AND DEVELOPMENT: THE PRESCRIPTIVE PROCESS

Learning outcomes

After working through this chapter, you will be able to:

- distinguish between the content and the process of the prescriptive approach;
- identify the six main criteria that might typically be used to evaluate the content of strategic options;
- outline the main prescriptive procedures and techniques used in selecting between strategy options;
- undertake an evaluation of strategic options in order to select the most appropriate option;
- apply empirical evidence and guidelines to the various options in order to assist the selection procedure;
- describe the main elements of the classic prescriptive process for developing corporate strategy;
- comment on the weaknesses in the classic process and suggest how these might be overcome.

INTRODUCTION

After identifying the options available, classical prescriptive corporate strategy has always argued that the next strategy task is to select between them.[1] The selection procedure is the subject of this chapter. It follows on from the options development process explored in Chapter 13.

Strategy selection involves two aspects that should be clearly distinguished: content and process.

- By *content* is meant the actual strategy that is finally selected to meet the objectives of the organisation. Content is about *what* is in the plan.
- By *process* is meant identifying the managers and others who will contribute to the task and outlining the way in which they will communicate and discuss with each other to make the selection decision. Process explores such questions as *who* develops the plan, *how* they undertake the task and *where* they are located in the organisation.

The first part of the chapter is about content and the second about process.

To select strategy content, the chapter begins by exploring in Section 14.1 the main criteria that might be used. It then identifies in Section 14.2 the main procedures and techniques that might be employed in selection. Finally, to assist the process, it also outlines in Section 14.3 some general guidelines and empirical evidence that might suggest which options would work best.

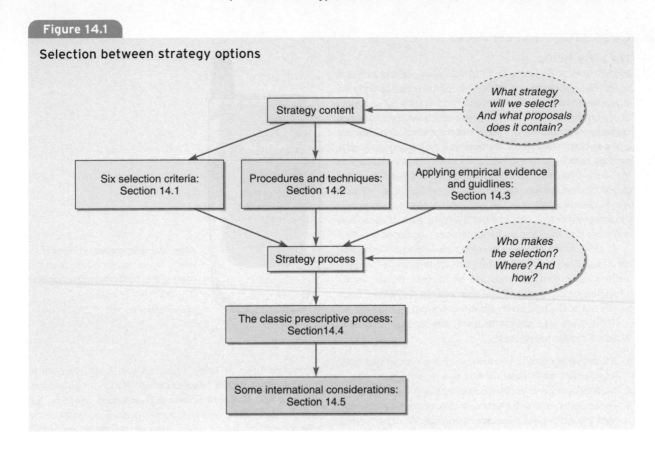

Figure 14.1

Selection between strategy options

To identify the strategy process, the classic prescriptive route is described in Section 14.4 and the main contributors and their responsibilities are identified. Finally, some international issues are explored in Section 14.5. In the next chapter, some alternative processes are presented and their implications examined.

Part 6b

In addition to the cases throughout the chapter, there is a longer case study at the end which sets out the various options available to a company and invites the reader to select one of them (or perhaps even reject all of them) using the techniques explored in the chapter. The structure of the chapter is shown in Figure 14.1.

CASE STUDY 14.1

Nokia – dialling global opportunities in mobile phones

Over the last 15 years, the Finnish company Nokia has built global leadership of the mobile telephone market. This case explores its strategic decision making and the risks that it now faces.

Background

In the late 1980s, the small Finnish company Nokia was involved in a wide range of businesses. For example, it made televisions and other consumer electronics in which it claimed to be 'third in Europe'. It also had a thriving business in industrial cables and machinery and manufactured a wide range of other goods from forestry logging equipment to tyres. It had been expanding fast since the 1960s and was beginning to struggle under the vast range of goods that it sold. Sadly, the group's chief executive at that time, Kari Kairamo, was so overwhelmed that he committed suicide. It is rare that strategic pressures are so intense but the impact on management of strategy evaluation and development is an important factor in generating stress.

▶

489

▶ **CASE STUDY 14.1 continued**

The early 1990s

In 1991 and 1992, Nokia lost FM482 million (US$120 million) on its major business activities. The company had to find new strategies to remedy this situation. It had already cut out some of its activities but was still left with a telephone manufacturing operation, an unprofitable TV and video manufacturing business and a strong industrial cables business. Nokia began the process by seeking a new group chief executive. Its choice was Mr Jorma Ollila, who had previous run the small Nokia mobile phone division, which was loss-making at the time. 'My brief was to decide whether to sell it or keep it. After four months, I proposed we keep it. We had good people, we had know-how and there was market growth opportunity', explained Mr Ollila.

In 1992, Nokia chose to develop two existing divisions that had related technologies: mobile telephone and telecommunications equipment (switches and exchanges). Subsequently, it focused mainly on the mobile business but did not pull completely out of the telecommunications equipment market.

There were four criteria to justify the strategic choice to focus on mobile telephones:

After dramatic growth in recent years, Nokia has faced problems in making the best strategic choice for continued growth.

Copyright © Nokia, 2005

1. It was judged that the mobile telephone market had great worldwide growth potential and was growing fast.
2. Nokia already had profitable businesses in this area.
3. Deregulation and privatisation of telecommunications markets around the world were providing specific opportunities.
4. Rapid technological change – especially the new pan-European GSM mobile system – provided the opportunity to alter fundamentally the balance between competitors.

Clearly, all the above judgements carried significant risk. In addition, the company's strategic choice was limited by constraints on its resources. The heavy losses of the group overall were a severe financial constraint. In addition, it was not able to afford the same level of expenditure on research and development as its two major rivals, Motorola (US) and Ericsson (Sweden). Moreover, although it had the in-house skills and experience of working with national deregulated telecommunications operators through competing in Nordic markets in the 1970s and 1980s, it would need many more employees if it was to develop the market opportunities. However, by selling off its other interests and concentrating on mobile telephones it was able to overcome some of the difficulties.

Looking back on that time, Mr Ollila commented: 'We were earlier than most in understanding . . . that in order to be really successful you have to globalise your organisation and focus your business portfolio . . . We have been able to grow and be global and maintain our agility and be fast at the same time.' What Mr Ollila did not say was that Finland is a small country, so to build any sizeable business, it is essential to think beyond the country's national boundaries.

1992–2000: building global leadership

One of Mr Ollila's first tasks was to build a management team. He chose two new, young executives as part of his team: Sari Baldauf as head of Nokia networks and Matti Alahuhta as head of Nokia mobile telephones. Mr Alahuhta had recently attended IMD Business School in Switzerland where he had written a dissertation on how to turn a medium-size technology-based company into a world-class enterprise against larger rivals with greater resources. He clearly had in mind how Nokia could compete with competitors like its Swedish rivals Ericsson, the Dutch company Philips, the French company Alcatel and the American company Motorola, all of whom had considerably greater resources in terms of finance and technical knowledge. Mr Alahuhta identified three important factors to help Nokia: first, it was important to find a new technology that would change the rules of the game and turn all existing competitors into beginners; second, it was essential to move fast internationally and respond flexibly as international markets developed; third, the company had to assess and deliver what customers really wanted from mobile telephones.

Mr Alahuhta did not especially identify one technology development that proved highly valuable in the early 1990s. This was the agreement within the European Union to adopt the GSM technical standard for mobile telephones. This allowed a company like Nokia to have access to a large market where the technology was standardised and major economies of scale were therefore possible. Such a development was important because the GSM standard was subsequently used worldwide, with around 500 million of the world's 700 million mobiles using this standard by 2000. This was fortunate for companies like Nokia: 'Good luck favours the prepared mind,' was Mr Alahuhta's cryptic comment some years later.

Benefits and problems of strategic choice

In fact, Nokia was highly successful in its expansion. It moved rapidly to design phones that would appeal to global customers by designing mobile phones that offered flair, reliability and ease-of-use. This meant that it had to invest heavily in software development and it formed an alliance with the British company, Symbian, subsequently taking a majority share in order to ensure that developments remained on track. Nokia was also single-minded in its investment in factories in order to deliver economies of scale, reduce costs and raise profit margins.

Nokia was particularly good at reading what customers wanted and then moving quickly into the market place with new telephones: it realised that the mobile phone during this period was almost a fashion accessory and designed phones to reflect this. It made the important judgement that the market during the 1990s was moving from being a high-tech market into a mass-market, where cheaper, entry-level phones were required. This was in sharp contrast to its Nordic competitor, Ericsson, who had remained with high-tech phones: 'We had the wrong profile in our portfolio,' was the later comment from Kurt Hellström, Ericsson's chief executive. By 2000, Nokia had developed a range of mobile telephones that were both attractive to look at and innovative in their use of the new digital technology that had become available. The result was that by 2000 Nokia was world leader in mobile telephone manufacture, with 35 per cent global share.

2000-2005: Coping with new challenges

Having concentrated its resources into mobile telephones, Nokia then had to cope with a major downturn in the world market 2000–2002 which occurred for three main reasons. The first reason was that the market became saturated in some parts of the world – for example, 80 per cent of people in the EU had mobile telephones. Other markets were also becoming saturated – only America lagged behind because of the profusion of mobile standards in that market. Even in countries like China and India, around 30 per cent of the population had mobiles and the take-up was much higher in Asian countries like Singapore, Australia and Japan, though the latter country had developed its own technical standards outside the GSM system – see Figure 14.2.

Figure 14.2

Percentage of population with mobile phones in selected countries in 2002

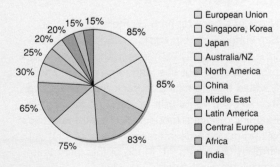

- ☐ European Union
- ☐ Singapore, Korea
- ☐ Japan
- ☐ Australia/NZ
- ▨ North America
- ☐ China
- ▨ Middle East
- ☐ Latin America
- ▨ Central Europe
- ☐ Africa
- ▨ India

Source: Author's estimates from references at end of chapter.

The second reason for problems was that the technology bubble of the late 1990s came to an end in 2001. This left the leading telecommunications companies overburdened with debt and wanting to slash their costs – *see* Case 15.2. Sales in Nokia's telecommunications equipment division – related to mobile phones but more associated with the surrounding infrastructure of telephone exchanges, masts, etc. – dropped 50 per cent over three years. Nokia itself had to make some 7,500 workers redundant in order to recover the situation.

In the mobile phone division of Nokia, there was a third additional problem for Nokia. The telephone service providers like Vodafone and Orange were delaying the introduction of the next generation of mobile telephone technology – *see* Case 15.2 – for reasons of technical feasibility and lack of funds through paying too much for the licences. The '3G' pure digital technology would introduced a whole new market for telephone services that would need a totally new series of product designs. In turn, this would require new manufacturing processes inside companies like Nokia. The result was that all the mobile telephone manufacturers, including Nokia, were hit by falling profits in 2001–2002.

The early markets for the new 3G technology were in Japan and Korea, where the GSM standard was not used. In addition, some of the Asian electronics manufacturers like Samsung and Sony realised that the new technology gave them another chance to enter the global mobile markets, particularly if they had missed out on the benefits of the GSM standard. Sony combined with Ericsson to launch a new joint venture and Samsung invested heavily in new 3G technology. The result was that Samsung had built a global market share of 14 per cent by 2005 and Sony Ericsson had a share of 6 per cent. However, Motorola still kept its second position with 17 per cent of the market. Competition was therefore increasing for Nokia.

New challenges and new management

At this point, Nokia lost its way slightly. It failed to read customer demand correctly around the year 2003/2004. The new 'clam shell' folding designs and mid-price photo imaging screens from its competitors proved popular in the market place. Nokia did not move to match these but stuck with its existing 'stick' designs. There was some suggestion that this may partly have been because Nokia's economies of scale were more associated with its existing designs. Certainly, Nokia had easily the highest profit margins in the industry and was reluctant to reduce these. Eventually, Nokia decided that its dominant world market share was highly valuable and it would be preferable to reduce its prices, take a loss of profit margin and also introduce new 'clam shell' designs. At the end of 2004, the company's share had begun to rise again and was back around 35 per cent.

More generally around 2004, Nokia realised that it needed to review its position. It had taken a hit from its competitors and it had failed to read the market changes fully. Importantly, it also faced new challenges that would come as 3G digital technology became the accepted medium of telephony. Essentially, this would open up opportunities that were ▶

▶ **CASE STUDY 14.1 continued**

Figure 14.3

Nokia 10-year sales and profits

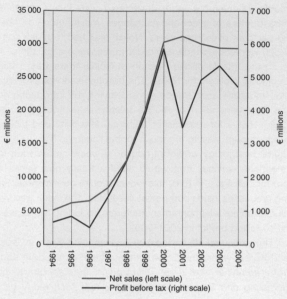

Net sales (left scale)
Profit before tax (right scale)

Source: Annual Report and Accounts.

unclear but potentially important – live transmission of television to mobile phones, new games to mobile phones, instant web access, etc. All these were technically feasible but still remained to be exploited fully. New mobile phones needed to be multimedia and also needed to consider the extent to which they would converge in terms of performance with other consumer electronics like the highly successful Apple iPod – see Case 1.1.

There was also another new trend that Nokia needed to master. The world market for mobile telephone providers was becoming more concentrated. Companies like Vodafone, Orange, Telekom and others were Nokia's major customers. The mobile telephone service customers were buying around 65–70 per cent of all the world's mobiles, which they were then selling or offering free to customers. The Japanese electronics company Sharp had been able to move into mobile telephones from nothing in the early 2000s by doing a deal to supply Vodafone with some of its models. This was a serious matter for Nokia since such large customers required more than the standard models: customers like Vodafone wanted *customised* phones that would deliver competitive advantages over their rivals and large orders meant real bargaining power. Nokia needed to introduce a whole new area of customer management for such large customers. 'It's a very different era in terms of management requirements, in terms of skills, know-how, how you build your customer relationship,' explained Nokia's chief executive, Mr Ollila.

The outcome of all the above was the introduction of new management at Nokia in December 2004. 'From a management point of view, it began in spring or summer 2003 when we in the management team started discussing the need to look at the organisation afresh,' said Mr Ollila. In a period of change in the industry, Nokia needed to adapt and restructure its management team. The result was that both Sarib Baldauf and Matti Alahuhta left Nokia. Mr Alahuhta went to a leading position at another Finnish company and Ms Baldauf to do something 'completely different'. Hence, as Nokia faced up to the new challenges, it decided that a new organisation structure and a new management team would be needed. Mr Ollila commented: 'You don't make generational changes easily . . . It's a big change. But change allows you to reposition, to rethink.' Nokia's profitability had stabilised in the short term – see Figure 14.3 – but the company needed to think carefully about new technologies, new trends and new strategic choices.

Just as this book was going to press, it was announced that Nokia's widely admired Chief Executive, Mr Jorma Ollila, would be leaving this position in May 2006 but would remain non-executive Chairman. The Nokia Management team that guided the company to world leadership in mobile phones would largely have left the company.

Case questions

1 *Why did Nokia select only one area for development? What is the strategic risk involved in selecting one area out of four?*

2 *What was the significance of the introduction of the new GSM system for Nokia's chosen strategy? Do companies always need such a technological development to ensure strategic success? Do they need other factors as well as technology – if so, what?*

3 *How important was the management team to strategic choice? Did it really have to change in 2004?*

STRATEGIC PROJECT

Nokia has been hit hard by the strategies of Samsung, Motorola and Sony Ericsson. At the time of writing, Nokia has responded with a new product range but has lost some market share. It would be interesting to track this market over the next two years from a strategy perspective. Examining prices, models and market initiatives will produce some interesting insights into strategy development. Much of this information is available on the web.

14.1 PRESCRIPTIVE STRATEGY CONTENT: EVALUATION AGAINST SIX CRITERIA

Prescriptive strategy has taken the approach that a rational and fact-based analysis of the options will deliver the strategy that is most likely to be successful: logic and evidence are paramount in choosing between the options. The content of strategy options therefore needs to be evaluated for their contribution to the organisation. We need to be able to understand in a structured way such comments as, 'Plausible . . . but not very likely'.[3] We need *evaluation criteria*.

In practice, each organisation will have its own criteria – for example, those for Nokia were outlined in the case above. However, and as a starting point, we can identify six main criteria[4] that can be used in evaluating strategy options: consistency, suitability, validity, feasibility, business risk, stakeholder attractiveness. This section examines each of these.

14.1.1 Criterion 1: consistency, especially with the mission and objectives

If the main purpose of the organisation is to add value, then the way that this is defined for the purposes of corporate strategy is through the organisation's mission and objective – Chapter 12 explored this in detail. In a non-profit-making organisation, the prime purpose may be better defined in terms of some form of service. Whatever the purpose of the organ-

Definition ➤ isation, a prime test of any option has to be its consistency: whether it is in agreement with the objectives of the organisation.

In a business context, this is likely to be the mission and its ability to deliver the agreed objectives of the organisation. If an option does not meet these criteria, there is a strong case for:

- either changing the mission and objectives, if they are too difficult or inappropriate;
- or rejecting the option.

If the mission and objectives have been carefully considered, then the rejection option is the most likely course. For example, the European consumer products company Reckitt Benckiser has a net revenue growth rate of 5–6 per cent for all areas of its business at constant exchange rates.[5] This means that strategy options that do not deliver this *in the long term* are rejected by the company. The qualification 'in the long term' relates to the fact that there may well be a period in the very early years of a new option when the project will fall short, but it must deliver over a longer period.

14.1.2 Criterion 2: suitability

In addition, some options may be more suitable for the organisation than others: how well does each option match the environment and resources and how well does it deliver com-

Definition ➤ petitive advantage? Suitability means to be appropriate for the context of the strategy of the organisation both internally and externally.

The environment can be explored from the mixture of opportunities to be taken and threats to be avoided. Competitive advantage can be built on the organisation's strengths, especially its core competencies, and may try to rectify weaknesses that exist.

The SWOT analysis at the beginning of Chapter 13 summarises the main elements that have been identified here. Strategy options can also be examined for their consistency with the elements of the SWOT analysis. For example, Nokia mobile telephones have strengths in marketing to the main telecommunications distributors across Europe. A new option that ignored these strengths and pursued a policy of new mobile outlets, such as grocery supermarkets, would need careful study and possibly (but not necessarily) rejection. In fact, this option has been picked up with vigour because it represented a way for Nokia to extend its market penetration.

14.1.3 Criterion 3: validity

Definition ➤

Most options will involve some form of *assumptions* about the future. These need to be tested to ensure that they are valid and reasonable, i.e. that they are logically sound and conform with the available research evidence. Validity means that the calculations and other assumptions on which the plan is based are well-grounded and meaningful.

In addition, many options will use *business information* that may be well grounded in background material or, alternatively, doubtful in its nature. For example, some of the information that Nokia has about its competitors is soundly based, e.g. the market share data, but some is likely to be rather more open to question, e.g. information on the future plans and intentions of Motorola.

For both the above, it will be necessary to test the validity of the assumptions and information in each option. In practice, there is some overlap between suitability and validity. Because of the element of judgement in such issues, this is done under the general heading of applying business judgements and guidelines.

14.1.4 Criterion 4: feasibility of options

Definition ➤

Feasibility means that the proposed strategies are capable of being carried out. Although options may be consistent with the mission and objectives, there may be other difficulties that limit the likelihood of success. An option may, in practice, lack feasibility in three areas:

1 culture, skills and resources *internal* to the organisation;

2 competitive reaction and other matters *external* to the organisation;

3 *lack of commitment* from managers and employees.

Constraints internal to the organisation

As we explored in Chapters 7, 8 and 9, an organisation might not have the culture, skills or resources to carry out the options. For example, there might be a culture in the organisation that is able to cope with gradual change but not the radical and sudden changes required by a proposed strategy option. For example, the difficulties experienced by the highly centralised company Metal Box (UK) when it merged with the decentralised company Carnaud (France) were largely in this area and caused the group major problems.[6]

Equally, an organisation may lack the necessary technical skills for a strategic option. It may not be possible for a variety of reasons to acquire them by recruiting staff.

In addition, some organisations have insufficient finance for an option to succeed. For example, the French computer company Groupe Bull had real problems financing its strategic development during the mid-1990s as it struggled to survive after a series of over-ambitious strategy initiatives earlier in the decade.[7]

Exhibit 14.1 summarises some of the main internal feasibility issues.

Exhibit 14.1

Ten-point checklist on internal feasibility

1 Capital investment required: do we have the funds?

2 Projection of cumulative profits: is it sufficiently profitable?

3 Working capital requirements: do we have enough working capital?

4 Tax liabilities and dividend payments: what are the implications, especially on timing?

5 Number of employees and, in the case of redundancy, any costs associated with this: what are the national laws on sacking people and what are the costs?

6 New technical skills, new plant and costs of closure of old plant: do we have the skills? Do we need to recruit or hire temporarily some specialists?

7 New products and how they are to be developed: are we confident that we have the portfolio of fully tested new products on which so much depends? Are they real breakthrough products or merely a catch-up on our competition?

8 Amount and timing of marketing investment and expertise required: do we have the funds? When will they be required? Do we have the specialist expertise such as advertising and promotions agency teams to deliver our strategies?

9 The possibility of acquisition, merger or joint venture with other companies and the implications: have we fully explored other options that would bring their own benefits and problems?

10 Communication of ideas to all those involved: how will this be done? Will we gain the *commitment* of the managers and employees affected?

Constraints external to the organisation

Outside the organisation, there are four main constraints that may make a strategic option lack feasibility: customer acceptance, competitive reaction, supplier acceptance and any approvals from government or another regulatory body.

In Chapter 5, we observed that customers need to find a new strategy attractive. In addition, competitors who are affected by a strategy option may react and make it difficult to achieve. For example, the US software company Microsoft has around 90 per cent of the world market for personal computer software with its Windows operating system. In the past, it has been accused by competitors of deliberately pre-announcing some of its products to stall sales of new, competing software products.[8] The likelihood of competitive response is an area that must be assessed.

There may also be other constraints outside the organisation that make strategy options difficult if not impossible. For example, Nokia had to consider carefully the implications of the reduction in government control over telecommunications markets. This was not only an opportunity but also a problem because governments were still sensitive over their national interests in this area.

The questions that might probe this area are summarised in Exhibit 14.2.

Exhibit 14.2

Four-point checklist on external feasibility

1 How will our *customers* respond to the strategies we are proposing?

2 How will our *competitors* react? Do we have the necessary resources to respond?

3 Do we have the necessary support from our *suppliers*?

4 Do we need government or regulatory approval? How likely is this?

Lack of commitment from managers and employees

If important members of the organisation are not committed to the strategy, it is unlikely to be successfully implemented. For example, the major US toy retailer Toys 'Я' Us had major problems implementing its business strategy in Sweden some years ago because the local managers and employees considered it to be inconsistent with the Swedish approach to labour relations.[9]

This constraint may arise because some organisations make a clear distinction between strategy development by senior managers and day-to-day management by more junior managers.[10] Hence in such organisations, junior managers and employees are unlikely to have been involved in the strategy development process: in essence, they have the results communicated to them and they may not feel *committed* to its implications.

Some strategic decisions may need to be made by a senior management centralised group – for example, the Nokia decision at the beginning of the 1990s to divest some companies. In spite of Nokia's commitment to an open Finnish culture, the key decisions on the new strategy were taken by a group of *senior* managers. The more junior managers and employees were not really consulted. Since the proposals included divesting part of Nokia, this is not really surprising.

14.1.5 Criterion 5: business risk

Definition ➤ Most worthwhile strategies are likely to carry some degree of risk. In this context, risk means that the strategy does not expose the organisation to unnecessary hazards or to an unreasonable degree of danger. Such areas need to be carefully assessed. Ultimately, the risks involved may be unacceptable to the organisation.

There are countless examples in corporate strategy of organisations taking risks and then struggling to sort out the difficulties. For example, Germany's largest industrial company, Daimler-Benz, took considerable risks with its expansion strategy during the 1990s (*see* Chapter 10). In 1998, the company chose to merge with the US car company Chrysler, involving significant risk if the benefits were to be achieved.[11]

It is easy to see business risk only as a major strategic constraint. The Japanese strategist Kenichi Ohmae comments that this may stop a company from breaking out of the existing situation.[12] Yet some degree of business risk is likely in most worthwhile strategy development. The important aspects are:

- to make an explicit *assessment* of the risks;
- to explore the *contingencies* that will lessen the difficulties if things go wrong;
- to decide whether the *risks are acceptable* to the organisation.

There is no single method of assessing risk in the organisation, but there are a number of techniques that may assist the process. Two are explored below – financial risk analysis and scenario building – and other techniques are examined in Sections 14.2.4 and 14.2.5.

Financial risk analysis[13]

For most strategy proposals in both the private and public sectors, it is important to undertake some form of analysis of the financial risks involved in strategy options. There are a number of types of analysis that can be undertaken:

- *Cash flow analysis*. This analysis is essential. An organisation can report decent levels of profitability at the same time as going bankrupt through a lack of cash. Each option needs to be assessed for its impact on cash flow in the organisation.
- *Break-even analysis*. This is often a useful approach: it calculates the volume sales of the business required to recover the initial investment in the business. The important point about such a result is to explore whether this volume is reasonable or not – *see* Exhibit 14.4. Break-even analysis at Eurofreeze on the main options, discussed later in the chapter, would be useful.
- *Company borrowing requirements*. The impact of some strategies may severely affect the funds needed from financial institutions and shareholders. This area was explored in Chapter 8 and represents a real area of risk for strategy analysis.

● *Financial ratio analysis.* Liquidity, asset management, stockholding and similar checks on companies can be usefully undertaken. It might be argued that they are not needed since the company should know in detail about these areas. But what about key suppliers? And key customers? The knock-on effects of bankruptcy in one of these, when the company itself is stretched financially, deserve consideration (*see* Chapter 8).

For international activities, there is one other area that is also important: *currency analysis.* A major shift in currencies can wipe out the profitability of an overseas strategy option overnight (or, more optimistically, increase it). A number of major companies have discovered the impact of this over the last few years. Specialist help may be required.

Scenario building

This is a most useful form of analysis and would be regarded as part of the basic strategy proposals in many organisations. Essentially, it explores the 'What if?' questions for their impact on the strategy under investigation. The basic assumptions behind each option, e.g. economic growth, pricing, currency fluctuation, raw material prices, etc., are varied and the impact is measured on return on capital employed, cash and other company objectives. The key factors for success may be used to identify the major points that need to be considered.

The sensitivity of each these factors, as they are moved up or down by arbitrary variations, is then assessed in order to determine which are crucial. Those variations that turn out to be particularly sensitive can then be re-examined carefully before the strategy is accepted. They can also be monitored after it has been put into operation.

For example, the key assumptions of the Nokia mobile telephone expansion might be tested by examining what would happen if they varied:

● What impact would there be if Nokia carried on without the new rate of investment? This is quite specific and the result could be used to assess the strategy.

● What impact would there be if Nokia only limited cost savings as a result of its new plans? Perhaps only another 10 per cent cost savings instead of the 20 per cent assumed in the plan? Again a specific calculation could be undertaken to test the sensitivity of this change.

● What impact would there be if Nokia lost its market leadership? Perhaps the simplest calculation would be to assume that the three main companies – Nokia, Motorola and Ericsson – ended up with equal shares and the result was recalculated. The sensitivity to share variation could then be assessed.

Clearly, the results of all sensitivity analyses can provide those selecting the strategies with a useful estimate of the risks involved.

14.1.6 Criterion 6: attractiveness to stakeholders

Definition ➤ Attractiveness to stakeholders means that the strategy is sufficiently appealing to those people that the company needs to satisfy. As we explored in Chapter 12, every organisation has its stakeholders, such as the shareholders, employees and management. They will all be interested in the strategic options that the organisation has under consideration because they may be affected by them. But stakeholder interests and perspectives may not always be the same. For example, an option might increase the *shareholders'* wealth but also mean a reduction in *employees* in the organisation. Hence, stakeholders may not find all the strategic options equally attractive.

One way of resolving this issue is to *prioritise* the stakeholders' interests – for example, by putting the shareholders' interests first and raising dividends, cutting costs and possibly even sacking some workers. Some writers and companies would have no hesitation in pursuing this route. However, it may be oversimplistic for corporate strategy.

Key strategic principles

- Evaluating strategy options relies on criteria for the selection process. There are six main criteria: consistency, especially with the organisation's mission and objectives, suitability, validity, feasibility, business risk and attractiveness to stakeholders.

- Consistency with the purpose of the organisation is a prime test for evaluating and selecting strategies.

- Suitability of the strategy for the environment within which the organisation operates is clearly important.

- Validity of the projections and data used in developing the option must be tested.

- In examining whether an option is feasible, there are three main areas to explore: first those that are internal to the organisation, which are mainly those that arise from a lack of resources; second, those external to the organisation, such as customer acceptance and customer reaction; finally, special consideration needs to be given to employee and manager acceptance and commitment.

- The risks that a strategy option may bring to an organisation also need to be assessed because they may be unacceptably high. Such risks can be assessed under two broad headings: financial risk and sensitivity analysis.

- Stakeholders also need to be assessed for their reactions to major strategy initiatives. It may be necessary to prioritise the interests of stakeholders: shareholders may or may not come first. Stakeholder reactions need to be assessed under five headings, each of which is related to the prime interests of the stakeholder group in question.

CASE STUDY 14.2

Eurofreeze evaluates its strategy options: 1

With sales in 2003 of US$1.05 billion, Eurofreeze is one of Europe's larger frozen food companies. However, it was being squeezed between two major competitive forces: its larger rival Refrigor, and the grocery supermarket own brands, which were becoming increasingly powerful across Europe. The time had come for a complete strategic rethink at Eurofreeze: the company was part of a large multinational and the group headquarters had turned up the heat.

This case begins the process by exploring the objectives, the environment and the resources of the company. At the end of the chapter, there is a follow-up case that examines the options identified by Eurofreeze.

Mission and objectives

As a starting point for the exploration of its options, Eurofreeze decided to re-examine its mission and objectives. It decided that it still wished to remain strong in European frozen food and therefore defined its mission as: 'To be a leading producer of frozen food products in the European Union'. This mission was based on its core strengths, its competitive position as the second largest in the EU, and the way it envisaged freezing technology would retain its position in preserving food over the next five years. Within this context, it then reviewed its current profitability, shareholder performance and market share position and defined its objectives over the next five years as being:

- to raise its return on capital from the current level of 12 per cent by 0.5 per cent per annum with the aim of reaching 15 per cent after six years;
- to raise its contribution to its earnings per share at a similar rate over time, but allow for some lag as it reinvested in the immediate future;
- to hold its overall market share but to move from low-value-added items (like frozen vegetables) to higher-value-added (like prepared pizza dishes).

To understand fully the implications of these demanding objectives, it was necessary for Eurofreeze to explore the background to the frozen food market and the competitive trends that were operating.

Some areas of frozen food are becoming increasingly like a commodity, with little competitive advantage and the main competition being based on price.

Frozen food products and added value

The first products to be frozen commercially were vegetables and fish in the 1940s. For many years, the higher food quality resulting from the freezing process allowed such products to be sold at premium prices to the competition from cans, glass jars and other forms of preserved food. But by 2000, freezing was old technology – there was no sustainable competitive advantage in this as such. Specifically, this meant that products like frozen vegetables and frozen meat, whether carrying a nationally recognised brand or not, had little value added to them before arriving in the shops.

Thus, the major supermarkets negotiated their own branded versions of many basic products and obtained keen prices from suppliers such as Eurofreeze. By the mid-1990s, the profit margins on basic vegetables and other commodities were very low: added value was minimal.

Over the same period, household incomes had risen across Europe, home freezers were more widespread, and tastes had become more international. For example, people across Europe had come to know and like a wider range of fresh recipe dishes and international products, everything from 'quattro stagioni' pizza to double layer chocolate gateaux. Such products had much higher added value. They were sold as branded items, usually under a name that had been well established over the years: Birds Eye, Dr Oetker, Heinz Weight Watchers and Findus were examples of the brand names that had become familiar in this context. The brand name was used across all products from the company so that it supported the strong, well-advertised products along with the weaker ones – a group branding policy.

Key factors for success

The following factors were considered to be critical to success in the industry:

● experienced and talented buyers to negotiate price and quality on low-value-added items;

● fast and efficient freezing processes coupled with good freezer storage and distribution;
● excellent relationships with the main supermarket chains;
● strong and consistent group branding;
● vigorous and innovative new product development programmes.

Eurofreeze core resources

As a result of its history and present market position, the company had core competencies in the following areas:

● purchase of raw materials such as vegetables, including the buying function;
● freezer technology;
● recipe development for new frozen dishes;
● frozen food distribution;
● supermarket negotiating and service;
● developing branded food products (it had a well-known brand name across Europe).

Within these areas, its key resource advantages over its leading rival were its brand names, its European market leadership in branded meat and fish products, and its corporate parent, which was one of the world's leading fast-moving consumer goods companies, with extensive financial resources.

The competition

During the 1990s, companies such as Eurofreeze sought new strategies to avoid the low-priced competition – the own-branded supermarket sales of vegetables and other low-value-added items had become a real problem. Profit pressures were such that Eurofreeze was even considering phasing out its range of branded vegetables. The giant supermarket companies like Tesco, Carrefour and Aldi had much of the bargaining power in basic frozen food.

In addition, many large grocery chains wanted *only one* market-leading frozen brand to put alongside their own brands. In this context, Eurofreeze faced a specific problem: in some European product categories, it was not the market leader. Eurofreeze was second in its markets to its major rival, Refrigor.

Refrigor had invested heavily in frozen food brands, manufacturing and grocery distribution over the last few years at a rate in excess of Eurofreeze. However, the company had been rather less profitable. It had much the same grocery customers as Eurofreeze. Both competitors offered a full range of frozen branded food products and, at the same time, supplied own-label versions to the leading grocery chains.

In total, Eurofreeze faced four competitive threats, the first two below being particularly strong:

1 The market leader, Refrigor, the low-cost leader.
2 In many supermarkets such as Sainsbury (UK) and Albert Heijn (part of Ahold, the Netherlands), increasing freezer space was given to supermarket chains' own-branded products at the expense of the manufacturer's branded product.
3 In other supermarkets with strong cut-price positioning, such as Aldi and Netto, the same freezer space was used

▶ CASE STUDY 14.2 continued

for local or regional branded products that had no national advertising or promotional support but were low-priced.

4 In some specific product lines, such as French fries or gateaux, specialised companies such as McCain (US) and Sara Lee (US), respectively, sold branded products that had a significant share of that particular market segment.

Overall, the market was becoming volume-driven and highly competitive in many sectors. It was also becoming increasingly difficult to afford the investment in advertising and promotions to support branded lines.

© Copyright Richard Lynch 2006. The case is based on real companies, which have been disguised to protect confidentiality. Market share and financial data have also been changed.

Case questions

1 What is your assessment of the mission and objectives of Eurofreeze? How do they stack up against the pressures of the highly competitive market? Are they too demanding?

2 Should the objectives be expanded? What about branded and non-branded items, for example? Clearer on the competitive threat? Further reference to financial objectives such as the precise relationship with headquarters? Specific reference to other matters such as ecological issues and employee job satisfaction? If your answer is yes to any of these questions, then what considerations should Eurofreeze take into account in making its decision? If your answer is no, then what are the implications for strategy selection?

3 What are the possible implications of the customer and competitive trends on the development of strategy options for Eurofreeze? You may wish to undertake some of the analyses contained in Chapter 13 in preparing your answer.

14.2 PRESCRIPTIVE STRATEGY CONTENT: PROCEDURES AND TECHNIQUES

In examining the many criteria that can be employed, it is sometimes useful to consider whether some criteria are more important than others. It is possible that no useful prioritisation can be undertaken in this case.

14.2.1 Criteria in commercial organisations

For most organisations, the criteria will be prioritised by the mission and objectives. Within these, the following three questions represent the areas that may need exploration:

1 Is each strategy option consistent with the mission of the organisation? How well does it deliver the objectives? For example, at Eurofreeze how does each option meet the stated desire for a return on capital of 15 per cent and rising? How does each option contribute to the shift to higher-value-added products?

2 Does each option build on the *strengths* of the organisation? Does it exploit the *opportunities* that have been identified? And the *core resources* of the organisation? Thus at Eurofreeze, it should be possible to test the option for its usefulness in contributing to freezer technology or to supermarket opportunities. If it is not consistent with these issues, then there *may* be a case for rejecting it. However, it should be noted that rejection is not automatic.

3 Does each option avoid, or even overcome, the weaknesses of the organisation? And does it do the same for the threats that have been identified? At Eurofreeze, an option that involved development of its basic vegetable business would move the company further into this weak area and would invite rejection.

Question 3 has *lower priority* than questions 1 and 2.[14] It is much more important to deliver the organisation's mission and objectives and to build on its strengths than to worry about its weaknesses. However, there will be occasions when the weaknesses cannot be ignored and strategy options need to consider these.

It would be a great mistake to consider only those criteria that can be put into numbers. For example, many organisations will have guidelines related to *customer quality and satisfaction*; others will include *service to the broader community*. These may not be easy to quantify but are no less important in spite of this. All of them need to be reflected in the criteria for selection of strategy options. Such matters simply underline the importance of carefully defining the purpose of the organisation.

14.2.2 Criteria in not-for-profit organisations

Great care needs to be taken in such organisations that any quantified criteria do not come to dominate the selection between strategies when such selection measures are inappropriate. All not-for-profit organisations will need to create added value. However, beyond this, the criteria may need to reflect strongly the important aspects of the service or the value to the community appropriate to the mission.

Criteria in not-for-profit organisations also need to take into account the different decision-making processes and beliefs that motivate many such organisations. The reliance on voluntary support, the strong sense of mission and belief in the work of the organisation, and the style of the organisation may not lend themselves to a simple choice between a series of options.

Not-for-profit organisations may involve high loyalty to a mission, which is often clear, but the organisation may be decentralised, with local decision making. If this is the case, then a centralised evaluation of options is difficult. A comparison of the objectives with commercial organisations is shown in Exhibit 14.3. The evaluation of strategy options in not-for-profit organisations may be more diffuse and open-ended.

Exhibit 14.3

Comparison of possible criteria in commercial and not-for-profit organisations

Commercial organisation	Not-for-profit organisation
● Quantified	● Qualitative
● Unchanging	● Variable
● Consistent	● Conflicting
● Unified	● Complex
● Operational	● Ambiguous
● Clear	● Non-operational
● Measurable	● Non-measurable

14.2.3 Taking the first steps in selection

Before exploring the problems associated with strategic options, it is usual to make some initial selection of one or more options. To some extent, the initial evaluation will depend on the type of organisation. In commercial circumstances, the selection might start with the *profitability* of the venture. In a not-for-profit situation, other factors, such as the ability to *deliver the service*, might be more important. These are the reasons that make careful exploration of the mission and objectives so important. Sometimes, it is useful to eliminate the obvious strategic options that have no hope of long-term success. The steps that might be involved in the initial evaluation are summarised in Exhibit 14.4.

Ten steps towards an initial strategy evaluation

1 Screen out any *early no-hopers* that are highly unlikely to meet the objectives.
2 Estimate the *sales* of each of the remaining options based on market share, pricing, promotional support and competitive reactions.
3 Estimate the *costs* of each of the remaining options.
4 Estimate the *capital and other funds* necessary to undertake each option.
5 Calculate the *return on capital employed* for each option.
6 Calculate the *break-even* of each option.
7 Calculate the *net cash flow* effects of each option.
8 Evaluate whether the *projected sales levels* imply exceptional levels of market share or unusually low costs. Are these reasonable? Real strategic weaknesses can emerge here.
9 Assess the likely *competitive response* and its possible impact on each strategy option.
10 Assess the *risks* associated with each option.

14.2.4 Evaluation techniques: financial[15]

Having removed any options that have no hope of meeting the basic evaluation criteria, the next step is to undertake a financial evaluation of the remaining options. As a first step, most evaluations of strategic options in commercial organisations attempt to analyse the profit against the capital employed. In this case, it is important to note that extra capital will be needed in most organisations[16] *as soon as sales rise*, not just when new buildings or plant are bought. This arises because of the need to fund new debtors and pay for the extra stocks required for the new business activity. There are at least five main financial techniques:

1 return on capital employed (ROCE);
2 net cash flow;
3 payback period;
4 discounted cash flow (DCF);
5 break-even.

There are some important words of caution to note in the use of any financial evaluation of strategic options. These are summarised in Exhibit 14.5.

Caution on the use of financial criteria

Following on from the discussion in Chapter 8, there are some clear difficulties with these methods of appraisal of strategic options:

● The cost of capital is a vital element in two of the calculations above. The difficulties associated with its calculation were explored in Chapter 8. It is especially difficult to estimate where investment takes place over a lengthy period.

● There are real problems in estimating the future sales accurately up to ten years away, which is a typical period in many DCF calculations, even in consumer goods companies. However, direct costs can usually be estimated satisfactorily. The projections are therefore doubtful. Payback may be better here.

- With shorter product life cycles and greater product obsolescence in some product categories such as computers, the DCF process may rely on an overextended time span. Payback may again be better here and this is the justification used by some Japanese companies for using this approach.

- Comment was made above on the difficulty of isolating incremental from ongoing capital. This applies not only to ROCE calculations but to all such appraisals.

- Because of the emphasis on cash generated in the project itself, the appraisal tends to concentrate on the quantified financial benefits and may ignore some of the broader strategic benefits that are more difficult to quantify – for example, synergies and value chain linkages.

- ROCE is by definition an accounting calculation that looks back at a project's past rather than forward to its future potential. It may therefore not be suitable for strategic use.

Return on capital employed (ROCE)

Definition ➤ This is a measure of the profitability of a strategic option. ROCE is defined as the ratio of profits to be earned divided by the capital invested in the new strategy. Profits are usually calculated *before* any tax that might be charged, because tax matters go beyond the assessment of individual strategy options.

This ratio is commonly used to assess strategies. The expected operating profit is assessed after the strategy has been in operation for an agreed number of years, usually defined before tax and interest. It is divided by the capital employed in the option, which is commonly averaged across a year, given the tendency of capital to vary during the course of a year.

One of the major difficulties is defining the *incremental* capital used purely for that strategy. It is easy where a new piece of plant has been installed, but more difficult where the strategy involves using existing plant or a service where the capital involved cannot be easily distinguished from more general trading.

For ongoing business investments, companies often have *hurdle rates* for ROCE: if they do not earn at these rates then there is serious discussion about abandoning that strategy. Such rates are usually set in relation to the company's *cost of capital*: if capital is cheap, then a lower rate can be set. Readers are referred to Chapter 8 for a more detailed exploration of this area.

Net cash flow[17]

Definition ➤ The net cash flow is the profit *before* depreciation less the periodic investment in working capital that is required to undertake the project. The importance of this calculation of cash flow lies in the ability of a negative cash flow to bankrupt a company. It is perfectly possible to deliver significant profits in the distant future, so that the return on capital looks good. However, there may be major negative outflows of cash in the short term, with the implication that the firm will go bust – the company may be unable to pay its current bills while waiting for its distant profits. An approximation of the net cash flow calculation is obtained by regarding it as the sum of pretax profits from the new strategy option, plus depreciation, less the capital to be invested in the new strategy.

Payback period

Payback period is used where there is a significant and specific capital investment required in the option. In the early years of the option, capital is invested in it. As the company earns Definition ➤ profits from the venture, it recovers the capital that has been invested. Payback is the time it takes to recover the initial capital investment and is usually measured in years. The cash flows in payback are not discounted but are simply added and subtracted equally, whatever year they occur.

Typically, payback on a capital project in the car industry will be around three to five years. This is because of the large amounts of capital involved (often into US$ billions) and the competitive nature of the industry, which makes profit margins low. In consumer goods, the period may be shorter, not because markets are any less competitive but because the profit margins on some items are higher, e.g. in fashion clothing and cosmetics. By contrast, the payback period may be 20–60 years for some highly capital-intensive items such as telecommunications infrastructure and roads.

Discounted cash flow (DCF)

Definition ➤ Discounted Cash Flow is the sum of projected cash flows from a future strategy, after revaluing each individual element of the cash flow in terms of its present worth using the cost of capital of the organisation. DCF is now used extensively for the assessment of strategic options. Essentially, DCF takes account of the fact that cash in five years' time is worth less than cash today, unlike payback above. It begins by assessing the net cash flow for each year of the life of the option, as in payback above. The cash is usually assessed after subtracting the taxation to be paid to the government. Each annual cash amount is then discounted back to the present using the organisation's *cost of capital* (discussed in Chapter 8). It is probably negative in the early years as capital is expended and then positive as the option increases its sales. There are discounting tables or computer spreadsheet programs that make this process relatively easy. The net present value (NPV) is the sum in today's values of all the future DCFs. Case study 14.4 shows the procedure for some Eurofreeze options – the analysis is typical of that undertaken by many organisations when exploring the consequences of strategic options.

Break-even analysis[18]

Definition ➤ Break-even is defined as the point at which the total costs of undertaking the new strategy are equal to the total revenue. It is often restated as the number of units of a product that need to be sold before the product has covered all its fixed costs.

Break-even analysis is directed at the break-even point, i.e. that point where fixed and variable costs equal total revenue. It is based on a number of assumptions that make its use in practice rather crude in strategy options analysis:

● Costs can easily be split into fixed and variable elements.

● Fixed costs are constant.

● Variable costs and revenue are linear in their relationship with volume over the range used in the analysis.

● Variable costs vary proportionately with sales, within given limits.

● It is possible to predict the volume of sales at various prices.

In spite of these problems, break-even has the great merit of being easily understandable and therefore communicable across an organisation. Used with caution, it can therefore be a useful tool in strategy options analysis.

14.2.5 Evaluation techniques: shareholder value added (SVA)[19]

In Chapter 8, we undertook a more detailed review of the above topic. This section presents a brief reprise, with readers being referred back to the earlier chapter for the more detailed examination. Although many Western companies continue to use DCF techniques in their evaluation of strategies,[20] they became conscious in the 1980s of the difficulties of ignoring the broader strategic benefits. There were also two other developments:

1 Professor Michael Porter's work emphasising the value chain and its relevance in strategy development – *see* Chapter 6.

2 Other writers[21] began to doubt the wisdom of seeking a steady increase in earnings per share as a measure of shareholder wealth. Such wealth can be measured in terms of a company's share price. It was shown empirically that share price was more closely correlated with long-term cash generation in a business than it was with earnings per share.

Taking the goal of a public company as being to maximise shareholder value, the concept of shareholder value added (SVA) was developed from DCF techniques and these difficulties. Its purpose is to develop corporate strategy, 'maximising the long-term cashflow of each SBU [strategic business unit]'.[22] Thus SVA evaluation differs in the following areas from the profitability approaches above:

● SVA takes the concept of cash flow but applies it to the complete business rather than to individual strategy options.

● It takes into account the cost of capital of the company and measures shareholder return against this benchmark.

● It lays particular emphasis on the critical factors for success in that business, defining them as being those that are particularly important in generating cash or value added. It calls these critical factors *value or cost drivers*. Such critical factors may bear some relationship to the key factors for success in an industry explored in Chapter 6. However, the value or cost drivers are different in that they relate to the *individual* business, not the *industry*.

● It supports the interrelationship of value or cost drivers in the development of cash generation. In this sense, it differs from the simpler DCF view that an option can be analysed by itself.

Comment

Although SVA represents an advance on some simpler DCF techniques, it still relies on a prescriptive view of strategy projections – a projection of future profit over an extended period of time is required. Moreover, it makes the crucial assumption that maximising shareholder value is the prime objective of strategy development. This may be true in UK and US companies but does not necessarily apply in some other leading industrialised countries. Other criticisms of this prescriptive approach were covered in Chapter 8.

14.2.6 Evaluation techniques: cost/benefit analysis[23]

Definition ➤ Cost/benefit analysis evaluates projects especially in the public sector, where an element of unquantified public service beyond commercial profit may be involved, by attempting to quantify the broader social benefits of such a project. Ever since cost/benefit analysis was used to assess the justification for building London Underground's Victoria Line in the 1960s, this has been an appraisal method favoured when the benefits go beyond simple financial benefits: for example, they might include lower levels of pollution or greater use of recycled materials. It is regularly used in public service investment decisions. It attempts to quantify a much broader range of benefits than sales, profits and costs.

When the benefits of some forms of public service go beyond simple financial appraisal, cost/benefit analysis may be used. It may be especially valuable where the project delivers value to users who are not directly investing their own funds. Thus, for example, in the analysis of the new Victoria Line on the London Underground, it attempted to assess:

● the faster and more convenient travel to be enjoyed by passengers on the London Underground;

● the ability of road transport to move more freely because roads were less congested.

As well as the benefits, there may also be social costs that need to be assessed. In the case of Underground transport, these might include building subsidence or inconvenience while the line is being built.

The key point in cost/benefit analysis is that all such broader benefits and costs are still assessed in monetary terms. Much of the research in this area is concerned with the quantification of such benefits and the costs that may be associated with them. The direct investment costs are usually rather easier to determine and form another element in the equation.

The difficult part of such a cost/benefit analysis is usually where to place the limit on the possible benefits and costs. For example, it might be argued that easier travel would mean that there would be less atmospheric pollution, more healthy people and therefore a need to quantify the health benefits. There might also be benefits in terms of a more stress-free lifestyle that need to be quantified, and so on. In spite of this difficulty and the more general problem of quantifying the intangible, cost/benefit analysis does serve a useful function in the appraisal of public projects and strategy initiatives.

Key strategic principles

- In making an initial selection of the best option, it is important to clarify the basis on which this is to be done. Evaluation against the mission and objectives is important but needs to be rigorous and precise if it is to provide real benefit. Non-quantified objectives may be just as important for some organisations.

- Additional criteria for evaluation include the ability to build on the strengths and core competencies of the organisation and avoid its weaknesses. Generally in evaluation, strengths are more important than weaknesses, but occasionally a weakness cannot be ignored.

- Different parts of an organisation, such as the HQ, the strategic business unit (SBU) and those involved in individual projects, will have different perspectives on the evaluation process. There is a need to recognise this in selection.

- In not-for-profit organisations, the criteria need to reflect the broader aspects of their service or contribution to the community. They also need to take into account the different decision-making processes and beliefs that motivate many such organisations. This may make the evaluation of strategy options more diffuse and open-ended.

- To undertake the initial evaluation in commercial organisations, it may be worth eliminating any options that have little chance of success. It is then usual to calculate initially for each option the profitability, break-even and net cash flow.

- Beyond this, ten steps can be undertaken to make an initial evaluation. From a *strategic* perspective, it is particularly useful to examine whether the projected sales levels of each option imply *exceptional* levels of market share or low costs in order to achieve their targets. If these occur, then it may imply that the option has real weaknesses.

- Evaluation usually employs common and agreed criteria across the organisation, such as contribution to value added and profitability. The strengths and weaknesses of these criteria need to be understood.

- The shareholder value approach (SVA) takes a broader perspective on evaluation than that provided by the specific project. It seeks to determine the benefit of such developments in the context of the whole SBU in which the project rests. However, it still relies on the assumption that shareholders are always the prime beneficiaries.

- Cost/benefit analysis has been successfully employed in public sector evaluation, where it is important to assess broader and less quantifiable benefits. The main difficulty is where to place the limit on such benefits and costs.

14.3 APPLYING EMPIRICAL EVIDENCE AND GUIDELINES

In addition to the logic of strategy development covered in the previous section, there is also empirical evidence of strategies adopted by other organisations in the past that have succeeded or failed. Such evidence also provides guidance that can be used to select the optimal strategy from the options available. We will consider this under three headings:

1 Generic industry environments;
2 Evidence on the link between profitability and three key strategic issues;
3 Mergers and acquisitions.

14.3.1 Generic industry environments[24]

Some strategies have been shown through logical thought to provide a higher chance of success than others. Such insights may aid the selection of strategy options. Exploration and

Definition ➤ understanding of the main concepts is called the study of *generic strategy environments:*[25] this proposes that strategies can be selected on the basis of their ability to cope with a particular market or competitive environment. One of the best-known examples of this general approach is the *ADL matrix*. The well-known management consultants Arthur D Little (ADL) developed the matrix during the 1970s. It relies on matching an organisation's own strength or weakness in a market with the life cycle phase of that market. Specifically, it focuses on:

- *stage of industry maturity* – from a young and fast-growing market through to a mature and declining market;
- *competitive position* – from a company that is dominant and able to control the industry through to one that is weak and barely able to survive.

It would be wrong to oversimplify the strategies that can be adopted depending on a company's competitive position in the above. As a starting point, the matrix shown in Figure 14.4 was developed in order to illustrate some of the choices that might be made. For example, if a company was in a *strong* position in a *mature* market, then the strategic logic of the matrix would suggest that it:

- sought cost leadership *or*
- renewed its focus strategy *or*
- differentiated itself from competition

while at the same time growing with the industry.

Hence, if other strategy options for this market and competitive combination were presented and they did not conform with one of the above proposals, there would be a case for rejecting them. However, it will be evident from the Nokia case that such analyses can be flawed where major technological change and marketing initiatives are introduced.

14.3.2 Profitability and three key strategic issues[26]

According to some research evidence, profitability in commercial organisations is linked to three key strategic issues:

1 the role of quality as part of strategic decision making;
2 the importance of market share and marketing expenditure as a contributor to strategy development;
3 the capital investment required for new strategic initiatives.

The evidence in this area comes from the Strategic Planning Institute (SPI), located in the US. For the last 20 years, the SPI has been gathering data on about 3,000 companies (some 600 of which are located in Europe). The information collected covers three major areas:

Figure 14.4

Evaluation using the life cycle portfolio matrix

Maturity \\ Competitive position	Embryonic	Growing	Mature	Ageing
Clear leader	**Hold position** Attempt to improve market penetration *Invest slightly faster than market dictates*	**Hold position** Defend market share *Invest to sustain growth rate (and pre-empt potential competitors)*	**Hold position** Grow with industry *Reinvest as necessary*	**Hold position** *Reinvest as necessary*
Strong	**Attempt to improve market penetration** *Invest as fast as market dictates*	**Attempt to improve market penetration** *Invest to increase growth rate (and improve position)*	**Hold position** Grow with industry *Reinvest as necessary*	**Hold position** *Reinvest as necessary or reinvest minimum*
Favourable	**Attempt to improve position selectively** Penetrate market generally or selectively *Invest selectively*	**Attempt to improve position** Penetrate market selectively *Invest selectively to improve position*	**Maintain position** Find niche and attempt to protect it *Make minimum and/or selective reinvestment*	**Harvest, withdraw in phases, or abandon** *Reinvest minimum necessary or disinvest*
Defensible	**Attempt to improve position selectively** *Invest (very) selectively*	**Find niche and protect it** *Invest selectively*	**Find niche or withdraw in phases** *Reinvest minimum necessary or disinvest*	**Withdraw in phases or abandon** *Disinvest or divest*
Weak	**Improve position or withdraw** *Invest or divest*	**Turn around or abandon** *Invest or disinvest*	**Turn around or withdraw in phases** *Invest selectively or disinvest*	**Abandon position** *Divest*

Note: The boxes indicate suggested strategies depending on life cycle and share position held by the company. They can be used both to stimulate options and to *evaluate proposed options* to ensure that they are consistent with the company's strategic position.

Source: Reproduced with permission from Arthur D Little. © Copyright Arthur D Little 1996.

1 the *results* of strategies undertaken (profits, market share, etc.);

2 the *inputs* by the company to this activity (plant investment, finance, productivity, etc.);

3 the *industry conditions* within which the company operates (market growth, customer power, innovation, etc.).

The data are often described as the *PIMS Databank* (PIMS is short for Profit Impact of Market Strategy), which is unique in the extent of its empirical database on corporate strategy coupled with its inputs and outputs. It collects data and calculates statistical correlations between various elements; whether such relationships have any real meaning has been the subject of fierce academic debate.[27] This book takes the view that it has made a useful contribution to empirical strategy research. The overall results have been published and a few of the key findings are explored below. In addition to its general work, the results are also fed back to contributing companies on a detailed and more confidential basis for them to assess their performance and draw relevant conclusions. From the results of these extensive studies, three key factors emerge – namely: quality, market share and marketing spend, and capital investment.

Quality

In the long run and according to the PIMS Databank, the most important single factor affecting a business unit's performance is the quality of its products and services, relative to those of its competitors. Strategy options that seek to raise quality are more likely to be successful than those that do not. This supports much of the activity described in Chapter 12 in this area on the subject of TQM, etc. Strategy options that consider quality in relation to the price charged are more likely to have a greater chance of success.

Market share and marketing expenditure[28]

In Chapters 3 and 5, we explored the strategic importance of a company having significant power in the market place. This is usually measured using market share and will be related, at least in part, to the marketing expenditure by the company on the product or service. PIMS monitors market share and has shown a strong correlation with return on investment. It also monitors marketing expenditure, where the results depend on whether the company already has a high or low market share.

The PIMS evidence suggests that there is a correlation between high levels of marketing activity and market share.[29] For those companies that already have a high share, there is merit in maintaining their levels of expenditure. For those companies with low market share, the correlation implies that it may not be the best strategy to spend funds on marketing activity to increase market share. Strategy options that attempt to buy market share with additional marketing activity may result in low return on investment.

However, it should be noted that the evidence is circular in the sense that, if high-share firms have higher profits, then they have more funds to invest in cost-saving devices, higher quality and more marketing activity. This will, in turn, raise their market share and profitability even further. Moreover, such evidence may be of little strategic help to the majority of companies that do not have a high share: what can they possibly do to catch up? It may be prohibitively expensive to invest in marketing and plant economies. However, Japanese car and electronics companies were in much that position in the 1960s, but have developed to become a major force in the world car industry. Innovation and the mistakes of the market leaders provide clues on the strategies needed.

Capital investment[30]

In the context of the operations strategies reviewed in Chapter 9, it might be argued that it will usually be worthwhile to invest in extra mechanisation to improve productivity and thus return on investment. The PIMS Databank suggests that this does not necessarily follow. Companies that have *high* levels of capital investment as a percentage of their sales tend also to have *lower* profitability. The higher productivity gained from such capital investment may not completely offset the damage.

There are several reasons for this: capital-intensive plant usually needs to be run at high production capacity to make profits, as the European steel industry case demonstrated in Chapter 3. Such production requirements need steady or increasing sales to deliver the profits and, as we have seen, this may be a dubious assumption. There may even be a temptation to keep production running at capacity by offering special deals to customers, stealing sales from competitors and so on, all of which will reduce profitability. By contrast, direct labour is more flexible and can be switched around when demand fluctuates. Moreover, if the company decides to leave the industry, the investment in fixed capital may make it more difficult, as we also saw in the European steel industry case in Chapter 3. Such companies may be tempted to reduce prices in order to survive, which will in turn reduce the profitability of all companies in the industry, even those that have invested in the latest capital-intensive equipment.

Strategy options that rely on heavy capital expenditure to generate profits need to be examined carefully. In some industries, there may be no choice. But there is no automatic likelihood that such expenditure will always deliver higher profitability.

14.3.3 Mergers and acquisitions[31]

Mergers and acquisitions often form part of the strategy options that are expected to transform company performance. Chapters 12 and 13 summarised the main reasons for seeking these routes, particularly as part of corporate strategy and as a means of entry into new markets. However, it should be stated that these activities are mainly confined to the UK, France and the US. They are less common in the rest of Europe and the Far East. Although there are clear reasons for seeking mergers and acquisitions, the empirical evidence on their performance suggests that they add little value to the companies undertaking the activity.

Given the amount of energy and publicity expended, this conclusion may be regarded as somewhat disappointing. Various researchers have reviewed the main evidence, which is summarised in Table 14.1. Essentially, they concluded that: '. . . The typical effect of merger and acquisition (M&A) activity on firm performance has been well documented and, on average, M&A activity does not lead to superior financial performance . . . Despite decades

Table 14.1

The performance of mergers

Method of evaluation	Examples of studies	Conclusions
1 Cumulative studies of research findings	King *et al.* (2004) Datta (1992)	On average, mergers do not lead to superior financial performance
2 Whether acquired business is held in the long term	Ravenscraft and Scherer (1987)	More divested than retained
3 Impact of acquisitions remains 'inconclusive'	Roll (1988); Haspeslaugh and Jemison (1991); Sirower (1997)	No clear evidence of benefits
4 Benefits of M&A to acquirors often resource-based or market-based	Anand and Singh (1997); Ahuja and Katila (2001); Hayward (2001)	Benefits possible but not fully proven: note the relationship with resource-based (Chapter 6) and environment-based strategy (Chapter 3)

Source: Compiled by the author from various research papers. The full references can be found by examining two papers: (1) King, D R, Dalton, D R, Daly, C M and Covin, J G (2004) Meta-Analysis of Post-Acquisition Performance: Indications of Unidentified Moderators, *Strategic Management Journal*, Vol 25, pp187–200. (2) Hayward, M L A (2002) When do Firms Learn from their Acquisition Experience? Strategic Management Journal, Vol 23, No 1, pp21–40. There is a useful summary of the broader issues in M&A activity by Professors Michael Hitt, R Duane Ireland and Jeffrey S Harrison in Chapter 12 of Hitt, M A, Freeman, R E and Harrison, J S (2001) *Handbook of Strategic Management*, Blackwell Business, Oxford.

of research, what impacts the financial performance of firms engaging in M&A activity remains largely unexplained'.[32]

None of the evidence suggests that it is impossible for mergers or acquisitions to succeed in adding value. What the evidence does suggest is that many do not and the main reason would appear to be over-optimistic and vague objectives rather than some deeper inherent flaw.[33] Generally, they are more likely to be successful where the partners are of similar size. In addition, cost cutting and asset downsizing may not be the most effective ways of improving performance. It may be more useful to consider ways of transferring competencies and exploiting revenue synergies.[34] Beyond this, such options have no proven record of success in terms of delivering value.

Key strategic principles

- Business judgement needs to be applied to selection because no one can be certain about the outcomes of strategy proposals.

- Generic industry environments have been analysed to provide some guidance on strategy evaluation. They are based on two broad categories: the *stage of industry maturity* and the *competitive position* of the organisation involved. After identifying where the organisation fits on these two parameters, simple choices then suggest themselves.

- Beyond this general work, further guidance on appropriate strategies has been developed for specific types of industry situation: fragmented industries, emerging industries, mature markets, declining markets have all been identified.

- Empirical evidence based on the PIMS Databank also exists on the connection between strategic actions and the results in terms of profitability and other criteria.

- According to PIMS, high quality and strong market share can make a positive contribution to profitability. High capital intensity is less likely to have a positive impact. Some researchers doubt the cause and effect relationships here.

- Acquisitions and mergers have also been studied for their impact on profitability. The evidence is, at best, mixed and, at worst, suggests that many are unsuccessful.

CASE STUDY 14.3

Where now for Unilever's 'Path to Growth' strategy?

Unilever is one of the world's largest food and consumer goods companies. In 1999, it introduced its new 'Path to Growth' strategy with the objective of focusing on its leading brands in order to deliver new profitable growth. This was classic product portfolio strategy – cutting weak brands in low-growth markets – but Unilever's profits were hardly higher in 2004 than in 2000. Why? And where now?

Unilever in the new millennium

Unilever has some areas of significant market strength: for example, it is the world's largest maker of ice cream products, tea beverages, margarine and cooking oils and some soap products – *see* Exhibit 14.6. Its major competitors worldwide include Procter & Gamble (US) and Nestlé (Switzerland). They are both equally dominant in related product areas, with Unilever often in second position. Although Unilever has been trading successfully over the last few years, it has been operating in relatively mature markets. As a result, the executive

committee decided in the late 1990s to weed out underperforming areas and focus on strengths. To understand the circumstances leading to such prescriptive strategic solutions, it is useful to begin by exploring Unilever's history.

Background – strategy as history

Unilever began as a merger between the British soap and detergent manufacturer Lever Brothers and the group of Dutch margarine and food oil companies Van Den Bergh and Jurgens, after the First World War. Both parents already had ▶

▶ **CASE STUDY 14.3 continued**

Unilever's acquisition of Hellmans Mayonnaise and Knorr Soups, including its Russian range, gave the company added presence in major branded products. But competition is fierce and retail pressures high. Some strategists have argued that Unilever would have been better acquiring in the personal products market where the profit margins are higher.

extensive international activities which they sought to consolidate and extend through the new joint company. But the national sensitivities were such that the new company had some special characteristics that still affect the way that Unilever operates in the twenty-first century: it has two worldwide headquarters and two chairpersons – specifically, in 2000 Antony Burgmanns (Dutch) and Niall Fitzgerald (Irish/UK). Especially in the 1970s and 1980s, it also had a strong tradition of international co-operation and human resource development between the semi-autonomous national companies that made up the group.

In the early years, the various national companies were allowed to manage their own affairs. In the 1960s, global co-ordination was introduced at the joint headquarters in product areas like detergents. But national companies were still allowed to keep their own national brands, strategies and

> ### Exhibit 14.6
>
> ## Unilever's key statistics
>
> - Worldwide turnover €40.2 billion in 2004 with operating profit €2.9 billion
> - Over 230,000 employees in over 100 countries worldwide
> - Leading food brands include Flora/Becel, Knorr, Hellmanns, Iglo/Birds Eye/Findus, Rama/Blue Band, Bertolli, Slimfast and the ice cream 'heart' logotype
> - Leading personal care and cleaning brands include Rexona, Dove, Lux, Pond's, Axe/Lynx, Sunsilk, Omo, Radion
> - Since 'Path to Growth' strategy launched in 1999, Unilever has reduced the main brands from 1,600 to 400 leading brands with another 250 smaller brands

manufacturing facilities. Thus, for example, Unilever's detergent activities across Europe in the period 1965–90 were a patchwork of national brands – Persil in the UK, Skip in France and Portugal, Omo in the Netherlands, Austria and parts of Africa – each with its own production operation. By contrast, its rival Procter & Gamble (P&G) was developing a more focused pan-European branding and manufacturing operation under the brand name Ariel. Profit margins at P&G were consequently significantly higher than at Unilever. However, there was more co-ordination in some newer Unilever product areas – for example, Dove skin care, Liptons Tea and ice cream products like Cornetto and Magnum were encouraged to develop worldwide under the heart-shaped logo.

Unilever's prescriptive approach

In the late 1990s, the relative independence of Unilever's national companies gave way to much greater international co-ordination and global strategy, at least in some product areas. The executive committee drove such a change from the centre with two major initiatives.

In 1997, Unilever announced a new organisational structure that had several specific objectives:

- to clarify worldwide management responsibilities and stimulate growth;
- to inject some new life into a company whose culture had become worthy but dull;
- to increase product co-ordination with a view to stimulating greater responsibility and innovation across the group.

In 1999, it coupled this reorganisation with a new, bold strategy: the 'Path to Growth'. This would concentrate the company's resources on its 400 leading brands. It would either sell or slowly run down its other 1,200 brands. Marketing, research and personnel were focused on its leading power brands. The objective was to achieve annual sales growth of 6 per cent by 2004 and to boost profit margins from 11 to 15 per cent. Major costs savings would result from simplifying operations and reducing suppliers – over US$1 billion per annum. The sales growth would come from investing more in marketing and advertising.

Subsequently, and in spite of approving a mission statement that was both bland and boring ('Our purpose at Unilever is to meet the everyday needs of people everywhere'), the small executive committee at the centre took some bold strategic decisions:

● It sold the speciality chemicals division for US$4.6 billion.
● It divested a range of national brands such as John West fish products in the UK, Mazola cooking oil in the US, Oxo cooking ingredients in the UK and a range of European soups: Batchelors in the UK, Royco and Lesieur in France and Heisse Tasse in Germany. Some of these brands were market leaders in their national markets.
● It bought new ice cream companies in Brazil, the US, Mexico and China – including the US superpremium ice cream company Ben & Jerry for US$125 million.
● It acquired the major slimming foods company, Slim Fast, for US$2.3 billion. This was just before the 'Atkins Diet' became popular, which was quite different from Slim Fast. Unilever's acquisition proved unsuccessful in the sense that it never covered the cost of capital.
● It acquired the global food company, Bestfoods, which owned Hellmans Mayonnaise and Knorr Soups and Sauces, for US$20 billion. Unilever's acquisition was successful in that it more than covered the cost of capital. However, with hindsight, some commentators felt that the company might have been better investing in the faster-growing personal products category rather than slow-growing foods.

Equally, Unilever decided to reorganise its entire operation to give more emphasis to key product groups and brands. Globalisation, even with local variations, meant that each national company could no longer go entirely its own way. The group's new structure was announced in 2000 and included the following:

● Business product groups would now have more power. National companies would continue but the business groups would be pre-eminent.
● Some seven starred product groups were identified with significant international growth potential for the first time: laundry, ice cream, yellow fats, personal wash, tea-based beverages, prestige products, skin care. These were considered to have real growth potential and would receive priority investment accordingly.
● Another three categories were also identified as established world products: hair care, oral hygiene, deodorants. However, these did not have quite the growth potential of the categories above and would receive investment accordingly.
● Innovation officers were appointed for each company.
● Unilever would work on a time horizon of eight to ten years for its basic category planning.

Results to 2004 and another reorganisation

As Figure 14.5 shows, the 'Path to Growth' strategy produced operating profits in 2004 that were hardly any higher than in 2000. There were some good reasons that were outside the control of the company – poor weather for ice cream sales in

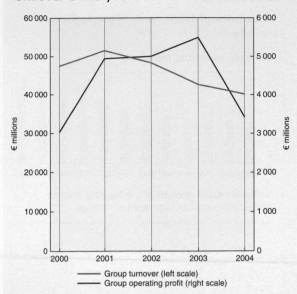

Figure 14.5

Unilever's five years since 'Path to Growth'

—— Group turnover (left scale)
—— Group operating profit (right scale)

Source: Annual Report and Accounts 2004.

2004 and the temporary success of the Atkins Diet hit Unilever's Slim Fast brand hard. But other areas also performed poorly – especially parts of the Liptons Tea range and some of the North American products.

Admittedly, sales margins had increased and there was some sales growth in the leading brands – see Figure 14.6. However, the overall picture suggested that the 'Path to Growth' strategy was, at best, a 'path to high margin' strategy, with the sales target being badly missed. Even earnings per share had slipped back in 2004. The difficulty was not that the company had failed to remove its brands but that its focus on the remaining brands was not producing the results. At the time of writing, Unilever did not have a full explanation of the strategy failure. But it did announce another reorganisation in early 2005 of its business from which it is possible to gain some insights into what went wrong.

Unilever's reorganisation was announced in February 2005. A new, smaller executive team replaced the previous executive committee, the two divisions and 11 business groups. The new team would have three regional presidents for Europe, the Americas and Asia/Africa. It would also have two product category presidents, one for the food division and one for the home and personal care division. The new executive team would be completed by a chief finance officer, a chief human resources officer and one group chief executive (not two as previously). The new chief executive, Patrick Cescau, commented: 'I am excited to have been entrusted with this new challenge. These changes are designed to make us more competitive in the market place. The fusion of our businesses under three regional presidents gives us the ability to truly leverage our scale and to service our customers more

▶

▶ **CASE STUDY 14.3 continued**

Figure 14.6

The results of Unilever's 'Path to Growth' strategy

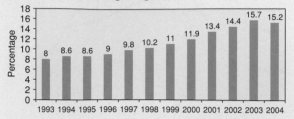

(a) Unilever: operating margin %

(b) Unilever: sales growth of the leading brands 2002–2004 – percentage annual change

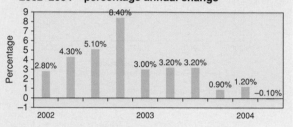

Source: Company Annual Report and Accounts.

effectively. The two category (product) presidents will concentrate on brand management and activation driven by consumer needs and aspirations.'

Some commentators argued that the company still had much to do. It was beginning to face up to the challenge of investing in its main brands, being more productive in terms of innovation and reacting to the rise of supermarket bargaining power in the more advanced economies. Although the new Unilever strategy appeared to lack the detail of the previous 'Path to Growth' strategy, this was quite deliberate: Mr Cescau expained: '[With Path to Growth] we boxed ourselves in. We wanted to be transparent. But in doing so, we created a straitjacket for ourselves.'

Case questions

1 *In what way is the Unilever strategic planning process prescriptive? How, if at all, does it help innovation?*

2 *To what extent is Unilever's strategic decision-making process a result of its history?*

3 *Given the size of the operation, would you make any changes to Unilever's strategic decision-making process? Are you convinced that the new structure will be any better at delivering results?*

14.4 THE CLASSIC PRESCRIPTIVE MODEL OF CORPORATE STRATEGY: EXPLORING THE PROCESS

Having made our choice of the *content* of a strategic plan, we now turn our attention to the related issue of who will make the choice and how it will be made – the strategic *process*. Clearly, in practice the two topics of process and content will be interlinked, but it is useful to separate them in our exploration here. The aim of this section is not merely to describe the process but also to evaluate its usefulness because it is important to be aware of such issues. We consider the matter under three headings:

1 The prescriptive process of corporate strategy

2 Some problems with the prescriptive process

3 Solutions within the prescriptive process to its problems.

14.4.1 The prescriptive process of corporate strategy

In describing their version of the classic prescriptive model, Wheelen and Hunger[36] state that the process of corporate strategy involves five major elements:

1 *environmental scanning* – the external opportunities and threats of the SWOT analysis;

2 *internal scanning* – the strengths and weaknesses of the SWOT analysis;

3 *strategy formulation* – mission, objectives, strategies and policies;

4 *strategy implementation* – including programmes, budgets and other procedures;

5 *evaluation and control* – to ensure that the strategic process remains on its predicted path.

Table 14.2

The prescriptive model of the corporate strategy process

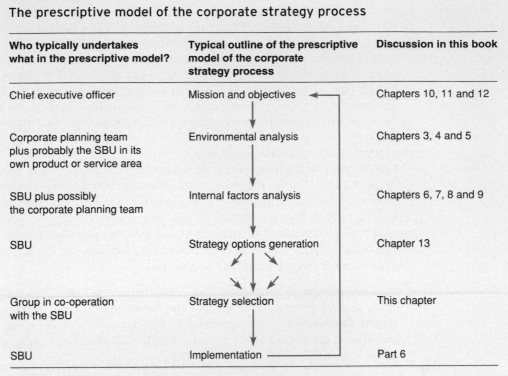

Who typically undertakes what in the prescriptive model?	Typical outline of the prescriptive model of the corporate strategy process	Discussion in this book
Chief executive officer	Mission and objectives	Chapters 10, 11 and 12
Corporate planning team plus probably the SBU in its own product or service area	Environmental analysis	Chapters 3, 4 and 5
SBU plus possibly the corporate planning team	Internal factors analysis	Chapters 6, 7, 8 and 9
SBU	Strategy options generation	Chapter 13
Group in co-operation with the SBU	Strategy selection	This chapter
SBU	Implementation	Part 6

Note: The process is largely linear but with feedback mechanisms at various points to ensure that the objectives, analysis and strategies are all consistent with each other. This is shown by the directions of the arrows, whose significance will become clearer when we examine alternative processes in Chapter 15.

For example, at Unilever the company is constantly scanning its major competitors such as Procter & Gamble (US) and Nestlé (Switzerland) – environmental scanning. It is also examining its own resources – internal scanning. It then considers its business objectives and develops new strategies such as its investment in global ice cream markets – strategy formulation. It implements such strategies by building or acquiring ice cream companies as described in Case study 14.3 – strategy implementation. After it has begun its strategies, it will monitor their profits to ensure that they meet group strategic objectives and it will then take corrective action if necessary – evaluation and control.

Some commentators on the classical model, such as Jauch and Glueck,[37] put the mission and objectives before environmental scanning. This book puts the objectives after the environmental and internal scanning for the reasons given in Chapter 1. However, in practice, the process is circular, with no firm rule at this point. Table 14.2 sets out a typical sequence for the classical model with, in this case, the objectives first.[38]

Just as important as the precise sequence of events in the process is *who* undertakes them. This becomes particularly acute when the organisation consists of a group of industries that are possibly unrelated. In these circumstances, it is likely that there will be a corporate centre that might undertake some tasks and strategic business units (SBUs) that will undertake others. But who does what tasks? There is no single answer to this question. For example, Unilever's approach described in Case study 14.3 is unique to the opportunities, history and products of that company.

Although there are dangers in generalising, several commentators have identified which groups are particularly likely to be involved at each stage.[39] In a large multinational like Unilever, the group's SWOT analysis is usually undertaken at the corporate level and it is also the corporation that defines the overall mission and objectives. The reason is that only the corporation can have the overview needed to direct the main strategic thrusts and the resources to fund them. The results are then passed down for the strategy *option* process to be developed by the SBUs. In the case of Unilever, some SBUs would be given specially favoured treatment – such as ice cream and tea-based beverages – while others would have a tougher evaluative regime. The strategy *selection* might then be undertaken at corporate headquarters, in consultation with the SBU and in the context of the available funds that the group has at its disposal. The SBU then implements the agreed strategies.

The process is therefore usually driven by corporate headquarters, on the basis that it is the only part of the organisation to have a complete picture of all aspects. However, individual businesses are often given considerable freedom within the guidelines to develop their strategy, as is the case at Unilever.

Such a relationship between the headquarters and the SBUs has been in operation at General Motors (US) since the 1920s when Alfred Sloan was brought in from one of the subsidiaries to rescue and reorganise what became one of the world's largest companies. He was one of the early strategy pioneers to propose such a process. His work is recorded in his own writing[40] and that of Alfred Chandler.[41] As well as examining General Motors, Chandler also conducted a historical survey of three other large companies in the early twentieth century to discover what made US industry so powerful.

> *Strategic plans can be formulated from below, but normally the implementation of such proposals requires the resources which only the general office [i.e. the corporate HQ] can provide. Within the broad policy lines laid down by that office and with the resources it allocates, the executives at the lower levels carry out tactical [i.e. day-to-day, non-strategic] decisions.*

However, it should be pointed out that, in the late twentieth century, more strategy decision-making freedom was given to the subsidiaries than described by Chandler. Although many companies around the world have adopted the classical prescriptive process, there are a number of well-documented problems with this approach. We now explore them.

14.4.2 Some problems with the prescriptive process

There are a number of assumptions or simplifications in the prescriptive process that may not be valid in reality. We summarise four here but should note that other difficulties have been identified.

1 *Environment*. It is assumed that this is predictable, so that a clear direction can be used to develop the opportunities and threats to the organisation. There have been numerous instances of major variations in the environment that make this difficult to sustain.

2 *Clear planning procedure*. The major strategic decisions are initiated by this procedure that, once set in motion, can arrive at a clear and simple decision point: the strategy selection. In many companies, planning procedures are complicated by the need to persuade managers to undertake specific strategies. They may be reluctant for a variety of reasons, from a loss of power to a personality clash.

3 *Top-down procedures*. These procedures from corporate HQ to the SBUs represent the most efficient method of developing new and innovative strategies. It is assumed that they can cope with the environment and gain commitment from the managers who will implement them. Many research studies have shown that managers find such a process demotivating. By contrast, the Japanese Honda case, with its frequent consultation and dialogue, may be far more effective.

4 *Culture*. The culture of organisations will allow the classical model to operate. Culture here has two meanings: the style, beliefs and practices of the *organisation itself* and, more broadly, the culture of the *country* in which the organisation operates. Both of these are assumed to be consistent with the top-down classical model. In practice, some cultures

are clearly more suited to a dominant top-down approach than others. The ABB case at the end of Chapter 16 provides an example of how the company's culture was actually changed.

Hence, all the above assumptions have been shown to have significant flaws.

Marx[42] quotes the former chairman of the giant US corporation General Electric, Mr Jack Welch, on the problems encountered in strategic planning in the 1960s using the classical process:

> *Our planning system was dynamite when we first put it in. The thinking was fresh, the form mattered little – the format got no points. It was idea-oriented. We then hired a head of planning and he hired two vice-presidents and then he hired a planner, and the books got thicker and the printing got more sophisticated, and the covers got harder and the drawings got better. The meetings kept getting larger. Nobody can say anything with 16 or 18 people there.*

Welch became increasingly concerned about the whole planning process in General Electric and moved to change it. Mr Welch was concerned about three areas:

1 the *bureaucracy* that may breed under classical strategy processes;

2 the *judgement* required to make choices, which may not be as rational as the simple options and choice selection process suggests;

3 the need to encourage a *culture of ideas* rather than a top-down approach as in the classical strategy process.

14.4.3 Solutions to problems within the prescriptive process

To explore the solutions available within the prescriptive process, it is useful to do a careful survey of the difficulties encountered. One such survey in the early 1980s observed that the prescriptive model had become excessively rational, bureaucratic and formalised.[43] There are a number of ways to overcome these problems. They involve a more open strategic planning culture with less emphasis on quantification of data. Stress can also be laid on two aspects of the actual process:

1 exploring with the proposers of the strategy the *assumptions* on which the strategy is based. When such assumptions are incorrect, the whole strategy is open to doubt;

2 during the strategy review sessions, requesting a simple *verbal summary* of the main proposals. If this cannot be done, then the proposals themselves may be suspect.

The whole process and system by which a strategy is developed should also be re-examined periodically in companies: this is a *planning process audit*. The aim would be to remove the impediments that creep in over time. It was just such an audit that led Unilever to rethink its strategy decision-making processes during 1996–97. The company felt the need to redefine its direction, highlight key business areas and clarify the procedures that linked them together. It is notable that it also coincided with the appointment of a new co-chairman, Niall Fitzgerald. Two specific aims were to gain greater individual ownership of strategic decisions and more emphasis on innovation. It is then notable that, when the 'Path to Growth' appeared to falter in the mid-2000s, the company made changes to its *management team* and *organisation structure* as well as to its products.

14.4.4 Conclusion

Overall, it will be evident that prescriptive strategists are aware of the problems that the process causes. They may attempt to overcome them by revising the process and renewing it. They may try to undertake this by more radical measures to change the culture of the company. But there are still residual problems and some strategists favour more radical solutions than the prescriptive process, as we will see in Chapter 15.

Key strategic principles

- The prescriptive model of the strategic *process* is largely linear. It has feedback mechanisms at various points to ensure that objectives, options and strategy choice are consistent with each other.

- Problems with the prescriptive approach cover four main areas: environment unpredictability, planning procedures, top-down approaches driven by the centre, and the culture of the organisation that will allow the model to operate.

- Specific criticisms include the need for more dialogue, a greater flow of ideas and more adaptation to the environment.

- It may be possible to solve these problems within the prescriptive process but some strategists take a more critical view.

14.5 INTERNATIONAL CORPORATE STRATEGY SELECTION[44]

Strategy selection across international boundaries is more complex because additional factors such as currency, national cultures, tariff barriers and other matters need to be considered. These aspects have been explored in previous chapters.

Probably the single most important aspect from a selection perspective is to clarify the *objectives* for international expansion. The reason is that these will provide the direction for the development and selection of the relevant international activities. In practice, there are many variations. Exhibit 14.7 contains some examples of possible links between international objectives and strategic choice.

Exhibit 14.7

Two examples of the connection between international objectives and strategy selection

Example 1

- *Objective*: international expansion because the home market is mature

- *Key factors for success*: include economies of scale

- *Implication*: retain home-based production to obtain increased economies of scale

- *Strategy choice*: select low-cost strategy based on production economies of scale from home-base factory and then export production

- *Example*: BMW car production is still based largely in Germany, but sales are international

Example 2

- *Objective*: international expansion because trade barriers are high

- *Key factors for success*: need to obtain distribution inside the barrier, as well as economies of scale in production

- *Implication*: need to set up manufacturing operation inside trade barrier

- *Strategy choice*: select country that represents a useful entry point behind the trade barriers, but also allows good communications with the home country

- *Example*: Nissan and Toyota cars have set up operations in the UK and Spain behind the trade barriers represented by the EU

The difficulty in international strategy is that the linkage between objectives and strategy selection may be more complex than simple business logic. The presence of international subsidiaries, each with its own culture, history and resources, may make this more difficult. Such companies may have conflicting views on objectives, strategy options and the practicality of their implementation. The writer clearly remembers having an international food launch – a powdered orange drink made up with water and called Apeel in the UK and Tang in the rest of Europe – imposed on a UK subsidiary by corporate headquarters in the US. But it was part of a 'Europe-wide strategy' and was therefore deemed to apply everywhere. It was only after it had generated substantial losses that the group headquarters was able to accept that the strategic choice was incorrect.[45] There are dangers therefore in the centre imposing its strategic choice on subsidiaries outside the home country. Further discussion on strategy choice, particularly in a global context, is contained in Chapter 20.

Key strategic principles

- International strategy selection is more complex. The starting point is clarity on the objectives and reasons for international expansion.

- Conflicting views on objectives, resources and cultures may exist between different international subsidiaries of an organisation. Such differences may make it more difficult to make strategic choices. There are dangers in the centre imposing its choice on subsidiaries.

CASE STUDY 14.4

Eurofreeze evaluates its strategy options: 2

After developing its mission and objectives, Eurofreeze began to examine the strategy options that were available and the important strategic decisions that would follow. Importantly, the case presents the strategic options in the form used by many companies to reach strategic decisions.

Future strategy options for Eurofreeze

The company was now considering a number of strategy options. It had undertaken the basic analysis using a cost of capital of 9 per cent. To help analyse the options, it gathered basic market data for its own products and those of its main competitor, Refrigor. The information covered all its main European markets and is shown in Table 14.3. Within the product groups, there was little useful additional information: product sales data were available on individual items, but varied so much by country and by store chain that there was little to be gained from analysing the data.

Refrigor was market leader in vegetables and fruit. Eurofreeze was market leader in branded meat and fish dishes, with Refrigor second. Neither company was market leader in savoury dishes (including pizza) or gateaux. (McCain was leader in savoury dishes, with a 30 per cent share, and Sara Lee in gateaux, with a 25 per cent share.)

The company undertook a portfolio analysis in 2003. This is shown as Figure 14.7. The calculation of the relative market shares for this analysis is shown in the Appendix at the end of the chapter.

Eurofreeze then proceeded to consider each of the options that were available to it. The results are outlined below. (There could be some further combination of options but it was felt that the following reflected the main routes available to the company.)

Eurofreeze options

The strategic options available to Eurofreeze are summarised in Table 14.4; their financial implications are then explored in the following text.

Option 1
Stop supplying all basic frozen products, including its branded and own brand (i.e. with the retailer's private brand name) vegetables. Dropping this range would mean that the overhead contribution made by carrying these products would no longer be available to the group. The financial implications are shown in Table 14.5.

Option 2
Cancel its current branded range of basic frozen food products such as vegetables, but continue to manufacture own brand ▶

▶ CASE STUDY 14.4 continued

Table 14.3

Market data on the European frozen products market 1999

| | Eurofreeze | | Refrigor | | Market growth of product category | |
	Sales (US$m)	Market share of product category (%)	Sales (US$m)	Market share of product category (%)	2003	2012
Branded vegetables vegetables and fruit	400	10	800	20	+2%	–
Private label vegetables and fruit	200	5	300	7.5	+2%	–
Branded meat and fish	300	30	200	20	+4%	+6%
Private label meat and fish	150	15	100	10	+4%	+6%
Branded savoury dishes including pizza	30	6	80	16	+7%	+5%
Private label savoury dishes including pizza	none	–	40	8	+7%	+5%
Branded cakes and gateaux	25	12	25	12	+8%	+6%
Private label cakes and gateaux	none	–	20	9.6	+8%	+6%

Figure 14.7

The European frozen foods market: portfolio matrices for Eurofreeze and Refrigor

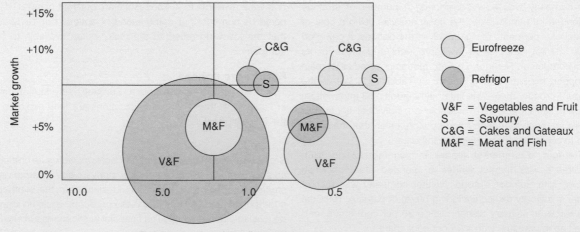

Diameter of circle proportionate to size of sales
for each company in that product category.

Table 14.4

Summary of the Eurofreeze strategy options

Option	Implication for sales
1 Stop selling branded and own label vegetables and fruit	Sales decline US$400 million in Year 1, US$200 million in Year 2
2 Stop selling branded vegetables and fruit but continue own label	Sales decline US$400 million in Year 1
3 Extend specialist branded food ranges, e.g. pizza and gateaux	Sales gain US$50 million each year
4 Major cutback of range in first two years, then rebuild specialist areas from Year 4 onwards	Sales decline US$205 million in Year 1, US$300 million in Years 2 and 3 Sales gain US$50 million in Year 4, US$100 million in each year from Year 5 onwards
5 Become lowest-cost producer through major investment	Build sales by at least US$100 million per annum

Table 14.5

Financial projection for Option 1
(US$ million)

	Projected from company base year in 2003											Option 1
	2003	2004	2005	2006	2007	2008	2009	2010	2011	2012	2013	NPV[a]
Sales	600	200	–	–	–	–	–	–	–	–	–	–
Incremental profit impact	24	(5)	(8)	(8)	(8)	(8)	(8)	(8)	(8)	(8)	(8)	(48.6)[b]
Capital impact: working capital	–	10[c]	20[c]	–	–	–	–	–	–	–	–	26.0[d]
Capital impact: fixed capital	–	–	–	–	–	–	–	–	–	–	–	–

Note: Current position shows the situation for the option only. All other sales and profits operate as previously.
(a) NPV = Net Present Value at 9 per cent cost of capital 2003 = (5) × 0.917 + (8) × 0.842 + (8) × 0.7721 etc.
(b) Net effect of lower sales and some lower overheads, but freezer transport and warehousing would still be needed for other products.
(c) Working capital no longer required to support sales.
(d) US$26 million working capital released from lower sales when discounted back to base year 2003.

versions. This would keep some overhead contribution but would have very low added value. At the same time, the company would keep and slowly extend its range of higher-added-value branded items. (See financial implications in Table 14.6.)

Option 3
Drive hard to redevelop and substantially extend some specialist branded ranges; for example, its range of frozen cakes and gateaux and its market-leader range of meat and fish

products. This would take time and resources but would produce higher added value. It would keep its broader range of branded products, including its low-value-added items, as long as they made a contribution to overheads. (See financial implications in Table 14.7.)

Option 4
Become a specialist producer. This would be done by dropping almost all of its low-added-value basic range, closing a number of freezer factories, contracting out its freezer

▶ CASE STUDY 14.4 continued

Table 14.6

Financial projection for Option 2
(US$ million)

| | Projected from company base year in 2003 | | | | | | | | | | | Option 2 |
	2003	2004	2005	2006	2007	2008	2009	2010	2011	2012	2013	NPV[a]
Sales	600	200	200	200	200	200	200	200	200	200	200	–
Incremental profit impact[a]	24	(5)	(6)	(6)	(6)	(6)	(6)	(6)	(6)	(6)	(6)	(37.6)
Capital impact: working capital	–	8[b]	12[b]	–	–	–	–	–	–	–	–	17.4
Capital impact: fixed capital	–	–	–	–	–	–	–	–	–	–	–	–

Note: Current position shows the situation for the option only. All other sales and profits operate as previously.

(a) Highly efficient to deliver own label to few supermarkets with no branded advertising. However, this is offset by the need to continue to deliver branded savoury, meat and fish dishes to all outlets.

(b) Reduction in working capital proportionately larger on smaller outlets: US$17.4 million released.

Table 14.7

Financial projection for Option 3
(US$ million)

| | Projected from company base year in 2003 | | | | | | | | | | | Option 3 |
	2003	2004	2005	2006	2007	2008	2009	2010	2011	2012	2013	NPV[a]
Sales	1 105	1 150	1 200	1 250	1 300	1 350	1 400	1 450	1 500	1 550	1 600	–
Incremental profit impact[a]	80	(5)	(5)	4	6	8	10	12	14	14	14	35.7
Capital impact: working capital	–	(2.5)[b]	(2.5)	(2.5)	(2.5)	(2.5)	(2.5)	(2.5)	(2.5)	(2.5)	(2.5)	(16.0)
Capital impact: fixed capital[c]	–	–	(5)	–	(10)	–	–	–	–	–	–	(11.3)

Note: In this option, the current column considers total sales and profits because they will all be affected by the option.

(a) Net effect of increase in sales less the branded expenditure needed to achieve this.

(b) Steadily increasing sales so extra working capital required.

(c) Some new capital investment required in plant and equipment to handle extra sales.

distribution, investing heavily in specialist menu ranges, advertising these ranges only. Clearly this is a more radical solution, but would emulate the success of several US companies across Europe, such as McCain and Sara Lee. (*See* Table 14.8 for financial implications.)

Option 5

Becoming the lowest-cost producer. This would be done by building on existing sales to all major customers: major invest-ment in new factories, new warehouses and new transport networks would be needed. This would be coupled with major (and largely unknown) manufacturing innovation, all with the aim of reducing costs, so that they would move below those of its competitor, Refrigor. Although this option was available in theory, it was based on three assumptions that carried some risk:

1 Refrigor would slow down its current rate of investment and allow itself to be overtaken.

Table 14.8

Financial projection for Option 4
(US$ million)

| | Projected from company base year in 2003 | | | | | | | | | | | Option 4 |
	2003	2004	2005	2006	2007	2008	2009	2010	2011	2012	2013	NPV[a]
Sales	1 105	900	600	600	650	700	800	850	900	1 000	1 200	–
Incremental profit impact[a]	80	(50)	(100)	(40)	(20)	10	30	100	225	250	300	258.7
Capital impact: working capital	–	10	30	–	(2.5)	(2.5)	(5)	(2.5)	(2.5)	(5)	(10)	19.0
Capital impact: fixed capital[b]	–	(50)	(100)	(50)	–	(50)	–	–	–	–	–	(201.1)

Note: In this option, the current column considers total sales and profits because they will all be affected by the option.
(a) Quite difficult to calculate the profit impact with certainty: need to explore detailed projections for each major product area but not presented above for reasons of space.
(b) Need to provide for factory closure costs and, in year 2008, for factory reinvestment.

Table 14.9

Financial projection for Option 5
(US$ million)

| | Projected from company base year in 2003 | | | | | | | | | | | Option 5 |
	2003	2004	2005	2006	2007	2008	2009	2010	2011	2012	2013	NPV[a]
Sales	1 105	1 400	1 500	1 600	1 800	2 000	2 200	2 400	2 600	2 800	3 000	–
Incremental profit impact[a]	80	5	5	10	12	20	30	40	50	60	70	160.0
Capital impact: working capital	–	(15)	(5)	(5)	(10)	(10)	(10)	(10)	(10)	(10)	(10)	(60.7)
Capital impact: fixed capital[b]	–	(100)	(300)	(150)	(50)	(50)	–	(200)	–	(200)	–	(729.4)

Note: In this option, the current column considers total sales and profits because they will all be affected by the option.
(a) Profit attempts to take into account the increased move to build higher-value-added products less the extra advertising and promotional costs to support these, especially in the early years.
(b) Substantial investment in new factories and other facilities will be required.

2 Major cost savings of the order of 20 per cent below existing costs were still available in the industry.
3 Market leadership could be gained through a low-cost route.

For this option, it was recognised that it would also be necessary to provide substantial extra advertising and promotional support to sustain and build the brands. Overall, this was the option with the highest investment. (See Table 14.9.)

Case questions

1 *What are the relative merits and problems of each option?*
2 *In what way does the use of the portfolio matrix help the strategic debate? And in what way might it mislead the strategic decisions?*
3 *Consider what other strategic analytical tools, if any, might provide useful insights into the strategic choice debate: you might wish to consider a PESTEL analysis, a Five Forces Analysis, generic strategies, a market options matrix, value chain, innovations checklist (in Chapter 11).*
4 *Which option, if any, would you recommend to Eurofreeze? Give reasons for your choice and explain the strengths and weaknesses of your choice.*

CRITICAL REFLECTION

Should companies engage in strategic plans?

This chapter has focused on prescriptive strategic decision making, which is widely used in many companies. It has explored both the strengths and weaknesses of such an approach, pointing out the many difficulties. Some strategists believe that prescriptive strategic planning has so many problems that it is not worth undertaking: in other words, it is counterproductive to produce a 'strategic plan'. What is your view? Should companies engage in strategic plans?

SUMMARY

- In evaluating strategic options, it is useful to distinguish between the content of the option (What strategy will we select?) and the process by which the selection will be undertaken (How will we undertake the selection task?).

In considering strategy content, the chapter provides an overview of the classic prescriptive evaluation approach. Such an approach relies on developing criteria as a starting point for selection. These need to be developed bearing in mind the nature of the organisation: for example, commercial and non-profit-making organisations will clearly require different criteria.

- There are six main criteria usually employed in commercial organisations: consistency (especially with the organisation's mission and objectives), suitability, validity, feasibility, business risk, attractiveness to stakeholders.

1 Consistency with the purpose of the organisation is a prime test for evaluating and selecting strategies.

2 Suitability of the strategy for the environment within which the organisation operates is clearly important.

3 Validity of the projections and data used in developing the option must be tested.

4 Feasibility will depend on two factors: constraints internal to the organisation, such as technical skills and finance; constraints external to the organisation, such as the response of competitors.

5 Business risk also needs to be assessed because it may be unacceptable to the organisation.

6 Attractiveness to stakeholders such as shareholders and employees is important: some options may be more attractive to some stakeholders than others.

- There may be international variations in evaluation criteria, depending on national differences in the roles and values of stakeholders and governments.

- In making an initial selection of the best option, it is important to clarify the basis on which this is to be done. Evaluation against the mission and objectives is important but needs to be rigorous and precise if it is to provide real benefit.

- Financial criteria can also be used as the basis of selection. The shareholder value approach takes a broader perspective on evaluation than that provided by the specific project. It seeks to determine the benefit of such developments in the context of the whole company against the cost of the company's capital. Major weaknesses are that it still relies on the assumption that shareholders are always the prime beneficiaries. In addition, it makes the dubious prescriptive assumption that revenue and profit streams can be forecast with accuracy some years into the future.

● Cost/benefit analysis has been successfully employed in public sector evaluation, where it is important to assess broader and less quantifiable benefits. The main difficulty is where to place the limit on such benefits and costs.

● Beyond the issues of criteria to aid strategy selection, business judgement is important. General empirical evidence is available through a number of routes. The ADL matrix summarises some broad decision-making parameters. It is based on two broad categories: the stage of industry maturity and the competitive position of the organisation involved. After the position of the organisation on these two parameters has been identified, simple choices then suggest themselves.

● Empirical evidence based on the PIMS Databank also exists on the connection between strategic actions and the results in terms of profitability and other criteria. According to PIMS, high quality and strong market share can make a positive contribution to profitability. High capital intensity is less likely to have a positive impact. Some researchers doubt the cause and effect relationships here. Acquisitions and mergers have also been studied for their impact on profitability. The evidence is, at best, mixed and, at worst, suggests that many are unsuccessful.

● International strategy selection is more complex. The starting point is clarity on the objectives and reasons for international expansion. The difficulty in international strategy is to find some basic pattern and logic for such developments in order to facilitate their selection. There may be some conflict between corporate headquarters and the individual international operating companies as a result of different competitive pressures, differing customer tastes and different cultures.

● After exploring the likely *content* of the selected strategy above, it is important to consider the *process* by which the selection is undertaken. The prescriptive model of the strategic process is largely linear. It has feedback mechanisms at various points to ensure that objectives, options and strategy choice are consistent with each other.

● Problems with the prescriptive approach cover four main areas: environment unpredictability; planning procedures; top-down approaches driven by the centre; and the culture of the organisation that will allow the model to operate. In addition, there are some specific criticisms which include the need for more dialogue, a greater flow of ideas and more adaptation to the environment. It may be possible to solve these problems within the prescriptive process model but some strategists take a more critical view.

QUESTIONS

1 Using Section 14.1, what criteria would you consider were particularly important if you were evaluating strategy options in the following organisations: a small chain of petrol stations; a large multinational developing a global strategy; a government telecommunications company that was about to be privatised; a student career planning service?

2 If you were developing strategy for a small company with 50 employees and a turnover of around US$5 million, would you use all the selection criteria outlined in Section 14.1 or would you select only some for this purpose? Give reasons for your answer and, if only choosing some, explain which you would pick.

3 Japanese companies have tended to favour payback criteria while US/UK companies have been more inclined to use DCF criteria in evaluating strategic options. What are the merits of the two approaches? Can you suggest any reasons why one might be preferred to another?

4 *'Discounting techniques rest on rather arbitrary assumptions about profitability, asset deterioration and external investment opportunities.'* (Professor Robert Hay)

Explain the implications of this comment for strategy evaluation and comment on its application in strategy selection.

5 What are the dangers, if any, of using quantified and precise evaluation criteria in strategy selection?

6 *'Strategy evaluation is an attempt to look beyond the obvious facts regarding the short-term health of a business and appraise instead those more fundamental factors and trends that govern success in the chosen field of endeavour.'* (Professor Richard Rumelt)

Discuss.

7 A well-known German company is primarily engaged in supplying motor components such as car radios and gearboxes to car companies in the EU, such as Ford and Toyota. It is considering acquiring a medium-sized US company as the basis for its first expansion outside Europe. What would you advise in this relatively mature and fiercely competitive industry?

8 With regard to new, fast-growing markets such as that for mobile telephones, the ADL matrix would suggest that weak and dominant companies face quite different strategic opportunities and problems. Is this really true when the market is changing so rapidly?

9 *'Merger and acquisition is the most common means of entry into new markets.'* (Professor John Kay)

What is the evidence of success from such ventures? What are the strategic implications of your answer for organisations considering this option?

10 *'Most firms rarely engage in explicit formal strategy evaluation . . . rather, it is a continuing process that is difficult to separate from normal planning, reporting and control.'* (Professor Richard Rumelt)

Discuss the implications for the evaluation criteria explored in this chapter.

APPENDIX

Calculation of relative market shares for portfolio analysis in association with Case study 14.4

For Eurofreeze

Vegetables and fruit: $(10\% + 5\%) \div (20\% + 7.5\%) = 0.54$

(Note that these could be redefined as separate branded and private product categories. Given the low added value from both routes, this has not been undertaken here. There are no clear rules.)

Meat and fish: $(30\% + 15\%) \div (20\% + 10\%) = 1.5$

Savoury dishes: $6\% \div 30\% = 0.2$

(Note that McCain is market leader in this category and it is this share that has been used.)

Cakes and gateaux: $12\% \div 25\% = 0.48$

(Note that Sara Lee is market leader in this category and it is this share that has been used.)

For Refrigor

Vegetables and fruit: $(20\% + 7.5\%) \div (10\% + 15\%) = 1.1$

Meat and fish: $(20\% + 10\%) \div (30\% + 15\%) = 0.67$

Savoury dishes: $(18\% + 16\%) \div 30\% = 0.8$

Cakes and gateaux: $(12\% + 9.6\%) \div 25\% = 0.86$

Further reading

On criteria for selection, *see* Day, G S (1987) *Strategic Market Planning*, West Publishing, St Paul, MN; Tiles, S (1963) 'How to evaluate business strategy', *Harvard Business Review*, July–Aug, pp111–22; Rumelt, R (1980) 'The evaluation of business strategy', originally published in Glueck, W F, *Business Policy and Strategic Management*, McGraw-Hill, New York, but republished in two more recent texts: De Wit, Bob and Meyer, R (1994) *Strategy: Process, Content and Context*, West Publishing, St Paul, MN; Mintzberg, H and Quinn, J B (1991) *The Strategy Process*, Prentice Hall, New York.

On financial evaluation, Glautier, M W E and Underdown, B (1994) *Accounting Theory and Practice*, 5th edn, Pitman Publishing, London, is a useful summary of the main areas. *See* also Arnold, G (1998) *Corporate Financial Management*, Financial Times Pitman Publishing, London, which provides an excellent review of the topic.

For a rational view on the use and abuse of investment criteria: Hay, R (1982) 'Managing as if tomorrow mattered', *Harvard Business Review*, May–June, pp72–9.

Feasibility is explored along with other criteria in Professor Richard Rumelt's article on 'The evaluation of business strategy' mentioned above.

For a more recent view of the problems of planning versus autonomy *see* Anderson, T J (2000) 'Strategic planning, autonomous actions and corporate performance', *Long Range Planning*, Vol 33, pp184–200, which contains some interesting empirical data.

Notes and references

1 *See*, for example, Gilmore, F and Brandenburg, R (1962) 'Anatomy of corporate planning', *Harvard Business Review*, Nov–Dec, pp61–9.

2 References for Nokia Case: Carnegy, H (1995) 'Scared of growing fat and lazy,' *Financial Times*, 10 July, p11. *See* also *Financial Times*, 30 Oct 1998, p18; 24 March 1999, p12; 9 July 1999, p21; 31 July 2000, p28; 8 December 2000, p16; 13 March 2001, p32; 29 May 2001, p29 (Ericsson interview); 14 June 2001, p18; 20 June 2001, p13; 22 June 2001, p13; 20 November 2001, p29; 7 December 2001, p32; 26 September 2002, p27; 18 November 2002, p21; 29 October 2003, p17; 27 September 2003, pM6; 6 December 2003, pM1; 16 December 2003, p29; 5 February 2004, p10; 10 February 2004, p26; 8 April 2004, p25; 20 April 2004, p21; 29 April 2004, p1; 15 June 2004, p30; 28 August 2004, p23; 1 October 2004, p14; 6 December 2004, p30; 20 December 2004, p11; 28 January 2005, p21; Nokia Annual Report and Accounts 1997, 2000 and 2004. For earlier data and comment on Nokia see Lynch, R (1994) *European Business Strategies*, 2nd edn, Kogan Page, London, p151.

3 Used with some effect to dismiss options by the late Professor 'Mac' MacIntosh in 1967 in London Business School MBA lectures and case discussions.

4 Different commentators have employed other criteria. Those used here have been developed from Day, G S (1987) *Strategic Market Planning*, West Publishing, St Paul, MN; Tiles, S (1963) 'How to evaluate business strategy', *Harvard Business Review*, July–Aug, pp111–22; Rumelt, R (1980) 'The evaluation of business strategy', originally published in Glueck, W F, *Business Policy and Strategic Management*, McGraw-Hill, New York, and republished in two more recent texts: De Wit, Bob and Meyes, R (1994) *Strategy: Process, Content and Context*, West Publishing, St Paul, MN; Mintzberg, H and Quinn, JB (1991) *The Strategy Process*, Prentice Hall, New York.

5 Reckitt Benckiser Presentation to Financial Analysts 9 February 2005, available on the web at www.reckitt.com.

6 *See* Lynch, R (1993) *Cases in European Marketing*, Kogan Page, London, Ch16.

7 *See Financial Times*, 15 Apr 1995, p9; 13 Oct 1994, p2; 1 Mar 1994, p29; and Lynch, R (1994) Op. cit., p84. Groupe Bull is a company with some real strategic problems that would make an interesting strategy project.

8 Kehoe, L (1995) 'Restrictive practice claims put Microsoft back in firing line', *Financial Times*, 6 Feb, p6.

9 Carnegy, H (1995) 'Bitter Swedish dispute to end,' *Financial Times*, 3 Aug, p2.

10 *See* Chapter 2 for details.

11 Munchau, W and Norman, P (1995) 'Planes, trains and automobiles,' *Financial Times*, 7 Nov, p19.

12 Ohmae, K (1982) *The Mind of the Strategist*, Penguin, Harmondsworth, p86.

13 For a more detailed treatment of this topic, *see* Arnold, G (1998) *Corporate Financial Management*, Financial Times Management, London, Chs2–6.

14 This is consistent with the emphasis on core competencies in Chapter 13.

15 Further detailed exploration of the financial techniques outlined in this chapter is contained in Glautier, M W E and Underdown, B (1994) *Accounting Theory and Practice*, 5th edn, Pitman Publishing, London and Arnold, G (1998) *Corporate Financial Management*, Financial Times Pitman Publishing, London.

16 The main exceptions are the large grocery multiple retailers which sell for cash to the general public and buy on credit from the manufacturers. Retailers have relied on their suppliers to fund increased sales for many years, but they do need careful stock control procedures to handle the situation.

17 *See* Arnold, G (1998) Op. cit., Ch3.

18 This section is based on the example in Chapter 31 of Glautier, M W E and Underdown, B (1994) Op. cit., p540.

19 This was essentially proposed by Rappaport, A (1983) *Creating Shareholder Value*, The Free Press, New York. *See* also Rappaport, A (1992) 'CEO and strategists:

forging a common framework', *Harvard Business Review*, May–June, p84. A clear and careful discussion of this area is also contained in Ellis, J and Williams, D (1993) *Corporate Strategy and Financial Analysis*, Pitman Publishing, London, Ch10.

20 It is not true of some Japanese companies according to the work of Williams, K, Haslam, C and Williams, J (1991) 'Management accounting: the Western problematic against the Japanese application', *9th Annual Conference of Labour Progress, University of Manchester Institute of Science and Technology*. The authors examined car and electronics companies only and made no claim to have extended their research to the *whole* of Japanese industry. Professor Toyohiro Kono also comments that 'DCF is not used very often' in his interesting survey of Japanese practice, which is more broadly based: Kono, T (1992) *Long Range Planning of Japanese Corporations*, de Gruyter, Berlin, pp277, 281.

21 Rappaport, A, quoted above, and Woolridge, G (1988) 'Competitive decline and corporate restructuring: Is a myopic stock market to blame?', *Continental Bank Journal of Applied Corporate Finance*, Spring, pp26–36, quoted in Ellis, J and Williams, D (1993) Op. cit.

22 Quoted from the UK chemist retailer Boots plc definition of strategy: Buckley, N (1994) 'Divide and thrive at Boots', *Financial Times*, 4 July, p12.

23 *See*, for example, Rowe, A, Mason, A and Dickel, K (1985) *Strategic Management and Business Policy*, 2nd edn, Addison-Wesley, New York.

24 This section is based on Porter, M E (1990) *Competitive Strategy*, The Free Press, New York, Chs9 to 13. The comments on leaders and followers also draw on Kotler, P (1994) *Marketing Management*, 8th edn, Prentice Hall International, Englewood Cliffs, NJ, Ch15.

25 Porter, M E (1990) Op. cit., p191.

26 This section relies heavily on Buzzell, R and Gale, B T (1987) *The PIMS Principles*, The Free Press, New York, and other researchers who are individually acknowledged below.

27 Described in Buzzell, R and Gale, B T (1987) Ibid.

28 Described in Buzzell, R and Gale, B T (1987) Ibid.

29 PIMS (1991) 'Marketing: in pursuit of the perfect mix', *Marketing Magazine, London*, 31 Oct.

30 Described in Buzzell, R and Gale, B T (1987) Op. cit.

31 This section relies essentially on the work and data in Kay, J (1993) *The Foundations of Corporate Success*, Oxford University Press, Oxford, Ch10.

32 King, D R, Dalton, D R, Daly, C M and Covin, J G (2004) 'Meta-Analysis of Post-Acquisition Performance: Indications of Unidentified Moderators', *Strategic Management Journal*, 25, pp187–200.

33 Ghemawat, P and Ghadar, F (2000) 'The dubious logic of global mega-mergers', *Harvard Business Review*, July–August.

34 Capron, L (1999) 'The long-term performance of horizontal acquisitions', *Strategic Management Journal*, November, 20, pp987–1018.

35 References for the Unilever case: Unilever press release 10 February 2005 available on the web at www.unilever.com Unilever 1997, 2001 and 2004 Annual Reports and Accounts. *Financial Times*, 10 June 1997, p26; 1 July 1997, p27; 27 Sept 1997, p19; 3 Oct 1997, p24; 23 Dec 1997, p9; 6 Jan 1998, p18; 11 Feb 1998, p28; 12 Mar 1998, p1; 15 Mar 1998, p22; 17 Mar 1998, p25; 22 Apr 1998, p10; 28 Apr 1998, p14; 15 May 1998, p15; 4 June 1998, p15; 10 July 1998, p33; 19 Jan 1999, p32; 24 Feb 1999, p31; 22 September 1999, p25; 24 September 1999, p27; 25 November 1999, p25; 11 December 1999, p15; 23 February 2000, p27; 30 May 2000, p29; 30 October 2000, p28; 22 January 2001, p1; 30 January 2001, p27; 9 February 2001, p24; 27 April 2002, p13; 8 May 2003, p25; 30 October 2003, p25; 29 April 2004, p21; 29 July 2004, p21; 23 August 2004, p15; 11 February 2005, p21.

36 Wheelen, T and Hunger, D (1992) *Strategic Management and Business Policy*, 4th edn, Addison-Wesley, Reading, MA.

37 Jauch, L R and Glueck, W F (1988) *Business Policy and Strategic Management*, 5th edn, McGraw-Hill, New York.

38 The prescriptive model presented in this chapter is shown in a number of texts in one format or another. In addition to references 2 and 3 above, similar versions of the model are also to be found in the well-known text by Thompson, A and Strickland, A (1993) *Strategic Management*, 7th edn, Irwin, Homewood, IL. The leading and well-respected European text is that by Johnson, G and Scholes, K (2002) Op. cit., and is also essentially built around the options-and-choice model of prescriptive strategy with implementation of the agreed strategic choice.

39 *See*, for example, Andrews, K (1987) *The Concept of Corporate Strategy*, Irwin, Homewood, IL; also Chakravarthy, B and Lorange, P (1991) *Managing the Strategy Process*, Prentice Hall, Englewood Cliffs, NJ.

40 Sloan, A P (1963) *My Years with General Motors*, Sedgewick and Jackson, London.

41 Chandler, A (1962) *Strategy and Structure*, MIT Press, Cambridge, MA.

42 Marx, T (1991) 'Removing obstacles to effective strategic planning', *Long Range Planning*, 24 Aug. This research paper is reprinted in De Wit, Bob and Meyer, R (1994) *Strategy: Process, Content and Context*, West Publishing, St Paul, MN.

43 Lenz, R T and Lyles, M (1985) 'Paralysis by analysis: Is your planning system becoming too rational?', *Long Range Planning*, 18 Aug. This is also reprinted in De Wit and Meyer (1994) Op. cit.

44 This section is based on Porter, M E (1990) Op. cit., Ch13; Thompson, A and Strickland, A (1993) Op. cit., pp136–7; Lynch, R (1994) Op. cit.

45 Such a record did not stop the US president moving several years later to a well-known pharmaceutical company, where he made a real contribution to its international development.

Chapter 15

FINDING THE STRATEGIC ROUTE FORWARD: EMERGENT AND PRESCRIPTIVE APPROACHES

Learning outcomes

When you have worked through this chapter, you will be able to:

● understand the importance of context in the development of strategy;

● explain five approaches to strategy development that go beyond the classic prescriptive approach;

● identify the relevance of a survival-based route forward in the context of the circumstances of the organisation;

● outline the importance of the uncertainty-based route forward and comment on its relevance, depending on the organisation's context;

● explain the two main elements of the network-based route forward and comment critically on its usefulness;

● outline the main elements of game theory and comment critically on its usefulness;

● decide the extent to which a learning-based strategy is needed as part of an organisation's strategy process;

● assess the implications for the strategy process where an organisation operates internationally.

INTRODUCTION

Part 7a

Although the classic prescriptive model is probably the most widely used approach in strategy development, its simplifying assumptions have long been recognised. In this chapter, we explore alternative approaches to strategy development. Some alternative routes are still prescriptive, but the majority have an emergent aspect.

In Chapter 14, we distinguished between the *content* (What?) of strategy development and the *process* (Why? Who? How?). In this chapter, we add a third element that helps to move beyond the simplifying assumptions of the classic prescriptive approach: the *context* within which strategy is developed.

Context means the circumstances surrounding and explaining the way that strategy operates and develops. For classic prescriptive strategy, context is assumed to involve slow, steady circumstances which are easy to predict.[1] However, this may be an oversimplification of real strategic situations: for example, context may contain periods of upheaval and rapid growth. Context is therefore developed further in the opening section of this chapter to explore some of the realities and uncertainties of real situations. Five routes forward for strategy development are identified; each of them relies on different contexts and implies alternative strategic approaches. All of them include this more complex view of context but also consider other aspects of the strategic process and content. The five routes forward are shown in Figure 15.1.

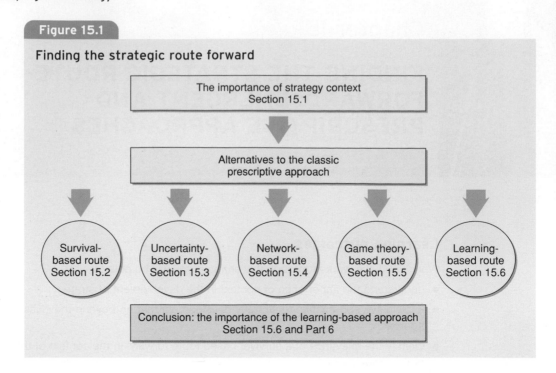

Figure 15.1

Finding the strategic route forward

The importance of strategy context
Section 15.1

Alternatives to the classic
prescriptive approach

Survival-based route
Section 15.2

Uncertainty-based route
Section 15.3

Network-based route
Section 15.4

Game theory-based route
Section 15.5

Learning-based route
Section 15.6

Conclusion: the importance of the learning-based approach
Section 15.6 and Part 6

Amongst the five routes, the chapter argues that the learning-based approach can usefully be added to the classic prescriptive approach developed in Chapter 14 in order to find the strategic route forward for all organisations. The other routes may also be useful depending on the context within which the strategy is being developed.

CASE STUDY 15.1

How Honda came to dominate two major motorcycle markets

This case study describes how Honda Motorcycles achieved its dominant market share of the US and UK markets. Although the strategic approach was originally seen as prescriptive, it was shown that, in reality, the strategies were much more emergent in their development.

During the period 1960–80, Honda Motorcycles (Japan) came to dominate motorcycle markets in the US and UK. Professor Richard Pascale has researched and described two perspectives on the process that Honda used to develop its strategies over this period.[2] They resulted in Honda moving from zero market share to domination of the US and UK markets, leaving the home-based industries with only small, niche-based market shares.

Professor Pascale first examined a study undertaken by Boston Consulting Group for the UK motorcycle industry in 1975 on the strategic reasons for the success of Honda. Two key factors for the success of Honda were identified:

1 an advantage in terms of Honda's economies of scale in technology, distribution and manufacturing;
2 the loss to other companies of market share and profitability as a result of the Honda attack.

The diagnosis appeared to be an example of the classical model and its prescriptive solutions in action.

Professor Pascale then interviewed the Honda executives who had actually launched the motorcycles in the US and subsequently in the UK. He discovered that Honda's strategy had at first been a failure and that it was as a result of sheer desperation that they had stumbled on the strategy that proved so successful. The executives at Honda had a full range of motorcycles that could be imported into the US. They ranged from small scooters to very large machines. All were more reliable and had higher performance than equivalent US competitors.

Honda US initially tried to compete head-on against the US main competition by using their large machines. However, Japanese motorbikes lacked credibility in the US market against the well-known US brands, even though the Honda bikes were better. The launch programme was unsuccessful.

By chance, Honda then tried to sell some small scooters into the US market purely for local transport. They were immediately successful and provided the platform for Honda to launch its attack on the main motorbike market several years later.

If corporate strategists had listened to the consulting company, they might have concluded that a major strategic initiative had been undertaken by Honda, based on careful strategic analysis and evaluation of options. But the reality was more haphazard and opportunistic, especially in the early days of the programme.

In conclusion, Pascale commented that Japanese managers at Honda and elsewhere did not use the term *strategy* to outline a *prescriptive* strategic plan. They were more inclined to see the process as providing an emerging process of trial and error, with the strategy evolving from experimentation as the process unfolded. According to his findings, Japanese companies were unlikely to develop a single strategy that was set to guide the company unerringly forward into the future.

In the Honda case, the strategy was developed from the managers in the market experimenting to find the most effective strategy. As each success was obtained, the Honda managers reported this back to Japan, with their ideas and suggestions for the next phase. There was frequent dialogue between Japan and the individual markets, with consensus being far more important to the emergence of the final strategy. Professor Pascale concluded that strategy needed to be redefined as:

For many years, Honda has dominated the motorcycle market, both in its home country – Japan pictured here – and around the world by a combination of segmented products, quality and competitive prices.

All the things necessary for the successful functioning of an organisation as an adaptive mechanism.

It should be noted, however, that during the 1980s Professor Toyohiro Kono repeatedly surveyed strategic planning in Japanese companies.[3] His conclusions suggested that, in large Japanese companies at least, there is rather more strategic planning than was observed by Professor Pascale. Other recent examples also exist that suggest that Japanese companies have now adopted some aspects of the prescriptive process, although there is still a strong element of experimentation and consensus in deriving the final plans.

Case question

Does prescriptive strategy need to be modified or would it be better, as Pascale suggests, to redefine the strategic process completely?

Figure 15.2

Breakdown of Honda Group sales 2005

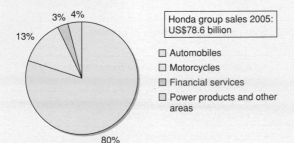

Honda group sales 2005: US$78.6 billion

3% 4%
13%
80%

☐ Automobiles
☐ Motorcycles
☐ Financial services
☐ Power products and other areas

15.1 THE IMPORTANCE OF STRATEGY CONTEXT

Definition ➤ Strategy context means the circumstances surrounding and influencing the way that a strategy develops and operates. As the Honda case demonstrates, the company's success in the US motorcycle market was the result of three interrelated strategic factors:

1 *strategy content* – Honda's use of small machines as an entry point, followed by its launch of the larger machines;

2 *strategy process* – the way this strategy was developed by a combination of luck, product performance and management persistence in the face of initial difficulties;

3 *strategy context* – the historical dominance of the US manufacturers initially led to the failure of Honda's prescriptive entry strategy, but the industry's relative weakness in the small market provided an opening for Honda.

Although all three elements are important in strategy development, this section of the book concentrates on context (Chapter 14 explored the other two).[4] Strategy context is concerned with the circumstances surrounding and influencing the way that a strategy develops and operates. The definition of context covers three main elements:

1 *factors outside the organisation* – customers, competitors and other areas that may also be important;

2 *factors inside the organisation* – its resources, particularly the way that they interact through leadership, organisational culture and management decision making;

3 *strategy as history* – the situation that the organisation finds itself in at the time of the strategic decision: its procedures, pathways, culture and history.

To make sense of these aspects of context, it is useful to begin by considering some problems of context associated with the classic prescriptive strategy route explored in Chapter 14. We then explore the relationship of context with the other two aspects of strategy development – process and content – before finally using context to identify five alternative strategic routes forward.

15.1.1 Some context problems with the classic model of prescriptive strategy

In some circumstances, the classic approach works adequately. However, it assumes that growth or decline is largely linear, continuous and predictable. Such simplifying assumptions enable new strategy to be developed and implemented. The difficulty is that there are a number of circumstances, particularly involving a more turbulent or uncertain context,

Exhibit 15.1

How context can weaken classic prescriptive strategy

Typical outline	Some assumptions and characteristics of classic prescriptive strategy	Some resulting problems of context
Mission and objectives	• Objectives can and should be identified in advance	• Objectives may need to be more flexible in fast-moving markets
Environmental analysis	• Environment sufficiently predictable	• Technology, war and economic disaster may make this assumption meaningless
Resource analysis	• Resources can be clearly identified and developed	• Tacit knowledge needs to be seen in the company context in which it was developed (*see* Chapter 11) • The context of a leadership change may fundamentally alter resources (*see* Chapter 10)
Strategy options generation	• It is only necessary to identify options once • It is possible to identify options clearly	• May want to keep options open where the context is unclear • Competitor reactions may be unknown, context will alter
Strategy options selection	• Only one option can be chosen • It is possible to make a clear choice between options	• Why choose only one option? Surely this depends on the context of the time, resources, etc.
Implementation	• Implementation only needs to be considered at this late stage in strategic development	• Context may make this highly dubious (*see* opening sections of Part 6 and Chapter 17)

where such assumptions are incorrect. In these circumstances, prescriptive strategic solutions are, at best, suboptimal and, at worst, irrelevant. Exhibit 15.1 outlines some typical contextual problems that can arise from the use of the classic prescriptive approach. They do not mean that the model is 'wrong', but (like all models) it may oversimplify the strategic context in some important circumstances.

15.1.2 The importance of context and its relationship with strategy process and content

Strategy context is important because it suggests that those alternatives to classic prescriptive strategy that include a fuller treatment of context may work better. There are two main reasons:[5]

1 *The external context.* This may be particularly uncertain – for example, internet banking may revolutionise the retail banking industry in ways that remain essentially unknown at the time of writing. This makes the prescriptive route, which relies on predicting the environment, largely meaningless.

2 *The internal context.* The organisation's resources and decision making are undoubtedly more complex than the simple options and choice of the classic prescriptive strategy model – for example, organisational politics, formal and informal networks, styles of leadership and many other issues all undermine the assumptions of the classic approach.

The *context* in which the strategy is developed may thus influence the *process* of strategy development. For example, an uncertain context may make a simple decision-making process irrelevant. As a result, the *content* of the strategy may therefore differ from that suggested by classic prescriptive strategy. For example, it will be difficult to decide the content of a strategy if the context within which it is being developed remains uncertain. It is this *combination* of context, process and content that will guide us in the search for alternative approaches to strategy development.

15.1.3 Alternative approaches to strategy development

Corporate strategy is not rocket science – combining context, process and content involves judgement that may go beyond the simple logic of classic prescriptive strategy. There is no well-tried and generally agreed scientific formula for finding the strategic route forward. As a consequence, there are many alternative approaches to strategy development.

Some approaches still have a strong prescriptive element, while others are more emergent in their exploration of strategic issues. The difficulty is how to explore the many alternative ways forward that have been suggested by strategy writers. This book has chosen five main routes for reasons of contrast and because each provides an insight into strategy development:[6]

1 *Survival-based.* This route puts heavy emphasis on organisations being able to survive in a hostile and highly competitive context. It does this through an *emergent* process, seeking out opportunities in strategy content as they occur.

2 *Chaos-based.* This route also emphasises the importance of context, treating the environment as uncertain and the processes as opportunistic and transformational. The process is therefore *emergent*.

3 *Network-based.* This route has two related elements: network externalities and network co-operation. The first element examines the way that networks for a product can be self-reinforcing and benefit members. The second element explores the ability of markets, industries and companies to form co-operative networks. Both these aspects of the route have *emergent* elements because they have evolving outcomes and unknown elements during the process.

4 *Game-theory-based*. This explores how to reach optimal strategic decisions by treating them as a competitive game. Because of the careful structuring of the process, it is at least partly *prescriptive*. However, in practice, there are so many judgements and qualifications that it also has strong *emergent* elements.

5 *Learning-based*. This route lays heavy emphasis on the context and the process derived from the existing knowledge and experience of the organisation. This essentially involves learning from the past and from the contributions of those involved at present. Thus both the historical context and the current process will influence strategy content – the process is, essentially, *emergent*.

This book places special emphasis on the learning-based route above. The reason is that most organisations will benefit from its insights on the strategy process. However, all five (and more not covered in this text) have their place in finding the most appropriate strategic route forward for the organisation.

Key strategic principles

- In developing strategy, it is important to distinguish three distinct elements: the content of the strategy, the process by which it has been derived and the context in which it has been developed.

- In the classic prescriptive model, context is assumed to be largely linear and predictable. This is not always the case, particularly when the context is turbulent and uncertain. Alternative approaches to strategy development may therefore be required.

- The context, process and content of a strategy are interconnected and it is this combination that is important in strategy development.

- There are a number of alternatives to the classic prescriptive approach to strategy development. Five are explored in the remainder of this chapter, but others may also be relevant.

CASE STUDY 15.2

Europe's leading telecom companies: overstretched and under threat

As a result of paying too much for acquisitions, all Europe's leading telecommunication companies were overstretched financially in 2002. In addition, they were under a competitive threat from new technologies that could potentially undermine their future profitability. This case traces the strategies that produced this muddle.

Privatisation in the 1980s and 1990s – the old telcos still dominated their national markets

Up to the 1990s, most European countries had one monopoly supplier of telephone services (called a 'telco' for short), often owned by the government. Even in the UK, where British Telecom had been privatised in 1984, the company still dominated services, with around 90 per cent market share. Then, during the 1990s, European governments decided to privatise their leading telcos. However, each national operator continued to dominate its national market, thus delivering high profits, good cash flow, stable business and often a steady programme of equipment and service modernisation – for example, investment in new digital telephone exchange equipment.

Starting in 1992, the European Union began to take an interest with the liberalisation of *data* telephone services – the transmission of data along telephone lines. This was followed in 1998 by the liberalisation of *voice* telephone services. This was meant to open up European markets to some real competition. In practice, Europe was still a closed shop, with each national company attempting to keep rival telcos out of its markets. The more ambitious companies like British Telecom (BT) were forced to seek expansion elsewhere, especially the US. At various times in the 1980s and 1990s in North America, BT acquired a mobile telephone company, a telecommunications equipment company and an alliance with a major US telecoms operator – MCI. But all of this failed to deliver any

How the technology has changed in mobile phones: 1990 mobile phone with a separate charger; 1998 mobile phone but without 3G; 2005 mobile phone with 3G digital options.

real profit and in 2000 BT was still reliant on its UK operations for 90 per cent of its profits. Only in Scandinavia was there some successful co-operation between the national telcos and that was in the area of mobile telephones. Even here, the proposed merger of two telcos did not materialise, with national interests being dominant.

The expansion of mobile telephone services – a new competitive threat

During the 1990s, a new competitive threat to the national telcos emerged: mobile telephone licences were awarded to small rival companies that often had no previous experience of telecommunications. For example in Germany, a new licence was awarded to the German engineering company, Mannesmann. At the same time, a licence was also awarded to the main German telco, Deutsche Telekom, but there was at last some competition. Importantly, although mobile call prices were initially high, customers liked mobile telephones. They were no longer tied to a fixed telephone line; mobiles were convenient, trendy and useful in an emergency. By 2002, the European Commission estimated that mobile telephone services made up 38 per cent of the Euro telecoms market, up from 23 per cent in 1998. In Portugal, Finland, Austria and Spain, mobile services generated more revenue than fixed lines.

Potentially, this was a major competitive threat to the former national telcos which had invested billions over the years in their fixed line systems. The customer base formed from such network connections constituted one of the principal areas of sustainable competitive advantage for such companies and it was being undermined by the new mobile operators. The competitive threat was even greater because, unlike fixed lines, mobile services had the potential for extra cost savings through economies of scale in procurement, engineering and branding.

The national telcos solved the competitive threat in almost every European country by setting up their own mobile services. The only exception was the UK, where the government realised the importance of encouraging competition in order to reduce telephone call prices and refused to allow BT to own such a service outright until the late 1990s.

By 2002, the former national telcos had taken a grip of their national mobile markets, with market shares of over 60 per cent. In addition, the leading European telcos were well placed to dominate the pan-European mobile services market outside their home territories: they achieved this strong strategic position by a series of acquisitions that are discussed in the next section. Table 15.1 shows the leading pan-European market shares – the only non-national European operator was

Table 15.1

Pan-European market shares of the six leading mobile telephone operators

Company	Home country	Pan-European market share (%)
Vodafone	UK	24
France Telecom – Orange	France	12
British Telecom – now a separate company called MMO2	UK	12
Telecom Italia – TIM	Italy	10
Deutsche Telekom	Germany	8
Telefónica	Spain	6

Source: McKinsey analysis – See references.

▶ CASE STUDY 15.2 continued

Table 15.2

Levels of net debt in leading European telecommunications companies – US$ billion

Company	2000	2001	2002
France Telecom	54	55	57
Deutsche Telekom	50	56	57
Telefónica	24	26	23
British Telecom	42	23	23
Telecom Italia	18	22	21
KPN – Holland	20	15	14

Note: In practice, the levels of indebtedness above need to be compared with the stock exchange valuations of the equity of the listed companies. Equity valuations vary, but at the time of compiling the above data debt was significantly higher than equity.

Source: See references.

the UK-based company Vodafone, which had also built its market position largely by acquisition.

The consequence of unbridled acquisition – massive debt

The eight leading European telcos expanded across Europe by a series of acquisitions of their rivals over the years 1998–2001. For example, France Telecom bought Orange in the UK, British Telecom acquired Viag in Germany and so on. The consequence of this major buying spree was that the leading eight European telcos borrowed between them US$800 billion over the years 1998–2002. Such a level of debt was unsustainable. Some companies like British Telecom were rapidly forced to sell some of their assets to reduce their debts during 2001–2002. As Table 15.2 shows, other European telcos were not so quick to shed their debt. At the time of writing, such companies remained severely handicapped in terms of their ability to expand further as a result of their high debt levels.

Part of the reason that the companies paid such high prices for shares was that European stock exchanges gave inflated values to European telco shares during this period – a stock market 'bubble' – and that the European telcos had optimistic views of their future prospects. In some cases, the problem was compounded because companies only acquired minority shareholdings in the target companies – what British Telecom once called a 'family of alliances'. This meant that the acquirer was unable to benefit from a controlling interest that might have delivered economies of scale.

In addition to acquisition, there was another reason for the high levels of debt – the need to bid for the new '3G' mobile telecoms licences.

Bidding for '3G' licences – piling on the debt

Ever seeking new ways of raising money, European governments decided in the late 1990s that the new frequencies needed for a new generation of mobile telephone services should be auctioned to the highest bidder. The third generation mobile services – '3G' for short – would deliver full webcasts and moving pictures so callers could see each other on their mobile telephones. They would require a new generation of mobile telephones, new transmitters and other equipment, along with technology, which was totally untested when the auctions took place during the period around 2000. Each country had its auction and each national operator, along with some new telephone companies, was encouraged to bid. Most of the auctions, except in France, involved secret bidding, such that the European telcos felt the need to outbid each other. The result was to raise the price of the new 3G licences to the extent that US$79 billion was raised by the auctions in the UK and Germany alone. The total cost across Europe was over US$100 billion – note that this is smaller than the cost of acquisitions outlined earlier. But it was a significant contributor to the debt mountains of the leading European telcos. In addition to this cost, there was then the need to develop, install and maintain the new equipment that would operate the 3G network. One estimate of the roll-out costs for Germany, Italy and the UK alone was an additional US$36 billion. This would be spread over the years 2001–2005 as the new 3G services were launched.

At the time when all these debts were being incurred, there was no substantial evidence that customers actually wanted 3G services. Thus the above investment had a degree of risk and experimentation that would challenge some strategists.

Market growth prospects – maturing except in mobile and data services

After growing at around 20 per cent per annum in the late 1990s, it is likely that overall industry revenue growth will slow down. It is predicted to barely exceed growth in gross domestic product over the next few years. Thus, the national European telcos are engaged in a relatively mature industry with very high levels of debt. This means that their future strategies need to take into account the lower growth prospects:

1 cost cutting to reduce staff costs where possible;
2 marketing to exploit the well-known brand names;
3 exploitation of new 3G technology – in practice, some older technology is also available.

Competition increasing – including mobile and cable operators

The fundamental difficulty is that the sustainable competitive advantages of the existing national telcos are being undermined by the new mobile and other services. In former years, the national telcos had a monopoly of the final access to individual households through the fixed line that delivered the telephone signal – the so-called 'local loop'. This meant that

Table 15.3

The benefit of broadband technology

Home–telco link	Time taken
Traditional 56 Kbps modem – the type linked to many home computers in 2005	2 minutes
Digital ISDN line with 128 Kpbs link	30 seconds
ADSL broadband technology	1 second – connection constantly live

such a telco was able to exclude competitors either by refusing to carry their signals or, more likely in practice, making it excessively expensive or inconvenient. However, not only can mobile operators overcome this problem, but the national telcos now face new competition from television cable operators that are able to carry telephone signals as well. In addition, many cable operators are able to deliver faster internet connections than traditional telcos and therefore pose a real threat in terms of data services. By 2005, most cable connectors across Europe were beginning to offer some form of fast connection.

Competition – the opportunity of broadband and other technologies

At the time of writing, the national telcos still control the local loop. As a result, one strategy that has become increasingly attractive for such operators is to develop the new technology of broadband digital services. Data transmission is vital to the development of the Internet and the World Wide Web. Such data can only be transmitted slowly with the traditional local loop: see Table 15.3 for an example. Germany's national telco, Deutsche Telekom, introduced a new broadband service in 2000 and by attractive pricing and good marketing

it had signed up 10 million subscribers by 2005. The next largest European supplier was British Telecom with 6 million subscribers, following a rapid extension of its service in this area during 2003. Alternative suppliers were also beginning to deliver, but claimed to be hampered by BT's pricing strategy that was designed to delay their progress as long as possible.

The strategic difficulty here is that telecommunications technology is changing all the time. This means that innovating through broadband might shortly be overtaken by some new technical system. Already parts of Asia and North America were introducing WiFi and other technologies. However, all such technologies were expensive to install and commit the telcos towards one specific technology, even if this proved not to be the best technology.

Case questions

1 *Given the lower levels of market growth, coupled with the grip of the existing telcos on their national markets, what are the advantages and problems with adopting the classic prescriptive strategy process to develop strategies in this market?*

2 *Some strategists argue that it is useless to predict what will happen, given that technology is uncertain. What would be the consequences, if any, of following this advice in the European telecommunications market and not making any predictions? What implications does your answer have for a prescriptive strategy process that is built on the need to make predictions?*

3 *Can smaller companies attempting to find opportunities in this market also employ the prescriptive process? Or would they be better to use a process that is more radical and innovative to structure their approach? If so, do you have any suggestions on the process that might be employed?*

15.2 THE SURVIVAL-BASED STRATEGIC ROUTE FORWARD

Definition ➤ Survival-based theories of strategy regard the survival of the fittest in the competitive market place as being the prime determinant of corporate strategy. As the European mobile telephone market has grown, competition has increased. Companies have entered each other's markets on a limited basis and made the necessary investments. Markets have shown reasonable growth rates but are now beginning to mature. Hence, the sales increases from such growth are unlikely to satisfy the objectives of the major companies. Moreover, in spite of high levels of debt finance, some European telecom companies still wish to expand. One important conclusion that some strategists have therefore drawn about the European telephone industry is that by the year 2010 only five major global companies will remain. The rest will have been swallowed up in a shakeout of the industry. The contrast with the relative stability of the state monopoly companies of the 1980s and 1990s is striking. Survival-based strategy processes provide one explanation of the likely outcome after liberalisation.

15.2.1 The nature of survival-based strategies

Essentially, the survival-based process begins with the concept of *natural selection* first introduced in the nineteenth century by Charles Darwin to explain the development and survival of living creatures. He argued that survival was a constant battle against the environment. The species most likely to survive were those best suited and adapted to their surroundings. On this basis, adaptation to the environment is the main strategy that needs to be developed in a business context. Those that fail to change quickly enough will be the ones that select themselves for extinction.[8] The fittest companies survive because they are selected on the basis of the demand for their goods or services and the profits that they make.[9]

In the survival-based process there are two mechanisms in operation:

1 adaptation to the environment;

2 selection among those present for survival.

Using these two processes, together with principles and concepts from sociology, researchers have analysed the way that some industrial companies have developed.[10] They noted that, of the top 500 companies listed in *Fortune* magazine in 1955, only 268 were still listed in 1975: 46 per cent had disappeared, merged or otherwise declined over the 20-year period. They suggested that *adaptation to the environment* was the preferred mechanism for change in many companies because it was less painful than selection. This was influenced by a built-in inertia with regard to change in many industrial situations (*see* Exhibit 15.2).

Exhibit 15.2

Examples of inertia towards change in company environments

Internal inertia

● Existing investment in plant and machinery

● Previous experience and history of the company

Example: in European telephone companies the existing bureaucracy, which had been built up during many years in government ownership, was very difficult to shift.

External inertia

● Barriers to entry and exit from an industry

● Difficulty and cost of acquiring information on how the environment itself might be changing

Example: European telephone companies' existing investment in exchanges and telephone equipment, coupled with external government restrictions that would prevent new companies entering until 1998, had created an inertia towards change within the industry.

Most strategy literature takes an *adaptive* perspective as its starting point in developing strategy options. Importantly, some survival-based strategists argue that this may not be sufficient. It may be necessary to add a *selection* perspective. There may come a time, precisely because of the inertia in the industry, when some organisations do not or cannot adapt quickly enough to the changes in the environment, and will not survive against the powerful forces ranged against them. Nevertheless, there may be an element of chance in selecting precisely who will disappear. For example, some European telephone companies may adapt to the changed environment of the new millennium, while others will change too slowly, and the pressures on them will be so great that they will not survive in their present form and will have to amalgamate with more efficient or luckier enterprises.

From a strategy *selection* perspective, the industry environment is the main determining factor of strategy development and survival. There is only a limited amount that individual companies can do in the time available before changes arrive. The only companies for which this may not apply are those that already have substantial market power and can influence the way their markets develop. However, even these may be overtaken by events – for example, in the case of European telecommunications, the advent of new communications technologies such as 3G mobile or the World Wide Web.

15.2.2 Consequences for the corporate strategy process

On this basis, corporate strategy has a limited ability, if any, to influence the environment. Moreover, an organisation may not be able to adapt quickly enough to change. In addition, the techniques recommended by the prescriptive process will be so well publicised that they will provide no competitive advantage to individual companies. As a result, and for those companies without real market power, Williamson[11] has recommended that the best strategy is to develop the most cost-effective operation possible, which he calls *economising*. He distinguishes this from new strategic moves beyond basic cost-effectiveness, which he calls *strategising*.

> *I aver that, as between economizing and strategizing, economizing is much the more fundamental . . . A strategizing effort will only prevail if a program is burdened by significant cost excesses in production, distribution or organisation. All the clever ploys and positioning, aye, all the king's horses and all the king's men, will rarely save a project that is seriously flawed in first-order economizing respects.*[12]

What, therefore, can be done? Table 15.4 summarises the main strategies that can be undertaken if this view of the strategy process is correct. It is clearly important to be cautious. It will also be necessary to seek clues from the environment on possible change and what is needed to survive. Finally, it will be useful to generate plenty of options so that whatever happens in the environment can be accommodated by the organisation.

Overall, if this view of the strategy process is correct, then the organisation is severely restricted in its strategies. Arguably, the way in which the European telephone companies

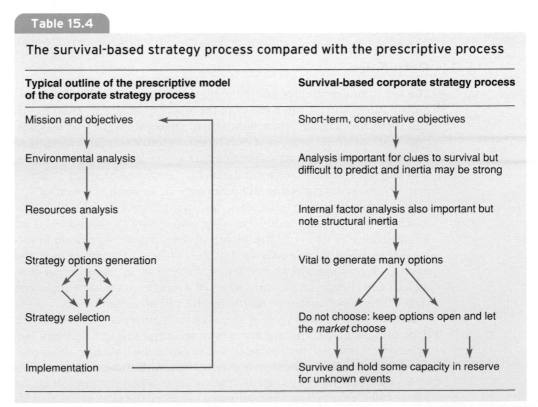

Table 15.4

The survival-based strategy process compared with the prescriptive process

Typical outline of the prescriptive model of the corporate strategy process	Survival-based corporate strategy process
Mission and objectives	Short-term, conservative objectives
Environmental analysis	Analysis important for clues to survival but difficult to predict and inertia may be strong
Resources analysis	Internal factor analysis also important but note structural inertia
Strategy options generation	Vital to generate many options
Strategy selection	Do not choose: keep options open and let the *market* choose
Implementation	Survive and hold some capacity in reserve for unknown events

have been building alliances and cross-shareholdings suggests that they cannot see the way ahead clearly and have chosen these mutually supportive strategies as the best protection.

Comment

This is a pessimistic view of the role of corporate strategy and the ability of organisations to shape their destiny. It rejects the insights offered by the prescriptive process but offers little alternative. It is useful in rapidly changing and turbulent environments, but offers only limited solutions in other circumstances.

Key strategic principles

- Survival-based strategies emphasise the importance of adapting strategies to meet changes in the environment. The ultimate objective is survival itself.

- The approach adopted is to develop options for use as the environment changes. Options that seek low costs are particularly useful.

- Beyond taking the precaution of developing strategic options, there is little that the individual organisation can do. There is an element of chance in whether it will survive or not.

15.3 THE UNCERTAINTY-BASED STRATEGIC ROUTE FORWARD

Definition ➤ Uncertainty-based theories of strategy regard a prescriptive, defined strategy as being impossible to develop because the strategic process is unpredictable, unstable and liable to chaotic outcomes. According to uncertainty-based strategists, Europe's telephone companies are wasting their time developing corporate strategies to cope with the events of the new millennium. They would argue that the environment is too uncertain and the outcomes largely unknown. Even striving for survival-based efficiency is useless. To understand the reasoning behind this, we need to examine the origins and thinking behind this approach.

15.3.1 Rationale

The key to understanding this route forward is its assumption about the purposes of most organisations: success will come from the ability of an organisation to survive by *innovating* and *transforming* itself.[13] Uncertainty-based strategists argue that it is not enough for most organisations simply to co-exist with others. In today's rapidly changing world, renewal and transformation towards new directions are key tasks for corporate strategy. To paraphrase the title of the strategy director at the mobile telephone company Orange, strategy is at least partially about 'imagineering and futurology' in an unknown world.[14]

Given this definition of success, the strategic process by which this is achieved will inevitably involve uncertainty. However, uncertainty can be modelled mathematically and its consequences set out in the science of *chaos theory*[15] – a system of modelling originally applied to scientific processes such as flow of liquid through a tube and subsequently to weather forecasting. The theory demonstrates that, in certain types of uncertain environment, *small* changes in the early stages of a process can lead to *major* variances in the later stages. This is not unlike the multiplier effect in macroeconomics.

In the classic strategy process, there is a mechanism of cause and effect that controls the dynamics of change. *Feedback* arises from an initial strategic decision, but goes *beyond* such a decision by multiplying its effects. *Uncertainty* is the unknown result of a strategic decision which may be affected by chance events along with those that are more predictable.

An example will help to clarify the concept. When the price of an item such as a telephone call is raised relative to competing products, the sales of the item are predicted to fall.

According to uncertainty-based theory, this simple process may not represent the *full* outcome of events. The *feedback mechanism* suggests that the rise in telephone prices may not only affect sales but may also feed back into a lower level of loading at the telephone exchange. This may in turn influence the ability of the company to recover overheads from the exchange. Thus, the exchange loading, overheads and overall profitability may all be influenced by the one pricing decision. As soon as these items are affected adversely, there may be some attempt to recover profitability by a *further* price increase, i.e. the initial problem has fed back on itself. This will have a deleterious effect on the organisation, and so is usually referred to as *negative feedback*.

Conversely, in the above example, a reduction in price might have the opposite effect. It might cause profitability to rise more than the initial move in pricing, as a result of other consequences in the organisation. This is called *positive feedback*.

Uncertainty theory then adds another possibility. It can be proved mathematically that, where positive and negative feedback mechanisms operate, the system can *flip* between the positive and negative states. Importantly, it is not possible to predict in advance which of these three outcomes – that is, positive, negative or flip – will occur. The long-term consequences are therefore unknown and cannot be foreseen.

15.3.2 Consequences for the corporate strategy process

Uncertainty-based strategists argue that there is little to be gained by predicting the future, because virtually all strategy is composed of feedback mechanisms and involves uncertainty; therefore the outcome cannot be predicted. If the future is unknown, the effects of long-term strategic actions will also be unknown and the classical prescriptive process has little meaning.

This does not mean that uncertainty-based strategists believe that nothing can be done. They take the view, however, that actions should be much shorter-term in nature. Organisations must be able to learn and adapt to changed circumstances. Thus workers and managers in organisations are capable of assessing the results of their actions – in the example above, the effects of raising or lowering the price of telephone calls. They are also capable of learning to adapt to the consequences. More generally, for strategy purposes, they are capable of experimenting and innovating in the organisation and assessing the results of their work.

The implications of such theories are profound for corporate strategy. The majority of organisations need to innovate in order to survive and they exist in the increasingly turbulent world of the early twenty-first century, and yet uncertainty-based strategists would suggest that it is not possible to predict how innovation will succeed in the long term. According to these strategists, however, new ideas and new directions are necessary to survival and growth and should be pursued using the learning mechanisms mentioned above in order to refine and adapt strategies to a rapidly changing environment.

As an example of uncertainty-based strategy in action, you might like to consider the consequences of the launch of Sky television by News Corporation in 1990 and its later dominance of digital television broadcasting in the UK – *see* Case study 13.4. Such an outcome was clearly impossible to predict at the time of the launch. According to the uncertainty-based theorists, corporate strategy based on, for example, a prescriptive approach would have been largely irrelevant in these circumstances.

For the uncertainty-based strategist, long-term strategy is a contradiction in terms. The only possible objectives are short-term, possibly with a strong innovative content.[16] There is no point in undertaking environmental analysis because it is essentially unpredictable, but it is useful to understand the organisation's resources in order to assess their contribution to the innovative process. As for strategy options and selection, this has no relevance to the strategy process that actually occurs. What is important is the way the company is organised to learn and respond to its changing environment: loose, informal networks of managers are required, rather than rigid functional divisions. Exhibit 15.3 presents some of the implications suggested by Stacey.[17]

Exhibit 15.3

Some practical implications of uncertainty for the corporate strategy process

Basic objectives: develop new strategic directions and innovate.

Eight actions consistent with the uncertainty-based approach are:

1 Loosen control – let things happen.

2 Reconfigure power in groups to make them less competitive and more co-operative.

3 Allow groups to develop and set their own challenges, objectives and processes.

4 Encourage new organisational cultures in order to develop new perspectives.

5 Set open challenges ('Develop a new initiative in . . .') rather than defined objectives ('Your job is to double our profits in . . .').

6 Expose the business to demanding and challenging situations.

7 Spend time and resources developing the learning skills of groups in the organisation.

8 Develop time and space for managers to experiment.

Table 15.5

Comparison of the uncertainty-based strategic route with the prescriptive process

Typical outline of the prescriptive model of the corporate strategy process	Uncertainty-based strategy process	Flow process
Mission and objectives	Short-term only: possibly some strategic intent with innovation as a stated aim	?
Environmental analysis Resources analysis	Unpredictable: waste of time Important to be aware of internal factors but the analysis will not have the predictive thrust of the prescriptive approach	No clear flow process ?
Strategy options generation	Options generation is irrelevant since the outcomes are unknown and unpredictable	Chaotic only with constant monitoring of the environment
Strategy selection	Strategy selection is also irrelevant but spontaneous small groups and learning mechanisms might be involved in short-term selection	?
Implementation	Informal, destabilising networks are useful. It may also be worth holding some resources in reserve because of the unknown	Flexible response from informal groups depending on the opportunities that emerge

Overall, there is no clear flow process, unlike in prescriptive strategy – only constant monitoring of the environment in order to take advantage of opportunities that occur. Table 15.5 makes a comparison between the prescriptive and uncertainty-based processes.

Comment

The approach may be useful when market conditions are turbulent, but it has few insights into some of the areas of strategic decision making, such as the short-term pressure to deliver profits or service. However, the approach is still in its early stages of development.

Key strategic principles

- Renewal and transformation are vital aspects of strategy. Inevitably, they will involve uncertainty. Such uncertainty can be modelled mathematically. However, the long-term consequences are unknown and cannot be foreseen or usefully predicted.

- Uncertainty-based approaches therefore involve taking small steps forward. Management needs to learn from such actions and adapt accordingly.

- Because of the uncertainty about the future, strategy options and selection between them using the prescriptive approach are therefore irrelevant.

CASE STUDY 15.3

How GEC Marconi used game theory to make an extra US$3 billion

In a series of negotiations in late 1998, the UK company GEC Marconi sold its defence interests for US$12 billion – some US$3 billion more than they had been valued several months earlier. This case explains how the company used strategic game theory to help improve the outcome.

Background – worldwide consolidation in defence industries

With the end of the Cold War in the early 1990s, many world governments were keen to reduce their defence spending. Moreover, the cost of developing new defence weapons was continuing to rise. The result of falling sales and rising costs was pressure on the world's leading defence companies to merge and share the costs of development and production. The first merger moves came in the US, with a shake-out in the mid-1990s that produced three big players: Lockheed Martin, Boeing and Raytheon. Table 15.6 shows the contracts that the leading companies had with the US government in 1997. It should be noted that most companies also had civil (non-defence) contracts which are not listed in the table.

European defence industry: political background

Although some European companies had defence sales in the US, their largest sales were in Europe and outside North America. All defence companies need to make sales outside their home markets because national territories provide insufficient revenue. The main customers are national governments so the tendency in Europe has been for combinations of such governments to commission new equipment – for

The cost of modern defensive weaponry, such as that used by the British Navy, is substantial, so only the largest defence contractors are able to deploy sufficient resources to bid for defence contracts.

example, the new European fighter aircraft involves the governments of the UK, Germany, Italy and Spain. France has had a long tradition of independent manufacture and sale and Sweden has also remained outside the usual consortia.

▶ **CASE STUDY 15.3 continued**

Table 15.6

Top US defence contractors in 1997

(value of contracts with the US Department of Defense, US$ billion)

Contractor	Value of contracts
Lockheed Martin	12.4
Boeing	10.9
Raytheon	6.5
Northrop Grumman	4.1
GEC	2.2
General Dynamics	2.1
United Technologies	1.9
Litton Industries	1.8
Science Applications	1.1
ITT	0.9

Source: Government Executive Magazine.

Table 15.7

The main companies in the European defence industry

British Aerospace	UK
GEC Marconi	UK
Deutsche Aerospace: Dasa	Germany
Aerospatiale	France
Dassault	France
Thomson-CSF	France
Matra (subsidiary of Lagardère)	France
Casa	Spain
Alenia	Italy
Agusta	Italy
Saab	Sweden

In the late 1990s, the three major European governments of Germany, France and the UK were keen to see consolidation in the European defence industry. There were three main reasons:

1 The US defence consolidation meant that US companies were well ahead of Europe in terms of the potential cost savings and rationalisation that were possible.
2 The European governments were determined as a matter of policy to ensure that their European defences were supplied by European-manufactured equipment. The alternative was that they would be reliant on the US, which was strategically much weaker. This meant that it was vital to secure a continued defence manufacturing base in Europe.
3 Defence manufacture in Europe continued to employ large numbers of workers – roughly one million across the EU. It was important to preserve these jobs.

However, it should be noted that there was some cross-Atlantic defence co-operation. For example, GEC itself was able to acquire the US defence company Tracor in 1998 for US$1.4 billion and become the fifth-largest contractor to the US government. Equally, the main US companies all had some manufacturing facilities in Europe, even though some were for civil rather than military use.

In 1997, Germany, France and the UK began to put pressure on their respective companies to combine. However, apart from the French government, they did not own the companies so their direct negotiating power was limited.

European defence industry: company perspectives

Naturally, the defence companies themselves could also see the case for consolidation. From their perspective, the issue was not whether this should be done, but how. During the course of 1997–98, a series of discussions and negotiations were undertaken amongst the leading players. Virtually any combination was possible but some companies already had minority stakes or strong technical links with others – useful but not conclusive. The main players are shown in Table 15.7. However, there were three companies that would have to be involved if the final concept of a consolidated European defence company was to be achieved: British Aerospace, Dasa and Aerospatiale.

British Aerospace, Dasa and Aerospatiale: core companies in any European defence consolidation?

These three companies already co-operated on the European Airbus – *see* Case study 5.3 – and were thus used to working together. The aerospace activities of each were roughly of equal size in terms of turnover and numbers employed – *see* Table 15.8. But they each had very different ownership structures which made combination difficult. British Aerospace had been privatised many years earlier and its shares were widely held. Dasa was still a subsidiary of the German/US DaimlerChrysler car company and it had no separate share quotation at all. Aerospatiale was majority-owned by the French government but being prepared for privatisation so that it could form part of a larger European company. The main effect of such ownership variations was to complicate any negotiations and therefore slow them down.

Nevertheless, British Aerospace had entered into detailed discussions with Dasa during 1998. There was a strong willingness to combine the two companies and agreement had been reached on many issues, including the combined company split of 60 per cent to British Aerospace and 40 per cent to Dasa. By December 1998, the main sticking point was the problem that such an ownership split would have given effective control to Dasa: the fragmented shareholdings in British Aerospace would have meant that Dasa was the largest single shareholder.

However, operating in parallel with this unresolved battle was a related strategy from GEC Marconi – and this company had its own objective.

Table 15.8		

Three main players in European consolidation

Daimler-Benz Aerospace (Dasa): Germany	Aerospatiale: France	British Aerospace: UK
Ownership: 100% DaimlerChrysler by parent	Ownership: French government 48%, Lagardère 30%, private shareholders the rest	Ownership: private, quoted on London Stock Market. The best profit record of the three leading players
Sales 1997: US$7.7 billion	Sales 1997: US$11.6 billion	Sales 1997: US$12.8 billion
Number of employees: 43,500	Number of employees: 56,000	Number of employees: 43,000
Partner in Airbus and Eurofighter. Also produces other military and civil aircraft, space systems, satellites and electronic systems.	Partner in Airbus but no pan-European defence interests. Also produces satellites, missiles, space systems. Owns 46% of Dassault, which produces Mirage and Rafaele fighter aircraft.	Partner in Airbus and Eurofighter. Also produces other military and civil aircraft, missiles, electronic systems, munitions; 36% share in Saab, Sweden. Also links with Alenia, Italy.

GEC Marconi: UK

When George Simpson took over as the chief executive of the GEC Group in 1996, he decided that it needed to have greater worldwide market share in a limited number of ventures. Up to that time, the company had been involved in a whole range of ventures, some of which were profitable, but they were all rather disparate. For example, it was involved in the manufacture of petrol vending machines, computer printers and power generation equipment. It also owned the large defence electronics company GEC Marconi. Simpson and his colleagues decided that the group needed more focus so it disposed of its shareholdings in some companies and concentrated on others, such as those producing telecommunications equipment.

Initially, the group decided to develop GEC Marconi. In 1998, as part of this strategy, it acquired the US defence company Tracor for US$1.4 billion. This made it one of the largest defence contractors in the US (see Table 15.6) and raised its ambitions for further developments. It began discussions with the French defence electronics company Thomson-CSF but the acquisition was blocked by the French government. As it cast around for further growth in the worldwide defence market, it made a fundamental strategic decision: either it would grow larger or it would exit the industry with a good price for its company. By mid-1998, it was again in discussions with Thomson-CSF but it had also opened up negotiations with British Aerospace, Northrop Grumman and Lockheed.

At least, it *said* that it was in discussion with these companies but there may have been an element of bargaining in this signal to the market. The purpose of such announcements would have been to make the real targets, British Aerospace and Thomson-CSF, more anxious to complete a deal. In fact, by late 1998, the GEC Group was using game theory to operate a special strategy called Project Superbowl. The object was to sort out GEC Marconi. It knew that its subsidiary was

valued at US$9 billion and entered into discussion with this as the minimum price. From these negotiations, it became clear that British Aerospace and Dasa were close to doing a deal. The GEC Group realised that this would substantially weaken its negotiating position because GEC Marconi would then become a much smaller player in a larger pool. Thus George Simpson decided to sell GEC Marconi to the highest bidder while the company still had real negotiating power. It gave the story to the *Financial Times* which ran the headline:

> BAE given ultimatum over Marconi: GEC sets end-of-week deadline for bid as other companies signal interest in defence electronics arm.

After further discussion, GEC Marconi was sold to British Aerospace for US$12 billion five days later in January 1999.

British Aerospace: also a game player

What the GEC Group did not know was that British Aerospace was also using strategic game theory to plot its moves in the consolidation battle. It had worked out that by combining with GEC Marconi it was able to ensure that it had a dominant interest in any further consolidation that would then take place. Moreover, it expected any subsequent moves towards consolidation to be more limited as a result. For these reasons, it was willing to pay rather more than the initial valuation of GEC Marconi – US$3 billion more, to be precise.

Outcomes – not always predicted by game theory!

After the deal was agreed, European governments were not very happy because the solution was a purely UK affair. However, British Aerospace took the view that this problem could be sorted out later. Its market position was enhanced by its new acquisition, even after paying an extra US$3 billion.

After divesting its defence interests, GEC was renamed Marconi. It went on to acquire a whole series of ▶

▶ CASE STUDY 15.3 continued

telecommunications equipment companies during 2000 and 2001 – just before the market for telecommunications equipment went into steep decline. By mid-2002, GEC had used up its extra US$3 billion and was in deep trouble – both the chairman, George Simpson, and all his senior colleagues were forced to resign.

© Copyright Richard Lynch 2006. All rights reserved. This case was written by Richard Lynch from published information only.[18]

Case questions

1 *What are the strengths and weaknesses of using game theory to plot this strategic battle?*

2 *To what extent were other negotiations involved that went beyond game theory? Were these significant?*

3 *What lessons can we draw from the case on the usefulness of game theory in strategy development?*

15.4 THE NETWORK-BASED STRATEGIC ROUTE FORWARD

Definition ▶ The network-based strategic route forward explores the links and degree of co-operation present in related organisations and industries and places a value upon that degree of co-operation. There are two major aspects of networks from a strategy perspective covered in this section:

● Network externalities
● Network co-operation.

In order to understand these, it is useful to explore the British Aerospace case from these two perspectives.

Network externalities[19]

Network externalities arise when an organisation is part of an external network that is seeking to standardise some aspect of operations across an industry. Benefits arise for all those in the network when the standardisation has been achieved and they will increase as more organisations adopt the standard. The benefit is *external* to an individual organisation in the network. For example, after British Aerospace completed its acquisition of GEC Marconi (*see* Case study 15.3), one form of further development would involve *networks* involving British Aerospace and other companies in the industry. The outcome of such network might be an agreement on a standard for an item of defence equipment – perhaps on agreed design for a military aircraft like the Eurofighter. This represents a real benefit to those taking part in the agreement because it allows those that are part of the network to develop new items of equipment based on the standard. Such an agreed standard may result in shared development costs and perhaps even economies of scale in production. If others join the network and adopt the standard, then all the existing members of the network will benefit even further. We explore this relatively new aspect of strategy development in Section 15.4.1.

Network co-operation

Network co-operation arises when companies engage in formal and informal agreements with each other for their mutual benefit. For example, even after British Aerospace completed its acquisition of GEC Marconi (*see* Case study 15.3), it was important from a strategy perspective to see this as only the beginning of a new phase in European defence industry alliances and consolidation. Further developments will involve negotiation between British Aerospace and others involved in the defence industry. The purpose will be to extract the full added value from the takeover and develop other forms of co-operation, while at the same time developing the sustainable competitive advantage of the enlarged British Aerospace company. We have previously explored some aspects of this in Chapter 4 in our analysis of co-operation. However, we are now seeking new strategies, so it is important to return to this network co-operation at this point. This is examined further in Section 15.4.2.

15.4.1 Network externalities[20]

Definition ➤ Network externalities refer to the development of an overall standard for a network that allows those belonging to the network to benefit increasingly as others join the same network. It is called an *externality* because the concept is driven not by an activity internal to the company but by the external membership of all that belong to the network. Probably the best-known example of an industry *network externality* is that owned by Microsoft: its Windows operating system is used in 90 per cent of all personal computers around the world. Those using this computer system gain increased benefits because many other users also use the same system. In other words, *the value of the system is enhanced because it can be shared with others who are part of the same external network.*

Importantly, the network has a benefit as the total number of users increases and reaches a critical mass of users – this is sometimes called the *'tipping point'*. Essentially, the tipping point is reached when the installed base of network users moves towards one company supplying the network and away from rival suppliers. This is quite different from the normal micro-economic concepts of supply and demand, which assume that the sale and price of each product or service is independent of other purchases. Under network externalities, the more of one product that is purchased, the more valuable it becomes.

Comment

Although this is a useful concept, it applies mainly to organisations that have a high and formal co-operative content, for example the need for consumer electronics companies to agree a common standard for DVD players. Once the standard has been agreed, there will usually be some winners and losers, but strategy then needs to move on to its many other dimensions. In other words, network externalities have a role but they will often apply only once in the technological lifetime of a product and will have more limited relevance where a single technology standard is less important in strategy development.

15.4.2 Network co-operation

Definition ➤ Network co-operation refers to the value-adding relationships that organisations develop *inside* their own organisation and *outside* it with other organisations. For example, European telecommunications companies have their own telephone exchange resources and employees that generate profits. In addition, they compete with each other in some national European telephone markets while, at the same time, developing co-operative linkages with other telephone companies in global markets. It is this complex web of internal and external activities that constitutes the network and delivers added value to the organisation.

From a strategic perspective, the issue is how to optimise the value added from such internal and external activities. As a starting point, we can refer to the two principles explored in Chapter 6:

1 *The benefits of owning and managing resources, rather than buying them in from outside.*[21] This can be used to identify the important relationships that organisations have both inside and outside their own organisation.

2 *The value chain and value linkages.*[22] The chain provides a picture of networks inside the organisation and the linkages do the same for the outside relationships.

In order to develop network-based strategy, these general principles need to be used to map out the networks that exist in and with every organisation. A largely prescriptive approach to this task is shown in Exhibit 15.4.

Exhibit 15.4

How networks can add value to the organisation

From *internal networks*, value added can be increased by:

- economies of scale and scope;
- development of superior, even unique, knowledge and technologies;
- investment in customer service, marketing and reputation;
- skills, knowledge and expertise in cash handling, financial transactions and other financial instruments.

From *external networks*, value added can be increased by:

- cost-effective logistics, stock handling and other outside transport facilities;
- superior purchasing from suppliers;
- skilled external sourcing of new technical developments, licensing of new technologies and other technical advances;
- strong and stable relationships with government and other influential organisations.

Note that these are only examples of the many networks that exist in and between organisations.

As a result of optimising value added, network co-operation also influences sustainable competitive advantage. For example, at the European telephone companies, those with superior value-added activities, based on an attractive combination of keen prices and high-quality service, are also likely to be able to compete strongly with competitors: high profits are likely to be associated with sustainable competitive advantage. However, such a combination of price and service will probably also derive, at least in part, from the valuable co-operative linkages that such superior companies have with others.

In more general economic terms, the 'invisible hand' of market competition should drive companies to greater efficiency in the use of their internal resources. At the same time, the 'visible hand' of co-operative linkages will generate real, and perhaps unique, external networks and value for organisations. In a sense, networks rely both on invisible and visible guidance in the generation and maintenance of relationships – a relationship more like a 'continuous handshake' than an intermittent hand clasp.[23]

Thus in network co-operation strategy, value is added and competitive advantage is developed by the precise *combination* of competition and co-operation that organisations have with others. As a result, organisations will construct a unique network of relationships both inside and outside their own organisation. For example, over time salespeople may strike up relationships with customers, purchasing managers with suppliers and so on. Long-term relationships with outsiders may be a crucial element of the company's strategy, as those in the aerospace, defence, telecommunications equipment and other industries negotiating with government will quickly confirm.

Negotiation is a vital strategic aspect of such relationships and the process becomes effectively one of the key determinants of success. Thus, for example, in the case of mobile telephones, governments may well be involved in the purchase or specification of such items. More generally, direct government control may be achieved by access to preferential credit, joint ownership, a threat to call in new suppliers, the allocation of R&D contracts and assistance in export sales.[24] Developing corporate strategy without negotiating with a government may be an expensive luxury. The bargaining power that each side has in such negotiations will depend on the maturity of the market and the technology involved.

In many respects, therefore, the organisation can be seen as a *network of treaties* both outside and inside the company.[25] Moreover, if such agreements are important for the development of strategy, then it follows that it is important to understand the dynamics of these networks in order to develop optimal strategy.[26] Because of the sheer complexity of this task, it may be better to use critical success factors to focus attention on the important areas of the process (*see* Chapter 3).

Comment

Some strategists argue that what matters is not the *combination* of competitive and co-operative networks but the *primacy* of one or the other:

● either competitive relationships are paramount: 'The essence of strategy formulation is coping with competition', according to Professor Michael Porter;[27]

● or co-operative networks represent the main scope for strategic development: 'The real-isation is growing that cooperative behaviour is at the root of many success stories in today's management', to quote J Carlos Jarillo.[28]

Such a choice is profoundly misleading.[29] All organisations both compete and co-operate and there is no 'strategic paradox' between these two that needs to be resolved. The only issue is the *balance* between the two. This will depend on the context within which the strategy is being developed. For example, in the European telephone companies in the late 1990s, *competition* was the main driving force. It was increasing inside countries like the UK and Germany, though co-operation was also important in providing international tele-phone networks. By contrast, in the European defence industry in the late 1990s, increased *co-operation* was being developed on a pan-European basis in order to allow European com-panies to compete more successfully in the global market place against the big US defence companies.

15.4.3 Consequences of all these aspects for corporate strategy

Essentially, networks are fluid and may change. Members of such networks can often leave without cost. In this sense, nothing is fixed and everything is open to negotiation. Therefore, objectives may need to be revised and selection may be compromised by the need to persuade groups to join or remain in the network. In a sense, the implementation process itself is now part of the selection process and part of the strategy.

Table 15.9 illustrates the major implications of such a network-based route forward. It should be noted that the timetable for any strategic change may need to be lengthened to accommodate this process. It is not possible to show this adequately in the table.

Comment

There can be little doubt that networks are a part of many organisations, both large and small. However, there is still a need to drive the strategy process forward. This is where *leadership* is probably vital. Network-based strategies are unlikely to represent a complete route in them-selves, but need to take place alongside prescriptive and learning-based strategy processes.

Key strategic principles

● *The network-based strategic route forward* explores the links and degree of co-operation present in related organisations and industries and places a value upon that degree of co-operation. The route has two aspects – network externalities and network co-operation.

● Network externalities refer to the development of an overall standard for a network that allows those belonging to the network to benefit increasingly as others join the same network.

Key strategic principles *continued*

● In such externalities, the key moment is the 'tipping point', which is reached when the installed base of network users moves towards one company supplying the network and away from rival suppliers.

● Network co-operation explores the links and degree of co-operation present in related organisations and industries and places a value upon that degree of co-operation.

● In network co-operation strategy, value is added and competitive advantage is developed by the precise *combination* of competition and co-operation that organisations have with others. Such a strategic approach also needs to be seen in the context of negotiations with powerful customers and suppliers where bargaining and trade-offs will take place.

Table 15.9

Comparison of the network-based process with the prescriptive process

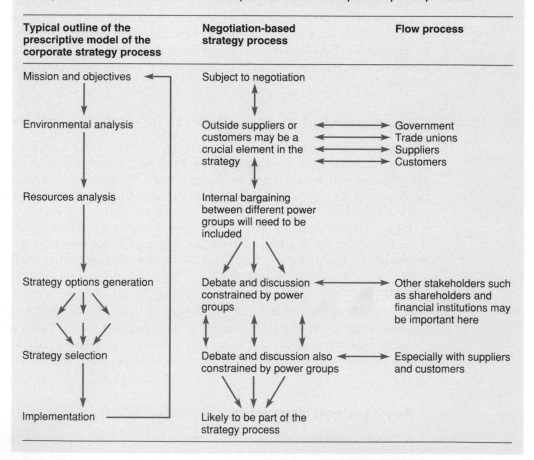

Typical outline of the prescriptive model of the corporate strategy process	Negotiation-based strategy process	Flow process
Mission and objectives	Subject to negotiation	
Environmental analysis	Outside suppliers or customers may be a crucial element in the strategy	Government Trade unions Suppliers Customers
Resources analysis	Internal bargaining between different power groups will need to be included	
Strategy options generation	Debate and discussion constrained by power groups	Other stakeholders such as shareholders and financial institutions may be important here
Strategy selection	Debate and discussion also constrained by power groups	Especially with suppliers and customers
Implementation	Likely to be part of the strategy process	

15.5 THE GAME THEORY-BASED ROUTE FORWARD

Definition ➤ The game-theory route forward refers to structured methods of bargaining with and between customers, suppliers and competitors of the organisation, such structuring involving the quantification of possible outcomes at each stage of the strategy decision-making process.

For example, Case 15.3 described how British Aerospace used game theory to complete the negotiation of the successful acquisition of GEC Marconi by British Aerospace. This was undertaken using an approach that quantified the various possible outcomes of different stages of the bidding and negotiating process, the purpose being to determine what and how British Aerospace should bid at each stage.

During the 1940s, mathematical models were first developed to handle in a structured way the commercial decisions that are involved: they are known under the general title of *game theory*.[30] Game-based theory is concerned with the immediate negotiation and its related strategy: it says little or nothing about the implementation stages that follow once the negotiation has been concluded. Game theory has two clear advantages for strategy development:

1 It clarifies the *nature of the negotiation*, identifying the players, setting out their options, identifying the outcomes of each option and the sequence of events that need to take place.

2 It can predict the *optimal outcomes of some games*, particularly by permitting the manipulation of the payoffs to the players. It does this by providing insights into the nature of the relationships that exist between players, including the identification of the competitors and co-operators.[31]

Game theory attempts to predict competitor reactions in the negotiating situation. The circumstances may be regarded as being similar to a game of chess, where anticipation of the opponent's moves is an important aspect of the challenge. Much of game theory has been modelled mathematically, with the rules specifying how the scarce resources of the company can be employed and what benefits will be obtained by particular moves or a combination of moves – the benefits are often called *payoffs*.[32]

● In a *zero-sum game*, there is ultimately no payoff because the gains of one member are negated by the losses of another.

● In a *co-operative game*, the benefits may add up to a positive payoff for all.

● In a *negative-sum game*, the actions of each party undermine both themselves and their opponents.

Although game theory has provided a useful basis for structuring negotiations and the consequences of each move, it has proved difficult to model strategic options and decisions which are often highly complex and interrelated. Probably the most interesting strategic insights provided by game theory are in the likely outcomes of various stages of the negotiation process. For example, when British Aerospace was negotiating the restructuring of the European defence industry, it used game theory to show that it was useful to acquire GEC Marconi for two reasons:

1 The increased size gave it much greater influence on the final shape of the pan-European consolidation game.

2 The acquisition reduced the number of options available in the industry, thus lowering the number of moves that it would take to achieve the consolidation required.

Given these advantages, the issue is how to make use of game theory to analyse and conduct competitive strategic games. There are six essential steps in what is essentially a prescriptive process; these are shown in Exhibit 15.5.

More generally, the mechanics and logical decision-making aspects of game theory are well represented in the various theoretical descriptions. But they say little about other vital aspects of most strategic negotiations. The leadership of the teams involved, the personalities and cultures of their members, the ambitions and the history of the players are not covered at all. The strategic context in which negotiations are taking place can lead to consequences that go well beyond the mathematics of game theory. For example, in the European defence industry case, the various personalities of the leading chief executives and

Game theory: six steps to playing strategic games in the European defence industry

Step 1

Identify the players. It is important to identify the potential as well as the actual players in any game. The main players are listed in the European defence industry case, but the Americans are excluded (perhaps unwisely).

Step 2

Analyse their strengths and weaknesses. Include potential links to outside influencers and complementors – *see* Chapter 3. For the European defence industry, some pointers are given in Case study 15.3 but more information would be needed in practice.

Step 3

Establish the extent to which the game will be played with sequential or simultaneous moves. In practice, most games are played with both. The significance of this analysis lies in its consequences for the way that the game will develop:

● Sequential moves mean that one of the players acts and then another responds, e.g. a game of golf or serving in tennis.

● Simultaneous moves mean that the players act without knowing what action the others are taking at the same time, e.g. a swimming tournament.

In the European defence industry, there were some simultaneous negotiations taking place – for example, between Dasa, British Aerospace and GEC Marconi. But once the British Aerospace bid for GEC Marconi had been tabled, the others backed off and it became sequential.

The next step depends on whether simultaneous or sequential moves represent the main way forward.

Step 4A: Sequential moves only

For sequential moves, plot out the consequences of each move – often called a game tree – and choose the best outcome. Then reason backwards from this on the best way to achieve this outcome.

At the time of writing on the European defence industry, the immediate best outcome for British Aerospace had been established. However, other companies would be plotting their next moves – for example, Dasa was signalling that it was willing to consider combining with a US company, but this may have been bluff.

Step 4B: Simultaneous moves only

For simultaneous moves, plot out all the possible outcomes in the form of a table – often called a payoff table – and then undertake the following in order:

1 Identify any *dominant strategy*, i.e. one that is clearly better than the competition. If one can be found, play it.

2 If no dominant strategy can be found, identify any *dominated strategy*, i.e. one that is clearly worse than the competition. If it can be identified, eliminate it from further analysis.

3 If there is no dominant or dominated strategy, seek other outcomes – often called a *Nash Equilibrium* – that represent each player's best judgement of its own interests. Essentially, here, each player understands the strategies of the opponent but cannot improve on his or her own position by making an alternative choice.

In the case of British Aerospace, the dominant strategy was clearly to become larger than its competitors. By this means, it was able to improve its negotiating position in subsequent negotiation moves. The best move for Aerospatiale might then be to become equally large through a merger with one of its French rivals such as Thompson-CSF or Dassault. Notice here that the best move for one company might not be the best for another.

Step 5

Consider how to signal moves to the other players. The best play may not be an open bidding process against an opponent because this invites an aggressive direct response which may be expensive. Even in simultaneous games, a better outcome may be possible if players are not presented with simple stark choices – many supposedly impossible games can be solved by allowing the players to signal to each other.

In the European defence industry at the time of writing, many signals were being made to other players. Companies were expressing their willingness to consider further consolidation, but on their own terms.

Step 6

Begin playing. It is vital to reassess the status of the game and its outcomes because the essence of the game is that it will alter as it progresses.

The *Appendix* at the end of this chapter provides some more detail.

their other responsibilities influenced the outcome of the game: George Simpson was determined to sort out the GEC Group that he had inherited, while Jürgen Schrempp at Daimler was preoccupied with the massive merger with Chrysler.

To capture some of these practical complexities of negotiation, the *negotiation checklist* at the end of the chapter has been constructed. Readers may care to note that it can be used not only for acquisitions but for many other negotiation situations, including personal strategies. There are four aspects of game theory in the checklist that are worth highlighting here:

1 *Viewpoint of the game.* It is important to assess the game not just from one player's perspective of the outcome. It is essential to gauge what rivals expect to take out of the game and possibly make some attempt to accommodate this.

2 *Rewrite the rules of the game.* The outcome of some games can be altered by totally rewriting the way that the game is played, even part-way through the game. In this sense, game theory is not like chess or football. This can provide a real opportunity.

3 *Reassessment of the game.* It is usually worth reconsidering whether a game is worth pursuing part of the way through the game. Some negotiations can simply be a waste of time and resources.

4 *Reassurance about the final outcome.* In any game, even where there are multiple winners, it is worth remembering that people are involved. Players need to be reassured after the outcome that it was the best that could be achieved.

Although game theory can be helpful in certain limited circumstances, it focuses mainly on one small area of the strategic process – the *options and choice* part of the prescriptive process. Game theory has nothing substantial to offer with regard to the earlier analysis phase or the later implementation phase of the prescriptive process. Table 15.10 makes the comparison with the prescriptive process.

Comment

There are three main problems with game theory in negotiation-based strategy:[33]

1 The mathematical complexity makes the analytical results useful but limited. Moreover, it assumes that a dynamic and interacting environment can be modelled by a series of static equilibria. This is a dangerously simple approximation of reality.

2 Many of its conclusions, especially about Nash equilibria, are ambiguous and based on a narrow view of context. For example, game theory largely excludes all psychological insight. Game theory has so far proved incapable of handling the many complexities of real business situations.

3 Importantly, game theory focuses on a small fraction of the strategic process. For example, it provides no insight whatsoever into the development of the competitive resources of the organisation, nor any useful guidance on the massive task of implementing whatever has been negotiated.

Key strategic principles

- Game theory attempts to predict the outcomes of customer reactions or, in some cases, to show how the outcome of negotiations may well produce a suboptimal solution unless both sides of the negotiations realise the consequences of their actions.

- Game theory has some value in negotiations but suffers from three difficulties: mathematical complexity; ambiguous conclusions; being only one small part of the strategy process.

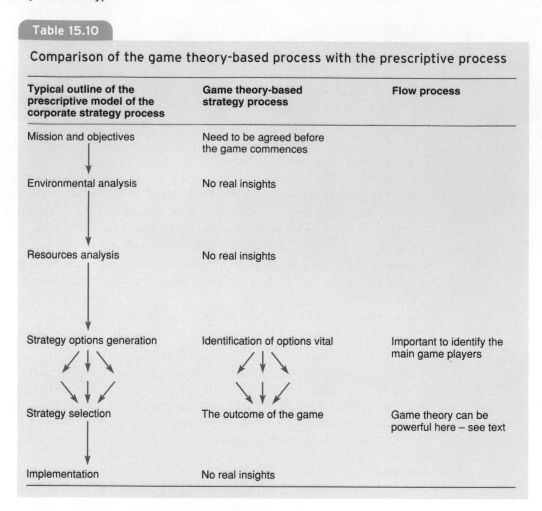

Table 15.10

Comparison of the game theory-based process with the prescriptive process

Typical outline of the prescriptive model of the corporate strategy process	Game theory-based strategy process	Flow process
Mission and objectives	Need to be agreed before the game commences	
Environmental analysis	No real insights	
Resources analysis	No real insights	
Strategy options generation	Identification of options vital	Important to identify the main game players
Strategy selection	The outcome of the game	Game theory can be powerful here – see text
Implementation	No real insights	

15.6 THE LEARNING-BASED STRATEGIC ROUTE FORWARD

Definition ➤

Part 7b

The learning-based strategic route forward emphasises learning and crafting as aspects of the development of successful corporate strategy. It places particular importance on trial and feedback mechanisms. Learning can take place at the *personal* level and at the *group* level: corporate strategy focuses mainly on *group* learning because this is the most relevant aspect in the context of organisational development. When there is considerable uncertainty, as in the European mobile telecommunications market, it may not be possible or prudent to develop a strategy that is firmly fixed for some years ahead. It may be better to have some basic business objectives, possibly even a vision of the future (*see* Chapter 10), but also be prepared to experiment and react to market events. These might include the launch or disappearance of rival companies. The process of adopting a flexible, emergent strategy that monitors events, reacts to them and develops opportunities is at the heart of learning-based strategies.

15.6.1 The role of learning in an organisation

In a persuasive article in 1987, Mintzberg argued that the rational analysis of such areas as markets and company resources was unlikely to produce effective strategy. A much more likely process was that of *crafting strategy* where 'formulation and implementation merge into a fluid process of learning through which creative strategies evolve'.[34] Mintzberg was not denying the need for planning and formulation of strategy. However, he argued strongly for the flexibility that comes from learning to shape and reshape a strategy as it begins to be implemented. This was particularly important because strategy occasionally had to address a major shift in the market place or in internal practice – a *quantum leap*. At such a time, those strategists who had really *learnt* how the organisation operated would be better able to recognise the need for change and respond quickly to the signals of the major shift.

As an example to clarify the process, we can examine Royal Dutch/Shell, one of the world's leading oil companies. The company provided an example of the quantum leap and the learning process during the 1980s.[35] In 1984, oil was priced around US$28 per barrel. Against this background, the company's central planning department developed a speculative scenario based on the price dropping to US$16 per barrel. Purely as an exercise, they urged senior management to speculate on the consequences of such a radical price drop. Some senior managers felt it was unlikely but were willing to enter into the spirit of the exercise. The consequences were explored well enough so that, when the price actually dropped to US$10 per barrel in 1987, the company was well prepared.

One of Royal Dutch/Shell's leading planners later concluded:

> *Institutional learning is the process whereby management teams change their shared mental models of their company, their markets and their competitors. For this reason, we think of planning as learning and of corporate planning as institutional learning.*

The key words here are *change their shared mental models* and the process of *learning*. Most companies explore strategic issues not just as individuals but also as a management team or group that meets together. It is this *group* that develops assumptions about the company and its environment: these need to be made explicit and shared. These may then need to be changed, depending on the circumstances – for example, a quantum leap as mentioned above.

15.6.2 The relationship of learning with knowledge – the contributions of Argyris and Garvin

Learning may be seen as the process of expanding the knowledge of the organisation. It involves a *loop* of activity consisting of acquiring new knowledge, checking this against reality and then feeding back the result – for example, reading the room temperature on a thermostat, checking the room temperature to ensure comfort and adjusting the thermostat if required. The learning process may involve study, tuition and practical experience. In the complex world of business and not-for-profit organisations, learning will involve all three mechanisms and thus become complex.

For organisations, learning has a further degree of difficulty because periodically it needs to embrace a fundamental review of the organisation's purpose and objectives. This will involve the managers of the organisation asking difficult questions and will place demands on them that go beyond mere data gathering and checking against reality. It was Professor Chris Argyris of Harvard Business School who first coined the term *double-loop learning* to explain this extra complexity. In addition to the first learning loop described in the paragraph above, there is a second learning loop which questions the whole mechanism served by the first loop. To take the example from the previous paragraph, he likened it to checking whether a thermostat was really needed and whether a completely different temperature control mechanism would produce better and cheaper results.[36] It is this fundamental reappraisal that is important to corporate strategy and to the process by which companies learn in organisations – *see* Figure 15.3. Hence, double loop learning consists of a *first* loop of learning that checks performance against expected norms and adjusts where necessary, coupled with a *second* loop that reappraises whether the expected norms were appropriate in the first place.

Given some imprecision over the criteria for the first and second loops, it is not surprising that there is no agreed definition of the learning organisation. Most people accept that

Definition ➤

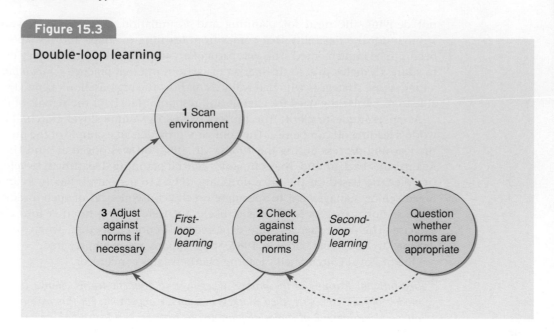

Figure 15.3

Double-loop learning

organisations learn over time and that increased knowledge will deliver increased perform-ance, but the processes beyond this are open to dispute. Some argue that organisations must change the way that they behave for true learning to occur, whereas others argue that simply acquiring new ways of thinking is sufficient. Recognising these difficulties, Professor Daniel Garvin, also from Harvard University Business School, has provided the following definition:[37]

> *A learning organisation is an organisation skilled at creating, acquiring and transferring know-ledge, and at modifying its behaviour to reflect new knowledge and insights.*

It is the second part of this definition, 'and modifying its behaviour', that constitutes the second learning loop. The mechanisms identified by this definition – knowledge creation, acquisition, transferral and modification – were explored in Chapter 11 with regard to knowledge creation. Importantly, the latter point that organisations will only show that they have learnt when they have modified and changed their past behaviour is one that was developed by Peter Senge.

15.6.3 How groups can learn better – the contribution of Senge

The contribution of Professor Peter Senge was to extend the learning concept from the *indi-vidual* as a learning unit to the *group*. To understand this contribution, we begin by review-ing the main elements of the emergent strategy process and the theory of learning.

As explained above, the concept of *double-loop learning* was to prove highly influential in learning approaches to strategy development.[38] Essentially, it involved not only learning by comparison with accepted standards but also questioning the standards themselves. In 1990, Peter Senge, Professor of Organisational Systems and Learning at the Massachusetts Institute of Technology, employed the learning principles but added to them significantly by using operations research feedback mechanisms and by suggesting that the most power-ful learning was by *groups or teams*, not individuals. He applied the group learning concept to strategy development, referring to:

> *[t]he Learning Organization . . . where people continually expand their capacity to create the results they truly desire, where new and expansive patterns of thinking are nurtured, where collective aspiration is set free and where people are continually learning how to learn together.*[39]

Importantly, Senge draws an important distinction between two types of learning. These are:

1 *adaptive learning* – understanding changes *outside in the environment* and adapting to these;
2 *generative learning* – creating and exploring new strategy areas for positive expansion *within the organisation itself.*

Both types of learning will come from experimentation, discussion and feedback within the organisation. Rigid, formal, hierarchical organisations are unlikely to provide this. New, more fluid structures are needed, according to Senge. It is interesting to note that, in the high-growth economies of Japan in the 1970s and 1980s and in South-East Asia in the 1990s, one of the major distinguishing features has been participation in the planning process, coupled with flexibility and adaptability, rather than rigid, formal plans.[40,41]

Senge went on to argue that learning is intimately involved with knowledge, which was best acquired by setting interesting and challenging targets and by encouraging group interaction. These ideas move strategy generation forwards from simply searching for simple, prescriptive solutions. A key point of Senge's text was that strategy development involved the *knowledge creation* process, which was best undertaken by groups. The aim was to develop a new 'mental model' of an issue through the group dynamic.

There are a number of well-recognised mechanisms for developing and sharing mental models as part of the learning process.[42] Probably the best known of these are the five learning disciplines of Peter Senge.[43] They are crafted to help organisations and individuals learn. However, *learning* here does not mean memory work or even merely coping with a changing environment. Learning has a more positive and proactive meaning: *active creativity* to develop new strategies and opportunities. The five learning disciplines developed to achieve this are summarised in Exhibit 15.6.

Exhibit 15.6

The five learning disciplines

1 *Personal mastery* – not only developing personal goals but also creating the organisational environment that encourages groups to develop goals and purposes

2 *Mental models* – reflecting and speculating upon the pictures that managers and workers have of the world and seeing how these influence actions and decisions

3 *Shared vision* – building commitment in the group to achieve its aims by exploring and agreeing what these aims are

4 *Team learning* – using the group's normal skills to develop intelligence and ability beyond individuals' normal abilities

5 *Systems thinking* – a method of thinking about, describing and understanding the major forces that influence the group

Source: Based on the writings of Peter Senge.

To survive in today's turbulent business climate, it has been argued that strategy must include mechanisms that transfer learning from the individual to the group.[44] There are then three advantages from the learning process for the group and for the whole organisation:

1 It will provide fresh ideas and insights into the organisation's performance through a commitment to knowledge.

2 Adaptation through renewal will be promoted so organisations do not stultify and wither.

3 It will promote an openness to the outside world so that it can respond to events – for example, the quantum change of an oil price shock or the rapid developments in the European mobile telephone market.

It is often the well-educated, highly committed senior professional in an organisation who has the most difficulty with this process.[45] Such an individual may misunderstand the meaning of the word 'learning' and interpret it too narrowly as being purely about problem solving. It may also not be understood that the *process* of learning is about more than just instructions from the teacher or the senior management. The implications for corporate strategy are that learning is a two-way process and is more open-ended than prescriptive strategy would suggest.

15.6.4 Learning and the problem of dominant logic

The essence of the learning model is to explore widely and without pre-conceived ideas about a particular strategic issue, experimenting and trying various options. After time, one or more solutions will prove to be more successful than others. Resources will then be allocated according to the results of such experimentation. This will become the basis of more general decision-making in the organisation and a model emerge of how the business should operate. That model is the dominant logic. Dominant logic is 'the way in which managers conceptualise the business and make critical resource allocation decisions.'[46]

Definition ➤

Although learning organisations can be interesting and demanding, there is evidence to suggest that learning can sometimes become stale and rely on past knowledge.[47] Managers evolve their mental models of how profits are made in a business or how procedures deliver good levels of service in a public organisation. The difficulty is that such mental models can fail to sense the new circumstances that may subsequently influence the organisation. Such models are rooted in the past and provide a set of answers for past strategic decisions.

When a logic becomes dominant, then it can become a barrier to the organisation continuing to learn. The difficulty is not only that such logic may no longer be appropriate but that it can become embedded in the routine tasks and procedures of the organisation. It may even be that managers are rewarded on their ability to deliver the dominant logic. The organisation may even revert back to single-loop learning and will only be jolted out of its actions when performance declines to the point that its survival is threatened. A new learning experience is then essential.[48]

15.6.5 The myopia of learning – the contribution of Levinthal and March

Reviewing Senge's contribution and other papers on learning, Levinthal and March[49] explored the myopia (short-sightedness) of learning. They acknowledged that learning has many virtues but argue that the learning process also has a number of limitations. They argued that learning has to maintain a difficult balance between developing *new knowledge* – exploring – and at the same time exploiting *current competencies* with the balance often tilting in favour of one or the other. They identified three constraints on organisational learning:

1 *Temporal myopia*: Learning tends to sacrifice the long run to the short run. As we learn about new competencies and market niches, we simultaneously focus on these and exclude other areas outside these competencies and niches. Clearly an organisation cannot survive in the long run if it is unable to survive its immediate future. But learning does present a problem here.

2 *Spatial myopia*: Learning tends to favour effects that occur near to the learner. Organisations tend to focus on the issues surrounding survival in the near future rather than the broader issues that will help the organisation to grow over time.

3 *Failure myopia*: organisational learning over-samples successes and under-samples failures. By its nature, learning tends to eliminate failure and focus on success. Learning does not easily correct such biases in experience and may even make organisations overconfident of future success.

For these reasons, learning may not be as useful as sometimes suggested. Learning organisations can have difficulty in sustaining adequate exploration. Organisations should be conservative in their expectations from learning: 'Magic would be nice, but it is not easy to find.'

15.6.6 Improving an organisation's ability to learn

Clearly, the leaders of the organisation can ensure that such a trap is avoided by being aware of the danger of dominant logic. Senge himself was concerned to emphasise the role of the leader in building the shared vision, challenging mental models and helping those involved in the organisation to develop their group learning in many different ways.

Three other mechanisms can help to overcome the difficulty of dominant logic:

- Organising an occasion to take managers away from their daily routines in order to undertake a fundamental review of the business.

- Storytelling, i.e. converting strategy development into a series of stories, can also assist by emphasising the creative aspect of the learning, by highlighting the more dramatic aspects of the strategy development, and by presenting the rich detail that brings alive the relationships and breaks down the barriers that preclude sharing knowledge.[50]

- Developing a 'no blame' culture that encourages and supports critical informed comment.

Underpinning all such initiatives and others is the realisation that organisations will improve their strategic decision making if they challenge existing ways of thinking and provide a supportive, 'no-blame' environment in which to undertake such a task. We return to this theme in Chapter 16.

15.6.7 Consequences for the corporate strategy process

In the learning process, the concept of 'top-down' management handing semi-finished objectives to the more junior managers and employees clearly carries no meaning. Generative learning needs to have a greater element of co-operation and discussion. Nevertheless, the analytical element of the process can proceed, though perhaps more openly and with more people involved. This will inevitably slow it down but it may be a small price to pay for the greater commitment achieved and the alternative insights on strategy from group members. Strategy options and selection are still conceivable but the process may be more complex and multilayered than the prescriptive route. However, it is clearly possible that the implementation phase may actually be faster because people will be better informed and more committed to strategies that they themselves have helped to form.[51]

Table 15.11 outlines the main elements of the learning-based process. The key point is that the learning process itself is part of the strategy, not something added after the strategy has been developed. This means that the fully developed strategy only emerges over time.

Comment

The learning-based route has real value in the development of corporate strategy. However, it has to be said that it is sometimes vague and non-operational in its proposals, beyond the need to consult everyone. Moreover, there is still a need in some circumstances for senior managers to take decisions *without* consultation (*see* Case study 14.1 on Nokia and Case study 16.3 on Asea Brown Boveri). More generally, *how* and *when* organisations should adopt the learning-based approach has been the basis for fully justified criticism of this route forward.[52] In spite of these weaknesses, the route does not preclude the use of the prescriptive process. It will be explored further in later chapters of this book.

Table 15.11

Comparison of the learning-based process with the prescriptive process

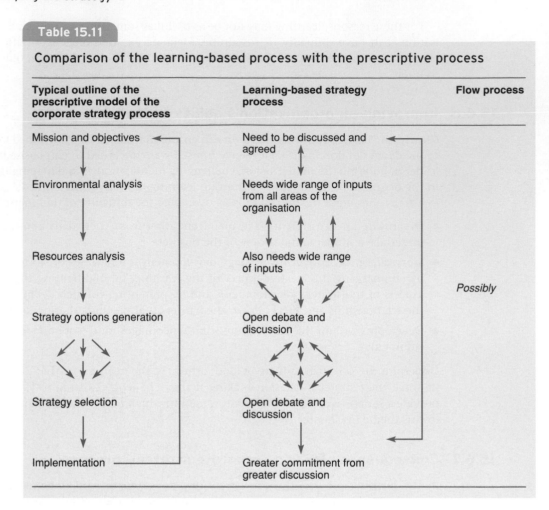

Typical outline of the prescriptive model of the corporate strategy process	Learning-based strategy process	Flow process
Mission and objectives	Need to be discussed and agreed	
Environmental analysis	Needs wide range of inputs from all areas of the organisation	
Resources analysis	Also needs wide range of inputs	Possibly
Strategy options generation	Open debate and discussion	
Strategy selection	Open debate and discussion	
Implementation	Greater commitment from greater discussion	

Key strategic principles

- The learning-based strategic route forward emphasises learning and crafting as aspects of the development of successful corporate strategy. It places particular importance on trial and feedback mechanisms in developing unique strategies. Learning is not concerned with memory work, but with active creativity in developing new strategic opportunities.

- Double-loop learning consists of a *first* loop of learning that checks performance against expected norms and adjusts where necessary, coupled with a *second* loop that reappraises whether the expected norms were appropriate in the first place.

- In strategy development, group dynamics are more important than individuals in developing new, experimental strategies. There are five principles to group learning: personal mastery, group mental models, share vision, team learning and systems thinking.

- One of the dangers associated with learning is that the 'successful solution' at the end of the process becomes the 'dominant logic' and this stops the organisation continuing to learn. There are ways of overcoming this including good leadership, story-telling and organising opportunities for a thorough reappraisal of an organisation's strategy.

- Within the learning concept, there is a difficult balance to be struck between the learning that comes from developing new knowledge and the learning that comes from exploiting existing competencies. There are three fundamental problems with the learning concept: *temporal myopia* – learning tends to sacrifice the long run to the short run – *spatial myopia* – learning tends to favour effects that occur near the learner – and *failure myopia* – organisational learning over-samples success and under-samples failure.

- Group and individual learning have real value as concepts but can be vague and lack operational guidance in practice.

15.7 INTERNATIONAL CONSIDERATIONS

Differences around the world in cultures, social values and economic traditions mean it is possible that some strategy processes may be difficult, if not impossible, to introduce and manage in certain countries. For example, the learning process of Section 15.6 requires a relaxed and open relationship between superior and subordinate that is available in some Northern European countries but much more rare in Malaysia and India.[53] Some writers have promoted the idea of the *borderless world* and the *global corporation*. Undoubtedly, in terms of common customer tastes and sourcing of production, there are real commonalities, but in terms of the strategy process, which is more detailed and requires more commitment, real differences still exist.[54]

International considerations may impact on the strategy process during every stage. However, they do not influence the process in a single, consistent fashion. Thus there is no 'international strategy process'.

15.7.1 Stakeholders

As we have seen, stakeholders and their relative power vary throughout the world: shareholders, employees, managers, financial institutions, governments and other interested groups. Importantly, their ability to influence the strategy process will also vary:

- In some areas of the Far East and Africa, government influence will be important in guiding strategy development.

- In the UK and North America, shareholders are often given the first consideration in developing strategy.

These differences have arisen for historic, cultural and economic reasons. In each country, different sets of values, expectations and beliefs will influence the strategic process: companies may not hold the simple economic, rational views that have been used to guide strategic processes in some Western countries. The influences may be more complex and embedded in culture and social values.[55] Explicit awareness of stakeholders' expectations is an important part of the strategic process.

15.7.2 Mission and objectives

Strategic goals and processes are likely to reflect the social systems of the country in which the strategy is developed. Thus, the missions and objectives of companies need to be seen in the context of their countries of origin. However, it should be recognised that even within countries there will be major variations in ambitions, ideas and values. The importance of socio-cultural elements should, therefore, not be overemphasised. As

Whittington commented: 'Societies are too complex and people too individualistic to expect bland uniformity.'[56]

15.7.3 Environment

In one sense, the international environment is the same for all companies: they will all be subject to the same trends in economic growth as they compete in world markets, the same major shifts in political power and the same social changes and technological developments. However, because the *base country* of the stakeholders may differ, their responses to and expectations of environmental changes may give rise to major variations in strategy. For example, the mid-1990s saw a significant rise of the Japanese yen against the US dollar. The impact of this environmental change on the world car industry is entirely different, depending on the base country of the stakeholders: Japanese car companies have suffered and US car companies benefited.[57]

15.7.4 Options and choice

The whole concept of the rational choice between options may be Western, even Anglo-American, in its cultural and social background. For example, some cultures place more emphasis on preordained fate as an important element of life, including business matters. If events are decided by fate, then this may significantly influence the options and choice process.[58]

Options and choice also require some basic agreement on the *method* and *criteria* by which they will be discussed and judged. These are also culture-specific, as one researcher has described:[59]

- *Anglo-Saxon* style is comfortable with open debate about different perspectives, and sees compromise as the best outcome from disagreement.
- *Teutons and Gauls* both like to debate but prefer to undertake this with those from the same intellectual and social backgrounds. This makes for less antagonism but for a more limited exposure to different expectations. Teutons seek rigour in the debate before the elegance of the theories, whereas the Gauls take the reverse viewpoint, preferring the aesthetic nature of the argument itself rather than the conclusion.
- *Japanese* do not debate, partly because they have no tradition and partly because of a desire not to upset the social relationships that have already been established.

It is perhaps not surprising that there are problems when it comes to operating strategic decision-making processes across international boundaries.

Key strategic principles

- International considerations may impact on the strategy process during every stage. The ability of stakeholders to influence the process will vary from country to country for historical, political and cultural reasons.
- The mission and objectives are likely to be rooted in the social and cultural systems of the country in which the strategy is developed. The environment may also be important to another aspect of strategy development: the *home country* of an organisation will influence the way in which its international strategy is developed and managed.
- Options and choice in the selection process will be governed by the culture and social systems of the people involved in the process.

CASE STUDY 15.4

Buying travel on-line: choosing a strategy for the internet age

Internet technology is revolutionising the US$100 billion global market for travel booking. This case explores the changes and the uncertainty. It raises the question of which strategic route to choose when developing a strategy, especially for smaller travel companies.

Travel agencies and package tours

For much of the last 50 years, many travellers have used independent travel agencies to book their tickets and accommodation for national and international travel. Such agencies have the relevant networks and contacts with the hotels, airlines, rail operators, car hire agencies and other companies engaged in providing travel services. They are knowledgeable in the complicated arrangements required and can take the pain out of booking a two-week holiday or a week-long business trip. Travel agents are located in town shopping centres or at the end of a telephone. More recently, they are available on-line through the internet.

In North America, travel agencies are largely independent of the companies offering particular aspects of the travel itinerary – air tickets, hotels, etc. In Asia, Africa and the Middle East, travel agencies are also largely independent. However, travel agencies in Europe are often connected with a particular travel organisation offering the complete holiday package covering flights, transfers, hotels and other activities – this approach is often called the 'package tour'. The package tour is particularly popular in some European countries like the UK and Germany. It is also important in China and Japan. Major European travel companies – like Thomas Cook, My Travel and Kuoni – were built on such business.

Even today, package tour companies are big business because they offer good value for money, especially where clients just want a single-location holiday destination. For example, package trips accounted for 49 per cent of all booked holidays in 2003 in the UK. However, this figure was down from 54 per cent in 1998, five years earlier. This suggests that independent travel is growing, but it has not reached the levels of North America, where it accounts for 80 per cent of the business. Part of the reason for this higher percentage is that more North Americans holiday in their home countries: domestic travellers are more confident about booking independently than those who take holidays in new countries with different languages, laws and travel facilities.

Package tour operators across Europe expect package holidays to survive over the next few years but they will need to adapt their products – offering holidays that are complicated for individuals to organise, all-inclusive of children's activities, accompanied by comprehensive travel insurance and guaranteed hotel quality, perhaps through the operator owning the hotel. Such measures will provide protection against the advance of those booking independent holidays. It is the *independent* traveller (or travellers) who is more likely to be attracted to use the internet. Typically, such travellers include two groups:

- the young travellers who have limited time and cash – perhaps on a 'gap' year combining work and travel;
- the retired independents who have plenty of time and rather more cash.

More generally, independent travel represents the major focus of internet travel booking.

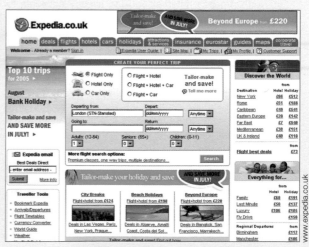

www.expedia.co.uk

Whether you are travelling to the Taj Mahal in India, Hurrah's Casino in Las Vegas, USA or the Pudong area of Shanghai, China (pictured), internet on-line booking opens up the possibilities.

▶ **CASE STUDY 15.4 continued**

Exhibit 15.7

The main providers of internet on-line travel services

- *Primary providers*: these include the main airlines, the budget airlines, the main hotel chains, the main car rental companies and the main rail companies. It is time-consuming for individuals to search each of these internet sites for prices, availability and special deals. However, some of the leaders buy headline space on the main internet search engines like Yahoo and Google.

- *On-line travel agencies*: they include those that offer a wide range of travel services – like Expedia, Travelocity and Orbitz – and those that have been primarily driven by a specialist sector like Opodo, which was set up by the airlines to sell travel tickets (but now also offers hotels and car hire through internet links). Some of the leading companies are shown in Exhibit 15.8.

- *Metasearch travel websites*: these are relatively new and use sophisticated search engine technology to trawl across all available prices and make price comparisons. Some of these are listed in Exhibit 15.8. Some main brand name hotel and travel sites block metasearch activity.

Independent travellers and the internet

For independent travellers – perhaps on short-break destinations, perhaps on long-distance business travel, perhaps backpacking around the world – individual journey plans are often required. However, it does not follow that individual travellers will immediately turn to the internet – the STA student travel agency and Trailfinders are examples of travel agents offering individually tailored travel itineraries. Travel agencies, telephone bookings and postal bookings still account for the majority of such activity. For example in the UK in 2005, it has been estimated that bookings via the internet still only accounted for 20 per cent of the total spent by the independent traveller. But the figure was growing fast and was expected to be 40 per cent of the total within three years. The figures were slightly lower in Germany, but in Scandinavia internet usage was much the same as in the UK. In France, a simplified form of on-line booking has been operated for many years – the French Minitel service – and this continues to be important in that country.

In North America, internet booking already accounts for around 30–40 per cent of all bookings, but this depends on good internet access. For countries without widely available private, individual internet access – such as parts of Africa, China and India – travel agencies were still the main method of making travel arrangements. In spite of such barriers, however, the internet has become a significant source of booking for such travel services around the world. Although internet booking only began about ten years ago, it was estimated in 2005 to account for US$5–10 billion worth of travel bookings every year around the world.

In a sense, there is nothing new in travel booking using telecommunications. Travel agencies have been using direct telephone links to central computers to book airline tickets on-line for at least 20 years. For example, Air France, Lufthansa and Iberia set up the Amadeus airline computer booking system and British Airways, KLM and Sabena responded with the Galileo system around 20 years ago to allow travel agencies and tour operators to buy airline tickets on behalf of individual customers and groups. Similar telephone booking systems have been used for many years by hotel chains, car rental companies and train companies.

What has changed in the last ten years is that the internet has allowed such linkages to take place at the level of *individual* customers: the travel agencies have been cut out of the value chain. In addition, computer software has been developed to allow such access to be handled easily by individual travellers. Internet booking began with airline ticketing but has now extended into car hire, hotel booking and other aspects of travel service. Independent booking on-line has been revolutionised by the internet but is not yet complete: for example, some people do not have access to the internet and others are still reluctant or do not have time to use it for a variety of reasons.

In 2005, internet booking still only accounts for 5–10 per cent of all travel bookings but it is growing fast. For example, internet booking now accounts for over 90 per cent of the travel business of the budget airlines like Ryanair and easyJet. Such companies actually impose price penalties on those customers who do not use the internet. Even among the older airlines, internet booking accounts for at least 40 per cent of all bookings and this share is increasing. Travel companies therefore need a strategy to cope with this opportunity.

Internet travel market – on-line booking

With a large and growing internet travel booking market, it is difficult to gain a complete picture of the various services and booking agencies that are available. Moreover, they are in continual change and development as this is being written. Exhibit 15.8 attempts to set out some of the leading internet players in 2005, but the picture will almost certainly have changed subsequently. In order to provide some focus to internet activity, it is useful to divide the internet travel service providers into three broad categories: primary providers, on-line travel agencies and meta-search travel websites. Each of these has different methods of operating – see Exhibit 15.7.

Profits from internet travel

Hotel chains like Accor, Peninsula Hotels and InterContinental Hotels sell spare rooms at discount prices to the on-line internet travel agencies – like Expedia and Travelocity. These room prices are then raised by 20 to 30 per cent by the on-line agency and the rooms offered to the individual traveller. In one sense, the hotel operator is losing profits but, if the hotel room would otherwise be empty, then any revenue is useful extra business – essentially, this is called *yield management* in the hotel business. However, the hotel companies are now beginning to realise that they may be able to claw back the profit passed on to the travel agencies by offering rooms through their own websites and bypassing the agencies.

For example, InterContinental Hotels has developed several internet strategies to counter the effect of the on-line travel agencies. In 2002, it began offering the lowest guaranteed prices on the internet for its rooms. It also started asking for significant sums from operators who wanted to use the InterContinental brand names – which also cover Crowne Plaza and Holiday Inn in the US – on their websites. InterContinental has also registered apparently independent travel-sounding internet agency names that in practice direct the searcher to the hotel group. Finally, the company began registering foreign language websites – German, French, Spanish, Japanese, Chinese, amongst others – with the aim of making it easy for travellers in those countries to book with InterContinental. Other hotel groups like the world's largest hotel group – Accor, with brand names like Sofitel and Novotel – now also guarantee that prices offered directly on their websites are the lowest available.

The large international airlines like American, British Airways and Air France/KLM sell tickets directly, if possible. Again the purpose is to cut out any profit margin that would be taken by the on-line travel agencies. However, in addition to developing their own websites, some airlines jointly offer

Exhibit 15.8

Some specialist internet companies

All the main hotels, airlines and train companies operate internet booking sites: these are not listed here.

Parent company	Internet travel company	Internet subsidiary of travel company	Comment
Sabre Holdings	Travelocity	Travelchannel.de At the time of writing, Sabre has just made a bid for Lastminute.com	Blocks metasearch
Leading European airlines – see text	Amadeus airline ticketing	Opodo	
Interactive Corporation	Expedia Hotwire	Hotels.com	60% US market Subsidiary acquired for US$ 665 million
Cedant	Days Inn and Ramada Inns hotels Avis car rental Budget car rental Orbitz Galileo airline ticketing eBookers		Cedant blocks metasearch 25% share of US market Subsidiary acquired for US$1.25 billion
Lastminute.com	Lastminute.com	Acquired seven companies in recent years	
Priceline	Active hotels		
Metasearch companies	SideStep Mobissimo Kayak – minority stake held by AOL CheapflightsUK		

Source: see references for case

▶ CASE STUDY 15.4 continued

a website in Europe called Opodo. These airlines are also beginning to operate the sophisticated computer pricing software used by the budget airlines – *see* below.

For the budget airlines like Ryanair and easyJet, there is a strong desire to keep costs to a minimum and therefore such companies only offer seats on their own websites. However, they have a sophisticated computer pricing mechanism that alters the seat prices on a daily, even hourly, basis as and when the aircraft fills up. It pays independent travellers to book early with such airlines, but not all travellers have the flexibility to make early choices.

Metasearch internet sites operate in a different way. They generate revenue by collecting a small commission when they direct traffic to a hotel or travel website. In addition, they make – or at least hope to make – much higher profits from sales of sponsored links from hotel chains and internet travel agencies on their websites.

All this suggests that the profits from internet operations depend on the nature of the business involved:

● *For the primary providers* like hotels and airlines, the opportunity to fill empty hotel rooms or airline seats provides one source of profitability. There is a particular benefit if travellers book directly with the provider since the profit is then retained by the provider rather than passed on to a travel agent.

● *For the on-line travel agencies*, the profit comes from charging a margin beyond the basic cost of the travel service. Such margins can be quite small – not always the 20 to 30 per cent quoted earlier.

● *For the metasearch travel companies*, the profit margins are very small from each actual transaction but can be significant from sponsored advertising on the site. In addition, the high volume of searches – even at a low profit per search – will generate significant profits in total.

Internet travel opportunities for smaller companies

What about new companies thinking of setting up travel websites? The cost of registering and maintaining a new internet website is actually quite small. But this is not the key to internet travel strategy. The real success is attracting enough customers to be able to generate sufficient business. The chief executive officer of Lastminute.com, Brent Hoberman explains: 'This is a scale game and you're always facing global competition. I've always said that you need £1 billion (US$1.9 billion) of bookings to be able to carry the right amount of technology, marketing and branding spend.' However, Mr Hoberman would be the first to acknowledge that his own company is young and began only a few years ago with nothing like US$1 billion of business.

Moreover, the internet offers three great advantages in the travel business. The first is that the fixed costs of operation in the early days of a small internet travel business are quite small – despite the comments of Brent Hoberman above. There are no expensive office premises, no major colour printing and brochure costs, direct contact with potential customers, etc. Such arrangements are ideally suited to small business start-ups. For this reason, many small travel companies are beginning to develop, especially those specialising in particular types of holiday – exclusive chalet skiing holidays, specialist adventure travel holidays and so on.

The second great benefit of the internet is the wide, *even global*, reach of the internet. This makes it much easier for a small business in a specialist area to find sufficient clients for a profitable operation by offering its services across national boundaries.

The third benefit is that business activities can be monitored constantly and changes in pricing, packaging and other services automated to reflect traffic flows. For example, seat prices on Ryanair and easyJet budget airlines are adjusted using computer modelling from constant monitoring of internet booking.

The internet has opened up the new opportunities, but what strategy process should small businesses adopt?

Case questions

1 *If you were moving into the market for internet travel as a small company, which, if any, of the five routes described in this chapter would you employ? You can also consider the use of classic prescriptive strategy if you wish.*

2 *Are there any strategic routes that you would definitely not employ as a small company? Why?*

3 *If you were an established internet provider, which strategic routes would you select to develop your presence further? Why? Give examples of current practice where possible.*

4 *How will the internet impact on travel in the future? Would it be more beneficial to use emergent strategies – if so, which strategies and how should they be used?*

STRATEGIC PROJECT

There are so many opportunities for both large and small companies that internet on-line strategy presents a most interesting challenge. Research opportunities exist because of the worldwide accessability of the web in terms of pricing, product, presentation and market positioning. One approach would be to start with the companies identified in the case and explore how they have developed. Another approach would be to take an area of travel – for example, adventure travel or cruise liners – and explore their use of the internet and possible future strategies. Another approach would be to consider likely future changes in the internet – text messaging, mobile telephone booking, more sophisticated presentation technology, etc. – and explore their impact on travel company strategy.

CRITICAL REFLECTION

Does the learning-based strategic route forward really help?

In considering alternatives to prescriptive strategy, this chapter has argued that the learning-based strategic route forward has particular merit. It delivers flexibility in strategy development and, particularly when coupled with group dynamics, can assist in initiating powerful new strategic insights.

However, the concept has also been criticised for being vague and lacking operational guidance. Companies need to take decisions on important matters and cannot wait for a learning process to commence with clear outcome. What do you think? Just how useful is the 'learning-based' approach?

SUMMARY

● This chapter first explored the importance of strategic *context* in the development of strategy. In the prescriptive model of strategy development, context is assumed to be linear and predictable, whereas, in reality, it may be turbulent and uncertain. Because of this difficulty, alternatives to the prescriptive process have been developed. The chapter then examined four models out of the many that are available. Particular emphasis was given to the *learning-based strategy* approach as one that has a contribution to make in conjunction with prescriptive approaches.

● *Survival-based* strategies emphasise the importance of adapting strategies to meet changes in the environment. The ultimate objective is survival itself. The approach adopted is to develop options for use as the environment changes. Options that seek low costs are particularly useful. Beyond taking the precaution of developing options, there is little that the individual company can do. There is an element of chance in whether the company will survive.

● *The uncertainty-based approach* concentrates on the difficult and turbulent environment that now surrounds the development of corporate strategy. Renewal and transformation are vital aspects of such strategy. Inevitably, they will involve uncertainty. Such uncertainty can be modelled mathematically. However, the long-term consequences are unknown and cannot be foreseen or usefully predicted. Uncertainty approaches therefore involve taking small steps forward. Management needs to learn from such actions and adapt accordingly. Because of the uncertainty about the future, it is argued that the prescriptive approach of looking at strategy options and selecting between them is irrelevant.

● *The network-based strategic route forward* explores the links and degree of co-operation present in related organisations and industries and places a value upon that degree of co-operation. The route has two aspects – network externalities and network co-operation.

● Network externalities refer to the development of an overall standard for a network that allows those belonging to the network to benefit increasingly as others join the same network. In such externalities, the key moment is the 'tipping point', which is reached when the installed base of network users moves towards one company supplying the network and away from rival suppliers.

● In network co-operation, value is added and competitive advantage is developed by the precise *combination* of competition and co-operation that organisations have with others. Such a strategic approach also needs to be seen in the context of negotiations with powerful customers and suppliers where bargaining and trade-offs will take place.

● *The game theory strategic route forward* attempts to predict the outcomes of customer reactions or, in some cases, to show how the outcome of negotiations may well produce a suboptimal solution unless both sides of the negotiations realise the consequences of their actions.

● Game theory has some value in negotiations but suffers from three difficulties: mathematical complexity; ambiguous conclusions; being only one small part of the strategy process.

● *The learning-based strategic route forward* emphasises learning and crafting as aspects of the development of successful corporate strategy. It places particular importance on trial and feedback mechanisms in developing unique strategies. Learning is not concerned with memory work, but with active creativity in developing new strategic opportunities. Double loop learning consists of a *first* loop of learning that checks performance against expected norms and adjusts where necessary, coupled with a *second* loop that reappraises whether the expected norms were appropriate in the first place.

● In strategy development, group dynamics are more important than individuals in developing new, experimental strategies. There are five principles to group learning: personal mastery, group mental models, share vision, team learning and systems thinking.

● One of the dangers associated with learning is that the 'successful solution' at the end of the process becomes the 'dominant logic' and this stops the organisation continuing to learn. There are ways of overcoming this, including good leadership, story-telling and organising opportunities for a thorough reappraisal of an organisation's strategy.

● Within the learning concept, there is a difficult balance to be struck between the learning that comes from developing new knowledge and the learning that comes from exploiting existing competencies. There are three fundamental problems with the learning concept: *temporal myopia* – learning tends to sacrifice the long run to the short run – *spatial myopia* – learning tends to favour effects that occur near the learner – and *failure myopia* – organisational learning over-samples success and under-samples failure.

● Group and individual learning have real value as concepts but can be vague and lack operational guidance in practice.

● *International considerations* may impact on the strategy process at every stage. The ability of stakeholders to influence the process will vary from country to country for historical, political and cultural reasons. The mission and objectives are likely to be rooted in the social and cultural systems of the country in which the strategy is developed. The environment may be important in another aspect of strategy development: the home country of an organisation will influence the way in which the international strategy is developed and managed. Options and choice in the selection process will be governed by the culture and social systems of the people involved in the process.

QUESTIONS

1 Professor Charles Handy has described recent technological breakthroughs in global development as discontinuous. He commented:

'Discontinuous change required discontinuous upside-down thinking to deal with it, even if thinkers and thought appear absurd at first sight.'

Can discontinuities be handled by the prescriptive process or is an emergent process required? If so, which one?

2 Why does context matter in strategy development? What are the main elements of context in the case of European telecommunications? How do they influence strategy development?

3 Take an organisation with which you are familiar and consider to what extent it plans ahead. How does it undertake this task? Is it reasonably effective or is the whole process largely a waste of time? To what extent does any planning process rely on 'people' issues and negotiation? What model from this chapter does the process most closely follow, if any?

4 Is it possible for the prescriptive strategy process to be creative?

5 Some have argued that the survival-based strategic route is overpessimistic in its approach. Do you agree?

6 For organisations, such as the telecommunications companies, involved in lengthy investment decisions that take many years to implement, the uncertainty-based route forward, with its very short time-horizons, appears to have little to offer. Can this strategic route provide any useful guidance to such companies?

7 Why is negotiation important in corporate strategy? Why is it not better to have a strong leader who will simply impose his/her will on the organisation?

8 The learning-based strategic route emphasises creativity in strategy development. Why is this important and how might it be achieved?

9 'Management theories are judged, among managers at least, by the demonstrable results that they deliver,' comments Professor Colin Egan.

Apply this comment to the strategic routes described in this chapter and outline your conclusions.

10 If you were advising Honda Motorcycles about its strategies in the 1990s, what strategic approach or combination of approaches would you adopt? Give reasons for your views.

APPENDIX

Negotiation checklist for a two-player game

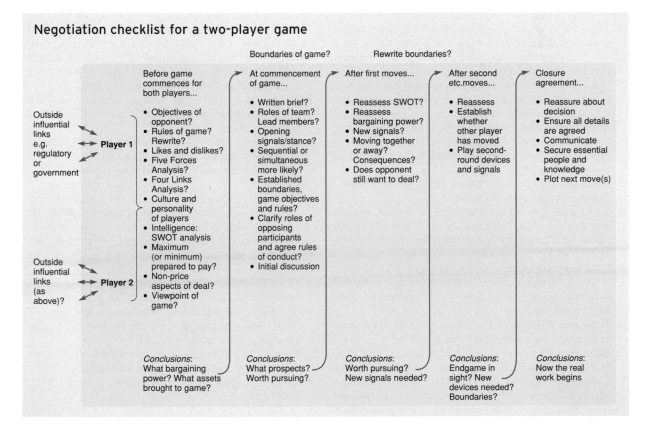

Further reading

For a comparative review of strategic approaches, the book by Dr Richard Whittington remains one of the best: Whittington, R (1993) *What is Strategy – and Does it Matter?*, Routledge, London.

For a discussion of survival-based approaches, *see* Rumelt, R, Schendel, D and Teece, D (1991) 'Strategic management and economics', *Strategic Management Journal*, 12, pp5–29. This is a very useful general review and would provide a good link for those who have already studied economics.

For a description of the uncertainty-based approach, *see* Stacey, R (1996) *Strategic Management and Organisational Dynamics*, 2nd edn, Pitman Publishing, London.

For a useful discussion of learning approaches, *see* Senge, P (1990) *The Fifth Discipline: the Art and Practice of the Learning Organisation*, Century Business, London. For a critical examination of learning, Professor Colin Egan's book is strongly recommended: Egan, C (1995) *Creating Organisational Advantage*, Butterworth–Heinemann, Oxford.

One of the best papers on learning is Levinthal, DA and March, JG (1993) 'The myopia of learning', *Strategic Management Journal*, Vol 14, Special Issue, Winter. Don't be put off by this academic journal. Unlike some of its research papers, this one is easier to read and it has some major insights. It won the *SMJ* best paper prize 2002.

An interesting more recent paper is one comparing strategic planning (prescriptive) and learning (emergent) processes: Brews, PJ and Hunt, MR (1999) 'Learning to plan and planning to learn: Resolving the planning school/ learning school debate', *Strategic Management Journal*, Vol 20, pp889–913. A particularly interesting paper on learning versus performance goals: Seijts, GH and Latham, GP (2005) 'Learning versus performance goals: When should each be used?', *Academy of Management Executive*, Vol 19, No 1, pp124–31.

For an exploration of game theory, *see* Dixit, A and Nalebuff, B (1991) *Thinking Strategically*, W W Norton, New York. *See* also Nalebuff, B and Brandenburger, A M (1997) *Co-opetition*, HarperCollins Business, London.

Notes and references

1 Thus, for example, classic prescriptive strategy might explore 'Gap analysis': *see* Jauch, L R and Glueck, W F (1988) *Business Policy and Strategic Management*, 5th edn, McGraw-Hill, New York, pp24–6.

2 Pascale, R (1984) 'Perspectives on strategy: the real story behind Honda's success', *California Management Review* XXVI, 3, pp47–72. This article was extracted in Mintzberg, H and Quinn, J B (1991) *The Strategy Process*, 2nd edn, Prentice Hall, Englewood Cliffs, NJ, pp114–23. This is well worth reading to illustrate the problems of the classical model.

3 Kono, T (1992) *Long Range Planning of Japanese Corporations*, de Gruyter, Berlin.

4 *See* Chapter 1 for a basic discussion on context, process and content. Also Pettigrew, A and Whipp, R (1993) *Managing Change for Competitive Success*, Blackwell, Oxford, Ch1.

5 For a fuller exploration, *see* Chaharbaghi, K and Lynch, R (1999), 'Sustainable competitive advantage: towards a dynamic resource-based strategy', *Management Decision*, 37(1), pp45–50.

6 These four routes were identified and set in the context of other strategic approaches in Chapter 2.

7 References for European telcos case: Isern, J and Rios, M I (2002) 'Facing disconnection – Hard choices for Europe's telcos', *McKinsey Quarterly*, No 1; Annexes to Seventh Report on the implementation of the telecommunications regulatory package, Commission Staff Working Paper, SEC (2001) 1922 Brussels – 26 November; *Financial Times*: 1 August 1998, p5 Weekend Money; 24 April 1999, p21; 27 January 2000, p1; 3 February 2000, p24; 1 May 2000, p11; 3 June 2000, p15; 28 March 2001, p23; 3 April 2001, p26; 2 May 2001, p15; 11 May 2001, p22; 13 June 2001, p27; 7 September 2001, p13; 13 October 2001, p16; 17 October 2001, p23; 18 December 2001, p23; 11 January 2002, p20; 12 January 2002, p11; 6 February 2002, p19; 8 February 2002, pp20, 24; 13 February 2002, p16; 23 February 2002, p19.

8 Alchian, A A (1950) 'Uncertainty, evolution and economic theory', *Journal of Political Economy*, 58, pp211–21, first proposed this.

9 Hofer, C W and Schendel, D (1986) *Strategy Formulation: Analytical Concepts*, 11th edn, West Publishing, St Paul, MN. This book used the same approach in the 1970s and 1980s.

10 Hannan, M and Freeman, J (1977) 'The population ecology of organisations', *American Journal of Sociology*, 82, Mar, pp929–64.

11 Williamson, O E (1991) 'Strategizing, economizing and economic organisation', *Strategic Management Journal*, 12, pp75–94.

12 This represents one particular view of the relationship between economics and strategy. For a more general discussion, see Rumelt, R, Schendel, D and Teece, D (1991) 'Strategic management and economics', *Strategic Management Journal*, 12, pp5–29.

13 Stacey, R (1993) *Strategic Management and Organisational Dynamics*, Pitman Publishing, London, p211.

14 Roberts, D (2000) 'Orange renegade', *Financial Times*, 3 June, p15.

15 Gleick, J (1988) *Chaos: the Making of a New Science*, Heinemann, London.

16 Lloyd, T (1995) 'Drawing a line under corporate strategy', *Financial Times*, 8 September, p10. This provides a short, readable account of some of the consequences of this strategic approach.

17 Stacey, R (1993) 'Strategy as order emerging from chaos', *Long Range Planning*, 26(1), pp10–17.

18 References for GEC Marconi case: General Electric Company plc Annual Report and Accounts for 1998; *Financial Times*, 27 June 1998, p6, Weekend Money section; 24 July 1998, p21; 4 September 1998, p11; 5 December 1998, p21; 9 December 1998, p26; 10 December 1998, p15; 19 December 1998, p6 Weekend Money section; 14 January 1999, p31; 19 January 1999, pp1, 25, 27; 21 January 1999, p21; 23 January 1999, p2; 26 February 1999, p19.

19 Katz, M and Shapiro, C (1985) 'Network externalities, competition and compatibility', *American Economic Review*, Vol 75, pp424–40.

20 This section has benefited from McGee, J, Thomas, H and Wilson, D (2005) *Strategy – Analysis and Practice*, McGraw-Hill, Maidenhead, Ch 12.

21 This refers to the work of Coase and Williamson described in Chapter 6, Section 6.3.2.

22 This refers to the work of Porter described in Chapter 6, Sections 6.5.1 and 6.5.2.

23 Gerlach M (1992) *Alliance Capitalism*, University of California Press, Berkeley, CA. Quoted in De Wit, R and Meyer, R (1998) *Strategy: Process, Content and Context*, 2nd edn, International Thomson Business Press, London, p512. But note my rephrasing of this relationship.

24 Doz, Y (1986) *Strategic Management in Multinational Companies*, Pergamon, Oxford, pp95, 96.

25 Reve, T (1990) 'The firm as a nexus of internal and external contracts', in Aoki, M, Gustafsson, M and Williamson, O E (eds), *The Firm as a Nexus of Treaties*, Sage, London.

26 Johanson, J and Mattson, L-G (1992) 'Network positions and strategic action', in Axelsson, B and Easton, G (eds), *Industrial Networks: a New View of Reality*, Routledge, London.

27 Porter, M E (1985) *Competitive Advantage*, The Free Press, New York.

28 Jarillo, J C (1988) 'On strategic networks', *Strategic Management Journal*, June–July.

29 This choice is presented as the prime focus of the 'debate' in De Wit, R and Meyer, R (1998) Op. cit., Ch7.

30 Useful introductory texts include: Nalebuff, B and Brandenburger, A M (1997) *Co-opetition*, HarperCollins Business, London; Schelling, T C (1980) *The Strategy of Conflict*, 2nd edn, Harvard University Press, Cambridge, MA; also Dixit, A and Nalebuff, B (1991) *Thinking Strategically: the Competitive Edge in Business, Politics and Everyday Life*, W W Norton, New York.

31 Nalebuff, B and Brandenburger, A M (1997) Op. cit., Ch2.

32 Dixit, A and Nalebuff, B (1991) Op. cit.

33 Amongst the critical comments on game theory, it is worth consulting: Camerer, C F (1991) 'Does strategy research need game theory?', *Strategic Management Journal*, 12, Winter, pp137–52. Postrel, S (1991) 'Burning your britches behind you', *Strategic Management Journal*, Special Issue, 12, Winter, pp153–5. *See* also Fisher, F M (1989) 'The games economists play: a noncooperative view', *RAND Journal of Economics*, 20, pp113–24.

34 Mintzberg, H (1987) 'Crafting strategy', *Harvard Business Review*, July–Aug.

35 De Geus, A (1988) 'Planning as learning', *Harvard Business Review*, Mar–Apr, p70.

36 Argyris, C (1977) 'Double loop learning in organisations', *Harvard Business Review*, Sept–Oct.

37 Garvin, D (1993) 'Building a learning organization', *Harvard Business Review*, July–Aug. The precision and care of its wording make this article particularly valuable.

38 Argyris, C (1977) 'Double loop learning in organizations', *Harvard Business Review*, May–June, pp99–109.

39 Senge, P (1990) *The Fifth Discipline: The Art and Practice of the Learning Organisation*, Century Business, London, Ch1.

40 Pucik, V and Hatvany, N (1983) 'Management practices in Japan and their impact on business strategy', *Advances in Strategic Management*, 1, JAI Press Inc, pp103–31. Reprinted in Mintzberg, H and Quinn, J B (1991) Op. cit.

41 World Bank (1994) *World Development Report 1994*, Oxford University Press, New York, pp76–9.

42 *See The Economist* (1995) 'The knowledge', 11 Nov, p107.

43 Senge, P (1990) 'The leader's new work: Building learning organisations', *Sloan Management Review*, Fall, and Senge, P (1990) *The Fifth Discipline*.

44 Quinn, S, Mills, D and Friesen, B (1992) 'The learning organisation', *European Management Journal*, 10 June, p146.

45 Argyris, C (1991) 'Teaching smart people how to learn', *Harvard Business Review*, May–June, p99.

46 Prahalad, C K and Bettis, R A (1986) 'The dominant logic: a new linkage between diversity and performance', *Strategic Management Journal*, Vol 7, pp485–501.

47 Bettis, R A and Prahalad, C K (1995) 'The dominant logic: retrospective and extension', *Strategic Management Journal*, Vol 16, pp5–14.

48 Bettis, R A and Prahalad, C K (1995) 'The dominant logic: retrospective and extension', *Strategic Management Journal*, Vol 16, pp5–14. See also: Cote, L, Langley, A and Pasquero, J (1999) 'Acquisition strategy and dominant logic in an engineering firm', *Journal of Management Studies*, Vol 36, pp919–52.

49 Levinthal, D A and March, J G (1993) 'The myopia of learning', *Strategic Management Journal*, Vol 14, Special Issue, Winter.

50 Shaw, G, Brown, R and Bromiley, P (1998) 'Strategic stories: how 3M is rewriting business planning', *Harvard Business Review*, May–June, pp41–50.

51 Burgoyne, J, Pedler, M and Boydell, T (1994) *Towards the Learning Company*, McGraw-Hill, Maidenhead.

52 Jones, A and Hendry, C (1994) 'The learning organisation: adult learning and organisational transformation', *British Journal of Management*, pp153–62. *See* also a thoughtful critique of the learning approach in Egan, C (1995) *Creating Organisational Advantage*, Butterworth–Heinemann, Ch5. Finally see the major review of learning: Levinthal, D A and March, J G (1993) Op. cit.

53 *See* the Hofstede research and the *power/distance* data in the last section of Chapter 7 of this book.

54 Hu, Y S (1992) 'Global or stateless firms with international operations', *California Management Review*, Winter, pp115–26.

55 Granovetter, M (1985) 'Economic action and social culture: the problem of embeddedness', *American Journal of Sociology*, 91(3), pp481–510.

56 Whittington, R (1993) *What is Strategy – and Does it Matter?*, Routledge, London, p37.

57 *Financial Times* (1995) 'Hollowing out in Japan', 28 March, p21; Nakanoto, M (1995) 'Knocked off the road again', *Financial Times*, 20 April, p25.

58 Kluckhohn, C and Strodtbeck, F (1961) *Variations in Value Orientations*, Peterson, New York.

59 Furnham, A (1995) 'The case for cultural diversity', *Financial Times*, 8 December, p11. The author was Professor of Psychology at University College, London, at the time the article was written.

60 References for Case 15.4: On-line travel: *Financial Times*: 16 November 2001, p24; 21 May 2003, p15; 6 August 2003, p21; 19 April 2004, p10; 21 May 2004, p28; 25 June 2004, p28; 3 September 2004, p26; 30 September 2004, p30; 9 November 2004, p13; 9 February 2005, p11.

Chapter 16

ORGANISATIONAL STRUCTURE, STYLE AND PEOPLE ISSUES

Learning outcomes

When you have worked through this chapter, you will be able to:

- evaluate critically the arguments that strategy and structure have a more complex relationship than that suggested by the early strategists;

- understand the basic principles involved in designing the structure of an organisation to meet its chosen strategy;

- evaluate the importance of changing an organisation's management style at the same time as changing its strategy.

- outline the six main types of organisation structure and assess their advantages and disadvantages in relation to a particular strategy;

- develop the special organisation structures that are more likely to lead to innovative strategies;

- explain the formal organisation needed to motivate staff and implement the chosen strategies;

- outline the additional considerations that apply when developing structures for international organisations, especially at headquarters level.

INTRODUCTION

Alongside a well-considered strategy, there exists the need for an organisation, management team and people to deliver the strategy. One important academic debate in the past has been whether the strategy is planned first and then the organisation developed to implement that strategy. This book takes the view that it is preferable to consider both elements at the same time: that is why we examined aspects of human resource strategy back in the analysis phase in Chapter 7. Nevertheless, the argument for putting strategy first and organisation structure second needs to be understood. We begin this chapter with this topic.

The more general principles associated with developing the organisation structure are then explored. One particular aspect that deserves highlighting is the choice of management style. Having considered these matters, we then explore how to design organisation structures in different types of business. Given the importance of innovation in successful strategy – especially from an emergent strategy perspective – we examine this topic separately. We explore the role of effective reward structures and selection procedures in providing capable and well-motivated senior managers to implement strategy successfully. Finally, in the light of these considerations, an appropriate organisation structure can then be developed, as summarised in Figure 16.1.

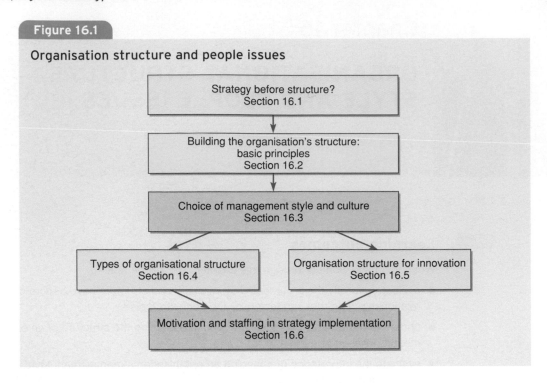

Figure 16.1

Organisation structure and people issues

Strategy before structure?
Section 16.1

↓

Building the organisation's structure:
basic principles
Section 16.2

↓

Choice of management style and culture
Section 16.3

Types of organisational structure
Section 16.4

Organisation structure for innovation
Section 16.5

Motivation and staffing in strategy implementation
Section 16.6

CASE STUDY 16.1

PepsiCo: organising to integrate its acquisitions

Over a three-year period from 1998 to 2001, the US food and drink company PepsiCo made two major acquisitions. Each purchase was bought for a price premium that could only be repaid by finding new synergies and economies of scale. This required PepsiCo to develop new organisation structures designed to deliver these benefits in the years that followed.

Background – the company itself

PepsiCo is probably best known for its carbonated cola drink, Pepsi-Cola, which it sells in most countries around the world, often in second place to its great rival Coca-Cola. However, in terms of total sales, PepsiCo is actually much larger than Coca-Cola – sales of US$29 billion in 2004 compared with Coke's US$22 billion. The main reason for the greater size is that PepsiCo is also the world's largest snack and crisp manufacturer, with a series of brands in regions of the world – including Frito-Lay in North America and Walkers in the UK. However, the company also has some other famous brand names like Gatorade, Tropicana fruit juices and Quaker breakfast cereals. Table 16.1 sets out some of its leading products, including those that arrived through its acquisition strategy in the six years to 2004.

Company major acquisitions – Tropicana and Quaker

Both the Tropicana range of fresh fruit drinks and the Quaker range of products came from PepsiCo acquisitions in the period 1998–2001. Tropicana was bought from Seagram for US$3.3 billion in 1998 and Quaker for US$15 billion in 2001. In both cases, PepsiCo paid a significant premium over the asset book value of the companies. It took the view that there were significant synergies and economies of scale to be gained from these two acquisitions. With regard to Quaker, PepsiCo was particularly interested in the sports drink Gatorade, which delivered the market leader in a new and fast-growing segment of the beverage market. The same purchase came with the Quaker cereal range, which was under heavy competitive pressure from Kellogg and General Mills – *see* Case study 2.1. However, the Quaker brand also brought the possibility of new snack products. PepsiCo then began to organise the company to exploit this advantage, not only in North America but also in Europe.

PepsiCo company reorganisation to exploit the full acquisition potential

Building on its strong competitive resources was the prime starting point in developing the revised organisation structure

Table 16.1

PepsiCo's top ten products at retail prices

Brand	Worldwide sales – US$ bn	
Regular Pepsi	17.0	
Diet Pepsi	6.0	
Mountain Dew	5.5	
Gatorade Sports Drink	5.2	Acquired 2001
Lays Potato Chips	5.0	
Doritos Tortilla Chips	3.0	
Tropicana Juice Drink	2.9	Acquired 1998
7Up Drink (outside the USA)	2.4	
Aquafina bottled water	2.3	
Cheetos Cheese Flavored Snacks	2.0	
Quaker Cereals	1.5	Acquired 2001

Source: Company Report and Accounts 2004.

for PepsiCo. Such resources included its major network of contacts with supermarkets across North America and, to a lesser extent, other countries. They also included its existing brand franchises in names like Pepsi and Frito-Lay, Quaker, Gatorade and Tropicana. The company had a specialist distribution structure designed to deliver fresh and fragile snacks every week directly to 15,000 outlets across the US and indirectly to around 500,000 outlets. It also had a strong network of bottlers who were responsible for delivering Pepsi. The company had a record of product and packaging innovation which came from its Pepsi and Frito-Lay technical development units, the Gatorade Sports Science Institute and the Tropicana Nutrition Center. All were skilled at developing new products and packaging. Such units were kept centrally at headquarters on behalf of all operating companies.

Because PepsiCo was particularly strong in North America in virtually every product category, it was decided to set up North American divisions and separate these from its other, international operations. In addition, although the sports drink Gatorade and the Quaker cereal products were important in North America, they had a more limited franchise internationally – especially Gatorade, which was largely unknown outside the American continent. It was decided to combine these product areas internationally with some of its other product groups.

PepsiCo main organisation structure – 2001

In 2001, PepsiCo therefore had the following organisational divisions, each reporting to headquarters:

- *Pepsi-Cola North America* – responsible not only for the largest brand but also for building a new product range of non-carbonated drinks such as bottled water. The company was not expecting this area to yield major savings from its two acquisitions. In 2004, this was combined with Tropicana/Gatorade – see below.

- *PepsiCo Beverages International* – contained the combined international operations of Pepsi-Cola, Tropicana and Gatorade. It was planned to combine general and administrative functions and gain 'very substantial cost savings'. One of the problems here was that, although the Pepsi brand was strong in the US, its international brand share was weaker – especially in parts of Europe. It was therefore more cost-effective to combine it with Tropicana (Gatorade was too small to be important) and gain cost savings from shared overheads. In 2004, this was combined with Frito-Lay International – see below.

- *Frito-Lay North America* – had part of the Quaker range of sweet cereal bars, energy bars and similar products, combined with its existing savoury crisps and snacks. The aim was to gain substantial cost savings and at the same time to offer the broader range of products to its existing outlets, thus increasing sales.

- *Frito-Lay International* – the snack and crisp products were sold across some 40 countries. The company already had some strong market positions, e.g. 80 per cent of the Mexican snack market and 40 per cent of the UK snack market with Walkers Crisps. The aim here was to add the Quaker food distribution and gain major cost savings on distribution. The Quaker international cereal product range was also included in this area – probably because it was convenient and PepsiCo had to buy this product range in order to obtain Gatorade, as mentioned above. In 2004, this was combined with PepsiCo Beverages International.

- *Gatorade/Tropicana North America* – These two major product areas – sports drinks and fruit juices – were combined as a separate area from cola drinks because they were used and sold in different ways and through different outlets. More specifically, there was a common 'hot-fill' manufacturing process that could be used to deliver substantial cost savings. In 2004, this was combined with PepsiCo North America – see below.

- *Quaker Foods North America* – PepsiCo decided to keep the Quaker cereals and related products, like Aunt Jemima syrup and mixes, together in North America. Some commentators suspected that this separate division would also allow the product range to be sold more easily at some later stage – it simply did not fit in with the main strengths of PepsiCo and faced strong competition in both North America and internationally. The well-established warehouse distribution capabilities of Quaker and Gatorade brought important new scale to a new delivery/distribution system for PepsiCo.

PepsiCo further re-organisation – 2004

By 2004, PepsiCo had decided to combine several of the above divisions – see Figure 16.2. The reasons for this change in organisation structure were:

- *PepsiCo Beverages International was combined with Frito-Lay International*. The new division was called PepsiCo International. The logic here was to build on the company's different international strengths in different international

▶ CASE STUDY 16.1 continued

Figure 16.2

How PepsiCo reorganised in 2004

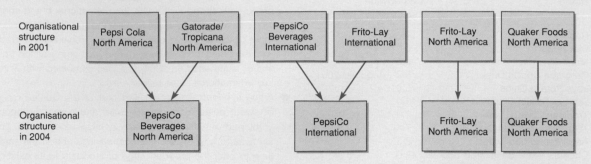

markets. For example, its snack brands were particularly strong in Mexico with the Sabritas brand, in the UK with Walkers brand and in Australia with the Smiths brand. In other countries, Pepsi-Cola was stronger and the snacks brands were relatively weak. Whatever was the strongest product category would be the lead brand and would then support the other weaker brands. This could best be done if there was one organisation rather than separate organisations.

● *Gatorade/Tropicana North America was combined with Pepsi Cola North America for financial reporting.* The new division was called PepsiCo Beverages North America. The reasoning here was to allow the company to exploit its strengths in non-carbonated and healthy fruit drinks across a wider range of outlets. Coca Cola was leader in the *carbonated* drinks market, but Pepsi with Tropicana and Gatorade was easily the market leader in the *total* soft drinks market. To exploit this leadership, it was essential to drive the various brands as part of one team. This was particularly important given the increased bargaining power of the large retail supermarket chains like the world's largest

retailer, Wal-Mart – PepsiCo Beverages became 'the No 1 liquid refreshment beverage company in measured channels.'

Case questions

1 *Why was PepsiCo essentially organised into North American and international divisions? Why were there some variations in this structure? Examining the organisation structures outlined in this chapter, in which category would you put PepsiCo?*

2 *What benefits was the company seeking from its acquisitions? How did the change in organisation structure contribute to such benefits? In order to achieve such benefits, what actions would have to be taken? Would they have any human consequences? If so, what?*

3 *What lessons, if any, on strategy and organisation structure can be drawn from the approach of PepsiCo in developing its new organisation structure?*

16.1 STRATEGY BEFORE STRUCTURE?

A major debate has been taking place over the last 30 years regarding the relationship between the strategy and the structure of the organisation. In the past, it was considered that the strategy was decided first and the organisation structure then followed. Recent research has questioned this approach and taken the view that strategy and structure are interrelated. In this section we examine the reasons why views have changed: strategy no longer comes before structure.

16.1.1 Strategy before structure: Chandler's contribution

To understand the logic behind this prescriptive approach to the development of organisational structures, it is helpful to look at the historical background. Prior to the early 1960s, the US strategist Alfred Chandler Jr studied how some leading US corporations had developed their strategies in the first half of the twentieth century.[2] He then drew some major conclusions from this empirical evidence, the foremost one being that the organisation first needed to develop its strategy and, after this, to devise the organisation structure that delivered that strategy.

Chandler drew a clear distinction between *devising* a strategy and *implementing* it. He defined strategy as:

> [t]he determination of the basic long-term goals and objectives of an enterprise, and the adoption of courses of action and the allocation of resources necessary for carrying out these goals.[3]

The task of developing the strategy took place at the centre of the organisation. The job of implementing it then fell to the various functional areas. Chandler's research suggested that, once a strategy had been developed, it was necessary to consider the structure needed to carry it out. A new strategy might require extra resources, or new personnel or equipment which would alter the work of the enterprise, making a new organisational structure necessary: 'the design of the organisation through which the enterprise is administered', to quote Chandler.

The principle that strategy came before organisational structure was formed, therefore, by considering the industrial developments of the early twentieth century.[4] Whether such considerations are still relevant as we move into the new millennium will be considered next.

16.1.2 Changes in the business environment and social values

To understand why it is no longer appropriate to develop an organisation structure after deciding a strategy, the earlier theory needs to be placed in its historic strategic context. Since Chandler's research on early twentieth-century companies, the environment has changed substantially.[5] The workplace itself, the relationships between workers and managers, and the skills of employees have all altered substantially. Old organisational structures embedded in past understandings may therefore be suspect. Exhibit 16.1 summarises how the environment has changed.

Exhibit 16.1

A comparison of the early twentieth- and early twenty-first-century business environments

Early twentieth century	Early twenty-first century
• Uneducated workers, typically just moved from agricultural work into the cities	• Better educated, computer-literate, skilled
• Knowledge of simple engineering and technology	• Complex, computer-driven, large-scale
• The new science of management recognised simple cause-and-effect relationships	• Multifaceted and complex nature of management now partially understood
• Growing, newly industrialising markets and suppliers	• Mix of some mature, cyclical markets and some high-growth, new-technology markets and suppliers
• Sharp distinctions between management and workers	• Greater overlap between management and workers in some industrialised countries

16.1.3 Managing the complexity of strategic change – the contribution of Quinn

Much of the prescriptive approach is built around the notion that it is possible to choose precisely what strategies need to be introduced. The issue then becomes one of building the organisation and plans to achieve the chosen strategy. From empirical research, Professor J B Quinn[6] has suggested that this grossly oversimplifies the process in many cases:

- Simple strategic solutions may be unavailable, especially where the proposed changes are complex or controversial.
- The organisation structure may be unable to cope with the 'obvious' solution for reasons of its culture, the people involved or the political pressures.
- Organisational awareness and commitment may need to be built up over time, making it impossible to introduce an immediate radical change.
- Managers may need to participate in the change process, to learn about the proposed changes and to contribute specialist expertise in order to develop the strategic change required.

Exhibit 16.2

Quinn's logical incremental strategy process and its organisational implications[7]

Strategic stage	Organisational implications
1 Sensing the need for change	Use informal networks in organisation
2 Clarify strategy areas and narrow options	Consult more widely, possibly using more formal structures
3 Use change symbols to signal possible change	Communicate with many who cannot be directly consulted: use formal structure
4 Create waiting period to allow options discussion and newer options to become familiar	Encourage discussion of concerns among interested groups: use formal and informal organisational structures
5 Clarify general direction of new strategy but experiment and seek partial solutions rather than a firm commitment to one direction	General discussion without alienation, if possible, among senior managers. Use formal senior management structure
6 Broaden the basis of support for the new direction	Set up committees, project groups and study teams outside the formal existing structures. Careful selection of team members and agenda is essential
7 Consolidate progress	Initiate special projects to explore and consolidate the general direction: use more junior managers and relevant team members from the existing organisation
8 Build consensus *before* focusing on new objectives and associated strategies	Use informal networks through the organisation. Identify and manage those people who are key influencers on the future strategic direction
Over time, possibly years	
9 Balance consensus with the need to avoid the rigidity that might arise from overcommitment to the now successful strategy	Introduce new members to provide further stimulus, new ideas and new questions
10 New organisation	Reorganise the organisation's formal structure to consolidate the changes: at last!

Quinn suggests that strategic change may need to proceed *incrementally*, i.e. in small stages. He called the process *logical incrementalism*. The clear implication is that it may not be possible to define the final organisation structure, which may also need to evolve as the strategy moves forward incrementally. He suggests a multistage process for senior executives involved in strategy development: this is shown in Exhibit 16.2. Importantly, he recognises the importance of informal organisation structures in achieving agreement to strategy shifts (*see* Chapter 7). If the argument is correct, it will be evident that any idea of a single, final organisation structure – after deciding on a defined strategy – is dubious.

Comment

The description of the process certainly accords with the evidence of other researchers. Formal organisation structures are important for day-to-day responsibilities and work, but are only part of the strategy process when it comes to implementing complex and controversial strategic change. The validity of the above description relies on the extent to which radical change is required. Quinn's assumption that change needs to be radical enables him to conclude that the final organisational structure may have to emerge at the end of this period.

16.1.4 Specific criticism of strategy before structure

According to modern strategists, strategy and structure are interlinked. It may not be optimal for an organisation to develop its structure *after* it has developed its strategy. The relationship is more complex in two respects:

1 Strategy and the structure associated with it may need to develop *at the same time* in an experimental way: as the strategy develops, so does the structure. The organisation *learns to adapt* to its changing environment and to its changing resources, especially if such change is radical.

2 If the strategy process is emergent, then the learning and experimentation involved may need a *more open and less formal* organisation structure.

In recent years, it has been suggested[8] that the impact of process and organisation on strategy has been constantly underplayed. The contribution of employees in energising the organisation and promoting innovation may often be underestimated. Moreover, the quality of management and the organisational structure itself will all have an impact on strategy and may even be a source of competitive advantage. In this sense, it cannot be said that people and process issues arise after the strategy has been agreed.

It has also been pointed out that there are some companies that have broadly similar resources but differ markedly in their performance. The reasons for this disparity may be associated with the way that companies are organised and conduct their activities, rather than with differences in strategy. The five main weaknesses of the strategy before structure approach are summarised in Exhibit 16.3.

> **Exhibit 16.3**
>
> ### Summary of the five main criticisms of the strategy-first, structure-afterwards process
>
> 1 Structures may be too *rigid, hierarchical and bureaucratic* to cope with the newer social values and rapidly changing environments of the 1990s.
>
> 2 *The type of structure* is just as important as the business area in developing the organisation's strategy. It is the structure that will restrict, guide and form the strategy

Exhibit 16.3 *continued*

options that the organisation can generate. A learning organisation may be required and power given to more junior managers. In this sense, strategy and organisational structure are interrelated and need to be developed at the same time.

3 *Value chain configurations* that favour cost cutting or, alternatively, new market opportunities may also alter the organisation required.

4 *The complexity of strategic change* needs to be managed, implying that more complex organisational considerations will be involved. Simple configurations such as a move from a functional to a divisional structure are only a starting point in the process.

5 *The role of top and middle management* in the formation of strategy may also need to be reassessed: Chandler's view that strategy is decided by the top leadership alone has been challenged. Particularly for new, innovative strategies, middle management and the organisation's culture and structure may be important. The work of the leader in empowering middle management may require a new approach – the organic style of leadership.

16.1.5 Implications of strategy and structure being interlinked – the concept of 'strategic fit'

Although it may not be possible to define which comes first, there is a need to ensure that strategy and structure are consistent with each other. For example, PepsiCo reorganised its North American business to ensure that its strengths in the growing non-carbonated drinks market could be exploited across its full range of drinks – *see* Case 16.1. For an organisation to be economically effective, there needs to be a matching process between the organisa-

Definition ➤ tion's strategy and its structure: this is the concept of *strategic fit*.[9] Strategic fit is the matching process between strategy and structure.

In essence, organisations need to adopt an internally consistent set of practices in order to undertake the proposed strategy effectively. It should be said that such practices will involve more than the organisation's structure. They will also cover such areas as:

● the strategic planning process (see Chapter 17);

● recruitment and training (see later in this chapter);

● reward systems for employees and managers (see later in this chapter);

● the work to be undertaken (see later in this chapter);

● the information systems and processes (see Chapter 17).

This means that issues of strategic fit may not be fully resolved by considering only strategy and structure. It may be necessary to revisit strategy, even when the implementation process is formally under consideration (*see* Chapter 17).

There is strong empirical evidence, both from Chandler and Senge, that there does need to be a degree of strategic fit between the strategy and the organisation structure.

Although the environment is changing all the time, organisations may only change slowly and not keep pace with external change, which can often be much faster – for example, the introduction of digital technology. It follows that it is unlikely that there will be a perfect fit between the organisation's strategy and its structure. There is some evidence that a minimal degree of fit is needed for an organisation to survive.[10] It has also been suggested that, if the fit is close early on in the strategic development process, then higher economic performance may result. However, as the environment changes, the strategic fit will also need to change.

Key strategic principles

- According to some modern strategists, Chandler's concept of strategy first and then structure to deliver it may oversimplify the situation. There have been five major criticisms.

- Changes in the business environment and social values of the late twentieth century suggest that others beyond top management may need to contribute to strategy. This is called empowerment of the middle and junior ranks of managers. This can best take place before the organisation structure is finalised.

- New processes for developing strategy are adaptive and involve learning mechanisms. They also need open, fluid structures that may not be best served by simple functional structures.

- When strategic change is radical, it may not be possible to define clearly the final organisation structure. It may be necessary to let the structure emerge as strategy changes and develops.

- If strategy and structure are interlinked, then it is essential that they are consistent with each other – the concept of 'strategic fit'.

16.2 BUILDING THE ORGANISATION'S STRUCTURE: BASIC PRINCIPLES

16.2.1 Consistency with mission and objectives

The organisation's structure is essentially developed to deliver its mission and objectives. Building the organisation structure must therefore begin at this point. Before considering the possible structures in detail, it is useful to explore some basic questions in the context of the analysis and development undertaken in Chapter 12.

- *What kind of organisation are we?* Commercial? Non-profit making? Service-oriented? Government administration? (These questions are not an exhaustive list.)

- *Who are the major stakeholders?* Shareholders? Managers? Employees?

- *What is our purpose?*

- *What does our purpose tell us in broad terms about how we might be structured?*

There is no simple or 'right' answer to the last question; it deserves careful thought. Every organisation is unique in size, products or services, people, leadership and culture. Exhibit 16.4 shows some of the possible implications for designing organisation structures. It can be useful to think in this general unformed way before plunging into the detail of organisation design, which is explored in the next section.

16.2.2 The main elements of organisation design

Before embarking on the design process, it is worth reviewing the analysis of the organisation undertaken in Chapter 7. We will be using the work and insights described in that earlier analysis. It is important to remember that many organisations have existing structures and that the primary task of organisation design is usually not to invent a totally new organisation but to adapt the existing one. These matters are reflected in the nine primary determinants of organisation design:

Exhibit 16.4

Examples of the connection between purpose and organisation design

Purpose	Implications for organisation design
'Ideas factory' such as an advertising or promotions agency	Loose, fluid structure with limited formalised relationships. As it grows in size, however, more formal structures are usually inevitable
Multinational company in branded goods	Major linkage and resource issues that need carefully co-ordinated structures, e.g. on common suppliers or common supermarket customers for separate product ranges
Government civil service	Strict controls on procedures and authorisations. Strong formal structures to handle major policy directions and legal issues
Non-profit-making charity with a strong sense of mission	Reliance on voluntary members and their voluntary contributions may require a flexible organisation with responsibility devolved to individuals
Major service company such as a retail bank or electricity generating company	Formal structures but supported by some flexibility so that variations in demand can be met quickly
Small business attempting to survive and grow	Informal willingness to undertake several business functions such as selling or production, depending on the short-term circumstances
Health service with strong professional service ethics, standards and quality	Formalised structure that reflects the seniority and professional status of those involved while delivering the crucial complex service provisions
Holding company with subsidiaries involved in diverse markets	Small centralised headquarters acting largely as a banker, with the main strategic management being undertaken in individual companies

1 *Age.* Older organisations tend to be more formal: for example, *see* Greiner in Chapter 7.

2 *Size.* Essentially, as organisations grow, there is usually an increasing need for formal methods of communication and greater co-ordination, suggesting that more formal structures are required.

3 *Environment.* Rapid changes in any of the *Five Forces* acting on the organisation will need a structure that is capable of responding quickly (*see* Chapter 3). If the work undertaken by the organisation is complex, then this will make its ability to respond to the environment more difficult to organise and co-ordinate.[11]

4 *Centralisation/decentralisation decisions.* To some extent, most organisations have a choice over how much they wish to control from the centre. In summary, there are four main areas that need to be explored:

● the nature of the business, e.g. economies of scale will probably need to be centralised;

● the style of the chief executive: a dominant leader will probably centralise;

● the need for local responsiveness;

● the need for local service.

5 *Overall work to be undertaken.* Value chain linkages (*see* Chapter 6) across the organisation will clearly need to be co-ordinated and controlled. They may be especially important where an organisation has grown and become more diverse. Divisional or matrix structures may be needed, with the precise details depending on the specific requirements and strategies of the organisation.

6 *Technical content of the work.* In standardised mass production, the work to be undertaken controls the workers and their actions.[12] However, Japanese production methods have recently shown that flexibility may be highly desirable in mass-production (*see* Chapter 9).

7 *Different tasks in different parts of the organisation.* It is clear that the tasks of operations (production) are not the same as those of the sales and marketing areas. Different organisations have different balances of such functions – for example, the strong role of *research* in a major pharmaceutical company versus the dominance of *creative* people in some media companies: the different tasks need to be reflected in the way the organisation structure is designed.

8 *Culture.* The degree to which the organisation accepts change, the ambitions of the organisation and its desire for experimentation are all elements to be considered.[13]

9 *Leadership.* The style, background and beliefs of the leader may have an important effect on organisation design. This will be particularly true in *innovative* and *missionary* organisations which are explored later in this chapter.

In bringing all the above elements together, there is a danger of overcomplicating the considerations and arguments. *Simplicity in design* should guide the proposals because the structure needs to be understood and operated after it has been agreed. We return to this area later in this chapter.

It is usual in undertaking such an analysis to consider the *responsibilities* and *powers* of the main individuals and groups involved, even if they are deliberately left vague in some structures. Responsibility and power need to be *controlled* and *monitored* and this needs to be built into the organisational structure. However, the control systems of the organisation can usually be considered after the proposed structure has been resolved (*see* Chapter 17).

16.2.3 External environment and internal organisation – Mintzberg's contribution

According to Mintzberg,[14] there are four main characteristics of the environment that influence structure (*see* Exhibit 16.5).

Exhibit 16.5

Environmental types and their impact on organisational structure

Type of environment	Range		Consequences for organisational structure
Rate of change	Static ⟷	Dynamic	As rate increases, the organisation needs to be kept more flexible
Degree of complexity	Simple ⟷	Complex	Greater complexity needs more formal co-ordination
Market complexity	Involved in single market ⟷	Involved in diversified markets	As markets become more diversified, divisionalisation becomes advisable
Competitive situation	Passive ⟷	Hostile	Greater hostility probably needs the protection of greater centralisation

1 *Rate of change.* When the organisation operates in a more dynamic environment, it needs to be able to respond quickly to the rapid changes that occur. In static environments, change is slow and predictable and does not require great sensitivity on the part of the organisation. In dynamic environments, the organisation structure and its people need to be flexible, well co-ordinated and able to respond quickly to outside influences. The dynamic environment implies a more flexible, organic structure.

2 *Degree of complexity*. Some environments can be easily monitored from a few key data movements. Others are highly complex, with many influences that interact in complex ways. One method of simplifying the complexity is to decentralise decisions in that particular area. The complex environment will usually benefit from a decentralised structure.

3 *Market complexity*. Some organisations sell a single product or variations on one product. Others sell ranges of products that have only limited connections with each other and are essentially diverse. As markets become more complex, there is usually a need to divisionalise the organisation as long as synergy or economies of scale are unaffected.

4 *Competitive situation*. With friendly rivals, there is no great need to seek the protection of the centre. In deeply hostile environments, however, extra resources and even legal protection may be needed: these are usually more readily provided by central HQ. As markets become more hostile, the organisation usually needs to be more centralised.

Using these principles, Mintzberg then developed six major types of organisational structures that combine:

- the environment;
- the internal characteristics of the organisation (age, size, etc.) discussed earlier;
- the key part of the organisation in delivering its objectives; and
- the key co-ordinating mechanism that binds it together.

He then gave each of these combinations a name that would characterise its main features. The configurations are shown in Exhibit 16.6.

Exhibit 16.6

Mintzberg's configuration of organisations and the way they operate

Mintzberg's strategic configurations	Background: see Part 2 of this book		Structures and linkages		Example
	Environmental analysis	Resource analysis	Key part of organisation	Key co-ordinating mechanism	
Entrepreneurial organisation	Simple/dynamic	Small, young Duplication of jobs	Strategic apex: the boss or owner	Direct supervision	Small computer service company
Machine organisation	High growth or cyclical	Older, large Defined tasks, techno-structure	Techno-structure	Standardisation of work	Computer assembly or car plant
Professional organisation	Stable, complex, closed to outsiders	Professional control by managers	Operating core	Standardisation of skills	Management consultancy or hospital
Divisionalised structure	Diverse	Old and large Strong links possible Standard criteria for resource allocation	Middle line	Standardisation of outputs	Fast-moving consumer goods group
Innovative organisation*	Complex and dynamic	Often young, complex work, experts involved	Support staff	Mutual adjustment	Advertising agency
Missionary organisation	Simple, static	Ideologically driven co-operative Small groups within total	Ideology	Standardisation of norms	Charity or social work

* *Note*: Innovative organisation is called an *adhocracy* in some texts and versions of the above.

Source: Mintzberg, Henry, Lampel, Joseph B, Quinn, James Brian, Ghoshal, Sumantra, *The Strategy Process*, 4th Edition, © 2003, pp209–225. Adapted by permission of Pearson Education, Inc., Upper Saddle River, NJ.

The importance of Mintzberg's configuration lies in the light it throws on the types of *organisation* needed to deliver types of *strategy*. Two examples will make the point:

1 *The machine organisation* is typified by work standardisation. Such an organisation may not wish to seek higher-value-added work in small market segments because this would not be consistent with its current resources and work methods.

2 *The innovative organisation* is typified by mutual adjustments between members of the organisation rather than standardisation of work, skills or output. An organisation structured in this way is unlikely to be able to start turning out standardised items, unless it changes radically, invests in totally new resources and learns new skills.

On this basis, when an organisation's structure is defined in broader terms than merely its reporting structure, then such a structure will guide the strategy options open to the organisation. In this way, *strategy is linked to structure*.

It should be noted that most organisations will rarely match Mintzberg's six configurations precisely. However, they do provide guidelines that link the earlier characteristics with their strategy and structure implications. Moreover, they could be used to show the implications of what might happen as the organisation changes – for example, becoming larger, with a more complex product range.

Comment

Mintzberg's configurations clearly oversimplify the possible organisational combinations. There are a number of more fundamental criticisms of the approach:

● It might be argued that Mintzberg's version of the *divisionalised structure* is so vague as to be limited in value: there may be a number of other different configurations contained inside the divisionalised configuration. In a sense, it is not discriminatory and could include a number of the other categories, each in its own division.

● It might also be said that some companies do not just standardise one variable as above, such as work or processes, but standardise several and that the distinctions that Mintzberg draws between them may not reflect reality. In these cases, there is no single key co-ordination mechanism.

● There may be connections between the innovative and entrepreneurial organisation types: the way some entrepreneurial companies grow may involve a strategy of innovation.

● Chapter 9 showed how manufacturing innovation has made some real contributions to strategy over the last few years. However, in Mintzberg's categorisation, manufacturing is probably a *machine* rather than an *innovative* organisation.

● This book takes the view that all companies need to include innovation as part of all their strategies. To confine it to one configuration is dubious at best.

Overall, Mintzberg's configurations provide some useful guidelines on organisation structure and its relationship with strategy, but they need to be treated with caution.

16.2.4 The strategy to be implemented

Every organisation is to some extent unique – the result of its past, its resources and its situation. In addition, the key factors for success (*see* Chapter 6) and the major strategies chosen by whatever process will depend on the situation at that time. It is difficult to specify clear and unambiguous rules to translate strategy into organisational structures and people processes. Thompson and Strickland[15] recommend five useful steps that will assist this process but they caution against certainty:

1 Identify the tasks and people that are crucial to the strategy implementation.

2 Consider how such tasks and people relate to the existing activities and routines of the organisation.

3 Use key factors for success to identify the chief areas around which the organisation needs to be built.

4 Assess the levels of authority needed to action the identified strategies.

5 Agree the levels of co-ordination between the units in the organisation necessary to achieve the strategy.

The above are all rather generalised but this is inevitable in view of the unique nature of each organisation.

16.2.5 Consequences for employment and morale

People implement strategies, not plant machinery nor financial resources. New organisational structures can provide new and interesting opportunities for managers and employees. Alternatively, structures may deliver a threat to their scope for work and possibly even their employment. Developing new organisational structures without considering the consequences for those who will be affected is clearly unsatisfactory. This is a major task for any strategy and is considered separately in Chapter 21.

Key strategic principles

● In building the organisation's structure, it is essential to start by considering its purpose. This will often provide some basic guidance on the structure required.

● There are eight main elements of organisational design: age; size; centralisation/decentralisation; overall work; technical content; tasks in different parts of the organisation; culture; leadership. All these elements will be interrelated with the organisation's strategy.

● Environmental factors such as market change and complexity will impact on the proposed structure. In general, increased change and complexity suggest more flexible, less centralised structures. There are six main types of structure – entrepreneurial, machine, professional, divisionalised, innovative and missionary – but they need to be used with caution.

● Each organisation is unique and so it is difficult to develop unambiguous rules to implement strategy in terms of organisation structure and people issues.

● The impact of strategic change on employees and managers is a major consideration that deserves separate and detailed work.

16.3 THE CHOICE OF MANAGEMENT STYLE AND CULTURE

Alongside the issues of organisational purpose and design, there is also a choice to be made with regard to the style of management organisational culture. The organisation's leadership and culture, previously covered in Chapters 7 and 10, are relevant here. We revisit them now because of their potential impact on strategy development.

16.3.1 Background

In addition to the discussions that have taken place over the last few years on the relationship between strategy and structure, there has been another equally vigorous debate about management style and culture. This has spanned both practitioner books and academic journals. Early writers included Professor Peter Drucker, who started writing in the 1950s but was still producing books of interest in the 1990s.[16] In the 1980s, Peters and Waterman wrote their influential book *In Search of Excellence*, though Tom Peters has subsequently repudiated some of the guidance.[17] The writings of Charles Handy also represent a significant contribution.[18] Most are a good read but they also present research on how to operate companies, especially from the viewpoint of culture and style.

16.3.2 Culture, style, leadership and the relationship with strategy

Although every organisation is the result of its history, products and people, it periodically has the chance to renew itself. In other words, it is able to change its management culture and style. Inevitably, this will have an impact on strategy – both in obvious ways, such as the attitude to risk taking, and in more subtle ways, such as the ability of the company to innovate.

To some extent, an organisation will evolve in response to its continually changing environment. Furthermore, the leadership and top management at any point in time will clearly influence the organisation's culture and style. Nevertheless, organisations can also make the deliberate choice to change their culture and style as part of a major shift in strategy. The issues are therefore:

● Should the organisation change its culture and style?

● If so, in what way should the company change these?

It should be noted that this is not just an issue of implementation *after* the strategy has been chosen, but a fundamental choice available as part of the process.

Most of the writers and researchers quoted earlier in this section would argue that a shift in culture and style is essential if a fundamental change in strategy is proposed. They would support this view for three reasons:

1 Fundamental strategic change needs to impact on people in the organisation as well as on decision making. People issues are essentially summarised in culture and style.

2 Leadership is usually important for major changes in strategy. This is likely to encompass some shift in style and, occasionally, a change of leader.

3 Such a shift in culture and style is a *powerful symbol* of the related change in strategy.

16.3.3 The choice of a new culture and style

As a starting point in exploring this area, the reader is referred back to the discussion of culture in Chapter 7 and leadership in Chapter 10. In addition, the final decision will clearly

---

Exhibit 16.7

Strategy and style options

Descriptors	Command	Symbolic	Rational	Transactive	Generative
Style	**Imperial** Strategy driven by leader or small top team	**Cultural** Strategy driven by mission and a vision of the future	**Analytical** Strategy driven by formal structure and planning systems	**Procedural** Strategy driven by internal process and mutual adjustment	**Organic** Strategy driven by the initiatives of those empowered in the organisation
Role of top management	**Commander** Provide direction	**Coach** Motivate and inspire	**Boss** Evaluate and control	**Facilitator** Empower and enable	**Sponsor** Endorse and sponsor
Role of organisational members	**Soldier** Obey orders	**Player** Respond to challenge	**Subordinate** Follow the system	**Participant** Learn and improve	**Entrepreneur** Experiment and take risks

Source: Adapted from Hart, S (1992) 'An integrative framework for strategy-making processes', *Academy of Management Review*, Vol 17, pp327–51. Copyright 1992 by Academy of Management. Reproduced with permission of Academy of Management in the format Textbook via Copyright Clearance Center.

be related to the proposed strategic changes. There will also need to be a degree of *strategic fit* between the strategy and the style, just as there was between strategy and structure earlier in the chapter.

More generally, Hart has suggested a range of styles from which the choice can be made: they vary from the *imperial* to the *organic* and are shown in Exhibit 16.7. The content of each style can be matched to how the organisation sees itself developing over the period of the strategy.

Comment

Culture and style can rarely be changed overnight: it is often possible to introduce a new strategy more quickly than bring about a related change in style. Culture and style take time to develop so the strategic fit may need some adjustment. Hence, the process of introducing a new style needs careful thought.

16.3.4 Coping with pressure for change: the new organic leadership style

To cope with the uncertainties of strategy development, those who lead the organisation have a key role in guiding, controlling, initiating and employing considered value judgements to move the strategy process forward.[19] The work of leadership is crucial in the development of strategy and the optimal organisational framework. The *imperial* leader will continue to decide strategy and then define the organisation to achieve this. However, for leaders who have a different, more organic style,[20] strategy and organisation have more complex interrelationships.

In the words of Peter Senge:[21]

> *The old days when a Henry Ford, Alfred Sloan or Tom Watson [the founder of IBM] learned for the organisation are gone. In an increasingly dynamic, interdependent and unpredictable world, it is simply no longer possible for anyone to 'figure it all out at the top'. The old model 'the top thinks and the local acts' must now give way to integrative thinking and acting at all levels. While the challenge is great, so is the potential payoff.*

If these comments are accurate, then it is possible that the structures of the early twentieth century are no longer appropriate. There may need to be a process of discussion *before* strategies and structures are finalised.

According to Senge,[22] there are three key dimensions to the role of the more organic leader in strategic change:

1 *Creative tension.* The tension that exists as a new leader moves to close the gap between his/her vision of the future and the current position of the organisation.

2 *New leadership role.* The former role of the imperial decision-maker may be too simplistic for the new millennium. The new role will involve:
   ● building the core values and purpose of the organisation;
   ● allowing strategy to emerge (see Mintzberg, Handy and others, Chapter 15);
   ● putting in place processes that allow an organisation to develop and renew itself;
   ● motivating, inspiring and coaching others in the organisation;
   ● adopting the role of custodian or steward of the organisation's people and its purpose.

3 *New skills.* None of the above will be achieved unless new skills are developed and employed, both by the leader and others in the organisation. The four main skill areas are:
   ● building a shared vision so that members of the organisation are committed to its future purpose;
   ● challenging deeply held assumptions without causing individuals to become overly defensive, so that new ideas can surface;

- identifying the key interrelationships and the factors critical to the success of the organisation (*see* Chapter 6);
- distinguishing the complex but unimportant details from the dynamic and important events that really shape strategy in the organisation.

The new role and skills imply more flexible relationships between the leader and the organisation. Such changes will include not only the organisational relationships but also the strategies associated with them: it is not possible to be a 'listening' leader while at the same time holding fixed, preconceived views on the strategic consequences. Hence, it follows that strategy, structure and leadership have more complex interrelationships. Naturally, the authoritarian leader can define the organisation structure that will implement his/her chosen strategies but, for other leadership styles, the position is more complicated.

Comment

Although the above values and comments may appear more in tune with some of the management thinking of the new millennium, caution is required in three areas:

1 It is not easy or necessarily appropriate to move quickly from a more imperial structure to a more organic organisation. Informing middle managers that they now have greater freedom may simply make older-style managers perplexed: they may have little experience, knowledge or skills in the new areas. It is too easy to underestimate the changes required in the *attitudes* and *skills base* to operate such an approach. Such changes involve both the leader and all the members of the organisation learning new roles and relationships over time periods, which are sometimes lengthy.

2 According to Hofstede (*see* Chapter 7), some national cultures need greater certainty and dominance from their leaders. Learning and adaptive cultural solutions may not be appropriate in these circumstances. The problems may outweigh the benefits.

3 The resource-based view of strategy development and some other theories of strategy have still not fully considered the implications for organisational structures.[23]

Key strategic principles

- Every organisation has the choice of changing its culture and style when it changes its strategy.
- In many cases, a change of style is essential when a fundamental change of strategy is proposed.
- The content of the culture and style depends on the strategies proposed. There needs to be a degree of strategic fit between the two areas. Importantly, culture and style take time to change and may move more slowly than the proposed strategy.

16.4 TYPES OF ORGANISATIONAL STRUCTURE

From all the above considerations, it is possible to identify some basic types of organisational structure that can serve to implement the chosen strategy:

- small organisation structure;
- functional organisation structure;
- multidivisional structure (sometimes shortened to *M-form* structure);
- holding company structure (sometimes shortened to *H-form* structure and discussed in Chapter 12 as the *corporate* headquarters company);

- matrix organisation structure;
- innovative organisation structure.

Each of these is explored in this section.

16.4.1 Small organisation structure

Definition ➤ The small organisation structure consists of the owner/proprietor and the immediate small team surrounding that person. In small organisations, there will often only be limited resources. Individuals will need to be flexible and undertake a variety of tasks. The informality of the structure will allow fast responses to market opportunities and customer service requirements. However, problems may be caused by the duplication of roles, confusion of responsibilities and muddled decision making, and it may not be realistic to draw up a clear organisational structure. Depending on the management style of the owner/leader, there may be many people or only the leader contributing to the organisation's strategy. Examples of such a company are a small family business or a specialist local computer service supplier.

16.4.2 Functional organisation[24]

Definition ➤ The functional organisation is based on locating the structure around the main activities that have to be undertaken by the organisation, such as production, marketing, human resources, research and development, finance and accounting. As the organisation grows from being a small company, the functional organisation structure is often the first structure that is adopted (*see* Figure 16.3). It allows experts in a functional area to be grouped together and economies of scale to operate. For example, a single product range production or service company, such as a regional bus company, is likely to have a functional structure. Exhibit 16.8 lists some of the advantages and disadvantages of this type of organisation structure.

Exhibit 16.8

Advantages and disadvantages of the functional organisation structure

Advantages	Disadvantages
• Simple and clear responsibilities	• Co-ordination difficult
• Central strategic control	• Emphasis on parochial functional areas in strategy development rather than company-wide view
• Functional status recognised	• Encourages interfunctional rivalry
	• Strategic change may be slow

Figure 16.3

The functional organisation structure

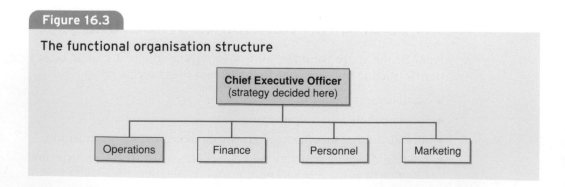

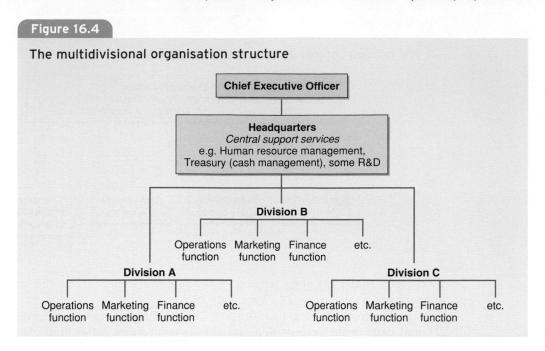

Figure 16.4

The multidivisional organisation structure

16.4.3 Multidivisional structure

Definition ➤ The multidivisional organisation is structured around separate divisions formed on the basis of products, markets or geographical areas. This form of organisational structure was developed in the early 1920s by the future head of General Motors, Alfred Sloan, and was recorded by Alfred Chandler,[25] as explored in Section 16.1.1.

As organisations grow, they may need to subdivide their activities in order to deal with the great diversity that can arise in products, geographical or other aspects of the business (*see* Figure 16.4). For example in Case 16.1, there would be little to be gained by PepsiCo combining its Quaker Foods North America division with its PepsiCo International division because they have different product ranges, different customers and different strategic priorities. Chandler argued that strategy was decided at the centre, but in modern companies it is often partially determined by the divisions. However, the centre does influence strategy and allocate resources. *See* also Exhibit 16.9.

Exhibit 16.9

Advantages and disadvantages of the multidivisional organisation structure

Advantages	Disadvantages
• Focuses on business area	• Expensive duplication of functions
• Eases functional co-ordination problems	• Divisions may compete against each other
• Allows measurement of divisional performance	• Decreased interchange between functional specialists
• Can train future senior managers	• Problems over relationships with central services

16.4.4 Holding or corporate company structure

Definition ➤ A holding company is a company that owns various individual businesses and acts as an investment company with shareholdings in each of the individual enterprises. The holding

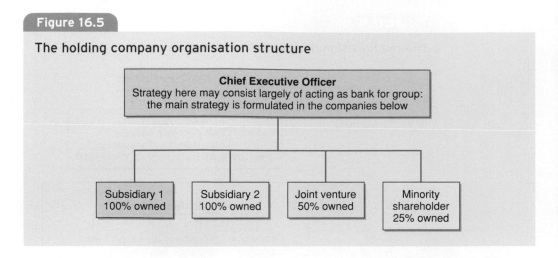

Figure 16.5

The holding company organisation structure

Chief Executive Officer
Strategy here may consist largely of acting as bank for group:
the main strategy is formulated in the companies below

| Subsidiary 1 100% owned | Subsidiary 2 100% owned | Joint venture 50% owned | Minority shareholder 25% owned |

company strategy is often referred to as a *corporate strategy* across the range of individual businesses – *see* Chapter 12 for more detail.

Further growth in organisations may lead to more complex arrangements between different parts of the organisation and outside companies. For example, joint ventures with totally new companies outside the group, alliances, partnerships and other forms of co-operation may be agreed. As a result, the original company may take on the role of a central shareholder for the various arrangements that may be set up: it becomes a holding company (*see* Figure 16.5). Its role becomes one of allocating its funds to the most attractive profit opportunities. The holding company structure became more prominent in the period from 1970 onwards and was explored by Williamson. *See* also Exhibit 16.10.

Exhibit 16.10

Advantages and disadvantages of the holding company organisation structure

Advantages	Disadvantages
• Allows for the complexity of modern ownership	• Little control at centre
• Taps expertise and gains new co-operations	• Little group contribution beyond 'shareholding/banking' role
• New market entry enhanced	• Problems if two partners cannot co-operate or one partner loses interest
• Spreads risk for conglomerate	• May have very limited synergy or economies of scale

Siemens and General Electric (described in Case study 12.1) is an example of a larger company that is well known for such arrangements:[26] it has extended its involvement into new markets and products. Some small companies have also become increasingly involved in such strategies in order to develop rapidly and exploit new opportunities. This is also seen in some of the large Japanese, Hong Kong and South-East Asian conglomerates.

16.4.5 Matrix organisation structure

Definition ➤ A matrix organisation is a combination of two forms of organisation – such as product and geographical structures – that operate jointly on all major decisions. In some cases, it may be advantageous for a large company to organise for its separate divisions or product groups to co-operate on business strategy with another method of organising the company, often

Figure 16.6

The matrix organisation structure

Chief Executive Officer

	Product group 1	Product group 2	Product group 3
Geographical area 1			
Geographical area 2		*Strategy perhaps decided in each of the matrix groups and perhaps at the centre*	
Geographical area 3			

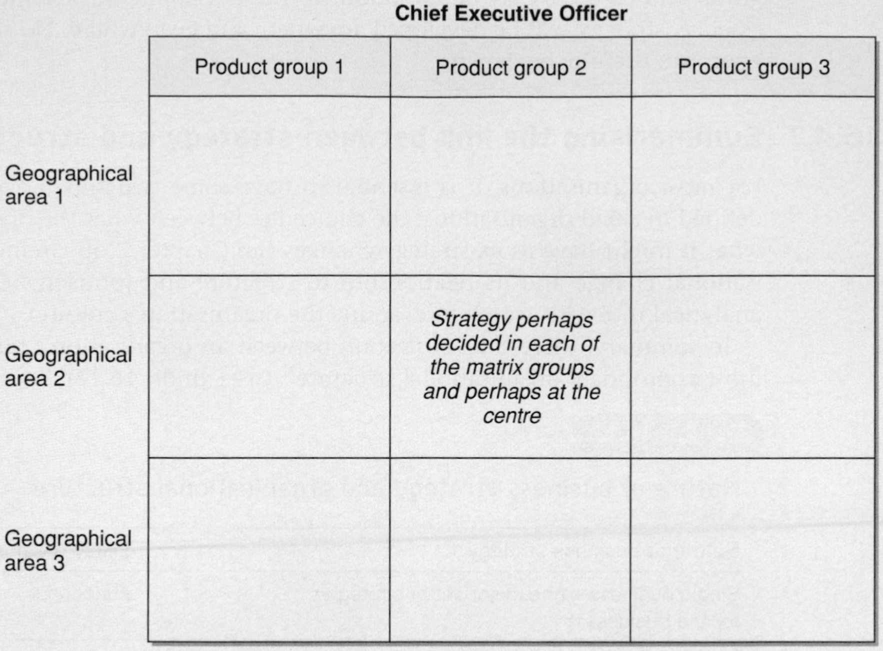

a geographical one. For example, an oil company such as Royal Dutch/Shell may need to take strategic decisions not only for its oil, gas and chemical *products* but also for *countries* such as the UK, Germany, the US and Singapore. It may be necessary to set up an organisation which has responsibilities along both product and geographical dimensions. Such dual-responsibility decision-making organisation structures are known as *matrix organisations*. The two dimensions do not necessarily have to be geography and product: any two relevant areas could be chosen (*see* Figure 16.6). Readers are referred to Case study 16.3 on Asea Brown Boveri for the problems in a matrix structure. *See* also Exhibit 16.11.

Exhibit 16.11

Advantages and disadvantages of the matrix organisation structure

Advantages	Disadvantages
• Close co-ordination where decisions may conflict	• Complex, slow decision making: needs agreement by all participants
• Adapts to specific strategic situations	• Unclear definition of responsibilities
• Bureaucracy replaced by direct discussion	• Can produce high tension between those involved if teamwork of some parts is poor
• Increased managerial involvement	

16.4.6 Innovative organisation structures

Definition ➤ Innovative organisation structures are characterised by their creativity, lack of formal reporting relationships and informality. In some cases, large organisations need to lay special emphasis on their creativity and inventiveness – for example, advertising agencies, some service companies and innovative design companies. In these circumstances, there is a case for having strong teams that combine experts with different skills and knowledge, work without much hierarchy and have an open style of operation. The free-flowing nature of the group and its ideas may be important in the development of some aspects of strategy. In essence, strategy will be developed anywhere and everywhere. No simple organisation diagram can usefully be drawn.

16.4.7 Summarising the link between strategy and structure

For most organisations, it is essential to have some structure – even if it is fluid and ill-defined in small organisations; the choice lies between what the organisation has now and what it might have as its strategy changes (*see* Chapter 7 on Greiner's depiction of organisational change and its relationship to structure and Johnson's *Cultural Web* – a useful analytical tool with which to examine the organisation's culture).

In summary, there is a connection between an organisation's business strategy and the most appropriate organisational structure[27] (*see* Exhibit 16.12).

Exhibit 16.12

Nature of business strategy and organisational structure

Nature of business strategy	Likely organisational structure
Single business – one major set of strategies for the business	Functional
Range of products extending across a single business – several strategies for each product area but business still run as one entity, perhaps with some common functions	Functional but monitor each range of products using separate profit and loss accounts
Separate businesses within group with limited links – assuming that each business is not related and operates in a separate market	Divisional
Separate businesses within group with strong links needed across parts of the group	Matrix (or divisional with co-ordination if matrix is difficult to manage)
Ideas factory – strategy needs to be strongly experimental and emerge	Innovative structure
Unrelated businesses – series of businesses each with its own strategic issues	Holding company
Related businesses owned jointly or by minority shareholdings – series of businesses where each needs to have its own strategies and be managed separately	Holding company

---

Key strategic principles

- There are six main types of organisational structure, each having advantages and disadvantages.
- The small organisation has limited resources but an informal structure, allowing flexibility in response, but giving unclear lines of responsibility.
- The functional organisation has been used mainly in small to medium-sized organisations with one main product range.
- As organisations develop further ranges of products, it is often necessary to divisionalise them. Each division then has its own functional structure, with marketing, finance, production, etc.

- As organisations become even more diverse in their product ranges, the headquarters may just become a holding company.
- An alternative form of structure for companies with several ranges of products is the matrix organisation, where joint responsibility is held by two different structures, e.g. between product divisions and another organisational structure such as geographical or functional divisions. This type of organisation has some advantages but is difficult to manage successfully.
- Innovative organisations may have cross-functional teams.
- The place where strategy is developed depends on the organisational structure.

CASE STUDY 16.2

Cisco Systems: benefits of a highly structured organisation?

In 1999, Cisco Systems, the international telecommunications company, operated a highly structured organisation that claimed to cut bureaucracy and costs. But was every part of the company truly centralised? And what happened when Cisco made a loss in 2001?

In 1999 on the outskirts of San José, California, there was a collection of 35 virtually identical brown office blocks that could be told apart only by the letters on the doorways. Inside each building, the floors were divided into cubicles and offices. The cubicles came in two sizes and the offices were all 10ft × 12ft. None had windows. The floor plans displayed on the walls looked more like computer circuits than maps of where to find people. These were the offices of Cisco Systems, one of the world's leading telecommunications equipment companies. For some years, the company outperformed the competition and won new business with relentless efficiency. The company was proud of its lean and highly structured organisation as the case below explains.

How did the company work in 1999? How was it organised?

In 1999, Mr Larry Carter was the company's chief financial officer and took personal pride in the company's Spartan surroundings. Every chair at Cisco, he said with satisfaction, was the same. Mr Carter joined the company in 1995, having spent most of his life in the semiconductor industry. He dedicated himself to building a system of computerised accounting and management controls that cut out every dollar of unnecessary cost. But he insisted he was not a bean-counting control freak. His main aim, he saids, was to create a system that operated with the minimum of bureaucracy and allowed the greatest flexibility to employees.

Take expenses. At Cisco, any employee could travel anywhere without prior approval. The employee entered the travel request into the system and as long as it met company policy – coach (tourist) class air tickets only – he or she would be automatically reimbursed within 48 hours. The point, Mr Carter explained, was to ensure that employees were free to do whatever was necessary for the customer rather than wasting time on bureaucracy. 'There will always be some who will abuse it,' Mr Carter said, 'but we do not slow down the whole company because of that 1 or 2 per cent. I will catch those who abuse it.'

The result was a company that claimed the highest level of revenues per employee in the industry and spent only 1 per cent of those revenues on its finance department. The cost control system contributed, in large part, to Cisco's success. From his desk each morning, Mr Carter was able to track exactly how much money his company was making, how each division was doing around the world, and even how each salesperson was performing against his or her target. He called up a page showing sales and margins for every region of the world: the information was no more than 24 hours old. He was able to review the figures by region, by product line, or by customer. He clicked on the US to get sales by state; then on Arizona for the figures for each salesperson. If anything looked amiss he was able to instantly fire off an e-mail to the individual concerned.

Working under such close scrutiny is not to everyone's liking. Those who were uncomfortable with the system generally did not last long at the company. 'We aim to take out the bottom 5 per cent constantly,' said Mr Carter. Cisco's modus operandi was unforgiving of people who were less than 100 per cent committed to their work and the company. But for those who were committed, the rewards were bountiful. The company's 17,000 employees were paid in part with options on Cisco stock which rose 10-fold in the four years 1996–99, making them extremely wealthy. (Although the shares declined early in the new millennium, they have since recovered.)

▶ CASE STUDY 16.2 continued

Mr Carter's system was probably impersonal, but it was undoubtedly efficient. Purchasing, sales, marketing and even the hiring of staff were managed through a co-ordinated network. About 70 per cent of Cisco's sales arose from direct orders over the internet, making it one of the largest e-commerce operations in the world. Mr Carter believed his system gave him an almost complete view of how the company was trading at the end of every day. This cut down the likelihood of nasty surprises when company results were published and it meant that the company was able to take action earlier if results were falling short of plan. The results were so impressive that Mr Carter said that he had calls from his peers at Dell and Texas Instruments who wanted to copy the Cisco system. Mr Carter believed that, one day, all companies would be run his way.

Cisco Systems restructuring from year 2000

Around the year 2000, the company's competitive environment worsened dramatically. Cisco Systems went into loss, in common with many other telecommunications companies. Arguably, the 1999 structure did not help the company to read market trends correctly. Nevertheless, the company rapidly recovered its market position and sales – see Figure 16.7. This was achieved by restructuring its businesses, including some reorganisation. This second part of the case explains the restructuring and explores the consequences for Cisco's organisation structure.

By 2000, it was obvious to senior managers in Cisco – including Mr Carter – that the company was in serious trouble. The market for telecommunications network equipment was Cisco's main line of business. This was down substantially because the telecommunications service companies – like Bell South in the US and British Telecom in Europe – were no longer placing major orders for new equipment because they were in trouble themselves, as explored in Case 15.2. Cisco's first recovery strategy therefore was to pursue new markets for related equipment, like security and net phones. It was able to respond rapidly because it was highly centralised.

The company also took some other decisions that were perhaps more surprising. It concluded that its engineering research division had previously been too widely scattered in its choice of research projects. Cisco therefore centralised engineering research: it is perhaps surprising that this was not centralised in the earlier organisation. As a result, the company cut its product line by 27 per cent to focus on the most successful models. In turn, this helped the company gain volume discounts from its customers.

Cisco also moved to centralise its company purchasing. Mr Carter explained: 'In the past, each unit could choose its own suppliers and manufacturers. Now a committee oversees all such decisions . . . [with the result that] . . . more than 3,000 resellers and 800 suppliers were squeezed out as Cisco reduced its partnerships to cut costs.' The company also began to put pressure on its suppliers to lower their prices and give more time for Cisco to pay.

At the same time, Cisco decided to limit the freedom of subsidiaries to make acquisitions. The company had previously allowed parts of the group to purchase small start-up companies in the 'dot.com' boom. But it now changed this policy to increase central permission for acquisitions, with one criterion being profitability from the outset of the purchase. Arguably, Cisco was similar to many other companies here in that it originally believed the hype surrounding the internet revolution. Its relatively centralised structure allowed it to move quickly to exert more control.

Finally, Cisco introduced an incentive scheme for its senior executives that was designed to encourage team working. The new compensation policy linked 30 per cent of annual bonuses to working with other peer managers. Essentially, this reinforced the centralised Cisco culture where arguably it had been too decentralised previously.

First part of case adapted by Richard Lynch from an article by Roger Taylor in the *Financial Times*, 12 April 1999, p13. © *Financial Times* 1999. Reproduced with permission. Second part of case written by Richard Lynch.[28]

Figure 16.7

Cisco Systems five-year record

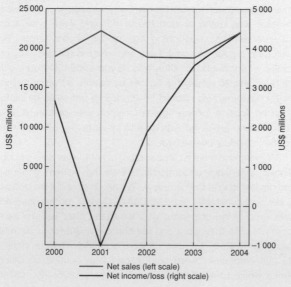

Source: Company Annual Report and Accounts 2004.

Case questions

1 *What are the advantages and disadvantages of working in such an organisation?*

2 *To what extent, if at all, does the organisation allow room for personal initiative and innovation? Could it do more to support innovation? If so, how? If not, would you change the organisation structure? If so, how?*

3 *Would you like to work in such a company? (We are all entitled to make choices about where we would like to work.)*

16.5 ORGANISATIONAL STRUCTURES FOR INNOVATION

Innovative structures and processes were introduced in the previous section, but innovation is too important to the whole corporate strategic process for it to be described as only suitable for some specialist organisation types. *Every* organisation needs an element of innovation: hence, *every* organisation needs structures capable of producing this, even if these structures are only temporary, e.g. a team is formed for a particular project and disbanded once the work is completed.

16.5.1 Innovation needs to be commercially attractive

Before exploring how an organisation can best structure itself to be innovative, it is useful to examine what is required. In a competitive market place, it is not enough to be innovative: the new product or service has to be commercially attractive to potential customers, i.e. it must offer value for money compared with existing products and services. Gilbert and Strebel[29] call this the *complete competitive formula*.

It may be desirable to include a broader range of benefits in addition to the innovation itself. Often, the real breakthrough comes not with the technical development but with the extended package of promotion, distribution, support and customer service. All of these elements are geared towards making the innovation user-friendly and more commercially attractive. This requires an *integrated* organisation structure across all functions of the business. For example, one of the reasons that the World Wide Web has taken off on the internet over the last few years has been the introduction of innovative user-friendly software such as Netscape. However, the real breakthrough for the company came when it arranged for free distribution through computer magazines of certain types of its software for evaluation by personal use. The result has been that, at the time of writing, Netscape has become the dominant software on this new, growing medium. From the organisational viewpoint, such developments need integration and co-ordination across all the functions if innovative solutions are to be obtained.

16.5.2 The nature of the innovative process

In Chapter 11, we examined Quinn's use of the concept of 'controlled chaos' to describe the innovative process. Innovation is flexible, open-ended and possibly without a clearly defined or fixed objective. The process needs to be free-wheeling and experimental. Within this, it is useful to distinguish between:[30]

- *simple innovation*, which might be possible in any organisation and relies on one person or a small group, and
- *complex innovation*, which may require experts drawn from a variety of business functions to form project teams. This is likely to involve larger resources and greater organisational complexity.

Guidelines for organising innovative project teams

1 *Flexible structures* are needed that allow experts not just to exercise their skills but to break through conventional boundaries into *new* areas.

2 *Co-ordination* within the team needs to be undertaken by experts with a technical background in the area, rather than a superior with authority from outside.

3 *Power* in the team needs to be distributed among the experts, where appropriate. Much of the activity will consist of liaison and discussion among the experts as they progress their innovative ideas.

Mintzberg's comments on the innovative process had complex innovation particularly in mind when outlining three guidelines for organising project teams, which are summarised in Exhibit 16.13.

Ultimately, the strategy that emerges from the innovative process may remain vague and ill-defined. This has the advantages of being flexible, responsive and experimental. However, the disadvantages associated with a lack of definition may not satisfy the culture of organisations wanting quick and precise results.

16.5.3 Organisational structures and procedures for innovative companies

Kanter[31] surveyed a number of US companies in the 1970s and 1980s in an attempt to identify the organisation structures and processes that were most conducive to innovation. Among her conclusions were:

- *The importance of matrix structures.* These were more likely in innovative companies. They tended to break down barriers and lead to the more open reporting lines that were important to the innovative process. Decision making may have been slow and complex in matrix structures, but it provided the network for individuals to move outside their own positions and make the interconnections useful to innovation.

- *The need for a parallel organisation.* A separate group to run in tandem with the existing formal hierarchy was often highly valuable. It was specifically tasked with finding innovative solutions to problems, especially where a matrix structure was not in operation. It was able to act independently, without the day-to-day pressures and politics of the existing structure. It was then left to the existing organisation to define routine jobs, titles and reporting relationships. Instead of contacts and power flowing up and down the existing structure, the parallel organisation allowed new relationships and ideas to develop.

- *The work of a parallel organisation.* This had to be problem solving, possibly focused on a single business problem and structured around the team. The work was integrative, flexible and with little hierarchical division. The function of such a group was often to re-examine existing routines and systems, concentrating especially on areas that were partially unknown and needed challenging. It often provided a means of empowering people lower down in the organisation.[32]

- *Participative/collaborative management style.* This was often employed to encourage innovation. It involved persuading rather than ordering, seeking advice and comments and sharing the favourable results of successful initiatives.[33]

From her research, Kanter recommended five pointers to action that could be taken to encourage innovation in weaker organisations[34] (*see* Exhibit 16.14). The most successful

---

Exhibit 16.14

Five pointers to encourage innovation

1 Publicise and take pride in existing achievements.

2 Provide support for innovative initiatives, perhaps through access to senior managers, perhaps through project teams.

3 Improve communication across the enterprise by creating cross-functional activities and by bringing people together.

4 Reduce layers in the hierarchy of the organisation and give more authority to those further down the chain.

5 Publicise more widely and frequently company plans on future activity, giving those lower down in the organisation a chance to contribute their ideas and become involved in the process.

global companies, such as Toyota and McDonald's, have been particularly successful at pursuing such policies.

Comment

All of Kanter's ideas were researched and proposed in the context of the North American corporation. Some may not work at all or may need to be substantially modified in other national cultures. Moreover, the problems that were observed in terms of innovation may not be the same in other countries. What they do illustrate is that, for strategic innovation at least, the flexible, *open structure* of the organisation may need to come before the *innovatory strategies* that subsequently emerge.

Key strategic principles

- All companies need to be able to innovate as part of the strategic process.

- Such innovation needs to be commercially attractive if it is to be viable. An organisation structure that integrates and co-ordinates all the functional areas of a business is desirable.

- Innovation is open-ended and flexible, so the process needs to be experimental, with flexible structures, close co-ordination and power distributed throughout the innovating group.

- In terms of structure, a matrix organisation may be more effective because it is more integrative. In some circumstances, a separate, parallel organisation tasked with developing innovative solutions can be usefully employed.

16.6 MOTIVATION AND STAFFING IN STRATEGY IMPLEMENTATION

Capable and well-motivated people are essential to strategy implementation, especially at senior management level. This section explores the *formal organisation* needed to achieve this:

- reward systems that can increase motivation;
- staff appraisal, training and selection procedures for a successful strategy.

The *informal* aspects of this subject, associated with strategy implementation, such as leadership and culture, are left to Chapter 21.

16.6.1 Reward systems

Definition ► Rewards systems are the structured benefits paid to individuals and groups who have delivered strategies that add value to the organisation consistent with its agreed purpose. The measurement of achievement and the reward for good performance against the organisation's objectives can be powerful motivators for the delivery of corporate strategy. The linkage between reward and motivation has been extensively researched over the last few years and the connection well established.[35] Rewards need to be seen more broadly than simple payment: they may involve other forms of direct remuneration but also promotion and career development opportunities.

In designing reward systems to achieve strategic objectives, several factors need to be considered:

● *Strategic objectives.* These tend to have a longer-term element, whereas managers may well need to have short-term rewards. Hence, there may be a conflict between rewarding achievement of strategic objectives and a personal desire for short-term recompense. Moreover, not all strategic objectives are easily measurable, thus making accurate assessment difficult. To some extent, these problems have been resolved by rewarding individuals with shares in the enterprise but this incentive may not be available to all organisations and is still subject to manipulation.

● *Rewards focusing on individual performance.* These may not be appropriate when group objectives have been identified as crucial to strategy. Careful consideration of the impact of reward systems may therefore be required.

● *Rewards encouraging innovation and risk taking.* These may need to move beyond quantitative measures of performance, such as an increase in return on capital or earnings per share, to qualitative assessments based on the number and quality of the initiatives undertaken. There may well be a greater element of judgement involved, which may in turn lead to accusations by others of unfairness unless handled carefully.

In recent years, reward systems have been given new emphasis by the introduction of *performance contracts*. Some companies have developed a system whereby strategy implementation is split into a series of measurable milestones. Individual directors and senior managers then sign contracts to deliver these targets and their performance is reviewed accordingly. Case study 21.1 describes the use of this procedure at the UK company BOC Group.

16.6.2 Formal staff appraisal, training and selection procedures

New strategies may well call for new business approaches, new skills and new knowledge. Existing members of staff will not necessarily have these. It may be necessary therefore to introduce formal structures and procedures to appraise and train existing staff or to recruit new people in order to implement the strategy successfully.[36]

For motivational reasons, it is often appropriate to begin with existing staff members and assess their suitability for new positions – called appraisal. However, they may not possess the required knowledge and skill levels required, in which case training or outside recruitment becomes essential.

In corporate strategy, staffing issues primarily concern the most senior managers in the organisation. In cases of major strategic crisis, the chief executive officer may need to be replaced: there are countless cases during recent years of this one act being crucial to strategic change. However, it should be said that this may only be the *beginning* of a new strategy, rather than its implementation. When Lou Gerstner was recruited to head IBM after its spectacular profit problems in 1994 (*see* Chapter 1), he was hired on the basis that he had complete freedom to identify the main strategic problems, solutions and strategies. In this case, the first stage of the new IBM strategy was to hire an outsider to rescue the company. However, it should be pointed out that the previous chief executive was also aware of the difficulties and the need for change. It will be evident that, in general, recruiting senior talent to implement identified strategies can be a crucial element in an organisation's continued success or failure.

For the many companies that do not experience major crises, the provision of a sound *performance appraisal system* will be a major contribution to successful strategy implementation. Staff training and broader staff development programmes to build up the people elements in corporate strategy may accompany this. These are part of the area of human resource management strategy for the company. Coupled with recruitment and reward, they underline the crucial importance of this functional area at the highest levels of corporate strategy development.

Key strategic principles

- Measurement of achievement and the subsequent reward for good performance can be powerful methods for directing corporate strategy.

- However, reward systems may be difficult to develop that fully coincide with the organisation's strategic objectives for a variety of reasons.

- Staffing issues, such as recruitment, appraisal and training, are essential to the implementation of strategy. Formal procedures need to be built into the consideration of new or revised human resource management procedures.

16.7 STRATEGY AND STRUCTURE IN INTERNATIONAL ORGANISATIONS - THE ROLE OF HEADQUARTERS

As organisations become more international, their structures become more complex. Country and regional divisions join the product and functional interests in the organisation structure. Some aspects of international structure need to be considered in the context of international strategy development: these matters are explored in the next chapter. However, since the case studies in this chapter touch on the role of headquarters in directing subsidiary staff it is relevant to consider this matter now.

For reasons of history, leadership and national cultural attitudes, different companies have different approaches to their foreign operations. This can be characterised by examining the role of the headquarters of the organisation in relation to its various operations. In the late 1960s, Professor Howard Perlmutter identified four different types of relationship that have stood the test of time:[37]

1 *Ethnocentric*. In this case, the role of headquarters is to represent the parent company's approach to strategic development. Culture, style and strategy formulation are largely decided at the centre. The home country dominates and foreign operations are mainly run as they would be back home.

2 *Polycentric*. In this case, the role of headquarters is diminished, with each foreign operation running its own affairs and developing its own strategy. National cultures will therefore predominate and each country will largely decide its performance objectives within the purpose defined by headquarters.

3 *Regiocentric*. In this case, the headquarters seeks to negotiate with its foreign subsidiaries on mutually acceptable objectives. There are likely to be regional activities, i.e. for an area of the world such as Europe or South America.

4 *Geocentric*. In this case, the headquarters is the centre of a global web of activity. It will co-ordinate global production and markets but also encourage appropriate local product variations. We will explore this aspect further in the next chapter.

Although such characterisations may oversimplify reality, they are useful because they help to identify a key aspect of management in international operations. They also assist in the process of implementing strategy because they raise questions about the appropriate method of seeking change in international organisations.

Key strategic principles

- The role of headquarters in relation to its subsidiaries can be classified into four main types: ethnocentric, polycentric, regiocentric and geocentric.

- Each involves a different working relationship between the HQ and its subsidiaries and different degrees of freedom for such subsidiaries.

How ABB empowered its managers and then reversed the process

When the world's largest electrical engineering company, ASEA Brown Boveri (ABB), was formed in 1987, one of its earliest strategic decisions was to reorganise and move power from the centre to its operating companies: empowerment. In the beginning, this was hailed as being a classic example of modern management under its famous chairman, Mr Percy Barnevik. By 2004, the empowerment strategy was regarded as being a complete failure. This case explains what happened at ABB.

Rise and fall of ABB

With 2004 revenue of over US$20.7 billion and 100,000 employees around the world, ABB was one of the world's largest traditional electrical engineering companies. Its products included electrical power transmission and distribution, building technologies and automation. It operated in global markets and competed against such major companies as General Electric (US), Westinghouse (US), Siemens (Germany) and Alsthom (France) as well as with the major Japanese groups Mitsui and Mitsubishi. But ABB was not profitable during the latter part of this period.

After success in building its turnover during the 1990s, ABB's sales and profits hit their peak in 1999. The company then made a loss in the four years 2001–2004, though the loss was very small by the end of this period. Its staff dropped by 57,000 employees between the years 2000 and 2004 as a result of the closure and sale of subsidiaries. The reasons for this decline included fierce competition and a weak world economy. The company was also hit by one of its subsidiaries having to bear the considerable costs associated with the medical liabilities of asbestos products. However, ABB's manufacturing costs were also higher than those of its competitors: many commentators judged that its whole organisation structure needed simplifying and further costs taking out. Figure 16.8 shows the whole difficult record.

Company history

ABB was formed in 1987 from the engineering interests of the Swedish company ASEA and the Swiss engineering company Brown Boveri. Over the period 1988–90, the company was completely reorganised by its new chairman, Percy Barnevik. The central HQ in Switzerland was reduced to a total of 150 people, with a matrix management structure introduced worldwide. The company was split into 1,300 smaller companies and around 5,000 profit centres, functioning as far as possible as independent operations. Several layers of middle management were stripped out and directors from the central HQ moved into regional co-ordinating companies. Costs were not necessarily lower because many of the central headquarters operations had to be duplicated in each company.

At the same time, the company engaged in a major programme of acquisitions that grew the order intake of ABB from US$16 billion to US$25 billion over two years. Major companies were purchased in the US, Spain, Italy, the UK, France, Spain and Germany. All the negotiations for these

Figure 16.8

ABB's sales and profit record

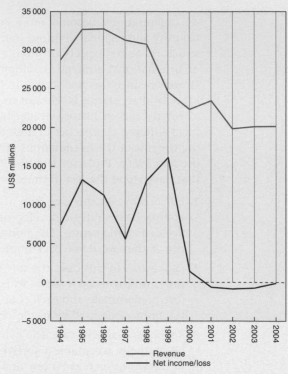

Source: Annual Report and Accounts from various years.

major decisions were handled centrally by ABB. A period of consolidation then followed from 1991 to 1993.

Company strategy to empower management

Under the direction of its chief executive (later chairman), Percy Barnevik, ABB pursued its bold initiative of breaking up the company into 1,300 smaller units, each with profit responsibility. The company became a well-known strategy case for business school study during this period. The moves were essentially aimed at empowering managers to move closer to their customers and at giving them the incentives to act as smaller and more entrepreneurial units. Even research and development was decentralised, with the new operating companies controlling 90 per cent of the group's US$2.3 billion budget. This made the centralised sharing of knowledge more difficult but the company judged that this was more than compensated by the empowerment of individual companies. Importantly, central finance and cash management were excluded from the decentralisation process and then used to monitor the performance of the empowered companies across the world.

Barnevik considered that the greatest strategic challenge in running a group of this size was motivating middle and lower managers and shifting entrenched corporate values. As he explained, previously managers had been happy to coast along with 2 per cent gross margins when a 5 per cent margin was possible with more commitment.

By 1991, the company was able to show that empowerment had become the norm for many of its managers. However, it was still necessary to reinforce the message: 'Now the problem is that they get too happy when they see profit doubled; they think 4 per cent margin is fantastic, and you have to tell them that American competitors can make 10 per cent.' Central management therefore continued to devote much of its time to 'indoctrinating' managers.

Inevitably there were problems. Goran Lindahl, one of ABB's top-level executive team, was given the key role of identifying areas where ABB managers had become complacent or allowed their units to drift. He was given the power 'to shake things up to create an environment of learning'. Five other problems emerged over the next few years:

● The small, empowered units of ABB were not well adapted to handling the big global companies who wanted one centralised negotiating and decision-making unit.
● It was difficult to find sufficient trained, experienced managers in Eastern Europe and Asia where some of the subsidiaries were located.
● There were major strains on central staff from the need to manage a complex, decentralised global operation.
● Extra costs were incurred in duplicating management positions in a large number of small companies.
● Small companies were not always able to gain the economies of scale that would be available to larger, more centralised organisations.

New leadership and new organisation structure – 1997

In 1997, Percy Barnevik gave up his position of chief executive. His successor was Goran Lindahl. Their leadership styles were quite different: Barnevik was eloquent, conceptual and led from the front, whereas Lindahl was more down-to-earth, consensual and interested in detail. Nevertheless, Barnevik stayed on as non-executive chairman.

In 1998, Lindahl announced two major strategic moves. First, he accelerated the shift to using Asian labour. Another 10,000 jobs would be lost in Europe and the US and be replaced by the same number of jobs in Asia. The cost for shareholders was estimated at US$1 billion. Second, he scrapped the group's matrix organisational structure and brought in some new, younger executives to the group's managing board. This was later followed by the sale of two

unprofitable divisions – power generation and transport – over the next eighteen months. Then, in 2000, Lindahl suddenly gave up his job. His explanation was that he believed ABB should be led by someone who 'understands how to exploit the IT revolution' and he was not that person. It is fair to say that his sudden departure halfway through his expected term caused some shock among outside observers.

New leadership and new organisation structure – 2000 onwards

The new chief executive, Jorgen Centermann, lost no time in completely restructuring ABB. He developed an organisation with four worldwide customer segments, coupled with two backup product segments. He cut the number of subsidiaries form over 1,000 to 400, thus having the effect of undoing the 'empowerment' strategy of the early 1990s. He gave three reasons:

1 the need to focus more on ABB's main large, global customers;
2 the need to cut costs, especially those associated with the duplication of management essential to decentralisation;
3 the need to exploit the power of the internet.

In addition, he appointed two new main board directors, one with responsibility for 'corporate processes' and the other for 'corporate transmission'. These were both associated with his desire to turn ABB into an 'agile, knowledge-based company' and to develop 'brain power' as a corporate motto.

Mr Centermann decided that ABB could not compete successfully in its power-related businesses so he scaled them back. He also sold the ABB nuclear power business to British Nuclear Fuels. In 2002, Mr Centermann negotiated the sale of the ABB's financial services division to one of its main competitors, General Electric of the US. The funds raised by this latter sale helped ABB, which was in significant financial difficulties at that time. The company had been hit by the downturn in the world economy, the asbestos claims against two of its subsidiaries and strong competition. Having undertaken this restructuring, Mr Centermann felt that he should resign. He was replaced as chief executive of ABB by Mr Jurgen Dormann. It was Mr Dormann who had previously taken over the chairmanship of ABB from Percy Barnevik in 2001 when it was obviously in trouble. Around this time and after adverse public criticism, Messrs Barnevik and Lindahl returned US$82 million in controversial pension benefits that they had received from ABB.

Mr Dormann remained chief executive until 2004 during a difficult business period. He oversaw major cutbacks at the company from the centre and then handed over this position to Mr Fred Kindle, who remained chief executive at the time of writing this case. With such a series of senior management changes, the company had clearly gone through a period of considerable turmoil. However, ABB claimed at the end of 2004 that, 'The company is now in good health.' The previous decentralised structure had been largely dismantled, with key decisions reverting to the centre of the company.

▶ CASE STUDY 16.3 continued

Case questions

1   *How important to the strategy of empowerment is a sophisticated financial control system? And how vital is the central monitoring (e.g. Lindahl)? What does this mean for empowerment?*

2   *If the world is becoming increasingly global, do you think that ABB's unit empowerment ever stood any chance of success?*

3   *To what extent, if at all, can large, global companies empower local managers? What are the implications for strategy development – centralised or decentralised?*

STRATEGIC PROJECT

This is a particularly interesting company because it was presented as a revolutionary new form of organisation in the 1990s and a model for other companies. You might like to use the references for this case to look back and see how the company has changed. You might also like to consider how the company should now move forward. It still faces significant difficulties that will need considerable effort and skill from all its employees.

CRITICAL REFLECTION

Should organisations put stronger emphasis on human resources issues much earlier in strategy development?

This chapter has explored the issues surrounding an organisation's culture, leadership style and structure *after* the previous chapters have considered the development of the organisation's strategy. The chapter has argued that strategy and structure are interrelated and, in that sense, suggested that the human aspects of the organisation need to be considered *earlier* in strategy development.

However, many of the leading strategy theorists seem to suggest that strategy is mainly concerned with competitive and customer issues, not human resource issues. But might human resource aspects – like leadership, organisation structure, culture and style – be more important? Should they perhaps come much earlier in strategy development? What are the consequences of your views for the way you would develop an organisation's strategy?

SUMMARY

● According to modern strategic thinking, Chandler's concept of strategy first and then structure to deliver it may oversimplify the situation. There have been some major criticisms of Chandler. First, changes in the business environment and social values of the late twentieth century suggest that others beyond top management may need to contribute to strategy. This is called empowerment of the middle and junior ranks of managers. This can best take place before the organisation structure is finalised. Second, new processes for developing strategy are adaptive and involve learning mechanisms. Third, such processes also need open, fluid structures that may not be best served by simple functional structures. When strategic change is radical, it may not be possible to define clearly the final organisation structure. It may be necessary to let the structure emerge as strategy changes and develops.

● If strategy and structure are interlinked, then it is essential that they are consistent with each other – the concept of 'strategic fit'.

● In building the organisation's structure, it is essential to start by reconsidering its purpose. This will often provide some basic guidance on the structure required. In addition, there are eight main elements of organisational design: age; size; centralisation/decentralisation; overall work; technical content; tasks in different parts of the organisation; culture; leadership. All these elements will be interrelated with the organisation's strategy. There are six main types of structure – entrepreneurial, machine, professional, divisionalised, innovative and missionary – but they need to be used with caution. Each organisation is unique and so it is difficult to develop unambiguous rules to implement strategy in terms of organisation structure and people issues. The impact of strategic change on employees and managers is a major consideration that deserves separate and detailed work.

● Every organisation has the choice of changing its culture and style when it changes its strategy. In many cases, a change of style is essential when a fundamental change of strategy is proposed. The content of the culture and style depends on the strategies proposed. There needs to be a degree of strategic fit between the two areas. Importantly, culture and style take time to change and may move more slowly than the proposed strategy.

● There are six main types of organisational structure, each having advantages and disadvantages. The *small organisation* structure is self-explanatory. The *functional organisation* structure has been mainly used in small to medium-sized organisations with one main product range. As organisations develop further ranges of products, it is often necessary to *divisionalise*. Each division then has its own functional structure – marketing, finance, production, etc. As organisations become even more diverse in their product ranges, the headquarters may just become a *holding company*. An alternative form of structure for companies with several ranges of products is the *matrix organisation*, where joint responsibility is held between the products structure and another organisational format such as the functional structure. This type of organisation has some advantages but is difficult to manage successfully.

● In building the most appropriate organisation structure, it is important to keep in sight the need for simple, cost-effective structures. Environmental factors, such as market change and complexity, will also impact on the proposed structure. In general, increased change and complexity suggest more flexible, less centralised structures.

● All organisations must be able to innovate as part of the strategic process, but such innovation needs to be commercially attractive if it is to be viable. An organisation structure that integrates and co-ordinates all the functional areas of a business is desirable. Because innovation is open-ended and flexible, the process needs to be experimental, with flexible structures, close co-ordination and power distributed throughout the innovating group.

● In terms of innovative structures, a matrix organisation may be more effective because it is more integrative. In some circumstances, a separate, parallel organisation tasked with developing innovative solutions can be employed.

● Measurement of achievement and the subsequent reward for good performance can be powerful methods for directing corporate strategy. However, it may be difficult to develop reward systems that coincide fully with the organisation's strategic objectives. Staffing issues, such as recruitment, appraisal and training, are essential to the implementation of strategy. Formal procedures need to be built into the consideration of new or revised human resource management procedures.

● In international structures, the role of the headquarters in relation to its subsidiaries can be classified into four types: ethnocentric, polycentric, regiocentric and geocentric. Each involves a different working relationship and different degrees of freedom for foreign subsidiaries.

QUESTIONS

1 Explain the structure of an organisation with which you are familiar, using the elements outlined in Sections 16.2 and 16.3 as your guide.

2 What structure would you expect the following organisations to have?

   (a) A small management consultancy company based in one country only.

   (b) A voluntary group providing volunteers to visit the elderly and house-bound

   (c) A medium-sized company with 1,500 employees, two factories and a separate headquarters.

   (d) A leisure park business owned and operated by a family company.

   (e) A medium-sized computer company with 80 employees which writes software for games machines.

3 *'If structure does follow strategy, why should there be a delay in developing the new organisation needed to meet the administrative demands of the new strategy?'* (Alfred Chandler)

How would you answer this question?

4 If you were asked to make Cisco Systems more innovative, what would you do? In answering this question, you should take into account the existing culture of the company.

5 *'Every organisation needs an element of innovation'* (see Section 16.4). Is this correct?

6 *'All any company has to do to explore its own potential to become a more innovatory organisation is to see what happens when employees and managers are brought together and given a significant problem to tackle.'* (Professor R M Kanter)

Discuss.

7 Why is it difficult to develop reward systems to deliver the organisation's objectives? How might such difficulties be overcome in a small entrepreneurial business venture?

8 The managing director of a large company making bicycles has become worried by the lack of growth in sales, believing the company has lost its earlier innovative spark, and has turned to you for advice. What would you recommend?

9 *'The hallmark of many successful business organisations is the attention given to the human element.'* Laurie Mullins, author of the well-known text *Management and Organisational Behaviour*.

Is the human element more important than competitive strategy?

Further reading

Professor Henry Mintzberg has a useful discussion on organisation structure and strategy in 'The structuring of organisations', in Mintzberg, H and Quinn, J B (1991) *The Strategy Process*, 2nd edn, Prentice Hall, New York, p341.

Laurie Mullins (1996) *Management and Organisational Behaviour*, 4th edn, Pitman Publishing, London, can be consulted for an extended discussion on organisational issues.

Professor Gerry Johnson's paper (1989) 'Rethinking incrementalism', *Strategic Management Journal*, Jan–Feb, is worth reading. It is reprinted in De Wit, B and Meyer, R (1994) *Strategy: Process, Content and Context*, West Publishing, St Paul, MN.

Professor Rosabeth Moss Kanter (1985) *The Changemasters*, Unwin, London, has a useful empirical study of innovative practice. Note there was a major and timely retrospective on Kanter's work in *Academy of Management Executive* (2004), Volume 18, No 2, pp92–110.

There was a special issue of *Long Range Planning* in 2000 on executive pay and recruitment: five papers including the editorial, Vol 33, No 4, pp478–559.

Notes and references

1 Sources for PepsiCo Case: Tropicana website 2002 and 2004; PepsiCo Annual Report and Accounts 2001 and 2004; *Financial Times* 22 July 1999, p2; 28 February 2000, p25; 15 March 2001, p20; 5 April 2002, p16.

2 Chandler, A (1987) *Strategy and Structure: Chapters in the History of the American Industrial Enterprise*, MIT Press, Cambridge, MA, pp8–14.

3 Chandler, A (1987): Op. cit., pp13–14.

4 Pugh, D (1984) *Organisation Theory*, Penguin, London. This book brings together various papers, including those of other influential theorists of the early twentieth century such as Taylor and Fayol.

5 This section has been adapted from the ideas of Kanter, R M (1983) *The Change Masters*, Unwin,

London, pp42–3 and pp398–9. This is a well-researched, thoughtful and provocative book.

6 Quinn, J B (1980) 'Managing strategic change', *Sloan Management Review*, Summer. Reprinted in Mintzberg, H and Quinn, J B (1991) *The Strategy Process*, Prentice Hall, New York and De Wit, B and Meyer, R (1994) *Strategy: Process, Content and Context*, West Publishing, St Paul, MN.

7 *Source*: Lynch, R, based on reference 6.

8 Prahalad, C K and Hamel, G (1994) 'Strategy: the search for new paradigms', *Strategic Management Journal*, Summer Special Issue, p11.

9 Galbraith, J R and Kazanjian, R K (1986) *Strategy Implementation*, 2nd edn, West Publishing, St Paul, MN, Ch7.

10 Galbraith, J R and Kazanjian, R K (1986) Op. cit., p113.

11 Laurence, P R and Lorsch, J W (1967) *Organisation and the Environment*, Richard D Irwin, Burr Ridge, IL, contains a full discussion of this important area.

12 Mintzberg, H (1991) 'The structuring of organisations', p341 in Mintzberg, H and Quinn, J B (1991) Op. cit.

13 Johnson, G (1989) 'Rethinking incrementalism', *Strategic Management Journal*, Jan–Feb. Reprinted in De Wit, B and Meyer, R (1994) *Strategy: Process, Content and Context*, West Publishing, St Paul, MN.

14 Mintzberg, H (1979) *The Structuring of Organisations*, Prentice Hall, New York.

15 Thompson, A and Strickland, A (1993) *Strategic Management*, 7th edn, Irwin, Homewood, IL, p220.

16 Examples: Drucker, P (1961) *The Practice of Management*, Heinemann/Mercury, London, and (1967) *Managing for Results*, Pan Books, London.

17 Peters, T (1992) *Liberation Management*, Macmillan, London.

18 Handy, C (1989) *The Age of Unreason*, Business Books, London, and (1991) *The Gods of Management*, Business Books, London.

19 These comments arise directly from the writings of Quinn quoted in reference 6. They are also consistent with the conclusions of Chandler earlier in the century.

20 *See* Hart, S and Banbury, C (1994) 'How strategy making processes can make a difference', *Strategic Management Journal*, 15, p254 and Ch17.

21 Senge, P (1990) 'The leader's new work: building learning organisations', *Sloan Management Review*, Fall. Reprinted in De Wit, B and Meyer, R (1994) pp132–41.

22 Senge, P (1990) Op. cit.

23 Moingeon, B, Ramanantsoa, B, Métais, E and Orton, J D (1998) 'Another look at strategy–structure relationships: the resource-based view', *European Management Journal*, 16(3), June, pp297–305.

24 Mintzberg, H (1979) Op. cit.

25 Chandler, A (1962) *Strategy and Structure*, MIT Press, Cambridge, MA. *See* also Channon, D (1973) *The Strategy and Structure of British Enterprise*, Macmillan, London, for evidence in the UK.

26 Bouygues moved from construction into media and mobile telephones in the 1990s.

27 Developed from Galbraith, J R (1987) 'Strategy and organisation planning', *Human Resource Management*, Spring–Summer. Republished in Mintzberg, H and Quinn, J B (1991) Op. cit., pp315–24.

28 References for second part of Cisco Systems Case: Annual Report and Accounts for 2001, 2002, 2003 and 2004, especially the chief executive's comments. See also an article in *Business Week*, 24 November 2003.

29 Gilbert, X and Strebel, P (1989) 'From innovation to outpacing', *Business Quarterly*, Summer, 54, pp19–22. Reprinted in De Wit, B and Meyer, R (1994) Op. cit.

30 Mintzberg, H (1991) 'The innovative organisation', Ch13 in Mintzberg, H and Quinn, J B (1991) Op. cit., pp731–46.

31 Kanter, R M (1985) *The Changemasters*, Unwin, London, p146.

32 Kanter, R M (1985) Ibid, p205.

33 Kanter, R M (1985) Ibid, p237.

34 Kanter, R M (1985) Ibid, pp361–2.

35 Galbraith, J and Kazanjian, R (1986) Op. cit. Chapter 6 contains a thoughtful review of the evidence.

36 Hunger, J and Wheelen, T (1993) *Strategic Management*, 4th edn, Addison Wesley, Reading, MA, Ch9.

37 Perlmutter, H V (1969) 'The tortuous evolution of the multinational corporation', *Columbia Journal of World Business*, 4(1), pp9–18.

38 ABB Case study references: Ghoshal, S and Bartlett, C (1995) 'Changing the role of top management: beyond structure to process', *Harvard Business Review*, Jan–Feb; *Financial Times*, 15 Nov 1989; 21 Mar 1990, p27; 5 Apr, 1991, p11; 15 Nov 1991; 20 Aug 1993, p15; 25 Aug 1993, p19; 15 Mar 1994, p32; 12 Aug 1994, p17; 18 Aug 1994, p18; 13 Aug 1998, p27; 24 Aug 1998, p8; 24 March 1999, p26; 1 March 2000, p28; 26 October 2000, p28; 30 October 2000, p16; 12 January 2001, p24 (Lex) and p29; 18 January 2001, p13; 25 April 2001, p24 (Lex); 25 July 2001, p28; 19 September 2001, p30; 25 October 2001, p28; 22 November 2001, p22 (Lex) and p28; 23 November 2001, p28; 31 January 2002, p30; 14 February 2002, p30; 21 February 2002, p29; *ABB Annual Report and Accounts*, 1993, 1994 and 2001; video interview with Percy Barnevik on Tom Peter's 1993 video film: *Crazy Times Call for Crazy Organisations*. *See* also reference 17 above and the interview with Mr Barnevik.

Chapter 17
Resource allocation, strategic planning and control

- What is the process of implementation?
- How are tasks and objectives set?
- How are resources allocated?
- How is strategic planning conducted and what is its influence on strategy?
- How is strategy controlled?
- What is the role of information processing and systems?

Chapter 18
Government, public sector and not-for-profit strategies

- What are the main strategy principles in this sector?
- How do such strategies differ when profit is no longer the major part of the objective?
- Is it possible to use the concepts developed for business strategy? Or do they need to be modified?
- What are the implications for strategy implementation?

Chapter 19
International expansion and globalisation strategies

- What is meant by international expansion and globalisation? How are they implemented?
- What are the main theories involved and how do they relate to individual countries and companies?
- What are the benefits and problems of company globalisation strategy?

Chapter 20
The dynamics of strategy development and entrepreneurial growth

- What is the relationship between an organisation's changing purpose and the dynamics of its strategy?
- How do the various elements of strategy interact?
- What are the implications of strategy dynamics for entrepreneurs?

Chapter 21
Managing strategic change

- Why do people resist strategic change?
- What are the main principles involved in strategic change?
- How can we devise a programme to manage such change?

Chapter 22
Building a cohesive corporate strategy

- How can the various elements of strategy be brought together?
- How are relationships changing between stakeholders?
- How is strategic management changing?

Part 6

THE IMPLEMENTATION PROCESS

This part of the book addresses implementation – the process by which the organisation's chosen strategies are put into operation. It may involve planning new activities, developing an organisational structure to undertake them and considering how to persuade stakeholders that their best interests will be served by undertaking the strategy.

However, empirical research has shown that the implementation process itself may influence the organisation's strategy. In other words, the distinction between the implementation process and the strategy choice may be overstated. Nevertheless, many organisations consider planning and control separately from the generation of strategy, while also recognising the interaction between the two. These issues are fully explored in the following chapters.

In addition, some special areas of strategy are explored in three chapters: strategy in government and not-for-profit organisations, international and global strategy and the dynamics of strategy. The issues explored include implementation, but range more broadly through the special situations described.

The prescriptive strategic process

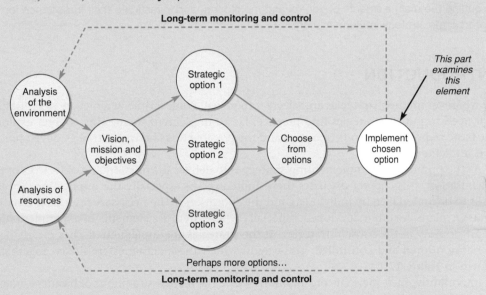

The emergent strategic process

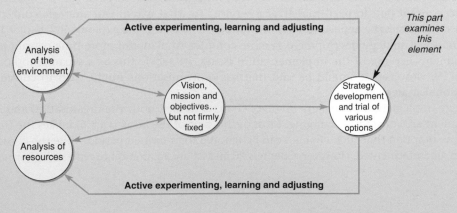

Chapter 17

RESOURCE ALLOCATION, STRATEGIC PLANNING AND CONTROL

Learning outcomes

When you have worked through this chapter, you will be able to:

- outline the nature and limitations of the implementation process;
- identify the interrelationships between strategy and implementation;
- understand the way that the objectives, tasks and timing are implemented;
- describe how resources are allocated between parts of the organisation;
- explore how strategic planning can be conducted and critically evaluate its merits;
- outline the main elements of control and monitoring, and investigate their importance for corporate strategy implementation.

INTRODUCTION

By whatever method strategies are selected, there will come a time when every organisation will need to put its strategies into practice, i.e. to implement them. This chapter explores the basic steps involved in this process and the possible links between strategy development and implementation.

As the prime aim in implementing strategy is to deliver the mission and objectives of the organisation, this chapter discusses these and considers especially the implications for the tasks to be undertaken by individuals and the allocation of the necessary resources. Detailed strategic plans are often developed, especially where there are elements of experimentation or uncertainty in the chosen strategies. As the strategies are implemented, they clearly need to be monitored and controlled. The way in which these activities are linked together is shown in Figure 17.1.

Importantly, there are some organisations where the main assumptions of business strategy may not apply. Governments undertake strategy, but they do not have to deliver a profit. Other public sector bodies like hospitals and the police deliver a service but do not directly compete against each other. In addition, not-for-profit institutions like charities do not have to deliver a profit but do need to deliver a service. To what extent can strategic concepts developed in business be applied to such institutions? These areas are explored in Chapter 18.

International strategy development is more complex to plan and more time-consuming to implement. Because of the implementation issues, we tackle this as a separate topic in Chapter 19. However, it should be said that some organisations might wish to consider international strategy earlier.

Strategy implementation usually involves change. In fact, both the organisation and its environment are constantly changing. Most of this part of the book (Part 6) makes the simplifying assumption that such changes can be ignored for a limited period while the chosen strategies are implemented. However, Chapters 20 and 21 are an attempt to redress the balance.

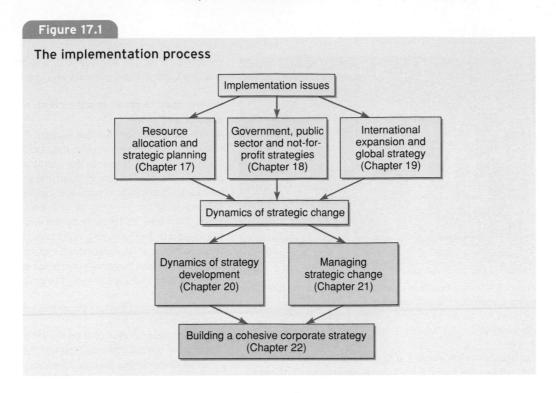

Figure 17.1

The implementation process

Chapter 20 explores the dynamics of change on the purpose, resources and environment of the organisation. In particular, it examines the way that the dynamics interact with the concept of implementation itself. It also explores entrepreneurial strategies.

Chapter 21 concentrates on the *people aspects* of change, such as change in responsibilities, work practices and the balance of power. *Strategic change* can be either a major opportunity or a significant threat to the people in the organisation and therefore to the implementation of strategy itself. To some extent, change can be managed positively to achieve the desired implementation.

Chapter 22 then briefly explores some areas of modern strategic activity that form part of the implementation process and contribute also to current strategic debate. In particular, it attempts to draw together the various strands of strategy development and implementation.

CASE STUDY 17.1

European football:* viable strategy badly implemented? Or does the whole strategy need a rethink?

Many of Europe's leading football clubs are in financial trouble as a result of changes in the way that football strategy has developed over the last 20 years. Yet the money pouring into the leading football clubs has soared over the same time. This case explores the strategic issues.

There are real difficulties across European football: for example, the famous Italian club Lazio, the 2002 European Championship Spanish club Real Madrid and the top English club Leeds United have all reported significant losses in recent years. Even clubs like Manchester United had a poor season for profits in the year ended 2004. Beyond the leading clubs,

---

* Readers in North America and parts of Asia need to know that football is what you might call 'soccer'. It has many of the same strategic issues as American baseball teams like Seattle Mariners and Canada's Toronto Blue Jays and American Football teams like Pittsburgh Steelers and Miami Dolphins – stars paid vast sums, strong competition between clubs and private sector finance that never seems to be sufficient.

▶

▶ **CASE STUDY 17.1 continued**

Football strategy has been revolutionised by the considerable sums earned from television rights and, in the case of Chelsea FC, by sums from its wealthy owner – Mr Roman Abramovich.

the situation is far worse – at the time of writing, some 30–40 English League football clubs have either gone into administration or are threatened with financial difficulty.

What is the basic strategic problem?

Even wealthy football clubs, like Manchester United, have to watch their profits carefully. But from a strategy perspective, they cannot survive by themselves – they need other clubs to make up a league to play against. Moreover, such a league must inevitably have winners and losers if the game is to be interesting. This means that clubs will go through periods when they achieve success and then periods when success may be more elusive. Arsenal were English League Champions in 2004 but were beaten by Chelsea in 2005. During the losing periods, strategic game theory can be used to show that this is likely to have financial consequences.

If this is correct then it follows that football clubs will always face strategic uncertainty. But does it mean that the losing clubs will always make losses and can never recover the situation? For example, the English League club Bradford City was relegated from the Premiership in 2001. In the following football year 2001/02, Bradford lost revenue from television and other sources amounting to around US$45 million and simply could not cut its costs fast enough. Its alternative strategy was to fund the loss from its bank for one year, hope that it would gain promotion in the season ending in 2002 and then pull in the funds again. In practice, it ended up filing for administration in May 2002 with the prospect that this proud club could totally disappear. The club then went on to survive – at least in the short term – but it was still in financial difficulties. More generally, other clubs faced similar financial difficulties, not only in the UK but across Europe.

Is this endemic to football strategy across Europe at the present time? Or just a feature of a few foolish clubs who have not realised that any strategy needs to be implemented

carefully? To explore this question, it is useful to explore the way that football clubs generate and use their funds.

Where does football money come from and where does it go?

Across Europe's main football leagues, the sources of funds will vary, depending on whether the club has a rich patron like Chelsea; whether it is famous like InterMilan and has a loyal fan base; the extent of television deals and the size of the league: for example, the Belgian league is inevitably smaller than the Bundesliga or UK Premiership and therefore generates less funds. Even after its takeover by the American Glazer family, Manchester United has strong obligations to the banks that have financed the deal; Real Madrid is a mutual company owned by its 50,000 fans and therefore not able to raise funds in the same way. However, there are broadly five main sources of funds:

1 *Gate money*: typically, this makes up 10–15 per cent of a club's total income.
2 *Transfer fees*: these could be anything between 10 and 40 per cent of total income. Some of the smaller clubs have survived by selling players. Even large clubs can benefit: Italy's Juventus sold Zinedine Zidane for US$70 million in 2001 to Real Madrid and Filippo Inzaghi to AC Milan for US$25 million. (And then the money was promptly spent on Pavel Nedved from Lazio, Lilian Thuram from Parma and Gianluigi Buffon from Parma.)
3 *Television rights*: typically, these could account for up to 40 per cent of total income for some leading clubs but much less for the smaller clubs. For example, BSkyB spent US$1.8 billion buying the rights to three years of live games in the English Premiership – shared equally between the clubs that survive each year. The Italian Serie A television rights for three years cost around US$450 million in 2001. It is widely believed that such television payments across Europe will be lower in the future.
4 *Merchandising and sponsorship*: typically, this could be worth around 10–20 per cent of total income for many clubs. Clearly, the most famous clubs are able to negotiate much larger deals.
5 *Wealthy owners*: these could be responsible for anything from zero to 80 per cent of total income. For example, the Agnelli family (who control Fiat cars) have ploughed well in excess of US$100 million into Juventus over the years and Mohamed Al Fayed (who owns the London department store Harrods) has invested some US$90 million into the English league club Fulham in recent years.

Where is the money spent? Apart from administration and management, there are obvious costs like football training and medical fees, hotel accommodation costs and travel costs. Some funds are also taken by the national and European leagues to invest and develop the game. But the majority of the funds go in players' wages – for instance, David Beckham's 2002 contract pays him nearly US$7 million per year for three years. With a typical squad of some 40 players, the leading clubs can easily spend most – perhaps all – of their income in this area. It might be argued that Beckham and his colleagues are overpaid, but his wages can be justified by the concept of economic rent – *see* Chapter 6.

How will the strategy change?

Nothing stands still in strategy, including football. Already, Juventus and Real Madrid have negotiated individual broadcasting deals for their games, rather than negotiate as part of their respective national football leagues. This means that individually these clubs earn more than the others in the same league and are beginning to pull away from the others in their respective leagues. By 2005, these two clubs were actually earning more than Manchester United, which remained part of

the English Premier League collective television contract. But the issue still hinged on what would happen to the funds generated by such deals and whether such funds could continue to rise indefinitely. European football was moving into a new era of funding without having resolved some basic issues.

Case question

Is this a problem of the correct strategy – finances and costs essentially sound but the implementation – players' wages and so on – needing some adjustment? Or does the strategy itself need to be changed in the face of fundamental problems across European football?

17.1 THE IMPLEMENTATION PROCESS

17.1.1 Basic elements of the implementation process

Whether the organisation faces the strategic problems of European football or the opportunities of new technologies such as the internet, it will have to draw up plans to carry out its strategies. Essentially, these implementation issues need to address the following questions:

- What activities need to be undertaken in order to achieve the agreed objectives?
- What is the timescale for the implementation of these plans?
- How will progress be monitored and controlled?

To turn general strategies into specific implementation plans involves four basic elements:[2]

1. *Identification of general strategic objectives* – specifying the general results expected from the strategy initiatives;
2. *Formulation of specific plans* – taking the general objectives and turning them into specific tasks and deadlines (these are often cross-functional);
3. *Resource allocation and budgeting* – indicating how the plans are to be paid for (this quantifies the plans and permits integration across functions);
4. *Monitoring and control procedures* – ensuring that the objectives are being met, that only the agreed resources are spent and that budgets are adhered to. Importantly, monitoring also takes place against the projections on which the strategies are based – for example, national economic change and competitive activity.

The relationship between these activities is shown in Figure 17.2.

17.1.2 Types of basic implementation programme

Implementation programmes will vary according to the nature of the strategic problems which the organisation faces. These problems will range from the extreme and urgent need for change, such as at a bankrupt European football club, to the more ongoing strategic development processes of Canon or Nestlé (described in the case studies later in this chapter). The two essential causes of variation in implementation programmes are:[3]

1. the degree of uncertainty in predicting changes in the environment;
2. the size of the strategic change required.

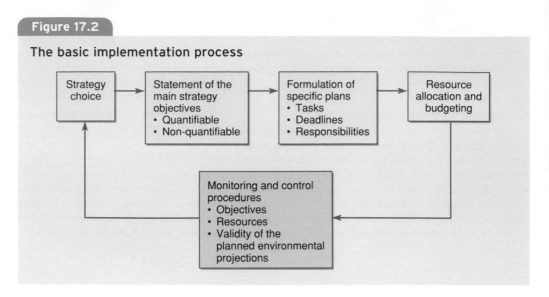

Figure 17.2

The basic implementation process

In response to these issues, several types of basic implementation programme can be carried out. At one extreme, there is the *comprehensive implementation programme* for fundamental changes in strategic direction. At the other extreme, there is the *incremental implementation programme*, where implementation is characterised by small changes and short time spans within the general direction implied by the strategy. Both these approaches have their difficulties, so a compromise may be chosen in practice: the *selective implementation programme*.

● *Comprehensive implementation programmes* are employed when the organisation has made a clear-cut, major change in strategic direction, as in the crisis faced by bankrupt European football clubs at the beginning of this chapter. Other reasons might include a new competitive or new technological opportunity. Implementation then becomes a matter of driving through the new strategies, regardless of changes in the environment and the reactions of those affected. Close co-ordination across the organisation is usually essential for success.

● *Incremental implementation programmes* may be used where there are conditions of great uncertainty – for example, rapidly changing markets or the unknown results of R&D. As a result, timetables, tasks and even objectives are all likely to change, depending on the outcome of current activities. Important strategic areas may be left deliberately unclear until the outcome of current events has been established.[4] Essentially, the uncertainty is handled by a flexible strategic approach.

● *Selective implementation programmes* may be used where neither of the above represents the optimal way forward. Comprehensive programmes involving radical change may require such fundamental changes that they encounter substantial resistance, such as negative reactions from fans to the collapse of their favourite European football club. Incremental programmes may be inappropriate when it is necessary to make a significant change that needs the impetus generated by a single, large step. Selective programmes represent the compromise required: a major programme developed in selective areas only.

Readers will recognise that the above two extremes are related to the prescriptive and emergent strategic approaches explored throughout this book.

To determine the type of implementation programme required, the following three criteria can be employed:

1 Are clear and substantial advantages to be delivered in a specific area, e.g. investment in a new drug that will provide competitive advantage?

2 Are there large increments that cannot be subdivided, e.g. a new factory with long lead times for construction?

3 Is it important to protect some future step that may be required but cannot be fully justified on the basis of current evidence, e.g. an investment in a new distribution facility that will be needed if development programmes proceed according to plan?

For many organisations, it is useful to draw a basic distinction between:[5]

- *ongoing, existing activities* with higher certainty and more predictable strategic change, barring a major cataclysm;
- *new activities* with higher uncertainty and possibly major strategic change.

17.1.3 Implementation in small and medium-sized businesses

The basic elements of the implementation process – the identification of general strategic objectives; the formulation of specific plans; resource allocation and budgeting; monitoring and control procedures – are equally applicable to smaller organisations. All organisations need to specify the tasks to be undertaken and monitor progress. Moreover, choosing the correct type of implementation programme – comprehensive, incremental or selective – according to the nature of the problem and the particular environment of the organisation is also important to small and medium-sized businesses. Indeed, any small or medium-sized business that attempts to obtain finance for a new venture will be asked to supply the essential information outlined above. Banks and other lending institutions no longer rely on vague promises and good intentions.

Key strategic principles

- Implementation covers the activities required for an organisation to put its strategies into practice. There are several basic elements to this process: general objectives, specific plans and the necessary finances, coupled with a monitoring and control system to ensure compliance.

- Within the implementation process, it is useful to draw a distinction between different types of implementation. There are three major approaches: comprehensive, incremental and selective.

- Implementation in small and medium-sized businesses may be less elaborate but needs to follow the same general principles.

17.2 RELATIONSHIP BETWEEN IMPLEMENTATION AND THE STRATEGY DEVELOPMENT PROCESS

Although many strategy researchers and writers have fully supported implementation as a separate stage after strategy choice,[6] over the last 20 years others have expressed significant and well-founded doubts. Their concerns have been based on empirical research into the way that strategy actually develops.

In the light of this research, it is important to view the basic implementation process as a series of steps over time, with complex learning and feedback mechanisms between implementation and strategy. This does not mean that Section 17.1 on basic implementation is incorrect; it does mean that implementation needs to be seen as a process over time that may well alter strategy. Consequently, it may even alter the organisation's vision and purpose.

The main areas of research that contributed to this alternative view of the implementation process were:

- the empirical research of Pettigrew and Whipp;
- the concepts of bounded rationality and minimum intervention;
- the Balanced Scorecard of Kaplan and Norton;
- the work of emergent theorists, such as Quinn and Senge.

17.2.1 The empirical research of Pettigrew and Whipp

In a series of research studies between 1985 and 1990, the UK-based researchers Pettigrew and Whipp analysed how strategic change occurred in four sectors of UK industry.[7] Their evidence did not extend beyond the UK but their conclusions are likely to be applicable to other geographic areas. They suggested that strategic change can most usefully be seen as a *continuous* process, rather than one with distinct stages, such as the formulation of strategy and then its implementation. In this sense, they argued that strategy was not a linear movement with discrete stages but an experimental, iterative process where the outcomes of each stage were uncertain. A first small step might be actioned and then the strategy itself adjusted, depending on the outcome of the actions.

Comment

The empirical evidence to support this view is significant. The description of the continuous process is similar to, but not necessarily the same as, the incremental implementation programme described in Section 17.1.2. According to this interpretation, strategy implementation at bankrupt European football clubs outlined in Case study 17.1 might have been better served by a series of separate smaller actions, conducted on an experimental basis, rather than one major restructuring announcement. Chapter 21 will explore further the research of Pettigrew and Whipp.

17.2.2 Bounded rationality and minimum intervention

In exploring how managers develop their implementation plans, the strategists Hrebiniak and Joyce[8] have suggested that the implementation process is governed by two principles: bounded rationality and minimum intervention.

- *Bounded rationality* derives from the work of researchers Cyert and March (*see* Chapters 2 and 7). They showed that managers in practice have difficulty in considering every conceivable option. They therefore reduce their logical choices to a more limited, 'bounded' choice. Arguing in a similar way, Hrebiniak and Joyce suggest that implementation is also likely to be limited: managers will act in a rational way but will reduce the overall task to a series of small steps in order to make it more manageable. Thus the strategic goals and implementation are likely to be split into a series of smaller tasks that can be more easily handled but may not be optimal.

In addition, the authors suggest that *individuals* will make rational decisions but will include in this process their *personal* goals which are not necessarily the same as those of the organisation itself. Implementation needs to ensure that there is consistency between personal and organisational goals.

- *Minimum intervention* has been summarised by the authors as follows:

  In implementing strategy, managers should change only what is necessary and sufficient to produce an enduring solution to the strategic problem being addressed.

Practising managers might recognise this principle as the rather more basic sentence: 'If it ain't broke, don't fix it.' The implication here is that implementation may be constrained by the need to consider the impact on the strategy itself.

Comment

Both approaches represent useful, if somewhat simple, guidance on strategy implementation. They suggest that implementation, strategy and goals are interrelated, which needs to be taken into account in the development of implementation plans.

17.2.3 The Balanced Scorecard: the contribution of Kaplan and Norton

Definition ➤ The Balanced Scorecard uses strategic and financial measures to assess the outcome of a chosen strategy. It acknowledges the different expectations of the various stakeholders and it attempts to use a 'scorecard' based on four prime areas of business activity to measure the results of the selected strategy.

During the course of researching and implementing strategy at a number of US corporations in the early 1990s, Professor Robert Kaplan of the Harvard Business School and David Norton of the international strategy consultants Renaissance Solutions developed the *Balanced Scorecard*. 'The scorecard is not a way of formulating strategy. It is a way of understanding and checking what you have to do throughout the organisation to make your strategy work.'[9]

The Balanced Scorecard arose from their perceptions about two significant deficiencies in the implementation of many corporate strategic plans:

1 *Measurement gap.* Although most companies measure performance ratios, quality and productivity, these are mainly focused on historical figures – for example, 'How are we doing, compared with last year?' The two authors discovered that such measures may have little to do with future success. In addition, although such ratios were important, they did not measure other important aspects of future strategy, especially those that were more difficult to quantify. For example, future strategy might stress the importance of customer satisfaction and loyalty, employee commitment and organisational learning, but none of these might be measured.

2 *Strategy gap between general plans and managerial actions.* The authors claimed that many companies began major new strategic initiatives but that these often had little impact on the organisation. The reason was that the strategic plans were often not translated into measures that managers and employees could understand and use in their daily work.

Kaplan and Norton were particularly keen to move beyond the normal financial ratio data such as return on capital employed and earnings per share. They claimed that these are essentially functional measures and that what really matters in strategy implementation is the process: 'Processes have replaced (or are replacing) departments and functions.'[10] They identified three main types of process that are important:

1 *management* – how the leader runs the organisation, how decisions are made and how they are implemented;

2 *business* – how products are designed, orders fulfilled, customer satisfaction achieved and so on;

3 *work* – how work is operationalised, purchased, stored, manufactured and so on.

They argued that these are the activities that implement the agreed strategies but they are not the same as return on capital, market share and growth data and the other measures that often summarise the outcome of a corporate strategy.

Kaplan and Norton developed the Balanced Scorecard to overcome these problems.[11] The Balanced Scorecard combines quantitative and qualitative measures of the selected strategy. It acknowledges the different expectations of the various stakeholders and it attempts to link scorecard performance measures to the chosen strategy. There are four key principles behind the scorecard:

1 *translating the vision* through clarifying and gaining consensus;

2 *communicating and linking* by setting goals and establishing rewards for success;

3 *business planning* to align objectives, allocate resources and establish milestones;

4 *feedback and learning* to review the subsequent performance against the plan.

While recognising that every strategy is unique, they then identified four strategy perspectives that need to appear on every scorecard. These are summarised in Exhibit 17.1. The four areas are:

1 *Financial perspective.* This translates the purpose of the organisation into action through clarifying precisely what is wanted and gaining commitment to it. For example, if the survival of the business is important, then cash flow features prominently on the scorecard.

2 *Customer perspective.* Purpose needs to be seen in the context of customer-oriented strategy. This should include not only market share data but also areas explored in Chapter 5, such as customer retention, customer profitability measures and customer satisfaction. For example, if the strategy highlights the introduction of a new product, then the scorecard might go beyond sales and share data to explore the extent of customer satisfaction and repeat business.

3 *Internal perspective.* This concerns internal performance measures related to productivity, capital investment against cost savings achieved, labour productivity improvements and other factors that will indicate the way that the organisation was undertaking the strategy inside the company. This might also involve setting internal strategy targets and establishing milestones for the implementation of the strategy. For example, the development of a new website will involve not only the customer satisfaction mentioned above but also registration of the web page, design of the site, maintenance of the site – all of these elements might be specified and targeted with dates and costs.

4 *Innovation and learning perspective.* This provides feedback and learning through strategy reviews and sharing comments on the outcome of events. It has the effect of highlighting the importance of communicating and linking people with the purpose through education, goal setting and rewards for achieving the required performance. For example, the achievement of a market share objective might be accompanied by a review of what was done well and what could be improved next time.

Exhibit 17.1

Balanced Scorecard: summary of strategy perspectives

Strategy perspective	Example	Example of scorecard measure – called a Key Performance Indicator (KPI)
Financial perspective	Shareholders' views of performance	• Return on capital • Economic value added • Sales growth • Cost reduction
Customer perspective	Customer satisfaction	• Customer satisfaction • Customer retention • Acquisition of new customers
Internal perspective	Assess quality of people and processes	• Manufacturing cost • Job turnover • Product quality • Stock turnover and inventory management
Future perspective	Examine how an organisation learns and grows	• New product development record • R&D core competencies • Employee retention • Employee profitability

These four strategy perspectives are then translated into Key Performance Indicators – called KPIs for short – for each of the areas as shown in the right-hand column of Exhibit 17.1. The KPIs are numerical measures of the target that will deliver the organisation's objectives from that particular perspective. There are therefore four steps, of which the KPI is the second, which we can examine with reference to a football club like the famous English soccer club, Manchester United (ManU) from Case 17.1. Readers in other countries and followers of other sports can easily substitute their own favourite sports teams and individual sports stars for the example that follows.

1 *Step 1*: Take a *strategy objective* from the ManU strategic plan – for example, let us assume that a strategic objective is to raise the profitability of the club. ManU had low profitability in 2005 – it spent a large sum on the young, talented footballer Wayne Rooney and was not sufficiently successful in the European Football Championship. Its takeover by the Glazer family in 2005 has only increased the pressure to raise its profitability.

2 *Step 2*: Decide how the company is going to *measure* this particular objective – for example, the ManU profitability might be measured by the club's ability to deliver a return on capital that exceeds its cost of capital. A specific measure needs to be agreed – this measure is called the KPI in the Balanced Scorecard. Note that KPI measures are often relatively easy for the *financial* part of the Balanced Scorecard but much more difficult to define in other areas – for example, how do you agree a KPI for 'customer satisfaction' or 'innovation processes' at Manchester United Football Club?

3 *Step 3*: Translate this specific measure into a specific *numerical target* for the next period of the strategic plan – for example, ManU does not publish figures for its cost of capital, but let us assume that it is currently 7 per cent. The numerical target might be to achieve a return on capital of 8 per cent (versus the 7 per cent cost of capital).

4 *Step 4*: Generate some specific *initiatives* to achieve this numerical target.

Setting out the steps in this way raises many implementation issues that need in practice to be resolved. Taking each step in turn, *Step 1* is valuable in that it links the strategic plan with the implementation actions of the company. But there will be other objectives as well as a profitability objective and it will require some judgement to strike a balance between them.

The KPI identified in *Step 2* then becomes important because it will indicate whether Step 1 has been achieved. The scorecard will return to the KPI at various times throughout the life of the strategic plan to judge whether it has been achieved. There are a whole range of issues here: for example, there may be more than one way of measuring the objective and the KPI itself may represent a distortion of the underpinning strategy from Step 1. Careful thought therefore is needed but the KPI has the great merit that it takes the strategic plan into the realm of what can be measured and controlled.

Step 3 takes the KPI and translates this into targets for the coming period of the strategic plan. Such targets require considerable judgement in practice and the Balanced Scorecard offers no substantive guidance on such matters – readers are referred back to the discussion on objective setting in Chapter 12 for some insights into this difficult area.

Step 4 is easy to summarise but more difficult to achieve in reality for two reasons. The first is that not all strategic initiatives will be successful, so judgement will be involved. The second reason is that each initiative is likely to have a cost that needs to be set against the likelihood and benefits of achievement. To take an extreme example, ManU might choose to achieve the financial KPI by copying the Chelsea Football Club strategy 2002–2004. This consisted of Chelsea buying every expensive, highly skilled football player that becomes available in the world. This would certainly be an initiative, but the cost might be beyond the financial reach of ManU, which has became a heavily indebted private company without the private financial resources of Chelsea's owner, Roman Abramovich. In addition, such an initiative might carry unacceptable levels of risk, especially in the uncertain world of sport and football.

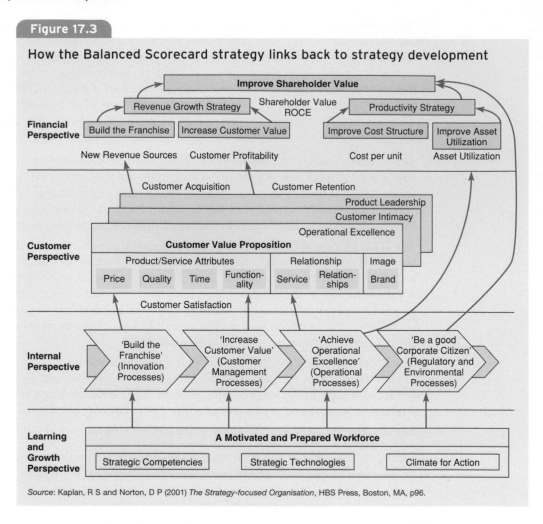

Figure 17.3

How the Balanced Scorecard strategy links back to strategy development

Source: Kaplan, R S and Norton, D P (2001) *The Strategy-focused Organisation*, HBS Press, Boston, MA, p96.

Importantly, the Balanced Scorecard does not have just one KPI. Typically, there may be 20 KPIs for each organisation, possibly more. Each KPI in each of the main areas – financial, customer, internal and learning – needs to be identified from the strategy, measured, targeted and the initiatives identified. This is a substantial task for any organisation but some have found it beneficial.

The real benefit of the Balanced Scorecard is that it provides a link between strategy and implementation. Kaplan and Norton argue that the final purpose of any strategy is to increase value to the shareholders of the organisation – a form of shareholder value added explored in Chapter 8. This is reflected in the way that the two writers have presented their approach, linking all the elements back to 'improve shareholder value' – *see* Figure 17.3. The four strategy perspectives shown in Figure 17.3 are linked with possible examples of the areas that might be chosen as KPIs for a particular company.

Comment

With reference to Figure 17.3, some strategists will disagree that the definition of purpose is mainly to 'improve shareholder value'. Moreover, we have seen that the Balanced Scorecard is complex to manage and some KPIs are difficult to define in practice.

In addition, some of these areas represent nothing new: educating, obtaining feedback, setting targets and milestones have been known for many years. Furthermore, as Norton himself has acknowledged, the danger of the scorecard is that it lays strong emphasis on what is measurable, which is not necessarily what is important strategically, rather than on gaining commitment and action. The scorecard may also lead to excessive measurement in larger companies, turning the whole process into a bureaucratic nightmare. However, the scorecard does represent a useful attempt in two major areas:

1 translating the abstract vision of strategic purpose into practical and useful action areas;

2 moving the strategy beyond a few overly simple measures such as earnings per share and return on capital employed.

For these reasons, it is worthy of serious exploration in many organisations.

17.2.4 Further emergent approaches to implementation

In Chapter 15, the work of Quinn, Senge and others on the strategy process was examined. They suggest quite clearly that implementation needs to be considered not just as a single event with fixed and rigid plans but rather as a series of implementation activities whose outcome will shape and guide the strategy. The full strategy will not be 'known' in advance but will 'emerge' out of the implementation.

This work has been complemented by that of Pettigrew and Whipp[12] who concluded that there were three interlinking aspects to strategic change:

1 *Analytical aspects*. Implementation must involve many aspects of the organisation. These are the areas that have been emphasised in various strategic models and frameworks and are explored in Parts 2 and 3 of the book.

2 *Educational aspects*. 'The new knowledge and insights into a given strategy that arise from its implementation have to be captured, retained and diffused within the organisation' (Pettigrew and Whipp). Thus implementation cannot be regarded as immutable and unchanging. The organisation will learn about its strategies as it implements them.

3 *Political aspects*. 'The very prospect of change confronts established positions. Both formulation and implementation inevitably raise questions of power within the organisation. Left unattended, such forces can provide obstacles to change . . . Indeed, in the case of Jaguar [Cars] in the 1970s, ultimately such forces can wreak havoc' (Pettigrew and Whipp).

Comment

Educational and political aspects (examined further in Chapter 21) are important elements of the implementation process and again suggest that implementation and strategy formulation are interlinked. The three emergent perspectives that ask for implementation are summarised in Exhibit 17.2.

Exhibit 17.2

Three emergent perspectives on the implementation process

1 Implementation must involve many parts of the organisation.

2 Implementation needs to be seen as an ongoing activity rather than one major event with a finite outcome.

3 Implementation needs to be flexible and responsive to outside and internal pressures.

Key strategic principles

- According to Pettigrew and Whipp, implementation is best seen as a continuous process, rather than one that simply occurs after the formulation of the strategy.

- Hrebiniak and Joyce placed boundaries on implementation in terms of the ability of managers to consider every choice rationally and to evaluate the impact of implementation on strategy itself.

▶

Key strategic principles *continued*

- Emergent approaches to strategy imply that implementation needs to be considered not just as a single event but rather as a series of activities, the outcome of which may to some extent shape the strategy.

- The Balanced Scorecard was developed as a method of translating abstract strategy into specific areas of company action to help strategy to work. The Balanced Scorecard combines quantitative and qualitative measures of the selected strategy. It acknowledges the different expectations of the various stakeholders and it attempts to link scorecard performance measures to the chosen strategy.

- There are four key principles behind the scorecard: translating the vision through clarifying and gaining consensus; communicating and linking by setting goals and establishing rewards for success; business planning to align objectives, allocate resources and establish milestones; feedback and learning to review the subsequent performance against the plan.

- The four strategy perspectives that appear on every scorecard are: financial, customer, internal, future. These are translated using four steps – strategy objectives, setting targets, identifying measurement criteria and developing strategy initiatives – that are summarised as Key Performance Indicators (KPIs).

- The main benefits lie in the focus of the scorecard on turning strategy into implementation and the development of objectives that go beyond simple financial measures.

CASE STUDY 17.2

Strategic planning at Canon with a co-operative corporate style

Since 1957, the Japanese company Canon has operated strategic planning. However, it has not been a rigid, inflexible process imposed by top management. Instead, it has been a free-flowing, open approach, driven by the strategic vision of Canon's senior and other managers. This vision covered the values of the company, the market position it expected to hold over many years and the resources needed to develop and sustain it. The strategies and their implementation have proved highly successful. This case study examines the planning process in more detail.

Canon's sales have grown from Y4.2 billion in 1950 to Y3,468 billion in 2004 (US$26 billion). The company has developed a strong market share in its leading products: for example, 70 per cent of the world laser beam printer engine market, 40 per cent of the world bubble jet printer market, second only to Hewlett-Packard. Overall, it has a strong global base in its major product areas: photocopiers, computer peripherals, computer and fax equipment, cameras, video recorders and optical products. The main business areas are shown in Figure 17.4. In terms of profitability, Canon has excellent ten-year record, which is shown in Figure 17.5.

As an example of its strategic vision, Canon identified the world photocopying market back in the 1960s as an area for growth. Xerox Corporation (US) had been the world leader since the 1950s, with its exclusive, patented technology. However, this did not stop Canon declaring its intention in 1967 of taking 30 per cent of the world market by the 1980s and its vision 'to catch Xerox through technological differentiation'.

Canon EOS 20Da Digital SLR Camera.
Courtesy of Canon (UK) Limited.

The patented optical and miniaturisation core competencies employed in Canon cameras have underpinned the company's strategic planning for many years.

Figure 17.4

The main areas of Canon's business

(a) Revenue by product area 2004

- 32% — Business machines: office imaging
- Business machines: computer peripherals
- Business machines: information products
- Cameras
- Optical and other products

9%, 32%, 34%, 3%, 22%

(b) Revenue by region 2004

13%, 25%, 31%, 31%

- Japan
- Americas
- Europe
- Other

Source: Annual Report and Accounts 2004.

Figure 17.5

Ten year record of Canon Inc

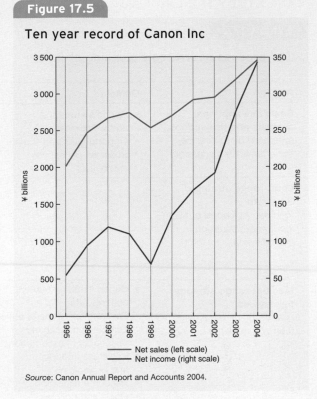

Net sales (left scale)
Net income (right scale)

Source: Canon Annual Report and Accounts 2004.

Through the 1960s and 1970s, it went about this by developing technology that was totally different from the Xerox patents and pursuing the small photocopier market niche, which remained poorly served by Xerox. Today, Canon is world market leader and has developed its core competencies out of photocopiers into laser printers, digital scanners, colour bubble jet printing, digitised optical images and other areas. It will be noted that printing was only one of Canon's areas of competence by the 1990s (*see* Table 17.1).

Strategic planning at Canon, however, is not just a matter of vision and the identification of core competencies.

Exhibit 17.3 outlines the strategic planning process at Canon. It is driven initially by the centre and its strong belief in customer satisfaction. Typical of large Japanese companies, the centre has also defined its main growth plan under the headline 'Excellent Global Corporation Plan'. Some Western companies might find this title vague and lacking in commercial directness, However, the detail from Canon is clear with its focus on 'gaining and maintaining top market shares. At Canon, top share and profitable operations must go hand in hand.' In other words, there is no question of driving for market share at the expense of profits.

Table 17.1

Canon's core competencies and product development

	1950s	1960s	1970s	1980s	1990s
Core competencies	• Optical • Precision mechanical	• Electronics • Fine optical	• Printing • Materials technology • Communications	• As 1970s but more advanced	• Biotechnology • Energy saving
Additional new products	• Still camera • Movie camera • Lenses	• Reflex camera • Calculators	• Copier • Laser printer • Word processing • Fax	• Office automation • Video recorders • Computers	• Audio visual • Energy saving • Information systems • Medical equipment

▶ **CASE STUDY 17.2 continued**

Exhibit 17.3

The process of strategic planning at Canon

Activity	Content		Example in 2004
Basic assumptions, analysis and projections *(prepared by the centre, but after open discussion)*	• Canon's strengths and weaknesses • Opportunities and threats • Business philosophy and beliefs		• Customer satisfaction • Cost reduction • Competitive products
Long-range strategy: Six years *(decided by centre but with input and discussion from division)*		• Vision • Long-term objectives • Key strategic projects	• Maintain No 1 position • World class • Develop global markets • Reduce cost base • Digital cameras • New screen displays and rear projectors
Medium-range strategy: three years *(started by divisions and then consolidated at HQ)*	• Canon itself: resources, cultures, etc. • Environment: general outlook; competition; scenarios if major shift in assumptions • Basic assumptions and projections • Resource allocation • Goals and policies • Contingency • Timetables		• Specific quantified goals developed • Resources include capital projects, human resources and the key strategic projects • Invest in R&D
Short-term plan: one year *(developed by the divisions)*		• Budgeting: financial goals are stressed • Build on the medium-range plan	

Such elements appear regularly in strategic planning in Japanese companies and are employed in order to shape the approach to strategy development in its early stages. They appear in the basic analysis along with the assumptions and projections about the future (as explored in Parts 2 and 3 of this book). In developing its long-range plan, Canon has to be directed and constrained by the distinctive features of its business. It is these characteristics that determine the nature of the strategic planning process at the company:

● *Highly automated manufacturing plant* that takes years to design, install and bring to full efficiency. Planning therefore needs to be developed over a number of years, not just the short term. It also needs to take into account the possibility that new designs will need further work and detailed co-operation from all those working to install them.

● *High-technology products* that take years to develop and perfect, including the possibility of some failures. Planning will again need to be experimental but will also need to be open and not involve criticism of failure to implement a new, experimental product.

● *Synergy and core competencies* that provide linkages across a number of product areas. These take time and resources and rely on strong co-operation across different divisions. Planning will act as co-ordinator and will also direct the divisions towards the areas that have been identified: it is likely to be centralised.

Although the centre sets the long-term strategy, the product divisions begin the *medium-range planning* within the constraints set by the centre. Considerable emphasis is placed on scenarios and contingency planning so that Canon is not caught out by an unexpected event, such as a sudden rise in the value of the yen. These plans are then consolidated by the centre.

For the short-term plan, financial objectives take greater precedence. They are usually prepared as budgets which are derived from the medium-term plan. Each division prepares its budget and these are then consolidated by the centre. From this amalgamation, the corporate HQ then prepares short-term plans on personnel, capital investments and cash flow. The data are also used to build the balance sheet and profit and loss account.

Although this might appear bureaucratic and unwieldy, Canon actually operates the process in an open, friendly and challenging fashion. Employees are encouraged to debate the issues, to take risks and to present new ideas. Strategy planning is regarded as an opportunity and a challenge, rather than a chore driven by hide-bound company rules.

Finally, Canon published some of the main elements of its latest corporate plan in presentations to financial analysts on the web – www.canon.com. These were the objectives for its global corporate plan for the years 2001–2005:

1 Becoming number one in the world in all of Canon's core businesses.
2 Building up the R&D capabilities to continually create new businesses.
3 Achieving a strong financial structure.
4 Fostering employees that are enthusiastically committed to achieving their ideals and take pride in their work.

1 *What are the main problems of large companies such as Canon in managing the strategic planning process?*

2 *How has Canon succeeded in remaining innovative? Could it do even better? If so, how?*

STRATEGIC PROJECT

In strategic terms, Canon was made famous by Hamel and Prahalad for its use of core competencies to develop into new product areas – their book *Competing for the Future* used Canon as an important example. An interesting strategic project would be to follow up Canon's recent progress and test to see just what the company is now doing. The Canon website is quite helpful, with several presentations made to financial analysts that go further than is possible in the case. There is much material for future exploration of this interesting and important company.

17.3 OBJECTIVES, TASK SETTING AND COMMUNICATING THE STRATEGY

It is important to set out and agree clear guidelines with those individuals who will implement the strategies: typically, this process of task setting and communications will cover what is to be done, by what time and with what resources. This is a significant implementation issue and involves five basic questions, which are summarised in Exhibit 17.4.

Exhibit 17.4

Task setting and communications: the basic questions

1 Who developed the strategies that are now being implemented?
2 Who will implement the strategies?
3 What objectives and tasks will they need to accomplish?
4 How can objectives and tasks be handled in fast-changing environments?
5 How will the implementation process be communicated and co-ordinated?

In reality, the answers to these questions will depend primarily on the way that the strategies have been developed. In this sense, the strategy development phase and the strategy implementation phase are interconnected.

17.3.1 Who developed the strategies that are now being implemented?

In the past, some strategy writers have taken the view that the strategies in large corporations will be largely developed at the centre:

Most of the people in the corporate centre who are crucial to successful strategy implementation probably had little, if anything, to do with the development of the corporate strategy.[14]

If this is the case, then the implementation process is very different from one where there has been a lengthy debate and agreement on the strategies. In this latter case, managers will know that they are likely to be responsible for implementing something that was discussed with them some weeks or months earlier. For example, if strategies have been produced using the procedures described in the Canon Case study 17.2, then most managers will be clear on who will be doing what because they will have been closely involved in developing them. Ignorance will be higher and commitment to the new strategy will be lower among those managers who have had no involvement in developing the strategy.

It is important therefore to address the question of who developed the strategy, rather than simply the question of who will implement it. For example, was it just a central team or was there full consultation? The response to this question will shape the implementation process.

17.3.2 Who will implement the strategies?

This question is important because it will define who is responsible for implementing a specific strategy. It is difficult to review progress at a later stage if no one is accountable for the way the strategy is being carried out. In many small companies, it is possible that a number of managers will be involved in the strategy development process because of the small size. The question needs more elaboration as organisations grow in size.

One important issue here is who makes the decision: is it the centre telling the managers or is the matter open for discussion and negotiation? Generally, this book takes the view that discussion is preferable because it is more motivating and rewarding all round. However, it may occasionally be necessary to instruct those involved.

17.3.3 What objectives and tasks will they need to undertake?

In Chapter 12, we examined the concept of the hierarchy of objectives – corporate, divisional and functional – cascading down from the top of the organisation. The main objectives and activities for implementation can also be considered as following a similar process. The overall corporate objectives need to be translated into objectives for each of the main areas of the business and then these objectives need to be reinterpreted into the tasks and action programmes that need to be undertaken in order to achieve them.

Figure 17.6 gives an example in a functional company of how the overall objective is reinterpreted in this way. The corporate objectives are translated into functional objectives that are each designed to make a contribution to the whole. This is not necessarily a simple task and may require several iterations before a satisfactory result is achieved. The marketing, operations and other tasks are defined from the functional objectives. These are then broken down into plans: timetables, resources to achieve the objectives and other matters. Deadlines are usually set to indicate the date for completion of a particular task, as are *milestones* – interim indicators of progress so that those monitoring events can review implementation while there is still time to take remedial action.

In practice, the definition of objectives, tasks and plans may be simpler in smaller companies and more complicated in larger companies. For example, at Canon three sets of objectives and plans are prepared: on six-year, three-year and one-year time-horizons. They do not all have the same degree of detail but they are all fully co-ordinated across the company.

17.3.4 How can objectives and tasks be handled in fast-changing environments?

When environments are changing fast, it may be exceptionally difficult to specify satisfactory objectives and tasks: by the time they have been agreed and communicated, the environment may have changed. As changes occur, the objectives may rapidly become impossible or straightforward, depending on the nature of the changes. In this situation, it makes little sense to adhere to objectives developed for earlier situations. Three guidelines can be applied:

Figure 17.6

An example of translating corporate objectives into tasks in a functional organisation

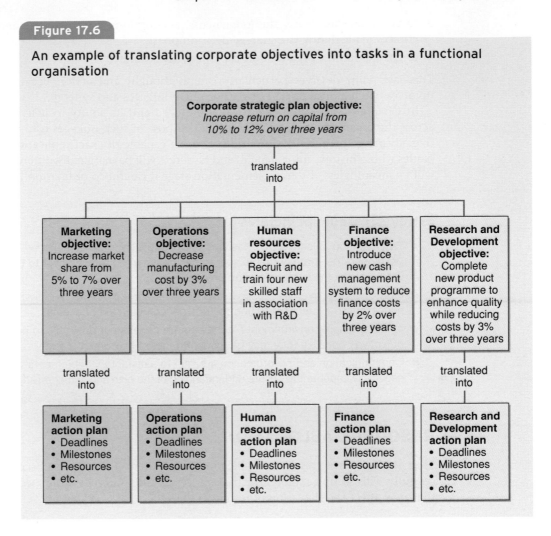

1 flexibility in objectives and tasks within an agreed general vision;

2 empowerment of those closest to the environment changes, so that they can respond quickly;

3 careful and close monitoring by the centre of those reacting to events.

The purpose of such surveillance is to ensure that actions taken do not expose the centre itself to unnecessary strategic or financial risk. This is vital if the organisation wishes to avoid the fate of companies such as Barings Bank in 1995, which crashed with debts of over US$1.5 billion, partly as a result of inadequate controls in such a rapidly changing environment.

17.3.5 How will the implementation process be communicated and co-ordinated?

In small organisations, it may be unnecessary, overcomplex or inappropriate to engage in the elaborate communication of agreed strategies. People who have explored the strategic tasks together during the formulation of the strategy and meet each other on a regular basis may not need lengthy communication during implementation. However, in larger enterprises, it is likely to be essential for four reasons:

1 to ensure that everyone has understood;

2 to allow any confusion or ambiguity to be resolved;

3 to communicate clearly the judgements, assumptions, contingencies and possibly the choices made during the strategy decision phase;[15]

4 to ensure that the organisation is properly co-ordinated.

This last point deserves particularly careful thought and action because co-ordination involves two major strategic areas: value chain linkages and synergy.

In Chapter 6, the value chain was introduced and its ability to deliver *unique linkages* across the organisation was discussed. The purpose of such linkages is to develop competitive advantage because they are unlikely to be capable of exact replication by other companies whose history, competencies and resources will be marginally different. Such linkages will be meaningless at the implementation stage if careful co-ordination is lacking.

> ## Key strategic principles
>
> - When setting objectives and tasks, the first question to be established is that of who developed the strategy that is now to be implemented. The answer to this question will influence the implementation process.
>
> - Individual objectives and tasks follow from the agreed overall objectives. It may be necessary to experiment to find the optimal combination of events.
>
> - In fast-changing environments, it may not be possible or desirable to have rigid objectives because they may be made redundant by outside events.
>
> - Communication and co-ordination are vital to satisfactory implementation. These are especially important to ensure understanding of the plan and its underlying assumptions.

17.4 RESOURCE ALLOCATION

Most strategies need resources to be allocated to them if they are to be implemented successfully. This section explores the basic processes and examines some special circumstances that may affect the allocation of resources.[16]

17.4.1 The resource allocation process

In large, diversified companies, the centre plays a major role in allocating the resources among the various strategies proposed by its operating companies or divisions.[17] In smaller companies, the same mechanism will also operate, although on a more informal basis: product groups, areas of the business or functional areas may still bid for funds to support their strategic proposals.

There are three criteria which can be used when allocating resources.

1 *The contribution of the proposed resources towards the fulfilment of the organisation's mission and objectives.* At the centre of the organisation, the resource allocation task is to steer resources away from areas that are poor at delivering the organisation's objectives and towards those that are good. Readers will recognise this description as being similar to that employed when considering the movement of funds in the BCG *product portfolio matrix* in Chapter 4: in that case, cash was diverted from cash cows towards stars and so on. The principle is similar here but relies on centrally available funds rather than the diversion of funds.

2 *Its support of key strategies.* In many cases, the problem with resource allocation is that the requests for funds usually exceed the funds that are normally available. Thus there needs to be some further selection mechanism beyond the delivery of the organisation's mission and objectives. This second criterion relates to two aspects of resource analysis covered in Chapter 6:

   - *the support of core competencies*, where possible, in order to develop and enhance competitive advantage;

● *the enhancement of the value chain*, where possible, in order to assist particularly those activities that also support competitive advantage.

Although both of these should underpin the organisation's objectives in the long term, they can usefully be treated as additional criteria when resources are allocated.

3 *The level of risk associated with a specific proposal.* Clearly, if the risk is higher, there is a lower likelihood that the strategy will be successful. Some organisations will be more comfortable with accepting higher levels of risk than others so the criterion in this case needs to be considered in relation to the risk-acceptance level of the organisation.

17.4.2 Special circumstances surrounding the allocation of resources

Special circumstances may cause an organisation to amend the criteria for the allocation of resources. Still on the basis of the common principle of *bargaining* for the centre's funds, some organisations will consider the following:

● *When major strategic changes are unlikely.* In this situation, resources may be allocated on the basis of a *formula*, e.g. marketing funds might be allocated as a percentage of sales based on past history and experience. The major difficulty with such an approach is its arbitrary nature. It may, however, be a useful shortcut.

● *When major strategic changes are predicted.* In this situation, additional resources may be required either to drive the strategic process or to respond to an expected competitive initiative. In both cases, *special negotiation* with the centre is required rather than the adherence to dogmatic criteria.

● *When resources are shared between divisions.* In this situation, the centre may seek to enhance its role beyond that of resource allocation. It may need to establish the degree of collaboration and, where the areas disagree, *impose* a solution. The logical and motivational problems associated with such an approach are evident.

17.4.3 Caution regarding the resource allocation process

Hamel and Prahalad have reservations about the whole resource allocation process.[18] They view it as offering the wrong mental approach to the strategy task, arguing that it is more concerned with dividing up the existing resources than with using the resources more effectively and strategically.

> *If top management devotes more effort to assessing the strategic feasibility of projects in its resource allocation role than it does to the task of multiplying resource effectiveness, its value added will be modest indeed.*

They make an important cautionary point.

Key strategic principles

● The resource allocation process is used to provide the necessary funds for proposed strategies. In circumstances of limited resources, the centre is usually responsible for allocating funds using various decision criteria.

● Criteria for allocation include the delivery of the organisation's mission and objectives, its support of key strategies such as core competencies and its risk-taking profile. Some special circumstances such as unusual changes in the environment may support other resource allocation criteria.

● There is a risk that the resource allocation process will ignore the need to use resources more effectively and strategically.

CASE STUDY 17.3

Informal strategic controls at Nestlé

Because of the diversity of its product portfolio, Nestlé has chosen in the past to devolve strategy to its main operating areas and control them informally from the centre. This case study describes the strategic planning procedures, but also shows how they are becoming more centralised as the company attempts to improve its performance and operational efficiency.

With sales of over US$72 billion, Nestlé (Switzerland) is the world's largest food and consumer goods company. Its main product areas include coffee (Nescafé), milk and baby foods, confectionery, pet foods and frozen foods. It operates globally through a series of geographical zones and a set of product *strategic business units* (SBUs). For example, zone 1 is Europe and there is an SBU for the confectionery and ice cream product area operating on a worldwide basis. Figure 17.8 shows the true global nature of the company and its main product areas. Figure 17.7 shows the Nestlé revenue and profit record for four years to 2004 – somewhat patchy with no significant growth in revenue and earnings.

Because of the wide variation in the SBUs in its portfolio, Nestlé has chosen to give *strategic* control of its operations to the individual SBUs. Each SBU has a full range of functional expertise in its business area: marketing, production, research and so on. However, *operational* decisions rest with the zones and below them the national companies. In the past, the role of the centre has been to co-ordinate and to allocate resources and this continues to the present with some modifications,

Nestlé's food range is founded on two major areas – milk products and instant coffee – Nescafé. The company's strategy has been to expand from this base into other food areas with a carefully planned series of acquisitions and in-house technology developments.

Figure 17.7

Nestlé four-year revenue and profit record

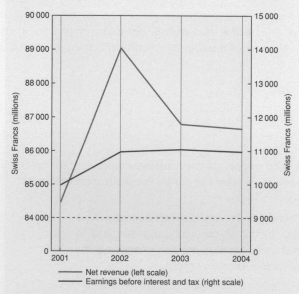

— Net revenue (left scale)
— Earnings before interest and tax (right scale)

Source: Annual Report and Accounts 2004.

described later in the case. The Nestlé structure for strategic planning, budgets and reporting is shown in Figure 17.9. The centre begins the process by issuing instructions to the SBUs for the next planning cycle. The SBUs then work on their three-year long-term plans (called LTPs). Every SBU prepares an LTP each year but some are merely updates from previous years. In order to promote strategic discussion with the centre, the LTPs are then circulated. They will include such areas as brand positioning, market share and competitive activity, pricing, capital proposals and new product development. However, as from 2000, the centre has initiated an additional layer of co-ordination and control on an experimental basis that will take some five years to be fully implemented.

Because the company operates in relatively mature markets, it is able to operate a system of checks and balances with more lengthy debate between the centre and the SBUs than might be appropriate where markets are changing fast and quick decisions are required. Hence, following the LTP preparation early in the year, discussions are held on content in

Figure 17.8

Nestlé activities around the world and by product group

(a) Nestlé revenue by area 2004

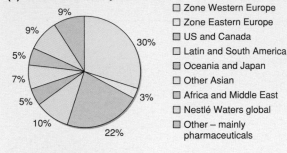

☐ Zone Western Europe
☐ Zone Eastern Europe
☐ US and Canada
☐ Latin and South America
☐ Oceania and Japan
☐ Other Asian
☐ Africa and Middle East
☐ Nestlé Waters global
☐ Other – mainly pharmaceuticals

(b) Nestlé revenue by product group 2004

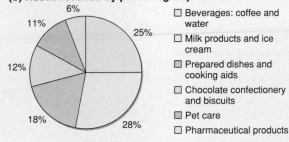

☐ Beverages: coffee and water
☐ Milk products and ice cream
☐ Prepared dishes and cooking aids
☐ Chocolate confectionery and biscuits
☐ Pet care
☐ Pharmaceutical products

the period from April to June between the SBUs, zones and the centre. The Nestlé executive committee has to give its approval. Later in the year, there is an investment and revenue budget review. The strategies and activities can be changed at this point if the market situation or competitive positions have altered significantly.

However, the controls and balances do not simply take the form of the official committees described above but are more subtle. A Nestlé manager commented on the control procedures: 'You could achieve your monthly budget targets by disturbing the strategy; for example, by repositioning brands or chang[ing] media expenditure. But if you did so, it would quickly be noticed by the product group director at the centre. This would not be through a formal report, but through informal contacts with the country in question.'

In a similar way, although the SBUs and zones are separated in decision-making terms from the centre, most are located in the same geographical location – at Nestlé's HQ in Vevey, Switzerland. Here is a senior manager talking about the chocolate strategy group, which was at one time located in York, England. 'I got increasingly sucked into Vevey because of the need to talk to the various zone managers, and to all the corporate functions and services . . . I don't believe in electronic communication: face-to-face discussions are vital, especially in a group the size of Nestlé.' This principle of direct informal contact is encouraged, even if it means that some managers have extensive travel commitments. The aims are to produce an integrated team and to maintain the informal

communications that provide the real checks and balances to the Nestlé style of strategic planning.

Nestlé believes that such informal approaches to planning and monitoring by the centre are useful in guiding and developing corporate strategy. They are probably just as effective as the formal reporting against strategic objectives. Financial rewards for achieving strategic targets are not an important aspect of the strategic process. Peer pressures, promotion and personal competitiveness are greater incentives in ensuring that strategies are delivered. A longer-term view is taken of management performance and competence by the centre rather than specific achievement against targets. This is reflected in the tendency for managers to serve the company for many years in long and stable relationships.

However in 2000, the company realised that its devolved approach to planning meant that it was not able to take full advantage of the benefits of globalisation – economies of scale, shared R&D expenditure and so on. Hence, the company introduced a new information technology programme called GLOBE. The aim was 'to improve the performance and operational efficiency of our businesses worldwide. In the process, we will revisit all aspects of our business practices to shape new ways to run Nestlé.' Thus the company was introducing common computer coding around the world for items such as raw and packaging materials, finished goods and customers.

The aim of GLOBE was to consolidate information, leveraging the company's size, and to communicate better across the world. There would also be an exchange of best practice and data: common information systems would be developed to achieve this. The whole project was expected to cost US$1.9 billion and, by 2006, deliver cumulative savings of the same magnitude. It would be introduced progressively throughout the company, starting with Switzerland, part of South America and Malaysia/Singapore. Clearly, the new project represented a shift from the informal controls of the current system, even though the new system would not replace that approach. The GLOBE IT system was implemented around the world by 2005.

In 2004, Nestlé then decided to move further in terms of its *regional* as well as its *global* activity. The company took the view that its real strength in some product groups was not global but in certain regions of the world, which it called zones. Such businesses could be managed globally to some extent, but would be even better if managed on a regional basis. 'Regional' here meant a region of the world like Western Europe or Africa. The company introduced a new manager called a zone executive officer (ZEO). The responsibility of the ZEO was to manage its regional businesses alongside its global management of some parts of Nestlé. For example, its ice cream business described in Case 4.4 had ambitions to be global but was particularly strong in certain parts of the world. The ZEO would have accountability for zone business strategies and for global strategies in so far as they impacted on that particular zone. The manager would also have responsibilities for the achievement of broader company policies in the particular zone. Importantly, the ZEO would also have clear ▶

◀ CASE STUDY 17.3 continued

Figure 17.9

The Nestlé structure for strategic planning, budgeting and functional organisation

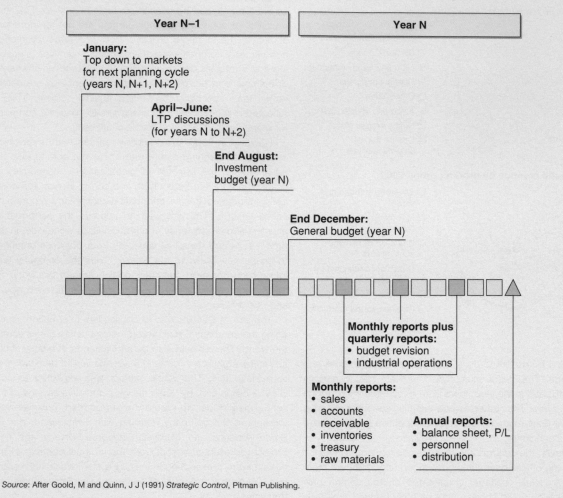

Source: After Goold, M and Quinn, J J (1991) *Strategic Control*, Pitman Publishing.

responsibility for innovation and be accountable for the 'launch plan of new global/regional products/technologies/brands'. In other words, the zone executive officer would have a broad general management role within a specific part of the world.

© Copyright Richard Lynch 2006. All rights reserved. This case was written from published information by Richard Lynch.[19]

Case questions

1 *What characterises the Nestlé style of strategic planning? To what extent is this a function of its large size? Its product range? Its geographical spread?*

2 *What, if any, are the dangers of informal strategic controls such as those operating at Nestlé?*

17.5 STRATEGIC PLANNING

17.5.1 What is strategic planning?

The purpose of strategic planning is to use a *formal planning system* for the development and implementation of the strategies related to the mission and objectives of the organisation. Importantly, strategic planning is no substitute for strategic thinking; it merely formalises

Figure 17.10

The basic strategic planning process

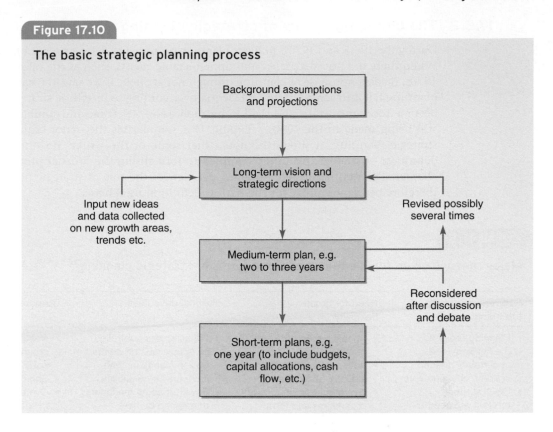

the strategy process in some organisations. More specifically, the plan will *integrate* the activities of the organisation and specify the *timetable* for the completion of each stage.

Professor George Day is right when he suggests[20] that strategic planning should not be an isolated event that culminates in a clear-cut decision. Instead, it should be an ongoing activity that responds simultaneously to the pressure of events and the dictates of the calendar. To ensure organisational commitment, involvement in the planning process must come from many levels of the organisation – each with a distinct role in formulating the strategy and ensuring the integration of corporate resource allocations, strategies, objectives and action plans.

Many companies believe that, in undertaking the strategic planning process, it is important to establish first the background assumptions and the basis on which business is conducted, including the key factors for success (*see* Chapter 3). Following this, the company will explore its *long-term vision* and broad strategic direction: these might be only achieved over a number of years and would be expected to include the input of new technologies and ideas. A *medium-term plan* can then be developed for the next two or three years, where the environment is sufficiently stable. *Short-term annual plans* and budgets consistent with the medium term are then developed. It is important to see this process as not just happening in sequence but involving much iteration and revisiting before each stage is finalised. Figure 17.10 illustrates the basic process.

Sometimes such a cycle is repeated by the company every year – Case study 17.3 describes such a process at Nestlé. However, because of the potential complexity and length of such investigations, it would be most unusual if *every* aspect of the business were reviewed every year from a long-term perspective. Product groups, special topics, core competencies, different group objectives are often chosen as starting points for exploring strategic issues and fed into the long-term review. As Arie de Geus, the former head of planning at Royal Dutch/Shell, wrote:[21]

The real purpose of effective planning is not to make plans but to change the . . . mental models that . . . decision makers carry in their heads.

17.5.2 The changing status of strategic planning

During the 1960s and 1970s, strategic planning promised to deliver superior financial returns. When these did not materialise and unpredictable events, such as the oil price crises of the 1970s, made a nonsense of planning (though not at Shell, as we saw in Chapter 15), strategic planning fell into some disarray.[22] Essentially, according to its critics, strategic planning had become too bureaucratic and rigid in its application.[23,24] These and similar comments were still being made in the 1990s.[25] Exhibit 17.5 summarises the major critical onslaught on strategic planning. It should be noted that some of the writers do not use the narrow definition of strategic planning, confined to formalising the broader process, used in this chapter. Their criticisms rely on a broader view of the role of strategic planning and may therefore be inappropriate for the narrow definition used here.

Exhibit 17.5

Major reasons given for the failure of some forms of strategic planning[26]

Poor direction from top management	Need for greater flexibility	Political difficulties	Corporate culture
• Planning replaced the flexibility and uncertainty needed in some environments • Deep strategic thought replaced by planning formulae • Short-term focus and financial emphasis • Poor discussion of key issues • Inadequate resources allocated for plans • Whole process of resources allocation	• Annual budget took priority • Accepted existing industry boundaries • Overemphasis on procedures and form filling • Tests for 'fit' between resources and plans rather than stretches for new resources • Better to introduce improved systems to cope with flexibility rather than stick with rigid plan	• Planning was controlled by specialist staff and not by line managers who have the responsibility • Power of some managers threatened by new procedures • Ability of entrenched interests to delay decisions	• Need to develop organisation that can cope with uncertainty • Short-termism • Overemphasis on financial results • Lack of risk taking and entrepreneurial flair • Little toleration of the occasional failure

Note: Some comments might be regarded as applying to any form of strategy development rather than strategic planning as such. Note also the comment in the text on the research evidence used to support some of the comments.

Given all these considerations, it might be argued that strategic planning is no longer appropriate as a means of formalising the strategy process. However, many companies still need to look beyond the short term and to co-ordinate their main activities, especially where significant commitments have to be made over lengthy time spans. Attitudes to strategic planning are beginning to change again and Nestlé and Canon which form the focus of the two main case studies in this chapter have been chosen from successful companies which still use some form of strategic planning. Even Mintzberg, who has been highly critical of strategic planning in the past, has now conceded that it does fulfil a useful function within certain limits.[27]

Comment

Mintzberg is right in his emphasis on the need for innovative thinking, which may not be best served by a strongly bureaucratic strategic planning process. Overall, this book takes the view that Mintzberg is correct in his identification of the role for strategic planning: it summarises the decisions taken elsewhere and is useful for making strategy operational. Strategic planning is no substitute for careful and innovative thinking on the main strategic issues.

17.5.3 Planning strategies and styles

Although a large number of companies undertake some form of strategic planning, it is important to understand that there are many variations in the way that it is conducted. The reasons for this include:

- *Environment.* Stable environments lend themselves to longer time-horizons. Stability also favours a more centralised approach to planning, because there is less need to respond to rapid variations in the market, e.g. Nestlé.

- *Product range.* As products become more diverse across a company, it becomes more difficult to develop coherent core competencies, synergies and linkages across the value chain. In these circumstances, the planning style may move from one seeking co-operation across divisions to one based on simple financial linkages, e.g. the more unrelated parts of Siemens and General Electric described in Chapter 12.

- *Leadership and management style.* Particularly in smaller companies, this will inevitably guide the approach to the development of strategy and its co-ordination across the company. It may also apply in some larger companies, e.g. Richard Branson at Virgin, Jürgen Schrempp of DaimlerChrysler and Rupert Murdoch of News Corporation.

There has been no wide-ranging international study on the range of management styles. However, Goold and Campbell conducted such a study during the 1980s on 16 diversified UK companies.[28] They distinguished several different styles for conducting strategic planning. The purpose of identifying the different approaches was to define the manner in which the *centre* added value to the company's separate businesses. The researchers suggested that there were two main ways in which value could be added:

1 The centre could help to shape the plans of each business – the *planning influence*.
2 The centre could control the process as the plans were being implemented – the *control influence*.

From the empirical research, three main styles of strategic planning were then identified as being most common:

1 *Strategic planning.* The centre is involved in formulating the *plans* of the various businesses. Then the emphasis is on long-term objectives during the *control* process. Canon is an example that conforms approximately to this, although there is more collaborative effort at Canon than is perhaps implied by the definition. *See* Case study 17.2.

2 *Financial control.* The centre exercises strong short-term financial control but otherwise the businesses are highly decentralised and able to operate as they wish. The individual businesses are able to develop longer-term plans if they judge that it is useful. It should be noted that there is little attempt to co-ordinate across companies in such an arrangement. Synergies, value chain linkages and core competencies are largely absent. Relatively few companies operate rigidly this way in the new millennium. Cisco Systems' financial controls have some of these characteristics. *See* Case study 16.2.

3 *Strategic control.* This lies between strategic planning and financial control. In planning terms, the company is not as centralised as a strategic planning company, nor as decentralised as a financial control company. Greater initiative is given to the individual businesses. In *control* terms, long-term strategic objectives are used but short-term profits are also required. Nestlé is a possible example here, except that the centre is closely involved at various stages of the strategy development process. *See* Case study 17.3.

A further style was also identified but not analysed in depth in the research: *the centralised style*. In this style, all the major strategy decisions are held at the centre, with day-to-day implementation being delegated to the various businesses.

Within these broad types of planning, there were then further variations. The purpose of the research was not to choose between the styles but rather to explore how the resulting strategic process could be more successful. The researchers drew four conclusions:

1 Style should be matched to the circumstances of the business: technology, product range, speed of environmental change, leadership and so on.

2 Some styles demand greater understanding of the businesses than others: for example, the debate between the centre and its subsidiaries in the strategic control style is much more keen than that to be found in the distant monitoring of financial performance in a financial control style.

3 Successful styles benefit from openness and mutual respect between those involved across the company. Suspicion and lack of trust between the centre and the parts of the business will cause real problems.

4 Shared commitment to work together to implement the agreed strategies is vital. This may come from inspired leadership or it may derive from the clarity of the objectives.

Comment

This research presents a useful and unique insight into strategic planning, but its attempt to categorise planning into a few distinct types is based on a sample of only 16 companies. There are other possible styles, e.g. entrepreneurial, that were not part of the sample. Moreover, styles change as companies, their environments and leaders change.

Exhibit 17.6 speculates on some possible styles in the public and not-for-profit sectors, where strategic planning is also possible.

Exhibit 17.6

Possible styles of strategic planning in the public and not-for-profit sectors

1 **Bureaucratic** (e.g. civil service)
   - Clear goals
   - Great reliance on rules
   - Decisions follow standard operating procedures

2 **Organised anarchy** (e.g. some charitable trusts)
   - Unclear goals, difficult to quantify
   - Very decentralised organisation
   - *Ad hoc* decisions
   - Haphazard collection and use of information
   - Decisions not linked to goals, but rather to the intersection of persons, solutions and problems

3 **Political power** (e.g. university)
   - Goals consistent with social role but pluralistic in organisation
   - Shifting coalitions of interests
   - Disorderly decision making but becoming less so
   - Information used strategically or withheld strategically
   - Decisions bargained among interested parties

17.5.4 Strategic planning in small companies

By comparison with large diverse companies, there is a much narrower product range in smaller companies. By definition, the scope of the issues may also be narrower. Hence, there may be less need to go through a formal planning process and resource allocation procedure. Planning systems may also be simpler and shorter. Changes in the environment will be less of an issue in the planning sense: small companies should be able to react more quickly and responsively.

Nevertheless, the same basic planning process will apply: background assessment, vision for the future plus long-term aims, and then medium-term and short-term plans. The time-horizon may differ and the planning style is likely to be more informal. As soon as external finance is needed to support or expand the business, however, basic plans will be required. Such plans will need the same strategic logic, evidence and justification as apply to larger organisations.

Key strategic principles

- Strategic planning operationalises the strategy process in some organisations. It is no substitute for basic and innovative strategic thinking.

- The basic process may well cover background assumptions, long-term vision, medium-term plans and short-term plans. Importantly, new ideas are input into the process and revisions are a significant element of its development.

- Strategic planning has been heavily criticised by some researchers as being too bureaucratic and rigid in its approach, but attitudes are beginning to mellow as long as the process is narrowly defined.

- There are a number of different styles for conducting the strategic planning process: for example, strategic planning, strategic control and financial control. The selection of a style depends on the circumstances of the company.

- Formal strategic planning in small companies may also prove beneficial, especially where external finance is being sought.

17.6 INFORMATION, MONITORING AND CONTROL[29]

17.6.1 Why are monitoring and controls important?

Monitoring and control procedures are an important aspect of implementation because information can be used:

- to assess resource allocation choices;
- to monitor progress in implementation;
- to evaluate the performance of individual managers as they go about the achievement of their implementation tasks;
- to monitor the environment for significant changes from the planning assumptions and projections;
- to provide a feedback mechanism and the fine-tuning essential for emergent strategy implementation, especially in fast-changing markets.

More generally, monitoring becomes increasingly important as the *concept* of strategy moves from being an isolated event towards being an ongoing activity.

> *Strategy creation is seen as emerging from the way a company at various levels acquires, interprets and processes information about its environment.*[30]

For all these reasons, companies like Nestlé and Canon spend significant resources on monitoring their activities. Because of the vast range of potential information, they may concentrate on the *key factors for success* as a first step (*see* Chapter 6). Some major companies have complete departments whose sole task is to monitor competitors. It is also a characteristic of some small businesses that they are acutely aware of their immediate competitors and customers, the market prices and other forms of strategic activity.

17.6.2 What are the main elements of a strategic control system?

Strategic control systems monitor the main elements of the strategy and its objectives. The crucial point of this is to obtain information in time to be able to take action. Information for its own sake has limited value: the real test is whether it is useful and timely in revising the implementation process, where required. Strategic control systems will include some financial measures but will also involve:

- customer satisfaction;
- quality measures;
- market share.

It may also be necessary to apply such indicators externally to monitor competition in order to assess the *relative* performance of the organisation against others in the market place.

It is important to distinguish between *financial monitoring* (cash flow, earnings per share, etc.) and *strategic controls* which may include these financial elements but will also have a broader perspective.

17.6.3 How can strategic controls be improved?[31]

To some extent, this question cannot be fully answered unless the precise strategy style has been established. Nevertheless, there are some useful guidelines designed to obtain the best from such systems:

- *Concentrate on the key performance indicators and factors for success.* There is a real danger that too many elements will be monitored, with resulting information overload.
- *Distinguish between corporate, business and operating levels of information and only monitor where relevant.* For example, not everyone at the centre needs to know that a minor product has just achieved its sales target. Equally, a division may have limited interest in market share data from another division, even if this is important at the centre.
- *Avoid overreliance on quantitative data.* Numbers are usually easier to measure but may be misleading and simplistic. Qualitative data and information that is difficult to quantify in such areas as service may be far more relevant to strategy monitoring.
- *As controls become established, consider relaxing them.* Eventually, they may interfere with the most important task of clear and insightful strategic exploration. For example, it was for this reason that Jack Welch at GE reduced controls, but he did not do so until the principles had been learnt. Every organisation may need to go through this stage of learning before controls are relaxed.
- *Create realistic expectations of what the control system can do as it is being introduced or upgraded.* Some managers may regard strategic controls as a waste of time. Their reasoning is that it is difficult to see early results because of the long time scales involved. Such an objection cannot be avoided but can be anticipated. It is better to acknowledge that the benefits in terms of improved strategy, resources and results will not be immediately obvious.

17.6.4 Strategy control, budgets and cost accounting

Bungay and Goold[32] state that it is 'vital' to link strategy monitoring into the budget process. They argue that, if the two processes are controlled by two different departments, there is a danger that short-term budget considerations will take precedence over longer-term important strategic decisions. This is a realistic but short-term Anglo-American view of the way that business operates. It is particularly associated with the financial control style described in Section 17.5. It holds the real danger that *strategy controls* and *budgeting variances* will be confused. Budgeting is concerned with the achievement of targets planned monthly or quarterly on the basis of revenue and costs. Strategy rarely concerns itself with such short-term matters.

Key strategic principles

- Monitoring and control systems are important for their contribution to assessing how strategies are being implemented and how the environment itself is changing.
- The important point about information and control is the necessity of obtaining information in sufficient time to take action, where required.
- There are a number of ways in which strategic controls can be improved. All of them rely on the establishment of simple, cost-effective and useful information about the organisation and its environment.
- It has been argued that strategy control and budgeting should be linked. This is not recommended because strategy monitoring is more concerned with exploration, while budgeting is more focused on achieving specific short-term targets.

17.7 IMPLEMENTATION OF INTERNATIONAL STRATEGY

International aspects of implementation are more complicated because of factors such as culture and geographical diversity. However, they essentially follow the principles already outlined in this chapter and the special comments elsewhere in this book.

CRITICAL REFLECTION

Strategic planning: to what extent is it needed?

Most senior managers and some strategists would agree that some form of strategic planning is essential in an organisation. The plan can be useful in setting out strategic and financial targets, as identified in the Balanced Scorecard, and in allocating resources between different parts of the business. Moreover, the analysis and logical process involved in devising and debating the strategies that underpin the plan is arguably of some benefit to the organisation, even if part at least is left to emerge from new innovations.

Nevertheless, the chapter has shown that there has been considerable scepticism about the benefits of strategic planning over the last ten years. Some strategists have rejected the whole notion of strategic planning. While this may go too far, it does raise the question of precisely what is meant to be achieved by a strategic plan, especially one that is developed to operate in the uncertain environment of many businesses at the present time.

To what extent is strategic planning useful? What constraints, if any, should be put on the process? And who should be responsible?

SUMMARY

- Implementation covers the activities required to put strategies into practice. The basic elements of this process are: general objectives; specific plans; the necessary finances; and a monitoring and control system to ensure compliance.

- There are three major approaches to implementation: comprehensive, incremental and selective. Implementation in small and medium-sized businesses may be less elaborate but should follow the same general principles.

- According to Pettigrew and Whipp, implementation is best seen as a *continuous* process, rather than as one following the formulation of the strategy. Hrebiniak and Joyce placed *boundaries* on implementation, depending on the ability of managers to consider every choice rationally and to evaluate the impact of implementation on the strategy itself. Emergent approaches to strategy imply that implementation needs to be considered not just as a single event but as a series of activities whose outcome may to some extent shape the strategy.

- The Balanced Scorecard was developed as a method of translating abstract strategy into specific areas of company action to help strategy to work. The Balanced Scorecard combines quantitative and qualitative measures of the selected strategy. It acknowledges the different expectations of the various stakeholders and it attempts to link scorecard performance measures to the chosen strategy. The main benefits of the scorecard lie in its focus on turning strategy into implementation and the development of objectives that go beyond simple financial measures.

- There are four key principles behind the scorecard: *translating the vision* through clarifying and gaining consensus; *communicating and linking* by setting goals and establishing rewards for success; *business planning* to align objectives, allocate resources and establish milestones; *feedback and learning* to review the subsequent performance against the plan.

- The four strategy perspectives that appear on every scorecard are: financial, customer, internal, future. These are translated using four steps – strategy objectives, setting targets, identifying measurement criteria and developing strategy initiatives – the targets are summarised as Key Performance Indicators (KPIs).

- When setting objectives and tasks, first establish who *developed* the strategy that is to be implemented. This will influence the implementation process. Individual objectives and tasks will follow from the agreed overall objectives. It may be necessary to experiment to find the optimal combination of events. In fast-changing environments, rigid objectives may be made redundant by outside events. Communication and co-ordination are vital to satisfactory implementation, and are especially important to ensure understanding of the plan and its underlying assumptions.

- The resource allocation process provides the necessary funds for proposed strategies. Where resources are limited, allocation of funds is usually from the centre of the organisation, using various decision criteria. Criteria for allocation include the delivery of the organisation's mission and objectives, the support of key strategies and the organisation's risk-taking profile, together with special circumstances, such as unusual changes in the environment. There is a risk that the resource allocation process will ignore the need to use resources more effectively and strategically.

- Strategic planning makes the strategy process operational in some organisations, but it is no substitute for basic and innovative strategic thinking. The basic process of strategic planning may well cover background assumptions, long-term vision, medium-term plans and short-term plans. Importantly, the input of new ideas and revisions to the process are significant elements of its development. Strategic planning has been heavily criticised by some researchers as being too bureaucratic and rigid in its approach, but attitudes towards it are beginning to mellow as long as the process is narrowly defined.

- There are a number of different styles of conducting the strategic planning process, including strategic planning, strategic control and financial control. The selection of a style depends on the circumstances of the company – for instance, formal strategic planning in small companies may help when external finance is being sought.

- Monitoring and control systems are important in assessing strategy implementation and how the environment is changing. The necessity of obtaining information in sufficient time to take the required action is crucial. There are a number of ways in which strategic controls can be improved. All rely on having simple, cost-effective and useful information about the organisation and its environment. It has been argued that strategy control and budgeting should be linked. This is not recommended because strategy monitoring is concerned with exploration, while budgeting is focused on achieving specific short-term targets.

● International aspects of strategy implementation follow the same principles but are complicated by culture, geographical diversity and other factors.

QUESTIONS

1 Compare the Canon and Nestlé styles of strategic planning and discuss why they are different. Is one better than the other and, if so, which?

2 Does a small company need a formal strategic plan?

3 Apply the basic implementation process outlined in Figure 17.2 to the current procedures of an organisation with which you are familiar. Where does it differ and where is it the same? What conclusions can you draw about the process?

4 'Nothing chastens the planner more than the knowledge that s/he will have to carry out the plan.' (General Gavin, quoted by Professor George Day)

Discuss this comment in the context of the implementation process.

5 What are the implications of bounded rationality and minimum intervention in developing the strategic process?

6 How can objectives and tasks be communicated from senior management while at the same time motivating those who have to implement them?

7 'If top management devotes more effort to assessing the strategic feasibility of projects in its allocational role than it does to the task of multiplying resource effectiveness, its value added will be modest indeed.' (Professors Gary Hamel and C K Prahalad)

Discuss.

8 Devise a strategic plan for an organisation with which you are familiar and identify the main elements that you would control during the period of the plan. Consider whether you yourself can be wholly responsible for devising such a plan or whether you would, in practice, not only need to consult with others but to gain their agreement to the plan.

9 Explain briefly why strategic controls are necessary and indicate how they might be improved. Consider an organisation with which you are familiar and assess its strategic controls with reference to your explanation.

Further reading

Hrebiniak, L and Joyce, W (1984) *Implementing Strategy*, Macmillan, New York is worth reading. An abridged paper based on this book appeared in the following: De Wit, B and Meyer, R (1994) *Strategy: Process, Content and Context*, West Publishing, MN, pp192–202. For a more recent review, *see* Miller, S, Wilson, D and Hickson, D (2004) 'Beyond planning: strategies for successfully implementing strategic decisions', *Long Range Planning*, Vol 37, pp201–218.

Kaplan, D and Norton, R (1996) *The Balanced Scorecard*, Harvard Business School Press, Boston, MA is important for this topic. *See* also Kaplan, D and Norton, R (2001) *The Strategy-focused Organisation*, Harvard Business School Press, Boston, MA. Also worth reading are Ahn, H (2001) 'Applying the Balanced Scorecard concept: an experience report', *Long Range Planning*, Vol 34, Issue 4, pp441–62. Veen-Dirks, P and Wijn, M (2002) 'Strategic control: meshing the critical success factors with the Balanced Scorecard', *Long Range Planning*, Vol 35, pp407–27. *See* also: Braam, G and Nijssen, E (2004) 'Performance effects of the balanced scorecard: a note on Dutch experience', *Long Range Planning*, Vol 37, No 4 pp335–50 and Papalexandris, A, Ioannou, G and Prastacos, G (2004) 'Implementing the Balanced Scorecard in Greece: a software firm's experience', *Long Range Planning*, Vol 37, No 4, pp351–66.

The classic study of different types of strategic planning is that by Goold, M and Campbell, A (1987) *Strategies and Styles*, Blackwell, Oxford and is well worth reading.

Arie de Geus wrote a useful article on strategic planning: (1988) 'Planning as learning', *Harvard Business Review*, Mar–Apr.

Professor H Mintzberg has changed his views on strategic planning: (1994) 'The fall and rise of strategic planning', *Harvard Business Review*, Jan–Feb, pp107–14. *See* also his book, Mintzberg, H (1994) *The Rise and Fall of Strategic Planning*, Prentice Hall, New York. Note that Professor Colin Egan provides a logical and well-argued critique of Mintzberg's work in Egan, C (1995) *Creating Organisation Advantage*, Butterworth–Heinemann, Oxford, Ch7.

Notes and references

1 Sources for this case are the author's life-long support for Portsmouth Football Club and *Financial Times*, 6 August 1998, p32; 11 March 1999, p25; 21 July 2001, p9; 22 July 2000, p13; 29 July 2000, p17; 18 August 2000, p13; 27 October 2000, p20; 29 March 2001, p14; 11 August 2001, p14; 24 August 2001, p9; 2 September 2001, p11; 6 October 2001, p16; 7 December 2001, p16; 23 February 2002, p13; 1 March 2002, p15; 9 March 2002, pp12, 14. 3 May 2005, p4 of 'Creative Business' special supplement. Manchester United Annual Report and Accounts 2004 – available on the web at www.ir.manutd.com/manutd/findata/kfd.

2 Day, G S (1984) *Strategic Market Planning*, West Publishing, MN, Ch8.

3 Yavitz, B and Newman, W (1982) *Strategy in Action: The Execution, Politics and Payoff of Business Planning*, The Free Press, New York. It should be noted that Hrebiniak and Joyce (1984) also describe similar distinctions in *Implementing Strategy*, Macmillan, New York.

4 Day, G S (1984) Op. cit., Ch8.

5 Author's experience based on strategy development in fast-moving consumer goods, telecommunications and consultancy.

6 For example: Wheelen and Hunger, Jauch and Glueck, Thompson and Strickland, Johnson and Scholes, Hofer and Schendel.

7 Pettigrew, A and Whipp, R (1991) *Managing Change for Competitive Success*, Blackwell, Oxford, pp26, 27.

8 Hrebiniak, L and Joyce, W (1984) Op. cit. An abridged paper based on this book appeared in: De Wit, B and Meyer, R (1994) *Strategy: Process, Content and Context*, West Publishing, MN, pp192–202.

9 Leadbeater, C. (1997) 'Flying with a clear view', *Financial Times*, 1 April, p17. Direct quote from David Norton.

10 Kaplan, D and Norton, R (1996) *The Balanced Scorecard*, Harvard Business School Press, Boston, MA, p77.

11 Kaplan, D and Norton, R (1996) Ibid.

12 Pettigrew, A and Whipp, R (1991) Op. cit., p176.

13 Harvard Business School Case (1983) *Canon Inc (B)*, reference number 9-384-151, and *Note on the World Copier Industry in 1983*, reference 9-386-106; Kono T (1992) *Long Range Planning of Japanese Corporations*, de Gruyter, Berlin; *Financial Times*, 16 Feb 1996, p31; *Canon Inc.*, Annual Report and Accounts 1994, 1998 and 2004 (English version); Hamel G and Prahalad C K (1994) *Competing for the Future*, Harvard Business School Press, Boston, MA.

14 Hunger, J and Wheelen, T (1993) *Strategic Management*, 4th edn, Addison-Wesley, Reading, MA, p238.

15 Day, G S (1984) Op. cit., p186.

16 Galbraith, J and Kazanjian, R (1986) *Strategy Implementation*, 2nd edn, West Publishing, MN, p98.

17 Goold, M and Campbell, A (1987) *Strategies and Styles*, Blackwell, Oxford, p21.

18 Hamel, G and Prahalad, C K (1994) *Competing for the Future*, Harvard Business School Press, Boston, MA, p159.

19 References for Nestlé case: *Financial Times*, 6 May 1992, p16; 15 May 1992, p13; 20 Apr 1994, p19. Goold, M and Quinn, J (1990) *Strategic Control*, Hutchinson Business Books, London, pp118–19. Nestlé Annual Report and Accounts 2004 available on the web at www.ir.nestle.com. The same website has a major power point presentation to investors on 15 June 2004, which detailed the latest Nestlé thinking on its global organisation and was used in the preparation of this case.

20 Day, G S (1984) Op. cit., p189.

21 De Geus, A (1988) 'Planning as learning', *Harvard Business Review*, Mar–Apr.

22 Marx, T (1991) 'Removing the obstacles to effective planning', *Long Range Planning*, Aug, Pergamon Press, Oxford.

23 Loasby, B (1967) 'Long range formal planning in perspective', *Journal of Management Studies*, Oct.

24 Lenz, R and Lyles, M (1985) 'Is your planning becoming too rational?', *Long Range Planning*, Aug, Pergamon Press, Oxford.

25 Hamel, G and Prahalad, C K (1994) Op. cit. p283

26 Exhibit 17.5 is developed from references 22, 23 and 24.

27 Mintzberg, H (1994) 'The fall and rise of strategic planning', *Harvard Business Review*, Jan–Feb, pp107–14. See also his book (1994) *The Rise and Fall of Strategic Planning*, Prentice Hall, New York. Note that Egan provides a logical and well-argued critique of Mintzberg's work in Egan, C (1995) *Creating Organisation Advantage*, Butterworth–Heinemann, Oxford, Ch7.

28 Goold, M and Campbell, A (1987) Op. cit.

29 This section has benefited from Galbraith, J and Kazanjian, R (1986) Op. cit., pp85–7.

30 Pettigrew, A and Whipp, R (1991) Op. cit., p135.

31 This section has benefited from the paper by Bungay, S and Goold, M (1991) 'Creating a strategic control system', *Long Range Planning*, June, Pergamon Press, Oxford.

32 Bungay, S and Goold, M (1991) Op. cit.

Chapter 18

GOVERNMENT, PUBLIC SECTOR AND NOT-FOR-PROFIT STRATEGIES

Learning outcomes

When you have worked through this chapter, you will be able to:

● explain why public sector strategy is different and why it is important;

● outline the two main public sector models and explain the concept of public value;

● analyse the public sector environment;

● analyse the resources of a public sector institution;

● explain how the purpose of a public sector institution can be developed and defined;

● outline the development of strategy in the public sector from the perspectives of context, content and process;

● develop either a plan to implement the selected strategy or an incremental approach for an emergent strategy.

INTRODUCTION

This chapter focuses on the special considerations that apply to strategy in the government, public and not-for-profit sectors. 'Government' means areas like defence and the law, which are the responsibility of the nation state. 'Public' means the provision of health, transport, energy and other services which may be the responsibility of the state or may have been privatised, depending on the political views of the government. 'Not-for-profit' means institutions that work for the common public good but are independent of the state – for example, charities, trusts and similar institutions. In order to avoid unnecessary repetition throughout this chapter, these organisations are simply called 'public' institutions and their strategies are called public strategies to distinguish them from the 'private' strategies of commercial businesses. The differences between the three different types of public sector institutions are discussed where required.

Why does public sector strategy deserve a separate chapter? There are two main reasons. The first is that the public sector in every nation around the world is important. Even for high-income countries such as the US, where many services are devolved to the private sector, the wealth expended on the public sector is over 34 per cent of gross domestic product.[1] In other words, every country spends considerable sums on its public sector. Public sector strategy therefore matters and deserves to be explored in depth.

The second reason for a separate chapter is that the public sector is more complex and involves factors that do not apply in the private sector.[2] For example, companies like Kelloggs and Cereal Partners compete in the private sector breakfast cereal market. A measure of their success is their ability to deliver profits to shareholders and offer value for money products to customers. But in a public sector example like the local or national police force, there is no question of delivering a 'profit' on the police budget and a 'value for money' policing service needs considerable clarification if it is to have any meaning at all.[3]

If public sector strategy is so different, then it follows that the principles that have been explored for business strategy in the rest of this book may not apply in public sector strategy. For example, Chapter 4 explored competitive strategies like 'head-on' and 'flanking' attacks against a dominant competitor. These have little meaning where the state runs a monopoly such as its defence or police force.[4] We therefore need to reconsider the elements of business strategy in a public sector context.

An additional difficulty faces the business strategist in redefining its concepts for the public sector. Theories on *public sector administration* have been around for longer than those in business strategy.[5] This means that there is another stream of intellectual thought that needs to be considered in re-examining business strategy. It is not possible in one chapter to explore *all* the many public sector administration theories that have been developed. The approach of this chapter has been to focus only on those that have a direct connection with the rest of this book. However, the chapter contains sufficient references to allow the reader to follow up those areas that deserve greater depth. Interestingly, theories in public sector administration in the last 20 years have been moving closer to private sector concepts – as we shall see when we explore the *new public management* concepts later in the chapter.[6]

In order to explore public sector strategy, we will follow the basic structure of the book as developed for business strategy. We begin by analysing the environment within which public sector strategy operates and the resources that are deployed by the public sector organisation. We then consider the purpose of public sector strategy before exploring strategy development using three fundamental strategic concepts – namely, context, content and process as they apply in the public sector. We finally consider issues of public sector strategy implementation. This approach is summarised in Figure 18.1.

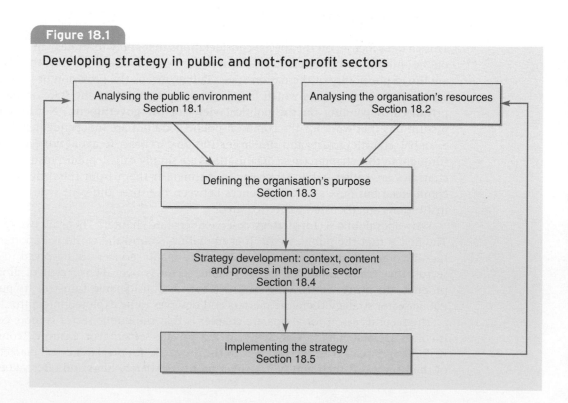

Figure 18.1

Developing strategy in public and not-for-profit sectors

Analysing the public environment
Section 18.1

Analysing the organisation's resources
Section 18.2

Defining the organisation's purpose
Section 18.3

Strategy development: context, content and process in the public sector
Section 18.4

Implementing the strategy
Section 18.5

The World Bank: juggling the strategic environment

The World Bank is one of the world's largest sources of development assistance. It provided over US$20 billion for 245 projects in developing countries in 2004. Yet it is part of the United Nations and is 'owned' by its 184 member countries. This case explores how this complex public sector institution juggles its various pressures and delivers results.

Sources of funds at the World Bank

The World Bank is not a 'bank' in the sense of providing cash and credit transactions for individuals and businesses. It is a specialised agency of the United Nations located in Washington DC, just a few blocks from the White House. Its members are the sovereign nations that make up the United Nations, the headquarters of which are in New York. The purpose of the World Bank is to 'bridge the divide' between the rich and poor countries of the world. Essentially, the 40 richest countries in the world provide contributions to a central fund every four years. For example, the fund was given US$9 billion in 2002 by the rich countries and, in addtion, sourced another US$6.6 billion from other bank resources. Such funds are therefore dependent in part on the political willingness of the rich countries to provide them. They are also dependent on the World Bank being able to raise its additional finance from other sources with whom it needs to maintain good relations.

In addition to the funding grants, the World Bank can also raise loans on the world's money markets. For example, it raised US$13 billion in 2004 at very low interest rates because the World Bank is regarded as highly credit-worthy, with an AAA credit rating. Importantly, its credit rating is far higher than that of some developing countries. This means that the World Bank can raise finance at lower cost than such countries. It is then able to make loans to such countries at a much lower cost of capital than they would be able to obtain for themselves. However, it also means that the World Bank loan system is subject to changes in money market rates and funding availability.

To summarise, the World Bank is able to make outright *grants* that can be used to assist projects, and *loans* which need to be repaid but at low rates of interest.

How is the World Bank organised?

The World Bank is run like a co-operative with the 184 nations as shareholders. The number of shares held by each member is based roughly on the size of that country's economy. Thus the US has 16.4 per cent of the votes, Japan 7.87 per cent, Germany 4.49 per cent, the UK 4.31 per cent and France 4.31 per cent of the votes. The rest of the shares are divided amongst the other members.

Shareholders are represented by a board of governors – often in practice the finance ministers of the individual countries – and the board meets annually. For much of the year, the World Bank is run by a committee of executive directors who are permanently located at its Washington headquarters.

The World Bank, located close to the International Monetary Fund Building in Washington DC, is a major source of funds for development assistance.

There are 24 directors, 5 from the countries above and the other 19 to represent the rest. The Bank's president is by tradition from the US and is effectively nominated by the US Government for a period of 5 years. More generally, the bureaucratic organisation structure suggests that informal contacts are important, as well as formal procedures, for leading positions within the Bank.

(Some anti-global commentators argue that the US Government unduly influences the World Bank. They say that the Bank 'rips off the poor and enslaves them in debt'. It is beyond the scope of this short case to explore this issue but such comment is heard from those who favour a radical restructuring of global trade.)

Below the executive directors, the Bank employs some 9,300 staff as economists, educators, environmental scientists, financial analysts, anthropologists, engineers and in many other roles. Employees come from 160 countries and over 3,000 of the total work in country offices rather than in Washington.

The World Bank has five major subsidiary agencies, each of which has responsibility in a specific area within the overall purpose of the Bank. These are outlined in Exhibit 18.1.

How does the Bank decide on projects?

The purpose of the World Bank is to provide development assistance to developing countries to build schools and health

▶ CASE STUDY 18.1 continued

Exhibit 18.1

The five main agencies of the World Bank

Agency	Role
International Bank for Reconstruction and Development	Since its beginnings in 1945 this institution has lent cumulatively US$394 billion with the aim of reducing poverty. It has a separate 24-member governing board representing 184 countries. There are 5 appointed members and 19 elected members to represent the countries. It promotes sustainable development through loans and non-lending analytical and advisory services.
The International Development Association	The IDA makes interest-free grants to poor countries of around US$9 billion per annum. It focuses particularly on those countries that have little or no capacity to borrow on money market terms. The grants are applied to poverty reduction strategies in key areas like raising productivity, improving the investment climate and access to health and education.
International Finance Corporation	The IFC works differently in that it invests with *business partners* in developing countries. It provides shareholders' funds, loans and other finance in areas that would be too risky for commercial operators acting alone. It funded nearly US$5 billion of activities in 2004.
The Multilateral Investment Guarantee Agency	This helps to promote foreign direct investment (FDI – *see* Chapter 19 for more) by providing guarantees to underwrite currency and other non-commercial risks – rather like an insurance policy for such risks. It made guarantees of US$1.1 billion in 2004.
The International Centre for Settlement of Investment Disputes	This agency provides facilities to settle the inevitable disputes and misunderstandings that can occur in international trade. There were 30 cases registered with the Centre in 2004.

Source: World Bank website – web.worldbank.org.

centres, to provide clean water and electricity, to fight disease and protect the environment. Hence, all the bids for project funds need to contribute to these activities.

In practice, the executive directors draw up work programmes for the year based on their main areas of interest and responsibility and in accordance with the priority areas agreed with the board of governors annually. They meet every week and report twice a year. Typical activities then work under a number of different headings, the following being examples only:

Investment climate area:

● Doing Business project
● Global development finance
● Global economic outlook

Trade area:

● Current developments in the world cotton market
● Leveraging trade for development
● Progress on Doha world trade negotiations

HIV/AIDS

● Progress report on critical next steps
● Global fund to fight AIDS, tuberculosis and malaria

Each of these (and more topics not covered above) has a regular schedule of committee meetings, reports, conclusions and follow-up activities. Thus the whole process is highly structured, recorded and bureaucratic. The World Bank considers such processes to be essential when dealing with the disbursement of large funds and the need to deliver recorded accountability to the donor countries.

© Copyright Richard Lynch 2006. All rights reserved. Case written by Richard Lynch from published information only.[7]

Case questions

1 *What changes in the environment are particularly likely to impact on the work of the World Bank? Use the strategic environmental analysis structure outlined in Section 18.1 in exploring this question.*

2 *Strategy at the World Bank is officially decided by the shareholders: is such a system appropriate and relevant? Is the system too complex? Are there any alternatives?*

3 *Who decides 'public interest' issues at the World Bank? How are such decisions taken? Are they typical of practice elsewhere?*

4 *What lessons, if any, on public sector strategy can be drawn from the way that the World Bank conducts its affairs?*

18.1 ANALYSING THE STRATEGIC ENVIRONMENT IN PUBLIC SECTOR STRATEGY

In public sector strategy, the analysis of the strategic environment is more complex than in the private sector. The main reason is that public sector strategy involves the wide-ranging

Definition ➤ and ill-defined subject of the *public interest*: the public interest concerns both the objectives and the institutions that make and implement public decisions. This basic concept in public sector strategy has two elements: the 'public' referring to citizens in general and 'interest' referring to the individual[8] wishes of the public.[9] The public interest is quite different from a company operating in a competitive market place. For example, the World Bank case shows that the public interest – as interpreted by national governments and various international agencies on behalf of their citizens – is important and quite different from a company selling its products in the market place. There are four main environmental factors that deserve to be analysed:

- the extent of the market mechanism in public service;
- the concept of public value;
- stakeholder power and complexity;
- special issues in not-for-profit organisations.

After exploring these factors, this section then concludes by analysing the public sector environment.

18.1.1 The extent of the market mechanism in public service

We can explore this under three main headings:

- The benefits of the market mechanism in the public sector
- The costs of the market mechanism in the public sector
- The balance between laissez-faire and dirigiste policies of national governments.

The benefits of the market mechanism in the public sector

In public sector administration theory, governments are assumed to take decisions on behalf of *all* their citizens, rather than a few. For example at the World Bank, the funds are made available to *all* relevant citizens associated with that application: everyone receives the grant. If public goods and services must be available to everyone, then public sector theorists have argued that this is most effectively and efficiently achieved through government agencies with centralised decision-making:[10] for example, one agency to manage police services. In public administration theory, centralised decision making is regarded as being beneficial.

Taking decisions on behalf of all citizens is quite different from private markets where the 'buyer' can choose whether to buy a product from a 'seller'. The citizen has no such choice in public administration theory and, in market terms, the centralised public bureaucracy is effectively a monopoly. For many economists, a monopoly is unresponsive and inefficient as a service supplier. Centralised decision making is therefore not beneficial. Hence, there is a basic conflict in public service between *public administration* theory and *market economic* theory.[11] For many countries in the last 20 years, the view has shifted towards introducing market forces to reduce the price of public goods. For such countries, public administration theory has therefore moved closer to market economic theory.

The public sector approach accompanying this shift towards market forces has been to break up the state monopoly supplier of such goods into several companies, which then compete against each other on price and service levels in the market place. Competition is likely to reduce the costs of the former monopolistic state enterprise and therefore the prices paid by the customer: in essence, this is the *privatisation* of former state monopolies. Even in countries with a strong socialist tradition like China, there have been moves to privatise former state monopolies like civil air transport. The underpinning principle of privatisation is that market competition – often referred to as the *market mechanism* – is more efficient than monopoly in the management of state resources.

In some countries, this market-based approach has taken an additional form: co-operation between the public interest and private enterprise – called *public private partnerships* – with private finance and management being used to develop and subsequently administer public services. For example, private finance might be raised to develop a new state hospital in the public sector and then a private company appointed for a period of years to manage all the hospital services on behalf of the public. This co-operative approach remains controversial – particularly the allegedly high level of fees paid for the management contract – but is an example of another form of market mechanism in the public sector.

The costs of the market mechanism in the public sector

In addition to market-based benefits in public sector strategy, there are also costs associated with such an approach. There are two main areas: first, there are clear *limits* to how far the market approach can be implemented. Market theory suggests that failed products disappear from markets because they are not meeting demand. In principle, this would therefore suggest that any public sector body that is subject to market pressures and fails to deliver on its public sector objectives should be closed. Whilst this may be possible for a failing school because there may be other schools, it is clearly not possible to allow a large regional hospital with specialist staff and equipment to fail. There is a cost to keeping such organisations open in terms of efficiency and lack of market pressures.

There is a second problem associated with introducing the market mechanism – the *transaction costs* of privatisation. There is a need to set standards, monitor progress, evaluate performance and other activities associated with giving former monopolies the freedom to undertake public services. If this were not done, such organisations might not deliver the full level of service previously provided by the monopoly: the market mechanism is powerful and can potentially distort performance. Setting such standards and monitoring the outcome has two main costs:

● the public monitoring organisations needed to check on the activities of the newly privatised public sector organisations and ensure that they continue to deliver their public service obligations;

● the administrative costs at the newly privatised organisations involved in providing data on their performance and related activities.

In theory, the benefit of the market mechanism should outweigh the two costs outlined above. In practice, there is some disagreement over such matters. Importantly in public sector strategy, it is essential to consider carefully the monitoring mechanisms, performance targets and their related costs in the development of strategy. It is also appropriate to build network contacts with those involved in the monitoring process – the public regulators – and discuss proposed strategy change with them.

The balance between laissez-faire and dirigiste policies of national governments

Definition ➤ In public sector policy, the market mechanism is the means by which the state uses competition between suppliers, market pricing and quasi-market mechanisms to determine the supply and demand of goods that were previously state monopolies. In both the EU and the US, there are differing views on the extent to which the state should become involved in markets. In France, Italy and Greece, it has long been the tradition that state-owned companies and state intervention are important elements of the national economy. In the UK, New Zealand and the US, the opposing view has been taken. The approach adopted is essentially a *political* choice made by those in power. The two approaches – often referred to as *laissez-faire* and *dirigiste* – are summarised in Table 18.1. Adam Smith, Karl Marx and many other political commentators have all contributed to the important political debate in this

Table 18.1

Two models of the public sector environment

Laissez faire: free-market model	Dirigiste: centrally directed model
• Low entry barriers	• High entry barriers
• Competition encouraged	• National companies supported against international competition
• Little or no state support for industry	• State ownership of some key industries
• Self-interest leads to wealth creation	• Profit motive benefits the few at the expense of the many
• Belief in laws of supply and demand	• Failure in market mechanism will particularly affect the poor and can only be corrected by state intervention
• Higher unemployment levels	
• Profit motive will provide basis for efficient production and high quality	• Need to correct monopolies controlled by private companies

area. Table 18.1 is intended merely to summarise areas that are the most relevant to the development of corporate strategy.

In practice, the distinctions drawn in Table 18.1 are very crude. Some countries offer a *balance* between strong state-sponsored policies in some areas – for example, education, favoured industries (as in Singapore), investment in roads, power and water – and then couple this with a free-market approach in other areas – for example, privatisation of state monopolies or lower barriers to entry to encourage investment by multinational enterprises (MNEs). (MNEs are the large global companies such as Ford, McDonald's and Unilever.) Each country will have its own approach, so any public sector environmental analysis will have to be conducted on a country-by-country basis.

18.1.2 The concept of public value

Definition ➤ Public value refers to the benefits to the whole of the nation from owning and controlling certain products and services. For example, the national defence forces and the police service have a clear benefit to all the citizens of a country. The government, on behalf of the nation, takes the decision of which public goods and services should be under national control and which services should be controlled privately by business. In practice in many countries, there are some grey areas which are neither totally in government control nor totally private; the public value is therefore mixed. Figure 18.2 gives some examples.

Given the concept of public value, there are three important consequences for public sector strategy analysis:

● Unlike a private sector market for a car or a hotel room, the public service for defence forces or clean air needs to be a binding collective decision for it to be effective. Public sector strategy needs to be enacted and supported by a *legal framework* and laws that bind, govern and distribute the public value. This legal framework needs to be analysed.

Figure 18.2

Public value is highest in the public domain

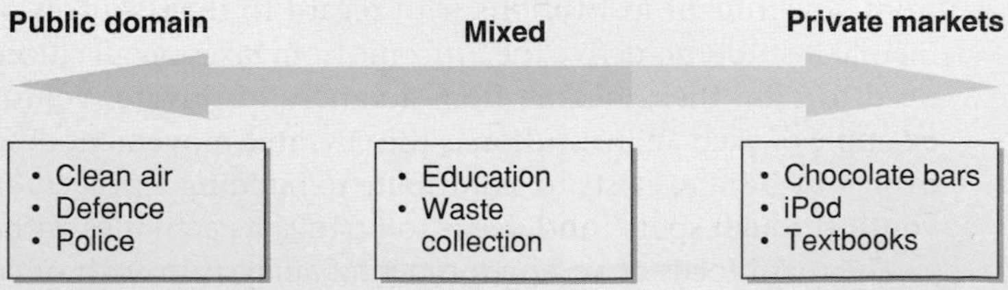

Public domain	**Mixed**	**Private markets**
• Clean air • Defence • Police	• Education • Waste collection	• Chocolate bars • iPod • Textbooks

● There is a need to ensure that the public value is genuinely available to all citizens, with everyone having a fair share or an equal opportunity – the concept of *equity*. This is fundamentally different from business strategy. The extent and nature of public equity needs to be analysed in developing public sector strategy.

● Occasionally, there is a need to remedy problems in distributing the public value: the market mechanism may fail after privatisation has occurred. Market failure can take many forms: for example, the newly privatised companies may attempt to control the market and keep their prices artificially high. The government may therefore appoint a special independent *public regulator* to oversee the results of privatisation and ensure full and fair distribution of the benefits of the public value arising from the privatisation. This is particularly important where public value is mixed with private wealth – for example, in a privatised telecommunications company. The mechanism for ensuring the fair distribution of public value therefore needs to be analysed.

As an example of the implications of the areas above, we can examine the World Bank. The *legal framework* environment analysis will cover the basic legal articles of association setting up the Bank, the membership of its board and their responsibilities. The *equity analysis* will need to examine the way that funds are actually distributed by the Bank and the mechanisms to ensure equality of all citizens without preference. In the case of the World Bank, a *public regulator* is probably irrelevant because there is no substantive element of competition involved in its distribution of funds and because the directors of the Bank have a legal duty to ensure fairness.

18.1.3 Stakeholder power and complexity

In the public sector, stakeholder power is possessed by those citizens who are able to influence the decisions of the state. In practice, this may be through democratic elections, with a change of government leading to substantial changes in the services provided by the state. But it may be through other forms of state structure that do not rely on democracy. The difficulty here is that all such changes can be short-term and involve quite substantial and unpredictable changes in public sector strategy. Such uncertainty deserves to be analysed in developing public sector strategy.

In addition, there are other ways for citizens to exert their influence – pressure groups, campaigns, even riots and disturbances. At the World Bank, the annual meeting can exert pressure for change but views are more likely to be expressed through committees and similar meetings. This is important because it shows how public bodies can be lobbied and pressured in their decision making. A stakeholder power analysis can be undertaken – *see* Chapter 12 – but this may only show that the stakeholder group is more powerful than the politician who is theoretically directing the public service. We return to this matter in Section 18.3 on power and democracy.

18.1.4 Special issues in not-for-profit organisations

Although the definition of not-for-profit organisations is very broad, it will certainly cover charitable, voluntary and other public interest bodies that are not owned by the state. Such organisations are not concerned with the distribution of public value in the sense of delivering this equitably to all citizens. In addition, not-for-profit organisations are quite different from government institutions with regard to their sources of funds. Public sector governmental institutions derive their income from taxes on all citizens. Not-for-profit organisations need to raise their income from a variety of private, voluntary and variable sources. An example of such an institution is the Olympic movement described in Case 18.2. This is not owned by a state, exists to 'contribute to building a peaceful and better world by educating youth through sport', and needs to finance its activities without state support.

The main focus of an environmental analysis in such organisations will need to explore two main areas:

1 *The precise role and purpose of such organisations*: the role will define the environment in which the not-for-profit organisation exists and with whom it is engaged. For example, the role of the international Red Cross organisation (and Red Crescent in Muslim countries) is to bring humanitarian and disaster relief to those in distress around the world. Its environment is therefore that of other relief agencies, governments and countries needing such relief and the individuals in those countries benefiting from such work. In practice, this needs careful definition to ensure that the environment is adequately described.

2 *The fund-raising mechanism of the organisation*: virtually every not-for-profit organisation needs financial support to undertake its work. Such organisations may even compete against each other for public support and public funds. For example, the public funds raised around the world in 2005 for the Asian tsunami disaster meant that some other public charities had difficulty in raising sufficient funds for their own activities. This suggests that an environmental analysis needs to examine carefully the current and future sources of funds of the organisation and the implications in terms of related, similar organisations. It also needs to explore the more general mood and public acceptance of the country or region in which the organisation operates, since this will impact on its ability to generate adequate funds.

18.1.5 Analysing the public sector strategy environment

We can summarise the implications of the discussion above by returning to the basic strategic environmental analysis undertaken in Chapter 3 and considering its implications for public sector analysis. This is shown in Table 18.2.

Table 18.2

Analysing the public sector strategic environment[12]

Stage	Business strategy techniques	Can they be used in the public sector?
1 Environment basics – an opening evaluation to define and explore basic characteristics of the environment (*See* Section 3.2)	Estimates of some basic factors surrounding the environment: • Market definition and size • Market growth • Market share	Possibly but they need to be redefined: • Demand for a public service • Political will to supply the public service • The relevant funding and costs of supplying the service
2 Consideration of the degree of turbulence in the environment (*See* Section 3.3)	General considerations: • Change: fast or slow? • Repetitive or surprising future? • Forecastable or unpredictable? • Complex or simple influences on the organisation?	Yes, but perhaps not so easy to analyse. It will need judgement, especially on the influence of political and pressure groups • Is the environment too turbulent to undertake useful predictions? • What are the opportunities and threats for the organisation?
3 Background factors that influence the competitive environment (*See* Section 3.4)	PESTEL analysis and scenarios	Yes, definitely • Predict, if possible • Understand interconnections between events
4 Analysis of stages of market growth (*See* Section 3.5)	Industry life cycle	Possibly but not really clear what this could mean beyond the natural rhythm of country change
5 Factors specific to the industry: what delivers success? (*See* Section 3.6)	Key factors for success analysis	Yes in the sense that KFS will help identify issues with regard to the *priorities* needed for successful public sector strategy
6 Factors specific to the competitive balance of power in the industry (*See* Section 3.7)	Five Forces analysis	• Possibly for 'customers' and even 'competitors' (many public sector institutions compete for funds) • 'Supplier' analysis is also relevant because governments should be powerful buyers • But difficult to see relevance of 'substitutes' and 'new entrants' in a monopoly

Table 18.2 *continued*

Stage	Business strategy techniques	Can they be used in the public sector?
7 Factors specific to co-operation in the industry (*See* Section 3.8)	Four Links analysis	• Definitely worth undertaking this analysis – the World Bank example shows its importance • Network analysis will also be useful
8 Factors specific to immediate competitors (*See* Section 3.9)	Competitor analysis and product portfolio analysis	• Difficult to envisage any significant benefit here
9 Customer analysis (*See* Section 3.10)	Market and segmentation studies	Customer analysis is useful but needs to be considered in relation to the broader concepts of public value and choice in the public sector

Key strategic principles

- In public sector strategy, the analysis of the strategic environment is more complex than in the private sector. The main reason is that public sector strategy involves the wide-ranging and ill-defined subject of the *public interest*: the public interest concerns both the objectives and the institutions that make and implement public decisions. There are two main public sector models – centrally directed (*dirigiste*) and free-market (*laissez-faire*).

- The *market mechanism* is the means by which the state uses market pricing and quasi-market mechanisms to determine the supply and demand of goods that were previously state monopolies. In practice, over the last 20 years many states have moved to greater use of the market through privatising state-owned companies. Each individual country will have its own approach to the use of such mechanisms. A public sector environmental analysis will have to be conducted on a country-by-country basis. There are also two costs associated with the market mechanism: first, the cost of being unable to close inefficient services because they provide vital public services; second, the cost of administering the market mechanism to ensure that it serves the agreed public objectives.

- Public value refers to the benefits to the whole of the nation from owning and controlling certain products and services. But such value needs to be considered within the legal framework that binds and governs the value. In addition, public value requires the concept of equity to make sure that the value is distributed to all citizens. In some circumstances, public value needs a regulator to deal with any market imperfections.

- In the public sector, stakeholder power is possessed by those citizens who are able to influence the decisions of the state. Such power may be expressed through democratic elections but these can lead to short-termism in strategic decisions. Power can also be exercised through pressure groups and other forms of interest. Such power needs to be analysed.

- In the not-for-profit sector, an environmental analysis needs to consider the role and purpose of the organisation. It also needs to identify its actual and potential sources of funds. Such organisations cannot rely on public taxes to pay for their activities and need to seek voluntary contributions that will vary with a range of factors.

- The nine stages in environmental analysis used for business strategy can be adapted for use in public sector strategy analysis, though they need to be treated with caution.

18.2 ANALYSING RESOURCES IN THE PUBLIC AND NOT-FOR-PROFIT SECTORS

As we saw in Chapter 6, the concept of sustainable competitive advantage underpins resource-based analysis in business strategy. However, the public sector has traditionally been regarded as not engaging in competitive activities – for example, the public fire and rescue service is non-competitive. If there is no competition in the public sector, then resource analysis will be quite different from its equivalent in business strategy. The first issue therefore is whether sustainable competitive advantage has any meaning in the public sector. If there is 'competition', then what form does this take?

The second issue with regard to public sector resources is the broader one of the *nature* of such resources beyond competitive issues and compared with business resources. By 'nature' is meant the range of resources available to the public sector strategist and the costs associated with public sector resources. The third issue is to identify the analytical tools for such work.

18.2.1 Does sustainable competitive advantage have any meaning in the public sector?

The World Bank case suggests that the Bank is unique and does not compete with other institutions. However, governments can withhold funds if the Bank is underperforming and, in a sense, the World Bank therefore has to compete for funds. The Olympic bargaining case later in this chapter deals with five cities bidding to host the Summer Olympics in 2012. It explores five competing bids from public bodies and demonstrates that public organisations *can* compete – *see* Case 18.2. But is this perhaps a special case? Do most public sector bodies conform to the monopolistic view of government and rarely engage in competition? The answer depends on the type of public administration model adopted by the nation – the *public sector administration* model or the *new public management* model. Resource analysis needs to begin by identifying which model is used by the state.

Definition ➤ For many years, the *public sector administration model* was that of an organisation that did the bidding of its political masters.[13] In this model, a professional civil service enacted government legislation and administered the activities of the state on behalf of the government. The same public sector also contained public sector enterprises, such as electricity or telecommunications, that made the public pay for their monopolistic services.[14] Competition played a relatively minor role in such a scheme: for example, one regional police force did not normally compete with another to make arrests. However, the annual budget of the police force – perhaps – 'competed' for funds from the government against the budget for other public services like defence and, in this sense, there was a small element of competition. Importantly, in this description of public services, there was little incentive for public employees to reduce their costs and increase their efficiencies because their services were essentially monopolistic.[15] More generally, such a model of public sector decision-making did not lend itself to the rigorous economic logic of competitive advantage.

For many national governments around the world over the last 20 years, the situation has changed from the model outlined above, which has been replaced, at least in part, by Definition ➤ the *new public management (NPM) model*.[16] New Public Management is a model of public sector decision-making where the professional civil service operates with more market competition coupled with former state monopolies being divided and competing against each other for business from citizens. However, the nation retains some areas under state control, like the defence of the nation. The new model offered a set of ideas about how government can operate based to a much greater extent on the efficiencies derived from market competition.[17] There are six core issues in NPM[18] – productivity, marketisation, service orientation, decentralisation, policy and accountability – but from a strategy perspective the key issue is marketisation, so that is the issue explored here. This means that this section is not a full discussion of the many other aspects of NPM, which can be explored through the books listed at the end of this chapter.

NPM is based on two main assumptions.[19] The first is that demand for government services can be separated from the supply of those services. The second is that it is possible to introduce competition into the supply of such services. We can explore these assumptions by examining what has happened in those countries that have sold into the private sector previously nationalised industries. Examples of such state companies sold into the private sector include electricity generation and telecommunications services. After privatisation, demand for such services has not fundamentally changed, so the assumption that supply can be separated from demand has proved correct. Moreover, privatisation has taken place in such a way that the monopolies have been split into several competing companies, thus introducing competition into supply.

From a resource analysis perspective, it follows that competition does exist when a nation has adopted NPM policies. It is not possible to set out all the evidence in this brief review, but many researchers in both public sector administration[20] and strategy development in the public sector[21] support such a conclusion. This means that it is relevant to consider resource-based competitive analysis in the public sector. Such competitive advantages as tangible and intangible resources, core competencies, architecture, reputation, innovative capability and knowledge may all be explored in the public sector. The reader is referred back to Chapter 6 for a more comprehensive view of this area. It also follows that a SWOT analysis can be employed to summarise such issues – Chapter 13 sets out the main elements.[22]

Although the above argument has focused largely on government organisations, the same basic principles can be applied in not-for-profit organisations. The Olympics case later in the chapter demonstrates their validity here. This is explored more fully in Section 18.2.3.

18.2.2 The special nature of public sector resources

In addition to issues of competitive advantage, public sector resource analysis also needs to explore the special nature of public sector resources in four areas:

- Sufficient and appropriate resources for purpose
- Public power as a resource
- The costs and benefits of public resources
- Persuasion and education as a public resource.

Sufficient and appropriate resources for purpose – trade-offs and balances

As we have seen, some parts of the public sector are essentially monopolies – for example, defence forces and the fire and rescue service – and therefore do not compete amongst themselves. Nevertheless, such services do need to deliver the service identified by the nation and its politicians and they need to do this at 'reasonable' levels of cost (with 'reasonable' usually being defined by the governing politicians of the country). Nevertheless, many recent government initiatives in many countries have been directed at achieving greater efficiencies, higher levels of service and lower costs with the same service[23] – Pollitt and Bouckaert call these 'trade-offs and balances'.

Definition ➤ In order to undertake such tasks, public sector resource analysis needs to assess whether sufficient and appropriate resources are available to deliver the purposes set by the state. The first step in analysing resources is therefore to examine the objectives set by the state – for example, if a public sector ambulance is required to answer an emergency within 15 minutes, appropriate numbers of ambulances and trained medical staff need to be available. Public sector resource analysis then needs to set the service levels and other requirements of the state against the available resources.[24] Such an approach to resource analysis goes beyond the identification of competitive advantage and similar concepts from business strategy.

In analysing the required resources to deliver public sector objectives, one of the main difficulties rests with the words 'sufficient and appropriate'. The reason is that many state institutions will be able to make a case for more resources. To overcome this difficulty, careful exploration of the defined purpose and the tasks to be undertaken, coupled with comparisons from past experience and similar activities in other areas will provide at least some of the answers. In practice, one of the main deciding factors is likely to be a government policy decision on 'trade-offs and balances' based on the political judgement of the public governing body. The case on the Kings Theatre at the end of this chapter captures many of the dilemmas and policy decisions required: public sector expertise, political pressure for re-election, pressure groups from within the local community. Resource analysis needs to consider these many complex aspects.

Public power as a resource

In corporate strategy, resource analysis often focuses on economic power, with cash and profitability as the dominant outcome. Even human resources like leadership and knowledge are often assessed by their ability to deliver profits or some form of added value to employees or management. In contrast, public resources have another dimension.

By definition, the nation state has an authority that is lacking to an individual business, however large. The state can be considered as having three distinctive, interactive systems that are not present in business: politics, a market economy and a system of public administration and the law.[25] Each of these is set within the larger context of a civil society of the nation – *see* Figure 18.3. The citizens of that nation both participate in and form judgements upon the legitimacy of that society and its institutions – not necessarily through a democracy.

From a public strategy perspective, this view of the state implies that citizens give their open or tacit approval to the events and decisions of the state. In this sense, citizens give power to public servants – for example, power to the defence forces to defend the state and support to the police and judiciary to uphold the law. This power can be mobilised at various times and forms a significant part of public sector strategy.[26] For example, the state can decide that it should lay increased emphasis on environmental 'green' issues in a way that

Figure 18.3

A simplified representation of the three main elements of the nation

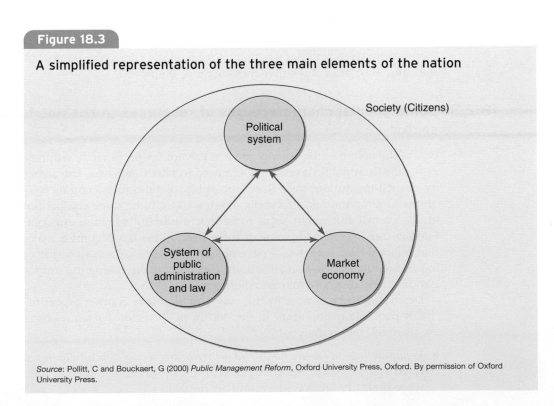

Source: Pollitt, C and Bouckaert, G (2000) *Public Management Reform*, Oxford University Press, Oxford. By permission of Oxford University Press.

Definition ➤ is beyond that of individual businesses. Public power is a resource possessed by nation states and consists of the collective decision-making that derives from the nation state. The analysis of such a resource is important in developing public sector strategy.

The costs and benefits of public resources

Coupled with the state's exercise of power, there are also costs. Costs arise as the state goes about its business, investing in defence, in legal institutions and other areas of governmental activity.[27] They also include the costs associated with the misuse of power and the unintended side effects of political decisions[28] – for example, the higher costs associated with sorting waste when recycling becomes part of government policy in order to preserve the environment for future generations. Importantly, the state does not have unlimited funds for such activities because of the limitations on raising taxes.

Definition ➤ Public resources need to be analysed for their ability to deliver the maximum benefit for the least cost. 'Benefit' here has a broader social definition than simply delivering shareholder profitability in the private sector – for instance, social benefits associated with improvements in public health. This means that the task of the public sector manager has some similarities to that in the private sector but has a far wider brief and consequences. In practice in the public sector, this may require a strategic choice between making cost resource savings and improving performance through resource investment. It has been suggested that this can be resolved if there is some spare capacity in the governmental system or the possibility of employing new technology to improve efficiency.[29] Other resource-based solutions have included privatisation, as explored earlier, and setting public sector service quality and service standards in order to make comparisons across a part of the public sector – comparisons of health treatment in various parts of a country, perhaps.

Persuasion and education as a public resource

Unlike individual businesses, the state has the opportunity to help individuals and groups improve their own lives by persuasion and education.[30] For example, the state can set up a public education programme to show citizens how to prevent fires. This may be just as useful and productive as the fire fighting service itself. This role for the state implies a public sector resource that is not readily available to individual businesses and needs to be considered in any resource-based analysis of public sector activity. Public sector resource analysis therefore needs to consider whether persuasion and education are possible resources of the state and, if so, how and where they might be employed.

18.2.3 Some special characteristics of resources in the not-for-profit sector

Unlike the public sector, the resources of the not-for-profit sector will require funds that do not come from public taxes: there is a need to raise funds from private sources. The majority of such institutions need to rely on public donations and commercial business support of one kind or another. Inevitably, there is likely to be some competition to obtain those funds, even if this might seem somewhat distasteful to those engaged in such activity. Fund-raising expertise for some of these institutions has become a major area of resource that requires careful analysis – covering such resource areas as networks of contacts, branding and reputation, and organisational capability in energising the supporters of the organisation, many of whom may be volunteers.

Describing the resources in this way also identifies another aspect of resource analysis that is particularly important in the not-for-profit sector: *human resources*. Typically, there are three relevant resources here:[31]

● *Voluntary help in raising funds and delivering the service.* Such helpers can be highly dedicated and provide a real strength to an organisation. But they can also be fickle in the sense that they are volunteers and are unpaid.

- *Specialist technical knowledge in delivering the service.* The purpose of some types of not-for-profit organisations is to deliver highly specialised expertise – for example the highly respected organisation Médecins sans Frontières provides high quality medical relief for refugees. Such specialist levels of expertise require careful resource analysis.

- *Leadership and governance*: each institution is unique but benefits over time from leaders who have the imagination and the ability to carry their workers, supporters and outside institutions with them as they develop and deliver their services. Arguably, this resource is even more important than in the public sector, because there is no acceptance and tradition of the public bureaucracy that is usually available to government institutions.

18.2.4 Analysing resources in the public sector

To summarise, the analysis of public sector resources will need to consider the main areas covered in Chapter 6 for business strategy: tangible, intangible and organisational resources; core competencies; architecture, reputation and innovative capability; knowledge. In addition, the areas covered in more depth in this section need to be explored – public power, costs and benefits, persuasion and education – as possible resources available in the public sector. In not-for-profit organisations, this needs to be supplemented by an analysis of fund-raising and human resources.

The outcome of the resource analysis will identify the public organisation's strongest abilities and most effective actions and policies. From an administrative viewpoint, it will also set out the resources that it employs on a regular basis to perform well.[32] This latter point is important because the public sector is often involved in delivering an efficient administration with its routine tasks and legal frameworks that go beyond much of private sector activity.

One final aspect of public sector resource analysis also deserves to be emphasised – the necessary and appropriate resources to deliver the purpose of the organisation.[33] We explore purpose in the next section.

Key strategic principles

- Public sector resource analysis needs to begin by examining which of the two public sector models – public sector administration or new public management – is adopted by the state. The *public sector administration* model consists of a professional civil service bureaucracy that enacts government legislation and administers the activities of the state on behalf of the government alongside state monopolies that supply services to the citizens. The *new public management* model is a model of public sector decision-making where the professional civil service operates with more market competition while former state monopolies are divided and compete against each other for business from citizens. However, the nation retains some areas under state control, such as the defence of the nation

- The former does not support competitive advantage while the latter is underpinned by concepts of market competition in what was formerly the monopolistic state sector. Resource-based analysis in the public sector for the second approach will include similar concepts to those in business strategy – tangible, intangible and organisational resources, etc.

- There are four additional considerations that apply in analysing resources in the public sector – appropriate and sufficient resources for purpose; public power as a resource; the costs and benefits of public resources; persuasion and education as a public resource.

Key strategic principles *continued*

- Public sector resource analysis needs to assess whether sufficient and appropriate resources are available to deliver the purpose and objectives set by the state. This means that resource analysis needs to identify public purpose and then assess resource requirements against this.

- Public power is a resource possessed by nation states and consists of the collective decision-making that derives from the nation state. The analysis of such a resource is important in developing public sector strategy.

- With regard to costs and benefits of public resources, the task of the public sector manager is often that of obtaining the maximum benefit for the least cost. 'Benefit' here has a broader social definition than simply delivering shareholder profitability in the private sector. Such a balance needs to be considered in resource analysis in the public sector.

- Public sector resource analysis also needs to consider whether persuasion and education are possible resources of the state and, if so, how and where they might be employed.

- In not-for-profit organisations, there is a need to examine the fund-raising resource of the organisation. In addition, there is a specific need to examine human resources of such organisations in three areas: voluntary help, specialist technical knowledge and the leadership and governance.

- The outcome of the resource analysis will identify the public organisation's strongest abilities and most effective actions and policies. From an administrative viewpoint, it will also set out the resources that it employs on a regular basis to perform well.

CASE STUDY 18.2

Olympic Games 2012: five cities bid to host the games

The Olympic movement is the public sector organisation that awards the Olympic Games every four years. Five cities bid to host the 2012 Games. This case examines the intense competition to pick the winning city.

Background

According to the Olympic Charter, established by Pierre de Coubertin, the purpose of the Olympic movement is to 'contribute to building a peaceful and better world by educating youth through sport'. The movement includes the International Olympic Committee (IOC) which chooses the location of the Games, and also involves the national Olympic committees, international federations and other bodies responsible for organising international sport.

Benefits of the Games to the cities and to the IOC

For the winning city, the Olympic Games can bring mixed benefits. On the positive side, they brought prestige and millions of visitors to cities like Barcelona in 1992, Sydney in 2000 and Athens in 2004. Countries also benefited from the billions of US dollars of investment in new transport, housing and hotel accommodation. Millions of visitors come to the Games and spend large sums during their time in the host city and

London's bid for the Olympic Games was judged alongside those of four other cities in a competitive spirit that would have done credit to any business.

television coverage is global. In many ways, the award of the Olympic Games is a form of international recognition that allows a city to establish itself finally on the world map: Beijing will be the next city to benefit, in 2008.

However, the Games experience has not always been so positive. Some earlier Olympics did not fully recover their costs. They were also hampered in some cases by Cold War boycotts and problems associated with drug taking in sport. The Athens Olympics caused concern for some years because the work to build the new venues was behind schedule and was likely to go over its budget. In spite of such problems, the five host cities were convinced that the benefits for them would outweigh the costs.

In addition to benefits to the host city and country, the Games also bring benefits to the Olympic movement itself. In the period 2001–2004, the summer and winter Games provided US$4.2 billion to support the work of the movement. By far the greatest part of this income is from broadcasting rights to the Games – *see* Figure 18.4 – with the IOC becoming very skilled at negotiating higher fees to broadcast the Games over the years. It was back in 1984 when the first bidding war was set in motion by the then President of the IOC, Juan Samaranch, for the bidding rights to the 1988 Winter Games in Calgary. The movement was in trouble financially after some Western countries had boycotted the Moscow Olympics. He set about restructuring the games to become more media-friendly – for example, by running the Games across two weekends – so that he could attract the big US television networks to bid for the broadcast rights and improve the Olympic movement's finances. He was successful and the Games have since developed a broadcast-led marketing strategy. Public sector institutions have not hesitated to seek sources of funds from commercial bodies where this did not conflict with their ideals.

The Olympic bidding process

After a preliminary process to select a group of leading cities, the IOC invites the selected candidate cities to develop detailed bids to explain how they would conduct the Games. The IOC has developed a set of detailed criteria in a number of areas to decide the winner – government support, public opinion, general infrastructure, security, venues, accommodation and transport to the various sporting sites. The candidate cities then develop detailed plans that are inspected by an evaluation commission on behalf of the IOC. The inspectors prepare a detailed report on each bid but do not make the final selection. In the case of the 2012 Games, the report was circulated to the IOC in June 2005, with the final choice being made by all IOC members in Singapore at a meeting in early July 2005.

Candidate cities were not allowed to approach members of the IOC during the evaluation phase on threat of exclusion from the process. However, it was known that some IOC members were not totally happy with this non-contact approach. Some commentators suggested that candidate city delegates could just 'happen to meet' IOC members at various public gatherings. The reason for this elaborate procedure was that delegates were accused of significant bribery during the bidding process for the Salt Lake City Winter Games of 1992. There were many apocryphal stories: an IOC delegate was reported to have complained to hotel reception that he could not enter his hotel room because it was jammed with gifts from candidate cities; another delegate was reported to have received a pet pedigree dog because she was rumoured to like dogs; sexual favours were also reported as being available. All this led the IOC to ban such attempts at influence and develop an independent review procedure for all the bids.

Winning the bid for the 2012 Games

All the candidates made their presentations to the evaluation committee during March and April 2005. The five cities are listed in Exhibit 18.2. It is important to note that it was not the national or local government that made the bid but a separate local committee made up of representatives from many in the local sporting and wider community. Nevertheless, the national and local governments were firm supporters of the bid because of the major changes in local and national infrastructure that were being proposed. In line with the earlier guidance on not accepting local favours, the evaluation committee were not allowed to accept any gifts and could only attend one reception given by each candidate nation: for example in France, this was hosted at the Elysée Palace by the French president and in the UK by the Queen at Buckingham Palace.

▶

Figure 18.4

Income to the Olympic movement

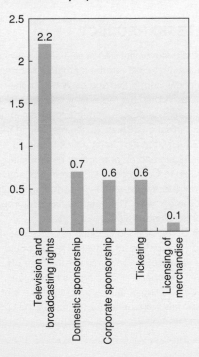

▶ **CASE STUDY 18.2 continued**

Exhibit 18.2

The five candidate cities for 2012 in the order visited by the evaluation committee

Candidate city	Total proposed investment US$ billion	Proposed facilities
Madrid	3.5	'Respect for the environment governs all aspects of the project.' Major facilities close to each other and the city centre
London	4.6	Main zone on regenerated site in East London with some events at famous venues in the city centre
New York	2.7	Athlete's village on the East River, Stadium in West Manhattan with floating warm-up track on Hudson River
Paris	5.0	Most venues already built and 80 per cent of all sports within 10 minutes of Olympic Village
Moscow	5.0	Most events within five sites along the Moscow River – 71 per cent of venues already built

Winning the bid has therefore been severely constrained in recent years. Nevertheless, it was considered that network contacts made over a number of years were vital to bid success. France had an advantage here because its team had made numerous contacts during their unsuccessful bid for the 2008 Games. Many of its venues were also well advanced. The London and Madrid bids were viewed with favour because they involved more radical sporting facilities and one of the criteria was to leave a legacy of buildings and facilities that had not previously been present. The New York bid had some excellent venue proposals, including the use of the Yankee Stadium, Giants Stadium and Flushing Meadow. Unfortunately, there was a problem over planning permission for one of the new venues. The Moscow bid used many venues that had been prepared for previous sporting events and was particularly compact in terms of sports and transport facilities.

During the actual bidding process in Singapore, one city was eliminated during each of the rounds of bidding. The final winner was London. Although the International Olympic Committee (IOC) did not give its reasons, it is likely that London presented a bid that more clearly met the IOC requirement for a new, lasting regeneration project. It is also likely that the intense lobbying of members of the IOC by the London bid team was more effective than the more discreet persuasion of the French team.

© Copyright Richard Lynch 2006. All rights reserved. Case written by Richard Lynch from published information only.[34]

Case questions

1 *Use the resource-based view of strategy development to analyse the Olympic bidding process.*

2 *Is it appropriate for public sector bodies to bid for benefits?*

3 *What lessons, if any, on public sector strategy can be learnt from the Olympic movement?*

STRATEGIC PROJECT

The Olympic movement began as a small international organisation that celebrated the amateur sportsperson. It was friendly, supportive and essentially non-commercial. Today, the movement has become a massive global enterprise, with the involvement of sports organisations, cities, governments and many others. Equally, the movement relies totally on television rights and other forms of commercial sponsorship to fund around US$4 billion of activities for the four years 2001–2004 – a budget of roughly US$1 billion per year. The amateur has been replaced by the professional athlete.

Has it all become too commercialised? If so, how would you restructure it? What strategies would you employ? How would you persuade the Olympic movement members – including the prestigious, gold medal winning countries and athletes – that your proposals were better for them than the current arrangements?

EXPLORING THE PURPOSE OF PUBLIC AND NOT-FOR-PROFIT ORGANISATIONS

Public sector organisations face a difficulty that does not apply to business organisations. They are directed, at least in part, by politicians who need to be re-elected – unlike business leaders. This means that the purpose of a public sector body may change significantly after an election. It also means that long-term strategic direction can be difficult to sustain in the public sector. It was for this reason that one of the criteria for the selection of the Olympic city – *see* Case 18.2 – was that *all* political parties had to support the bid, thus ensuring some continuity in the event of a political change.

In not-for-profit organisations, the reliance on voluntary, often unpaid assistance also means that such help is relatively unpredictable: it can even be withdrawn without warning for a variety of reasons. Moreover, unlike business organisations, many public sector bodies do not have shareholders expecting dividends and capital gains from their investments. Particularly in the not-for-profit sector, the objectives may well involve – perfectly justifiably – objectives that are more imprecise than shareholder value added. Such objectives may be difficult to measure and measurement may even be inappropriate: for example, the many voluntary groups that help the sick and dying deserve to be more than just a series of statistics. So how do public organisations develop their purpose? We examine this under three headings:

● Stakeholders and the will of the people

● Exploring and restating the purpose

● Dilemmas and conflicts.

18.3.1 Stakeholders and the will of the people

In developing the purpose of public sector organisations, 'the key to success for public and non-profit organisations (and for communities) is the satisfaction of key stakeholders'.[35] The starting point in exploring the purpose has to be the opinions, views and judgements of the stakeholders. We explored stakeholder concepts in Chapter 12 and emphasised the need to analyse the influence of *stakeholder power*. The reader is therefore referred back to the earlier material on this important topic.

In addition to stakeholder theory, the public sector also relies on citizens expressing their opinions to politicians, arguably – though not necessarily – through their votes in public elections. This applies particularly to government organisations but can also apply to some not-for-profit bodies. Such a choice has its antecedents in the underlying principles to ascertain the will of the people developed by such scholars as Rousseau[36] and John Stuart Mill.[37] However, as pointed out by Nobel Laureate Amartya Sen,[38] similar thinking can be traced back to leaders in other non-Western countries including India and Japan, and some Muslim thinkers. He argues that 'democracy is best seen as the opportunity of participatory reasoning and public decision-making – as government by discussion'. On this definition, democracy goes beyond voting in national elections every few years.

From a public sector strategy development perspective, there is a problem because some strategic decisions are complex and rely on expert knowledge. Sometimes it is difficult for the public to be fully informed about such matters, even if they participate in the 'participatory reasoning' of Sen above.[39] The relationship between informed public choice and its public sector consequences is therefore underpinned by an unavoidable tension. Namely, there is the need for the public debate and decision-making to be mature and insightful while at the same time allowing citizens – even the ignorant – to express their opinion and even vote.[40] Britain's former prime minister Winston Churchill's observation that 'democracy is the worst form of government except for all the others' expresses the difficulty neatly.

In forming public sector strategy, there are times when ignoring the will of the people can invite problems. Hence, it is essential to attempt to understand the public perspective in developing purpose in public sector strategy. However, there are many ways to engage and represent the people around the world.[41] Churchill's comment on the weakness of democracy can be extended to the need for a range of methods to ascertain the will of the people in deciding the purpose of public sector strategy.

18.3.2 Exploring and restating the purpose

The starting point in defining the purpose of the strategy must lie with the basic mandate of the public sector organisation – What precisely is the organisation meant to do? Who is it meant to serve? There needs to be an identifiable social or political need that the organisation seeks to fill. This should be clarified, if necessary, by revisiting the formal charter or other legal, constitutional device that was agreed at the outset. This will lead to the mission of the organisation that, ideally, needs to be stated in a paragraph, using the principles explored in Chapter 12. An exploration of the strategic context in which the organisation is operating at a particular time will then suggest its purpose. For example, the mission of the World Bank to relieve suffering, coupled with the context of the HIV/Aids epidemic in Africa, has led the bank to redefine its purpose with regard to providing finance in this particular area of assistance.

For many public and not-for-profit organisations, the mission may also need to remind the stakeholders of the *inspiration* that originally led to the foundation of the organisation – in the case of volunteer organisations in particular, this may be what will drive them forward.[42] Such a purpose sometimes requires restating in strategy development.

18.3.3 Dilemmas and conflicts

One of the problems in public sector purpose is that many statements of purpose have to consider objectives that may conflict with each other.[43] For example, the World Bank is being urged to find further funds to support development in certain countries while at the same time the Bank itself is critical of some of these countries for the way that they spend their funds.[44] More generally, we can usefully identify two dilemmas that regularly impact on public sector strategy development:

- *Steering versus rowing*:[45] some commentators have argued that, in the setting of purpose in government strategy, government would work better if it concentrated on *steering* – setting policy, providing suitable funding to relevant public bodies and evaluating performance – rather than *rowing* – delivering the services. We do not need to resolve this matter here but simply recognise that this conflicting view of the role of government will impact directly on the ability to define strategic purpose.

- *Improving public sector performance versus cost saving*: commentators have varied in the emphasis they lay on these two different areas.[46] Performance improvements take as their starting point the need to adapt to the changing needs of society, new cultures and technologies. Cost saving begins by emphasising the need for the state to do less, cut back on public services and let market demand decide what is really needed. Again, we do not need to resolve this conflict here but recognise that such conflicts need to be identified and explored in the context of purpose.

In practice, these and other conflicts will vary with the strategic context of the time and the beliefs of the stakeholders. They need to be recognised and discussed. If they remain unresolved then it will be difficult for the purpose to be defined with sufficient clarity for strategy to be developed.

Key strategic principles

- When developing the purpose of public sector organisations, the key to success for public and non-profit organisations is the satisfaction of main stakeholders. It is essential to conduct a stakeholder power analysis and seek the views of leading stakeholders.

- In addition to stakeholder theory, the development of public sector purpose also needs to reflect the general will of the people. Pubic opinion therefore needs to be identified and explored. It is sometimes difficult for citizens to develop an informed choice on complex issues but such difficulties need to be recognised and resolved.

- The starting point in defining the purpose of strategy in the public sector must lie with the basic mandate of the public sector organisation, its role and its reason for its existence. This will lead to the mission of the organisation and a definition of its purpose in the context of the issues that it faces at that time.

- Many public sector organisations receive conflicting objectives. These need to be resolved if purpose is to be successfully defined and strategy developed.

18.4 CONTEXT, CONTENT AND PROCESS IN PUBLIC SECTOR STRATEGY

Having defined and clarified purpose, we are now in a position to develop strategies to deliver that purpose. It is possible to employ prescriptive models such as the options-and-choice approach of Chapters 13 and 14.[47] The outcome, with some variations, is similar to that explored in the earlier chapters and is outlined briefly under the 'content' section below. However, given our focus on public sector strategy and the need to avoid repetition of areas covered previously, this section concentrates on the *differences* from business strategy. We examine this under three familiar strategy headings: context, content and process.

18.4.1 Strategic context

From the environmental and resource analyses, we established the chief differences in strategic context between public and business strategies:

- the change over the last 20 years from a public administration model of public sector strategy to a market-driven model in many countries;

- the dilemmas and contradictions that often exist between different policy directives in the public sector;

- the short-term and shifting nature of the political environment;

- the difficulty of raising funds and the reliance on specialist and voluntary human resources in parts of the not-for-profit sector.

Resource pressures to reduce numbers, privatisation of state monopolies and cost reduction policies all contribute to strategic context in the public sector. Shifting public attitudes on political, moral and social issues may determine the not-for-profit context. Such issues also need to be coupled with more radical changes in world environments when analysing strategic context in the public sector. For example, global warming, poverty and diseases, war and conflict, the increasing power of the internet and the ethical issues arising from biological advances all provide challenges in the public sector that may be important. Each public sector organisation will have its own list of factors against which to develop its strategy. The point here is that strategic context is arguably *broader* in the public sector than in business because of the wider role of government and not-for-profit institutions. The danger is that strategic context becomes over-complex. It can be focused by at least three methods:

- *Developing some priorities with regard to strategic purpose*: identifying, possibly through group meetings, what will have a substantial impact on purpose and strategy.

- *Using scenarios to develop some possible outcomes for the leading strategic context issues*. This will help to examine the consequences of particular situations.

- *Keeping the strategic context analysis simple*. Complex and elaborate procedures are more likely to confuse than produce workable strategies.

18.4.2 Strategic content

Just as in business strategy, public sector content development can employ prescriptive strategy concepts of options-and-choice approaches.[48] In developing such options, Bryson recommends developing options that are both 'practical alternatives and dreams' for achieving the strategic purpose of the organisation.[49] He suggests that a useful procedure is to identify the barriers to achieving those outcomes and then ways of overcoming the barriers. Finally, he recommends that the chosen options are developed into specific proposals. Such an approach is not greatly different from business strategy, though the word 'dreams' might not appear in the latter.

In developing the strategic options, the question will arise as to whether the business strategy options outlined in Chapter 13 can be employed. The options fell into two distinct areas – options associated with the strategic *environment* – such as Porter's generic strategies – and options associated with strategic *resources* – such as cost reduction and the resource-based options. Can public sector strategy use these concepts?

Dealing first with environment-based options, Porter is probably the dominant strategist in this area. It is unlikely that business strategy environment options can be used in public sector strategy. To quote Professor Ewen Ferlie of London University: 'With its strong focus on markets, profitability and competitiveness, [Porter's] models are difficult to apply literally, as prices, markets and profits all remain underdeveloped in the public sector.'[50] Nevertheless, Ferlie concludes that Porter's approach does have some merit where market-based concepts have been introduced into the public sector: 'Porterian models may prove especially useful for public sector regulators and purchasers, guiding them in their market development tasks.'[51] Such approaches may therefore be more appropriate in *new public management* treatments of public sector strategy. In addition, strategy in the not-for-profit sector may benefit from options that identify the possibility of competition in the environment for funds and people.

Resource-based strategic options offer the opportunity to focus on those competitive resources that allow some public sector bodies to offer superior public service to others.[52] To quote Professor Ferlie again: 'Resource-based models can be applied to public sector organisations, as their profile of intangible assets is surely closely correlated with their performance in such important managerial tasks as the management of strategic change.'[53] Hence, options based on public sector resource analysis are worth pursuing, including cost reductions where relevant.

We explore emergent approaches to options development in the next section.

18.4.3 Strategic process

Because of the uncertainties involved in the public sector – regime change at the political level and unforeseen cataclysmic events at the general level – some public sector strategists favour the *controlled chaos* or *logical incrementalism* of J B Quinn, explored in Chapters 11 and 16.[54] This consists of a series of small decisions within the overall purpose of the organisation, with the outcome of each step determining the next steps – in other words, an emergent process for strategy development. Beyond this concept, there seems to have been little exploration of the 'Learning-based strategic route forward' of Chapter 15. Nevertheless, the extended strategic options process called the *Oval Mapping Process*, developed by Professor

Colin Eden of Strathclyde University along with Professor Bryson and others,[55] would seem to derive much of its basis from learning-based approaches.

An alternative to logical incrementalism that has found favour with some public sector strategists[56] is the approach recommended by Lindblom. He wrote a theoretical paper – it quoted no empirical evidence – some 50 years ago called 'The Science of Muddling Through' that is still quoted with approval today.[57] Essentially, Lindblom argued that it is impossible in public sector strategy to analyse fully all the options that are available: there are just too many factors involved, from political ideas through economic pressures to social trends. He set out an alternative strategic process that was more realistic and concentrated particularly on small-scale, incremental decisions. It differs from logical incrementalism in that Lindblom made no reference to using the outcome of one stage to decide the next. 'Muddling through' is more basic in that regard. Professor Bryson argues that Lindblom's approach can have real merit in some circumstances: it reduces risk, breaks a project into small do-able steps, eases implementation, quickly makes real change, provides immediate reward and preserves gains.[58]

Professors Pollitt and Bouckaert take a similar approach and favour small steps over major change in many situations in the public sector

> To launch, sustain and implement a comprehensive strategy for reform requires certain conditions and these are seldom satisfied in the real world of public management reform . . . Thus talk of 'strategy' is usually an idealization, or post hoc rationalization of a set of processes which tend to be partial, reactive and of unstable priority.[59]

This all argues in favour of the realism of a small-scale, incremental process in public sector strategy development.

Comment

The strategic context of public sector strategy is relatively uncertain for a variety of reasons and it is also complex. There is little to be gained by speculating about whether it is *more* complex than business strategy. The essential point is that public sector strategy development has a number of dimensions that make it difficult to manage. This all suggests that radical change in public sector strategy needs to be treated with some caution – it can be done, but it requires a very clear vision, strong leadership and substantial resources which may need specialist training.[60] Incrementalism in public sector strategy may be the better option in many cases.

Key strategic principles

- For a variety of reasons, the strategic context of public sector strategy is broader than its counterpart in business strategy. The danger is that it becomes more complex and difficult to handle. There are three main mechanisms to simplify the process: priorities, scenarios and simplicity.

- Strategic content in public sector strategy can follow the options-and-choice route commonly used in some business strategy. However, options associated with the strategic environment need to be treated with considerable caution because the market mechanism is still lacking in much of the public sector. Nevertheless, options derived from resource-based analysis can be employed.

- With regard to strategic process, the uncertainties of the public sector favour the use of 'logical incrementalism' as a process. An alternative is the 'muddling through' approach which reduces public sector strategy to a series of small decisions.

- Importantly, a number of strategists argue that major strategic decisions in public sector strategy usually require substantial commitment in terms of resources and leadership. Such an approach is not so easy in practice.

18.5 IMPLEMENTATION IN PUBLIC SECTOR STRATEGY[61]

As with business strategy, effective implementation of proposed strategies is essential in the public sector. Such activity needs to be carefully planned and is best undertaken quickly and smoothly. Beyond this, the form of implementation depends upon the scale of changes planned:

● *Major changes in strategic direction*: These need a strong group of supporters and implementers, a clear agreement on the change that is required, an understanding of the main elements of that change and adequate resources to carry out the task.

● *Incremental changes in strategic direction*: These represent the better option when some of those affected hold reservations about – even objections to – the proposed strategic change. It may be possible to undertake pilot projects, use learning-based approaches, circulate the results of first initiatives so others can analyse the consequences and so that adjustments can be made.

Beyond these basic matters, strategic implementation in the public sector needs to develop specific, testable plans in a number of specific areas:

● *Explanation and understanding of the value added*: if successful strategies add value, as has been argued throughout this text, then it follows that those implementing the strategy must clearly understand this added value, its purpose and the strategies by which it will be achieved. An education and explanation phase is therefore desirable. Agreement by those involved may also be necessary in order to overcome objections to such a strategy.

● *Fixing difficulties*: in most implementation procedures, problems will arise. It is important that such difficulties are recognised as they occur. This means building monitoring mechanisms and milestones into the process.

● *Summative evaluations*: it is desirable to find out if the purpose of the strategy has been achieved. This needs to be built into the implementation process. Bryson draws a useful distinction between two aspects of such a process: *outputs*, which are the actions produced by the strategies, and *outcomes*, which are the larger ramifications of such changes – especially the symbolic changes that occur.[62] He suggests that such an evaluation can be difficult and lengthy but it is important to establish whether things are 'better' as a result of a new strategy. However, such an approach has also been used recently to justify an army of managers who do little beyond evaluating the results of strategic change – an obvious recipe for over-bureaucratic management.[63]

● *New organisations and culture*: it may be necessary to reorganise existing public sector areas and possibly to recruit or redefine management responsibilities. It may even be necessary to develop a new organisational culture to ensure long-lasting changes. These areas need to form part of the overall plan at the outset but it should be recognised that they may take years to implement. Some recent public sector strategies in the UK have underestimated the difficulties here.[64] In both the public and business sectors, people need to be given time to learn, adjust and adapt to new situations. The principles involved in this approach are explained in Chapter 21.

● *Recognise the need for flexibility*: there are very few public sector strategies that have a single, clear outcome. Many strategies will be challenged and others will need to adapt as events – including political changes – occur in the surrounding strategic context. Implementation therefore has to be alert to such issues and respond as they occur.

In the public sector, budget allocations for a period of time can often be a crucial factor in strategy implementation – 'no money, no strategy'. The difficulty is that such budgets are subject to political pressures and are often short-term, incremental and reactive. There are no simple ways to overcome this problem but it is desirable if the strategic planning stage comes *before* budget setting. In addition, it may be important to recognise the importance of individual leaders in developing the strategy – agreement and ownership of a strategy are important factors in strategy development and are not confined simply to the 'implementation phase'. In this sense, this whole section on implementation needs to be reevaluated as being part of a broader, ongoing strategy development process, rather than an add-on process after the strategy has been decided.

Comment

Finally, it is important to make the point that public servants involved in the development of strategy have an important responsibility with regard to strategy development. To quote Robert Reich:

> *The core responsibility of those who deal in public policy – elected officials, administrators, policy analysts – is not simply to discover as objectively as possible what people want for themselves and then to determine and implement the best means to satisfying these wants. It is also to provide the public with alternative visions of what is desirable and possible, to stimulate deliberation about them, provoke a re-examination of premises and values, and thus to broaden the range of potential responses and deepen society's understanding of itself.*[65]

Key strategic principles

- Strategy implementation in the public sector needs to be carefully planned and is best undertaken quickly and smoothly.

- The form of implementation depends on the scale of what is proposed. Major changes need substantial support. Smaller changes are probably best treated incrementally.

- In implementing public sector strategy, it is important to identify the value added and then explain this to those involved in its implementation. It is also necessary to have a mechanism that can fix the inevitable difficulties that will arise as new strategies are implemented.

- It may be appropriate to have a summative evaluation of the strategy after it has been implemented to find out whether the planned improvements have been achieved. However, such an approach can be lengthy and time-consuming. It can also be overbureaucratic.

- A new organisational structure and culture may be necessary for some new strategies. This will take time that needs to be built into the process from the beginning. Such processes should not be underestimated and may require years to complete. There is also a need to build some degree of flexibility into the implementation process as circumstances change.

- The budget process can be crucial for new strategies and should ideally be undertaken after the strategy has been agreed. Importantly, this is only a part of a broader implementation process that needs to include the agreement of key decision-makers. Arguably, implementation needs to be re-evaluated as being part of a broader, ongoing strategy development process, rather than an add-on process after the strategy has been decided.

'Should we close the Kings Theatre?'

A tough strategic decision for Portsmouth City Council

Portsmouth city councillors had a difficult strategic decision to make in July 2003: should they withdraw the city's financial support for the Kings Theatre, Portsmouth, UK?

The theatre had only been relaunched in 2001 but its subsidiary commercial operating company went bankrupt in early 2003 with over £200,000 debts. Closure would cause immense local anger and negate the 'Two Theatres' strategy of the city. But keeping the theatre open would be fraught with many financial problems and major risks. This case explores the strategic options available to the city.

City councils are not required to make profits. They have a broader responsibility to their electorate – to provide a range of services from education and social services to the arts and sporting activities. They operate within limits defined by the national government on the services that *must* be provided locally – like education and social welfare – and services over which the council has some *choice* – like selecting the level of support for local libraries or local sport. The difficulty comes in balancing the various demands on the council's limited budget. The decisions are more difficult when activities have been underfunded in the past and when local pride and passion are involved. Local councillors are politicians and, understandably, want to be re-elected. This case explores this typical mix of strategic decisions in one particularly acute case – the possible closure of a well-loved local theatre and its sale to a national brewery chain as a public house.

> '*A city with cultural ambitions like ours must be seen to do something with its theatres. That is the challenge.*'
> (Former council leader, Frank Worley, April 2003)

With over 170,000 people and an annual budget of around £200 million, it might be thought that Portsmouth was well placed to provide live theatre for its citizens. The city is a major tourist venue as well as offering employment in a range of local companies from IBM European headquarters to small local manufacturing companies. But Portsmouth's theatres are a victim of its past – it had four live theatres in 1950 that were packed every week. By the late 1990s, there were only two remaining major theatres – the Kings Theatre and the New Theatre Royal – plus a small Arts Theatre for experimental plays that was to be relocated to save money in mid-2003.

The reasons for this decline were not hard to find – television, the mobility to visit more distant theatres, that came from mass car ownership, the demand for nightclubs and more intimate entertainment. There was nothing unusual in Portsmouth with regard to these trends, which were the same across the UK. Many regional theatres were struggling to survive and relied on local councils to provide a subsidy. However, the fact was that the majority of people in Portsmouth had lost the habit of going to live theatre – there was limited customer demand. In addition, the demand that existed was for 'fun' entertainment rather than serious live theatre such as opera, major drama or ballet.

Portsmouth's Kings Theatre became a major focus for political pressure with the threat of total closure.

It was against this background that the city council drafted its 'Two Theatres in Portsmouth' strategy in 1999 – *see* Figure 18.5. The concept was one theatre for major popular musicals, entertainment and drama – the Kings Theatre, with around 1,500 seats – and another theatre for smaller commercial productions such as small-scale experimental drama and concerts – the New Theatre Royal, with around 500 seats. (In addition, there was another small theatre, with around 100 seats, on a different site for amateur plays and readings, but this was not considered to be a major part of the strategy.) Thus the 'Two Theatres' strategy was aimed at filling some 2,000 seats each week of the year, but without identifying a specialist market audience. There was a pool of local loyal and enthusiastic theatre-goers in the Portsmouth area, but this group was too small in itself to fill this capacity.

The 'Two Theatres' strategy relied on using its two major theatres for two different audiences. The concept was for the larger Kings Theatre to focus on the major UK touring productions, with the smaller New Theatre Royal being used for smaller-scale productions. This strategy alone would stretch the council's arts budget across two theatres. The main elements of the strategy are summarised in Figure 18.5 – the Arts Council for England did not agree with the strategy. They judged that there was insufficient customer demand for two

Figure 18.5

Kings Theatre – the 'Two Theatres in Portsmouth' strategy

Kings Theatre

- 1,500 seats, to be used for major touring companies plus local amateur companies needing a large venue.

- Grade II* listed early twentieth-century beautiful building – never been modernised – poor car parking, away from city centre.

- Was relaunched by city council in 2001 as a non-profit theatre trust.

- Trust set up a limited company in 2001 with new manager/proprietor appointed – bankrupt with over £20,000 debts by early 2003 – company then liquidated.

- Needs minimum £7.5 million capital spend to modernise – possibly as much as £13 million to bring to the standard of competitors such as Mayflower Theatre, Southampton.

New Theatre Royal

- 500 seats, to be used for smaller touring companies, local drama education projects, Portsmouth University drama and music venue.

- Grade II* listed early twentieth-century beautiful building – never been modernised – partly burnt down so cannot take large scenery; city centre location, good parking.

- Needs minimum £5 million capital spend to modernise and create flexible performance space.

major theatres. They also noted that neither theatre was positioned to appeal to a specialist 'niche' theatre market.

'We have been supporting the New Theatre Royal because a study we did some years ago demonstrated that there wasn't sufficient audience capacity in Portsmouth to support two theatres . . . [The New Theatre Royal] offers potential in the city centre and like the Kings is a beautiful theatre.'

(Richard Russell, director of external relations and development for the Arts Council England South East Region, April 2003)

As Figure 18.5 also shows, the city's strategy across its two main venues was particularly difficult because both its major theatres were old and unmodernised. Portsmouth is unique in the UK as the only city with two beautiful old theatres designed by the great theatrical architect, Frank Matcham – there were only 23 Matcham theatres left in the whole of the UK in 2003. But the two unmodernised theatres were also an immense financial burden on the city, which the central government had

done nothing to alleviate. Financial support was supposedly available for the fabric of both buildings from a national fund called the Heritage Lottery Fund for the repair of the roof, rebuilding walls and undertaking plaster repairs. However, no grants were available from that fund for any major related expenditure such as the provision of disabled facilities and the introduction of modern lighting equipment. This meant that a grant of £3–5 million from the Heritage Lottery Fund to modernise the fabric of the Kings would need to be matched by another £3–4 million from the people of Portsmouth to pay for new access arrangements for the disabled, new electrical wiring and lighting, new sound systems, etc.

An alternative source of capital funds was the Arts Council England (ACE). Such funds were not for preserving architectural heritage but for developing new arts provision in the local community. For example, ACE would fund local educational dance and drama programmes, experimental theatre and so on. ACE was not interested in the commercial theatre activities of the Kings Theatre, but it had looked favourably on the local educational initiatives of the New Theatre Royal in the past. It was able to offer grants for capital and revenue items amounting to several million pounds, but in practice ACE had never actually given any money to any of the two Portsmouth theatres.

The result was that both theatres were badly in need of complete renovation, part of which would have to be funded by the city council. But the city also had other demands on its leisure funds – for example, a major new swimming pool and a replacement for its City Museum and Records office – possibly amounting to £13 million over the next five years. Such issues were important when considering the possible closure of the Kings Theatre, which might free up funds for such other activities. They were typical of the complex strategic balance that needed to be struck between the various demands for council funds over time.

More specifically with regard to the Kings Theatre, there was disagreement on the capital expenditure needed for renovation. One estimate was £3 million by David Rixon, whose company – Kings Theatre Southsea Limited – had been brought in to manage the Kings in 2001: it was this company that went bankrupt in 2003 (see below for more on this matter). Another estimate provided to the council in May 2003 was for a figure of £7.5 million, while an earlier estimate from a company willing to take over the Kings as a full commercial venue had quoted £13 million. Any decision on the future of the Kings could not ignore these demands for significant items of capital refurbishment. In addition to the capital, a significant annual revenue subsidy by the city council would be needed for at least ten years.

In the 'Two Theatres Strategy', it was the larger Kings Theatre that would be the main commercial theatre in the city. Over time, it was hoped to attract major national touring companies that needed a large theatre. However in July 2003, the Kings Theatre was unable to take such companies because its facilities were old and needed major investment – *see* Figure 18.6. Importantly, neither of the two main competitors to the Kings Theatre required such capital expenditure. Both the Mayflower Theatre in Southampton and the Festival Theatre in Chichester had the benefit of substantial monies being spent on them in the 1980s. Essentially, they were already modern ▶

▶ CASE STUDY 18.3 continued

Figure 18.6

Kings Theatre, Portsmouth – the competitors

Mayflower Theatre, Southampton

- 1,800 seats, regular audience developed over years.

- Fully modernised theatre – compare to Kings Theatre, which is still using scenery handling built nearly 100 years ago.

- Takes top London musicals – King's Theatre will *never* compete here.

- City centre location, plenty of parking – compared with Kings Theatre, which is located away from Portsmouth town centre with poor parking for cars.

Festival Theatre, Chichester plus adjacent small experimental theatre

- 1,600 seats, strong local audience built over years.

- Modernised theatre, runs own productions – some transfer to London.

- Located on own site with good parking – just outside city centre.

Plus Portsmouth Guildhall Concert Hall and Portsmouth night clubs, comedy clubs plus other major venues in other local towns – e.g. Fareham, Havant.

'The [Kings] theatre could be solvent and operated successfully with continued subsidy at the present level.'
(Sam Shrouder, theatre consultant, after studying the Kings bankruptcy in April 2003)

Partly because of the competition, the city council faced an important question in the future – could the Kings meet its annual financial targets? This was particularly difficult because the Kings went bankrupt in March 2003 after relaunching in 2001. This suggested that its business breakeven model might never be viable – even with an annual subsidy from Portsmouth city council of £135,000.

As part of the 'Two Theatre' strategy, Portsmouth city council had decided to relaunch the Kings Theatre in 2001. The theatre had previously been in the ownership of Hampshire County Council and leased to two local Portsmouth people, who had done their best to keep the theatre alive. The city bought the Kings Theatre for £1 from Hampshire, who also gave a 'dowry' of £150,000. The city then invested some £300,000 in urgent capital funds and set aside an annual revenue subsidy of £135,000. The city recognised that it would take some time to test which theatre productions were likely to be particularly successful.

In 2001, the council leased the Kings Theatre to a trust, who in turn appointed an existing commercial limited company called Point 6 Productions to run the theatre. Its director was Mr David Rixon, who had some experience in running provincial theatres. Such a person is especially important in any such theatre strategy because commercial judgements are required on which shows to bring to the theatre and on what commercial terms. He then set up a new operating company, Kings Theatre Southsea Ltd, with a theatre producer Vanessa Ford, and with himself as managing director. It was this company that went bankrupt in 2003.

As background to the difficulties of developing a new theatre, it was always accepted that the first few years of the Kings Theatre after its relaunch would be experimental. Hence, Mr Rixon was given some freedom to test local customer demand during the period 2001–2003. However, no one bargained for the theatre actually going out of business in March 2003, with Mr Rixon resigning through ill-health.

To understand the bankruptcy and judge its relevance to the long-term impact on the Kings Theatre, it is necessary to understand how provincial theatres make profits in the UK. Precise figures are not available, but it is likely that the Kings had an annual turnover of around £550,000. It was not open every week – probably around 30 weeks of the year. Some weeks there would be a full week of activity, perhaps with a local amateur theatrical company or with a touring opera or drama company. Other weeks, there might be just one or two nights with a well-known comedian or singer. It was the responsibility of the theatre's managing director – in this case, Mr Rixon – to negotiate commercial terms with each touring company or individual artist. Typically in a modern theatre, the touring company would take 70 per cent or more of the revenue from that week – *see* Figure 18.7.

In order to attract productions, the managing director might need to take risks – for example, taking only 10 per cent

theatres that were able to offer touring companies vastly superior front and back-stage facilities compared to both Portsmouth theatres. For example, the Kings still relied on hemp ropes to pull up scenery while it was all done automatically in the Mayflower. The New Theatre Royal did not have any such facility at all: it had been burnt down in a fire started by two schoolboys in the 1970s and never replaced.

In addition to the immediate competition from Southampton and Chichester, the Kings Theatre also faced broader competition from a variety of other Portsmouth venues – numerous comedy clubs, night clubs, sporting venues and the city-owned Guildhall Concert Hall in Portsmouth city centre. Even the famous and wide-ranging theatres of central London were only two hours away by train.

As a result of possessing more modern buildings and facilities, the rival theatres in Southampton and Chichester were able to operate more attractive, popular programmes. This meant that their seat prices were higher than the Kings Theatre – typically a yield of £12–14 per head compared to around £6–10 per head at the Kings. The competitors had developed loyal audiences over many years from a wide geographical area and would provide formidable competition to any refurbished Kings Theatre, Portsmouth.

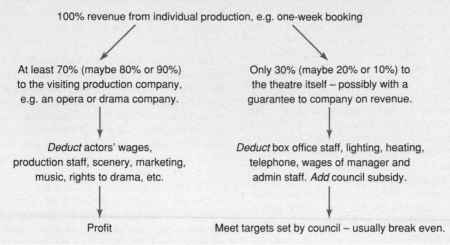

Figure 18.7

Kings Theatre – How local council-owned theatres achieve financial targets

100% revenue from individual production, e.g. one-week booking

At least 70% (maybe 80% or 90%) to the visiting production company, e.g. an opera or drama company.

Only 30% (maybe 20% or 10%) to the theatre itself – possibly with a guarantee to company on revenue.

Deduct actors' wages, production staff, scenery, marketing, music, rights to drama, etc.

Deduct box office staff, lighting, heating, telephone, wages of manager and admin staff. *Add* council subsidy.

Profit

Meet targets set by council – usually break even.

of revenue where the staging was attractive and the demand might be high. Occasionally, the director might be tempted to offer a guarantee with regard to revenue – regardless of how much money was taken at the box office during the week. Clearly, this could be particularly risky since the sums involved could easily be £30,000 for a week – compare this with the annual subsidy from the city council of £135,000. Nearly a quarter of the annual grant might be risked in only one week.

When the city council relaunched the Kings Theatre in 2001, it set three major targets for the Theatre Trust and, in turn, the public limited company of Mr Rixon. They were:

1 To raise £150,000 from local people as a contribution to the regeneration fund and a measure of local support for the Kings Theatre project. This objective was met in late 2002.
2 To achieve several business plan targets set by theatre company itself – to operate at 70 per cent of capacity, with six months open and six months closed. This was coupled with an understanding that the Kings Theatre would stay within its budget of £135,000 subsidy per annum from the city council. These targets were not met – the theatre went bankrupt in early 2003.
3 To make a successful bid to the UK Heritage Lottery Fund in late 2002 for around £3 million to fund the upgrading of the theatre. This target had not been met at the time of the bankruptcy and looked unlikely, even if the theatre had not gone bankrupt.

More than 200,000 seats were sold for 350 performances at the Kings Theatre during its 18 months of operation from late 2001 to early 2003. This was seen as satisfactory over this period. But the crucial matter to impact on the targets was the bankruptcy of the limited operating company in March 2003. What precisely happened during the 18 months of operation that led to this situation remains unclear. It is probable that some guarantees were given to touring companies – it will be obvious from the overall turnover and the level of council subsidy that

such guarantees are highly risky. In addition, the theatre did not regularly reach its operating audience capacity target of 70 per cent – it probably came closer to 50 per cent over the year.

In addition, there is some suggestion that the general management did not keep costs under sufficiently tight control. For example, it appeared that the annual pantomime made a loss at the Kings Theatre in December/January 2002/03. This is most unusual – it would be more typical at a provincial theatre for this highly popular annual event to make a significant profit and thus subsidise other activities through the year. However, the pantomime loss might also be due to the theatre being insufficiently full. It was unclear whether this latter was the case – this was particularly important because any such lack of demand would imply that the city was unable to sustain two major theatres. In turn, this would suggest that one theatre needed to be closed.

In March 2003 after the limited company had gone bankrupt, the Kings Theatre Trust called in an independent theatre expert, Mr Sam Shrouder, to examine the situation. He concluded that the Kings Theatre could be successfully operated at the level of subsidy originally set by the council. But such an approach would still require the recruitment of a new theatre general manager and would not overcome the problem of the need to spend a substantial capital sum to improve the building.

'If only one theatre can be preserved, I would have to plump for the Kings because it is the more complete, with backstage and fly tower. Volunteers have also done an enormous amount of work on the dressing-rooms and would be devastated if that went to waste.'

(Ms Paddy Drew, who has masterminded the local campaign for the survival of the Kings Theatre)

Unquestionably, there would be tremendous sadness among some members of the local and national theatre community if the Kings Theatre were to close as a theatre venue. 'Over my dead body' was how one well-known theatre expert expressed his views on the possible closure. Funds had been raised and excitement generated about the theatre's centenary in 2006. Importantly, only the Kings Theatre had the full stage facilities – fly tower and backstage – needed for many theatre productions. If the Kings were to close, then the city would be without such theatre facilities until such time as new ones could be built – possibly at the New Theatre Royal after several years of delay, though the current plans for that theatre did not include a fly tower.

There was an alternative use for the theatre, however. Back in 1999 a UK national pub chain company – J D Wetherspoon – had expressed interest to Hampshire County Council in purchasing the Kings Theatre as a public house entertainment venture. It said that it would preserve the fabric, spend funds to restore the interior and honour the grade II* listed status of the building. Importantly, the company had developed a proven tradition of preserving the fabric of historic buildings that it had acquired. But there would no longer be any live theatre for the general public.

The influential local newspaper, The News, had come out in favour of such a pub sale:

It will be a painful decision. The theatrical equivalent of separating Siamese twins. Allowing one to die to save the other. But for too long Portsmouth has been a second-division city in theatre terms, a long way behind Southampton and Chichester, despite having two buildings that are both architectural gems. And cutting off the supply lines to the Kings seems to be the sensible way to make a difference.

The Arts Council of England was also in favour of this option. This was important because its views could influence the award of substantial capital grants and it could support local arts activity.

By contrast, Portsmouth city councillors were also faced with a strong local lobby that wanted to see the theatre preserved. 'No political party is going to want to be seen as the one that closed the Kings' was how one observer summed up the local political pressure. This pressure was particularly acute because the local council was a hung council – each of the three main political parties had approximately equal representation – leaving decision making by one party open to easy attack by the other two.

As the possibility of closing the Kings Theatre became clear, the Kings Theatre Trust produced its own plan to keep the theatre open on a limited basis with just local productions – like a local amateur dramatic society production – for a three-year period with a modest annual subsidy from the council of around £130,000. Essentially, the theatre would not compete with Southampton or Chichester and the situation would be reviewed after three years.

The main strategic options for the Kings Theatre were clear:

● find significant additional sums and a new managing director to keep the theatre going on a full commercial basis;

● sell the theatre to an interested outside party and direct the council's limited funds towards the New Theatre Royal;

● keep the theatre open on a limited local basis for three years with an annual subsidy from Portsmouth city council of £130,000.

Importantly, the three options had significant political implications and involved a fine judgement over the best outcome for the local community. After careful consideration, the city council's leisure officer – David Knight – recommended to the council that the Kings Theatre should be closed and sold to the highest bidder. He argued that the council's limited funds would be better deployed in developing the New Theatre Royal and such a policy was much more likely to find favour with the Arts Council.

Portsmouth city council debated the leisure officer's report at a major meeting on 22 July 2003. Some city councillors were heavily lobbied by members of the Kings Theatre Trust. Theatre supporters also staged street demonstrations and protests. After a lengthy debate, the Council decided to adopt option three – the continuation of the Kings Theatre on a limited basis for another three years with an annual subsidy from the council. They argued that it was better to keep this beautiful theatre alive on a limited basis in spite of lack of clear demand, the risks involved and the possible impact on the further development of the New Theatre Royal.

Case questions

1 *What are the key strategy issues here? Political pressure and local choice? Customer demand? Theatre run with innovative flair on a tight budget? You may wish to use the strategy concepts of context, content and process to structure your answer.*

2 *What are the sustainable competitive advantages of the Kings Theatre? Are they strong or weak? You should use well-established resource-based strategy concepts – like reputation and core competencies – to develop your answer.*

3 *What would you recommend to the city council? Which strategic option would you choose? Why?*

4 *Having chosen an option, what is the strategic process that should then be adopted to implement that option? You may wish to identify the key players with whom the city council will need to bargain and what game plan will be required.*

CRITICAL REFLECTION

Public sector strategy: increased service or lower costs?

One of the underpinning themes throughout public sector strategy in recent years is where to focus the effort. Some argue that it is important for the public sector to increase the quality of the service that it offers to citizens. Others argue that the public sector has become too large and it would be better to make cutbacks, even if this reduces the services offered to the public. Such a conflict needs to be resolved if strategy is to be developed, so an answer is needed. Where do you stand on this issue? What is your view?

SUMMARY

- In public sector strategy, the analysis of the strategic environment is more complex than in the private sector. The main reason is that public sector strategy involves the wide-ranging and ill-defined subject of the *public interest*: the public interest concerns both the objectives and the institutions that make and implement public decisions. There are two main public sector models – centrally directed (*dirigiste*) and free-market (*laissez-faire*). The *market mechanism* is the means by which the state uses market pricing and quasi-market mechanisms to determine the supply and demand of goods that were previously state monopolies. In practice over the last 20 years, many states have moved to greater use of the market through privatising state-owned companies. Each individual country will have its own approach to the use of such mechanisms. A public sector environmental analysis will have to be conducted on a country-by-country basis. There are also two costs associated with the market mechanism: first, the cost of being unable to close inefficient services because they provide vital public services; second, the cost of administering the market mechanism to ensure that it serves the agreed public objectives.

- Public value refers to the benefits to the whole of the nation from owning and controlling certain products and services. However, such value needs to be considered within the legal framework that binds and governs the value. In addition, public value requires the concept of equity to make sure that the value is distributed to all citizens. In some circumstances, public value needs a regulator to deal with any market imperfections.

- In the public sector, stakeholder power is possessed by those citizens who are able to influence the decisions of the state. Such power may be expressed through democratic elections but these can lead to short-termism in strategic decisions. Power can also be exercised through pressure groups and other forms of interest. Such power needs to be analysed.

- In the not-for-profit sector, an environmental analysis needs to consider the role and purpose of the organisation and also its actual and potential sources of funds. Such organisations cannot rely on public taxes to pay for their activities and need to seek voluntary contributions that will vary with a range of factors.

- The nine stages in environmental analysis used for business strategy can be adapted for use in public sector strategy analysis. But they need to be treated with caution.

- Public sector resource analysis needs to begin by examining which of the two public sector models – public sector administration or new public management – is adopted by the state. The *public sector administration* model consists of a professional civil service bureaucracy that enacts government legislation and administers the activities of the state on behalf of the government coupled with state monopolies that supply services to the citizens. The *new public management* model is a model of public sector decision-making where the professional civil service operates with more market competition, while former state monopolies are divided and compete against each other for business from citizens. However, the nation retains some areas under state control, such as the defence of the nation.

● The former does not support competitive advantage while the latter is underpinned by concepts of market competition in what was formerly the monopolistic state sector. Resource-based analysis in the public sector for the second approach will include similar concepts to those in business strategy – tangible, intangible and organisational resources, etc.

● There are four additional considerations that apply in analysing resources in the public sector – appropriate and sufficient resources for purpose; public power as a resource; the costs and benefits of public resources; persuasion and education as a public resource. Public sector resource analysis needs to assess whether sufficient and appropriate resources are available to deliver the purpose and objectives set by the state. This means that resource analysis needs to identify public purpose and then assess resource requirements against this.

● Public power is a resource possessed by nation states and consists of the collective decision making that derives from the nation state. The analysis of such a resource is important in developing public sector strategy. With regard to costs and benefits of public resources, the task of the public sector manager is often that of obtaining the maximum benefit for the least cost. 'Benefit' here has a broader social definition than simply delivering shareholder profitability in the private sector. Such a balance needs to be considered in resource analysis in the public sector. Public sector resource analysis also needs to consider whether persuasion and education are possible resources of the state and, if so, how and where they might be employed.

● In not-for-profit organisations, there is a need to examine the fund-raising resource of the organisation. In addition, there is a specific need to examine the human resources of such organisations in three areas: voluntary help, specialist technical knowledge and the leadership and governance.

● The outcome of the resource analysis will identify the public organisation's strongest abilities and most effective actions and policies. From an administrative viewpoint, it will also set out the resources that it employs on a regular basis to perform well.

● When developing the purpose of public sector organisations, the key to success for public and non-profit organisations is the satisfaction of main stakeholders. It is essential to conduct a stakeholder power analysis and seek the views of leading stakeholders. In addition to stakeholder theory, the development of public sector purpose also needs to reflect the general will of the people. Public opinion therefore needs to be identified and explored. It is sometimes difficult for citizens to develop an informed choice on complex issues but such difficulties need to be recognised and resolved.

● The starting point in defining the purpose of strategy in the public sector must lie with the basic mandate of the public sector organisation, its role and its reason for its existence. This will lead to the mission of the organisation and a definition of its purpose in the context of the issues that it faces at that time. Many public sector organisations receive conflicting objectives. They need to be resolved if purpose is to be successfully defined and strategy developed.

● For a variety of reasons, the strategic context of public sector strategy is broader than its counterpart in business strategy. The danger is that it becomes more complex and difficult to handle. There are three main mechanisms to simplify the process: priorities, scenarios and simplicity.

● Strategic content in public sector strategy can follow the options-and-choice route commonly used in some business strategy. However, options associated with the strategic environment need to be treated with considerable caution because the market mechanism is still lacking in much of the public sector. Nevertheless, options derived from resource-based analysis can be employed.

● With regard to strategic process, the uncertainties of the public sector favour the use of 'logical incrementalism' as a process. An alternative is the 'muddling through' approach which reduces public sector strategy to a series of small decisions. Importantly, a number of strategists argue that major strategic decisions in public sector strategy usually require substantial commitment in terms of resources and leadership. Such an approach is not so easy in practice.

● Strategy implementation in the public sector needs to be carefully planned and is best undertaken quickly and smoothly. The form of implementation depends on the scale of what is proposed. Major changes need substantial support. Smaller changes are probably best treated incrementally.

● In implementing public sector strategy, it is important to identify the value added and then explain this to those involved in its implementation. It is also necessary to have a mechanism that can fix the inevitable difficulties that will arise as new strategies are implemented.

● It may be appropriate to have a summative evaluation of the strategy after it has been implemented to find out whether the planned improvements have been achieved. However, such an approach can be lengthy and time-consuming. It can also be overbureaucratic.

● A new organisational structure and culture may be necessary for some new strategies. This will take time that needs to be built into the process from the beginning. Such processes should not be underestimated and may require years to complete. There is also a need to build some degree of flexibility into the implementation process as circumstances change.

● The budget process can be crucial for new strategies and should ideally be undertaken after the strategy has been agreed. Importantly, this is only a part of a broader implementation process that needs to include the agreement of key decision-makers. Arguably, implementation needs to be re-evaluated as being part of a broader, ongoing strategy development process, rather than an add-on process after the strategy has been decided.

QUESTIONS

1 Take your own country and analyse the extent to which it employs *laissez-faire* or *dirigiste* policies in the public sector. How does this compare with other countries?

2 What public sector strategy would you expect the following organisations to have?

   (a) A public library based in a small town.

   (b) A voluntary group providing volunteers to visit the elderly and house-bound.

   (c) A prosperous town with 100,000 inhabitants and a range of industrial activities from manufacturing to leisure.

   (d) The police force associated with a region of a country.

3 *'The need to improve service quality has been and remains a major pre-occupation for many public sector organisations and those who fund their activities'* (*Exploring Public Sector Strategy*, p250)

Take an organisation with which you are familiar and consider this comment: is the comment correct for your chosen organisation? How has it been tackled? How should it be approached?

4 If you were asked to make the World Bank more responsive to world pressures, what would you do? In answering this question, you should take into account the existing structure of the institution.

5 Winston S Churchill commented: 'Democracy is the worst form of government except for all the others' (*see* Section 18.3). Is this correct? What are the implications for public sector strategy?

6 Undertake a stakeholder power analysis for a public sector organisation of your choice: it could be a voluntary organisation like a student society or club. What are the implications of your analysis for the development of strategy in that organisation?

Questions *continued*

7 Why is it difficult to apply Porter's market-based concepts in public sector strategy? Do they have any relevance at all in a city-based fire and rescue service?

8 The chief executive of a not-for-profit charity serving those who are terminally ill has become worried by declining levels of income, believing the organisation has lost out to others that have a stronger public presence, and has turned to you for advice. What would you recommend?

9 *'To launch, sustain and implement a comprehensive strategy for reform requires certain conditions and these are seldom satisfied in the real world of public management reform.'*

This is the view of Professors Pollitt and Bouckaert – see Section 18.4. Are they being too gloomy about the prospects for radical reform of public sector strategy? Does this mean that major reform in the public sector is almost certainly doomed to failure?

Acknowledgements

This chapter breaks new ground in strategy textbooks. The author is therefore particularly grateful to three people who have commented on earlier drafts of this chapter: Dr Paul Baines of Middlesex University, Dr Paul Hughes of Loughborough University and Marc Coleman, Economics Editor of the *Irish Times*. Any remaining errors and omissions remain solely the responsibility of the author.

Further reading

Bryson, J M (1998) *Strategic Planning for Public and Non Profit Organisations*, Jossey Bass, San Francisco, CA is one of the leading texts in this area and has strong, practical advice.

Two books on public administration are Lane, J-E (2000) *The Public Sector: Concepts, Models and Approaches*, 3rd edn, Sage, London and Frederickson, H G and Smith, K B (2003) *The Public Administration Theory Primer*, Westview, Oxford. Both provide useful summaries of the basics of theories that follow a completely different academic tradition from strategic management.

A text with substantial cross-country empirical comparisons and interesting comment is Pollitt, C and Bouckaert,

G (2000) *Public Management Reform: A Comparative Analysis*, Oxford University Press, Oxford, which is well written and thought-provoking.

Three recommended texts on strategic management in the public sector are:

Joyce, P (1999) *Strategic Management for the Public Services*, Open University Press, Buckingham; Bovaird, T and Loffler, E (eds) (2003) *Public Management and Governance* Routledge, London; Johnson, G and Scholes, K (eds) (2001) *Exploring Public Sector Strategy*, Pearson Education, Harlow.

Notes and references

1 Ferlie, E (2002) 'Quasi strategy: Strategic management in the contemporary public sector, in Pettigrew, A, Thomas, H and Whittington, R (eds) *Handbook of Strategy and Management*, Sage, London.

2 Lane, J-E (2000) *The Public Sector: Concepts, Models and Approaches*, 3rd edn, Sage, London.

3 Frederickson, H G and Smith, K B (2003) *The Public Administration Theory Primer*, Westview, Oxford.

4 Reference Lane, J-E (2000) Op. cit.

5 Reference Lane, J-E (2000), Op. cit; Frederickson, H G and Smith, K B (2003) Op. cit. and many other public strategy texts.

6 *See* many reviews. For example: Hood, C (1987) 'British administrative trends and the public choice revolution', in Lane, J-E (1987) (ed) *Bureaucracy and Public Choice*, Sage, London; Joyce, P (1999) *Strategic Management for*

the Public Services, Open University Press, Buckingham; Pollitt, C (1990) *The New Managerialism and the Public Services: The Anglo-American Experience*, Basil Blackwell, Oxford; Pollitt, C (1993) *Managerialism in the Public Services*, 2nd edn, Blackwell, Oxford; Boyne, G A (2002) 'Public and private management: What's the difference?', *Journal of Management Studies*, Vol 39, No 1, pp97–122.

7 Sources for World Bank Case: The information for this case is mainly taken from the World Bank website which contains much material on the principle of open access information.

8 Some readers will detect a contradiction here but that is beyond the scope of this strategy text. You can explore it in: Lane, J-E (2000) Op. cit.

9 Lane, J-E (2000) Op. cit., p6.

10 Frederickson, H G and Smith, K B (2003) Op. cit., p193.

11 Back in the 1950s, Charles Tiebout attempted to resolve this problem by arguing that a theoretical competitive market could be created in a nation. It would need citizens to be mobile and different levels of public service to be offered in different parts of their country. If such citizens were able to shop around between local government areas for their preferred package of services and pay the taxes related to the choice that best suited their preferences, then such mobility would deliver 'the local public goods counterpart to the private market's shopping trip'. In essence, he was proposing a theoretical market in public services. Tiebold's hypothesis was that it was more efficient to have alternative government agencies competing rather than a centralised bureaucracy. For a fuller treatment, see Frederickson, H G and Smith, K B (2003) Op. cit., pages 193–4.

12 Bryson, J M (1998) *Strategic Planning for Public and Non Profit Organisations*, Jossey Bass, San Francisco, CA.

13 Frederickson, H G and Smith, K B (2003) Op. cit., p113, Lane, J-E (2000) Op. cit., p2.

14 Lane, J-E (2000) Op. cit., p305.

15 Lane, J-E (2000) Op. cit., p304.

16 Pollitt, C and Bouckaert, G (2000) *Public Management Reform: A Comparative Analysis*, Oxford University Press, Oxford.

17 Frederickson, H G and Smith, K B (2003) Op. cit. has a comparison of the two systems on p113.

18 Kettl, D (2000) *The Global Public Management Revolution: A Report on the Transformation of Governance*, Brookings Institute, Washington, D.C.

19 Lane, J-E (2000) Op. cit., p307.

20 See extensive reviews in Lane, J-E (2000) Op. cit. and Pollitt and Bouckaert (2000) Op. cit.

21 See for example, Ferlie, E (2002) 'Quasi strategy: strategic management in the contemporary public sector', in Pettigrew, A, Thomas, H and Whittington, R (eds) *Handbook of Strategy and Management*, Sage, London; Bryson, J M (1998) Op. cit.; Bovaird, T (2003) 'Strategic management in public sector organizations', in Bovaird, T and Loffler, E (eds), *Public Management and Governance*, Routledge, London.

22 Bryson, J M (1998) Op. cit. uses SWOT extensively with many examples in both the public and non-profit sectors in his text.

23 Pollitt, C and Bouckaert, G (2000) Op. cit. Ch7.

24 Brygon, J M (1998) Op. cit., Ch5.

25 Pollitt, C and Bouckaert, G (2000) Op. cit. p173.

26 *See*, for example, Hood, C (1983) *The Tools of Government*, Macmillan, London; Heymann, P (1987) *The Politics of Public Management*, Yale University Press, CT; Moore, M (1995) *Creating Public Value: Strategic Management in Government*, Harvard University Press, Cambridge, MA.

27 Lane, J-E (2000) Op. cit.

28 *See* for example, Bardach, E and Kagan, R (1982) *Going by the Book: The Problem of Regulatory Unreasonableness*, Temple University Press, PH; Wolf, C (1988) *Markets or Governments*, MIT Press, Cambridge, MA.

29 Pollit, C and Bouckaert, G (2000) Op. cit. p170.

30 Osborne, D and Gaebler, T (1992) *Reinventing Government: How the Entrepreneurial Spirit is Transforming the Public Sector*, Plume, NY; Alford, J (1998) 'Corporate Management', in Shafritz, J *International Encyclopedia of Public Policy and Administration*, Vol 1, Westview Press, Boulder, CO.

31 Readers may care to note that this area remains somewhat under-researched. The author has therefore developed these comments from personal observation with the usual words of caution that derive from such an approach – partial, incomplete and a biased sample.

32 Bryson, J M (1998) Op. cit., p30.

33 Bryson, J M (1998) Op. cit., Ch5.

34 Sources for Olympics bidding case: International Olympic Committee website – www.olympic.org; BBC website: news.bbc.co.uk?sport/hi/other_sport/Olympics; *Financial Times* editorial 19 February 2005, p10; Michael Payne (2005) *Olympic Turnaround*, London Business Press, London.

35 Bryson, J M (1998) Op. cit., p27.

36 Cranston, M (1968) (Trans and ed) *Jean-Jacques Rousseau – The Social Contract*, Penguin, Harmondsworth.

37 Mill, J S (1962) *Utilitarianism – Edited with an Introduction by Mary Warnock*, Collins/Fontana, London.

38 Sen, A (2005) 'The diverse ancestry of democracy', *Financial Times*, 13 June, p19.

39 Lynch, R (2004) When majority opinion conflicts with expert judgment – the case of the Kings Theatre', *British Academy of Management Conference Paper*, St Andrews.

40 Lynch, R (2004) Loc. cit.

41 Wolf, M (2005) 'A more efficient Union will be less democratic, *Financial Times*, 15 June, p19. This has an informed, if complex, discussion on such issues in the European Union. According to this argument, 'democracy' is more than just voting for European politicians every few years.

42 Bryson, J M (1998) Op. cit., p27.

43 Pollit, C and Bouckaert, G (2000) Op. cit. Ch7 has a long and interesting list of such conflicts and dilemmas which they discuss in detail.

44 World Bank (2000) *World Development Report 2000*, Oxford University Press, NY.

45 Osborne, D and Gaebler, T (1992) *Re-inventing Government*, Addison Wesley, Reading, MA.

46 Bryson, J M (1998) Op. cit., p.159.

47 Bryson, J M (1998) Op. cit. Ch7 provides a long and useful description in this area.

48 Bryson, J M (1998) Op. cit., p33.

49 Bryson, J M (1998) Op. cit., p33.

50 Ferlie, E (2002) Op. cit., p289.

51 Ferlie, E (2002) Op. cit., p289.

52 Bryson, J M (1998) Op. cit., Ch5.

53 Ferlie, E (2002) Op. cit., p289.

54 See, for example, Bryson, J M (1998) Op. cit., Ch7.

55 Outlined in some depth with extensive references in Bryson, J M (1998) Op. cit.; Bryson, J M, Ackermann, F, Eden, C, Finn, C B, 'Resource C – Using the *Oval Mapping Process* to Identify Strategic Issues and Formulate Effective Strategies', pp257–275

56 See, for example, Bryson, J M (1998) Op. cit., p147 and Pollit, C and Bouckaert, G (2000) Op. cit., pp183–7.

57 Lindblom, C (1959) 'The science of muddling through,' *Public Administration Review*, Vol 19, No 2, pp79–88.

58 Bryson, J M (1998) Op. cit., p147.

59 Pollitt, C and Bouckaert, G (2000) Op. cit., p185.

60 Several research studies have shown that while the Margaret Thatcher privatisation reforms of the 1980s may have been presented as radical change, in practice, they were much more gradual and incremental, with the final outcomes being unknown at the start of the process. Quoted and referenced in Pollit, C and Bouckaert, G (2000) Op. cit.

61 This section of the chapter has benefited particularly from Ch9 of Bryson, J M (1998) Op. cit.

62 Bryson, J M (1998) Op. cit., p167.

63 One inevitable consequence of the introduction of the market mechanism into the public sector is the pressure for public servants to be accountable. This can 'distort priorities, consume time and effort in form-filling and produce changes locally that make no sense' – *Financial Times* Editorial, 31 January 2005, p18. But, as the *FT* goes on to argue, there is good evidence that they have their uses and what is the alternative?

64 As one example, see Timmings, N (2005) 'Flagship hospital hit by barrage of changes', *Financial Times*, 31 January 2005, p8.

65 Reich, R (1988) (ed) *The Power of Public Ideas*, Ballinger, Cambridge, MA. Quoted in: Alford, J. (2001) 'The implications of "publicness" for strategic management theory', Ch1 of Johnson, G and Scholes, K (eds) *Exploring Public Sector Strategy*, Pearson Education, Harlow. More generally, Ch18 of *Corporate Strategy, 4th Edition* has benefited from Alford's introductory chapter to this edited book. It has also gained from the contributions of the other authors and the editors of this text.

66 Sources for the Kings Theatre Case: The author, Professor Richard Lynch, has known the theatres of Portsmouth all his life. He declares an interest in the Kings Theatre, having made a small donation to its renovation fund in 2002. Other sources – *The News*, Portsmouth: 17 April 2003, p5; 24 April 2003, pp6, 8–9; 25 April 2003, p22; 28 April 2003, p5; 30 April 2003, p6; May 9 2003, p11; 26 June 2003, p6; 27 June 2003, p10; 1 July 2003, p6; 3 July 2003, p5; 7 July 2003, p5; 10 July 2003, pp8 and 9; 10 July 2003, p6; 11 September 2003, p22; 21 February, 2004, p7. Interviews as outlined in the acknowledgements at the end of the case.

Chapter 19

INTERNATIONAL EXPANSION AND GLOBALISATION STRATEGIES

Learning outcomes

When you have worked through this chapter, you will be able to:

- explain what is meant by globalisation and distinguish it from international expansion;
- outline the main theories of international trade and explain their relevance to corporate strategy;
- identify the main institutions involved in international trade and investment and their influence on corporate strategy;
- explain the importance of trade blocks and their relationship with the development of corporate strategy;
- explore the main benefits and problems of globalisation strategies and comment critically on theories of globalisation;
- understand the main organisation structures needed to operate global strategy successfully;
- outline the main development routes and methods for global expansion.

INTRODUCTION

For some companies, international expansion and globalisation have become a vital aspect of strategy development and implementation. They present new opportunities to generate extra value added which deserve exploration. They may also entail increased competitive risk: international expansion may expose a company to new and sophisticated competitors. However, international strategy is not the same as global strategy, so the starting point is to explore what is meant by the two.

To understand international expansion, it needs to be viewed in the strategic context of international trade and investment development over a number of years. This involves the theories of international trade and the institutions that govern such activities.

Within the context of foreign trade and investment issues, international and globalisation strategies then need to be explored – the benefits and problems need to be understood if such strategies are to be successful. Because of the increased scope of international operations, issues of organisational structure are particularly important. In addition, the routes to international development also need careful exploration since they may vary, depending on the markets and the countries. Finally, the relationships between the companies seeking global strategies and the sovereign countries providing the markets need to be investigated because they are mutually dependent. Figure 19.1 summarises the structure of this chapter.

International trade has its origins and theoretical foundation in the prescriptive topic of international economics. Thus some parts of international strategy seek prescriptive solutions. However, some of the more recent areas have taken more experimental routes which

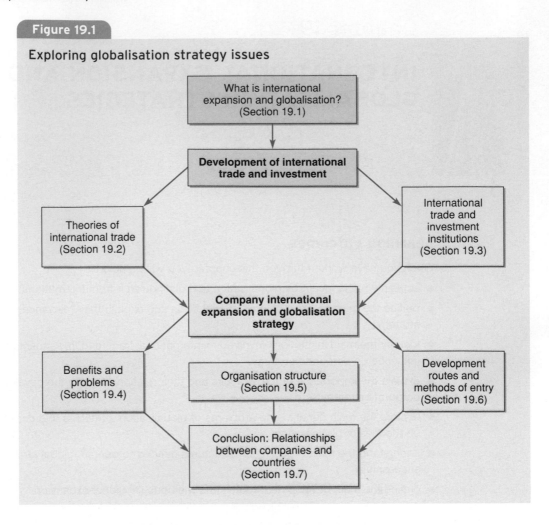

Figure 19.1

Exploring globalisation strategy issues

would fit more naturally within emergent strategic perspectives. Thus the early part of the chapter – on trade development – is more prescriptive, with emergent approaches being more appropriate later, in the section on company international expansion.

CASE STUDY 19.1

MTV: more local than global?

Around 1 billion people around the world see MTV every day, according to its American parent Viacom. Although there are global stars, like Madonna and Eminem, MTV mainly broadcasts through 40 national or regional music channels, each with a distinctive chart sound. This case explores the reasons why MTV's strategy is more local than global.

Programme content

When MTV began in 1981, it broadcast largely to its American home audience and its programme content was primarily music videos. By 2005, the US was still MTV's largest and most profitable market. But the programming had moved from simply music to include reality television programmes like the activities of *The Osbournes* and the baiting of celebrities on *Punk'd*. Nevertheless, music was still the central theme

and the MTV Annual Music Awards were still able to cause controversy.

MTV pioneered the reality television format in 1992 with a programme called *The Real World*. It was about a group of young people living in an apartment in New York. It was originally planned to use actors but the company did not have sufficient funds, so it observed real people at zero cost instead. The company had the same low-budget, free-wheeling

http://www.mtveurope.com

MTV's European headquarters co-ordinates individual country strategies but allows considerable flexibility within the overall station's vision and purpose.

culture in 2005 – except for the vast sum it paid the Osbournes to have television cameras follow them for months. This was all part of the way of staying creative and in touch with its young target audience.

MTV was a major part of the global media company Viacom and it was under pressure to deliver profits. Tom Freston, 45-year-old chief executive of MTV Networks, was aware of the need to keep MTV away from the pressures of the large, global corporation: 'The bigness thing has been a problem. It's not going to make you a better record or a better TV show. Quite often it means more people get in the way or more people have to agree things.' Importantly, the relaxed approach allowed MTV to be more flexible and employ staff who were much nearer the age of the target audience than the parent company managers: 'The question is how do we connect with these specialist groups we go after? The focus is really on that connection and trying to compensate for the fact that we're a big company.'

Growth strategy

As the US has seen the launch of more TV stations and advertising begin to slow, MTV has been seeking growth from its international interests. By 2005, MTV International accounted for 80 per cent of viewers but only 15 per cent of revenues.

But international activity was the future, with the company launching services to high-growth markets like India and China. In 2005, MTV launched its first African channel, MTV Base. The main task of Bill Roedy, president of MTV International, was to turn the high growth into a profitable business. 'Africa we expect to be a big contributor. People look at Africa and see problems, but we also have to look at the positives. Its GDP growth is the second highest in the world behind growth in East Asia.'

China and India also represented major opportunities. 'The epicentre is shifting to the Far East and India,' commented Mr Roedy. 'They are amazing markets but it's important not to get too euphoric about the numbers.'

Competition

Music downloading over the internet was becoming a major threat: Apple had led the way with its legal music site to millions of customers. In addition, the technology of broadband telecommunications would extend downloading to videos and mobile phones. MTV therefore needed to offer more than just music videos. In addition, it needed to take into account new ways of delivering its product. Japanese customers already accessed MTV more frequently by mobile telephone than by TV channel. Equally, in Korea, most homes had broadband and could download videos quickly and legally.

As a result, MTV was continuing to change its programme content with non-music offerings like *Jackass* and *Dirty Sanchez* and it was making all this available through the new media channels. But it faced the problem that much of this material was mainly American in humour and style. Its target audiences might be young and international, but they still mainly listened to national and ethnic recording artists – hence the need for local material alongside the global MTV brand name.

© Copyright Richard Lynch 2006. All rights reserved. This case was written from published sources only.[1]

Case questions

1 *What are the benefits of operating a global media strategy and what are the difficulties?*

2 *What are the market trends that will make it more difficult for MTV in the future?*

3 *Should MTV become more global with more programmes like* Jackass, *or more local with little global content?*

19.1 INTERNATIONAL EXPANSION AND GLOBALISATION: THEIR MEANING AND IMPORTANCE

For a series of structural reasons which we will explore later, international trading activities – *country exports and imports* – have increased substantially over the last 50 years. Moreover, in addition to trading, companies have also invested substantial capital sums in countries outside their home nation to set up factories and other facilities. The world is becoming more international and this has significant implications for corporate strategy. International expansion and globalisation issues are amongst the most important factors in the business environment influencing strategy development in the twenty-first century.

The early years of MTV show that such expansion is not just an issue for the major multi-national enterprises (often abbreviated to MNEs) like the Ford Motor Company (US) and Coca-Cola (US). It may also be a significant issue for many rather smaller companies involved in international trade. It has also become increasingly important in not-for-profit activities such as international aid agency work and international rescue. However, this chapter concentrates on commercial activities for reasons of space.

As background to our understanding of globalisation, this section begins by looking at recent trends in world trade activity. It then uses this strategic context to explore the meaning of globalisation. Words like 'globalisation' and 'internationalisation' are used interchangeably to explore the strategic issues, but they are not the same. The distinction between them is important because it may lead to different strategic activities. Finally, the main strategic implications of globalisation are then examined in terms of the activities of both countries and companies.

19.1.1 The importance of world trade and investment: the strategic context

Definition ➤ In 1994, world merchandise trade amounted to US$4,000 billion and grew by over 9 per cent over the previous year:[2] *foreign trade* means the exporting and importing activities of countries and companies around the world. At the same time, world output of goods increased by 3.5 per cent: *output* is the total production of goods by companies and public organisations aggregated together across the world. In fact, as shown in Table 19.1, world merchandise trade outstripped world output during the period 1970–90.[3] Countries are trading more with each other and faster than they are increasing their output. This should present continuing opportunities for the development of corporate strategy.

The reasons for the major increase in world trade are shown in Exhibit 19.1.

Exhibit 19.1

The reasons for the major increase in world trade

- *New or enhanced trade blocks* have been agreed over the last 20 years, e.g. the Single Europe Act 1986 certainly encouraged and supported trade across the EU. The ASEAN pact has been extended because benefits have been identified. New trade agreements are expected to keep this momentum for the next few years. There are several recent examples:

  1 The Uruguay Round of the General Agreement on Tariffs and Trade (GATT) was signed in December 1993 and was projected at the time to increase global welfare by between US$213 and 274 billion in 1992 dollars by the year 2002.[4]

  2 The Mercosur Treaty has brought together Brazil, Argentina, Paraguay and Uruguay in South America to form a new regional trade pact.

  3 The North American Free Trade Agreement (NAFTA) was signed in late 1994 and brought increased trade between the US, Mexico and Canada.

- *World and regional trade organisations* have themselves been strengthened and reformed: for example, the European Bank for Reconstruction and Development (EBRD) has been renewed following a difficult early period and has now begun to offer significant funds for development in Eastern Europe. The WTO, the World Bank and the IMF have also been strengthened. These institutions are explained in Section 19.3.

- *Multinationals* have become an important source of world sales and investment. According to UN estimates,[5] foreign sales by transnational corporations reached US$5,500 billion in 1992. The same companies have accumulated US$2,000 billion worth of foreign direct investment.

- *New technology* has made telecommunications, travel and media and all international communications much easier. This has brought countries together and influenced political and economic decision making.

Table 19.1

Comparison of world exports and world manufacturing value added

	1960–70 (%)	1970–80 (%)	1980–90 (%)
Annual growth in world trade	9.2	20.3	6.0
Annual growth in manufacturing value added (1990 US$)	n.a.	3.1	2.1

Source: UNIDO.[6]

In many respects, world merchandise trade has come to be an important *driver* of country economic growth around the world. Corporate strategy has played a significant part in achieving this and, equally, has benefited from it. We are concerned here with the way international markets and industry structure interact with international company activity. Some industries cannot survive without overseas trade: for example, aerospace and defence companies such as Boeing (US), Aerospatiale (France) and British Aerospace (UK) need sales beyond their home countries to make a profit. MTV, featured in Case study 19.1, needs international sales since its national market in the US is beginning to mature. Other industries simply benefit from being able to sell their products or services internationally.

19.1.2 The distinction between foreign trade and foreign direct investment

In addition to engaging in trading activities, companies may also engage in foreign direct investment (often abbreviated to FDI). It is important to distinguish between the two:

● *Foreign trade* means the exporting and importing activities of countries and companies around the world – for example, MTV's export of *The Osbournes* TV programme from the US.

Definition ➤ ● *Foreign direct investment (FDI)* is the long-term investment by a company in the technology, management skills, brands and physical assets of a subsidiary in another country. Such investment is then used to generate sales in that country, quite possibly replacing exports from the home country – for example, the FDI by MTV in its television network in South Africa.

The role of overseas trade and foreign direct investment has changed significantly for many companies and has come to be a direct part of corporate strategy. But an increase in *international* activity is not the same as an increase in *globalisation*.

19.1.3 Defining and exploring different types of international expansion

In analysing international company activity, Bartlett and Ghoshal distinguished between three different types:[7]

Definition ➤ 1 *International* – when a significant proportion of an organisation's activities are outside the home country and they are managed as a separate area. For example, a small company engaged in exporting some of its product beyond its home country would be international according to this definition. The focus of such a business is its domestic operation, with international activity being an appendage to this.

Definition ➤ 2 *Multinational* – when a company operates in many countries, though it may still have a home base. One purpose of such operations is to respond to local demand. For example, the MTV music television company has many different operations to suit different music traditions, but they are all owned by its home-base operation in the US. The business consists of a series of semi-independent operations, under a global brand name like MTV – *see* Case 19.1.

Definition ➤ 3 *Global* – when a company treats the whole world as one market and one source of supply. There is only limited response to local demand – for example, Rolex watches or Disney's Mickey Mouse – *see* Case 13.1 for the latter. The focus of the business is one world market, with each of the operations delivering contributions to that activity.

These distinctions are important because they have different strategic implications:

● With the international activity, the primary strategic driver is the home market and the competitive advantage that it delivers, with international sales being subsidiary to this.

● With the multinational business, the competitive advantage is separately determined for each of the various national or regional markets in which the organisation is engaged.

● With the global business strategy, competitive advantage usually comes from common global brands and from concentrated production activity that has been sited to deliver significant economies of scale and resource sourcing. There may be some adjustment of the product or service for local needs but essentially it is the same around the world. The whole world is treated as one market.

In addition to the above on *company* activity, the term 'globalisation' is also used to cover three other topic areas:[8]

1 *Globalisation of economies, trade activities and regulatory regimes*. World economies are slowly coming together, with barriers to trade being lowered. We will explore this in Sections 19.2 and 19.3 below.

2 *Globalisation of industries*. Whole industries like the car industry, the aerospace industry and the paper and pulp industry are beginning to trade as one market rather than as a series of regional markets. We will explore this in Sections 19.4 and 19.5 below.

3 *Morality of globalisation*. It is argued by some commentators that the globalisation process has led some companies to pillage the environment, destroy lives and fail to enrich poor people as promised.[9] These are important issues that are beyond the scope of this text. However, the underlying principle of this book is that companies will act responsibly and in the interests of the wider community, as well as those of the owners of the organisation. These issues deserve our serious attention.

Comment

Those organisations that fail to distinguish between international, multinational and global strategy miss important elements of strategic development. Many companies that claim to be 'global' are not global in the sense set out above – they are merely selling in many parts of the world. This means that such companies are international or multinational, but it does not mean that they are global. In practice, as we will see later, the distinctions between these areas are not as clear as set out above, but they serve as a useful starting point in exploring global strategy.

19.1.4 International expansion and globalisation: the C–C–B Paradigm

In order to explore the relationships between companies and the many countries within which they operate, it is useful to identify the essential elements. These are set out in the C–C–B Paradigm shown in Figure 19.2. It is developed from an earlier paradigm by the international economist Professor John Dunning, but has been substantially altered to concentrate on corporate strategy issues.[10] The main elements of the paradigm are:

Figure 19.2

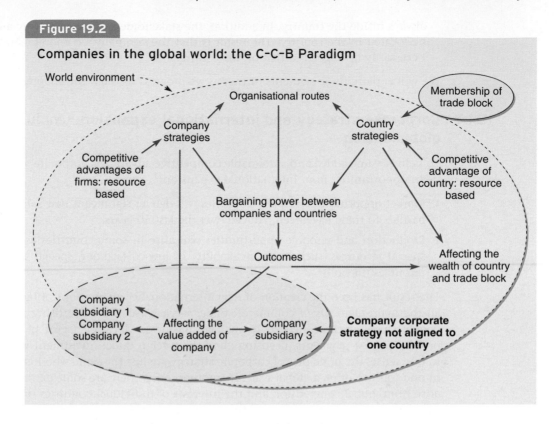

Companies in the global world: the C–C–B Paradigm

- *C–C–B.* This refers to three essential components of the paradigm: the Company, the Country in which the company is operating and the Bargaining that will take place between the company and the country.

- *Underlying assumption of the paradigm.* Companies have different interests from countries. The conflict between these interests is resolved through bargaining between the two parties. The main areas of advantage can be identified by exploring the concept of competitive advantage – *see* Chapter 6 for companies and Section 19.2 below for countries.

- *Company.* Each company will have sustainable competitive advantages, based on its resources. For example, MTV has expertise in television programme development, local content development and its global brand name. These advantages will be used in developing its international strategy for individual countries.

- *Country.* Each country will have some competitive advantages, based on its resources. For example, these might include its physical location, such as Singapore's position on shipping routes between Europe and Asia. However, resources will also include the country's investment in education, such as Singapore's substantial investment in this area over the last 20 years, and its technical knowledge, such as Singapore's financial and electronics expertise developed over this period.

- *Bargaining power.* Companies and countries will negotiate with each other on the basis of customer market size, investment required, availability of investment incentives, country infrastructure and so on.

- *Outcomes.* The results of such bargaining will deliver *wealth* to the country receiving the trade and the foreign direct investment and *value added* to the company.

- *Value added of the company.* There may be more than one subsidiary of the company involved. Moreover, some subsidiaries may have other relationships with each other, not always inside the country. In addition, the stakeholders of the company are unlikely to be located in the country. The result is that the company's corporate strategy will not necessarily be aligned to that of one country.

We will explore these elements further as we progress through the chapter.

19.1.5 Corporate strategy and international expansion – including globalisation

To deliver value added and sustainable competitive advantage, corporate strategy seeks two main opportunities from international expansion:

1 Market opportunities in many countries will deliver significant new sales, particularly as barriers to trade have been reduced over the last 50 years.

2 Production and resource opportunities will arise in some countries as a result of their special resources, such as the availability of low-cost labour, special skills and natural resources (like oil).

The result has been the creation of new international configurations of business that cover all the main elements of commerce: trade; services (such as advertising and technology); people (such as those needed to manage businesses locally); factor payments (such as profits, interest payments, licensing); and the foreign direct investment referred to above. In one sense, the principles of corporate strategy are just the same whether they are applied in one country or on a global scale. In another sense, there are some extra dimensions that arise from global competition and the interests of individual countries or groups of countries. We begin our exploration of these additional dimensions by exploring country issues in the next three sections of this chapter. We then turn to company issues in the following three sections of the chapter.

Key strategic principles

- International expansion and globalisation are amongst the most important strategic influences in the business environment in the twenty-first century.

- International expansion has become an important driver of country economic growth. Companies have contributed to this and benefited from it.

- It is important to distinguish between foreign trade – exports and imports – and foreign direct investment – the investment in capital, factories and people in foreign locations.

- It is important also to distinguish between three types of international and global expansion: *international*, where a significant proportion of an organisation's activities take place outside its home market but it is still the domestic market that is the prime focus of strategy; *multinational*, where a company operates in many countries and varies its strategy country by country; *global*, where a company treats the world as one market.

- Significantly, each of the three areas above implies a different international expansion strategy.

- The *C–C–B Paradigm* explores the resource relationships between the Company, the Country in which it operates and the Bargaining that takes place between the two. The twin purposes of such bargaining are to deliver increased value added to the company and increased wealth to the country.

CASE STUDY 19.2

Tate & Lyle plc: globalisation to sweeten the profit line

As one of the world's largest producers of sweeteners and starches, the UK-based company Tate & Lyle should be well placed to generate profits from its global operations. Yet its profitability declined as it became more global. This case explores some of the problems of international expansion, including a new twist at the end.

Greater globalisation, lower profits

Over the period 1988–97, Tate & Lyle grew from a UK/European food company into one of the largest producers of sweeteners and starches in the world. Expansion came from two large acquisitions – Staley Industries in the US in 1988 and Bundaberg in Australia in 1991 – and a series of smaller purchases, joint ventures and other co-operative deals in many parts of the world. For example, in May 1998 the company purchased the well-known citric acid company Haarman and Reimer from the German chemical giant Bayer for US$219 million (£130 million).

In spite of this major expansion programme, Tate & Lyle has not been able to generate a similar increase in profits. Table 19.2 compares its turnover and profits in 1991, 1994 and 1997. Over the period, the company generated £1.4 billion extra turnover, largely outside Europe, but profits were down £60 million.

Products: global reach but low value added

Tate & Lyle's operations are mainly involved in two world markets:

1 *The world market for nutritive sweeteners.* This covers agricultural crops such as sugar cane and sugar beet, but also includes sweeteners made from cereals such as maize and wheat. The sweeteners are used in a wide variety of food products, including drinks, cakes and cooking ingredients.

Europe and the US account for nearly 20 per cent of world consumption of these basic food products. The market is mature, with annual growth being only around 2 per cent.

2 *The world market for starch products.* This is derived mainly from cereals but also from potatoes. The products form a staple and versatile ingredient of many processed foods. Europe and the US account for around 40 per cent of world consumption: this is higher than for sugar because starch-type products are more suited to Western tastes and also because they are used in the greater amount of processed food that is sold in Western countries. The market is mature in Europe and the US, with annual growth of around 3 per cent, but growth is higher in other areas of the world, at around 5 per cent.

Essentially, Tate & Lyle's companies take agricultural crops and process them into the sweeteners and starches outlined above. This means that the company is involved in adding value to commodity agricultural products that are subject to price fluctuation, natural disasters and the many currency problems that are outside the company's control. For example, the company reported in 1997 that its profits were reduced in the UK by £16 million as a result of EU/Green Pound changes and another £25 million from currency translation changes elsewhere in the world. In addition, there were unquantified competitive pressures on profit margins for some products in the US. They were also reduced by poor cane sugar prices in Australia and several other difficulties.

Global strategy: spread the risk of downturn and move to higher-added-value products

The company's strategy has been to extend its operations worldwide. The purpose has been twofold:

1 to reduce the impact of individual geographic markets;
2 to balance downturns in some markets with favourable movements in both prices and growth in other world markets.

The result has been major global expansion over the last ten years, the results of which are shown in Table 19.3.

In spite of the wider geographic spread, most of these activities remain in product categories that have low profit margins. For these reasons, the company has also been investing in new products with higher value added, such as its recent development of a new low-calorie sweetener, sucralose. This gained US Food and Drug Administration approval for use in 15 food and drink categories in early 1998. The product is more stable than other sweeteners, which lose their sweet properties with time or when used at high

Table 19.2

Tate & Lyle: higher turnover. Pity about the profits

	1991	1994	1997
Turnover £m			
UK	790	828	772
Rest of Europe	690	905	931
US	1 358	1 648	1 863
Rest of world	424	840	1 085
Total	3 262	4 221	4 651
Profit before interest £m			
UK	48	71	24
Rest of Europe	58	64	30
US	154	147	127
Rest of world	20	31	39
Total	280	313	220

Source: Annual Accounts for various years.

▶ CASE STUDY 19.2 continued

Table 19.3

Globalisation at Tate & Lyle: some examples of its far-reaching spread of activities

Europe	• UK: Tate & Lyle • Belgium, Holland, France: Amylum • Spain: Alcantara • Russia: T&L International • Hungary: Kaka • Slovakia: Junhocukor
North and Central America	• US: Staley • US: Domino • Canada: Redpath • Mexica: Occidente
Africa and Middle East	• Zambia: ZSR • South Africa: Booker Tate • Saudi Arabia: United Sugar
Australasia and Pacific	• Australia: Bundaberg • Vietnam: Nghe T&L • Thailand: UFIC Group • China: T&L Swire

Note: Some of the above are joint ventures with local or regional companies. The information is sourced from various Annual Reports of the company.

temperatures. In previous years, Tate & Lyle has developed other new products that can also command higher prices and therefore contribute to the company's competitive advantage. The difficulties with such a specialist strategy are the length of time and considerable investment needed to achieve success. Moreover, such activities often have only a limited impact on the basic commodity nature of much of the company's volume production. Low-cost strategies are also required.

Global strategy: drive down manufacturing costs and compete on price

Because of its involvement in the wayward shifts of agricultural commodity markets, Tate & Lyle, like many companies, has little control over its raw material costs. In addition, such companies can develop little competitive advantage and the rates of growth in the market are low. All this means that the only way to increase profits is to drive down the costs of processing the basic commodity products and compete on price. This strategy has been pursued relentlessly by Tate & Lyle over the last few years. Examples of its 1997 activities include the following:

● continued investment programme of over £500 million in totally new plant at its Belgian operation, Amylum (66 per cent owned);
● North American Business Improvement Project pursued at a cost of £82 million. This will bring together five separate businesses and save on overheads;

● £45 million investment in new projects in India, Hungary and the Czech Republic;
● construction of the first new sugar cane mill for 70 years in Queensland, Australia.

The difficulty with such developments is that competitors are also making similar investments. At the same time, new entrants are coming into the market. In addition, the new production capacity is only truly effective when it drives out older, less efficient companies. This takes time and means that there is often excess production capacity in the market in the interim period, which in itself will push down prices. Moreover, there are uncertainties in the commissioning process for new plant that often mean that it takes time for the new lower costs to be realised: this has had a significant impact on Tate & Lyle in recent years. A related difficulty is that production needs to be sited close to the crop. Hence, it is not possible to obtain the centralised economies of scale and the close co-ordination of product sourcing that can reduce costs in other global industries. All this means that it is tough for a company like Tate & Lyle to drive down manufacturing costs.

In addition to the production problems, there are difficulties with customers in the food industry. They are often sophisticated and aggressive, global, branded food and soft drink manufacturers. These customers are able to drive prices down and attempt to ensure that such prices never fully recover. For example, in 1997 Tate & Lyle reported that customer pressures had hit its HFCS business in the US. In the early 1990s, HFCS products used to contribute 75 per cent of the total profits at its US subsidiary, Staley Industries. However, by 1997, customer pressures had driven down prices to the extent that the HFCS business contributed under 10 per cent of profits.

In the context of global strategy, low-cost manufacturing and pricing therefore have significant problems. The overall result of such a cycle of investment, competitive pressure and erratic commodity prices is the decline in profitability at Tate & Lyle, as shown in Table 19.4.

Table 19.4

Decline in profitability at Tate & Lyle

Return on capital before interest (%)	1993	1994	1995	1996	1997
Sweeteners and starches					
• North America	14.9	20.3	20.7	12.9	14.5
• Europe	25.8	23.5	24.5	20.9	9.3
• Rest of world	15.2	14.8	11.3	11.7	(0.8)
Animal feed and bulk storage	27.4	26.0	23.6	22.0	6.9
Total for group	18.1	20.1	20.5	16.1	10.5

Source: Author, calculated from Annual Report and Accounts.

Global strategy: unscrambled and then revived

For several years after the above activities, the group's profitability continued to decline due to unexpected events. For example, Staley's starch profits had improved in 1998 but the US business was hit by disease in the sugar beet harvest. The American operations were sold to a local farmers' group in 2002 and Tate & Lyle largely pulled out of North America. There were also extra costs in commissioning the massive new plant at Amylum, Belgium, and for other plants around the world. All this led the company to abandon its global strategy when new management took over in 2000 – many activities outside Europe were sold or closed. For example, the Australian venture Bundaberg was sold in 2001.

Global strategy appeared to be dead at Tate and Lyle. Then suddenly demand for its sweetener sucralose began to expand rapidly, especially in North America, where it was regarded as a better-tasting alternative to saccharin and aspartame. Even Coca Cola was preparing to launch a sucralose version. And Tate & Lyle had a product that was protected by patents – at least for a time. Worldwide demand was beginning to grow – maybe it was time to think again about a global strategy.

Early part of case © Financial Times Business Limited 1998.

This case was adapted by Richard Lynch from an article written by him for *Financial Times Food Business* in 1998. He then wrote the latter part to bring the case up to date.

Case questions

1 *How do Tate & Lyle's globalisation strategies fit with the globalisation advantages outlined by Levitt?*

2 *To what extent are the company's difficulties specific to commodity markets like sugar and starch? Will companies in other industries also experience such problems? What, if any, are the implications for a strategy of globalisation?*

3 *What strategies would you now recommend for the company? Should it continue along its current trajectory or rethink its whole position?*

19.2 WORLD TRADE AND THE INTERNATIONAL EXPANSION STRATEGIES OF COMPANIES

To understand the basis of company international expansion and globalisation, it is essential to explore why and how national markets have become increasingly global over the last 50 years. Between 1950 and 1996, world trade in merchandise goods increased by 1,500 per cent. Virtually all of this increased activity has been channelled through companies engaged in international activities. Globalisation is therefore capable of delivering major company strategic opportunities.

However, globalisation is also dependent on national government strategy. For example, the world sugar industry would be totally unable to operate without the willing permission of governments to allow sugar exporting and importing when such countries have their own sugar-producing agricultural industries. We begin by exploring the theories of world trade, which have been mainly developed at the *country* rather than the *company* level. After setting the theories in historical context, we pick out some leading theories and then examine their strategic implications.

Until recently, world trade was mainly in commodities like agricultural products.[11] It turned down in the 1930s as countries attempted to protect their new industrial ventures. From the late 1940s, it has grown dramatically as countries have lowered barriers to trade and developed institutions to encourage international trade. The reasons for this growth are clearly relevant to corporate strategy but are complex and not easy to resolve.

Over the last 200 years, economists in particular have been developing theories to explain the growth and advantages of international trade. They have explored the benefits and problems in the context of empirical evidence that increased trade has generally been beneficial to those countries that have engaged in it.[12] The importance of such theories for corporate strategy is threefold:

1 They explain the way that nation states view their *bargaining position* with companies wanting to expand internationally.

2 They provide a *framework* in which to analyse the corporate strategy relating to international opportunities and threats.

3 They help to identify the *sustainable competitive advantages* of the nations that might be selected by companies to form part of an international corporate strategy.

Amongst the many theories of international economic growth, three can usefully be identified and contrasted for their impact on corporate strategy. They are explored in the sections that follow. There is no agreement amongst economists on the 'correct' theory: they all have some merit but all fail to capture the complexity of the full international strategic implications.

19.2.1 Theories of trade based on the resources of the country – the comparative advantage of nations

Definition ➤ The comparative advantage of nations consists of the resources possessed by a country that give it a competitive advantage over other nations. In the theories of the nineteenth century to the present day, some economists have argued that free trade between nations will deliver increased wealth. Early theories to support this argument relied on simple views of comparative labour costs between nations. More recent theories have concentrated on the economies of scale that arise as companies inside nations produce on a larger scale and thus reduce their costs. In both cases, these theories will depend on the resources of the country – such as the availability of raw materials and energy – along with the resources of the individual companies and industries within the country. They are often called *theories of the comparative advantage of nations*. None of these theories provides a complete explanation of the complex reasons for the growth in world trade.[13]

Whatever the reasons, evidence of the effects of removing some trade barriers during the period 1965–95 came from the experience of Eastern Asia.[14] Singapore, Hong Kong and, later, South Korea and Taiwan lowered some trade barriers rather than protect their home industries. The four Asian newly industrialised nations raised their average real incomes per head from 20 per cent of those of the high-income countries (like the US and the EU) in 1965 to 70 per cent by 1995. Contrasts were drawn between North and South Korea, mainland China and Hong Kong, West and East Germany. From the mid-1980s, mainland China itself began to take a different path, with successful results, especially in Shanghai and Guandong Province. In the late 1990s, even countries like India that had feared the effects of trade liberalisation on their own national industries began to think again.

From a corporate strategy perspective, the significance of this theory is that it stresses the importance of identifying the resources of a country or region within a country as part of international strategy development.

19.2.2 'Diamond' theory of competitive advantage of nations – the contribution of Porter

Definition ➤ Porter's diamond theory of international competitive advantage identifies a 'diamond' of four interrelated areas within a nation that assist that country to be more competitive in international markets – the four areas being factor conditions, competing firms within the country, support industries of the country and home demand. In the late 1980s, Michael Porter embarked on a major empirical study of ten nations and four major world industries. His purpose was to identify those factors that contributed to national success in international markets. The countries surveyed were: Denmark, Italy, Japan, Singapore, South Korea, Sweden, Switzerland, the UK, the US and West Germany. The industries were German printing presses, US patient-monitoring equipment, Italian ceramic tiles and Japanese robotics. The result was a diamond formed from four interrelated factors, as shown in Figure 19.3.

The four factors are as follows:

1 *Factor conditions*. Porter emphasised that competitiveness was not just a matter of comparative advantage. Resources can also be 'home-grown' and specialised. Thus, the provision of education, universities, excellent telecommunications goes well beyond natural resources but can assist in delivering national competitiveness. The success of countries

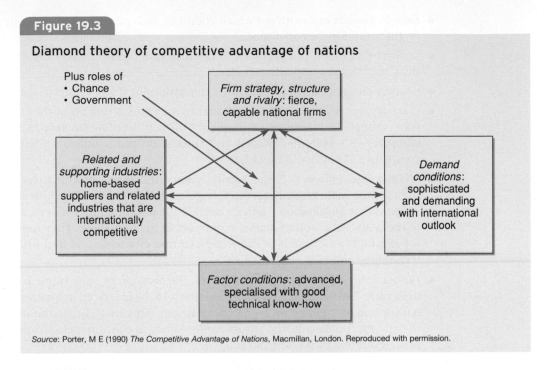

Figure 19.3

Diamond theory of competitive advantage of nations

Source: Porter, M E (1990) *The Competitive Advantage of Nations*, Macmillan, London. Reproduced with permission.

like Singapore and Malaysia has depended, at least in part, on the national government's willingness to invest in these areas over long periods of time.

2 *Related and supporting industries.* Internationally competitive *suppliers* and other related industries represent a critical resource for international success. Clusters of such industries, each offering expertise and world-class service, can be vital. For example, Hollywood USA relies for its world success not just on film studios but on a range of other related companies in film recording, electronics, design and music.

3 *Firm strategy, structure and rivalry.* Fierce national *competition* will drive innovation, force down costs and develop new methods of competing that can then be used internationally by the same companies. For example, Porter argued that the global strength of the Japanese consumer electronics companies like Mitsubishi and Hitachi was directly related to the strength of the highly competitive home market for such goods.

4 *Demand conditions.* Highly sophisticated and demanding *customers* in a nation's home market will drive up innovation and quality. Porter pointed to the sophistication of Japanese cameras, like Canon, and the quality of German cars, like BMW, being the result of demanding national customers.

In addition, Porter identified two other factors that are important:

1 *the role of government*, which can influence any of the above by subsidies, regulation, investment in education and so on;

2 *the role of chance events*, which can shift competitive advantage in unpredictable ways: for example, war, inventions, oil price rises and so on.

From a corporate strategy perspective, this significant theory helps identify and select countries for production investment. It also provides evidence on the nature of customers and competitors in such countries. Importantly, it suggests that the size of a market matters less than its characteristics.

Comment

In spite of its clear relevance to the development of international and global strategy, Porter's theory has a number of difficulties:[15]

- *Sample*. Readers can work out which countries and industries were left out and what this might mean for the conclusions.

- *Government*. This is not included in the diamond but is crucial to many elements of it, such as national competition policy.

- *Chance*. This appears to be the only explanation for many events that may be crucial.

- *Company, not country, competition*. Porter took as his starting point the concept that countries compete in international markets. This is misleading because it is companies that compete – for example, Sweden and Finland do not compete on paper and pulp but companies like SCA and Stora Enso do.

- *Multinational influence*. Porter totally ignores the major multinational companies, yet they are the main contributors to foreign trade and foreign direct investment. Dunning suggests that multinational enterprises (MNEs) accounted for between 25 and 30 per cent of the GDP of the world's market economies in the mid-1980s. They were also responsible for around three-quarters of the world's commodity trade and four-fifths of the trade in technology and managerial skills.[16]

- *Home country advantage*. For some MNEs, the location of their home countries is largely irrelevant. The fact that ABB – *see* Case study 16.3 – is located in Switzerland and Sweden has almost no bearing on its global strategies. This means that the basis of the Porter thesis – the 'home country' advantage (of Japanese consumer electronics, for example) – is irrelevant for such companies.

These and other criticisms suggest that the theory is only a partial explanation of complex issues. However, it does alert companies to important country issues that need to be addressed.

19.2.3 Theory of limited state intervention – attributed to the World Bank

In its work in supporting investment in developing countries over the last few years, the World Bank has had the opportunity to examine the areas of investment that deliver real increases in the wealth of countries. It has never published the results as a 'theory' as such but its empirical findings can be found in its annual reports. It is these that have been summarised as the limited state intervention theory outlined in Figure 19.4.

Definition ➤   Essentially, the theory of limited state intervention suggests that companies gained from national government investment in the early years in such areas as telecommunications and roads, but that as nations become more wealthy the state should withdraw its support and allow free market pressures to operate. This means that state support for home-grown industries should be reduced if companies are to compete internationally.

Figure 19.4

Theory of limited state Intervention

⟵─────────────────────────────────────⟶

Early stages of development
- Economic stability
- Low inflation
- Stable finances and currency
- Export support for selected areas
- Quality civil service and training institutions
- Agricultural development policies

Later stages of development
- Maintain openness to international trade
- Allow free markets to operate
- Continue to invest in infrastructure but privatise where possible
- Low tariff barriers

Company strategy should be seeking evidence of the above

From a corporate strategy perspective, the findings indicate the attitudes that companies should have towards government intervention. They indicate that companies should be wary of governments that deny open market access. Governments should also be seeking to stabilise the economy of a country and its currency as a matter of policy and should invest in its infrastructure and education. This provides clear guidance to companies on country selection for market potential and for production plant location.

19.2.4 Implications of international trade theories for corporate strategy

Overall, they point to the important role of government policy in several areas:

- *Developing basic infrastructures.* These concern such areas as water supplies, telecommunications and roads. It is difficult for company corporate strategy to make much headway in a country if the government is unwilling to invest in these areas.

- *Training and the quality of education.* These too are also vital. The stock of human capital is an important element in the development of new investments because of the need to recruit and train nationals to work for the company. In selecting countries for international strategic development, this may be a major factor.

- *Economic stability and selected export stimuli.* Most organisations are able to work better if inflation is low and the economy is stable. In the early stages of development, there is also some evidence that governments can usefully support certain industries in terms of export assistance to stimulate early growth.

- *Competitive and open home market.* Although there is a risk that home industries may be swamped by large international companies entering the home market, this is not what has tended to happen in practice. When the home market is open, it has stimulated new entrants to open factories, created jobs and thus wealth. For example, India has for years had home markets that were partially closed to international trade. Singapore and Malaysia have opened up their markets and benefited accordingly. And so have companies like Sony (Japan) and Philips (Netherlands) that have invested in such countries.

More specifically from a company perspective, it is important to examine the extent and nature of the main barriers that might exist to the opportunities associated with free trade: these are shown in Exhibit 19.2. In the short term, some barriers may be small and outside the more fundamental scope of corporate strategy. However, at a deeper level, such barriers may be fundamental to company survival and development. For example, the production plant investment by the Japanese car companies Nissan, Toyota and Honda inside the EU in the 1980s and 1990s was a direct strategic response, at least in part, to trade barriers and EU sensitivities in this area.

Exhibit 19.2

The main barriers to trade

- *Tariffs*: taxes on imported goods. They do not stop imports but do make them less competitive.
- *Quotas*: a maximum number placed on the goods that can be imported in any one period.
- *Non-tariff or technical barriers*: local laws or other technical means imposed by governments to make it difficult for imports to enter the country.
- *Financial subsidies for home producers*.
- *Exchange controls*: government control of the access its citizens have to foreign currency so that it becomes difficult to pay for imports.

Key strategic principles

- Early theories of international trade concentrate on the *resources of the country*. They suggest that a reduction in trade barriers can be coupled with the economies of scale available to companies in explaining the growth of international trade over the last 50 years.

- Porter's *diamond theory of the competitive advantage of nations* identified four home country factors that explained why some countries were particularly successful internationally: factor conditions; related and supporting industries; firm strategy structure and rivalry; demand conditions. In addition, he identified two outside factors – government policy and chance – that were also significant.

- The *theory of limited state intervention* was attributed to the World Bank and identified the role of government in different stages of economic growth. As countries become more wealthy, governments should let free markets operate.

- Theories of international trade identify the role of government in encouraging international investment. They also help companies select which countries offer the best international prospects.

19.3 INFLUENCE OF INSTITUTIONS INVOLVED IN INTERNATIONAL TRADE

In any development of international and global strategy, it is useful to have some background knowledge of the main institutions involved and their roles in its development. Corporate strategists may meet them directly and will certainly encounter their policy decisions indirectly over time. It should be noted that the United Nations is not identified separately below. However, it has come to have an important policy role in a number of areas such as education, health and agriculture, which will have relevance to specific product strategy initiatives.

19.3.1 Three international trade institutions

In order to promote free trade after the mistakes of the 1930s, the major Western nations decided during the 1940s that they would need new bodies to oversee international trade. They attempted to establish three international institutions that would be directly relevant to companies involved in international trade:

1 *The International Monetary Fund* (IMF). The IMF is designed to lend funds to countries in international difficulty and to promote trade stability through co-operation and discussion. It has also provided a forum for the regulation of currencies up to 1973.

2 *The International Bank for Reconstruction and Development*. This is often called the World Bank. It was set up to provide long-term capital aid for the economic development of nations – roughly US$10 billion per annum. It still provides lending for infrastructure, tourism and other projects, with the aim of long-term improvement in growth. *See* Case 18.1.

3 *The International Trade Organization* (ITO). This was to be set up to regulate trade activity and sort out the trade disputes that had been so disastrous during the 1918–39 period. It was never allowed to operate but the World Trade Organization, which was formed in 1995, was its direct successor.

The IMF and the World Bank were successfully inaugurated and continue to the present. Unfortunately, the US failed to ratify the treaty setting up the ITO in 1948. As an interim

Definition ➤ measure, GATT was signed by 23 signatory countries in 1947. GATT is the General Agreement on Tariffs and Trade. It is a treaty between nations that is designed to encourage and support world trade by providing an agreed set of trade rules and a means of adjudicating breaches of those rules. It continued as the main mechanism to ensure free trade up to 1995. Exhibit 19.3 shows the main GATT principles. By the late 1990s, over 140 countries had signed the GATT because the results were seen to be beneficial.

Exhibit 19.3

The main principles of the GATT

There are three major principles:

1 *Non-discrimination*. Each country will give all other countries the same rates on import duties. Giving more to one country means giving more to all signatories (called *most favoured nation* status).

2 *Consultation*. When disputes arise, GATT brings the parties together and encourages compromise, rather than the squabbles of the 1930s.

3 *Sanctions for non-compliance*. Where no compromise is possible, then the WTO is empowered to adjudicate and impose a solution. It has semi-judicial status.

Over the period from 1947, GATT has sponsored eight major rounds of tariff and other trade barrier reductions to encourage world trade (barriers to trade are explored in the next section). Each negotiation round is named after the country or town where it was begun. The latest completed round was the Uruguay Round which started in 1986 and was signed in 1993.[17]

The World Trade Organisation (WTO) was set up in 1995 to administer the GATT and to undertake the functions originally envisaged as being part of the ITO.[18] It has become a prime mover in the continued development of international trade and highly beneficial to those companies developing international corporate strategy. For example, the 'Banana War' between the US and the EU in 1998–99 was eventually decided under the GATT rules. The WTO judged that the US was entitled to complete access for its banana exports and could apply sanctions against a range of EU companies if such entry was denied. The corporate strategy of a large number of firms, including many that had no involvement with bananas, was affected by this move.

19.3.2 Third World countries and the GATT

Although GATT gave important protection to poorer and smaller countries when they reduced their barriers to large and powerful partners, such countries still felt that it assisted industrialised countries. They pointed to the fact that their share of world trade was declining. They therefore encouraged the United Nations to form the United Nations Conference on Trade and Development (UNCTAD). This body has been concerned with highlighting the trade concerns of the developing nations. It has a more limited role in the development of corporate strategy.

19.3.3 Institutions involved in currency regulation

In addition to trade, another major area of concern in 1945 was *exchange rates for currency* between countries: there is little point in fixing a price, regardless of tariffs, if the unit in which it is quoted then collapses. This will clearly have an immediate impact on company profitability. There had been real problems in this area in international trade in the 1930s. A system of largely fixed exchange rates was agreed internationally in 1944: the 'Bretton

Woods' Agreement. This lasted until 1973 but was then replaced by floating exchange rates around the world. The International Monetary Fund (IMF) was set up to oversee the fixed system but did not disappear when the fixed system was discontinued. Today, it has more of a background role. It lends funds to countries in balance of payments difficulties and helps to support international trade stability through co-operation and discussion.

19.3.4 Importance of trade blocks

To pursue international strategy, companies usually need to negotiate with national governments. At its most basic level, this means that the company will need to assess the political attitudes of the government – *see* Chapter 3. This section concentrates on the international dimensions only.

In addition to individual countries, various *trade blocks* have also developed around the world. A trade block is a group of countries that have agreed to give each other preferential international trading terms. The purpose of a trade block is to encourage trade between its members on the basis of the theories related to trade barriers and economies of scale. Because it is conducive to free trade, such a block may also help in stabilising a country's political and economic environment.

Definition ▶

Some trade blocks have already been mentioned, one of the best known being the EU. Other well-known ones include ASEAN (Association of South East Asian Nations) and NAFTA (North American Free Trade Agreement). Each block is governed by its own rules: for example, the EU has a tight set of rules and relatively close degree of co-operation, while ASEAN is a looser grouping of countries, each having a stronger degree of independence.

For companies engaged in international expansion, the main tasks are to assess the opportunities in specific countries and the trade blocks to which such countries belong.

19.3.5 Conclusions for corporate strategy

At a senior level, there is increasing contact between the leading multinational companies and the main institutions outlined above. For smaller companies, there is always the possibility of *lobbying* to gain benefits and influence decisions that might be taken. For example, the world's leading banks are usually represented at the biannual conferences of the IMF and individual companies have made representations to the WTO. These are important areas of strategic influence for the senior officers of any company.

Key strategic principles

● Three major international institutions have significant influence on international trade. The International Monetary Fund (IMF) oversees international payments. The World Bank provides long-term capital aid. The World Trade Organisation (WTO) regulates trade activity and resolves trade disputes between nations.

● The General Agreement on Tariffs and Trade (GATT) is the general treaty covering trade between many nations of the world. Various rounds of tariff reductions have been sponsored under the GATT. They have opened up world markets over the last 50 years and significantly increased international trade.

● The United Nations Conference on Trade and Development (UNCTAD) represents the interests of Third World countries in international negotiations.

● Trade blocks consist of countries that agree to give each other preferential trading terms. Corporate strategy will need to consider such blocks and their impact on trade.

Global automotive vehicles – strategy in a mature market

This case explores the background to this major international industry. In particular, it examines the way that strategy has altered as market growth has slowed in many parts of the world.

Competition in the global automotive market

The world's largest vehicle producer is the US company General Motors (GM). This company produced 8.5 million vehicles in 2003 and had a world market share of around 15 per cent. The Japanese company, Toyota, was the second-largest producer, with nearly 7 million vehicles and a share of around 12 per cent. Ford was just behind Toyota, with a market share also around 12 per cent. The next two companies were both German – Volkswagen and DaimlerChrysler. Table 19.5 shows that Toyota has been putting pressure on the two largest companies in recent years. To quote John Devine, GM's chief financial officer: 'I'm the first to admit it is a tough environment but the sky is not falling in. We are in a much stronger position today than we were in the early 1990s.'

US manufacturers have been working hard for many years against the Japanese competition by modernising plants, cutting the costs of parts and introducing new vehicle designs. But the Japanese companies have not been standing still. 'GM, Ford and Chrysler are rapidly catching up with Toyota,' says Fujio Cho, the president of Toyota. 'So we must go back to the origin of the new vehicle in an effort to improve quality.'

Outside the top five companies, competition is also fierce amongst the next group of companies. This latter group includes:

- the Italian company Fiat (in which GM has a 20 per cent shareholding);
- the two French companies PSA Peugoet Citroen and Renault;

The global automotive market is mature and fiercely competitive. But the differences in wealth around the world mean that customer preferences vary widely across the globe.

- the two Japanese companies Honda and Nissan (in which Renault has a 38 per cent shareholding and close co-operation on vehicle design and parts-sharing);
- the Korean company Hyundai.

Included in these companies, there are some other famous brand names – *see* Table 19.6.

Many of these companies have areas of regional strength around the world: for example, Volkswagen, Fiat and Renault are important in their home countries – Germany, Italy and France respectively. Volkswagen is the top-selling car company in the whole of the European Union (EU). However, it is important to note that large market share does not necessarily mean high profitability. The largest sales were achieved in the volume market segments – like the small cars segment with models such as the Twingo and Fiesta – where the profit margins were low. Smaller sales were achieved in the large, luxury segments – like those for luxury saloons from BMW and Mercedes – where the profit margins were substantial.

Global car, truck and commercial vehicle markets

In analysing world automotive markets, the data can be confusing. Some companies – such as Renault – publish information on their sales and market shares based on the market for 'passenger cars'. Other companies – such as GM – define their markets to include trucks and commercial vehicles like buses and heavy lorries. This makes a comparison of data from the companies potentially confusing – for example, the world market for *passenger cars* in 2002 was over 37 million units, but the market for *all* automotive vehicles was over 57 million

Annual global sales of cars, trucks and buses – GM is still the leader

Data in millions of vehicle units

Year	General Motors	Toyota	Ford	Volkswagen	DaimlerChrysler
2001	8.60	5.28	7.01	5.08	4.48
2002	8.58	6.17	6.97	4.98	4.54
2003	8.52*	6.78	6.72	4.85*	4.60*

* Estimated data by author

Note: The above sales exclude units from other companies where the above company has a minority shareholding. For example, the above Ford figures exclude the 1 million unit sales of the Japanese company Mazda, where Ford has a 30 per cent shareholding and co-operates in the common sourcing of car parts.

Source: Company accounts.

▶ **CASE STUDY 19.3 continued**

Table 19.6

Brand names and models of some of the leading car companies

Ranked by approximate total vehicles sold in 2002

Company	Home country	Total vehicle sales*	Brand names and models include:
General Motors	US	8.6	Opel, Vauxhall, Saab
Ford Motor Company	US	7.0	Aston Martin, Jaguar, Land Rover, Volvo
Toyota	Japan	5.7	Daihatsu, Lexus
Volkswagen	Germany	5.0	Audi, Lamborghini, Bentley, Skoda, Seat
DaimlerChrysler	Germany	4.5	Freightliner (trucks), Mercedes-Benz, Setra (trucks), Sterling (trucks), Western Star (trucks) Thomas Built (buses)
PSA Group	France	2.7	Peugeot, Citroën
Fiat	Italy	2.6	Alfa Romeo, Ferrari, Iveco (trucks), Lancia, Maserati
Hyundai	Korea	2.5	Kia
Nissan	Japan – but Renault has effective control	2.4	Infiniti
Honda	Japan	2.4	Acura
Renault	France	2.4	Dacia, Mack (trucks)
Mitsubishi	Japan	1.0	
Mazda	Japan	1.0	(Ford owns 30%)
BMW	Germany	1.0	Mini, Rolls Royce

* Approximate numbers in millions based on company Annual Reports.

units. Even though commercial vehicles have different industrial customers and different methods of distribution, most world companies are involved in both passenger and commercial markets because the technology and production methods are similar. This case therefore defines the market as that for *all* automotive vehicles, including buses and trucks.

From a global perspective, North America is still the world's largest automotive market – see Table 19.7. Western Europe is the second largest and Japan third, with these three geographical areas accounting for over 80 per cent of world sales. Importantly, many markets hardly grew over the period 2000–2003 and no substantial growth was expected over the next few years. However, this was not true of the Asia-Pacific region, especially the People's Republic of China (PRC). Although PRC sales were small in 2004, manufacturers were impressed by the economic growth of that country and its large population and investment in new roads. All vehicle companies expected substantial growth in sales volume over the next few years in the PRC and were therefore investing heavily in that country.

Production strategy: productivity and quality

From a strategy perspective, the automotive industry has the production capacity to produce 70–80 million units per year. In practice, most companies only produce what they are able

to sell during a year, but there have been some exceptions as companies attempt to keep their plant operating during periods of low demand. The spare production capacity in the industry is particularly relevant because automotive companies rely on economies of scale and scope to deliver profits.

Labour productivity has become one of the classic measures of cost reduction in such companies using techniques like just-in-time, Kaizen and supplier relationships – see Case 9.2 for an example from Toyota. The Japanese companies like Honda, Nissan and Toyota have the most experience in this area and, as a result, often have the lowest costs and highest productivity in the industry. Table 19.8 makes some comparisons amongst European companies.

Productivity is not the only important production strategy: *build-quality* has also become vital over the last 20 years. The three largest Japanese companies – Toyota, Honda and Nissan – have been amongst the leaders globally. They have developed competitive advantages in this area that have put them ahead of their American rivals, GM and Ford. The advantages are sustainable in the sense that it takes several years to invest in new plant that makes cars of a higher quality and probably longer to change workforce practices to those associated with higher quality. Importantly, when companies build to a higher quality, they also reduce their manufacturing costs because there is less waste and fewer rejects that have to be recycled.

Table 19.7

Geographical sales of automotive vehicles

Thousands of units

	2002	2000	Comment
North American Free Trade Area	20 118	20 595	The three traditional companies – GM, Ford and Chrysler – are important. Chrysler was acquired by Daimler-Benz in 1998 – *see* Case 10.1
Europe including Eastern Europe	19 172	20 158	Volkswagen, Fiat, PSA Citroen Peugeot and Renault are important companies in addition to Ford and GM. Fiat dominated the Italian market but was loss-making for several years 2000–2003
South and Latin America, Africa and the Middle East	3 673	3 664	Several of the major manufacturers had production facilities – for example, Ford in Mexico and Volkswagen in Brazil
Asia-Pacific, including Japan and Korea	14 373	12 880	Toyota is the largest company in its home market with Honda second. Hyundai is the leader in Korea

Source: GM and industry estimates by the author.

Table 19.8

Ranking of European car companies by the productivity of its leading factory during 2003

Automotive productivity is defined as 'vehicles produced per person working at the factory'

Ranking 2003	Manufacturer	Plant	Country of named plant	Models produced in factory
1	Nissan	Sunderland	UK	Primera, Almera, Micra
2	Renault	Valladolid	Spain	Clio
3	Toyota	Valenciennes	France	Yaris
4	Ford	Saarlouis	Germany	Focus
5	GM	Antwerp	Belgium	Astra
6	Honda	Swindon	UK	Civic, CR-V, Accord
7	Peugeot Citroen	Aulnay	France	106, Saxo, C3
8	Fiat	Melfi	Italy	Punto, Ypsilon
9	Volkswagen	Pamplona	Spain	Polo
10	DaimlerChrysler	Rastatt	Germany	A-Class

Note: The World Markets Research Centre, London, produces a better and more complete list, which is available on its website – www.wmrc.com. For example, it shows that the leading Volkswagen plant – at Pamplona – was actually ranked in productivity at number 27 in 2002, with many other plants from other manufacturers before the first VW plant. Similarly, the leading DaimlerChrysler plant – Rastatt – was ranked at number 34. It is perhaps not surprising that these companies have lower profitability. However, this data is not essential for an understanding of this case.

Source: Based on data and comment in company Annual Reports.

The labour productivity of car plants is also related to the capital investment in new machinery and other design features at individual plants – newer machinery is likely to make workers more productive. However, numerous studies have also shown that the *way* that the workers are employed and managed in the factory is also important – for example, the Toyota manufacturing system is described in Chapter 9. Other companies have now adopted such approaches and invested heavily in new plant to improve productivity.

In manufacturing strategy, supplier relationships are also important. Every company only manufactures some parts of the car – for example, no major vehicle company makes tyres or batteries. If the outside suppliers are high-cost then this increases the costs of manufacture of the automotive companies. Toyota has traditionally been different from other manufacturers in that it has bought in more products from outside the company than a company like Ford, which has made more internally.

While not strictly manufacturing strategy, research and development (R&D) is also important in business strategy at automotive companies. Although the petrol engine and car technology are relatively mature, new developments can be a

▶ **CASE STUDY 19.3 continued**

source of competitive advantage. The greatest cost reductions often come from redesigning components rather than seeking cost reductions on the factory floor.

Recent advances in R&D have come from new electronic devices in the vehicle – electronic diagnostics, electronic sensors, etc. In addition, other more fundamental developments are beginning to emerge. For example, Toyota has developed a totally new model of car – the new Prius (the word means 'ahead of time'). It is a hybrid power vehicle involving two forms of technology combined into one engine. There is a high-efficiency *petrol engine* for low speeds in town coupled with a zero-emissions *electric motor* for higher steady speeds on motorways – all combined into one engine. Honda has also been developing similar technology. Other vehicle companies like Ford and GM are reported to be starting to use the Toyota patents under licence from Toyota. These developments are significant because of increased concern amongst environmentalists over exhaust emissions and energy usage of all vehicles over the next few years.

Customers, market segmentation and branding

Given that the majority of sales are in the three wealthiest regions of the world – namely, North America, Western Europe and Japan – it is not surprising that most marketing activity is focused on these areas. Companies have various sophisticated methods of segmenting their markets but, in essence, the markets can be divided into the segments shown in Table 19.9, with pricing pitched to each as appropriate. The main developments over the last few years have been twofold:

● the development of new, specialist vehicle market segments – like sports utility vehicles, large people-carriers and 4-wheel-drive off-road carriers. Such segments are often accompanied by higher prices and therefore higher profit margins.

● the introduction of higher quality and add-on features as standard items – for example, electronic alarms, electric windows, extra safety bars and crash panels. For companies like Toyota with lower manufacturing costs, such vehicles have been priced the same as their rivals but they have been able to offer more value for money.

Although vehicle manufacturers have worked to standardise their brands in one region of the world, they use different brand names in other markets. For example, Toyota has the Yaris, Corolla and Avensis in Europe, but its five brands in the Japanese market – the ist (sic), Noah, Vitz, Estima and Alphard – are largely unknown in Europe. Equally, the Ford motor company has brands in North America that are unfamiliar in Europe – for example, the Lincoln Navigator and the Mercury Monterey and Marauder.

The only segment of the market where branding is truly worldwide is the luxury segment. Well-known marques like Rolls Royce (now owned by BMW), Bentley (now owned by Volkswagen), Mercedes (part of DaimlerChrysler) and Lexus (a Toyota subsidiary) are available worldwide through exclusive dealerships. The quality and finish on such cars is high and the profit margins substantial. The profit margins have recently been increased through a new strategy: the luxury models use some standard parts that are available from cheaper cars of the parent company, thus benefiting from economies of scale. Occasionally, such parts prove to be inappropriate – for example, the new £110,000 Bentley Continental was launched in 2004 and was delivered with the same plastic ignition key used on the £12,000 Volkswagen Golf. Although the unit sales of luxury cars are lower, they have still been important for

---

Table 19.9

Example of market segmentation – the UK car market for Ford and Toyota 2004

Prices in £ sterling

	Toyota		Ford	
	Model	Price range depending on specification	Model	Minimum price – may be higher depending on specification
Small car segment	Yaris	6 900–12 600	Ka Fiesta	6 775 8 415
Medium car segment	Corolla	10 800–16 100	Focus	10 995
Large car segment	Avensis	14 200–22 700	Mondeo	14 995
Off-road, 4-wheel-drive, sports car specialist segments	RAV-4 MR2 Land Cruiser	17 000–18 500 17 000–18 500 24 300–37 200	Maverick Galaxy	18 000 19 460
Luxury	Lexus	35 000 upwards	Jaguar	35 000

Source: Author from company websites 2004.

The Ford dealer network in 2003

	Ford	Lincoln	Mercury	Mazda*	Aston Martin	Jaguar	Volvo	Land Rover
Markets served worldwide	137	38	15	145	25	66	100	142
No of dealers worldwide	13 000	1 561	2 141	6 131	100		787	2 500	1 808

* Mazda shares some activities with Ford but the US company only has a minority stake.

Source: Ford Company Annual Report 2002.

some companies. For example, the Mercedes car range has been a major source of profits to its parent, DaimlerChrysler, while the parent was grappling with its highly unprofitable North American Chrysler car and truck operations.

With respect to brand support, all major companies spend extensively on advertising and other forms of promotion around the world. For example in the UK, the five vehicle companies Ford, Renault, GM (through its Vauxhall brand in the UK), Volkswagen and Toyota were amongst the top 20 advertisers in 2003. Between them, these five companies spent £300 million (US$450 million) on media advertising in 2003 and, in addition, spent substantial sums on mailshots, promotion and sponsorship. Branding and new product introductions are important parts of company strategy.

Service strategy and dealer networks

After-sales of spare parts and vehicle regular servicing are also an important part of business strategy. There are two main reasons: they allow the companies to control the prices and promotion of their products and they can be a major source of continuing profits through high prices for servicing and spare parts. Customers of new cars are forced to continue to use the manufacturers' dealer networks for servicing or face the threat of invalidating their new car guarantees. All the major manufacturers have developed substantial networks and support organisations to undertake such tasks. Table 19.10 outlines the main elements for the Ford company as an example.

Future trends

With a global industry, it is always difficult to identify worldwide trends – some parts of the world will be more affected than others. However, there are three trends that may be generally relevant:

- *Higher oil prices*: the major increases of the last few years will put increased pressure on the main vehicle manufacturers to make more fuel-efficient cars. The same prices may also persuade customers – even those driving giant American sports utility vehicles and trucks – to buy more fuel-efficient cars.
- *Global warming*: some countries still regard this as being another country's problem and even deny that it is a serious issue. However, Europe at least is beginning to wake up to the consequences of sending excessive carbon emissions into the atmosphere. Over time this will bring demand for engine redesign.
- *Economic slowdown in America, Japan and Western Europe*: the years 2002–2005 have seen static market growth in parts of the world that account for the majority of world vehicle sales. This will have major implications for sales and profitability.

Case questions

1 *What are the benefits and costs of a global strategy in the vehicles industry? What difference, if any, has the maturity of the industry made to global strategy?*

2 *Given the mature state of the industry and the future trends, what strategies would you recommend to the leading car companies for the next five years?*

19.4 INTERNATIONAL AND GLOBAL EXPANSION STRATEGIES: THE COMPANY PERSPECTIVE

We now move from issues concerning country competitive advantages to those relating to the company. This section explores basic issues surrounding international and global expansion strategies: the basic business case, the case for global strategy, the case for a global and local strategy, and some other international considerations. The following two sections explore organisational structures and specific entry routes and problems.

19.4.1 The basic business case for international expansion

In exploring international expansion, the starting point has to be the strategic business case and the impact on the company of any significant form of international expansion.

The contribution of Hymer

Although some basic products have been sold internationally for centuries,[19] the business logic for international expansion relied on two main arguments:[20]

- a mature home market meant that higher growth might be achieved abroad;
- higher rates of return could be earned outside the home country.

These two benefits needed to be set against the extra risks and costs of moving internationally – currency risks, political risks, economic risks and so on. Most economists thought for some years that a positive balance – rates of return from international expansion being greater than the risks and costs – was the reason that companies expanded internationally.[21] Hymer suggested that the reason for international expansion by companies investing in a country was more subtle. He pointed out that some companies chose to go further than simply take the low-risk option of exporting from their home countries. Why did they risk foreign direct investment (FDI) in another country? The reason was to exploit the benefit of some hard-to-replicate competitive advantage of the company that could be used beyond the home country: brand, technology, patent, efficiency due to size, etc. He argued that this would enable the company to dominate a foreign market in the way that it dominated a home market. Professor Richard Caves then developed the arguments further but the initial concept came from Hymer.[22] If a company has such a competitive advantage, then it may benefit from international expansion.[23]

19.4.2 The case for global strategy – the contribution of Ghoshal[24]

Global strategy means treating the world as one market and one interconnected source of supply. Some markets may be regional rather than global. For example, Toyota treated the European car market as having different customer tastes from the North American market – *see* Case study 19.4. Companies need to explore the business case for extending this into operating a global market. Ghoshal set out a framework to explore the business case for a global strategy. He argued that there are three main areas of potential competitive advantage that will come from pursuing a global strategy:

- *Exploitation of the comparative advantage of nations*: explored in Section 19.2.1 earlier in this chapter.
- *Developing of economies of scale*: marginal cost improvements as a company increases in size.
- *Achieving economies of scope*: cost savings achieved by transferring skills from one part of a business to another.

He suggests that there are three main outcomes to be obtained from a global strategy:

- *Achievement of increased efficiency* from such areas as low cost leadership and differentiation – maximising the economic outputs of a company while minimising the inputs.
- *Better management of risks* – offsetting the risks of one country by being involved in others can be beneficial in both economic and political terms. There may also be competitive and resource risks that can be lessened by a global strategy – for example, sourcing supplies from more than one country may have real benefits if a problem arises in a particular country.
- *Stimulation of innovation and learning* may arise from sharing knowledge, ideas and insights across international barriers.

He then combined these into a matrix, which is shown in Exhibit 19.4. It structures the logical reasoning behind the development of a global strategy, but does not claim to provide simple answers. It should be seen as outlining areas for consideration rather than providing definitive guidance.

Exhibit 19.4

Global strategy – the logic behind the principle

		Competitive advantages of global strategy		
		National comparative advantage	Economies of scale	Economies of scope
Strategic outcomes from global strategy	Achieved increased efficiency of current operations	Benefiting from differences between nations on wages and cost of capital	Developing potential economies of scale in every area of business	Sharing of activities and costs across products and subsidiaries
	Better risk management	Managing different areas of risk arising from changes in the comparative advantages of different countries	Balancing the advantages of scale with strategic and operational flexibility	Diversifying product portfolios and spreading risks of options
	Stimulation of innovation and learning	Learning from different parts of world, different organisations and managerial systems	Benefiting from experience of cost reduction and new innovation	Shared learning and knowledge across different markets and businesses

Source: Based on the late Professor Sumanthra Ghoshal's 1987 paper on global strategy – 'Global Strategy: an organising framework', *Strategic Management Journal*, Vol 8, pp425–440.

Comment

Some strategists – particularly Ghemawat, Rugman and Verbeke – now suggest that there are real difficulties in developing a truly global strategy.[25] They argue that the major investment required, the need to downplay local customer tastes and the organisational and co-ordination difficulties associated with global strategy all suggest that such a strategy would be better replaced by strategies of 'semi-globalisation'. There is evidence to support such arguments, particularly in the more mature product areas such as food and drink.[26] We return to this topic in Section 19.4.5 below.

As Chapter 5 explained, Professor Theodore Levitt argued that global strategy can deliver extra value added and sustainable competitive advantage. There were two main factors that needed to be present to justify a global strategy:[27]

1 *Resources*. These may be more economically manufactured and sourced on a global basis.[28] This was explored in Chapter 9. It is a factor commonly used in the consumer electronics industry, where there are both economies of scale and considerable cost savings by manufacturing labour-intensive items in countries with efficient production equipment and low labour costs, such as some Asian countries. Companies such as Sony (Japan) and Philips (Netherlands) now operate in this way.

2 *Customer demand*. This is essentially the same around the world for some products. Companies such as Gucci (Italy, though actually owned by a French company), Rolls Royce Cars (UK, though actually owned by a German company) and Nike (US) make products that are essentially branded in the same way in all countries. In so far as there are any differences, then customers will be prepared to compromise as a result of the lower prices gained by the economies of scale from the global manufacturing operation outlined above. This was explored in Chapter 5.

Professor George Yip has further developed the arguments in favour of globalisation.[29] He suggests that some organisations may fear being left behind. Moreover, the adoption of 'Western' values and customs has also contributed to globalisation because it promotes common customer demand. He lays particular emphasis on the ability of global products to spread the considerable costs of research and development across more countries – for example, the costs of drug development explored in Chapter 6.

Fundamentally, Yip argues that globalisation may increase the competitive leverage of a company, i.e. it may increase its competitive advantage as a result of its global scope. This presents the clear opportunity of globalisation. But it also raises the question of the number of markets that are truly global: even McDonald's has had to adjust parts of its menu to suit local tastes and dispense with the Big Mac completely in India. Rolex watches and Yves St Laurent clothing will arguably be global, but many other products may have to be significantly adapted to local needs.

19.4.3 The case for a global/local strategy

In arguing the case for a global strategy, Levitt's arguments largely stopped with the two considerations outlined above. However, for many organisations the global considerations have to be balanced by the need to respond to variations in local demand: the case for the global/local strategy. This is sometimes summarised in the phrase: 'Think global, act local.'

About three years after Levitt produced his paper in favour of globalisation, Professors Susan Douglas and Yoram Wind delivered a suitably robust response.[30] For most companies, there is likely to be a need for some local variation: even supposedly global companies like Nike – *see* Chapter 11 – need to have local variations simply because body sizes vary in different countries.

Local responsiveness clearly pulls in the opposite direction to the pressure for global activity. There are four main reasons behind this:

1 Customer tastes and conditions of usage may vary between countries. This was examined in Chapter 5.

2 National governments may be concerned that the interests of their countries are better served by some variation special to that country. This was explored earlier in this chapter.

3 Different technical standards, different legislation and other social issues may make it essential to produce products especially for a particular country. For example, it is still necessary for domestic electrical plugs and sockets to be produced for specific EU countries because of the different electrical connections (two- or three-pin) in each country.

4 Different national competitors may make it difficult to offer precisely the same competitive advantage in every market. For example, the UK chocolate company Cadbury has had difficulty selling some of its chocolate block products in France and Spain because it faces stronger competition from Kraft Jacobs Suchard (part of Philip Morris, US) in these markets than in its home UK market.

If local responsiveness is required, then this will dilute the value added that might be gained by the scale benefits of globalisation. However, many companies have found that such local issues can be accommodated within global expansion.

In practice, therefore, many supposedly global initiatives also need to accommodate significant national responsiveness. Even companies like Coca-Cola, Walt Disney and McDonald's provide some local variations in tastes, languages or national menu items respectively. The difficult strategic choice is often to find the *balance* between global expansion and local responsiveness. The global/national balance is summarised in Table 19.11.

19.4.4 Four prescriptive strategic options for international expansion

Considering the issues explored above, companies have at least four options for international expansion.[31] They are essentially prescriptive in their approach and arise from a consideration of the benefits to be obtained by the two main factors: global strategy and national (or regional) demand.

Table 19.11

The balance between global expansion and national responsiveness

Pressure for global strategy*	Pressure for international strategy but still responsive to national variations*
• Global or multinational competitors	• Differing competitors or distributors by nation or region
• High levels of investment or technology that need large sales for recovery, e.g. in production, branding or R&D	• Need to adapt product extensively to meet national needs
• Economies of scale in production and purchasing	• Product life cycle at a different stage in local country
• High levels of investment in marketing and brand building	• High skill levels in local country that will permit product adaptation to that country
• Desire by customers for a global 'image'	• Differing conditions of usage, e.g. climate
• Need to cut costs by seeking low labour sources	• Pressure from governments for national activity, e.g. tariff or quota restrictions on global activity
• Global sourcing of raw materials or energy	• National purchasing of key supplies essential

* These are not mutually exclusive.

1 Some companies may decide to undertake purely global expansion, e.g. Gucci or Rolls-Royce cars.

2 Some companies opt for a global strategy *and* for national responsiveness, e.g. Toyota cars and Hewlett-Packard printers.

3 Some companies may need to be largely responsive to national demands and gain little from any form of global activity, e.g. Bata shoes.

4 Some companies may face *neither* of these pressures but still see opportunities to sell their products or services internationally, e.g. any domestic company that is willing to export some of its products.

The four options have been given names and are shown in Figure 19.5. However, it is important to note that the choice of one option does not preclude the choice of another at a later stage. For example, Yip argues that companies do not immediately choose the global option.[32] The global process will go through three stages that will take time and, arguably, some companies will not move beyond the first two stages. Yip's three-stage global process is:

● *Stage 1: Develop the core strategy* – the basis of competitive advantage. This is often developed for the home country first.

Figure 19.5

Four prescriptive options for international expansion

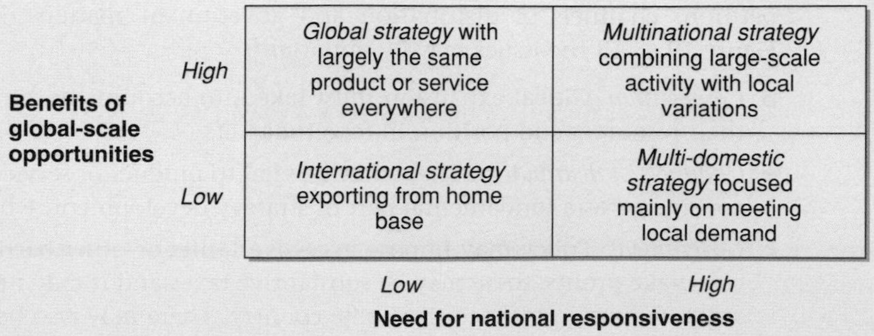

Benefits of global-scale opportunities

	Low ← **Need for national responsiveness** → High
High	*Global strategy* with largely the same product or service everywhere | *Multinational strategy* combining large-scale activity with local variations
Low	*International strategy* exporting from home base | *Multi-domestic strategy* focused mainly on meeting local demand

● *Stage 2: Internationalise the core strategy* – by launching it across a number of countries.

● *Stage 3: Globalise the strategy* – by seeking out the integration benefits that come from having one global market.

In practice, various other international strategy options have been identified. They are given various titles, with the following being representative:

● *Multicountry strategy.* This targets individual countries or groups of countries according to their customer potential and competitor presence. International co-ordination is secondary to a country-by-country expansion programme. For example, Danone (France) has marketed biscuits across Europe according to the local expansion opportunities rather than using a pan-European brand.

● *Global low-cost strategy.* This sources production where production costs are lowest and then sells globally. For example, Philips (Netherlands) manufactures radios in Hong Kong and sells them in Europe.

● *Global niche strategy.* The same product is sold in the same market niche in all countries of the world. For example, Dunhill (UK) and Yves St Laurent (France) products are presented in the same up-market fashion in all countries.

● *International regional strategy.* Regions of the world will have their own production and there will be some regional or national variation in the products made and marketed, but the *global underpinning* of strategy is clear. For example, most car companies, such as Toyota (Japan) and General Motors (US), follow such a strategy.

There are many other strategy variations that may also be chosen. The final decision will be *specific* to the product group and the organisation but it may be assisted by the summary arguments presented in Table 19.11.

19.4.5 Recent developments in global and international strategic thinking

As outlined earlier in Section 19.4.2, some strategists have begun to doubt the simple benefits of a global strategy. These developments remain to be fully proven but rest on the fact that many industries are neither fully domestic nor fully global. For this reason, some strategists have now begun to explore more subtle ways of international expansion. One method is to categorise companies into four groups: *country-centred players, geographical niche players, international opportunistic players and continental leaders*.[33] The first two groups have primarily a defensive stance against foreign competition, with the latter two seeking opportunities either temporarily or on a long-term basis.

19.4.6 Some other considerations in international expansion and global strategy

The global/local debate is not the only one that will guide international expansion. Two major issues are explored in the sections that follow: organisation structures and entry methods. However, there are issues in three other areas that need to be explored: competition, channels of distribution and government matters. These are summarised in Figure 19.6. All the issues may be important:

● *Competition.* Global expansion must take into account the activities of rival companies, their resources and position in target markets.

● *Channels of distribution.* These may be vital to product or service success. They need to be considered as a fundamental part of strategy development, where relevant.

● *Government.* Policy may impose excessive tariffs or other barriers. Even if the company can make profits, there may be substantive taxes and it may not be possible to repatriate any remaining profits to the home country. There may also be restrictions on the transfer of technology and poor country infrastructure – *see* earlier in this chapter.

Figure 19.6

Three other considerations in global expansion

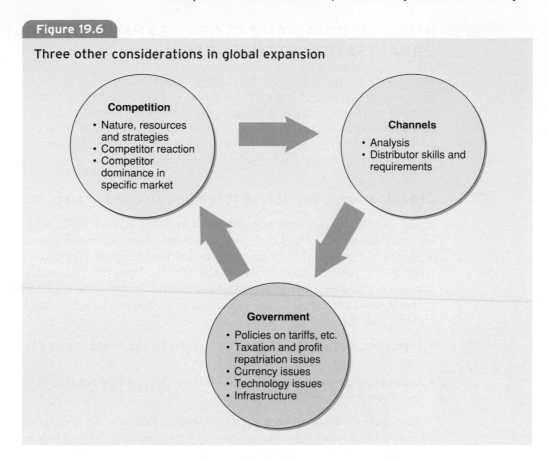

Key strategic principles

- International strategy expansion will follow the basic principles of strategy development. However, its greater complexity and uncertainty may mean that a staged development process is employed and selection is more complex. The starting point is clarity on the objectives and reasons for international expansion.

- Organisational history and culture, often based on home country senior management, also need to be considered.

- The case for a global strategy rests on two major elements: resources may be more economically procured and manufactured on a global basis. In addition, customer demand may be essentially the same around the world, thus allowing the world to be treated as one market.

- The case for a strategy that is both global and local derives from the need to gain the benefits of a global market while responding to the needs of national market variations. Local variations may arise as a result of customer demand and conditions of usage, national governments, differing technical standards and different national competitors.

- In practice, there is often a need to balance both global and local issues in strategy development.

- At least four prescriptive options emerge from such considerations: global, international, multinational and nationally responsive. In practice, many other variations in international expansion strategies have been developed.

- Other considerations in international expansion include careful consideration of competitors, investigation of distribution channels and a full analysis of national government restrictions and requirements.

INTERNATIONAL AND GLOBAL EXPANSION STRATEGIES: ORGANISATION STRUCTURES

Much of the thinking so far in this chapter has taken a prescriptive approach. This is probably because the background and foundation lie in the prescriptive routes adopted by international economic analysis and marketing strategy development. However, we also know that some organisational theorists like Mintzberg and Quinn have approached strategy development from an emergent perspective. This is reflected in some of the more recent work on organisational structures for international expansion.

19.5.1 Organisational development leading to a matrix structure

In the early 1970s, research was published by Stopford and Wells suggesting that organisational structures evolved over time as international expansion proceeded: their model is shown in Figure 19.7.[34] In the early period international expansion was handled by a separate international division which was often isolated from the main areas of strategic decision making. As international sales and business activity continued to grow, the organisational structure changed. The next stage depended on whether the dominant strategic problem was that of:

- organising across different geographic parts of the world, leading to the *area division* structure;
- or organising across increasingly diverse product groups, leading to a *worldwide product group* structure.

Subsequently in the 1980s, the globalisation/localisation debate explored in the previous section led to a new organisational structure: the *matrix structure* where both area divisions and product divisions were employed.[35] This form of organisational structure was explored in Chapter 16 – the criticisms made then also apply here:

Figure 19.7

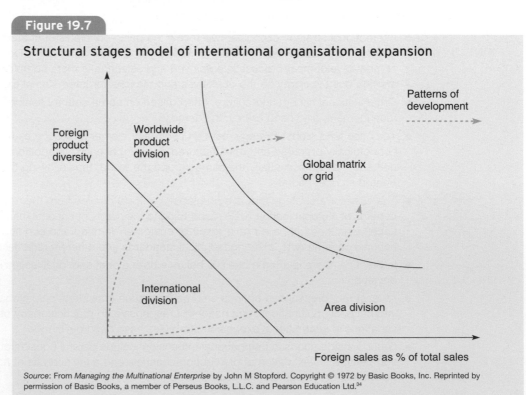

Structural stages model of international organisational expansion

Source: From *Managing the Multinational Enterprise* by John M Stopford. Copyright © 1972 by Basic Books, Inc. Reprinted by permission of Basic Books, a member of Perseus Books, L.L.C. and Pearson Education Ltd.[34]

- Dual responsibilities, e.g. area and product, are difficult to manage.
- The matrix amplified differences in perspectives and interests by forcing issues through a dual chain of command.
- Management became slower, more costly and possibly even acrimonious.

As a result, some larger companies, such as Unilever, tried and then abandoned the matrix organisation structure. At the end of the 1980s, along came a new organisational solution – the 'transnational structure'. It should be noted that this was *not* a new organisational form, but rather a way of conducting the business of a large international organisation.

19.5.2 Organisational structure: the transnational solution

In the late 1980s, Bartlett and Ghoshal published the results of a study of nine multinational companies that focused on the way that they organised their business and their ability to be both global and locally responsive. This placed considerable emphasis on the importance of innovation and technology development which was disseminated rapidly through the company.[36] The nine companies were grouped into three product areas:

1 branded packaged goods: Unilever (UK/Netherlands), Kao (Japan) and Procter & Gamble (US)

2 consumer electronics: Philips (Netherlands), Matsushita (Japan) and General Electric (US)

3 telecommunications switching: ITT (US), NEC (Japan) and Ericsson (Sweden).

From an extensive study of the strategic requirements of these businesses and the way that each handled its main resources, the two authors identified both existing problems and the methods that these companies had developed to overcome them.

According to Bartlett and Ghoshal, the basic problem with a matrix structure was that it focused on only one variable – the formal structure – that could not capture the complexity of the international strategic task. They defined this task as being to reshape the core decision-making systems and management processes of large MNEs: their administrative systems, their communications channels and their interpersonal relationships. The authors argued that, in the complex and fast-moving environment of global business, it was difficult to use a simple 'structural fit' between strategy and structure in the way suggested by Chandler – *see* Chapter 16. What was needed was to build in *strategic and organisational flexibility*. They therefore developed the transnational form, which would have the following characteristics:

- Assets and liabilities: dispersed, interdependent, with different parts of the organisation specialising in different areas. Thus, one country/company might take the lead on one product, another on another product, but all would co-ordinate and co-operate fully.
- Role of overseas operations: within an integrated worldwide structure, each country or product group would make a differentiated contribution.
- Development and diffusion of knowledge: this would be developed jointly and shared around the world. Chapter 11 explored this concept.

The two authors commented that the Transnational Form was 'not an organisational form but a management mentality.'[37] They suggested from their empirical evidence that the locus of decision making was likely to vary:

- across functions like finance and marketing (some might need to be more centralised than others);
- across different product categories (some might be more global than others). Figure 19.8 is an attempt to capture the approach.

It was Kogut who later added an important word of caution: new organisational structures take longer to diffuse across MNEs than technological innovations.[38] This has the

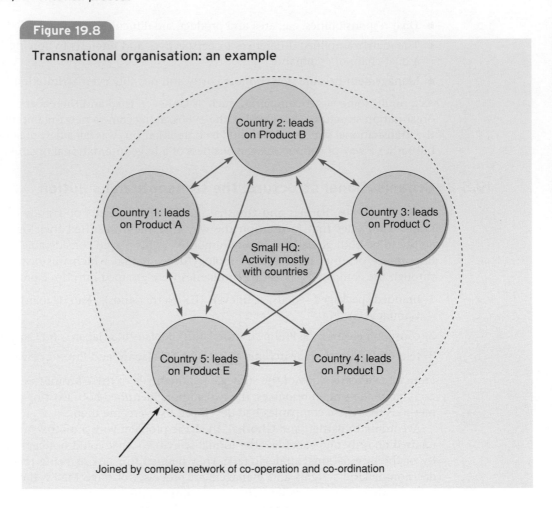

Figure 19.8

Transnational organisation: an example

Country 2: leads on Product B

Country 1: leads on Product A

Country 3: leads on Product C

Small HQ: Activity mostly with countries

Country 5: leads on Product E

Country 4: leads on Product D

Joined by complex network of co-operation and co-ordination

implication that the transnational form cannot simply be introduced overnight into a company. More recently, the internet has aided such developments and led to 'netchising' in which firms create a network of related businesses that are highly integrated on an international scale.[39] Such network contacts have also been explored to allow international R&D centres to exchange knowledge in various configurations.[40]

Comment

This research has been highly influential in many large, international companies in terms of their style of operation. Essentially, it is emergent in its approach and emphasises the knowledge and learning aspects of organisational development in a way that is not captured in other models. Yet it was developed from observations on only nine companies. Moreover, its proposals remain essentially vague and without clear guidance on pressing issues like the relative roles of national companies and product groups. The reorganisation at Unilever in the late 1990s – *see* Case study 14.3 – clearly borrows something from the approach but it was not enough to show the company how to balance the individual elements of its far-flung interests.

19.5.3 The history and culture of the organisation

The former head of the management consultants McKinsey in Japan, Kenichi Ohmae, has argued persuasively that company culture is also an important area in the development of organisational structure.[41] In summary, the organisation's culture needs to be considered in developing organisational structures. For example:

- A company that has acquired another outside its home country may have to live with the need to continue to satisfy its newly purchased local management and therefore provide some local autonomy to its new subsidiary.

- By contrast, the company that has set up an overseas operation from the beginning may have taken longer over the process, but will have been able to recruit, train and develop its people in exactly the way that it wishes, without any previous history. Hence it may be easier to develop an integrated structure.

In some of the literature, there is little consideration of the real strategic difficulties faced by organisations as a result of company historical and cultural influences. These can have a significant effect on strategic choice and organisational development. For example, even in international companies like Walt Disney pictures and Renault cars, the senior management is largely North American and French respectively. More recently, several authors[42] have produced useful analyses on this subject. The general conclusion seems to be that much of the key strategic decision making still remains centred on the home country, even if national responsiveness is needed. There is a need to consider these matters when international organisations are being designed.

Key strategic principles

- Organisational structures for international expansion often start by creating a separate division for international activities. As they grow in importance, such activities may the be reorganised either into a geographical area structure or one based on product divisions. This may then lead to a matrix structure with all its difficulties.

- The transnational solution to international organisation structure has been used by some companies. It involves dispersed and interdependent subsidiaries that are integrated into a worldwide operation.

- Organisational culture and past history are also important considerations.

19.6 DEVELOPING INTERNATIONAL RELATIONSHIPS SUCH AS ALLIANCES AND JOINT VENTURES

Many companies involved in international expansion have been rethinking their relationships with other companies as customers, suppliers and associates. Many different outside relationships are possible – Chapter 13 outlined some of the major options. Two are explored in this section because they have particular relevance for international expansion: joint ventures and alliances. Exhibit 19.5 sets out some basic questions that need to be examined for both areas.

Exhibit 19.5

Some basic questions on the nature of international relationships

- *Nature*: who with?
- *Purpose*: what for?
- *Strategy*: how does it fit with the MNE's objectives and strategies?
- *Bargaining*: who gains what?
- *Verticality*: how are risks shared?
- *Behaviour*: what is expected of the venture by governments?

Source: Dunning, J H (1993) *Multinational Enterprises and the Global Economy*, Addison Wesley, Wokingham, p240.

19.6.1 Basic forms of external relationships

In many circumstances, companies will decide that international expansion is best served by some form of external relationship with other companies. An external relationship means a contractual relationship between the *home* company and a *host* company in a foreign location. Essentially, the home company no longer has complete ownership of some aspect of its international strategy. There are three main reasons for developing external relationships:

1 *learning* – about the country and its culture, about the technologies contributed by the home and host companies and about the organisation and resources of its new host company;

2 *cost minimisation and risk reduction* – for example, lower-cost production sources, research, different regulatory systems and project economies;

3 *market factors* – international market access and distribution, competitive positioning, customer service.

The nature of the relationship is clearly important in determining the success of a new venture: *ownership* is an important starting point. Should the new venture be *wholly owned*, with the external relationships then applying to other elements of the value chain, such as suppliers and distributors? Or should it be a *joint venture*, in which both the home and host companies have shares? Or should it be simply an *alliance* with no shareholding involved and some rather weaker form of co-operation? The answers to these questions will vary with each company and its strategic situation. However, it is possible to provide some general guidelines on the factors that will determine the likely success of external relationships – *see* Exhibit 19.6.

Exhibit 19.6

Factors determining success of external relationships

- *Complementarity*. The partners should bring different resources to the relationship.
- *Agreement on objectives*. If this cannot be achieved, then the relationship will be difficult.
- *Compatible strategies and cultures*. They do not have to be the same but there should be some degree of empathy.
- *No surrender of key resources or core competencies*. The home partner must keep control of important strategic elements.
- *Stakeholder agreement*. There must be no conflict here.
- *Low risk of the host becoming a competitor*. It has occasionally been the case that a strong position has been established only for the host to set up in competition with the home partner.

19.6.2 Joint ventures[43]

Definition ➤ A joint venture involves two or more companies creating a legally independent company to share some of of the parent company's resources with the purpose of developing competitive advantage. Joint ventures can take many forms, the most obvious one being a 50/50 shareholding in a joint company. An example of a recent successful operation has been that of the Cereal Partners joint venture. This is a joint company set up by the multinational food companies Nestlé (Switzerland) and General Mills (US) – *see* Chapter 2 – with 50 per cent of the joint venture being owned by each of the two parents. It was formed to attack the breakfast cereal market around the world outside North America and has had some significant success. Such a share arrangement may not be appropriate in a different strategic context and with different strategic resources and competitors. It is essential to research well both the market and the chosen partner.

The main benefits that can arise from joint ventures between a large multinational and a local company are:

● risk reduction through sharing the project;

● rapid market access and speedy profits;

● the local firm's involvement and contacts, which may make the multinational more acceptable in the local community.

However, problems can arise from such joint venture activity:

● domination of the local market by the local partner so that the multinational remains insulated from direct customer contact;

● inability to work with the local partner for reasons of organisational culture, trust and national culture;

● the global objectives of the multinational may be in conflict with those of the national objectives of the local partner.

There is no simple way to determine the long-term success of joint ventures. Dunning is cautious, pointing to the difficulties of researching a topic with so many different variables.[44] Kogut is more pessimistic, commenting that they may succeed in mature markets but success is less likely in fast-growing markets. The reason for the problem is that high growth is usually accompanied by the need for a rapid extra cash injection and at least one partner often has a problem with such demands.[45] Tomlinson is probably right to emphasise the *partnership nature* of a joint venture.[46] He argues that the joint venture must involve an opportunity for reciprocal benefits to both parties. Moreover, there needs to be mutual trust and forbearance to make the association work. This will ultimately mean compatible goals. It is also likely to imply a clear definition of asset ownership and specific areas of contribution so that the partners are clear on their respective resource contributions.

19.6.3 Strategic business alliances[47]

Definition ➤ A strategic business alliance (SBA) is some form of contractual relationship designed to secure an international venture without involving a shareholding. Recent years have seen a substantial growth in SBAs for several reasons: first, because the increasing cost of R&D has brought pressures to share such costs; second, because SBAs were found to deliver lower costs through shared economies of scale and scope; third, because SBAs brought other cost benefits as a result of the SBA partners specialising or rationalising their operations. Dunning has commented that: 'SBAs are deliberately designed to advance the sustainable competitive advantage of the participating firms.'[48] Here are some examples of SBAs:

● European and North American pharmaceutical companies have been operating SBAs to distribute new drugs without the expense of setting up totally new marketing networks.

● Telecommunications companies have been setting up world SBAs to deliver seamless telephone services to their major multinational customers around the world without being present in every country – *see* Case study 15.2.

● National airline carriers have agreed SBAs to offer seamless ticketing across continents to their customers without opening offices in every airport.

In practice, the broad nature of such relationships suggests that there will be many reasons for SBAs. Exhibit 19.7 summarises the main reasons.

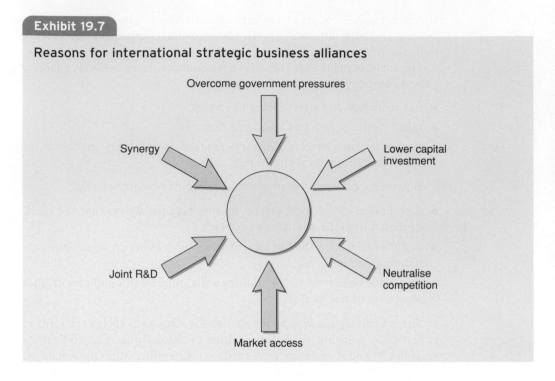

Exhibit 19.7

Reasons for international strategic business alliances

Overcome government pressures

Synergy

Lower capital investment

Joint R&D

Neutralise competition

Market access

Professors Yves Doz of INSEAD and Gary Hamel of the London Business School investigated alliance relationships in the early 1990s.[49] They concluded that they were more likely to be successful when each partner was clear about the intent of the other and accepted that such relationships were likely to evolve over time. They also suggested that it was preferable for the governance relationships of the two parties in such alliances to be similar. The reason was that this would avoid conflicting objectives. It was important, too, that any national or organisational differences in culture were respected as part of the SBA. They also found that it was better if the participants were able to balance their needs inside the SBA with their other interests outside the partnership.

Although the above conclusions are useful, SBAs are difficult to research because they can take so many forms. It is therefore appropriate to be cautious about the long-term success of SBAs in international strategy development.

Key strategic principles

- In developing international relationships with other companies, ownership issues need to be investigated. Joint ventures and alliances represent differing degrees of closeness in international co-operation.

- A joint venture between a multinational and a local company can provide rapid market access and local market involvement. However, the differing objectives of the two partners may lead to problems.

- Strategic business alliances cover relationships that do not involve a cross-shareholding. Benefits include cost savings and market access, but the nature of the linkage is essentially weak and it may not survive in the long term.

CASE STUDY 19.4

Global automotive vehicles – the battle between Ford and Toyota

In March 2004, the Japanese automotive company Toyota announced that it had sold 6.78 million cars and trucks around the world in the year 2003. This total was 60,000 higher than the American company Ford. It was the first time ever that Toyota had beaten Ford. It made Toyota second only to the American company General Motors in world automotive sales.

This case explores competition in the global automotive industry. It needs to be read in conjunction with Case 19.3.

Toyota strategy – stand alone

In around 2000, Toyota identified its purpose as being to take global market leadership by 2010. It called this its '2010 Global Vision Strategy'. During the 1980s and 1990s, the company targeted North America as its prime strategic focus. Along with Honda, Toyota launched cars of superior quality and with lower manufacturing costs than its US competitors. During the years 1991–2002, the main three US companies – GM, Ford and DaimlerChrysler – lost over 21 percentage share points of the American car market to Japanese and European competition. The combined losses of the three major US companies in 1991 alone were US$7.5 billion. The US car manufacturers were only saved by three changes:

1 the launch by each of the three companies of specialist vehicles – like sports utility vehicles, minivans and pickups;
2 a severe economic recession in Japan, which made Toyota's Japanese home base difficult;
3 a substantial rise in the Japanese yen, which made Japanese exports to the US less profitable.

Bob Lutz, vice chairman of GM explains: 'As we look at our market share performance, we have been enormously successful in the light truck business and the secular market share losses have occurred in the passenger car business, where the Europeans and Japanese have been the strongest.' Nevertheless by 2003, Toyota was selling the most popular single car model – the Camry – in North America. Toyota also now produces many of its basic models in North America so it is unlikely to be affected again by changes in the Japanese yen. Toyota now has six manufacturing plants in North America that produce over 1,250,000 units per year. It has announced plans for Mexican and Texan plants in the years 2005 and 2006. The company has now become a major employer in North America and is not merely outsourcing work to Japan.

In the 1990s, Toyota decided to attack the Western European market, which is the next largest market in the world. They had been selling vehicles in Europe for many years but decided to build their first factory – at Burnaston in the UK – in 1995. This was then followed by other factories and a design facility in France in the late 1990s. Toyota was cautious about Europe for many years for two reasons: first, because the European vehicle industry was protected by trade barriers; and, second, by a voluntary agreement by the Japanese car companies to restrict their European sales. However, the EU removed such barriers in the mid-1990s and Toyota

© Royalty-Free/Corbis

In the global car market, one strategy relies on economies of scale to reduce costs. But the market is mature and supply outstrips demand for standard car models. Excess cars are then stored in massive car parks for possible future sale. Perhaps a new global strategy is needed?

responded by a major drive into the region. Much of Toyota's world growth (*see* Table 19.5 earlier in the chapter) has come from this European expansion. According to one commentator, 'The main reason for the success is the decision by Toyota to be a major player in Europe. Before that, Toyota focused on America and gave second priority to Europe.'

In earlier years, Toyota based its European strategy on selling cars that were reliable but were not perhaps the most attractively designed – arguably even dull. However, European car manufacturers like Volkswagen were rapidly able to replicate any competitive advantage based on quality. More recently, Toyota has begun to design cars specifically for EU markets: Shuhie Toyoda, head of Toyota's EU operations explains: 'In Europe styling and performance is generally high. European people enjoy driving their cars more than, for example, Americans. In 1999, we introduced the Yaris. That is a vehicle designed specifically for Europe. Until then, although we tried to develop a vehicle that would suit Europe, the main target was not Europe.'

But all is not completely satisfactory with Toyota Europe's strategy. Its factories are still not as efficient as Nissan – *see* later section. Its customers do not recognise Toyota quality as being the highest, reserving that accolade for Volkswagen. Moreover, profit margins on its European operations are small – but it built a new plant jointly with PSA Citroen in the Czech Republic, where labour costs are lower, to make the Yaris.

▶

▶ CASE STUDY 19.4 continued

Table 19.12

Profit record at Toyota Motor Corporation – includes some other smaller trading activities like construction – but mainly automotive activity

Billions of Yen ¥ and US$

	Comparison for 2003 in US$ billions	Toyota results 1999–2003 Yen ¥ billions				
	2003	2003	2002	2001	2000	1999
Net sales	134	16 054	15 106	13 424	12 880	12 749
Net income	8	945	615	471	407	356
Total assets	173	20 742	19 889	17 519	16 469	14 533

Source: Company accounts – Toyota does not separate out its automotive trading or its financial activities from its vehicle trading in its financial accounts.

In spite of such difficulties, Toyota has enjoyed substantial growth in both sales and profits over the period 1999–2003. Its market share, its assets and its worldwide influence have impacted on other companies and, at the same time, delivered real growth – see Table 19.12 for the main figures. Apart from some production co-operation with competitors – it shared a manufacturing plant with GM in North America and built a manufacturing plant with PSA Peugeot Citroen in the Czech Republic – Toyota never co-operated or acquired another company outside its home market. This strategy was quite different from that of Ford – see below.

Importantly, Toyota always had some doubts about a simple global strategy. It used basic model designs for its volume car ranges but essentially produced cars that were designed for major regions of the world. For example, the Yaris small car was designed purely for the requirements of the European market in 2002 and there were no plans to develop the model as a global car.

GM strategy – build alliances and hold market share

Ford's main North American rival – General Motors – has often followed a strategy of building alliances, minority shareholdings and joint ventures outside its traditional North American and European markets. Over recent years, it has also followed a policy of reducing its prices in order to hold its market share, especially in its home country. The alliance strategy is described first, followed by the market share strategy.

GM's alliance strategy

GM's home country is the US where it has some of the strongest established brand names like Buick, Cadillac, Chevrolet and Pontiac. Its North American operations include around 100 manufacturing, assembly and warehousing facilities. It has also been involved for many years in Europe, where its brands include Opel (Germany), Vauxhall (UK) and Saab. It has 10 production and assembly facilities in seven European countries.

In addition to investment activity in its existing plants, GM has taken minority shareholdings in a number of world vehicle companies – for example, it owns 20 per cent of the shares of Fuji Heavy Industries, the owner of the Japanese brand Subaru; it has 10 per cent of the shares of Fiat, Italy, but has declined to purchase the remainder. The only company bought outright by GM was the Swedish company Saab. GM spent around US$4.7 billion to build such minority stakes over the period 2001–2004.

Essentially, GM has built a series of alliances and minority shareholdings and then co-operated with such companies in order to gain purchasing savings from extra scale. Thus it has obtained benefits in diesel engines from its links with Isuzu and Fiat; it has sold Chevrolets in Japan through its co-operation with Suzuki; it has sold a Suzuki-designed car as one of its own brands in European markets. 'We could have bought 100 per cent of somebody, but that probably wouldn't have been a good use of capital,' says Rick Wagoner, chairman and chief executive of GM. 'We have gotten better at getting synergy value out. Could we have got more from taking control? We might have done, but think about the extra capital we would have had to put in.' Essentially, such a strategy derives from serious doubts about the benefits of mergers and acquisitions in the car industry – both Ford below and DaimlerChrysler are examples of companies that have struggled with outright acquisitions.

One drawback of such GM-type links is that the biggest benefits often go to their smaller partners, who benefit from access to GM's size and negotiating power without making much difference to the overall GM purchasing power base. For example, Suzuki has put only 5 per cent of its purchasing bill through GM's worldwide purchasing network, which is insignificant for GM. Suzuki has then been able to benchmark the GM prices and see if its own supply network – mainly in Japan, where GM is weak – can offer a better deal.

In addition, some links are not easy to manage. An investment banker commented: 'The good part is that [GM] has not spent much, and it doesn't have the DaimlerChrysler problem of integration [of the Daimler and Chrysler companies – see Case 10.1]. The minuses are that managing all these alliances is exceedingly complex, and the synergies it can extract, while significant, are limited.'

GM's market share strategy – reduce prices

In 2004, GM spent US$6.5 billion on developing new car and truck designs with the aim of changing its reputation for poor quality and indifferent design. It sold its vehicles at an average price in the US of $18,891 – exactly $1 less than the price in 2003. In other words, GM was investing more in R&D at the same time as reducing its prices. It was offering cash buyers rebates up to US$1,400 per vehicle. The company actually sold 50,000 fewer vehicles in 2004 than in 2003. In other words, GM was following a strategy of holding its market share by selling at lower prices. The company had rejected a strategy that would have focused primarily on reducing unproductive costs in favour of a market-oriented approach.

GM's problem of 'legacy costs'

At the same time, GM – along with Ford – faced another major problem that did not apply to Toyota. It was paying contributions to its employee health insurance and pension scheme that amounted to US$6 billion per year and these were growing at an additional US$500 million per year. Two-thirds of the payments were not even to present employees but to GM's former employees who outnumbered current staff by two-and-a-half to one. These were the so-called 'legacy costs' associated with the American method of paying its employees, including those who had retired or otherwise left the business. No chief executive would wish to deny former employees their rights. But GM was in danger of putting its current employees and its shareholders at risk by such a strategy. In early 2005, GM's debt on the financial markets was reduced to 'junk' status.

Ford strategy – first a global strategy, then acquisitions and then 'back-to-basics'

Global strategy

For many years, Ford has been both a leading company in North America and in Europe. Its strategy during much of the 1990s was to gain the benefits of a global strategy. It made substantial attempts to integrate its operations on a global scale in the period 1995–98. Core engineering and production operations were simplified and combined with common parts, common vehicle platforms and common sourcing from out-side suppliers. The purpose was to achieve annual cost savings of around US$42 billion through economies of scale and through the spread of the development costs of a specific model across the sales in more countries – see Case Study 7.1 for more detail. Substantial savings were achieved and Ford's profits then rose – Table 19.13 shows the figures for 1998.

Acquisitions strategy

Following this success, the company then embarked on what it called a 'global niche' strategy. The company judged that world market demand was moving towards *niche* car markets – like off-road vehicles, people carriers – and this meant that the company should invest in these areas. The company therefore invested heavily by *acquiring companies* in its specialist brands in these areas – Jaguar cars, Lincoln luxury cars, Volvo cars, Land-Rover vehicles, Aston Martin sports cars. The strategy of acquiring rival companies in some cases – see Case Study 7.1 for more information – carries the major risk that it becomes difficult to gain sufficient economic benefits from the acquisition premium paid to buy such companies.

Table 19.13

Profit record at Ford Motor Company – but are the profits really so much worse than those of some other car companies?

US$ Million

	2002	2001	2000	1999	1998
Ford automotive sector – manufacturing and selling cars and trucks					
Sales	134 425	130 827	140 777	135 029	118 017
Income/ (loss) before tax	(1 156)	(8 862)	5 323	7 292	5 842
Total assets	107 790	88 319	94 312	99 201	83 911
Ford financial services sector – providing finance for purchases of cars and trucks					
Revenues	28 161	29 927	28 314	25 162	25 011
Income/ (loss) before tax	2 109	1 440	2 976	2 565	2 460
Total assets	187 432	188 224	189 078	171 048	148 801
Ford total company data including automotive sector and financial sector					
Net income after tax and interest	(980)	(5 453)	3 467	7 237	22 071*
Total assets	295 222	276 543	283 390	270 249	232 712

* Note: The dramatic increase in after-tax profit in 1998 included a 'non-cash gain of US$15,955 million' that resulted from the successful spin-off of one of its subsidiaries. The accounts do not name the company but it was probably the profit on the sale of Visteon, its car parts business.

Source: Company accounts.

▶ **CASE STUDY 19.4 continued**

An additional danger with the acquisition strategy was that the company was distracted by the need to integrate its acquisitions. Ford failed to invest sufficiently in its basic car ranges – like the Mondeo and the Fiesta in Europe – during the period 1999–2001. This allowed other companies to move ahead in these areas. The outcome was a profit disaster in 2001 – Table 19.13 shows the detail.

Back to basics strategy

With the benefit of hindsight, Ford's global niche acquisition strategy was considered to be wrong and the Ford chief executive of that period, Jac Nasser, was sacked. A new strategy of 'Back to Basics' was introduced under the guidance of one of the members of the Ford founding family, Mr Bill Ford. Ford was attempting to introduce basic new models, improve quality and reduce costs across its main passenger car ranges. The company was also part-way through introducing 'flexible manufacturing' systems. This meant that the company was able to allow different models to be made simultaneously on the same assembly line without the need for expensive tooling and robot changes. In addition, Ford was also developing a series of production designs that would allow a variety of models to be made using one basic vehicle template, thus saving across a range of models. However, GM, Chrysler, Toyota were also introducing such systems – indeed, Toyota has had much of this in place for some years.

Importantly, Ford had switched its efforts to redesigning its mid-sized cars to improve quality and equip them with many of the features found on more luxury models – higher driving positions, more storage space, etc. 'Redefining the North American saloon is a tall order, but that is what we set out to do,' says Phil Marten – Ford's group vice-president of product creation. The Ford company relaunched some of its American models in early 2004 with such a strategy and had plans to follow this up with more products in later years. It was undertaking a similar range of activities across its European models over a similar time-period. More launches would follow in subsequent years as it attempted to regain its former position.

The company also had similar 'legacy cost' problems to its American rival, General Motors. Ford was also deeply engaged in a price-cutting strategy in its main North American markets in order to protect market share. Both Ford and GM faced a major competitive threat from rivals, including Toyota.

Case questions

1 *Which of the three companies, if any, has a truly global strategy? Do you think that global strategy is important for companies in the world vehicle industry?*

2 *How would you recommend that GM and Ford tackle the Toyota '2010 Global Vision Strategy'?*

3 *What lessons, if any, can other companies learn about the benefits and problems of a global strategy?*

STRATEGIC PROJECT

You might like to follow up the strategic battle between the three market leaders to see how it develops. Both GM and Ford have been trying to catch up with Toyota for some years. Considerable data is available on the car market from the web, starting with the car companies themselves. The case references will point to further web data that would allow you to analyse the immediate past strategies of each of the three companies. It would then be possible to assess their present levels of success.

CRITICAL REFLECTION

Global strategy: is it sufficiently attractive?

The costs of globalisation run into many millions of US dollars – beyond the scope of all but the largest companies. The benefits of a global strategy are often constrained by the need to make local variations to suit local demand, thus losing some of the scale benefits associated with global strategy.

At the same time, some companies would have difficulty surviving without a global strategy – for example, the cost of new drugs might be prohibitive if their R&D costs could only be recovered from a small part of the world. Equally, companies like Walt Disney and Coca Cola thrive on the benefits of their global strategies.

There is much strategic debate about developing a global strategy. But does this make sense for the majority of companies? Or would they be better opting for an international or multinational strategy?

SUMMARY

● International expansion and globalisation are amongst the most important strategic influences in the business environment in the twenty-first century. International expansion has become an important driver of country economic growth. Companies have contributed to this and benefited from it.

● It is important also to distinguish between three types of international and global expansion: *international*, where a significant proportion of an organisation's activities take place outside its home market but it is still the domestic market that is the prime focus of strategy; *multinational*, where a company operates in many countries and varies its strategy country by country; *global*, where a company treats the world as one market. Significantly, each of the three areas above implies a different international expansion strategy.

● The *C–C–B Paradigm* explores the resource relationships between the Company, the Country in which it operates and the Bargaining that takes place between the two. The twin purposes of such bargaining are to deliver increased value added to the company and increased wealth to the country.

● Theories of international trade identify the role of government in encouraging international investment. They also help companies select which countries offer the best international prospects. A number of theories can usefully be identified: some theories concentrate on trade barrier reduction and company economies of scale. Two theories are particularly useful: Porter's *diamond of national competitive advantage* and the *theory of limited state intervention* attributed to the World Bank.

● Three major international institutions have significant influence on international trade. The International Monetary Fund (IMF) oversees international payments. The World Bank provides long-term capital aid. The World Trade Organisation (WTO) regulates trade activity and resolves trade disputes between nations.

● A trade block is a group of countries that have agreed to give each other preferential trading terms. Some blocks have stronger ties than others. All influence trade development.

● The case for a global strategy rests on two major elements: resources may be more economically procured and manufactured on a global basis. In addition, customer demand may be essentially the same around the world, thus allowing the world to be treated as one market. The case for a strategy that is both global and local derives from the need to gain the benefits of a global market while responding to the needs of national market variations. Local variations may arise as a result of customer demand and conditions of usage; national goverments; differing technical standards; and different national competitors. In practice, there is often a need to balance both global and local issues in strategy development.

● Organisational structures for international expansion often start by establishing a separate division for international activities. As they grow in importance, such activities may then be reorganised either into a geographical area structure or one based on product divisions. This may then lead to a matrix structure with all its difficulties. The *transnational solution* to international organisation structure has been used by some companies. It involves dispersed and interdependent subsidiaries that are integrated into a worldwide operation. Organisational culture and past history are also important considerations.

● In developing international relationships with other companies, ownership issues need to be investigated. Joint ventures and alliances represent differing degrees of closeness in international co-operation.

1 If international expansion is the most important strategic trend of the twenty-first century, should every organisation, even the smallest, develop international strategies? If so, what strategies might be adopted by (a) a medium-sized engineering company based primarily in one part of the world, such as Europe, and (b) a major grocery retailer whose sales are mainly in one country?

2 What different international expansion strategies are implied by international, multinational and global approaches to strategy development? Give examples to support your explanation.

3 Do theories of international trade help to explain why and how companies like MTV, General Motors and Tate & Lyle have developed internationally?

4 How do the major institutions of world trade influence strategy development?

5 Name two trade blocks and show how each of them influences the development of international strategy. In particular, identify any factors that are unique to each trade block.

6 How useful is Porter's diamond of national competitive advantage in the development of a company's business strategy?

7 'Whether to globalize and how to globalize have become two of the most burning strategy issues for managers around the world.' (Professor George Yip)

Comment critically on the usefulness of such generalisations in the development of international business strategy.

8 Does the 'transnational organisation' offer a solution to the difficulties facing major companies when they organise their international operations?

9 What are the problems with using alliances and joint ventures in international strategy development? How might they be overcome?

10 'The adoption of a global perspective should not be viewed as the same as a strategy of global products and brands. Rather, for most companies, such a perspective implies consideration of a broad range of strategic options of which standardisation is merely one.' (Professors Susan Douglas and Yoram Wind)

Do you agree with this comment? What, if any, are the implications for international business strategy?

Further reading

Kogut, B (2002) 'International management and strategy', Ch12 in Pettigrew, A, Thomas, H and Whittington, R (eds) *Handbook of Management and Strategy*, Sage, London is very readable and has a useful summary of global strategic thinking.

Professor Alan Rugman's text – Rugman, A M (2000) *The End of Globalization*, Random House, London – provides a more sceptical view of globalisation in his usual lively style. Read also the papers by Professor Ghemawat listed in the references below.

Dunning, J (1993) *Multinational Enterprises and the Global Economy*, Addison Wesley, Wokingham has a very strong academic foundation and is a top-quality text if you are an economist.

Robock, S H and Simmonds, K (1989) *International Business and Multinational Enterprises*, Irwin, Homewood, IL is now out of print but is strong readable account of the main issues.

For a different approach to organisational issues on a global scale: *see* Saunders, C, Van Slyke, C and Vogel, D R (2004) 'My time or yours? Managing time visions in global virtual teams', *Academy of Management Executive*, Vol 18, No 1, pp19–26.

Jones, G (1996) *Evolution of International Business*, Routledge/International Thompson, London is an excellent text for providing a historical context.

Notes and references

1 References for the MTV Case: Viacom and MTV websites. *Financial Times*: 10 October 2003, p12. Times OnLine site www.timesonline.co.uk – 15 April 2005 – 'MTV grows into far more than music television.'

2 United Nations Industrial Development Organisation (UNIDO) (1993) *Industry and Development Global Report 1993/94*, Vienna, p81. Interesting and thoughtful material with additional references useful for essays and assignments.

3 Williams, F (1995) *Financial Times*, 4 Apr, p3.

4 Woolf, M (1993) *Financial Times*, 16 Dec, p19.

5 UNIDO (1993) Op. cit., p81.

6 UNIDO (1993) Op. cit., pp88, 89.

7 These are based on Bartlett, C A and Ghoshal, S (1989) *Managing Across Borders: The Transnational Solution*, Century Business, London, Ch3.

8 I am grateful to one of the anonymous reviewers of the second edition of this text for prompting these important distinctions.

9 Harding, J (2001) 'Globalisation's children strike back', *Financial Times*, 11 September, p14.

10 Dunning, J H (1993) *Multinational Enterprises and the Global Economy*, Addison Wesley, Wokingham. *See* also: Dunning, J H (1995) 'Re-appraising the electic paradigm in an age of alliance capitalism', *Journal of International Business*, 3rd Quarter, pp461–91.

11 One of the best books at tracking these developments is Kennedy, P (1992) *The Rise and Fall of the Great Powers*, Fontana Press, London.

12 Kennedy, P (1992) Op. cit., Ch7.

13 Jepma, C J, Jager, H and Kamphnis, E (1996) *Introduction to International Economics*, Netherlands Open University/Longman, London, Ch3.

14 World Bank (1993) *The East Asian Miracle*, Oxford University Press, New York.

15 Useful critiques are contained in Rugman, A and Hodgetts, R (1995) *International Business*, McGraw-Hill, New York, Ch10; Dunning, J H (1995) *The Globalization of Business*, Routledge, London, Ch5.

16 Dunning, J H (1993) Op. cit., p14.

17 *See Financial Times*, 16 Dec 1993, for a summary of the new Uruguay Round deal that had been negotiated over many months.

18 A useful short history of the WTO was published by the *Financial Times* as a supplement on the WTO's 50th birthday in 1998: 'The World Trade System at 50', *Financial Times*, 18 May 1998.

19 Kennedy, P (1992) Op. cit.

20 Chandler, A (1986) 'The evolution of modern global competition', in Porter, M E (ed) *Competition in Global Industries*, Harvard Business School Press, Boston, Mass.

21 Kogut, B (2002) 'International management and strategy', Ch12 in Pettigrew, A, Thomas, H and Whittington, R (eds) *Handbook of Management and Strategy*, Sage, London.

22 Caves, R E (1971) 'International corporations: the industrial economics of foreign investment', *Economica*, Vol 38, pp1–27.

23 For more recent work, see the special issue of *Long Range Planning*, October 2000, Vol 33 No 5, pp619–754.

24 Ghoshal, S (1987) 'Global strategy: an organising framework', *Strategic Management Journal*, Vol 8, pp425–40. This paper is often difficult to access because it is more than ten years old and not always archived in libraries. However, it was reprinted in: Segal-Horn, S (1998) *The Strategy Reader*, Blackwell Business, Oxford.

25 Ghemawat, P (2003) 'Semiglobalization and international business strategy', *Journal of International Business Studies*, Vol 34, pp138–52. Ghemawat, P and Ghadar, F (2000) 'The dubious logic of global megamergers', *Harvard Business Review*, July/August, Vol 78, Issue 4. Rugman, A M (2000) *The End of Globalization*, Random House, London. Rugman, A M and Verbeke, A (1992) 'A note on the transnational solution and the transaction cost theory of multinational strategic management', *Journal of International Business Studies*, Vol 23, No 4, pp761–77. Rugman, A M and Verbeke, A (2003a) 'Regional multinationals: the location-bound drivers of global strategy', in Burkinshaw, J, Ghoshal, S, Markides, C, Stopford, J, Yip, G, (eds) *The Future of the Multinational Company*, Wiley, Chichester.

26 Lynch, R (2003) 'Glitches in global strategy? Some evidence from the food and drink industry', *Paper presented at the Academy of Management*, Seattle, August.

27 Levitt, T (1983) 'The globalization of markets', *Harvard Business Review*, May–June.

28 This argument is also supported by Hout, T, Porter, M E and Rudden, E (1982) 'How global companies win out', *Harvard Business Review*, Sept–Oct, p98; Hamel, G and Prahalad, C K (1985) 'Do you really have a global strategy?', *Harvard Business Review* July–Aug, p139.

29 Yip, G S (1989) 'Global strategy – In a world of nations?', *Sloan Management Review*, Fall, pp29–41. This article represents the clearest exposition of globalisation.

30 Douglas, S and Wind, Y (1987) 'The myth of globalization', *Columbia Journal of World Business*, Winter.

31 Prahalad, C K and Doz, Y (1986) *The Multinational Mission: Balancing Local Demands and Global Vision*, The Free Press, New York.

32 Yip, G S (1989) Op. cit., p29.

33 Calori, R, Atamer, T and Nunes, P (2000) *The Dynamics of International Competition*, Sage, London. *See* also the paper by Leknes, H M and Carr, C. (2004) 'Globalisation, international configurations, and strategic Implications: The case of retailing', *Long Range Planning*, Vol 37, pp29–49. This latter paper provides interesting empirical evidence to explore these issues.

34 Stopford, J M and Wells, L M (1972) *Managing the Multinational Enterprise: Organization of the Firm and Ownership of Subsidiaries*, Basic Books, New York.

35 For an extended discussion of this trend, *see* Turner, I and Henry, I (1994) Op. cit., pp417–31.

36 Bartlett, C A and Ghoshal, S (1989) *Managing Across Borders: The Transnational Solution*, Century Business, London.

37 Bartlett, C A and Ghoshal, S (1989) Op. cit., p17.

38 Kogut, B (1990) 'The permeability of borders and the speed of learning amongst countries', *Globalization of Firms and the Competitiveness of Nations, Crafoord*

Lectures, University of Lund, Lund. Quoted in Dunning, J H (1993) Op. cit., Ch8.

39 Morrison, A, Bouquet, C, Beck, J (2004) 'Netchising: the next global wave?', *Long Range Planning*, Vol 37, No 1, pp11–28.

40 Burkinshaw, J (2002) 'Managing internal R&D networks in global firms', *Long Range Planning*, Vol 35, pp245–67.

41 Ohmae, K (1990) *The Borderless World: Power and Strategy in the Interlinked Economy*, Collins, London, Ch6.

42 *See* Bartlett, C and Ghoshal, S (1989) *Managing across Borders: The Transnational Corporation*, Harvard Business School Press, Boston, MA. *See* also Turner, I and Henry, I (1994) 'Managing international organisations: Lessons from the field', *European Management Journal*, 12(4), p417.

43 Dunning, J H (1993) Op. cit., Ch9, has a comprehensive survey of joint venture research. *See* also Kogut, B (1997) 'Globalization and alliances in high technology industries', *Financial Times Mastering Management*, Pitman Publishing, London, pp491–4.

44 Dunning, J H (1993) Op. cit., p245.

45 Kogut, B (1997) Op. cit., p493.

46 Tomlinson, J W L (1970) *The Joint Venture Process in International Business*, MIT Press, Cambridge, MA.

47 Dunning, J H (1993) Op. cit., Ch9, also has a useful survey of alliances. For a more recent review, see the three papers in *Long Range Planning*, Vol 36, No 6, pages 533–78.

48 Dunning, J H (1993) Op. cit., p250.

49 Doz, Y and Hamel, G (1993) *The Competitive Logics of Strategic Alliances*, The Free Press, New York.

50 Sources for Cases 19.3 and 19.4: General Motors, Ford and Toyota Annual Report and Accounts. *Financial Times*: 8 May 1998, p23; 19 March 2003, p14; 15 April 2003, p15; 9 June 2003, p19; 29 December 2003, p20; 5 January 2004, p13; 8 January 2004, p6; 14 January 2004, p29; 28 January 2004, p22; 2 February 2004, p9; 4 February 2004, p32; 16 February 2004, p10; 19 February 2004, p18; 20 February 2004, p26; 2 March 2004, pp12, 30; 9 March 2004, p19; 25 March 2005, p19; 29 March 2005, p6. See also www.gm.com; www.ford.com; www.toyota.com.

Chapter 20

THE DYNAMICS OF STRATEGY DEVELOPMENT AND ENTREPRENEURIAL GROWTH

Learning outcomes

When you have worked through this chapter, you will be able to:

- outline the relationship of the organisation's purpose with the dynamics of its development;
- explain the dynamics of resource development and comment upon the quality of its insights;
- identify the dynamics of environmental development and comment critically on the main elements;
- explore the dynamics of fast-moving environments, especially in the context of innovation and the opportunities available for small and medium-sized enterprises;
- outline the dynamics of entrepreneurial development.

INTRODUCTION

Both organisations and the strategies that they pursue change continuously over time. They alter as the environment shifts and they may change as the organisation's own resources grow or decline. The mechanisms by which these processes occur are not fully understood because they are complex and our knowledge of the various elements requires further development. This chapter on the dynamics of strategy development explores the current state of knowledge.

In particular, it seeks to examine how an organisation can enhance its value added and its competitive advantage in the context of the dynamics of strategic change. It also seeks to address the implications for small and medium-sized enterprises (often abbreviated to SMEs) because fast-moving dynamics may present such organisations with particular opportunities and threats. SMEs often involve entrepreneurial strategic decisions so we will examine these specifically. We begin our exploration of the topic by considering the purpose of the organisation, We then examine the dynamics of change *inside* the organisation. Specifically, we examine the dynamic relationship between competitive advantage and the changing resources of the organisation.

In addition to resource-based change, the environment of the organisation is also changing, sometimes in ways that are turbulent and unpredictable. Such *outside* pressures in the environment will also influence strategy development, perhaps in unpredictable ways. These need to be assessed and techniques developed for monitoring and coping with the dynamic changes arising from them. To consider the strategic consequences thoroughly, we explore two environmental situations in more depth: fast-moving markets and the special characteristics of strategy associated with entrepreneurial activity. These areas are summarised in Figure 20.1.

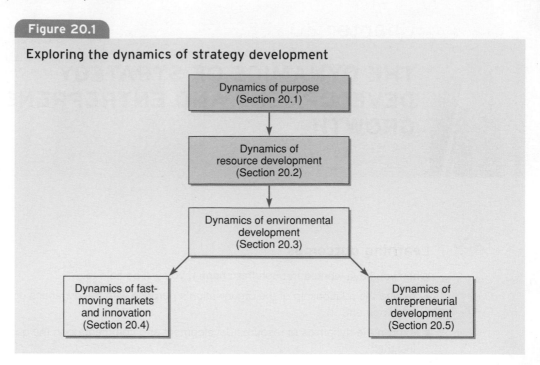

Figure 20.1

Exploring the dynamics of strategy development

Dynamics of purpose
(Section 20.1)

↓

Dynamics of
resource development
(Section 20.2)

↓

Dynamics of environmental
development
(Section 20.3)

Dynamics of fast-
moving markets
and innovation
(Section 20.4)

Dynamics of
entrepreneurial
development
(Section 20.5)

CASE STUDY 20.1

eBay – the auction market that spans the world

In spite of the 'dot.com disaster' suffered by many companies, there is at least one internet site that is actually making good profits. It is eBay – the site where it is possible to buy products and services both by auction and by paying a fixed price. This case explores the strategy of the company, including its ability to deliver business opportunities to small and medium-sized companies.

eBay began back in 1997 as a small internet start-up in California. While its peers burned their start-up cash, eBay became a phenomenon – a Silicon Valley company that has always made a profit. It is the world's most successful internet group, with 70 million customers making deals at the rate of US$34.2 billion in 2004, of which eBay takes just under 10 per cent net. The profit potential is huge because eBay has almost no cost of goods, no inventories, few marketing costs and no large capital expenditure. Basically, the company simply acts as a computer internet medium between buyer and seller. The growth in e-Bay's profits is shown in Table 20.1.

The figure of US$34.2 billion, according to Meg Whitman, chief executive of eBay since 1998, continues to grow. In 2002, she promised that by 2005 deals would have more than tripled to US$35 billion and eBay revenue would have also have tripled to around US$3 billion. She was right on the eBay revenue and only slightly wrong on the gross trading revenue – *see* Table 20.1. To put this into perspective, this meant that eBay was handling the same revenue as the big US retailers JC Penney and Kmart, which achieved turnover of US$33 billion and US$37 billion in 2001 respectively.

To achieve this, Meg Whitman faced a massive challenge. To achieve her targets, she had to transform eBay. She

Table 20.1

eBay financial results: extraordinary growth over five years

	1999	2000	2001	2002	2003	2004
Gross trading revenue (US$ billions)	2.8	5.4	9.3	14.9	23.8	34.2
Net company revenue (US$ millions)	225	431	749	1 214	2 165	3 271
Operating profit margin	3%	11%	24%	31%	32%	35%

Note: 'Gross trading revenue' means the business that eBay handles over the year. Most of this revenue is passed between buyer and seller. 'Net company revenue' means the commission that eBay earns on each transaction that it carries on the web: these are the real 'earnings' of the company.

Source: Company Annual Report and Accounts – available on the web at www.investor.ebay.com

eBay has succeeded in establishing a new method of selling and buying products with its internet community. Innovative strategy can still lead to substantial growth.

These materials have been reproduced with the permission of eBay Inc.

There is no doubt that eBay has been transformed over the last few years from a site that held auctions in 300 categories to a global enterprise, operating in 18 countries and offering 16,000 categories. The journey has not been easy – possibly the worst moment was when the internet site went down for 22 hours in June 1999 – no site, no income. But the proposed drive to expand the business will run two significant risks:

1 The strategy of attracting large corporate sellers – such as IBM, now its biggest supplier – has raised fears among smaller, traditional clients. Such a move risks antagonising the 'power sellers' – the army of entrepreneurs that have formed the bedrock of eBay's sellers and make their living trading on its site.

2 The possibility that competitors such as Yahoo and Amazon can take advantage of the disquiet amongst such sellers. Yahoo is particularly aggressive. It makes no secret of going after eBay and its 30 per cent operating margins. The group claims to be listening harder to its sellers and is undercutting eBay heavily on price. Amazon is also trying to convert its 23-million-strong active customer base to the lucrative area of person-to-person selling.

For the moment, the competitive threat is remote. Neither company can match the number of buyers on eBay. 'I'm not concerned about competitors trying to undercut eBay transaction prices,' says one outside commentator. 'Buyers want to be where the most sellers are. The economies of scale ensure more transaction completions and higher average selling prices, so, even though the fees might be a bit higher, they are more than compensated.' Thus, if the eBay CEO Meg Whitman can keep her user base, she could conceivably achieve even more ambitious goals over the next few years.

© Copyright *Financial Times*. Case heavily adapted, reorganised and supplemented by Richard Lynch from an original article by Paul Abrahams and Thorold Barker, 11 January 2002, p24. Quote from an eBay article by Patti Waldmeir in the same paper on 16 May 2002, p15. Both used with permission.

You might like to look at the website – **www.eBay.com** . . . and the rivals . . . **Amazon.com** and Yahoo.com.

needed to expand the number of different audiences the company served, and move into sectors with higher average selling prices, such as cars. She needed to increase the range of formats, shifting increasingly from auctions to fixed-price sales – without alienating traditional customers. She also needed to attract more large sellers, particularly corporations. And she had to do this without giving her competitors – like Yahoo and Amazon – an opportunity to expand market share. Finally, she had to reinforce eBay's international sales.

eBay started as a small internet site that allowed people in California to exchange and sell unwanted items. Thus the culture of eBay has been one of trust. This was reinforced by the company setting up a system of feedback: the aim was to give buyers and sellers an idea of each other's good faith and reliability. Each seller has a scorecard showing positive, neutral and negative feedback for each transaction, as well as detailed comments. 'That is very powerful. If you saw the comments of everyone who shopped in a store, it would completely change the way you shopped,' explains Rajiv Dutta, the chief financial officer of eBay.

Alternative sites do not have the right format or sense of community, explains Geoff Giglio, who has a small company selling computers and IT equipment on eBay. 'Other companies just can't figure it out. I have tried Yahoo and Amazon and didn't sell a thing.' In fact, eBay has rapidly grown into an important channel for SMEs to sell their goods – anything from painted furniture to baby clothes. But this is both the strength and the weakness of the site – it will be difficult to move from the local relationships that characterised the old eBay to its new more sophisticated self. Patti Waldmeir, a devotee of the site, commented in May 2002:

For the past year, eBay has been increasingly acting the part of Big Brother, closely monitoring auctions for fraud. Now citizens of eBay will also have to carry what amounts to a national identification card . . . I write to mourn the demise of the civilisation called eBay.

Case questions

1 *What delivers profits in this company and how is the situation changing?*

2 *To what extent are the competitive and supplier threats real? Would they alter your view of the future goal of this company? Do you believe that the goal will be achieved?*

3 *Are there any lessons for other companies with regard to developing successful internet sites?*

STRATEGIC PROJECT

Clearly, with substantial growth still to come, there are real strategic opportunities for both large and small companies. You might like to investigate this area, probably using emergent strategic processes. A good way to start would be to consult the *Financial Times* survey on e-Commerce, 10 June 2004, p17, plus updating all the business figures in this case using web-based sources.

20.1 THE DYNAMICS OF PURPOSE

The purpose of an organisation can and probably will change over time – eBay is an example of how companies can start with a simple objective and then expand.[1] Purpose is subject to the judgement and priority setting of senior management, which may also vary over lengthy periods. The balance of influences that will be taken into account in arriving at the purpose of the organisation was outlined in the *polygon of purpose – see* Figure 12.3. This represents a shifting coalition that will alter depending on two factors:

1 *The choice and activities of the organisation.* For example, the recruitment of a new chief executive at eBay in 1998 was crucial to its present success – *see* Case 20.1.

2 *The activities and choices of others outside the organisation.* For example, the increased competitive activity of Yahoo in the internet auction market is already having some influence on the purpose of eBay.

More generally, some of the dynamic factors influencing the purpose of an organisation are shown in Exhibit 20.1. Their relationships with each other and their influence on the overall direction of the organisation remain largely uncharted. This means that their dynamics at this stage of our knowledge remain essentially unknown.

Exhibit 20.1

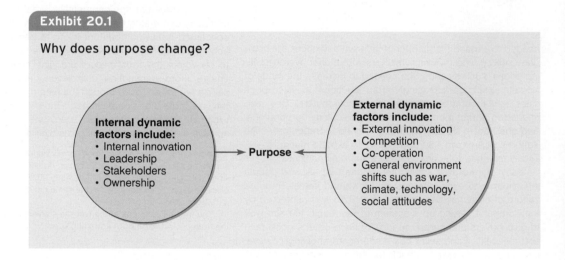

Why does purpose change?

Internal dynamic factors include:
• Internal innovation
• Leadership
• Stakeholders
• Ownership

→ **Purpose** ←

External dynamic factors include:
• External innovation
• Competition
• Co-operation
• General environment shifts such as war, climate, technology, social attitudes

Importantly, although purpose may be a shifting coalition, the dynamics of purpose are, at least partially, in the control of the organisation itself. In principle at least, every organisation has the *choice* to change its purpose. For example, it may wish to reconsider its attitude to the key topics of added value and sustainable competitive advantage. These are matters of judgement that will influence the purpose and therefore the dynamics of purpose. For example, entrepreneurs may reach different conclusions on the direction of purpose from senior managers of large, stable multinationals like Unilever in Chapter 14.

Equally, it is sometimes claimed that every organisation should make growth part of its purpose. The management writer Tom Peters says: 'A firm is never static – it is either growing or stagnating.'[2] However, it should be noted that such generalisations are not necessarily true of every organisation: they involve a normative judgement about the importance of growth that some will not share. Thus every organisation will develop its own response to the concept of growth as part of purpose and there are no absolute rules.

More generally, every organisation will bring judgement, values and ambitions to its definition of purpose. Small businesses without public shareholdings may have more scope for flexibility in purpose. Medium-sized enterprises like eBay with public share quotations may find that this reduces their room for manoeuvre.

Given the complexity of purpose, this book has chosen to concentrate on two aspects – value added and sustainable competitive advantage – in the development of strategy. This is important because if purpose cannot be made explicit then it is difficult to explore its dynamics. However, it needs to be acknowledged that this is a simplifying assumption, with all the weaknesses that this implies.

Key strategic principles

- The purpose of an organisation can and will change over time. The coalition of interests that defines and develops purpose will be influenced by factors both inside and outside the organisation.

- Importantly, the purpose of the organisation is at least partially in the control of the organisation itself.

- Although purpose is complex, it is usual in strategy to concentrate on two common elements: value added and sustainable competitive advantage.

20.2 THE DYNAMICS OF RESOURCE DEVELOPMENT

In Chapter 6, the resources of the organisation were classified into four main areas and the concept of the *hierarchy of resources* was explored. However, the balance between the four areas does not stay static over time.[3] Figure 20.2 illustrates how resources might be expected to alter dynamically over time. This section explores how and why such changes might occur.

Resources will change as the organisation's purpose changes. In addition, they will also be influenced by what is happening outside in the environment. For example, even if the eBay internet auction house had made no decision to expand its resources by including larger suppliers like IBM, it would still face resource decisions on its internet sites as a result of the aggressive actions of its competitors like Yahoo and Amazon. Thus competitive resources will also be influenced by the outside activities of competitors and by the internet expanding over time. However, as a starting point, this section will concentrate primarily on resource dynamics, with the next section exploring the environment.

Given that an organisation has made the normative and reasonable choice to increase its value added, the dynamics of resource development can be considered as having three main dimensions:[4]

Figure 20.2

How resources alter dynamically

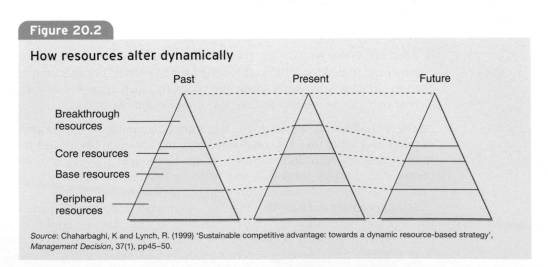

Source: Chaharbaghi, K and Lynch, R. (1999) 'Sustainable competitive advantage: towards a dynamic resource-based strategy', *Management Decision*, 37(1), pp45–50.

1 *time* – resource configurations developed and destroyed over time;

2 *early-mover advantages* – resource developments when moving into a new market place;

3 *imitation pressures* – resource changes related to the existing resources.

20.2.1 Resource configurations developed and destroyed over time: the contributions of four leading economists

Four leading economists have explored aspects of resource dynamics, each making their own contribution:

- Penrose: the two sources of new resource growth;
- Nelson and Winter: the delaying effect of routines in companies;
- Schumpeter: the mechanism that destroys resources over time.

In exploring the future growth of the firm, Professor Edith Penrose was very clear. It would partially come from the resources already present in the company: 'In planning expansion, a firm considers two groups of resources – its own previously acquired or "inherited" resources, and those it must obtain from the market in order to carry out its production and expansion programmes.'[5] The clear implication of this statement is that the starting point of resource dynamics will be these two aspects, which we can extend to any organisation rather than just the firm. It also follows that organisations may be constrained by their previous resources: this is an example of *strategy as history* as explored in Chapter 2.

Writing originally in the 1950s, Penrose considered the dynamics of the resources only in the context of the growth of the firm. Some 20 years later, Professors Richard Nelson and Sidney Winter developed a view of evolutionary economics that examined how firms changed over time, possibly but not necessarily with growth as the objective. They identified the *routines* of the firm as being the basis of its resources and its strategic decision making.[6] They defined such routines as the well-practised patterns of activity inside the firm: for example, the Toyota production system described in Chapter 9 and the European branding policy introduced by Unilever on its ice cream products explored in Chapter 5. It is these routines that deliver some distinctive resources to the firm and therefore provide some of its competitive advantage. The concept of routines has three implications for resource dynamics:

1 Many routines have to be learned and take long periods to establish. This means that these resources will change relatively slowly. Such resources are *sticky*.

2 In so far as routines dominate the pattern of activity in an organisation, they may limit the innovative capacity of the firm to develop totally new resources. Such resources are relatively *blind* to new developments.

3 Routines often employ tacit knowledge and informal networks of people. This is beneficial in making it difficult for outsiders to imitate, but this imprecision will make it more difficult to replicate inside the company. Such resources will *require investment* so that they can be relearnt or they may atrophy and die.

The overall result of this view of resource dynamics is that resource configurations develop over time, they are constrained by what has gone before and they require investment if they are to continue. Now it might be thought that resource development could continue in this way for ever. It was Professor Joseph Schumpeter who argued that such a pattern was inherently unlikely over long time periods.

Schumpeter explored the dynamics of resource development.[7] In particular, he identified the way that innovation and entrepreneurship operate over lengthy time periods. He said that there were patterns of development in all markets, with periods of comparative calm, during which firms develop superior products and reduce costs, followed by periods of shock or discontinuities. It was during these latter times that new technologies, new services and totally new ways of operating were introduced. He was writing in the early 1940s during the upheaval of the Second World War and was also able to look back to the First World War and the relatively calmer period in between. He had no knowledge of the 'dot.com' boom-and-bust scenario of the period 1999–2000, but this is a more recent example of his concept. He argued that entrepreneurs who were able to exploit the market opportunities during such periods of shock would benefit during the subsequent periods of calm. At the time of writing, it is not clear who the 'dot.com' winners will be – perhaps eBay in Case 20.1. Schumpeter called this process *creative destruction*.

From the perspective of resource dynamics, the significance of creative destruction is that all resources should have a limited shelf-life. They cannot go on for ever and will be superseded by innovatory new products. Thus Schumpeter would argue that Bill Gates and his colleagues at Microsoft may have made a fortune with the Windows computer operating system, but it will ultimately be overtaken by some new development. Competitive resources will become uncompetitive over time as a result of innovation and new organisational knowledge.

If Schumpeter's argument is correct, then the strategic problem is that competitive resources never stand still. The strategic solution is to develop new resources before the competition. We examine this in the next section.

Comment

It is interesting to note that it took Microsoft several years to see the potential threat of Netscape's Internet Browser as an alternative means of delivering computer software services. No wonder Microsoft reacted so vigorously to the opportunities presented by the internet.[8] On this evidence, Schumpeter's view of *creative destruction* is useful in high-technology markets.

However, creative destruction may have less relevance as a resource dynamic in relation to more traditional markets. For example, the substantial worldwide market for chocolate products like Nestlé's KitKat or Mars' Milky Way does not seem, so far, to have been subject to creative destruction. In some product categories, evolutionary resources may continue for substantial periods without destruction.

20.2.2 The early-mover advantage: resource developments when moving into a new market place

In some markets, the firm that acquires a competitive advantage early in the life of a market may find that this sets in motion a resource dynamic that preserves the advantage during the life of the market: *the early-mover advantage*. For example, by being one of the early companies into the market for computer operating systems and by co-operating with the market leader at the time, IBM, Microsoft was able to establish a user base for its Windows system that other companies have been unable to match – *see* Case study 1.2. Equally, by being one of the early companies to producing mobile telephones on a global scale, Nokia has established itself as one of the leaders in that market and delivered sustainable competitive advantages based on economies of scale and product design – *see* Case study 14.1.

Importantly, being the early mover does not necessarily mean being *first* into a new market. The very first companies can make mistakes from which they never recover – perhaps from poor technical performance, perhaps in marketing. Learning from what others have already done may be useful, while still being one of the early-but-not-first movers may be all that is required.

There are at least five resource advantages delivered by an early move into a market:

1 *Establishment of the benchmark technical format.* Innovation may introduce a basic technology that will set the standard for the market. It may not even be the most efficient technology but it may still deliver useful advantage. The example usually quoted is the

QWERTY typewriter layout which was introduced in 1899 and is still used in keyboards today. Although this configuration of letters on the keyboard is technically not as fast as some others, it has become the dominant design.[9]

2 *Building networks of complementors.* For some products, such as computers, computer games and sound systems, it is not just the product itself that matters but the complementors who supply the software, the new games and the recording artists. These networks take time to establish and early movers have an advantage in terms of an installed base of suppliers and users that becomes difficult to shift. For example, in the early 1990s, both Sega and Nintendo video games companies placed considerable emphasis on gaining and keeping their installed base of games users. Nintendo made a major strategic mistake when it introduced its 16-bit machine in the 1990s and made no attempt to build on its previous users of its 8-bit machine.[10]

3 *Early move down the learning curve.* Early production experience should allow a company to learn before its competitors and move down the learning curve – *see* Chapter 13.

4 *Usefulness of reputation when buyers are uncertain.* When new products cannot be assessed fully by customers before they are purchased, the reputation of the company launching such a product becomes a useful customer guide to subsequent performance. For example, a new format video camera from Sony is more likely to carry conviction than the same product from an obscure brand name.

5 *Costs to the buyer from switching products.* When new products are launched, buyers may be reluctant to switch to them if the costs involved are high. For example, switching retail bank accounts used to be an immense administrative task with high costs. In the era of telephone banking, rivals have attempted to reduce such costs by using new technology, but there is still a resource advantage for those banks with an established customer base.

Thus the dynamics of resources are conditioned by the early-mover advantages. However, there are also obvious problems with being the early mover: most companies have to make a bet on the new technology and this may turn out to be incorrect. They may *choose the wrong technology*. For example, Sony took the view that its Betamax technology would become the dominant tape format for television videotape machines, but JVC ended up with the more widely accepted format and Sony was eventually forced to withdraw its system.[11]

Moreover, companies may be unable to understand or afford the organisational and administrative back-up that is necessary to support the introduction of a totally new technology: they may lack the *complementary assets*. For example, when it was first introduced, the EMI scanner was technically the most advanced machine of its kind for scanning human bodies. But the company's resources were primarily engaged in recorded music and television rental and it simply lacked the resources to develop the market.[12] EMI was forced to withdraw and sell out to General Electric (US) which had the relevant resources.

20.2.3 Imitation pressures: resource changes related to existing resources

For existing products and services, the luxury of being an early mover does not apply. Resource dynamics are driven by the need to deter rivals from imitation. The dynamics of gaining and improving resources that cannot be imitated lie in five main areas:

1 *Incremental improvements in the product or service.* Probably the most widely used way of preventing resources being imitated is a regular programme of product improvement. Consumer companies like Procter & Gamble (US) in household detergents like Ariel, and PepsiCo (US) in its Walkers and Frito-Lay snack products have ongoing activities designed to keep their products one step ahead of the competition. None of the resource changes is radical in itself but all represent genuine improvements that allow these companies to maintain their competitive advantage. The dynamic is slow, steady resource change.

2 *Legal barriers to imitation.* Patents, copyrights and trademarks all represent means of reducing the ability of competitors to imitate products. For example, The Disney Corporation (US) not only owns the exclusive rights to Disney characters like Mickey Mouse but has also acquired rights to other characters such as Winnie the Pooh. The resource dynamic is powerful and one-way, as long as the resources remain relevant to the customer.

3 *Developing superior relationships with suppliers and customers.* Networks that involve customers and suppliers have been explored extensively in this text – *see* Chapters 3, 4, 9 and 15. Good supply networks can provide lower costs and higher quality from suppliers. Equally, strong and loyal customer networks can provide larger sales and greater profitability over time. The resource dynamic here is most likely to be broken if technology changes or the balance of power alters.

4 *Exploiting market size and scale economies.* Imitation will clearly be more difficult when profits are derived, at least in part, from a minimum size and economies of scale. Thus Asian car companies like Daewoo (Korea) and Proton (Malaysia) have had difficulty moving into European markets because of the need to provide adequate levels of service support. There are ways around this problem, so the resource dynamic tends to slow the rate of change rather than stop it completely.

5 *Developing intangible barriers to imitation.* There are a whole series of barriers here that have been explored in Chapters 6 and 11. They include *tacit knowledge*, which is difficult for the company to codify, let alone for competitors to imitate; *innovative ability*, which is difficult to define but represents a real resource in companies like 3M; *causal ambiguity*, which makes it difficult for competitors to understand how a firm has developed a competitive advantage. The resource dynamics here can present real and practical barriers to imitation.

Conclusion

The purpose of much of the investigation of resource dynamics has been to identify those areas that provide sustainable competitive advantage and increase added value. The above areas provide some important guidance on this task. However, their weakness is that they remain lists of possible areas rather than providing more specific strategic conclusions. They also clearly need to be related to the changing environment within which the organisation is operating. We tackle this topic next.

Key strategic principles

- From a dynamic perspective, resources in organisations are developed and destroyed over time. There are three main dimensions: time, early-mover advantages and imitation pressures.

- When exploring the time dimension, there are three main considerations: the two sources of new resource growth; the delaying effect of routines in companies; the mechanism that destroys resources over time.

- In terms of early-mover advantages, there are five main areas: the establishment of the benchmark technical format; the building of networks of contacts; the early movement down the learning curve; the usefulness of reputation; the subsequent costs to the buyer when switching from the early mover.

- The pressures that arise from imitating an existing product or service can be countered by five resource activities: incremental improvements in the product or service; legal barriers to imitation, such as patenting; developing superior relationships with customers and suppliers; exploiting market size and scale economies; developing intangible barriers to imitation.

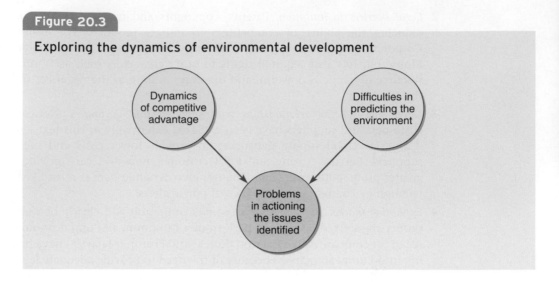

Figure 20.3

Exploring the dynamics of environmental development

20.3 THE DYNAMICS OF ENVIRONMENTAL DEVELOPMENT

Throughout this book, we have analysed the main environmental factors that influence strategy, including general policies and events, competitors, customers and suppliers. All such factors are continuously changing, both in relation to each other and to their influence on the organisation. This section explores the dynamics of such continuous change on the strategy of the organisation. The two sections that follow select some particular circumstances for further consideration.

Although there are many dimensions to the environment, it is useful to divide our consideration of the dynamics into three related areas (*see* Figure 20.3):

1 *The dynamics of competitive advantage.* Although it is generally accepted that this concept is important in strategy development, it is often treated as if it is fixed at a point in time. In reality, it will be changing continuously.

2 *The predictability of the environment.* When the environment is growing or declining steadily, the dynamics may be easy to predict. However, not all environments are predictable, so the issue needs to be explored.

3 *Resource responsiveness to environmental change.* Even though the dynamics of the environment may be *understood*, this does not necessarily mean that the organisation is able to *act* on that understanding. The relationship between the two areas needs to be investigated.

20.3.1 The dynamics of competitive advantage

Amongst strategists, there is a widely held view that the search for competitive advantage is fundamental to strategic success. To quote Professor Michael Porter:

Competitive strategy is the search for a favourable competitive position in an industry . . . Competitive strategy aims to establish a profitable and sustainable position against the forces that determine industry competition.[13]

There are two difficulties acknowledged by Porter in this statement:

1 The forces determining industry competition are changing all the time.

2 The firm itself will not only respond to such forces but will also attempt to '*shape* that environment in a firm's favour [my italics].'[14]

In other words, Porter argues that the dynamics of competitive advantage have at least two dimensions:

1 the nature of the competitive advantage operating in an industry;

2 the degree to which a firm is able or willing to shift the balance of competitive advantage towards itself by its new strategies in that industry.

However, according to Professors Gary Hamel and C K Prahalad, this misses an important element in the dynamics because it concentrates on the *current* industry boundaries:

> *Strategy is as much about competing for tomorrow's industry as it is about competing within today's industry structure. Competition within today's industry structure raises such issues as: What new features should be added to a product? How can we get better channel coverage? Should we price for maximum market share or maximum profits? Competition for tomorrow's industry structure raises deeper questions such as: Whose product concepts will ultimately win out? How will coalitions form and what will determine each member's share of power? And, most critically, how do we increase our ability to influence the emerging shape of a nascent industry?*[15]

Although Hamel and Prahalad were addressing their remarks primarily to new industry opportunities like satellite television and internet record distribution, the same logic can be applied to existing and more mature markets. To quote Baden-Fuller and Stopford on mature market strategy: 'The real battles are fought among firms taking different approaches, especially those that counter yesterday's ideas.'[16] In other words, the dynamics of competitive advantage need to be viewed not just as a battle between the existing firms but also as an attempt to break out of the existing competitive framework. This carries the significant difficulty of shaping such a dynamic so that it is still manageable within the resources of an organisation. Exhibit 20.2 shows a three-stage process that might elucidate the dynamics and identify the opportunity.[17]

Exhibit 20.2

Investigating the dynamics of competitive advantage

Three possible steps:

1 *Develop a vision about the future direction of an industry and related areas.* For example, the Ford Motor Company has taken the view that strategy in the global car industry will involve control of distributors, second-hand cars and servicing in addition to car manufacturing. This is the organisation identifying the opportunity.

2 *Manage the paths that will service this vision.* This will involve building before rivals such areas as the key resources, the new products and services, the relevant networks and alliances. For example, the UK retailer Tesco was amongst the first to establish a home shopping service using the internet which required both a website and a well-organised home delivery service. This is the organisation shaping the strategy.

3 *Compete within the chosen market for market share.* This will involve such areas as the level of service, the marketing mix and the reduction in costs through operations strategies.

Keypoint: it is this last stage that is often portrayed as the conventional battleground of sustainable competitive advantage, whereas it may be the two earlier areas that contain the most useful dynamic opportunities.

20.3.2 The predictability of the environment

From a strategic management perspective, the dynamics of the environment can be managed better if the environment can be predicted. The changes are known in these circumstances and the strategic implications can therefore be actioned. We examine this issue by first exploring some of the types of prediction that can be and have been undertaken. We then explore the argument of Mintzberg that much of this activity is a waste of time.

The purpose of prediction

The objective of undertaking prediction is to cope better with uncertainty in the environment. There will always be some residual risk but prediction should help to reduce this and increase the chance of success. In other words, the dynamics of the environment may be at least partially controlled, if they can be predicted.

According to some strategists,[18] the key to tackling strategic prediction is to understand that some environments are more predictable than others. For example, the market for ice cream – *see* Case studies 4.1 and 4.4 – can be predicted with some certainty. Some revolutionary new technology might invalidate this prediction, but this is unlikely. By contrast, the internet recording market – *see* Case study 20.2 – cannot be so easily predicted, because the future direction is highly uncertain. However, although the second is more open, there are some techniques that will reduce the uncertainty and make the environment partially predictable.

For our purposes, it is useful to identify three types of environment and the techniques that might be employed in their prediction: these are shown in Exhibit 20.3. This book has explored the main techniques elsewhere so they are not repeated here. The main point is that, even where there is strong residual uncertainty, some prediction of the environment may be possible within broad limits.

Exhibit 20.3

Coping with different levels of environmental uncertainty

Environment 1 Reasonably predictable, barring catastrophe	**Environment 2** Alternatives clear, but precise outcome remains unknown	**Environment 3** Many possible outcomes with no clear idea of way ahead

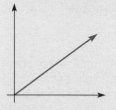 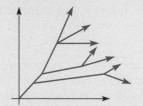 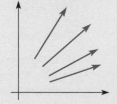

Techniques: market and competitor projections – *see* Chapters 3 and 14

Techniques: market projections, decision analysis plus options from game theory – *see* Chapters 3, 14 and 15

Techniques: market outlook, technology forecasting and scenario planning – *see* Chapters 3, 14 and 15

Prediction: single outcome with upside and downside

Prediction: series of discrete outcomes that will encompass the main future possibilities

Prediction: some possible outcomes that provide a general sense of direction only; even this may be of only limited value

Example: Nestlé's food markets – *see* Case study 17.3

Example: Prediction of the likely outcomes to the consolidation of the European defence industry – *see* Case study 15.3

Example: The outcomes of the opportunities that will arise from the internet record industry – *see* Case study 20.2

The fallacy of prediction?

Within the context of this conclusion, we now turn to the comments of Professor Henry Mintzberg. He has argued that prediction is often a complete waste of time.[19] He describes how traditional prescriptive strategic planning will make a prediction about the environment and then expect the world to stay on this predicted course while the strategy is developed and implemented.

As an example of what he regards as the fallacy of prediction, Mintzberg quotes from one of the early pioneers of corporate strategy, Professor Igor Ansoff, who wrote in his book on *Corporate Strategy*: 'We shall refer to the period for which the firm is able to construct forecasts with an accuracy of, say, plus or minus 20 per cent as the planning horizon.' Mintzberg comments:

> *What an extraordinary statement! How in the world can any company know the period for which it can forecast with any accuracy? . . . While certain repetitive patterns, such as seasons, may be predictable, the forecasting of discontinuities, such as technological innovation or a price increase, is virtually impossible.*

Thus Mintzberg argues that, where environmental prediction really matters, for example in predicting innovations, it is largely worthless. He dismisses the value of future visions of markets, explaining that they arise from essentially personal and intuitive approaches.

Comment

What does this mean for environmental dynamics? Mintzberg is right to dismiss the value of precise predictions in areas of great uncertainty. Thus financial DCF calculations based on predictions about the size of the internet record industry in ten years' time – *see* Case study 20.2 – have little value, beyond the general implication that considerable growth is likely. However, Mintzberg takes his argument too far when he suggests that nothing can be done: scenarios, options and general forecasts may prove beneficial, as outlined in Exhibit 20.3. Moreover, where the environment is more stable, environmental dynamics can benefit from prediction.

20.3.3 Acting on the dynamics of the environment

Even though organisations are able to see and understand changes in the environment, they are not always able to act upon them. There is an inertia in organisations that arises from the difficulties, costs and risks implied by such change. The result is that the dynamics of the environment will not necessarily be translated immediately into actions inside the organisation, especially in terms of resource-based change. The economist Professor Richard Rumelt has suggested that there are five reasons for this:[20]

1 *Distorted perception.* Although individuals in organisations may be able to see the environment clearly, the organisation taken as a whole may have more difficulty. The reasons may include a desire to stay with short-term certainties, a fear of what the future might bring or a selective desire to stay with current habits.

2 *Dulled motivation.* Even though organisations understand the environment, they may not perceive with sufficient clarity the threat that it poses. Thus they will not be sufficiently motivated to act on the information.

3 *Failed creative response.* The organisation may be unable to find a creative way out of the threat posed, even though it perceives it accurately.

4 *Political deadlocks.* Organisational politics may make it impossible to develop the best strategy to cope with the perceived opportunity or threat.

5 *Action disconnects.* Leadership, organisational routines and stakeholder interest groups may all make it impossible to react to environmental change.

We explore some of these areas in more depth in Chapter 21, but it is appropriate here that we acknowledge the difficulty of connecting the environment with the resources of the organisation.

Key strategic principles

● The dynamics of environmental development have many dimensions but can usefully be considered from three perspectives: the maintenance of competitive advantage; the predictability of the environment; the ability of the organisation's resources to respond to changes in the environment.

● The maintenance of competitive advantage will depend on the nature of the advantages operating in an industry. It will also involve the willingness of a firm to shape new advantages and the nature of the future advantages that might operate in an industry.

● If the environment is predictable then it allows the dynamics of the environment to be managed more easily. Although no environment is entirely predictable, some strategists argue that the process is largely a waste of time, with no meaningful results where it matters.

● Although an organisation may have understood the nature of environmental change, it may not be able to act upon it. Five major reasons have been identified for this: distorted perception; dulled motivation; failed creative response; political deadlocks; action disconnects.

CASE STUDY 20.2

Recorded music on the internet: only the beginning of the broadband revolution?

Over the seven-year period 1999–2008, recorded music sales through the internet are predicted to grow from US$50 million to US$8 billion. And there are expectations that the spread of broadband technology and third generation mobile phones will extend this to computer games and films.

Recorded music sales in the year 2003: the Big Five dominate

Around the time of the new millennium, five leading record producers dominated the global record industry: they accounted for nearly 75 per cent of the total sales of US$345 billion – see Table 20.2. Although the main area of market demand was pop music, there were also substantial segments in such areas as classical and country and western music. Pop music itself also had many sub-segments, with the main record companies being represented in most of the leading areas.

The competitive advantages of the Big Five come from three related areas:

1 *Recording contracts.* Most of the world's top artists are signed up to one of the leading record producers. For example, Elton John, Cher, Michael Jackson and Madonna all have exclusive contracts that provide sustainable competitive advantage for their record companies. George Michael's very public dispute with his record company only highlighted the control that generally exists in the industry.

2 *High promotional barriers.* Entry barriers for new artists are high because of the marketing funds needed to promote

Table 20.2

The leading global record producers 2003

Company	Market share 2003 (%)	Comment
Universal	23.5	Sold by Vivendi to independent group in 2002. Also includes the market share of Polygram acquired in 1998. Seeking to launch shares and then link with EMI below in 2005
Sony	13.2	Part of Sony multimedia empire
Warner	12.7	Part of AOL Time Warner
BMG	11.9	Owned by German media parent Bertelsmann
EMI	13.4	UK-based group – possible link with Universal in 2005/6
Others	25.3	Many specialist smaller groups

Source: Author from trade sources.

international stars. In addition, considerable expertise and networks are employed to promote and distribute records.

3 *Record sales through retail stores*. The majority of sales are through the leading recorded music stores. These prove a barrier for the smaller companies and an opportunity for the large record producers because the latter have the bargaining power to handle such important customers.

Competitive threat from the Internet: new and growing fast

Although existing record companies dominate traditional distribution, the internet is beginning to change this. Already thousands of teenagers routinely download music from internet sites through MP3 computer files. On-line music delivery can take place in a number of ways, including:

- Legitimate internet sites selling CDs and cassettes in competition with the high-street retail outlets. These sites will be supplied by the Big Five above; indeed, several either own or are in the process of setting up their own sites. The danger is that they upset their traditional retail outlets.

- Digital juke boxes run by small, independent music companies like IUMA and MP3.com. These have been specially set up to distribute the music of new groups unable to get contracts from the Big Five. Each music group pays only US$250 to put a recording on the site. Consumers can listen for free and download for only 99 cents. By 2005, IUMA had extended this activity from its base in the US to Europe and Asia.

- Underground internet sites playing music illegally from the Big Five without paying royalties, thus allowing others to download without buying the recordings. Napster was probably the most famous but was only one of many and has now been made legal. One estimate claims that 150,000 songs were available on MP3 files by the end of 1998 and 3 million by 2002. Portable MP3 recorders led the way in the late 1990s, with the iPod and other players following in the new millennium.

It is this last route that has, so far, alarmed the Big Five recording companies. They have been developing a new pirate-proof internet system to distribute their own music in response. But after five years of development, the joint technical standard was still not finalised in 2003 between the leading producers and the developer, the world's largest computer company IBM. The record companies have therefore taken two different approaches:

- First, to identify some leading download sites and seek to close them down. They have had some success here but can hardly be said to have stopped the activity completely.

- Second, they have licensed their music to legitimate websites, the pioneer being the Apple iTunes site explored in Case 1.1.

Extension via broadband to film and computer games – even mobile phones

Now, there is a new threat. The internet has made it much easier for individuals and small groups to bypass the traditional record companies and gain distribution for their music. The widespread introduction of broadband technology (*see* Case study 15.2) has increased the speed of transfer – 3 minutes to download a complete CD. Importantly, the spread of broadband at home is already having broader effects in some countries – for example, Korea already has wider use of broadband than much of Europe and it is being used to transmit computer games, which were previously too slow on the older internet technology. It cannot be long before films are exchanged over the internet using broadband technology – just as illegal as distributing copyright recorded music, and just as much a threat to the leading film companies.

However, some companies see broadband as a business *opportunity*: for example, Microsoft is developing applications for its new X-box games player. Microsoft is also exploring a deal with the Nokia mobile phone company to play music on handsets. The new 3G technology is opening up even further business scope. All companies recognise that the technology presents new opportunities, especially for the smaller companies. The real issue is how to exploit them.

Case questions

1 *What characteristics of the internet threaten the Big Five record companies? What are the advantages for small companies of using the internet? And what are the problems?*

2 *One estimate of the internet record market puts the size at US$4 billion in 2006. What reliance would you place on this figure? What implications does this have for any strategy proposals that you might have for the industry? And for other industries like computer games and films?*

3 *What lessons can be drawn from the case on the opportunities presented by new technology in the dynamics of strategy development?*

STRATEGIC PROJECT

Explosive growth in the internet will provide major strategic opportunities over the next few years for small and medium-sized enterprises (SMEs); Case study 20.2 describes one example for the record industry. Identify further internet opportunities and use the concepts explored in this chapter and other parts of this book to develop strategies for SMEs to exploit them.

20.4 THE DYNAMICS OF FAST-MOVING MARKETS

Fast-moving markets present real opportunities and challenges for strategists. The dynamics of the internet record industry above show just what scope there is for strategic development, including real opportunities for small and medium-sized enterprises (SMEs). The dynamics of such fast-moving markets are mainly governed by the pace and change of innovation.

By its nature, innovation is difficult to define. Thus some innovations are relatively small, while others revolutionise whole industries. For example, the compact disc method of recording was innovative in producing increased sound quality in the record industry but was hardly revolutionary, whereas the possible distribution of music by the totally new technology of the internet may cause the market to open up significantly. This latter development will be both innovative and revolutionary. In exploring innovation dynamics, there are several interrelated areas that need to be explored: these are shown in Figure 20.4.

20.4.1 Innovation dynamics: market dominance issues

Where an industry is subject to rapid technological change, then there are two problems facing a company that dominates an industry and has *already* committed its resources to a specific technology:

1 *Sunk cost effect*. Firms that have already committed substantial resources to a specific technology may be reluctant to change. Resources and organisational abilities will have been developed for that technology and will be less valuable in any new technology. Such resources represent costs sunk into that technology: for example, the massive investment

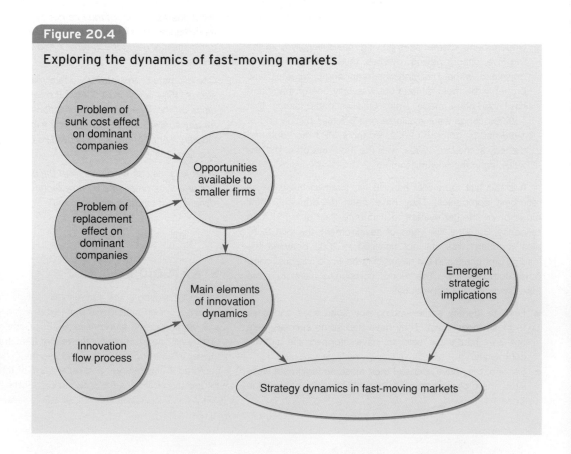

Figure 20.4

Exploring the dynamics of fast-moving markets

in record promotion networks to retail shops by the Big Five would be largely useless on the internet. In deciding whether to switch to new technology, the sunk costs should be ignored because they have been spent. But inevitably such costs may bias firms like the Big Five against making the innovative change.[22]

2 *Replacement effect.* Existing large firms have less incentive to innovate than new companies. The reason is that new companies might expect to gain market dominance by innovation, whereas existing large firms gain no further dominance by such a process. For existing large firms, their market dominance by one technology is simply replaced by that of a new technology – the replacement effect.[23]

20.4.2 Innovation dynamics: the opportunities available to smaller companies

In fast-moving markets, SMEs that do not dominate the market should have significant opportunities. They should be faster and more flexible. Their cultures should be more entrepreneurial and seek out the opportunities presented by the market dynamics. For example, it is the smaller, independent record companies that have developed new artists over the years: as they have benefited from their growth, so they have been acquired in many cases by the Big Five.

Innovation is about process as well as product. For example, in the record industry it is not only about new artists and music (product) but also about new forms of internet distribution (process). Small companies that do not have vested interests in existing processes will also gain by new process methods, such as using the internet.

20.4.3 Innovation dynamics: the innovation flow process

Clearly, it is the substantive, major innovation that will provide important opportunities for SMEs to transform an industry and gain substantial new added value. Professor James Utterback of the Massachusetts Institute of Technology has explored innovation and its dynamics. In particular, he studied how substantial innovation has revolutionised a number of industries.[24] Other writers have also investigated the importance of innovation in revolutionising the structure of industries, especially the way that new firms come to dominate industries.[25]

From the various empirical studies, it is possible to identify the elements of the way that innovation changes whole industries over time: this is shown in Figure 20.5. Essentially, innovation starts with the existing resources of an organisation and an influx of new ideas from outside. In the early stages, there is often no dominant technology or design. This has the advantage of allowing many companies to participate but the disadvantage of making cost reduction of such a design difficult. Once a dominant design has emerged, then a small group of firms may come to dominate that market and cost reduction begins. After a period of time, a totally new technology emerges and the process begins all over again. The significance of this is that it highlights the opportunities for small, new companies to come to dominate an industry as a result of innovative change: the classic example is the Microsoft dominance of personal computers with its Windows operating system – *see* Case study 1.2.

20.4.4 The emergent strategic implications of fast-moving dynamics

When a market is new and fast growing, it is not clear how it will develop. Technology may still be in its early stages, with little agreement on industry standards. Companies will still be low on the experience curve (*see* Chapter 13, Section 13.7.2) and will be operating emergent strategies to find the best route forward.

Dominant market shares will have less meaning because the market is changing fast. New customers will still be entering the market and will need to be introduced to the products.

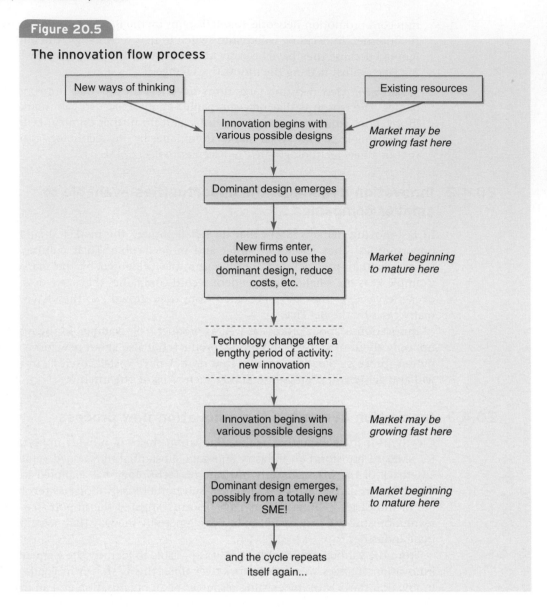

Figure 20.5

The innovation flow process

New ways of thinking

Existing resources

Innovation begins with various possible designs

Market may be growing fast here

Dominant design emerges

New firms enter, determined to use the dominant design, reduce costs, etc.

Market beginning to mature here

Technology change after a lengthy period of activity: new innovation

Innovation begins with various possible designs

Market may be growing fast here

Dominant design emerges, possibly from a totally new SME!

Market beginning to mature here

and the cycle repeats itself again...

Competitors should all be experiencing significant sales growth, with the problem being to provide adequate finance for this and for further research at the same time. For example, some of the small record companies mentioned in Case study 20.2 were swallowed up by the Big Five because they were unable to generate sufficient cash: that was how the group U2 came to Universal and Oasis ended up at Sony. Exhibit 20.4 summarises some of the strategic implications of the strategy dynamics of fast-moving markets.

Exhibit 20.4

Strategy dynamics in fast-moving industries

- *Bold initiatives* to capture market share and build on cost experience effects.
- Significant investment to develop the *basic technology* and adapt it to customer tastes.
- Search for a viable *customer base* beyond the initial trialists, e.g. a market segment.

Examples of such markets in the new millennium include the new 3G technology for mobile telephones and some new uses for the Internet.

Key strategic principles

- In fast-moving markets, the dynamic process is dominated by innovation.

- Companies that already dominate their markets and have committed resources to a specific technology are less likely to innovate for two reasons: the sunk cost effect and the replacement effect.

- Small and medium-sized companies should have more opportunities in such markets if they are faster, more flexible and entrepreneurial.

- The dynamics of innovation go through a series of phases that depend on one technical design becoming dominant.

- Emergent strategic processes are more appropriate in fast-moving markets.

CASE STUDY 20.3

Chocolate maker savours its sweet desserts

FT

Mary-Ann O'Brien has built her company by targeting the 'volume luxury' domain of the Belgians and Swiss.

Oh, to have been a fly on the wall at Lindt when the venerable chocolate maker found out it has lost an important long-term contract to supply British Airways. To lose to the Belgians would have been understandable – but not to a small Irish company, run by a woman who just five years previously had bought her first set of chocolate moulds in a South African flea market for £12. 'Ah God, that was sweet. You can't imagine how I felt,' says Mary-Ann O'Brien. 'Here was Lindt, the grand-daddy of them all, nearly 150 years old and steeped in so much tradition, and here's me, barely getting into my stride and pinching the contract from right under their noses.'

Ms O'Brien had been eyeing the airline market after winning a contract with Aer Lingus. 'I just thought the Lindt brand looked tired, so I rang up British Airways and said it was all a bit dated and suggested we meet, saying I had a new, exciting range of chocolates and designs to offer. I asked the team to come up with a range of beautiful contemporary designs for packaging and our R&D department to come up with a range of "dessert-like" sweets.' Soon, BA passengers were being served sticky toffee pudding, lemon meringue pie, raspberry mousse and lemon brulé as sweets. All these chocolates contained natural ingredients similar to those in desserts, be they lemon curd, or real raspberries. 'The chocolates were an instant hit and we soon landed more airline contracts. As well as BA, we have Aer Lingus, Virgin, Continental, United and US Air.'

There was a wobble when the airline industry went into a bit of a tailspin after September 11 2001 and slashed spending, but Ms O'Brien hung in there, cutting costs with new designs, and eventually regained most of the business.

The airlines themselves lost substantial business and this impacted on their suppliers, such as Lily O'Brien's. The company responded by developing a new flow-wrapped airline chocolate product to replace the more expensive two-chocolate format. This innovation saved the airlines money and subsequently won the company the Mercury prize for cost-saving innovation on an airline. In 2004, Lily O'Brien's Chocolates (named after her daughter) shipped 8 million pieces on airlines alone. Lily O'Brien's employs more than 100 people in Newbridge, Co Kildare, Ireland and had a turnover in 2004 of about €10 million (US$11 million). The company exported to dozens of countries but mainly to those that serve the 'sweeter palate' – the UK, the US, Canada

www.lilyobriens.ie. Lily O'Brien's homepage 2005, designed by Lily O'Brien's MD Mary Ann O'Brien, managed by Curratech Internet Consultancy.

Lily O'Brien's Chocolates exploit the power of the internet for small entrepreneurial businesses.

▶ **CASE STUDY 20.3 continued**

Exhibit 20.5

Words of wisdom from the woman who ate Lindt's lunch

Mary-Ann O'Brien has learnt a series of commonsense lessons during her 12 years in the chocolate-making business. Here are the main ones:

● The relationship between you and your financial controller is vital. But try to avoid allowing them to be 'penny wise and pound foolish'.

● Keep your ego in a basket under the desk and do not show it in the company of others. Too many good companies are seriously harmed by megalomaniac bosses strutting around.

● Don't let your fear get the better of you. Use it to your advantage, no matter what you are facing. It is a cliché, but true, that fear can be a great creative motivator. Lily's found this out after September 11 2001, when it thought it was facing ruin. Instead, it developed other markets and eventually got its old ones back.

● Don't shy away from confrontation. The longer you leave it the worse it so often becomes. But never show anger to anyone in the business, be it a supplier, an employee or, in particular, a customer.

● Stay close to your competitors and never get smug. The day you are pleased with yourself is the day your rival is stealing a march on you.

● Travel, and keep travelling, particularly in the US. The number of ideas to be found there is staggering.

● If you don't know, do not be afraid to ask, and do not be afraid to hook up with a mentor.

and Australia. In the trade, her company was among the '55 per-centers', chocolate makers with a minimum of 55 per cent cocoa in their products, which are described as 'luxury'. Some of the lessons learnt by the company over the last twelve years are summarised in Exhibit 20.5.

The company's long product list is headed by Ms O'Brien's trademark Chocolate Crispy Hearts, her first commercial product, later augmented by dozens of handcrafted products from crèmes brûlées, mousses and pralines to truffles and nuts, all in milk, dark and white chocolate. 'We are a volume luxury chocolate maker, but all our products are hand-crafted,' she says. By volume, she means about 10–12 tonnes per week though that can rise to as much as 25–30 tonnes 'in a good week'. And good weeks there have been. So much so that a mezzanine extension was built at the factory over Easter 2004 to allow extra production.

This is all a far cry from Ms O'Brien's first chocolate mak-ing experience. While on holiday in South Africa in 1992, she

became friendly with the daughter of the owner of the hotel. At the time, she was recuperating from the debilitating illness myalgic encephalomyelitis or ME. One afternoon she was in the hotel kitchen, where a woman was stirring chocolate in a bowl. It turned out she was 'tempering' the chocolate – cool-ing it and removing air bubbles – before it was folded into moulds for setting. Ms O'Brien was transfixed and the next day she bought a set of chocolate moulds. On her return to Ireland, she tried different recipes to see what worked. Often it was people such as her hairdresser who formed the tasting panel and, later, her first customers. 'Initially, I just worked in the kitchen of our flat and drove round delivering chocolates to customers.'

She took chocolate-making lessons in Belgium and became adept at the fiddly processes that make the difference between success and failure – often no more than 1°C either way in temperature. In 1993, she borrowed £30,000 for her first 'industrial scale' chocolate machinery and moved into a catering kitchen. Slowly, a business started to emerge – but it was still being run as a cottage industry. Later, a friend from the meat industry invested £40,000 in return for a significant share of the equity and encouraged her 'to stop thinking in kilos and start thinking in tonnes'. Funds from a Business Expansion Scheme allowed the company to spend nearly £1 million on modern machinery for the production line. 'I got my first big contract from Ireland's version of Waitrose which is called Superquinn. They said "We won't let you make our truffles. The Belgians are doing that, but you can make our crocodiles and pigs." So I did. It started very small but, within a year, I had the whole of the Superquinn group and the Belgians were gone.' Lily's now supplies most of the British supermarket chains.

However, Ms O'Brien realised her limitations. She does see herself as a seller, first and foremost. 'Give me a glass of vodka at lunchtime, and I'll talk all afternoon, it doesn't matter to whom: buyers, companies, you name it.' But chocolate-making is a scientific, complicated process with little room for the talk. So she has hired the best food tech-nologists, designers and production, operational, financial and development staff she can find. 'They are all a class act, seriously, all of them,' she says. The learning curve has been all the more steep because chocolate-making is relatively new to Ireland (Lir and Butlers are fellow Irish chocolate businesses). The companies have benefited from the expertise of Bord Bia (the Irish Food Board) which has helped expand their markets overseas and helped the producers tailor products to meet demand. Early research by Bord Bia uncov-ered an untapped sector of the market as 'self-indulgence'. This was where people wanted to buy luxury chocolates to treat themselves and wanted something better than Cadbury's but not quite as rarefied (or expensive) as the top Belgian brands.

In 2004, the company was hoping to see the opening of a Lily O'Brien's café, selling own-brand coffee as well as a new range of chocolates. 'I think the brand is strong enough now to expand in that area,' Ms O'Brien says. She has come a long way since buying those first chocolate moulds. Not even Lindt could quibble with that.

This case was adapted by Richard Lynch from an article in the *Financial Times*, 20 April 2004, page 13, written by Eamonn Rafferty. Professor Lynch is grateful to Lily O'Brien's for correcting some data and adding some new information for this case.

© Copyright *Financial Times* 2004. All rights reserved. Used with permission.

Case questions

1 *What do the dynamics of purpose, resources and the environment suggest about the strategic issues facing the company?*

2 *Did Ms O'Brien develop a strategic plan or did she allow the company to develop in a more experimental way? Was her strategy prescriptive or emergent?*

3 *What lessons can entrepreneurs learn from a company like Lily O'Brien's Chocolates?*

20.5 THE DYNAMICS OF ENTREPRENEURIAL ACTIVITY

As Mary-Ann O'Brien demonstrates, entrepreneurship becomes the major focus of an individual's life. It involves seeking and developing opportunities – such as a demand for high-quality chocolates – and then finding outlets for them such as the airlines. Very often, entrepreneurs create opportunities – even new ones like the latest coffee shop concept at Lily O'Brien's Chocolates – and they usually take risks. In Ms O'Brien's case, she clearly took a number of years of experimentation to develop products and there must have been times – like the period around September 11, 2001 – when she wondered if the business would survive. The key to taking risks in entrepreneurial activity is to shift them in your favour, balancing the risk and potential reward.[26]

Entrepreneurship is a major area of business activity that has developed its own literature and research. The purpose of this brief section is not to replace the long and respected intellectual tradition developed elsewhere but to show how such thinking links back and in to corporate strategy. Thus, the approach here is to use the structure developed throughout the book to highlight some basic concepts and then point the interested reader to further research in other areas.

Definition ➤ For many SMEs, the most attractive strategic opportunity comes from entrepreneurial activity. Entrepreneurship is a way of thinking, reasoning and acting that focuses on the identification and exploitation of business opportunities from a broad general perspective driven by the leadership of individuals or small groups. The main elements of the entrepreneurial have both prescriptive and emergent elements but the opportunism of entrepreneurs is probably best captured by an emergent process. A possible model is shown in Figure 20.6. This section explains and explores the different aspects of the model.

20.5.1 Organising framework for entrepreneurial process

Most small companies remain small[27] and the high growth firm that creates real wealth is unusual.[28] In spite of this slightly discouraging beginning, many of us have knowledge of people who have made significant wealth from entrepreneurial activity. We have even identified some already in this book – Sir Richard Branson at Virgin and Rupert Murdoch at News Corporation. In developing the entrepreneurial process, the starting point is the business opportunity. This is clearly external to the company – demand for superior, hand-made chocolates, for example. Thus the organising framework needs to begin by identifying the business opportunity.

According to McGrath,[29] the next step is to form a business to exploit that opportunity. Two further stages develop from this: the growth and development of the business and, finally, the closure of unprofitable business activity. This last aspect is often overlooked in

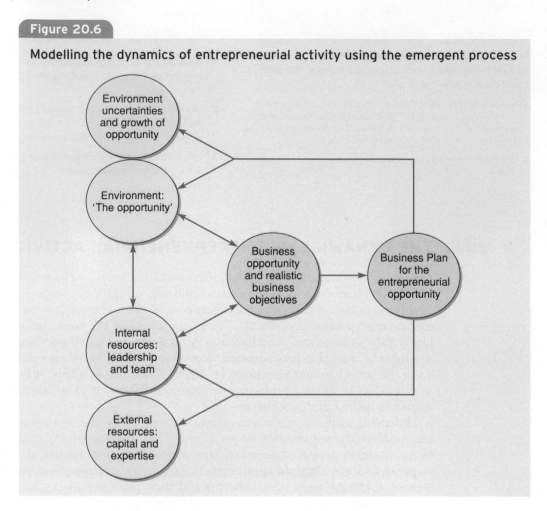

Figure 20.6

Modelling the dynamics of entrepreneurial activity using the emergent process

the enthusiasm of entrepreneurial activity but it is important that business people learn how to walk away from failure and, if necessary, build up a totally new business venture.[30] However, from a strategy development perspective, this eventuality only occurs later. The model therefore needs to begin by focusing on the business opportunity in the strategic environment.

20.5.2 Exploitation and development of resources to exploit the opportunity

After identifying the opportunity, the most important and difficult task is then to develop the team to exploit the opportunity. For example, Mary-Ann O'Brien clearly needed to build a team to manufacture and sell the business opportunity in chocolate in Case 20.3. Over several years, the team had grown to 140 people. In describing the lessons that she had learnt over that time, Ms O'Brien went out of her way to mention several that were clearly related to team building – selection of members, handling of tensions, etc. More generally, most small companies will not have all the resources inside the organisation. It is for this reason that a separate 'External Resource' area is identified in Figure 20.6. For example, Ms O'Brien clearly used the resources of the outside organisation *Bord Bia* to help identify new market niches to be tackled. Such resources are often in the areas of specialist expertise and in the provision of new capital to develop the opportunity.

20.5.3 Development of realistic business objectives and a business plan

Once the initial resources are in place, there is then a need to develop the specific entrepreneurial opportunity and a business plan. A sense of realism coupled with some enthusiasm is important here in order to make the process happen.[31] Importantly, some financial institutions will expect to have a 'business plan' that will look more like a prescriptive approach to strategy than an emergent one – five-year projections of sales, profits, cash flow, etc.

The key is to ensure that such a plan remains flexible and able to learn from what happens in the market place. It is for this reason that Figure 20.6 has a strong feedback mechanism to the 'environment' with specific, separate recognition of two points:

- The chance outside events that can make or break an opportunity;
- The need to be adopt a learning-based approach with regard to ways of serving and developing the business opportunity. As Ms O'Brien clearly indicated in the case study, the customer is crucial to any such opportunity.

Key strategic principles

- Entrepreneurship is a way of thinking, reasoning and acting that focuses on the identification and exploitation of business opportunities from a broad general perspective driven by the leadership of individuals or small groups.

- There are four main phases of entrepreneurial development: the identification of the business opportunity, the development of a business to exploit the opportunity, the growth of the business and, finally, the closure of businesses that are not sufficiently attractive.

- In terms of the resources needed to develop an entrepreneurial opportunity, there is a need to begin by developing the team that will exploit the opportunity. This is likely to be supplemented by outside resources in specialist areas and in the provision of capital because small businesses are unlikely to have such resources.

- Beyond the initial building phase, businesses need to identify the specific opportunity and develop a business plan to meet this. It is also important to monitor the environment in order to identify any chance events that might impact on the business and to ensure that feedback is obtained on the acceptability of the business opportunity.

CRITICAL REFLECTION

Does entrepreneurship have to be unstructured?

Some strategists argue that entrepreneurs need to seize market opportunities, wherever they arise. This means that they are essentially unstructured and opportunistic. However, when raising finance, many banks and other institutions insist that they need a prescriptive plan before they will risk their funds on such ventures. Who is right? Does entrepreneurship have to be unstructured?

SUMMARY

- The purpose of an organisation can and will change over time. The coalition of interests that defines and develops purpose will be influenced by factors both inside and outside the organisation. Importantly, the purpose of the organisation is at least partially in the control of the organisation itself. Although purpose is complex, it is usual in strategy to concentrate on two common elements: value added and sustainable competitive advantage.

● From a dynamic perspective, resources in organisations are developed and destroyed over time. There are three main dimensions: time, early-mover advantages and imitation pressures. When exploring the way that resources change over *time*, there are three main considerations: the two sources of new resource growth, the delaying effect of routines in companies and the mechanism that destroys resources over time.

● Some strategists argue that moving early into a market will help to establish a particular type of sustainable competitive advantage: it is called the *early-mover* advantage. There are five main benefits associated with this, many of them being built on the assumption that such a move will be accompanied by a technical breakthrough that competitors will find difficult to match. The *imitation pressures* that arise from competitors attempting to match an existing product or service can be countered by five resource activities: incremental improvements in the product or service; legal barriers to imitation, such as patenting; developing superior relationships with customers and suppliers; exploiting market size and scale economies; developing intangible barriers to imitation.

● The dynamics of environmental development have many dimensions but can usefully be considered from three perspectives: the maintenance of competitive advantage; the predictability of the environment; and the ability of the organisation's resources to respond to changes in the environment. The maintenance of competitive advantage will depend on the nature of the advantages operating in an industry. It will also involve the willingness of a firm to shape new advantages and the nature of the future advantages that might operate in an industry.

● If the environment is predictable then it allows the dynamics of the environment to be managed more easily. Although no environment is entirely predictable, some strategists argue that the process is largely a waste of time, with no meaningful results where it matters. Although an organisation may have understood the nature of environmental change, it may not be able to act upon it. There are five major reasons that have been identified for this. They are based on the difficulties that organisations and individual managers have in perceiving and acting upon the changes in the environment.

● In fast-moving markets, the dynamic process is dominated by innovation. Companies that already dominate their markets and have committed resources to a specific technology are less likely to innovate for two reasons: the sunk cost effect and the replacement effect. Small and medium-sized companies should have more opportunities in such markets if they are faster, more flexible and entrepreneurial.

● The dynamics of innovation itself go through a series of phases that depend on one technical design becoming dominant. At a time of rapid change in the early stages of the dynamics, emergent strategic processes are more appropriate. Entrepreneurship is a way of thinking, reasoning and acting that focuses on the identification and exploitation of business opportunities from a broad general perspective driven by the leadership of individuals or small groups. There are four main phases of entrepreneurial development: the identification of the business opportunity; the development of a business to exploit the opportunity; the growth of the business and, finally, the closure of businesses that are not sufficiently attractive.

● In terms of the resources needed to develop an entrepreneurial opportunity, there is a need to begin by developing the team that will exploit the opportunity. This is likely to be supplemented by outside resources in specialist areas and in the provision of capital because small businesses are unlikely to have such resources. Beyond the initial building phase, businesses need to identify the specific opportunity and develop a business plan to meet this. It is also important to monitor the environment in order to identify any chance events that might impact on the business and to ensure that feedback is obtained on the acceptability of the business opportunity.

QUESTIONS

1 Using Exhibit 20.1, identify how purpose has changed in an organisation of your choice and explain why these changes occurred. What have been the implications for the strategy of the organisation?

2 What are the main reasons for resource changes in an organisation? How do they affect sustainable competitive advantage and value added? Give examples to support your explanation.

3 Does the early-mover advantage have any relevance from the perspective of strategy development in more mature markets, like those for chocolate and beer?

4 If you were attempting to defend an existing pharmaceutical product against the announcement by a rival of a similar new drug, which of the five resource-based imitation strategies would you employ? Use Section 20.2.3 to assist you. Give reasons for your approach.

5 Why is it sometimes difficult for an organisation to act upon the changes that it sees taking place in the environment? What can it do to overcome such problems? Give examples to support your views.

6 *'A successful business strategy is affected by many amplifying feedback processes that are outside the control of its managers and produce effects that they did not intend.'* (Professor Ralph Stacey)

Discuss this comment in the context of the dynamics of the environment.

7 Take a fast-moving market with which you are familiar – such as the provision of services on the World Wide Web – and investigate the strategies that might be available for entering such a market. Identify those strategies, if any, that are more likely to deliver sustainable competitive advantage.

8 In entrepreneurial markets that are served by the internet, what strategies are available for the smaller business to gain market share and value added (*see* Case studies 20.1 and 20.1)? You should consider whether such companies are exploiting all the available strategic opportunities.

9 Think of a small business opportunity – perhaps one of which you are aware or one that you would like to develop – and consider what steps you might employ to develop it. Use Figure 20.6 to help you in this process.

Further reading

Utterback, J M (1996) *Mastering the Dynamics of Innovation*, Harvard Business School Press, Boston, MA is an interesting read that has some excellent examples.

Peter Drucker's text might be old – Drucker, P (1961) *The Practice of Management*, Mercury Books, London – but it still has many valuable insights. It was the subject of a retrospective by the *Academy of Management Executive* in 2003.

Tom Peters is always stimulating – Peters, T (1989) *Thriving on Chaos*, Pan Books, London – if somewhat over the top on occasions.

Rita McGrath's chapter – McGrath, R G (2002) 'Entrepreneurship, small firms and wealth creation' in Pettigrew, A, Thomas H and Whittington, R, *Handbook of Strategy and Management*, Sage, London – provides a useful structure on entrepreneurship.

There is a special issue in *Long Range Planning* on Boundaries and Innovation – six papers covering topics from resource allocation to acquisition: guest editors – Gibbert, M and Valigangas, L (2004) Boundaries and Innovation: Special Issue, *Long Range Planning*, Vol 37, No 6, pp493–601. *See* Day, G S and Schoemaker, P (2004) 'Peripheral vision: sensing and acting on weak signals', *Long Range Planning*, Vol 37, No 2, pp117–23 plus many other well-known strategy writers for this special issue including Sidney G Winter and C K Prahalad.

Notes and references

1 Drucker, P (1961) *The Practice of Management*, Mercury Books, London, p74.
2 Peters, T (1989) *Thriving on Chaos*, Pan Books, London.
3 Chaharbaghi, K and Lynch, R (1999) 'Sustainable competitive advantage: towards a dynamic resource-based strategy', *Management Decision*, 37(1), pp45–50.
4 Parts of this section have benefited from Chs14 and 15 of Besanko, D, Dranove, D and Shanley, M (1996) *The Economics of Strategy*, Wiley, New York.
5 Penrose, E (1995) *The Theory of the Growth of the Firm*, Oxford University Press, Oxford, p85.
6 Nelson, R R and Winter, S G (1982) *An Evolutionary Theory of Economic Change*, Belknap Press, Cambridge, MA.
7 Schumpeter, J (1942) *Capitalism, Socialism and Democracy*, Harper & Row, New York.
8 At the time of writing, Microsoft is the subject of a US Federal and State Government investigation into its competitive reaction against Netscape's browser success.

9 Utterback, J M (1996) *Mastering the Dynamics of Innovation*, Harvard Business School Press, Boston, MA, pp10, 30.

10 Nalebuff, B J and Brandenburger, A M (1997) *Co-opetition*, HarperCollins Business, London, p241.

11 Utterback, J M (1996) Op. cit., p28.

12 There is a Harvard Business School case that explores this well.

13 Porter, M E (1985) *Competitive Advantage: Creating and Sustaining Superior Performance,* The Free Press, New York, p1.

14 Porter, M E (1985) Op. cit., p2.

15 Hamel, G and Prahalad, C K (1994) *Competing for the Future*, Harvard Business School Press, Boston, MA, p42.

16 Baden-Fuller, C and Stopford, J (1992) *Rejuvenating the Mature Business*, Routledge, London, Ch2.

17 Based loosely on Hamel, G and Prahalad, C K (1994) Op. cit., p47.

18 Courtney, H, Kirkland, J and Viguerie, M (1997) 'Strategy under uncertainty', *Harvard Business Review*, Nov–Dec, pp67–79.

19 Mintzberg, H (1994) 'The fall and rise of strategic planning', *Harvard Business Review*, Jan–Feb, pp107–14.

20 Rumelt, R (1995) 'Inertia and transformation', in Montgomery, C A (ed) *Resource-based and Evolutionary Theories of the Firm*: *Towards a Synthesis*, Kluwer Academic, Boston, MA, pp101–32.

21 References for the record industry case: Ghosh, S (1998) 'Making business sense of the Internet', *Harvard Business Review*, Mar–Apr, p180. Also *Financial Times*,

25 June 1996, p17; 24 May 1997, p7; 23 Aug 1997, p2; 15 May 1998, p28; 2 June 1998, p22; 19 Nov 1998, p8; 27 Nov 1998, p6; 13 Jan 1999, p18; 8 Apr 1999, p34; 16 September 2003, p27; 23 September 2004, p21; 16 February 2005, p27; 28 February 2005, p1; 8 March 2005, p4.

22 Besanko, D, Dranove, D and Shanley, M (1996) *The Economics of Strategy*, Wiley, New York, p581.

23 Concept originally developed by Professor Kenneth Arrow: Arrow, K (1962) 'Economic welfare and the allocation of resources for inventions', in Nelson, R (ed) *The Rate and Direction of Inventive Activity*, Princeton University Press, Princeton, NJ. Concept outlined in Besanko, D, Dranove, D and Shanley, M (1996) Op. cit., p584.

24 Utterback, J M (1996) Op. cit.

25 For example, see the references in the discussion on innovation in Chapter 11.

26 Timmons, J A (1999) *New Venture Creation – Entrepreneurship for the 21st Century*, 5th edn, McGraw Hill, Boston, MA, p27.

27 Aldrich, H (1999) *Organizations Evolving*, Sage, Newbury Park, CA.

28 McGrath, R G (2002) 'Entrepreneurship, small firms and wealth creation', in Pettigrew, A, Thomas H and Whittington, R *Handbook of Strategy and Management*, Sage, London.

29 McGrath, R G (2002) Op. cit. Table 14.1, p301.

30 Lynch, R (2003) 'Can young firms use the RBV?' Working paper, Middlesex University, 2003.

31 Timmons, J A (1999) Op. cit.

Chapter 21

MANAGING STRATEGIC CHANGE

Learning outcomes

When you have worked through this chapter, you will be able to:

- understand the nature of strategic change and its implications for strategy development;
- analyse the causes of change;
- outline the main approaches to managing strategic change;
- link a strategic change programme with the type of change required;
- draw up a programme of strategic change appropriate to the strategic task.

INTRODUCTION

Corporate strategy invariably involves change for people working in organisations. Sometimes they resist such proposals and make strategy difficult to implement; sometimes they are enthusiastic and make a significant contribution to the proposed developments. Understanding and exploring the impact of change on people is therefore important for strategy implementation.

Figure 21.1

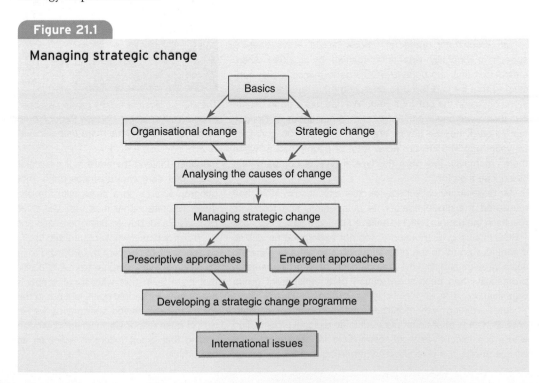

Managing strategic change

As a starting point, it is useful to analyse the causes of strategic change. It is also important to understand the dynamics of the change process in the context of the strategies proposed. These can be used to suggest how such a change process can be managed in principle. Finally, a strategic change programme can be developed either on a one-off or permanent basis. The main areas to be explored are summarised in Figure 21.1.

CASE STUDY 21.1

Shock tactics at BOC

After years of underperforming, a new managing director forced BOC along the path of strategic change. Then he left the company just as it received a highly attractive takeover approach.

BOC's attempt to end years of lacklustre performance began by shocking the top management into silence. It was May 1998 and the UK industrial gases group's most senior executives had gathered in Chantilly, Virginia, for their annual get-together. 'There was none of the usual cosies: "Did you have a nice flight?" and all that,' recalls Danny Rosenkranz, the chief executive. 'It was right between the eyes. I really rattled them.'

The process, known as Project Renew, culminated in March 1999 when the final parts of the group's new structure were put into place. A few weeks earlier Mr Rosenkranz had signed performance contracts with the 19 managers chosen to head the business units that are key to the new BOC. In the intervening ten months, the group had begun a £120 million (US$180 million) cost-cutting plan involving 5,000 redundancies at group and associate companies; reorganised along global business rather than regional lines; and put hundreds of managers through an arduous reselection programme.

Mr Rosenkranz opted for 'shock tactics' – his opening speech in Chantilly was accompanied by a video where critical City analysts berated BOC's performance – after concluding that he had failed to drive home his message on the same occasion the previous year. 'We had had a good debate but then everyone went home and forgot about it. No one really heard me,' he says. 'We were a FTSE 100 company 20 years ago and still are now. A lot of people had a "we're there" mentality. We were the typical type of company that could lose the plot.'

Mr Rosenkranz, who became chief executive in 1996, had measured the group against its competitors and found its results in the bottom half. He believed the core gases business – BOC is also in distribution – was not performing as well as it should. Central to the project, which also aims to generate sales growth and lay the foundations for improvements in profitability, has been the creation of a transparent group organisation.

After working with McKinsey, the management consultants, BOC has abandoned its traditional regional organisation where top executives were responsible for continents, with all operations in a given country reporting to a locally based

The BOC Industrial Gases group has been through a period of enforced strategic change through which its strategic purpose has been little more than survival.

manager. Instead there are four main global lines of business (LOB) that comprise business units, most of which cover a geographic area. In a break with the past, it is the heads of these 19 units, rather than the LOB chiefs, who are primarily responsible for day-to-day operations and profitability.

The group as a whole committed itself to achieving a return on assets of 16 per cent by 2000 and to increasing turnover to £5 billion in five years, up from £3.33 billion in 1998 – targets that have been met with some scepticism in the City. Unit heads have individual goals laid out in their performance contracts, to be reviewed quarterly by Mr Rosenkranz. 'The idea was to push responsibility lower down the company,' he says, adding that group incentive schemes are being widened to reflect this.

Barry Beecroft, one of the architects of Project Renew and an LOB head, adds: 'Before we had a vertical, top-down approach, with the division boss deliberately interventionist and sometimes quite autocratic. LOB chiefs can't do that any more, they don't have the staff.'

Previously, regional divisions, and country managers, had their own support service teams, ranging from information technology and finance to health and safety. Now LOB heads have just a handful of staff and share enabling functions grouped in service centres. Many of the redundancies are being made among support staff. A uniform IT system, for example, is replacing the differing systems used in the group. 'The regional chiefs have been used to having their own army of staff,' says Mr Beecroft, who was formerly head of BOC's European gas operations. 'Some anxieties have been working through that resources are further away and less directly controlled.' His new role, he says, is about setting strategy and coaching the heads of his LOB's four business units: 'We have to bring on tomorrow's management stock.'

While LOB chiefs have to adjust to a less hands-on approach, some of the unit heads find the new structure liberating. 'We have greater responsibility and more autonomy and influence than before,' says John Bevan, an Australian who leads a unit in Beecroft's LOB and was previously head of BOC's Thai operations. 'Having the enabling functions taken away has freed up quite a lot of time. This way you are closer to the customer and able to adjust and compete more quickly.'

Despite having worked for BOC for more than two decades, Mr Bevan, like the other unit heads, had to go through a rigorous reselection process. BOC brought in Egon Zender, the headhunter and management appraisal firm, to interview the 45 staff who had applied to be unit heads and the 25 hoping for the top positions in support services. Other consultants carried out a less intensive process with more than 300 staff seeking positions in the next two levels of management.

'No job was sacrosanct. There were no sitting tenancies,' says Mr Rosenkranz, adding that BOC followed most, but not all, of the consultants' recommendations. 'The new structure will also help us see the next group who will lead the company. On the management board, we are all around the same age.'

The new divisions are organised on similar lines, making it easier to compare performance. 'Before there were different structures in the different geographies. This made it hard to get people with similar concerns and responsibilities around the table,' says Jim Ford, another of the new unit heads. 'Looking on a global basis now, it's also easier to see which the important contracts are, to make sure the prize is big enough.'

Playing to the organisation's increased transparency, Mr Rosenkranz has also developed what he calls a 'peer process'. The unit heads have been divided into small groups, across divisions and around the world, that meet and talk (via video link) regularly to share ideas, evaluate each other and swap best practice. Mr Rosenkranz expects the process to take up 20–25 per cent of the time of those involved. 'In time, once we've got to know each other, this process could be quite powerful,' says Mr Ford. 'I've been looking at an acquisition and my peer group is involved in reviewing the decision. There's an element of challenging each other.'

What happened next?

Two major changes occurred in 1999. First, the company was the subject of a major takeover bid by its two international rivals – Air Products of the US and Air Liquide of France. The two competitors made a joint bid of US$14 billion to acquire BOC and then split the company between them. BOC shareholders accepted the bid because they would have made a significant profit on the sale of their shares. However, the acquisition would have severely restricted competition in the market for industrial gases. It was surprisingly cleared by the European Commission but turned down after much negotiation by the US competition authorities. The latter judged that it would severely reduce competition in the US over gas prices and was therefore anti-competitive. In 2000, BOC was still an independent company.

Second, Mr Rosenkranz left the company in 1999 around the time of the bid. The reasons for his departure were not publicly clear but he had not made himself popular with some colleagues at BOC. In addition, the prospect of the agreed acquisition made the position unattractive. He was replaced on a 'temporary' basis by Mr Tony Isaac. The new chief executive then had to cope with some ten months of waiting while the competitive authorities cleared the bid. In the meantime, it was important to communicate with shareholders, customers and employees. 'The only way to keep people motivated and reassured during a bid period was to communicate,' explained Mr Isaacs later. By May 2000, BOC became concerned over progress with the competition authorities: 'That last month I began to worry more about what was going to happen but, up to the last minute, many people thought [the May 12 deadline set by the companies] would be extended again. I started to think what would be done if there was a BOC post-May 12.'

After the bid collapsed, BOC had to rethink its strategy. It had to face the fact that it had failed to deliver major projects profitably during the 1990s – Mr Rosenkranz had been right. BOC therefore needed to tighten up its project management and work hard to regain its position. During the interim acquisition period, staff had left for other jobs. Equally important, BOC had been unable to recruit new staff – who would want to join a company that was about to be taken over?

Nevertheless, the acquisition had delivered one major advantage to BOC. The directors and employees had received a major shock, but they still had their jobs. The company then needed to develop a new strategy as an independent company. Mr Isaacs commented: 'The agenda was to talk our way through why we got ourselves into the situation [of being acquired] and why we as a board accepted the bid.' Over the next five years, BOC's directors developed new strategies in a number of areas. It acquired companies, moved into China, developed new product areas and tightened up its management of new projects.

▶ **CASE STUDY 21.1 continued**

Figure 21.2

BOC Group: five-year record

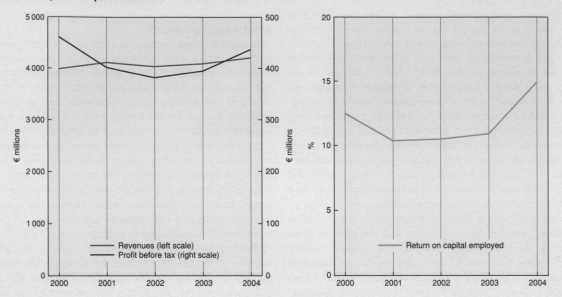

Mr Isaacs was still chief executive in 2005: 'When I look at what we've got now, I believe we are a significantly stronger and better company than we were five years ago. We never wanted to go through a period like that ever again.' Figure 21.1 shows how BOC has managed over the five years since the acquisition.

The first part of this case was adapted by Richard Lynch from an article by Virginia Marsh in the *Financial Times*, 29 April 1999, p22. © Copyright the *Financial Times*.

The second part of the case was written by Richard Lynch from the published Annual Report and Accounts of BOC and from other published sources. © Copyright Richard Lynch. All rights reserved. Sources for second part of case: See reference.[1]

Case questions

1 *Why were shock tactics necessary at BOC in 1998? What are the problems with this approach?*

2 *What were the main elements of the 1998 BOC change programme? Are they consistent with any of the models outlined in this chapter? Why did the failed acquisition benefit the company?*

3 *Are there lessons for other companies from this approach to change? Would you recommend other companies to adopt the same process?*

21.1 THE BASIC CONCEPT OF STRATEGIC CHANGE

In this section, the concept of strategic change is explored and its importance for strategy implementation is explained. A distinction needs to be made between *organisational change*, which happens in every organisation and is inevitable, and *strategic change*, which can be managed.

21.1.1 Organisational change

Change takes place continuously within organisations. The pace of change can be represented by two extremes:

1 *Slow organisational change.* This is introduced gradually, and is likely to meet with less resistance, progress more smoothly and have a higher commitment from the people involved.

2 *Fast organisational change*. This is introduced suddenly, usually as part of a major strategic initiative, and is likely to encounter significant resistance even if it is handled carefully. However, some prescriptive change may be unavoidable, e.g. factory closure as part of a cost-cutting project.

Organisations usually prefer to choose slow change, where possible, because the costs are likely to be lower. In fact, much change follows this route, otherwise organisations would be in perpetual turmoil. Where there is a faster *pace* of change, it may be associated with strategic change, which is *proactive* in its approach.

21.1.2 What is strategic change?

Strategic change is the *proactive management of change* in organisations to achieve clearly identified strategic objectives. It may be undertaken using either prescriptive or emergent strategic approaches.

Because strategy is fundamentally concerned with moving organisations forward, there will inevitably be change for some people inside the organisation. However, strategic change is not just a casual drift through time but a *proactive search* for new ways of working which everyone will be required to adopt. Thus strategic change involves the implementation of new strategies that involve substantive changes *beyond the normal routines* of the organisation. Such activities involve:

> the induction of new patterns of action, belief and attitudes among substantial segments of the population.[2]

Thus the chief executive of BOC altered the responsibilities and activities of his senior managers. They then changed when his replacement arrived.

Many researchers and writers have explored the important topic of *organisational change*.[3] This text concentrates on those who have examined such concepts from a *strategic* perspective. Within this subject area, some researchers have seen the management of change as clear and largely predictable: the *prescriptive* approach (the actions of BOC would probably fall into this category). Other researchers have formed the view that change takes on a momentum of its own and the consequences are less predictable: the *emergent* approach. (Emergent strategists might argue that in the BOC case, although the initial consequences of Mr Rosenkranz's actions were well known, the longer-term results were more difficult to predict and were taking time to emerge. In fact, it took nearly a year for the process to settle down.) In the emergent sense, change is not managed, but 'cultivated' (*see* Handy).[4]

It should be noted that emergent theorists may use the word *change* in a different way from prescriptive theorists:

● In prescriptive theories, change means the *implementation actions that result* from the decision to pursue a chosen strategy. In extreme cases, it is probable that the changes will be imposed on those who then have to implement them (such as the managers being forced to reapply for their jobs at BOC and later to redevelop the BOC strategy).

● In emergent theories, change can sometimes mean the *whole process of developing the strategy*, as well as the actions that result after it has been developed. This may involve experimentation, learning and consultation for those involved in the change.

We will return to this distinction in Sections 21.3 and 21.4.

21.1.3 Pressure points for strategic change

Strategic change is primarily concerned with *people* and the *tasks* that they perform in the organisation. They undertake their work through *formal organisation structures*, explored in Chapter 16. Groups of like-minded people also form *informal organisation structures* to pursue particular common interests: sometimes social groups, like the company sports club, sometimes commercial groupings, such as a group seeking a minor change in working practices. All such groups inevitably discuss, formally or informally, any new developments that affect their lives – for instance, the announcement or the rumours of strategic change. Importantly, such informal groups can abide by, interpret or change any element of the strategy implementation process: this can be advantageous but it can also be a focus for problems if the group does not like the proposed strategies.

Whether the groups are formal or informal, they provide a channel of opportunities for senior management to influence strategic change and to be influenced by the comments of those affected by such changes. In the BOC case, Mr Rosenkranz was engaged in this task when he introduced the 'peer process'. This used video conferencing to encourage senior managers to exchange views around the world and share best practice. Mr Isaacs was engaged in a similar process when he described the way the board had a long review of why it accepted the bid.

Identification of such groups and individuals – for example, the BOC board – constitutes an analysis of the *pressure points for influence* in the organisation (*see* Figure 21.3). The pressure points provide important links between the basic strategic change process and the people involved.

In more general terms, strategic change borrows from a number of academic disciplines and does not have a clearly defined set of boundaries.[5] The basic issues were outlined in Chapter 7 and the main themes will be explored during the course of this chapter.

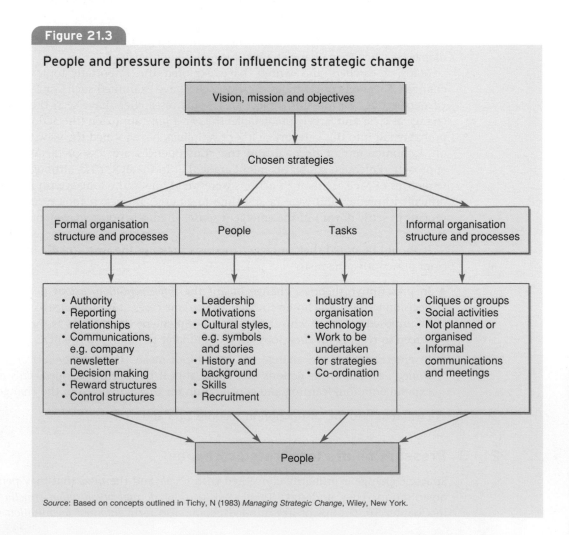

Figure 21.3

People and pressure points for influencing strategic change

Source: Based on concepts outlined in Tichy, N (1983) *Managing Strategic Change*, Wiley, New York.

21.1.4 Why is strategic change important?

In many cases, strategic change is accompanied by a degree of risk and uncertainty. Although risk assessment can be undertaken in an impersonal way at the corporate level,[6] uncertainty cannot be assessed in the same way at the *personal* level in an organisation.

In some organisational cultures, individuals do not like the consequences of strategic change and seek to resist the proposals that are the cause of their problems. Strategic change may spark objections, thus making it difficult to implement. For example, initial indifference at BOC to the call for action was a typical response of those unconvinced of the need for strategic change.

In other organisational cultures, where learning and open debate have been part of the management process, change may be welcomed. However, even here, change will take time

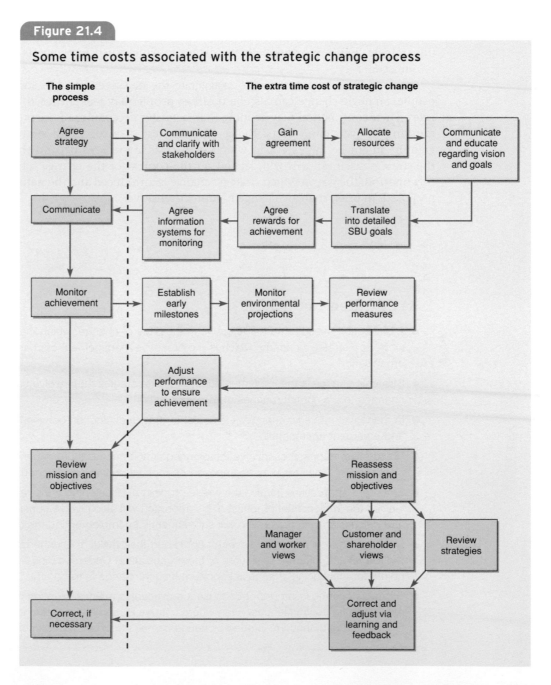

Figure 21.4

Some time costs associated with the strategic change process

and will involve careful thought. Moreover, it will also be recalled from Chapter 16 that, even in a classic learning organisation such as the ABB of the late 1990s, there may still be some managers who do not like change.

To overcome problems associated with resistance to change, strategic change is therefore often taken at a slower pace – 'strategy is the art of the possible', to quote from Chapter 7. More consultation, more explanation and more monitoring of reactions are therefore involved in these circumstances. Figure 21.4 illustrates how the apparently simple process of strategic action is complicated by the reality of the many factors involved in successful strategic implementation.

All such discussion takes time and resources. For example, the cost at BOC can be measured by the length of time – two years – it took to implement the new style of working and then another ten months waiting for the bid to be accepted. Hence, strategic change is important because even successful change has an *implementation* cost for the organisation to set against the *direct benefits* identified from the new strategies. Although there are costs involved in strategic change, it may be possible to reduce them. A partial test of a successful strategic change programme is the extent to which such implementation costs can be minimised.

However, it is important not to exaggerate the negative effects of strategic change on people. Strategic change can also be positive: people may feel enthused by the new strategies. Their contribution may be more than a passive acceptance of the proposed strategies, resulting in even lower costs. Hence, another test of a successful strategic change programme might be the extent to which such costs are *reduced* beyond those identified in the strategy itself. All this will depend on the context of the change – the culture of the organisation, the way in which strategic change is introduced and the nature of the changes proposed. In brief, strategic change is context-sensitive.

Key strategic principles

- A distinction needs to be made between the pace of change, which may be fast or slow, and strategic change, which is the proactive management of change in an organisation.

- Strategic change is the implementation of new strategies that involve substantive changes to the normal routines of the organisation.

- In managing strategic change, it is useful to draw a distinction between prescriptive and emergent approaches.

- Prescriptive approaches involve the planned action necessary to achieve the changes. The changes may be imposed on those who will implement them.

- Emergent approaches involve the whole process of developing the strategy, as well as the implementation phase. This approach will also involve consultation and discussion with those who will subsequently be implementing the change.

- Strategic change is concerned with people and their tasks. It is undertaken through the formal and informal structures of the organisation. Understanding the pressure points for influencing change is important if such change is to be effective.

- Strategic change is important because it may involve major disruption and people may resist its consequences. Even where change is readily accepted, it will take time and careful thought. Strategic change carries important hidden costs.

21.2 ANALYSING THE CAUSES OF STRATEGIC CHANGE

In order to manage strategic change effectively, it is important to understand its causes. Strategic change can arise for all the reasons explored in Parts 2 and 3 of this book. Analysis of the specific causes is useful because it may provide clues to the best means of handling the change issues that arise. The two main classifications of the causes of change are:

1 Tichy's four main causes of strategic change;

2 Kanter, Stein and Jick's three dynamics for strategic change.

21.2.1 The four main causes of strategic change

Tichy[7] identified four main triggers for change:

1 *Environment.* Shifts in the economy, competitive pressures and legislative changes can all lead to demands for major strategic change.

2 *Business relationships.* New alliances, acquisitions, partnerships and other significant developments may require substantial changes in the organisation structure in order to take advantage of new synergies, value chain linkages or core competencies.

3 *Technology.* Shifts here can have a substantial impact on the content of the work and even the survival of companies.

4 *People.* New entrants to organisations may have different educational or cultural backgrounds or expectations that require change. This is especially important when the *leadership* of the organisation changes.

The implications of the above need to be considered in the context of the organisation's dynamic and complex structure. Tichy suggests that change is not only inevitable in such circumstances but can be managed to produce effective strategic results. This is explored later in the chapter.

21.2.2 Three dynamics for strategic change

Kanter, Stein and Jick[8] identified three causes of strategic change, one of which is the same as in the Tichy classification:

1 *Environment.* Changes in the environment compared with the situation in the organisation can lead to demands for strategic change.

2 *Life cycle differences.* Changes in one division or part of an organisation as it moves into a phase of its life cycle that is different from another division may necessitate change. For example, in a telecommunications manufacturer such as Nokia, mobile telecommunications would still be growing while network telecommunications might be in a more mature market phase. Typically, change issues relate to the size, shape and influence of such parts and involve co-ordination and resource allocation issues between them.

3 *Political power changes inside the organisation.* Individuals, groups and other stakeholders may struggle for power to make decisions or enjoy the benefits associated with the organisation. For example, a shift in strategy from being production-oriented to customer-oriented would be accompanied by a shift in the power balance between those two functions.

The description of such changes suggests that they relate not only to strategic change but also to other complex factors, such as the interplay between people and groups. The researchers suggested that the causes were constantly shifting, sometimes slowly and at other times faster. Essentially, such causal effects prompted the need at various points for substantive strategic change.

21.2.3 Analysis of causality

In practice, there is a need to define more *precisely* the causes that apply to a particular organisation. The above interpretations may supply some general pointers but precision will prove more useful when it comes to managing strategic change. Equally, the causes described above raise important issues regarding how strategic change then takes place. This is examined in Sections 21.3 and 21.4 from the prescriptive and emergent change perspectives.

Key strategic principles

- To manage strategic change, it is important to understand what is driving the process. There are numerous classifications of the causes, two of which are explored in this text.

- Tichy identifies four main causes of strategic change: environment, business relationships, technology and new entrants to the organisation, especially a new leader.

- Kanter, Stein and Jick identify three dynamics for strategic change: environment, life cycle differences across divisions of an organisation and political power changes.

- Precision regarding the causes of change is important in order to manage the change process effectively.

CASE STUDY 21.2

Counting on Carly: part 1

CEO Carly Fiorina directs strategic change at Hewlett-Packard

From the moment she joined the company as chief executive officer in 1999, Carly Fiorina began forging a new strategic direction for the US computer company Hewlett-Packard: she reorganised its organisational structure and reoriented its organisational culture in her first two years. This case explores the way the company has changed since her arrival – both in organisational culture and business strategy.

The story is picked up again in Case 20.4 at the end of this chapter. It ended in 2005 with Ms Fiorina being sacked. But to understand the reasons, you need to know what happened in her first three years.

The HP Way: the 'old' organisational culture?

Soon after Carly Fiorina arrived at Hewlett-Packard in 1999, she gave a presentation of her plans to the surviving joint founder of the company, Bill Hewlett. At this time, Bill was in a wheelchair and dying of cancer. But he remained fiercely (and rightly) proud of what he and his late partner, Dave Packard, had created: one of the world's largest computer and office equipment companies with a turnover of US$42 billion and over 100,000 employees.

Named after its two founders, Hewlett-Packard had started in a converted garage in Palo Alto, California, in 1939 making audio oscillators for Walt Disney's *Fantasia* and scientific instruments for the US Navy. It grew steadily during the war years of the early 1940s on the back of US government contracts and then branched out into the areas of business and consumer electronics in the 1950s and 1960s. Table 21.1 outlines some of the company's history in more depth.

Essentially, the company's two founders were particularly skilled at encouraging, supporting and then driving skilled employees to develop new products – moving into hand-held electronic calculators, personal and business computers, scientific instruments, electronic measurement devices and computer printers. The organisational culture of Hewlett-Packard was crucial to this rapid growth: it was called the 'HP Way'.

According to the founders' philosophy, the 'HP Way' encouraged and supported individual and small group engineering initiatives to develop business ideas. The whole atmosphere was ideas-driven and supportive, but it also had a hard-edged results side. Dave and Bill could often be seen walking individually around the Hewlett-Packard factories and offices – 'managing by walking around' as they used to call it. It was personal, friendly and socially aware. Its public face was summarised by HP – see Table 21.2 – but it is important to keep such an approach in perspective: some key growth

Table 21.1

The Hewlett-Packard timeline

Year	Brief company history
1939	Company founded with US$538 – Bill Hewlett was the prime mover in terms of ideas, with Dave Packard responsible for management. Both believed that finding the right people was more important than developing market opportunities.
1940–43	Sales rose from US$34 000 to US$1 million
1957	Company sold shares to the public
1957	Bill and Dave meet with a few senior executives in the aptly named hotel Mission Inn, California, to develop the principles that would shape the new company: the HP Way – see text.
1959	Opened first plant outside US in Germany, marketing office in Switzerland.
1961	Moved into medical market by company acquisition of Sanborn, analytical instrument business.
1965	Purchased F&M Scientific to consolidate medical instrument business.
1969–71	Dave Packard becomes US deputy defense secretary for two years.
1972	Launched world's first handheld scientific electronic calculator.
1970s	First PCs developed, first desktop mainframe plus the LaserJet printer: all reputed to be more rugged than competitors but also more expensive. John Young named chief executive officer by the two founders in 1978.
1981–86	Invested over US$250 million in R&D to develop new range of HP computers based on reduced instruction computing (RISC) architecture: particularly suited to business computing.
1987	Bill Hewlett retires: sons of both Hewlett and Packard appointed to the HP board. Family still retains strong minority shareholding.
1989	Acquired Apollo Computers to become market leader in computer workstations – merging the technologies loses HP around US$750 million worth of business.
1992	Acquired UNIX-based computer product range from Texas Instruments: business-oriented market served by purchase.
1992	New cost saving drive announced.
1992	Lewis Platt named as president and chief executive – formerly executive vice president.
1993	Dave Packard retires: died in 1996.
1995	HP combines its various computer operations, including its personal and business computing divisions.
1996–1999	Complete changeover of HP senior vice presidents – see text.
1999	HP forms a separate company, Agilent Technologies, for its scientific testing and measurement business activities: 15% shares sold direct to public immediately, with remaining shares sold in year 2000. HP concentrates solely on its computing-related businesses. This explains the sudden drop in turnover and employees in Table 21.3.
1999	Lewis Platt retires and Carly Fiorina arrives from Lucent – see text.
2001	HP purchases two companies to move HP more firmly into business computing market segment: application server specialist Bluestone Software and StorageApps.
2001	HP announces 6 000 jobs to be cut.
2001	Bill Hewlett dies.
2002	HP finally acquires Compaq after months of heated exchanges between company senior executives – see text.
2003	First 15 000 job cuts achieved in combined company to produce desired cost savings.
2005	Ms Carly Fiorina leaves HP. A new chief executive is appointed.

Source: Company documents, press reports plus company histories listed in references.

▶

▶ CASE STUDY 21.2 continued

initiatives were achieved by acquisition, as shown earlier in Table 21.1. Considerable efforts were made to bring such newly acquired companies into the 'HP Way', resulting in some delays to planned merger benefits.

Although the HP Way was originally developed in the 1950s, it was still relevant 50 years later according to Hewlett-Packard's CEO, Carly Fiorina. In the HP Annual Report 2001, she wrote: 'We are now entering a period of computing that defies all limits and crosses all borders, in which everything works with everything else, everywhere, all the time.' She continued: 'Since I arrived at HP, we've taken aim at the heart of this transformation, and set a goal to re-invent this great company: to restructure and revitalize ourselves to recapture the spirit of invention that is our birthright, and apply it to meeting customer needs. . . . As Bill and Dave understood, the real genius of the HP Way is that it's a legacy built on innovation, bold enough to embrace change and flexible enough to absorb it. The spirit of these original seven principles continues to guide us to this day.'

Although Carly Fiorina claimed that the company was still following the 'HP Way', it was not clear that the surviving founder, Bill Hewlett believed her. New competitors and new technologies had entered the market place – IBM reborn, Sun Microsystems, Dell Computers, the Japanese company Canon – and Hewlett-Packard was beginning to lose its way. Certainly in 1999, the dying Bill Hewlett's only reaction to Carly Fiorina's presentation was a terse request to his nurse: 'Get me out of here.' And this was only just the beginning of Carly's battle with the old guard at HP.

Photo: © Reuters/Corbis

There can be few people who have been more charismatic as company leader in the last few years than Carly Fiorina of Hewlett-Packard.

Early impact of Carly: the need to streamline the organisation

When Carly Fiorina arrived at Hewlett-Packard in early 1999, she quickly decided that there were fundamental problems with the company's organisation structure. The company was still organised as a series of separate divisions that allowed strong, decentralised, local initiative but meant duplication of valuable resources. The group had 83 product divisions, each of which was headed by a general manager with complete responsibility for all aspects of a business area from new product development to marketing. Importantly, the organisational culture of HP was also imbued with this long tradition of autonomy. The view was taken that duplication increased costs, so greater centralisation would reduce costs and increase profits.

'We have a lot of soloists in this company and what we need is an orchestra,' said Carly Fiorina. One of her best examples was the inefficiency created by the fact that HP had no fewer than 750 internal websites for employee training. 'Now why do we have that?' she asked.

The company had long recognised that there were major disadvantages with its decentralised structure. In his book *The HP Way*, Dave Packard himself told of an incident in the 1970s when working capital had suddenly started to rise for reasons that top management could not understand: it emerged that big customers were 'buying products from several HP entities to combine into a system. They were not paying for any of the products until they received the last one needed. We changed the procedure so that we were able to put the system together

---

and check it before it was delivered.' Although decentralisation encouraged entrepreneurial activity and specialisation excellence, such an approach meant that the group co-operated badly. Moreover, it meant that even obvious benefits of co-operation, such as ensuring that the same company made the different parts of a personal computer (storage, drives, central processor, etc.) were not undertaken. Thus, simple economies of scale became increasingly difficult to achieve and this put HP at a major cost disadvantage against its competitors.

Carly Fiorina had previous experience of managing a fundamental reorganisation when she was chief executive of Lucent Technologies, the telecommunications equipment subsidiary of the major US telephone service company AT&T. She made her reputation at Lucent and was voted in 1998 'The Most Powerful Woman in American Business' on the cover of the American business magazine, *Fortune*. She joined HP in 1999 and came with a strong marketing and sales reputation that did not fit well with the organisational culture of the company. Essentially, the senior managers there were all engineers with a production-led approach to strategic issues. Ms Fiorina was fearful on her arrival that she would be seen as 'marketing fluff' – someone who lacked strong operational skills. In fact, she was subsequently praised for her accomplished sales style and for bringing an important marketing approach to a high-technology company proud of its engineering history.

Two years after she arrived at Hewlett-Packard, she introduced a similar structure to that at Lucent. She combined the various operating companies into a very simple 'front end/back end' structure – see Figure 21.5. The front end would be customer-oriented and was essentially split into business and personal customers, with a separate section covering ongoing services. The back end would contain all the production and research functions, structured around product groups. In addition, there was a separate section devoted to services delivering ongoing and fee-earning relationships with major customers, who were not just buying products as such. The key to making such an organisation structure work is to develop the *links* across the company so that the front end and back end co-ordinate their efforts. HP attempted to solve this in three ways:

1 Keeping the structure simple – only three customer-oriented divisions.
2 Appointing a group of managers that reported to both front and back end executives.
3 Ensuring that back end units are not profit centres and therefore cannot sell their products direct to end-customers.

Perhaps not surprisingly, this reorganisation was not received well by some of the long-serving members of HP: 'The way it was done left a lot of product people feeling like the back end of the pantomime horse.' Some engineers complained that they were in danger of losing touch with customers. More fundamentally, as one external business school professor commented: 'They are trying to reach synergies between divisions when all their traditions are about autonomy.'

Even after the subsequent reorganisation, the company's profitability did not improve – arguably for other reasons, such as a downturn in its markets – and the management response was that the situation might have been even worse if the reorganisation had not occurred. But this did not help Carly's case with those that opposed the changes. Carly was clearly fighting some fundamental attitudes at HP but the battle was about to intensify further.

Figure 21.5

The new 2001 organisational structure of Hewlett-Packard

Front end:

- *Business Customer Organisation*: selling technology solutions to corporate customers – 20 000 employees

- *Consumer Business Organisation*: selling consumer items – 5 000 employees

- *HP Services*: delivering customer education, consulting and outsourcing – 30 000 employees

Back end:

- *Computing Systems*: makes servers, software and storage – 13 000 employees

- *Imaging and Printing Systems*: builds new printing and imaging products – 15 000 employees

- *Embedded and Personal Systems*: makes appliances, PCs and embedded solutions – 1 450 employees

- *HP Labs*: provides technological leadership for HP and invents new technologies – 850 employees

Group of managers reporting to both front and back end organisations

▶ **CASE STUDY 21.2 continued**

Table 21.3

Long-term perspective at HP – major changes needed in 2001

	1987	1988	1989	1990	1991	1992	1993	1994	1995	1996	1997	1998	1999	2000	2001
Sales (US$ billion)	8.1	9.8	11.9	13.2	14.5	16.4	20.3	25.0	31.5	38.4	42.9	47.1	42.3*	48.8	45.2
Net income (US$ million)	644	816	829	739	755	881	1 177	1 599	2 433	2 586	3 119	2 945	3 491*	3 697	408
Number of employees '000	82	87	95	92	89	93	96	98	102	112	122	125	84*	89	86

* After demerger of Agilent Technologies – *see* Table 21.1.

Source: Company Annual Report and Accounts

What strategy for the next five years? A new battle with the old guard at HP

Although there was clear business logic to the 2001 reorganisation, it was not enough in itself to solve the profit pressures that were now beginning to hit all computer and related companies around the world. The reorganisation had come at a time when three external factors were making business even more difficult for Hewlett-Packard:

- There was a downturn in the world economy during the period 2001 onwards. Large companies and small customers were tempted to delay investment in new computers, printers and related services.
- The after-effects of the dot.com bubble. During the late 1990s and early 2000, companies associated with the internet revolution had seen their share prices rise sharply and then fall as it was realised that the benefits of the worldwide web would take longer to emerge and would not necessarily favour small, new web-based companies. The result was a sudden drop in demand for telecommunications products, including associated computer-related equipment.
- Increased competition from companies such as IBM, Dell Computers and Sun Microsystems.

The results of these pressures were evident in the 2001 results of Hewlett-Packard: the worst set of profit figures for many years – *see* Table 21.3. The company needed a new

strategy and it needed to do something fast. The result was a battle between two groups:

- the old guard at HP – some of the earlier managers and the original Hewlett and Packard family trusts that still owned substantial blocks of shares in the company;
- the new guard at HP – represented by Carly Fiorina and her immediate colleagues who judged that there were no easy strategic solutions.

The old and new guard were to clash fundamentally on the new strategic directions for Hewlett-Packard in 2001.

Sources: See references at end of Hewlett-Packard Case study 21.4.

Case questions

1 *What were the main problems at Hewlett-Packard? Analyse the organisational culture and the power balance using concepts from Chapter 7. Identify also the business problems: strategic change needs to be seen in the strategic context of the business issues facing the company.*

2 *How would you categorise the strategic change analysis here?*

3 *What would you do at this point if you were chief executive?*

21.3 ## PRESCRIPTIVE APPROACHES TO MANAGING STRATEGIC CHANGE

In developing and implementing strategy, managers will need to consider how to *manage* the change process. For example, in the Hewlett-Packard case, the company clearly set out to manage its major organisational changes in 2001. Specifically, it undertook the following actions:

● It reassured its employees by careful announcements and explanations.

● It explained the reasoning behind making the new organisation structure more customer-focused.

● It promoted willing managers and ignored those who were against such change.

Two *prescriptive* routes for the management of change are examined in this section and then two *emergent* routes are examined in Section 21.4. The overall argument from the two sections is that the choice of prescriptive or emergent change is context-sensitive.

21.3.1 The three-stage prescriptive approach

During the late 1980s and early 1990s, research into change management by Kanter and her colleagues identified three major *forms* taken by the change process.[9] They linked these three forms with three *categories of people* involved in the change process, to produce a *three-stage process for managing change*. Their three forms were:

1 *The changing identity of the organisation.* As its environment changes, the organisation itself will respond. For example, it may need to react to a shift in the political stance of a national government. The dynamic is likely to be slow rather than fast, unless a political or other major revolution occurs.

2 *Co-ordination and transition issues as an organisation moves through its life cycle.* Relationships inside an organisation change as it grows in size and becomes older. Chapter 7 examined Greiner's depiction of the four stages of organisation development, with each being associated with a 'crisis'. Whether such a precise event occurs or not, the dynamic shifts associated with such change are predictable with regard to their pressures on groups and individuals. For example, the decision to create a separate division for a product range that is growing increasingly wide will give rise to change issues that are well known, but need management.

3 *Controlling the political aspects of organisations.* This results directly from the political pressures outlined in Section 21.2.2. Sometimes an orderly shift in power can be made but, occasionally, a more radical move is required – for example, the sudden departure of a chief executive 'after a clash over strategy and structure'.[10]

The three major categories of people involved in the change process were also identified:

1 *Change strategists.* Those responsible for leading strategic change in the organisation. They may not be responsible for the detailed implementation.

2 *Change implementers.* Those who have direct responsibility for change management (the programmes and processes that are explored later in this chapter).

3 *Change recipients.* Those who receive the change programme with varying degrees of anxiety, depending on the nature of the change and how it is presented. They often perceive themselves to be powerless in the face of decisions made higher up the organisation. In extreme cases they may object – for example some of the managers at Hewlett-Packard.

Essentially, the researchers observed that, in their sample, managing change was a top-down, prescriptive process. Emergent strategists would point to the obvious weakness in such an approach: the lack of knowledge and co-operation in advance is quite likely to cause anxiety and resistance. Prescriptive strategists would counter this by pointing to the difficulty of exploring a hostile acquisition with the change recipients before the acquisition takes place. Prescriptive strategists might cite a famous case from 1993, in which contact was made with future employees prior to acquisition, resulting in the workers eventually rejecting the offer. Volvo Car workers joined its Swedish management and a majority of shareholders in repudiating the proposed joint venture with the French car company, Renault.[11]

Comment

Kanter, Stein and Jick offer one way of structuring and managing aspects of the change process. However, their categories of people only give limited indicators of how to manage the process. Their model may also be more suited to major changes than the more common ongoing strategic process.

21.3.2 Unfreezing and freezing attitudes

In the 1950s, Lewin developed a three-step model to explain the change process:[12]

1 *Unfreezing current attitudes*. For change to take place, the old behaviour must be seen to be unsatisfactory and therefore stopped. Importantly, this need for change must be felt by the person or group themselves: it is a *felt need* and cannot be imposed. This process might be undertaken by leaking relevant information or openly confronting those involved.

2 *Moving to a new level*. A period of search for new solutions then takes place. This is characterised by the examination of alternatives, the exploration of new values, the changing of organisational structure and so on. Information continues to be made available to confirm the new position.

3 *Refreezing attitudes at the new level*. Finally, once a satisfactory situation has been found, refreezing takes place at the new level. This may well involve positive reinforcement and support for the decisions taken. For example, good news about the new position might be circulated, along with information about changes in status, changes in culture, re-organisation and reconfirmation of investment decisions.

Comment

This apparently simple model has been widely used to analyse and manage change. It tends to treat people as the objects of manipulation and does not involve them in the change process at all. However, it can be useful on occasions (see, for example, Figure 21.6 where the Hewlett-Packard case has been interpreted using the Lewin model).

21.3.3 Comment on prescriptive models of change

There are other similar models that take a prescriptive approach to organisational change.[13] We have explored the criticisms of the prescriptive approach elsewhere in this book and can summarise the issues here with regard to change models.

● The assumption is made in prescriptive models that it is possible to move clearly from one state to another. This may not be possible if the environment itself is turbulent and the new destination state therefore unclear.

● Where major learning of new methods or substantial long-term investment is needed for the new situation, it may not even be clear when the new refrozen state has been reached – the situation may be soft-frozen (as it probably was at Hewlett-Packard, judging by the back-room comments afterwards).

● The assumption is also made that agreement on the new refrozen state is possible. This may be unrealistic if the politics within the organisation remain in flux. Given that prescriptive models involve only limited consultation, this assumption can be shown to have real weaknesses in some cultural styles characterised by competition and power building.

● Such models rely on the *imposition* of change on the employees concerned. This may be essential in some circumstances, e.g. factory closure, but, where the co-operation of those involved is needed or the culture works on a co-operative style, the prescriptive models may be totally inappropriate.

Figure 21.6

Hewlett-Packard reorganisation using the Lewin model

Typical activities in the organisation	Lewin model	Hewlett-Packard case study example
• Realisation among group of need for change • Signals from top management that 'all is not well' (perhaps even exaggerated news circulated) • Data on nature of the problem made known throughout the organisation	**Unfreezing current attitudes** ↓	• Information about the current situation given to all employees after takeover • News that profitability and performance have fallen to unacceptable levels
• Specific call for change coupled with discussion of what is required • Views gathered on possible solutions • Information built on preferred solution • Experiment	**Moving to a new level** (State of flux: reactions tested to proposed solutions; organised debate and discussion) ↓	• Emotional reactions • Profit pressures • Use of 'soft' management contacts to probe feelings • Senior managers present at social activities • Decentralised structure leading to duplication and higher costs
• Make announcement • Reassure those affected • News circulated to show that new solution is working	**Refreezing attitudes at the new level**	• Introduction of customer-orientated organisation • New emphasis on HP innovation • Reconfirmation of the 'HP Way' set of values

Key strategic principles

● There are a number of prescriptive routes for the management of change: two were examined in this section.

● Kanter, Stein and Jick recommend a three-stage approach involving three forms of change and three categories of people involved in the change. Essentially, the route is a top-down guide to managing planned change and its consequences throughout the organisation.

● Lewin developed a three-stage model for the prescriptive change process: unfreezing current attitudes, moving to a new level and refreezing attitudes at the new level. This model has been widely used to analyse and manage change.

● Prescriptive models of change work best where it is possible to move clearly from one state to another. In times of rapid change, such clarity may be difficult to find and such models may be inappropriate.

CASE STUDY 21.3

StanChart chief swept out by culture clash

Tensions within Standard Chartered Bank came out into the open in late 2001 when chief executive Rana Talwar was ousted and the bank became a takeover target.

Rudyard Kipling once wrote: 'East is East and West is West and never the twain shall meet.' The ousting in December 2001 of Rana Talwar, the Indian-born chief executive of Standard Chartered Bank (or StanChart as it is known), may have proved the colonial author's insight right. Those who know the history of StanChart might have seen it coming: it has always been the bank where cultures have clashed.

When it was created in 1968 after the merger of Standard Bank, one of the leading banks in Africa, with Chartered Bank, its rival in India and East Asia, the two halves failed to integrate on the most basic levels. The Standard Chartered executives would eat lunch in the Eastern canteen, while their Chartered counterparts ate in the Western canteen. In recent years, the collision of the cultures is between the old and the new. The City of London was surprised, but insiders at the bank were not. Tensions between Sir Patrick Gillam, the StanChart chairman, and Mr Rana Talwar had been simmering for most of 2001 and had come to the boil in April 2001 at a remuneration committee meeting. The two men found themselves engaged in a shouting match over incentives, which left their fellow directors in no doubt that the relationship would not last.

StanChart, however, continued to maintain its British reserve. At the beginning of November 2001, rumours started to surface about Barclays Bank, one of the leading UK banks, considering a takeover bid for StanChart. As expected, StanChart insisted: 'We have a great future as an independent bank.' But behind the scenes, it was nervous. At the same time, tensions were growing between Sir Patrick and Mr Talwar. On a Tuesday evening in late November 2001, Mr Talwar was hosting a cocktail party for business analysts, accompanied by Nigel Kenny, the finance director, and Christopher Keljik, an executive board member. Meanwhile, a select group of board members had gathered in StanChart's cheerless City of London headquarters to decide Mr Talwar's fate. The meeting lasted one and a half hours. 'There was a clear divide between the executives who believed Patrick should step down and the non-executives who complained about Rana's management style,' said one board member present. However, Sir Patrick, who was not present at the board meeting, denied this. 'The non-executives were unanimous,' he said. Furthermore, he refuted suggestions that the tension was between himself and his chief executive: 'There was a culture clash between Mr Talwar and his bank colleagues.'

Reaction to Mr Talwar's departure

Mr Talwar's departure both surprised and angered some of StanChart's biggest shareholders. He was the second chief executive to leave in less than three years at a time of stiff

The Standard Chartered Bank is located in the City of London's financial district with its strategic network of financial contacts and knowledge, all able to influence decision making.

competition from rival banks. His predecessor, Malcolm Williamson, left abruptly after it emerged that he had held informal discussions with Martin Taylor, chief executive of Barclays, over a merger that Sir Patrick strongly opposed. 'Malcolm was not ousted,' Sir Patrick said. 'He had reached retirement age and had agreed to go to Visa.' The City, aware of Sir Patrick's domineering management techniques, found it difficult to understand why it was Mr Talwar who was asked to leave. Sir Patrick, aged 69, had already announced his retirement for 2003. Not known for his modesty, he claimed that his management style had never been questioned: 'I may be old, but I'm not old-fashioned. I am a dynamic, modern manager, even if I say so myself.'

But investors and analysts did also express concern over the board's choice of successor, Mr Mervyn Davies. First, they argued, was it right to hire from inside the bank? Second, if Sir Patrick disliked Mr Talwar's abrasive US-style of management, why had he chosen yet another executive who learnt his trade at Citigroup, the US financial giant where Mr Talwar had spent more than 30 years? 'This would not have happened in a world of true corporate governance,' said one large institutional shareholder in StanChart. 'What Patrick has done is appoint a chief executive who will toe the party line,' he added. Indeed, this is a view shared by many in the City of London. Mr Talwar was clearly ready to take on his chairman. One advisor said he had clashed with Sir Patrick and other old StanChart hands over his determination to promote locals to run the Asian and Asia–Pacific operations. This was not liked by the old guard, who wanted to deploy head office executives abroad.

Analysts were also familiar with these tensions. 'Rana used to tell them that they could not succeed in Asia if they had so many middle-aged white faces running the bank. He was right – how could he compete against HSBC or Citigroup in Asia with English bank executives? Times have changed,' one said. Sir Patrick refuted this, citing the cultural diversity of the bank: 'We have a Greek-American running the Emirates, Pakistan and Sri Lanka, an Indian running India, and Singapore run by a Singaporean, to name a few.' The cultural clash between Sir Patrick and Mr Talwar also started to concern the bank's financial advisers, Dresdner Kleinwort Wasserstein and Goldman Sachs, as well as their brokers, Cazenove and UBS Warburg.

Some directors were not convinced about a move to acquire Grindlay's Bank for US$1.3 billion, which had been initiated by Mr Talwar. However, given the lacklustre Asian markets on which StanChart had come to depend, expansion was necessary to find new growth opportunities. Others took a more measured view, suggesting that Mr Talwar was unlucky to be hit by a second economic recession in five years. But if economic conditions were to worsen and shareholders felt the impact, their patience was unlikely to stretch much further. In those circumstances, Mr Talwar's departure would force StanChart at least to consider a takeover approach. StanChart was now considered to be vulnerable to takeover, despite Sir Patrick's mission to keep it independent.

© Copyright *Financial Times*. Article slightly shortened by Richard Lynch from 'StanChart chief swept out by culture clash' *Financial Times*, 1 December 2001, p14 by Lina Saigol. All opinions and conclusions expressed in the case study are those of the *Financial Times* and its editorial team.

Case questions

1 *Undertake an analysis of the changes that have taken place in the culture and power balance across the company. What conclusions can you draw for employees and management?*

2 *With hindsight, would you have managed the essential changes at the merchant bank differently from the senior managers who undertook them at the time?*

3 *Is the company likely to come through the change period with success or will there be permanent problems?*

21.4 EMERGENT APPROACHES TO MANAGING CHANGE

From Section 21.3, it will be clear that there are occasions when prescriptive approaches to strategic change are essential, usually where some major shift in strategy is under discussion, such as in the Standard Chartered case. However, the human cost may be high in terms of resistance to the changes and the consequences that follow from this. Emergent approaches therefore deserve to be investigated.

Within emergent theories, there is no one single approach. Some emphasise the need for responsiveness in an increasingly turbulent world. Others concentrate on the longer-term need to change an organisation's skills, style and operating culture fundamentally and over long time periods. It is these latter theories that are explored in this chapter, since they are more closely related to issues of strategic change. The two emergent areas chosen for examination have already been explored:

1 learning theory, as developed by Senge and others;[14]

2 the Five Factors theory of strategic change, as developed by Pettigrew and Whipp.

21.4.1 Learning theory

According to Senge,[15] the learning organisation does not *suddenly* adopt strategic change but is *perpetually* seeking it. The process of learning is continuous: as one area is 'learnt', so new avenues of experimentation and communication open up. In addition, the learning approach emphasises the following areas:

● team learning;

● the sharing of views and visions for the future;

- the exploration of ingrained company habits, generalisations and corporate interpretations that may no longer be relevant;
- people skills as the most important asset of the organisation; and, most importantly,
- systems thinking – the integrative area that supports the four above and provides a basis for viewing the environment.

It will be evident that the learning approach can work well where the company has the time and resources to invest in these areas. The objective is for the people in the organisation to shape its future over time. (The Hewlett-Packard case included elements of this in Carly Fiorina's comment, 'Since I arrived at HP, we've taken aim at the heart of this transformation.')

Arguably, learning would not be so applicable where there was a sudden change in strategic direction – for example, the HP reorganisation. The gradual assimilation of change and the ability of employees to guide their own destiny is limited, if rapid change is imposed for outside commercial reasons. The learning approach appeared to offer little in the short term for Hewlett-Packard's 2001 predicament, for example.

Comment

The principle of the learning organisation appears to have a significant difficulty: precisely how and when companies should be developed into 'learning' organisations.[16] The outline concept is clear enough but the practicalities of how this is achieved are vague and lacking in operational detail. Egan has commented on the definitional and conceptual ambiguity in the learning concept 'which has stifled the practical adoption of what could otherwise be an extremely powerful idea'.[17] Garvin has attempted to answer these difficulties by exploring the management and measurement of such new processes.[18] He suggests some first useful steps that might be adopted to begin the process, e.g. *learning forums* or discussion groups in the organisation to tackle specific change issues.

21.4.2 The Five Factors theory of strategic change

Pettigrew and Whipp[19] (*see* Chapter 17) undertook an in-depth empirical study of strategic change at four companies: Jaguar cars, Longman publishing, Hill Samuel merchant bank and Prudential life assurance. They also undertook a more general examination of the industries in which the four companies were operating. Their conclusions were that there were five interrelated factors in the successful management of strategic change (*see* Figure 21.7):

1 *Environmental assessment*. This should not be regarded as a separate study but a separate function. All parts of the organisation should be constantly assessing the competition. Strategy creation emerges constantly from this process.

2 *Leading change*. The type of leadership can only be assessed by reference to the particular circumstances of the organisation. There are no universal 'good leaders'. The best leaders are always constrained by the actual situation of the firm. They are often most effective when they move the organisation forward at a comfortable, if challenging, pace: bold actions may be counterproductive.

3 *Linking strategic and operational change*. This may be partly prescriptive in the sense of a specific strategy for the organisation – 'This is my decision.' It may also be partly emergent in that the strategy may allow for evolution over time – 'But naturally our new strategy will evolve as we implement it.'

4 *Strategic human resource management – human resources as assets and liabilities*. These resources constitute the knowledge, skills and attitudes of the organisation in total. Crucially, some people are better than others at managing people. It is a skill acquired over time and needing a learning approach (*see* Section 21.3.1). Long-term learning is essential for the organisation to develop its full potential.

Figure 21.7

The five factors in the successful management of strategic change

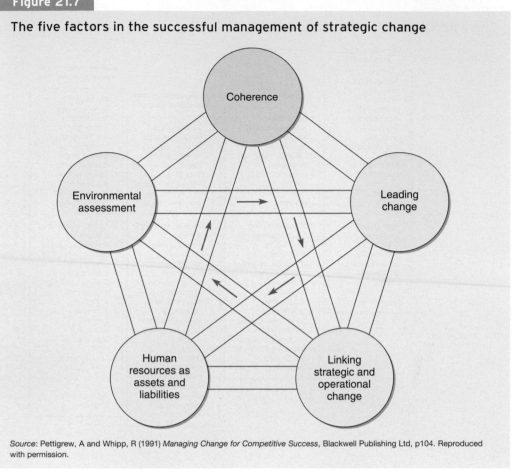

Source: Pettigrew, A and Whipp, R (1991) *Managing Change for Competitive Success*, Blackwell Publishing Ltd, p104. Reproduced with permission.

5 *Coherence in the management of change.* This is the most complex of the five factors. It attempts to combine the four above into a consistent whole and reinforce it by a set of four complementary support mechanisms:

- *consistency* – the goals of the organisation must not conflict with each other;
- *consonance* – the whole process must respond well to its environment;
- *competitive advantage* – the coherence must deliver in this area;
- *feasibility* – the strategy must not present insoluble problems.

Note that the five factors relate to the whole strategy development process, not just to the implementation process.

Overall, the organisation needs to be able to develop a *balanced approach* to change that is both focused and efficient internally, while adapting successfully to external changes. To assist this process, the researchers included two additional components for each factor:

1 *the primary conditioning features*;

2 *the secondary actions and mechanisms* which can only come into effect once the primary conditioning features are present.

These additional components are shown in Figure 21.8.

To illustrate how the five factors might be used, the Hewlett-Packard reorganisation (*see* Case study 21.2) has been analysed using this approach. The results are shown in Table 21.4. The model provides a useful way of taking the facts from a strategic change situation and

Figure 21.8

Characteristics of the five central factors

| | | Environmental assessment | Leading change | Linking strategic and operational change | Human resources as assets and liabilities | Coherence |

PRIMARY CONDITIONING FEATURES

Environmental assessment
1 Availability of key people
2 Internal character of organisation
3 Environmental pressures and associated dramas
4 Environmental assessments as a multi-function activity

Leading change
1 Building a receptive context for change; legitimation
2 Creating capability for change
3 Constructing the content and direction of the change

Linking strategic and operational change
1 Justifying the need for change
2 Building capacity for appropriate action
3 Supplying necessary visions, values and business direction

Human resources as assets and liabilities
1 Raising HRM consciousness
2 Use of highly situational additive features to create positive force for HRM change
3 Demonstrating the need for business and people change

Coherence
1 Consistency
2 Consonance
3 Advantage
4 Feasibility

SECONDARY MECHANISMS

Environmental assessment
5 Role of planning, marketing
6 Construction of purposive networks with main stake-holders
7 Use of specialist task-forces

Leading change
4 Operationalising the change agenda
5 Creating the critical mass for change within senior management
6 Communicating need for change and detailed requirements of the change agenda
7 Achieving and reinforcing success
8 Balancing continuity and change
9 Sustaining coherence

Linking strategic and operational change
4 Breaking emergent strategy into actionable pieces
5 Appointment of change managers, relevant structures and exacting targets
6 Re-thinking communications
7 Using the reward system
8 Setting up local negotiation climate for targets
9 Modifying original visions in light of local context
10 Monitoring and adjustment

Human resources as assets and liabilities
4 *Ad hoc*, cumulative, supportive activities at various levels
5 Linking HRM action to business need with HRM as a means not an end
6 Mobilising external influences
7 Devolution to line
8 Construction of HRM actions and institutions which reinforce one another

Coherence
5 Leadership
6 Senior management team integrity
7 Uniting intent and implementation
8 Developing apposite knowledge bases
9 Inter-organisational coherence
10 Managing a series of inter-related changes over time

Source: Pettigrew, A and Whipp, R (1991) *Managing Change for Competitive Success*, Blackwell Publishing Ltd, p104. Reproduced with permission.

Table 21.4

Analysing the five factors for change at Hewlett-Packard

Factor	Hewlett-Packard analysis
Coherence	• Defined by the single act of reorganisation • The arrival of the new chief executive • Restatement of the 'HP Way'
Environment assessment	• Drivers of the business were identified – customers, etc. • Emphasis on customer-facing staff plus careful co-ordination with the back end staff
Strategic human resource	• Clear understanding of the old engineering culture of some employees • Communication emphasis, especially core messages management • Careful presentations to staff across the group
Linking strategic and operational change	• Links between back and front end staff • Attendance of senior managers at informal functions • Motivation and customer focus
Leading change	• Individual responsibility: the role of Ms Fiorina • Accessibility of senior managers • Focus on key factors for success: customer focus, more centralisation, new innovation

Note: The factors are in the order relevant to the Hewlett-Packard reorganisation.

structuring them to highlight the important items. Where data have not been gathered on one of the five elements of change, it highlights this area. The model may also suggest additional areas that need to be explored in the organisation in order to understand the dynamic of change, especially in the area of coherence.

Comment

Although the comprehensiveness of the model is its greatest strength,[20] it is also its most significant weakness. Some of the factors represent truths that most would agree with, but contain areas that are so generalised that they may provide only limited guidance on the difficult issues involved in strategic change. Thus, some of the five factors needed to be treated with caution.

- *Environmental assessment* is a well-known factor requiring constant monitoring. However, the more detailed comments against this heading in the model provide more limited guidance than those in Part 2 of this book.

- *Linking of strategic and operational change* is an important area of study, but many would regard this as being the same as the 'implementation' process discussed by other writers and explored in this book.

- *Leading change* and its complexity has been recognised as a change factor for many years.[21]

However, the emphasis on *human resource assets and liabilities* is a welcome emphasis not present in some other analyses, such as Porter's generic strategies or portfolio matrices. Moreover, the identification, definition and logic of *coherence* as a major factor is also useful.

21.4.3 Comment on emergent models of change

Both the StanChart and the Hewlett-Packard cases illustrate the difficulties of using emergent models of strategic change. For whatever reasons, both companies found themselves being forced to undertake completely different approaches to their strategy:

- Hewlett-Packard under pressure to raise profit margins by increased centralisation.

- StanChart's need to remove the chief executive in order to change strategic direction.

It could certainly be argued that both companies had signalled the difficulties they were facing in computer markets and in international banking services, both to the Stock Exchange and to employees. However, the *emergent* models of strategic change, with their long-term approach to learning, provide only limited clues to interpreting the difficulties and suggesting how they might be tackled over this period. Nor, for example, is the abrupt departure of the StanChart chief executive handled well by emergent models of change – such departures are sudden by their nature. By contrast, the three-phase Lewin *prescriptive* model does provide a means of interpreting the events and their meaning for change. For instance, at Hewlett-Packard, the unfreezing came from Carly Fiorina's comments about the need for revitalising the company; the moving to a new level from the questioning of every aspect of the decentralised structure; the re-freezing from the announcement of the new reorganised structure.

Emergent models of strategic change have a number of weaknesses that may make them difficult to employ:[22]

- The 'long-term learning' approach of Pettigrew and Whipp[23] necessary to achieve emergent strategies may have little practical value where an organisation faces a short-term unforeseen crisis. There is no guarantee that the 'learning' that has already taken place will be relevant to the crisis. Arguably, the crisis may partly have arisen because the learning was incorrect.

- In some emergent models, increased turbulence of the environment is assumed as a justification for the emergent strategies. Such generalisations about the environment need empirical evidence. There are a number of environments that are generally predictable.

- A reliance on a learning culture may be counterproductive for some managers and employees. Some managers may refuse to learn because they realise that such a process will reduce their power.[24] Empowerment of some employees may mean that others will have less power and may react accordingly.

Overall, the way forward proposed by some emergent strategists often amounts to the need to introduce change earlier so that the organisation is better able to adapt. This may not be sufficient at the time when a sudden change hits the organisation.

21.4.4 The choice between emergent and prescriptive strategic change

The choice between the prescriptive and emergent routes is context-sensitive. Potentially, organisations may wish to choose emergent strategic change management because it is less disruptive and therefore has a lower cost. However, there may be occasions when the strategic circumstances force prescriptive change. The choice depends on the situation facing the organisation at the time.

Key strategic principles

- There are a number of emergent approaches to strategic change. The two explored in this section concentrate on the longer-term, learning culture routes to change.

- According to Senge, the learning organisation does not suddenly adopt strategic change but is perpetually seeking it. Hence, the organisation is using its learning, experimentation and communication to renew itself constantly. Strategic change is a constant process.

- Pettigrew and Whipp's empirical study of strategic change identified five factors in the successful management of the process. They were environmental assessment, leadership of change, the link between strategic and operational change, human resource aspects, and coherence in the management of the process.

- Emergent models of strategic change take a long-term approach and may have limited usefulness when the organisation faces short-term strategic crisis.

- The choice between prescriptive and emergent strategic change processes will depend on the situation at the time: ideally, emergent change should be chosen because it is less disruptive and cheaper. In reality, a prescriptive approach may be necessary.

21.5 DEVELOPING A STRATEGIC CHANGE PROGRAMME

The starting point for any programme of strategic change is *clarity* regarding the changes required. These will relate back to the organisation's objectives explored in Chapter 12 but may include a more experimental element as well. They may also need to be modified by some aspects of the implementation programme – 'the art of the possible' from Chapter 7. A strategic change programme might also include the introduction of a 'learning culture' as part of its way forward.

Furthermore, most programmes of strategic change concentrate on certain key tasks: for example, they may identify individuals or groups with particular power to make or break a proposed change. In this context, the organisation has the ability to make changes among many variables and would be well advised to consider all of these before making its selection. Since one of the main problems may be the resistance to changes that are proposed and another will be the need to persuade people to support the proposals, it is also important to give these matters serious consideration at the commencement of the programme. The change programme needs to address four questions:

1 What areas of change are available?

2 What areas will we select and why?

3 Will people resist change? If so, how can this be overcome?

4 How will people use the politics of an organisation?

21.5.1 What areas of change are available?

In Section 21.1, four general areas of activity associated with people, referred to as pressure points for influence, were identified – formal organisation structure, people, tasks and informal organisation structure. These can be coupled with three main areas of strategic change activity[25] to produce the *change options matrix* shown in Figure 21.9. In practice, every organisation undertaking change will need to develop activities in most of these options. However, for most organisations, there will be a need to concentrate effort and monitor results. Hence, it will be useful to *focus and direct activities more tightly*: selection among the options will be a priority.

Figure 21.9

Change options matrix

		Areas of people activity			
		Formal organisation structure	People	Tasks	Informal organisation structure
Three main areas of strategic change	*Technical and work changes* from the strategy to be undertaken	• Organisation of work and reporting • Strategy and structure	• Selection, training • Matching of management style with skills • Routines	• Consider environment, technology, learning, competitor activity • Learn and carry out new tasks	• Understand and monitor • Feed with 'good news'
	Cultural changes Style of company, history, age, etc.	• Managerial style • Mintzberg's subcultures (Chapter 15) • Handy's cultures (Chapter 7)	• Individual and corporate values matched • Management of groups and teams • Leadership choice	• Symbols, stories • Unfreezing • Make role models of key people • Clarify values • New recipes	• Awards, symbols • Develop networks • Encourage useful groups • Develop social activities
	Political changes Interactions and power inside the organisation	• Formal distribution of power • Balance of power between departments	• Use available skills and networks • Match with new strategies • Incentives and rewards	• Lobbying • Develop structures • Influence formal and informal groups	• Attempt to manage • Make contacts • Network and circulate

21.5.2 What areas will we select from the change options matrix and why?

The response to these questions will depend on the organisation, its culture and leadership. For example, organisations that have a history of top-down management might select items from the change options matrix that match this style of operating – that is, organisation of work and formal distribution of power – whereas organisations that have selected an open-learning, co-operative style of operating might select as their starting point team building and training and education. The clear implication is that it is essential to review the organisation's culture analysis: Johnson's *Cultural Web* from Chapter 7 should provide a useful guide here.

There are no universal answers. As we have seen, some researchers have recently tended to favour the more co-operative, learning organisation approach. However, it should be recognised that this may be a fashion of the turn of the century: only time will tell.

Whatever route is chosen, a more detailed answer to the question then needs to be followed through. As an illustration of the issues that can then arise, the *assumption* is made here that the co-operative, learning approach has been chosen. Within this route, Beer, Eisenhort and Spector[26] provide a detailed six-point plan on how to proceed, beginning by stressing that the areas to be selected for change should be chosen not by top management but by *those involved in the implementation process*. The six overlapping areas are:

1 *Mobilise commitment to change through joint diagnosis of business problems arising from the change objective.* One or more task forces might be employed here. They should represent all stakeholders in the organisation and be directed at specific aspects of the change objective.

2 *Develop a shared vision of how to organise and manage for competitiveness.* Senior management may lead the process but the identification of the new roles and responsibilities is undertaken by those involved in implementation. Typically, this will be through the task forces.

3 *Foster consensus for the new vision, competence to enact it and cohesion to move it along.* This book has already explored vision, competencies and cohesion. The key new word is *consensus*, which the researchers suggest needs to come from strong leadership at the top. New competencies may be required, resistance may build and some individuals may turn out to be more reluctant than others. Difficulties may be overcome by teamwork coupled with training to provide support. However, it is likely that leadership will also be needed.

4 *Spread revitalisation to all departments, pushing it from the top.* Change is spread to the departments that supplied the members of the task force. However, such change cannot be forced onto departments. They must be allowed some freedom, but they can be guided and revitalised by top management.

5 *Institute revitalisation through formal policies, systems and structures.* Up to this stage, the process has contained a degree of freedom of choice, experimentation and action. Now the time has come to 'refreeze' the procedures, both to ensure commitment and understanding and to provide the basis for future monitoring and controls.

6 *Monitor and adjust strategies in response to problems in the revitalisation process.* Having 'learnt' an area, the organisation should be able to repeat the process as the environment continues to change and more is understood about the changes already introduced.

With the emphasis on joint task forces and learning through doing, it might well be asked what role senior management can perform. The researchers suggested they had three prime tasks:

1 *To create the prime conditions for change* – forcing recognition of the need, setting the standards and monitoring performance. Hewlett-Packard senior management is a good example here.

2 *To identify those teams and organisation units that had achieved successful change and then praise them as role models for the rest.* Exploring why there were so many websites at HP is one example here.

3 *To identify individuals and promote them on the basis of their success in leading change.*

Finally, it should be emphasised again that this approach is suitable for one type of organisation but may not be appropriate for other types.

21.5.3 Will people resist change and how can this be overcome?

In practical terms, the issue of resistance to change is probably the chief obstacle to the successful implementation of strategic change. The reasons are many and the ways of overcoming them will depend on the circumstances. Exhibit 21.1 presents a list of some of the more common areas of resistance and suggests ways of overcoming them.

Exhibit 21.1

Resistance to change

Why people resist change	Overcoming resistance
• Anxiety, e.g. weaknesses revealed or loss of power or position • Pessimism • Irritation • Lack of interest • Opposition to strategy proposals • Different personal ambitions	• Involving those who resist in the change process itself • Building support networks • Communications and discussion • Use of managerial authority and status • Offering assistance • Extra incentives • Encouraging and supporting those involved • Use of symbols to signal the new era

---

More positively, resistance will be less if the change is not imposed from outside but developed by those involved in the change procedures. Change will be more welcome if it is seen to reduce, rather than increase, the task of those involved and to be consistent with the values that they hold. Change is also more likely to be accepted if it offers an interesting challenge and a change from existing routine. Importantly, change is more likely to be appreciated if the outcome is genuinely valued by senior management, who have wholeheartedly supported the process as it has developed.

21.5.4 How will people use the politics of an organisation?

In the context of strategic change, politics starts by *persuading* people to adopt a new strategy. It may not be a question of meeting open resistance but rather one of different priorities, different power blocks or differences of opinion on the way forward. The first step is usually to establish the organisation's 'ground rules': that is, any criteria that it has for the acceptance of projects, such as minimum levels of profitability and so on.

The more difficult aspects of politics usually begin when these criteria have been met but there is still resistance. Politics then becomes *discussion, negotiation* and even *cunning* and *intrigue*. The Florentine diplomat and writer Nicolo Machiavelli (1469–1527) remains well known to this day for his insights into the ways that people use the politics of the organisations to which they belong.[27] His writing appears cynical, devious and self-serving but he certainly understood management politics at its worst:

> *It is unnecessary for a good prince to have all the qualities I have enumerated but it is very necessary to appear to have them.*

On the subject of change:

> *There is nothing more difficult to take in hand, more perilous to conduct, or more uncertain in its success, than to take the lead in the introduction of a new order of things.*

Machiavelli saw little benefit in persuasion, except as a means of avoiding the alternative, which was to use direct force and possibly end up making enemies. His attitude was that reason mattered less than power, and human nature was best considered as acting for the worst possible motives. He would have chuckled cynically at such strategic change concepts as communication, discussion and empowerment.

In some organisations, Machiavelli still remains relevant today. Certainly, it is highly unlikely that major strategic change can be implemented if it meets strong political barriers. Strategists therefore have to be skilled not only at devising their proposals but also at building support for them through the organisation's political structure. Hence, it is important to understand how the *decision-making system* works in the organisation: this will include not only any final presentation but also the preceding discussions, consultations and lobbying. It may be useful to call for advice from those who have had previous experience of its processes.

Inevitably, the politics of an organisation will take time to understand. It will include the activities of other people and their interaction with strategy across a whole range of activities. People will have many motives: some good and some less attractive. They may employ many different types of activity that could loosely be described as political. Table 21.5 lists some that have been shown by empirical research to be important.

By definition, change involves moving from a previous strategy and therefore the starting point for the persuasion process might appear to be an attack on the existing strategy. However, politically this may be a mistake. It may force those who introduced the previous strategy to defend their decisions and therefore raise barriers to the new proposals. The people who are antagonised by the new strategies may be the very individuals whose support is vital for them.

Table 21.5

Politics in organisations[28]

Objective	Activities undertaken to achieve the objective	Reaction by superiors or rivals to the activities
Resist change of resist authority	• Sabotage • Rebellion	• Fight back • Institute new rules and regulations
Build power	• Flaunt or feign expertise • Attach oneself to superior • Build alliances with colleagues • Collect subordinates: empire build • Control resources	• Call bluff • Find heir • Reorganise department • Reclaim control of resources
Defeat rival	• Battles between units • Battles between staff and line managers • Expose mistakes (we all make them)	• Good leadership should provide balance
Achieve fundamental change in strategy, authority and leadership	• Form power group of key executives • Combine with other areas above • Inform on opponent • Leak damaging material to public media	• Intelligence essential • Recognise and cultivate those who are particularly influential • Seek out rival power groups • Respond with own leaks

Beyond these considerations, the person(s) responsible for seeking agreement to a new strategy will need to undertake several important tasks:

- identify potential and influential supporters and persuade them to support the new strategy;
- seek out potential opposition and attempt to change opinions or, at least, to neutralise them;
- build the maximum consensus for the new proposals, preferably *prior* to any formal decision meeting.

Finally, it is important to keep political matters in perspective. They are important but this book has hopefully shown that strategy does not deal in certainties. It is an art as well as a science. This means that there is room for differing views and the use of judgement and debate in arriving at decisions. Strategy is the art of the possible.

Key strategic principles

- The change options matrix sets out the main areas where change is possible: it is important within this to focus and select options.
- Selection from the matrix needs to be undertaken. This can best be undertaken by an understanding of the culture of the organisation: the Cultural Web can be useful here. A more detailed process to achieve change can then be planned out, with six overlapping areas providing a starting point.
- Resistance to change is probably one of the chief obstacles to successful strategy implementation. It is likely to be lower if strategies are not imposed from the outside.
- The politics of strategic change needs to begin by attempting to persuade those involved to adopt the new strategy recommendations. Beyond this, a Machiavellian approach may be necessary to ensure the desired changes are achieved. More generally, strategic change activities may include identifying supporters, attempting to change opposition views and building the maximum consensus for the new proposals. Preferably, this should be undertaken prior to any decision meeting.

CASE STUDY 21.4

Counting on Carly: part 2

The rise and fall of CEO Carly Fiorina at Hewlett-Packard

Following her earlier clash with the old guard at Hewlett Packard, the chief executive, Carly Fiorina needed to work out a new strategy to take the company forward for the next five years. This case describes the main market data and the choice made. It then describes how Carly was forced to leave the company in early 2005.

Strategic options available to Hewlett-Packard in 2001 – the strategic content of the debate between the old and the new managers

As a starting point to understanding the debate about the future strategic direction of Hewlett-Packard in 2001, it is relevant to explore the strategic options available to the company at that time. The options that follow are not the only way to segment the computer and printer markets but, rather, they present the options as Hewlett-Packard saw them. The four options explored below follow the way that the company reports its business activities in its Annual Report and Accounts – *see* Table 21.6 – with one exception. 'Computing systems' has been split into two subsections – personal computers and computer servers – because these two areas represent largely different market segments. Arguably, the presentation of only four options ignores other options that ▶

▶

Table 21.6

Hewlett-Packard: Segment information – printing systems are crucial to profitability

All data in US$ billions

	2001	2000	1999
Net revenue			
Imaging and printing systems	19.4	20.5	18.6
Computing systems, e.g. home and office computers	17.8	20.6	17.4
IT services, e.g. consultancy	7.6	7.1	6.3
Other	1.0	1.6	1.3
Adjustments	(0.6)	(1.0)	(1.1)
Total HP consolidated revenue	45.2	48.8	42.4
Net earnings before extraordinary items			
Imaging and printing systems	1.8	2.7	2.4
Computing systems, e.g. home and office computers	(0.4)	1.0	1.0
IT services, e.g. consultancy	0.3	0.5	0.5
Other	(0.3)	(0.1)	(0.1)
Corporate adjustments, including tax	(1.0)	(1.6)	(1.6)
Total HP consolidated earnings	0.6	3.6	3.1

Source: Hewlett-Packard Report and Accounts – note that numbers have been rounded so there may be some minor differences in totals.

might be available to Hewlett-Packard because it uses the company's existing segment definitions. More radical options involving a more fundamental redefinition of the market might be more beneficial.

1. *Imaging and printing systems: the competitive advantage of Hewlett-Packard?*

The basic printer market is mature. It has several distinct segments:

● the low-end, low-price inkjet printers, where Epson and Canon are the market leaders; HP introduced a new range to counter this in the late 1990s;
● the middle-range market, where Hewlett-Packard is market leader;
● the high-end, high performance volume printers where companies like HP, Brother and Canon have involvement.

The biggest printer segment is the middle market – *see* Table 21.7 – where customers range from home users to businesses. The method of distribution varies from direct telephone sales through retail stores to independent office

suppliers. HP is represented in all these areas with good quality, reliable products that perform well. Historically, HP's dominance of the printer market derives from the company investing over US$250 million in the 1970s and 1980s in the first laser jet printers. More recently, HP's development of combined printer/scanner/copiers has provided continuing evolution in the market. The company is now targeting the replacement film processing market as digital photography grows. New digital cameras no longer use film that has to be inserted and then developed but connect directly to a computer for printing. This has opened up a new printing opportunity for companies like Hewlett-Packard. One strategic option, strongly favoured by the old guard at HP, was to focus even more on the computer printer market.

2. *Low-end, domestic and small office personal computer market – HP is just one of a clutch of companies in the market*

Although the market is large and still growing worldwide, it is now mature, with relatively few major technological advances and much of the value added taken by the branding and related strategies of the leading computer chip and software suppliers – Intel and Microsoft respectively – *see* Chapter 1 and Table 21.8 below. Back in the mid-1970s, Hewlett-Packard pioneered the personal computer and was one of the early manufacturers with a desktop PC. By year 2000, the main PC manufacturer strategy for survival had become cost cutting. Dell began this process through its use of direct telephone selling, which cut out the *distributor's* margins and costs. Dell has subsequently followed this with a low-cost *manufacturing* strategy – using just-in-time procedures and flexible manufacturing to make PCs only for actual orders received rather than holding stock – *see* Case 9.1. PC customers have become increasingly value-conscious. Hewlett-Packard's products were seen as a reliable and well-engineered, but not notably better than others.

One strategic option for Hewlett-Packard was to reduce costs and build economies of scale through acquiring a competitor. It would then be necessary to rationalise the combined production and product ranges of HP and the acquired company in order to achieve the strategic benefits. For example, Compaq Computers bought two smaller rivals during the 1990s – Tandem and DEC – then employed this strategy. However, Compaq found that it needed time to undertake such a rationalisation strategy and lost momentum in the market place during the cost-cutting process. Nevertheless, by 2000, the Compaq Presario was claimed to be the largest selling range in the personal computer market and Compaq also had a well-integrated product range in the computer server market. The new guard at Hewlett-Packard were highly attracted to this strategic option, in spite of its difficulties.

3. *High-end computer server market – HP is significant but substantially smaller than the market leader, IBM*

Large customers, such as major businesses and national governments, have important computer requirements that are

Table 21.7

Worldwide computer printer market – HP dominates middle segment with rapid growth likely in digital imaging – before buying Compaq

	Printer and imaging market – worldwide	Market potential – five-year horizon
Total market size	US$50 billion	US$80 billion (by replacing film processing market and extending printer usage)
Market growth	+2% But imaging segment growing much faster	Market maturing in existing uses +15% in imaging segment *Long-term potential only*: Possible move into commercial printing: US$600 billion – currently served by other, related technologies
Market segment – imaging	US$18 billion (included in total market above)	HP developing this area along with rivals
Market segment – low cost printers	US$6 billion (included in total market above)	Canon, Epson important here
Market segment – middle market	US$26 billion	HP dominates this segment
Market shares HP Epson Lexmark Canon Xerox	 43% 14% 9% 9% 8%	 Xerox has now pulled out of the market for basic printers to focus on 'office services'
Others, e.g. Brother, IBM, Ricoh, Minolta	17%	IBM made losses on its printer product group in 2001 Dell does not sell its own printers

Sources: See references at end of case.

Table 21.8

Worldwide personal computer market – mature with relatively small HP involvement – before the purchase of Compaq

	Worldwide PC market 2001	Comment
Total market size	Around US$120 billion	
Market growth versus year 2000	+3%	Annual growth reduced steadily during the 1990s
Market shares Compaq	 12%	 Compaq grew via the acquisitions of Tandem and Digital during 1990s
IBM	9%	
Dell	6%	Dell cost-cutting strategy via new production methods – *see* Case 9.1. Company growing fast
HP	5%	Historically, HP has always been a 'follower' in market
Others	68%	Market fragmented beyond those above

Note: PC manufacturers have become assemblers of computer parts and software, with significant value added shift to Intel and Microsoft – *see* Case 1.2.

Source: See references at end of case.

▶

▶ CASE STUDY 21.4 continued

Table 21.9

The high-end computer server market – HP is significant even before buying Compaq

	Computer server and IT consultancy market 2001	Comment
Market size	US$47 billion	
Market growth	+5%	Market growth slowed because world economy has slowed and dot.com bubble burst in 2000
Market shares		
IBM	29%	Dominates market – uses proprietary and open systems
Sun Microsystems	23%	Important with proprietary systems – *see* text
Compaq	15%	Acquisition of DEC enhanced its market share in 1995
HP	6%	Has always had presence – has chosen open rather than proprietary systems
Dell	5%	Growing fast with cheap, reliable, open-source systems

Source: See references at end of case.

met partially by large computers. However, computer servers are also required: these route data within and between companies, they process data and they operate internal and external internet networks. In addition, such networks often require specialist design, set-up and maintenance advice in order to produce optimum performance. Such large customers have strong price expectations but also have even stronger performance requirements. Thus the high-end computer server market can also be coupled with the market for information technology (IT) consultancy. The combined market consists of the sale of computer server equipment and, in addition, the on-going provision of technical advice: this complex and multi-faceted nature makes the market size difficult to define precisely. Table 21.9 focuses on the computer server market.

An important complicating factor in the computer server market is related to the type of product being purchased – 'proprietary or open system'. Traditionally, the products sold by IBM and Sun Microsystems used computer chips and software that were developed exclusively by the companies themselves: *proprietary* systems. Such systems clearly deliver competitive advantage to the companies concerned because the customer is tied to that system and that manufacturer for any upgrades in the future – provided the systems perform well. Although a company such as Sun has competitive advantage from this route, there is also a cost: the ongoing need to invest in new chip and software development – typically US$250 million every three years. Some commentators argued that such investment would need to rise and proprietary technology would therefore become less attractive over time. Figure 21.10 outlines the options.

In recent years, some computer software developers (and more recently some companies) have taken the view that there should be more open competition in the market place. They have therefore developed systems that can be shared with

rivals: 'open systems'. Probably the most famous system is the Linux system, which can be accessed by any major software developer in the world. The main rival to the Linux system is that produced by Microsoft – Windows NT. It is important to note that part of the incentive for the development of open products has been a groundswell of feeling amongst software developers that Microsoft has become too dominant and restrictive in the market place – naturally, Microsoft rejects this argument and is fighting to preserve its presence here.

Figure 21.10

Options available for selected computer server manufacturers

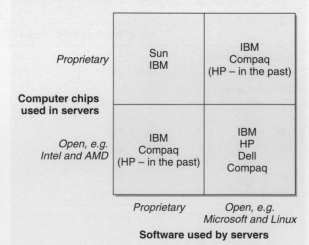

By 2001, shared software had taken off for two main commercial reasons. The first reason was that it was potentially much cheaper for the customers – all development is shared and openly available via the internet. The second reason was that IBM was willing to devote significant resources (over US$1 billion plus the use of its computer programmers) to its development and to its installation on its systems. It might seem strange for IBM to undermine its competitive advantage in this area. But IBM does not *need* this specific competitive advantage – because it has other advantages – and its support of open systems undermines the advantage of leading competitors, Sun Microsystems in servers, and Microsoft in software. An important company in the market place, Compaq, had also moved towards open systems, though part of its range still employed some proprietary systems.

What is the Hewlett-Packard policy with regard to open and closed systems? Essentially, the company has for some years supported an open policy. As a relatively small player in this market, it has had little option but to work with systems that will attract potential customers not tied to proprietary systems. The strategy meant that HP had to work closely with companies such as Intel and Microsoft to develop suitable products. For the new guard, an attractive strategic option was to acquire a competitor that would give Hewlett-Packand more scale in the server and IT market.

4. The computer IT consultancy market – the competitive dominance of IBM

Data on market size and growth in this market is not readily available. However, the market was worth approximately US$100 billion in 2001 and annual growth was around 5 per cent. For many years, IBM has been the dominant player in both the IT and the server markets. IBM has size, research facilities, skilled and knowledgeable staff and product range. In 2002, the company purchased the PricewaterhouseCoopers' (PwC) consulting group for US$3.5 billion to extend its grip on the IT market. This added another 30,000 consultants to the existing IBM staff of 150,000 operating in this market. It should be noted that Hewlett-Packard explored the acquisition of PwC in 1999 but could not agree commercial terms. IT Services have become the most profitable part of IBM's total business – see Table 21.10. Although it failed with PwC, the new guard at HP were keen to find another strategic option to move further into IT consultancy.

Choice between the strategic options at HP and the consequences for strategic change – the acquisition of Compaq

HP decided that the company simply did not have the scale of its rivals and needed to undertake a major acquisition. The big business opportunity would come from major customers, who required single suppliers to provide comprehensive technology systems and services. Moreover, the industry was expected to slow down in terms of market growth and new technology – cost savings, rather than new technology, would therefore be the focus of strategy. The acquisition candidate would have to be large and possess heavy involvement in

Table 21.10

IBM segment information – the importance of IT services

All data in US$ millions

	2001	2000	1999
External revenue			
Global Services/IT	34 956	33 152	32 172
Hardware, including servers and printers	33 695	37 811	37 453
Software	12 939	12 598	12 662
Global financing[a]	3 407	3 500	3 219
Enterprise investments/Other[b]	1 118	1 369	1 651
Total	86 115	88 430	87 157
Pre-tax income/(loss)			
Global services/IT	5 161	4 517	4 464
Hardware	1 303	2 702	2 058
Software	3 168	2 793	3 099
Global financing[a]	1 143	1 176	1 047
Enterprise investments/Other[b]	(317)	(297)	(697)
Total	10 458	10 891	9 971

[a] Sales of second-hand computer equipment and some leasing/finance deals

[b] Other business activities not relevant to IBM's major lines of business

Source: IBM 2001 Annual Report and Accounts – p102.

the IT sector to provide service for large customers. 'This is an industry that will consolidate and will required sustainable business models,' explained Carly Fiorina.

The search produced one candidate – Compaq Computers. This company was almost as large as HP and would bring a new dimension to the HP consultancy services. It was also strong in servers, personal computers and related businesses. Thus, Carly Fiorina launched a US$21 billion takeover bid for Compaq in late in 2001.

After discussion, the Compaq managers and shareholders resolved to accept the bid in early 2002. Carly Fiorina's problem was that some of the shareholders of her own company – especially the members of the original Hewlett and Packard families – were against the deal. Led by Walter Hewlett, the son of Bill, they fought the acquisition of Compaq for months. The opponents issued three reports attacking the acquisition, including a specially commissioned survey that showed that large computing company mergers have consistently failed. Mr Hewitt commented: 'HP optimistically assumes it can succeed where others have failed before. Given that past computer mergers failed during the greatest IT spending boom in history, it is far riskier to attempt a complex global integration during the current severe recession in technology spending.' However, it would be wrong to simply see this just as a personal battle between the old guard and the

▶

▶ CASE STUDY 21.4 continued

new at HP: there were important strategic arguments that deserved to be understood.

After a protracted battle, Carly won the backing of 51 per cent of the shareholders of Hewlett-Packard in May 2002. Compaq was to be absorbed into HP. But this was only the beginning of the strategic change that was then required to achieve the benefits of the Compaq acquisition: 'Fiorina wins the battle but now faces the war,' was how the UK newspaper, the *Financial Times*, summed up the situation. Hewlett-Packard had spent months working on the new merger organisation so was able to act quickly. It began by producing a combined new board of directors for the larger group, many of whom came from Compaq, including its chief executive Michael Capellas. The strategic change compared to five years earlier was remarkable. All the heads of the various divisions of Hewlett-Packard were new, with only the two senior staff directors remaining from the previous era – *see* Table 21.11.

With the senior managers in place, the next task was to gain the benefits of the acquisition. Walter Hewitt had repeatedly argued during the battle to secure the deal that technology mergers rarely work in practice – they were disruptive and involved too many painful cuts. Moreover, the merger would

have to take place against the backdrop of a downturn in the computer industry.

Hewlett-Packard's early merger strategy was to focus on customers: the company was keen to ensure that it lost no more than 5 per cent of its revenue base from such customers. Thus the company made early announcements regarding its combined product ranges, its branding policy, its combined website and drive to reassure major customers. HP needed to sort out such issues as overlapping product ranges without losing customers. Ultimately, the new HP needed to have the scale and service associated with an industry leader with a product range that would, in particular, serve the largest customers. At the time of writing this case study, this process was still ongoing.

In order to achieve the acquisition benefits, the combined company announced that it also needed to cut around 15,000 jobs – some 10 per cent of the combined workforce. It planned to undertake this task by the end of 2002 and expected to save US$2.5 billion costs on an annualised basis. There were also some difficult organisational decisions to be taken – labour laws, software system incompatibility and tax issues made it difficult to achieve some quick savings. For example,

Table 21.11

Senior directors at HP – the changing of the guard between 1996 and 2001

1996		2001 After acquisition of Compaq	
Chairman, President and Chief Executive	Lewis E. Platt, age 55	Chairman and Chief Executive	Carleton S. Fiorina, age 47
President and Director	None	President and Director	Michael D. Capellas, age 47 (from Compaq – see text)
Executive Vice President Finance and Administration	Robert P. Wayman, age 51	Executive Vice President Finance and Administration	Robert P. Wayman, age 56
V. P. Human Resources	Susan D. Bowick, age 49	V.P. Human Resources	Susan D. Bowick, age 53
Executive V.P. Computer Organization	Richard E. Belluzzo, age 43	Executive V.P. Enterprise Systems Group	Peter Blackmore, age 54
Executive V.P. Test and Measurement Organization	Edward W. Barnholt, age 53	Executive V.P. Imaging and Printing Group	Vyomesh Joshi, age 47
Senior V.P. Research and Development	Joel S. Birnbaum, age 59	Executive V.P. Personal Systems Group	Duane E. Zitzner, age 54
Senior V.P. Corporate Affairs and General Counsel	S.T. Jack Brigham, age 57	Executive V.P. HP Services	Anne Livermore, age 43
Senior V.P. Measurement Systems Organization	Douglas K. Carnahan, age 55	Executive V.P. Worldwide Operations	Michael J. Winkler, age 56
Senior V.P. European Strategic Initiatives	Franco Mariotti	Senior V.P. Information Technology	Robert V. Napier, age 55
Director Internet Program	William Murphy	Senior V.P. Corporate Strategy and Technology	Shane V. Robison, age 48

Note: V.P. = Vice President.

some national labour laws required consultation before any redundancies. In some cases, this meant that the Compaq and Hewlett-Packard sales teams were still in competition with each other until the merger was achieved. More generally, such cost cutting and major change was expected to impact on company morale. HP planned to move quickly in order to reduce such problems, but they were expected to take several years, given the additional problem of depressed conditions in the computer industry.

One person close to HP was quoted in the *Financial Times* as saying that the acquisition was never going to be easy but that Carly Fiorina had the full support of her new board. Turning around the company's entrenched culture would always be difficult and would attract criticism in some quarters. Continued board support for Carly now depended on her delivering the benefits of the merger. In truth, Carly had risked her job twice – first, in pursuing the merger against the old guard; second, in delivering the results of a new, larger and more streamlined Hewlett-Packard. Strategic change can sometimes carry real risks.

What happened next?

The cost savings were achieved, with US$2.5 billion taken out of the costs of merged group. The difficulty was that Dell Computers continued to force the pace in the personal computer market. At the time of the takeover, Hewlett-Packard's combined share of the worldwide PC market was 15.1 per cent and Dell's share was 14.5 per cent. In late 2002, Dell cut its prices but was able to cope with this because it had the best profit margins in the business. HP did not immediately follow because this would have swallowed up the profit margin gains from its merger. Eventually, HP was forced to reduce some prices. The result was that Dell's global market share climbed during 2003 to 17.2 per cent and Hewlett-Packard's share rose only slightly to 15.7 per cent.

Although HP regained some ground in 2003, Dell recovered market leadership with over 18 per cent of the market in 2004 and HP was struggling. Its strategy of taking on the low-cost market leader, Dell, was doomed to failure in a price-conscious commodity market. However, Hewlett-Packard's printing business was doing well. It had also been helped by the Compaq computer server business that filled a gap in its range. But Hewlett-Packard was still small in IT and consultancy services, which was the other booming area. By late 2004, it was in strategic trouble.

At HP headquarters, there were various changes in the main board of directors in early 2005. The people who had backed Carly Fiorina's appointment in 1999 resigned and were replaced by others who were more sceptical. It was only a matter of time before the position of Ms Fiorina herself was reviewed. On 10 February 2005, Hewlett-Packard made the announcement that had been expected: Carly Fiorina was sacked.

The London *Financial Times* thundered: 'Hewlett-Packard's decision to sack Carly Fiorina robs the corporate world of one of its most charismatic and articulate leaders and its most senior female executive. For all that, it was the right decision and one the board probably should have been made much earlier. Ms Fiorina's strategy had reached a dead end.' But that was not the view of the Hewlett-Packard board – they still felt that the basic strategy was correct. But a new chief executive was needed to drive the company forward: Mark Hurd from the American company NCR was appointed from 1 April 2005.

Case Questions

1 *What were the main changes made by Carly Fiorina? Analyse the changes using the models outlined in this chapter and use Case 21.2 as well.*

2 *If you were appointed as chief executive at HP, what would you do now?*

STRATEGIC PROJECT

Follow up the Hewlett-Packard cases of strategic change outlined in this chapter. What has happened since and with what results? Has there been any fundamental change in the management and its style?

CRITICAL REFLECTION

How important is ongoing strategic change in companies?

From the cases presented in this chapter, it is clear that one of the problems with the companies was that they only made changes after they were forced to change. Might it be better if all organisations were constantly engaged in some form of emergent change process?

Would this produce better strategy? And a better place to work?

SUMMARY

● In the management of strategic change, a distinction needs to be made between the *pace of change*, which can be fast or slow, and *strategic change*, which is the proactive management of change in an organisation. Strategic change is the implementation of new strategies that involve substantive changes beyond the normal routines of the organisation.

● In managing strategic change, it is useful to draw a distinction between prescriptive and emergent approaches. Prescriptive approaches involve the planned action necessary to achieve the changes. The changes may be imposed on those who will implement them. Emergent approaches involve the whole process of developing the strategy, as well as the implementation phase. This approach will also involve consultation and discussion with those who will subsequently be implementing the change.

● Strategic change is concerned with people and their tasks. It is undertaken through the formal and informal structures of the organisation. Understanding the *pressure points* for influencing change is important if such change is to be effective. Strategic change is important because it may involve major disruption and people may resist its consequences. Even where change is readily accepted, the changes will take time and careful thought. Strategic change carries important hidden costs.

● To manage strategic change, it is important to understand what is driving the process. There are numerous classifications of the causes, two of which are explored in this text, those of Tichy and Kanter, Stein and Jick.

1 Tichy identifies four main causes of strategic change: environment, business relationships, technology and new entrants to the organisation, especially a new leader.

2 Kanter, Stein and Jick identify three dynamics for strategic change: environment, life cycle differences across divisions of an organisation and political power changes. Precision regarding the causes of change is important in order to manage the change process effectively.

● There are a number of *prescriptive routes* for the management of change, two of which are examined.

1 Kanter, Stein and Jick recommend a three-stage approach involving three *forms* of change and three *categories of people* involved in the change. Essentially, the route is a top-down guide to managing planned change and its consequences throughout the organisation.

2 Lewin developed a three-stage model for the prescriptive change process: unfreezing current attitudes, moving to a new level and refreezing attitudes at the new level. This model has been widely used to analyse and manage change.

● *Prescriptive models* of change work best where it is possible to move clearly from one state to another: in times of rapid change, such clarity may be difficult to find and such models may be inappropriate.

● There are a number of *emergent* approaches to strategic change. The two explored in this chapter concentrate on the longer-term, learning culture routes to change. According to Senge, the learning organisation does not suddenly adopt strategic change but is perpetually seeking it. Therefore, the organisation is using its learning, experimentation and communication to renew itself constantly. Strategic change is a constant process.

● Pettigrew and Whipp's empirical study of strategic change identified five factors in the successful management of the process. These were environmental assessment; leadership of change; the link between strategic and operational change; human resource aspects; and coherence in the management of the process. Emergent models of strategic change take a long-term approach and may have limited usefulness when the organisation faces a short-term strategic crisis.

- The choice between prescriptive and emergent strategic change processes will depend on the situation at the time: ideally, emergent change should be chosen because it is less disruptive and cheaper. In reality, circumstances may make a prescriptive approach necessary.

- In developing a change programme, the *change options matrix* sets out the main areas where change is possible: it is important to focus and select options from the matrix. This can best be undertaken by an understanding of the culture of the organisation: the *Cultural Web* can be useful here.

- A more detailed process to achieve change can then be planned out, with six overlapping areas as a starting point. Resistance to change is probably one of the chief obstacles to successful strategy implementation. It is likely to be lower if strategies are not imposed from the outside.

- The politics of strategic change first require the persuasion of those involved to adopt the new strategy recommendations. Additionally, a Machiavellian approach may be necessary to ensure the desired changes are achieved. More generally, strategic change activities may include identifying supporters, attempting to change opposition views and building the maximum consensus for the new proposals. Preferably, this should be undertaken prior to any decision meeting.

QUESTIONS

1 How would you characterise the strategic changes at the three companies in this chapter – fast or slow? How would you describe their strategic management process – as prescriptive or emergent?

2 'The twin tasks for senior executives are to challenge misconceptions among managers and to foster a working environment which facilitates rather than constrains change.' (Professor Colin Egan)

   Discuss.

3 Identify the pressure points for influencing strategic change in an organisation with which you are familiar.

4 If strategic change is important, why do some people find it difficult to accept and what are the consequences of this for the change process? How can these difficulties be overcome?

5 'The sad fact is that, almost universally, organisations change as little as they must, rather than as much as they should.' (Professor Rosabeth Moss Kanter)

   Why is this and what can be done about it?

6 Given the problems associated with prescriptive change, why is it important and what can be done to ease the process?

7 Does the comment in this chapter that the way forward proposed by some emergent strategists often amounts to the need to start earlier mean that emergent approaches have little useful role?

8 Examining Hewlett-Packard in 2001 (*see* Case study 21.2), use the change options matrix to determine what areas of change were available. What areas would you select to enact the proposed changes and why?

9 Analyse the politics of an organisation with which you are familiar. If you were seeking significant strategic change in the organisation, how would you approach this?

10 Leadership may be important for strategic change, but is it essential?

Further reading

Bernard Burnes (1996) *Managing Change*, 2nd edn, Pitman Publishing, London, has a most useful broad survey of the areas covered in this chapter. *See* also Goodman, P S and Rousseau, D M (2004) 'Organizational change that produces results: The linkage approach', *Academy of Management Executive*, Vol 18, No 3, pp7–21 and Mezias, J M Grinyer, P and Guth, W D (2001) 'Changing collective cognition: A process model for strategic change', *Long Range Planning*, Vol 34, pp71–95.

Professor Charles Handy (1993) *Understanding Organisations*, Penguin, Harmondsworth, is still one of the best available reviews of organisational change.

Kanter, R M, Stein, B and Jick, T (1992) *The Challenge of Organisational Change: How Companies Experience it and Leaders Guide it*, The Free Press, New York, has some thoughtful guidance on strategic change.

A most useful article is that by Garvin, D (1993) 'Building a learning organisation', *Harvard Business Review*, July–Aug, pp78–91.

Professors A Pettigrew and R Whipp (1991) *Managing Change for Competitive Success*, Blackwell, Oxford, has some important strategic evidence and insights.

Notes and references

1 Sources for second part of BOC case: BOC Annual Report and Accounts 2004 available at www.boc.com. *Financial Times*: 9 May 2005, p26 interview with Mr Isaacs.

2 Schein, E H (1990) *Organisational Psychology*, 2nd edn, Prentice Hall, New York.

3 Burnes, B (1996) *Managing Change*, 2nd edn, Pitman Publishing, London. Part 1 of this book presents a useful broad survey of this area.

4 Handy, C (1993) *Understanding Organisations*, Penguin, Harmondsworth, p292 (see Chapter 7 for further discussion of Handy and note that his view is emergent rather than prescriptive).

5 Burnes, B (1996) Op. cit., p173.

6 Ansoff, I (1987) *Corporate Strategy*, 2nd edn, Penguin, Harmondsworth.

7 Tichy, N (1983) *Managing Strategic Change*, Wiley, New York, pp18–19.

8 Kanter, R M, Stein, B, Jick, T (1992) *The Challenge of Organizational Change: How Companies Experience it and Leaders Guide it*, The Free Press, New York.

9 Kanter, R M, Stein, B and Jick, T (1992) Op. cit.

10 *Financial Times* (1996) 24 Apr, p1.

11 *Financial Times* (1993) 1 Nov, p19; 6 Dec, p17.

12 Lewin, K (1952) *Field Theory in Social Science*, Tavistock, London.

13 Burnes, B (1996) Op. cit., pp179–86 has a useful summary.

14 For other writers, such as Levinthal and March, and a wider review of the research, see the references on the learning-based strategic route forward in Chapter 18.

15 Senge, P (1990) *The Fifth Discipline: the Art and Practice of the Learning Organization*, Doubleday, New York.

16 Jones, A and Hendry, C (1994) 'The learning organisation', *British Journal of Management*, 5, pp153–62. Egan, C (1995) *Creating Organizational Advantage*, Butterworth–Heinemann, Oxford, pp131–8, also has a useful critical discussion.

17 Egan, C (1995) Ibid, p135.

18 Garvin, D (1993) 'Building a learning organization', *Harvard Business Review*, July–Aug, pp78–91.

19 Pettigrew, A and Whipp, R (1991) *Managing Change for Competitive Success*, Blackwell, Oxford.

20 Egan, C (1995) Op. cit., p178.

21 *See*, for example, Handy, C (1993) Op. cit., Ch4.

22 Burns, B (1996) Op. cit., pp194–5.

23 Pettigrew, A and Whipp, R (1991) Op. cit., p237.

24 Whittington, R (1993) *What is Strategy and Does it Matter?*, Routledge, London, p30.

25 Tichy, N (1983) Op. cit., pp126, 135, 131.

26 Beer, M, Eisenhart, R and Spector, B (1990) 'Why change management programs don't produce change', *Harvard Business Review*, Nov–Dec, pp158–66.

27 Machiavelli, N (1961) *The Prince*, Penguin, Harmondsworth. There is a short article that summarises his work: Crainer, S (1994) *Financial Times*.

28 There are four sources for this table: Machiavelli, N (1961) Op. cit.; Mintzberg, H (1991) 'Politics and the political organisation', Ch8 in Mintzberg, H and Quinn, J B (1991) *The Strategy Process*, 2nd edn, Prentice Hall, New York; Handy, C (1993) Op. cit., Ch10; and the author's own experience.

29 Sources for both Hewlett-Packard cases: Company Annual Report and Accounts of Hewlett-Packard, Compaq, IBM, Dell, Sun, Microsoft and Intel. *Financial Times*: 28 March 1996, p6; 14 November 1997, p12; 21 January 1998, p1; 9 November 1998, p13; 13 April 1999, p20; 20 July 1999, p24; 16 November 1999, p35; 7 December 1999, p36; 1 December 2000, p22; 19 April 2001, p26; 9 May 2001, p29; 22 August 2001, p10; 9 January 2002, p28; 31 January 2002; p31; 1 February 2002, p12; 21 March 2002, p20 and 28; 9 May 2002, p27; 3 September 2002, p28; 10 September 2002, p27; 17 September 2002, p28; 12 November 2002, p27; 22 November 2002, p32; 19 December 2002, p12; 10 February 2003, p9; 11 March 2003, p28; 8 June 2004, p29; 13 August 2004, p12; 15 January 2005, pM5; 18 January 2005, p31; 9 February 2005, p24; 10 February 2005, p16 and 26; 11 February 2005, p15; 30 March 2005, p27, 29.

Chapter 22

BUILDING A COHESIVE CORPORATE STRATEGY

Learning outcomes

When you have worked through this chapter, you will be able to:

- explain how emergent and prescriptive approaches are part of one cohesive strategy process;
- understand how the organisation's various elements can combine to form the organisation's corporate strategy;
- evaluate critically whether there is one standard of excellence for all corporate strategy situations;
- examine the contention that contradictions and tensions assist the corporate strategy process;
- focus on longer-term strategy issues including purpose, value added and sustainable competitive advantage.

INTRODUCTION

Although corporate strategy has been explored as a series of separate elements – such as the resource-based view of strategy development and the consideration of learning-based strategy routes – the topic needs also to be considered as a whole. The purpose of this chapter is to bring these elements together in order to build a cohesive strategy.

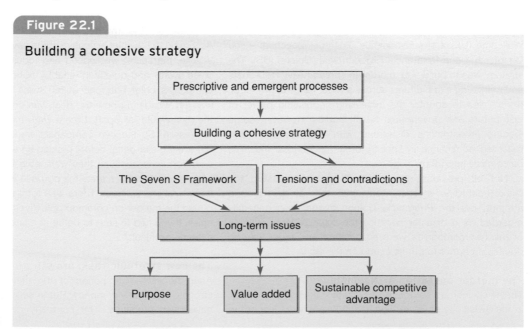

Figure 22.1

Building a cohesive strategy

One of the key distinctions running through the text has been that of prescriptive and emergent strategic processes: we need to explore whether these two areas can be combined.

One way of bringing the various strategy elements together is the *Seven S Framework*. This will lead us to consider the contention of some strategists that there is a standard of excellence – 'one best way' – to develop and implement corporate strategy: this deserves critical evaluation. Finally, there is a need to focus on some longer-term strategic issues such as purpose, value added and sustainable competitive advantage. The structure of the chapter is summarised in Figure 22.1.

CASE STUDY 22.1

Next steps for Novartis

In March 1996, two major Swiss companies, Ciba and Sandoz, agreed to merge their worldwide operations under the new company name Novartis. The immediate merger was successful but the company then faced the challenge of developing the next stage of its strategy.

Background

With 1995 sales of US$26 billion, Ciba was a medium-sized competitor in the global markets for pharmaceuticals and agricultural chemicals. In the same year, Sandoz had sales of US$18 billion and was more heavily involved in pharmaceutical markets with a range of products that complemented those of Ciba. Together, after the merger, the two companies formed the world's second-largest drugs company, with a market share of 4.4 per cent: at the time, only Glaxo Wellcome was larger, at 4.7 per cent. Subsequently, other mergers have taken place and Novartis has dropped down the list to number four, with around 4 per cent share. Both Ciba and Sandoz also had non-drug businesses that were subsequently demerged so that Novartis became essentially a drug and agribusiness company.

In their merger, the two companies were following recent trends in the pharmaceutical industry, which had seen some global consolidations over the previous five years: for example, Smith Kline (US) with Beecham (UK), Glaxo (UK) with Wellcome (UK) and subsequently SmithKleinBeecham – *see* Chapter 6 – and Pharmacia (Sweden) with Upjohn (US). The strategy was to build size in order to spread heavy R&D costs and marketing expenditures across a wider range of products. It was also to counter the increasing negotiating power of distributors and government health bodies. However, some leading industrialists disagreed with this approach and regarded dominance in specific drugs and critical mass as being more important.

Not all previous mergers had been successful: the GlaxoSmithKline merger went smoothly at the second attempt, but the Pharmacia Upjohn merger was generally regarded as a disaster because the organisational cultures of the two companies were so different and there was no dominant partner to put its stamp on the other.

The merger operation at Novartis

The newly merged company was located, like its two parents, in the Swiss city of Basle. Some 10,000 jobs were lost out of a combined workforce of 130,000 over the following two years. These occurred mainly in Basle but also in New Jersey, where both companies had their US headquarters. The restructuring cost around US$2.5 billion but was expected eventually to save US$2.2 billion annually. In subsequent years, this proved to be the case, with significant savings being made.

Ciba and Sandoz arranged the deal through an exchange of shares and so avoided the need to raise heavy debt to finance the merger. They then faced the problem of making the deal work in human terms. Although they were both Swiss companies headquartered in the same city, their backgrounds were very different. Sandoz was the faster-growing of the two, with a greater product concentration in drugs. Ciba had slower sales growth and had a stronger portfolio in some lower-growth chemical products. In the past, the two companies had not been direct competitors but they had been rivals in terms of culture and local civic pride.

However, the merger turned out to be a success. According to the chief executive of the new Novartis, Dr Daniel Vasella, the secret was speed and focus. Negotiations took place swiftly and quietly in 'shabby hotels' so that even the company's chief pharmaceutical Swiss competitor, Roche, was left wondering how the deal was completed. 'We knew the deal would fall apart if there were market rumours,' said Dr Vasella. So the two companies went ahead and sorted out every major detail before making an announcement. They were fortunate because they were able to agree on what is often the real problem area: the purpose and objectives of the newly merged venture. 'There was total agreement achieved during the merger on common objectives and common strategies. If you had to start to battle at a later stage, it becomes extremely difficult.'

The new strategic task: growth

After the immediate period of the merger, sales held up strongly in the new company. But in subsequent years, there have been problems. The company needs new drugs to

Figure 22.2

Novartis – performance of the company since the merger

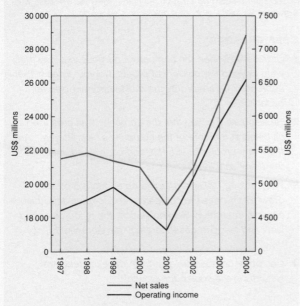

Source: Novartis Annual Report and Accounts 2004. Available on the company website at www.novartis.com – page 133 of the Annual Accounts – difficult to find on this website.

Figure 22.3

The main areas of Novartis's business

(a) Novartis net revenue by product 2004

6% 2%
9%
54%
29%

☐ Pharmaceuticals
☐ Consumer health
☐ Sandoz generics
☐ Over the counter
☐ Animal health

(b) Novartis net revenue by region 2004

17%
36%
47%

☐ Europe
☐ The Americas
☐ Asia/Africa/Aust

reinvigorate its portfolio of products. It is investing around US$2–3 billion each year in research and development, which is amongst the largest budgets in the pharmaceutical industry. The company had a wide range of drug products but for some years had no real blockbuster that would set it apart. For example, the company launched five new medicines in February 2001, but some did not live up to expectations. However, further drug approvals were gained in August 2001 so that the double-digit sales growth was still possible for at least another year. This has continued in later years with the success of new drugs such as Diovan for hypertension, Lotrel for cardiovascular treatments and Glivec for leukaemia. The company's record is summarised in Figure 22.2 and the source of its sales in Figure 22.3.

Organisation and purpose

According to Dr Vasella, there is another important aspect to growth: organisation and purpose. He believes that drug companies conducting research in a number of countries and subsidiaries often lack the knowledge-sharing necessary for the new breakthrough. A small advance in one subsidiary might be ignored by that company. Yet, if the same development was shared around the group, it might represent the final element in a major drug development for another part of the company. 'That is why I hate fiefdoms,' says Dr Vasella. 'They are extremely bad for companies like ours. With decentralisation

and strong local managers, there is always that danger . . . and there are small pockets of resistance.' However, this approach to central co-operation and knowledge sharing has upset some senior managers who feel that there may be too much centralisation: 'He's sometimes a bit too controlling,' commented one of his boardroom colleagues.

Dr Vasella responded by pointing to the importance of developing the purpose of Novartis. 'Being a good manager is to formulate a purpose of the company, to picture a future [that] people can imagine and embrace.' He saw purpose not only in sales and profit terms but also as a means of communicating the good things about working for the new company. But that still left him and his colleagues with the task of developing a viable strategy that would go beyond the immediate cost savings of the merged company. He needed to develop a growth strategy.

Strategic move into generics

Although pharmaceutical companies are struggling to maintain their growth rates in new drugs, there has been one major growth area over the last ten years – generic pharmaceuticals. These are the drugs that were invented at least ten years ago and then came out of patent. They can be up to 80 per cent cheaper after the patent has expired and any pharmaceutical company can make them. In practice, what has happened is that specialist drug companies have been set up to manufacture and distribute such products. The market for generics has been growing at over 20 per cent per annum for some years. Around US$69 billion sales of patented drugs will lose protection by 2009.

The difficulty for the major drug manufacturers is that generic drugs can be 80 per cent cheaper than the original product, i.e. the profit margins drop dramatically. In other words, generics are just commodity products that rely on low-cost, high-quality manufacturing techniques. They require core competencies that are different from the large R&D-oriented drug manufacturers typically spending US$800 million to get a new drug to market. The benefit is that there are large customers – the major hospitals and health care providers – who are looking to cut prices and are therefore willing buyers of such drugs.

Why is this relevant to Novartis? Essentially because Novarits – unlike most of the other major pharmaceutical companies – took a strategic decision several years ago to move into generics. It used its Sandoz brand as the basis of its activity and acquired two companies for a total purchase price of US$8.3 billion in 2005. The deal will make Novartis the largest generics company in the world.

Note: The case of Novartis's Swiss competitor, Roche, is considered later in this chapter.

Case questions

1 Dr Vasella defined the company's purpose in a way that went beyond the delivery of profits. Do you agree with this approach? Or are profits the most important element by far?

2 He also saw the way that the company was organised as being at the core of the company's new strategy. Are there any problems with this approach? And, if so, are there any solutions?

3 Will a strong R&D programme be enough to provide growth? Or does the company need to consider other aspects of strategy like knowledge, the resource-based view and learning-based strategy development? If so, how?

4 Can other companies learn from the experience of Novartis in the search for growth?

22.1 COHESION IN PRESCRIPTIVE AND EMERGENT PROCESSES

During the course of this book, both prescriptive and emergent processes have been used to explore various strategic issues. At the same time, it has been pointed out that these two headline words are just shorthand for a broader range of strategic approaches that have been favoured by different strategic writers. The two particular approaches were identified because they are representative of those broader routes and because they provided a convenient contrast in the treatment of the issues of strategic content, process and context.

Having reached this stage in the text, it is now appropriate to consider whether there really are a number of different approaches to strategy development or whether they would be better considered as aspects of the same strategic development task.

22.1.1 Two contrasting approaches?

In Parts 2 and 3 both prescriptive and emergent approaches were used at different times to develop corporate strategy. For example, in Case study 22.1 the environment and resources at Novartis can be analysed in prescriptive terms – such an analysis would show that the market was becoming more competitive and, at the same time, the company was forced to invest substantial funds on research into new products to attract new customers. However, some of this expenditure was inevitably experimental and unlikely to be successful, which has an emergent aspect.

In Part 4, the purpose of the organisation included prescriptive elements – such as the definition of the mission and objectives – and emergent elements such as the exploration of knowledge and innovation. This contrast can be seen in a company like Novartis, which chose not only to define its purpose in terms of profit but also to acknowledge other aspects of the purpose that involved sharing knowledge amongst its subsidiaries.

In Part 5, the process of developing strategy first considered the prescriptive route of options and choice and then considered the emergent process in Chapter 15. Part 6 has used both approaches, where appropriate. Thus at Novartis, it was possible to identify the prescriptive solutions that were used for the cost-cutting task essential to gain the benefits of the merger. However, it was also possible to identify broader, emergent strategies related to new drug developments that were also being pursued and were more experimental in their results.

In strategic terms, it is possible to develop prescriptive and emergent approaches to strategy development. While acknowledging the reality of a broader range of strategic routes, this book has chosen to concentrate on these two generic approaches as a device to explore the main issues. This is useful in highlighting various important issues that arise in the development of strategy, especially those contrasting the analytical – *prescriptive* – with the more entrepreneurial – *emergent*.

22.1.2 Better combined: one approach with a number of facets

Some strategists might recommend that corporate strategy concentrates on one approach rather than another: many strategy texts only explore one route – the prescriptive – in any depth. However, this book has demonstrated that an eclectic approach is more productive. Both prescriptive and emergent routes have their contributions to make: one is logical and follows from the evidence of markets, financial criteria and specific targets; the other is more creative, open-ended and experimental. In many respects, these two routes reflect the modern trend in scientific development to consider both rational and post-modern approaches.

To concentrate on just one approach would be to miss important elements of the other. This book takes the view that there is one corporate strategy process but it has *at least* two facets: prescriptive and emergent.

In reality, strategic content, process and context have a number of facets: knowledge-based, learning-based, negotiation-based and so on – *see* Chapters 14 and 15 for some of the routes. In essence, the development of corporate strategy is better aided by combining the various strategic processes, rather than concentrating on one of them.

Key strategic principles

- Although prescriptive and emergent processes have been one of the themes of this text, they have been used as shorthand for a number of approaches to strategy development.

- It is possible to analyse many strategic tasks from prescriptive and emergent perspectives. This is useful in highlighting various important issues that arise in the development of strategy, especially those contrasting the analytical with the entrepreneurial.

- This book has demonstrated that an eclectic approach is preferable. The combination of a number of strategic approaches allows different aspects of the strategic problem to be explored.

- The strategic process has a number of facets which go beyond prescriptive and emergent approaches. All of them provide insights and guidance in the development of corporate strategy.

22.2 COMBINING THE ELEMENTS OF CORPORATE STRATEGY: THE 'SEVEN S FRAMEWORK'

One way of building a cohesive strategy is to use the 'Seven S Framework'. This is explored in the early parts of this section. The concept led to the proposition that there was 'one best way' of developing corporate strategy. Such an approach deserves to be evaluated critically.

Finally, an alternative to the 'Seven S Framework' is explored; this examines the contradictions in strategy development and attempts to bring them together. Again, this approach to cohesive strategy deserves to be examined critically.

22.2.1 Background

Back in the 1970s, the well-known US consultancy company Boston Consulting Group was highly successful with its launch of the product portfolio matrix of problem children, cash cows, dogs and stars. One of its chief rivals, McKinsey & Co, charged four of its consultants with the task of finding a rival model to analyse organisations. The result was the *Seven S Framework*. The four consultants were Richard Pascale and Tony Athos (who published the diagram in their book *The Art of Japanese Management*), and Tom Peters and Bob Waterman (who published the same diagram in their book *In Search of Excellence*).[2]

The purpose of the model was to show the *interrelationships* between different aspects of corporate strategy. It was developed out of a realisation that the effective corporate strategy was more than merely a group of analytical tools, organisation structures and strategies: this is the disadvantage of the dissecting approach that has been adopted throughout this book. The elements need to be brought together. For example, the way that Novartis is now being combined into one company will involve a large number of elements, all of which are important in themselves but together will forge a totally new company.

22.2.2 The 'Seven S Framework'

The framework has no obvious starting point: *all the elements are equally important*. Moreover, all the elements are interconnected, so that altering one element may well impact on others. Fundamentally, the framework makes the point that effective strategy is more than individual subjects such as strategy development or organisational change – it is the relationship between strategy, structure and systems, coupled with skills, style, staff and superordinate goals.[3]

● *Strategy* – the route that the company has chosen to achieve competitive success (*see* Chapters 14 and 15).
● *Structure* – the organisational structure of the company (*see* Chapter 16).
● *Systems* – the procedures that make the organisation work: everything from capital budgeting to customer handling (*see* Chapter 17).
● *Style* – the way the company conducts its business, epitomised especially by those at the top (*see* Chapters 10 and 16).
● *Staff* – the pool of people who need to be developed, challenged and encouraged (*see* Chapter 7).
● *Skills* – not just the collection of skills that the organisation has but the particular combinations that help it to excel. The resource-based view was a concept invented after the framework but may at least partially capture the special nature of skills (*see* Chapters 6 and 13).
● *Superordinate goals*. This means goals 'of a higher order' and expresses the values, concepts and vision that senior management brings to the organisation (*see* Chapters 10, 11 and 12).

The framework is shown in Figure 22.4.

As a minimum, the framework provides a checklist of important variables for evaluation of proposed strategy developments. More fundamentally, it provides a structure for the network of interrelationships that exist between the various elements, especially when an organisation is ensuring that they are all *coherent* during the strategy process. For example, its application to the Novartis merger would show the many varied links that need to be developed in the new combined organisation.

Figure 22.4

The Seven S Framework

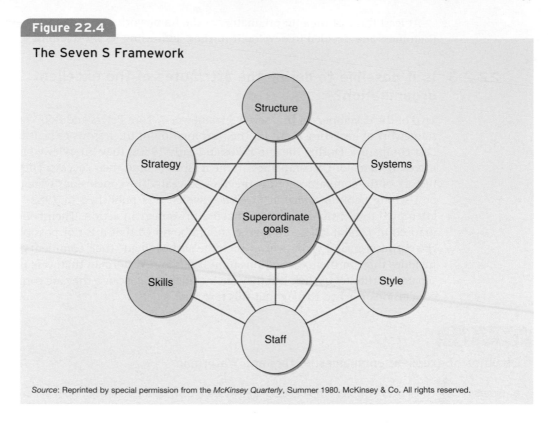

A particularly useful distinction is drawn by the developers of the framework between its *hard* elements – strategy, structure and systems – and its *soft* elements – style, skills, staff and superordinate goals. The hard elements are more tangible and definite, and so they are often the ones that gain the greater attention, even in some books. However, the soft elements are equally important, even if they are less easy to measure, assess and plan. The comments of some Novartis workers on not wishing to wait and see if they had jobs in the new, merged company is a good example of soft issues at work: certainly Novartis fully accepted that the way the company treated its workers was just as important as its merger strategy.

Comment

The framework provides a way of examining the organisation and what contributes to its success. It is good at capturing the importance of the *links between the various elements* and, for this reason, it appears at this point in the text. However, Peters and Waterman used it only as the *starting point* for their search for more detailed interconnections. The framework shows that relationships exist and it provides some limited clues as to what constitutes more effective strategy and implementation. Beyond this, however, it is not precise: for example, *strategy* is just that and nothing more. Essentially, the framework says little about the *how* and the *why* of interrelationships. The model is therefore poor at explaining the logic and the methodology in developing the links between the elements.

A further weakness is that the model does not highlight or emphasise other areas that have subsequently been identified as being important for corporate strategy, such as:

- innovation;
- knowledge;
- customer-driven service;
- quality.

At least three of the four originators of the framework were not entirely satisfied with its usefulness and decided to develop it further, addressing its shortcomings.

22.2.3 Is it possible to define the attributes of the excellent organisation?

Two of the developers of the 'Seven S Framework', Tom Peters and Bob Waterman, used the framework as a starting point for their exploration of the lessons to be learnt from the US's best companies. During the late 1970s and early 1980s, they interviewed many senior executives in 43 major US companies on the reasons behind their success. They also tracked the history of the companies for the previous 25 years. The conclusions were presented in their best-selling book *In Search of Excellence*, which was published in 1982.[4] Essentially, they attempted to identify the best US practice of strategy in action. Their conclusions are summarised in Exhibit 22.1, although it should be noted that it is not possible to do justice to the enthusiasm and vigour with which the authors made their comments. Exhibit 22.1 also includes three further observations from Peters and Waterman that were not highlighted as separate attributes in their list: they are included here because they are consistent with other conclusions reached throughout this text.

Exhibit 22.1

Qualities of excellent companies: Peters and Waterman

- *Operate on loose–tight principles*. The best companies were both tightly controlled from the centre and yet, at the same time, encouraged entrepreneurship.

- *Incline towards taking action*. There may be analysis, but there is always a bias towards practical and fast solutions where possible.

- *Close to the customer*. The best companies offered customers quality, reliability and service.

- *Innovative autonomy*. Responsibility is moved to individuals, who are encouraged to be as innovative as possible.

- *Simplicity of organisational form*. Organisation structures work better when they are clear and simple and have well-defined lines of authority and responsibility. Matrix management structures were not to be encouraged because they were too complex. When organisations were organised simply, they were more able to combine quickly into effective teams, task forces and project groups.

- *The importance of the people resource, not just as an abstract concept but as individuals to be respected*. The better companies not only made tough demands on employees but also treated them as individuals to be trained, developed and given new and interesting challenges.

- *Clarity regarding the organisation's values and mission*. In the best companies, many employees were clear both about the company's values and about why such values had been chosen. Better companies made a significant attempt to communicate, debate and seek to inspire all within the organisation.

- *Stick to the knitting*. Organisations may diversify into other related areas but the companies that do best are the ones that concentrate on their core skills. Companies should not move into unrelated areas.

In addition, three other elements of excellent companies can be identified from the Peters and Waterman research that are consistent with other areas of this book:

- *Excellent companies have flexible organisation structures*. This flexibility enables them to respond quickly to changes in the environment.

- *Excellent companies have quite distinctive cultures*. The company culture integrates the organisation's desire to meet its defined mission and objectives with two other important areas: serving customers and providing satisfying work for its employees.

- *Successful strategy emerges through purposeful, but essentially unpredictable, evolution*. Excellent companies are learning organisations that adapt their strategy as the environment changes through experimentation, challenge and permitting failure.

Source: See reference[5].

Without doubt, Peters and Waterman took the view that it *was* possible to define the attributes of the excellent organisation. They identified eight attributes that characterised the excellent, innovative companies. 'Most of the attributes are not startling. Some, if not most, are motherhoods.'[6] Not all the eight were present or conspicuous to the same degree in all of the excellent companies, but in every case a preponderance was present. The authors noted that, when they presented the material to students who had no business experience, the response was occasionally boredom[7] because students felt that some of the conclusions were self-evident. In such cases, the authors pointed out that their empirical evidence showed that many US companies *did not follow* such 'self-evident' best practice.

Comment

Unfortunately, as Tom Peters himself pointed out in 1992,[8] many of the excellent companies described in this book, *In Search of Excellence*, went through major strategic difficulties during the 1980s. For example, the original sample included extensive and enthusiastic endorsement of IBM's strategies: Chapter 1 showed what happened to that company in the 1980s and 1990s. The overall result has been to cast doubt on the evidence and conclusions of the original research. This has not stopped Mr Peters pursuing some of the major conclusions in his later research and writings. He remains one of the major gurus of the early twenty-first century (*see* the Key Reading later in this chapter). Essentially, he has focused even more on empowerment, innovation and the use of local initiatives rather than central direction in strategy.

One of Peters' original co-developers of the 'Seven S Framework', Richard Pascale,[9] pointed out that, within five years of publication, two-thirds of the 'excellent' companies had slipped from their pinnacle, with some in serious trouble, e.g. Atari Computers and Wang Office Systems. He also criticised the *methodology* of the research:

> *Simply identifying attributes of success is like identifying attributes of people in excellent health during the age of the bubonic plague . . . The true path to insight required a study of both the sick and the healthy.*

Two issues arise from the above:

1 *How reliable are the conclusions of Peters and Waterman?* Pascale is correct: the methodology is flawed. However, the conclusions are not inconsistent with other areas covered in this book. For example, it was Lawrence and Lorsch who first produced empirical evidence of the *loose–tight* principle.[10] The conclusions are largely reliable because, as Peters and Waterman said, the recommendations are 'not startling'. In truth, they support some important areas of strategy development and perhaps oversimplify others. Moreover, their research is being assessed with hindsight. In fairness, it is easier to be wise after the events have taken place.

2 *Is it possible to identify universal recipes for excellence?* This is one of the essential questions that we have been exploring throughout this book. Much of strategy development is context-sensitive, resource-sensitive and environment-sensitive. At best, this makes it difficult to derive universal solutions such as *recipes for excellence*; at worst, it is most unlikely.

Importantly, the *excellence* research was widely praised in the 1980s. Part of the reason for its inclusion here is to encourage the reader to review *critically* new evidence and theories in strategy development. A number of corporate strategy texts claim to offer the universal recipe. We examine another in Section 22.2.4.

22.2.4 Building a cohesive strategy through contradictions and tensions

One of Peters' colleagues in the development of the 'Seven S Framework', Richard Pascale, worked independently of the others to produce his own insights in 1990 into the development of corporate strategy, *Managing on the Edge*. He reviewed the main areas of strategy research and development in a similar way to that of Chapter 2 of this book. He concluded that:

> A common thread runs through almost all . . . organisational theories: each is predicated on seeking or maintaining order. Weber, Taylor and Chandler clearly belong to this school. The same is true of the writings of . . . Herbert Simon and the Hawthorne Experiments as reported by . . . Mayo. The contingency theorists, such as Lawrence and Lorsch, while acknowledging fluctuations in the environment, propose multiple strategies to retain coherence in the face of environmental uncertainty.

Readers will also recall the theory of Pettigrew and Whipp in Chapter 21 that laid great emphasis on *coherence*.

Pascale did not agree that organisations should seek stability. He argued that every organisation had inherent tensions and contradictions that needed to be recognised in the development of corporate strategy, especially where change was the main objective. Strategy must *contend* with these contradictions and not try to reduce them. Thus coherence or the maintenance of order was not always appropriate.

Pascale highlighted what he described as 'compelling and surprising' research from Miller and Friesen.[11] They had established from empirical research into 26 companies over a prolonged period that *significant* change occurs in *revolutionary* ways. It does not just evolve and there is no question of 'seeking or maintaining order'. There is a wall of inertia that naturally blocks important new strategic initiatives. Pascale concluded from this that the way to encourage major strategic change was to seek a major disturbance of the existing state in an organisation, i.e. to seek to destabilise it by *managing on the edge*. It takes 'a concerted frontal assault to break through the wall'.[12] He then proceeded to produce his own evidence to support this contention with a study of six major US companies: Ford, General Motors, General Electric, Citicorp, Hewlett-Packard and Honda, US.

Overall, Pascale concluded that strategy must *transcend* these difficulties and create opportunities with a *new vision* that will transform the organisation (*see* Chapter 10). Importantly, the outcome is not entirely predictable. There will always be uncertainties that have to be taken as they come. The management itself will have to change as it enacts its new strategies. It will have to learn, experiment and adapt along the way.

Exhibit 22.2

Factors that drive strategic stagnation and renewal (Pascale)

Fit – *the consistencies, coherence and congruence of the organisation*. Specifically, this is the fit between objectives, strategies and identified elements of change. For example, a strategy of increased customer service will not 'fit' if funds are withdrawn from the customer service department and reward systems are defined simply by short-term profits. This is similar to the concept of *coherence* explored in Chapter 21.

Split – *the variety of techniques that can be employed to develop and sustain the autonomy and diversity of large organisations*. An example would be setting up profit-accountable subsidiaries or profit centres. This concept includes both divisionalisation and the multifunctional task forces to encourage innovation, as described in Chapter 18.

Contend – *the constructive conflict that every organisation needs*. For example, conflict generated between different functional areas needs to be channelled productively, not suppressed. Resolution of such conflicts is an ongoing management task.

Transcend – *given the inevitable complexities of the above three areas, organisations need an approach to management that will cope with the difficulties*. This cannot be achieved by compromise but needs a totally different mindset (or paradigm) that copes with conflict and uses it to move the organisation forward.

Source: Adapted from Pascale, R (1990).[13]

To manage strategic transformation, Pascale suggested that there were four factors that influenced stagnation and renewal in organisations: *fit*, *split*, *contend* and *transcend*. All four are summarised in Exhibit 22.2.

Comment

Having criticised Peters and Waterman for the inadequacy of their research, Pascale then proceeded to base his main conclusions on a sample of six companies that are not representative of the whole of US industry. It is possible that a wider sample would have produced some different evidence on the strategy development process.

Pascale argued that a totally new mindset or paradigm is needed to cope with the inevitable complexities and tensions of strategy development. He described this as *transcending* the existing difficulties and opportunities. However, it might be argued that this recipe for transformation is vague and unconvincing in terms of its usefulness. He describes no tests, gives no clear guidance and develops a concept that is difficult to define clearly, let alone manage.

Key strategic principles

- The 'Seven S Framework' can be used to bring the elements of strategy together. Each element is equally important and all need to be considered in the development of corporate strategy: strategy, structure, systems, style, staff, skills, superordinate goals. However, the model does little to explain the logic and the methodology of developing the links between the elements.

- Peters and Waterman used the 'Seven S Framework' as the basis for an empirical study on the attributes of the excellent US companies in the 1980s. They emerged with eight qualities, some of which were very basic and some more demanding. Included among the latter was an emphasis on innovation and on the devolution of power to individuals and groups.

- Pascale also used the 'Seven S Framework' when he investigated apparent tensions and conflicts between the various elements. His research established what he described as four factors that would drive stagnation or renewal in the strategic process: fit, split, contend and transcend.

- *Fit* relates to the coherence of strategy. *Split* describes the need to devolve responsibility in large organisations. More controversially, Pascale concluded that there would always be some tensions and contradictions in strategic development: he called this the *contend* factor. His research also suggested that the strategic challenge was to attempt to manage such difficulties: he called this the *transcend* factor. Some parts of the theory appear to suffer from a lack of operational usefulness.

22.3 LONGER-TERM STRATEGY ISSUES

22.3.1 Implementation

As Chapter 1 pointed out, the separation in prescriptive strategy between analysis, options and choice and implementation is useful but does not really capture much of the ongoing strategy work that occupies organisations on a regular basis. Even where major upheaval occurs, such as the creation of Novartis, the success of the venture will depend on how it is implemented over a relatively short space of time. Such issues will remain part of the longer-term strategic task of the organisation.

In general terms, *milestones* and *controls* need to be set up to oversee implementation issues:

● *Milestones* are used to measure precisely what progress of the strategy towards a final implementation goal has been made at some intermediate point. They are important because it is only by assessing activity while it is still in progress that useful corrective actions can be taken.

● *Controls* are employed to ensure that financial, human resource and other guidelines are not breached during the implementation process. For example, they might include cash flow, cost expenditures against budget, training programme achievement, plant installation procedures and many other tasks. They differ from milestones in that they are more detailed, ongoing and function-specific.

Some further guidelines on implementation issues are shown in Exhibit 22.3.

Exhibit 22.3

Some key guidelines on strategy implementation and control

Problems of successful implementation tend to focus on how well or badly the organisation's reporting proves to be.

Problems arise:
● where implementation cuts across traditional organisational units;
● when information monitoring is poor;
● when an organisation resists change;
● when rewards for performance are geared to past performance rather than future action.

For successful implementation:
● allocate clear responsibility and accountability;
● pursue a limited number of strategies;
● identify the required actions and gain agreement from those who will implement them;
● produce 'milestones' so that it is clear earlier rather than later if implementation is off-course;
● above all, secure the active support of the chief executive.

22.3.2 Re-examining the future environment

In developing a coherent strategy, organisations may take the view that it is useful to identify the main trends that are likely to affect them over the next few years. Both Novartis and other pharmaceutical companies have clearly found the need to re-examine the future pharmaceutical market as part of their development of strategy.

However, one of the most respected management writers, Peter Drucker, cautions against such predictions:

It is not very difficult to predict the future. It is only pointless. Many futurologists have high batting averages – the way they measure themselves and are commonly measured. They do a good job foretelling some things. But what are always far more important are fundamental changes that happened though no one predicted them or could possibly have predicted them.[14]

In general, there are real problems with predicting the future. Yet there is no denying its importance. It has even been argued that strategy should attempt to shape the future.[15] Some emergent strategists believe the process of prediction to be largely a waste of time (*see* Chapter 2). Possibly a useful route forward for those who believe in prediction is to adopt a scenario-building approach (*see* Chapter 3). However, it will be recalled that part of the reasoning for scenario building was not *prediction* but rather *preparation* in the event of the unpredictable happening.

22.3.3 Re-examining the organisation and its purpose

As well as examining their environment, organisations will need to reconsider their vision, purpose and mission. Organisations rarely stand still: some grow fast, like the producers of Xbox and other computer games. Some grow more slowly, such as major multinationals, unless they make a major strategic shift, like Novartis. Some decline for a whole variety of reasons. Some are changing beyond all recognition: the case of Novartis is an example.

The changes that take place raise fundamental questions about the purpose of the organisation. These were explored in Chapters 10 to 12 but deserve to be raised again here because they are part of the longer-term implementation programme, which becomes the *starting point* for the next round of corporate strategy. The four areas that deserve re-examination are:

1 *The purpose of the organisation.* Does it actually matter if we decline? How important is it that we achieve our stated growth targets? The answers to these questions will relate to the values of the organisation and those of its management, employees and shareholders.

2 *Sustainable competitive advantage.* How and where will we retain or develop this? What are the implications for the resources of the organisation?

3 *The culture and style of the organisation.* How do we undertake our work? What style do we wish to adopt? Again, these are fundamental questions that go beyond immediate implementation issues to the underlying philosophy of the business.

4 *The values and ethical standards.* What values do we hold? Why? How do we wish to conduct ourselves? How do we measure up to these ideals? As organisations move into the new millennium, some have questioned previously held views on sustaining the environment, equal treatment for minorities, political affiliations and so on. These are legitimate matters of corporate strategy and deserve to be revisited.

This book has argued in favour of customer-driven quality, innovation and the learning organisation. It has also simplified purpose down to value added and strategy down to the search for sustainable competitive advantage. Such considerations will not necessarily be appropriate for all organisations, but all will need to determine their long-term perspectives, whatever they are.

22.3.4 Conclusions on corporate strategy issues

Coupled with changes in the environment and in the organisation, new issues are constantly emerging in corporate strategy itself. The research papers, journals, books and magazines quoted throughout this book will provide guidance on the subjects that are currently under study[16] – the subjects that make corporate strategy dynamic, stimulating, controversial and relevant to our future.

Finally, it should not be forgotten that, in spite of all the corporate strategy attempts to guide and cope with the future, there are always the *unpredictable* elements that are beyond strategic theory. In the words of the German chemical company, Henkel, 'To succeed in business, you need skill, patience, money . . . and a bit of luck.'[17]

Key strategic principles

- When implementing corporate strategy, it is useful to identify the tasks that need to be undertaken. These will include setting *milestones* to measure the progress along the way and establishing *controls* to ensure that overall guidelines on finance and other resources are not breached as the implementation proceeds.

- Many organisations attempt to re-examine the future environment. However, the most important elements may be difficult to predict. A useful route forward may be to adopt the scenario-building approach. Part of the reasoning for scenario building is not *prediction* but rather *preparation* in the event of the unpredictable happening.

- Organisations rarely stand still: it may also therefore be appropriate to re-examine the vision, purpose and mission of the organisation and also its culture and style. The values and ethical standards also deserve to be reappraised, along with an examination of stakeholder relationships.

- There will always be an element of chance in corporate strategy. Luck will make a contribution to the development of workable proposals.

CASE STUDY 22.2

Side-effects of age leave Roche reeling

When the 105-year-old Swiss pharmaceutical group discovered Novartis had bought one-fifth of its voting stock, it was one more on a growing list of problems that had seen the decline of a once-great company.

Franz Humer replaced the handset slowly. The Roche chairman was still in a state of shock as he tried to make sense of what he had heard. Mr Humer, 54, had just taken a call from Daniel Vasella, his younger, more suave counterpart at Novartis, the drugs group that faces Roche across the Rhine in Basel, Switzerland. Mr Vasella had told him that Novartis – a company with a five-year history compared with Roche's 105-year one had just put the finishing touches to a transaction: buying one-fifth of Roche's voting shares. A chunk of Roche had somehow slipped into the hands of its arch-rival.

Mr Vasella's call could not have come at a worse time. Roche was in turmoil. Two of Mr Humer's senior lieutenants, including the head of the vital US operations, had quit. Fritz Gerber, whom Mr Humer had replaced as chairman only days before, still loomed large – both as a board member and the spokesman for the Hoffmann families that controlled Roche. Mr Humer was having blazing rows with another senior executive, Anton Affentrager, his recently appointed finance director. Mr Affentrager was to be fired within a week. And that was the good news.

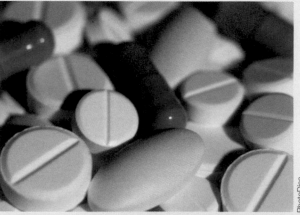

Deeper malaise

The personnel problems were symptomatic of a much deeper malaise. Martin Ebner, the Swiss corporate raider who sold his stake to Novartis, had been complaining for years about Roche's archaic share structure. Senior executives warned that the pharma (short for pharmaceutical) division lacked

a clear strategy and that swift, decisive action was needed. In March 2001, Roche had released a dreadful set of results. Although diagnostics was performing well, the flagship pharmaceuticals division was a disaster. Sales of prescription drugs had fallen 2 per cent – quite a feat in an industry where double-digit growth was the norm. No fewer than three of Roche's biggest-selling drugs were nearly two decades old, rapidly nearing the end of their life. More alarming still, sales of Xenical, the slimming pill on which Mr Humer had staked much of his reputation, had stalled in only in its third year on the market.

At about the time of Mr Vasella's call, Mr Humer had been finalising a cost-cutting exercise that would see 3,000 pharma jobs go. Losses would be heavy in Roche's subsidiary in the US, where most drug companies were frantically expanding. But facts had to be faced. Roche was no longer the company of a mere five years earlier, when it was vying with Merck of the US for the industry's top slot – it had fallen to eleventh place. What had gone wrong? As with most corporate stories – especially in pharmaceuticals where it takes at least a decade to invent a medicine – there was a long- and a short-term answer.

Long-term strategic problems

Back in 1985, Roche faced a major problem: the 1985 patent expiry of Valium. This drug and its precursor, Librium, were the medicines that made Roche great. Librium was a sensation from the moment of its launch in the early 1960s as the drug that could tame lions and tigers. Valium quickly became the biggest-selling medicine of all time. As the patent expiry loomed, the company began to revamp its strategy, shedding non-core assets and regrouping into four divisions. In 1985, under its then celebrated R&D director Jurgen Drews, it started pouring billions into research towards the next block-buster. Fifteen years later, nothing – certainly nothing that remotely compared with Valium.

Instead, the company embarked on a decade-long acquisition spree that saw it buy, among other things, Genentech, a San Francisco-based biotechnology pioneer, and Syntex, another Californian start-up. In 1997, it splashed out a further US$10.2 billion for a diagnostics group, Boehringer Mannheim. Without these acquisitions, Roche's portfolio would be practically empty in 2001. But, astute as these deals were, the company was substituting then for self-generated growth. 'Once you start going down the track of buying, maybe you lose your soul as a company,' says a chief executive of a rival group. 'You just buy something, strip out the costs and then buy the next one. Ultimately, you run out of steam.'

Most of the acquisitions were engineered by Henri Meier, the brilliant finance director who had another means of compensating for the pharma division's shortcomings. He seemed to be able to produce cash from thin air. Under his stewardship, Roche made such fabulous returns that it became known as a bank with a pharma business attached – in 2000 for example, financial income was nearly 30 per cent of group profits.

One of the reasons Roche became so reliant on acquisition and financial conjuring tricks stemmed from its archaic share structure. This prevented it from participating fully in the consolidation that was transforming the industry in the 1990s. Founded by Fritz Hoffmann in 1896, the company was still controlled by his descendants, who had 50.1 per cent of the voting shares, with only 10 per cent of the capital. Thus, while companies like Novartis were being formed by smaller rivals, Roche shareholders were reluctant to take part because they might lose control of the combined group.

Roche's short-term strategy in the late 1990s

Mr Humer had become chief executive in 1996. He had arrived in 1995 from Glaxo and had observed how such companies had grown fat by exploiting the primary care market: selling drugs for asthma, blood pressure and other chronic conditions directly to doctors. He decided that Roche needed to join this gravy train. Mr Humer's team scoured Roche's labs for drugs that could be turned into blockbusters. They found two.

One was Posicor, a molecule for high blood pressure intended as a specialist drug. The new Roche team thought it could become a medicine for medical general practice. The only problem, as some employees pointed out, was that Posicor could cause dangerous side-effects if taken with other medications. That was a big drawback for a mass-market drug and, sure enough, Posicor was withdrawn in June 1998, less than a year after launch.

The second possible blockbuster was Xenical. Mr Humer's team rescued the obesity pill after it had languished in the laboratory for several years. Obesity was a huge problem. Surely this was the drug on which to build Roche's future? After a few teething problems, Xenical was launched with great excitement in 1999, a few months after Viagra, Pfizer's impotence pill, had created a craze for life-style drugs. Xenical got off to a flying start, garnering sales of SF940 million in its first year. But then it stalled. The main problem was a side-effect delicately referred to as 'rectal leakage' by the company. People were trying Xenical for a few months and then giving up. In addition, Roche's marketing strategy was not clear. On the one hand, Roche said that Xenical should be positioned as a serious drug with real health benefits, not a casual slimming drug. On the other, it piled millions of dollars into a huge American TV campaign that played down the unpleasant side-effects.

Additional problems at Roche

As Xenical's problems were becoming clear, Roche was hit again. In May 1999, US trust-busters fined the Roche vitamins division a record US$500 million for organising a price-fixing cartel. A former Roche executive was jailed and the company took SF2.4 billion in charges to cover law suits. It was an episode unlikely to boost morale at a time when the pharma division was drifting. No fewer than nine drugs had fallen at the last hurdle – a failure rate that raised eyebrows throughout the industry. Given Xenical's disappointing performance, there were simply not enough new drugs to replace the cash cows. That left Mr Humer with little option but to scale back costs – which he did in 2001.

But some fellow executives, including the departed Mr Affentrager, thought that more drastic action was needed. Any further move, such as an acquisition or even a merger, would almost certainly be tougher with the Novartis shareholding in place. Importantly, power ultimately rested with the secretive descendants of Fritz Hoffmann, Swiss billionaires who have stuck with Roche through 100 years of ups and downs. Mr Humer needed at all costs to retain their support.

Case adapted by Richard Lynch from an article by David Pilling, with additional reporting by William Hall, in the *Financial Times*, 1 June 2001, p25. © Copyright *Financial Times* 2001. Reproduced with permission.

▶ **CASE STUDY 22.2 continued**

Case questions

1 *What are the main strategic problems at Roche? How would you overcome them?*

2 *Is another acquisition the answer? Or do you accept the arguments of the commentator quoted in the case?*

3 *What lessons, if any, can other companies learn from Roche's difficulties?*

STRATEGIC PROJECT

Follow up the changes in the pharmaceutical industry. The cases in this chapter indicate the scope for strategic development. The *Corporate Strategy* website (www.**booksites.net/lynch**) has an article with basic data on companies in the industry.

CRITICAL REFLECTION

Just how important is luck?

Towards the end of this summary chapter, the German company Henkel was quoted: 'To succeed in business, you need skill, patience, money . . . and a bit of luck.' If luck is a factor, then does this perhaps negate the value of the strategic content and process developed throughout the text? What is your experience? Does luck matter? What are the implications of your view for the development of corporate strategy?

SUMMARY

● Although prescriptive and emergent processes have been one of the themes of this text, they have been used as shorthand for a number of approaches to strategy development. It is possible to analyse many strategic tasks from these two perspectives. However, this book has demonstrated that an eclectic approach is preferable. In reality, the strategic process has a number of facets which go beyond prescriptive and emergent approaches. All of them provide insights and guidance in the development of corporate strategy.

● The 'Seven S Framework' can be used to bring the elements of strategy together. Each element is equally important and all need to be considered in the development of corporate strategy: strategy, structure, systems, style, staff, skills and superordinate goals. However, the model does little to explain the logic and the methodology of developing the links between the elements.

● Peters and Waterman used the 'Seven S Framework' as the basis for an empirical study on the attributes of the excellent US companies in the 1980s. They emerged with eight qualities, some of which were very basic and some more demanding – the latter including an emphasis on innovation and on the devolution of power to individuals and groups.

● Pascale also used the 'Seven S Framework' when he investigated apparent tensions and conflicts between the various elements. His research established what he described as four factors that would drive stagnation or renewal in the strategic process: fit, split, contend and transcend. *Fit* relates to the coherence of strategy. *Split* describes the need to devolve responsibility in large organisations. More controversially, Pascale concluded that there would always be some tensions and contradictions in strategic development: he called this the *contend* factor. His research also suggested that the strategic challenge was to attempt to manage such difficulties: he called this the *transcend* factor.

● In implementing corporate strategy, it is useful to identify the immediate tasks that need to be undertaken: they will include setting *milestones* to measure the progress along the way and establishing *controls* to ensure that overall guidelines on finance and other resources are not breached as the implementation proceeds.

● Many organisations attempt to re-examine the future environment, but the most important elements may be difficult to predict. A useful route forward may be to adopt the scenario-building approach. However, part of the reasoning for scenario building is not *prediction* but rather *preparation* in the event of the unpredictable happening.

● Organisations rarely stand still: it may also, therefore, be appropriate to re-examine the vision, purpose and competitive advantages of the organisation and also its culture and style. The values and ethical standards also deserve to be reappraised, along with an examination of stakeholder relationships. There will always be an element of chance in corporate strategy. Luck will make a contribution to the development of workable proposals. Finally, it is the conclusion of this book that both prescriptive and emergent approaches should be used in the development of corporate strategy.

QUESTIONS

1 Use the 'Seven S Framework' to analyse the proposed changes at Novartis.

2 Is it possible to have excellent companies against which to compare performance?

3 What is your assessment of Pascale's theory of strategic change? Will there always be tension and is this intrinsic to change?

4 Examine a strategic decision with which you are familiar, and use the various strategic processes explored in this text – prescriptive, learning-based, knowledge, etc. – to plot the way the decision was derived and comment on the usefulness of each process.

5 This book has highlighted 'customer-driven quality, innovation and the learning mechanism' as being particularly important in the development of corporate strategy. Are there other areas that you would wish to select and, if so, what are they and why would you select them?

Further reading

It is worth examining Peters, T and Waterman, R (1982) *In Search of Excellence*, Harper Collins, New York. The main argument was reprinted in De Wit, R and Meyer, B (1994) *Strategy: Process, Content and Context*, West Publishing, St Paul, MN, pp176–82. Any of Tom Peters' books also repays examination. Try Peters, T (1992) *Liberation Management*, Macmillan, London.

Richard Pascale's book (1990) *Managing on the Edge*, Viking Penguin, London, is also valuable.

To look into the strategic future, you might read Hamel, G and Prahalad, C K (1994) 'Strategy as a field of study: why search for new paradigms?', *Strategic Management Journal*, Special Issue, 15, pp5–16. The 'Special Issue' of *Long Range Planning*, April 1996, also has a most interesting review of this area. For a more recent perspective: Cummings, S and Angwin, D (2004) 'The future shape of strategy: Lemmings or chimeras?', *Academy of Management Executive*, Vol 18, No 2, pp21–28, which contains some interesting ideas and comparison between the 'old' and the 'new.'

Finally, for an approachable comparison between the resource-based view, hypercompetition and complexity *see* Lengnick-Hall, C and Wolff, J (1999) 'Similarities and contradictions in the core logic of three strategy research streams', *Strategic Management Journal*, Vol 20, pp1109–32.

Notes and references

1 References for Novartis case: Novartis Annual Report and Accounts 2004 – available on the web at www.novartis.com *Financial Times*, 8 Mar 1996, pp1, 17, 28; 19 Mar 1996, p25; 11 Apr 1996, p18 (Dr Håken Mogren's comments); 12 Oct 1998, p15; 16 July 1999, p27; 18 February 2000, p26; 11 July 2000, p34; 16 February 2001, p25; 8 May 2001, p19; 14 May 2001, p27; 22 August 2001, p20; 28 November 2001, p23; 21 January 2004, p12; 22 February 2005, pp1, 28. *See* also Lynch, R (1994) *European Business Strategies*, 2nd edn, Kogan Page, London, pp31–2, for an earlier exploration of global strategies in the drugs industry.

2 Handy, C (1993) *Understanding Organisations*, 4th edn, Penguin, Harmondsworth, p187. *See* also: Pascale, R and Athos, A (1982) *The Art of Japanese Management*, Allen Lane, London, and Peters, T and Waterman, R (1982) *In Search of Excellence*, HarperCollins, New York.

3 In the original publication by McKinsey & Co, the central 'S' was for 'Superordinate goals'. This was later changed by Peters and Waterman to 'shared values', which they interpreted as meaning culture when they repeated the diagram in their book *In Search of Excellence*. This appears to have been not just a semantic change but to alter the fundamental meaning of the model. In the original publication, the authors coupled the word 'style' with culture and left 'superordinate goals' to mean the mission and purpose of the organisation. To avoid confusion, the original wording has been adopted in this book. *Original reference*: article reprinted in De Wit, R and Meyer, B (1994) *Strategy: Process, Content and Context*, West Publishing, St Paul MN, pp176–82. *Revised reference*: Peters, T and Waterman, R (1982) *In Search of Excellence*, HarperCollins, New York, p9.

4 Peters, T and Waterman, R (1982) Ibid.

5 *Source*: Adapted by the author from Peters, T and Waterman, R (1982) Ibid, pp13–15. The last three areas have been summarised from pp308, 103 and 110 respectively.

6 Peters, T and Waterman, R (1982) Ibid, p16.

7 Peters, T and Waterman, R (1982) Ibid, p17.

8 Peters, T (1992) *Liberation Management*, Macmillan, London.

9 Pascale, R (1990) *Managing on the Edge*, Viking Penguin, London, pp16, 17.

10 Lawrence, P R and Lorsch, J W (1967) *Organisation and Environment*, Harvard University Press, Cambridge, MA.

11 Miller, D and Friesen, P (1982) 'Structural change and performance: Quantum versus piecemeal-incremental approaches', *Academy of Management Journal*, pp867–92. Quoted in Pascale, R (1990) Op. cit., pp113, 295.

12 Pascale, R (1990) Op. cit., p115.

13 Adapted by the author from Pascale, R (1990) Op. cit., p24.

14 Drucker, P (1995) *Managing in a Time of Great Change*, Butterworth–Heinemann, Oxford, pvii.

15 Whitehill, M (1996) 'Introduction to foresight: exploring and creating the future', *Long Range Planning*, Apr, p146. This issue has a range of articles that tackle this subject from a number of perspectives, including those that believe it is a waste of time.

16 *See*, for example, Hamel, G and Prahalad, C K (1994) 'Strategy as a field of study: why search for new paradigms?', *Strategic Management Journal*, Special Issue, 15, pp5–16. *See* also *Long Range Planning*, Apr 1996.

17 Henkel, A G, Annual Report and Accounts: 1987.

Glossary

Added value The difference between the market value of the output and the cost of the inputs to the organisation.

Architecture The network of relationships and contracts both within and around the organisation.

Attractiveness to stakeholders Strategy evaluation criterion associated with the strategy being sufficiently appealing to those people that the company needs to satisfy.

Backward integration The process whereby an organisation acquires the activities of its inputs, e.g. manufacturer into raw material supplier.

Balanced Scorecard This uses strategic and financial measures to assess the outcome of a chosen strategy. It acknowledges the different expectations of the various stakeholders and attempts to use a 'scorecard' based on four prime areas of business activity to measure the results of the selected strategy.

Benchmarking The comparison of practice in other organisations in order to identify areas for improvement. Note that the comparison does *not* have to be with another organisation within the same industry, simply one whose practices are better at a particular *aspect* of the task or function.

Bounded rationality The principle that managers reduce tasks, including implementation, to a series of small steps, even though this may grossly oversimplify the situation and may not be the optimal way to proceed.

Branding The additional reassurance provided to the customer by the brand name and reputation beyond the intrinsic value of the assets purchased by the customer. A specific name or symbol used to distinguish a seller's product or services.

Break-even The point at which the total costs of undertaking a new strategy are equal to the total revenue from the strategy.

Bretton Woods Agreement System of largely fixed currency exchange rates between the leading industrialised nations of the world. In operation from 1944 to 1973.

Business ethics *See Ethics.*

Business process re-engineering The replacement of people in administrative tasks by technology, often accompanied by delayering and other organisational change. *See also Delayering.*

Capability-based resources Covers the resources across the entire value chain and goes beyond key resources and core competencies.

Capacity utilisation The level of plant operation at any time, usually expressed as a percentage of total production capacity of that plant.

Cash cows Products with high relative market shares in low-growth markets. *See also Portfolio Matrix.*

Change options matrix This links the areas of human resource activity with the three main areas of strategic change: work, cultural and political change.

Changeability of the environment The degree to which the environment is likely to change.

Channel strategy *see Distribution strategy.*

Collusive alliances Co-operative strategies in which firms seek to share information in order to reduce competition or raise prices. They are illegal in many countries.

Comparative advantage of nations This consists of the resources possessed by a country that give it a competitive advantage over other nations. *See also Diamond theory.*

Competitive advantage The *significant* advantages that an organisation has over its competitors. Such advantages allow the organisation to add more value than its competitors in the same market.

Competitor profiling Explores one or two leading competitors by analysing their resources, past performance, current products and strategies.

Complementors The companies whose products add more value to the products of the base organisation than they would derive from their own products by themselves – for example, Microsoft software adds significantly to the value of a Hewlett-Packard Personal Computer.

Complete competitive formula The business formula that offers both value for money to customers and competitive advantage against competitors.

Concentration ratio The degree to which value added or turnover is concentrated in the hands of a few firms in an industry. Measures the dominance of firms in an industry.

Consistency Strategy evaluation criterion associated with the strategy being in agreement with the objectives of the organisation.

Contend The constructive conflict that some strategists argue is needed by every organisation.

Content of corporate strategy The main actions of the proposed strategy.

Context of corporate strategy The circumstances surrounding and influencing the way that a strategy develops and operates.

Contingency theory of leadership Argues that leaders should be promoted or recruited according to the needs of the organisation at a particular point in time. *See also Style theory* and *Trait theory*.

Controls Employed to ensure that strategic objectives are achieved and financial, human resource and other guidelines are not breached during the implementation process or the ongoing phase of strategic activity. The process of monitoring the proposed plans as they are implemented and adjusting for any variances where necessary.

Co-operation The links that bring organisations together, thereby enhancing their ability to compete in the market place. *See also Complementors*.

Co-operative game Has positive pay-off for all participants.

Co-operative strategy A strategy in which at least two companies work together with rivals or other related companies to achieve an agreed objective or to their mutual benefit.

Core areas of corporate strategy Strategic analysis, strategy development and strategy implementation.

Core competencies The distinctive group of skills and technologies that enable an organisation to provide particular benefits to customers and deliver competitive advantage. Together, they form key resources of the organisation that assist it in being distinct from its competitors.

Core resources The important strategic resources of the organisation, usually summarised as architecture, reputation and innovation.

Corporate governance The influence and power of the stakeholders to control the strategic direction of the organisation in general and, more specifically, the chief executive and other senior officers of the organisation.

Corporate-level strategy The value-added contribution of the central headquarters of a group of diversified businesses, each with its own strategy.

Corporate purpose The purpose and contribution of the central headquarters of a diversified group of companies.

Corporate social responsibility The standards and the conduct that an organisation sets itself in its dealings within an organisation and outside with its environment. *See also Ethics*.

Corporate strategy This has at least three definitions. First, the identification of the *purpose* of the organisation and the plans and actions to achieve that purpose. Second, the identification of market opportunities, coupled with experimenting and developing competitive advantage over time. Third, the pattern of major objectives, purposes or goals and the essential policies or plans for achieving those goals.

Cost/benefit analysis Evaluates strategic projects, especially in the public sector, where an element of unquantified public service beyond commercial profit may be involved. It attempts to quantify the broader social benefits to be derived from particular strategic initiatives.

Cost of capital The cost of the capital employed in an organisation, often measured by the cost of investing in a risk-free bond outside the organisation coupled with some element for the extra risks, if any, of investing in the organisation itself. *See also Weighted average cost of capital*.

Cost-plus pricing Sets the price of goods and services primarily by totalling the costs and adding a percentage profit margin. *See also Target pricing*.

Cultural Web The factors that can be used to characterise some aspects of the culture of an organisation. Usually summarised as stories, symbols, power structures, organisational structure, control systems, routines and rituals.

Culture *See Organisational culture* and *International culture*. It is important to distinguish between these two quite distinct areas of the subject.

Customer-competitor matrix Links together the extent to which customers have common needs and competitors can gain competitive advantage through areas such as differentiation and economies of scale.

Customer-driven strategy The strategy of an organisation where every function is directed towards customer satisfaction. It goes beyond those functions, such as sales and marketing, that have traditionally had direct contact with the customer.

Customer profiling Describes the main characteristics of the customer and how customers make their purchase decisions.

Cyclicality The periodic rise and fall of a mature market.

Delayering The removal of layers of management and administration in an organisation's structure.

Demerger The split of an organisation into its constituent parts, with some parts possibly being sold to outside investors.

Derived demand Demand for goods and services that is derived from the economic performance of the customers. *See also Primary demand.*

Diamond theory of international competitive advantage Identifies a 'diamond' of four interrelated areas within a nation which assist that country to be more competitive in international markets – the four areas being factor conditions, competing firms within the country, support industries of the country and home demand. *See also Comparative advantage of nations.*

Differentiation The development of unique benefits or attributes in a product or service that positions it to appeal especially to a part (segment) of the total market. The products of the organisation meet the needs of some customers in the market place better than others and allow higher prices to be charged. *See Generic strategies.*

Dirigiste policy Describes the policies of a government relying on an approach of centrally directed government actions to manage the economy. *See also Laissez-faire policy.*

Discontinuity Radical, sudden and largely unpredicted change in the environment.

Discounted cash flow (DCF) The sum of the projected cash flows from a future strategy, after revaluing each individual element of the cash flow in terms of its present worth using the cost of capital of the organisation.

Disruptive innovation This takes an existing market and identifies existing technologies that will offer simpler, less expensive products or services than have been offered previously. *See also Innovation.*

Distribution or channel strategy The strategies involved in delivering the product or service to the customer.

Division A separate part of a multi-product company with profit responsibility for its range of products. Each division usually has a complete range of the main business functions, such as finance, operations and marketing.

Dogs Products with low relative market shares in low-growth markets. *See also Portfolio matrix.*

Dominant logic The way in which managers conceptualise the business and make critical resource allocation decisions.

Double-loop learning Consists of a *first* loop of learning that checks performance against expected norms and adjusts where necessary, coupled with a *second* loop that reappraises whether the expected norms were appropriate in the first place. *See also Learning-based strategy.*

Economic rent Any excess that a factor earns over the minimum amount needed to keep that factor in its present use.

Economies of scale The extra cost savings that occur when higher-volume production allows unit costs to be reduced. For example, a new, larger production plant produces products with the same quality but using fewer operatives, thus reducing unit costs. *See also Economies of scope.*

Economies of scope The cost savings developed by a group when it shares activities or transfers capabilities and competencies from one part of the group to another – for example, two products sharing the same sales team. *See also Economies of scale.*

Emergent change The whole process of developing a strategy whose outcome only emerges as the strategy proceeds. There is no defined list of implementation actions in advance of the strategy emerging. *See also Prescriptive change.*

Emergent corporate strategy A strategy whose final objective is unclear and whose elements are developed during the course of its life, as it proceeds. *See also Prescriptive corporate strategy.*

Empowerment The devolution of power and decision-making responsibility to those lower in the organisation.

Entrepreneurship A way of thinking, reasoning and acting that focuses on the identification and exploitation of business opportunities from a broad general perspective driven by the leadership of individuals or small groups.

Environment Everything and everyone outside the organisation: competitors, customers, government, etc. Note that 'green' environmental issues are only one part of the overall definition. *See also Changeability of the environment* and *Predictability of the environment.*

E-S-P Paradigm This analyses the role of government in strategy development along three dimensions: Environment, System and Policies.

Ethics The principles that encompass the standards and conduct that an organisation sets itself in its dealings within the organisation and with its external environment. *See also Corporate social responsibility.*

Expansion method matrix Explores in a structured way the methods by which the market opportunities associated with strategy options might be achieved.

Experience curve The relationship between the unit costs of a product and the total units *ever produced* of that product, plotted in graphical form, with the units being cumulative from the first day of production.

Feasibility Strategy evaluation criterion associated with the strategy being capable of being implemented.

Fit The consistencies, coherence and congruence of the organisation.

Floating and fixed exchange rates Currency exchange rates, such as the rate of exchange between the US dollar and the Yen, are said to *float* when market forces determine the rate, depending on market demand. They are *fixed* when national governments (or their associated national banks) fix the rates by international agreement and intervene in international markets to hold those rates.

Focus strategy Occurs when the organisation focuses on a specific niche (or segment) of the market place and develops competitive advantage by offering products especially developed for that niche (or segment) *See also Generic strategies.*

Foreign trade The exporting and importing activities of countries and companies around the world.

Foreign direct investment (FDI) The long-term investment by a company in technology, management skills, brands and physical assets of a subsidiary in another country.

Formal organisation structures Those structures formally defined by the organisation in terms of reporting relationships, responsibilities and tasks. *See also Informal organisation structures.*

Forward integration The process whereby an organisation acquires the activities of its outputs, e.g. manufacturer into distribution and transport.

Franchise A form of co-operative strategy in which a firm (the franchisor) develops a business concept and then offers this to others (the franchisees) in the form of a contractual relationship to use the business concept. Typically, the franchisee obtains a tried-and-tested business formula in return for paying a percentage of its sales and agreeing to tight controls from the franchisor over the product range, pricing, etc.

Functional organisation structure Structure based around the main activities that have to be undertaken by the organisation such as production, marketing, human resources, research and development, finance and accounting.

Game-based theories of strategy These focus on the decisions of the organisation and its competitors as strategy is developed – the *game* – and the interactions between the two as strategic decisions are taken.

Game theory Structured methods of bargaining with and between customers, suppliers and others, both inside and outside the organisation. Such structuring usually involves the quantification of possible outcomes at each stage of the strategy decision-making process.

Gearing ratio The ratio of debt finance to the total shareholders' funds.

General Agreement on Tariffs and Trade (GATT) International agreement between various countries around the world, designed to deal with trade disputes and support world trade.

Generic industry environment The study of those strategies that are particularly likely to cope with a particular market or competitive environment.

Generic strategies The three basic strategies of cost leadership, differentiation and focus (sometimes called niche) which are open to any business.

Global and national responsiveness matrix This links together the extent of the need for global activity with the need for an organisation to be responsive to national and regional variations. These two areas are not mutually exclusive.

Global product company This will often involve the global integration of manufacturing and one common global brand. There is only *limited* national variation. *See also Transnational product company.*

Global strategy When a company treats the whole world as one market and one source of supply. *See also International strategy* and *Multinational strategy.*

Growth-share matrix *See Portfolio matrix.*

Hierarchy of resources The four levels of resource that are the full resources of the organisation. The distinguishing feature of the higher levels is an increased likelihood of sustainable competitive advantage.

History *See Strategy as history.*

Holding company organisation structure (sometimes shortened to *H-Form* structure) Used for organisations with very diverse product ranges and share relationships where a central (holding) company owns various businesses and acts as an investment company with shareholdings in each of the individual enterprises. The headquarters acts only as a banker, with strategy largely decided by the individual companies.

Horizontal integration When an organisation moves to acquire its competitors or make some other form of close association.

Human resource audit An examination of the organisation's leadership, its people and their skills, backgrounds and relationships with each other.

Human resource-based theories of strategy These emphasise the importance of the people element in strategy development. *See also Emergent corporate strategy, Negotiation-based* and *Learning-based strategic routes forward.*

Implementation The process by which the organisation's chosen strategies are put into operation.

Informal organisation structures Those structures, often unwritten, that have been developed by the history, culture and individuals in an organisation to facilitate the flow of information and allocate power within the structure. *See also Formal organisation structures.*

Innovation The generation and exploitation of new ideas. The process moves products and services, human and capital resources, markets and production processes beyond their current boundaries and capabilities. *See also Disruptive innovation.*

Innovation and knowledge-based theories of strategy privilege the generation of new ideas and the sharing of those ideas as being the most important aspects of strategy development.

Innovation organisation structure Characterised by creativity, lack of formal reporting relationships and informality.

Innovative capability The special talent possessed by some organisations for developing and exploiting innovative ideas.

Intangible resources The organisation's resources that have no physical presence but represent real benefit to the organisation, like reputation and technical knowledge. *See also Tangible resources* and *Organisational capability.*

Intellectual capital of an organisation The future earnings capacity that derives from a deeper, broader and more human perspective than that described in the organisation's financial reports.

International culture Collective programming of the mind that distinguishes one human group from another. *Distinguish from Organisational culture.*

International Monetary Fund (IMF) International body designed to lend funds to countries in international difficulty and to promote trade stability through co-operation and discussion.

International strategy When a significant proportion of an organisation's activities are outside the home country and are managed as a separate area. *See also Multinational strategy* and *Global strategy.*

Joint ventures Co-operative strategies where two or more organisations set up a separate jointly owned subsidiary to develop the co-operation.

Just-in-time System that ensures that stock is delivered from suppliers only when it is required, with none being held in reserve.

Kaizen The process of continuous improvement in production and every aspect of value added (Japanese).

Kanban Control system on the factory floor to keep production moving (Japanese).

Key factors for success (sometimes called *critical success factors*) Those resources, skills and attributes of the organisations in an industry that are essential to deliver success in the market place. Note that the emphasis is on *all* the companies in an industry. (Key factors for success are *not* about those factors that apply to an *individual* company.)

Knowledge A fluid mix of framed experience, values, contextual information and expert insight. It accumulates over time and shapes the organisation's ability to survive and compete in markets. Note that knowledge is *not* 'data' or 'information'.

Knowledge creation The development and circulation of new knowledge within the organisation.

Knowledge management The retention, exploitation and sharing of knowledge in an organisation that will deliver sustainable competitive advantage.

Laissez-faire policy Describes the policies of a government relying on an approach of non-interference and free-market forces to manage the economy of a country. *See also Dirigiste policy.*

Leadership The art or process of influencing people so that they will strive willingly and enthusiastically towards the achievement of the group's mission.

Learning The strategic process of developing strategy by crafting, experimentation and feedback. Note that learning in this context does *not* mean rote or memory learning.

Learning-based strategic route forward Emphasises learning and crafting as aspects of the development of successful corporate strategy. It places particular emphasis on trial and feedback mechanisms. *See also Human resource-based theories of strategy* and *Double-loop learning.*

Leasing A form of debt where the organisation hires an asset for a period, possibly with the option of buying it at the end of the period.

Leveraging The exploitation by an organisation of its existing resources to their fullest extent.

Life cycle Plots the evolution of industry annual sales over time. Often divided into distinct phases – introduction, growth, maturity and decline – with specific strategies for each phase.

Logical incrementalism The process of developing a strategy by small, incremental and logical steps. The term was first used by Professor J B Quinn.

Logistics The science of stockholding, delivery and customer service.

Long-term debt A loan repaid over a period longer than a year. *See also Short-term debt.*

Loose-tight principle The concept of the need for tight central control by headquarters, while allowing individuals or operating subsidiaries loose autonomy and initiative within defined managerial limits.

Low-cost leader in an industry Has built and maintains plant, equipment, labour costs and working practices that deliver the lowest costs in that industry. *See Generic strategies.*

Macroeconomic conditions Economic activity at the general level of the national or international economy.

Market equilibrium The state that allows competitors a viable and stable market share accompanied by adequate profits.

Market mechanism The means by which the state uses market pricing and quasi-market mechanisms to determine the supply and demand of goods that were previously state monopolies in public sector strategy.

Market options matrix Identifies the product and the market options available to the organisation, including the possibility of withdrawal and movement into unrelated markets.

Market segmentation The identification of specific groups (or segments) of customers who respond to competitive strategies differently from other groups. *See also Market positioning.*

Market positioning The choice of differential advantage possessed by an organisation that allows it to compete and survive in a market place. Often associated with competition and survival in a segment of a market. *See also Market segmentation.*

Mass marketing One product is sold to all types of customer.

Matrix organisation structure Instead of the product-based multidivisional structure, some organisations have chosen to operate with two overlapping structures. One structure might typically be product-based, with another parallel structure being based on some other element, such as geographic region. The two elements form a *matrix* of responsibilities. Strategy needs to be agreed by both parts of the matrix. *See also Multidivisional organisation structure.*

Milestones Interim indicators of progress during the implementation phase of strategy.

Minimum intervention The principle that managers implementing strategy should only make changes where they are absolutely necessary.

Mission Outlines the broad general directions that the organisation should and will follow and briefly summarises the reasoning and values that lie behind it. *See also Objectives.*

Mission statement Defines the business that the organisation is in or should be in against the values and expectations of the stakeholders.

Monopoly rents Economic rent deriving from the markets in which the organisation operates. Such rents are associated with a company's unique position in the market place enabling it to influence market prices in its favour. *See also Economic rent.*

Multidivisional organisation structure As the product range of the organisation becomes larger and more diverse, similar parts of the product range are grouped together into divisions, each having its own functional management team. Each division has some degree of profit responsibility and reports to the headquarters, which usually retains a significant role in the development of business strategy. Sometimes this is shortened to *M-Form* structure. *See also Matrix organisation structure.*

Multinational enterprise (MNE) One of the global companies that operate in many countries around the world – for example, Ford, McDonald's and Unilever.

Multinational strategy When a company operates in many countries, though it may still have a home base. *See also International strategy* and *Global strategy.*

Negative-sum game Actions of each party undermine both themselves and their opponents.

Negotiation-based strategic route forward Has both human resource and game theory elements. Human resource aspects emphasise the importance of negotiating with colleagues in order to establish the optimal strategy. Game theory aspects explore the consequences of the balance of power in the negotiation situation.

Net cash flow Approximately, the sum of pre-tax profits plus depreciation, less the periodic investment in working capital that is required to undertake the project.

Network-based strategy Explores the links and degree of co-operation present in related organisations and industries. It places a value upon that degree of co-operation.

Network co-operation Refers to the value-adding relationships that organisations develop *inside* their own organisation and *outside* it with other organisations.

Network externalities Refer to the development of a overall standard for a network that allows those belonging to the network to benefit increasingly as others join the network.

New public management model Consists of a model of public sector decision-making where the professional civil service operates with more market competition and former state monopolies are divided and compete against each other for business from citizens. *See also Public Sector Administration Model.*

Niche marketing Concentration on a small market segment with the objective of achieving dominance of that segment.

Objectives or **goals** Take the generalities of the mission and turn them into more *specific* commitments. They state more precisely than a mission statement what is to be achieved and when the results are to be accomplished. They may be quantified. *See also Mission.*

Oligopoly A market dominated by a small number of firms.

Organisational capability The skills, routines, management and leadership of its organisation. *See also Tangible resources* and *Intangible resources.*

Organisational culture The set of beliefs, values and learned ways of managing in an individual organisation. Note that it is important to distinguish this from *national* cultures.

Outsourcing The decision by an organisation to buy in products or services from outside, rather than make them inside the organisation.

Paradigm The recipe or model that links the elements of a theory together and shows, where possible, the nature of the relationships.

Parenting The special relationships and strategies pursued at the headquarters of a diversified group of companies.

Payback The time that it takes to recover the initial capital investment, usually measured in years.

Payoffs The results of particular game-plays. *See also Game theory, Zero-sum game, Co-operative game, Negative-sum game.*

PESTEL analysis Checklist of the political, economic, socio-cultural, technological, environment and legal aspects of the environment.

Plans or **programmes** The specific actions that follow from the strategies. Often a step-by-step sequence and timetable.

Politics Concerned with the exercise of authority, leadership and management in organisations.

Portfolio matrix Analyses the range of products possessed by an organisation (its portfolio) against two criteria: relative market share and market growth. It is sometimes called the growth-share matrix.

Predictability of the environment The degree to which changes in the environment can be predicted.

Prescriptive change The implementation actions that result from the selected strategy option. A defined list of actions is identified once the strategy has been chosen. *See also Emergent change.*

Prescriptive corporate strategy A prescriptive strategy is one whose objective is defined in advance and whose main elements have been developed before the strategy commences. *See also Emergent corporate strategy*, where such elements are crafted during the development of the strategy and not defined in advance.

Pressure points for influence The groups or individuals that significantly influence the direction of the organisation, especially in the context of strategic change. Note that they may have no *formal* power or responsibility.

Primary demand Demand from customers for themselves or their families. *See also Derived demand.*

Problem children Products with low relative market shares in high-growth markets. *See also Portfolio matrix.*

Process of corporate strategy How the actions of corporate strategy are linked together or interact with each other as strategy unfolds.

Profit-maximising theories of strategy Emphasise the importance of the market place and the generation of profit. *See also Prescriptive corporate strategy.*

Profitability The ratio of profits from a strategy divided by the capital employed in that strategy. It is important to define clearly the elements in the equation, e.g. whether the profits are calculated before or after tax and before or after interest payments. This is often called the *return on capital employed*, shortened to ROCE.

Public interest Concerns about the objectives of the institutions that make and implement public decisions in public sector strategy.

Public power The resource possessed by nation states and consisting of the collective decision making that derives from the nation state.

Public sector administration model Consists of a professional civil service bureaucracy that enacts government legislation and administers the activities of the state on behalf of the government, coupled with state monopolies that supply services to citizens. *See also New public management model.*

Public sector resource analysis Needs to assess whether sufficient and appropriate resources are available to deliver the purpose and objectives set by the state.

Public value Refers to the benefits to the whole of the nation from owning and controlling certain products and services in public sector strategy.

Quota A maximum number placed by a nation state on the goods that can be imported into the country in any one period. The quota is defined for a particular product category.

Reputation The strategic standing of the organisation in the eyes of its customers and other stakeholders. It is the sum of customer knowledge developed about an organisation over time, including its brands among many other factors.

Resource allocation The process of allocating the resources of the organisation selectively between competing strategies according to their merit.

Resource-based strategy Stresses the importance of an organisation possessing some resources that deliver its competitive advantage over its rivals in the market place.

Resource-based view Stresses the importance of resources in delivering the competitive advantage of the organisation. It is often shortened to 'RBV'. *See also Prescriptive corporate strategy.*

Retained profits The profits that are retained in an organisation rather than distributed as dividends to shareholders. These can be used to fund new strategies.

Return on capital employed Defined as the ratio of profits to be earned divided by the capital invested in the new strategy.

Reward The result of successful strategy, adding value to the organisation and the individual.

Reward systems The structured benefits paid to individuals and groups who have delivered strategies that add value to the organisation consistent with its agreed purpose.

Ricardian rents Economic rent deriving from the resources of the organisation. They are derived from resources that possess some real competitive advantage and allow the company to earn exceptional returns. *See also Economic rent.*

Risk Strategy evaluation criterion associated with a strategy that does not expose the organisation to unnecessary hazards or to an unreasonable degree of danger.

ROCE *See Profitability.*

Scenario Model of a possible future environment for the organisation, whose strategic implications can then be investigated.

Schumpeterian rents Economic rent deriving from new and innovatory products and services that allow the organisation to charge significantly above the costs of production. *See also Economic rent.*

Seven S Framework The seven elements of superordinate goals: strategy, structure, systems, skills, style and staff. In some later versions, the first item was replaced by share values.

Share issues New shares in an organisation can be issued to current or new shareholders to raise finance for new strategy initiatives. The word 'equity' is sometimes used in place of shares and the process is then called 'equity financing'.

Shareholder value added The difference between the return on capital and the cost of capital multiplied by the investment made by the shareholders in the business.

Short-term debt A loan repaid in less than one year. *See also Long-term debt.*

Small organisation structure Consists of the owner/proprietor and the immediate small team surrounding that person.

Socio-cultural theories of strategy Focus on the social and cultural dimensions of the organisation in developing corporate strategy. *See also Prescriptive corporate strategy.*

Split The variety of techniques that can be employed to develop and sustain the autonomy and diversity of large organisations.

Stakeholders The individuals and groups who have an interest in the organisation and, therefore, may wish to influence aspects of its mission, objectives and strategies.

Stars Products with high relative market shares operating in high-growth markets. *See also Portfolio matrix.*

Strategic alliances Co-operative strategies where organisations combine or share some of their resources without involving an exchange of shares or other forms of joint ownership.

Strategic business unit (SBU) The level of a multi-business unit at which the strategy needs to be developed. The unit has the responsibility for determining the strategy of that unit. An SBU is not necessarily the same as a division of the company: there may be more than one SBU within a division and SBUs may combine elements from more than one division.

Strategic change The proactive management of change in organisations in order to achieve clearly defined strategic objectives or to allow the company to experiment in areas where it is not possible to define strategic objectives precisely. *See also Prescriptive change* and *Emergent change*.

Strategic environment Everything and everyone outside the organisation: competitors, government, etc.

Strategic fit The matching process between strategy and organisational structure.

Strategic groups Groups of firms within an industry that follow the same strategies or ones that have similar dimensions and which compete closely.

Strategic planning A formal planning system for the development and implementation of the strategies related to the mission and objectives of the organisation. It is no substitute for strategic thinking.

Strategic space The identification of gaps in an industry representing strategic marketing opportunities.

Strategies The principles that show how an organisation's major objectives or goals are to be achieved over a defined time period. Usually confined only to the *general logic* for achieving the objectives.

Strategy as history The view that strategy must, at least in part, be seen as a result of the organisation's present resources, its past history and its evolution over time.

Style theory of leadership Suggests that individuals can be identified who possess a general style of leadership that is appropriate to the organisation. *See also Contingency theory of leadership* and *Trait theory of leadership*.

Suitability Strategy evaluation criterion associated with the strategy being appropriate for the internal and external context of the organisation.

Survival-based theories of strategy These regard the survival of the fittest in the market place as being the prime determinant of corporate strategy. *See also Emergent corporate strategy*.

Sustainable competitive advantage An advantage over competitors that cannot be easily imitated. Such advantages will generate more value than competitors have.

SWOT analysis An analysis of the strengths and weaknesses present internally in the organisation, coupled with the opportunities and threats that the organisation faces externally.

Synergy The combination of parts of a business such that the sum is worth more than the individual parts – often remembered as '2 + 2 = 5'.

Tangible resources The physical resources of the organisation like plant and equipment. *See also Intangible resources* and *Organisational capability*.

Target pricing Sets the price of goods and services primarily on the basis of the competitive position of the organisation, the profit margin required and, therefore, the target costs that need to be achieved. *See also Cost-plus pricing*.

Targeted marketing *See Market segmentation*.

Tariffs Taxes on imported goods imposed by a nation state. They do not stop imports into the country but make them more expensive.

Taylorism Named after F W Taylor (1856–1915). The division of work into measurable parts, such that new standards of work performance could be defined, coupled with a willingness by management and workers to achieve these. It fell into disrepute when it was used to exploit workers in the early twentieth century. Taylor always denied that this had been his intention.

Tiger economies Countries of South-East Asia exhibiting exceptionally strong economic growth over the last 20 years, including Singapore, Malaysia, Hong Kong, Thailand and Korea.

Total Quality Management (TQM) Emphasises the need for the whole company to manage quality at every stage of the company.

Trade barriers The barriers set up by governments to protect industries in their own countries.

Trade block Agreement between a group (or block) of countries designed to encourage trade between those countries and keep out other countries.

Trait theory of leadership Argues that individuals with certain characteristics (traits) can be identified who will provide leadership in virtually any situation. *See also Contingency theory of leadership* and *Style theory of leadership*.

Transcend Given the inevitable complexities of corporate strategy, some strategists argue that every organisation needs an approach to management that *transcends* these problems and copes with such difficulties.

Transfer price The price for which one part of an organisation will sell its goods to another part in a multidivisional organisation.

Transnational product company This usually involves some global integration of manufacturing coupled with *significant* national responsiveness to national or regional variations in customer demand. *See also Global product company.*

Uncertainty-based theories of strategy These regard prediction of the environment as being of limited use because the outcomes of any strategy are essentially complex and unpredictable, implying that long-term planning has little value. *See also Emergent corporate strategy.*

United Nations Conference on Trade and Development (UNCTAD) A trade body set up to highlight the trading concerns of the developing nations of the world and promote their interests.

Validity Strategy evaluation criterion associated with the strategy and its related calculations and other assumptions being well-grounded and meaningful.

Value chain This identifies where the value is added in an organisation and links the process with the main functional parts of the organisation. It is used for developing competitive advantage because such chains tend to be unique to an organisation.

Value system The wider routes in an industry that add value to incoming supplies and outgoing distributors and customers. It links the industry value chain to that of other industries. It is used for developing competitive advantage.

Vertical integration This occurs when a company produces its own inputs (backward integration) or when a company owns the outlets through which it sells its products (forward integration).

Vision A challenging and imaginative picture of the future role and objectives of an organisation, significantly going beyond its current environment and competitive position. It is often associated with an outstanding leader of the organisation.

Weighted average cost of capital The combination of the costs of debt and equity capital in proportion to the capital structure of the organisation. *See also Cost of capital.*

Zero-sum game Has no pay-off because the gains of one player are negated by the losses of another.

Name index

Aaker, D R 89, 98, 130, 134
Abernathy, W 481
Abrahams, P 725
Amit, R 195, 216
Andrews, K 40, 450
Ansoff, I 5, 36, 38, 40, 49, 50, 83, 462
Argenti, J 16
Argyris, C 44, 555
Athos, A 792

Baden-Fuller, C 455, 733
Baker, M 89, 98, 397
Baptista, J P 345
Barker, T 725
Barney, J 216, 221
Bartlett, C A 683, 709
Beer, M 774
Bennis, W 353, 359
Berle, A A 420
Besanko, D 198
Bouckaert, G 654, 665
Brown, A 249
Brown, S L 121
Bryson, J M 665, 666
Bungay, S 638
Butler, (Lord) R A 260
Buzzell, R D 130

Campbell, A 6, 436, 635
Cannon, T 420
Caves, R 702
Chaharbaghi, K 220, 347, 414, 727
Chakravarthy, B 40
Chandler, A 49, 62, 242, 516, 576,
    577, 580, 591
Child, J 54
Christensen, C 398
Christopher, M 325
Clausewitz, C von 40
Coase, R 198
Coleman, H J 257
Collis, D 218
Connor, K 216
Cool, K 52, 216
Cyert, R M 16, 36, 44, 50, 59, 616

Darwin, Charles 538
Davenport, T H 378, 386
Day, G S 134, 462, 633
de Geus, A 243, 633
Dean, J 287
Deming, W E 51, 434

Dhalla, N Y 89
Dierickx, I 52, 216
Douglas, S 179, 704
Doyle, P 158, 160
Doz, Y 714
Dranove, D 198
Drucker, P 5, 51, 344, 377–8, 430,
    586, 798
Dunning, J H 684, 711, 713

Eden, C 665
Egan, C 106
Eisenhardt, K M 54, 121
Eisenhort, R 774
Ellis, J 289
Evert, G 435

Faulkner, D 54
Fayol, H 34, 35
Ferlie, E 664
Ford, Henry 35, 51, 239, 260, 479
Freeman, J 50
Friesen, P 59, 796

Gale, B T 130
Garvin, D 556, 768
Garvin, J 287
Gertz, D 345
Ghemawat, P 703
Ghoshal, S 683, 702, 703, 709
Gilbert, X 597
Glautier, M W E 288
Gleick, J 59
Gluck, F 403
Glueck, W F 16, 515
Goold, M 632, 635, 638
Grant, R 216
Grant, R M 287
Greiner, L 257, 258, 594

Hall, R C 57
Hall, W 801
Hamel, G 50, 163, 216, 218, 225, 226,
    352, 378, 389, 391, 473, 625, 629,
    714, 733
Handy, C 248, 249, 260, 291, 587,
    753
Hannah, M T 50
Harrison, J S 510
Harrison, R 248
Hart, S 587, 588
Harvey-Jones, J 98

Hayes, W 287
Henderson, B 57
Hendry, J 455
Hill, T 310, 312, 320, 321
Hitch, C J 57
Hitt, M 510
Hofstede, G 249, 262, 263, 589
Hoopes, D G 216
Hrebiniak, L 616
Hunger, D 49, 514
Hunt, J 353
Hymer 702

Inkpen, A C 54
Ireland, R D 510
Ishikawa, K 51, 434

Jacobsen, R 130
Jarillo, J C 549
Jauch, L R 16, 515
Jick, T 757, 763
Johnson, G 44, 248, 594, 774
Joyce, W 616

Kanter, R M 598, 757, 763
Kaplan, R 617, 620
Kay, J 50, 52, 120, 129, 173, 195, 216,
    218, 224, 225, 455, 479, 481, 510
Kluckhohn, C 262
Kogut, B 709, 713
Kono, T 531
Koopman, K 140
Kotler, P 125
Krishna, G 329

Lawrence, P R 795
Leonard(-Barton), D 226, 388
Levinthal, D A 558
Levitt, T 105, 158, 179, 332, 703, 704
Lewin, K 764
Liddell Hart, B H 40, 126
Lindblom, C 665
Little, Arthur D 507, 508
Lorange, P 40
Lorsch, J W 795
Luerhman, T 288
Lynch, R 139, 207, 220, 325, 347,
    414, 468, 727

McDonnell, E 83
McGahan, A 217
McGrath, R G 743

Subject index

Note: case studies are indicated by **emboldened page numbers**; glossary terms are listed on pp 805–14

accounting profit 289
  economic rent and 210
Acer computers 217
acquisitions 466–7, 510–11
  automotive industry 240, 348–51,
    698, 716, 717
  computer industry 65, 759, 781–3
  defence industry 544, 545
  food industry 146–7, 466–7, 513,
    574, 687
  as means of expansion 466–7, 468
  media industry 448, 460, 470, 471
  pharmaceuticals 192, 312, 467, 801
adaptation to environment 538
adaptive learning 557
added value, definition 201, 805
adding value 8–9, 137, 190, 201–2,
    320–1
  resource analysis and 201–2
  see also value
Adidas sports shoes and clothing 171,
    179
ADL matrix 507, 508
advertising 173
Aerospatiale 177, 180, 544, 545, 683
aggressive competitive strategies
    125–9
  analytical process 125
  attack strategies 127–8
  attack/defend options 129
  choosing the enemy 126–7
  competitors' objectives clarified
    126
  innovatory strategies 128–9
  market intelligence used 126
Air France 24, 25, 27
Airbus 42, 163, 171, 177, **180–3**
airline case studies **23–8, 42–3**
Aldi retailing 126, 146, 148, 175, 196,
    499
Alitalia airline 23, 24, 25
alliances
  automotive industry 716
  as means of expansion 467, 468
  see also co-operative strategies;
    strategic business alliances
AmBev brewing 298, 299
analyser organisation 256, 257
Anheuser-Busch brewing 299, 300
Ansoff matrix see market options
  matrix

Apple computers **3–5**, 5–6, 7, 8–9,
    110, 196, 217, 309, 681
Arbed steel 90, 91, 92, 196
Arcelor steel 91, 92, 95
architecture (of resources) 224, 476, 805
Arts Council England 669, 672
ASEA Brown Boveri (ABB) engineering
    196, 403, **602–4**
assets, sale of 278
Association of South-East Asian
    Nations (ASEAN) 327, 696
Aston Martin sports cars 701, 717
Astra Pharmaceuticals 96, 191, 192
Atari computers 11, 231
attack strategies 127–8
  attack/defend options 129
attractiveness-to-stakeholders
    criterion 497, 805
Austrian Airlines 25

backward integration 417, 465, 805
Bajaj motorcycles **328–30**
balanced portfolio 130
Balanced Scorecard 617–21, 805
  comments on 620–1
  example 619
  Key Performance Indicators 618,
    619–20
  rationale 617–18
  reason for developing 617
  strategy perspectives 618
bank shareholdings 430, 437
banking **389, 766–7**
bankruptcy
  effects 497
  factors causing 130
bargaining power
  of buyers/customers 95
  of suppliers 94–5
Barings Bank 627
barriers to entry 95–6, 146
barriers to trade 693
  lowering/removal of 682, 689,
    690, 715
base resources 220
Bata shoe company 125
Bayer chemicals 223
BCG growth–share matrix 40, 130–2,
    628, 792
  alternatives 132–3
  limitations 132

Ben & Jerry's ice cream 87, 115, 116,
    118
benchmark technical format, early-
    mover advantage 729–30
benchmarking 229, 805
Benetton clothing 101, 179, 198–9,
    455
Bentley cars 700
biotechnology
  developments/companies 392
BMG records 736
BMW cars 457, 465, 698
BOC industrial gases **750–2**, 753,
    754, 756
Body Shop cosmetics 417
Boeing aerospace and defence 171,
    180–3, 683
Boo.com **122–3**, 124
borrowing requirements, as risk
    criterion 496
Boston Consulting Group
  product portfolio matrix 40, 130–2,
    628, 792
  survey on motorcycle industry 530
  see also BCG growth–share matrix
bounded rationality 616, 805
Bouygues construction and media
    200–1, 226
Bradford City football club 612
brand analysis 171
branding 164, 170–1, 173, 174, 805
Brazilian steel companies 100
break-even analysis 496, 504
break-even point 504, 805
breakfast cereals **33**, 36, 40, 52, 136,
    467, 712–13
breakthrough resources 220
Bretton Woods Agreement 695–6,
    805
brewing industry case studies **273–5,
    298–301**
British Aerospace 177, 180, 544, 545,
    551, 552, 683
British Airways (BA) 23, 24, 25, 27,
    162
British Petroleum (BP) 363, 364, 366,
    386
British Rail 210
British Steel 91, 92
British Telecom (BT) 534, 535, 536,
    537